Also by Virginia and Lee McAlester

A Field Guide to American Houses

Great American Houses and Their Architectural Styles

A Field Guide to America's Historic Neighborhoods and Museum Houses

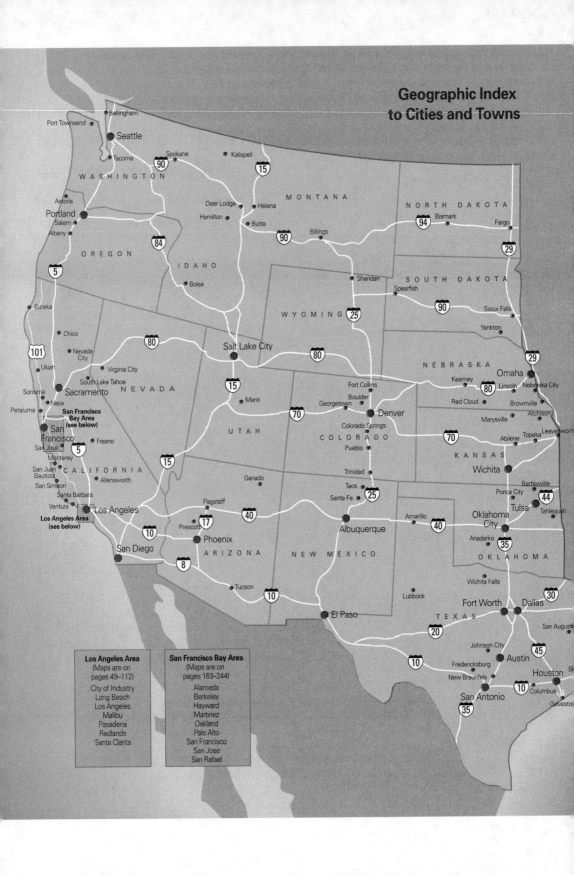

Geographic Index
to Cities and Towns

WASHINGTON

Bellingham
Port Townsend
Seattle
Tacoma
Spokane
Kalispell

MONTANA

Astoria
Portland
Salem
Albany

OREGON

Deer Lodge
Helena
Hamilton
Butte
Billings

Boise

IDAHO

NORTH DAKOTA
Bismark
Fargo

SOUTH DAKOTA
Sheridan
Spearfish
Sioux Falls
Yankton

WYOMING

Eureka
Chico
Nevada City
Ukiah
Virginia City
South Lake Tahoe
Sonora
Sacramento
Petaluma
Napa

NEVADA

Salt Lake City

UTAH

Manti

Fort Collins
Boulder
Georgetown
Denver
Colorado Springs
Pueblo

COLORADO

NEBRASKA
Kearney
Lincoln
Omaha
Nebraska City
Red Cloud
Brownville
Marysville
Atchison

KANSAS
Abilene
Topeka
Leavenworth
Wichita

San Francisco
Bay Area
(see below)
San Francisco
San Jose
Monterey
Fresno
San Juan Bautista
San Simeon
Allensworth
Santa Barbara
Ventura

CALIFORNIA

Ganado

Flagstaff
Prescott

Los Angeles Area
(see below)

Los Angeles

Phoenix

San Diego

ARIZONA

Taos
Santa Fe
Trinidad

Albuquerque

NEW MEXICO

Amarillo

Anadarko

Bartlesville
Ponca City
Tulsa
Tahlequah

Oklahoma City

OKLAHOMA

Tucson

El Paso

Lubbock

Wichita Falls

Fort Worth
Dallas
San Augus

TEXAS

Johnson City
Fredericksburg
New Braunfels
Austin
San Antonio
Houston
Columbus
Galvesto

A Field Guide to America's Historic Neighborhoods and Museum Houses

The Western States

Virginia and Lee McAlester

With maps by Terry Guyton and Greg Malphurs; Jerry Guthrie, map editor; drawings by ArchiTexas

Alfred A. Knopf   New York   1998

This Is a Borzoi Book
Published by Alfred A. Knopf, Inc.

Copyright © 1998 by Virginia and Lee McAlester
All rights reserved under International and Pan-American
Copyright Conventions. Published in the United States
by Alfred A. Knopf, Inc., New York, and simultaneously
in Canada by Random House of Canada Limited, Toronto.
Distributed by Random House, Inc., New York.

www.randomhouse.com

Library of Congress Cataloging-in-Publication Data
McAlester, Virginia.
A field guide to America's historic neighborhoods and museum
houses : the western states / by Virginia and Lee McAlester.
p.   cm.
Includes index.
ISBN 0-679-42569-1 (hc.); 0-375-70172-9 (pbk.)
1. Architecture, Domestic—West (U.S.)—Guidebooks.
2. Historic buildings—West (U.S.)—Guidebooks.   3. West
(U.S.)—Guidebooks.   I. McAlester, A. Lee (Arcie Lee).
NA7223.M33   1998
728'.0978—dc21   97-48419   CIP

Manufactured in the United States of America
First Edition

For those who own and preserve the homes in America's historic neighborhoods, and for the professionals and volunteers who care for our country's museum houses. Their dedicated and often-unsung efforts provide enjoyment and enlightenment for us all.

Contents

Preface

This book has grown out of the authors' efforts, over many years, to find, study, and enjoy our nation's historic residential neighborhoods. Early in this process we discovered that there was no simple and efficient way to locate or obtain background information about a great many such neighborhoods. There are a number of fine guides to our nation's historic sites, but these tend to focus on individual landmarks and, at best, treat only a small handful of residential districts. State or local architectural guides with comprehensive neighborhood information are also relatively uncommon (important exceptions for the western states, which have proved invaluable in preparing this book, are listed in the "For Further Reference" section, page 707). With this book, and projected future volumes covering the central and eastern states, we hope to make accessible a much larger sample of our nation's fascinating, and often still underappreciated, historic residential districts.

One of the high points of visiting historic towns and neighborhoods is the opportunity to supplement the viewing of evocative facades and streetscapes by touring the *interiors* of historic houses that are open to the public. Introductions to numerous such museum houses are thus included along with the neighborhood descriptions.

The book is organized geographically by state. The chapters treating individual cities and towns within each state are arranged alphabetically (the frontispiece map provides a geographic index to all of these city and town chapters). The book's introduction gives a chronological overview of the entire West and includes graphic summaries, adapted from our *Field Guide to American Houses*, of the West's principal styles of pre-1940 domestic architecture. Also included are lists of the museum houses in each style that are discussed later in the book. An appendix provides an introduction to some of the geographic and design factors that contribute to the overall character of differing western neighborhoods.

The core of the book is its city and town chapters, which typically have several components. The intended scope and limitations of each of these can be summarized as follows:

Towns included: The towns and cities treated in the book were determined during three years of intensive research and travel, which included one or more visits to every sizable western city as well as to hundreds of prospective smaller towns and villages. Our goal in each town was to evaluate all reasonably intact neighborhoods of early homes and to visit all prospective local museum houses. From these we chose for inclusion the ones we believed would be of most interest to visitors from elsewhere whose time was limited, a clearly subjective matter made essential by our desire to provide some depth of coverage within a book of manageable size. Dozens of charming and instructive neighborhoods and museum houses had to be omitted; some are described in the local guidebooks listed in the "For Further Reference" section.

Any city or town with at least one selected neighborhood or museum house is included in the book. Among these are all of the West's twenty-three cities with a 1990 population of more than 300,000, as well as eighty-two important smaller towns. A number of additional small towns have not been given a separate "town" chapter but are treated instead under a larger, and usually related, nearby town in order to save space (see table on page vi). Note that three of these nearby towns (Council Bluffs, Iowa; Moorhead, Minnesota; and Mesilla, New Mexico) are across a state line from their larger neighbors. Note also that Moorhead and Council Bluffs are in states not otherwise included in this volume. Rather than truncate a metropolitan area, we have chosen to include such satellite towns with their larger neighbors. This means that the important historic resources of Kansas City, Kansas, will be treated along with Kansas City, Missouri, in a projected future volume covering the central states.

Smaller Towns Included under Related Nearby Towns

town	included under	page		town	included under	page
CALIFORNIA				**NORTH DAKOTA**		
Belmont	Palo Alto (Ralston Hall)	202		Moorhead, Minn.	Fargo (Comstock House)	469
Campbell	San Jose (Ainsley House)	242		**OREGON**		
Ferndale	Eureka	38		Oregon City	Portland	523
Grass Valley	Nevada City (Bourn Cottage)	130		**SOUTH DAKOTA**		
Hillsborough	Palo Alto	197		Deadwood	Spearfish	539
Pacific Grove	Monterey	122		**TEXAS**		
Santa Fe Springs	City of Industry (Clarke Mansion)	55		Mesilla, N.M.	El Paso	585
Saratoga	San Jose (Villa Montalvo)	243		Orange	Beaumont	559
Wilmington	Long Beach (Banning Residence)	62		Seguin	San Antonio (Sebastopol)	636
Woodside	Palo Alto (Filoli)	204		Waxahachie	Dallas	578
COLORADO				**UTAH**		
Idaho Springs	Georgetown	321		Copperton	Salt Lake City	654
Manitou Springs	Colorado Springs	295		Spring City	Manti	645
Silver Plume	Georgetown	320		**WASHINGTON**		
NEBRASKA				Ferndale	Bellingham (Hovander Homestead)	660
Council Bluffs, Iowa	Omaha (General Dodge House)	418		Port Gamble	Port Townsend	666
NEW MEXICO				Puyallup	Tacoma (Meeker Mansion)	688
Corrales	Albuquerque (Casa San Ysidro)	439				

Town introductions: Each town chapter begins with a box showing the date the town was founded and its later populations, where appropriate, in the years 1840, 1860, 1900, and 1940, and in the latest official census, that of 1990 (noncensus estimates of town populations can be notoriously inaccurate). The first four dates are the approximate endings of the four great design eras of pre-1940 American houses—Colonial (in the western states), Romantic, Victorian, and Eclectic. The principal western housing styles of each of these eras are summarized on pages xiv, xxii, xxx, xxxi, xxxvi, and xxxvii of the introduction. A town's relative populations in these years provide a simple index to its periods of most rapid growth, an important clue to the styles and relative abundance of pre-1940 houses that might be found there. Most promising are towns with rapid growth in some earlier era and relative population stability or decline in succeeding years. Less promising, in general, are those that have experienced explosive population growth in the decades since 1940. This usually means that commercial core expansion will have destroyed much of the city's earlier residential fabric. Unfortunately, many of the larger cities of the West fall into this category.

The main body of each town introduction tries to answer such questions as: Why was the town located here in the first place? What were the later economic and social factors that contributed to its having, and keeping, important historic neighborhoods and museum houses? For towns where we found unusually instructive commercial historic districts, or other sites that help explain the town's economic and social history, these are also mentioned in the introduction, or sometimes elsewhere, in boldface type. The sites are

also shown on the appropriate maps, where they are located and labeled in black, rather than in the colors used for featured neighborhoods and museum houses. These sites should be considered as more or less random visiting suggestions, since we did not attempt a systematic analysis of nonresidential historic resources.

Town maps: We consider the maps, which show the locations of every neighborhood and museum house included, to be the heart of the book. They bring together, for the first time, a wealth of scattered local data in a form that should make it possible for house watchers to visit any of almost four hundred important western neighborhoods and museum houses with maximum efficiency. The maps attempt to show all the streets within each neighborhood and also to relate it, and each museum house, to the relevant local thoroughfares and highways. To facilitate visits by cross-country travelers, we have particularly emphasized access routes from interstate highway junctions. Note, however, that outside the featured areas, most secondary streets and roads are omitted from the maps. In addition, the maps were compiled from base maps of differing ages and styles, which despite our best efforts undoubtedly introduced errors. Supplementary local street maps are thus highly recommended, particularly in the larger cities.

Local experts will note that the neighborhood boundaries shown on our maps may not be the same as the official limits of formally designated historic districts, when present (many important neighborhoods lack such designations). This is intentional, for, particularly in large districts, we sometimes emphasize smaller areas that we feel will be the most rewarding to house watchers on tight schedules. All such boundaries are arbitrary, and we strongly encourage further neighborhood exploration when time permits. Note that two different intensities of color are shown within a featured neighborhood on some maps: the darker color shows the principal area of interest; important secondary areas with more scattered historic houses are shown in the lighter color. Note also that some maps include suggested driving routes for more efficient viewing of widely separated concentrations of historic houses. These routes correspond to the order of presentation in the neighborhood descriptions.

Neighborhood descriptions: In choosing the neighborhoods to include, we have favored those with at least some intact historic blocks that have relatively few inappropriately modified historic facades. These are far less common than historic neighborhoods in which the earlier houses are overshadowed by later intrusions (usually apartments or commercial buildings), or that have many unsympathetically remodeled dwellings (some of the latter are, of course, in transition as owners progressively restore the early facades). This policy, and space limitations, required us to exclude many fine but relatively isolated landmark dwellings. Some of these are treated in local guidebooks (see the "For Further Reference" section).

The neighborhood descriptions usually have two components. The first summarizes what we were able to learn about the neighborhood's history—when and by whom it was developed, how long it took to fill with houses, subsequent changes, and so forth. Such data, where they exist at all, are usually scattered in rather obscure local publications or, in larger cities, arcane government planning documents. Where little information is provided, it means that we were unsuccessful in finding such sources. This section may also include our own subjective comments about the neighborhood's overall appearance.

Following these neighborhood introductions, in smaller type, are descriptions giving our impressions of the facades of a number of "featured houses" that demonstrate some of the diversity of styles and design details that can be seen in the neighborhood. These are based only on our streetside impressions, not on close inspection or archival research. They will be of most interest to those with a concern for the subtleties of rapid stylistic analysis. We would like to stress that *all of these houses are private homes that should be viewed only from public streets or sidewalks.* Please be considerate of their owners' privacy.

Museum house descriptions: In choosing museum houses for inclusion, we have generally favored examples having much of their early architectural character either intact or accurately restored; interiors, when not

of the approximate period of the house itself, at least reflecting pre-1950s design fashions; and public or private ownership that seemed committed to permitting public visitation for the foreseeable future. For houses of unusual interest we readily abandoned one or more of these preferences.

We have not attempted to include such essential, but constantly changing, visiting details as the days and times the houses are open and the charges, if any, for visits. It has been our experience that such information, when published in relatively long-lived books such as this one, are more often than not inaccurate. We *have* included current telephone numbers for every site and hope to keep these updated in future printings. *We strongly urge a preliminary phone call before planning a visit to any of the museum houses.* While some are open daily, most are closed during a part of each week; some open only one or two days a week. Hours of opening are equally variable; some houses can be visited for only a few hours each day, or on certain days. *A handful of houses, including some of unusual interest, require advance reservations for visits; we have tried to note all of these in the text.* Be aware, too, that some houses are open "seasonally." These are mostly in the northern states or in the mountains, and typically are open only during the warmer months.

Space limitations prevented the inclusion of the West's many "museum villages," those that have been created by moving onto a single site houses of differing ages that were originally built somewhere else. While these can be very instructive, they also create artificial "neighborhoods" that often bear little resemblance to the real thing. Exceptions have been made for three such villages that carefully re-create or preserve now mostly vanished types of folk dwellings. These are Indian City U.S.A. in Anadarko, Oklahoma (page 472); the Tsa-La-Gi Ancient Cherokee Village in Tahlequah, Oklahoma (page 493); and the Ranching Heritage Center in Lubbock, Texas (page 616).

A final note regarding the term "museum house": Some curators of historic houses prefer the alternative word sequence "house museum," which emphasizes "museum" as the noun and makes "house" its adjectival modifier. We agree that this is often the appropriate connotation. In this book, however, we have also included a number of houses, many of them of rare quality, that permit limited public visitation but are not full-time museums. Instead they have been adaptively reused, with much of their original architectural character still intact, as schools, art museums, restaurants, offices, conference centers, and such. For this reason we prefer the more inclusive phrase "museum house," which reverses the emphasis of the two words.

Introduction
A Brief History of the West

The several hundred houses and neighborhoods that are the subject of this guide are organized in the traditional manner—by geographic location. The fundamental geographic units used are cities and towns, the natural habitat of residential neighborhoods, as well as of most museum houses. The hundred-plus cities and towns included are, in turn, grouped by the states in which they occur. The principal disadvantage of such a geographic organization is that the unfolding chronology of social, economic, and political changes that affect the entire region—in this case, the American West—is easily lost in a maze of local details. This introduction attempts to put such details into a broader context by providing an overview of events influencing the growth of western towns and cities during each of the four principal pre-1950 eras of fashion change in American architecture—the Colonial, Romantic, Victorian, and Eclectic eras. Not surprisingly, these eras reflect not only an easily observed sequence of preferred housing styles, but also periods of more fundamental change in the nation's social, economic, and political fabric. (Note: Boldfaced names in the following discussion indicate towns and neighborhoods described more fully in the main body of the book.)

THE COLONIAL-ERA WEST
(1600–ca. 1850)

Figure 1 (see page x) shows the principal towns of the American West in 1840, a time near the end of its culturally defined Colonial era. Much of the West was then still dominated by its heritage from more than two centuries as the northernmost outpost of Spain's once-vast New World empire. Only nineteen years earlier, after a long period of conflict, Mexico had won independence from Spain to become the new Republic of Mexico. These events had been inspired, at least in part, by the similar struggle for independence by its Anglo neighbors almost a half century earlier.

This remote northern frontier area had only one per-

ceived value to the rulers of first Spanish, and then independent, Mexico—as a buffer zone to protect its gold-, silver-, and agriculture-rich heartlands, centered around Mexico City, from the territorial ambitions of France, England, Russia, and later the United States. After early Spanish exploring expeditions reported that the Indians of the region entirely lacked the gold and silver ornaments of the Aztecs and Incas, further Hispanic activity was mostly limited to token settlements intended to maintain Spain's political hold on this vast buffer.

The Laws of the Indies

Strict laws for governing their American colonies had been prescribed by Spanish kings since the 1500s. These were later codified into a single book known as the *Laws of the Indies,* a sort of how-to-do-it manual for Colonial expansion that was published in 1680. Among the countless topics included were precise instructions for establishing new settlements in frontier regions. The initial cores of such settlements were to be *missions,* large agricultural and teaching complexes whose primary goal was to convert the local Indians into loyal and productive citizens of Catholic Spain. Such local recruiting was necessary to build substantial new settlements, because relatively few Spanish nationals voluntarily chose to trade the comforts of central Mexico, or elsewhere, for the rigors of frontier life. Each mission was to be founded and governed by one or more specially trained friars; initially, these were from the Jesuit order and later from the Franciscan order.

Accompanying these selfless friars were small contingents of salaried Spanish soldiers. They lived outside the mission grounds and had dual responsibilities—protecting the mission from hostile Indians and also acting as policemen to ensure that the Indian converts obeyed the rules established by the friars. In some strategic locations, such as near important harbors or in areas subject to raids by hostile neighbors, the sol-

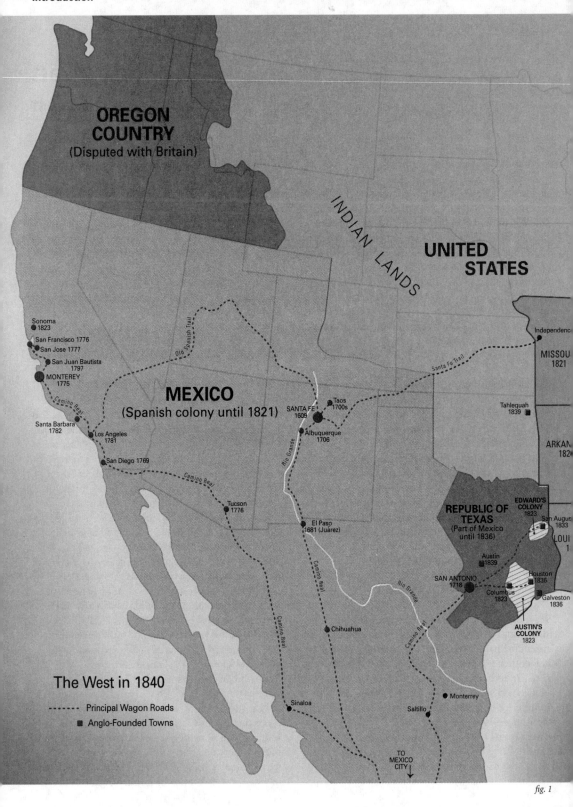

OREGON
COUNTRY
(Disputed with Britain)

INDIAN LANDS

UNITED
STATES

Independenc

MISSOU
1821

Sonoma
1823
San Francisco 1776
San Jose 1777
San Juan Bautista
1797
MONTEREY
1775

Old Spanish Trail

Santa Fe Trail

Tahlequah
1839

MEXICO
(Spanish colony until 1821)

Taos
1700s
SANTA FE
1609

Santa Barbara
1782
Los Angeles
1781

Camino Real

Albuquerque
1706

ARKAN
182

San Diego 1769

Camino Real

Rio Grande

Tucson
1776

El Paso
1681 (Juárez)

REPUBLIC OF
TEXAS
(Part of Mexico
until 1836)

EDWARD'S
COLONY
1823

San Augus
1833

LOUI
1

Austin
1839

Camino Real

SAN ANTONIO
1718

Houston
1836

Columbus
1823

Galveston
1836

AUSTIN'S
COLONY
1823

Camino Real

Rio Grande

Chihuahua

The West in 1840

- - - - Principal Wagon Roads
▪ Anglo-Founded Towns

Sinaloa

Camino Real

Saltillo

Monterrey

TO
MEXICO
CITY

fig. 1

diers were also responsible for constructing defensive forts called "presidios."

The *Laws of the Indies* also stipulated that after a ten-year period of religious training and exposure to European-style culture, the mission's agricultural lands would be assigned to the new Indian converts/citizens and the mission transformed into the nucleus of a new civilian town. The mission chapel would then become a church staffed by a parish priest, and the missionary friars would go elsewhere to repeat the process. Needless to say, the ten-year schedule was wildly optimistic for accomplishing such massive changes in the complex cultures of native peoples. A long-postponed version of this process did ultimately begin in 1824, when the new Republic of Mexico established a long-term plan to "secularize" the missions and distribute most of their lands and buildings to local residents. Even today, some of the former mission churches still serve their surrounding parishes. Among these are Missions Conception, Espada, and San Juan near San Antonio, many in northern New Mexico, and such California examples as those at Sonoma, San Francisco, San Juan Bautista, and Santa Barbara.

Chains of Missions

Spanish missions were established in the American West in beadlike chains along a single wagon road that linked them with each other and with larger towns farther to the south. From there similar roads led south to Mexico City. All of these official roadways, mandated by the king, were called El Camino Real (the Royal Road), a name that suggests more than their rugged surfaces usually delivered. Three such road-linked mission chains, each begun at a different time and headed for a different destination, were built in the American West.

New Mexico—Earliest, most ambitious, and ultimately the most successful at blending Spanish and Indian cultures were those missions established near the Rio Grande in northern New Mexico beginning in 1598, which makes them the second-oldest European settlements in what is now the United States (the Spanish presidio town of San Augustine, in modern Florida, was founded in 1565). Here the Spaniards were attracted by the towns of the sedentary, agricultural Pueblo tribes who lived in communal, mud-walled dwellings. These had a familiar similarity to mud-walled houses imported into southern Spain from northern Africa by the Moors several centuries earlier. Seemingly an ideal setting for applying the *Laws of the Indies,* these advanced Pueblo cultures instead long resisted Spanish control. Their initial brutal conquest

thus bore scant resemblance to the idealized patterns outlined in the *Laws of the Indies*. In spite of these early conflicts, by the mid-1700s thirty-two missions had been established adjacent to Pueblo villages that stretched down the Rio Grande for more than a hundred miles southward from the most northerly Pueblo village at **Taos.** Farther southward, an important way-station mission was established on the Camino Real at El Paso del Norte; this became the nucleus for the modern city of Juárez, Mexico.

Texas—The next chain, begun in 1716, was a result of provocations to Spanish Texas that originated in adjacent Louisiana, then a colony of France. To meet this threat, Spanish authorities planned a sequence of missions reaching across the province from the Rio Grande on the southwest to the Sabine River, Spain's unofficial boundary with Louisiana. By 1718 the first four missions had been established in the pine forests of easternmost Texas. There the local Caddo tribes, a sedentary agricultural people, seemed promising for conversion.

A fifth mission was located three hundred miles westward as a convenient way station on the route to the eastern missions. Here, in the more arid west, a series of massive springs created a clear and swift-flowing river bounded by lush grasses that revitalized travel-weary horses and oxen. The river was named for the idyllically sited new mission, **San Antonio de Valero,** universally shortened to just "San Antonio." This was soon to become the focal point of Spanish Texas. As the French threat subsided, and the Caddo proved indifferent to conversion, the eastern missions were abandoned. Some of their friars, and others from elsewhere, brought their small contingents of converts to the bountiful San Antonio River to make a new start. By 1731 the original mission had been joined by five others as well as by a small civilian town, all of them protected from the horseback raids of nomadic tribes by a large contingent of soldiers.

California—The youngest of the three mission chains was that of coastal California. Fearing the tenuous intrusions of Russian fur-trapping expeditions along the region's then-undefended and largely unexplored shores, in 1767 Spanish authorities began expanding into Alta (Upper) California, a coastal chain of missions and forts established earlier in Baja (Lower) California. By 1776 seven new missions extended from **San Diego de Alcala** on the south to **San Francisco de Asis** on the north, a distance of more than five hundred miles. By 1804 twelve additional missions had been founded between the two terminal points. These ensured that no mission was more than about twenty-five miles, a day's horseback ride, from its neighbors. Still later, two more missions were added to the north of San Francisco—**San Rafael Archangel** in 1817 and San Francisco Solano in the new town of **Sonoma** in 1823. About five hundred miles to the southeast of San Diego, an important way-station mission on the California-bound Camino Real provided the early nucleus for the town of **Tucson.**

These California missions had less difficulty with the local Indians than did their counterparts in New Mexico and Texas, for the region's benign climate and abundance of fish, game, and edible plants, had created native cultures unlike those farther to the east. Instead of large, and often-conflicting, tribes of either nomadic hunter-gatherers or sedentary agriculturists, here the population consisted of hundreds of small hunter-gatherer "tribelets." Each of these occupied a rather-small area with relatively little interference from its neighbors. The Spanish friars and soldiers had little difficulty in making converts, either by reason or, if necessary, by force, of these peaceful natives.

Here, as throughout the New World, a principal cause of failure in the relatively humane Spanish mission system, which attempted to assimilate, rather than eliminate, the local Indians, was the natives' great susceptibility to such routine European diseases as measles and smallpox. Isolated from their Eurasian forebears for many thousands of years and thus lacking any natural immunity, the Native Americans died of these ailments in appalling numbers after their first close encounters with Europeans.

Hispanic Towns

Figure 1 (see page x) illustrates fourteen of the most important Hispanic towns that dominated the urban West in 1840. All of these had grown at or near the sites of one of the early missions. Now officially designated pueblos (small towns) after the Mexican secularization of the missions, by 1840 most had only a few hundred inhabitants. Most important were the early capitals of their respective provinces: **San Antonio** in Texas (whose population of about 2,000 now included some Anglos), **Santa Fe** in New Mexico (population about 5,000), and **Monterey** in California (population about 700). Many of these modest towns were destined to play important roles in the massive Anglo domination of the region that unfolded in the next decade (see figure 8, page xviii).

Anglo Texas

The first seeds of Anglo domination of the Hispanic Southwest were planted by a new approach on the part of Mexican authorities to a potential threat from a foreign neighbor. They noted with alarm the growing Anglo presence and restlessness along the border of what before 1803 had been the remote French wilderness of Louisiana. Some bold Anglos had gone so far as becoming illegal squatters on Mexican territory. To counter this trend, the government made a boldly preemptive move. Rather than continuing the already-unenforceable prohibition against Anglo entry onto Mexican soil, the government now decided to *encourage* it, but under terms it felt would benefit both parties.

Thus in 1821 the Mexican government issued the first of what were to be a number of grants of Texas land to Anglo *empresarios*. To obtain permanent title to, and full authority over, this land, the grantee was required to bring in several hundred financially and morally responsible Anglo families, whose members would swear to become loyal Mexican citizens. The first, and by far most successful, of the *empresarios* was a talented and visionary young Missouri lawyer named Steven F. Austin, who later became the revered "Father of Anglo Texas." As the site for his colony, Austin chose the fertile coastal region drained by the Colorado and Brazos Rivers, which lies between the appropriately named later towns of Austin and Houston. By the 1830s, Austin's Colony, skillfully and faithfully managed by its founder, had about eight thousand Anglo settlers. Its principal town was called **Columbus,** a name honored by both Hispanics and Anglos.

Most of the would-be *empresarios* that followed Austin lacked his talents and ultimately defaulted on the terms of their grants, usually for failure to attract enough settlers. One of these was Haden Edwards, whose grant centered around several existing Hispanic villages, some of which dated back to the abandoned East Texas missions founded a century earlier. Because of these, Edwards was unable to obtain clear title to his lands and abandoned the grant. The area nevertheless became an important center of early Anglo settlement. **San Augustine** was among its principal towns.

The Mexican-authorized Anglos brought in by Austin and the other successful *empresarios* were mostly former southern cotton farmers, who transported their Texas-grown bales to small coastal ports either by wagon or by floating them downriver in small boats. There they were transferred to coastal schooners for shipment to the cotton-marketing center of New Orleans. By 1835 these authorized Anglo immigrants were outnumbered, by about two to one, by illegal squatters, many of whom were rustic and restless frontiersmen that lived mainly by hunting and subsistence farming. Both groups played important roles in the dramatic events that were about to unfold.

Texas Revolution

In 1835 the increasingly prosperous Texas Anglos, resenting taxes and other regulations imposed by a new Mexican governing regime, began exploring other options. Joined by many sharpshooting illegal immigrants, they decided to follow the precedent set by their 1776 British forebears—they declared independence from Mexico. The result was an American Revolution in miniature.

In October a volunteer army of about 500 Anglo planters and frontiersmen, most of them expert marksmen, surrounded and sealed off San Antonio for a five-week siege. Then they began to fight their way, house by house, through the town's streets with such ferocity that the Mexican commander surrendered his entire force of 1,100 professional soldiers. Texas's provincial capital and largest town had been captured by Anglo rebels.

Mexico responded by rushing northward a 4,000-man army of elite troops that were personally commanded by the country's new president, General Antonio López de Santa Anna, the self-styled "Napoleon of the West." Resolutely brutal Anglo defeats soon followed at San Antonio's Alamo fortress and at the nearby mission town of Goliad. Then came an improbable change of luck for the reduced Anglo army, which had been fast retreating toward safety in American Louisiana. Led by General Sam Houston, the George Washington of Texas, the troops staged a brilliant surprise attack on their pursuers at San Jacinto, near the present-day city named for the general. In this the 700 Anglos managed to kill 630 of Santa Anna's troops and capture the remaining 730, which included their commander. The Napoleon of the West then prudently signed documents giving the rebels their independence in exchange for the right to return to Mexico. Thus, in 1836, the continent gained a new nation called the Republic of Texas.

Newly independent Texas established its first capital at Harrisburg, soon renamed **Houston,** an Austin's Colony village a few miles inland from Galveston Bay on a short but dependably navigable river. Reachable only by small boats, this was supplemented by a deep-water port on a nearby island. Oceangoing vessels arriving at this port city of **Galveston** unloaded and then reloaded their cargo and passengers into smaller boats for the trip up shallow Galveston Bay and along Buffalo Bayou to Houston. This arrangement bypassed a wide belt of muddy coastal marshes that restricted direct wagon access to the coastline. In 1839 the leaders of the Texas Republic chose a more central location for a new capital city. On a hill overlooking the scenic Colorado River they founded **Austin,** named for the father of Anglo-American Texas.

Colonial-Era Houses

Almost four hundred years have elapsed since Spanish pioneers established their provincial capital at Santa Fe in 1609. Rather miraculously, large parts of the dwelling and administrative center they built in that year still survive today as a sort of evocative time machine that transports visitors back to the very beginnings of our nation's European cultural heritage. Equally notable are other surviving houses and neighborhoods scattered throughout the West that allow us to similarly re-create, in our mind's eye, the actual settings in which many of the epochal events described in the preceding paragraphs took place.

America's Spanish pioneers erected dwellings similar to those that housed their ancestors in Spain. These venerable building traditions are preserved today in the West's surviving houses constructed in what modern historians call the Spanish Colonial style. Figure 2 (see page xiv), adapted from our book *A Field Guide to American Houses,* illustrates the subtypes of this style. It also includes a tabulation of the important Spanish Colonial museum houses that are more fully described under the town in which they occur in this book.

In addition to the West's many Spanish Colonial museum houses, figure 2 also shows two rare western museum houses that reflect the quite different building traditions of the early French and English colonists who were concentrated farther to the East.

Colonial-Era Neighborhoods

As was the case for rules of governance, Spain's *Laws of the Indies* also spelled out how each new town was to be planned. Clear rules were given for siting the towns; laying out their street grids and building lots; size, shape, and location of the mandatory central plaza; and numerous other such details. In practice, however, the application of these rules was relatively lax, particularly in remote frontier regions. Wagon-road communications between Mexico City and the far northern provinces were very time-consuming and, in the end, the missionary friars and Spanish soldiers who settled the American Southwest generally built far less formally organized communities than those prescribed in the laws. This can be clearly documented in the case of San Antonio. Figures 3 and 4 (see page xv) contrast the formal plan drawn for the town before it was settled (this plan already deviated from the *Laws of the Indies* in many details) with a later plan of the town as it was actually built. Note that it has *two* squares rather than one and irregular angles in the street "grid."

One planning element that was universal in the

Colonial-Era Styles and Museum Houses

SPANISH COLONIAL

Pitched Roof

California   Monterey: Cooper-Molera Complex, 1830 and later
San Diego: Old Town, ca. 1821–1872
SF Bay Area/San Jose: Peralta Adobe, ca. 1797
Santa Barbara: Casa de la Guerra, 1820s
Santa Barbara: Trussell-Winchester Adobe, 1854
    and later

Pitched Roof with Anglo-Influenced Porches

California   LA Area/Long Beach: Rancho Los Alamitos, early 1800s with many
    additions
LA Area/Long Beach: Rancho Los Cerritos, 1844 and 1930s
Monterey: Casa Soberanes, 1840s
Monterey: Cooper-Molera Complex, 1830 and later
Monterey: Larkin House, 1835
Monterey: Stevenson House, 1830 and later
Petaluma: Petaluma Adobe, ca. 1836–1846
SF Bay Area/Martinez: Martinez Adobe, 1849
San Juan Bautista: Castro-Breen House, ca. 1838
Ventura: Olivas Adobe, 1847–1853

Flat-Roof Tradition

Arizona   Ganado: Hubbell Home, 1902
Tucson: La Casa Cordova, 1850s and 1879
Tucson: Sosa-Carrillo-Frémont House, 1880

Colorado   Trinidad: Baca House, 1870

New Mexico   Albuquerque vicinity: Casa San Ysidro, ca. 1875 and later
Santa Fe: Palace of the Governor, ca. 1610 and later
Santa Fe vicinity: El Rancho de las Golondrinas, 1700s and later
Taos: Blumenschein Home, ca. 1800 and later
Taos: Kit Carson Home, 1825
Taos: Martinez Hacienda, 1804 and later

Texas   El Paso vicinity: Barela House, 1860 and 1878
El Paso: Magoffin Home, 1875
San Antonio: Spanish Governor's Palace, ca. 1749

FRENCH COLONIAL

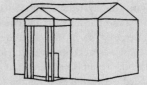

Texas   Austin: French Legation, 1841

EARLY CLASSICAL REVIVAL

Oklahoma   Tahlequah: Murrell Home, ca. 1844

fig. 2

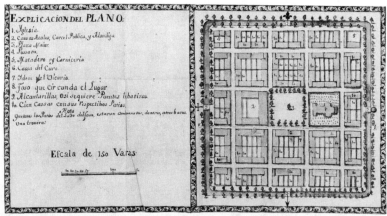

Proposed plan
of San Antonio,
Texas, ca.1777

fig. 3

Actual plan of
San Antonio,
Texas, 1873

fig. 4

Spanish Colonial Southwest was at least one central parklike plaza with the parish church facing it on one side. At first the other three sides were mostly lined with houses and, where appropriate, barracks for the local military garrison. The streets around the one or more plazas rarely formed a right-angled grid; indeed, their irregular street patterns are today considered a primary contributor to the picturesque character of most Hispanic-era neighborhoods. Figure 5 (see page xvi), an actual 1862 map of Tucson, shows three separate plazas, each with its own function, and the typical pattern of angled streets and irregular lots that surrounded them. Most of the early plazas had small shops in some of their surrounding residences. As the towns grew, these early houses were typically replaced by Hispanic or Anglo two-story structures with shops below and residential rooms above. This pattern still survives in the **Historic Core** of **Sonoma** (California), **Old Town** in **Albuquerque**, the **Rancho des Taos Plaza**, and the **Main Plaza** in **Taos** (New Mexico), and in **Mesilla**, New Mexico (discussed under El Paso, Texas). Similar but much more heavily restored examples are **Old Town** in **San Diego** and the **El Pueblo Historic Monument** in **Los Angeles**.

A second distinctive feature of most Hispanic towns is that the houses are generally sited directly on the sidewalks, with outdoor spaces confined to private rear yards. Figure 6 (see page xvi) illustrates these differ-

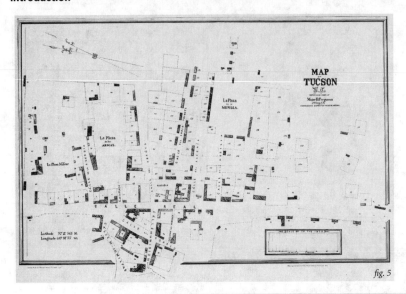

Plan of Tucson, Arizona, 1862

fig. 5

Hispanic and Anglo Neighborhood Differences

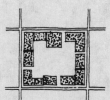

Closely spaced houses sited on sidewalk with private courtyards behind are most typical.

Hispanic Neighborhood

Detached houses surrounded on all sides by open space are most typical.

Anglo Neighborhood

(Adapted from University of Arizona, College of Architecture)

fig. 6

ences as seen in **Tucson's Barrio Historico,** one of the West's most intact early examples of an urban Hispanic-style neighborhood. Other survivors suggesting something of their original character are parts of **Tucson's El Presidio Historic District; Santa Fe's Barrio Analco** and **Canyon Road** neighborhoods; and **San Antonio's La Villita.**

American Indian Dwellings

North America's first European colonists did not, of course, enter into an uninhabited, Antarctica-like continent. Instead, they found native peoples whose cultures were even older and more diverse, in their complex customs and adaptations, than those of western Europe. What the natives lacked was European technology—the sailing ships, compasses, armor, guns, and beasts of burden—that allowed most of the immi-

grants to eventually subjugate and destroy the native cultures. When deemed desirable, as in gold- and silver-rich central Mexico, this process moved very swiftly. Mostly it crept along slowly, fueled by endless waves of immigrants spreading to occupy an ever-decreasing expanse of land left relatively undisturbed by European intrusions.

In 1840 this process had yet to enter its final phase in the American West. Most of the vast lands beyond the tenuous threads and circles of Hispanic and Anglo settlement shown in figure 1 (see page x) were still occupied by relatively undisturbed Indian tribes of diverse languages and cultures. All of this was to end over the next fifty years.

Mirroring their great cultural diversity, the western Indians lived in houses of differing styles and complexity. Some of the principal types, adapted from a more

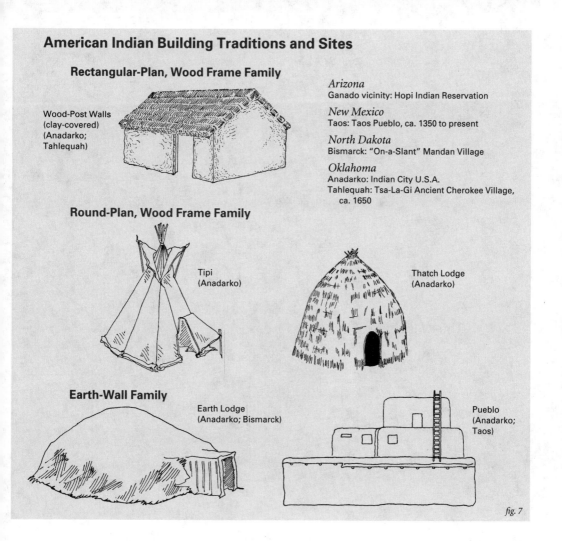

American Indian Building Traditions and Sites

Rectangular-Plan, Wood Frame Family

Wood-Post Walls
(clay-covered)
(Anadarko;
Tahlequah)

Arizona
Ganado vicinity: Hopi Indian Reservation

New Mexico
Taos: Taos Pueblo, ca. 1350 to present

North Dakota
Bismarck: "On-a-Slant" Mandan Village

Oklahoma
Anadarko: Indian City U.S.A.
Tahlequah: Tsa-La-Gi Ancient Cherokee Village,
ca. 1650

Round-Plan, Wood Frame Family

Tipi
(Anadarko)

Thatch Lodge
(Anadarko)

Earth-Wall Family

Earth Lodge
(Anadarko; Bismarck)

Pueblo
(Anadarko;
Taos)

fig. 7

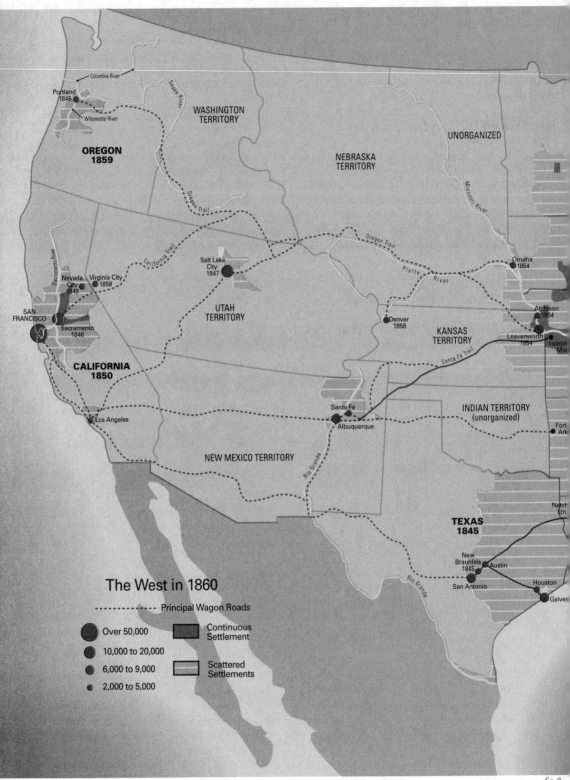

The West in 1860

- - - - - - Principal Wagon Roads

● Over 50,000

● 10,000 to 20,000

● 6,000 to 9,000

● 2,000 to 5,000

Continuous Settlement

Scattered Settlements

fig. 8

complete discussion of Native American dwellings in our *Field Guide to American Houses,* are shown in figure 7 (see page xvii). Note that, just as in European dwellings, the Indians used two basic structural systems—either wooden frames covered by some kind of protective sheathing or masonry-walled structures with wood-supported roofs.

THE ROMANTIC-ERA WEST (1840–ca. 1880)

Figure 8 (see page xviii) shows the principal towns of the American West in 1860. That year marks the approximate boundary between the nation's preference for new "Romantic" styles of architectural design, which had replaced the transplanted European fashions of the preceding Colonial era, from yet a third phase of design preferences that were to dominate the country after the Civil War. A comparison of figures 1 (see page x) and 8 makes clear the momentous political, social, and economic changes that took place in the West in the two decades between 1840 and 1860.

Whereas formerly the West was shared by four sovereign nations—Britain, Mexico, the Republic of Texas, and the United States—in a period of only three years, from 1845 to 1848, the United States had expanded its boundaries to the approximate limits of the present Lower Forty-eight. Equally dramatic changes had taken place in the West's principal cities. In 1840 the West was dominated by very small towns that had been associated with three northward-thrusting chains of missions established by Spain in the 1600s and 1700s. By 1860 several of these had been transformed into much larger, Anglo-dominated urban centers; these were now joined by several newly founded and rapidly growing Anglo cities.

The Oregon Trail

The first large Anglo migrations across the West began in 1846 when a long-simmering dispute with Britain over the status of the Oregon Country (see figure 1, page x) was finally resolved with the international boundary between the United States and Canada fixed at its present position along the forty-ninth parallel. This set the stage for an epidemic of "Oregon fever" in the northeastern states, as hundreds of land-hungry settlers headed west to a new life. Most arrived via a difficult, two-thousand-mile wagon route that became the legendary Oregon Trail.

A small trickle of settlers had come earlier, in the 1830s, with the not-unreasonable hope that their new homes would eventually become a part of the United States. They were attracted by the fertile and sheltered valley of the Willamette River, a small tributary of the mighty Columbia River that was located sixty miles inland from the Columbia's junction with the rocky, windy, and foggy Pacific coastline (see figure 8, page xviii). Lewis and Clark had reached the Pacific by following the Columbia River to its mouth, where they spent the winter of 1805 on the inhospitable coast. On their return, they had been lavish in their praise of the sheltered Willamette Valley's virtues for settlement.

The 1830s trickle of Willamette-bound immigrants became a steady stream after the 1846 boundary settlement. The principal urban beneficiary of this migration was a new riverside town, aptly named **Portland,** founded in 1845 near the head of large-ship navigation on the Willamette. Three years later, when the California gold rush created an urgent, and unusually high-value, demand for the food products of the valley's farms, Portland boomed as the main shipping center. It quickly became the largest city in the Pacific Northwest, a position it held until slipping to second place behind its upstart rival **Seattle** in 1910.

Mormon Zion

In 1846 another large group of agriculturists moved westward searching for a different sort of promised land—one that "nobody else wanted." These were the Mormons, who, since the 1830 founding of their religion in western New York, had steadily moved westward to escape the sometimes-brutal persecutions of them by their intolerant neighbors.

The final blow had come in Nauvoo, Illinois, a prosperous town founded by the group in 1840. There in 1844 Mormonism's founder, Joseph Smith, was arrested and murdered by Illinois militiamen. The new leader, Brigham Young, then led a long westward trek to a new and much more isolated promised land. Crossing the Nebraska Territory along the route of the Oregon Trail, the party diverted southward into Mexican territory to reach the arid wilderness near the Great Salt Lake. There they founded **Salt Lake City** and began energetically constructing dams and irrigation systems to harness the fresh waters of nearby mountain streams. Soon they had converted the barren Utah desert into a bountiful agricultural oasis.

Brigham Young also organized a well-trained militia to defend his new homeland of Deseret from *all* hostile intruders, whether they be Mexican authorities, unfriendly Indians, or, most threatening of all, bigoted non-Mormons from the United States. In this, after many conflicts and political compromises, he succeeded. Augmented by a steady flow of new converts to Mormonism, by 1860 remote Salt Lake City had a population of ten thousand and was the largest town in the entire interior West.

The Santa Fe Trail

Another important route westward was the Santa Fe Trail, which first flourished soon after Mexican independence from Spain in 1821. Unlike the Oregon and Mormon Trails, this route was established not to accommodate westward immigration, which was forbidden by the Mexican authorities, but to permit trade between Mexican Santa Fe and Anglo merchants in the Missouri River towns of Independence and St. Louis. Spain had forbidden such trade, but it was now encouraged to provide tax revenue to cash-poor independent Mexico. Only after the Hispanic Southwest became a part of the United States in 1848 did the trail become a significant route for passenger travel as a small number of Anglo immigrants began arriving in the region's early Hispanic towns. There they added Greek Revival detailing and English-style double-hung windows to the indigenous adobe folk houses to create charming Territorial dwellings, some of which still survive in and near Santa Fe.

Texas Annexation

Relations between the United States and Mexico deteriorated rapidly after Texas's Anglo immigrants revolted and became an independent nation in 1836. The Anglo leaders of that conflict confidently expected that Texas would quickly become a new state in their native United States. Many congressional leaders welcomed that prospect, but it soon bogged down in the larger controversy over slavery. Most of Texas's Anglo cotton planters owned slaves, making northern members of Congress reluctant to upset the delicate political balance by adding another proslavery state to the Union.

This impasse was broken by the 1844 election of President James K. Polk of Tennessee. Polk had adroitly sidestepped the slavery issue by campaigning on a platform of manifest destiny, the nation's inevitable right to expand its limits from the Atlantic to the Pacific. After his victory, Polk lost no time in carrying out his campaign promises. In 1845 his supporters in Congress passed a resolution making Texas the nation's twenty-eighth state. In 1846, after a period of saber-rattling brinksmanship on both sides, the United States and Britain agreed to the present international division of the disputed Oregon Country. The stage was now set for the final, and most difficult, chapter of Polk's expansionist plans.

The Mexican War

Texans had disagreed with Mexico about the western boundary of their new country ever since winning their independence in 1836. Mexico considered it to be the Nueces River, which lies just west of San Antonio. By this definition, Texas included only the large settled area shown in figure 8 (see page xviii). The Texans believed, with little justification, that the boundary should be the Rio Grande, a border that included a much larger hunk of Mexican territory. Polk and his expansionist colleagues agreed with the Texans. The infuriated Mexican government broke off diplomatic relations and prepared for another war against its land-hungry northern neighbors.

When his attempts to negotiate a diplomatic settlement were rebuffed, Polk sent American troops to entrench themselves across the Rio Grande from Matamoros, which lay deep in Mexican-claimed territory near the river's mouth. Thus provoked, Mexico sent 1,600 troops across the river to capture a small contingent of American soldiers, killing eleven of them in the process. Three weeks later, Congress declared war, and Polk ordered American troops to Santa Fe to take possession of New Mexico. These then proceeded to California to link with naval forces that had previously occupied Monterey and San Francisco. Still other troops were dispatched farther south to capture the important northern Mexican towns of Monterrey and Saltillo.

With much of northern Mexico now occupied by American troops, Polk dispatched his chief of the army, General Winfield Scott, on a bold amphibious mission to capture the important Mexican port of Veracruz and then march inland to occupy Mexico City itself. After much hard fighting, that goal was achieved in September 1847. For the first time in the nation's history, its flag flew over a foreign capital. On February 2, 1848, Mexican officials and the American diplomat who accompanied Scott's army signed the pivotal Treaty of Guadalupe Hidalgo. In return for a payment of $15 million, this ceded to the United States the disputed western part of Texas, California, and what became the territories of New Mexico and Utah. Unknown to any of the signatories was the discovery, made only five days earlier in northern California, of gold deposits that had eluded its Mexican occupants for more than three centuries. This new wealth proved to be comparable in scale to the Aztec and Inca treasures that had long made Spain Europe's most powerful nation. Small wonder that the California discovery and its aftermath were to dominate the American West for many decades.

The Forty-niners

The massive wealth and profound human displacements created by the gold rush to northern California quickly changed the area from a pastoral Mexican backwater to a frantically growing focus of worldwide attention. **San Francisco,** in 1848 a sleepy Mexican hide-shipping village adjacent to the Bay Area's best deepwater anchorage, became in the next two years a worldly metropolis with thirty-five thousand inhabitants. It would remain the largest city of the American West until overtaken by Los Angeles in 1920. As San Francisco burgeoned, so did its gold-rich hinterlands. By 1850 California's population had reached ninety-three thousand, and it was admitted to the Union as the nation's thirty-first state.

About half of the gold seekers that flooded California arrived at San Francisco after a long sailing-ship voyage either in a single vessel that circled the tip of South America or in the second of two vessels, the voyage separated by a difficult land crossing of Central America. The other half of the gold seekers came overland, mostly via the California Trail, which branched southwestward from the older Oregon Trail in what is now southern Idaho. More adventurous souls avoided the crowds by braving a variety of less established trails, both old and new.

Most of those arriving by land went directly to the goldfields, which lay in the Sierra Nevada foothills about 120 miles east of San Francisco (see map page 159). The booming city, however, benefited from all arrivals. More miners meant more demand for tools, machinery, clothing, and other manufactured goods that they could only receive via San Francisco's wharves and merchants. Even much of the food, for miner and merchant alike, had to be imported, as did all the hardware and much of the lumber for the area's mushrooming towns. Equally important was the return flow from the mines—most of the precious gold ended up in San Francisco banks.

Because oceangoing sailing ships could not traverse the mostly shallow waters of San Francisco Bay, almost all of the passengers and freight that arrived at the city's wharves en route to the distant goldfields had to be transferred to smaller boats for transport first across the Bay and then up either the Sacramento or San Joaquin River to inland ports closer to the goldfields. The most important of these river ports was **Sacramento,** near the headquarters of the earlier John Sutter ranch, some of whose workmen had made the original 1848 gold discovery. San Francisco and Sacramento thus developed a symbiotic seaport/river-port partnership similar to the one established more than a decade earlier between the Texas port towns of Galveston and **Houston.**

Sacramento's early growth mirrored, on a smaller scale, that of its oceanside partner. Founded shortly after the gold discovery, only two years later it had a population of seven thousand. In 1854 it was made the permanent capital of the young state of California.

Even more remarkable, the town soon became the incubator that hatched the next great development in the history of the American West—the building of the first transcontinental railroad during the 1860s.

Gold Rush Beneficiaries

While San Francisco, Sacramento, and **Nevada City,** California, a deep-shaft mining center high in the Sierra Nevada foothills, lay at the heart of the gold rush storm, most of the urban West received substantial, if less direct, benefits from its outflowing energies. Not only did the struggling agricultural settlements along Oregon's Willamette River receive a much needed market for their food, but the thrifty and efficient Mormon farmers of Utah could now trade their surplus crops for gold, the most solid of currencies. New farms also sprouted in formerly sleepy **Los Angeles,** which had the advantage of being the first California stop on the principal southern route to the goldfields.

Farther east, in 1854 local merchants founded the new towns of **Atchison** and **Leavenworth,** Kansas, and **Omaha** on what were formerly Indian lands on the western side of the Missouri River. Located near the previous Iowa and Missouri points of origin for the Oregon and California Trails, these new river ports avoided the cumbersome necessity of crossing the wide Missouri in heavily laden wagons. They soon boomed as outfitting centers providing late-arriving gold seekers, and a flood of western-bound traders, with steamboat-delivered wagons, tools, hardware, cloth, and the many other factory-made necessities and luxuries of frontier life.

In New Mexico the Hispanic village of **Albuquerque** gained a new role as the last supply stop on the most-used southern trail to California. Situated directly on the banks of the Rio Grande, Albuquerque became the preferred New Mexico way station rather than the historic capital of Santa Fe, which was located away from the river at a higher elevation and thus required a rugged northward detour from the more direct low-level route westward.

Least directly affected by gold rush activities were the Hispanic and Anglo towns of Texas, which were themselves the centers of a less dramatic but more permanent boom. The climate and soils of eastern Texas were ideal for growing cotton, and thus it became the final westward extension of the southern Cotton Belt. The belt stopped here because the lands farther west mostly lacked the dependable summer rainfall needed to grow this high-value crop. The importance of this cotton boom can be seen in the populations of the three western states in 1860. Texas led with just over 600,000 inhabitants. Despite its gold rush hordes, California

Romantic-Era Styles and Museum Houses

Greek Revival

California   LA Area/Long Beach vicinity: General
Phineas Banning Residence, 1864

Nebraska   Nebraska City: Nelson-Taylor-Bickel House, 1857

Oregon   Portland: Bybee-Howell House, 1856

Texas   Austin: Neill-Cochran House, 1855
Austin: Texas Governor's Mansion, 1856
Beaumont: John Jay French House, 1845
Columbus: Dilue Rose Harris House, 1858
Galveston: Menard Home, 1838
Galveston: Samuel May Williams House, 1839
San Antonio vicinity: Sebastopol, 1854
San Augustine: Ezekiel Cullen House, 1839

Utah   Salt Lake City: Beehive House, 1854

Washington   Port Townsend: Rothschild House, 1868

Italianate

California   Chico: Bidwell Mansion, 1868
SF Bay Area/Martinez: John Muir House, 1882
SF Bay Area/Oakland: Camron-Stanford
House, 1876
SF Bay Area/Oakland: Pardee Home Museum, 1868
SF Bay Area/Palo Alto vicinity: Ralston Hall, 1864
SF Bay Area/San Jose: Fallon House, ca. 1858

Colorado   Denver: Byers-Evans House, 1883 and later

Kansas   Abilene: Eisenhower boyhood home, 1887
Abilene: Lebold-Vahsholtz Mansion, 1880
Topeka: Ward-Meade House, 1870

Nebraska   Brownville: Carson House, 1860, 1864, and 1872
Lincoln: Kennard House, 1869
Omaha: General Crook House, 1878

Nevada   Virginia City vicinity: Bowers Mansion, 1864
Virginia City: The Castle, 1868
Virginia City: Mackay House, 1860

Oregon   Salem: Bush House, 1878

Texas   Galveston: Ashton Villa, 1859

Washington   Tacoma vicinity: Meeker Mansion, 1890

Gothic Revival

California   LA Area/City of Industry: Workman House,
1840s and 1870s
SF Bay Area/San Rafael: Boyd Gatehouse, 1879
Sonoma: Lachryma Montis, 1852

Colorado   Colorado Springs vicinity: Briarhurst Manor,
1888
Colorado Springs: McAllister House, 1873
Fort Collins: Avery House, 1879 and later
Georgetown: Hamill House, 1867 and 1879–1885

Kansas   Atchison: Amelia Earhart birthplace, 1861
Marysville: Koester House, ca. late 1850s
and 1874

Nebraska   Brownville: Captain Bailey House, 1877
Brownville: Governor Furnas House, 1868
Nebraska City: Wildwood, 1869

Octagon

California   SF Bay Area/San Francisco: Octagon House,
1861

fig. 9

followed well behind with 380,000, and Oregon was a distant third with only 52,000.

Two recently founded mining towns shown in figure 8 (see page xviii), **Virginia City, Nevada,** and **Denver,** were destined to play pivotal roles in the West's about-to-begin Victorian era.

Romantic-Era Houses

In 1840 the West had about 115,000 non-Indian inhabitants, most of them of Hispanic origin except for about 40,000 Anglo Texans. Twenty years later, the West's population had surged to 1.4 million. Most of the newcomers were Anglos, attracted, either directly or indirectly, by the California gold rush. Those who actively worked the gold deposits lived in crude, temporary dwellings made of logs, boards, sticks, stones—anything that was conveniently available to provide basic shelter. Many miners excavated partial or full dugouts into hillsides, which minimized the problems of roof and wall construction. As the gold-bearing stream gravel was depleted at one site, the shelters were abandoned and new ones constructed elsewhere.

More substantial Anglo dwellings were built by farmers in Oregon, Utah, Kansas, and Texas, as well as by the urban residents of the many towns and cities that served the scattered mining and agricultural districts. In this prerailroad frontier, most lived in simple but sturdy folk houses built of local materials. Stylish houses were understandably scarce in a land where long-distance transport was still dominated by animal-drawn wagons traveling over primitive roadways.

Given these obstacles, it seems extraordinary that many western homes were also built in the fashionable Greek, Gothic, and Italianate styles of the nation's Romantic era. These are shown in figure 9 (see page xxii), adapted from our book *A Field Guide to American Houses.* Not surprisingly, such stylish houses were most common in San Francisco, the region's principal seaport and largest city. Other prerailroad examples are most frequent in the Missouri River ports at the West's eastern edge. Nevertheless, as the many surviving museum houses tabulated in figure 9 demonstrate, fashionably stylish homes were not infrequent in most of the larger towns of the West, as well as in some village-sized communities. (It should be noted that many of the more grand Italianate and Gothic Revival houses listed in figure 9 were built in the late 1870s and 1880s, after railroads reached their towns.)

Prerailroad Anglo Folk Houses

Most Anglo residents of the West in the prerailroad decades, before 1870, lived in simple folk dwellings made of local materials. Designed to provide basic shel-

ter, these lacked the fashionable architectural features of the more pretentious "styled" houses. The pioneer Anglo settlers of the eastern half of the country had, much earlier, developed three principal types of such folk dwellings, and these became the favored housing types in the prerailroad West. The three types, or building "traditions," as they are called, originated along the Atlantic seaboard and are summarized in figure 10 (see page xxiv), adapted from *A Field Guide to American Houses.* Each of the three building traditions are represented by important museum-house survivors. (The adobe- and stone-walled dwellings of the Spanish Southwest, which long preceded that area's Anglo settlement, are discussed on page xiii.)

Romantic-Era Neighborhoods

Anglo neighborhood planning in the wagon-road West of the prerailroad era mostly consisted of the simple platting of regular street grids with either square or, more commonly, rectangular blocks. When a new town was located on a riverfront or shoreline, the grid was usually oriented to parallel this feature; otherwise, developers sometimes used north–south/east–west grids, sometimes other orientations. Except in crowded San Francisco, these grids usually had many more lots than houses. The houses tended to be rather widely spaced even where the lot sizes were relatively small, which was usually the case. Exceptions to the rather-haphazard town plans in most of the West during this era were the carefully planned Mormon towns in Utah and adjacent states. Towns such as **Manti** and **Salt Lake City** featured large, square blocks, very wide streets, and a provision for infill building as the towns grew.

Those early western towns that prospered in the railroad-based population boom that began in the 1870s soon had their vacant lots filled with Victorian-era, and sometimes later, dwellings. For this reason neighborhoods, and even single blocks, dominated by the principal Romantic-era styles—Greek Revival, Gothic Revival, and Italianate—are very rare throughout the West. Perhaps the region's best surviving collections of Romantic-era houses are the Italianate blocks of San Francisco and, at the opposite side of the West, assemblages found in two early Missouri River ports that were later bypassed by the railroad boom—**Brownville,** Nebraska, and **Yankton,** South Dakota.

Mining Towns

Most early town-site and neighborhood developers in the West, like those elsewhere, preferred relatively flat sites because of the difficulty of scaling steeper hills with animal-drawn wagons and carriages. There was one necessary exception to this rule—mining towns,

Prerailroad Folk Building Traditions and Museum Houses

Frame Tradition: New England

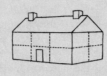

Montana
Deer Lodge: Grant-Kohrs Ranch, 1862 and later

Oregon
Portland: McLoughlin House, 1846

Frame Tradition: Tidewater South
Similar forms also built of stone and *fachwerk* (half-timbering) by German settlers, particularly in central Texas

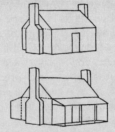

Hall-and-Parlor

Texas
Lubbock: Ranching Heritage Center
New Braunfels: Lindheimer House, 1852
San Antonio: La Villita, ca. 1835 and later

Extended Hall-and-Parlor

Texas
Fredericksburg: Kammlah House, 1849–1910
Lubbock: Ranching Heritage Center
New Braunfels: Breustedt House, 1858
San Antonio: Casa Navarro, ca. 1850 and later
San Antonio: Yturri Edmunds House, 1840
 and 1860

Log Tradition: Middle Colonies

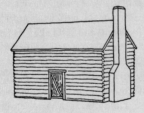

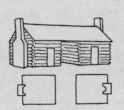

Arizona
Prescott: Arizona Governor's Mansion, 1864

Texas
Columbus: Alley Log Cabin, ca. 1836
Johnson City: Sam Ealy Johnson Log House,
 ca. 1867

fig. 10

whose economic base was mostly located in mountainous areas. Here the high-value product, and the need for workers to extract it, led to irregular town plans. These typically included only a few long blocks of streamside grid-pattern streets, surrounded by curved streets that followed the contours of the hills in the most expedient manner—a street pattern we call contour curves. This is to distinguish these from the curves designed for smooth and sinuous beauty found in Olmstedian planned developments. These did not become popular in the West until after 1900.

Most mining towns were geared primarily toward male miners, not family home owners. The miners lived in everything from tents and shacks to rooming houses and hotels; single-family houses were the exception in all but the most long-lived and prosperous towns. Among the exceptions discussed in the book are **Butte,** Montana; **Georgetown** and its neighbors **Idaho Springs** and **Silver Plume,** all in Colorado; **Nevada City,** California; and **Virginia City,** Nevada.

THE VICTORIAN-ERA WEST (1860–ca. 1900)

Figure 11 (see page xxv) shows the nineteen largest cities of the West in 1900, when the Victorian houses that dominated the nation in the post–Civil War decades were beginning to give way to the more diverse and broadly based housing fashions of the following Eclectic era. A comparison of figures 11 and 8 (see page xviii) shows that the West was transformed once again during the Victorian decades. Hispanic culture dominated the Colonial-era West, and the Anglo gold rush shaped its Romantic era. During the forty years of the Victorian era, yet-another theme took over—the westward spread of the nation's railroad network, which brought to an end the West's long and cumbersome wagon-road era. But before the first transcontinental railroad was completed across the West in 1869, almost a decade of new gold and silver discoveries helped to pave its way.

Bonanzas Spread Eastward

As the easily exploited stream-gravel gold deposits of California played out through the 1850s, many seasoned prospectors took their newly gained knowledge and began to move eastward, to explore the West's other mountain ranges for deposits that had been by-

passed in the hectic scramble to California. In 1859 the first spectacular fruit of these efforts was found in what is now westernmost Nevada, ironically not very far from the California Trail along which countless forty-niners had begun their ascent of the rugged Sierra Nevada to the goldfields just beyond (see figure 8, page xviii). This new discovery was the fabled Comstock Lode, a massive silver deposit so large that it both energized further eastward prospecting and revitalized San Francisco's flagging economy. As one 1860s journalist noted, **Virginia City,** Nevada, the booming center of the Comstock discovery, had become San Francisco's "most essential suburb."

In 1858 excitement had been generated farther eastward by reports of gold in the foothills of Colorado's Front Range. This could be reached from the populous East by a relatively short and safe journey across the

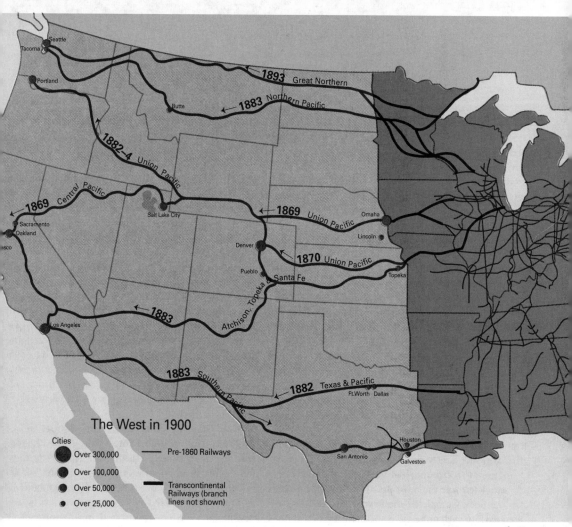

fig. 11

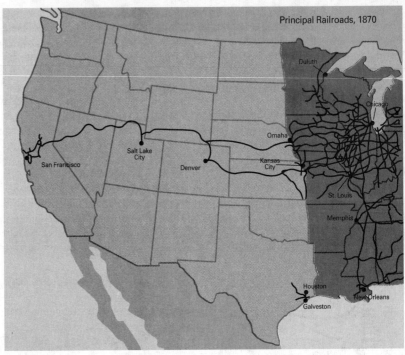

Principal Railroads, 1870

fig. 12

Kansas or Nebraska plains. Soon the western trails were flooded by a wave of new "Pikes Peak or Bust" gold seekers from the East, as well as by a steady stream of experienced prospectors arriving from farther west. The initial Colorado discoveries proved disappointing, but later strikes deeper in the mountains established **Denver** as the trade and supply center for a rich mining hinterland. By 1860 the new city's population of five thousand made it the fifth-largest in the interior West.

Most other prerailroad Anglo towns in the mountainous West had their roots in early gold and silver discoveries. Among the most important survivors of these are **Georgetown,** Colorado (gold and silver, 1859); **Boise,** Idaho (gold, 1858–1862); **Helena,** Montana (gold and silver, 1864); and **Butte,** Montana (gold and silver, 1864–1874).

The Railroad Explosion

In the mid-1840s, when the nation's boundary first reached from the Atlantic to the Pacific, the northeastern states already had a rapidly expanding railroad network. Public sentiment soon began to grow for a new transcontinental rail line that would link the populous East with the largely undeveloped West. In response, Congress in 1853 authorized the Pacific Railroad Surveys to determine the most practical westward routes for rail lines. Completed the next year, these recommended four such routes, two northern and two south-

ern. None could be agreed upon by legislators already deeply divided by the slavery issue.

President Lincoln solved the impasse in 1863. With the Civil War in progress, he recommended and Congress authorized construction along a fifth route that would connect Omaha with Sacramento. Six years later, the joining of the eastward- and westward-building segments of this first transcontinental line near Salt Lake City launched changes in the West that would far exceed even those of the monumental gold rush twenty years earlier. Now a several-month wagon-road journey from Omaha to California had been reduced to a several-day train ride.

The results of the western railroad-building boom of the next twenty years can be seen in figures 12 and 13. By the 1890s five separate rail systems, shown in figure 11 (see page xxv), spanned the West, each with its own terminals on the Pacific coast. The building of these systems effectively completed the nation's trunk railroad network; with relatively minor changes it still remains in use today.

In addition to showing the largest cities of the American West in 1900, figure 11 also shows the railroad systems that served them. Not surprisingly, these were built through most of the important earlier wagon-road cities shown in figure 8 (see page xviii). At first these provided the only important sources of, and destinations for, passengers and freight throughout

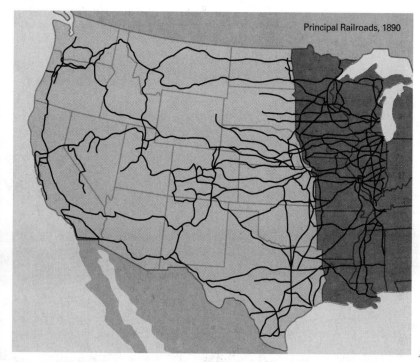

Principal Railroads, 1890

fig. 13

most of the vast interior West. One of the principal goals of the railroad builders was to change this pattern by establishing new towns, mostly agricultural trade centers, along their routes. To this end, the railroad's construction costs were mostly financed by selling bonds secured by wide bands of federally granted land that paralleled both sides of the privately built tracks.

The interior West's best agricultural land lay in the plains that make up its eastern third. Here land-hungry farmers and ranchers, anxious to push westward the frontier of continuous settlement shown in figure 8, provided ready purchasers for some of the federally granted railroad land. Only one obstacle stood in the way of this ideal scenario. The U.S. government had already assigned the Great Plains to the Plains Indians for "as long as the rivers flow." The horse-based culture of the Plains tribes gave them, in the words of one U.S. Army officer, "the world's best light cavalry." These warriors did not respond passively to broken promises.

The Indian Tragedy

By the 1870s two centuries of expanding Anglo agriculture had pushed the eastern Indians, mostly woodland tribes with relatively localized territories (see map, page 473), progressively westward. By 1860 much of the land of the interior West, previously valueless to Anglos, was dominated by either displaced Indians from farther east or by indigenous western tribes. The building of the western railroads through this region accelerated the previous cycles of Indian persecution and removal and precipitated the final brutal phase of Indian-Anglo conflict.

The nomadic Plains tribes of the western interior had long before mastered the taming of wild horses, the descendants of early Spanish animals that had escaped and multiplied on the western grasslands. These they used not only to hunt and kill buffalo, which provided them with shelter, clothing, and much of their food, but also for lightning fast raids to gather animals, food, and captives who became servants from their more sedentary neighbors. Skilled bowmen, they could shoot several arrows with deadly accuracy from fast-running horses while a mounted soldier or settler reloaded his single-shot musket or rifle. They had also became expert in the use of captured firearms.

Wild West folklore to the contrary, the Plains Indians seldom attacked pioneer wagon trains, mining camps, or even railroad builders unless seriously provoked. On the other hand, large-scale occupation of their hunting lands by buffalo-killing hunters and fence-building farmers threatened the economic basis of their culture, which they fought heroically to preserve. When the Civil War ended in 1865, these superb mounted warriors still controlled most of the western plains. The U.S. government then adopted a two-pronged strategy to confine the Plains tribes to reservations in Oklahoma and the Dakotas.

Large contingents of Civil War–seasoned troops were dispatched to transport the tribes to their assigned reservations. This led to open warfare that peaked in the late 1860s and early 1870s but continued sporadically in the northern plains through the 1880s. All told, this involved about a thousand battles and skirmishes in which 932 soldiers were killed and more than 1,000 wounded. The Indian dead and wounded were not counted.

In addition to pursuing the Indians themselves, the government encouraged market hunters to destroy the vast buffalo herds that sustained their culture. By 1880 all but a scattered handful of the millions of buffalo that once roamed the plains were gone. By then, too, most survivors of the Plains tribes had joined their more sedentary eastern neighbors on supervised reservations. These still occupy large blocks of the West, particularly in Arizona, Montana, and South Dakota (see figure 14).

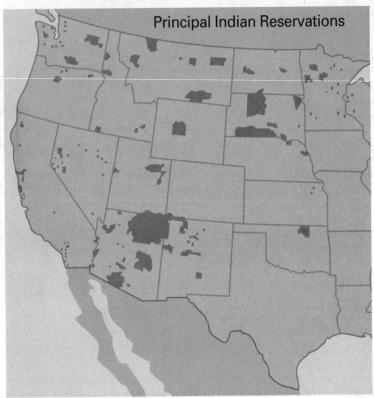

Principal Indian Reservations

fig. 14

Farmers and Ranchers Spread Westward

As the Indian threat receded in the 1870s, railroads began converting the interior West into a vast agricultural province whose long-term riches would far exceed its scattered bonanzas of gold and silver.

At its eastern edge was a six-hundred-mile-wide belt of grass-covered prairies and plains—most of present-day Texas, Oklahoma, Kansas, Nebraska, the Dakotas, and eastern Montana—where rainfall in most years is sufficient for dryland crops. The northern part of this huge area was ideal for growing wheat, among the most basic of human foods, while to the south high-value cotton thrived. Still farther west lay endless semiarid grassy basins and lush mountain meadows suitable for grazing valuable cattle or sheep, as well as mountain-fed river valleys suitable for irrigated crops. As new agriculturists, many recruited by the railroads themselves, moved into the region, they required new towns to serve as their marketing and trade centers. The

trackside sites for these were also conveniently provided by the railroads. The railroads normally platted and developed the most favorably located town sites themselves. Other sites were sold for third-party development.

Thus, in addition to serving the scattered prerailroad towns of the West, the transcontinental rail lines created countless new "railroad towns." These provided gathering points for the export of grains, cotton, and livestock and other products of farm and ranch as well as distribution centers for rail-transported tools, lumber, hardware, cloth, coffee, sugar, tobacco, lumber, and the myriad other imported items needed by the region's farmers and ranchers. More than half of the cities and towns included in this book either were founded by the railroads or were transformed from small villages when the tracks were built through or near them. In a few particularly favored locations—for example, at important railroad junctions or where the rail lines crossed the region's larger rivers, the towns grew to become regional centers for finance, trade, and government. Among the most important of these are **Dallas, Fort Worth, Lincoln, Oklahoma City, Omaha, Phoenix, Sioux Falls, Spokane,** and **Topeka.**

Railroads Reach the Pacific

The railroad-based spread of agriculture extended across the interior West to also include much of the Pacific coast states of California, Oregon, and Washington. Here, just as farther east, countless new rail-side towns grew up to serve new rail-based agricultural provinces. A new factor entered the scene, however, as the transcontinental railroads chose their final destinations on the Pacific Ocean shore. There each of the five principal western rail systems held enormous trump cards. Any location, among the hundreds of possibilities, that was picked as a site for an oceanside terminus was virtually guaranteed to become a nationally important metropolis. There, rail-transported passengers and freight would interface with oceangoing ships serving the entire Pacific Rim and beyond.

The western division of the first transcontinental line, the Central Pacific Railroad authorized by Congress in 1863, chose the small residential town of **Oakland,** located directly across the Bay from San Francisco, as its principal terminus. This had a large and undeveloped waterfront where the line's Big Four owners could build their own docks, warehouses, and terminal facilities. As a result, Oakland eventually became the principal industrial city of northern California.

The four additional transcontinental lines completed in the early 1880s located their principal oceanside terminals in **Portland** (Union Pacific), the small town of **Tacoma** in Washington (Northern Pacific), and **Los Angeles** (Atchison, Topeka, and Santa Fe and the Southern Pacific), a Big Four spin-off of the original Central Pacific. The final line was the Great Northern, completed in 1893 with **Seattle** as its terminus. All of these western rail-seaport junctions were to quickly prosper from their new roles. By 1900 Los Angeles, Portland, Seattle, and Oakland were four of the seven largest western cities. Oakland's neighbor San Francisco retained its long position as number one, while distant Denver and Omaha rounded out the top seven.

Victorian-Era Houses

By 1900 the West's railroad explosion had increased its population eightfold since 1860—from 1.4 million to just over 11 million inhabitants. As before, many of these new arrivals lived in simple folk houses that made little or no attempt to appear stylishly fashionable. With the exception of the adobe dwellings that still dominated the older Hispanic towns and villages, most postrailroad folk houses were no longer built of local materials but were constructed of inexpensive and convenient presized lumber delivered by the railroads from distant sawmills. Most used one of the half-dozen or so preferred shapes of the National Folk houses that spread westward across the country with the advancing railroad network.

Railroad-delivered lumber, trim, and hardware also made it much simpler to construct the elaborately detailed styled dwellings that dominated the Victorian era. These were built in six principal styles, which are illustrated, along with the museum houses of each style that are described in this book, in figure 16 (see pages xxx–xxxi), adapted from our *Field Guide to American Houses*. Most of the large cities shown in figure 11 retain at least scattered fragments of their postrailroad heritage of fine Victorian dwellings. Some of these, as well as a handful of smaller towns not shown in figure 11, also retain delightfully intact blocks or neighborhoods of Victorian houses that are summarized in the following section.

Victorian-Era Neighborhoods

As in the preceding Romantic era, little formal neighborhood planning, other than grid street platting, was done in the West during the Victorian era. The more imaginative neighborhood plans that were springing up in the northeastern and midwestern states during these years did not generally make an appearance in the western states until after 1900. The primary factor that affected neighborhood development during the Victorian era was new forms of urban transportation that first made possible commuter suburbs filled with large-lot single-family houses.

Cable Cars and Electric Trolleys

As long as urban transportation depended on animal-drawn vehicles, most residential neighborhoods were developed on flat or rolling sites with relatively small lots to minimize the distances to the town's commercial

Typical horse-drawn trolley

fig. 15

Victorian-Era Styles and Museum Houses

Second Empire

California
Sacramento: Governor's Mansion, 1877
Sacramento: Stanford Mansion, 1857 and 1871

Colorado
Trinidad: Bloom Mansion, 1882

Nebraska
Omaha vicinity: General Dodge House, 1869

Texas
San Antonio: Steves Homestead, 1876

Stick

California
SF Bay Area/Hayward: McConaghy House, 1886
SF Bay Area/Oakland: Cohen-Bray House, 1884

North Dakota
Bismarck: Former Governor's Mansion, 1884

Oregon
Astoria: Flavel House, 1885

South Dakota
Yankton: Cramer-Kenyon Heritage Home, 1886

Texas
Columbus: Seftenberg-Brandon House, ca. 1860s
    and 1890s

Victorian Stylistic Mixtures

California
Santa Barbara: Fernald House, 1862 and 1880

Kansas
Atchison: Evah C. Cray Historical House Museum, 1882
    and later
Leavenworth: Carroll Mansion, 1867 and 1882

Montana
Helena: Original Governor's Mansion, 1888

Shingle

California
South Lake Tahoe: Tallac Historic Site, 1894 and later
South Lake Tahoe vicinity: Ehrman Mansion, 1902

Montana
Kalispell: Conrad Mansion, 1895

Nebraska
Kearney: Frank House, 1889

Utah
Salt Lake City: McCune House, 1901

heart. This did not change with the widespread introduction of horse- or mule-drawn trolleys (figure 15) in the 1860s and 1870s, which had the advantage that one or two animals could move much heavier loads in cars moving along low-friction tracks. Some fifty thousand of these horse-drawn trolley lines were operating by 1880, according to Blake McKelvey's *The Urbanization of America*. This rapid growth was principally a response to the need to house more and more people near their work in the rapidly expanding industrial cities. Many such lines also operated in the larger towns of the West.

In 1872 the nation's first fully mechanized system for urban transport, Andrew Hallidie's cable cars, was installed in **San Francisco,** and soon its steepest, and previously inaccessible, hills were sprouting new developments of Victorian houses. Other cities around the country then began installing cable cars, among them **Portland,** Oregon, where they made the **Portland Heights** neighborhood accessible for development.

Folk Victorian

Queen Anne

Nebraska
Red Cloud: Willa Cather Childhood Home, 1879

Texas
Columbus: Lura, 1872 and 1890s
Fredericksburg vicinity: Sauer-Beckmann Farm, 1869
  and 1915
Johnson City: Lyndon Baines Johnson Boyhood Home,
  ca. 1900

Washington
Bellingham vicinity: Hovander Homestead, 1901

Arizona
Phoenix: Rosson House, 1895

California
Fresno: Meux Home, 1889
San Diego: Villa Montezuma, 1887
SF Bay Area/Hayward vicinity: Patterson House,
  1889
SF Bay Area/San Francisco: Haas-Lilienthal House,
  1886
SF Bay Area/San Jose: Winchester Mystery House,
  1884–1922
SF Bay Area/San Rafael: Falkirk, 1888

Richardsonian Romanesque

Colorado
Georgetown: Bowman-White House, 1892

Kansas
Atchison: Muchnic Art Gallery, 1888

Montana
Butte: W. A. Clark House, 1888

North Dakota
Fargo vicinity: Comstock House, 1882

Oklahoma
Oklahoma City: Harn Homestead, 1904

Oregon
Salem: Deepwood Estate, 1894

South Dakota
Sioux Falls: Pettigrew Home, 1889

Colorado
Denver: Molly Brown House, 1889
Pueblo: Rosemount, 1893

Texas
Beaumont vicinity: W. H. Stark House, 1894
Dallas: Wilson House, 1898

Texas
Galveston: Moody Mansion, 1895

fig. 16

Cable cars were, however, expensive and troublesome to operate and achieved their greatest success in areas too hilly for access by horse-drawn trolleys.

In 1881 Thomas Edison invented the electric motor, and in 1887 this was adapted by Frank Sprague, one of his early technicians, to power the first electric-trolley-car system, which was installed in Richmond, Virginia. Sprague trolleys eliminated many of the disadvantages of the cable car, and other lines soon followed (twenty-five had opened within a year). According to *The Ur-*

banization of America, by 1897 the nation had fifteen thousand miles of trolley lines owned by nine hundred companies, operating forty-eight thousand cars. Although these were concentrated in eastern and mid-western cities, the larger western cities also began installing electric trolleys. By 1900 trolley lines and "streetcar suburbs" had become the primary "planning" factor in the development of new urban neighborhoods throughout the country.

Most of the neighborhoods included in this book

were once served by one or more trolley lines. Among those where the trolley's influence is most obvious are **Mesa Junction** in Pueblo, Colorado, and **Waxahachie,** near Dallas, Texas, which have large-lot Victorian homes made accessible from the central city via trolley, and **Willamette Heights** in Portland, Oregon, which was made accessible by an early hillside trolley. Although San Francisco still has some of its early cable-car lines, we know of only one western city, **Fort Collins,** Colorado, that still has a historic trolley operating through its original, in this case mostly Eclectic-era, residential neighborhood.

Alameda, located on a narrow peninsula across the Bay from crowded San Francisco, was one of the West's earliest, pre-trolley commuting suburbs. Two steam-railroad lines ran the length of the peninsula, delivering passengers to fast steam ferries that crossed the Bay to San Francisco's downtown docks.

It is ironic that during the Victorian era, main streets with streetcar lines leading out from town were considered the most desirable homesites because of their easy accessibility to the commerical core. With the advent of automobiles, these main streets usually became heavily traveled thoroughfares or even highways. Their desirability plummeted, and the grand Victorian homes that lined many such streets have now disappeared almost without a trace. **Broadway** in **Galveston,** Texas, still the location of three particularly fine Victorian and Romantic-era museum houses, is a prime example. Once lined with grand homes, it is the main entry to the island from Houston, and the pressures of traffic and commercial uses have significantly eroded its original fine turn-of-the-century residential character. Fortunately, some nearby Galveston neighborhoods still contain Texas's finest concentration of Victorian houses. **Montana Avenue** in **El Paso** is a rare example of a main trolley-line street with most of its early houses still in-

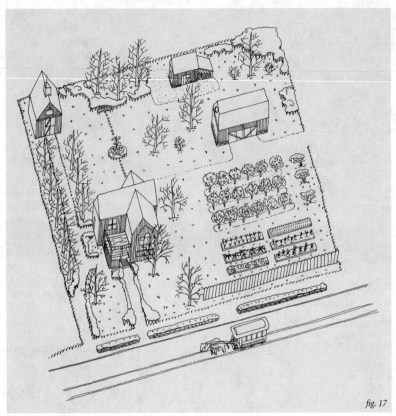

fig. 17

Typical Victorian mini-farm

tact; many of these date from the early Eclectic era, and a number have been converted to office use.

Large-Lot Suburbs

Most Victorian-era residential suburbs were "planned" only to the extent that they were often platted with oversize lots that provided enough space for a "mini-farm" (figure 17). This might include a chicken house, vegetable garden, orchard, horses for transport, and perhaps even a cow or two. Some lot buyers bought several—not uncommonly a single house (whether large or small) might occupy a half block or even a full block. Easy access provided by animal-drawn or electric trolleys made these widely spaced homes feasible. Later, as the mini-farms became less important and the land more valuable, the large lots and tracts were subdivided and infilled with younger houses. For this reason it is rare to find entire western streetscapes filled with Victorian-style homes except in crowded **San Francisco,** which was, by far, the West's largest Victorian city. Thus in **Eureka,** California, most of the Victorian homes on its hillside streets are scattered one or two to a block, rather than providing complete Victorian streetscapes.

Port Townsend, Washington, and **Astoria,** Oregon, display similar patterns of widely spaced Victorian houses. **Waxahachie,** Texas (near Dallas), provides an excellent example of Victorian homes scattered along early mule-car trolley lines.

Potwin Place, in **Topeka,** Kansas, is a rarity for the West—a planned neighborhood from 1885 (with broad sidewalks and street intersections featuring rounded mini-parks) filled mostly with Victorian-era homes. **Colorado Springs** was an early planned town with three long north–south boulevards, a device rarely used in the West before 1900. However, most of its Victorian blocks have had later apartment infill added, while the homes in the still-intact residential blocks date mostly from after 1900.

THE ECLECTIC-ERA WEST
(ca. 1890–1940)

In many respects the four-decade interval from 1900 to 1940 was merely an elaboration of the West's railroad-based agricultural revolution accomplished in the Victorian era. Figure 18 shows the similarity in the West's principal cities in 1900 and 1940, when the Second World War would soon interrupt the building of all but the most essential war-related housing. When large-scale civilian house construction resumed around 1950, the nation's taste for the prewar Eclectic styles had faded, and a new era dominated by simpler, "modern" designs took over. This change is treated only in passing in this book, whose principal theme is pre-1950 western neighborhoods and houses. A brief overview of some later housing fashions can be found in the final chapter of our *Field Guide to American Houses.*

The comparison of the principal western cities of 1940 with their 1900 counterparts shown in figure 18 illustrates the persistence of the railroad-based urban patterns established in the Victorian era. Fifteen of the twenty largest western cities in 1940 were also among the top twenty in 1900. Eleven of 1900's top twenty were still among the West's twenty-largest cities almost a century later in 1990. Between 1900 and 1940 the growth rate decreased in five of the smaller 1900 towns, and they dropped to lower rankings. Three of the newcomers to the 1940 list—**Oklahoma City, Tulsa,** and **Wichita**—played major roles in a new series of western bonanzas that began in **Beaumont** in 1901. These involved the discovery and development of rich deposits of oil and natural gas, which were to be the principal economic additions to the West's expanding agricultural wealth during the Eclectic-era decades.

Principal Western Cities in 1900 and 1940

(* = cities not on both lists)

	1900	Population	1940	Population	Top 20 rank of 1940 cities in 1990
1.	San Francisco	343,000	Los Angeles	1,500,000	1st
2.	Denver	134,000	San Francisco	635,000	11th
3.	Omaha	103,000	Houston	385,000	2nd
4.	Los Angeles	102,000	Seattle	368,000	9th
5.	Portland	90,000	Denver	322,000	11th
6.	Seattle	81,000	Portland	305,000	15th
7.	Oakland	67,000	Oakland	302,000	19th
8.	Salt Lake City	54,000	Dallas	295,000	4th
9.	San Antonio	53,000	San Antonio	254,000	6th
10.	Dallas	45,000	Omaha	222,000	
11.	Houston	45,000	*Oklahoma City	204,000	14th
12.	*Lincoln	40,000	*San Diego	203,000	3rd
13.	Tacoma	38,000	Fort Worth	178,000	13th
14.	*Galveston	38,000	Salt Lake City	150,000	
15.	Spokane	37,000	*Tulsa	142,000	
16.	*Topeka	34,000	Spokane	122,000	
17.	*Butte	30,000	*Wichita	115,000	
18.	Sacramento	29,000	Tacoma	109,000	
19.	*Pueblo	28,000	Sacramento	106,000	20th
20.	Fort Worth	27,000	*El Paso	97,000	10th

fig. 18

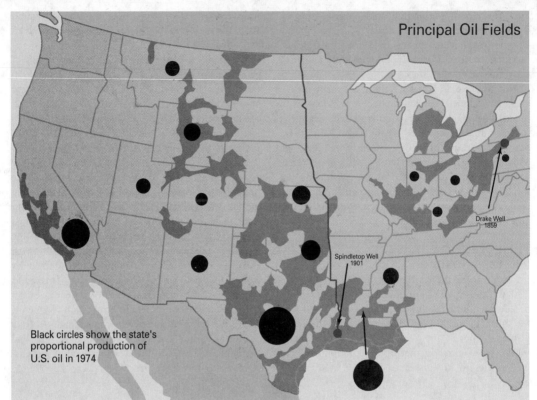

Principal Oil Fields

Drake Well
1859

Spindletop Well
1901

Black circles show the state's
proportional production of
U.S. oil in 1974

fig. 19

Black Gold

Several of the northeastern states had a Victorian-era oil boom after the original 1859 Drake Well discovery in western Pennsylvania (see figure 19). At that time the principal use for crude oil was not for power production in engines and for space heating, as in the twentieth century, but as a fuel for lighting building interiors. Refined into kerosene and burned in simple lamps, this new fuel quickly replaced more expensive candles, whale oil, and refined "coal oil" as the principal means of interior lighting throughout much of the world.

Most of this late-1800s oil came from shallow, low-volume wells that individually produced only a few barrels a day. Drilled in large numbers, these wells supported an entire industry of crude-oil production, refining, and kerosene marketing. All of this changed abruptly on January 10, 1901, when a wildcat well, drilled about seventy miles east of Houston near the small town of **Beaumont,** blew out with what was probably the most enormous flow of oil the world had ever seen. Known as Spindletop, this single well gushed more than 100,000 barrels of oil a *day,* more than the monthly or even yearly production of most of all the oil *fields* of that era.

Spindletop launched many decades of oil booms in the western states as prodigious new discoveries spread from coastal Texas and Louisiana northward into the midcontinent fields of Oklahoma and Kansas and farther north and westward into the fabled Permian Basin of western Texas and adjacent New Mexico, and beyond to southern California (see figure 19).

Many new towns sprang up to serve the West's burgeoning petroleum industry, but most of these, like the

Entry gates to the Munger Place development,
1905, Dallas, Texas

fig. 20

mining camps that had preceded them, faded in size and importance as the nearby oil was depleted and the boom moved elsewhere. A few, like **Amarillo** and **Tulsa,** grew to become regional financial and trade centers. In addition, some of the older cities of the West took on new, petroleum-related functions. **Houston** became not only a refining center, but also a principal supplier of oil-drilling equipment and services, a role in which it is today the world leader. **Dallas** banks were among the first to make loans for developing new oil discoveries, and the city became a financial center for the new industry, while nearby **Fort Worth** was an early refining, distribution, and supply center for fields in its region, as were **Denver, Oklahoma City, Long Beach,** and **Wichita.** This oil-based prosperity is reflected in each city by unusually fine Eclectic-era houses and neighborhoods from the 1920 to 1940 period.

Eclectic-Era Houses

Between 1900 and 1940 the population of the western states more than doubled, from 11 million to 23 million. Much of this growth took place in new "streetcar suburbs" added to the region's already-established towns and cities. What the Eclectic-era West lacks in newly founded urban centers, it more than makes up for in the number and diversity of its fine suburban neighborhoods and houses, which mostly reflect the region's agriculture- and oil-based prosperity of the 1900 to 1929 period before the Great Depression of the 1930s brought most new building to a halt. Exceptions occur mostly in cities that benefited from recently discovered oil fields, among them Dallas, Tulsa, and Los Angles; the latter's movie industry also boomed during the 1930s because of the then-recent perfection of "talking" motion pictures.

Throughout the nation the Eclectic era saw the country's previous preference for only about a half-dozen fashionable housing styles per era bloom into a veritable smorgasbord of stylistic choices for the design of new houses. These styles are summarized, along with the museum houses of each style treated in this book, in figure 22 (see pages xxxvi–xxxvii), which is adapted from our *Field Guide to American Houses.*

Eclectic-Era Neighborhoods

By about 1900 some western neighborhoods began to be laid out with street plans that went beyond traditional grids of square or rectangular blocks. These more advanced neighborhood-planning systems, which had been introduced in the northeastern states several decades earlier, were of two principal types— formal City Beautiful designs, which emphasized one or more grand boulevards with landscaped medians, and informal, Olmstedian designs, whose curved streets and naturalistic landscaping created a "house in the country" atmosphere. As automobiles began replacing trolley lines for urban transport of affluent residents, two other types of planned neighborhoods with curving streets also became common. On relatively flat sites, symmetrical, "geometric" street patterns, incorporating both straight and curving streets, were sometimes used to avoid the monotony of the traditional grid. The automobile also made possible the development of steeper hillsides with "contour" street plans, determined largely by the local topography.

All of these types of upscale "planned neighborhoods" were commonly governed by protective covenants (sometimes called deed restrictions) that typically required their houses to be built with uniform setbacks from the street, generous side yards, open front lawns without fences, and streetside trees, all intended to give the neighborhood a pleasing visual unity. Additional requirements might include minimum building costs for each lot, which generally served to group a neighborhood's most expensive homes along certain streets and blocks. Developers also often added amenities like

Residential boulevard in the Munger Place development, 1905, Dallas, Texas

fig. 21

Eclectic-Era Styles and Museum Houses

ANGLO-AMERICAN AND ENGLISH PERIOD HOUSES

Neoclassical

Colonial Revival

California
SF Bay Area/Alameda: Meyers
House, 1897
SF Bay Area/Palo Alto vicinity:
Filoli, 1917

Colorado
Boulder: Harbeck-Bergheim House,
1900

South Dakota
Spearfish: Hatchery Superintendent's
House, 1905

Tudor

California
LA Area/Los Angeles: Greystone,
1928
Nevada City vicinity: Bourn Cottage,
1897
SF Bay Area/San Jose vicinity:
Ainsley House, 1925

Colorado
Colorado Springs vicinity: Glen
Eyrie, 1904

Washington
Spokane: Campbell House, 1898
Spokane: Glover Mansion, 1888

Wyoming
Sheridan: Trail End, 1913

California
SF Bay Area/Oakland vicinity:
Dunsmuir,1899

Kansas
Abilene: Seelye Mansion, 1905

Montana
Hamilton: Daly Mansion, 1910

Nebraska
Nebraska City: Arbor Lodge, 1903
and earlier

Oklahoma
Bartlesville: Frank Phillips Home,
1909 and 1931
Oklahoma City: Hefner House,1917
Tulsa: Gilcrease Home, 1914

Texas
Amarillo: Harrington House, 1914
Beaumont: McFaddin-Ward House,
1906
Fort Worth: Thistle Hill, 1903

FRENCH PERIOD HOUSES

Chateauesque

California
Fresno: Kearney Mansion, 1903
LA Area/Redlands: Kimberly
Crest, 1897

Montana
Billings: Moss Mansion, 1903
Butte: C. W. Clark House, 1899

Oklahoma
Oklahoma City: Overholser
Mansion, 1904

Texas
Austin: Littlefield House, 1894
Fort Worth: Eddleman-
McFarland House, 1899
Galveston: Bishop's Palace,
1893

Utah
Salt Lake City: Utah Governor's
Mansion, 1902

Beaux Arts

California
LA Area/Pasadena: The Huntington,
1910

French Eclectic

California
LA Area/Pasadena: Cravens
House, 1929

Kansas
Topeka: Cedar Crest, 1928

Oregon
Portland: Pittock Mansion,
1914

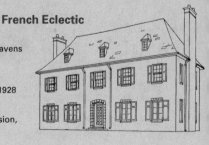

MEDITERRANEAN PERIOD HOUSES

Italian Renaissance

California
LA Area/Los Angeles: Virginia Robinson Home, 1911
LA Area/Pasadena: Fenyes Mansion, 1905
LA Area/Pasadena: Tournament House, 1914
SF Bay Area/San Jose vicinity: Villa Montalvo, 1912

Oklahoma
Ponca City: First Marland Home, 1916
Ponca City: Marland Mansion, 1928
Tulsa: Philbrook, 1927
Tulsa: Travis Home, 1921

Monterey

California
LA Area/Los Angeles: Will Rogers Home, 1928

Mission

Arizona
Tucson: Corbett House, 1907

California
LA Area/Los Angeles: Wattles House, 1907

Colorado
Colorado Springs: Orchard House, 1907

Other Eclectic-Era Houses

California
South Lake Tahoe: Tallac Historic Site, 1894 and later
South Lake Tahoe vicinity: Vikingsholm, 1929

Oklahoma
Bartlesville vicinity: Frank Phillips Lodge, 1927
Tulsa: Mackey House, 1926

Texas
Houston: Bayou Bend, 1928

Washington
Port Townsend: Commanding Officer's House, 1904
Spokane: Patsy Clark Mansion, 1897

Pueblo Revival

New Mexico
Taos: Fechin Home, 1927–1933
Taos: Luhan House, 1922 and earlier

Spanish Eclectic

Arizona
Phoenix: Wrigley Mansion, 1930

California
LA Area/City of Industry: La Casa Nueva, 1927
LA Area/Malibu: Adamson House, 1930
LA Area/Santa Clarita: William S. Hart House, 1927
San Simeon: Hearst Castle, 1919–1947
Santa Barbara: Casa del Herrero, 1925

Texas
Dallas: De Golyer House, 1939
San Antonio: McNay Art Museum, 1928

MODERN HOUSES

Prairie

Kansas
Wichita: Allen-Lambe House, 1918

Other Modern Houses

California
LA Area/City of Industry vicinity: Clarke Mansion, 1921
LA Area/Los Angeles: Hollyhock House, 1921

International

California
LA Area/Los Angeles: Schindler Home and Studio, 1922

Craftsman

Arizona
Flagstaff: Riordan Mansion, 1904

California
LA Area/Pasadena: Gamble House, 1908
San Diego: Marston House, 1905
Ukiah: Sun House, 1911

Washington
Bellingham: Roeder Home, 1908

fig. 22

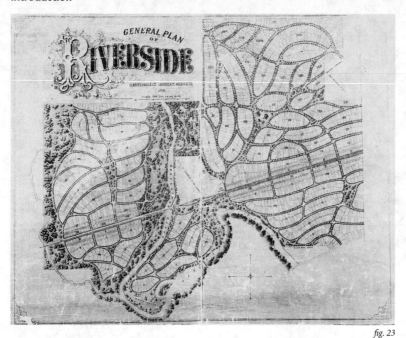

Olmsted, Vaux & Company
plan for Riverside, Illinois,
1869

fig. 23

alleys, underground or rear-yard utilities, streetlights, and such. Handsome entry gates (figure 20) were a favored way of announcing that you had arrived at one of these "special" neighborhoods.

City Beautiful Plans

Divided residential streets with landscaped medians (usually called either boulevards or parkways; see figure 21) became quite popular after 1900 and are found in most of the larger western cities. Inspired by the axial Beaux Arts planning of the 1893 World's Columbian Exposition in Chicago, these provided a relatively affordable way of introducing drama into a neighborhood, because they could be easily adapted to the grid street system already in use in most towns. **Denver** and **Colorado Springs** have the most extensive use of such boulevards in the West. In Colorado Springs, these were introduced by the original founder of the town, who set out to design a model community from its inception in 1871, making it an extraordinarily early use of planning and of boulevards. Denver's many boulevards (called parkways there) may have been inspired by Denverites' familiarity with the Colorado Springs example. Whatever the reason, an extensive series of parkways were suggested by planner George Kessler in his 1907 Parks and Parkways Plan for the city, most of which, like the **Seventh Avenue Parkway,** were actually built. **Swiss Avenue** in Dallas, Texas, is another example planned at about the same time. Some boulevards were also principally designed to accommodate a trolley or railroad.

West Mountain Avenue in Fort Collins, Colorado, is an example where the trolley line still remains; **Huntington Boulevard** in Fresno, California, has had the original tracks removed and replaced with median plantings.

Olmstedian Plans

Naturalistic Olmstedian plans required relatively large tracts of land to achieve their curving-street, rural-type atmosphere and thus were usually full-scale suburban villages. It is important to note that even though many of these were distinctly suburban in the early 1900s, today most are close-in neighborhoods surrounded by later city growth. In 1871 the pioneering landscape designer Frederick Law Olmsted described suburbs as "detached dwellings with sylvan settings yet supplied with a considerable share of urban convenience." Urban historian Robert Fishman, in his 1987 work *Bourgeois Utopias,* elaborates further: "The distinguishing feature of classic suburbs was not such common institutions as churches or country clubs, but the landscape. The pattern of tree shaded streets, broad open lawns, substantial houses set back from the sidewalk with a pattern of propriety, family life, and union with nature that represents the culmination of suburban style." Cynthia Girling and Kenneth Helphand, in their innovative 1994 book *Yard, Street, Park,* describe suburbs as "on the one hand, nostalgic and pastoral in reflecting a desire for country living and contact with nature, and, on the other hand, profoundly modern in their dependency on the technologies of transportation, electricity, and communications that enabled the new patterns and ways of life to emerge."

The nation's first planned naturalistic suburbs were apparently Glendale, Ohio, which opened near Cincinnati in 1851, and Llewellyn Park, New Jersey, developed six years later near New York City. The first of Olmsted's many designs was for Riverside, Illinois, a Chicago suburb that opened in 1869. All three of these projects were true suburban towns built at a distance of several miles from the cities they were designed to serve and were linked to them by railroads. Olmsted's creative plan for Riverside was widely publicized, and ultimately its smoothly curving streets and ribbons of parkland (figure 23) were imitated in hundreds of later developments, both large and small. The curving streets were most readily adapted to gently rolling land, but could also be used on flat sites.

The Olmstedian **Oak Knoll** neighborhood in Pasadena, California, laid out in 1886, is the earliest *designed* example in this book—most of its houses were not actually built, however, until after 1900. Other examples of Olmstedian "suburbs" include **Mount Baker** in Seattle, Washington; **St. Francis Wood** in San Francisco; **Beverly Hills** in Los Angeles; **Westboro** in Topeka, Kansas; **Happy Hollow** and **Fairacres** in Omaha, Nebraska; **Sheridan Place** in Lincoln, Nebraska; **Old Highland Park, Volk Estates, Lakewood,**

Plan of the El Encanto subdivision, 1928, Tucson, Arizona

fig. 24

and **Hollywood Heights** in Dallas; **River Oaks** in Houston; **Olmos Park** in San Antonio, Texas; and **Laurelhurst** in Portland, Oregon.

Geometric Plans

Subdivisions with streets curved into symmetrical geometric shapes were favored by a few developers, particularly during the 1910s and 1920s. These often combine straight and curved streets and usually have a very distinctive bull's-eye look on maps (figure 24). They are fun to explore, although frequently the planning proves more impressive than the individual houses. Two examples are included in this book—**El Encanto** in Tucson, Arizona, and **Encanto-Palmcroft** in Phoenix, Arizona.

Contour Plans

The widespread use of private automobiles by about 1920 made it possible to build homes on steep and previously inaccessible hillside sites. To reach these, irregularly curving streets dictated by the contours of the steep sites were normally required. The **Hillside Sampler** route in Los Angeles, California, traverses several such neighborhoods, among them the upper reaches of **Bel Air, Hollywood Hills** north of West Hollywood, and Glendower Drive and other streets in **Los Feliz.** Because the suggested route of the Sampler was planned to allow easy access, it does not generally venture up into the higher reaches of the hills north of the Los Angeles Basin—places where the curves are tortuous, the roads wickedly narrow, the drops steep, and street signs fairly worthless because of the odd angles. When exploring an area where roads go where they must in order to fit with the topography, one often must simply head either uphill or downhill at every turn. One positive aspect of exploring the hills north of Los Angeles is that (as long as you have not reached Mulholland Drive at the mountain crest) after working your way uphill, if you then go downhill at every turn, you will eventually find your way back to the main spine of the Sampler route. This approach to navigation generally works better than map reading in serious contour-plan neighborhoods.

Zoning

Planned neighborhoods in which the developers put "protective covenants" in their deeds to ensure visual and functional unity first became popular in the West about 1900. These proved so successful that some city and state governments began to wonder if municipalities could successfully *legislate* such protection from intrusions for all of their neighborhoods. The idea evolved remarkably quickly. Protective covenants had commonly relied on individual home owners to enforce them (in some cases an official home owners' group was established for this purpose). This meant that when someone ignored a covenant, his neighbors had the expense of taking him to court to enforce compliance. Lower-income neighborhoods were less often protected by such covenants and, even when they were, found it harder to enforce such restrictions because of the cost involved. If zoning was adopted by municipal law, the burden of enforcing compliance would fall to the city. Thus, at least in theory, the same protections would be provided to all of the citizens.

Two initial steps in this direction were taken when Boston imposed height restrictions in 1904 to 1905 and Los Angeles divided itself into residential and industrial sections in 1909. Then in 1914, the New York state legislature adopted a statute that made it legal for towns in New York State to provide more comprehensive restrictions on development within their boundaries. In 1916 New York City became the first city in the country to adopt a zoning code. The idea of zoning legislation spread quickly, and by 1922 twenty states had already adopted statutes allowing their cities to make and enforce zoning restrictions; fifty cities had already taken advantage of this right. By 1926 twenty-three more state legislatures passed zoning statutes, and cities across the country were rushing to adopt zoning codes for their towns. In that year the United States Supreme Court upheld the legality of such efforts in a landmark decision.

Today, zoning laws are almost ubiquitous in American cities, and few people realize how recent an innovation these are (Houston remains one of the few large cities that does not have a zoning code; protective deed covenants remain its principal means of controlling de-velopment). While some recent critics have rhapsodized about the wonderful years when everyone "agreed" what a city should look like, this was before the realities of the industrial revolution rapidly changed the kinds of buildings, the scale of buildings, and the kinds of transportation that make up a city. The industrial revolution brought large factories to cities, made possible new structural systems and elevators that allowed high-rise buildings, produced railroads that cut the downtowns of many cities into sections, and then introduced, with the twentieth-century popularity of automobiles, an entirely new set of problems. All of this change evolved rapidly beginning about 1850 and culminated with the proliferation of the automobile in the 1910s. The old "agreement of how cities should look" was swept aside during these sixty years of massive change. No wonder that the ability to regulate the location of all of these new uses through zoning ordinances swept the country in just ten short years.

An ironic side effect of the adoption of zoning laws is that major real estate interests quickly became very active in city government, either in supporting development-oriented candidates or serving on city councils themselves. Thus, in many cases, enforcement of existing zoning restrictions was made even more difficult for neighborhoods than it had been before with protective covenants.

A second, and even more far-reaching, side effect is that the zoning regulations themselves have today evolved in ways that virtually legislate urban sprawl, thus creating new problems of the same magnitude as those they were intended to solve. It is the rewriting of these zoning codes that recent "Neotraditional" urban planners have emphasized as an important first step in preventing future sprawl.

A Field Guide to America's Historic Neighborhoods and Museum Houses

Arizona

FLAGSTAFF

FOUNDED 1876
Population Growth:
1900 1,300
1940 5,000
1990 46,000

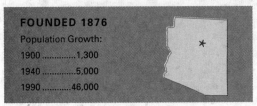

Situated at an altitude of 6,900 feet on the high, pine-forested plateaus of northern Arizona, Flagstaff was a tiny village serving scattered trappers and ranchers until the Atchison, Topeka, and Santa Fe Railroad arrived in 1882 en route to California. The railroad facilitated Flagstaff's emergence as a center for processing and shipping lumber from northern Arizona's vast pine forests. Despite its newfound importance, Flagstaff remained a small town until the 1950s; since then it has grown exponentially, with its original lumber-based economy now mostly replaced by tourism, retirees, federal research facilities, and Northern Arizona University. The town's principal historic architectural attraction is a rare, large-scale museum house in the early Craftsman style.

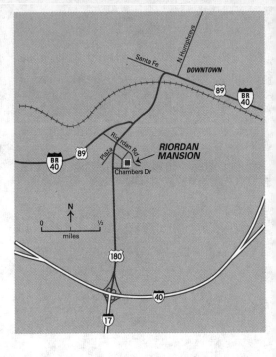

Riordan Mansion, 1904

1300 Riordan Ranch Street, Riordan State Historic Park; 520-779-4395;
Charles Whittlesey, Albuquerque, architect.

This unusual dual dwelling is two separate houses joined together by a large and rustic one-story Rendezvous Room, much like Siamese twins. The homes were jointly commissioned by two brothers—Timothy Riordan (1858–1946) and Michael Riordan (1865–1930)—whose wives were also sisters (Caroline Metz,

who married Timothy in 1889, and Elizabeth Metz, who married Michael three years later). In 1903 the siblings began this unique thirteen-thousand-square-foot double house for their large families.

As architect they chose Charles F. Whittlesey, then also chief architect for the Santa Fe Railroad. Whittlesey was best known for designing the dramatically rustic El Tovar Hotel at the nearby Grand Canyon, which was under construction from 1902 until 1905. This was

Riordan Mansion, photographed in 1925

Riordan Mansion

an early and sophisticated interpretation of the naturalistic log dwellings being advocated for "summer camp or permanent country home" by the furniture maker and writer Gustav Stickley (1858–1942) in his influential *Craftsman* magazine, which began publication in 1901. Many of the dwellings that followed these precepts were lodges in New York's Adirondack Mountains, one of the locations that Stickley mentioned as being particularly appropriate for his log homes. During the next decade Stickley's writings were to become a principal vehicle for popularizing both Craftsman-style houses as well as the clean-lined, handcrafted furniture Stickley produced in his Syracuse, New York, workshops (furniture designs that today are often popularly referred to as "Mission style"—see "Corbett House," page 22). Architect Whittlesey, in his rustic designs for the Santa Fe Railroad's western stations and hotels, was a strong advocate of this emerging design trend. His Riordan house is thus an early precursor of the countless Craftsman dwellings that were soon to dominate entire neighborhoods throughout the country.

The style was particularly appropriate to the forested Flagstaff area—as well as for the Riordan brothers, who, with a third older brother, had built a pioneering lumber business there in the 1880s. Thus, both the Riordans and their architect were experts at building with wood—Whittlesey in designing rustic wooden structures, the brothers in supplying quality raw materials. The outside cuts from huge logs were used to give the house a loglike wood cladding in places. Totem faces were carved into the ends of some protruding logs. Entire massive timbers were used to support the roof and were left exposed. Following Stickley's precepts, stonework was used to great effect in the entrances to each home and for the wall that surrounds a central garden. These exterior details were brought inside in the intriguingly named Rendezvous Room, a grand

space that connects the two homes and features the same exposed roof timbers and stonework in the fireplace and log walls. The remainder of each house has more typical finishes, such as paint, wallpaper, and fabric over plaster.

Stickley's greatest strengths were interior design and furnishings; in the Riordan homes, his influence was profound. The Riordan brothers have been credited with contributing many of the ideas for their houses, and they must have been very up-to-date with this avant-garde design movement—Stickley's magazine began publishing just as the Riordans were beginning to build.

Only Timothy's side of the structure and the connecting Rendezvous Room are currently open to visitors. But these abundantly document the Riordans' innovative interiors, which include many rare pieces of Stickley-built furniture. The living room also doubles as a library, a favorite Stickley concept. Rather than the traditional sofa, a large "swinging couch" (a glorified porch swing) playfully hangs from the ceiling in the middle of the living room. (One could swing facing the fireplace in the winter and rehang the swing to face the entry garden in the summer.) The windows in the Rendezvous Room have huge early photographic images of Arizona sandwiched between twin sheets of glass, created by developing a photographic image with emulsion directly on one side of a glass pane and then protecting the exposed fragile emulsion with a second pane of glass. Examples of this delicate technique are extremely rare.

Most of the light fixtures and sconces are original to the house, and many have Tiffany-style glass, as do the fine tulip-design transom windows. Fireplaces are of differing design and materials, but most of their surrounds were covered with a mixture of cement and pebblelike pieces of local volcanic ash. Stickleyesque built-in cabinetry is found throughout. Among the most striking Stickley-made furnishings are a number of handcrafted chairs inlaid with pewter, copper, and brass. (These were actually designed by architect Harvey Ellis during his tenure at the Stickley studio.)

Only the Riordans and their descendants ever occupied the houses. They all respected the innovative early interiors and made relatively few changes over the years. In 1980 the family generously gave the house and furnishings to the Arizona State Parks, a state agency that plans to restore and open the second Riordan home by the year 2000. The Riordan homes are important both as rare and unique expressions of the American Arts and Crafts movement and as a pristine interpretation of the early-twentieth-century lifestyles of the Riordan families.

GANADO

FOUNDED CA. 1870

Population Growth:

1900 ....ca. 100

1940 200

1990 3,400

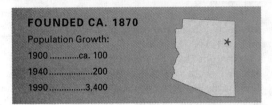

Ganado is one of several dozen small towns that have grown up since the 1880s to serve the almost 170,000 occupants of the vast Navajo Nation, the country's largest reservation, which covers 15 million acres of northeastern Arizona and adjacent New Mexico and Utah. Most of the Navajo Nation's small towns grew up around early Anglo-managed trading posts where the rural Indians brought their cash crops—mostly wool and lambs from herds of sheep they tended in grassy stream bottoms or wooded mesas—which were exchanged for coffee, flour, sugar, cloth, hardware, and a host of other goods brought to the posts by wagon trains from the rail-junction town of Gallup, New Mexico. Ganado was such a town, which, unlike most of the others, still retains its early trading post as a rare and important survivor from the past.

The Navajo (who arrived about five hundred years ago) are relative newcomers to this area, which has been inhabited for over two thousand years by the ancestral Puebloans and their descendants, who today form such communal tribes as the Hopi of Arizona and the Pueblo of New Mexico. These two tribes are accomplished agriculturists who long lived in compact communal dwellings called pueblos (the Spanish word for "town"), from which they walked to their nearby fields. The Navajo, in contrast, are descendants of nomadic hunting tribes from western Canada and the Great Plains. Although they soon learned agriculture and other customs from their pueblo-dwelling neighbors, the Navajo never accepted communal living, preferring instead to dwell in isolated family units housed in single-room hexagonal or octagonal structures called hogans. These were usually built with walls of logs or mud-covered sticks and were widely scattered across the landscape in much the same way as typical Anglo farmhouses. Many Navajo still live in such dispersed dwellings, with the traditional hogans situated side by side with Anglo-style houses. One Navajo hogan survives on the Hubbell Trading Post, along with the home of trader John Hubbell.

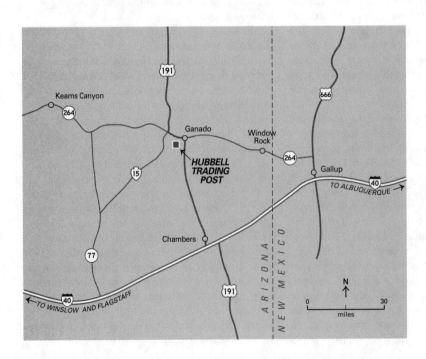

Hubbell Trading Post National Historic Site, early 1870s and later, and Hubbell Home, 1902

Arizona Highway 264, one mile west of Ganado; 520-755-3475.

This unique complex of folk buildings centers around a stone-walled trading-post building that began as a two-room structure in 1883 and was later expanded. Adjacent is an adobe home built in 1901 by the post's longtime owner, John Lorenzo Hubbell (1853–1930). Among the many outbuildings are an 1897 stone barn and a 1934 stone guest house built in the form of a hexagonal Navajo hogan.

Hubbell's father was a Connecticut Yankee soldier in the 1846 to 1848 Mexican War, who, finding himself stationed in remote New Mexico, fell in love with both the romantic countryside and an aristocratic Hispanic girl whose grandfather was a former governor of that Mexican province. The young couple made their home near Albuquerque, where their bicultural son John Lorenzo, the future Navajo trader, was educated in both Spanish and English. As a teenager, Lorenzo began learning the complex Navajo language, as well as the business of frontier trading, by helping his father deliver hay for the horses and mules at the army's Fort Wingate, 125 miles west of Albuquerque in the Navajo country. Soon the energetic and now-trilingual young man found himself in demand as an assistant to the first Anglo merchants setting up trading posts on the reservation. In 1878, at age twenty-five, Hubbell purchased one of these early trading posts, now the Ganado complex, which was to become the focal point of his fifty-year career as adviser, friend, and business partner to the Navajo people. At their best, exemplified by Hubbell, Anglo Indian traders went far beyond the usual economic aspects of trade. They also acted as in-terpreters and teachers for the Indians and helped them to understand and profit from the Anglo culture that was being forced on them. Don Lorenzo, as Hubbell was universally called, went still farther by being among the first to deeply appreciate and actively encourage the high-value Navajo crafts of weaving, basketmaking, and silversmithing, skills the Indians first learned from the early Spanish colonists. Hubbell insisted on high standards of workmanship and helped the Indians understand which traditional designs and products would bring premium prices from Anglo buyers and thus maximum rewards to the highly skilled craftsmen.

Because most Navajo did not live in villages, the trading posts also became information centers—places to learn the latest news about friends and, perhaps, new requirements being issued from the Office of Indian Affairs. Money rarely changed hands, although some traders issued tin currency for local use. More commonly, the Indians traded their wool, sheep, and handicrafts directly for foodstuffs and other necessities. A typical trade might take two or three days to conclude.

These were times of social as well as economic interaction. Some posts even provided traditional hogans to house visiting customers (the Hubbell post had several, one of which still survives). Competition among traders was keen, and various attractions were added to help keep clients using a post. Small, free courtesies, like snacks and tobacco, were common. Special events were also popular, particularly "chicken pulls," the Navajo equivalent of a rodeo.

Hubbell was among the first traders to adopt such public relations techniques, but, far more important, his success as a trader was built on the fairness and honesty of his dealings and on the fondness and respect he showed to his Navajo clients. As a measure of Hubbell's ultimate success, the National Park Service's guide to the site notes that "he built a trading empire that in-

Trading post buildings from Hubbell Hill, 1904

cluded stage and freight lines as well as several trading posts. At various times he and his two sons, either together or separately, owned 24 trading posts, a wholesale house in Winslow, and other business and ranch properties. Beyond question he was the foremost Navajo trader of his time." In addition to his home at Ganado, Hubbell also owned urban residences in Albuquerque, Gallup, and his wife Lina's small hometown of St. Johns, Arizona. These served as bases not only for the purchase and sale of his trading goods, but also for educating his four children during their school-age years.

Don Lorenzo always spent much of the year supervising the Ganado post, and here the entire family spent its summers together. By 1901 the family had outgrown the post's rustic 1870s folk dwelling, and Don Lorenzo began to build a much larger new home. The result was a dwelling of traditional Hispanic design with thick adobe walls and a roof supported by massive timbers called vigas. (These were cut in a wooded canyon ten miles away and hauled, with great difficulty, by wagons across rocky arroyos and steep canyon slopes.) Completed in early 1902, the house centers around a traditional Hispanic zaguan, a large, all-purpose living room. Flanking the zaguan are two bedrooms on one side and three on the other. The furnishings and extraordinary artwork mostly date from the pre-1920 years of the house's occupancy. The furniture is of simple Anglo design, which provides an appropriately unobtrusive background for the Hubbells' extensive collection of art and Navajo craftsmanship—countless superb baskets adorn the ceiling and handsome rugs cover the floor. On the walls hang paintings and drawings of Indian subjects by some of the nation's finest early-twentieth-century artists, many of whom Hubbell invited to use his home as their studio. Among these were Eldridge Ayer Burbank, whose numerous red Conté crayon sketches capture the profiles of tribe members. In some places these sketches are hung so densely that they resemble fine wallpaper.

After Hubbell's death in 1930, his son and daughter-in-law continued to manage the trading post and, fully aware of its unique importance, carefully preserved its historic buildings and interiors. In 1965 the daughter-in-law, Dorothy Hubbell, sold the site to the National Park Service. The NPS still operates the post, which today continues to specialize in the sale of rare and valuable Navajo rugs, baskets, and silver jewelry. The historic Hubbell home can be visited on regular tours conducted by National Park Service rangers. This unusually important complex provides a time-warp glimpse at a period in which many Navajo artisans were producing and trading high-quality goods with a compassionate Anglo-Hispanic pioneer.

Hopi Indian Reservation

Begins 30 miles west of Ganado on Arizona Highway 264; visitor information provided at the Hopi Cultural Center in Second Mesa, about sixty miles west of Ganado on the same highway; 520-734-6650.

An instructive contrast between Navajo lifestyles and those of their pueblo-dwelling predecessors can be seen in the nearby Hopi Indian Reservation, which is surrounded by Navajo lands. Although many of the Hopi now live in modern villages with typical Anglo houses, several traditional villages with early stone-walled pueblo dwellings still survive on dramatic mesa-top settings. One of these, **Old Oraibi,** was founded about A.D. 1150 and is among the oldest continuously inhabited towns in the United States. Information on visiting these sites can be obtained at the Cultural Center. Also in the region are numerous archaeological sites featuring the prehistoric stone pueblo dwellings of the ancient Puebloans, the Hopi's ancestors, who once dominated the region. Outstanding among these are **Canyon de Chelly National Monument** (520-674-5436) and **Navajo National Monument** (520-672-2366). Visits to parts of these sites are limited, with difficult access; advance information and planning are advised.

PHOENIX

FOUNDED 1867

Population Growth:

1900 6,000

1940 65,000

1990 983,000

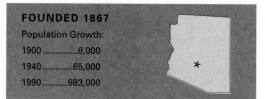

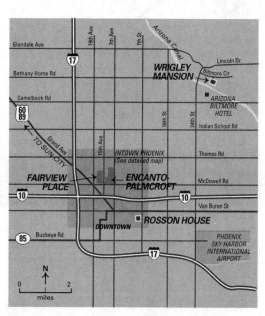

Phoenix, in 1990 the nation's ninth-largest city, is the youngest of America's great urban centers. Little more than a village in 1900, as recently as 1950 Phoenix's population of slightly more than 100,000 ranked it only sixty-sixth in size among the nation's cities.

Most of Phoenix's early growth was tied to the exceptional agricultural potential of the surrounding Salt River Valley—an unlikely name for a waterway that was to support some of the nation's richest farmlands. Shortly after Arizona gained territorial status in 1863 (see also "Prescott," page 15), early Anglo settlers were impressed by the valley's complex network of abandoned irrigation canals constructed by a long-vanished Indian culture known as the Hohokam (People Who Went Away), which dominated south-central Arizona between about A.D. 700 and 1400. Seeking to emulate these earlier residents, the Anglo settlers rebuilt some of the old irrigation canals, constructed larger new ones, and began raising crops to supply the mining camps and military forts that were springing up in the new territory. Soon several small trading centers grew up in the Salt River Valley. One of these, destined to ultimately dominate both the valley and all of Arizona, was named for the mythical phoenix bird, which, like the Hohokam people's agriculture, sprang up from the ashes to begin life anew after five hundred years.

Salt River Valley agriculture, now enhanced by a vast network of modern dams and canals, is still important to the region's economy but has been overshadowed since 1950 by an enormous Sunbelt boom based on light industry, tourism, and retirees—fifty thousand of whom have made nearby Sun City into one of the nation's premier retirement communities.

Not surprisingly, in view of its relative youth and recent growth, Phoenix is short on historic architecture. A fine Victorian museum house survives from the 1890s, and Eclectic-era high points include a geometric plan neighborhood and a fine Spanish Eclectic home, one of the nation's relatively few examples of that style that are open to the public. Conversely, the recent growth that gives Phoenix relatively few older landmarks also makes it an exceptional laboratory for viewing fundamental changes that have taken place in the planning and layout of American neighborhoods from 1920 to the 1970s.

Neighborhood Planning in Phoenix

A quick look at a map of Phoenix (see above) shows that the entire city has its major streets running due north–south or east–west at regular one-mile intervals. Such planning is a very visible legacy of the land-survey policies instituted by the federal government in the 1780s for developing the nation's sparsely populated western lands. Beginning with Ohio, federal agents carefully surveyed areas suitable for new settlement into a grid of one-square-mile blocks called sections, each of which contained 640 acres. Most of the surveyed sections were then ultimately sold or granted by the government to private owners for farming, ranching, and town-site development. The government also encouraged building public roads along the lines separating adjacent sections. Secondary roads were often found on the half-mile spacing that divided a full section into quarter sections. It is this early pattern of land division and road development that is still so evident in street maps of modern Phoenix and its satellite towns. A similar pattern can be seen in thousands of other towns from Ohio westward; what is unusual is the clarity and scale with which it can be seen in Phoenix.

The early town was concentrated in and around the modern downtown and included parts of six survey sections adjacent to the Salt River. This area is now bounded on the south and west by the prominent, right-angled bend in Interstate 17 near downtown. (These sections have the simple rectangular street grid that typified most nineteenth-century American town planning, see below.) Here, as elsewhere, the grid is interrupted primarily by railroad tracks, the lifelines of the local economy. Moving northward, the principal direction of the city's growth, one begins to see mile-square sections that are still dominated by the grid pattern but have occasional curved streets or cul-de-sacs added for variety. (Cul-de-sacs are dead-end streets designed to eliminate through traffic in residential neighborhoods.) They provide an instructive post-automobile planning twist. Before the 1920s, busy streets with streetcar lines for convenient transport were the *preferred* sites for upscale dwellings. Lot prices and house sizes dropped quickly with increasing walking distance to streetcar lines. (See also the discussion of Montana Avenue in El Paso, Texas, page 584.)

A bit farther from downtown are mile-square sections that feature an abundance of cul-de-sacs and curved streets, most often in combination. Finally note the "golf-course" communities, generally farther yet from downtown. In these the homesites are arranged around golf fairways that add highly desirable green space to the neighborhood. Many developers have found such convenient and scenic golf courses to be an ideal formula for adding value to upscale housing projects. The lots command a premium price that more than subsidizes the open space. At the same time, most residents pay dues for the privilege of belonging to the golf club, a long-term revenue source for the developer. Phoenix's retirement suburb of Sun City is an amazing example of *multiple* golf-course neighborhoods with unusual groups of concentric-circle streets each surrounded by a fairway.

Historic Preservation Pioneering

Most of Phoenix's intact earlier neighborhoods were developed after 1920, and the city is currently designating historic areas built as recently as the early 1950s. Phoenix is among the first American cities to formally recognize the significance of such neighborhoods, which illustrate the important transition from the Period houses of the 1920s and 1930s into the Neomodern designs, principally the Ranch and Contemporary styles, that dominated American home building in the 1950s. This transition was strongly influenced by programs created by the federal government, particularly President Franklin Roosevelt's Federal Housing Administration (FHA), one of his many initiatives to fight the 1930s depression. The staff of the city of Phoenix's Historic Preservation Office has been particularly innovative in emphasizing the impact of this, and subsequent federal housing programs, on the design of typical American houses and neighborhoods.

To put Roosevelt's influential FHA programs in con-

Phoenix Neighborhood Planning, ca. 1920–1980s

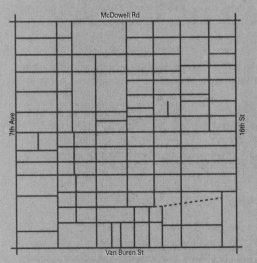

Square-mile section with grid streets (typical of western neighborhoods prior to 1940)

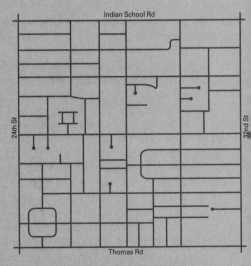

Square-mile section with grid modified by *occasional* curved streets and cul-de-sacs (typical of early attempts to follow FHA planning guidelines first issued in 1936)

text, it is important to understand that, throughout most of our country's history, potential homebuilders had to first save the entire cost of the home's site, whether a town lot or a larger rural tract. Such locations were then purchased before contracting with a builder to construct the house. Local banks often made mortgage loans to pay for some or all of these construction costs, with repayment usually involving periodic interest payments and with the entire principal amount falling due at some future date.

By the early twentieth century, some large home-building enterprises began to offer custom-designed homes that could be purchased along with the lot and paid for together with a long-term, installment-payment mortgage that included both interest and principal reductions. These were advertised as the "low down payment, low monthly payment installment plan." Americans now take this method of home financing for granted, but it is less than a century old, a revolutionary innovation that spurred the development of countless early-twentieth-century neighborhoods. Still a relatively new concept at the time of the great 1929 stock market crash, such private financing plans were almost killed by the Great Depression that followed.

As a result of the widespread financial crisis of the early 1930s, a great many Americans defaulted on their mortgage payments. The bank lenders then repossessed the houses but could not resell them at any reasonable price because of the depressed economy. Soon the banks themselves were suffering from the loss of mortgage payment revenues. In Phoenix, as in most of the country, housing construction had come to a virtual standstill by 1933. An entire industry ground to a halt.

The National Housing Act of 1934 was designed to combat this trauma. Enacted during the first hundred days of Roosevelt's administration, it set out to "improve nationwide housing standards, provide employment and stimulate industry, improve conditions with respect to mortgage financing, and realize a greater degree of stability in residential construction." Among other provisions, the act created the Federal Housing Administration (FHA), which was to have an enormous influence on the future of American neighborhoods. This government agency renewed private mortgage lending by *insuring* banks and other lenders against losses from new mortgage loans. In return, the FHA required that the houses so insured meet certain design and construction standards. The agency encouraged overall planning of neighborhood design—street layout, street plans, utilities, lot sizes and shapes—as well as simplified house designs. This led many home builders to become developers of large-scale neighborhoods rather than individual homes. In these they offered a limited selection of standardized house plans, building materials, and stylistic detailing.

The FHA's programs were a great success in stimulating new house construction and home ownership but were interrupted by the Second World War. From 1941 until 1945, only housing deemed necessary to the war effort was permitted. In 1944 another government

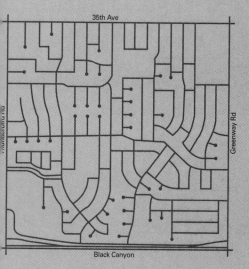

Square-mile section developed with *multiple* curved streets and cul-de-sacs (follows FHA suggested planning guidelines)

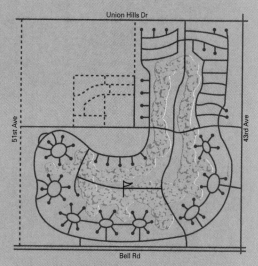

Square-mile section developed with golf course green space (an upscale, and generally later, version of curved street with cul-de-sac planning)

agency became involved with the housing industry when Congress passed the GI Bill of Rights. Among many other things, the legislation provided returning servicemen with loan guarantees that made possible the purchase of a new house with virtually no down payment. A nationwide housing shortage had developed during the war, caused principally by the hoards of former rural residents who had relocated to the nation's larger cities to work in war production plants. The GI Bill, administered by the Veterans Administration (VA), coupled with an expansion of the FHA's prewar programs, set the stage for an enormous housing boom after the war's end in 1945. An instructive look at the results of these federal policies can be seen in the small Phoenix neighborhood of Fairview Place.

Fairview Place, 1928–1947

This small subdivision northwest of downtown is filled with modest one-story houses, many of them originally financed under FHA or VA loan guarantees (see above). The neighborhood is of interest principally as an example of the government-influenced houses built during the trying decades of the 1930s and 1940s. These are not stately homes but small houses of relatively uniform character and simple design—typical of

countless others being built throughout the country at that time. Minimal Traditional and "French Provincial" Ranch houses (see "Encanto-Palmcroft," below) are the most prevalent styles.

The first twenty-seven houses on Fairview's 340 lots were completed between 1928 and 1932 and were financed by conventional bank loans. By 1933 the deepening depression brought construction to a five-year halt. In 1938 an improving local economy, coupled with FHA loan guarantees, led to renewed building activity—by the end of 1939 Fairview had seventy-four additional homes. The developer's advertising stressed that more were on the way, all "built and approved under FHA." These were soon to dwindle to a trickle as the Second World War curtailed all but the most essential home construction. Not until the postwar building boom were Fairview's lots finally filled with new FHA- and VA-approved dwellings.

Encanto-Palmcroft, ca. 1927–1939

This neighborhood, developed in the late 1920s, has streets lined with stately palm trees. It also has a geometric street plan—three rounded squares with irregular building lots lining them. The area was originally

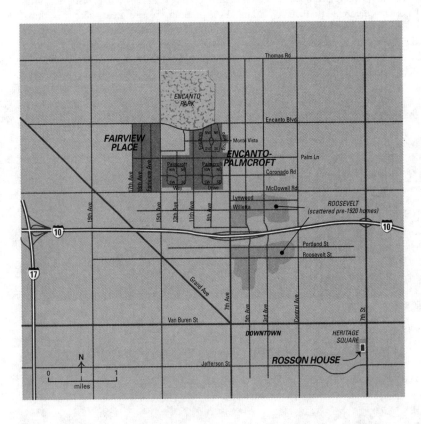

Encanto-Palmcroft

two separate subdivisions: the southernmost, called Palmcroft, includes two of the multiblock units that were opened in 1927 and 1929 and quickly began filling with Period house designs, Spanish Eclectic being the most common. New construction slowed to a trickle at the depth of the Great Depression in the mid-1930s. When building activity picked up in the late 1930s, the Period designs were joined by a variety of newly fashionable Ranch-style houses, which had increased in popularity as the neighborhood's last lots were filled in the 1950s.

Just north of the Palmcroft subdivision's two multiblock units is Encanto, opened in 1929 by another developer, who mimicked Palmcroft with a third rounded square of streets. A fourth square was planned to the west, but this was abandoned in the depths of the depression and the land purchased with federal relief funds to become the nucleus of a large municipal park.

In Palmcroft's first blush of late-1920s prosperity, two "model homes" were built to attract buyers—an unusual marketing strategy at that time. Both of these were Spanish Eclectic designs. The first, built in 1927, is at 1808 Palmcroft Drive NW (private); the second, built about 1929, is at 1615 Palmcroft Way SW (private).

1801 Palmcroft Drive Northeast (private). This is an excellent example of the neighborhood's predominant Spanish Eclectic style. Note the complex massing of varied roof levels and shapes, the deeply recessed and scalloped front door, the enclosed courtyard with the exterior stairway, the unusual placement of small arcades on the second story, the decorative tile vents and elaborated chimney tops, and the unusual window mullion patterns.

Ranch-Style Variations

The Encanto-Palmcroft neighborhood provides an instructive look at variations in Ranch-style designs, which were uncommon in the 1930s but quickly expanded to dominate postwar housing of the late 1940s and 1950s. Here again, Phoenix's Historic Preservation Office has taken the lead by providing an excellent

analysis of Ranch-house design in its 1992 book *Historic Homes of Phoenix.* Two concentrations of Encanto-Palmcroft houses illustrate their Ranch-style subtypes.

The first concentration is located along Palmcroft Way SW and the intersecting Coronado Road. Number 1315 West Coronado Road (private) is a French Provincial Ranch, complete with incipient Norman tower. Note the metal casement windows, including one that wraps around a corner, and the round vent in the front-facing gable; all of these features are typical of houses from the late 1930s and 1940s. Number 1309 West Coronado Road (private) is an "American Colonial" Ranch house, complete with broken pediment over the entry door. Number 1301 West Coronado Road (private) is a later and more fanciful French Provincial Ranch. Number 1609 Palmcroft Way Southwest (private) is a "California" Ranch with a wood-shake roof, open eaves with exposed rafters, and walls clad with a combination of brick and board-and-batten. Number 1605 Palmcroft Way Southwest (private) is another American Colonial Ranch.

A second concentration of Ranch houses is found along Palm Lane, a long street lined with formal rows of stately palm trees, which marked the dividing line between the original Palmcroft and Encanto subdivisions. Number 1115 Palm Lane (private) is a late example of the French Provincial Ranch; 1109 Palm Lane (private) is a "Spanish Colonial" Ranch; 946 Palm Lane (private) is a California Ranch; 934 Palm Lane (private) is an early example of the French Provincial Ranch; and 940 Palm Lane, 928 Palm Lane, 922 Palm Lane, and 905 Palm Lane (all private) are but four of many good examples of the Spanish Colonial Ranch along this picturesque street.

Rosson House, 1895

Sixth and Monroe Streets, Historic Heritage Square;
602-262-5071 or 602-262-5029;
A. P. Petit, Phoenix, architect.

This picture-perfect Queen Anne house sits on the only block of the original Phoenix town site that still retains its early historic buildings—Block 14, as it was designated by Phoenix's early surveyors. Four additional smaller homes, a duplex, and a carriage house, all from the early twentieth century, still occupy their original sites on the block. While the Rosson House is the only formal museum house, most of the smaller houses, now adapted for other uses, are also accessible to the public. Historic Heritage Square is not a typical enclosed museum village but rather a city amenity with the grounds open at all times. The only new additions to this historic block are a second carriage house, moved from nearby, and a pavilion built for outdoor events.

Rosson House

The block's showpiece landmark was built by Dr. Roland Rosson (1851–1898) and his wife, Flora Murray Rosson. Rosson graduated from the University of Virginia Medical School in 1873 to become a U.S. Army surgeon. Dismissed from the army in 1879, he moved to Phoenix, then a small frontier town with 1,700 inhabitants, to establish a private practice. Soon Rosson also became involved in civic affairs. In 1895, shortly before his new home was completed, he was elected mayor of Phoenix. Disagreements with the city council led to Rosson's resignation in 1896. The next year the family sold its home and moved to Los Angeles. Even before the family's departure for California, the home was rented out during the winter of 1895–1896 to Whitelaw Reid, the influential publisher of the *New York Tribune* who later became ambassador to England. Indeed, it is not certain that the Rossons ever actually lived in the house. But it is certain that, in building the elegant dwelling, the family left a superb legacy to the city.

Before building the house, the Rossons had lived nearby since 1882, the year Mrs. Rosson purchased

from her sister all of the city block on which the Rosson House now stands. The Rossons moved into a smaller, adobe-walled dwelling on the block before building their stylish new home. To design it, they chose architect A. P. Petit, a Pennsylvanian who had long practiced in the San Francisco Bay Area before moving to Phoenix in 1879.

The house's walls are pink-beige brick around which wraps an elaborate spindlework porch. The gables are sided with unusual metal panels pressed to resemble the usual patterned wood shingles. Iron cresting tops the many ridges of the roof, and a three-story octagonal tower adds a finishing touch to the overall composition.

When the city of Phoenix purchased the structure in 1974, it had long been used as a rooming house. Extra walls, painted woodwork, and layers of linoleum on the floors made the original features hard to determine. A restoration committee raised the funds to undertake extensive research as well as the restoration. Wallpaper patterns were duplicated from unearthed scraps, painted woodwork was returned to its original tones,

Rosson House block

the cranberry glass transoms and copper door hardware in an unusual winged pattern.

The furnishings are not original but have been carefully researched to be appropriate to the 1895 dwelling. A highlight is a room furnished as if it were Dr. Rosson's office (physicians at that time often practiced from home offices). This features a Victorian anatomic chart, early electric-shock equipment, and a portable embalming table.

Silva House, which faces Adams Street at the corner of Seventh Street, is typical of several smaller turn-of-the-century dwellings that survive on the block. It is a one-story Neoclassical cottage built in 1900. Its pyramidal roof and porch columns with elaborate Ionic capitals are both characteristic of this style. Inside is a small museum with two furnished rooms.

Wrigley Mansion, 1930

2501 East Telewa Trail, entrance off Twenty-fourth Street on Arizona Biltmore Circle; 602-955-4079; advance reservations required for visit, ask for detailed directions to parking area; Earl Heitschmidt, Los Angeles, architect.

This was the last of several elegant homes built by William Wrigley Jr., the chewing-gum magnate. It was built atop a small "mountain" just a few miles northeast of downtown Phoenix. The house's Spanish Eclectic style easily incorporates numerous exterior balconies and terraces that take full advantage of the site's many dramatic vistas of the city and surrounding country-

and the original pressed-tin ceilings were found to still be intact. Perhaps most spectacular was the discovery of the original wood parquet floors underneath the tar paper of the first linoleum layer. These have been restored and show that each downstairs room has a different border pattern. Other original finishes include

Wrigley Mansion

side. The eighteen-thousand-square-foot dwelling occupies most of the summit. It is reached by a narrow road that winds up the solitary hill to a small turnaround at the main entrance.

Inside is a round, two-story entry hall with painted ceilings and a curved staircase. The home has many original features both inside and out. All of the heavy brass hardware is still present—on every metal casement window, each door hinge, doorknob, and even the locks. Original ceilings remain throughout the house; many, hand-painted in egg tempera, are quite extraordinary. Bathrooms remain unchanged, finished with tiles in funky 1930s colors, some of them manufactured on Catalina Island, California, where Wrigley owned another home. A Moorish star pattern is found in the tiles and other decorative work throughout the house.

Although the house is now a private club, restaurant, and banquet facility, some original furnishings survive. Most have been moved into what were formerly upstairs bedrooms. A huge inlaid-wood Steinway grand piano, converted to a player piano and reputed to be the first such conversion done by this prestigious piano maker, is one of the more exceptional pieces.

PRESCOTT

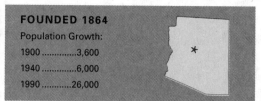

FOUNDED 1864
Population Growth:
1900 3,600
1940 6,000
1990 26,000

Prescott was one of the first two Anglo towns established in Arizona. In 1863, at the height of the Civil War, Congress created the new Arizona Territory from what was then the western half of the New Mexico Territory. President Lincoln appointed John N. Goodwin, a former congressman from Maine, as Arizona's first governor and sent him westward, along with other newly appointed officials plus a support contingent of laborers and soldiers, to establish a capital. Before Goodwin's arrival, Arizona's most important town was the old Hispanic village of Tucson. In the years leading up to the Arizona annexation, Tucson had also become pop-

ulated by Anglo miners and stage-line workers, some of whom were Confederate sympathizers. Lincoln's new appointees were, of course, staunch Union supporters from the northeastern states; they found it prudent to found a new capital city. Near the geographic center of the territory, they chose a picturesque mountain valley surrounded by pine-covered slopes, where promising gold strikes had recently been made. They must have viewed their mission in a somewhat-romantic light, for they decided to name their new town Prescott. It honors not the usual political or military figure but historian William H. Prescott, then a popular chronicler of the exploits of the early Spanish conquistadores.

Prescott's tenure as a capital city was to be short. Soon after the war's end, the capital was moved to the more accessible Tucson, located on the region's principal east–west roadway. Ten years later, in 1877, the territorial government voted to return the capital to Anglo-dominated Prescott, then at the height of a rela-

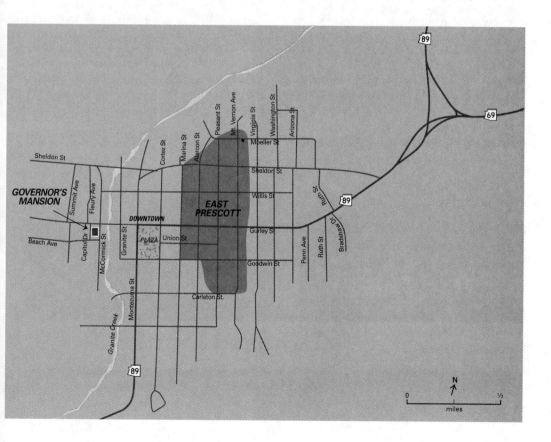

View of Prescott,
ca. 1885

tively short-lived gold-mining boom. Finally, in 1889, the capital made its last move, this time to Phoenix, where large-scale irrigation projects were beginning to turn the surrounding Salt River Valley into a rich agricultural oasis (see page 7).

Through all of these governmental moves, Prescott remained a small regional trade center for the surrounding mines, ranches, and lumber mills. In the decades since 1950, the town's growth has been accelerated by tourists and retirees, attracted by its scenic mile-high location with cool nights that provide relief from the region's oppressive summer heat.

Today, Prescott has the rare distinction of still retaining its very first building on its original site—a substantial, eight-room log structure built by Governor Goodwin as both his home and an administrative center for the new territory. A modest turn-of-the-century

neighborhood also survives, on the opposite side of town, which reflects the eastern origins of the town's early population.

Arizona Governor's Mansion, 1864

415 West Gurley Street, Sharlot Hall Museum complex; 520-445-3122.

After their long wagon trip from the East, Governor Goodwin's group scouted several locations before choosing this site for the first building of their new capital city (see page 15). Built of massive logs from the nearby stands of ponderosa pine, the eight-room structure took about three months to complete. Two large fireplaces and chimneys were constructed of adobe. These still miraculously survive; their preservation and that of the log walls have been facilitated by the dry

Arizona Governor's Mansion

mountain air. An excellent museum display shows how the house was built and includes examples of the frontier tools that were used. A further group of photos documents subsequent modifications of the house. Together, these displays form an instructive "museum-of-the-house," giving information that is rarely available about log-walled folk dwellings. The house's modern restoration and furnishings reflect its earliest years—from 1864 to 1867—when Governor Goodwin, and often some of his associates, lived and worked in the comfortably large structure.

After the territorial capital moved to Tucson in 1867, the Prescott "mansion"—a term it clearly deserved in a frontier village dominated by one- and two-room log structures—remained a center of community life for many years. Later, it became a neglected and deteriorating rental property before being rescued by a determined local antiquarian named Sharlot Hall (1870–1943). Miss Hall, who had moved with her family from Kansas to the remote Arizona Territory when she was twelve years old, was a tireless collector and preserver of the frontier history she had experienced as a girl. Her collections were moved into the old Governor's Mansion in 1928. Today, the mansion forms the centerpiece of a three-acre complex of modern historical museums and moved-in structures that surround the venerable log dwelling.

East Prescott, ca. 1890–1920

In 1900, Arizona had a population of 122,000, most of whom lived on ranches, farms, or in very small trading villages. Prescott's 3,600 inhabitants made it Arizona's third-largest town, exceeded only by Tucson (population 8,000) and Phoenix (population 6,000). Prescott's upscale residential district occupied a hillside near downtown, an area preserved today as the East Prescott Historic District, which includes Arizona's best assem-

blage of late-Victorian houses. On a national scale these are all relatively modest dwellings but were quite grand in a region still dominated by log or adobe folk houses. East Prescott's Victorian houses were built on scattered lots and are today interspersed with Eclectic-era homes. The latter group consists mainly of Craftsman- and Colonial Revival– (mostly of the gambrel-roofed Dutch Colonial subtype) style houses. The neighborhood also has many postrailroad folk houses, mostly of the pyramidal-roof form.

143 North Mount Vernon Avenue (private). This Queen Anne design, typical of the neighborhood's Victorian survivors, preserves many of its original details. Note the cutaway bay window in the wing to the right, the square panels above the main window in that bay, and the truncated hexagonal tower. The recessed balcony in the centered gable appears to have a new door and windows behind.

205 North Mount Vernon Avenue (private). This modest Tudor cottage gains its unique character from an exterior completely covered, top to bottom, by wood shingles. It retains what appears to be the original false-thatched roof of wood shingles; the front gable is clad with shingles applied in random wavy lines; even the porch supports are clad in multisized shingles. Altogether, an uncommon variety of complex shingle detailing to be applied to a relatively modest house. Its preservation is probably due to the dry mountain climate.

309, 313, 317, and 334 North Mount Vernon Avenue (all private). These are four good examples of pyramidal-roof, postrailroad folk designs.

202 South Mount Vernon Avenue (private). This inventive early Eclectic-era design combines features of several styles. Note the brick columns combined with short Ionic columns set on pedestals, the corner quoins, the hint of half-timbering in the large central dormer, the unusual smaller dormers, and the handsome front door with transom above and diamond-shaped panes in the right-hand window.

An instructive Neo-Victorian design is across the street and about ten houses south of 202. It can be distinguished from its older prototypes by, among other features, its vinyl siding (including a telltale "chimney" of boxed siding), built-in garage, and unadorned, absolutely flat side walls.

East Prescott

TUCSON

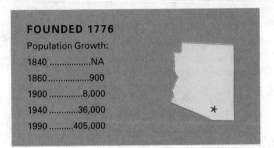

FOUNDED 1776

Population Growth:

1840 ....NA
1860 900
1900 8,000
1940 36,000
1990 405,000

Founded as a remote military post to protect Jesuit missionaries sent to convert the Native Americans on New Spain's northernmost frontier, for almost a century the small village of Tucson was the only urban center in what is now Arizona. Not until the region became a U.S. territory in 1864 did the venerable Hispanic town first have a rival—Anglo-dominated Prescott, established 175 miles to the north as capital of the new territory (see page 15).

Unlike most of the Southwest, the Tucson region was not part of the vast area ceded to the United States in 1848 at the close of the Mexican War. Instead, it was acquired six years later in the Gadsden Purchase from Mexico. This added a narrow strip of land to southernmost New Mexico and Arizona to facilitate the construction of a proposed transcontinental railroad across the southern United States. Interrupted by the Civil War, the southern Arizona railroad wasn't completed until 1880 when the Southern Pacific built through Tucson to link California with Texas and the southern states.

With the railroad came a boom, as Tucson's population jumped from 3,000 in 1870 to 7,000 in 1880. Now a rail-shipping point for the region's cattle, copper ore, and irrigated cotton crops, Tucson nevertheless remained a small regional trade center until the 1950s. In that decade, the city's population jumped a remarkable 400 percent, from 45,000 to 213,000, as new light industries, tourists, and retirees discovered Tucson's mild winters, scenic setting, and informal charm. Fortunately, this massive Sunbelt boom slowed somewhat in the following decades so that modern Tucson still has the feel of a small city rather than a vast urban complex.

Hispanic Tucson

In spite of its post-1950 growth, Tucson retains important remnants of its Hispanic origins. The original walled fort, or *presidio* in Spanish, occupied two blocks of what is now downtown Tucson—none of its original structures survive. The limits of the Spanish village that

Idealized depiction of the Tucson presidio, ca. late 1700s

grew up around the fort, loosely bounded by today's Sixth Street, Sixth Avenue, Seventeenth Street, and the Santa Cruz River, can still be seen in the area's irregular pattern of streets, a typical characteristic of Hispanic towns. This contrasts sharply with the surrounding regular grid of streets, the pattern favored by the Anglo settlers who arrived in a steady stream with the coming of the first railroad. Most of the prerailroad Hispanic town has been replaced by later Anglo buildings, but enough early structures survive to give a glimpse into Tucson's origins. These include early adobe dwellings in two modern historic districts: the El Presidio Historic District, which encompasses much of the north end of the early town near the site of the original fort, and the notable Barrio Historico, one of the nation's best surviving concentrations of simple Hispanic folk houses. These were located in the southernmost part of the early town. Two of early Tucson's Hispanic dwellings—La Casa Cordova (see the following entry) and the Sosa-Carrillo-Frémont House (see page 21)— are open to the public as museum houses.

Anglo Tucson

The city also has important historic neighborhoods and houses dating from the Anglo-dominated postrailroad decades after 1880. These include several fine turn-of-the-century dwellings in the El Presidio Historic District (among them the Corbett House Museum), the Armory Park Historic District, one of the city's first Anglo-style neighborhoods, and an instruc-

tive pair of Eclectic-era neighborhoods from the late 1920s.

La Casa Cordova, 1850s and 1879

175 North Meyer Avenue; 520-624-2333.
This Spanish Colonial–style museum house is part of an entire block of fine early homes that are operated by the adjacent Tucson Museum of Art. Most of the houses are now adapted to other uses, but all sit on their original sites, which once lay within the walls of the eighteenth-century Spanish presidio. Guided tours of the entire block are offered twice a week (summers excluded), and a self-guided walking tour is usually available at the museum.

La Casa Cordova, one of Tucson's oldest surviving buildings, is a typical Hispanic residence from the second half of the nineteenth century. The protective layer of hard-fired bricks that crown its adobe walls and its double-hung, multiple-paned windows mark it as the Territorial substyle, which added such Anglo-introduced details to traditional Hispanic folk buildings. The house is an L-shaped structure with five rooms and a zaguan (a central entryway) and illustrates the Spanish practice of building urban houses along the street line with an enclosed patio inside. Carefully restored in 1975, Casa Cordova's adobe-brick walls were not covered with the usual protective coating of mud or stucco but were chemically sealed and left exposed to reveal the underlying structure.

La Casa Cordova

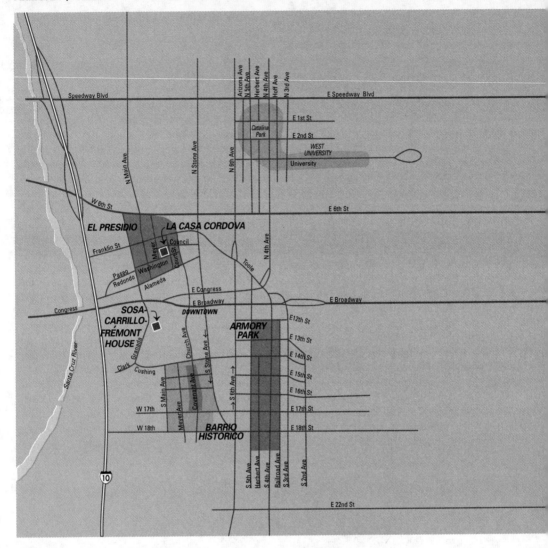

The flat-roofed design is typical of Spanish Colonial building practice in the arid Southwest. Heavy log roof beams called vigas are embedded near the top of the adobe walls. These support smaller strips of wood overlain by a thick covering of earth. An unusual Tucson-area feature is that the ribs of the local saguaro cactus are used atop the vigas to support the earthen roofs.

As with most Hispanic folk dwellings, Casa Cordova was built in stages. Here the first two rooms are the two in the rear, constructed during the 1850s. A single additional room was then added to these, and later, in 1879, the front three rooms were built along the street and the rear rooms reroofed. This created a sheltered outdoor area at the rear of the house that was used for gardens, chickens, and household chores.

The house is authentically furnished and instructively interpreted. The two earliest rooms give an unromanticized view of early Spanish frontier living conditions, complete with dirt floors. The newer parts of the house offer a combination of museum exhibits and two other furnished rooms, one showing upper-class lifestyles during the presidio period and the other illustrating a typical room from the 1880s, after the railroads arrived to provide a flood of factory-produced consumer goods.

A number of other early Territorial-style Hispanic dwellings survive in the vicinity of Casa Cordova. In the same block are the Fish House (private; 1867) and the Stevens House (private; 1866), both of which face on Main Avenue immediately west of the art museum. Others, many of them with later Anglo-style modifications, are scattered through the El Presidio Historic Dis-

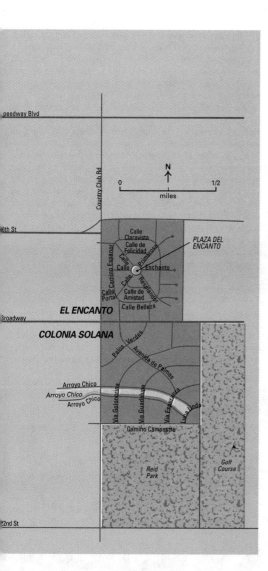

The "Sosa" part of the house's name comes from José María Sosa, the first owner of the property where the house stands. The "Carrillo" part of the name came in 1878 when Sosa sold his property to Jesús Suárez de Carrillo, a civic leader and merchant, who built this spacious home for his family in 1880. The house was quite grand for its day and was described by the wife of explorer and then territorial governor John C. Frémont as "one of the very best houses" in Tucson. The Frémont connection came when she rented the house in 1880, just after it had been completed. Both Governor and Mrs. Frémont returned to the East without ever living in the house. Only two servants and the Frémonts' daughter, Elizabeth, stayed there for a few months before also departing for the East Coast. After Elizabeth's departure, Carrillo family members lived in the house for almost ninety years.

The large and spacious interior is the best feature of the house. It has a large zaguan with other rooms that open off of it. The furnishings are mostly upscale, Anglo-influenced pieces—the sort that would have been uncommon in Tucson until after the railroads arrived in 1880, just as the house was being constructed.

Barrio Historico

This district occupied the southernmost part of Hispanic Tucson and is the only relatively intact part of the early town. Today, its 150 surviving adobe structures make up one of the nation's largest concentration of Spanish Colonial–style houses. Most date from the mid-1850s to 1880, the period after the Gadsden Purchase but before the first railroads brought a rapid shift to Anglo-style dwellings. Most of the district's buildings began as simple folk dwellings and have had various alterations, additions, and restorations during their long lifetimes. Although few individual houses thus closely resemble their prerailroad precursors, the combined effect of their close spacing and streetside siting

trict, which includes several additional blocks immediately north of the art museum complex (see page 22).

Sosa-Carrillo-Frémont House, 1880

151 South Granada Avenue; 520-622-0956.
This Spanish Colonial–style museum house is the sole survivor in what was once the midsection of Hispanic Tucson. This area was the site of a massive 1960s "urban renewal" project that demolished 250 homes and businesses to provide vacant land for new construction. Much of the land is now occupied by the vast Convention Center that dwarfs the early dwelling, which sits on its original site but now faces an empty, suburban-style green lawn rather than the lively sidewalks and streetscape it once enjoyed.

Barrio Historico

Barrio Historico

gives the neighborhood the decidedly non-Anglo feel of a village in Mexico or Spain.

A choice cluster of houses can be seen on Convent Street between Cushing and Seventeenth Streets. Original Spanish Colonial houses in the Southwest were built of adobe brick, with flat roofs and simple rectangular windows and doors; multiple doors opened directly onto the sidewalk (see page 21). After the region became a part of the United States in the mid-1800s, Anglo detailing began to be added to these basic Hispanic houses. Doors and windows had small triangular pediments added above and a row or two of hard-fired bricks were added to the top of the roof parapet to help protect the adobe walls from water seepage. These two additions created the "Territorial" variation of the basic Spanish Colonial house. With the railroads came even more Anglo influences—Folk Victorian front porches and hipped or gabled roofs, which were much easier to maintain than the traditional flat-earth roof. Any or all of these features might be added to an earlier house, incorporated into a later one, or restored to a previously modified house. Look for these features as you visit the Barrio.

El Presidio Historic District

In addition to Casa Cordova and its nearby Hispanic neighbors (see page 19), the El Presidio District, near the heart of the city, became a favored site for upscale, Anglo-style dwellings after the arrival of the railroad in 1880. Important survivors include:

241 West Franklin Street (private), McLeary House, ca. 1880, alterations ca. 1890 and later. This began as a simple Spanish Colonial design with flat roof and doors opening directly onto the sidewalk. Later alterations clearly demonstrate two ways that such houses were Anglicized. First, a Folk Victorian front porch was added, probably in the 1890s. Second, a hipped roof, with hipped dormer, was added over the flat roof. This served the dual purpose of better protecting the house and of adding what was, at the time, considered a more stylish look. This roof could have been added at the same time as the porch, but the hipped roof and dormer closely resemble those of the American four-square shape, which became popular shortly after 1900.

300 North Main Avenue (private), Steinfeld House, 1900; Henry C. Trost, Tucson, architect. This finely detailed Mission-style structure was originally built as the Owl's Club, an upscale residence for affluent young bachelors. It was converted to a private home in 1904. Note the bold arcaded porch and the elaborate Sullivanesque detailing between the semicircular arches, a legacy of architect Henry Trost's years spent working in Chicago. The elliptical windows under the eaves helped cool the house during Tucson's scorching summers. Trost, one of the Southwest's most creative designers, practiced in Tucson only from 1899 until 1903, when he moved to El Paso, Texas, where most of his surviving buildings are concentrated (see page 583). Before leaving Tucson he designed a second and larger Owl's Club down the street at 378 North Main Avenue (private) in 1902. For this he also used the popular Mission style.

405 North Granada Avenue (private), Hinchcliffe Court, ca. 1915. A bit north of the official historic district, this is a charming court of ten Craftsman bungalows. Such courts are occasionally found in southern California but are relatively unusual outside of that area. This one was restored in 1995 for the Designer Showcase sponsored by the Tucson Museum of Art.

El Presidio Historic District

Corbett House, 1907

180 North Main Avenue; 520-624-2333;
David Holmes, Tucson, architect.

When J. Knox Corbett and his wife, Elizabeth Hughes Corbett, decided to build their new home in 1905, they chose what was then called Snob Hollow, an area just outside of the original presidio walls, where well-to-do Anglos were building fine homes at the turn of the twentieth century. A part of this area is today included in the El Presidio Historic District, along with the earlier

Corbett House

Hispanic homes, which these later homes adjoined. The Tucson Museum of Art has played a major role in preserving the Spanish-era homes in the El Presidio District, all of which remain on their original site (see "La Casa Cordova," page 19). The museum's recent decision to open this house, the only postrailroad one in the museum's historic block, helps to give a fuller view of life in Tucson in the early twentieth century. Corbett House is particularly important, as it is one of only a few Mission-style house museums in the country. The interior detailing of this, and of most, Mission-style houses is identical to that found in contemporaneous Craftsman (or Arts and Crafts) houses. American Arts and Crafts furniture is sometimes called Mission furniture, as the designers imagined it sitting in the old missions of the West. In order to avoid confusion it is helpful to understand that the three terms—"Arts and Crafts," "Craftsman," and "Mission"—are often used somewhat interchangeably in *interior* design. However, in *exterior* architectural style there are two very distinct styles: the Craftsman (occasionally called Arts and Crafts) and Mission (see page 3).

The Corbett House has had its original interior restored. The handsome Craftsman woodwork (some recreated to match the original) includes ceiling beams, simple cased door openings, broad picture mold, and, in the dining room, a "skeleton" wainscot—all of a dark-stained wood. The living room has wonderful broad windows and an Arts and Crafts fireplace of light brick with a broad wood mantel shelf and built-in bookcases on each side. Today, a fine collection of Arts and Crafts furnishings is displayed in Corbett House, along with some of the Corbett family's personal belongings. Among them is a massive sideboard that one of Mr. Corbett's grateful employees made especially for this dining room.

The Corbett House interior detailing is similar to that of many of the one-story Craftsman bungalows built between about 1900 and 1920 (although it is a particularly fine example). Few of these homes have yet been opened to the public despite the fact that it was long a wildly popular style for middle-income homes across the nation. A visit to the Corbett House will be of particular interest to those restoring Craftsman-style houses. And a note of cheer for those engaged in such projects—even though Mr. Corbett was in the hardware, lumber, plumbing, and building-supply businesses, and had easy access to the kinds of supplies and finish materials needed for a house like this, erratic shipments of the desired items caused construction to take two years!

Armory Park

With the arrival of Tucson's first railroad in 1880, the old Hispanic town, with its irregular pattern of streets, was rapidly supplemented by new Anglo-style residential developments built with geometric grids of streets running either north–south or east–west. The railroads

23

also brought Anglo construction materials. Brick and lumber were in; adobe was out. Old-timers joked that the newcomers preferred to freeze in winter and stew in summer rather than live in one of those "ugly mud houses."

Armory Park, located directly east of the old Barrio Historico, was the first of these new neighborhoods, and many railroad employees were among those who chose to make their homes here. As in the adjacent Barrio, the district's principal interest lies not in its individual houses but in the contrast between the Barrio's closely spaced, streetside dwellings and Armory Park's larger lots. These permitted each house to be separated from its neighbors and set back from the street to provide space for what would, in less arid regions, be a front lawn (see figure 6, page xvi).

The lots are occupied by an interesting mixture of Anglo-influenced houses. Many are simple folk designs, usually with Anglo-style walls of hard-fired brick or stucco-covered wooden framing. More elaborate styled houses, mostly Folk Victorian or modest Queen Anne designs, also occur throughout the district. Arcaded front porches are common, some original and some later additions. Echoing a now-almost-vanished tradition of walking to a neighborhood grocery store, Armory Park retains several such structures (for example at **445 Fourth Avenue South** and at the **corner of Sixteenth Street and Fifth Avenue South**). Even an architecturally intact corner gas station survives.

Another early Anglo-style neighborhood can be seen in the **West University Historic District,** which contains houses built from about 1890 to 1930. The homes here are generally a bit larger than those in Armory Park. Some of the best are in the blocks surrounding **Catalina Park** (at the intersection of First Street and Fourth Avenue) and a handful of examples along University Boulevard, particularly 645 University (private), a Prairie-style design by Henry C. Trost (see page 22).

406 Fourth Avenue South (private). This pleasing brick house looks like it was built around 1905. All of the masonrywork is very nicely executed. Note the single band of brick that encircles the house and continues up over each window crown. The entry is designed in a Palladian motif and crowned with a row of rusticated stone trim.

544 Fourth Avenue South (private). As in the preceding house, this has unusually fine brickwork for a small house. The arcaded front porch is one of many found throughout the district. This one appears to be original to the house; some others look like later additions.

El Encanto and Colonia Solana

This contrasting pair of Eclectic-era subdivisions, both opened in 1928, provide a fascinating lesson in the crucial role that landscape and streetscape play in neighborhood ambience. Both subdivisions offered irregular lots, curvilinear streets, and dense vegetation, and both suffered the slowdown in development that came with the 1930s depression and Second World War. Individual houses in both run the stylistic gamut from late-1920s Period houses to 1950s Ranch-style houses to a scattering of new construction. Most of these, including the Ranch houses, display some Neo-Hispanic detailing. The two developments thus share similar house designs and street layouts, yet are startlingly different because of their landscaping.

Colonia Solana is an exquisite, and perhaps unique, neighborhood in which you feel as if you have driven directly into the surrounding desert and stumbled upon a few scattered houses. There is no street paving, no curbs, and no gutters. A line of rocks is used to delineate the boundary between road and yard. A natural arroyo running through the neighborhood has been left undisturbed. There are no "lawns" in the conventional sense. Instead, the neighborhood contains the fascinating native plants of the surrounding Sonoran Desert. With the native plants come small desert animals—quail, rabbits, ground squirrels, and hummingbirds. Although small, this neighborhood is easy to get lost in, but one doesn't care—you're exploring a life-size terrarium in the middle of the city. In this remarkable example of the long-term results of eco-friendly natural landscaping, only a few jarringly evident home owners haven't followed the "rules."

Adjacent to the north is El Encanto, less unusual but also charming. Here the curved streets and irregular lots are arranged in a symmetrical bull's-eye pattern, a type favored by those designing early-twentieth-century geometric neighborhoods (see figure 24, page xxxix). Although much native vegetation is used, the neighborhood is dominated by majestic imported palm trees, which accent the formal curves of the streets.

75 Calle Primarosa (private), ca. 1940. This is a pleasant Pueblo Revival house. Note the inward curve at the top of the walls that mimics adobe construction; the chimney has a similar shape. Details are very understated. The metal casement windows have an unornamented wooden lintel above and a line of bricks below. A simple wood balcony is above the front door.

California

ALLENSWORTH

FOUNDED CA. 1908

Population Growth:

1940 .... NA

1990 .... St. Park

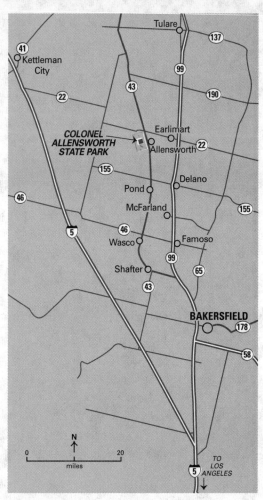

Colonel Allensworth State Historic Park, ca. 1908

California Highway 43, off County Road J22; thirty-eight miles north of Bakersfield, six miles west of Earlimart, off California Highway 99; 805-849-3433.

The Allensworth State Historic Park represents the rarest of western historic districts: a turn-of-the-century community planned, owned, and operated exclusively by African-Americans. The 1908 founding of Allensworth, California—by an idealistic army minister and former slave who gave his surname to the new village—constituted perhaps the first such venture in the West. But though its birth was testament to the utopian vision of one man, Allensworth's subsequent travails speak more to the difficulties facing an entire race—not to mention the obstacles hindering settlers in the dusty San Joaquin Valley. By 1969, when the California Department of Parks and Recreation began taking steps to rescue Allensworth from demolition, the communal ideal fostered by Colonel Allen Allensworth had been reduced to a few crumbling buildings, its settling families having long since abandoned the town. Today, a partially reconstructed Allensworth offers a compelling—if underdeveloped—reminder of a unique village.

Allen Allensworth (1842–1914) was born a slave near Louisville, Kentucky. His path to freedom evinced the kind of self-reliance that would mark his life's work. He was sold at age thirteen to a Mississippi slaveholder, reportedly for having committed the crime of learning to read and write. He subsequently ran away, was recaptured, sold in Kentucky for $960, resold in Memphis for $1,200, and transferred to New Orleans and eventually ended up in Louisville with an owner intent on training Allensworth to ride racehorses. Fortuitously, his arrival there occurred at the height of the Civil War, and the Union army arrived in Louisville shortly after Allensworth did. He escaped to their ranks and became

an army nurse. By 1863, he was a navy seaman aboard a riverboat.

After his postwar honorable discharge, Allensworth joined his brother William to open two restaurants in St. Louis. He quickly divested his interests in the venture to begin his formal education, enrolling in elementary school at the sprightly age of twenty-five. Over the next forty years, Allensworth became an ordained Baptist minister (1871); married his wife, Josephine (1877); and joined the army as minister to the all-black Twenty-fourth Infantry (1882). When he retired in 1906, he had risen to the rank of lieutenant colonel—both the first black and the first minister to have attained such honors. This ability to succeed in a white-dominated world would further inspire Allensworth after his retirement.

Upon his second discharge, Allensworth began preaching an ideal then popular among such African-American philosophers as W. E. B. Du Bois: black equality through education, economic empowerment, and self-help. As would be expected of any black in turn-of-the-century America, he dreamed of a locale where racial prejudice was nonexistent. He traveled to California and found no such place in Los Angeles. Determined to realize his goal, Allensworth teamed with locally esteemed black businessmen and civic leaders to form the California Colony and Home Promotion Association. The formation of this group led directly to the acquisition of twenty acres of land in southwest Tulare County, in the San Joaquin Valley, at a transfer point on the Santa Fe rail line between Los Angeles and San Francisco. On August 3, 1908, a township site plan was filed. The town of Allensworth, envisioned as a community where blacks could live, work, and raise families free of racism, was born.

The village's first few years were wildly successful. Eighty acres were added to the original plot. The city's economy was built on agriculture (cotton, grains) and livestock. The Santa Fe railcars stopped in town six times daily. The thirty-three-square-mile Allensworth school district was established; the original school-house, completed in 1910, was quickly replaced in 1912 by a bigger building to cope with the demands of a town that, at its peak, boasted some three hundred families. Several general stores and a hotel (nightly rate: seventy-five cents) sprang up. A glee club was established. The Allensworth Progressive Association ran the town in city-council fashion. With the establishment of the area as a judicial district, California's first African-American constable and justice of the peace were elected.

Sadly, the town's euphoria would be short-lived, and a series of events led to its ultimate demise. Perhaps most damaging was the 1914 death of Allensworth himself, killed on his way to Los Angeles by a motorcyclist in Monrovia, California. Much of the town's original success was obviously the result of Allensworth's determination, and his status as both army officer and minister doubtless garnered him added respect among whites. In the wake of his death, no Allensworth citizen managed the trick of equaling his vision, and none gained his status among an indifferent and disdainful white society. Without a minister and soldier at its helm, the town Allensworth had founded was probably condemned to falter.

Just prior to Allensworth's death, the township was forced to litigate with the Pacific Farming Company (which sold the original land to the settlers) over the in-

Colonel Allensworth State Historic Park

adequate irrigation system installed by the company. Though the system was eventually placed under control of Allensworth citizens, the town's water demands had been grossly underestimated when the land was originally sold—an oversight, intentional or not, that would come back to haunt the town: by 1925, the water supply was virtually gone, as the demand of surrounding areas rapidly lowered the water table. Those not driven away by lack of water—and, later, the depression and the World War II urban-factory boom—were finally forced to leave in 1966, when arsenic was discovered in the town's meager drinking-water reserves.

As developers moved to destroy the remnants of old Allensworth, the California Department of Parks and Recreation, recognizing the historic significance of the town, bought Allensworth and its surrounding lands, dedicating a state park in 1976 and promising to rebuild the area to its former glory. (Much of this work can be attributed to a park department draftsman named Cornelius Ed Pope, a childhood resident of the town.) Today, however, the project still stands half finished, as park placards announce numerous homes and buildings yet to be reerected. Enough such structures have been completed, however, to present a nice glimpse of Allensworth's heyday. Of note are the two school buildings, the Allensworth Hotel, and the original train station (with two wooden boxcars, much dilapidated but still infused with character and make-do spirit).

Only two homes, the Smith House and the Allensworth House, have thus far been reconstructed. This has been done with enough accuracy (such as old flooring and materials) that one can easily imagine (and even hope) that they are the originals. Both were prefabricated houses; of the two, the Allensworth House is more striking. Its interior is filled with period furniture indicative of the Allensworths' tastes.

Though the park is open daily, visitors should call ahead to arrange ranger-guided tours of the structures, which are open only on request.

CHICO

FOUNDED 1860

Population Growth:

1900 1,900
1940 9,000
1990 40,000

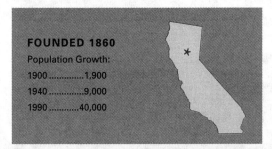

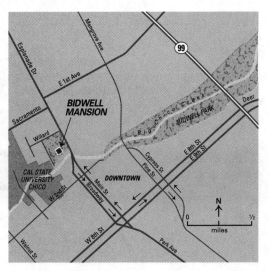

Located near the Sierra Nevada foothills, in the northern part of California's Central Valley, for much of its history Chico was a small market and trade center for a rich agricultural region specializing in fruit production. Then, in the twenty-year span from 1960 to 1980, the town's population jumped from fifteen thousand to forty thousand largely because of the expansion of popular Chico State University, which today enrolls more than sixteen thousand students each year. The city's principal historic landmark is the grand Victorian home of its founder, one of California's most talented and successful Anglo pioneers.

Bidwell Mansion, 1868

525 Esplanade Drive; 530-895-6144;
Henry W. Cleaveland, San Francisco, architect.

Born in western New York, John Bidwell (1819–1900) went west at age twenty to seek his fortune in frontier Missouri. Disappointed by his experiences there, and hearing of the wonders of Mexican California from a widely traveled Santa Fe trader, in 1841 young Bidwell and sixty-eight others made up the first large wagon train of Anglo settlers to depart for the Pacific Coast via the Oregon Trail (see page xix). Reaching southern Idaho, about half of the group proceeded northwestward to Anglo-controlled Oregon, while Bidwell and thirty others chose to head southwestward to California. After struggling across uncharted Nevada deserts, abandoning their wagons, and climbing through the icy Sierra Nevada barrier, they finally reached California's Central Valley in November 1841 as one of the first overland parties of Anglo immigrants to arrive in Mexican California.

Young Bidwell's boundless energy and quick intelligence soon caught the eye of the Central Valley's principal entrepreneur, an ambitious Swiss immigrant named John Sutter, who had established a prosperous irrigated-farming enterprise called New Helvetia, centered around what was later to become the city of Sacramento (see page 136). By 1845 the talented twenty-six-year-old Bidwell was Sutter's bookkeeper, general manager, and chief lieutenant.

Sutter's name is most remembered today for the event that was to destroy New Helvetia. In January 1848 his chief carpenter, constructing a new sawmill on a foothills stream about forty miles east of the settlement, discovered gold in the stream gravel. Soon an enormous flood of fortune seekers was overrunning New Helvetia, ruining its crops, slaughtering its livestock, and appropriating its lands as their own. American courts later denied Sutter's claims for compensation for these affronts.

Bidwell was to be more fortunate. Prospecting on his own he discovered Bidwell's Bar on the Feather River about seventy miles north of the Sutter headquarters. This was to become one of richest placer discoveries of the entire gold rush. Bidwell's first love was farming, however, not wealth for its own sake. A man of enormous self-discipline, when he had accumulated enough profits, estimated at several hundred thousand dollars, to buy and establish his dream farm on nearby Chico Creek, he left the prospecting to others and became one of California's most successful agricultural innovators. Bidwell's accomplishments at his twenty-five-thousand-acre Rancho Chico are succinctly summarized by the National Park Service: "The estate eventually included 20 subranches, each devoted to a particular product, ranging from wheat to fruit and from sheep to turkeys. Before Bidwell's death, the fruit and nut trees numbered

Bidwell Mansion

65,276, and the annual production of wheat sometimes ran as high as five million pounds" (Robert Ferris, editor, *Prospector, Cowhand, and Sodbuster,* 1967).

In 1865 Bidwell, still a bachelor at age forty-six, decided to replace Rancho Chico's rustic adobe headquarters with a more fashionable dwelling. His picture-book-perfect new Italianate home was designed by architect Henry Cleaveland, the author of a popular 1856 house-plan book called *Village and Farm Cottages.* Nothing in this thoughtful book on the construction of small houses even approached the grandeur of Bidwell's new home, which he may have commissioned with thoughts of seeking a bride.

From 1865 to 1867 Bidwell served a two-year term in the U.S. Congress. While in Washington, he met a young woman, Annie Ellicott Kennedy (1839–1918), whose talents and energy were a match for his own. Daughter of an important government official and descendant of Andrew Ellicott, who had helped Pierre L'Enfant plan the District of Columbia, Annie was a deeply religious woman committed to a number of social causes, among them women's suffrage. No acceptable suitor having appeared by age twenty-seven, Annie expected never to marry. She certainly had no intention of breaking the deep roots she had in her home city. The now-love-smitten Bidwell finished his term in Congress in the spring of 1866 and returned to California to campaign for nomination as a candidate for gov-

ernor. There he continued his courtship of the reluctant Annie by mail. To help woo her to the wilds of northern California, his letters gave regular reports on the progress of his grand, new home, stressing that it had the latest advances in gas lighting, in plumbing, and in water systems, which included a built-in washbasin with running water in every bedroom, a rarity even in the nation's capital at that time.

Bidwell's persistence and sincerity finally won out, and their high-society Washington wedding in April 1868 was attended by President Andrew Johnson; General, and future president, Ulysses S. Grant; and many other Washington notables. They returned to Chico to find their house nearing completion. Annie was reportedly charmed by its scenic setting adjacent to tree-lined Chico Creek and turned her considerable energies to furnishing their new dwelling. Here she and her devoted husband were to spend the rest of their long and productive lives.

Both of the Bidwells were interested in conservation of California's natural resources and were friends of John Muir and supporters of his pioneering efforts (see pages 184–187). Together they worked to protect and to educate the gentle Meechoopda Indians, whose ancestral homeland was included within Rancho Chico, for which they now supplied most of the labor. Annie taught them new skills and even became a licensed Presbyterian minister so that she could perform baptisms, marriages, and other ceremonies for Indian converts. She continued her interest in the woman suffrage movement and entertained Susan B. Anthony at the house.

The Bidwells' home was as solid and attractive as its owners. The double masonry walls were originally covered with a soft-pink-tinted stucco, and exterior details were executed in brown-toned wood trim, and this color scheme has been employed in the house's modern restoration. The overall effect is quite lovely, as one glimpses the soft pink tones through the towering trees that now surround it. Picturesque Chico Creek runs nearby, with a small footbridge leading across it to Chico State University, which was originally established in 1887 on a ten-acre site donated by the Bidwells.

The exterior of the house retains its original elaborate detailing. Small individual roofs, supported by brackets with handsome Eastlake detailing, are used above each second-floor window. A one-story porch wraps around three sides of the house. The tall centered tower has its original, see-through, clear-glass windows that, viewed from the ground at certain angles and times, make the roof above appear to be almost floating in the sky. This effect can rarely be seen today because in most surviving towers the windows are now shuttered or boarded up.

Inside, the rooms are large and lavish, with fourteen-foot ceilings on the first floor and twelve-foot on the second. The house has a wide central hall with the stairway off to the side, thus providing a clear, through-the-house view upon entering (and cooling ventilation in summer). The downstairs has four main rooms—living room, dining room, study, and office. There are five

bedrooms and two baths on the second floor. A ballroom, six additional guest bedrooms, and Bidwell's private office are on the third floor. All floors have additional service and servants' areas.

The interior finishes are less ornate than the exterior. Door and window surrounds are fairly simple. There are numerous Italianate mantels in front of coal-burning fireplaces. All are of "slate" with a remarkable variety of faux marble graining ornamenting them. Only about 20 percent of the furnishings are original to the Bidwells, but an excellent job has been done of gathering an appropriate collection of mid-to-late-Victorian items. There are many Eastlake and Renaissance Revival pieces.

The house was left by Annie to the Presbyterian church for a school. When the church could not afford to maintain the aging structure, it was sold to what was then Chico State College for a dormitory. In 1964, after strong citizen interest and pressure, the college turned the historic dwelling over to the California Department of Parks and Recreation for restoration and preservation as a house museum and memorial to John Bidwell, who founded the town in 1860, and, joined by his wife, Annie, left it with a remarkable legacy of philanthropic giving. Among the most important of these was Annie's 1905 gift of Bidwell Park in honor of her late husband. Stretching for ten miles eastward along Chico Creek, its 3,400 acres preserve one of the few surviving tracts of intact native plants in the Sierra foothills. It is also reported to be the third-largest municipal park in the nation and today provides Chico with superb hiking, fishing, golf, horseback riding, swimming, and picnic facilities.

Bidwell Mansion

EUREKA

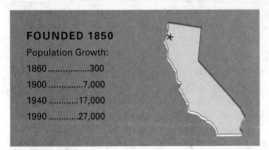

FOUNDED 1850

Population Growth:

1860 300
1900 7,000
1940 17,000
1990 27,000

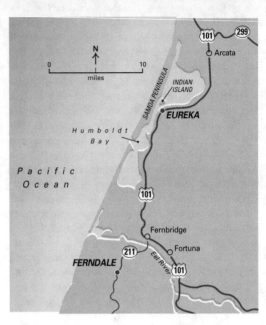

California's rugged, wave-pounded coastline has only three natural harbors—San Diego Bay on the south, San Francisco Bay near the middle, and Humboldt Bay on the mountainous and foggy northern coast. Unlike its two southerly neighbors, whose deepwater gateways provided shelter for Spanish sailing ships in the 1700s, the entrance to Humboldt Bay—a narrow channel between two barrier islands—was virtually invisible from the open ocean and was first entered by a Russian-American seal-hunting vessel in 1806. Forgotten for almost half a century, the bay was rediscovered in 1849 by explorers seeking new goldfields in California's coastal mountains.

Only a few modest gold strikes were made in the Humboldt Bay region, which soon proved to have a less glamorous but more substantial source of wealth—great forests of virgin fir, spruce, pine, and giant redwood trees to supply lumber to the rapidly expanding gold rush cities to the south. By 1854 the small town of Eureka, adjacent to the bay's best deepwater anchorage, had seven sawmills supplying 2 million board feet of lumber each month to the San Francisco Bay Area.

At first the output of Eureka's mills was delivered by fleets of small, shallow-draft coastal schooners that could maneuver through the treacherously shifting sandbar at the bay's entrance. By the 1880s improved transport facilities were making possible a manyfold increase in Eureka's lumber shipments. Dredging and jetty construction at the harbor entrance allowed large steamships to enter the bay and deliver their cargoes to ports as far away as Australia. At the same time a network of local railroads facilitated the movement of massive logs from distant forests to the Eureka mills. The town thus became the principal timber-processing center of the vast northern California forests, a role that grew steadily until the 1960s, when the nation's post–World War II building boom finally began depleting the region's old-growth timber. Today, replanted

stands of fast-growing species, particularly redwood that increases in height from one to three feet every year, are beginning to reach marketable size. With careful management such "tree farming" can provide indefinite yields of valuable logs to Eureka's mills.

A wide and rugged band of coastal mountains separated remote and seaward-focused Eureka from the rest of California, and overland routes were very slow to develop. Its local network of log-hauling railroads lacked outside rail connections until 1914, when the Southern Pacific completed a branch line—three years late and three times over budget—through the treacherous mountains to link the town with San Francisco. Even today, Eureka's principal access highway, U.S. 101, retains long stretches of narrow and winding two-lane roadway.

Eureka's geographic isolation, coupled with its modest post-1940 population growth and its long-prosperous lumber industry, makes it something of a time capsule of fine historic architecture. Most spectacular are its many surviving Victorian houses, among them one of the nation's most elaborately detailed and often-photographed Queen Anne landmarks, completed in 1885 for pioneer lumberman William Carson.

The Eureka area also retains many fascinating survivors of its early lumber industry, most of them emphasizing the inventiveness required to fell, transport, and process the large redwood trees. **Fort Humboldt State Historical Park,** on the south edge of town at 3431 Fort Avenue (707-445-6567), features an instructive small museum and large outdoor display of the heroic equipment used in logging the giant trees. **Samoa Cookhouse** (707-442-1659), formerly the dining facility of a large redwood mill and now a popular boardinghouse-style restaurant, has displays of small-scale logging equipment and fine historic photographs. It is located on the Samoa Peninsula, part of the barrier island that separates Humboldt Bay from the open ocean, and is reached by crossing the Samoa Bridge (California Route 255) from R Street, four blocks east of the Carson Mansion. Most spectacular of all are the region's numerous groves of old-growth redwoods that have been preserved as local, state, and national parks by farsighted conservation efforts that began in 1918 and continue today. These are scattered along U.S. 101 (the Redwood Highway) for seventy miles both north and south of Eureka.

Carson House Neighborhood, ca. 1870–1895

This small residential area adjacent to Eureka's waterfront and early downtown retains several fine Victorian houses built by affluent Eurekans who wished to live close to their mills, wharves, and offices. Chief among these is the remarkable dwelling that dominates the district.

Second Street at M Street (private), William Carson House, 1884; Samuel and Joseph Cather Newsom, San Francisco, architects. Built by pioneer lumberman William Carson (1825–1912) and his wife, Sarah Wilson Carson, this unique landmark is one of America's most-often-photographed Victorian houses. Dramatically sited on a rise at the eastern terminus of Second Street, the tall and flamboyantly decorated structure with its steeplelike tower quickly became a local icon—visible throughout the town and from passing ships far out in Humboldt Bay.

Like so many others, young Carson had set out for California in 1849 to seek his fortune in the newly discovered goldfields. By mistake, his party detoured through the

Carson House

Dolbeer and Carson Lumber Company wharves, ca. 1890s; the Carson House looms in the background.

Eureka area, where he marveled at the endless stands of giant trees rising around Humboldt Bay's fine natural harbor. He was already familiar with the opportunities and challenges this represented, for, as a youth in the Canadian province of New Brunswick, Carson had helped his father with logging that region's less heroic forests, the timbers destined for distant Liverpool by sailing ship.

Although he continued to try his luck in the goldfields, by 1852 several sawmills had been erected on Humboldt Bay, and experienced loggers were in demand to supply them with raw materials. In that year Carson purchased a team of oxen and became a contract logger for the mills. By 1854 he was managing one of the Eureka mills. In those first years, only fir and pine were being cut and shipped—no one had yet dared tackle the giant redwoods. Carson helped work out techniques for felling, moving, and processing the enormous logs, and his mill shipped the first redwood lumber from Humboldt Bay.

In 1863 Carson formed a partnership with John Dolbeer, the inventor of a portable steam engine that revolutionized logging by "snaking" the huge multiton logs out of the woods far faster than had the earlier ox teams. Dolbeer and Carson eventually co-owned mills, forests, and a fleet of lumber schooners; these were later joined by a spur railroad, banks, oil wells, mines, and commercial properties. On his death in 1912, Carson left an estate of almost $20 million, a long legacy of philanthropic works, and an enviable reputation for fairness and generosity among his many employees.

The Carson House was occupied by his descendants until 1950, when it was sold to the Ingomar Club, a nonprofit lumberman's organization, with stipulations that the home be carefully maintained in its original condition. Its massive and flamboyantly decorated wooden exterior, much of it redwood from Carson's nearby mill, thus became a kind of unique permanent monument to its builder's contributions to the town and region.

The inventive design that the Newsom brothers prepared for Carson was the crowning masterpiece of an unusually creative partnership that specialized in high-style houses, several of which survive both here and in San Francisco (see page 225; see also the following entry). The exterior is an original blend of influences that defies simple stylistic description. The basic hipped-roof-with-cross-gables shape is Queen Anne, as is the spindlework porch detailing and wall decoration of the main house. The tall and striking tower, in contrast, is ornamented with the narrow vertical stripes and brackets characteristic of West Coast Stick–style designs.

Both the Stick and Queen Anne detailings are oversize, multithemed, and crowded together in a seeming riot of strong vertical elements accented by bulbous floral curves. Unified by the simple two-color paint scheme, these potentially chaotic parts become a remarkably satisfying whole—a sort of American folk version of a European baroque church facade.

One can gain a deeper appreciation of the Newsoms' accomplishment by looking at the care they lavished on individual details of this complex facade. Start by focusing on the four differing treatments given the second-story windows across the front facade. At the left these begin with a broad window with an almost-Italianate segmental arch above and stylized columns on each side. Next come triple windows with a highly elaborated ogee pediment above and a swooping bracket to one side, similar to those at 837 Third Street (see page 35). Next is a pair of windows with a three-dimensional reinterpretation of a broken-ogee pediment above and turned spindles to each side. Finally, there is the right corner window, set at an angle, with its own unique crown and with long, textured brackets on each side that begin at the roof and continue down the sides of the window.

Next, focus only on the balconies on the front facade—a recessed one in the main gable, one in the upper floor of the tower, and one slightly recessed in the gabled dormer. And then comes the puzzle over whether the porch/balcony in front of the third-floor tower windows is indeed a porch or a balcony. (Even trying to concentrate on one small set of details leads to trouble in this house!) Other facade elements—roof and gable peaks, porch railings, eave levels, wall textures, and floral decorations—can be similarly isolated on each facade. Pity the poor draftsman who had to convert all of these complex elements into final working drawings for the millers and carpenters.

Second Street at M Street (private), Milton Carson House, 1889; Samuel and Joseph C. Newsom, San Francisco, architects. William Carson built this fine dwelling across the street from his own home for his eldest son. Here the Newsoms provided a quintessential towered Queen Anne design with spindlework detailing. Note the five different wood-shingle patterns on the front facade. On the side facade, notice the three downstairs windows with almost-identical surrounds; each is a different shape, and each features a central large pane of glass surrounded by smaller ones. After his father's death in 1912, Milton moved into the larger family home across the street.

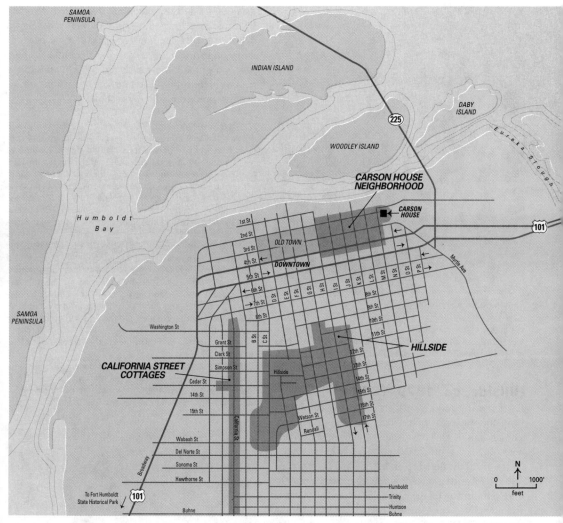

1033 Third Street (private), Carter House, 1981; built from 1884 plans by Samuel and Joseph C. Newsom, San Francisco, architects. This is a faithful modern rebuilding of a San Francisco house that burned in the fires that followed the 1906 earthquake. The original Newsom plans were followed for the exterior except for a bay window added in the entry. The dark brown color with red window muntins is quite striking. At first, and even second, glance this looks like an original pre-1900 house. On third glance you might notice that the brickwork in the chimney looks newish, but that might simply mean that the chimney had to be rebuilt or that the house had been moved. Overall, it is a rather-amazing job of re-creating a Queen Anne exterior.

837 Third Street (private), 1896. This more modest Queen Anne house, at least by the standards of Eureka and the Newsom brothers, still has a remarkable amount of surviving wooden detailing. Note the heavy use of wall texture in the second story. The downstairs right window has an exaggerated pediment above and swooping side brackets. These two uncommon elements are used in many variations on the Carson House (see page 33). The rebuilt Carter

House (see preceding entry) also has several of the Newsoms' distinctive swooping brackets.

314 L Street (private). This one-story, squared pyramidal roof shape is a very typical folk-house form in northern California. Also common in the American South, there this folk-house form usually has a very high-pitched roof and a full-width porch. The northern California version most often has a lower-pitched roof and smaller porch. The low roof pitch is probably borrowed from the Italianate designs that were prevalent in northern California during the 1870s and into the 1880s. Add a bit more roof overhang, a few modest cornice-line brackets, and slightly more pronounced window crowns or bay windows, and you would be looking at a small one-story Italianate cottage (see page 38).

1006 Second Street (private), Young House, ca. 1888. This Queen Anne cottage is one of a number of Victorian houses from elsewhere in Eureka that have been moved into this area (this one was originally built at 1528 Sixth Street). It has several unusual details—a triple-arched entry porch, a broad-arched window on the right side with a unique muntin pattern, and fan-ornamented brackets above

35

Carson House Neighborhood

the cutaway bay window. This house lost its second story after a fire, but an identical twin two-story version survives at 216 Hillsdale Street (see page 37).

Hillside, ca. 1870–1940

Eureka's early residential districts spread southward from the waterside commercial district up a gently sloping hillside that was originally covered with the dense forests that supplied the town's first lumber mills. By the 1870s the now-barren hillside had been platted into a street grid large enough to accommodate most of the town's growth for the next half century. Because the abundant lots were relatively inexpensive, many of the town's Victorian dwellings were built on large, multilot or even full-block tracts that provided room for gardens, small orchards, henhouses, and even stables and milk cows. As the town grew and lot values increased, the extra lots were gradually sold off as sites for new houses. As a result, most of the town's Victorian dwellings are now scattered within a matrix of younger houses, the majority dating from the first decades of the twentieth century. The map (see page 35) highlights an area with a relatively high concentration of Victorian houses, but many other fine examples occur dispersed throughout the early town grid shown on the map. Many of Eureka's larger homes of the early twentieth century were concentrated just beyond the southern edge of the map in an area loosely bounded by Buhne, Carson, D, and J Streets.

One feature of residential Eureka that strikes many visitors as peculiar is the scarcity of large trees on lawns or along the streets, which are dominated by utility poles as in early photographs of newly developed neighborhoods. The houses appear to have been set down on bare ground, almost like toy buildings on a Monopoly board. Most observers attribute this to the region's frequently foggy and cloudy weather—residents welcome every bit of sunshine!

828 G Street (private), Foster House, 1882. This very well-detailed Italianate design is of the simple-hipped-roof subtype. Note the pair of two-story slanted-side bay windows with hipped roof, the window hoods crowning the upstairs center window and those on the side facades. The handsome entry has double doors with a balcony above that is supported by large carved brackets. 1005 G Street (see below) is a one-story version of this house; 915 G Street (see the following entry) is also similar in form, but with Stick-style detailing.

915 G Street (private), Chamberlain House, 1892. This one-story-house form with a bay window on each side and a recessed porch between is common in Eureka. The house here is of West Coast Stick–style inspiration. The twin bay windows are squared and have gabled roofs above, the window tops are flat, and the cornice-line brackets line up with the vertical members of the windows and the corner boards. The only thing missing is that the builder did not bother to actually extend the brackets down to the vertical sides of the windows.

1005 G Street (private), Jacobson House, 1882. This one-story design is very similar in shape and form to 915 G Street (see the preceding entry) but has Italianate rather than Stick-style detailing. Note the slanted-side bay win-

Hillside Neighborhood

Hillside Neighborhood

dows, the slight arch of the window tops, and the way the brackets are paired along the cornice rather than arranged to line up with the window sides. Also note the typical Italianate bracketed and pedimented windows on the side facade.

1226 G Street (private), Brown House, 1888. The three preceding houses on G Street are all symmetrical designs with a bay window on each side of the entrance, a very common configuration in Eureka Victorians. Also common are houses such as this one, having an asymmetrical facade with a bay window on just one side. This example has a mixture of Italianate and Stick-style detailing. Italianate features predominate and include the low-hipped roofs, the slanted bay window on the side facade, the arched window tops, and the double entry doors. Stick-style features include the two-story squared bay window on the front facade, the pattern of short vertical strips along the cornice, and some roofline brackets that extend downward to become window frames.

1411 H Street (private), Johnson House, 1890. Like 1226 G Street (see the preceding entry), this is an asymmetrical design with a two-story bay window on one side. Here, however, the details are strictly West Coast Stick style—squared bay window with gabled roof, flat window tops, and brackets that align with vertical window framing below.

1635 G Street (private), Monroe House, 1889. This is an unusually inventive local interpretation of the Queen Anne style. The asymmetrical form with dominant front-facing gable, areas of patterned wall shingles, and a highly detailed entry porch are typical Queen Anne features. But also note the creative use of Eureka's ubiquitous squared and slanted-side bay windows. The slanted-side bay is topped with a broad, front-facing gable to create typical Queen Anne cutaway bay windows on the second floor. But if you run your eye down the length of this two-story bay window, you'll see that the area between the upstairs and downstairs windows doesn't have typical Queen Anne ornamentation at all but rather what we've been seeing on Italianate houses. A squared bay window has also been ingeniously incorporated, this set at an angle on the corner of the house so as to disguise the regularity of the window shape and make the design more asymmetrical.

1406 C Street (private), Clark House, 1888. It is hard to believe that this straightforward, nicely articulated, and appealing house does not fit neatly into any stylistic category. But that is the case. One of us (Virginia) describes it as "a

quite beautiful and highly elaborated pyramidal-roof Folk Victorian house. It has beautifully ornamented centered gables, a line of brackets under the eaves, and a handsome spindlework porch. Not typical of the Folk Victorian, but very typical of Eureka, are the pair of squared bay windows on the front and the slanted bay window on the side." Or you might prefer Lee's view of the house as "a unique interpretation of the Stick style which combines gables with Stick truss-work typical of the East Coast with variants of the squared bay windows typical of the West Coast." Or you might elect not to bother about such niceties and simply enjoy its unusual charm.

Hillsdale Street

The two blocks of this narrow street are just about the only part of Eureka to present a solid streetscape of Victorian facades. The fine local survey publication called *Eureka: An Architectural View* notes that the 200 block of Hillsdale "may be the most important streetscape in Eureka."

216 and 220 Hillsdale Street (private), Mowry Houses, 1893. This is a fine pair of spindlework Queen Anne designs, both built by Francis Mowry. Number 216 has a twin design at 1006 Second Street (see page 35, where some of its unusual features are mentioned).

303 Hillsdale Street (private), Baker House, 1893. You'll have no trouble deciphering this house if you've looked at 915 G Street (see page 36). If you haven't, just read that description, look at this house, and see that the builder put hipped roofs on the squared bay windows, but then compensated for it by adding a gable-on-hip to the main part of the house. And this builder *did* remember to connect the cornice-line brackets to the window verticals. The front door looks newer.

261 Hillsdale Street (private), Redmond House, 1890; A. A. Redmond, Eureka, architect. Designed by its owner, this is an example of the Queen Anne style with half-timbered decorative detailing. Note the stylized half-timbering in the gables and the solid brackets to the sides of the porch supports.

295 Hillsdale Street (private), Biord House, 1904; W. Skilling, architect. Shingle-style houses with very high-pitched front-gabled roofs, such as this design, are frequently seen in northern California. This example is easy to miss because the dominant front-facing gable has been resided. Note the eyebrow dormers on the sides. A similar house is found at 1103 California Street (private), where the front-facing gable has not had its original wood shingles obscured.

California Street Cottages, ca. 1870–1910

An early street railway line terminating near the waterside industrial district west of downtown ran down California Street, which became a favored site for workmen's homes. An instructive range of small-scale styled and folk houses lines the street, which retains much of the character of Eureka's more modest turn-of-the-century neighborhoods.

1451 California Street (private), Graham House, 1886. This is an excellent example of a one-and-one-half-story front-gabled Folk Victorian cottage.

1818 California Street (private), Smith House, 1904. This one-and-one-half-story front-gabled house is very similar in shape to that at 1451 California (see preceding entry). But the decorative detailing of patterned shingles, cutaway bay, and spindlework porch make it an unusually small example of a styled Queen Anne design.

1801 to 1819 California Street (all private), Willey Houses, 1889. This pair of double houses was reportedly built on the nearby Samoa Peninsula and later reassembled here. The square bays and brackets extending downward to become vertical window framing make these excellent small examples of the West Coast Stick style. Note the wide band of trim under the cornice.

2135 California Street (private), Steele House, 1901. This is the same typical northern California hipped-roof folk-house form described under 314 L Street in the Carson House Neighborhood (see page 35).

2202 California Street (private), McMillan House, 1895. This one-story Italianate cottage has a pair of slanted-side bay windows and modest brackets. Its relationship to the folk-house forms at 2135 California (see the preceding entry) and 314 L Street (see page 35) is described under the latter entry.

200 block of West Cedar Street (all private). Located just off of California Street, this block has several other variations of the one-and-a-half-story front-gabled house.

Ferndale

The wooded hillsides that surrounded Humboldt Bay offered its early settlers few level and fertile sites suitable for agriculture. Fortunately, only a few miles south of the bay lay the mouth of the large Eel River, whose frequent flooding over many thousands of years had created a broad and grassy delta with rich alluvial soils. Fields of potatoes and grains, as well as lush pastures and hay fields for livestock, were soon established here to become the principal local food source for Eureka and the Humboldt Bay timber industry.

In 1860 the small village of Ferndale (reached today by taking U.S. Highway 101 for seventeen miles south of Eureka to the village of Fernbridge, then turning four miles southwest on local Highway 211; see map, page 39) was established on a hillside adjacent to the flood-prone delta to provide a market and trade center for the area's many prosperous farmers, some of whom built fine Victorian dwellings in the village. By 1900 Ferndale was a thriving small town of 1,200 people, many of them immigrant agriculturists from Scandinavia, Italian Switzerland, and Portugal. By then, all of the fertile delta land was under intensive cultivation and remains so today, with its farmers, now concentrating on high-value dairy products, still served by picturesque Ferndale (1990 population 1,300), which has been called California's best-preserved Victorian village. Now a state historical landmark, modern Ferndale has added "heritage tourism" to its traditional role as an agricultural trade center. Particularly charming is its small-scale, turn-of-the-century Main Street, fea-

The Italianate and Stick Styles in Northern California

In northern California, and occasionally elsewhere along the Pacific Coast, houses of both the Italianate style and the Stick style have decorative brackets along the cornice line. This means that houses with these brackets, which are a principal identifying feature for Italianate designs in the rest of the country, must be otherwise distinguished from Stick-style houses in this region.

To further complicate matters, the Stick style in northern California generally looks quite different from its appearance in the rest of the United States. Elaborate bay windows become a principal design element and roof gables generally lack the characteristic decorative trusses found elsewhere. These designs are sometimes referred to as "West Coast Stick–style" houses.

In northern California, bay windows in two distinctive shapes become the primary distinguishing feature between Italianate- and Stick-style designs. The illustrations to the right summarize these differences in freestanding houses, which are particularly common in Eureka. (See pages 220–221 for San Francisco town house examples of these styles.)

Italianate (1870–ca. 1885)

Italianate-style examples tend to have bay windows with *slanted sides*. In addition, the bay window area most often has a *hipped* roof above it. The windows are more likely to have a slight curve above them. The decorative brackets along the cornice line are not generally placed in a line with the sides of the windows, but are more likely to be evenly spaced all along the cornice. Italianate houses built before 1880 do not typically have bay windows at all and look much like Italianate houses in the rest of the United States.

1. Bay windows with *slanted* sides

2. Hipped roof above bay window

3. Segmental arch common on upper window pane

4. Decorative brackets at cornice line (do not always align with corner boards and sides of windows)

Italianate (typical one-story form)

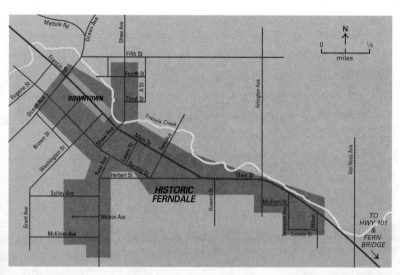

turing many carefully restored one- and two-story commercial buildings from the 1870s through 1920s. Among the town's many fine houses are:

703 Main Street (private), Shaw House, ca. 1850s. This handsome Gothic Revival cottage was the home of the town's founder, Seth Louis Shaw, and is the oldest home remaining in Ferndale. Shaw and his brother made their way to what is now called Francis Creek in 1852 and found it surrounded by giant ferns. Shaw claimed 160 acres of land and called it "Fern Dale." A farmer, he first discovered that pota-

toes grew well here. Note the one-story bay window, the "false shaping" that creates an illusion of a Gothic window in the centered gable, and the through-the-cornice dormers on each side wing. The house is surrounded by a picturesque white fence. Some of the trim looks like it may have been recently replaced.

1337 Lincoln Street (private), ca. 1895. This typical northern California Victorian-house form has an asymmetrical front facade with a single bay window. This example has a square-sided bay and West Coast Stick–style detailing (see below). Ferndale has several similarly shaped houses along Main Street, among them 824 and 835 Main. The former has

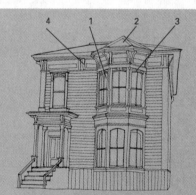

Italianate (typical two-story form)

Stick (1880–ca. 1895)

West Coast Stick-style houses usually have bay windows with *straight sides.* In addition, the bay window area most often has a *gabled* roof above it, and the windows are more likely to have flat tops. The decorative brackets usually line up with the sides of the windows and with the corners of the house and extend down into long vertical strips in these locations. There is sometimes a pattern of short verticals along the cornice line.

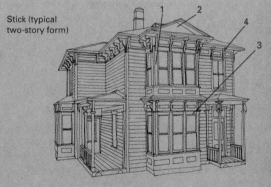

Stick (typical two-story form)

1. Bay window with *straight* (squared) sides

2. Gable roof above bay window

3. Flat tops common on upper window panes

4. Brackets align with window sides and corner boards

5. May have pattern of short verticals along cornice line

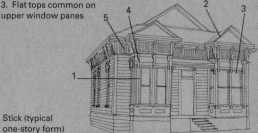

Stick (typical one-story form)

Ferndale

Ferndale

rather-spectacular windows in the upper sashes—large panes of cranberry-colored glass bounded by smaller panes.

455 Ocean Avenue (private), Berding House, 1875. Coast cypress trees trimmed into gumdrop shapes line the fence in front of this delightful house, which combines features of three Romantic-era styles. It is, at first glance, an asymmetrical Gothic Revival house characterized by the steeply pitched roof, the wall surface extending into the gable, the decorated vergeboards, and the one-story entry porch that, while it does not have flattened Gothic arches, at least has rounded arches. But then you notice that the windows, which extend both into the main front-facing gable and into the smaller secondary cross gable in the wing, are not Gothic in shape but rather have segmental arches more typical of Italianate houses. The one in the main gable even has a bracketed triangular pediment above it. This and the corner quoins are both typical Italianate features. The influence

of a third Romantic style is seen in the narrow line of transom and sidelights that surround the front door, a typical Greek Revival feature. The home's builder, Arnelle Berding, opened the first general merchandise store in Ferndale, and the house has long been in his family. There is a nice view of the side facade and of the rear stables from Berding Street.

400 Berding Street (private), 1898. This large and elaborate Queen Anne dwelling has, after a 1920 rear addition, been used as a hospital, rest home, and apartment building before its current reincarnation as a bed-and-breakfast inn. Notable features include the upstairs porch incorporated into the octagonal tower and the deep spindlework friezes above both the upper and lower porches. These feature beadwork and dramatic open fans with pendants hanging below. The windows are modern replacements.

The Italianate and Stick Styles in Northern California (continued)

Mixtures
The confusion and fudging begins when, as so often happens, these typical sets of features occur with slight variations or even together on the same house (for example, a straight-sided bay window on the front facade and a slanted-side bay window on the side facade). Or, an otherwise Stick-style house has slanted-side bay windows with a hipped roof. Or, a Queen Anne–shaped house has bay windows more typical of the Stick or Italianate styles. Because much of the wooden detailing was purchased ready-made from building-supply dealers and lumber yards, such stylistic mixtures can be thought of as the architectural equivalent of mix-and-match clothes. Many builders chose to ignore the "proper" stylistic choices by combining different elements that caught their fancy, or that were more readily or inexpensively available.

"Eastlake"
If you are looking at other guidebooks to Eureka or northern California, you'll notice that many houses are

described with "/Eastlake" after the basic style, as in "Stick/Eastlake," "Italianate/Eastlake," and "Queen Anne/Eastlake." Eastlake is not a *style*, but rather a family of trim inspired by the English furniture designer Charles Lock Eastlake. Typical features include spindles turned on mechanical lathes, incised floral detailing, and other kinds of textural surface details. In most parts of the country, Eastlake-inspired details are almost exclusively found on Queen Anne houses, where they make up the spindlework family of ornamentation that dominated that style from 1880 until about 1895. In most of the country, the Queen Anne style for houses replaced the Italianate and Stick styles in the early 1880s. But in San Francisco and northern California, both the Italianate and Stick styles continued to be built up until the early 1890s and were about as prevalent here as the contemporaneous Queen Anne during those prosperous years. Not surprisingly, beginning about 1880 these two styles also began to be embellished with much the same kind of Eastlake-inspired ornament as were spindlework Queen Anne houses.

FRESNO

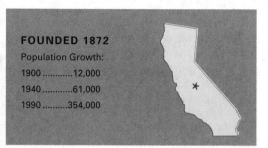

FOUNDED 1872
Population Growth:
1900 12,000
1940 61,000
1990 354,000

Fresno, the state's eighth-largest city, is the prosperous nerve center of one of the world's richest agricultural regions—California's dry but fertile Central Valley, where abundant sunshine and equally plentiful irrigation water, supplied both from wells and channeled from the snow-fed streams of the adjacent Sierra Nevada, produce an unparalleled bounty of high-quality fruits, vegetables, and grains. Today, these supply about one-fourth of the nation's food as well as a substantial surplus that commands premium prices on world markets. Fresno County lies at the heart of this bounty and ranks first in the nation in the value of its agricultural products.

Fresno County was also the birthplace of large-scale irrigated farming in California. Since Spanish Colonial days, most of the arid Central Valley had been considered suitable only as scrub pasture for scattered herds of cattle, sheep, and goats. In 1869 a Napa Valley sheep man named A. Y. Easterby, convinced that much of the Central Valley needed only water to become richly productive farmland, drilled a well in then-desolate Fresno County and used it to irrigate several acres of wheat. This thrived beyond his most optimistic expectations. By 1871 two thousand adjacent acres of wheat were being watered by irrigation canals dug to tap the distant Kings River. That same year, the first railroad line to traverse the length of the Central Valley was under construction. Builder Leland Stanford (see page 142), impressed by Easterby's lush green fields, ran his tracks nearby and the following year platted the new town of Fresno to capitalize on the area's agricultural potential. Stanford was not to be disappointed.

The new railroad provided Fresno-area farmers with ready access to distant markets, and soon the irrigated fields blossomed with experimental plantings of every kind of high-value fruit and vegetable crop. In 1874 a

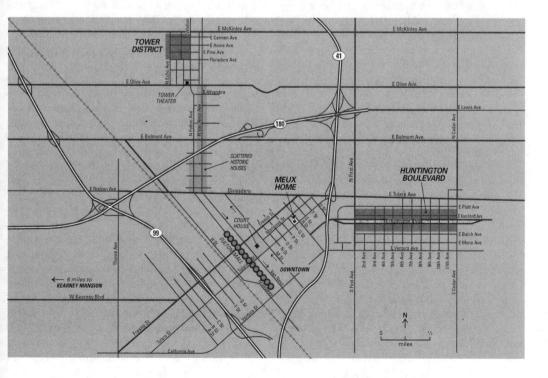

part of a vineyard, planted with undistinguished grapes intended for conversion to cheap wine, was inadvertently left unpicked. The ripe grapes quickly dried in the hot valley sun and were discovered to have become superb raisins, then a valuable delicacy produced in only a few favored and distant localities around the world. By accident, Fresno County had found its premier high-value crop.

By 1890 the small town of Fresno was surrounded by endless fields of raisin-grape vineyards, most of them planted on small, owner-operated farms of fewer than a hundred acres. Today, about one-fifth of the world's grapes are grown in Fresno County for conversion to raisins. These are then distributed on every continent by an efficient local marketing cooperative that uses the familiar brand name "Sun-Maid."

As in so many large western cities, Fresno's twentieth-century growth has left only scattered remnants of its Victorian past. Among these is a fine Queen Anne museum house built during the town's initial raisin-based population boom of the 1880s. Several important Eclectic-era neighborhoods also survive, along with a remarkable Chateauesque museum house built by one of the colorful pioneers of the local raisin industry.

Kearney Mansion, 1903

Rural Kearney Boulevard, seven miles west of
downtown Fresno; 209-441-0862.
This large Chateauesque structure may be the only French-château-inspired home in the world to be built of sun-dried adobe bricks. It is particularly appropriate that this worldly exterior was added over such down-to-earth underpinnings here, for that is exactly how the house's builder, Irish-English immigrant Martin Theodore Kearney (1842–1906), constructed his own life, which was to become closely intertwined with the development of Fresno's bountiful raisin industry.

Much of what is known about the personal life of this enigmatically private man is provided by a set of surviving notebook diaries that he kept from 1865 to 1903. These are well summarized in a short biography, *M. Theo Kearney, Prince of Fresno*, by S. Rehart and W. K. Patterson. Born in England as the son of a poor Irish laborer, Kearney immigrated with his family to Malden, Massachusetts, in 1854. About 1860 he moved to Boston, where he became a salesman for a luggage-manufacturing company. Eight years later he was the company's manager. During that interval Kearney also carried out a remarkable self-improvement plan that included lessons in German, French, elocution, dancing, and learning the manners of upper-class society. In 1868 the modestly affluent and self-made young aristocrat abruptly left Boston, perhaps because of some personal trauma, aboard a luxury steamer bound for San Francisco.

One of Kearney's shipmates, Dr. Edward B. Perrin, was to profoundly shape his future. In the words of Rehart and Patterson:

Dr. Perrin, a remarkable, foresighted man who had studied irrigation methods in Egypt, Spain, and Italy, had bought large tracts of land in Merced and Fresno counties. It was he who convinced Kearney that the San Joaquin Valley, if properly irrigated, could produce bountiful crops. . . .

Upon his arrival in San Francisco, Kearney deposited a substantial sum of money in a bank. He subsequently withdrew $8,000 to make a down payment on 8,640 acres of Fresno County land that he bought from . . . Perrin . . . sight unseen. This shipboard friendship would grow into a profitable business relationship for Kearney in the coming years.

Now a small-scale investor-landowner himself, the debonair Kearney was soon accepted into the social circles of wealthy San Franciscans, some of whom controlled hundreds of square miles of Central Valley desert that they hoped would someday become valuable farmland. They had been recently encouraged in this expectation by Easterby's successful irrigated wheat experiments and by the projected completion of the Central Valley Railroad. Seeking to supplement his own relatively modest financial resources through the expected run-up in value of Central Valley land, Kearney, the former luggage salesman, found a role that utilized his proven talents. He shrewdly devised a plan for subdividing the large tracts held by his wealthy investor friends, originally purchased for only a few dollars per acre, into improved twenty-acre "colony farms" complete with adjacent roads, fences, and irrigation ditches. These were then sold, with generous time-payment terms, to farmer-immigrants from the eastern states and Europe for fifty dollars per acre. Some measure of Kearney's ultimate success in these ventures can be seen in the growth of the town of Fresno, the central-marketing and raisin-processing center of the region, whose population surged from eight hundred in 1880 to eleven thousand in 1890.

As he had apparently done with his luggage salesman's earnings in Massachusetts, Kearney saved and shrewdly invested his substantial real estate commissions, this time in prime Fresno County farmland. Some of this he subdivided and sold, other tracts he farmed himself under the supervision of resident managers. By 1880 Kearney was independently wealthy, dividing his time between overseeing his Fresno County properties during the mild weather of spring and fall

Kearney Mansion

and participating in the winter social season in San Francisco, where he maintained his principal office. Summers were often spent in socializing with wealthy and influential friends in New York or the elegant resort towns of Europe.

Kearney's crowning achievement was to be his Fruit Vale Estate, a model 6,800-acre colony farm with Kearney's own 240-acre European-style country barony, which he called Château Fresno, as its centerpiece. The development commenced in 1891 with the construction of a large complex of service buildings near his future homesite. These served as the headquarters of the entire Fruit Vale venture and included workers' quarters, a general store, barns, stables, and even a post office. Nearby, a large wooden dwelling housed the estate superintendent and domestic servants. It also included a suite for Kearney's use when visiting the project.

Next came planting of Kearney's personal Château Fresno Park, which, in addition to large tracts of fruit trees, vineyards, and hay fields, included many acres of ornamental gardens with thousands of exotic trees and shrubs. The following year the roads and irrigation canals serving the first of the estate's colony farms were completed, as was the remarkable Château Fresno Boulevard (now called Kearney Boulevard), a three-lane, eleven-mile roadway lined with eucalyptus and palm trees linking the estate with urban Fresno.

Early in the planning for the Fruit Vale project, Kearney had commissioned a London architect to prepare preliminary plans for his future Château Fresno. Modeled after the Loire Valley's Château Chenonceaux, the plan rivaled the French original in scale and grandeur. By about 1900 the flourishing estate had completely outgrown the original wooden Superintendent's House. Preoccupied with his often-futile attempts to organize the region's many small raisin growers into an effective marketing combine, Kearney was not yet ready to begin his grand Château. Instead he compromised by constructing a larger Superintendent's Lodge, which would be a permanent part of the Château Fresno complex. Completed in 1903, this is the present adobe-walled Kearney Mansion.

Nearby, his workmen were finally working on the foundation for his grand, five-story château in May 1906 when Kearney departed for his usual summer in Europe. Three weeks later he died in his stateroom aboard a British luxury liner in the mid-Atlantic.

Kearney's estate today is a county park and remains much as it was at his death. The 1903 Superintendent's Lodge, now called the Kearney Mansion, lacks the classical splendor of his planned château but is nevertheless a large and impressive structure for its time and place. About half of its fine original furnishings remain, including French wallpapers emphasizing the bounties

of horticulture. Those in the large entry hall are original. About half of those elsewhere in the house have been reproduced from original samples. Not surprisingly, grapes are a recurring theme—bold clusters dominate the walls of the upstairs halls. Even the downstairs hall light fixtures have a grape-cluster theme. The large dwelling also includes a private suite for Kearney and a large general office, where the financial affairs of the estate were managed.

Kearney's self-composed epitaph, written sometime before his death, emphasized not his many triumphs, but his disappointments in persuading the region's numerous small growers, many of whom owned their profitable farms as a result of Kearney's efforts, to market their raisins only through a cooperative association he had organized. This would have prevented drastic drops in raisin prices in years of overproduction by aggressively seeking new markets and, when necessary, by buying and storing the excess raisins for future sale. He wrote:

Warning—here lies the body of M. Theodore Kearney, a visionary who thought he could teach the average farmer, and particularly raisin growers, some of the rudiments of sound business management. For eight years he worked strenuously at the task, and at the end of that time he was no further ahead than at the beginning. The effort killed him.

Kearney was actually to prove more successful than he predicted, for six years after his death, the California Associated Raisin Company (now the Sun-Maid Corporation) incorporated many of Kearney's farsighted ideas and became a major force in providing a stable raisin market for California growers. His beneficial influence still continues today, for the bachelor "Raisin King of California" left his entire estate to further the agricultural research efforts of the University of California.

Meux Home, 1889

Tulare and R Streets; 209-233-8007.

Reported in the local newspaper to be "the most elaborate residence in Fresno" when it was completed, this textbook Queen Anne home was built by Dr. Thomas Richard Meux (1838–1929). Meux had received his medical training at the University of Virginia and then served as an assistant surgeon in the Confederate army. For the next twenty years, he lived in Tennessee, where he and his wife, Mary Davis, had three children. The entire family moved to Fresno in 1887 in the hope that the dry climate would improve Mrs. Meux's poor health.

His practice must have flourished, for the next year he began this elegant new home that could have come straight out of the pages of an upscale Victorian pattern book. Indeed, Mrs. Meux and her builder are reported to have poured over such books until they finally found a one-story-cottage design she loved. The builder then simply added a second story. The signature Queen Anne roof (pyramidal hipped with lower cross gables), fish-scale shingling of the upper story, and spindlework porch (wrapped around the entire south and east facades) are complemented by a large picturesque tower. Mrs. Meux took full advantage of the large octagonal tower by making the bold decision to place the master bedroom in it. Dr. Meux conducted his medical practice both in a downstairs office as well as from a "downtown" location.

The grand house, with many modifications over the years, remained in the Meux family until 1970. Two years later, the city of Fresno, concerned about the loss of significant early homes, purchased the historic home and restored it as a Victorian house museum. Most of the original wallpapers and floor coverings had to be

Meux Home

replicated, although the original wallpaper remains in the dining room and the original floor covering in the library. Happily, the original gas- and electric-light fixtures are still in place. Six original coal-burning fireplaces with their handsome tiles and surrounds also survive. The furnishings are mostly donated pieces and include many small everyday Victorian items. Among them is an impressively barbaric and memorable women's waist-cincher.

Dr. Meux's Civil War uniform, bookcase, and writing set all remain in his home office. Many Victorian professionals practiced at home and usually, as here, had side entrances to accommodate their patients or clients.

Although there are now many intrusions into this once dominantly residential neighborhood (the very phenomenon that led the city to purchase the Meux House in the first place), early houses remain in the area, mainly along S and T Streets between Tulare and Fresno. Particularly impressive is the Brix House, (1911), at 2844 Fresno Street (private), by architect Edward Foulkes, San Francisco. This handsome Italian Renaissance design is now used for offices.

Huntington Boulevard, ca. 1914–1940

The Huntington Boulevard neighborhood was organized to supply new customers for early Fresno's struggling electric utility and streetcar companies. In 1903 a local businessman, Albert Graves Wishon, persuaded Los Angeles streetcar magnate Henry E. Huntington (the nephew of Collis Huntington, one of the Big Four builders of the historic Central Pacific Railroad, see page 213) to buy, along with two coinvestors, the unprofitable companies and then supply new capital to reorganize them under Wishon's management.

A long-range component of Wishon's plan was an upscale version of a classic streetcar company strategy. This involved "building a line to nowhere," that is, extending it through former fields and pastures at the edge of town, which were then simultaneously platted for sale as building lots with convenient adjacent trans-

Huntington Boulevard

portation (see also "Mission Hills," page 156). Wishon's version added two uncommon twists: the line would run down the center of a wide, landscaped boulevard lined with extra-large lots for prestigious houses, and, probably an important prerequisite for this expensive scheme, he controlled not only the street railway company and its adjacent land, but also the electric company that would serve the entire complex. Not surprisingly, Wishon named the principal street of his new development Huntington Boulevard, in honor of his key financial backer.

By 1914 the first houses were going up in the development, and the next year Wishon built his own new home at 3555 East Huntington Boulevard (private). During the 1920s the street became Fresno's most prestigious new address, its large lots filling with a full stylistic range of fine Eclectic-era houses. In 1939 the streetcar tracks, once a handy convenience but now, with the expansion of automobile ownership, a noisy nuisance, were removed after neighborhood protests.

Today, Wishon's original vision remains wonderfully intact. Huntington Boulevard is lushly planted and lined with tall palms. It and its adjacent streets are filled with dwellings ranging from large mansions to small cottages built in a multiplicity of styles during the period from 1914 to about 1940. At the end of Huntington Boulevard, farthest from downtown, Ranch-style houses from the 1950s and 1960s begin to dominate the streetscape. Adjacent Kerckhoff Avenue is lined with a superb collection of Craftsman designs, both large and small. Many of these have porch gables with open wood bracing or lattice designs, and some also have a very stylish low pitch to their gabled roofs.

3318 East Huntington Boulevard (private), Kahn House, 1922. This small stylistic jewel is an unusual and effective combination of Neoclassical and Italian Renaissance features. The stuccoed walls, arched windows, and flat roof are all typical of flat-roofed Italian Renaissance houses, while the handsome full-height curved entry porch and the squared side porch are Neoclassical in inspiration. Strongly symmetrical houses like this are common in both of these two styles, making them easy to blend.

The fringe of tile along the roof (unusual on flat-roofed Italian Renaissance houses and quite typical of flat-roofed Spanish Eclectic houses) and the tiled front steps (also typical of the Spanish Eclectic) complicate determining the dominant style of this delightful house. The strong symmetry and the arched first-floor windows lead one away from the flat-roofed Spanish Eclectic (which is usually asymmetrical and has no more than one arched window or door as a focal point) and toward the flat-roofed Italian Renaissance (which is usually symmetrical, has arched downstairs windows, and at least uses tile roofs on its other subtypes). All of these influences have been skillfully blended into a remarkable, one-of-a-kind house.

3406 East Huntington Boulevard (private), Turner House, 1938. This Neoclassical design has the same semicircular and full-height entry porch with a flat roof seen at 3318 (see the preceding entry). The skinny columns are typical of Neoclassical houses built after about 1920. Note the broad width of the wood siding, the balustrade above the entry porch, the mock-Federal fanlights over the two downstairs window groupings, and the recessed front door with a fanlight above.

3870 East Huntington Boulevard (private), Blum House, 1927. This is the largest of a group of related Spanish Eclectic houses, all of the combined gabled-and-hipped-roof subtype, that are scattered on corners throughout this neighborhood. Note the lower gabled wing that extends out toward the street. It has a long entry walk with a colonnade on the side that overlooks the front courtyard. The main house block has a tower at the entrance. This example has a rough-textured finish on the stucco and many typical stylistic details. Maisler House (1938), at 3606 East Huntington Boulevard (private), is a slightly smaller version with the same basic form of roof, colonnaded entry walk, front court-yard, and tower at the entry, but with fewer elaborations. At 3462 East Huntington Boulevard (private), Folsom House (1941), is a yet-smaller, one-story version with these same basic characteristics. Number 3301 East Huntington Boulevard (private) appears smaller still and has the same general characteristics, but no entry tower. Drew House (1936), at 3105 East Huntington Boulevard (private), is a final related house that has a simpler cross-gabled roof. It has the gable extended outward toward the front, the colonnaded entry walk, and the entry tower, but lacks the front courtyard. This has the advantage of making it easy to see the long colonnaded entry walk and towered entry that distinguish this set of related houses.

3839 East Huntington Boulevard (private), Lewis House, 1939. Note the unusual entry porch and bay windows made of metal. These details are occasionally found in houses built between about 1935 and 1955 and were almost certainly available from catalogs. Entry porches with this canopy-roof shape are often seen on the simplified Regency version of the Colonial Revival that was popular during these same years. Here the porch and matching bays are on a house that has small, arch-shaped breaks in the cornice line similar to those in the taller, through-the-cornice windows of French Eclectic houses.

3729 East Huntington Boulevard (private), Bekins-McClatchy House, 1926. This is a handsome and restrained Tudor design. Note the two parapeted gables of slightly different size, the flattened Tudor arches of the door and entry porch, and the unusual finish of the stucco wall cladding. Interestingly, the house lacks two of the most common features of Tudor designs—a prominent chimney and an area of casement windows.

3465 East Huntington Boulevard (private), Terrill House, 1934; Taylor-Wheeler, Fresno, architects. This is an unusually large and fine Monterey-style design. The tiled roof and the one-story gabled wing are both typical. A variant of the Monterey style was called Creole French by builders of the day. This is similar in form to the Monterey except that the characteristic cantilevered balcony has lacy cast-iron trim inspired by the balconies of the New Orleans French Quarter. This house sneaks bits of this lacy ironwork into its

balcony design. Note the broad metal windows downstairs, precursors of the large picture windows that were so popular in the 1950s.

3128 East Kerckhoff Avenue (private), 1915. This adorable Craftsman cottage has both the very low roof pitch and the open porch gable with wood bracing that are frequent features in Kerckhoff Avenue's Craftsman houses. This one is completely clad in wood shingles.

3136 East Kerckhoff Avenue (private), 1922. Note the distinctive curve at the apex of the gable in this Craftsman design. This same curve is seen in many of the Craftsman houses along Huntington Boulevard and Kerckhoff Avenue.

3204 East Kerckhoff Avenue (private), 1915. Craftsman designs with a single window-surrounded upstairs room, as seen here, were called airplane bungalows, perhaps because airplanes could be spotted in all directions. Note that porch supports rise from only the two outer pedestals of the balustrade while the pedestals to each side of the entry are "empty." It's easy to assume that the original supports were later removed from these, but many Craftsman houses were designed this way to allow an uninterrupted view from the porch. This house has been somewhat modified by the addition of modern iron detailing; other similar designs occur in the 3400 and 4000 blocks of East Kerckhoff.

Tower District, ca. 1915–1940

Contemporaneous with the Huntington Boulevard neighborhood east of town, this near-north-side district has generally smaller lots but a similar mix of both large and small houses illustrating a rich variety of Eclectic-era designs. The district takes its name from a favorite local landmark, an Art Moderne commercial block dominated by the streamlined **Tower Movie Theater.** Located at the corner of Olive Avenue and Wishon Street, this Tower Block is now the heart of a funky neighborhood-scale commercial district with many unusual shops and restaurants.

This north-side area began to develop around 1900 as the city outgrew its original, angled street grid and moved across Divisadero Street into a newly platted

Tower District

Tower District

grid of north–south and east–west streets. The most intact grouping of homes in the area is just north of the Tower Theater and was developed slightly later, from about 1915 to 1940. This area is highlighted on the map on page 41 and featured in the descriptions below.

North Van Ness Avenue was the main thoroughfare linking these northern neighborhoods with the city's downtown commercial core. South of Olive Avenue and the Tower Block, North Van Ness still retains scattered fine homes from the streetcar-dominated years of 1900 to 1915. This is now uncommon, for, as automobiles replaced streetcars in the decades after 1920, the large early dwellings that once lined such thoroughfares have mostly been demolished for automobile-oriented commercial structures fronted by parking lots (see also the discussion of Montana Avenue in El Paso, Texas, page 584). Note particularly the blocks from Divisadero Street to Alhambra Street. An adjacent street parallel to North Van Ness, North Fulton Avenue, also has some interesting remaining homes in the blocks between Divisadero Street and California Freeway 180.

1525 North Echo Avenue (private), Todd House, 1934. This delightful house is part of a row of six Spanish Eclectic dwellings built along North Echo Avenue, most of them in the 1930s. Spanish Eclectic houses typically have stucco walls, but here we see a distinctive brick pattern with the mortar extruding from the joints as if each brick were squashed down on an unusually large batch of mortar. There is a handsome stone arch at the recessed entry, which is also accented by a wrought-iron gate. The attached garage is made less dominant by recessing it a bit under a tile-covered shed roof. Note also the low stone walls and the handsome stonework that paves the driveway.

1487 North Echo Street (private), Everts House, 1920; Shorb and Meade, Fresno, architects. This simplified stucco Tudor design owes much to the work of contemporaneous English architects such as C. F. A. Voysey (1857–1941) and M. H. Baillie Scott (1865–1945), who reinterpreted English vernacular house designs with an "elegant simplicity." As here, some Craftsman (or Arts and Crafts) influence also was found in their work. Note the strong horizontal line and the bold, stylized chimney, both typical of Voysey's designs. Almost identical chimneys are found at 625 Home Street (private), which has some of the same simplicity of design, and at 1445 North Echo Street (private), which has more typical Tudor detailing.

667 East Home Avenue (private), Parlier House, 1918. This airplane bungalow (see page 47) has a slight Oriental flare at the tops of the gables.

601 East Pine Avenue (private), Johnson House, 1922. This unusual Mission-style design of the one-story, symmetrical subtype has an entry porch shaped a bit like the top half of the quatrefoil windows often found in this style.

640 East Pine Avenue (private), Gates House, 1931; Taylor-Wheeler, Fresno, architects. This picturesque French Eclectic design with tower would have been called a Norman cottage by its builder. Note the unusual false-thatched roof, which here wraps around the tower and also ends with a rolled effect at its corners.

LOS ANGELES AREA

Compared to the San Francisco Bay Area, where the discovery of rich Sierra Nevada goldfields near the Pacific coast's best natural harbor led to almost instant urbanization in the late 1840s (see page 159), urban Los Angeles had a very slow birth. The Los Angeles Basin (see illustration below) had only one natural advantage—it is by far the largest area of relatively flat, coastal land anywhere along the entire mountainous Pacific shoreline. This would have made it ideal for both agriculture and town sites except for two crucial problems. First, it is mostly surrounded by broad beaches and tidal flats that provide no natural harbor. Second, and even more important, most of the basin did not have a reliable, year-round water supply. Its subtropical Mediterranean-type climate receives most of its relatively meager annual rainfall during the winter. As a result, local rivers (which begin in the surrounding mountains and cross the basin to the sea) flow mostly in the winter and early spring—by summer most are dry and dusty channels called arroyos.

In the Colonial era the Spanish missions (see pages ix–xii) were served mostly by wagon roadways, and the lack of harbor was not important. The water problem was solved by locating Mission San Gabriel and the small agricultural town of Los Angeles at sites near the base of the mountains where spring-fed rivers normally provided enough year-round water for small-scale irrigated agriculture.

The first glimmering of the basin's urban future came with the arrival of the Southern Pacific Railroad in 1876. With the railroad came support for a dredged, man-made harbor on San Pedro Bay, part of the basin's southern shore. The railroads also brought the heavy machinery needed to dam nearby mountain streams and create lakes that provided a dependable water supply. By the 1880s the basin was in the first of a series of railroad-era booms based on irrigated crops grown in its fertile soils and mild, sunny climate. At first this was only modestly successful. By 1900 Los Angeles's population of 102,000 was less than a third of San Francisco's 343,000 inhabitants.

Los Angeles's own gold rush was to begin in the next decade and was based not on metallic nuggets but on growing high-value golden navel oranges. A nationwide campaign promoted the sale of irrigated "mini-orchards"; this was an unprecedented success. By 1910 the city's population tripled to 319,000 and surrounding Los Angeles County (where many of the new orchard developments were located) had also surged from 68,000 inhabitants in 1900 to 185,000 in 1910. The boom continued into the next decade; in 1920 the city's population was 577,000, exceeding San Fran-

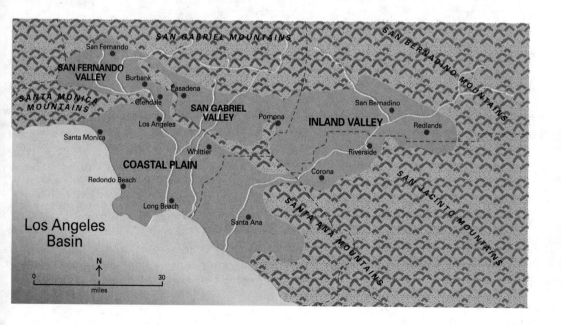

cisco's 507,000 to make it the largest city in the West, a title it has since maintained by ever-widening margins.

By 1920 mini-orchards of citrus trees, and small farms of other high-value intensive crops, occupied most of the Los Angeles Basin's Coastal Plain as well as large parts of the adjacent San Fernando, San Gabriel, and Inland Valleys (see illustration page 49). Spread over a region roughly thirty miles wide and seventy miles long, this concentrated agriculture generated numerous market and trading centers. These small towns

were connected with one another, and to the core city of Los Angeles, both by roadways and by an unusually extensive network of fast electric-trolley lines that carried both passengers and freight.

Just as San Francisco's initial gold rush boom was followed by the spectacular Comstock Lode silver bonanza (see page 202), in the early 1920s Los Angeles received two new economic windfalls that, in a single decade, more than doubled its population to 1.2 million and made it the nation's fifth-largest city. First

came the discovery of giant oil fields in the Long Beach area, fortuitously close to the region's large, man-made seaport. California, lacking important coal deposits and with relatively small petroleum reserves, had previously been energy starved. These new discoveries began the basin's role as a major industrial center. On a quite different note, in 1920 the small suburban town of Hollywood had recently become the nation's principal center for making newly popular, "feature-length" motion pictures. By 1930 moviemaking was the city of Los Angeles's largest industry.

Throughout the dramatic boom decades from 1900 to 1940, the commercial core of Los Angeles expanded steadily westward, along Wilshire Boulevard, from its original site near the early Hispanic-era plaza (see Near West LA and Far West LA on map opposite). The city's upscale residential districts generally moved in the same direction in a broad belt roughly bounded by Wilshire Boulevard on the south and the Santa Monica Mountains on the north.

Three of Los Angeles's early satellite towns, Pasadena (an early Los Angeles competitor in the San Gabriel Valley), Long Beach (near the site of the basin's man-made seaport), and Redlands (a fine survivor of the mini-orchard era), all have important concentrations of historic neighborhoods and museum houses. In addition, four once-rural dwellings, now important museum houses, are located within the more recent communities of Santa Clarita, Malibu, and City of Industry.

The Los Angeles Area Today

The summary above describes the urban expansion of the Los Angeles Basin up until about 1940. In succeeding decades the area's growth continued as industry and commerce replaced agriculture as the dominant elements of the economy. Today the region's mini-orchards have mostly been replaced by endless residential suburbs, which now cover most of the basin except for the farthest eastern reaches of the Inland Valley. This massive "urban sprawl" is often blamed on the automobile, which rather quickly replaced urban and interurban electric trolleys during the 1920s and 1930s. This is, however, only part of the story, for the earlier mini-orchard economy had already established a series of strong and independent satellite towns scattered throughout the basin. As the population increased and industrial expansion required new building sites, these became the nuclei of still another boom, this one based on neighborhood growth and a dispersed pattern of new, job-creating commerce and industry. In a very real sense, the area's much-maligned modern freeway system is the direct descendant of the interurban trolleys that served the dispersed mini-orchards and small-town trading centers of the Basin's agricultural boom years.

CITY OF INDUSTRY

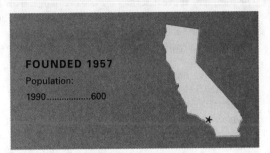

FOUNDED 1957
Population:
1990.................600

The two important museum houses described here, built as the successive seats of a large rural agricultural complex along San Jose Creek about twenty miles east of downtown Los Angeles, could hardly have ended up in a less appropriately named town than City of Industry. This municipality was founded after the Second World War as the farmlands along San Jose Creek became the site of a vast industrial park that stretches for many miles along the creek and its adjacent railroads. The good news is that the affluent new town, most of whose workers live elsewhere, decided to devote some of its tax revenues to making its principal historic sights into a first-class museum complex, emphasizing local history as demonstrated in these two carefully researched and restored houses, one each from the Romantic and Eclectic eras.

About eight miles to the southwest, in the town of Santa Fe Springs, is another important municipally owned house (see page 55) that preserves one of the few surviving larger commissions of the pioneering modernist architect Irving J. Gill.

Workman House, 1840s and 1870s, and La Casa Nueva, 1927

Homestead Museum, 15415 East Don Julian Road; 626-968-8492; Ezra F. Kysor, Los Angeles, architect for Workman House; Walker and Eisen, Los Angeles, and Roy Seldon Price, Los Angeles, architects for La Casa Nueva.

These two homes, which are featured on the same tour, tell the story of southern California in the 1840s and 1870s (when the first house was built and then remodeled) and in the 1920s (when the second was built). The story of these homes provides a microcosm of the history of the early Anglo West—and of fortunes won and lost by one California family.

Born in England, William Workman (1799–1876) came to the United States at the behest of his brother

David in 1822; he worked for his brother in a saddlery shop in Missouri for several years before joining a caravan to New Mexico. There, after a period as a mountain trapper, he opened a successful store in Taos with a partner, John Rowland. In order to become part of the community (and be allowed to marry), Workman became a naturalized Mexican citizen, converted to Catholicism, and in 1829 married Nicolasa Urioste (1802–1892), a Taos native.

Then came the successful Texas Revolution of 1836 (see page xii). After this, Anglos in other parts of northern Mexico were regarded with suspicion by authorities in Mexico City. Workman and Rowland were victims of this understandable shift in attitude. In 1840, the Republic of Texas named Workman and Rowland as the two agents who were representing Texas's interests in annexing New Mexico. (This may well have been done without either Workman's or Rowland's knowledge, and they did not accept this role they had been "given.") Nonetheless, in Mexico, as Taos was at the time, even a perceived affiliation with Texas was tantamount to treason. Workman and Rowland and their families decided to head to California overland, taking about forty other Anglos with them. Leaving in September of 1841, they traveled over the Old Spanish Trail and became the first Anglo immigrant party to enter southern California via an eastern overland route. (Although also part of Mexico, California was far from Texas and had so few Anglos that officials were not yet nervous.)

The two partners immediately applied for Mexican land grants in California and were initially given 18,000 acres (in Rowland's name only), and then in 1845 Mexican Governor Pio Pico revised this to 48,800 acres (11 square leagues) in both of their names. Workman built his first simple one-story adobe home here in 1842. He ranched and farmed and then, like other California ranchers, discovered in 1849 that the value of his cattle had multiplied almost thirtyfold. He became wealthy selling food to the miners during the next ten years. Luckily he had diversified his agricultural operation and so was able to weather the great flood and subsequent drought of the early 1860s. In 1867 Workman finally had the title to his Mexican land grant upheld by the courts (he had filed for this in 1852). It now seemed like a propitious time to enlarge his original adobe dwelling and give it a more stylish face.

By the early 1870s the Workman House had been enlarged with two new brick wings and the entire house

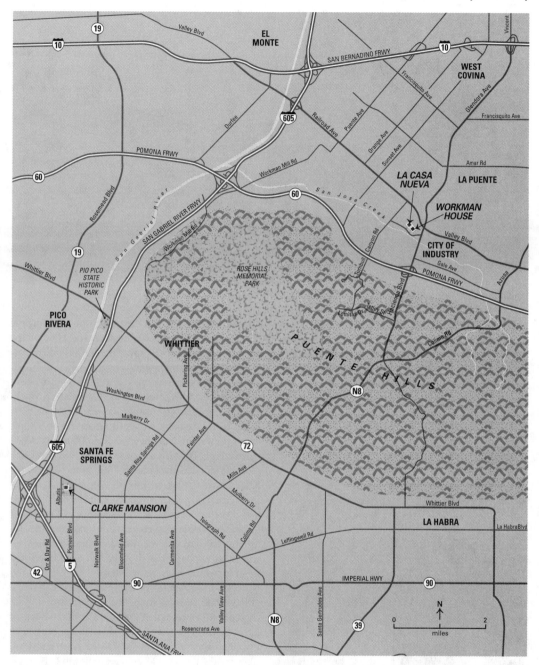

transformed to a new Romantic-era image—a Gothic Revival shape, but with Italianate details (a common stylistic mixture at the time). The house has a pair of steeply pitched front-gabled roofs, one on each of the two added wings; this gives it the distinctive look of a paired-gable Gothic Revival house. But rather than a Gothic pointed-arch window, the windows here are Italianate (round arched and hooded and with small Corinthian columns between). And rather than the decorated vergeboards or cross bracing of the Gothic Revival, the cornice line has closely spaced Italianate brackets. The porches were finished with plaster, which was painted and scored to look like blocks of granite.

Having weathered the crises of land title and the 1860s drought that put an end to so many of the Hispanic land grant ranches, the Workman family should

Workman House

now have had an easier life. But William instead entered into an ill-fated banking venture with his son-in-law, F. P. F. Temple (1822–1880), the respected husband of their daughter, Antonia Margarita (1830–1892). In 1868 Workman and Temple formed a banking partnership with Isaias Hellman (see page 274). Hellman pulled out in 1871 because he did not like the lending policies of the bank. But Temple pressed on and somehow convinced Workman to continue as his banking partner. The restructured Temple and Workman bank

Temple's hoganlike office

opened in 1871. Then, in the 1875 panic following the collapse of the Comstock Lode, there was a run on the bank (the same run that proved the end of William Ralston; see page 204). The only way to reopen it was to get a large loan from Lucky Baldwin (see page 270), who demanded that this be secured by a mortgage on Workman's home and ranch lands. Rather than being reassured when the bank reopened after the run, people continued to withdraw their funds, and the bank closed permanently. Baldwin foreclosed. After the bank sent a receiver to take possession of his home, Workman killed himself at age seventy-six. His son-in-law soon suffered a series of strokes and died in 1880. Baldwin allowed the women to stay in the homes and even sold the family back small pieces of land, but these were also lost. Indeed, almost all of Workman's and Temple's descendants' properties in the area had been foreclosed upon for various reasons by 1900.

In 1912 Workman's grandson, Walter P. Temple (1869–1938), then a struggling walnut farmer, purchased some of his father's old land from the estate of Lucky Baldwin. In 1914 oil was found in a pool of water left standing after a rain. By 1916 a lease had been signed with Standard Oil, and, beginning in 1917, some twenty-six producing wells were drilled on the land. Temple and his wife, Laura Gonzalez (1871–1922), promptly repurchased much of the old Workman Homestead and, after a bit of work restoring the old structures, proceeded with plans to build their dream house, La Casa Nueva, near their grandfather's old ranch house. Architects Walker and Eisen drew up the Temples' ideas, and then Laura Temple died a sudden

Temple House entry

Temple House courtyard

and unexpected death. Plans stopped, and it was a year before the family decided to continue with construction, dedicating the house to Laura.

They now hired architect Roy Seldon Price to proceed with the house. The design evolved in his hands into the present Spanish Eclectic home, which is built of lightly fired adobe bricks. The house is filled with architectural ornament. Beautiful stained glass, almost fifty pieces made using several different techniques, were incorporated into the home. The themes include the history of California, the history of the Workman and Temple families, and more generic subjects like portraits of authors for the library and painted flowering vines that meander across upstairs bedroom windows. The glass windows were carefully planned to look quite old. The studio that produced these is unknown, although it is believed they came from the Chicago area, and they resemble the style and type of glass made at the Munich Studios there between 1903 and 1932.

Wrought-iron fixtures and ornaments are also found throughout La Casa Nueva. Many of the heavy wood doors are hand carved, as are the handsome corbels in the front hall. The house also features numerous tiles: for floors and baseboards, in bathrooms and kitchen, and on the stairs and even the outdoor walks. There are three tile niches inside that cost fifty dollars each (when an average weekly family income was but twenty dollars). Many of the featured tiles were imported from Puebla, Mexico; others came from U.S. sources.

While the house has most of the original interior features, it has only a few pieces of Temple family furniture. Temple's original furnishings are in his office, a small detached Indian hoganlike structure, and other pieces are scattered throughout the home. All of the furnishings added to the home have been very carefully chosen.

Sadly, history was to repeat itself. Walter Temple, like his father before him, overextended himself and had to borrow money to cover his obligations. He was also required to mortgage his personal properties in order to do so. Temple was to lose everything, despite great attempts to save the old Workman Homestead itself. The mortgage on the Workman Homestead came due on October 29, 1929, and when he could not pay, Temple lost the property he had so proudly repurchased to reclaim the families' honor. After his family left, the home served as a military academy and then a convalescent home before being purchased by the City of Industry in 1963. During the next thirteen years, the city purchased the remainder of the six-acre park and undertook a lengthy and careful restoration.

Today, the Homestead Museum offers an intriguing story of fortunes won and lost and of a family whose history was intertwined with that of southern California from 1840 until 1930. In doing this it shows two important houses, one a lovingly updated early immigrant's adobe and the other a 1920s Spanish Eclectic home. In addition to the normal tour, there are also group tours that look in depth at some of the fine architectural decoration found in La Casa Nueva.

Clarke Mansion, 1921

South side of Telegraph Road, between Albutis Street and Pioneer Boulevard, Santa Fe Springs;
562-868-3876; Irving J. Gill, San Diego, architect.
Just down the road, by suburban Los Angeles standards, is the city of Santa Fe Springs, located about eight miles southwest of the Workman-Temple complex. Here the city has purchased the important Clarke Mansion, which is open for limited hours each week, even though the city of Santa Fe Springs uses it as a conference center. Built for Chauncey Dwight Clarke and his wife, Marie, this was the last of Irving Gill's major residential designs and is the only one of his large

Clarke Mansion courtyard

concrete homes to survive in almost-original condition. The Clarke House is constructed of poured-in-place reinforced concrete and built around a central courtyard with a simple colonnade on three sides. The finest of Gill's classic concrete homes that remain, it is a treasure that will be of interest to anyone interested in Gill or early modernism (even with its conference center furnishings). For more on Gill, see the more traditional Marston House in San Diego (page 153), which is one of his more traditional early works.

LONG BEACH

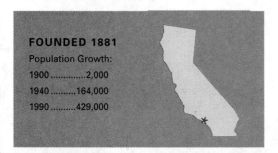

FOUNDED 1881

Population Growth:

1900 2,000
1940 164,000
1990 429,000

Long Beach is the youngest, and largest, of the three adjacent cities that contain Los Angeles's massive harbor facilities, today the nation's busiest seaport complex.

Landlocked Settlements

Los Angeles and other early settlements in the dry Los Angeles Basin were located away from the ocean to be nearer the basin's mountainous rim, whose streams gave them a dependable water supply for both domestic uses and for irrigated agriculture. Entirely fringed by wide beaches and shallow mudflats, the basin's shoreline also lacked the fine natural harbors found at San Diego and San Francisco; the only even semiprotected anchorage lay about twenty-five miles southwest of Los Angeles adjacent to the western margin of San Pedro Bay. Even there, arriving ships had to anchor far offshore and laboriously transfer their cargoes to smaller vessels for transport to shallow-water, beachfront wharves. This system was adequate during the Hispanic ranching era, when only occasional Yankee sailing ships arrived to trade manufactured goods for local cattle hides and tallow, but after the American takeover and San Francisco Bay–focused gold rush in the late 1840s (see page xx), it became clear that the Los Angeles region could never prosper without better harbor

facilities. Building and expanding these have been modifying the margins of San Pedro Bay ever since.

Phineas T. Banning and Wilmington

The principal architect of Los Angeles's early harbor and other transportation improvements was a far-sighted Yankee entrepreneur named Phineas T. Banning who, in 1858, founded the new port town of Wilmington, which lies immediately west of modern Long Beach (see page 62). Banning's early harbor played a key role in convincing the Southern Pacific Railroad to detour its main line, building from San Francisco southeastward toward Arizona and Texas, through the small town of Los Angeles in 1876. Now with both a deepwater harbor and transcontinental rail connections (via San Francisco at first, more directly when the Southern Pacific reached Texas in 1881), Los Angeles was poised for many decades of railroad-based booms (see page 66); by 1920 it had replaced San Francisco as California's largest city, a position it has retained ever since.

Phineas Banning in his early twenties, soon after his arrival in California in 1851

Long Beach, Oil, and the Navy

Long Beach, the most recent and largest of Los Angeles's seaport cities, was an early seaside resort community served, after 1902, by the efficient "Big Red Cars" of Henry Huntington's Pacific Electric Railway (see page 68). Now conveniently linked to both central Los Angeles and the older adjacent seaport cities of Wilmington and San Pedro, Long Beach became a popular seaside residential suburb. By 1920 it had a population of fifty-six thousand.

Beginning in the 1890s, several important oil fields had been discovered in the Los Angeles Basin, but these

Banning's wharf and railroad, ca. early 1870s

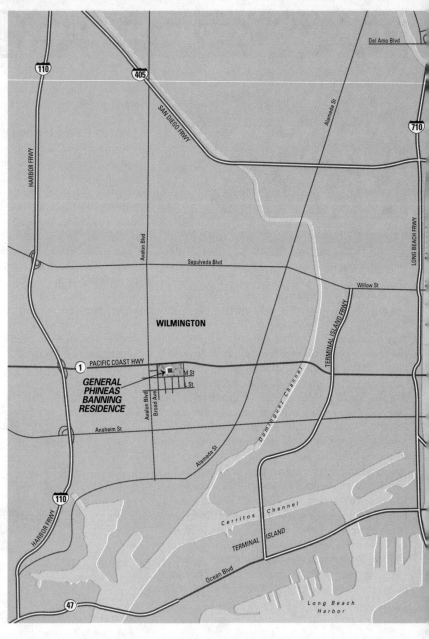

were mostly confined to its inland agricultural regions on the eastern side of the basin. In 1921 the largest oil discovery of them all was made at Signal Hill on the northern edge of Long Beach only three miles from the ocean. By then some relatively small-scale harbor improvements had attracted light industry to parts of the Long Beach waterfront. Soon the harbor was being massively expanded, both as a petroleum port and as the site of a major U.S. naval base, which had the advantage of abundant fuel supplies for its fleet conve-

niently at hand. These new activities caused Long Beach's population to almost triple, from 56,000 to 142,000, during the 1920s.

Long Beach naval base expansions, along with the construction of nearby shipyards and aircraft plants, accelerated during the Second World War and Korean War. These contributed to another surge in the city's population—from 164,000 in 1940 to 344,000 by 1960. All of this seaport-based activity, coupled with its role as the dominant office, shopping, and entertainment

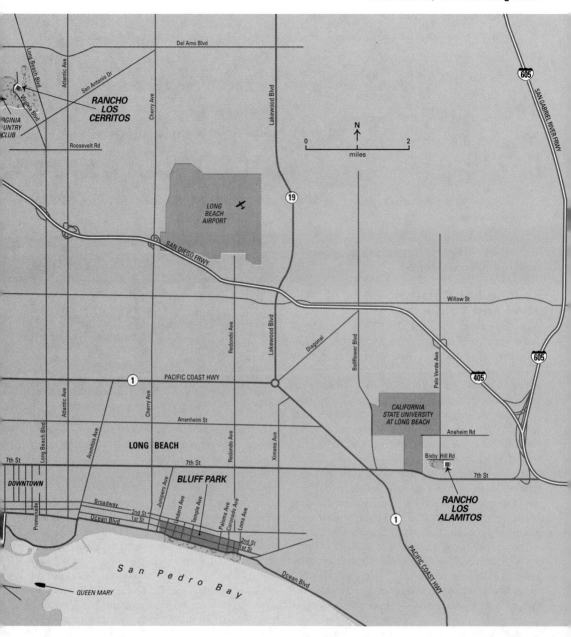

center for the entire harbor complex, has made Long Beach far and away the second-largest city in the Los Angeles area for many decades.

Modern Long Beach

In spite of its status as a major industrial seaport, many parts of Long Beach still retain the flavor of its original role as a residential suburb, a tribute to the city's enlightened policies on urban planning. Today, its revitalizing downtown adjoins a popular, tourist-oriented waterfront district whose most dramatic historic attraction is the carefully maintained **Queen Mary** (1126 Queen's Highway; 310-435-3511), the giant Art Deco British passenger liner launched in 1936.

In addition to the elegant Greek Revival Banning Residence in nearby Wilmington, Long Beach amazingly still retains the central Ranch houses, now surrounded by twentieth-century suburbs, of the two huge cattle ranches that occupied the entire area in the Mexican era and for many years afterward. Among the

Rancho Los Cerritos

most scenic of its Eclectic-era suburbs is the fine water-front Bluff Park neighborhood.

Rancho Los Cerritos, 1844 and 1930s

4600 Virginia Boulevard; 562-570-1755.
Today but 5 acres remain of the 27,000-acre Rancho Los Cerritos that Manuela Nieto de Cota inherited in 1804 from her father, Manuel Cota, a retired Spanish soldier. Her father's estate consisted of the 167,000-acre land grant he received upon retiring from the Spanish army; this was divided among Manuela and her four brothers. The eldest, Juan Jose Nieto, received a nearby tract which became Rancho Los Alamitos (see the following entry). Jonathan Temple and his wife, Rafaela Cota Temple, purchased Manuela's land in 1843 and built this historic house. Don Juan Temple, as Jonathan was more often called, was one of the pioneers of early Los Angeles, where he built the first merchandise store and the original courthouse and began the first library.

The Temples' home was built of adobe brick and red-wood. It had a two-story main block with Monterey-style porches on the rear and two 140-foot-long one-story wings, which created a front courtyard. The family lived in the two-story house, and the long wings housed various work and storage rooms for the rancho. The court-yard was kept clean-swept during the rancho's early years, when it was used as a working part of the ranch.

In 1866 the Temples sold Rancho Los Cerritos to the Flint-Bixby Company sheep ranchers. Jotham Bixby (died 1916) and his wife lived here overseeing the ranch, which supported as many as thirteen thousand sheep. After Jotham's death, the house was rented out for a number of years. Then in 1931, Jotham's nephew, Llewellyn Bixby Jr. (died 1942) and his wife, Avis Smith Bixby (died 1954), bought the house and five sur-rounding acres. They restored the house, 1930s style.

This included adding the present tiled roof, enlarging the parlor to two stories, adding a glassed-in sun porch, and many other improvements. They also converted the front courtyard to a rear garden and put the main entry on what had been the rear house facade.

Today, the house has been kept just as the Llewellyn Bixbys left it, complete with all of the 1930s interior changes and innovations. The Bixbys' furnishings do not remain, only the architectural changes. In some places furnishings reflecting the earlier years of the ran-cho have been set into the 1930s setting. Like its sibling, Rancho Los Alamitos, Rancho Los Cerritos has sur-vived from a much earlier era, but has been much changed in the process. The interpretation here stresses the many adaptations and changes made during the life of the rancho.

Rancho Los Alamitos, early 1800s with many additions

6400 Bixby Hill Road (enter through residential security gate at intersection of Anaheim Road and Palo Verde Avenue); 562-431-3541.
This home was originally part of the same Manuel Cota land grant as Rancho Los Cerritos (see the preceding entry). Manuel left this twenty-eight thousand-acre

section to his eldest son, who is believed to have built the original small adobe house sometime after 1805, making it one of the earliest homes in California. However, multiple later additions have covered up what are thought to be the home's modest beginnings, today revealed only in the deep window and door openings. Wings were later built on the north and south to form a courtyard. In 1925 a second story and two covered porches were added to the main portion, and the interior was redone. Today Rancho Los Alamitos appears as a pleasant and comfortable early-twentieth-century home. Its many additions leave it not as an example of any particular architectural style, but rather as a great example of a home that grew in stages, always with the emphasis on friendliness and utility rather than a highly fashionable facade. One of Los Alamitos's most pleasant aspects is its large and varied garden developed in the 1920s and 1930s and designed by Boston's prestigious Olmsted Brothers, among others.

The rancho has had a series of distinguished owners. In 1834 it was purchased by Governor Jose Figuerosa for five hundred dollars, less than five cents an acre. In 1842 Abel Stearns (1798–1871) bought it for six thousand dollars and lived there until his cattle herds were wiped out by the droughts of the early 1860s, and the spread went back to the mortgage holder, Michael Reese, a San Francisco financier. In 1878 John Bixby leased the home and in 1881 purchased it through a partnership with his cousin, Jotham Bixby (see the preceding entry) and I. W. Hellman, a prominent Califor-

nia investor. John Bixby and his wife, Susan Hathaway Bixby (died 1906), began the garden and the transformation into today's house. After Susan Bixby's death, their son, Fred Bixby (1875–1952), and his wife, Florence (died 1961), moved into the house and made many more additions and changes—such as adding skylights and also many built-in bookshelves, the latter with Florence's "egg money" (the money a wife received for tending the chickens and selling their eggs was traditionally money she could use for anything she wanted). Bathrooms were added and the garden enlarged. The discovery of oil on Bixby land at nearby Signal Hill added an infusion of funds with which to undertake ranch improvements. It was Fred and Florence Bixby's family that gave the remaining seven and a half acres of Rancho Los Alamitos to the city of Long Beach. Today, the house looks as it did when the Bixbys last lived here; their generous gift included most of the furnishings that the family had used during its many years at Rancho Los Alamitos.

Rancho Los Alamitos

General Phineas Banning Residence

General Phineas Banning Residence, 1864

401 East M Street, Wilmington; 310-548-7777.

This extraordinary Greek Revival home, one of the finest ever built west of the Rocky Mountains, symbolizes the life of its farsighted and entrepreneurial builder, General Phineas Banning (1830–1885). Banning, a native of Wilmington, Delaware, became fascinated with ocean shipping when he was but sixteen. He soon found a job on the wharves in Philadelphia, and by 1851, the year he departed for southern California, Banning had learned much about the business. He sailed from Philadelphia to Panama, walked and sailed across the isthmus, and then caught a ship to the then-small town of Los Angeles (population 1,600). Once there, Banning discovered that there was no decent port. Ships had to anchor far offshore in nearby San Pedro and unload onto flatboats to take their cargo ashore. From there, the cargo was loaded onto freight wagons and hauled overland to Los Angeles, over dusty, bumpy dirt roads.

Banning entered the business of "staging and freighting," as the chore of getting a ship's cargo to Los Angeles was called. He was a fierce competitor and was said to be able to drive a stagecoach over the poor roads faster than anyone else. These hours of driving rough roads gave Banning a fine appreciation for the crucial role played by good transportation and also provided him with plenty of time to reflect on the need for a proper port and integrated transportation system if Los Angeles was to flourish as a city. Banning took upon himself the role of creating such an integrated system. He pioneered stage routes from Los Angeles to Yuma, Arizona, and Salt Lake City, Utah; purchased land for a port on San Pedro Bay (which became the town of Wilmington, named in honor of Banning's childhood home); worked as a senator with the state government to get a railroad built between Los Angeles and San Pedro Bay (the Los Angeles and San Pedro Railroad, completed in 1869); worked with the federal government to create a deepwater channel and port; and finally successfully campaigned to bring the Southern Pacific Railroad through Los Angeles, becoming its land acquisitions agent through the Arizona and New Mexico Territories. Banning was the pivotal figure in creating the early transportation network that led to the development of today's Los Angeles.

In 1864, when Banning finished this fine home, he and his first wife, Rebecca Sanford Banning (died 1868), had two surviving sons with a third yet to be born. Banning's transportation empire was still in its infancy. The large home was designed not only to hold their growing family, but also to provide a setting in which he could convince politicians, business partners, and potential investors to carry out his masterful plans.

For this he chose a front-gabled, or "temple-form," Greek Revival house with a two-level porch stretched across the front facade and supported by squared columns. The front entry with an elliptical fanlight above is a later addition. A rooftop cupola was used by Banning to keep tabs on the harbor he was developing. After Banning's death in 1885, all three of his sons (William, born 1858; Joseph Brent, born 1861; and Hancock, born 1866) maintained his business enterprises. William had an interest in history and purchased some fine furnishings for the home. Joseph Brent and his wife, Katherine, lived here for a period. It was not until 1925, after the death of the youngest son, Hancock, that the house was finally sold by the family. Just two years later, the house and twenty surrounding acres were acquired by the City of Los Angeles for a park and house museum.

The Banning family has donated forty-two pieces of furniture that were used in the home by various Banning family members. This gives the house the distinctive look of a home that has been lived in by several generations. The furnishings acquired to complement the Banning pieces have been carefully selected. Among the Banning pieces are Phineas Banning's mahogany-veneered four-poster bed, an armoire given to Phineas by General Mariano Vallejo, and many family portraits. The fine fireplaces in the parlor and the family living room were hand-carved by William Stotzner, who was hired by William Banning to make some later improvements to the home. Another later addition is an 1876 bathroom. And today the carriage house holds a collection of early horse-drawn vehicles.

Bluff Park, 1903–1940s

The homes of the Bluff Park neighborhood were built mainly from 1900 to 1920, a period when Long Beach's population was growing rapidly. Located along a low bluff overlooking San Pedro Bay, the grandest homes were those along Ocean Boulevard, which looked out onto the water. The area was later zoned for high-rise apartments, and in 1966 and 1972 high-rise condominiums replaced a couple of the district's architectural gems. The residents worked hard to save the neighborhood from more such intrusions and in 1982 succeeded in gaining historic designation.

The traffic on Ocean Boulevard is so fast moving that nothing is featured on that street, but it is definitely worth looking at (carefully and quickly or else on foot). If you are walking, 2749 East Ocean Boulevard (private) was designed by Irving Gill in 1918. First Street is still intact and features a delightful mixture of houses and styles.

Bluff Park

2761 East First Street (private), Swartz House, 1926. A striking copper top ornaments the chimney on the right of this false-thatched-roof Tudor home. Note the use of both stucco and brick infill for the half-timbering and the arched driveway entrance. Roofed archways, sloping from the side of a Tudor house, are often used to provide an entry to a side garden; they are less often built in a scale to accommodate a driveway.

2621 East First Street (private), 1903. Almost everything about this front-gabled house looks original, as if it has come straight from the pages of a pattern book. Because Chicagoan William Radford's popular early-twentieth-century pattern books often advocate the use of the rock-faced concrete blocks used here for foundation and porch supports, we checked *The Radford American Homes* and found a design (number 518) with a similar distinctive roof and eave design (front gabled with cross gables ending in the same plane as the sides of the house and roof returns on each side of the gable front but with slightly different porch and window design. Of course this discovery simply raised further questions. Was there another, unpublished, plan that was identical? Or did the original builder use plan 518 and simply modify it? Is the interior floor plan the same or similar? Or are the similarities between this and the Radford designs coincidental?

This is a front-gabled folk house, as its details do not place it in any stylistic category. The patterned shingles in the gables are holdovers from the Queen Anne style, and the concrete-block porch supports can be found on several different styles. Sometimes simple front-gabled houses like this are called homestead houses, a name popularized by the *Old House Journal*.

2405 East First Street (private), 1911. An intricately crafted, shed-roofed composition of windows and wood trim located above the entry porch adds distinction to this front-gabled Craftsman house.

2319 East First Street (private), 1912. A side-gabled Craftsman house with a front-gabled entry porch and matching roof dormer. The 2300 block of East First Street has a particularly nice grouping of Craftsman-style homes clad with rectangular wood shingles, which makes it a great place to compare ways these can be applied to form varied cladding patterns. Here the shingles are of different widths, but are carefully applied to form alternating narrow and wide horizontal rows. Next door at 2329 East First Street (private), 1910, uniformly narrow wood shingles are applied to form alternating narrow and wide horizontal rows.

2320 East First Street (private), 1912. Pedestals and a porch of assorted-sized rocks are finished with a layer of brick. The shingles here are of a medium uniform width and are applied in a staggered manner to form wide, even horizontal rows.

2732 East First Street (private), 1905. Narrow clapboard siding gives this Craftsman house a quite different look from the shingle-clad examples above. Note the intricate design cut into the ends of the exposed rafters.

3048 East First Street (private), 1921. One-story, flat-roofed Italian Renaissance houses often occur in California (in the rest of the country, flat-roofed Italian Renaissance houses are more often large and architect designed). This one-story example is symmetrical, has an arched entry porch with a Palladian motif, has windows with blind arches above, and has a full-width terrace with a typical Italian Renaissance balustrade design.

3070 East First Street (private), Morris House, 1926. This large towered French Eclectic house has fine architectural details everywhere. Perhaps the most unusual are the pointed-arch windows and elaborate iron hinges on the garage doors. Three stepped, round-arched windows in the tower indicate that the stairway is located there. Also note the solid-wood-paneled front door, the castellations in the porch roof above it, a single through-the-cornice dormer, the elaborate chimney, bits of half-timbering, and a bas-relief plaque of a ship.

LOS ANGELES

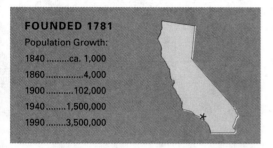

FOUNDED 1781

Population Growth:

1840	ca. 1,000
1860	4,000
1900	102,000
1940	1,500,000
1990	3,500,000

Los Angeles was one of two civilian villages established by Spanish authorities in the late 1700s as adjuncts to their long chain of California missions and forts (see page xi). It was to remain a small provincial trading center until the mid-1870s, when the first plans to bring a long-distance rail connection into the area were announced. The railroad's first arrival in 1876 and the completion of a direct link to Texas in 1881 set off a series of unprecedented population booms that by 1920 had transformed the small town into the largest city in the American West, a position previously held by San Francisco and one that Los Angeles has since maintained by ever-increasing margins. In 1990 Los Angeles and its immediate neighbors had a total population of 8,863,000, making it the largest central city in the nation, followed closely by the five boroughs of New York City with a total population of 8,547,00. Many demographers predict that Los Angeles's lead will have considerably widened by the year 2000 census.

Hispanic Agricultural Center

The broad, seaside plain of the Los Angeles Basin, which provided such an ideal site for the spread of the later megalopolis, was settled only along its inland margins in California's Spanish era. The region's Mediterranean climate, with rainfall concentrated in the winter months, meant that the mountain-fed rivers that crossed the wide plain in the winter and spring were commonly dry ditches by late summer and fall. Year-round water supplies were only available near the base of the plain's mountainous rim, and it was there that its first settlements were located. In 1771 Mission San Gabriel Arcángel, the fourth in the California chain (see page xi), was founded on a site near what was later to become the mountain-base town of Pasadena.

Ten years later the Spanish authorities established a new civilian pueblo (agricultural town) at a riverside site about ten miles west of Mission San Gabriel, Per-

haps to encourage new settlers, this was given a very grand name—El Pueblo de Nuestra Señora la Reina de los Angeles de Porciuncula (the Town of Our Lady the Queen of the Angels by the Porciuncula [River]). This was soon universally shortened to simply "Los Angeles."

Like its twin civilian pueblo established four years earlier at San Jose near San Francisco Bay (see page 237), the town was intended to supply food for the garrisons of Spanish soldiers assigned to defend the region's missions and coastal presidios (forts). The new town was a success and soon became a small but prosperous agricultural trade center. That was to remain its principal function for almost a century as its population grew slowly to about one thousand in the 1830s and to six thousand in the Anglo-dominated California of 1870.

Improbable Pacific Terminus

Leland Stanford and his San Francisco–based Big Four partners, who had completed the first transcontinental railroad in 1869 and then quickly consolidated their control of the Bay Area's rail network with their Southern Pacific line (see pages 139 and 213), began building rapidly southward in 1870 to seek a similar advantage in southern California.

The original Western Railroad Surveys of the 1850s had recommended two southerly transcontinental routes to California. One of these roughly followed the thirty-fourth parallel of latitude across northern New Mexico and Arizona; the other crossed these states about 150 miles farther south, near the thirty-second parallel. Interrupted by the Civil War, by 1870 various eastern financiers were seeking the capital to build these lines. The Big Four now boldly planned to head off such competition by themselves building the thirty-second parallel line, which would give them control of both the northern and southern railroad gateways to the state.

It had long been assumed that San Diego, whose magnificent harbor rivaled that of San Francisco Bay, would be the oceanside terminus of the southern routes. With their San Francisco Bay monopoly on Pacific Ocean shipping, the Big Four were particularly concerned with preventing a rival seaport from developing in southern California. The Los Angeles area, bounded only by beaches and mudflats with no natural harbor, had never received serious attention as a Pacific rail terminus. While building southward toward Ari-

Los Angeles town square, ca. 1875; the large building at the center right is the still-surviving Pico House, originally a hotel; the Los Angeles River is seen in the distance.

zona, Stanford and his Southern Pacific associates adopted another bold strategy that ensured that the previously ignored Los Angeles area, rather than San Diego, would become southern California's principal seaport.

This novel plan had been made possible by the visionary Los Angeles transportation entrepreneur Phineas T. Banning (see page 57). Arriving in the frontier town as an ambitious twenty-one-year-old in 1851, Banning soon began a small wagon-freighting company linking Los Angeles with a semisheltered anchorage for oceangoing ships in San Pedro Bay, twenty-five miles to the south. At first all cargoes had to be loaded into small boats for transfer across the mudflats to and from a small beachfront wharf, but Banning reinvested his profits in buying land to build improved waterfront facilities. Here a channel was dredged through the mudflats and a long wharf built so that smaller ocean-going vessels could be loaded and unloaded adjacent to his wagons. Later the wharf was enlarged and the channel deepened. In 1869 Banning replaced his horses, mules, and wagons with the region's first short-line railroad, which connected his wharves with Los Angeles.

As the Southern Pacific raced southward toward Arizona, Banning and other Los Angeles boosters persuaded the Big Four that they had much to gain by detouring their main line in a westward loop to Los Angeles and incorporating Banning's short-line railroad into their system. This gave the Southern Pacific an instant southern California seaport, with transcontinental connections to the rest of the nation via the San Francisco Bay Area. The plan worked, and Los Angeles's man-made harbor has been expanding ever since. Today, it is the nation's largest, while San Diego's fine natural harbor remains a minor player in maritime

commerce. It did later become the home port for much of the U.S. Navy's Pacific Fleet (see page 149).

First Railroad Boom, 1880s

The Southern Pacific's arrival in Los Angeles in 1876 gave that railroad a crucial advantage over its westward-building rivals but, because of the inconvenient and expensive access via San Francisco, brought only a modest influx of new activity to the Los Angeles area in the 1870s. Among the most important of these early arrivals were the affluent Indiana group that founded the upscale suburban town of Pasadena in 1874 (see page 94).

It was not until the eastward-building Southern Pacific reached a junction with a branch of the westward-building Santa Fe line at Deming, New Mexico, in 1881 that low-cost, direct train travel first connected the eastern states with balmy southern California. The railroad and other Los Angeles boosters had already been widely advertising the area as a mild-climate, agricultural paradise that, with irrigation, could grow almost any kind of crop. Not surprisingly, many of the first newcomers were not potential farmers but, in the usual pattern of western railroad growth, land promoters, attorneys, and salesmen who, following the "greater fool" theory, were delighted to buy quickly, mostly on credit, and then sell their holdings at substantial profits to the next wave of arrivals. Soon dozens of prospective new towns had been platted in the vast ranching lands that surrounded Los Angeles. This real estate boom escalated to its peak in 1887, when Los Angeles, a town of eleven thousand in 1880, had surged to eighty thousand inhabitants.

By that time the banks that financed the boom had begun to realize that much of the growth consisted of promoters selling to each other rather than to long-term owners. The bust quickly followed as new lending ceased and banks foreclosed on creditors unable to sell, or pay for, their landholdings. By 1890 the city's population had dropped by almost 40 percent, and the banks held a huge inventory of expensive, and now unsellable, real estate. Things hit bottom in 1893, when the worldwide collapse of silver prices threw the nation into a severe depression.

"California for Health, Oranges for Wealth," 1895–1920

In 1893 Los Angeles civic leaders, acting on the principle of "it's always darkest just before the dawn," decided that their city needed a new image to attract stable, long-term residents. In planning this, they discovered that, in spite of their massive previous advertising, most Americans still regarded the region as the dry and barren desert that it did, in fact, then closely resemble. A still-greater surprise came when they found that most of those that stayed on after the recent bust were not the typical migrants of the nation's previous westward expansions—adventurous youth joined by hard-pressed families escaping worn-out farm lands farther east or economic and social crises overseas. Instead, like the founders of nearby Pasadena, they were mostly "middle age, middle class, and Middle West." Now the civic leaders organized a well-financed new campaign to target just such immigrants.

As the unifying theme of their campaign, they shrewdly chose a recent arrival on the California agricultural scene—the Washington navel orange. Edible sweet oranges originated in ancient China and had spread to the Mediterranean by the time of the Roman Empire. They were brought to the New World, including both Florida and California, in the Spanish Colonial era. Small, very pulpy, and somewhat sour, these "Mission oranges" were all but inedible by modern standards. In 1873 the U.S. Department of Agriculture shipped from Brazil young plants of a remarkable new "navel" orange, which was large, sweet, juicy, seedless, and even thick-skinned for easy shipment. The trial plants were sent to growers in both Florida and at Riverside, forty miles east of Los Angeles. They died in Florida but flourished in California, and thus was born a new local industry that was but one of many California virtues extolled in the early advertising. Navel oranges, "the aristocrat of fruits," would now take center stage.

The Middle West was dominated by Corn Belt family farms that used simultaneous hog raising as a means of converting their corn into a more valuable end product. This involved intensive, year-round work through the rigors of very hot summers, very cold winters, and very long days. The slogan of the new campaign, "California for health, oranges for wealth," was the equal of

Los Angeles transit plan, 1925. The black lines show the routes of Henry Huntington's Pacific Electric Railway.

Madison Avenue's finest. In only six words, it conjured up visions of mild winters, cool summers, and a grove of fragrant, dark green, low-maintenance trees that, once planted, lived for more than fifty years, in each of which their high-value fruits might provide more income than the labor-intensive family farm.

Spread throughout the Middle West in a long-term media blitz of newspaper ads, billboards, exhibits at state fairs and national expositions, traveling railroad displays, and informative free literature, this campaign was an unprecedented success. As the nerve center of the resulting orange-grove boom, Los Angeles saw its population triple from 1900 to 1910 and then doubled again, to almost 600,000, by 1920 to make it the largest city in the American West. For much of the period from 1900 to 1940, the citrus industry also made Los Angeles County, and adjacent Orange County, the two richest agricultural counties in the nation.

Henry Huntington's "Big Red Cars"

Closely allied with the Los Angeles area's orange-grove boom was a remarkable interurban transportation system built by the wealthy nephew of railroad baron Collis Huntington, one of the Big Four founders of the Central Pacific and Southern Pacific lines (see pages 139 and 213). Henry E. Huntington had been his uncle's close associate in the management of his railroad empire for thirty years until the older man died in 1900. Unsuccessful in a bid to succeed his uncle as the Southern Pacific's president, Henry decided to turn his considerable talents, and the $40 million fortune he had just inherited, to opportunity-rich Los Angeles.

Huntington farsightedly sensed that the orange-grove boom, then just beginning, was destined to make the Los Angeles area into a new kind of urban complex. The typical, family-operated orange grove covered less than ten acres, much smaller than a normal farm and more like a large, prosperous residential estate. Clustered on favorable sites throughout the area, such estates required nearby towns to provide shops, banks, laundries, restaurants, and other services. Already by 1900 many such towns existed, and several had, during the preceding decade, been linked to central Los Angeles by high-speed electric trolley lines called interurbans. Undercapitalized and poorly managed, the fledgling interurban system was a financial failure.

Realizing that the already-sprawling metropolitan area's future rested on fast, dependable transportation, Huntington bought the ailing interurban lines and transformed them into the Pacific Electric Railway, a model system that over the next ten years grew to become the world's largest. Pacific Electric's Big Red Cars, traveling a smooth fifty miles per hour on carefully constructed roadbeds, linked fifty communities in four counties. Six hundred of the cars daily passed through Pacific Electric's Los Angeles Terminal, then the largest building west of the Mississippi. In the words of historian Kevin Starr in *Inventing the Dream*: "Electrical mass transit had made a new sort of urbanscape possible: a network of communities, separate yet joined at fifty miles an hour into a suburbanized conglomerate." Los Angeles's modern geographic sprawl is commonly blamed on automobiles and freeways. In reality, these only reflect the pattern already determined by its earlier orange-grove prosperity served by Huntington's interurbans.

In 1910, his transit network now completed and his inherited fortune almost doubled, Henry Huntington retired at age sixty to pursue his deepest passion—book collecting. Today his most visible legacy is the extraordinary Huntington Library complex near Pasadena (see page 106).

Black Gold

All of the Los Angeles area's first 140 years of population growth, from the riverside grain fields of its Span-ish founders to the aristocratic orange groves that dominated the area by 1920, were based on irrigated agriculture. During the decade of the 1920s the city's geometric population growth still continued, doubling to 1.24 million by 1930. This boom was different, however, for it was the first to be based on new economic underpinnings. Chief among these was the discovery of the region's first giant oil field near Long Beach in 1921 (see page 57), a development that set the stage for making the Los Angeles area the industrial center of the Pacific coast.

Oil seeps and tar pits (*breas* in Spanish) occur at many places in the Los Angeles Basin, and the tar, in particular, was used by both the native Indians and the Spanish colonials as a waterproof caulking for boats. In addition, the Spanish applied it over wooden planking to make waterproof roofs; drawings of early Los Angeles show the entire town made up of adobe buildings having flat tar-covered roofs.

The region's first important oil discovery, the Brea-Olinda Field, was made in 1880 near tar pits at the base of the Puente Hills, about twenty miles east of Los Angeles. Subsequent area drilling, concentrated around oil seeps and tar pits near the base of the mountain ranges to the north and east, turned up many similar fields over the next forty years, including several in the Los Angeles area (see "Greystone," page 80). Most were relatively small and difficult to produce because they contained only very thick and heavy oil. Such oil contains little of the lighter hydrocarbons that can be refined into high-value kerosene and gasoline and was mostly suited for use as a boiler fuel for steam production.

In 1920 the area's first discovery of a giant, high-value oil field was made at Huntington Beach, a small resort community about thirty miles south of Los Angeles. The next year the equally large discovery at Long Beach established the new coastal oil province that was to be the foundation of the city's industrial growth. This was further ensured in 1932 when a still-larger giant, the Wilmington Field, was discovered just offshore and running directly beneath the city's large man-made harbor. Still in production, by 1990 the Huntington Beach and Long Beach (originally called Signal Hill) Fields had each yielded more than a billion barrels of oil, and the Wilmington Field more than two billion.

Industrial development in California had long been limited by a shortage of fossil fuels. The state lacks significant coal deposits, and the early oil discoveries were too small to support a long-term industrial base. These new discoveries rapidly solved this problem and literally fueled much of the 1920s boom. By 1927 large oil refineries lined the Los Angeles waterfront, and the city had already become the nation's second-largest producer of automobile tires. In addition, a host of other new industrial plants had been established in the area to serve its burgeoning population. This population increase now included not only the usual agriculturists and retirees, but also a flood of factory workers attracted to Los Angeles both by its new industries and by its mild climate. Unlike the previous railroad-based booms, many of the newcomers were now arriving in their own automobiles via Route 66, the nation's first all-weather transcontinental highway (see page 435).

The Silver Screen

A quite different kind of industry, moviemaking, was also a major contributor to the 1920s boom. First perfected by New Jersey–based Thomas Edison in 1891, the earliest movies were made for individual viewing in coin-operated, peep-show-like devices. These employed fifty-foot "loops" of film containing about thirty seconds of action that was endlessly repeated. By 1895 short films were also being projected onto screens for multiperson viewing. In 1903 an Edison Company cameraman produced several ten-minute films featuring multiple short scenes that very effectively told simple stories. One of these was *The Great Train Robbery,* a classic that over the next ten years became the most popular and profitable early film.

By 1905 the operators of vaudeville theaters were discovering, much to their surprise, that people would actually *pay* to view such screen-projected stories in their theaters. Thus began the popular nickelodeons, small theaters in which, for five cents, patrons could view six different ten-minute (one-reel) films. To keep their audiences returning, the theaters needed a large supply of such films, which were soon being cranked out by numerous production companies scattered throughout the country.

In 1907 employees of a large Chicago production company, shooting a film called *The Count of Monte Cristo,* finished their interior, studio-based filming in the midst of a cloudy and wet Great Lakes winter. Apparently having experienced some of Los Angeles's balmy-climate media blitz, they headed west to complete the outdoor sequences for their film. This proved to be a historic decision. The owners of the production company were delighted with the completed film and in 1908 established a permanent Los Angeles base for outdoor shooting. Soon other companies were establishing similar branch offices in the area.

One of these was the New York–based Biograph Studios, whose star director, D. W. Griffith (1875–1948), was a former California resident. Between 1908 and 1910, he had brilliantly directed a staggering 288 films, mostly ten-minute one-reelers. Beginning in 1910 he moved his winter and spring operations to Los Angeles and began to incorporate romantic California themes and stories from its colorful Hispanic past, into some of his films. By 1914 Griffith had completed over 400 short films for Biograph; in these he had fully explored

Hollywood advertisement, ca. 1887

the artistic possibilities of film. In the authoritative words of the *Encyclopaedia Britannica:*

> The conscious discovery of the aesthetics of the motion picture begins with D. W. Griffith. To some extent, it also ends there. There was not one device of the visual, black-and-white cinema that Griffith did not master or point the way for others to control.

By 1914 Griffith, as well as others, were already experimenting with films that were longer than the ten-minute reel that dominated nickelodeon viewing. Refused permission to make such "feature" films by Biograph, Griffith resigned and immediately produced what was to become his masterpiece, a three-hour Civil War drama called *The Birth of a Nation.* Entirely made in Los Angeles, in 1915 it had its premiere showing in the city. The film received rave reviews. Here, at last, was a work that demonstrated the full potential of the motion picture as both art and entertainment.

The film's production had been centered around a small suburban town northwest of Los Angeles that was founded in the 1880s land boom. Called Hollywood, its large and inexpensive Victorian hotel had become a popular base of operations for the city's mostly seasonal movie colony. Historian Kevin Starr writes in *Inventing the Dream* that now

> Hollywood was supporting the production of a film masterpiece. Up until then Hollywood had been a Johnny-come-lately competitor against New York City and to a lesser extent Philadelphia and Chicago as a center of the American film industry. After the release of *The Birth of a Nation,* Hollywood attained a primary status it never surrendered. With *The Birth of a Nation,* the movies came permanently to Los Angeles.

The Birth of a Nation and the countless one-to-two-hour silent feature films that were soon to follow transformed not only Hollywood but also the entertainment habits of the entire nation. The ten-minute films of the nickelodeon era were a diverting novelty; feature movies, shown on large screens, could rival theatrical productions for drama, suspense, and comedy, and could far exceed them in variety of locations and visual effects. They could also attract a far larger audience. By 1920 nickelodeons had mostly been replaced by large and lavishly decorated theaters designed specifically for large-screen projection of silent movies. There, the showings were accompanied by appropriate music provided by an in-house organist or pianist.

As the nerve center of this entertainment revolution, Hollywood was, both directly and indirectly, a principal contributor to the Los Angeles boom of the 1920s. The town itself had only 4,000 residents in 1911 but jumped to 36,000 in 1920 and surged to 235,000 by 1930. Comparable growth also took place in Beverly Hills and other upscale residential neighborhoods to the west of Hollywood, which housed most of the movie industry's affluent new leaders. The boom was also indirectly stimulated by the many idyllic southern California settings seen around the nation both in the earlier one-reelers and in the newer feature films.

By 1930 the production of movies was Los Angeles's largest industry. With an added boost when "talkies," with directly recorded sound tracks, were perfected in the late 1920s, the industry retained its economic strength even through the depression years of the 1930s, a decade that some critics still consider to be the golden age of Hollywood filmmaking.

The Los Angeles Area Since 1940

The Second World War accelerated the region's economic transformation from agriculture to industry as aircraft plants, shipyards, and other war-related activities and workers flocked to southern California. Now with a seemingly endless source of energy in its prolific oil fields, and a huge and efficient man-made harbor, diversified industrialization has since replaced agriculture as the dominant force of the region's economy. Contributing to this trend is the city's position as the nation's industrial gateway to the accelerating trade with Japan and other Pacific Rim countries. In each decade since 1950, Los Angeles has added about a half million new residents to its population. The metropolitan area has grown even faster, increasing from 11.5 million to 14.5 million in the single decade of the 1980s. Los Angeles still remains the center of the nation's entertainment industry, but this now contributes less than 10 percent of the city's gross revenues.

Not surprisingly, Los Angeles's many decades of unprecedented growth have consumed most traces of its pre-twentieth-century past. Some unlikely survivors of the town's Hispanic origins, recently restored, remain around the original town square in the **El Pueblo de Los Angeles Historic Monument** (125 Paseo de la Plaza, 213-628-1274). Chief among these are the 1870 **Pico House,** a fine Italianate hotel built by Pio Pico, the last governor of Mexican California, and the much restored **Avila Adobe,** part of which may date back to 1818. Only a handful of Victorian dwellings survive, the best of which are on Carroll Avenue (see page 91). Even traces of the early-twentieth-century orange-grove boom have mostly disappeared; fortunately, one of the boom's most prosperous far suburban towns survives

Hancock Park

almost intact at Redlands, sixty miles east of Los Angeles (see page 108). Some of the fine houses and neighborhoods of nearby Pasadena also date from that era (see page 99). As if to compensate for earlier losses, modern Los Angeles has an extraordinary collection of Eclectic-era museum houses and neighborhoods, most of them dating from the 1920s boom years and later.

Hancock Park, 1910–1940s

This is the largest and most intact of the many upscale "flatland" neighborhoods that spread westward from the city's downtown core beginning with the 1880s boom (see map, page 82). Subdivided with large lots and broad tree-lined streets, it was built-out mostly in the movie-boom years of the 1920s and 1930s. Its many grid-plan blocks contain a seemingly bottomless reservoir of Eclectic-era designs, with the Italian Renaissance, Tudor, and French Eclectic styles most frequent.

434 South Windsor Boulevard (private), ca. 1920s. A textbook Italian Renaissance home that is being engulfed in ivy.

454 South Windsor Boulevard (private), ca. 1920s. Unusual cast-stone trim lends a refined air to this stucco Italian Renaissance design. Rarely seen stone "shutters" are on each side of the upstairs windows.

531 South Windsor Boulevard (private), ca. 1920s. Italian Renaissance designs dominate these blocks of South Windsor. This example is in the flat-roofed subtype. The entry porch has triple arches and extends out from the house. The fence around the broad open terrace is a later addition.

601 South Windsor Boulevard (private), ca. 1920s. Yet-another Italian Renaissance house, this one features slender Roman bricks and a triple-arched entry porch that is recessed into the body of the house. All of the rounded arches, windows, and dormers are concentrated in the central part of the facade.

356 South Lorraine Boulevard (private), ca. 1915. This early Tudor house has the almost-symmetrical look and squared porch supports that are common in pre-1917 examples of the style.

366 South June Street (private), ca. 1920s. This formal French Eclectic house is of the asymmetrical subtype. Note the very high pitched hipped roof and the tall skinny dormers.

191 Hudson Avenue (private), Smith House, 1930; J. C. Smale, architect. This is a rare example of an Art Deco single-family house. Note the art-glass window, the fluting along the parapet (topped with zigzags), and the overall feeling of verticality.

200 block of Wilton Avenue (all private) and *100 block of Ridgewood Place (all private).* These two blocks on the edge of the district are filled with charming, builder-designed Craftsman houses.

HILLSIDE SAMPLER

Most of Los Angeles's upscale residential neighborhoods of the 1920 to 1940 movie-boom era spread from Hollywood, the industry's original nerve center, westward along the base of the Santa Monica Mountains. These hillside neighborhoods have remained among Los Angeles's most desirable places to live ever since. As a result, their early homes have now been joined by countless post-1950 neighbors to make a continuous, fifteen-mile-long belt of fine dwellings. Finding the scattered clusters of important pre-1950 houses in this huge complex can be a daunting task. This "Hillside Sampler" offers a driving route that will, we hope, provide an accessible introduction to such clusters.

Many, but not all, of the area's streets and neighborhoods are familiar icons of the entertainment industry. Sunset Boulevard is the major spine for the more luxurious western parts of the route, which proceeds from west to east through residential suburbs with such fa-

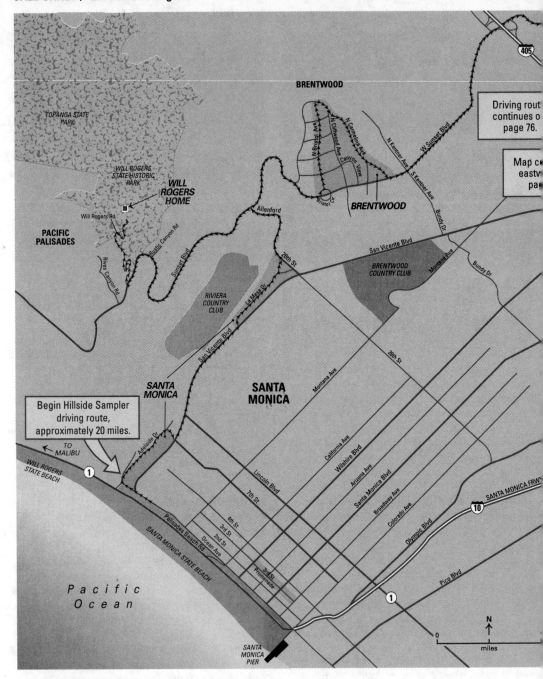

Driving rout
continues o
page 76.

miliar names as Santa Monica, Brentwood, Bel Air, and Beverly Hills before reaching the Hollywood area. East of Hollywood the route visits Los Feliz and Silver Lake, two less familiar movie-era neighborhoods, and then ends in Angelino Heights, the city's first residential suburb developed in the 1880s boom. Here the small Carroll Avenue Historic District preserves Los Angeles's most intact concentration of fine Victorian houses. (Note: The suggested route can, of course, be reversed and traveled from east to west; this will require some minor backtracking to gain access to a few steep and narrow one-way roads.)

For those who want to go beyond this brief introductory tour, we suggest two invaluable guide books.

David Gebhard and Roger Winter's *Los Angeles: An Architectural Guide* is the most complete, containing insightful introductions to every part of the metropolitan area followed by succinct and authoritative descriptions of countless landmark houses and buildings. Charles Moore, Peter Becker, and Regula Campbell's *The City Observed: Los Angeles* has fewer entries, but these provide a witty and in-depth analysis of the Los Angeles area's principal architectural treasures.

Santa Monica

Founded in 1875, Santa Monica was intended to be a competitor for the more distant Los Angeles area seaport on San Pedro Bay (see "Long Beach," page 57); by 1897 this plan had been abandoned, and the town took on a new life as a seaside resort focused around its superb beach. Much of the early town was platted in fifty-foot-wide lots for workers' houses, and these soon began filling with summer cottages, retirees' homes, boardinghouses, and small apartments. Streets nearest the beach became the site of numerous large hotels adjacent to the commercial district, now the **Third Street Promenade.** The town's principal upscale neighborhood centered around landscaped San Vicente Boulevard near its northernmost edge. Here can be seen many fine Eclectic-era dwellings. Among them are:

142 Adelaide Drive (private), Weaver House, 1911; Milwaukee Building Company (later Meyer and Holler), builders. Surely there was an apparently unidentified, and unusually creative, architect involved in the design of this Craftsman home. The wood detailing is meticulously executed. The porch supports are exquisite; their pedestals are accentuated with two horizontal courses and atop these is a composition of two squared pieces of wood with intricate interlocking detailing. Notice how the roof beams protruding from the front gable are stepped back in six stages. The large picture windows appear to be later additions (glance to your left for the magnificent view they overlook).

236 Adelaide Drive (private), Milbank House, 1911. Two low-pitched, front-facing gables give this house a look often found in one-story Craftsman designs. Here they are accentuated with protruding roof beams (single, paired, and tripled), all with multiple step-backs that read almost like sawteeth and that stand out dramatically because of their pale blue color. The upstairs porch looks inviting, even though it lacks a railing.

2012 La Mesa Drive (private), ca. 1925. La Mesa Drive is an excellent example of a street that gains beauty and distinction from its streetside trees, in this case Moreton Bay figs. This picturesque towered French Eclectic (Norman French) home has a front door constructed of heavy boards with a small window, which is typical of the style. Here the door is particularly well ornamented with large exposed nail heads and heavy metal hardware. Note how the line of the half-timbering on the left wing echoes the steep slope of the gabled roof on the right wing.

2034 La Mesa Drive (private), Byers House, 1924; John Byers, Santa Monica, architect. This talented architect chose

Santa Monica

Will Rogers Home

the Monterey style for his own home, with a balcony that continues around three sides of the front house block. A subtly curved walk leads through understated and appropriate landscaping to an arched wooden gate that opens onto a private courtyard. Byers also designed homes at 2101, 2153, and 2210 La Mesa (all private).

Will Rogers Home, 1928

Will Rogers State Historic Park, 1501 Will Rogers Road, Pacific Palisades; 310-454-8212; leaving Santa Monica the route reaches Sunset Boulevard, where it detours westward to visit the rural estate of humorist Will Rogers, now an important museum house complex.

Oklahoma may have made Will Rogers a charmingly rustic philosopher, but Los Angeles made him a star. Before moving to southern California in 1919, Rogers had found moderate success as a roper in a traveling rodeo and, later, as an entertainer in New York's Ziegfeld Follies. In the sixteen years between his westward move and his death in a 1935 plane crash, Rogers became internationally renowned as a humorist, writer, radio personality, and movie hero—the last in such fondly remembered films as *Connecticut Yankee* and *State Fair.*

It is a reflection of Rogers's unpretentious "I never met a man I didn't like" outlook that his 400-acre Pacific Palisades spread (the core 86 acres of which are now a state park) manages to retain a down-home character. Nowhere is this more evident than in his house, which stands as a testament to Rogers's personality. The two-story board-and-batten structure rambles about, connected by a covered porch along the left wing that becomes a pergola as it crosses the informal outdoor patio Rogers used for entertaining and then tucks under a Monterey balcony as it reaches the right wing. Rogers built the home piecemeal. The original

began as a modest cottage that was enlarged to encompass thirty-one rooms in the early 1920s when his family made it their primary residence. Though a few further additions were made in the next few years, the current structure largely reflects its 1928 to 1935 history. A large two-story living room, which Rogers filled with western art and Native American objects, adds character to the house.

Also present are numerous outbuildings and their surrounding landscapes. Particularly notable is the polo field, which once doubled as the Rogerses' front lawn, as well as the stables and barn north of the house. The large stable is a glorious affair, with two long wings of stalls radiating from a tall central rotunda. The grounds of the current state park (donated to California after Mrs. Rogers's death in 1944) also present a wealth of trails and picturesque views, an oasis of eucalyptus trees and tranquil scenery made all the more spectacular by its Sunset Boulevard location.

Brentwood

This is the most westerly of the "three B" residential districts favored by the affluent movie industry set (the others are Bel Air and Beverly Hills). First platted in 1906, it has relatively few houses from the 1920s and 1930s and was mostly built-out in the 1950s and later. Among its important earlier dwellings are several designed by Santa Monica–based architect John Byers (see "2034 La Mesa Drive" above).

526 Carmelina Avenue (private), 1989, Frank Gehry, Los Angeles, architect. This fine home, a modern reinterpretation of the International style, won a 1990 American Institute of Architects Honor Award.

436 North Carmelina Avenue (private), Murray House, ca. 1935; John Byers, Santa Monica, architect (with Edla Muir). This is how Colonial Revival–style houses typically looked from the mid-1930s to the mid-1950s. The form of this

Brentwood

Brentwood

house, with a lowish pitch to the gabled roof and a front-gabled wing on one side, is characteristic of that period. The use of brick for the first floor only and the very wide wood siding were typical details during this period, as were the paneled front door and shutters on every window.

428 Carmelina Avenue (private), Kerr House, 1930; John Byers, Santa Monica, architect (with Edla Muir). This represents a highly Anglicized version of Monterey Revival.

Westwood

Westwood is an exception among the area's neighborhoods in having a university, rather than Hollywood, as its economic focus. Charles Moore and his coauthors explain in *The City Observed*:

> In the 1920s the Janss Investment Company . . . performed the extraordinary coup of offering, at a discount, to the Regents of the University of California a small but highly developable site for UCLA. This insured the inordinately high value of the surrounding Janss-owned real estate for decades to come.

Our tour route next jogs south a short distance into northern Westwood to visit:

222 Loring Avenue (private), ca. 1930s. A small International-style design, probably erected by a builder. The curve and glass brick at the entry add a Streamline Moderne touch.

308 Loring Avenue (private), ca. 1950. An excellent example of a builder's Colonial Revival house that could have been built at almost any time from about 1935 to 1955. Just as at 436 North Carmelina (see page 74), a brick first story is paired with a wood second story. This one has an arched window over the entry and to the left are two typical ca.-1950 windows—a bay window and a small round window.

336 Loring Avenue (private), ca. 1950. This has the same mix of materials and looks like it could be by the same builder as 308 (see the preceding entry). The front door is crowned with a very minimal broken-ogee pediment, and there are two ca.-1950 Colonial Revivalized windows (one tripled and one single). Note the two teensy dormers and the mortar "oozing" out from between the bricks.

234 South Hilgard Avenue (private), Kaufmann House, 1937; Richard Neutra, Los Angeles, architect. Here Neutra, a

Westwood

pioneering modernist designer, produced a classic example of the International style. Most of the outdoor living spaces and views face the rear garden.

Bel Air

Developed about 1918 on a rugged hillside site, the determinedly upscale neighborhood featured estate-sized lots and narrow, winding, contour-curved roadways. A favorite of the movie industry, it contains numerous

Bel Air

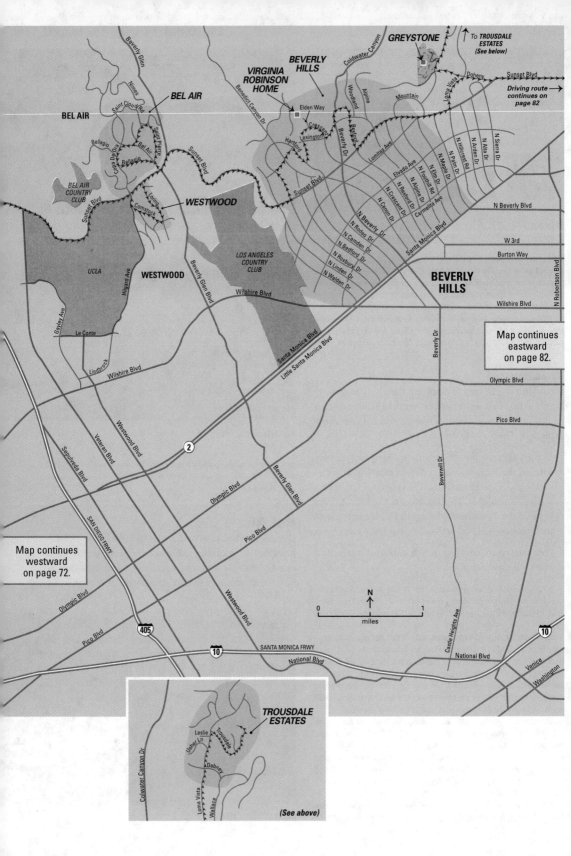

GREYSTONE

↑ To *TROUSDALE ESTATES* (See below)

BEVERLY HILLS

VIRGINIA ROBINSON HOME

BEL AIR

BEL AIR

Beverly Glen

Nimes Rd

Saint Cloud Rd

Benedict Canyon Dr

Elden Way

Coldwater Canyon

Loma Vista

Doheny

Sunset Blvd

Driving route continues on page 82

Woodland

Alpine

Mountain

Bellagio

Saint Pierre

Bel Air Rd

Bellagio

Cara De Oro

Hartford

Crescent

Lexington

Beverly Dr

Bedford

Sunset Blvd

Lomitas Ave

Elvado Ave

N Hillcrest Rd

N Sierra Dr

N Alta Dr

N Arden Dr

N Palm Dr

N Maple Dr

N Elm Dr

N Foothill Rd

N Alpine Dr

N Crescent Dr

Carmelita Ave

BEL AIR COUNTRY CLUB

Loma

Comstock

WESTWOOD

Sunset Blvd

N Canon Dr

N Beverly Dr

Santa Monica Blvd

N Beverly Blvd

UCLA

Hilgard Ave

WESTWOOD

Beverly Glen Blvd

LOS ANGELES COUNTRY CLUB

N Roxton Dr

N Camden Dr

N Bedford Dr

N Roxbury Dr

N Linden Dr

N Walden Dr

W 3rd

Burton Way

N Robertson Blvd

Gayley Ave

Le Conte

Lindbrock

Wilshire Blvd

Wilshire Blvd

Little Santa Monica Blvd

Santa Monica Blvd

BEVERLY HILLS

Beverly Dr

Wilshire Blvd

Map continues eastward on page 82.

Olympic Blvd

Pico Blvd

Beverwil Dr

Sepulveda Blvd

Veteran Blvd

Westwood Blvd

②

Olympic Blvd

Beverly Glen Blvd

Pico Blvd

Map continues westward on page 72.

Olympic Blvd

Pico Blvd

San Diego Frwy

405

Westwood Blvd

N

0   miles   1

Castle Heights Ave

10

10

SANTA MONICA FRWY

National Blvd

National Blvd

Venice

Washington

TROUSDALE ESTATES

Colgwater Canyon Dr

Leslie

Usher Ln

Trousdale

Dabney

Loma Vista

Wallace

(See above)

Bel Air

fine architect-designed dwellings, most of which are hidden on their large sites by mature landscape screening. Among its more easily visible early houses are:

214 Saint Pierre Road (private), ca. 1940s. This large Colonial Revival design with second-story overhang is based on post-Medieval precedents. Note the large chimney and simple entry with a round window to the side.

320 Saint Pierre Road (private), ca. 1940s. The very large redbrick Colonial Revival house has shutters, triangular pedimented entry, brick dentils, front-gabled dormers, and the round window so often found in examples built from the late 1930s through early 1950s.

10431 Bellagio Road (private), ca. 1930s. This is a lovely towered French Eclectic home.

Beverly Hills

Founded in 1906 and still a separate city with a 1990 population of thirty-two thousand, this is the largest and best known of Los Angeles's movie-boom residential suburbs. South of Santa Monica Boulevard is the city's upscale civic and commercial district, which, along Rodeo Drive, includes one of the nation's most elegant shopping strips. The residential district lies north of Santa Monica Boulevard and has two distinctive components.

Between Santa Monica and Sunset Boulevards are gently sloping flatlands made more interesting by a street grid composed of gentle arcs instead of straight lines—rather like a rectangular grid distorted by a trick mirror. To add to their distinctiveness, each street is lined by a different species of tree that, in some cases, is reflected in the name of the street, notably Linden, Elm, Maple, and Palm. Most dramatic are the plantings along residential Rodeo Drive, which feature alternating taller and shorter varieties of palm trees. This area south of Sunset Boulevard was designed by the New York landscape architect Wilbur David Cook (see page 575). North of Sunset Boulevard begin the actual "hills," whose naturalistic road pattern and landscaping were designed by Boston's renowned Olmsted brothers. These hills were the site of some of the city's grandest Eclectic-era houses and estates. Two of the latter are now important museum house complexes (see "Virginia Robinson Home and Gardens" and "Greystone," pages 78 and 80).

Beverly Hills: ca. 1930s, 1960s, 1990s, from bottom to top

Like its western neighbors, Beverly Hills has pre-1940 houses that now are far outnumbered by younger dwellings, many of which have replaced earlier structures. Perhaps the most recent of these post-1950 house designs are very large squared, two-story structures with light-colored stucco walls and front facades elaborated by an oversized, two-story doorway treatment of varying sorts.

1005 Rexford Drive (private), ca. 1990s. A new interpretation of the Beaux Arts style shows in this mansard-roof form. This house has lots of applied floral detail and segmental arched windows. Related two-story front-door compositions, with an arch above, are seen on almost every house under construction in Beverly Hills in the 1990s, whatever its other stylistic influences might be. Another 1990s Beaux Arts design, this with a flat roof and even more floriferous details, is located on North Crescent Drive, at the intersection with Elden Way (private).

921 Rexford Drive (private), ca. 1960s. Based on the post-1940 categories in our *Field Guide to American Houses,* this would be a Neoclassical Revival house. However, Marcus Whiffen in his 1969 classic, *American Architecture Since 1780: A Guide to the Styles,* discusses a style much used in other building types during the 1960s, which he calls "the New Formalism." This is a more appropriate stylistic designation for this home, which does not actually have Classical columns, even though its Classical inspiration is unmistakable. Faced in marble and with patterned grilles in front of the windows on each wing, this is a superb example of its kind, and it is nicely enhanced by the landscaping.

1006 North Crescent Drive (private), ca. 1930. This Neoclassical house has a full facade porch and front door surrounded by Adamesque (Federal) elliptical fanlight and sidelights. The expansive front lawn is a gift of open space to the neighborhood.

915 and 913 Hartford Way (both private), ca. 1960s. These are two nice examples of the Mansard style popular in the 1960s and 1970s. Note the through-the-cornice windows, tall arched entries, and rooftop urns. The Mansard was quite popular in Los Angeles and there are many other examples along this route.

933 Rexford Drive (private), ca. 1990. The Moorish Revival, 1990s version.

1001 Lexington Road (private), ca. 1930. A huge white-clapboard Colonial Revival home with cupola on top and a pleasant white wooden fence along the sidewalk.

516 Walden Drive, at Carmelita Avenue (private), Spadena House, 1921; Henry Oliver, architect. After seeing photos of this greatly exaggerated "Hansel and Gretel" house for years, we had great fun discovering its location and history in Gebhard and Winter's *Los Angeles: An Architectural Guide.* It was originally an office and sometime set for a movie production company. The structure was later moved here from Culver City, landscaped and fenced to match its dramatic form, and otherwise adapted for residential use.

Virginia Robinson Home and Gardens, 1911

Beverly Hills; 310-276-5367; address given when required advance reservations are made; Nathaniel Dryden, architect.

Virginia Dryden Robinson (1877–1977) and her husband, department store owner Harry Winchester Robinson (1876–1932), were two of the first residents of Beverly Hills. As Mrs. Robinson recalled, "Everyone was talking about the new Los Angeles Country Club, so one evening we started out to find it. We never did—but we found this piece of land. Just like that, my husband said, 'This is where we're going to live.' By ten the next morning we had bought it." They had purchased about nineteen acres directly from the developer of Beverly Hills, Eldon Green. At the time Beverly Hills was mostly a sea of vacant lots with one small sales shack. When a zoning code was adopted by the town,

Virginia Robinson gardens

the largest lot size allowed was six acres, so the Robinsons sold off parts of their original purchase.

For sixty-six years Virginia Robinson reigned as the first lady of Beverly Hills, although she would never accept that description (she always insisted that Mary Pickford was the first lady). Her home was used for constant entertaining, from Wednesday lunches for ninety people to Friday evening bridge with such gallants as Maurice Chevalier and Charles Boyer. Anthony Eden, Amelia Earhart, Clark Gable, and just about everyone else who counted in the motion-picture industry attended her constant parties.

From the street the Robinson House is a very understated one-story Italian Renaissance house with a flat roof. Inside it is large and welcoming and just as Mrs. Robinson left it. It has been presided over by three majordomos—one for forty years, one for twenty years, and the last, the intelligent and charming Bulgarian Ivo Hadjiev, for the last seven years of Mrs. Robinson's life. Ivo is still with the house, and because of his knowledge of how the home was used and exactly how things were done, it has been maintained in a state of pristine preservation. The Robinsons did not have children and everything in their house is at this point intact. However, there is a great need for a complete curatorial study of the house, of oral interviews, and of complete documentation of a unique era and way of life. The property, bequeathed to Los Angeles County in 1974 and opened to the public in 1982, is currently operated

and maintained by the county's Parks and Recreation Department.

One enters into a large living hall. A morning room and living room are to the right and a huge library to the left. Precisely at 10 a.m. each morning, Mrs. Robinson would open her mail in the corner of the sofa in the morning room, and for three or four hours each day she would sit and read in her favorite chair in the library. Daily trips were made to the Robinson's Department Store downtown, which she ran after her husband's death, looking only to an uncle for business advice. These trips were made in her Duesenberg, the only kind of car she ever had (she only needed seven new ones during her extraordinarily long lifetime). The rooms are filled with antiques that the Robinsons collected, all arranged amid comfortable chairs and sofas.

There are four parts to the private garden. A huge party lawn lies just behind the house; beyond this is a fountain and swimming pool with a delightful Italian Renaissance pavilion, providing a focal point from the house. To the left of the party lawn is a large Italian garden, which has three consecutive terraces stair-stepped down the hill. To the right of the party lawn is an awe-inspiring two-and-one-half-acre palm forest, designed by landscape architect Charles Gibbs Adams. This private paradise contains the largest grove of king palms found outside Australia and also includes the world's largest collection of Chamaidora palms, with more than sixty different varieties.

Greystone gatehouse

Advance reservations are required to visit the Robinson Home and Gardens.

Greystone, 1928

905 Loma Vista Drive, at Doheny Road, Beverly Hills; 310-285-1014; Gordon B. Kaufmann, Los Angeles, architect.

Although the interiors of Greystone can only be viewed through its multiple windows, the grounds are usually open during daylight hours, and one can stroll eighteen acres of what were once magnificent formal and informal gardens. Edward Lawrence Doheny (born 1856) and his friend Charles Canfield were the first to strike oil in Los Angeles. This discovery, along with a later one in Mexico, made them for a period of time the world's largest oil producers. Doheny built Greystone for his son Edward Lawrence Doheny Jr., better known as Ned (born 1893), and his wife, Lucy Smith. He began with a magnificent 12.5-acre site (part of a more-than-400-acre family estate); $3,166,578 was invested in construction, with $1,238,378 going to the house proper. The result was a 46,054-square-foot parapeted Tudor mansion, then the largest home in Beverly Hills, with three-foot-thick walls of reinforced concrete faced with Indiana limestone and a steeply pitched roof clad with thick slabs of Welsh slate. It is from the grayed tone of these materials that Greystone takes its name.

When walking down the hill from the parking area, you approach the rear of the house and must walk through an inner courtyard before reaching Greystone's automobile entrance. While in the auto court, note the central fountain and the heroic roof and chimneys and then peek in the doors of the entrance. Next walk through the forecourt and around the house, past a lily pond (usually empty) to explore the south terrace with its view of Los Angeles. Here you can imagine yourself a party guest outside for a breath of fresh air. And you'll be able to peek into all of Greystone's main front rooms. On most days you'll be almost alone (except for a remarkably efficient group of park rangers who emerge from nowhere should a dog, picnic, or camera appear on the scene).

Even through the windows you can see the many fine floors (the ones in the grand hall are black-and-white marble inlay). Beautifully crafted details abound: a different artist handmade each of the seven exterior chimneys, and the oak banisters, balustrades, and rafters of the interior were all hand-carved in place. A musician's balcony is visible through the living room windows. There was even live-in space for fifteen servants.

Paul G. Thiene was the landscape architect. Today, much of the garden "hardscape" (stairs, balustrades, swimming pool, and such) remain. The plantings are much simplified, with a formal garden and Eugenia Lane being the most intact (they are up the hill back toward the parking area). The grounds originally included many paths and trails, as well as numerous out-buildings. Of these, the elegant gatehouse remains at the base of the hill, as do a stable and garage.

Ned unfortunately died soon after the home was complete. Lucy stayed in the house with their five children, and she later married investor Leigh Battson. Members of the family lived in Greystone until 1954, when 410 acres were sold to the Paul Trousdale Company (see the following entry). In 1955 they sold the mansion, but it remained vacant until purchased by the city of Beverly Hills for a 19-million-gallon water reservoir. The city was persuaded to come up with a plan that left Greystone intact, roofed over the reservoir (it's beneath the parking area), and created a lovely park. The house is regularly used as a filming location.

Trousdale Estates

For an instructive change of pace from fortresslike Greystone, one can continue up Loma Vista Drive to one of the newest, and most architecturally unified, Beverly Hills neighborhoods, called Trousdale Estates. Until 1954 its 410-acre site was a part of the Greystone grounds. In that year the tract was sold to developer Paul Trousdale, who created what now seems like a perfect, time-warp example of the funky late-1950s housing fashions favored by some affluent Angelinos. No lawns were permitted. Instead the low-slung, one-story houses have wide, prominent driveways and carports in a landscape of beds and berms thickly planted with ground covers that are punctuated by small trees and fanciful topiary shrubs. The principal accents of the houses themselves focus around their tall front doors, some of which are enlivened by elaborate modern-design metalwork or stonework.

330 Trousdale Place (private), ca. late 1950s. This is a Contemporary house of the flat-roofed variety. Sheets of smooth dark granite cover the walls of the side wings and a

Trousdale Estates

Trousdale Estates

large patterned screen shades the central section. The deeply recessed front entrance is through a massive pair of wood-slab doors. The landscape perfectly complements the house with nonrepresentational topiary and a circular drive separated from the street by a massive and Orientalized berm.

385 Trousdale Place (private), ca. late 1950s. This understated flat-roofed Contemporary house has an open carport approached over a broad, patterned driveway. The sunscreen here is composed of vertical elements.

440 Trousdale Place (private), ca. late 1950s. This post-1940 Neoclassical Revival design has a distinct Los Angeles flair. Similar houses that are white with flat roofs, lots of columns, and varying amounts of statuary can be spotted in Westwood, Beverly Hills, Los Feliz, and even Hancock Park. The front door is a treasure—classic (though not Classical) 1950s design.

West Hollywood

Visitors to Hollywood, the legendary heart of the nation's entertainment world, have from its movie-era beginnings been surprised to find it a workaday industrial town that bears little resemblance to its more romantic products. Founded as a residential suburb in the failed 1880s boom (see page 66), it was "discovered" by the city's early movie colony precisely because it had so much vacant land for outdoor shooting, as well as a

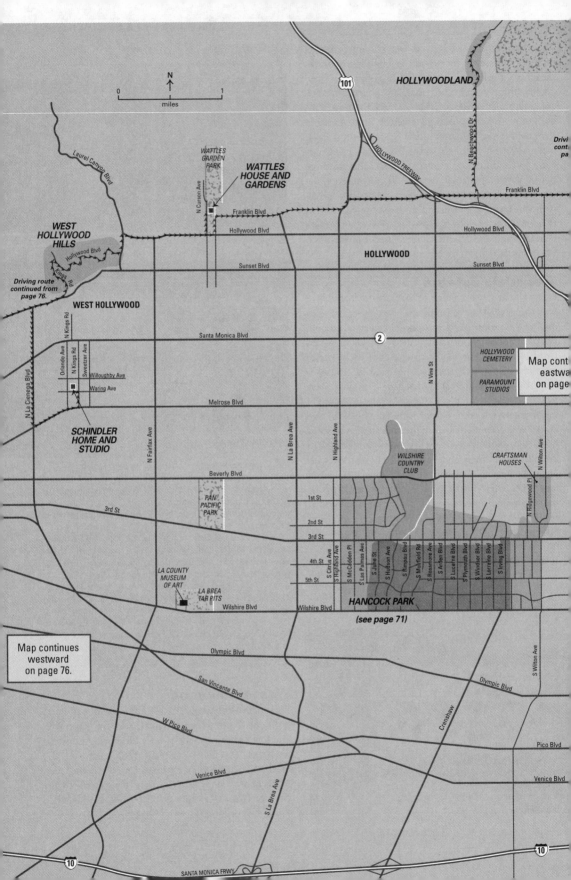

N

0   miles   1

HOLLYWOODLAND

Laurel Canyon Blvd

101

Hollywood Freeway

N Beachwood Dr

Drivi
cont
pa

WATTLES
GARDEN
PARK

WATTLES
HOUSE AND
GARDENS

N Curson Ave

Franklin Blvd

Franklin Blvd

WEST
HOLLYWOOD
HILLS

Hollywood Blvd

Hollywood Blvd

Hollywood Blvd

Kings Rd

Sunset Blvd

HOLLYWOOD

Sunset Blvd

Driving route
continued from
page 76.

WEST HOLLYWOOD

N Kings Rd

Santa Monica Blvd

2

N Vine St

HOLLYWOOD
CEMETERY

PARAMOUNT
STUDIOS

Map cont
eastwa
on page

N La Cienega Blvd

Orlando Ave

N Kings Rd

Sweetzer Ave

Willoughby Ave

Waring Ave

SCHINDLER
HOME AND
STUDIO

N Fairfax Ave

Melrose Blvd

N La Brea Ave

N Highland Ave

WILSHIRE
COUNTRY
CLUB

CRAFTSMAN
HOUSES

N Ridgewood Pl

N Wilton Ave

Beverly Blvd

PAN
PACIFIC
PARK

1st St

2nd St

3rd St

3rd St

Map continues
westward
on page 76.

LA COUNTY
MUSEUM
OF ART

LA BREA
TAR PITS

Wilshire Blvd

Wilshire Blvd

4th St

5th St

S Citrus Ave

S Highland Ave

S McCadden Pl

S Las Palmas Ave

S Julia St

S Hudson Ave

S Rimpau Rd

S Muirfield Rd

S Rossmore Ave

S Arden Blvd

S Lucerne Blvd

S Plymouth Blvd

S Windsor Blvd

S Lorraine Blvd

S Irving Blvd

HANCOCK PARK

(see page 71)

Olympic Blvd

San Vincente Blvd

Crenshaw

Olympic Blvd

S Wilton Ave

W Pico Blvd

Pico Blvd

Venice Blvd

S La Brea Ave

Venice Blvd

10

SANTA MONICA FRWY

10

large, and almost equally vacant, hotel with cheap rooms. When Hollywood unexpectedly became the center for the nation's production of new "feature-length" films in 1915 (see page 70), it suddenly became a *real* boomtown as movie production companies from around the country brought their writers, directors, actors, producers, cameramen, and equipment to the new heart of American filmmaking. Soon the town was filled with production studios, office buildings, workers' housing, and the providers of all of the multiple services needed by a rapidly expanding industrial town. As noted earlier, Hollywood's population soared from only 4,000 in 1911 to 235,000 by 1930. Long before then, anyone who could possibly afford it preferred to live elsewhere.

Many of the industry's most affluent workers commuted to Beverly Hills and beyond on the west or to Hancock Park farther south. To serve those wanting to live closer to their work, and not disturbed by steep, mountainside settings reachable only by the now almost-ubiquitous automobile, new upscale developments were opened in the Hollywood Hills, as the slopes of the Santa Monica Mountains to the north were renamed. Perhaps the most memorable of these developments is Hollywoodland, which opened in 1924 (see page 85).

The area immediately to the west of Hollywood attracted a different clientele. There, a large and undeveloped tract of land had not yet been annexed into the city of Los Angeles and was therefore not subject to the city's building code and the other usual urban restrictions. Soon this area was filling up with the modest houses of many of the movie colony's less affluent creative talents—writers, artists, architects, musicians, and such. Today, this area is the thriving and carefully regulated town of West Hollywood; its early history still gives much of it a small-scale character that is quite different from either industrial Hollywood on the east or affluent Beverly Hills on the west. It also gives the area many dwellings designed by pioneer modernist architects, among them the home of Rudolf Schindler, now an important museum house (see the following entry). The tour route here passes some upscale dwellings in hills just north of West Hollywood, with detours southward leading to the Schindler Home and northward to the Wattles House and Gardens (see page 85).

8437 Hollywood Boulevard (private), ca. 1930. The Spanish Eclectic home looks like a miniature hillside Spanish village.

8460 Hollywood Boulevard (private), ca. 1930. This Spanish Eclectic house, which hugs the hillside, has a prominent rounded tower with a high, open angular patio adjoining.

8161 Hollywood Boulevard (private), Storer House, 1923; Frank Lloyd Wright, architect. The second of Wright's textile

West Hollywood

block houses (La Miniatura in Pasadena preceded it; see page 95), this almost appears at first to be a part of the hill behind it. While Wright's earlier Prairie-style houses were long and horizontal, echoing the lines of the flat midwestern prairie, his textile block houses were inspired by the rugged, semibarren hills around Los Angeles. The gray concrete feels almost like stone, and the terrace and roof levels of the house step up, echoing a craggy hillside. The total effect is stunning, a unique home perfectly sited and carefully detailed.

Schindler Home and Studio, 1922

835 North Kings Road, West Hollywood; 213-651-1510; Rudolf M. Schindler, Los Angeles, architect.

Much of modernism's early energy emanated from California, and particularly southern California, with its generally mild climate. Los Angeles lies at about the same latitude as Charleston, South Carolina, on the Atlantic, yet the prevailing temperate winds off the Pacific give it a far more moderate climate. In Los Angeles the temperature almost never dips below freezing, while Charleston averages thirty-seven subfreezing days each

Schindler Home and Studio

year. Summer nights in Los Angeles are about ten degrees cooler than in Charleston; winter nights, about ten degrees warmer. This is why, if you've never spent time in California (and particularly southern California), some of modern architecture's integration of interior and exterior space can be puzzling. When cold north winds are creating waves of drafts off that large sliding glass door, or a burning western sun is hitting a large picture window in one-hundred-degree summer weather, it is hard to fully appreciate the indoor-outdoor lifestyle advocated by Schindler and so many of the early modern architects. But when in southern California it seems the only way to live.

It was with the region's mild climate in mind that Austrian émigré Rudolf M. Schindler (1887–1953) set out to build a "real California house" for himself and his wife, Sophie Pauline Gibling Schindler (1893–1977). They had just returned from a glorious fall camping trip to Yosemite Park, where they had experienced the very best of California climate and outdoor living. This recent adventure played a vital role in Schindler's design for his home and studio, which in turn helped chart a new direction for modern architecture.

The Schindlers had lived at the Frank Lloyd Wright Studio in Oak Park, Illinois, during the first year of their marriage and then had moved to Wright's Taliesen in rural Wisconsin in 1911. In both settings they were intrigued by the integration of work and play, building and landscape. They dreamed of someday building a

similar studio for themselves. So the Schindler Home and Studio is actually not a house at all, in the traditional sense. It is rather individual studio workspaces for four persons—Schindler; his wife, Pauline; her close Smith College friend Marian Da Camara Chace (1892–1978); and Marian's architect husband, Clyde Chace (born 1891). Their four separate spaces were built around a single utility area. Cooking was projected to be done at the table or in the individual fireplaces "like a social campfire." Work and living were integrally bound together—the concept that the Schindlers had experienced at Taliesen, where Pauline believed she had discovered life's four essentials, "work, play, love, and worship." Each studio was to open onto one of two outdoor courtyards, each defined by plantings and a lowered area that acted almost like a moat in enclosing the outdoor space. As another bow to the recent camping experience, sleeping was to be done in "sleeping baskets" on the roof of the house (their use was to be a relatively short-lived experiment).

In addition to the reinterpretation of a room's functions to fit an envisioned lifestyle, and the close integration of exterior and interior spaces, Schindler conceived a new construction system, partially inspired by learning about Irving Gill's slab-wall construction (Clyde Chace had worked with Gill). According to *R. M. Schindler House: 1921–22*, by Kathryn Smith, an exemplary booklet on sale in the Schindler house shop,

The design for Kings Road was a tour-de-force that anticipated by over a decade many of the innovations that Frank Lloyd Wright introduced with his first Usonian House for Herbert Jacobs (1936). These included:

- Building a flat concrete pad directly on the ground: using this pad as the surface for on-site prefabrication of the walls, as the final floor surface, and as an extension into the garden creating a direct connection between indoors and outdoors.
- Building the house in systematic stages from floor slab to solid walls to framing to glass infill.
- Elimination of layers of building materials and, consequently, the expense of conventional building trades; using the same materials, on the interior and exterior, left in their natural state.
- The intimate embrace of two wings of the building wrapping around the garden and opening to it through glass walls and a series of doors.
- The use of clerestory windows on several sides for ventilation and light, a flat roof, and the placement of plumbing at the hinge of the L plan for convenient access.

Wattles House

As his apprentice, Schindler had absorbed many of Wright's principles, but in his own studio-residence he was pioneering new ground.

Unfortunately, the utopian parts of Schindler's scheme went a bit awry. Both Pauline and Marian became pregnant as construction progressed (requiring the accommodation of young infants), a kitchen had to be installed, Pauline became depressed, and the Schindlers' marriage began to deteriorate. Marian and Clyde Chace moved out after two years, and in 1925, Richard Neutra (1892–1970) and his wife moved in. At first Neutra and Schindler worked together as partners, and together designed a handful of the most exciting early-International-style houses and buildings in the United States. During the years they worked together, 1925 to 1930, the house was a gathering place for the cultural and architectural avant-garde. But Pauline was still depressed and moved out in 1927. In 1930 Schindler and Neutra had a falling-out over clients and commissions. Neutra went his own way. Schindler continued to design fine International-style homes for many years. The two architects maintained a sort of friendship, but without the closeness of the initial years.

Today the Schindler House is functioning as a gallery space for the MAK Center for Art and Architecture. (Schindler's nearby Mackey Apartments are part of the same center, but are not generally open.) A visit here is a fascinating trip back to 1922, when most of the country was forgetting the popular early modern styles (Craftsman and Prairie) and becoming infatuated with Period house styles (Tudor, Italian Renaissance, Colo-

nial Revival, and French and Spanish Eclectic, etc.). As this was happening elsewhere, Schindler was building a house that served as a salon where artists, architects, and intellectuals gathered, and in the process spreading the ideals behind this small and deceptively simple home—ideals that helped chart the course of American modern architecture for many years to come.

Wattles House and Gardens, 1907

1824 North Curson Avenue; house open only by appointment; 213-874-4005; Myron Hunt and Elmer Grey, architects.

This former country estate is a rare survivor from Los Angeles's premovie colony, orange-grove boom era (see page 67). A large Mission-style dwelling is the centerpiece for many acres of dramatic gardens that mostly climb the hillside to the rear of the house. The house is no longer furnished, but some sense of the house's Mission-style interior detailing can be glimpsed through the windows that open onto the arcaded front porch.

Hollywoodland

The tour route traverses Hollywood along Franklin Avenue, the approximate northern limit of the 1880s development. Still farther north are the early developments carved out of the Hollywood Hills. A northward detour up the hills along Beachwood Avenue visits the most familiar of these developments, called Hollywoodland. Its founders erected a huge sign spelling out the name with illuminated metal letters fifty feet high on the mountainside above their subdivision. Later, the

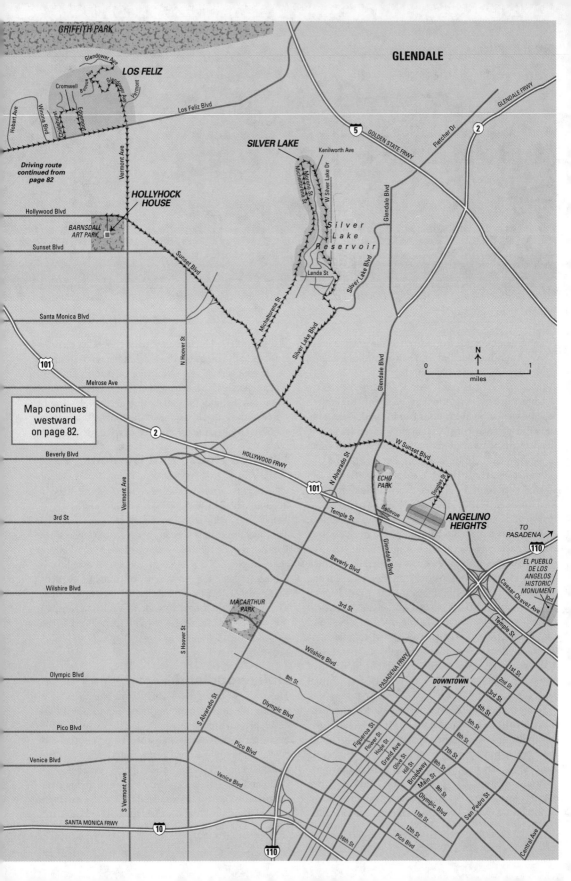

GRIFFITH PARK

GLENDALE

LOS FELIZ

Glendower Ave
Cromwell
Bryce Ave
Glendower Ave
Edgemont
Chislehurst
Vermont
Hobart Ave
Winona Blvd

Los Feliz Blvd

SILVER LAKE

Kenilworth Ave

GLENDALE FRWY

5

GOLDEN STATE FRWY

2

Fletcher Dr

Driving route
continued from
page 82

Vermont Ave

HOLLYHOCK
HOUSE

Hollywood Blvd

BARNSDALL
ART PARK

Sunset Blvd

Sunset Blvd

Santa Monica Blvd

Marino St
Michletorena St
W Silver Lake Dr

Silver
Lake
Reservoir

Glendale Blvd

Landa St

Silver Lake Blvd

N

0   1
miles

101

Melrose Ave

N Hoover St

Michletorena St

Silver Lake Blvd

Map continues
westward
on page 82.

2

Beverly Blvd

Vermont Ave

HOLLYWOOD FRWY

101

Temple St

W Sunset Blvd

ECHO
PARK

Bellevue

Douglas St

ANGELINO
HEIGHTS

TO
PASADENA

110

EL PUEBLO
DE LOS
ANGELOS
HISTORIC
MONUMENT

3rd St

Wilshire Blvd

Glendale Blvd

Beverly Blvd

Glendale Blvd

3rd St

Caesar Chavez Ave

ord

Temple St

MACARTHUR
PARK

S Hoover St

1st St

2nd St

DOWNTOWN

3rd St

Olympic Blvd

8th St

Wilshire Blvd

4th St

Pico Blvd

S Alvarado St

Olympic Blvd

5th St

6th St

PASADENA FRWY

Figueroa St

Flower St

Hope St

Grand Ave

Olive St

Hill St

7th St

Venice Blvd

Pico Blvd

Broadway

Main St

8th St

9th St

San Pedro St

S Vermont Ave

Venice Blvd

Olympic Blvd

9th St

11th St

SANTA MONICA FRWY

10

12th St

16th St

Pico Blvd

Central Ave

110

Hollywoodland

last four letters were removed; rebuilt in 1978 the "Hollywood Sign" remains a beloved Los Angeles icon.

2706 North Beachwood Drive (private), ca. 1920s. A large round tower and shed-roof sections add interest to the massing of this Spanish Eclectic house, the first you see as you enter the original gates to Hollywoodland. Nearby is the development's original real estate office, which still offers houses and lots for sale.

2837 North Beachwood Drive (private), ca. 1920s. This French Eclectic home combines two towers—a lowish angular one and a taller squared one that contains the pointed-arch front door.

2904 North Beachwood Drive (private), ca. 1920s. Built up on the hillside, this asymmetrical French Eclectic house has half-timbering, a high terrace, a stone retaining wall, and a garage featuring paired wood-plank doors and prominent hardware that are perfect for the style.

3036 North Beachwood Drive (private), ca. 1920s. A fine false-thatched-roof Tudor cottage. Note the rustic half-timbering, the prominent diamond-paned casement windows, and the picturesque stone-and-brick chimney.

Los Feliz

East of Hollywood the final segment of the Santa Monica Mountains is occupied by heroic **Griffith Park,** a seminaturalistic urban preserve of over four thousand acres given to the city in 1896 by wealthy mining engineer Griffith J. Griffith. It is the nation's largest urban park. The lower foothills and plains south of the park were subdivided into several turn-of-the-century housing developments that are now known as the Los Feliz neighborhood, named for the original Hispanic grantee of the large cattle ranch that once occupied the

area. The narrow foothills strip of Los Feliz, adjacent to Griffith Park and centered around landscaped Los Feliz Boulevard was developed into a small, upscale residential district much favored by some movie industry leaders for its closeness to Hollywood. Two short northward detours from Los Feliz Boulevard provide a sampling of its fine houses. Farther south, the Los Feliz area was originally filled with more modest dwellings, now mostly replaced by commercial buildings. Towering above these, atop one of the many small hills that lead southeastward to downtown Los Angeles, is an extraordinary survivor—the Frank Lloyd Wright–designed Hollyhock House (see the following entry), now a museum dwelling and the center of an art-oriented urban park.

Los Feliz

Los Feliz

2220 Chislehurst Drive (private), ca. 1930. The rounded stone entryway of this Spanish Eclectic design faces out toward the corner and is accentuated with four spiraled columns. Note the deeply recessed Spanish paneled door and the large parabolic art-glass window.

2201 Chislehurst Drive (private), ca. 1930. Ribbons of casement windows and clinker-brick accents adorn this large, brick-clad Tudor home.

4970 Cromwell Avenue (private), ca. 1930. Note how the two-story-high roof on the right side stretches all the way down to the first story, not even broken by a dormer. The broad expanse of roof in combination with the two front-facing gables (each with inventive half-timbering pattern at the midsection) give this Tudor home a distinctive look.

Glendower Avenue (all private). If you are feeling particularly adventurous and don't mind narrow winding streets, the most monumental of Frank Lloyd Wright's textile block houses, the Ennis House, built in 1924, is at 2607 Glendower Avenue (private). The house is perched high atop the hill, with a magnificent view; its owner is having to fight deterioration of the concrete blocks. A handout available in a holder by the entrance tells you about the rare days it is open (or call 213-668-0234). Just below at 2567 Glendower Avenue (private) is Schindler's Skolnik House, built in 1952 with later additions. At 2587 Glendower Avenue (private), ca. 1990s, is a strikingly modern design built on a very steep lot. Its carport is inventively placed on a high terrace sheltered by the house.

Hollyhock House, 1921

4808 Hollywood Boulevard; Barnsdall Art Park; 213-913-4157; Frank Lloyd Wright, Tokyo and Los Angeles (at this period), architect.

The Hollyhock House gains significance from the architect who designed it, the woman who commissioned it, and the relationship between the two. It was the first Los Angeles house designed and built by Frank Lloyd Wright (1867–1959), the innovative early-twentieth-century American architect. The woman for whom the home was built, oil heiress Aline Barnsdall (1882–1946), was a storied free spirit who originally commissioned the structure as part of a planned community devoted to avant-garde theater. These two forward-thinking characters came together in the 1910s in Chicago, where she directed a theater company and he was an established architect. Although their oft-rumored affair was probably one only of the mind, Hollyhock House is one of the most opulent and artistic love letters ever written.

Aline Barnsdall was the granddaughter of Pennsylvania oil magnate William Barnsdall. Her family fortune enabled her to live the life of an eccentric theater patron. When she arrived in Chicago as a young woman, she soon became influenced by the thinking of such political anarchists as Emma Goldman—an ideological shift no doubt bolstered by her artistic pursuits. Frank Lloyd Wright's *An Autobiography* said she was called a "parlor Bolshevik." By the time Barnsdall moved to Los Angeles around 1915, she had formulated a plan to construct a utopian theatrical community and turned to her good friend Frank Lloyd Wright to design it. She bought a thirty-six-acre tract called Olive Hill, for the olive trees covering it, and, together with Wright, devised a layout that included her home, several residences for actors and guests, and two theaters—one for films, the other for plays. This communal vision would never reach fruition; she and Wright had disagreements over the design and the costs, and only the house and two smaller guest houses were completed.

The design of Hollyhock House turned definitively away from the Prairie-style homes Wright had earlier built in the Midwest. Here he was hard at work beginning to create a house type he felt more appropriate for southern California. Wright's design used stylized concrete hollyhocks, Barnsdall's favorite flower, as an exterior and interior design motif. This is repeated in many different ways on a massive form somewhat suggestive of Mayan architecture. This unusual touch indicates the kind of innovation that Wright was willing to undertake. And it was this use of geometric floral forms in concrete that soon led Wright to begin his series of

Hollyhock House

textile block houses in the Los Angeles area (see pages 83 and 95).

Aline Barnsdall's home defies a quick description. A bold juxtaposition of style and ideas, it creates a thoroughly modern structure. Every major interior space is complemented by a matching exterior space; rooftop terraces offer beautiful views all the way to the Pacific Ocean; ceiling levels rise and fall with abandon (a pattern begun in Wright's Prairie homes); and a bold hollyhock arcade adorns the exterior. Donald Hoffman writes in *Frank Lloyd Wright's Hollyhock House:*

> Hollyhock House forms a quadrangle to sequester an inner garden court, but reaches outward to consort with as much of the world as it can. Wright can invest one and the same building with a profound sense of shelter and an exhilarating air of excursion into the American landscape. That is his great achievement. Hollyhock is not so much ambivalent as comprehensive; it can respond to every rhythm of the day, every slight change in spirit.

As was his custom, the interior finishes and furnishings for these exciting interior spaces were also strictly planned by Wright. He designed the dining room furniture, still in place, and living room furnishings that were beautifully replicated in 1990.

The house was completed in 1921, but Barnsdall

only lived in the main house a scant six years. In his autobiography, Wright explains that Barnsdall was a born wanderer, and "she stayed in [Hollyhock House] longer at a time than she ever stayed anywhere before." He devotes ten pages to the home in his autobiography and obviously was a great admirer of both the work and its occupant. "Up there on Olive Hill above hillsides furrowed with rows of gray-green olive trees, the daughter of one of America's pioneers had constructed a little principality, her very own, free to live as a queen. There was nothing like it anywhere in the world."

In 1927, Barnsdall donated her home to the city. It was the subsequent home of the California Art Club and a cultural research foundation, but it gradually fell into disrepair and for a time looked like it might be demolished. The city undertook a serious renovation in the 1970s, and today Barnsdall Art Park boasts theaters, galleries, and studios, as was originally intended. Barnsdall remained an important, if atypical, figure in Los Angeles cultural circles. In her later years Barnsdall lived in one of the two guest houses. Before her death in 1946, she helped found and promote the Hollywood Bowl. Along with the Hollyhock House, it constitutes the most tangible reminder of her cultural accomplishments in Los Angeles.

Silver Lake

Located north of Sunset Boulevard, about a mile southeast of Hollyhock House, the delightful Silver Lake neighborhood occupies the slopes of one of this area's many small hills. Filled mostly with small-scale, architect-designed dwellings, the entire effect is rather like a miniature, and more easily accessible, version of the Hollywood Hills. Particularly striking is the juxtaposition of many starkly simple designs by Los Angeles's pioneering modernist architects, with small Period house designs in various Eclectic-era styles.

1856 Micheltorena Street (private), Daniels House, 1939; Gregory Ain, Los Angeles, architect. As you drive uphill, the carport dominates the view of this International-style house; the better view is seen looking downhill after you've passed it (not to be attempted while driving). Note the flat plane of stucco that shields the entry, turns horizontally to

provide a cantilevered shelter over the carport entry, and then travels vertically to define to right corner of the house. Clerestory windows provide privacy to the occupants, yet allow light and air to enter from the street facade. The private garden and patio are not visible.

1926 Micheltorena Street (private), ca. 1950. Here is a small hillside version of the 1950s builder-type Colonial Revival home with the characteristic brick lower story and wide wood-clad upper story, seen earlier in Westwood and Brentwood. Note the broken-ogee pediment above the front door.

2236 Micheltorena Street (private), Olive House, 1933; R. M. Schindler, Los Angeles, architect. As with all the best International-style homes, you would have to be an invited guest in order to appreciate the private outdoor views and the interesting interior spaces of this home tucked into the hillside.

2404 Micheltorena Street (private), Orans House, 1941; Gregory Ain, Los Angeles, architect. This International-style design presents a particularly pleasing view to the street. Note how the gently curved left side of the smooth wall surface leads you into the flight of entrance steps, while the right side shields most of them from view.

Silver Lake

Silver Lake

Angelino Heights

Occupying yet another of the small hills that extend northwestward from the original Hispanic town of Los Angeles, Angelino Heights, only a mile from downtown, was the city's first suburb. Platted in the failed 1880s boom, it escaped the fate of its more distant contemporaries and was soon being filled with fine Victorian houses built on hillside lots that provided dramatic views of the surrounding countryside. Today, the early heart of the neighborhood is preserved in the **Carroll Avenue Historic District,** the city's largest intact concentration of Victorian dwellings.

Angelino Heights

1344 Carroll Avenue (private), Haskin House, ca. 1888. A particularly delicate spindlework Queen Anne design with an open tower above the wraparound porch.

1330 Carroll Avenue (private), Sessions House, 1888; Joseph Cather Newsom, San Francisco, architect. This exuberant Queen Anne house was designed by one of San Francisco's renowned Newsom brothers (see pages 180–181 and 225). Their houses always have a unique quality, and this is no exception. Note the Syrian arch above the porch entry and the carved creatures to each side and the "moongate" porch above.

1320 Carroll Avenue (private), Heim House, 1888. During the 1880s there was a craze for Japanese interior decor and decorative objects. This Japanesque influence sometimes extended to exterior details, such as the Japanesque fan motif seen on this fine Queen Anne home. Note the dramatic paired front doors in which two open fans face each other, their bottom panels with the same motif reversed and repeated in the glass windows above. It is repeated yet again below the lower-story windows and in a simplified geometric form in a stained-glass window (possibly later) to the left of the porch. The cornice and bracket design is a holdover from the earlier Italianate style.

1316 Carroll Street (private), Russell House, 1888. This Stick-style house is transitional to the Queen Anne. Among its Stick-style details are the king's post truss in the gable, the modified-picket-fence pattern along the cornice, and the vertical strips at the sides of the windows, which extend all the way from the cornice line down to the foundation. The hipped roof with a lower front-facing gable, shaped wood shingles in the gable, and spindlework porch detailing are all Queen Anne features.

1300 Carroll Avenue (private), Phillips House, 1887. An elaborately detailed spindlework Queen Anne design.

MALIBU

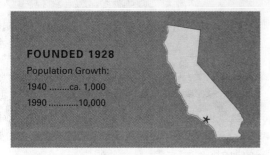

FOUNDED 1928

Population Growth:

1940 ....ca. 1,000

1990 10,000

Malibu, an upscale, beachfront community about twelve miles west of Santa Monica (see page 73), is best known for its surfing and its private developments of modern houses favored by media celebrities. Perhaps its most unusual distinction is in having, as one of its oldest and most historically significant buildings, a house built as late as 1930.

Adamson House, 1930

23200 Pacific Coast Highway, in the Malibu Lagoon State Beach Park; 310-456-8432; Stiles O. Clements (of Morgan, Walls, and Clements), Los Angeles, architect.

This pristine Spanish Eclectic house masterfully demonstrates the many uses of architectural decorative tiles. It contains a wealth of high-quality tilework and tile designs—all produced at the nearby Malibu Potteries. The company's wares were used lavishly throughout both house and garden: ceiling, floors, baseboards, walls, countertops, fireplaces, grilles, furniture, stair treads and risers, fountains, and patios—all were selectively enriched with this colorful hand-painted ornament. This

profusion is understandable, since Adamson House was built as a beach house for Rhonda Rindge Adamson (1893–1962) and her husband, Merritt Huntley Adamson (1888–1949), the daughter and son-in-law of May Knight Rindge (1864–1941), who owned Malibu Potteries.

May and her husband, Frederick Hastings Rindge (1857–1905), were the last owners of Rancho Malibu, an intact Spanish land grant that stretched twenty-two miles along the coast from Santa Monica to Zuma Beach and extended from the Pacific Ocean to the ridge of the Malibu Mountains (defined by the metes and bounds of natural landmarks, as was typical of Hispanic land grants). Frederick, who came from a wealthy New England family, purchased the grant in 1891 for about $130,000, and until his death the family owned and operated it as a ranch. Not long after his death, the state of California began to try to acquire the right-of-way for the Pacific Coast Highway. May, who now owned Rancho Malibu, was determined to protect the land's pristine beauty and fought the state fiercely for seventeen years, a legal battle that almost totally drained her resources. The state ultimately won in 1925, and it was probably in an attempt to recoup some of her dwindling fortune and to find a new direction for her life that May Rindge founded Malibu Potteries in 1926, right on the beach just east of Malibu Pier and adjacent to the dreaded roadway. When the highway opened in 1928, it at least provided her wares with easy transportation.

Malibu Potteries quickly became extraordinarily

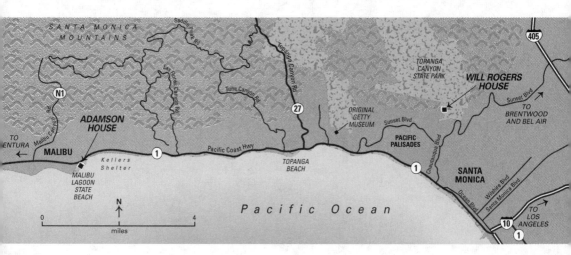

Adamson House

successful. The factory used high-quality clays that were available right on Rancho Malibu. Designs were taken from photographs, from information brought back from European expeditions, and from the creative work of the many artisans who worked there. Almost all of the Potteries' designs were created to complement and be installed in the Spanish Eclectic homes that were being built throughout California in the 1920s and 1930s. Most of the standard designs were called Moorish or Saracen. These were primarily complex geometric designs (because the Muslim religion forbade the pictorial representation of living creatures; see also Casa del Herrero, page 259) and occasionally were of stylized plants. Commonly, a six-inch-by-six-inch tile would have a diagonal design, which when put together with three other matching tiles would make a completed square pattern.

Custom-made designs could also be ordered, and these were highly varied and imaginative. The Adamson House holds a number of custom designs—among them are Oriental "rugs" executed in tile, oversize tiles hand painted with sailing ships, and large tiled murals featuring peacocks and other exotic birds. Unfortunately the Potteries had but a brief life; in 1932 the company fell victim to the depression.

Today Adamson House still sits on thirteen glorious acres overlooking Malibu's picturesque lagoon, with its sparkling beach and historic pier. The house contains most of its original fixtures, finishes, and furnishings and features view windows, balconies, and open porches overlooking the ocean. Wrought-iron light fixtures and sconces, some with their original parchment shades, are still intact. The original hand-painted ceilings and woodwork remain, and the furnishings, many of which were produced just for this house, are still in place. As might be expected in a house of tile—each bathroom is a small jewel.

The grounds are beautifully landscaped and filled with a profusion of flowers. Flagstone paves the large entry court and walkways. Two tiled fountains still operate, one a wall fountain and the other in a large Moorish pool in the shape of an eight-pointed star. Farther from the house you can visit the original swimming pool and beach house (and admire yet more tilework).

You will end your visit to Adamson House in awe of the many uses of this flexible architectural ornament—and perhaps with a new appreciation of a material that can add joyful color and design with such permanence.

PASADENA

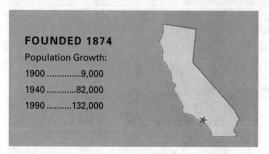

FOUNDED 1874
Population Growth:
1900 9,000
1940 82,000
1990 132,000

Pasadena was the Los Angeles area's original upscale suburban town; today, its fine early houses and neighborhoods are still among the region's most desirable places to live.

The town was founded in the initial railroad excitement of the 1870s (see page 65) by an Indianapolis doctor and some of his affluent friends, who decided "to get where the life is easy." For twenty-five thousand dollars the group purchased a four-thousand-acre tract about ten miles northeast of Los Angeles at the base of the San Gabriel Mountains. Situated almost one thousand feet higher than its older neighbor, on clear days the land offered scenic views over the adjacent plain and ocean beyond.

During its first decade, when railroad travel to southern California required a round-about and expensive journey via San Francisco, the town grew slowly. It was, however, developing a reputation as an idyllic paradise among other well-off but disaffected midwesterners who shared its founders yearning for a different lifestyle. When the Santa Fe Railroad arrived in Los Angles in 1885, Pasadena was a stop on its main-line route from Kansas City and Chicago. Furthermore, a railroad-fare war and subsequent rate competition between the newly arrived Santa Fe and the long-entrenched Southern Pacific Railroad soon reduced even first-class fares to a small fraction of their previous cost. Now those tempted by a climate mild enough to permit rose festivals on New Year's Day could hardly afford *not* to at least come for a visit to see such wonders firsthand.

A great many of the visitors decided to make Pasadena their new home, at least during the winter. Elegant residential hotels began springing up in the town, and house-lot buying began a swell that ultimately reached boomtown proportions. From 1900 to 1907 the year-round population surged from nine thousand to thirty thousand and by 1930 had increased to seventy-six thousand.

Modern Pasadena, scarcely larger today than it was in 1950, is still a delightfully self-contained small city dominated by pleasant residential neighborhoods served by a rare, fully functional downtown core that combines shopping, dining, and entertainment, concentrated in the Old Town area, with fine commercial, government, and educational buildings. The town is also a house watcher's delight, with some of the West's finest surviving Eclectic-era neighborhoods and five of its grandest dwellings open to visitors.

THE ARROYO SECO

In 1769 Miguel Constansó, cartographer with the Portolá expedition, described the then-beautiful Los Angeles River and also "another water-course or river-bed which formed a wide ravine, but it was dry. This water-course joined that of the river, and gave clear indications of heavy floods during the rainy season, as it had many branches of trees and debris on its banks." According to Jane Apostol in *Museums along the Arroyo,* this is "an accurate description of the Arroyo Seco, the usually dry streambed that originates in the San Gabriel Mountains and extends to the Los Angeles River." Filled with much native vegetation and also with characteristic stones that were worn smooth by many millennia of torrential rains and floods, this deep landscape feature became a favored location for fine homes that could overlook its rugged beauty from a safe height. The terms "Upper" and "Lower" Arroyo Seco are used locally in Pasadena; "Upper" refers to a location above, or north of, Interstate 210 (the Foothill Highway) while "Lower" refers to a location below, or south of, Interstate 210. While today separated by a freeway, the two areas are still connected by early Arroyo Boulevard that follows the course of the arroyo far beneath the freeway, which crosses above on dramatic bridges.

Orange Grove Boulevard, a favored early location for grand homes, runs generally north–south along the east side of the arroyo. Before about 1900, the gardens of these large homes extended down toward the arroyo, which itself remained almost a wilderness area. Today, most of these large early estates have been subdivided and, along Orange Grove Boulevard, often replaced with apartments. Despite this, four of the remaining grand homes can be viewed by the public.

The streets just off of Orange Grove still have a high proportion of fine and well-preserved houses. In their

Los Angeles: An Architectural Guide, authors David Gebhard and Robert Winter declare that "the entire Arroyo Seco should be declared a national monument. The architecture is as important as that of Charleston, South Carolina, and the scenery is much better."

Upper Arroyo Seco, 1900–1930

Three small but distinct neighborhoods are found in the Upper Arroyo. All boast homes designed by the extraordinary Greene brothers (see "Gamble House," page 99). The Gamble House itself is located on the one-block-long Westmoreland Place, a private street set back from Orange Grove with but four houses along it, two by the Greenes. In 1917 the brothers were hired to design the Westmoreland Gate at Rosemont Street, as the residents had become annoyed by tour buses.

Across Rosemont Street, the northeastern boundary of Westmoreland Place, is Prospect Park. This 1906 subdivision was protected with deed restrictions that required, among other things, minimum construction costs of five thousand to eight thousand dollars. Large lots and camphor trees line the broad, curving streets. The entrance from Orange Grove Boulevard onto Prospect Boulevard passes through handsome portals of boulders and clinker bricks, which were clearly inspired by Greene and Greene. Prospect Park has seventy-one houses, mostly built between 1907 and 1930. There is a nice mixture of Craftsman designs and homes of Period styles, principally Tudor, French Eclectic, Spanish Eclectic, and Colonial Revival.

At the southwestern end of Westmoreland Place is the Arroyo Terrace neighborhood with a streetscape of seven homes designed by the Greene brothers, including Charles Sumner Greene's own home and that of his sisters-in-law, the White sisters. It requires a walk to appreciate their subtleties.

Prior to the construction of Interstate 210, Grand Avenue went straight through to the Lower Arroyo area below, while today you must detour along Orange Grove Avenue or down through the picturesque Arroyo Boulevard.

Prospect Park: 645 Prospect Crescent (private), La Miniatura, 1923; Frank Lloyd Wright, architect. From Crescent Terrace you see the garage and rear entry of this stunning textile block house, the first of several that Frank Lloyd Wright built in the Los Angeles area. The textile blocks were precast concrete with geometric designs on the exterior sides; they were installed at the site with steel ties and poured concrete. This one was built for Mrs. George Millard primarily to house her book and art collection. For the classic view of this home, you will have to look at it through its gate on Rosemont Street.

Prospect Park: 445 Prospect Square (private), Hamilton House, 1924; Marston, Van Pelt, and Maybury, Pasadena,

Upper Arroyo Seco

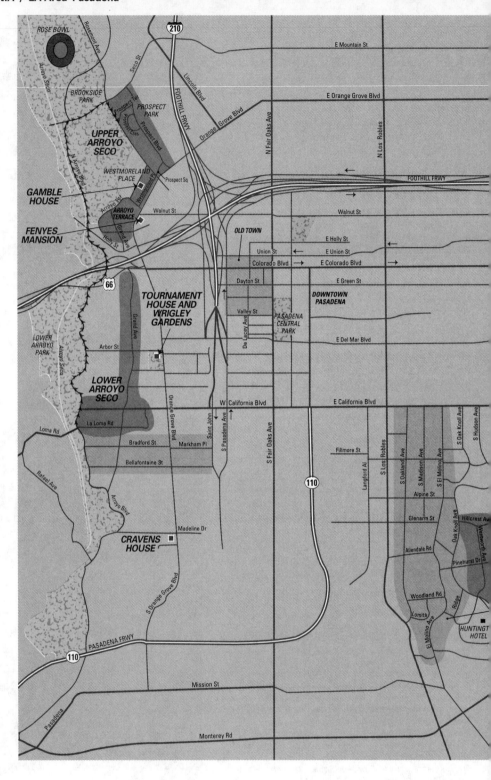

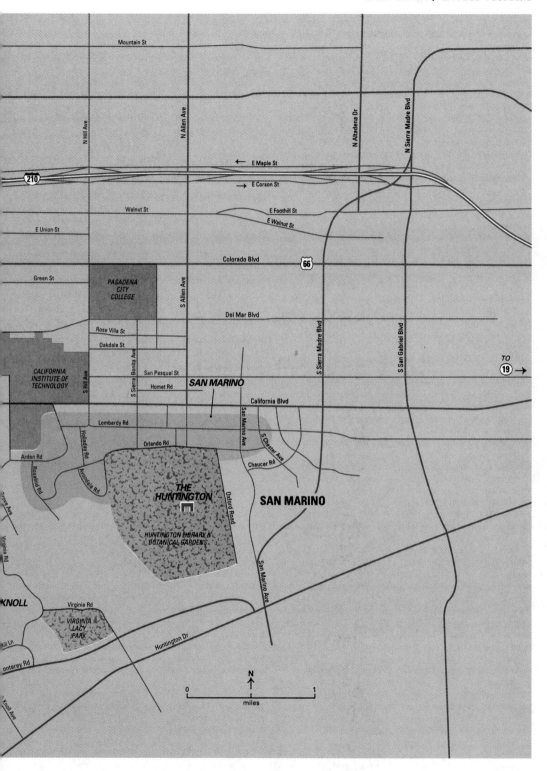

architects. This timeless Colonial Revival home, restrained but with lots of carefully detailed trimmings, has windows with multiple small panes and shutters; an entry surrounded with an elliptical fanlight and sidelights; a handsome portico; three dormers with round-arched windows; brick side walls with paired double chimneys; and a roof balustrade.

Prospect Park: 657 Prospect Boulevard (private), Bentz House, 1906; Greene and Greene, Pasadena, architects. John Bentz, one of the developers of Prospect Park, decided to build the first home in the neighborhood to encourage development. His wife wanted a home of the Swiss-chalet type, and this sedate interpretation is what the Greenes provided. Similar boxy, two-story-high, front-gabled Craftsman homes occur throughout Pasadena. Only occasionally is Swiss-chalet-type ornament added, such as that found at 572 (see the following entry).

Prospect Park: 572 Prospect Boulevard (private), Bartlett House, 1906. This whimsical Swiss chalet has most of the typical stylistic ornament—zigzag trimmed vergeboards, flat porch railing with cutouts, a window box with heart and diamond cutouts, and triangular braces (which here are made from unusual turned spindles).

Westmoreland Place: 2 Westmoreland Place (private), Cole House, 1906; Greene and Greene, Pasadena, architects. This house gains distinction from its front porte cochere with massive sloping stone supports and dramatic side chimneys.

Arroyo Terrace: 408 Arroyo Terrace (private), Hawks House, 1906; Greene and Greene, Pasadena, architects. This front-gabled Craftsman home used the same floor plans as the Bentz House (see above) but added a broader and more dramatic porch.

Arroyo Terrace: 400 Arroyo Terrace (private), Van Rossem–Neill House, 1903, 1906, 1913; Greene and Greene, Pasadena, architects. The most noticeable feature of this home is the distinctive wall of clinker bricks, boulders, and occasional see-through tiled elements. It was added when the original small rental house was expanded to the present structure.

Arroyo Terrace: 370 Arroyo Terrace (private), White House, 1903; Greene and Greene, Pasadena, architects. This home was built for Charles Greene's sisters-in-law and has been altered by the addition of stucco.

Arroyo Terrace: 368 Arroyo Terrace (private), Greene House, 1901, 1906, 1914, 1916; Charles S. Greene, Pasadena, architect. Architects often continually enlarge and improve their own homes and Charles Greene was no exception. His home was regularly expanded to serve his growing family.

Arroyo Terrace: 240 North Grand Avenue (private), Duncan-Irwin House, 1900, 1906; Greene and Greene, Pasadena, architects. This large home assumed its current appearance in 1906. Note the broad eaves with rafters extending beyond the roof, the beamwork above the porch, and the spacious terraces growing out of the ground.

Arroyo Terrace: 200 North Grand Avenue (private), Hunt House, 1905; Myron Hunt, Pasadena, architect. Myron Hunt, the architect for the Huntington (see page 106), built this unusual and understated Craftsman-style home for himself. The entrance porch, on the right side, is supported by the robust columns favored by the *Craftsman* magazine. These are echoed on the front facade by short engaged columns in between the three front windows. This triad of paired windows is beautifully composed. A narrow shed roof above is supported by triangular braces and has exposed rafter tails. Each window pair is topped by a row of dentils with a narrow band of geometric art glass above. The side entry facade features a subtle rounded arch above the windows and spanning between the porch supports.

Arroyo Terrace: 90 North Grand Avenue (private), Halstead House, 1905. This Tudor estate is complete with a gatehouse and a four-car garage with Tudor arches above each garage entrance. Note the elegant glass entry canopy on the main house.

Lower Arroyo Seco

Before 1900, the grand estates of Orange Grove Boulevard backed up to the arroyo. After about 1900, the two natural terraces on this, the eastern side of the arroyo, became desirable building sites for slightly smaller homes. As the large estates were subdivided, smaller lots were created along the arroyo, which appealed to many writers, artists, and craftsmen. This attraction was present not only in Pasadena but all along the length of the Arroyo Seco. An Arroyo Guild was formed and began a journal, the *Arroyo Craftsman*, devoted to "simple living, high thinking, pure democracy, genuine art, honest craftsmanship, natural inspiration and exalted aspiration." Despite the lofty goals, it only survived for one issue.

Today, interesting houses are found all along the Lower Arroyo, but a particularly good concentration of different styles, including a few 1890s homes, can be found along a several-block stretch of Grand Avenue. A group of fine smaller Craftsman homes is clustered in a several-block area of Arroyo Boulevard, La Loma Street, California Street, and Saint John Street. This small area can best be enjoyed by walking.

346 Markham Place (private), Blankenhorn House, 1893; Bradbeer and Ferris, architects. This perfect spindlework Queen Anne house, in the hipped-roof-with-lower-cross-gables subtype, is covered with embellishments typical of the style. The front-facing gable has a decorated triangular section at the top and a pent roof at the bottom. The porch has a frieze of beaded spindles and an embellished triangular pediment above the entry steps. Note also the cutaway bay window, the centered porch upstairs, the paired front doors with multiple small panels, and the rounded tower topped by a bulbous roof.

293 South Grand Avenue (private), ca. 1930. Asymmetrical French Eclectic houses come in two types—picturesque examples based on rambling French farmhouses as well as more formal houses similar to the symmetrical subtype, but with slightly off-center doorways and asymmetrical window placement. This example of the latter formal group has a tall chimney to each side and a very steeply pitched roof. The front entry is crowned with a bracketed cornice and has a handsome small elliptical window in the second story above.

325 South Grand Avenue (private), ca. 1895; Seymour Locke and Jasper N. Preston, architects. This ample Shingle-style house has a gambrel roof and broad squat tower

Lower Arroyo Seco

Lower Arroyo Seco

topped by a pinnacle. The wing to the right of the tower looks like it could be a well-matched later addition.

395 Grand Avenue (private), "Cobbleoak," 1893; Seymour Locke and Jasper N. Preston, architects. Designed by the same firm as 325 South Grand (see the preceding entry), this Shingle house has a cross-gabled roof and a first floor clad with small stones.

640 La Loma Road (private), ca. 1910. This broad front-gabled Craftsman home has an angled porte cochere, likely influenced by the one at Greene and Greene's Blacker House (see page 104).

626 La Loma Road (private), ca. 1910. This side-gabled Craftsman home is clad with wood shingles. The small roof above the entry is supported by three stepped-back beams that are separated by small wooden elements that resemble dumbbells.

475 La Loma Road (private), ca. 1910. This stucco-clad Tudor house has many Craftsman touches. The front entry has a Tudor-arched front door, while the gabled roof above combines an appearance of Tudor half-timbering with Craftsman openness and triangular braced supports.

626 South Arroyo Boulevard (private), Batchelder House, 1909, 1913; Ernest A. Batchelder, Pasadena, architect. Ernest Batchelder, who had studied at the Birmingham School of Arts and Crafts in England, wrote many articles for the *Craftsman* magazine and was one of the founders of the Minneapolis Guild of Handicrafts. Beginning with a small studio and kiln he built at the back of this property, Batchelder became one of the most respected Arts and Crafts tile makers in the United States. He designed this small Craftsman home for himself. Its distinctive asymmetrical chimney design features stucco carefully ornamented with arroyo stone, bricks, and four Batchelder tiles; it is incorporated into an equally carefully composed one-story front-gabled wing. Also note the tiled front sidewalk.

Gamble House, 1908

4 Westmoreland Place; 626-793-3334;
Greene and Greene, Pasadena, architects.

An immaculately preserved creation of pioneering modern architects Charles S. Greene (1868–1957) and Henry M. Greene (1870–1954), the Gamble House exudes a quiet power. Sometimes called an ultimate bungalow, it is hardly a bungalow, for that term was used by early-twentieth-century builders to mean simply "one-story house." (In essence, "bungalow" was a more modern and image-laden way of saying "cottage.") Bungalows came clothed in many different styles, of which the Craftsman style (sometimes called Arts and Crafts) was the most common. But this early modern style was also used for many large and luxurious homes, particularly in southern California. The Gamble House is the most fully realized and completely preserved of the grand Craftsman-style homes that are open to the public. Not only the house but most of its carefully crafted furnishings and interior detailing remain intact and in place.

Gamble House, garden facade

When David Berry Gamble (1847–1923) and his wife, Mary Huggins Gamble (died 1929), decided to build their new home in Pasadena, Mr. Gamble had just retired as an officer of Cincinnati's Procter and Gamble Company, which his father had cofounded. The couple chose the Greenes as their architects after just one meeting. They loved the brothers' ideas and current work, all of which reflected the ideals of America's Arts and Crafts movement. The Greenes responded with masterful skills. The Gamble House is a completely integrated project; the Greenes designed the house and the landscaping, the interior fixtures and finishes, and even much of the furniture. Tireless perfectionists, they oversaw every detail, from rug color to furniture manufacture to the finish of all the beams (which were sanded smooth to achieve an ageless look).

When you stop to think about it, being a modern architect in 1907, when the Greenes were drawing up their designs for this house, was incredibly challenging. Rather than being able to find inspiration and ideas in a sketchbook made on a European study trip, or from a pattern book written by Palladio or others, or from careful measured drawings of architectural landmarks (as builders had done for thousands of years), the early modern architects had to create almost every detail from scratch. Every nuance of every light fixture, screen door, piece of molding, window sash, cornice, stairway, and door had to come from deep within. This was particularly true of the early modernists, like Wright and the Greenes, who believed strongly in decorative detail, but eschewed that which relied on earlier precedents.

The Greene brothers had completed two years of architecture study at M.I.T. but were frustrated by the curriculum's dependence on the Beaux Arts movement; they yearned to be more creative. Their role as perfecters of the Craftsman style drew heavily on their high school training at the Manual Training School of Washington University. The school's motto was "The Cultured Mind—the Skillful Hand." Here, in addition to the usual academic studies, they spent two hours a day working with their hands—one year on wood, one on metals, and a third on tools. There could have been no better preparation for perfecting an architectural style that expressed the properties of wood and utilized all kinds of crafts in its execution.

A delightful art-glass entry provides a dramatic introduction to the Gamble House. Based on a gnarled tree-of-life design by Charles Greene, the doorway's subtly colored art-glass panels are held together by an innovative leading process that widens and narrows as needed to become an integral part of the overall design. The large, heavy central door is flanked by two smaller side doors with corresponding screens that allow ventilation even when the main door is closed. Beyond is a broad stair hall with walls of warmly stained teak and floors covered with Oriental rugs. The Greenes designed many fine stairways; the Gamble House example is among the most sensuous designs of the early modern movement. Meticulously crafted in dark teak, its rich sheen and rounded edges invite one to touch it.

The living room features a hand-carved redwood frieze, featuring bas-relief trees, flowers, bats, and birds. The Arts and Crafts tiles of the fireplace are embellished with a mosaic vine pattern that appears to grow through the background tiles (carefully created by the Greenes). The spaces of the downstairs flow one into the other—from living room to hall to dining room. Each has furniture designed by the Greenes especially for the spaces they occupy. The dining room has Honduras mahogany paneling and a handsome fixed-pedestal table that extends to seat fourteen. Over it hangs a coordinated art-glass light fixture. Above a built-in sideboard is a large window of sinuously lined art glass. During the day the glass gives off a warm glow, and at night it comes magically alive with iridescent mother-of-pearl accents.

The interrelationship between the house and the outdoors is as harmonious as that among its interior spaces. Low-walled terraces connect the house with the surrounding garden. Built up of boulders of gradually decreasing size, the walls of these terraces appear to grow out of the lawn. They are topped by clinker bricks, which are bricks placed too close to the hardening fire, causing them to become slightly misshapen and discolored but giving them great character. Upstairs, three open wood-beamed sleeping porches reach out to connect the family bedrooms with the out-of-doors.

Great credit goes to the clients, David and Mary Gamble, for giving the Greenes the freedom to create this masterpiece, and to their son, Cecil H. Gamble, and his wife, Louise, for appreciating its rare character and maintaining it intact for forty years. Upon Louise's death in 1963, their son, James N. Gamble, acting on behalf of the Gamble heirs, deeded the house to the city of Pasadena, which, in conjunction with the University of Southern California, maintains it as a permanent memorial to the Gambles, to the brothers Greene, and to their innovative Craftsman-style home.

The Gamble House warrants many return visits. And if you happen to be in Pasadena when the house is not open, you can still view the exquisite exterior and visit the fine bookstore located in the garage—it specializes in all aspects of the Arts and Crafts movement and is open during normal business hours.

Gamble House, entry

Fenyes Mansion (Pasadena Historical Society), 1905

470 West Walnut Street (also called Pasadena Historical Museum); 626-577-1660; Robert D. Farquhar, Santa Monica, architect.

The Fenyes Mansion was commissioned by New York City publishing heiress Eva S. Fenyes, whose father was Scott Publishing Company magnate Leonard Scott. Fenyes, a painter and an artist of some renown, planned her home as a place in which to gather and entertain and encourage the intellectual and artistic elite of Pasadena—which it became, virtually upon completion. This creative salon was complemented by the work of Eva's husband, Dr. Adalbert Fenyes, an esteemed entomologist whose insect collection can now be found in San Francisco's Academy of Sciences. The mansion's legacy as a place in which to nurture continued for three generations after Eva's death in 1930: her daughter, Leonora Curtin, authored books on Native American customs, and her granddaughter, Leonora Paloheimo, married a future Finnish consul, whose appointment in the late 1940s resulted in the home's temporary transformation into a Finnish consulate.

For her architect, Fenyes chose Robert D. Farquhar, an 1893 Harvard graduate who had studied architecture at the École des Beaux Arts and then worked for both Carrère and Hastings and Hunt and Hunt. Farquhar (who would later design such Los Angeles landmarks as the California Club and Beverly Hills High School) had recently moved to Santa Monica when he received the commission. He designed a simplified Italian Renaissance house (flat-roof subtype) with an ample entry porch supported by paired Beaux Arts columns and topped with a low balustrade. Originally, the house had a matching balustrade along the roof parapet, which added another touch of grandeur. The upper floor has slender round-arched windows, with a triple-window composition in the center. A two-story wing, containing a laboratory/study, solarium, and gallery, was added to the north facade in 1911 by architect Sylvanus Marston.

As the house remained with the family until its dedication to the Pasadena Historical Society as a museum in 1970, most of the original interior and furnishings remain intact, although some rooms were modified by the Fenyeses' offspring. The furnishings include a collection of cross-cultural antiquities purchased from antique dealers in New York and New Orleans and many Oriental rugs. Most of the artwork (including many family portraits) was painted by Fenyes and her contemporaries. Of practical interest are a typical fire escape of the era (a rope adorning the west wall of the

Fenyes Mansion

master bedroom) and an antique carpet beater in the kitchen hallway.

Tournament House and Wrigley Gardens, 1914

391 South Orange Grove Boulevard; 626-449-4100 (call in advance); G. Lawrence Stimson, Pasadena, architect.

The history of the Tournament House presents a fitting microcosm of California development at the turn of the century. Built by southern California real estate mogul George Stimson and designed by his architect son, the ornate home was constructed along the stretch of Orange Grove Boulevard dubbed "Millionaire's Row." After spending eight years constructing his new residence, Stimson promptly sold the home upon its completion for $170,000. The buyer was William Wrigley Jr., the Chicagoan behind the prosperous

chewing-gum business that bears his name. Though the family owned some six homes, Wrigley's wife spent much of her time here following her husband's death in 1932. The house was given to the Tournament of Roses Association upon Mrs. Wrigley's death in 1958.

The twenty-two-room Italian Renaissance home, built of concrete and steel, boasts a facade distinguished by a broad balustraded terrace, porch and porte cochere roof balustrades, and even a balustraded porch in front of the single-hipped dormer. A green tile roof and windows with balconets below and bracketed supported crowns above add a luxurious air to the facade. Coupled with the surrounding palm trees and the massive rose garden northeast of the home (on a separate plot acquired by the Wrigleys), the Tournament House seems perfectly designed for its southern California environs.

Tournament House

The exterior of the home and the gardens are open almost year-round. Start on the two-inch-thick Italian-marble steps and consider that this was once thought one of the more modest homes on Millionaire's Row. Then you can stroll the gardens, which consist of an expansive front lawn with many palm trees and a large Moreton Bay fig tree, the Fountain Garden to the south, and, appropriate for the home of the annual Rose Parade, a large rose garden on the north. A guide to the gardens is available upon request.

The interior has well-preserved details hinted at by the intricately detailed mahogany doors at the front entrance. We were there at the off-season, but it is reported that marble fireplaces and fine woodwork crafted from now-extinct woods abound. The home is available for tours only two hours a week, between February and August. Call ahead for times and further information.

Cravens House, 1929

430 Madeline Drive, just west of Orange Grove Boulevard; 626-799-0841, extension 101 (call in advance); Lewis P. Hobart, architect.

This gigantic twenty-four-thousand-square-foot French Eclectic mansion is today part of the San Gabriel Valley Chapter of the American Red Cross, which generously allows visitors to look about during its weekday office hours (please call ahead to let them know you are coming). Originally entered from a drive that led off of Orange Grove and through sixteen acres of gardens to the imposing home, today the Cravens House sits on a much diminished lot. It has a slate-covered, high-

pitched hipped roof with side wings. The roof is enlivened by two sizes of dormers and many chimneys. Inside, you will find marble and wood parquet floors, elaborate wood paneling, and a grand elliptical stairway.

EAST PASADENA

Pasadena east of the arroyo includes many fine neighborhoods; Oak Knoll and the San Marino area, two of the grandest, both bordered the large estate of Los Angeles financier Henry Huntington (see pages 67 and 106).

Oak Knoll, 1906–1930

This large neighborhood was laid out in 1886, during the height of the southern California real estate boom of the 1880s (see "Los Angeles," page 65). Not a single lot had been sold when the boom went bust, and the area reverted to pasture land. In 1905 William R. Staats purchased the tract and revived the original plans. His partners were Henry Huntington and A. Kingsley Macomber. They closely followed the 1886 plan, one of the earliest in southern California to abandon the grid plan and follow the precepts of Frederick Law Olmsted; its streets carefully followed the curves of canyon rims. Staats and his partners kept the plan, but changed the street names. Underground utilities were installed, and their early lots, now mostly subdivided, were almost as large as those along Orange Grove Boulevard.

Oak Knoll was marketed on the basis of its hundreds of huge live oaks and its proximity to the Wentworth Hotel (remodeled by Henry Huntington in 1916 to

Cravens House

become the Huntington Hotel) and to the Pasadena Country Club. Huntington ran one line of his Pacific Electric Railway down Oak Knoll Avenue to the Huntington Hotel, giving the neighborhood excellent transportation access to all of Los Angeles. Oak Knoll's promotional pieces proudly proclaimed: "Those who can afford to live in Oak Knoll cannot afford to live in any other place."

This extensive neighborhood has most of its larger lots and homes in the curved streets to the south and concentrates many fine midsized homes in the grid streets on the northwest. Today, the area still has a quiet country feeling despite a disturbing amount of remodeling in progress.

1177 Hillcrest Avenue (private), Blacker House, 1907; Greene and Greene, Pasadena, architects. One of Greene and Greene's masterpieces, this home received national attention several years ago when it was purchased with the disgraceful intent of ripping out its original fixtures and fittings for resale. A nationwide boycott on the purchase of these items was urged. The front facade is dominated by a massive angled porte cochere that Randell L. Makinson describes in *Greene & Greene: Architecture As a Fine Art*. The Greenes

Oak Knoll

designed an enormous, heavily timbered porte cochere which angled out from the central entry to rest on a clinker brick pillar beside a circular drive which swung in from the corner. The long bridge timbers necessary for the construction of the porte cochere were personally selected by Henry Greene who made special trips to the northern lumber areas to study the grain structure of the timbers. This porte cochere became the dominate feature of the overall design and served to relate the large two-story house to the surrounding grounds.

These grounds originally contained five and a half acres, which have been subdivided and today contain five houses—among them are 1200 Wentworth Avenue (private), originally the chauffeur's quarters of the Blacker House, and 1208 Wentworth Avenue (private), the Blacker House's groundskeeper's cottage, both designed by the Greenes. Today, the great Blacker House is in strong and sympathetic hands and is being restored.

1188 Hillcrest Avenue (private), Culbertson House, 1911; Greene and Greene, Pasadena, architects. One of the finest and most subtle of the Greenes' houses, this is far different from the wood Craftsman homes for which they are best known. This home has walls clad with gunite (a then-new stuccolike material applied with a pressure gun), and the roof is clad with Ludowici-Celodon tile. This long and dramatic roof, the most dominant element from the street, gains interest from its slight changes in level. The house wraps around a rear courtyard and garden.

1330 Hillcrest Avenue (private), Freeman House, 1913; Arthur S. Heineman, Pasadena, architect. This huge Craftsman house has lost the rolled edge to the roof (it has been replaced with a fascia board), but kept the graceful roofline curve that accompanied it. The refined entry echoes the same curve; the handsome door and sidelights incorporate

a variation of the Greenes' favorite "lift-line," a horizontal line with a slope up to a slightly higher level that mimicked cloud lines. The massing of this house is intriguing, with a large angled wing and small one-story angled bay window to the left of the entrance. A Batchelder tile plaque graces the chimney. Another Heineman house at 1233 Wentworth Avenue (private), 1913, has a similar curve to the roofline, which still has the curved "false-thatched-roof" edge.

1212 South El Molino Avenue (private), Van Pelt House, 1926; Garrett Van Pelt, Pasadena, architect. A very unusual French Eclectic house designed by Van Pelt, one of Pasadena's many fine architects, for his own home.

979 South El Molino Avenue (private), Crow House, 1909; Greene and Greene, Pasadena, architects. Designed by Henry Greene (brother Charles was usually the partnership's principal designer), the Crow House, with its low horizontal one-story form and side-gabled roof incorporating subtle changes in level, foreshadows the Culbertson home (see "1188 Hillcrest"). Note the three separate sets of doors opening out to the porch. It has a U-shape wrapping around a courtyard behind.

800 South Oakland Avenue (private), Flintoft House, ca. 1910; G. S. Bliss, Pasadena, contractor. Bliss was one of the many builders of outstanding Craftsman-style homes in Pasadena. South Oakland Street has examples of Craftsman-style houses that appear to have been built by a contractor from standard plans rather than being individually designed as were the homes of Greene and Greene. Numbers 903, 911, 869, 862 (an airplane bungalow), 812, 755, 737, and 726 South Oakland Avenue (all private) are cases in point, and many of these may have been built by Bliss.

965 South Oakland Avenue (private), ca. 1925. This is an excellent Colonial Revival of the gambrel-roofed subtype that is often called Dutch Colonial. Side-gambreled roofs like this one were typically built during the 1920s and 1930s. Here, there is an Adamesque door with an elliptical fanlight and sidelights, an entry porch with a balustrade above, and three shed dormers. At 874 South Oakland Avenue (private), ca. 1925, is another Dutch Colonial with a smaller entry porch crowned by a segmental pediment and with one broad shed dormer.

San Marino, 1920 to present

The separate town of San Marino was incorporated by Henry Huntington in 1925 from parts of his original estate. Huntington's own home attracted many wealthy neighbors to live nearby. San Marino is slightly later than the other neighborhoods around Pasadena and has a high concentration of Spanish Eclectic and Monterey-style homes, with early-Ranch-style homes occasionally interspersed.

1910 Lombardy Road (private), 1948; R. H. Ainsworth, architect. This Neoclassical house has a full-height entry porch and is a typical late example. The columns are slender and unfluted, with simplified capitals. The door has an Adamesque elliptical fanlight; a small octagonal window, a common feature on houses built in the late 1940s and 1950s, is added on each side of the entry. A similar house from 1941 by the same architect is at 1945 Lombardy Road (private).

2000 Lombardy Road (private), ca. 1990s. This postmodern interpretation of the Neoclassical style has stepped gables on the paired side wings. Note the interesting postmodern detailing of the full-height entry porch and triangular pediment above. The tiny square windows are intriguing.

2035 Lombardy Road (private), Bourne House, 1927; Wallace Neff, architect. This grand Spanish Eclectic home has a front auto court, parabolic arched entry, and inviting landscape designed by landscape architect Katherine Bashford.

1883 Orlando Road (private), Neff House, 1929; Wallace Neff, architect. The architect's own home is in a form he often used, placing an inset porch (or loggia) above a centered front entry. Based on Tuscan villas, they are by an architect thoroughly familiar with the wide range of early Italian domestic architecture and do not have the typical identifying features of early-twentieth-century American Italian Renaissance–style homes.

2115 Orlando Road (private), Bertololli House, ca. 1928; Wallace Neff, architect. Here is a slightly different interpretation of 1883 Orlando Road (see the preceding entry).

665 South Allen Avenue (private), Baldwin House, 1926; George Washington Smith, Santa Barbara, architect. This house presents a calm facade to the street, as did most of Smith's houses, reserving their drama for the rear. This is more lively than most of his front facades, with three balconies and many other subtle details.

Southwest corner of Orlando Road and San Marino Avenue (private), ca. 1950. The wings of this typical California Ranch house angle back to fit the curve of the corner lot. Note the board-and-batten wall cladding, the open eaves with gently rounded rafter ends, and the recessed porch with simple supports.

San Marino

The Huntington, 1910

1151 Oxford Road, San Marino; 626-405-2100;
Myron Hunt and Elmer Grey, Los Angeles, architects.

The Huntington offers a dazzling response to the question of what, exactly, a successful entrepreneur was to do with those millions of dollars earned building railroads, mining ores, drilling wells, and herding cattle. In the case of renowned railroad tycoon and southern California developer Henry Edwards Huntington (1850–1927; see also page 67), the answer was to buy a 550-acre ranch twelve miles northeast of Los Angeles, build an expansive Beaux Arts–style mansion, and start collecting things: housed within the boundaries of the current 207-acre tract can be found a 130-acre botanical garden, in which Huntington amassed both regional and exotic flora; an extensive art collection, now found in the former residence; and a library building containing some 4 million titles, including such rarities as a Gutenberg Bible and early editions of works from such authors as Shakespeare, Chaucer, and J. J. Audubon.

The tenacity and proficiency with which these collections were assembled amply reflect the kind of ambition that made Huntington such a success in the business world. In actuality, there were three fortunes used to build the Huntington and its collections. When Henry's uncle Collis Huntington died in 1900, he had left his fortune in two equal parts of approximately $40 million to his widow, Arabella, and to his nephew, Henry. (For more details on Collis Huntington, see page 139.) Henry then proceeded to accumulate an additional estate of about $30 million by developing the Pacific Electric Railway, a sophisticated interurban system (which helped determine the future shape of Los Angeles), and with related Los Angeles area real estate investments (see page 67 for further details). In 1913, Henry married Arabella (died 1924), the wealthy widow of his uncle Collis. They proceeded to build the Huntington collections together from that point on, with Arabella's interests reflected primarily in the fine and decorative arts and Henry's more in the library and gardens.

Huntington first visited the site of his future home in 1892, en route to San Francisco, where he was moving to manage the family's West Coast interests. Then the estate of James De Barth Shorb, the San Marino tract was acquired by Huntington ten years later. Between his uncle's death in 1900 and his retirement from the life of a full-time businessman in 1910, he began planning the San Marino acreage as his primary residence. Though he formulated rough sketches of his proposed mansion, he left the final design and execution to architects Myron Hunt and Elmer Grey, who rewarded him with a large, stately villa of Beaux Arts design. Note the symmetrical main house (now the art gallery) with paired columns, a broad terrace, projecting wings on each side of the main house block, roofline balustrade, and a balustraded upstairs open porch contained within the side wings. The roof is low pitched, hipped, and covered with tiles—a Beaux Arts roof type less common than flat and mansard versions. A handsome one-story loggia, supported by paired columns, is located to the side of the house.

Following Huntington's death in 1927, his former home was converted into the Huntington Gallery, which displays the extensive collection of British and French art acquired by him and Arabella. The main hall has a gently arched ceiling and is dominated by pairs of colossal fluted Ionic columns; the stairway, placed to the side, has a handsome curvilinear balustrade. There is a fine collection of primarily eighteenth-century French furniture and decorative art displayed throughout the gallery, but with the library being of particular interest. One room, the Quinn Room, features eighteenth-century British paneling and furniture donated by Florence M. Quinn in 1937. Most of the rooms in the gallery remain as they were when the Huntingtons resided here. The home was slightly modified in 1934 to create more space for the gallery, which augments the Huntington pieces with subsequent acquisitions and temporary exhibits. The major change was the replacement of the service wing with a gallery designed to display larger paintings in the collection to full effect. Among the notable works housed in the museum are

Henry E. Huntington, ca. 1925

The Huntington

Thomas Gainsborough's *The Blue Boy* and Thomas Lawrence's *Pinkie.*

Sitting two hundred yards to the east of the gallery is the Huntington Library, a massive, austere building completed in 1923 and inspired by the great libraries of the East. On the acreage south and west of the library and gallery can be found some spectacularly picturesque gardens, including the exotic twelve-acre desert garden (reportedly the largest assemblage of mature cacti in existence), the jungle garden, the beautiful rose garden, and the Japanese garden—the last of which bears a striking resemblance to the Giverny landscapes that Monet painted in his later years.

REDLANDS

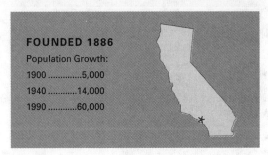

FOUNDED 1886

Population Growth:

1900 5,000

1940 14,000

1990 60,000

The character of this delightful small city at the far eastern edge of the Los Angeles area was well captured in a recent geography textbook:

Probably more than any other city in the Los Angeles Basin, Redlands still personifies the "prim and proper" orange belt town. Still retaining many acres of surrounding groves, it is the principal center in Southern California for packing and shipping navel oranges. Less affected by recent boom periods than many area cities, it has a substantial central district. . . . Redlands has been well regarded for its homes and gardens for decades. Its hillside section has impressive views of the San Bernardino Mountains. (Gary L. Peters et al., *California*)

Modern Redlands thus provides a rare time-warp sample of what much of suburban Los Angeles looked like during the area's orange-grove boom years, from about 1890 to the 1920s (see also page 67). Most of the city's prosperous neighborhoods from that era remain remarkably intact, with an exceptional number of fine homes built, either directly or indirectly, from orange-growing profits. In some blocks even the orange groves themselves survive, as if to bear witness to their long-term value. As an added delight, Redlands also has one of the nation's few museum houses in the elegant Chateauesque style, a favorite for grand dwellings built around the turn of the century.

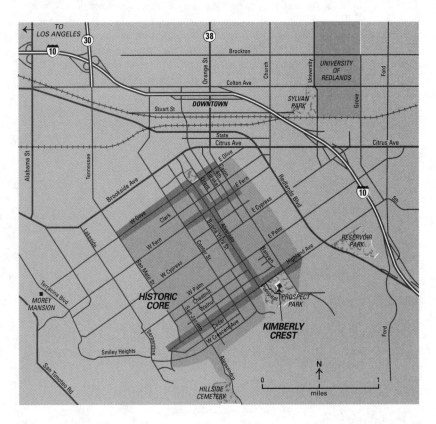

Historic Core, ca. 1890–1920

The older parts of Redlands have more than a thousand historic homes of many styles, ages, and sizes. Almost every block reveals at least one delightful surprise for the house watcher. The town's landscape qualities are particularly pleasant. Many of the curbs in the older neighborhoods are made of hand-cut stone, giving a distinctive look to the streetscape. Palm trees, now mature, were planted along many Redlands streets, such as Highland Avenue, and, as noted above, picturesque small orange groves still adorn several blocks.

The twin brothers Alfred H. and Albert K. Smiley, who moved to Redlands in 1889, are credited with much of the sophistication of the early town. They were notable educators and resort owners and helped to attract many wealthy persons from the East and Midwest to Redlands to build winter or retirement homes. The brothers encouraged landscaping programs for the town, planted their own acreage in the hills with many exotic plants, and even donated the town's library.

West Highland Avenue, from Cedar Avenue on the west to Cajon Street on the east, is the city of Redlands Historic District and has homes built as early as 1887. By 1900 this area of upscale houses was reportedly called the Butler's Belt. Today, it has the greatest concentration of easily viewable larger homes. It also makes a convenient dividing line between the hilly areas to the south, which contained many of Redlands larger estates (including that of the Smiley twins), and the grid pattern streets to the north. Today, most of the great estates in the southern hills have long since been subdivided, and these streets now have many post-1960 Neo-Mediterranean houses, making it harder to find the scattered older homes.

Almost all of the streets from Highland Avenue north to downtown have interesting small and mid-sized houses. Alvarado Street is of particular interest for its nice collection of Craftsman and Neoclassical cottages, while Olive Avenue displays many varieties of American four-squares and Victorian-era designs along its length.

1205 West Crescent Avenue (private), Burrage Mansion, 1901; Charles Bingham, architect. Just visible up a heavily landscaped hillside, this is one of the largest and most fully developed Mission-style homes in the nation. It has a lovely pair of bell towers and three elaborate-shaped front-facing parapets, one on the central house block and the others on the side wings. Multiple flights of steps form a long straight line from the sidewalk up to front entrance.

405 West Olive Avenue at Alvarado Street (private), Holt House, 1903 and 1905; Louis Cooper, architect. Architect Charles Moore and his coauthors poetically describe this Mission-style design as

> robust . . . something like the fancy-dress outfits of Mexican charros, contrast[ing] a basically simple form with generous doses of intricate ornament. The main distractions of the two-story rectangular block are the sinuously scalloped edges . . . along the many false-fronted Mission pediment walls and along the second-story railing of a wraparound porch. [The] stucco walls beneath . . . are made to seem three-dimensional with thick plaster cartouches, reveals and moldings of some unidentifiable exotic persuasion. . . . The porch, which becomes a porte cochere on the east, is made up of Romanesque arches. Nonetheless, the braidlike edges and the rows of dots around the arches bring us back to the charro costume, with its multiple silver buttons. (*The City Observed: Los Angeles*)

Note also the open squared tower with Sullivanesque trim along its cornice.

Redlands Historic Core

426 West Olive Avenue (private), Smith House, 1900. This Neoclassical design is in the full-height-entry-porch-with-lower-full-width-porch subtype. It has a lot of added Colonial Revival detail, including the elliptical fanlight over the front door, the roofline balustrade, and the copious use of floral garlands along the cornice line. The entry appears to have been modified.

731 Cedar Avenue (private), Hall House, 1895; Lynn and Lewis, architects. This Queen Anne house is unusual in combining a centered gable and symmetrical placement of windows and doors with a Queen Anne spindlework wrap-around porch, recessed balcony with spindlework trim, and half-timbered gable (which appears to be infilled with mosaic).

160 West Highland Avenue (private), Sweeney House, 1914; Robert Ogden, architect. This large cross-gabled Craftsman house has unique angular pedestals on each side of the front steps. Note how the shingle wall cladding is applied in alternating wide and narrow strips.

827 Alvarado Street (private), England House, 1893. This Queen Anne cottage features a dramatic curved sweep of windows with decorated transoms above; this is topped by a front-facing gable accentuated by an octagonal window. Note the low roof pitch and squared porch columns. This house gives you a feeling for the landscape of much of early Redlands—the house is surrounded by associated orange groves, which actually belong to a larger house around the corner.

515 Alvarado Street (private), ca. 1905. One of Alvarado Street's many Craftsman-style houses, this one has a front-gabled roof and battered (sloping) stone supports for the porch and porte cochere.

238 Alvarado Street (private), Michaels House, 1902. This is a typical one-story Neoclassical cottage, a house style and subtype found along Alvarado Street and also on West Olive Street, west of Alvarado. Here the porch is set under the main roof of the house, and there is a centered gabled dormer. Simpler one-story Neoclassical cottages are located to the right and the left of this house; both of these have the more usual hipped dormer. The door here looks original.

225 Alvarado (private), ca. 1910. This is a slightly less typical one-story Neoclassical cottage, as the porch does not cover the full width of the house. Note the two "special front sash" windows with different decorative glass designs above. This house also appears to have its original front door, which is different in design from the one at 238 (see the preceding entry).

140 Terracina Boulevard (bed-and-breakfast with occasional tours), Morey Mansion, 1890; David Morey, architect and builder. Shipbuilder and cabinet maker David Morey retired to Redlands in 1882, along with his wife, Sarah. When Sarah discovered that the baby trees for what was to be their twenty-acre orange grove would cost a dollar each, she promptly started sprouting seedlings herself. After four years she had grown ninety thousand trees and sold her nursery for a profit of twenty thousand dollars. With dollars earned in this second career, David Morey set about personally building this handsome new Queen Anne home. He used a foot-pedaled lathe to shape the many turned spindles found in the wraparound porch and staircase.

Perhaps the most distinctive feature is the home's onion-domed tower, roofed with shaped wood shingles. The unusual area of basket-weave trim below the onion dome is

Morey Mansion

formed by circular pieces of wood stacked atop each other. These are just two of the many creative details that builder-architect-owner Morey incorporated into his fine spindlework Queen Anne home.

Kimberly Crest, 1897

1325 Prospect Drive; 909-792-2111;
Dennis and Farwell, Los Angeles, architects.

This romantic Chateauesque home, perched atop a hill overlooking Redlands, looks so much like a miniature castle on the Loire River that it could easily be an illustration for a children's book of French folk tales. It has a rounded tower, two turrets, and many dormers, all with steeply pitched roofs topped with pinnacles and spires. Rather than having the stone-wall finish most typical of the Chateauesque style, it has frame walls covered with a smooth coat of stucco and trimmed with wood accents. Originally built as a retirement home by Mrs. Cornelia A. Hill in 1897, it was purchased by J. Alfred Kimberly (1838–1928) and his wife, Helen Cheney Kimberly (1843–1931) in late 1905 for their retirement home. Kimberly was one of the original founders of Kimberly-Clark and Company in 1872 and had served as president of the company.

Mrs. Kimberly proceeded to put her own stamp on the house. First, she gave the home a name as picturesque as its appearance, Kimberly Crest. Then, according to family members, she sought the advice of the Tiffany Studios in New York City and proceeded to redo the interiors. Silk fabrics, many still intact, were used to cover some walls. Glazes, accented with silver paint, were used in other areas. The fireplace in the main living hall was covered with an iridescent glass mosaic of water lilies, and many silver light fixtures were installed.

Mrs. Kimberly also decided to add a new Italian garden to replace a portion of the orange grove near the house. These gardens were designed in 1908 by one of

Kimberly Crest

her sons-in-law, George Edwin Bergstrom, a Yale and M.I.T.-educated architect. His creation flows down the hillside, with terraces, curved flights of steps, and cascading fountains. The featured front fountain was designed by J. L. Mott Company of New York, which produced fine garden statuary from 1875 until after 1919. Mott was considered by many as the leading manufacturer of outdoor statuary for much of this period, and Mott fountains and statues graced the gardens at the Coronado Hotel in San Diego, hotels at Coney Island in New York City, as well as those of fine homes all across the United States (the Winchester Mystery House gardens in San Jose have a number of Mott pieces). The edges of the estate continued (and still continue today) to hold orange groves, which were the main economic base of Redlands.

In 1919 Mary Kimberly Shirk (1881–1979), the youngest of the Kimberly's children, moved back to Kimberly Crest. Her husband had recently died, and Mrs. Shirk returned to Redlands to be near her elderly parents. After the deaths of both her parents, she continued to live there, maintaining the home and keeping it much as her mother had remodeled it in 1906 and 1907. In 1968 she pledged to give Kimberly Crest to the "people of Redlands" if they succeeded in raising the funds required to match a federal grant to acquire Prospect Park, located just next door. The funds were raised, and in 1969 the Kimberly-Shirk Association was founded to receive the house. In 1981 the association received the house along with six acres of grounds. In addition, the furnishings in the house, all of which had belonged to the Kimberly family, were generously donated and are displayed today.

Behind the house is a matching Chateauesque carriage house, later a garage, that holds a shop and a small exhibit about the house and family. This is where you discover that Kleenex, manufactured by Kimberly-Clark, was made possible by the invention of "cellucotton," an absorbent wadding, by one of the company's employees, Austrian chemist Ernst Mahler, who introduced it in 1924 as a product with which to remove cold cream. Kleenex didn't rocket to popularity until 1929, when it began to be marketed as disposable handkerchiefs. This campaign came just as changing economic conditions were beginning to make laundering and pressing cloth handkerchiefs a luxury of the past.

SANTA CLARITA

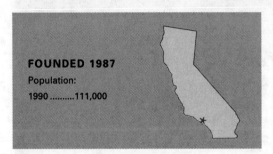

FOUNDED 1987
Population:
1990 111,000

Santa Clarita, at the northern edge of Los Angeles's urban growth, is one of the area's instant cities, formed by the incorporation of what were formerly smaller towns into a single larger unit of government. One of its early towns, now fast disappearing from city maps, was Newhall (population 9,000 in 1990, 1,100 in 1940), founded in 1876 as the site of California's first oil refinery and later the location of a fine Eclectic-era country estate that today includes an important museum house.

William S. Hart House, 1927

24151 San Fernando Road, in the William S. Hart Park; 805-254-4584; Arthur Kelly, Los Angeles, architect.

In trying to understand the West and its history, it is illuminating to visit the home of William S. Hart (1864–1946), a man who strongly influenced the entire genre of western movies, which first introduced much of America to the Old West. Hart had grown up moving around the Midwest with his family. This gave him firsthand contact with ranchers and cowboys, and he even learned a bit of the universal Native American sign language and the Sioux language from playmates. During these childhood years he gained a respect for the Native American culture and a love for the West.

Hart later became a well-known actor in the East and was the leading man in everything from Shakespearean plays to *Ben Hur*. In 1905, he played his first lead in a western play, "Cash" Hawkins in *The Squaw Man*. From that point on, Hart played mainly western roles onstage, including one in a triumphant production of *The Virginian*. When silent films first began to treat western themes, Hart was appalled at their quality. In his autobiography he called the early efforts "impossibilities or libels on the West." In 1914 he decided to go to Los Angeles and try to make western films. He later wrote, "I was an actor and I knew the West. . . . I had to bend

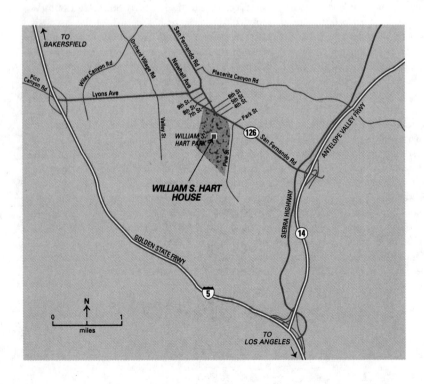

every endeavor to get a chance to make Western motion pictures."

He got that chance by playing parts in several films and collaborating on screenplays. He quickly developed, and played, an enormously popular cowboy hero, Two Gun Bill. Hart wrote, collaborated on, produced, or directed (and usually starred in) over sixty movies during the next eleven years, trying to imbue his films with a more realistic vision of the West than had been portrayed in earlier ones. He strove for more authenticity in costumes, locations, and plots. The result of his efforts was that Hart became one of the public's favorite leading men. He also "made a major contribution to film history by developing and embodying the prototype of the frontier hero," according to the visitors' brochure. This of course was Two Gun Bill; by Bill's side was usually Fritz, his feisty pinto pony and the cinema's first horse "hero."

Hart retired at the height of this second career, when he was sixty-one years of age. The Newhall area had been the setting for a number of his films, and he had bought this 265 acres of land. At first there was just a small house on it, but Hart commissioned Los Angeles architect Arthur Kelly to build a Spanish Eclectic house for him at the top of his favorite hill. He named the house La Casa de los Vientos, or the House of the Winds. Built into the side of the hill, the house is much larger than it looks, with ten thousand square feet and twenty-two rooms. It cost $100,000 when it was built.

Although the Hart House looks like it could be built of adobe bricks or bricks or hollow tiles covered with a coat of stucco, it is actually a balloon-frame house, covered inside and out with plaster stucco. The walls look thick, but that is because they are double framed to look like thick adobe. The entire interior is covered with rough-finished plaster, which has its original antique-wash finish. Almost everything in the house belonged to Hart. The furnishings are comfortable, but not lavish, and provide an appropriate background for Hart's art collection. He filled the house with a large collection of western art and Native American handicrafts. This includes many Charles Russell paintings along with the work of lesser-known western artists and illustrators. Illustrator James Montgomery Flagg's large painting of Hart astride his pony Fritz is a classic western painting. (Flagg is best known for the World War II UNCLE SAM WANTS YOU poster). Handwoven rugs and baskets, Hart's favorite Native American crafts, are scattered about. Hart wrote more than a dozen novels and books after he "retired," and first editions of these, and illustrations from them, are also on display.

Although Hart had a brief, and reportedly disas-

William S. Hart House

trous, marriage while in Los Angeles, this only lasted a year. Hart shared this home with Mary Ellen Hart, his unmarried sister, until her death in 1943. Despite Mary Ellen's presence in the house for many years, the Hart House feels like that of a bachelor who wants to be comfortable but is not overly concerned with the details. One who collects his few treasured objects, but is not obsessed with how they are displayed, just as long as he can enjoy each object in passing. Memorabilia are side by side with outstanding paintings. Hart's handmade parade saddle sits in the front hall, tucked under the stairway. A display of horseshoes from Hart's favorite cow ponies hangs in the living room. There is a nice, unstudied, casual spirit to Hart's home; you feel he has just stepped away for a moment and will be delighted to have you make yourself at home until he can return.

Hart went to great lengths for the comfort of Fritz and the other ponies from his movies that he brought with him to the ranch for their retirement. The road to the top of the hill remained unpaved as long as Hart was alive—because it was easier on the horses' hooves. He had a similar soft spot for his dogs, two giant spotted Great Danes. He started out sharing a bedroom with them, and when this seemed a bit overwhelming,

he simply built on a small adjoining bedroom for himself, leaving the old one for his pets.

Today, the Hart house is exactly as he left it, apparently even to his socks, still in the drawers. Hart decided to leave the house and its collections to his fans, to whom he was very grateful for making him wealthy: "While I was making pictures, the people gave me their nickels, dimes and quarters. When I am gone, I want them to have my home." The bulk of his estate was left to the county of Los Angeles, with strict stipulations about the preservation of the house as a museum and the ranch as a park for all to enjoy. This included explicit directions for planting shrubs (which in the last fifty years have now grown to a size he could not have imagined, obscuring the lovely views from the hilltop). Hart did not, apparently, stipulate a lot of signage. Be prepared for understated, indeed virtually nonexistent, signs (this lends a bit of the same casual charm to the park that one finds in the house). You may have to ask for directions or inquire at the small park office. The Hart House sits at the top of a hill reached via a nature trail. Inquire in advance to determine what days a shuttle is running, or else be prepared for a short hike. If you cannot make the climb, be sure to inform the rangers.

MONTEREY

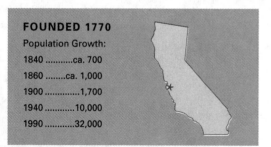

FOUNDED 1770

Population Growth:

1840 ....ca. 700
1860 ....ca. 1,000
1900 1,700
1940 10,000
1990 32,000

The small seaport town of Monterey was both the political capital and the social and economic center of Hispanic California from 1770 until the province became a part of the United States in 1848. Like most of California's Spanish settlements, Monterey began with the founding of a Catholic mission, whose friars were charged with the task of converting the local Indians into Christian citizens of New Spain. Seeking to establish a permanent Spanish presence in Alta (Upper) California to discourage incursions by British naval vessels and Russian whaling ships, in 1769 the Spanish viceroy in Mexico City sent a party of two hundred soldiers and friars northward from Baja (Lower) California, which had been settled earlier, to establish a chain of missions in Alta California (see page xi). Their final destination was Monterey Bay, which had been glowingly described by earlier Spanish naval expeditions. After much hardship, the group's survivors (over half had died en route) established their first mission near San Diego Bay in 1769 (see page 149) and in 1770 founded a second mission and presidio (fort) adjacent to Monterey Bay.

The following year the Franciscan friar in charge of mission development, Padre Junípero Serra (1713–1784), moved his new mission, called San Carlos Borromeo, about five miles southward to Carmel Bay, where he had found better agricultural land and more potential Indian converts. He most probably also wanted to shelter his Indian converts from the attentions of the soldiers at the bustling presidio, which was already becoming the Spanish administrative center of the region.

Over the next several years, the viceroy sent several additional small groups of soldiers, settlers, and friars to Monterey, both to establish more missions and to strengthen the new civilian town of Monterey, which soon was expanding beyond the walls of the original presidio. In 1775, Monterey was officially designated the capital of both Baja and Alta California.

The character of both California and its small capital city began to change after Mexico won its independence from Spain in 1821. The new government of Mexico, in need of revenues from import taxes, reversed Spain's ironclad policy of allowing its colonies to trade only with Spain itself. American and foreign merchant ships soon began anchoring at the coastal California towns to trade cloth, tools, and other manufactured items for cattle hides and tallow, the raw materials for shoe leather and candles.

To meet the seemingly limitless demand for hides to feed the newly invented shoe factories of both Old and New England, the leading families of Mexican California then greatly expanded their Spanish-era cattle ranches in an escalating trading partnership that enriched both the Anglo traders and their Mexican suppliers. This period, from about 1825 to the American takeover in 1846, was the romantic golden age of the vast California ranchos and their aristocratic "Californio" patrons.

As the financial and political center of this lucrative trade, Monterey prospered and also became the adopted home of several important Anglo merchants, some of whom married the daughters of wealthy Californios and became Mexican citizens. When California became a part of the United States (see page 265), the region's intermarried Hispanic-Anglo elite took the lead in drafting a progressive constitution for what they hoped would soon be the new state. Completed at Monterey in October 1849, one historian has called the signing of this farsighted document the town's "finest hour." Even as the Constitutional Convention was in progress, the region's frantic gold rush excitement was about to make Monterey an obsolete relic of the past.

The hordes of Anglo gold seekers largely ignored the constitution's provisions for joint Anglo and Hispanic governance of the new state. As the center of California's burgeoning population shifted to San Francisco, and to new river port towns near the goldfields, its capital was moved to more centrally located San Jose only two months after the new constitution was signed. In 1854, gold-rush Sacramento became the permanent capital; by then venerable Monterey was almost a ghost town.

In 1880 the town began a slow revival, this time not as a government center but as a destination for affluent tourists. Railroad magnate Charles Crocker, one of the Big Four whose fortunes, ironically, began in Sacra-

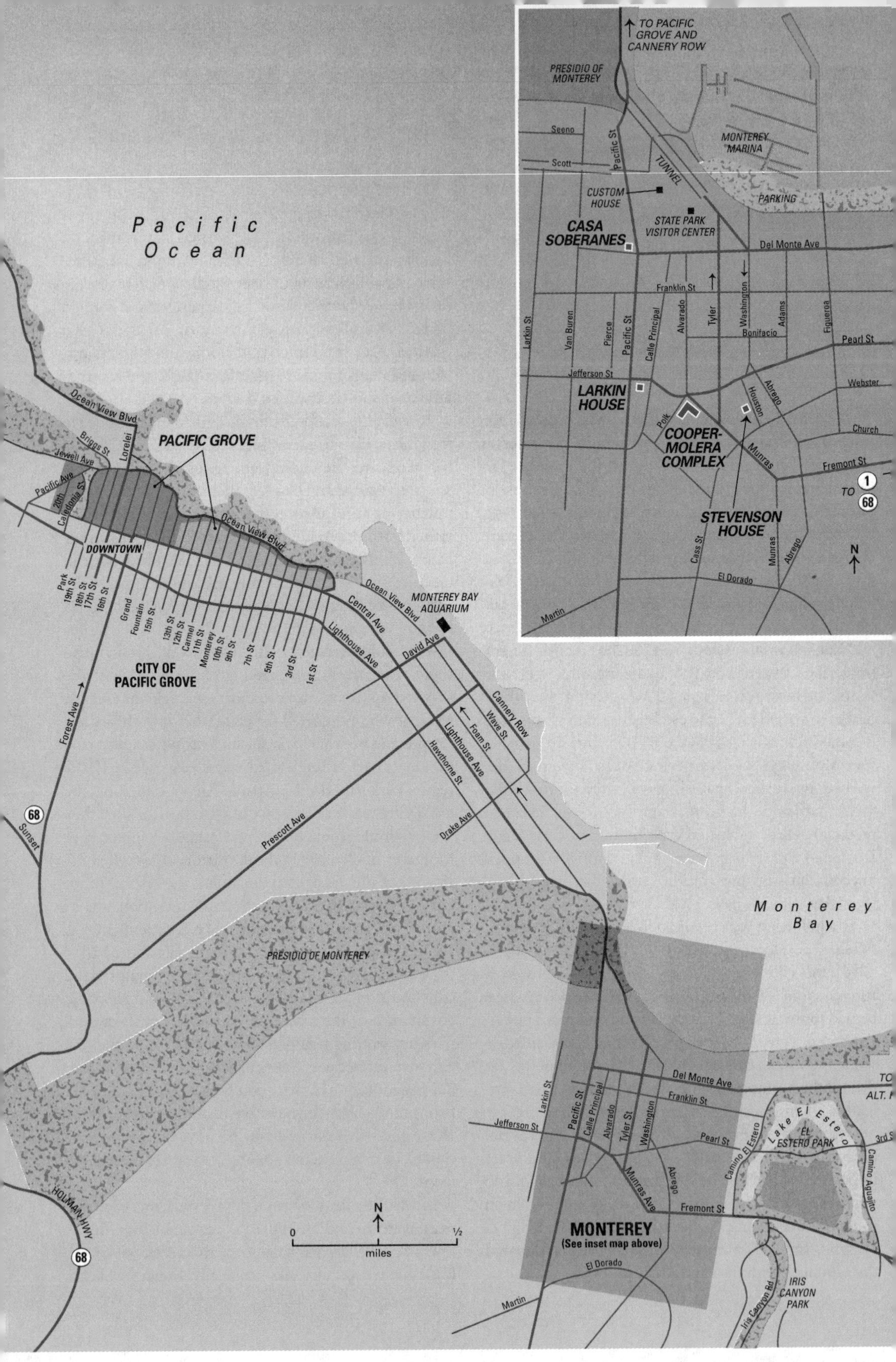

Pacific Ocean
Monterey Bay
PACIFIC GROVE
DOWNTOWN
CITY OF PACIFIC GROVE
Ocean View Blvd
Briggs St
Lorelei
Jewell Ave
Pacific Ave
20th
Caledonia St
Park
19th St
18th St
17th St
16th St
Grand
Fountain
15th St
13th St
12th St
Carmel
11th St
Monterey
10th St
9th St
7th St
5th St
3rd St
1st St
Central Ave
Lighthouse Ave
MONTEREY BAY AQUARIUM
David Ave
Cannery Row
Wave St
Foam St
Hawthorne St
Drake Ave
Prescott Ave
Forest Ave
Sunset
68
HOLMAN HWY
PRESIDIO OF MONTEREY
MONTEREY
(See inset map above)
Del Monte Ave
Franklin St
Jefferson St
Larkin St
Pacific St
Calle Principal
Alvarado
Tyler St
Washington
Pearl St
Munras Ave
Abrego
Fremont St
El Dorado
Martin
Camino El Estero
Lake El Estero
EL ESTERO PARK
Camino Aguajito
3rd St
TO ALT.
Iris Canyon Rd
IRIS CANYON PARK
N
0
½
miles
TO PACIFIC GROVE AND CANNERY ROW
PRESIDIO OF MONTEREY
Seeno
Scott
Pacific St
TUNNEL
MONTEREY MARINA
PARKING
CUSTOM HOUSE
STATE PARK VISITOR CENTER
CASA SOBERANES
Del Monte Ave
Franklin St
Larkin St
Van Buren
Pierce
Pacific St
Calle Principal
Alvarado
Tyler
Washington
Adams
Figueroa
Bonifacio
Pearl St
Jefferson St
LARKIN HOUSE
Polk
COOPER-MOLERA COMPLEX
Houston
Abrego
Webster
Church
Munras
Fremont St
TO 1 68
STEVENSON HOUSE
Cass St
Munras
Abrego
El Dorado
Martin
N

mento (see page 139), decided that the scenic Monterey Peninsula, with its quaint Hispanic village, would be an ideal site for a lavish resort hotel for the wealthy of San Francisco and elsewhere. On a 126-acre site just east of town, he built the grand Del Monte Hotel, served by a sixteen-mile branchline of the Southern Pacific that connected with the main line at Castroville.

The huge hotel could accommodate five hundred guests and featured luxurious furnishings, superb cuisine, four swimming pools, boating, billiards, bowling, and carriage tours of the scenic "seventeen-mile drive" along the coast, which is still a popular tourist attraction. Crocker's new resort was an immediate success and attracted national and international attention as the "Queen of American Watering Places." Twice the great hotel was destroyed by fires, once in 1887 and again in 1924, and each time it was rebuilt in grand style.

In the early 1900s Monterey received a new economic boost. Adjacent Monterey Bay had long been noted to have great schools of small fish that fed on plankton nourished by the nutrient-rich waters from the nearby Pacific depths, which rose to the surface along the coast. Between 1900 and 1910 Frank Booth, a small local canner of salmon, conceived and developed the idea of canning the nearby Monterey "sardines." With help from a Norwegian fisheries expert and an inventive Sicilian fisherman, who devised the first practical net for catching the small and elusive fishes, Booth opened Monterey's first sardine cannery at the foot of Alvarado Street. By 1913 the town had four canneries served by a motorized fishing fleet that could deliver up to twenty-five tons of sardines in a single night. By 1918, the food demands of the First World War were supporting twenty-seven plants along Cannery Row north of town, a district that was to be made famous by some of the writings of Nobel Prize–winning novelist John Steinbeck (1902–1968), who was born in nearby Salinas.

By 1939 the port of Monterey produced the world's third-largest tonnage of fish, which added an annual employee payroll of $4 million to the local economy, the equivalent of many times that amount today. As local historian Augusta Fink aptly notes, "Cannery Row was Monterey's Comstock Lode." Like that fabled Nevada silver bonanza, the sardines also proved to be a finite resource. Experts had repeatedly warned that overfishing could destroy Monterey's own bonanza. In 1945 the catch began to decline precipitously, and by the early 1950s the sardines were gone, apparently forever.

In the decades since 1950, Monterey has returned to its presardine emphasis on tourism, now focused around its extraordinary heritage of historic buildings, rather than on a single resort for the rich. It is almost miraculous that nearly every major structure shown in a detailed 1842 drawing of the town (see page 119) still survives today, now surrounded by a dense matrix of younger buildings that fill the spaces between the loosely scattered early structures. In addition to the four important Mexican-era museum houses (see the following entry and pages 119 and 122), other important survivors include the original **Custom House** (1827 and later), now a part of the **Monterey State Historic Park,** which has a visitor center in nearby Stanton Center (Custom House Plaza, 408-649-7173); **Royal Presidio Chapel** (1795 and later; 550 Church Street), the town's only Spanish-era structure, which was once a part of the long-vanished first presidio and survived as the local parish church; **Colton Hall** (1847; Pacific Street between Madison and Jefferson Streets, 408-646-5640), a distinctly Anglo public building built by the town's first American administrator—it was here that California's first constitution was drafted and signed; and the final, 1924 incarnation of the elegant **Del Monte Hotel** (Del Monte Avenue and Lake Drive), which since the 1940s has been the home of the U.S. Naval Postgraduate School. Even Cannery Row has taken on a new life as the home of the very popular **Monterey Bay Aquarium** (west end of Cannery Row, 408-648-4888), a state-of-the-art facility in a historic setting that emphasizes the marine life of the bay and nearby Pacific. Along the coast beyond Cannery Row is the Anglo town of Pacific Grove, founded as a Methodist summer resort in 1875; its many Victorian dwellings provide a striking contrast to the adobe structures of its older Hispanic neighbor.

Larkin House, 1835

510 Calle Principal at Jefferson Street, part of Monterey State Historic Park; 408-649-2904.

By all accounts Thomas Oliver Larkin (1802–1858) was an extraordinary man. Bright, entrepreneurial, and extremely capable, he played an important role in easing the transition of California from Mexican control to a United States territory. Born in Charlestown, Massachusetts, he was orphaned at age sixteen and had tried out various jobs before he sailed to California in 1831, where he planned to work for his half brother, Captain John Cooper. When he boarded the cargo ship *Newcastle,* the only other passenger was Rachel Hobson Holmes (born 1807), a beautiful young married woman. Rachel was a native of Lynn, Massachusetts, and had married a Danish sea captain in 1827. He left her in Massachusetts soon after they were married and ended up staying in California rather than returning to

Larkin House

the East Coast. In 1831 he had finally sent for Rachel to come to Monterey.

When Rachel and Larkin docked in Monterey in April of 1832, she learned that her husband had left on a voyage, and she would have to await his return. As there were no hotels, Rachel stayed in the home of Larkin's half brother. About six months later she learned her husband had died on a South American voyage, never having returned to Monterey. This must have given Rachel some sense of relief along with sadness. Larkin and Rachel had fallen in love and were soon married. Rachel thus became the first Anglo woman to settle in Alta California. Their first child was the first to be born in California of parents who were both natives of the United States.

By 1835 Larkin had gone into business for himself, and Rachel had received a small estate from her late husband. In April of that year Larkin began building this fine home, and by September the roof had been finished. Although the house was by no means complete, he soon opened a general store on the ground floor, and with his family moved into the upstairs. Larkin was immediately successful with his store and soon added a flour mill and a lumber mill to his holdings. He also began purchasing California real estate. In 1843 he was appointed the United States consul to Mexican California, and this house served as the United States consulate. It was from this influential post that Larkin worked to effect a peaceful transfer of California to the United States. He ended up as a delegate to the Constitutional Convention in 1849, during which Rachel had

to feed many of the other delegates in the Larkin House, as Monterey was not prepared for so many distinguished visitors at once. In 1850 the Larkins traded this house to a friend and moved to New York to be closer to their children, who were in eastern schools. He was now a wealthy man and could live comfortably. But he was unhappy in New York and made two voyages back to California to look after business interests. After three years he and Rachel moved back to San Francisco and lived there until Larkin died of typhoid fever just five years later.

The Larkin House is a classic—both handsome and innovative, it beautifully blends the Georgian symmetry of the New England homes of Larkin's childhood with two native California materials, adobe brick and redwood. It was probably the first two-story house in Monterey, and the two-room-deep floor plan reflects the Larkins' Anglo roots. Larkin had worked and traveled in the Carolinas for ten years before deciding to come to California, and he was undoubtedly familiar with the wide two-story verandahs that occurred in Charleston, Beaufort, and throughout the Carolina Low Country and West Indies. Once he arrived in Monterey, Larkin was displeased by the fact that "the houses are much disfigured by having the south ends lumbered up with boards or brush to keep off the rains from the south" as he described in an 1842 letter. He likely thought that the broad porches of the American South would serve the purpose of keeping rain off of the vulnerable adobe walls, although the same letter reveals that by 1842 the south end of the Larkin House had a

Monterey in 1842; the Larkin House is the large structure on the left.

scaffold to keep off the rain. The side porches and hipped roof were added to solve this problem.

Larkin reinforced the adobe-brick walls with a red-wood structural skeleton that made window placement and porch construction much easier. He protected the adobe walls with a coat of plaster and covered the roof with wood shingles. Inside, he added several fireplaces, while Hispanic homes of the day used coal braziers for heat. And the crowning touch was the multitude of large double-sash windows with multiple glass panes that gave his home light and airiness that were missing from the typical Hispanic home of the 1830s. The interior plan of Larkin House is that of a typical late New England Georgian or South Carolina plantation house. It features a centered front door that opens into a central stair hall. A dining room is to one side and parlor to the other, with each room having two windows on the front facade. It is not certain whether this interior stair hall is original or came when the entire house was converted into a residence. But as Rachel was never as fond of California as Larkin was, he may well have wanted to please her with a home with an East Coast interior.

Larkin's house and its many innovations did not go unnoticed. Other Monterey houses were soon built with second stories. Double porches such as Larkin's or cantilevered full-width upstairs balconies became frequent additions. This type of architecture long dominated the older parts of Monterey. Much later, in the 1920s, this type of house was revived to become a favored late-Eclectic-era house style in California and throughout the Southwest. It was now called the Monterey Revival style, and the cantilevered balconies were far more popular than Larkin's more southern double verandahs.

Larkin's youngest son, educated in New England, made his home in New Hampshire. He and his wife, Mary Louise, had only one daughter, Alice, who later married Henry Woughton Toulmin. The Toulmins purchased Larkin House in 1922, moved to Monterey, and lived there until Henry's death in 1952. Since they had no children, Alice decided to donate the house, which they had carefully preserved, and the Anglo antique furnishings, which they had together collected, to the state of California in 1957. Today, Larkin's house and his granddaughter's fine antique collection make a fitting tribute to Thomas Larkin and his contributions to both California politics and California architecture.

Cooper-Molera Complex, 1830 and later

525 Polk Street at Alvarado Street (in Monterey State Historic Park); 408-649-7109.

This enclosed complex of two homes, gardens, orchard, barns, corner store, and museum provides an accurate, in-depth look at life in Old Monterey. The two homes were originally one house—a long one-story adobe house with a courtyard, built by Captain John Cooper (1791–1872) for his family in 1830. Just three years later, Cooper found himself with a debt he could not pay and had to divide his new home and courtyard to form two attached smaller adobe houses with courtyards behind. Each half of the property has had differing additions that, when looked at together, tell much about early California history.

Cooper kept the interior half for his own home and gave the remainder of the property to John Jones in payment for his debt. Jones simply rented out the dwelling as well as an early warehouse that Cooper had built on the back of the property. In 1845 Manuel Diaz and his wife, Luisa Estrada Diaz, a prosperous Hispanic family, purchased the home and warehouse.

Four years after their purchase, the discovery of gold drastically changed Monterey, along with the rest of California. The Diazes' economic and political power declined dramatically, along with that of most Californios. Despite building and opening the corner store in the early 1850s, the Diaz family never fully recovered. Manuel Diaz died in 1867, and his widow lived in their home until 1900, alone and eking out a meager living from renting out the shop next door. She never changed the early Hispanic character of their home.

In the meantime, John Cooper's family next door was following a different course. Cooper had been born in Alderney, one of the English Channel Islands. His father, a sea captain, had died when he was about nine years old, and he and his mother moved to Massachusetts to be with her brother. There, his mother married Thomas Larkin, father of his half brother, Thomas Oliver Larkin (see page 117). Cooper had the nerves to his left hand severed while in Massachusetts, leaving it almost useless. Nonetheless, at age fourteen he went to sea with his uncle, a sea captain engaged in the China trade. He worked his way up to become captain of his own ship, the *Rover,* and he sailed it into the port of Monterey in 1823. It is said that on this trip he first saw his wife-to-be, Encarnacion Vallejo (1809–1902), the fourteen-year-old daughter of Ignacio Vallejo, a Castilian who was the *sargento distinguido* of the troops

Cooper-Molera Complex courtyard

in Monterey. One of her brothers was Mariano Guadalupe Vallejo, who was to become the last governor of Alta California (see page 265).

But Cooper and Encarnacion did not immediately marry, even though Californio women often married at a very young age. Instead, they waited until she was eighteen and John was thirty-six. In that year of 1827 Cooper converted to Catholicism, necessary to marry Encarnacion, and later became a Mexican citizen. From this position he accumulated California land, including a grant that encompassed much of the Big Sur; through the years he even did a bit more seagoing. At home Encarnacion was having and raising their six children. In the early 1850s Cooper sold a piece of land, and they used the proceeds to add a second story to house their growing family. At the same time they added many American Victorian features to the house. In 1864 the

Cooper-Molera Complex

Cooper family moved to San Francisco, but maintained their family home in Monterey. Over the years it became a repository for everything the family no longer needed. Dishes, furniture, photographs, decorative objects, and even magazines were simply stored in the house. In 1900 Cooper's daughter, Anita Wohler, was able to buy back the other half of the original house from the Diaz estate, and she kept the entire property intact. Her niece donated the land, the buildings, and all of the contents to the National Trust for Historic Preservation. In turn the Trust leased it to the state to be operated as part of the Monterey State Historic Park.

Together, the two houses tell the story of two cultures, one that ended about 1850 and the other that began to flourish at about the same time. The Diaz house was never modified. You enter into the *sala,* the main all-purpose room that would have been used for dining or for visiting guests to sleep in or, with the furnishings removed, for a fandango, or dance. All of the front rooms open directly onto the street, as was the Spanish custom. There are no interior halls. Furnishings are sparse, and nothing adorns the walls unless it is a religious object. There are no closets, and a camphor chest in the *sala* shows the kind of chest that belongings were stored in and gives a whiff of how they must have smelled when pulled out for wear. The mattress is made of layered wool blankets, reportedly quite attractive to fleas and other vermin. The Diaz home tells the story of an earlier time and a simpler culture with fewer material belongings and far removed from most of the rest of the United States.

Next door, the Cooper-Molera House was enlarged just as the Californio culture was being eclipsed. The family added a Victorian indoor staircase and turned one room into a stair hall. Victorian woodwork and double parlors were added. Doors that opened directly onto the street were converted into windows. Wallpaper adorns the walls, and furnishings are more lavish. Remarkably, nearly every item in this house belonged to someone in the Cooper family—even a rare specially made king-size bed in the master bedroom. Another rare item is a locally crafted pine-and-redwood chest, very unusual for Monterey, which had to import almost all of its fine furniture. A wide cantilevered balcony, typical of Monterey houses, was added, and from it the family could watch the gory Californio bear and bull fights.

One room of the house has been left unrestored, and it is of particular interest because it shows the kind of foundation that was needed under adobes built in northern California—a couple of feet of rock or stone material. The ground here is often so damp from coastal rains and fogs that without this foundation the adobe walls absorb dampness from the ground below, and the base of the walls simply begins dissolving away. Even in arid northern New Mexico a stone foundation is needed to prevent similar kinds of transmission of ground water to adobe walls.

Today, the Diazes' old store is the museum shop for the house, and the courtyard has been restored to function in much the way in which it was originally intended. This mix of uses in close proximity—warehouse, store, urban farm, and dwelling—was typical of early small towns in the days before there were so many material goods produced by the Industrial Revolution that groupings of "Main Street" storefronts became the norm. The remarkable group of structures at the Cooper-Molera complex is one of the most important historic sites in all of the West.

Stevenson House

530 Houston Street, in Monterey State Historic Park; 408-649-7118.

Although this house incorporates two small early adobes, one of which belonged to an important early Monterey official, its chief historic importance today is its association with Robert Louis Stevenson (1850–1894) and the fine collection of Stevensoniana that it now houses. Stevenson, the Scottish novelist, essayist, and poet, was plagued by ill health from childhood. In 1876, while living in Paris for the warmer climate, he fell in love with Fanny Van de Grift Osbourne, a Californian separated from her husband. In 1878 she had returned to California, and in 1879 Stevenson followed her, much against his parents' wishes. He rented an upstairs room in Stevenson House and eked out a living of two dollars a week writing pieces for the local paper while wooing Fanny. In 1880 the couple was finally able to marry. The marriage and Fanny's constant companionship improved Stevenson's health and spurred his creativity. He, Fanny, and her son, Lloyd Osbourne, returned to his native Scotland to reconcile with his parents. He soon began writing some of his best works—*Treasure Island* (1883), *The Strange Case of Dr. Jekyll and Mr. Hyde* (1886), and *Kidnapped* (1886). The couple constantly traveled, looking always for a climate good for his health. What was intended to be a cruise for health and pleasure to the South Pacific Islands in 1888 lasted more than two years and then led to a four-year stay in Samoa, which ended with his death from a cerebral hemorrhage. Stevenson had continued writing to the very end and on the day of his death had been working on one of his finest novels, *Weir of Hermiston,* an acknowledged masterpiece, even though unfinished.

This house was donated to the state of California in 1941 by Mrs. Celia Tobin Clark and Mrs. Edith Van

Casa Soberanes

Anthwerp. A large collection of Stevenson materials and furnishings was donated by Stevenson's step-daughter Isabel Field and other family members in 1948 as a memorial to Stevenson—and it is a fitting one, for his stay here and the marriage it produced were major turning points in Stevenson's life.

Casa Soberanes, 1840s

336 Pacific Street at Del Monte Avenue, part of Monterey State Historic Park; 408-649-7118.
Casa Soberanes was built in the early 1840s by Rafael Estrada, a half brother of Governor Juan Alvarado and nephew of General Mariano Guadalupe Vallejo. It is likely that these illustrious family connections helped him to obtain the large city lot on which the house stands today. Rather than building his home at the street line, as was typical of urban Spanish Colonial houses, he built it far enough up the hill to have a commanding view of the bay and also to avoid having more of the hill's water draining down into his home's foundations. The house has had a number of distinguished owners, including Jean and Rueben Serrano, who added the terraced front garden in the 1920s and 1930s. This house retains many original Hispanic details. Its one-room-deep floor plan is particularly typical of Spanish houses. It has a cantilevered balcony upstairs that is sheltered by the wide roof overhang above. Note how the heavy roof tiles end at the house wall, and the overhanging portion of the roof is clad with light-weight wood shakes. This house was given to the state of California by Mayo Hayes O'Donnell, who was a strong supporter of preserving Monterey's architectural heritage.

Pacific Grove, 1875–1910

Pacific Grove and the core of Old Monterey present the same kind of dramatic contrast as the two sides of the Cooper-Molera complex (see page 119). Monterey is the early Californio town, still full of the adobe homes and oddly angled streets that marked Monterey's days as the main port of entry to Mexico's Alta California. Catholicism was the only religion during Spanish and Mexican rule, and it long dominated Monterey. Right next door is Pacific Grove—an Anglo town through and through. It began as a Methodist summer camp and a place of worship. In 1875 its grid-plan streets were surveyed, and small lots among them were offered for sale. With the coming of the first chautauqua circuit

Pacific Grove

Pacific Grove

from the beach along the numbered streets, crossing first Central and then Lighthouse Avenues, Pacific Grove transitions from earlier houses to mostly Eclectic-era houses—with many Craftsman- and other style bungalows. Although not a part of the shaded area on the map, if small houses of this age interest you, you will easily find many blocks of them.

130 Forest Avenue (private). This is a recent Neo-Victorian, which is obvious by the built-in garage and the scale of the balustrades. Number 132 Forest Avenue (private), next door, is a harder call. At first glance it looks like an original Victorian but with some unusual features, like the porch with spandrels that support the upstairs balcony. Then you notice the sign that it won a 1990 design award and the newish windows. From the side you see the mansard roof behind the Queen Anne tower and see that some of the detailing actually looks new on close inspection—all suggesting that this is indeed a Neo-Victorian or at least a major renovation.

Near 127 Forest Avenue (private), Roe House, 1886. Across the street from the above and a bit toward the beach is a two-story hipped-roof Folk Victorian house clad in board-and-batten. The enclosure on the left side of the porch could easily be a closely matched later addition.

137 Sixteenth Street (private), Thorton House, 1883. A king-post truss completes the gable in this delightful Folk Victorian cottage. It is in the narrow one-story front-gabled form that is called a shotgun and is typical across the urban South.

135, 135½, and 137 Seventeenth Street (all private). A group of shotguns (see the preceding entry) that have had a variety of modifications.

132 Eighteenth Street (private). This one-and-one-half-story gabled-front folk house is the next step up in size from the shotgun form.

129 Pacific Avenue (private). Stevenson House, 1883. This board-and-batten-clad Gothic Revival house has a front gable facing Pacific Avenue and paired gables facing Caledonia. Note the simple vergeboard, spaced scallops with a bull's-eye cutout, which matches the low railing above the porch that has bull's-eyes in square panels. A matching carriage house is to the side.

104 Fifth Street at Ocean View Boulevard (private), ca. 1890s. This large and late–Gothic Revival house has now been converted to a bed-and-breakfast. Note the pointed arch at the entry and the decorated chimneys.

in 1879 (see page 284), it also became a center for cultural and educational events.

Today, many small houses line the blocks between Ocean View Boulevard, which runs along the beachfront, and Lighthouse Avenue. Most were originally designed to be summer cottages, and these include many folk and Folk Victorian homes as well as small examples of Queen Anne, Craftsman, and other Eclectic-era styles. A number of two-story Neo-Victorians have more recently been added to the district. Each street slants down toward the beach and terminates in a wonderful ocean view. When you really start to look closely at the individual houses, you begin to realize that a great number have had later modifications and additions—likely because of the original small size and because they were originally primarily for summer use. Some larger early houses are spaced out along the main east–west streets like Ocean View Boulevard, Central Avenue, and Lighthouse Avenue. As you drive away

NAPA

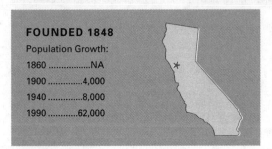

The quiet town of Napa has long been upstaged by its namesake river valley, which, for twenty miles northward from the town, is today lined with dozens of internationally famous vineyards and wineries. Located at the head of small-boat navigation on the Napa River, the town is older than the wine industry it now serves.

Food was in very short supply when the gold rush hoards began arriving in the formerly sleepy village of San Francisco in 1849. As a result, the lowlands around San Francisco Bay were rapidly converted from their Hispanic legacy of cattle grazing to the production of grains, vegetables, and fruits to feed the flood of hungry miners. Particularly productive were the lush valleys along the Napa and Petaluma Rivers at the northernmost extension of the Bay. The town of Napa, like its

neighbor Petaluma twenty miles to the west (see page 132), was founded here as a marketing and trade center where the local agricultural products were loaded onto small boats for transport downriver and across the Bay to San Francisco, or up the larger Central Valley rivers to the mining-supply river ports of Sacramento and Stockton.

The Napa Valley wine industry was slow in developing. Production of high-quality European wine grapes began in 1856 near the old Hispanic village of Sonoma, which lies about ten miles west of Napa on the opposite side of the low but rugged Mayacamas Range (see page 265). The first experimental Napa Valley vineyard was planted by German immigrant Charles Krug in 1861, but it wasn't until the 1880s that wine shipments became an important addition to the town of Napa's agricultural marketing functions. Interrupted by a vine-destroying insect plague in the 1890s, the Prohibition amendment that stopped most of the nation's production of alcoholic beverages from 1919 to 1933, and then the Second World War in the 1940s, wine remained only one of Napa's many agricultural underpinnings as the prosperous small town grew from four thousand inhabitants in 1880 to fourteen thousand in 1950.

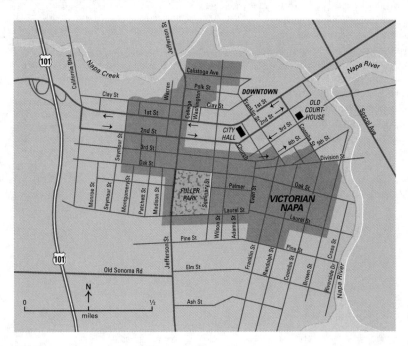

Victorian Napa

In the 1960s the American public began developing a new appreciation for quality table wines that has since led to an enormous boom in the domestic wine industry. This trend has been particularly magnified in the Napa Valley, the acknowledged crown jewel of American wine making, where the 28 wineries of 1970 had multiplied to 240 by 1988. Many of these attempt to outdo one another with elaborate guided tours and wine tastings to promote their products. As a result, the once romantically rural Napa Valley has become a sort of wine lover's Disneyland, its narrow highways and popular wineries often overcrowded with tour buses and automobile loads of visitors. Fortunately, the town of Napa itself, even though its population tripled from 1960 to 1990, still remains a peaceful oasis adjacent to this frenzied activity. More remarkable still, it retains many fine Victorian dwellings, which give a clear sense of the prosperous turn-of-the-century town.

Victorian Napa

Napa's Victorian-era houses are concentrated in a large neighborhood that wraps around the southern and western edges of downtown (see map, opposite). Lush plantings and mature trees add a feeling of permanence and character to the district. In some places, entire blocks of early dwellings survive to evoke the sense of being in a Victorian townscape. Many smaller dwellings fill the spaces between the larger homes. Although several wide streets serving downtown Napa disrupt the continuity of the neighborhood a bit, particularly to the west, the individual homes remain intact.

Napa's grid system of streets has sections canted at different angles. The first grid was laid out in 1848, and none of the sections added later aligned either with the original grid *or* with each other. As a further navigational challenge, none of the grids are lined up exactly north–south. The result, aptly described by David Gebhard et al. in *A Guide to Architecture in San Francisco and Northern California*, is that "Napa's street pattern presents the most picturesque assemblage which can be obtained through the use of the grid pattern." It is also confusing to drive through. Focusing on Oak Street as the main "east–west" street and on Jefferson Street as the main "north–south" street helps.

1211 Division Street (private), Parker House, ca. 1887. This excellent Stick-style design has a two-story squared bay set at an angle on the left-front corner. The gable above this angled bay window and the front-facing gable are both beautifully detailed. Note the picket-fence pattern used as a wide band of trim under the eaves. Many triangular brace supports are used here as well; notice how they are placed to align with the windows and corners. An old-house detective would wonder if the left side of the front porch was enclosed after the house was built.

443 and 485 Brown Street (both private), Manasse House, 1886, and Churchill House, ca. 1889. These side-by-side dwellings make an interesting pair, as both have had full-height Neoclassical porches added in the early twentieth century. Number 443 was originally built as a Stick-style house and 485 as a Second Empire design.

486 Coombs Street (private), Wilder-Churchill House, 1893; Ernest Coxhead, San Francisco, architect. This creative Shingle-style design experiments with different patterns of laying the shingles and features a squat entrance tower supported by four Classical columns as well as unusual roof and dormer shapes. In addition to the front view,

Victorian Napa

approach it down the side street to get a view of the unusual roof overhangs and inset dormers on the rear roof.

313 Franklin Street (private), Holden House, 1886. A rare tree tunnel of towering redwoods shelters the 300 block of Franklin Street. This large and ornate Italianate house sits at one end of it. There is an elegant recessed entry, approached by a flight of steps with a graceful outward curve that leads onto a one-story entry porch with mansard roof. Beyond, one enters the recessed portion, which has paneled sides before, finally, reaching the handsome double entry doors. Note the use of small triangular pediments over many of the windows and at the center of the entry porch. The two-story bay window on the right has fine detailing.

606 Seminary Street (private), ca. 1905. This cottage is an excellent example of a Queen Anne– to Craftsman-style transitional design. It has a Queen Anne roof shape—hipped roof with lower cross gables—combined with the low roof pitch, widely overhanging eaves, and exposed rafters and roof beams of the Craftsman style. It features a Free Classic Queen Anne wraparound porch with the typical Classical columns. The conical corner porch roof, typical of Queen Anne houses, has the very low roof pitch associated with Craftsman designs. The house faces Fuller Park, which is surrounded by small and midsized homes in a wide variety of styles.

1903 Oak Street (private), ca. 1925. This is a charming, one-story, stuccoed French Eclectic design. Towered subtype houses like this one are often called Norman cottages.

1930 Clay Street (private), Burford House, ca. 1877. This basic Italianate design has a simple hipped roof and a flat, three-bay facade unadorned by bay windows or elaborate detailing. Note the tall, narrow windows with simple bracketed pediments above.

1929 First Street (private), Smith House, 1875. This Second Empire house features a concave-shaped mansard roof. The entire exterior looks amazingly original.

1926 First Street (private), Francis House, 1900; Luther M. Turton, architect. Shingle-style houses with very steeply pitched, front-gabled roofs are common in northern California. Many subtle variations of window- and shingle-pattern detailing are seen in the dominant front gables. Here the two center windows in the lower row project out in a V shape. A false balustrade above echoes this same shape. The upper row of three windows has a triangular area inset above that echoes this same V shape. This is accentuated by a tall, skinny "keystone" with the shingle pattern curving into it.

NEVADA CITY

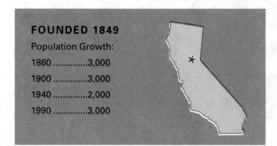

FOUNDED 1849

Population Growth:

1860 3,000
1900 3,000
1940 2,000
1990 3,000

This small gold rush community had the good fortune to become the center of California's richest and most long-lived gold production and is today one of the state's best-preserved mining towns.

Early Mining Camps

Most of the many hundreds of gold rush mining settlements that sprang up along promising streams throughout the Sierra Nevada foothills following the initial 1848 discovery at Sutter's Mill (see page 136) were called camps for good reason. Tents, dugouts, and crude cabins housed the mostly male, young, and single miners who, after the loose pieces of placer gold were panned from the easily worked stream-bottom gravel, moved on in search of richer "diggin's" elsewhere. This initial phase of the gold boom, in which individuals or small groups of miners had a reasonable chance of being well rewarded for their efforts, was remarkably brief. By the end of 1850, the tens of thousands of "forty-niners" had prospected, staked claims, and already removed much of the easily recovered gold from every productive stream in the region, which stretched for a remarkable 130 miles along the Sierra foothills.

Hydraulic Mining

Nevada City began as a typical mining camp, and, as with most of the others, its stream-bottom gold deposits soon played out. By that time, however, its miners had recognized that some of the surrounding Sierra Nevada foothills were themselves made up of rock formed from *ancient* stream gravel that, like their present-day counterparts, were rich with scattered particles of gold. Unlike the loose particles of the modern streambeds, however, these ancient gravels were partially cemented into rock and thus required laborious pick-and-shovel digging to excavate tunnels, called coyote holes, into the productive hillsides. The excavated rock then required sledge-hammer pounding to

break it apart for separation of the gold by the usual technique of flowing water over the particles in pans or flumes. The time and effort required for all of this meant that "coyoteing" miners working with simple hand tools could rarely do more than survive on the value of the gold they produced each day.

Seeking a more efficient means of recovering this ancient-gravel gold, in 1852 a Connecticut Yankee miner working near Nevada City conceived the idea of blasting the rock particles apart with high-pressure jets of water. The pressure was obtained by damning a stream higher in the foothills and then conducting the water downhill through canals, flumes, and pipes before releasing it from hoses or pipes equipped with jet nozzles. Enormous water pressures, sufficient to wash away entire hillsides, could be developed by this "hydraulic-mining" technique, which also made possible wholesale washing of the debris in long flumes where flowing water removed the lighter sand particles, leaving behind their small residue of heavier gold.

Hydraulic mining required a heavy initial investment for dams, flumes, pipes, hoses, and leases of mineral rights covering entire hillsides. Many of the late arrivals to the gold rush region during the 1850s ended up working as day laborers for large and well-financed hydraulic-mining companies rather than as independent prospectors working their own claims.

The region around Nevada City was ideal for large-scale hydraulic mining, and the town became a prosperous supply center for this activity as well as the seat of gold-rich Nevada County. Problems began to arise, however, as more and more hillsides were washed away and their remains dumped into the local streams. This enormous volume of washed-out sand and gravel was transported downslope by the rivers and streams and deposited in the adjacent dry Central Valley, where it overflowed rich agricultural lands and destroyed the carefully constructed irrigation dams and canals that watered the crops. In 1880 the California legislature outlawed most types of hydraulic mining, and this source of Nevada City's prosperity ended. Fortunately, still another type of local gold boom had already developed to take its place.

Quartz Mining

It had long been recognized that the gold fragments in the region's stream gravels originated, like the sand and pebbles in the gravels themselves, from the slow break-

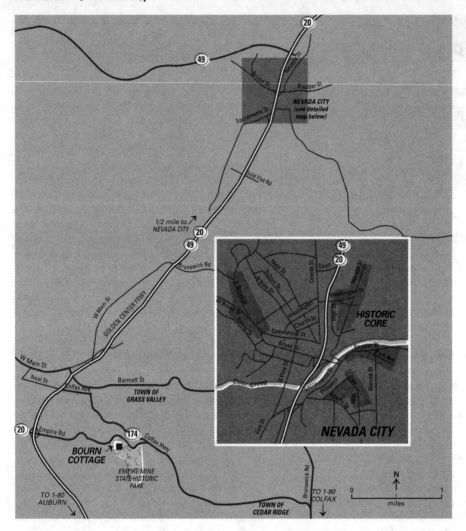

down of the massive granites and related "hard" rocks of the adjacent Sierra Nevada. Searches for these gold-bearing mother-lode rocks began with the gold rush itself and were soon successful. In some of the higher foothills, gold-bearing quartz veins were discovered in association with granite and other massive rocks. On the surface the veins appeared as low ledges, about a foot wide, made up of milky-white quartz with scattered inclusions of dust-to-sand-sized gold. Unlike the free gold particles found in stream-gravel deposits, this quartz gold was sealed within its hard, glassy matrix. Except for occasional large particles, this gold could not be released by simply breaking up the quartz. Furthermore, the long and narrow quartz ledges extended downward beneath the surface as thin veins surrounded by granite and related massive rocks. These required blasting and other hard-rock mining techniques

to separate the proportionally small quantity of gold-bearing quartz. Once released, the quartz ore then required machine crushing and complex chemical processing to release its included gold.

The forty-niners discovered several such quartz veins in the Nevada City area and tried with little success to work them with simple hand tools. They soon gave up and sold their claims to speculators and investors, many of whom formed mining companies to exploit the quartz gold. Most of these quickly failed, but by 1853 six such companies, each well financed, with knowledgeable supervisors, and located on particularly rich veins, were making a profit from their expensive underground operations. These were the vanguard of a hard-rock-mining complex that was to make the Nevada City area the heart of California gold production for the next hundred years.

Nevada City and Grass Valley

The richest of the area's quartz veins turned out to be clustered about four miles southwest of Nevada City (see "Bourn Cottage," page 131). Here the town of Grass Valley grew up to serve the rich underground mines. Such deep underground mining was new to California, so the mine owners imported large numbers of British miners experienced in working the deep and historic tin mines of Cornwall in southwesternmost England. Grass Valley soon became the center of a thriving colony of Cornish miners; by 1870 the town had almost twice the population of nearby Nevada City, which remained the area's principal financial, professional, and government center.

Modern Nevada City

Nevada City is one of the very few gold rush mining towns with the good fortune to be near the center of a long-prospering region of gold production. The town's important administrative and trading functions, however, never demanded a large population, so that Nevada City has remarkably maintained about three thousand inhabitants since shortly after its founding almost 150 years ago. The town's early prosperity led to the construction of numerous charming Victorian dwellings, many of which still survive. In addition, **Broad Street,** the town's business center, retains many rare commercial buildings from the 1850 to 1880

decades. The surrounding hills also retain several instructive gold-mining legacies. About fifteen miles northeast at the village of North Bloomfield is the **Malakoff Diggins State Historic Park** (916-265-2740), which preserves and interprets California's largest hydraulic-mining operation. Four miles south of Nevada City at the quartz-mining town of Grass Valley is the **North Star Mining Museum** (south of downtown on Allison Ranch Road; 916-273-4255), with a fine collection of the heroic machinery used in the deep-quartz mines. About a mile southeast of downtown Grass Valley is the **Empire Mine State Historic Park,** which preserves many of the buildings of California's richest and longest-producing deep-quartz gold mine. Among these is Bourn Cottage, a remarkable part-time dwelling for its wealthy San Francisco owner.

Historic Core, ca. 1850s–1900

Historic dwellings are found along almost every street in Nevada City, and on the map we have simply highlighted four areas of town that seemed to have particularly choice "diggin's." Probably the most common house style here is the Folk Victorian, most often front gabled. These houses occur in many different sizes and with varying details. Many have been modified to some extent over the years. Unfortunately, most of the residential parts of Nevada City are not covered by the city

Nevada City Historic Core

Nevada City Historic Core

preservation ordinance, which protects the architectural integrity of its downtown.

255 Boulder Street (private), Marsh House, 1873. This handsome Italianate dwelling is an excellent example of the simple-hipped-roof subtype with a central cupola added—a form often called a cube-and-cupola house. Martin Luther Marsh was a carpenter from Middletown, Ohio, who came to California in 1850 and worked in various mining towns before arriving at Nevada City in 1859. Here he was successful in several enterprises, among them owning a lumberyard.

Marsh met his wife-to-be, Emma Ann Ward, aboard ship on a return journey from the East in 1862. The couple married in 1864 and by 1867 had purchased this lot. Construction began in 1873. It could have been guided by the Eleventh Design in Samuel Sloan's 1852 pattern book, *The Model Architect,* which gave detailed instructions for "A Plain and Ornamented Villa" and showed two illustrations of how a simple three-bay cube like this house might have either more or less ornament as the owner's taste and pocketbook dictated.

The Marshes chose a middle path, ornamenting their own three-bay cube with Italianate brackets under the eaves, shallow triangular pediments above the upstairs windows, and simplified quoins on the corners. They also incorporated some features typical of the earlier Greek Re-

vival style, notably the narrow line of transom and sidelights surrounding the front door and the simplified Classical columns of the full-width porch. Lumberman Marsh used all native woods and materials in the house, including local bricks and stone in the foundation. The high quality of its construction has well served four generations of his family. The home must have been greatly admired when it was built, because in the late 1870s Marsh built a similar interpretation of the cube-and-cupola form at 208 Clay Street (private). This has the same Greek Revival door surround seen in Marsh's own house. The entry porch was redone in the 1970s.

204 Clay Street (private). This spindlework Queen Anne design is one and one-half stories high. The extra half story of height gives it the appealing but slightly ungainly look of a half-grown teenager. Note the small roof gable-on-hip and the unusual fish-scale shingles in the gable with the curved side facing upward rather than down. The diamond-shaped window next to the front entry could be a later addition.

309 Park Avenue at Nimrod (private), Shaw House, ca. 1890. This large and handsomely detailed Queen Anne design has a gable dominated by two exuberant sunbursts. All of the spindlework detailing and even the front door look original.

316 Nevada Street (private). This elegant asymmetrical Italianate house has a two-story bay window on one side, handsome brackets, inventive hooded windows, and a typical Italianate double door.

304 Nevada Street (private). The gable of this charming front-gabled Gothic Revival house has decorated vergeboards, elaborated cross bracing, and a typical Gothic Revival window with a slightly flattened pointed arch. These are joined by elements typical of other styles. The gable surface is clad with various shapes of patterned wood shingles typical of the later Queen Anne style, while the doorway reflects the earlier Greek Revival style (similar doorways can be seen at 255 Boulder Street and 208 Clay Street, see above). In remote places like Nevada City, such varied combinations of stylistic detail were frequent. Unless you were extremely wealthy and could bring in outside materials or design assistance, you were at the mercy of what was in stock at the local lumberyard and/or what the local carpenter knew how to build. And, as today, sometimes one didn't find out what the local carpenter actually knew how to build until he had already built it! For the house watcher, combinations like these in Nevada City provide delightful surprises.

Bourn Cottage, 1897

10791 East Empire Road, Empire Mine State Historic Park, Grass Valley; 916-273-8522; Willis Polk, San Francisco, architect.

San Francisco financier William Bourn Jr. (1857–1936) must have enjoyed working with that city's creative young architect Willis Polk (1867–1924), for he asked him to design two consecutive houses. In 1896 Bourn commissioned Polk to design his elegant San Francisco town house. The next year Polk was asked to design this summer home, or "cottage," as the family called it, located adjacent to the source of Bourn's wealth, the great Empire Mine (see page 129). Bourn must have been

Bourn Cottage

satisfied with these two homes, for he was to call upon Polk yet a third time ten years later to design his great country estate, called Filoli, south of San Francisco (see page 204). This cottage was by far the most modest of the three homes and was designed to be occupied mainly during short periods in the summer. The constant noise of the mine's nearby ore-crushing "stamp mill" ruled out considering this an idyllic country retreat.

Polk, always inventive, was squarely in the camp of those Eclectic-era architects who preferred "not to take things too straight." The cottage's exterior design combines numerous historical features into Polk's own unique expression of an informal country house; it is not a house that falls neatly into any of the popular styles of the day, but the overall effect suggests a French or English folk cottage. The light gray stone walls are uncut and uncoursed; the stone was salvaged from the mine excavations. This rough wall surface is then given a crisp look by finishing all corners, edges, windows, and doors with redbrick brought in from Sacramento.

The two materials are quite pleasing in this unusual combination.

The 4,600-square-foot house has a living room, dining room, writing room, and kitchen with related service rooms on the first floor. Above are four bedrooms arranged across the front of the house for family use and three additional bedrooms for the housekeeper and staff. The home's interior is paneled with hand-planed heart of redwood. The floors are oak, added in 1929, but now stained ebony to match the finish of the original floors. Furnishings are relatively sparse.

Thirteen acres of gardens surround the cottage. The broad front lawn has two round pools surrounded by forty-nine-jet fountains that spray water up and into them. Water also cascades from a lily pond down the slope to a reflecting pool. The Bourns' large rose garden has been restored to the period ca. 1905 and is planted with almost a thousand rosebushes in fifty-six early varieties. The arbor is planted with the Gold of Ophir climbing rose, the variety originally planted there.

PETALUMA

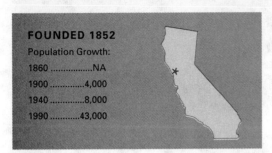

FOUNDED 1852

Population Growth:

1860 ....NA
1900 4,000
1940 8,000
1990 43,000

Like its neighboring town of Napa twenty miles to the east (see page 124), Petaluma was founded in the gold rush days as a food supply center for the endless flow of fortune seekers that poured into the state following the initial 1848 gold discovery. As with Napa, Petaluma is located at the head of small-boat navigation on a small river that flows into San Francisco Bay. This provided a convenient means of delivering the region's agricultural bounty to San Francisco and, via larger inland rivers, to the mining supply centers of Sacramento and Stockton.

By the 1870s both the Napa and Petaluma areas were developing more specialized agricultural functions. The Napa region was to become the nation's premier supplier of fine table wines, while Petaluma found national prominence in a less glamorous, but more fundamental, product. A local poultry man named Lyman Ryce first conceived and developed the idea of hatching chicks in artificial incubators rather than in the time-honored, but less controllable, nests of henhouses. By 1900 Petaluma-produced incubators were being shipped around the world, while the town's mass-produced eggs and chicks dominated the West Coast poultry industry.

Petaluma's poultry industry declined after the 1940s as more localized supply facilities developed throughout the country. Today, dairying is the town's principal industry, supplemented, in recent decades, by an influx of Bay Area retirees and long-distance commuters who enjoy the town's semirural atmosphere. Adding to the town's character are some remarkably intact turn-of-the-century neighborhoods whose survival is probably a result of Petaluma's mid-1970s decision to limit its growth. It was among the first towns in the country to make this choice, which was ultimately appealed all the way to the U.S. Supreme Court, which confirmed the decision's legality. Supplementing Petaluma's fine collection of Victorian houses is one of California's most

remarkable survivors from its Hispanic past—a massive adobe ranch headquarters built by the region's most influential Mexican-era soldier and statesman (see page 134).

The Alphabet Streets, ca. 1860s–1920s

This large neighborhood is chock-full of delightful historic houses. When looking at a map of Petaluma, one easily sees two distinct street grids arranged to follow a bend in the Petaluma River. This neighborhood occupies the second grid to be platted and has street names chosen by a less imaginative developer—A, B, C, D, etc., in one direction and First, Second, Third, Fourth, etc., in the other. Along these streets is a large and unusually intact neighborhood of fine houses dating from the Victorian and early Eclectic eras.

The tip of the district closest to downtown is called the A Street residential district and is featured on a local walking tour that highlights homes on Fifth and Sixth Streets from D to just past A. In addition to houses, this part of the district has several handsome churches. Most prominently sited is the **St. Vincent de Paul Catholic Church,** a large twin-towered Spanish Colonial Revival structure built in 1927 and ornamented with handsome mosaicwork that overlooks a triangular park bounded by Liberty and Howard Streets.

A second and equally fine church is **St. John's Episcopal** at the corner of Fifth and C Streets, a striking

The Alphabet Streets

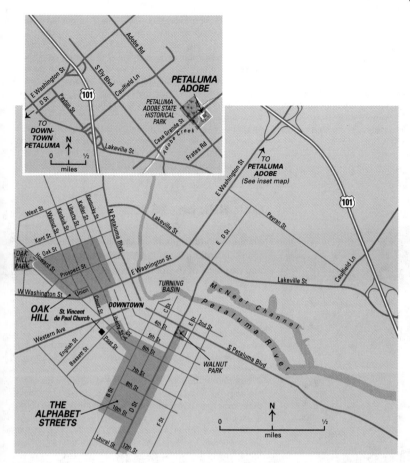

1890s Shingle-style building designed by Ernest Coxhead of San Francisco. Its most prominent feature is a voluminous shingled corner tower with a slightly incongruous Spanish Baroque entry. It would be interesting to know if this detail was the architect's idea or a concession to California tradition needed to get the avant-garde design passed by the church's building committee.

The small A Street District, easily viewed on foot, is only an introduction to the neighborhood's resources. A drive out from downtown along D Street takes one past a hundred-year span of fine homes enhanced by broad lawns and landscaping that give a delightful feeling of continuity and coherence. Although the largest homes tend to be grouped along D Street, adjacent streets feature many interesting small and midsized dwellings.

6 Sixth Street (private), Stewart House, ca. 1865. This Greek Revival design is of the front-gabled subtype favored along the Pacific coast. Note the corner pilasters and the wide band of trim. The Gothic windows in the upstairs were restored in 1994. Traces of them were found under layers of paint. Their design could have been original, as many houses were built that combined Greek and Gothic features, or it could have been the result of an early stylistic alteration. The front door looks much newer than the rest of the house.

48 Sixth Street (private). This would be a typical cross-gabled Craftsman design but for the addition of a squat tower topped by a low conical roof. There are a fair number of similar houses in northern California, where they are called simply Transitional houses because the tower is considered to be a holdover from the Victorian era.

758 D Street (private), Fairbanks House, 1890; William J. Cuthbertson, San Francisco, architect. This huge Shingle-style house is of the cross-gabled roof subtype. Note the use of typical Shingle trademarks, such as the large eyebrow dormer and the combination of tower and front-facing gable blended into a single elegant composition. The unusual detailing begins with a swirl of shingles at the gable peak. Beneath this is a frieze of stucco with decorative pebbles that ties together the gable and adjacent five-sided tower. Under this is an almost-Modernistic band of windows that begins at the left with three horizontal lines, then extends to include a Palladian window and the tower windows. Beneath this, the entire upper story of the house is covered with patterned shingles. The left side elevation is just as artistic and uses the same general trim elements but in slightly different ways.

1000 D Street (private), ca. 1930; Warren Perry, architect. This inventive interpretation of the Colonial Revival style is dominated by a broad centered gable. Although quite formal in composition, the house is clad with rather-informal wood shingles. Note the use of a shallow trellis all across the house facade; it reads almost like a belt course.

853 D Street (private), Anderson House, ca. 1925. This understated Colonial Revival design has superb brickwork laid in a Flemish bond (alternating headers and stretchers in every row). Note the same brick pattern in the chimney of the house to the left.

The Alphabet Streets

706 B Street (private), ca. 1900. This front-gabled form of Shingle-style house was common throughout northern California, and many variations of it are found in Petaluma. Two other examples are nearby at 715 B Street and 730 B Street (both private). Notice the wide lancet arch leading onto the porch. Identical arches appear on many houses in Petaluma and were likely stocked by a local lumberyard or were a favorite feature of a particular builder. Look for them throughout Petaluma, where they are used on several different house styles. Just down the block, on the southeast corner of Seventh and B Streets (private), is a Craftsman design with the identical lancet entry arch. Number 826 D Street (private) has a porch graced with four of these broad lancet arches.

Oak Hill, ca. 1880s–1910s

Oak Hill overlooks downtown and was favored by early Petalumans that preferred hillside homesites rather than the flatter land of the Alphabet Streets. The south and east faces of the hill were the first to be developed.

200 Prospect Street (private), Haubrich House, 1892. This handsome Queen Anne design, at the corner of Prospect Street and Keller Street, is built entirely of redwood. The original low iron fence still surrounds it. The home has a three-story corner tower with conical roof, cutaway bay windows, and large areas covered with fish-scale-patterned wood shingles.

316 Keller Street (private), ca. 1890s. Note the gable-on-hip roof on this Queen Anne cottage. There are several other examples of these small rooftop gables in the neighborhood.

301 Keokuk Street (private), Sweed House, 1892; Samuel Rodd, builder. This elegant Queen Anne home was built for Philip Sweed, a native of Bavaria who arrived in Petaluma in 1876. Sweed opened a successful dry-goods business and for over thirty years served as president of the Petaluma Board of Education. His son and daughter lived in this house until about 1962, and they, and subsequent owners, have kept the house remarkably intact. In architectural dictionaries, an overall pattern of small squares, usually painted or carved, is called diaperwork. Here, areas of traditional diaperwork decorate the gable peaks and are mimicked by the see-through woodwork in a repetitive square design that decorates the porch. Note the original paired front doors with the "fanned" areas; these are echoed by three "fan" panels in the roof gable.

Petaluma Adobe, ca. 1836–1846

3325 Adobe Road at Casa Grande, Petaluma Adobe State Historic Park; 707-762-4871.

This huge adobe structure is a unique survivor from California's long Hispanic era. It was built by a brilliant young Mexican army officer named Mariano Guadalupe Vallejo, who, in 1834, was the recently appointed commander of the small garrison of troops stationed at the presidio (fort) of San Francisco. In that year the Mexican government decided to close California's venerable chain of Franciscan missions, many of them then over a

Petaluma Adobe

century old and all suffering from the government's inability to provide support in the chaotic years that followed Mexico's gaining of independence from Spain in 1821. Wishing to encourage civilian development of the lush and sparsely populated grasslands north of San Francisco Bay, California's provincial governor sent Vallejo to establish the new town of Sonoma adjacent to the province's northernmost mission (see page 265). As an incentive to bring new settlers to the town and region, Vallejo was also personally granted a vast tract of some forty-four thousand prime acres of grassland between the Petaluma River on the west and Sonoma Creek on the east. As he set about building the town of Sonoma, Vallejo also began constructing, about twelve miles westward, this headquarters building for his vast new cattle ranch, which he called Rancho Petaluma.

California cattle in the Hispanic era were of value principally for their hides and for the tallow rendered from their fat. Sailing-ship captains of many nationalities purchased these products for delivery around the world as raw materials for leather goods and candle making. At its peak, Rancho Petaluma produced not only enormous numbers of cattle but also valuable herds of both horses and sheep. In addition, large quantities of wheat, corn, and barley were grown for the export trade. Other crops were produced mainly for local consumption. Skilled blacksmiths, carpenters, tanners, weavers, and other craftsmen made the rancho a remarkably self-sufficient operation. Day-to-day operations were overseen by Miguel Alvarado, Vallejo's majordomo. Vallejo himself lived in nearby Sonoma (see page 267) and spent only a few weeks a year at the rancho.

During its active era, the large structure that survives today was but one-half of the ranch headquarters complex; an almost-identical structure to the east completed an enclosed inner courtyard. This now-vanished structure lacked the permanent wood roof that protected the adobe walls of the surviving half of the building. Many of the individual adobe bricks, which appear to have never received a protective coating of mud or stucco, are easily visible today. Experts estimate that about 80 percent of the walls are original, as is about 20 percent of the structure's woodwork. This survival is due to the high-quality redwood used in construction, the efforts of the Petaluma Chapter of the Native Sons of the Golden West, who owned the historic structure from 1910 to 1951, and to the ongoing efforts of the California Department of Parks and Recreation since 1951. The department is now in the process of historically reinterpreting the furnishings and functions of the building's many rooms, some of which were given an overly romantic Old West flavor in earlier decades.

The state happily still owns forty-one acres of land around the adobe—enough that one can begin to imagine being in the midst of a vast Hispanic rancho in the heyday of the vaqueros.

SACRAMENTO

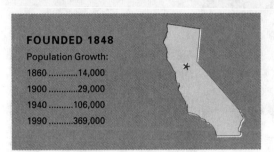

FOUNDED 1848

Population Growth:

1860 14,000
1900 29,000
1940 106,000
1990 369,000

In January 1848 the village that was to become Sacramento provided the spark that set off one of the most massive human migrations since the medieval Crusades—the great California gold rush. At that time California was a remote Mexican frontier whose non-Indian inhabitants, numbering about 14,000, were mostly long-established Hispanic cattle ranchers. Two years later the population had jumped to 92,000, and California became the nation's thirty-first state. Although the population was dominated by Anglos from the eastern states, this total included large contingents of fortune seekers drawn from every continent on the globe. By 1860 the count had swelled to a remarkable 380,000. Much of this immigrant horde reached destinations in the Sierra Nevada goldfields via the bustling river port of Sacramento (see map page 159).

Sutter's Fort

Sacramento's founder was a visionary German-Swiss entrepreneur and ex–army officer named John Augustus Sutter (1803–1880). Never a very careful money manager, Sutter had left Switzerland for New York in 1834 to avoid prosecution by creditors, a potentially serious crime in that bank-dominated country. He apparently arrived with a significant bankroll still intact, for he was to spend the next five years exploring North America in search of new opportunity. This restless odyssey took him to St. Louis, Santa Fe, Oregon, Alaska, and Hawaii before he arrived, in 1839, at Monterey, the capital of Mexican California.

Sensing the region's untapped potential, the talented and worldly Sutter persuaded California's provincial governor to grant him an enormous tract of forty-eight thousand riverside acres in the dry and unsettled Central Valley. In return Sutter promised to establish an irrigated agricultural center that would attract new settlement and commerce to the province and, not incidentally, enrich his personal fiefdom. This he accomplished with remarkable success. By 1847 the colony, which Sutter called New Helvetia in honor of his former homeland, was a thriving farming, ranching, and trade center whose prosperity rivaled that of the vast coastal cattle baronies of the aristocratic Mexican Californios.

The headquarters of New Helvetia was a walled complex of adobe shops, storerooms, and living quarters located on high ground near the junction of the Sacramento and American Rivers. The site is today surrounded by the eastern suburbs of Sacramento. Known simply as **Sutter's Fort,** it was from here that Sutter sent his trusted chief carpenter, James Marshall, on a fateful mission to establish a new sawmill on the American River in the Sierra Nevada foothills about forty miles east of the fort. What happened next is graphically summarized by historian John W. Reps in *Cities of the American West*:

When the mill was first tried, the mill wheel would not turn properly because the raceway—the channel needed to return the water to the river—had not been excavated to the proper depth. Marshall directed the Indian laborers to remove more earth from the tailrace and, to flush out the loosened rocks and soil, he opened the floodgate each night to allow the water to carry off the material. On the morning of January 24, 1848, Marshall came to inspect the ditch, noticed some small, dull, yellow particles at the bottom and, after hammering them to determine that they were malleable, realized . . . it was gold. Its discovery was to change the history of California and the nation.

Nine days later in distant Mexico City, the Treaty of Guadalupe Hidalgo was signed, ending the United States's two-year war with Mexico. In return for a payment of $15 million, Mexico ceded California and the adjacent Southwest to the United States (see page xx). Neither party to the treaty knew about Marshall's discovery.

The Rush Begins

Sutter and Marshall tried to keep their find secret, but all of the sawmill workers had witnessed it, and the news slowly spread. In May 1848 an enterprising Sutter's Fort merchant seeking new business went to San Francisco, then a seaside village of 850 inhabitants,

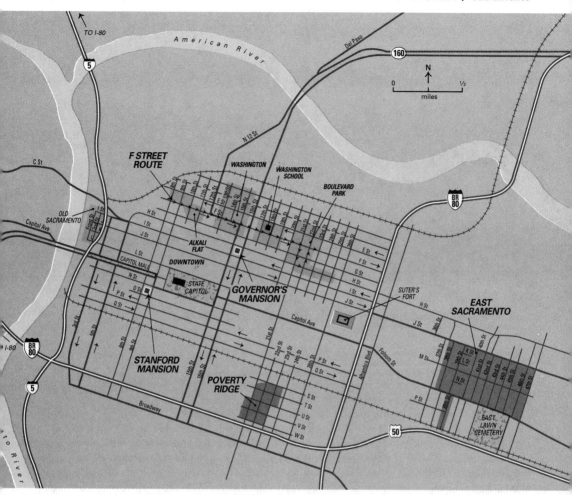

where he reportedly ran through the streets waving a small bottle of gold particles and shouting, "Gold! Gold! Gold from the American River!" Within a week San Francisco was a ghost town—all but a handful of its former inhabitants had departed for Sutter's Mill. As word of the richness of the gold-bearing gravels spread, California's coastal towns and rural ranches were similarly deserted. By July about 4,000 miners were digging and panning for gold along the American River, with more arriving every day.

These earliest gold rush participants were mostly Pacific coast residents. This was to change in December, when President James Knox Polk confirmed in his annual message to Congress that an "abundance of gold" had been discovered in the remote and newly acquired American territory of California. Even more provocative was the president's written report, which asserted that "a man could earn in one day's work mining gold twice the monthly pay of a private soldier." True for some but not for many, this official endorsement launched an international flood of about 100,000 forty-niners who sailed, rode, walked, and sometimes crawled to distant California the following year.

The River Port

Sutter's grand plan for New Helvetia, still mostly a paper plan when the first wave of gold seekers arrived from San Francisco in small boats, called for a new port city named Sutterville to be built on the Sacramento River at an elevated site about three miles south of its swampy, lowland junction with the suddenly famous American River. The frenzied crowds ignored Sutterville and landed as close as possible to the shallow American River before proceeding overland toward its upriver goldfields.

At the landing site, unauthorized squatters began to appropriate sites for stores, mostly in tents or crude wooden buildings, to help supply the passing crowds.

View of Sacramento, 1857

As the gold seekers moved inland, they passed Sutter's well-stocked fort and through his extensive farmlands and livestock-filled pastures. As the flood of arrivals increased, their insistent purchases soon depleted the fort's previously ample, but not quickly replaceable, stocks of food and supplies. At the same time, the passing throngs trampled his distant fields and "borrowed" from his large herds of cattle, sheep, and goats. Within a few months, Sutter's formerly prosperous agricultural empire was approaching ruin, and his vast landholdings threatened with seizure by creditors.

Things took a turn for the better in August when Sutter's twenty-two-year-old eldest son, John Sutter Jr., arrived from Switzerland to help his dispirited father. Between them they came up with a bold plan for survival. In October Sutter deeded his lands to his son, which protected them from the creditors. Sensing the inevitable, the son also persuaded his reluctant father, who farsightedly insisted that the site would be regularly flooded, to allow the platting of an enormous new port city of "Sacramento" around the squatters' shacks.

In January 1849, only a month after President Polk's address to Congress had briskly fanned the gold rush flames, John Jr. held the first auction of Sacramento lots. The proceeds from this and subsequent sales in the following months were enough to retire his father's debts. Retaining title to their vast Mexican-era land grants during the coming Anglo deluge was, however, to prove impossible. Neither father nor son was to

again profit from the region's enormous riches, whose development they pioneered.

Growing Pains

Sutter's predictions proved to be only too accurate as the initial wooden buildings of the booming port suffered not only the usual frontier fires, but also devastating floods when winter rains drenched the adjacent mountains and overflowed the Sacramento and American Rivers. A storm in January 1850, only a year after the first Sutter lots were auctioned, caused many drownings and covered 80 percent of the young city with water. Many others were to follow. Both problems were eventually subdued. In 1853 a fire-protection ordinance required new commercial buildings to have walls of brick, stone, or cast iron. In 1862, following an unusually destructive flood, Sacramento's citizens embarked on an ambitious and expensive grade-raising plan that was not completed until 1873. This involved jacking up the waterfront-area commercial buildings eight feet into the air, and then filling the space beneath, and the adjacent streets, with hauled-in dirt. Supplemented by tall riverside levees, this effectively minimized the flood threat.

In 1854 Sacramento defeated several rival contenders to become the permanent capital of the four-year-old state of California. Now an important center of government, the city also continued to flourish as a principal supply and trade center for the hundreds of mining camps that blossomed and faded in the nearby Sierra Nevada foothills (see page 127). By 1860, however, the mountains' easily mined surface gold was playing out, and Sacramento's boom years appeared to be over. Providentially, the city then became the birthplace of yet another great event that was to forever change the West—the nation's first transcontinental railroad.

The Central Pacific Railroad

Dreams and plans for such a rail line, to replace the long and dangerous wagon trails that wound across seemingly endless deserts and impenetrable mountain ranges, had fascinated Americans for decades. They were ultimately to be realized through the efforts of a visionary young civil engineer named Theodore K. Judah (1826–1863).

Born in Connecticut and trained in Troy, New York, young Judah was a precocious designer of early rail lines in New England and adjacent New York. In 1853 several Sacramento civic leaders hired him to design and build California's first railroad—a short line intended to replace some of the tedious wagon roads that connected Sacramento with the nearby Sierra Nevada goldfields. Two years later, when only twenty miles of the projected line had been completed, its backers ran out of money, and Judah found himself unemployed. Already, however, he had developed a bold new obsession.

It had long been assumed that the first transcontinental railroad would follow the low-level southern route, reaching California via the plains and deserts of Texas, New Mexico, and Arizona, thus avoiding a crossing of the seemingly impenetrable granite peaks of the massive Sierra Nevada farther north. Indeed, the federal government's 1854 Gadsden Purchase of southernmost Arizona from Mexico was made specifically to facilitate such a railroad. Judah had a better idea.

Realizing that a Sierra Nevada crossing east of Sacramento would far more directly link California's principal urban centers with the industrial Midwest, Judah set out to determine the feasibility of such a route. Both the Sierra Nevada's gentle western slope and its more precipitous eastern slope were cut by river gorges that, Judah demonstrated with preliminary surveys, could be graded and filled to make a conventional, if expensive, roadbed with the necessary gentle grades. The problems lay in the massive and steep granite crest of the range, which appeared to be passable only by blasting impossibly long tunnels beneath much of the summit. Finally, after visiting many unsuitably steep passes through the peaks, in the fall of 1860 Judah was shown a previously ignored, and more gently ascending, ridge

of granite near the early emigrant trail through Donner Pass, northwest of Lake Tahoe. Here, his practiced eye quickly noted, was the first practical railway passage through the granite barrier. Thrilled with the discovery, on his last night in the mountains Judah took out pen and paper and drew up a stock subscription agreement for his new Central Pacific Railroad.

The Big Four

For many years it had been clear that no transcontinental railroad could be built across the sparsely populated West without massive federal subsidies. Several bills in support of such lines had been introduced in Congress during the 1850s, but, with pre–Civil War sectional disputes heating up, northern delegates voted against any southern route and vice versa. Most of the bills stipulated that the railroad would be built by a private corporation that, after completing a stated number of miles using its own capital funds, would receive government loans to finance some of the construction costs of each subsequent mile. In addition, the corporation would receive outright grants of large blocks of federal land on either side of the completed tracks. These could either be sold or held for future profit.

The year was 1860, with Abraham Lincoln's election imminent and secession of at least some southern states a strong possibility. Judah felt that a bill supporting his partially surveyed Central Pacific route might soon win congressional approval. What he needed now were committed funds for a final engineering survey and initial construction costs. He first sought these in San Francisco, California's financial center, whose civic leaders had long favored the principle of a Pacific railway. In practice, Judah was to find, such a railway threatened their established stagecoach and freighting companies as well as their profitable shipping lines that served both the Bay Area and East Coast ports. All of these could be severely damaged by railroad competition.

Returning to Sacramento empty-handed, Judah had one last hope. Perhaps the business leaders of his adopted city, though less affluent than their San Francisco counterparts, would finance his dream. Much of the town's commerce was then dominated by four merchants whose prosperous businesses supplied the principal necessities of frontier life—groceries (Leland Stanford, 1824–1893; see also "Stanford Mansion," page 142); hardware (Collis Huntington, 1821–1900, and Mark Hopkins, 1813–1878); and dry goods, which were principally cloth and ready-made clothing (Charles Crocker, 1822–1888). Amazingly, each of these gold rush immigrants had once lived in the general vicinity of Troy, New York, Judah's hometown, and

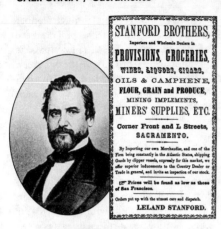

Sacramento's Big Four and their unlikely credentials for building one of the great engineering marvels of the nineteenth century. One historian has noted that Crocker, the Central Pacific's boisterously energetic construction supervisor, must have been particularly ill-suited for a life of "measuring out calico and ribbons for the ladies of Sacramento."

all had grown up watching the whirlwind development of the northeastern rail network that began nearby. Intrigued with Judah's proposal, they cautiously agreed to finance the detailed engineering survey and await its results before making further commitments.

When the attack on Fort Sumter began the Civil War in April 1861, Judah's surveys were still incomplete, but the Big Four, as they came to be known, hastily proceeded to incorporate their "Central Pacific Rail Road of California" with Stanford as president, Huntington vice-president, Hopkins treasurer, and Judah chief engineer. Crocker was one of several directors and also president of the new Crocker Construction Company, which was to build much of the line. All of this was a bold gamble, for, as Huntington was later to admit, the four's combined wealth was then only $159,000, about enough for five miles of level-ground track. The Donner Pass summit was ninety miles from Sacramento and almost seven thousand feet higher.

The Golden Spike

Judah's survey was completed in August 1861, and by September he had finished the detailed supporting maps, drawings, and figures needed to gain congressional support for the Central Pacific route. In October he boarded a steamboat in San Francisco, bound, via a Panama rail connection, for Washington, D.C., to present his case to influential congressmen. He was apparently very persuasive, for the following May, the House of Representatives passed a bill authorizing the long-sought transcontinental railroad by a vote of 79 to 49. In June it sailed through the Senate with a 35 to 5 vote. On July 1, 1862, President Lincoln signed into law the Pacific Railroad Act, authorizing the Central Pacific to begin building eastward from Sacramento and providing that a new "Union Pacific Rail Road Company" be organized to build a connecting line westward from Nebraska. Judah telegraphed the good news to his Sacramento colleagues with the words "We have drawn the elephant, now let us see if we can harness him."

The elephant proved difficult to harness. The Pacific Railroad Act provided that both the Central Pacific and Union Pacific must first build forty miles of track before qualifying for federal construction loans. These ranged from sixteen thousand dollars per mile in flat country to forty-eight thousand dollars per mile in rugged mountain terrain. The payments, which rarely covered more than about half of the actual building costs, were to be delivered after the completion of each forty-mile increment, excluding the first, which was a double payment on completion of the initial eighty miles of track. These terms presented no serious problems for the Union Pacific, which was to build westward across flat Nebraska plains. For the Big Four it meant risking all they had, including their hard-won reputations, by personally borrowing several million dollars while their workers, under Crocker's tireless leadership, laboriously dug, scraped, hacked, and blasted a roadbed through one of North America's most forbidding mountain ranges.

Almost miraculously, forty-one months later, in July 1868, the first Central Pacific work train descended the eastern slope of the Sierra Nevada to enter the flat Nevada desert and begin the fabled ten-month race toward its junction with the Union Pacific. This took place at Promontory Point, Utah, on May 10, 1869. Against all odds, four former Sacramento shopkeepers had succeeded in creating one of the great engineering marvels of the age. Regrettably, engineer Theodore Judah, whose visionary talent had given birth to the project, did not live to see it completed. During an 1863 trip to the northeastern states, he contracted yellow fever while crossing Panama and died several weeks later in Washington, D.C.

Railroad Boomtown

As headquarters for all of the frenzied activity of building the Central Pacific, Sacramento had a second boom that rivaled that of the gold rush a decade earlier. Remote California then lacked any heavy industry, so the enormous quantity of "hardware" needed for the railroad—rails, spikes, hammers, picks, shovels, locomotives, passenger cars, flatcars, telegraph wires, these and countless other items made in northeastern factories—had to be loaded onto oceangoing ships for a twenty-thousand-mile journey around the tip of South America to the San Francisco docks. There they were laboriously reloaded onto smaller boats for travel across San Francisco Bay and up the Sacramento River to newly constructed wharves, warehouses, and railroad yards on the Sacramento waterfront. A constant stream of work trains arrived to pick up these items, as well as food and other locally produced supplies, for transport to the eastward-pushing railhead. In addition, all of the railroad's thousands of workers, many of them Chinese laborers recruited in San Francisco or directly from China, passed through the city en route to and from their railhead jobs.

During the frantic effort to build the Central Pacific, the Big Four had often considered returning to less stressful lives as Sacramento merchants and civic leaders. Once success was assured, however, they decided that their work was only half complete. Having brought their elephant across trackless deserts and forbidding mountains to bountiful California, they realized that only here could it be harnessed to become truly useful. Soon they were applying their considerable talents to buying and expanding several short-line railroads that had recently sprouted around San Francisco Bay. Among these was the Southern Pacific, which was to become the flagship of the Big Four's new holdings. By 1873 its lines reached from Sacramento to San Francisco, where the Big Four moved their homes and the Central Pacific headquarters to begin a second career of railroad building. Remarkably, this was to culminate in another transcontinental line, this one stretching across the long-discussed Southern Route to connect Los Angeles with New Orleans (see page 65).

Modern Sacramento

The gold rush and Central Pacific Railroad were hard acts to follow. As new rail lines crisscrossed the state in the following decades, the venerable transportation hub of Sacramento settled into a more sedate role as state capital and marketing center for the irrigated crops of the richly fertile Central Valley, a tradition begun by John Sutter himself (see also "Fresno," page 41). As in other western cities, this complacency was broken by the demands of World War II, which brought new airfields and light industry to the city. The latter, particularly electronics, has expanded in recent decades to make the city the heart of a fast-growing metropolitan area.

In spite of this recent growth, Sacramento still has some of the feel of a small-town state capital. It has also retained a remarkably significant fraction of its architectural past. Included is Sutter's original 1840s headquarters building, now surrounded by reconstructions of some of its outbuildings, in **Sutter's Fort State Historic Park** (2701 L Street, 916-445-4422). Equally significant are many waterfront commercial buildings from the gold rush era that have miraculously survived fires and floods and are now preserved as **Old Sacramento,** bounded by I and L Streets, Interstate 5, and the Sacramento River (916-442-7644). Today, these house mostly tourist-oriented shops and restaurants. The district also includes re-creations of the original **Huntington and Hopkins Hardware Store** as well as of the 1875 **Central Pacific Passenger Station and Freight Depot.** Appropriately nearby is the enormous **California Railroad Museum** (111 I Street, 916-552-5252, extension 7245), which features historic Big Four locomotives and railroad cars. The 1860s **State Capitol** (Tenth Street between L and N Streets, 916-324-0333) was modeled after its federal counterpart in Washington, D.C. Much modified over the years, it was restored to its original Victorian splendor in 1982.

Unfortunately, later expansions of the central city's

commercial and government centers have consumed much of its Victorian residential architecture, but many scattered dwellings still survive, two of them preserved as important museum houses. Farther east are some instructive Eclectic-era neighborhoods.

Stanford Mansion, 1857 and 1871

Eighth and N Streets; 916-324-0575; Seth Babson, Sacramento, architect.

This is apparently the only surviving dwelling of any of the Big Four railroad builders (see page 139), three of whom built opulent San Francisco mansions in the late 1870s that were destroyed in the 1906 earthquake and fire. This house began as a row house, which in 1857 was expanded to a refined, center-hall Italianate structure for Shelton C. Fogus, a respected Sacramento merchant and politician. Designed by local architect Seth Babson, it was handsomely detailed, with elegant hooded windows, plaster quoins, and an exterior covered with plaster scored to look like stone. Five bays wide and two bays deep, the house also included a rear service wing. Downstairs, a large parlor occupied the west side of the central hall with a library and dining room on the east; four bedrooms were upstairs. A matching stable occupied the rear of the property.

Leland Stanford and his wife, Jane, bought this fine dwelling from Fogus for eight thousand dollars in July 1861, only a month after the Big Four had incorporated the Central Pacific Railroad. That as-yet-embryonic project, and even Stanford's prosperous grocery business, probably had less to do with the new purchase, however, than did his principal hobby, which was politics. Trained as a lawyer in his native Albany, New York, the gregarious and energetic gold rush grocer had quickly become a leader of Sacramento's small group of "Republicans," the new antislavery party that had begun to take shape in the 1850s. In 1860, with Abraham Lincoln the Republican Party's nominee for president, Stanford reluctantly agreed to become its nominee for governor of California, even though he faced certain defeat in the then-mostly-Democratic state.

Public sentiment in California changed dramatically with the outbreak of the Civil War in April 1861. California's governors were then elected for two-year terms, and there was now a ground swell of support for Lincoln's previously defeated protégé Leland Stanford. It was probably the realization that he would soon be California's governor that led Stanford to purchase his fine new home. As expected, he was elected. On the night of his inauguration in January 1862, Sacramento was struck by an enormous flood as its rivers rose to twenty-three feet above their normal low-water level.

The Stanfords had to travel from their partially flooded new home to the nearby festivities in a rowboat.

The house required extensive repairs after the water receded, and along with these, Stanford added a small, two-room office on the east side of the house, which became his Executive Office. Stanford served as governor for only one two-year term, for by 1864 his duties as president of the Central Pacific Railroad required constant attention and frequent travel. For the next four years the Stanfords vacated their large home to permit its use as Executive Mansion by his Republican successor, Governor Frederick Low.

When the Stanfords moved back into their home in 1867, Jane was pregnant for the first time after seventeen years of marriage. The couple's only child, Leland Stanford Jr., was born in the upstairs northeast bedroom in May 1868. It was a joyous event, to be followed by another almost exactly one year later, when Stanford traveled to Promontory Point, Utah, to drive the famous golden spike celebrating the completion of the first transcontinental railroad (see page 141). Now it took only four days to complete a journey that previously required nearly four months of laborious wagon travel.

By 1871 the Stanfords needed a larger home. They now had a young son, many extended family members who spent time with them, and a tremendous amount of entertaining to do on behalf of the Central Pacific. Rather than moving, they decided on a major expansion of their current house—one that contemporary newspaper accounts indicate took a remarkably short four months to complete.

A creative approach to the expansion left the original Italianate house mostly intact as part of the new structure. This was accomplished by jacking it up a full story and then adding a new ground floor beneath. Next, a fourth story was gained by adding a Second Empire mansard roof above the original Italianate house. Finally, a broad, new four-story wing and a rear-service wing were added at the rear to create a cross-plan house. The entire ground floor of the new wing was devoted to entertainment and featured a billiard room and a heroic twenty-by-seventy-three-foot ballroom. The downstairs rooms of the original house were now elevated as the front of a piano nobile floor with a grand exterior front stair leading up to it. All of these four rooms retained their original functions except the dining room, which became a library opening into a huge, twenty-by-fifty-one-foot dining room housed in the new rear wing. The third floor maintained three of the original bedrooms, while the fourth was split into two smaller rooms. Additional bedrooms and their associated closet, bath, sewing, and other small rooms were in the new rear wing. The new fourth floor, con-

Stanford Mansion

cealed within the mansard roof, held additional guest bedrooms as well as storage. A new three-story service wing with kitchens, laundries, and servants' rooms was added behind the main structure.

It is not surprising that the finished exterior of the main house looks as if it could have originally been built as a Second Empire design, for these typically look very much like Italianate houses from the roof cornice down. Matching the elaborate window hoods and scored plaster of the original house and adding a slightly heavier cornice to complement the mansard roof made possible a pleasingly stylish Second Empire exterior.

The irony of this massive undertaking is that only two years after its completion, Stanford and his Central Pacific colleagues moved the railroad's headquarters, and their homes, to San Francisco (see page 213). The Stanfords retained their grand Sacramento home, but spent little time there. Tragedy struck the Stanford family in 1884, when their beloved and talented sixteen-year-old son died from typhoid fever. This sad event led the now-childless couple to devote much of their large fortune to endowing Stanford University in his memory (see page 199). The university admitted its first class in 1891. Returning to his love of politics, Stanford was elected to the United States Senate in 1885, won re-election in 1891, and was serving in this capacity when he died at his Palo Alto country estate in 1893. Now

widowed and childless, Jane Stanford gave their Sacramento house to the Catholic Church in 1900 as a home for "friendless" children. It went through many variations of related usage under the Church's ownership until 1978, when it was purchased by the state of California for eventual restoration. Amazingly, through all of the property's changes in use and architecture, its original 1857 stable still survives at the rear, making it one of the oldest such structures anywhere in the West.

A full restoration of the uniquely significant Stanford Mansion is expected to get under way in 1998, a surprisingly long twenty years after its acquisition by the state to whose beginnings Stanford contributed so much. Those years have, however, been spent in careful documentation of the complex architectural and social history of the grand dwelling, resulting in superb "archaeology tours," which show the public the many steps involved before beginning final restoration of such landmark buildings.

Governor's Mansion, 1877

Sixteenth and H Streets; 916-323-3047;
Nathaniel Goodell, architect.

This elegantly detailed Second Empire home has a less direct connection to Sacramento's Big Four than does the Stanford Mansion. The house was built for Albert Gallatin, a junior partner in the local hardware firm of Huntington and Hopkins. As the firm's principal

Governor's Mansion

partners became more deeply involved in their Central Pacific Railroad project (see page 139), Gallatin managed their joint hardware business so successfully that he was also able to invest in early California agricultural and hydroelectric-power developments. His new wealth also built this imposing four-story mansion.

In 1887 the wealthy and influential Gallatin moved to San Francisco and sold his home to Joseph Steffens, a local businessman. Just six years later, in 1903, the state of California bought the house for use as the Governor's Mansion. It admirably served in this role through twelve governorships. In 1967, shortly after the state's thirteenth governor, Ronald Reagan, moved in, first lady Nancy Reagan declared the historic house unsafe and persuaded her husband to rent a more modern dwelling in suburban Sacramento. This turned out to be a fortunate day for old-house enthusiasts, since the home was converted into a museum and preserved almost exactly as it was the day the Reagans moved out. The result is an exceptionally well documented home that still reflects the changing needs and tastes of the thirteen families that lived there from 1877 until 1967.

The policies of the state of California that led to this remarkable chronology are described in the Sacramento Historical Society's 1973 publication *Families in the Mansion:*

Each First Lady walks into the Mansion like a bride into an alien community, like a preacher's wife moving into a parsonage. In effect, she is told, "Here it is. Make the best of it." Anything that has happened before she came is often to be a closed book. Each First Lady is told: This is State property. Nothing can be sold, or given away, or thrown out. Items may be stored out of sight, or "inventoried off." She is handed a budget within which she must operate. Sometimes, budgets are skimpy. When they are generous, often an accumulation of essential repairs has become imperative.

Thus, like the home of a very thrifty but ever industrious and changing large family, the mansion evolved and changed over the years. And each and every stage was uncommonly well documented.

Gallatin's original house had very fine detailing. The main floor features fourteen-foot ceilings and doors with pressed-wood cornices reflecting different themes—game birds and fruits in the dining room; pharaohs and writers in the original library; and famous explorers in much of the rest of the house. Reflecting Gallatin's business, the hardware throughout the house—every doorknob and hinge—is of high-quality cast ornamental bronze. There are eight coal-burning fireplaces, most of Italian marble. Four of the original large overmantel mirrors remain in place, as do the original velvet draperies in the two parlors.

Upstairs, the house retains an original full bath as well as one remaining example of the hand-painted sinks that were in the closet of each bedroom. The ceilings throughout are of scratchwork, a process in which delicate designs are created by squeezing wet plaster through a cone onto a nonstick surface—similar to applying ornamental cake frosting. Once hardened, the designs are glued to the ceiling and then gold leafed; today, gold paint replaces the original leaf.

Much of the fun in touring this house is seeing what different first ladies chose to do in different rooms. The principal downstairs rooms retain much of the Victorian spirit, but beyond is a house that has continuously evolved and changed. Despite the fact that so many families have lived here, it all seems remarkably homey.

Decor from the 1910s is well represented by overstuffed purple velvet furniture and matching draperies selected by the Hiram Johnsons for the Music Room in 1911. The Johnsons also "modernized" the mansion by painting all of its detailed walnut and mahogany woodwork.

The 1920s legacy includes most of the first-floor light fixtures, which were purchased by the C. C. Youngs in 1927. These replaced the single drop cords with one lightbulb that had been installed in 1897 and that, in turn, had replaced 1877 gas fixtures.

The 1930s dining room table, chairs, and draperies were chosen by the James Rolphs.

Ironically, the 1940s provided the room that is most Victorian in feeling, the Formal Parlor. In that decade, the Earl Warrens filled it with fine reproduction Victorian furniture. They also added many of the valuable Oriental rugs seen throughout the house at a wartime bargain price of ten thousand dollars. Such rugs were not often used in Italianate houses, but are very typical of fine houses from the first half of the twentieth century and look completely at home here.

The 1950s are memorably represented by nineteen truly remarkable "pitcher" lamps with highly inventive shades that were purchased for five dollars each by the Goodwin Knights. Found throughout the upstairs, they are particularly at home in the guest room, where they complement the soft pink curtains and bed-spreads selected by Mrs. Knight and the 1911 French Provincial furniture purchased by the Hiram Johnsons. Equally impressive are the blue "Scandinavian" kitchen left by Mrs. Knight and the fact that, in trying to be thrifty by re-covering the back stairs with carpet from the third-floor ballroom, she uncovered an intricate parquet floor and restored it.

In the 1960s, comfortable "family den" furniture was placed in the Victorian surroundings of the Second Parlor by the Edmund G. "Pat" Browns. This is joined by a typical 1950s wood-cabinet television set and window air conditioner, both purchased by the Goodwin Knights and still operational.

Most of the upstairs decor dates from the 1950s and 1960s and provides great examples of how "period," rather than "contemporary," family bedrooms looked during those decades. These will shock visitors who grew up in those years and haven't yet realized that their memories are becoming historic!

And the many kids who lived in the mansion left their own touches. Most practical are the enclosed porch and the small front addition added so children could sleep near their parents. Most whimsical are the jazzy painted "toenails" on the Victorian footed tub. Most daring are the tales of multiple families of children that slid down the handsome banister that curves downward for three floors. And most stereotypically California is the privately funded pool added in 1959 for the Pat Browns, who had just moved into the mansion with their fourteen-year-old daughter, the very same young lady who was immortalized by painting the bathtub's toenails!

F Street Route (Old City), 1850s–1915

John Sutter Jr.'s original 1849 plat of Sacramento, now called the Old City, runs from C Street to Broadway and from the Sacramento River to Alhambra Boulevard. Residential development of this large area proceeded gradually eastward in a roughly chronological sequence from the waterfront commercial district. It was to take half a century before the easternmost streets, around Sutter's original fort, began to fill with houses.

Scattered early houses and buildings occur throughout the Old City plat, where the city now recognizes twenty historic districts. Almost every street outside of the downtown core has its share of historic dwellings, and exploring for these can be great fun. An instructive overview can be had by driving eastward along F Street. Beginning at Eighth Street, this passes through five small historic districts—Alkali Flat, Twelfth Street commercial, Washington, Washington School, and Boulevard Park. Be sure to look down the cross streets

as you go. Although we discuss only Victorian examples, younger in-fill houses from the early twentieth century occur throughout these districts.

Alkali Flat, which begins at Seventh Street and ends just past Eleventh Street, is the city's oldest surviving residential district. Named for a lime deposit originally found here, it began as home to many of the city's business elite, but later expansion of the Central Pacific rail yards to the north changed it into a working-class neighborhood. The Twelfth Street commercial district crosses F at Twelfth. Twelfth Street has long been an important commercial and transportation corridor for the city and was a main route to the goldfields of the north.

Alkali Flat: 813 to 833 F Street (all private), ca. 1890. This pleasant row of raised Queen Anne cottages has simple spindlework detailing. In Sacramento this type of raised cottage was built from 1850 until the 1910s and was clothed in a variety of different styles over this long period. These are sometimes called Delta-type houses in Sacramento because their raised foundations helped to minimize damage in the city's frequent floods. Such houses continued to be built even after flood-control measures had much reduced the flood threat. Similar raised houses are found in flood-prone coastal areas throughout the country. Raised cottages built adjacent to inland river deltas are more unusual, since river towns were typically placed on high ground above expected flood levels.

Alkali Flat: 1024 F Street (private), Boehme House, 1869. This is a small but carefully detailed Italianate cottage. Note the segmental arches over the windows and door, the heavy scrolled brackets, and the delicate columns supporting the porch.

Alkali Flat: 1029 F Street (private), Johnson House, ca. 1854. Possibly the oldest surviving house in Sacramento, this front-gabled Greek Revival design is built of brick and was once owned by early California governor Peter Burnett and later by yet-another governor, J. Neely Johnson. The house originally had extensive gardens, which are now part of the adjacent park.

The **Washington District** begins just past Twelfth Street and extends almost to Sixteenth Street, where the

F Street Route through Old City

Washington School neighborhood starts and extends to just past Nineteenth Street. These two districts are quite similar to each other, with the main difference being the dominant school in the latter. Both are filled with the raised cottages that are so common in Sacramento; in these districts most date from about 1880 to 1900 and are typically Queen Anne or Folk Victorian in style.

Washington District: 1323 F Street (private). This simple front-gabled folk house is raised for flood protection. Just a tad narrower, and it would be a true shotgun.

Washington District: 1330 F Street (private), ca. 1905. Here the raised cottage is built with a front-facing gambrel roof. This house has shingled wall cladding, a solid-shingled porch balustrade, and triple columns for porch supports—all stylistic details that can be found on both late gambrel-roofed Shingle-style houses and on early gambrel-roofed Colonial Revival designs. The rest of the details on the house are rather subdued. If it had a Palladian window in the front gambrel, one would likely immediately say it was Colonial Revival. If it instead had shingles curving into a window in the front gambrel (as at 1931 Twenty-first Street, in Poverty Ridge, see page 148), one would probably immediately call it Shingle. Without such additional indicators it could pass for either style.

F Street Route through Old City

Washington School: 1706 F Street (private), George House, 1898. Frank George was a Southern Pacific Railroad conductor who chose to follow the prevailing fashion of the day with this lovely spindlework Queen Anne raised cottage.

Some of the youngest houses in the Old City are found in **Boulevard Park,** which extends from Twentieth Street to Twenty-third Street. It is a large district, and almost all of its houses date from 1905 to 1915. An old racetrack had been located here and had long blocked residential development. When the track was closed and lots made available, the entire neighborhood promptly filled up—primarily with that era's American four-square house shape with different stylistic details and with contemporaneous Craftsman bungalows. Boulevard Park features two impressive tree-lined boulevards along Twenty-first Street and Twenty-second Street, and the scale of the houses is generally larger than that in the earlier parts of the city. The most impressive homes tended to be located on the corners.

Boulevard Park: 2100 F Street (private). This large house is an unusual rendition of the hipped-roof-with-full-width-porch subtype of the Colonial Revival style. Note the remarkable chimney that pierces through a hipped-roof dormer. The intriguing capitals on the one-story porch supports and on the two-story corner pilasters are Art Nouveau in inspiration. The cornice combines a row of small dentils with very elaborate brackets.

Boulevard Park: 608–610 Twenty-first Street (private). This duplex has wide overhanging eaves and a pair of matching entry porches with dramatic Moorish arches.

Boulevard Park: 2131 H Street (private), Hart House, 1907. This is a unique symmetrical translation of the Shingle style with a rusticated stone porch and a combination of fish-scale and flat wood shingles cladding the second story. A dramatic lion presides over the entry to the front porch. Above is a recessed second-story porch and above that a gabled dormer with a second recessed porch. This has a Palladian motif and the entry lion's mate perches above the arch. Note the handsome art glass on each side of the front door and in several smaller shaped windows.

Boulevard Park: 627 Twenty-second Street (private). This American four-square design has Craftsman detailing; note the open eaves with exposed rafter tails and the slanting porch supports.

Poverty Ridge

Poverty Ridge, ca. 1900–1915

This small neighborhood, built on one of the Old City's few hills, has broad lots and some upscale houses.

1931 Twenty-first Street (private), Mason House, 1900. This is a superb example of the small fraction of Shingle-style designs that have Queen Anne–type hipped roofs with lower cross gables. Note the open tower area supported by simple Tuscan columns, the shingles curving into recessed windows in both front and side gables, and the many windows with lovely stained glass. The detailing under the side-facing gable is fun, a small V-shaped bay window supported by a single bracket is beside a Romanesque-arched recessed balcony (note the way the shingle pattern subtly changes above it). On the front facade don't miss the unusual exotic window with exaggerated keystones extending in all four directions.

2131 T Street (private), ca. 1900. This handsome Free Classic Queen Anne design features floral garlands around the cornice and a line of dentils used as a belt course above the first-floor windows.

East Sacramento, ca. 1915–1950

Most of Sacramento's Old City street grid had been built by 1915, and subsequent developments extended the grid beyond Alhambra Street, where much of the city's Eclectic-era housing is located. As in the Old City, grids with Eclectic-era houses are in rough chronological order—blocks with Craftsman bungalows, various styles of American four-squares, and early period styles lie closest to Alhambra, while by the time one reaches the vicinity of Forty-fourth Street, the earlier Craftsman and four-square homes are dying out and later period designs are found—Tudor, French Eclectic, Monterey, Colonial Revival (with many Dutch Colo-

nial), and others. Moving a few more streets eastward, Ranch houses from the 1950s begin to appear.

1301 Forty-fifth Street at M Street (private). This large and handsome French Eclectic house is clad in stone and has two important facades. On the M Street facade there is a Norman tower, prominent side entry, and large attached garage. The 45th Street facade is more formal and, with its dominant front-facing gable, looks almost Tudor. The through-the-cornice window on the far left gives you a clue that there might be some French influence lurking around the corner.

1341 Forty-fifth Street (private). This brick Tudor design underscores the playful mixing of styles used by some creative Eclectic-era architects. Note the very prominent Colonial Revival door right smack in the middle of the house's dominant front-facing gable. It sports a large broken triangular pediment just to make certain one doesn't miss its parentage.

1022 Forty-fourth Street (private). This small, two-story Italian Renaissance house has lots of fine detailing. Note the balconets supported with decorated brackets, the blind arches above the downstairs windows, the heavy brackets decorated with acanthus leaves along the cornice line, and the Palladian motif in front of the recessed entry. The design next door at 1040 Forty-fourth Street (private) is almost identical in shape, but the details have been simplified. There are no blind arches, no balconets, no modillions, no columns at the entry (although the shape of the entry is the same). It would be interesting to know if the house was built this way or if some original detailing has been removed.

1428 Thirty-ninth Street (private). This is an example of an early side-gambreled Colonial Revival design with heavy Craftsman influence. This roof shape, with a broad shed dormer, is the most common Dutch Colonial Revival form. The neatly rolled edges of the gambrel roof are very unusual. Craftsman features include the robust columns of the broad porch, the horizontal geometric-patterned stained-glass windows to each side of the front door, and the triangular braces under the window boxes.

East Sacramento

SAN DIEGO

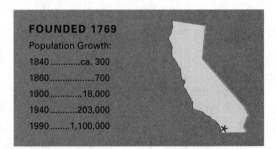

FOUNDED 1769

Population Growth:

1840	ca. 300
1860	700
1900	18,000
1940	203,000
1990	1,100,000

San Diego was the site of the first in the long chain of missions established in Alta California in the late 1700s to strengthen Spain's claims to this northern frontier region (see page xi). Here, too, was located one of the four Spanish presidios (forts) built to protect California's principal seaports from Russian and English naval intrusions; the others were at Santa Barbara, Monterey, and San Francisco, which was the most northerly of the early mission sites.

Hispanic San Diego

The presidio and original mission were located on a commanding hilltop site beside the San Diego River that looked out over sandy marshes and beaches to the ocean about two miles to the west. Five years after the mission's founding, it was moved six miles farther inland up the San Diego River, where the land was more suited to farming, and the Indian converts less accessible to the attentions of nearby soldiers. The presidio remained on its original hilltop site to become the center of a small settlement of farmers and military families.

The modest village of San Diego became more lively after Mexican independence in 1821. Now, for the first time, Yankee sailing ships were welcomed in California's ports to trade locally produced cowhides and tallow for hardware, cloth, and other goods produced by New England factories. It was in this era that the center of settlement moved from the hilltop to a more convenient riverside location on the adjacent flatland; this is today's Old Town.

Railroad Era Resort and Naval Center

After the American takeover of California in 1848, San Diego remained a remote small town until its first railroad arrived in 1885. Beginning in the 1850s, Anglo land promoters attempted to move the town from its original riverside site to a more scenic, beachfront "New Town" overlooking San Diego Bay. This met with

only modest success until the early 1880s, when, in anticipation of the railroad's arrival, New Town, site of the present downtown, experienced a dramatic real estate boom that emphasized its seaside location and mild climate. To attract visitors and potential lot buyers, a posh resort, centered around a grand hotel, was developed on the sandy Coronado Peninsula just across the bay from New Town. Still in operation today, the lavish **Hotel del Coronado** (1500 Orange Avenue in the town of Coronado, reached via the California Highway 75 bridge, south of downtown) is one of the rare survivors of many such grand hostelries favored by affluent Victorians. By 1890 San Diego was both a popular resort and the trade center for a prosperous agricultural hinterland specializing in groves of oranges, lemons, apples, pears, figs, and olives.

Following the Spanish-American War of 1898–1899, President Theodore Roosevelt began a large-scale expansion of the nation's naval forces and coastal defenses. San Diego, with its large, sheltered harbor, was a principal beneficiary of these efforts. By the 1920s it was the center of operations for much of the U.S. Navy's Pacific Fleet. Some indication of the scale of these facilities can be seen in the city's mostly-military-based population growth, which surged from 18,000 in 1900 to over 40,000 in 1910 and to 148,000 by 1930. The Second World War and Korean War brought another round of military expansions as the city's 203,000 inhabitants of 1940 swelled to 334,000 in 1950 and 573,000 by 1960.

Modern San Diego

By 1990 San Diego was the nation's sixth-largest city, but, unlike most Sunbelt boom towns, its older central city still retains some of the pleasant scale and density of a smaller metropolis. Traces of the small prerailroad town survive in Old Town, as do important Victorian and early-Eclectic-era museum houses and a charmingly diverse and intact Eclectic-era neighborhood.

Old Town, ca. 1821–1872

San Diego's plaza was established in the early 1820s as the town center for a growing agricultural community primarily populated by soldiers retired from the presidio. As was typical of Hispanic plazas, many houses were built around the plaza's perimeter. By the 1830s the small town had, according to Richard Henry Dana

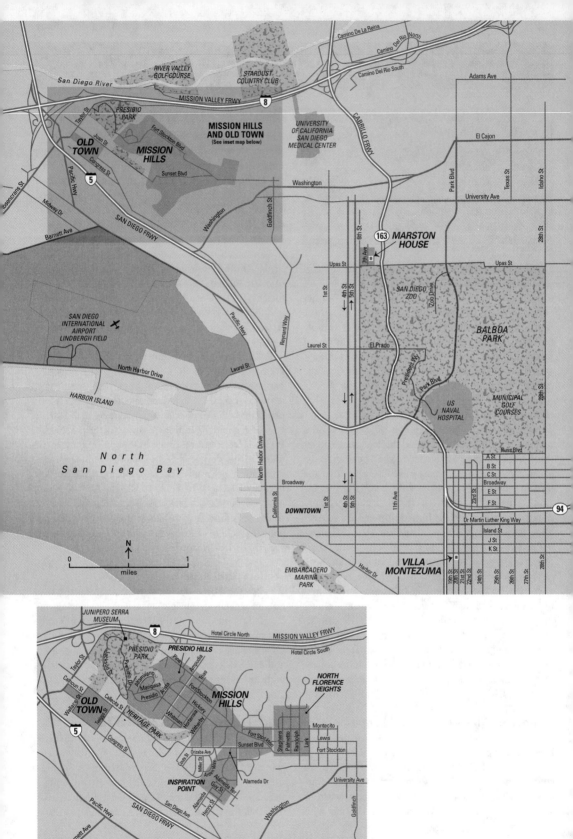

Jr.'s *Two Years before the Mast*, "about forty dark brown looking huts . . . and three or four larger ones, white-washed, which belonged to the *gente de razón* [upper class]." A combination of events led to population loss and deterioration of the original town around the plaza. San Diego was bypassed by the Butterfield stage-coach route in 1857; drought and problems with their land grants impoverished the formerly wealthy owners of ranches; and a fire swept the area in 1872, destroying many buildings. Finally, with the arrival of the first rail-road in the 1880s, the town's commercial core shifted three miles southward to its present Bay-side location. In 1968 the Old Town San Diego State Historical Park was established. The first priority was saving the remaining adobes.

Old Town: La Casa de Estudillo historic view

Today, several houses have been restored and are open to the public. The largest and most well known structure is **La Casa de Estudillo** (1829–1850s), a house museum located on the Mason Street side of the plaza. The house has been restored at least twice, and it has been furnished by the National Society of Colonial Dames, perhaps a bit too romantically. Casa de Estudillo has thirteen rooms that wrap around a full U-shaped courtyard, completely surrounded with a portal. It has features (some tiled areas and the garden courtyard) that would not have been present during its Spanish Colonial days. Away from the plaza, toward Congress Street, is the small **Machado-Stewart Adobe** (1830s), furnished as a more modest home. **La Casa de Machado y Silva** (1830–1843), on the San Diego Avenue side of the plaza, is interpreted as an 1850s restaurant run by a family in their house. The **Robinson-Rose Building** (1853), built to serve as both a residence and an at-home attorney's office and today housing the **Park Visitor Center** (4002 Wallace Street; 619-220-5422), is a good place to begin a tour and to obtain a guide that explains a bit more about which houses

Old Town: La Casa de Estudillo

Old Town: Whaley House

in the park are original and which are reconstructions. (Even the original houses have needed extensive restoration.)

Part of Old Town but not the state historic park is the **Whaley House** (1857), a simple brick Greek Revival town home of a type rarely seen in the West. The home's builder, early San Diego merchant Thomas Whaley (1823–1890), made the bricks for the house from river sand and clay in a new brickyard he constructed just three hundred yards away. The side wing of the house has seen many uses over the years. One was as the county courtroom in 1869 to 1870, and today it is furnished as such, although not with the courtroom furnishings originally used. Furnishings in the house are donated. Across Juan Street from Old Town is **Heritage Park,** a collection of Victorian homes and San Diego's first synagogue, which date from 1887 to 1896. These were all rescued from demolition by being moved here, and now house a variety of commercial activities, including a bed-and-breakfast. The **Sherman-Gilbert House** (1887) is an outstanding Stick-style house with a dramatic tower. It was designed by Comstock and Trotsche, the same architects who worked with Jesse Shepard on Villa Montezuma.

Villa Montezuma, 1887

1925 K Street; 619-239-2211;
Comstock and Trotsche, San Diego, architects.
"There is something so very peculiar, something so very striking, about even the exterior of the building that the passerby cannot but stop and admire its unostentatious eccentricity. . . . Enter the structure and even the air seems laden with the richness and elegance that is on every hand." So wrote the 1887 *San Diego Union* in its long front-page description of Villa Montezuma's Queen Anne styling. It is as apt today as in 1887—except that the word "unostentatious" applied to a home with two towers, one turret, and copious exterior detailing can only be explained by Villa Montezuma's lack of the showy wraparound porch, which is typical of the Queen Anne style.

Imaginatively designed by talented musician, writer, and spiritualist Jesse Shepard (in collaboration with architects Comstock and Trotsche), the house still has almost all of its original interior detailing. When built, the interiors were the epitome of the Queen Anne style, and today they are beautifully preserved and clearly interpreted. Villa Montezuma, a miraculous survivor of years of neglect and even an upstairs fire, today offers the best representation of an exuberant Queen Anne interior available in the West. (Although there are a number of other fine Queen Anne house museums, most of those with intact interiors have had a later stylish update in one or more major rooms—changes that today have their own historic significance.)

Shepard was an unusual person, mostly self-schooled in music and with a charm to match his talent. Through the early part of his life, he managed to float effortlessly from salon to salon, being supported by wealthy patrons. His ability to build Villa Montezuma

Villa Montezuma

was no exception. The High brothers, San Diego businessmen, met Jesse in Chicago and were so taken with his talent that they offered him the funds to build a house in San Diego. Their motive was not totally altruistic, as San Diego at the time had little to offer in the way of culture, and Shepard's home was to be a salon where he could entertain with his music, display fine art, and discuss literature. This in turn was expected to help attract cultured people to San Diego. It was a noble goal, but within two years San Diego was in a depression, and the peripatetic Shepard was again on the road. He soon sold the house—which then went through an amazing array of owners and hard times before being rescued by the San Diego Historical Society in 1970.

The entry hall introduces you to the kind of detail found throughout. It has walls paneled with redwood and walnut; a ceiling covered with Lincrusta Walton (an embossed, linoleum-like material), painted in silver tones, and accented with redwood strips; multiple pieces of art glass (used both as exterior windows and interior transoms); and a stairway of turned spindles, which create a diagonal pattern. A lovely "tile rug" of encaustic tile ornaments the wood floor. (Encaustic tiles, which became wildly popular in England after Prince Albert used them in a royal residence in 1843,

are tiles that gain their color and pattern not from a glaze but from color that suffuses the clays used to manufacture the tiles. This makes them doubly ideal for use on floors: the pattern does not wear away, and they are not slippery from a glaze.)

Throughout the house the same high level of detailing is found. Villa Montezuma has extraordinary art glass, all made by John Mallon of San Francisco and used lavishly and in varied ways throughout the house. Most of the designs feature the artistic, musical, and literary themes that appealed to Shepard. All of the fireplaces are original, with their 1887 tiles and overmantels intact. Where the original elaborate Lincrusta Walton and wood surfaces end, the original wallpapers have been reproduced.

The house is truly, in the words of longtime curator Lucinda Eddy, "a monument to the ornate and exotic tastes of the late nineteenth century." Every room offers its own unique delight. The Pink Room, Red Room, Music Room, dining room, Gold Room, Blue Room, and drawing room were each individually designed by Shepard to reflect his ideals and those of the late Victorian age.

Shepard's charm and music were eventually not enough to support him, and he died in poverty in Los Angeles, but with the same flair with which he had lived. After striking the final chord of a benefit performance in 1927, he did not move and stayed in the same pose for so long that his companion finally came up to the stage and discovered that Jesse was dead. Although he died without funds, Jesse Shepard left us all a rich legacy in his lovingly designed Villa Montezuma.

Marston House, 1905

3525 Seventh Avenue; 619-298-3142; William Hebbard and Irving Gill, San Diego, architects.

George White Marston (1850–1946) bestowed almost seventy-five years of his foresight, intelligence, and aptitude upon San Diego, the city he loved. In the privacy of his home, Marston was renowned for spontaneous song, practical jokes, and performances (such as a 1932 Christmas Eve rendition of the *Dance of Salome*—in full costume at the age of eighty-two); in public he presented a more dignified and understated persona. It must have been an effective one, for Marston left behind a remarkable string of accomplishments. One of his earliest projects was saving San Diego's large central urban park, **Balboa Park,** from developers. Later Marston was a key figure in organizing the 1915–1916 Panama-California Exposition, which gave Balboa Park its rich legacy of Spanish Colonial Revival exposition buildings. Marston spent $400,000 to privately develop the forty-acre **Presidio Park** and build the

Marston House

Junípero Serra Museum (later he donated the entire project to San Diego). The museum, in turn, served as home to the San Diego Historical Society, which Marston founded. He also financed and led the State-County Parks and Beaches Association, a group that succeeded in setting aside 500,000 acres of open space for parkland. In addition to his belief in the power of parks, Marston was interested in planning, and he sponsored two master plans for the city of San Diego, one in 1907 and another in 1926, both executed by John Nolen.

When Marston arrived in San Diego in 1870, he had almost nothing. He had accompanied his ailing father to San Diego's salubrious climate and immediately began working—first as a hotel clerk, then as a book-keeper, and finally in a general store. By mid-1893 he owned part of the store, and by 1900 he was the owner of the Marston Store, a department store with one hundred employees and a large, new four-story building with an elevator. On the side he invested in real estate (see page 156) and began his enormously long and productive civic life.

In 1878 he married Anna Lee Gunn (1853–1940), and they proceeded to have five children. As was typical of the times, Anna raised the children, took care of the home, handled the details of George's numerous house and dinner guests, worked with her church and various ladies' clubs, and enjoyed gardening and needlepoint

when time allowed. She provided the complex framework that allowed Marston to go on lengthy buying trips, run an extremely successful store, and still have time for civic life. By 1905 the couple decided to build a new home suitable for their central place in the community.

For the architect they chose the top San Diego firm of Hebbard and Gill, and plans began for what initially was to be an English Tudor–style home. But at some point, the firm's younger partner, Irving J. Gill (1870–1936), decided to do all of the interior detail and drawings himself; he further oversaw the construction of Marston House. And even more important, after the house had already been begun, Gill visited Chicago and saw the avant-garde Prairie houses that Frank Lloyd Wright and others were building there. (Gill had apprenticed briefly under Louis Sullivan and Wright in the early 1890s but moved to San Diego for his health.) His visit to Chicago instilled in him a renewed interest in modernism.

Gill was to go on to design some of the most avant-garde houses of the early modern movement. In partnership with Frank Mead, he designed the 1907 Russell Allen House, in Bonita, California, which Gill's biographer Bruce Kamerling believed "may be the first intentionally antiornament structure ever built." (Adolph Loos's 1910–1911 Steiner House in Vienna usually claims this accolade.) Henry Russell Hitchcock and even Frank Lloyd Wright (who was not given to praising other architects) believed he was one of the seminal modernist architects.

Gill's first step was to change some of the Marston House details. When he returned to San Diego, he removed the half-timbering (which had been planned to cover the second story) and simplified other details. The interiors he designed are beautiful renditions of the then-popular Arts and Crafts movement. Gill's elegant interiors (combined with a lack of original Marston furnishings and the fact that Marston's store was San Diego's sole distributor of Stickley furniture) led the San Diego Historical Society to furnish the interior with fine pieces of Arts and Crafts furniture. It is one of five museum houses in the West to feature such interior furnishings (the others are Corbett House, Tucson, see page 22; Sun House, Ukiah, California, see page 276); Gamble House, Pasadena, see page 99; and the Riordan Mansion, Flagstaff, see page 2. The collection here is excellent and includes furniture from the workshops of both Gustav Stickley and Elbert Hubbard, as well as a piece designed by San Diego architect Richard Requa. "Fumed" pieces (these look like they have been smoked by a fire, but in actuality their dark finish results from a chemical reaction to ammonia fumes) are included, along with many decorative arts objects. A child's bedroom is just beginning to be furnished, and this, along with the rest of the collection, is expected to continue to grow through donations.

The first thing one notices about this 8,500-square-foot home is that it has no prominent "front" entrance. The entrance is through an understated porch that extends to become the porte cochere. Inside the house, warm redwood tones predominate. At the far end of the long entrance and stair hall is a Gill trademark, a large glass door opening out to a terrace beyond. He used this device in many of his designs to ensure that one saw light upon entering; he did not want his clients or their guests to feel they were entering a dark house. Gill's stair design is an elegantly simplified interpretation of Arts and Crafts that wraps around a hall seat. It has solid rectangular balusters; a flat handrail; closed stringer with flat string board (which is a technical way of saying that you can't see the sides of the stair treads because they are hidden behind a flat piece of wood that runs diagonally up the stairs); and, rather than the usual newel post, there is a simple squared pier that stretches from floor to ceiling. Doors and windows are surrounded by extra-wide square-edge trim (which means wide, flat boards with no moldings attached). All are beautifully proportioned and finished.

Upstairs, Gill raised the floors of the closets and bathrooms four inches above the bedroom floor level in order to help keep dust out of those rooms. He hated places where dust and dirt could be entrapped. Two other examples of how he tackled this problem are found in the one original bathroom on the second floor. It still has the magnelite-encased bathtub and coved floor tiles that Gill used in many of his houses; he felt these were easier to clean and therefore healthier.

The house sits on four acres of grounds. On three sides it is surrounded by a garden in the English Romantic landscape tradition—a sloping lawn with layered shrubs delineating the edges, and trees providing accents for both the shrub border and the house itself. In the back, there is a formal walled garden completed between 1926 and 1928 in time for the Marstons' fiftieth wedding anniversary. It has a teahouse with decorative tiles, a wall fountain, and a pergola overlook, which features a view of informal native plantings on the steep hill that leads to a stream at the bottom of the canyon. Outbuildings include the carriage house (now used by the San Diego Parks Department) and the original incinerator.

This fine house and the gardens were given to the San Diego Historical Society in 1974 by Miss Mary G. Marston, the eldest daughter. She retained a life estate that lasted until she died in 1987 (just weeks before her 108th birthday). With her death the house was officially incorporated into Balboa Park, with gardeners maintaining the grounds and the San Diego Historical Society operating the house. The society has published an excellent booklet on the Marston House that includes a complete walking tour of Seventh Avenue and has well-researched articles on all aspects of the house. The Marston House bookstore specializes in books on the Arts and Crafts movement.

Nearby Houses

This group is important because, in conjunction with the Marston House, it shows Irving Gill moving rapidly toward his mature modern style.

3526 Seventh Avenue (private), Cossitt House, 1906; William Hebbard and Irving Gill, San Diego, architects. Here the house steps up from the street. In the front is a one-story inglenook with the chimney rising through a bank of windows on each side. The next step up is a living room with a high ceiling and clerestory windows. Behind this, the third step up in height is to the two-story house.

3534 Seventh Avenue (private), Barney House (George and Miriam), 1913; Frank Mead and Richard Requa, San Diego, architects. This house began as a small Pueblo Revival/Spanish-style home, but recent additions have added a second story and moved the entrance from the north to the south side of the house.

3536 Seventh Avenue (private), Elston House, 1908. When built, this house had dark wood shingles, which have since been painted over; and the white paint effectively disguises its brown-shingled First Bay Tradition (see page 170) beginnings. The prominent entry porch is the most noticeable part of a facade that, upon close inspection, is filled with subtle asymmetry. The house is Craftsman in style, which is typical of most later First Bay houses.

3560 Seventh Avenue (private), Teats Cottage, 1905; William Hebbard and Irving Gill, San Diego, architects. This house was built as part of a three-part plan, which included 3574 and 3578 (see the following two entries). It was modified by Gill in 1912 and his son in 1922, enclosing an original south-facing porch and extending the second story out over it. Yet, it still has the cubic look that was typical of most of Wright's smaller Prairie houses—the ones that spawned the hipped-roof, symmetrical, no-front-entry Prairie-style subtype discussed in *A Field Guide to American Houses.*

3574 Seventh Avenue (private), Lee House, 1905; William Hebbard and Irving Gill, San Diego, architects. This house, and its mates on each side (see the preceding and following entries), were the first of Hebbard and Gill's houses to reflect Irving Gill's trip to Chicago in 1905, where he had viewed Prairie-style homes. That influence is very obvious in these three homes. Note their low hipped roofs with broad overhanging eaves, the band of horizontal trim just under the base of the upper-story windows, and the rows of windows. Miss Alice Lee had been involved in real estate development in the East, and she desired (and likely was active in designing) the U-shaped plan, which linked her home with a smaller house to each side; all three houses shared the central garden and were connected by pergolas. This group of three houses may well be the earliest Prairie-style design in California.

3578 Seventh Avenue (private), Lee Cottage, 1905; William Hebbard and Irving Gill, San Diego, architects. Originally more cubic in shape (like 3560; see above), this house has had an addition on the right that added a second bay of windows. The upstairs porch, on the left, has also been enclosed. All of the work has been carefully matched to the original house, making it hard to tell the old from the new.

3575 Seventh Avenue (private), Arthur Marston House, 1909; Irving Gill, San Diego, architect. Designed for the Marstons' son and daughter-in-law, who apparently wished to have a brick house like his parents' next door. By 1909 Gill was actively engaged in designing concrete and stuccoed homes similar to those on the rest of the street. Apparently Gill sketched a number of stuccoed designs for the younger Marstons, but they elected to build this home, which combines warm brick tones and a round-arched entry with Gill's simplified details for the rest of the house.

Mission Hills, 1908–1930

This large neighborhood includes four primary early subdivisions: **Inspiration Point** (1887); **North Florence Heights** (1890); **Mission Hills** (1908, 1910, and 1911); and **Presidio Hills** (1923 and 1926). Although the late-nineteenth-century subdivision dates might indicate an earlier neighborhood, the area remained little more than peaceful hay fields until 1908, when the trolley first arrived, courtesy of Kate Sessions, an acclaimed San Diego horticulturist. San Diego was originally little more than a desert, and Kate Sessions

provided the early horticultural knowledge and leadership to turn it into the garden city it is today. She offered well-chosen plants at her nursery and also actively enhanced San Diego through the tree-planting programs she had undertaken for the city (in exchange, the city had offered her a rent-free nursery location).

In 1903 Sessions began to search for a new site for her nursery. Impending development and an expiring lease made the earlier location (on the edge of Balboa Park, close to the Marston House) no longer an option. After a long search, she settled on the Mission Hills area and proceeded to purchase or lease most of the as-yet-undeveloped North Florence Heights tract, as well as nearby pieces of land.

Sessions had watched her earlier location, with its verdant plantings, increase the property values around it. She had seen others reap the profits from their lands, which had been enhanced by her work. Although the prevailing theory is that she purchased land in Mission Hills far from the city in order to have a long-term nursery location safe from development, her next step makes another interpretation quite possible. In 1907 she coaxed John D. Spreckels, the owner of the local electric-streetcar company, to extend a streetcar line to the front door of her new nursery location. Then she spent hours with a friend driving a horse and carriage all over San Diego, gathering signatures on a petition requesting that the city approve the line. And in 1909, as requested, the streetcar line arrived at the corner of Lewis and Stephens. By 1913 it was extended to the corner of Fort Stockton and Trias; and along with the trolley, development came to Mission Hills.

If Sessions had wanted to protect her rural nursery site for the long term, this would have been a pretty naive move—since at the turn of the century new development almost inevitably grew up along well-placed streetcar lines. As Spreckels put it, "Transportation determines the flow of population." Since Sessions is reported to have been *anything* but dull, it seems likely that she may have had another goal in mind. In buying as much undeveloped land as possible for her nursery, and then attracting a streetcar line to her front door, she surely expected that this time around *she* would reap the rewards for the improved land values around her lush operation. The trolley made it easier for her to attract customers, and it greatly enhanced the ultimate value of all of her holdings. (Sessions did gradually sell off pieces of her land, using the proceeds to help support herself and her operation for many years.)

It can hardly be a coincidence that a group of investors that included George Marston, a longtime friend because of their mutual horticultural and park interests (see page 153), opened a new **Mission Hills**

subdivision right next door to her nursery in 1908, perfectly timed to the extension of the streetcar line. The **Mission Hills** subdivision added sections in 1910 and 1911. This large area (from which the entire neighborhood now derives its name) is today filled with a wonderful mixture of homes. The Craftsman style predominates, and with it are many Mission and early Spanish Eclectic houses (many in the flat-roofed subtype).

Sessions's **North Florence Heights** area developed a bit later, as she was running her nursery on the land. Today, it has a mixture of homes, including a number of Craftsman-style bungalows with a distinctive curved porch roofline—likely indicating that they were constructed by the same builder.

Some of the most intriguing Mission Hills homes are in **Inspiration Point,** first platted in 1887 as Johnston Heights by Sarah Johnston Miller. Her father, a sea captain, had owned the land and hoped to someday build on it. But it was to be his daughter who subdivided the tract and built the first home in Mission Hills for her family (in 1887, at 2036 Orizaba [private], and later remodeled into a Prairie-style home). Villa Orizaba stood alone in Johnston Heights until about 1910, when this area, which overlooks beautiful San Diego Bay, began to finally be developed, thanks to the nearby trolley line.

Marston had begun buying land around the old San Diego presidio in about 1903, the same year that Sessions had started to assemble her nursery location. His long-term goal was to create a park for the city in the location of the old presidio, but it was 1930 before the city accepted the gift of today's Presidio Park, which Marston lovingly assembled and even built the Junípero Serra Museum upon. In the meantime, Marston had prudently purchased the land overlooking his planned park and museum. In 1923 and 1926 he opened the **Presidio Hills** section of Mission Hills (it actually began as

Mission Hills

two subsections: Presidio Ridge and Presidio Hills). This part of Mission Hills, located just over the ridge from the rest of the neighborhood, is filled with late-1920s and 1930s Spanish Eclectic houses, which nicely complement the museum.

Mission Hills: 2658 Fort Stockton (private), ca. 1915. Mission style and Craftsman style are the two most common styles in the 1908 Mission Hills subdivision. This house, and its next-door neighbor (see the following entry), demonstrate these two styles on the midsized homes that make up this part of greater Mission Hills. Here the Mission style is expressed in the stuccoed walls, the tiled roof, and the porch supported with large squared piers with arches above. The wide overhanging eaves are open and have exposed roof rafters like the contemporaneous Craftsman style.

Mission Hills: 2652 Fort Stockton (private), ca. 1915. This front-gabled Craftsman-style home is clad with wood shingles; these are applied to form alternating wide and narrow horizontal bands. The porch railings, both upstairs and down, and the porch supports are made of stout squared wood pieces creatively combined to express the Craftsman aesthetic.

Mission Hills: 1965 Sunset Boulevard (private), ca. 1915. This is a hipped-roof Craftsman house with lots of triangular knee braces. Such braces rarely occur on hipped-roof houses; they ordinarily are used beneath the exposed roof beams found in Craftsman homes with gabled roofs. This builder has creatively added a "beam" under the exposed rafter tails and then used triangular knee braces to support this structurally superfluous element. This arrangement also ensures that there are lots of these distinctive braces.

Mission Hills: 1935 Sunset Boulevard (private), ca. 1915. This front-gabled Craftsman house is covered with wonderful details. Writers of the day sometimes referred to this kind of Craftsman house as being "of the California type." Houses so described typically included massive porch supports (and often chimneys) of smooth rounded pebbles such as are seen here. These characteristic rocks were readily available in the many arroyos of southern California and gave such houses a strong local feeling. Other elaborations include staggered application of the wood-shingle cladding; triangular wood pieces inserted above the sloping porch supports; a shed roof over the second-story window (with highly exposed rafter tails); window boxes; and an open structure in the porch gable.

North Florence Heights: 4121 to 4101 Randolph Street (all private), ca. 1920. Bungalows with this distinctive curve over the front entry are found through much of greater Mission Hills and likely are the product of one builder who adroitly varied the porch supports and other details to give some of his bungalows a Craftsman style and others, with arched porches, a strong Mission influence. This is a particularly nice grouping; one has an added second story.

North Florence Heights: 4150 Stephens Street (private), ca. 1920. Here is the same distinctive curved roofline seen in the 4100 block of Randolph Street (see the preceding entry), but with a full-width arched front porch, which its builder used to create its Mission-style look.

Inspiration Point: 1980 Alameda Terrace (private), ca. 1910. A fascinating "Early Eclectic What's It?" This one is particularly intriguing because it combines a Classical theme (portico design and balusters) with a strong early modern influence (heavy squared piers with exposed double beams above and a flat roof with the porch roof resting on top of it). The house is complemented by an unusual stuccoed fence with slivers of circles removed.

Inspiration Point: 2055 Sunset Boulevard (private), Miller House, 1921; Robert S. Raymond, architect. This large stuccoed Italian Renaissance home is set on a large lot enclosed by a stucco-and-iron fence. This house has the prominent dentiled cornice and roofline balustrade common to the flat-roofed subtype of this style. The house has smaller one-story wings on each side, but little other elaboration except for the centered Palladian window upstairs and simple door surround.

Inspiration Point: 2031 Sunset Boulevard (private), McKnight House, 1919; J. F. McKnight, architect. Another Italian Renaissance house, this one is in the simple-hipped-roof subtype. Note the round-arched entry with pilasters on each side, the low-pitched hipped roof, and the larger and more elaborate first-floor windows.

Inspiration Point: 2156 Guy Street (private), Gray House, 1928; William H. Wheeler, San Diego, architect. A large and ornate Spanish Eclectic house with Moorish influence in the front door and window above.

Inspiration Point: 4106 Alameda Drive (private), ca. 1915. This is just one of several intriguing flat-roofed (or almost-flat-roofed) homes in the Henry Street–Alameda Terrace–Alameda Drive–Alameda Place part of Inspiration Point. These are stuccoed, appear to be built of concrete or hollow tile, and represent an inventive interpretation of the Prairie style, probably by one local architect or builder.

Presidio Hills: 4395 Ampudia Street at Fort Stockton (private), ca. 1930. Glazed tiles (in geometric patterns) enliven the risers of the sidewalk steps. These, along with cast-iron balconies and window grilles and a cast-stone door surround, compose the main Spanish Eclectic elaborations bestowed on this midsized home.

Presidio Hills: 2441 to 2401 Presidio Drive (all private), ca. 1930. As you drive up from Presidio Park, this street presents an unusually picturesque and unified Spanish Eclectic streetscape.

SAN FRANCISCO BAY AREA

It was a happy accident of geography that the 1848 Sutter's Mill gold discovery was made in remote California's Sierra Nevada foothills only 120 miles east of San Francisco Bay, the U.S. Pacific coast's best natural harbor (see illustration below). While only about one-third of the ensuing flood of gold-seekers arrived by ship at the booming young port city of San Francisco (the rest came overland by various routes), virtually all of the miners' supplies and equipment, as well as much of their food, arrived via San Francisco's docks. From there these essentials were transferred to smaller boats that proceeded first northward, across the shallow open Bay waters, and then eastward, through a series of narrow salt-water straits and bays that bisected the coastal mountains. The boats then arrived at the mouths of two large rivers, the southward flowing Sacramento River and northward flowing San Joaquin River, which drain California's Central Valley. Both rivers were normally navigable by small boats for many miles upstream, which meant that cargoes could be unloaded at river ports located a short wagon-haul away from the vast Sierra Nevada goldfields. These were so rich that by 1850 San Francisco, the region's commercial nerve center, was the largest and wealthiest city of the West, a title it would retain until well into the twentieth century.

San Francisco's prosperity soon began to spread around the Bay. The south and southeast sides of the Bay were surrounded by large areas of flat grasslands. Formerly cattle ranches, these were quickly converted into high-value grain fields and truck farms to help feed the region's booming population. By 1900 the region's agriculture began changing to still-higher-value fruit orchards. Two of the region's principal trade centers were the small town of **Hayward,** in the southeast Bay Area, and the early Spanish town of **San Jose,** near the south end of the Bay.

San Francisco's largest satellite towns developed directly across the Bay on its eastern shore, where they were conveniently accessible by fast steam ferry boats. By 1880 **Oakland** was a city of thirty-five thousand inhabitants and a favored homesite for San Francisco commuters. It was also the western terminus for the first transcontinental railroad, and after 1900 it became increasingly industrial as factories moved from crowded San Francisco to new quarters in Oakland, and national companies opened West Coast branches there. The adjacent peninsular town of **Alameda** still retains much of its character as a turn-of-the-century San Francisco commuter suburb. Immediately north of Oakland, the hillsides of **Berkeley** centered around the original University of California, established there in 1868. After 1900 the town also became a popular homesite for San Francisco commuters. Northeast of Berkeley, the small town of **Martinez** was an early agricultural trade center and small-boat port on the narrow mountain-bound strait that led to the rivers of the Central Valley.

The low mountains that form the western edge of San Francisco Bay are broken into two peninsulas by the Golden Gate waterway. The southern peninsula is occupied by the city of San Francisco itself at its north end. The wooded hills and valleys south of the city, easily reached by an early railroad line, became favored

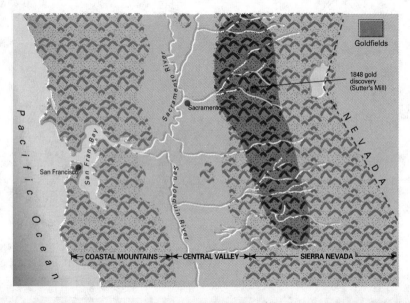

Goldfields

1848 gold
discovery
(Sutter's Mill)

Sacramento

San Francisco

Water routes
to the goldfields

◄— COASTAL MOUNTAINS —►◄— CENTRAL VALLEY —►◄— SIERRA NEVADA —►

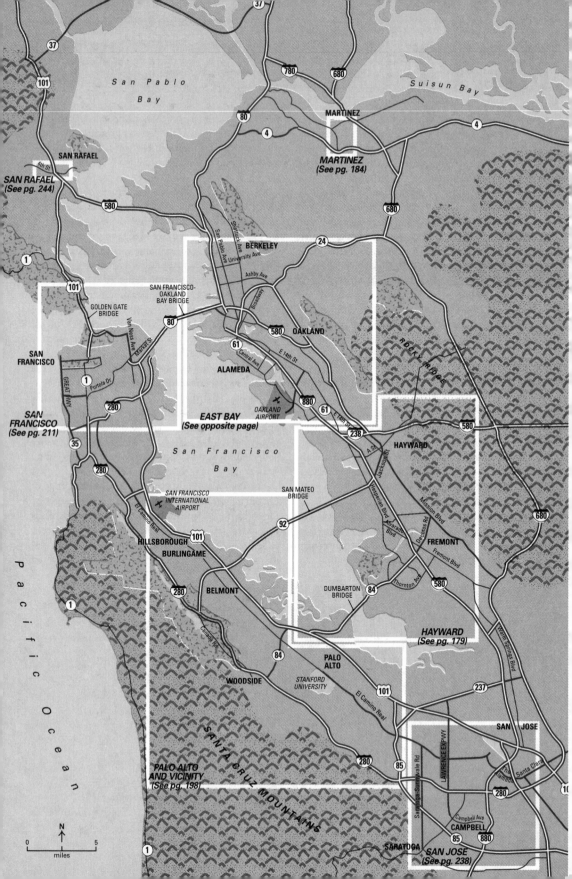

SAN RAFAEL
(See pg. 244)

MARTINEZ
(See pg. 184)

EAST BAY
(See opposite page)

SAN FRANCISCO
(See pg. 211)

HAYWARD
(See pg. 179)

PALO ALTO
AND VICINITY
(See pg. 198)

SAN JOSE
(See pg. 238)

San Pablo
Bay

Suisun Bay

MARTINEZ

BERKELEY

OAKLAND

ALAMEDA

SAN
FRANCISCO

GOLDEN GATE
BRIDGE

SAN FRANCISCO-
OAKLAND
BAY BRIDGE

San Francisco
Bay

SAN FRANCISCO
INTERNATIONAL
AIRPORT

OAKLAND
AIRPORT

ROCKRIDGE

HAYWARD

SAN MATEO
BRIDGE

HILLSBOROUGH

BURLINGAME

BELMONT

FREMONT

DUMBARTON
BRIDGE

WOODSIDE

PALO
ALTO

STANFORD
UNIVERSITY

SANTA CRUZ MOUNTAINS

Pacific Ocean

SAN JOSE

CAMPBELL

SARATOGA

N

0   5
miles

sites for the country estates of affluent San Franciscans. One of the largest, and most southerly, of these was the stock farm of railroad magnate Leland Stanford. In 1885 Stanford gave this nine-thousand-acre farm, and a huge cash endowment, to establish a Leland Stanford Jr. University in memory of his only child, who died in 1884 at age sixteen. Now served by the adjacent town of **Palo Alto,** named for Stanford's farm, the university has grown to become one of the nation's premier centers of higher education.

The peninsula north of the Golden Gate makes up Marin County, the most rugged and undeveloped corner of the Bay Area. Its steep hills were almost inaccessible prior to the automobile era and have since become a favorite site for back-to-nature living. **San Rafael** is the county seat and the region's principal commercial center.

The Bay Area Today

The summary above presents the relationship of some of the most important Bay Area towns to dominant San Francisco up until about 1940. The towns mentioned are those featured in the following pages (note that several of the towns also treat museum houses and estates in nearby smaller towns). In visiting these towns today it is important to remember that what were once scattered urban centers dotted around the Bay have now largely coalesced into one continuous metropolitan complex of large and small cities. In 1940 the Bay Area's combined population was 1.4 million, and its cities and towns were mostly linked by two-lane roadways and electric trolleys that traversed much open countryside. By 1990 the population had more than quadrupled to 6 million people served by a dense network of freeways and six cross-Bay bridges. Today the Bay Area is the nation's fourth-largest metropolitan complex, exceeded in population only by New York's 18 million, Los Angeles's 14 million, and Chicago's 8 million.

The Bay and Los Angeles areas (see page 49) have had many similarities in their post-1940 growth patterns but are fundamentally different in the modern roles played by their original urban cores. Early Los Angeles has all but disappeared with the explosive spread of its vast suburban satellites. In contrast, the city of San Francisco, isolated by water on three sides, much like New York's Manhattan, has remained the vibrant cultural and financial heart of the entire Bay Area.

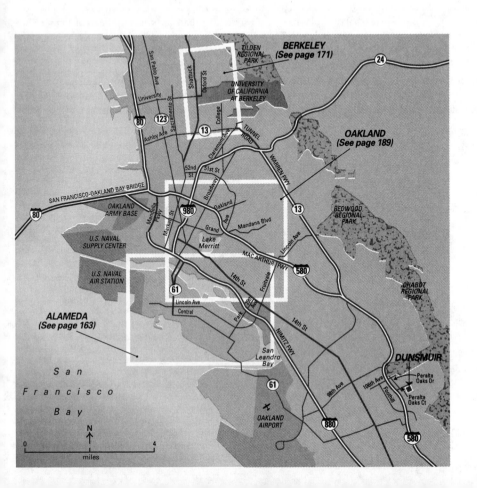

ALAMEDA

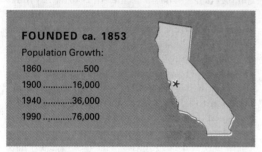

FOUNDED ca. 1853
Population Growth:
1860 500
1900 16,000
1940 36,000
1990 ...,........76,000

The island town of Alameda contains a fascinatingly intact collection of Victorian and Eclectic-era neighborhoods, where almost every block offers new delights for the house watcher. The site was originally a peninsula, about a mile wide and five miles long, separated from adjacent Oakland by the wide estuary of San Antonio Creek. At its eastern end, the peninsula was connected to the mainland along a one-mile strip at the inland termination of the estuary (see map below).

The Oakland side of the San Antonio Creek estuary was bounded by solid ground where wharves and warehouses were later constructed to make that city's Inner Harbor. Note in the map below that, in contrast, much of the Alameda side of the estuary was bounded by a wide expanse of tidal marshes. These not only made harbor construction difficult, but also created a formidable transportation barrier between early Alameda

and booming Oakland that, in 1869, the year after the map below was prepared, became the western terminus of the Central Pacific Railroad, the nation's first transcontinental rail line (see also page 139). This geographic isolation helps to explain the remarkable later contrast between industrial Oakland and tranquil Alameda, which has long been renowned as a City of Homes.

Early Commuter Suburb

The Alameda Peninsula's 1860s landowners, like many others around the Bay, hoped their property would become the oceanside terminus for the new transcontinental railroad. As the 1868 map below shows, three of the peninsula's owners had by then platted ambitious, and as yet largely unoccupied, town sites in anticipation of a coming boom. From west to east, the towns were Woodstock, Encinal, and Alameda. When nearby Oakland was chosen as the Central Pacific's terminus, these incipient towns were destined to boom more slowly. Rather than becoming the heart of a new industrial city, they became instead the nuclei for one of the West's first commuter suburbs, with the help of an early short-line railroad.

The most influential of the peninsula's early landholders was attorney and financier Alfred A. Cohen, who, along with many other properties, owned Fern-

1868 map of the Alameda Peninsula and adjacent Oakland

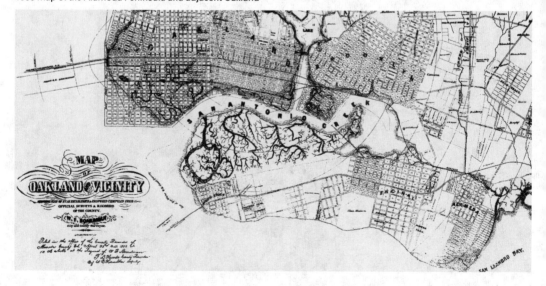

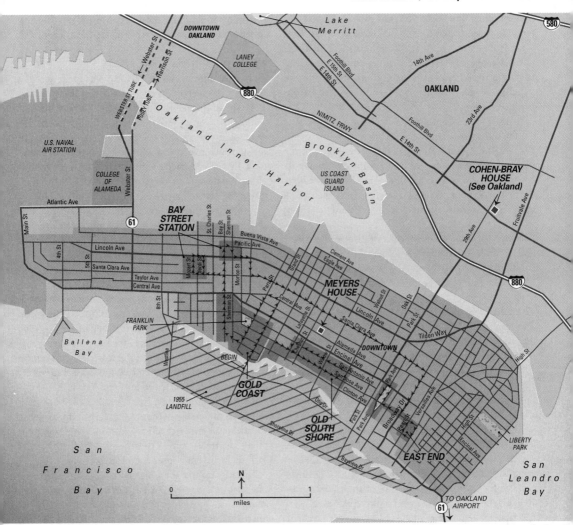

side, a large country estate near its northeastern corner (his son was the Alfred Cohen of Oakland's Cohen-Bray House; see page 192). In the early 1860s the elder Cohen began building a local railroad line linking his country estate, and other lands he owned at the eastern end of the peninsula, with his newly platted town of Woodstock at the western end. Completed in 1864, Cohen's Line, as it came to be called (its official name was the San Francisco and Alameda Railroad), picked up passengers at five stations spaced along what is now Lincoln Avenue. The trains delivered them to ferryboats bound for San Francisco via a long wharf that Cohen constructed across the shallow mudflats adjacent to Woodstock.

Coming before the invention of either cable cars or electric trolleys, Cohen's steam railroad, one of the first in California, gave the Alameda Peninsula the most im-

portant requirement for a successful bedroom community—a convenient means of commuting to work in a nearby urban center. The journey from Alameda to downtown San Francisco, by steam train and steam ferry, typically took less than an hour. Soon a trickle of commuters began buying lots and building homes on the peninsula. They were attracted by its level roads, rich alluvial soils, fine live oak trees, and sunny climate—all a welcome contrast to hilly, rocky, barren, and foggy San Francisco.

By 1870 Alameda's population had grown from a handful of prerailroad inhabitants to 1,600 residents, most of them commuters. A great many more were to arrive during the following decades as the town gained a reputation as a tranquil alternative to domestic life in hectic and booming San Francisco or Oakland. This trend was accelerated in 1878, when a second commuter railroad line was completed that connected to a ferry landing on its own, even longer, wharf built westward from the peninsula's tidal marshes. This line's narrow-gauge tracks extended along Encinal and Central Avenues, where ten local stations served the expanding neighborhoods on the southern half of the peninsula.

In 1872 the three original villages united into a single town, named Alameda, which was to enjoy many decades of slow but steady growth. By 1902, after thirty years of dredging operations to improve Oakland's Inner Harbor, a wide channel was finally cut through the peninsula's connection to the mainland, thus making Alameda a true "island city." By 1930 the relatively small island was completely filled by pleasant residential neighborhoods whose houses, of diverse ages, sizes, and styles, provided homes for thirty-five thousand inhabitants. This peaceful scene was soon to be changed by the demands of the Second World War.

The Island Grows Larger

Two large parts of modern Alameda Island, representing almost half of its area, were either unbuildable marshlands or covered by the waters of the Bay prior to 1937. Together these new areas, built up by dredging clay and sand from the surrounding Bay bottoms, were the sites of much of the town's population growth since 1940.

First and largest was a new naval air station at the island's northwestern end that, anticipating the coming conflict, was begun in 1937. When the war ended eight years later, the U.S. Navy had added about 1,250 new acres to the 2,000 occupied by all of the island's pre-1940 neighborhoods. The effect of this change has been described by geographer Imelda Merlin in her excellent 1977 book *Alameda, a Geographical History:*

> The Naval Air Station was commissioned on November 1, 1940, and the vast influx of people that followed . . . permanently altered the makeup of Alameda's population. To the predominantly property-owning population has been added a large number of transient families and many young sailors. It has markedly lowered the average age of Alameda residents. Many old-timers look back on the days "before Naval Air."

Not only the naval station but also wartime employment opportunities in nearby shipyards and other facilities added many new residents to Alameda. These filled an estimated 6,500 new housing units; by 1950 the town's prewar population had almost doubled to 64,400. Apartments originally built to help house the

wartime population explosion constitute the principal intrusion in the island's earlier historic character.

Modern Alameda

As in all communities adjacent to San Francisco Bay, Alameda has seen many proposals, in the decades since 1950, for additional landfill projects to relieve the burgeoning Bay Area's shortage of new building sites. Except for a few small projects, the city has generally resisted such expansion with one controversial exception. In 1955 Alameda voters narrowly approved the Utah Construction Company proposal to fill an additional 335 acres along the island's scenic south shore. As a result, the fine earlier neighborhoods along that shore—some of which formerly looked out over the Bay with a view of the San Francisco Peninsula in the distance—are now separated from the water by a huge new landfill covered by a shopping center, apartments, and houses.

In spite of such intrusions, and the usual losses from fires and demolition for newer buildings, Alameda still retains a remarkably high percentage of its pre-1940 houses. About 2,750, mostly in the Victorian styles, survive from the years between the town's incorporation in 1872 and 1904. More than 1,200 additional surviving dwellings, mainly early modern and Period house designs, date from the next five years. Equally important is the fact that many of these 4,000 early homes survive with little or no later alteration. Modern Alameda is thus a rare treasure trove of largely intact Victorian and early-Eclectic-era houses and neighborhoods.

Driving around the older parts of Alameda (those not part of the navy or Utah Construction Company landfills) also provides constant surprises because the town did not grow in typical fashion. Instead of having the usual downtown core from which neighborhood growth radiated in generally chronological bands, Alameda has houses built between 1870 and 1920 scattered throughout—a result of its three early villages and the total of fifteen train stops along two separate lines.

Each of these train stops provided an early nucleus for neighborhood growth in that preautomobile era. Thus Victorian houses, both large and small, can be found throughout most of Alameda's pre-1940 boundaries. Many of the larger Victorian homes originally occupied much of a city block and were surround by mini-farms with an orchard, a vegetable garden, a chicken house, and perhaps a small barn with horses and a milk cow. Later their owners gradually sold off lots for infill development, producing a mixture of Victorian and early-Eclectic-era houses, particularly Craftsman cottages, in most areas. Occasionally one also finds a block or two of houses of the same vintage. These are mostly the result of later subdivision of a large early estate.

All of early Alameda is a delight to explore, but to provide an introductory sample of its rich resources, the map includes a driving route through several important neighborhoods and concentrations of interesting homes. The island's highest concentration of large Victorian homes occurs in two adjacent south shore neighborhoods known as the Gold Coast and Old South Shore. The Gold Coast is the more intact neighborhood, while the island's only museum house, the 1897 Meyers House and Garden (see page 166), is located in Old South Shore. In driving these neighborhoods, one notices a particularly high percentage of Queen Anne houses with towers. The Bay Street Station neighborhood, located around a stop on Cohen's original steam railroad (see page 162), has a rare collection of small but ornate "high-basement" Victorian cottages, mostly in the Queen Anne style. But just as large Victorians are found throughout the island, so too are such smaller Victorian cottages. The East End neighborhood, near the original village of Alameda, has both one of the earliest houses on the island and an area of particularly funky stucco Craftsman bungalows.

Old South Shore

Old South Shore, ca. 1880–1910

This is the district that, prior to 1955, was located along the open southern coastline of Alameda Island. Its geographic orientation was changed precipitously in the 1950s when the Utah Construction Company dredged and filled 335 acres adjacent to the shore for new development (see page 164). Today this now-landlocked coastline neighborhood is known as the Old South Shore. In looking at this neighborhood, one must remember that Clinton Avenue originally looked out on beautiful San Francisco Bay, and Willow, Walnut, Chestnut, Lafayette, and Union Streets each provided scenic sight lines to the Bay. What are today the dead ends of these streets were then windows opening out to the beach and Bay.

The central third of Alameda Island, all of the area lying between today's Grand Street and Park Street, originally belonged to an American frontiersman named James Hibberd. In 1854 he platted his entire tract into the prospective town of "Encinal, which featured very large city blocks." These remained mostly unoccupied until the area's second commuter railroad was completed along Encinal Avenue to serve the southern part of the island in 1878. Commuter stations were located where Encinal intersected both Walnut and Chestnut Streets, thus opening this scenic part of the midisland to large-lot development on Hibberd's oversize blocks. The result was the Old South Shore neighborhood, where a pleasing mixture of both large and midsized Victorian homes were built. Unfortunately some of this neighborhood's houses have been replaced by later apartments, but these are scattered enough so that much of the original neighborhood character survives.

891 Union Street (private), Leonard House, 1896; C. H. Russell, architect. Owner J. A. Leonard was a local homebuilder who constructed all of the houses in this short block except number 898. He also built so many of the houses in the 1800 blocks of Clinton, San Antonio, and San Jose Streets that this small area was sometimes called Leonardsville. Although Leonard himself designed most of the houses he built, he hired another architect to prepare this fine Shingle-style design. Built at a cost of $20,000, Leonard intended to make this his permanent home. However, as often seems to be the fate of builders and their families, he sold it just four years later. Note the rusticated stone foundation and the shingled porch supports. The two towers are treated entirely differently. The one on the right is a broad, two-story, rounded tower with a shingled cove cornice; on the left is a three-story octagonal tower featuring an open cornice line with exposed structural elements. The roof running between the two towers extends outward to shelter the upstairs porch.

893 Union Street (private), Captain Morse House, 1891; J. A. Leonard, Alameda, architect. This Queen Anne design, which sold for $6,450 when new, has an elaborate spindlework porch. Notice how the tower and the front-facing gable are treated as separate elements, as is usually the case in Queen Anne houses, and compare it to the Shingle-influenced tower and gable treatment at 899 Union Street (see the following entry).

899 Union Street (private), Morrison House, 1891; J. A. Leonard, Alameda, architect. Alamedans apparently loved towers on their Queen Anne houses, and this spacious $9,000 home is no exception. It has both a tower on the Bayside and a lovely open balcony porch with a towerlike pointed roof. The tower roof bulges outward while the balcony roof slopes inward. This house is a spindlework Queen Anne design of the hipped-roof-with-lower-cross-gables subtype. The design also has several Shingle-style elements. The melding together of the tower and front-facing gable by a continuous band of shingles is very Shinglesque, as is the gable ornament, which consists of a single "wave" of shingles. Compare this with the tower and gable next door at 893.

2070 San Jose Avenue (private), Brehaut House, 1893; Charles S. Shaner, architect. Built for a reported $4,000 by contractor David S. Brehaut as his own home, this is a particularly elaborate spindlework Queen Anne design. Among its many handsome features are a tall octagonal tower with convex-curved octagonal roof; paired entry steps that embrace a one-story turreted porch and face the corner; and gables with multiple overhangs. Number 2103 San Jose Avenue (private) is another grand towered spindlework Queen Anne designed by the same architect and built by the same builder at a cost of $4,660.

Meyers House and Garden, 1897

2021 Alameda Street; 510-522-8897 (limited visiting hours); Henry H. Meyers, Alameda, architect.

This part of the Old South Shore neighborhood is called Chestnut Station, after the convenient train stop that was originally located just one block away from this Colonial Revival house. It was designed as his own home by architect Meyers and built by his father, Jacob Meyers. The house was originally located on just one lot, but Meyers purchased the Victorian house next door in 1916 and created a lovely side garden on its site. An unusually handsome vine-covered pergola and set of gates are built in line with the front facade of the house and separate the front lawn from the formal garden. Outbuildings include an early greenhouse and garage and a small Spanish Eclectic studio used by the architect and his daughter. This opens out onto a naturalistic garden that extends all the way through the block to Central Street.

The main house is an understated early Colonial Revival design with a subtly rounded, two-story bay window and a balustraded entry porch. The door and its transom are enhanced with an unusually handsome beveled glass pattern; because these are slightly recessed into the house, there is space for a pleasant built-in bench. Meyers's daughter Mildred was also an architect, and she lived in the house until 1981. Over the years the family made many small changes and additions to the home, but blended each so neatly into the original that it is hard to tell where one ends and the next begins. If you look carefully at the side facade facing the garden, you may be able to guess where a downstairs side extension and a small upstairs room were added.

Some parts of the interior date to the home's original construction and others to a major 1915 remodeling.

Many furnishings and fixtures, original either to 1897 or the 1915 remodeling, remain throughout. Original Victorian-type double parlors were combined into one large living room in 1915. The room's curly redwood wainscoting, fireplace, and wall sconces date from the remodeling. The couch, carpet, and piano are all original to the house, as is a lovely statuette, *Pauline Reclining*. The dining room still has its 1897 mantel and built-in sideboard, although the room was extended outward in 1909. At that time an extraordinary stained-glass scene of Monterey was added. The original square table and chairs are still in place, along with a chandelier acquired on a trip to Germany.

Nearby Houses

2044 Alameda Street (private), Siegfried House, 1875 and 1885. The fact that this handsome house was built in two stages may account for its interesting mixture of Italianate and San Francisco Stick features. The squared bay windows are typical of the Stick style, popular in the 1880s, but the roofline brackets do not line up with the sides of the windows and extend down as a line of trim that bounds the windows as is typical in West Coast Stick–style designs. Instead, the cornice-line brackets are evenly spaced in the manner of the Italianate style. Handsome crowns adorn the single, second-story windows.

1630 Central Street (private), Anthony House, 1876. This is considered the finest Italianate home on the island. It was built for John A. Anthony, the chief freight agent for the Central Pacific Railroad, and was lived in by him and his heirs for more than a century.

Gold Coast, ca. 1880–1910s

Franklin Park lies at the heart of this fine neighborhood of upscale homes that are built in Alameda's typical mixture of Victorian and Eclectic-era styles. Grand Avenue and Paru Street offer some of the best groupings of large houses in Alameda. A group of executives from the Southern Pacific Railroad purchased much of this area, called the Oak Park Tract, and divided it into large and spacious lots. As with the Old South Shore neighborhood, it is important to remember that before the 1950s the north–south streets here had sight lines that looked out over San Francisco Bay.

Some of the neighborhood's streets developed a bit later than the core area near Franklin Park. The three southernmost blocks of Bay Street, for example, have mainly houses built after 1900. In addition, some areas near the original Bay front, such as Dayton Street, appear to have been early estates that were later subdivided and filled with Period houses. Happily, the Gold Coast neighborhood has escaped the scattered later apartment houses seen in the Old South Shore.

815 Grand Street (private), Jacobi House, 1890; Charles S. Shaner, architect. The cost of building this Queen Anne design was $5,193. For this price, the new owner obtained a handsome home complete with a tower that is multisided on the first floor and rounded above; an unusual chimney that begins on the exterior of the house and then disappears behind the broad front gable; and a wraparound spindle-work porch with a side entry.

900 Grand Street (private), 1879. Built in the Italianate style that dominated the entire Bay region during the 1870s, this home has decorative quoins, a two-story slanted bay window, a fine entry portico complete with the original cresting, and an elaborate secondary entrance on the left side. The only exterior alteration appears to be the Queen Anne tower that was added to the right-rear corner.

1101 Grand Street (private), 1879 and 1907. Originally built as a typical northern California Stick-style design with a low-pitched roof, front-facing gable, and side wing (see page 39), this house had a complete stylish update in 1907, converting it to a credible rendition of the early Tudor style.

1114 Grand Street (private), 1901. Early Colonial Revival designs similar to this one were popular in Alameda around the turn of the century; the semicircular entry porch was particularly favored. This example also has corner pilasters, a single oval window, and a centered eyebrow dormer on the roof.

1000 Paru Street (private), Heberer House, 1893; Otto Collischonn, architect. A front-gabled, towered Queen Anne design built for $4,500, the house was later modified by adding shed dormers on each side of the roof. The tower begins with a squared bay window on the first floor and then enlarges to an octagonal shape on the second floor and roof. The broad front gable overhangs the second floor and has multiple brackets below.

1004 Paru Street (private), Duveneck House, 1896; E. Kollofrath, architect. This fine and unaltered Colonial Revival design cost its first owners $4,685. It is unusual in having a rounded bay window in the center of the front facade and the entrance recessed on the right. This house also documents an early appearance of the low-hipped-roof-with-centered-hipped-gable shape that dominated entire neighborhoods of American four-square homes during the early twentieth century.

1018 Paru Street (private), Victors House, 1889; A. R. Denke, architect. Moorish-shaped arches across the front porch give this Queen Anne house an exotic appearance. This effect is accomplished by arches that neck down slightly at their base and are sometimes called horseshoe arches. Here two such arches with pointed tops bound a third with a simple rounded top. The original cost of this home was $4,300.

800 Paru Street, at Dayton Street (private), Willison House, 1904. Built for $12,000, this is a very large Colonial Revival house, again with the semicircular entry porch that was so popular in Alameda. Although its address is on Paru, the home faces Dayton and undoubtedly had a fine view out to San Francisco Bay before the 1950s landfill. Note the handsome triple windows.

1100 Bay Street (private), Marriott House, 1907. This fine and unaltered side-gabled Craftsman cottage once had a lovely view out over San Francisco Bay. The house was built for $5,000, the architect using fieldstone to enhance the long winding sidewalk, as well as for the bold chimney and the pedestals supporting the pergola. The latter substituted for the more typical front porch.

1232 Bay Street (private), Walker House, 1909; Morgan and Hoover, San Francisco, architects. This fine Tudor home cost $9,755. Its architect, Julia Morgan, was particularly fond of turning her houses to have an entrance in the middle of the side facade, which gained her a nice central entry hall when used on the narrow lots of San Francisco. Here the owners were able to purchase an adjoining lot for a large broad side garden. The first story is of brick, and the stuccoed and half-timbered second story overhangs it.

Bay Street Station, ca. 1890–1900

This remarkable neighborhood, which grew up around the Cohen's Line (see page 162) Bay Street Station, retains a number of fine streetscapes filled with small but highly ornamented Queen Anne cottages. Many of the most ornate of these were built by Marcuse and Remmel, an extremely prolific building partnership that was founded in 1890 and survived for only nine years. Both partners were from early Alameda families. Julius Remmel was a piano tuner and teacher, and Felix Marcuse was a butcher when the pair decided to become homebuilders. Julius's brother Bert was a beginning architect and helped the partners with their designs. They set up their storefront office right across from the Bay Street Station, which gave them lots of visual exposure to potential home owners. This approach gained them

Bay Street Station

dozens of building contracts in the blocks around the station as well as elsewhere in Alameda. Marcuse and Remmel's small houses featured a riot of exterior ornamentation, much of it cut into the redwood facade as a sort of surface appliqué. As with other Victorian builders, sunbursts were a favorite decorative pattern.

Builders in this neighborhood commonly constructed what are known in Alameda as high-basement cottages, perhaps because this part of low-lying Alameda Island was prone to periodic flooding (similar designs are common along the hurricane-prone Gulf coast of the southeastern states, where they are called raised cottages). Here the basements were left unfinished to provide storage and work areas. Marcuse and Remmel provided an interior stair to the basement, although many other builders did not. Today many home owners have converted these areas into garages or finished interior living space.

The two most charming streets in the Bay Street neighborhood are Mozart and Verdi, names that, although chosen earlier, must have appealed to builder Remmel, the former music teacher. Their short blocks are lined with mature plane trees that today form wonderful tree tunnels that greatly enhance the character of the charming cottages.

1556 Verdi Street (private), Marcuse Home, 1893; Marcuse and Remmel, Alameda, architects. This handsome high-basement cottage cost builder Felix Marcuse $5,100, as much as many of the large, two-story homes in the Gold Coast neighborhood. The design, with its rounded corners and tower and its understated detailing, looks more like the Edwardian designs that were to sweep San Francisco in the next decade than it does the Queen Anne homes that builders were constructing all over Alameda in 1893. The house next door at 1552 Verdi Street (private) is a more typical 1893 cottage design and cost a more usual price of $2,225.

1531 Verdi Street (private), Leavitt House, 1906. This cottage, built by S. H. Wilson and Son, is a fine example of the front-gabled Shingle-style designs with very steeply pitched roofs that were then popular in northern California (see "295 Hillsdale Street," page 37).

1536 Mozart Street (private), Bell House, 1894; Marcuse and Remmel, Alameda, architects. This high-basement Queen Anne cottage has spindlework detailing and a hipped roof with lower cross gables. First owned by bookkeeper George Bell, it cost $2,800 and is a fine example of a typical Marcuse and Remmel home. This prolific pair constructed twelve additional houses in this one block. These ranged in original price from $1,650 for 1549 and 1553 Mozart Street (both private), which were built in 1892, to $2,900 for 1530 Mozart Street (private), which was built in 1894.

1548 Mozart Street (private), ca. 1910. This is a fine, small-scale Craftsman design. Note the shingle cladding, the wooden handrails that extend from inward-sloping brick pedestals, the use of clinker brick in the pedestals, and the careful detailing of the exposed roof beams.

1611 Bay Street (private), Pierce House, 1892; Marcuse and Remmel, Alameda, architects. This high-basement cottage, a front-gabled spindlework Queen Anne design, cost $1,950 to build. Marcuse and Remmel also built 1609, 1613, and 1615 Bay Street (all private) for similar amounts. All were in a prime location, only steps away from the Bay Street rail station.

1219 Pacific Avenue (private), David House, 1895; Marcuse and Remmel, Alameda, architects. This $2,500 high-basement Queen Anne cottage was first lived in by bookkeeper Edward David. The builder's typical redwood appliquéwork is found in the gable tops; the cornices appear to have plaster ornament. Other details include a gable-on-hip roof that echoes the ornament on the lower front-facing gable and a rounded entry porch with conical roof. The balustrades of the porch inventively give the look of more expensive, rounded balustrades but are fashioned from more easily shaped flat elements.

1615, 1619, 1623, 1627, and 1631 Sherman Street (all private), Walther Cottages, 1894; Marcuse and Remmel, Alameda, architects. All of the remarkably ornate and individualistic high-basement Queen Anne cottages in this row were built by Marcuse and Remmel and originally owned by Max Walther, who paid the builders $2,150 for each and probably used them as rental properties.

1549 and 1551 Benton Street (both private), 1896. The Alameda Land Company built both of these towered Queen Anne cottages, with their high basements, for $2,000 each. They also were responsible for several other homes in this block face.

1531 Benton Street (private), Mott House, 1894; Charles S. Shaner, architect. This high-basement spindlework Queen Anne cottage, like most of its neighbors, is complete with tower and originally cost $2,000.

East End, ca. 1850–1920s

The original town of Alameda was located here at the eastern tip of the early peninsula (see map, page 162). Today, this architecturally diverse neighborhood includes the island's oldest house as well as important later dwellings, among them some fine 1880s Stick-style houses along Park Avenue and several block faces of distinctive 1910s stucco-clad Craftsman bungalows. The latter were constructed by George Noble, a prolific builder of these easily recognizable houses during the 1910s and 1920s.

East End

Alameda streetscape

1201 Park Avenue (private), Smilie House, 1885. This high-basement Stick-style cottage has been nicely maintained and appears to be unaltered except for the new single-pane windows.

1193 Park Avenue (private), Harvey House, 1887; attributed to Charles S. Shaner, architect. One of the finest Stick-style dwellings remaining in Alameda, this has a variation of the upside-down-picket-fence pattern under the cornice, diagonal porch-support braces on the entry porch, brace supports under the eaves, and the squared bay window so popular on San Francisco examples of this style. Notice how the two-story squared bay window has its own little gable above it. All of this cost only $3,300 in 1887.

2721 San Jose Avenue (private), ca. 1915. This is a particularly fine example of the many stucco-clad Craftsman homes that line the 2700 blocks of San Jose Avenue and Washington Street, most of them constructed by homebuilder George Noble. This one has three very low pitched front-facing gables, each with a slight Oriental peak at its center, a feature that was typical of this builder's work. The massive porch supports begin at ground level and have inward-sloping sides, and the side chimney is ornamented by a geometric design that is emphasized by art-glass windows on both sides of the chimney. It is remarkable that Noble could pack so much drama into such a small Craftsman design—not by the more typical use of varied materials (like pebble or stone chimneys and porch supports), but rather by creating strong geometric forms in a single material. Similar homes by this builder are found along Versailles and Pearl Streets and scattered elsewhere throughout much of Alameda.

1238 Versailles Avenue (private), Webster House, 1854. This Gothic Revival cottage is the oldest documented house in Alameda. It is believed to have been prefabricated in the Northeast, shipped around Cape Horn, and then assembled here.

BERKELEY

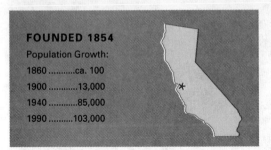

FOUNDED 1854

Population Growth:

1860 ....ca. 100

1900 13,000

1940 85,000

1990 103,000

Founded, like nearby Oakland, as a Bay-side agricultural trade center, the neighboring towns' destinies took divergent paths in 1868 when Oakland was chosen as the Pacific terminus of the soon-to-be-completed transcontinental railroad (see page 188); in the same year, Berkeley was named the site for the new University of California. Berkeley thus became the state's, and later one of the nation's, principal educational centers, which gave the town something of a split personality.

The university was built on a dramatic hillside site that lay miles inland from the earlier waterside trading center, which continued to grow as a mostly blue-collar town of docks, warehouses, factories, and workers' cottages. The hillside university, in contrast, was dominated by large and scenic tracts of land set aside for the more upscale houses of professors and administrators. Both the industrial and university districts were to prosper and expand, in their respective roles, over the succeeding decades but would also suffer more than the usual amount of "town-gown" friction. In the words of Berkeley historian Malcolm Margolin, the original town

> had not been settled by people who came to Berkeley to settle the "Athens of the Pacific," but by those who hoped to beat high rents, set up serviceable inns, grist mills, and lumber yards, and establish farms on cheap land with adequate water and ready accesss to a marketplace. This contrast between an idealistic and literary university, in which faculty and students alike would draw financial support from Sacramento . . . and the necessarily self-sufficient, working class community to the west . . . would be a dominant force in the shaping of Berkeley, and one which can be still felt today.

By 1900 Berkeley was still a small town whose thirteen thousand residents mostly lived in modest Victorian neighborhoods that filled the gently sloping plain that separated the waterfront industrial area from the hillside university. This semirural tranquillity was to end abruptly during the next twelve years as the city's population surged to over fifty thousand by 1912. Several factors contributed to this extraordinary flood of new residents.

In 1903 the Key Line, a state-of-the-art new trolley-and-ferry system, was completed with Berkeley as its hub. This cut in half, to thirty minutes, the previous cross-Bay commuting time and made Berkeley, rather than nearby Oakland or Alameda, the favored East Bay bedroom suburb of San Francisco's commuters. Then, just three years later, the 1906 San Francisco earthquake and fire sent about fifteen thousand homeless refugees to Berkeley, many of whom chose to become permanent residents.

Berkeley's reputation as a desirable homesite continued to bring new residents, although at a less spectacular rate, over the next three decades, and by 1940 the population had climbed to eighty-five thousand, a total that was to increase by only eighteen thousand over the next half century. During this period the city's earlier balance of prosperous blue-collar and white-collar workers had changed as its industrial west side suffered from the "postindustrial" factory closings and unemployment that had plagued similar districts throughout the nation. At the same time its formerly California-focused university grew into a vast and world-renowned "multiversity" with more than thirty thousand students and a faculty that included more than a dozen Nobel Prize winners. As a result of these changes, much of the town's central residential area is now dominated by apartment buildings and earlier homes subdivided for student housing.

Fortunately, much of the university's post-1950 physical expansion has taken place within its large campus grounds, rather than by destruction of its fine surrounding neighborhoods, most of which date from Berkeley's population-explosion years from 1900 to 1930. Three of these are described below, the most distinctive of which is closely associated with one of the nation's seminal movements toward architectural modernism.

The First Bay Tradition

Befitting the university's role as a center for innovative thinking, some of its adjacent neighborhoods contain

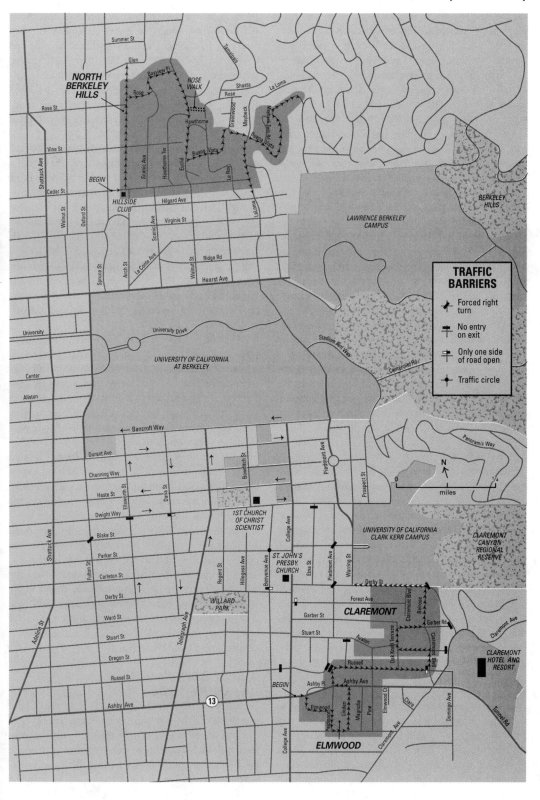

turn-of-the-century houses that experiment with simple, almost-rustic, livability as an alternative to what their designers regarded as the decorative excesses of typical Victorian homes. These unpretentious, avant-garde designs differed sharply from the Victorian- and Period-style homes that dominated nearby Oakland and Alameda, as well as much of the rest of Berkeley itself. Hardly shocking to modern eyes attuned to a half century of abstract building styles, these pioneering modern houses have come to be called the First Bay Tradition and were to influence the work of creative Bay Area architects for many decades.

Many of the house-building dictates of First Bay Tradition architects, including their emphasis on walls of dark-stained wood shingles, were similar to those advocated elsewhere by proponents of Arts and Crafts design. Most First Bay houses are thus related to two nationally popular housing fashions—either the Shingle style (most often these are the earlier and/or urban examples) or the Craftsman style (most often later and/or suburban examples). These same principles were revived in the Bay Area as a part of the all-pervasive architectural modernism that swept the nation after the Second World War. These designs came to be known as the Second Bay Tradition; northern California architects working in this mode were to provide much of the inspiration for the woodsy Contemporary-style houses that were built throughout the country during the 1950s and 1960s.

Maybeck Country

The creative leader of the First Bay Tradition movement was a young French-trained German-American architect named Bernard Ralph Maybeck (1862–1957), who moved to San Francisco in 1889 and became closely associated with Berkeley and the University of California for the rest of his long life. In 1892 Maybeck began remodeling a small cottage north of the university campus for himself and his bride of two years, and this was to become the first house of the First Bay Tradition. Soon a friend, the naturalist and author Charles Keeler, wanted a similar house, which so pleased Keeler that he became a dedicated convert to Maybeck's unpretentious design philosophy. In 1904 Keeler published an influential short book, *The Simple House*, which helped to popularize Maybeck's then-radical ideas.

Although earlier architects had built Shingle-style dwellings in San Francisco and other parts of the Bay Area, Maybeck's homes for himself and for Keeler were the first to have interior walls made of simple wood planks left with a natural wood finish. This interior simplicity became one of the things that distinguished

West Coast Shingle–style houses from their cousins on the East Coast, which had more elaborately finished interiors. In addition, many West Coast Shingle and Craftsman homes were smaller than their eastern counterparts, a reverse luxury made possible by the year-round mild weather. Indeed, Keeler described First Bay Tradition houses as being "landscape architecture with but a few enclosed rooms for staying out of the rain."

Maybeck was not, however, an architect who worked only in the Shingle or Craftsman styles. The son of a woodworker and a graduate of Paris's prestigious École des Beaux Arts, he had a restless intellect and constantly brought new and different influences into his work. Esther McCoy, in her important book *Five California Architects,* notes that "some of his houses were like little travelogues. The pagoda roof appeared in his style in 1895 and the chalet in 1900." In addition, Craftsman, Prairie, Spanish, Italian, Tudor, Classical, and early Gothic influences also appeared, all creatively reinterpreted through his remarkably informed and idiosyncratic eyes.

Maybeck had a perpetually youthful optimism coupled with an unconcerned approach to financial matters. The latter often left him on the brink of bankruptcy as he designed and redesigned his commissions. The former helped him to survive the tragic fire that swept through North Berkeley Hills in 1923, destroying in a single day much of his previous life's work (see page 173). Maybeck immediately set to work rebuilding his own vanished home and helping friends rebuild theirs—now often working in fire-resistant concrete rather than wood. Fortunately, his principal early masterpiece still survives elsewhere in town. This is the unique **First Church of Christ Scientist,** completed in 1912 at the corner of Dwight Way and Bowditch Street, a remarkable building that clearly demonstrates the power and individuality of Maybeck's best work. Nearby is another fine First Bay Tradition structure, the 1910 **St. John's Presbyterian Church,** designed by Maybeck protégé Julia Morgan (see page 251) in a Craftsman-like style. Now used as a theater, it is two blocks away from the Maybeck church at the corner of College Avenue and Derby Street.

North Berkeley Hills, ca. 1900–1930

Architect Bernard Maybeck owned four acres of land just east of La Loma Avenue along Buena Vista Way in the hills immediately north of the university campus. Here he built his own home and the studio from which he taught, designed houses, educated clients, and periodically sold off lots when money was scarce. In the surrounding neighborhood, served by an early street-car line along Euclid Avenue, Maybeck and his Bay Tradition followers were to design many houses for friends, neighbors, and others.

Adding to the early distinction of Maybeck's home neighborhood was a remarkably successful civic improvement organzation called the **Hillside Club.** Organized in 1898 as a women's group, it was expanded to include men in 1902 when it became obvious that males were needed to capture the attention of the Berkeley city government. Among the club's ambitous goals were ensuring unobtrusively narrow hillside roads that closely followed the contours of the land; building footpaths and steps for easier pedestrian access (see "Rose Walk," page 174); planting new trees while saving existing specimens; encouraging irregular lots and house placement; and instigating cooperative neighborhood landscaping that would emphasize the sweeping contours of the hills rather than punctuate the view with jarring demarcations between small, individual lots.

In addition to these general neighborhood concerns, the club held equally firm views about the appropriate type of house for its rustic environment. Houses should "hug the hill" and be parallel to the slope; should be built of natural materials "such as shingles, shakes, rough stone or clinker brick"; should have their exterior materials left with their natural finishes; should avoid unnecessary ornament, which, if present at all, was to be covered with "dull brown paint"; should "follow straight lines" appropriate to wood material rather than incorporating curves; should have overhanging eaves; should have simple inside finishes and furnishings; should have "hinged windows, swinging out" to afford picturesque, uninterrupted views; and should have curtains of simple materials such as denim or burlap. And, in case that wasn't enough, a conference with the board of directors of the club was recommended for further suggestions! Most were apparently followed, and the neighborhood developed a naturalistic integrity that was widely admired.

Unfortunately, many of its early houses, including Maybeck's own home, were lost in 1923, when a devastating fire swept through North Berkeley Hills, destroying over six hundred houses. A number of important dwellings, however, managed to escape serious damage, and others were rebuilt following the same principles as before, but with a new emphasis on fire-resistant walls of stucco or concrete. In addition to its many First Bay Tradition houses, the neighborhood also has more traditional Victorian and Eclectic-era styles. These are mostly concentrated on the lower parts of the hillside.

A driving route through the neighborhood has been included because house addresses are frequently obscured by the lush landscaping or are even absent altogether; the houses described here are listed in the order they occur on the tour, which will help in locating them. If one is in good physical shape, walking along steep and winding Buena Vista Way and narrow Maybeck Twin Road (which is not recommended for casual driving) will allow more leisurely appreciation for the integration of house, landscape, and view that was so much a part of the Hillside Club's philosophy. Note that the house numbers along Arch Street and all of the north–south streets in this neighborhood are not intuitive—they become smaller as you travel farther *up* the hill and *away* from the campus.

2286 Cedar Street (private), Hillside Club, 1906; Bernard Maybeck, Berkeley, architect; rebuilt 1924, Mark White, Berkeley, architect. This was the clubhouse for the influential Hillside Club and is thus an appropriate place to start a tour of the Berkeley Hills. The original clubhouse burned in the 1923 fire and was rebuilt along similar lines by Maybeck's brother-in-law.

1431 Arch Street (private), Gough House, 1886; Ira Boynton, Berkeley, architect. This cross-gabled Queen Anne design has a rather-unusual hexagonal "tower" above the porch that is actually all roof and no tower. One of the oldest houses in the area, this is the kind of Victorian dwelling that the Hillside Club, and indeed the entire Arts and Crafts movement, sought to replace with rustic simplicity.

1340 Arch Street (private), Wallace House, 1905; John White, Berkeley, architect. Designed by Maybeck's brother-in-law, this stucco-walled house is Swiss chalet in inspiration. It is heavily landscaped, but the massive stepped brackets under the front-gabled roof and a balcony with a flat wood railing featuring a typical cutout Swiss-chalet design are both visible.

1325 Arch Street (private), Schneider House, 1907; Bernard Maybeck, Berkeley, architect. This was one of a series of Swiss-chalet designs that Maybeck turned out, with his distinctive personal flair, beginning in 1901. This example, perched high up on the hillside, is among the finest. It has two broad front-facing porches with flat cutout railings

North Berkeley Hills

North Berkeley Hills

and a particularly wide roof overhang. The exaggerated roof overhang on the right-hand front appears to have been designed to shelter the downstairs porch. John McLaren, longtime superintendent of San Francisco's Golden Gate Park, designed the lovely hillside garden, likely in consultation with Maybeck. This house long belonged to Professor Alfred L. Kroeber, one of the fathers of modern anthropology, and his wife, Theodora, who wrote *Ishi in Two Worlds: A Biography of the Last Wild Indian in North America*. She later wrote of her husband, who rarely was interested in material possessions, "This house he wanted from the first moment of glimpsing it through its redwood-tree screen, nor did his satisfaction with it and his possessiveness toward it lessen over the years."

1321 Bayview Place (private), Senger House, 1907; Bernard Maybeck, Berkeley, architect. Here Maybeck shows his dexterity at combining diverse architectural elements into a single complex design that defies stylistic analysis. A complex interplay of gabled and shed roofs of varying pitch is emphasized by the house's near-sidewalk site on a corner lot that allows full views of both the front and side facades. The front facade features a one-story entry wing with a dramatic cross-trussed gable above the front door; broken-pediment wall dormers, one with a chimney ascending through the "break," accent the taller, side-gabled roof behind. On the side facade a second gabled roof with a one-story wing mirrors the front half of the house except for walls clad in dark wood shingles rather than the light stucco used for the front section. This change in material indicated the interior division between the formal and service portions of the house.

1322 Bayview Place (private), 1907; Henry Gutterson, Berkeley, architect. Partially hidden by lush landscaping, this large, side-gabled First Bay design by one of Maybeck's associates has the typical dark-wood-shingle exterior, here accented by rough stucco. Stenciled panels beneath a line of upstairs windows were likely influenced by Maybeck's house across the street (see the preceding entry).

Rose Walk, public walkway connecting Euclid and LeRoy Avenues (all houses private), 1912; Bernard Maybeck, Berkeley, architect. This is one of the pedestrian "walks" encouraged by the Hillside Club to provide access from the Euclid Avenue trolley to houses up the steep hillside. Maybeck designed an elaborate double-entry stairway and bench, made of concrete, for the walk's Euclid Avenue entrance. The original small houses that lined the walk were destroyed in the 1923 fire. Architect Henry Gutterson, in consultation with Maybeck, designed their replacements along the walk's north side. These were cleverly sited to provide both privacy and a shared public garden along the walkway. Houses along the south side were added later and designed by other architects.

1537 Euclid Avenue at Buena Vista Way (private), Kennedy House and Studio, 1914, 1923; Bernard Maybeck, Berkeley, architect. No address is visible; the house is on the northeast corner, across from 1540 Euclid Avenue. This remarkable Maybeck structure was built for a music teacher and then rebuilt by him, with some additions, after the 1923 fire. It uses strong Gothic imagery, including a heroic, cathedral-like central window that opens into a large studio/recital room. The medieval decorative elements are superimposed on an Italian Renaissance form with stucco walls and a low-pitched, red tile roof featuring Maybeck's favored broken-pediment gable.

2800 Buena Vista Way (private), Boynton House (Temple of the Wings), 1912; Bernard Maybeck, Berkeley, architect for initial phase. This house was designed for a somewhat-eccentric couple who, before it was constructed, had a falling-out with Maybeck and hired another architect to finish it. It was not planned to be a house in the traditional sense, but rather a two-part open pavilion with a roof supported by tall Corinthian columns. Large canvas "shades" between the columns could be lowered when the demands of weather or privacy made it necessary. One part of the pavilion was for living and the other for dancing, for the Boyntons were advocates of the "free dance" movement popularized by Isadora Duncan, who was then teaching in San Francisco.

The family ate only peanuts and dried fruit and dressed in togalike robes; such preferences may have led to the nickname "Nut Hill" that was once applied to this part of the neighborhood. The 1923 fire destroyed the roof, canvas, and furnishings, but left the thirty-four columns standing. A more traditional Neoclassical house was then built behind these Corinthian "ruins."

2753 Buena Vista Way (private), Brown House, 1914; William C. Hays, architect. This unusual and refined house has an Italian Renaissance form with walls covered not by Mediterranean-type stone or stucco, but with First Bay Tradition brown wood shingles. At the sidewalk entrance is a wooden entry gate with a small roof above, a favorite landscape feature of First Bay architects.

2711 Buena Vista Way (private), Maybeck Studio (Sack House), 1923 and later; Bernard Maybeck, Berkeley, architect. Shortly before the 1923 fire, Maybeck had begun to experiment with a kind of cellular concrete called Bubblestone, which had been patented by a friend, engineer and geologist John Rice, in 1923. It was sort of a frothy concrete that weighed as much as 75 percent less than normal concrete. To rebuild his home destroyed by the fire on this site, Maybeck built a large, one-room wooden frame on the surviving foundation and then covered the walls with a unique and inexpensive siding material—large burlap sacks that had been dipped in the wet Bubblestone mixture and allowed to dry. These were then nailed to the wooden frame to make large, fire-resistant "shingles," thus the nickname "Sack House." Industrial-type metal windows and doors were installed in the wooden framing through easily cut openings in the Bubblestone shingles. Maybeck and his family lived in lofts in the tall studio for many years; additional rooms, sided with other materials, were later added.

2704 Buena Vista Way, at La Loma Avenue (private), Mathewson "Studio" House, 1916; Bernard Maybeck, Berkeley, architect. In this large First Bay Tradition design, Maybeck echoed many features of the popular Craftsman style. Stuccoed lower walls give way to board-and-batten redwood under the eaves, which combine an unusually broad overhang with oversize triangular braces. Much of the two broad gables is filled with windows, a design element that was not widely used until the 1950s.

1598 Hawthorne Terrace (private), Van Deussen House, 1938; William Wilson Wurster, architect. This understated International-style design, unlike most examples of the style, tries not to call attention to itself, perhaps as a concession to its many naturalistic neighbors.

1515 La Loma Avenue (private), Lawson House, 1908; Bernard Maybeck, Berkeley, architect. The distinguished Berkeley geologist Andrew Lawson was best known for helping to make the 1930s Golden Gate Bridge earthquake-proof. Earlier in his career, Lawson had traced the path of the Hayward Fault to this site, where he was about to build a new home. He conferred with Maybeck, and they decided to build the house of massively reinforced concrete, a technique then rarely used for houses.

Maybeck modeled the home loosely on a Pompeian villa, but its simple, powerful massing anticipates some Modernistic designs of the 1930s. Tints of light red and buff, incised geometric patterns, and small colored tiles enliven and accent the concrete wall surfaces. Maybeck's versatility is demonstrated by comparing this house with the quite different, yet equally inventive, Senger House (see "1321 Bayview Place," page 174) and Schneider House (see "1325 Arch Street," page 173) designed at about the same time.

Claremont and Elmwood, ca. 1905–1920

South of campus are more traditional neighborhoods that feature a combination of First Bay Tradition homes with contemporaneous Period house styles. Claremont and Elmwood contain particularly fine examples of these. If you have the time and the desire to more fully explore the streets immediately around the Berkeley campuses, you had best stop in a map store and purchase a copy of *Professor Pathfinder's University of California: Berkeley Campus & Environs* map, as there is a maze of forced right and left turns and closed streets, installed in the 1970s and designed to keep the tens of thousands of daily commuter cars that pour into Berkeley via Tunnel Road out of the heart of its neighborhoods.

The adjoining Claremont and Elmwood neighborhoods are treated together, as they require a driving route because of these multiple street obstructions, which funnel traffic along Ashby Avenue, which runs through the heart of Elmwood, and along Claremont Boulevard/Belrose Avenue, one of the grander streets in Claremont. These two streets are almost always filled with rapidly moving, impatient commuter traffic that makes stopping to admire a house on either street somewhat foolhardy.

There is a major difference in the stylistic mix found in the early-twentieth-century neighborhoods of Berkeley (and indeed throughout much of California) and that found in other parts of the West. This is most pronounced in the two-story houses built for middle- and upper-middle-class families between 1900 and 1920. Where in other parts of the West, neighborhoods of this era and economic class are filled with American four-square homes interpreted in the Prairie, Colonial Revival, or Neoclassical styles, here these are much less frequently found. In their place are two-story First Bay Tradition/Craftsman-style houses, most often clad with wood shingles and of either front-gabled or gable-front-and-wing shape.

These two neighborhoods are great places to see this typical California stylistic mix. The large styled houses in Claremont are quite similar to those found in neighborhoods elsewhere. The more modest one-story Craftsman houses on Pine Street in Elmwood also resemble those seen throughout the country. What differ are the mid-price-range houses, between these two extremes, which here are typically larger, two-story Craftsman designs clad in brown wood shingles.

Claremont

Claremont was developed in 1905 by the real estate firm of Mason-McDuffie as an exclusive neighborhood of large homes called a "private residence park." One source attributes the culs-de-sac and connecting walking paths in Claremont to the Olmsted brothers' landscape firm, and another to Duncan McDuffie, who was an early member of the Sierra Club. Whoever was responsible, the use of a cul-de-sac was somewhat unusual at this early date, and the use of connecting footpaths may have been influenced by the precepts of the Hillside Club (see page 173). This neighborhood takes its name from the fine Claremont Hotel, which has been restored and sits majestically on an adjacent hillside. John Galen Howard designed entry gates and other street improvements for Claremont in 1905, and they give a fine sense of arriving at something special, as you will note when you turn onto Claremont Boulevard from Russell Street. This southern portion of Claremont Boulevard (and Belrose Avenue, which it turns into) has many fine homes—with Italian Renaissance ones being most conspicuous. But none are featured here because of the fast-moving traffic!

Elmwood

The Elmwood neighborhood, just to the south of Claremont, has generally smaller houses built along grid-pattern streets. The heart of this neighborhood is Elmwood Center, with its rows of small shops along College Avenue at Ashby. Within the neighborhood is a rich mixture of First Bay Tradition and early Eclectic-era houses of many different sizes. Piedmont and Elmwood Avenues have generally larger homes, and the average home size gradually decreases as you move east onto Linden Avenue and Magnolia Street, which feature many American four-squares, clad either with stucco or brown shingles. Pine Avenue, farthest to the east, has a collection of small stuccoed Craftsman homes. Russell Street on the north has the largest homes in Elmwood and makes a perfect transition between Elmwood's generally smaller-scale lots and the larger lots and homes of Claremont. This street features a rich mixture of house styles and varied-size lots; it connects through to Claremont with two walking paths.

Elmwood: 2729 Elmwood Avenue (private). A fine example of an "Early Eclectic What's It?"—those homes built from about 1895 to 1910 that include a number of different stylistic influences combined so that none really dominates. This makes it impossible to handily identify them as houses of a particular style with only secondary influences from other styles. This house is clad in rough-finished stucco and has unusual exposed double roof "beams" along the cor-

nice. Each "beam" (and "beam" is in quotation marks because these may well not be the ends of the actual roof beams, but instead be added outside trim that looks like it could be a continuation of the roof beam) is composed of three layers of wood laminated together, with the two outside pieces cut into a pattern with a jigsaw. The front door has a strong Renaissance flavor and is crowned with a large overhang supported on each side by an oversize bracket. The downstairs windows have diamond lights in the thresholds and an overly deep cornice with large dentils above. This gives an unusual effect because the threshold window and the deep cornice combine to create an area almost as deep as the lower windowpanes. The two-story front-gabled Craftsman house across the street has a double vergeboard of the type described under 2960 Piedmont (see the following entry).

Elmwood: 2960 Piedmont Avenue (private), ca. 1910. One of a row of three fine First Bay Tradition homes—all are shingle-clad Craftsman houses—this one is cross gabled, and the second story overhangs the first story; the overhang has a slight outward flare of shingles above and is supported by heavy wood beams below. The front-facing gable has two vergeboards, one below the other and each supported by a separate level of projecting roof "beams." This kind of double vergeboard is seen on a number of Berkeley houses. This house is relatively narrow, and the entrance is placed to the side. Next door, 2962 Piedmont Avenue (private) is also a cross-gabled shape, but it is wider, allowing a front entry. It also sports a shed dormer and a fashionable trellised front porch with a second-floor open porch supported over part of it. The third house in this row, 2970 Piedmont Avenue (private), is front gabled in shape and, like 2960, has its entry to the side. The second floor overhangs the first, and there is a slight outward flare of the shingle cladding at the first-floor level. This slight flare is found on many of Berkeley's First Bay Tradition houses, marking the base of a gable or the transition between stories, as at 2960 Piedmont. A large bay window accents the center front of this home. Intriguingly, the upstairs windows are casement windows but with a pattern of muntins that mimics double-hung windows with multiple panes in the upper sash and a clear pane in the lower sash.

Elmwood: 2948 Magnolia Avenue (private), ca. 1910. Here is a good example of a brown shingled house with a side entry and a front chimney enlivened with clinker bricks

Elmwood

Claremont

(bricks misshapen by being placed close to the heat source during firing). Note the characteristic outward-flaring shingles marking the transition between the first and second stories and again between the first floor and the foundation.

Elmwood: 2827 Russell Street at Kelsey Street (private), Marquis House, 1909. An outstanding Mission-style home. Note the use of three shaped parapets across the full-width front porch with another along the side. At the roofline, a shaped parapet is used on the left side, while castellations with a visor roof below are on the right. The house is wonderfully set off with the original palm trees.

Elmwood: 2929 Russell Street (private), Burke House, 1914; Julia Morgan, San Francisco, architect. Julia Morgan, the first woman to graduate from the École des Beaux-Arts (see page 251), designed almost seven hundred structures during her very productive professional career. Many of these were houses, and, during the first years of her career, they were often clad with natural wood shingles, as here. This house has the side entrance that she favored for narrow lots because it allowed a spacious living room to stretch across the front of the house. Here the detailing is Shingle rather than Craftsman. Note the boxed eaves and dentils. The one-car front garage, built into the hillside, has detailing that matches the house and looks like it was built quite early.

Claremont: 2801 Oak Knoll Terrace (private), ca. 1910. Another "Early Eclectic What's It?" that looks like it could have been designed by the same architect as 2729 Elmwood Avenue (see page 176). Houses of this type are often enticing because everything about them looks familiar yet is somehow different. This one has a Medieval feeling, even though it lacks most of the Tudor identifying features. A high-pitched roof, steeply gabled dormers, and second-story overhang all contribute to this effect. The four large bay windows with leaded-glass panes seem related to the diamond-paned casement windows so often found on Tudor houses, yet there are four of them all symmetrically placed. Another interesting touch is the curiously placed band of trim that wraps around the house in line with the horizontal rail of the upstairs windows. The oversize cornice brackets contribute to this effect with a flat portion that lies just at the trim line. Note the Gothic-inspired arches between the porch supports with their hanging pendant and the extruding diamond panels of the front door.

Claremont: 2927 Garber Road (private), ca. 1910. This stuccoed Tudor house is symmetrical, quite common in Tudor houses built before 1915. Unlike 2801 Oak Knoll (see the preceding entry), which gives only subtle hints of its Medieval inspiration, this house leaves absolutely no doubt about its stylistic allegiance—much of the facade is covered with half-timbering. A very dramatic full-width balcony has a railing design that matches the half-timbering pattern used beneath the bay windows on the right side of the house.

HAYWARD

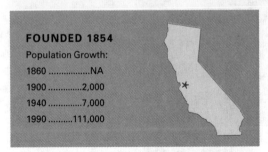

FOUNDED 1854

Population Growth:

1860	NA
1900	2,000
1940	7,000
1990	111,000

Founded as a gold rush stagecoach stop on the principal East Bay wagon road, Hayward later became an important marketing and trade center for the region's rich farms and orchards. Much of the spirit of these early farms can still be felt at the Ardenwood Historic Farm, located about nine miles south of Hayward, whose centerpiece is a fine Queen Anne museum house.

Hayward itself remained a small agricultural trade center until the 1940s, when the demand for workers' housing for the Bay's burgeoning shipyards and other wartime industries led to new residential developments on the town's surrounding farmlands. By the 1950s, the postwar suburban boom took over entirely as Hayward began annexing its surrounding suburbs along with potential Bay-side industrial areas. The latter were intended to increase the local tax base by providing nearby jobs for its commuter-dominated citizenry. Because of these actions, the city's population surged from 14,000 in 1950 to 73,000 in 1960. Today, most of the formerly rural East and South Bay is a continuous belt of urban sprawl. One lone reminder of Hayward's agricultural beginnings survives in the city's center—a fine Stick-style museum house whose early history closely parallels that of the still-rural Patterson House preserved on the Ardenwood Historic Farm.

Patterson House, 1889

34600 Ardenwood Boulevard, in Ardenwood Historic Farm of the East Bay Regional Park District, about 10 miles south of Hayward off of California Highway 84; 510-791-4196; Samuel Newsom, San Francisco, architect.

George Washington Patterson (1822–1895) lived a life that perfectly mirrored California's early Anglo development. Arriving from Indiana with the forty-niners, he failed at finding gold but became one of northern California's most successful farmers, amassing almost 6,500 acres of land during his lifetime. He married

quite late, and with his wife, Clara Hawley (1853–1917), built a fine Queen Anne house designed by Samuel Newsom, one of the Newsom brothers, San Francisco's famed Victorian-era architects. Today, the house is preserved as part of a living farm that tells the important story of the fertile East Bay farmers and farming tradition. And thanks to an unusually thorough 1995 biography by Keith E. Kennedy, *George Washington Patterson and the Founding of Ardenwood*, we have an in-depth historical look at the farm and its owner.

Patterson was born in Pennsylvania and moved westward with his family along the National Road to Greene County, Ohio, when he was two years old. The family again moved west to Americus, Indiana, when George was ten, and it was here he spent his formative years watching, and no doubt helping, his father sharecrop land. George was twenty-six when news of the great California gold discoveries hit, and he banded together with many other young men from the area and became part of a business organization, the Lafayette-California Mercantile and Mining Company. Each member paid five hundred dollars, and supplies were ordered from New York to be waiting for them upon their arrival in San Francisco. The supplies had a lengthy wait. The group left in mid-March, choosing an unusual California route—steaming downriver to New Orleans, sailing across the Gulf of Mexico to Port Lavaca, Texas, and from there going overland, via San Antonio, Texas, and Durango, Mexico, to the Mexican port of Mazatlán. From there they sailed to San Francisco aboard the *Louisa*, an English-owned boat that joined a multitude of eerily abandoned ships crowding San Francisco Harbor as their captains and crew headed to the goldfields. Patterson's journey to California was almost six months of hardship that included the loss of a boyhood friend to cholera and the breakup of the company.

But miraculously their supplies were still waiting in San Francisco, and the group arrived near the fork of the American River in early fall, fully outfitted and just in time to endure a tough fall and winter season. George met with some success, and exactly one year after leaving Americus, he sent twenty-one ounces of gold back home. But then gold became harder to find, and by late 1850 George had left the goldfields and sought work as a farmhand with an old friend. By 1854 he had saved enough and learned enough to sharecrop

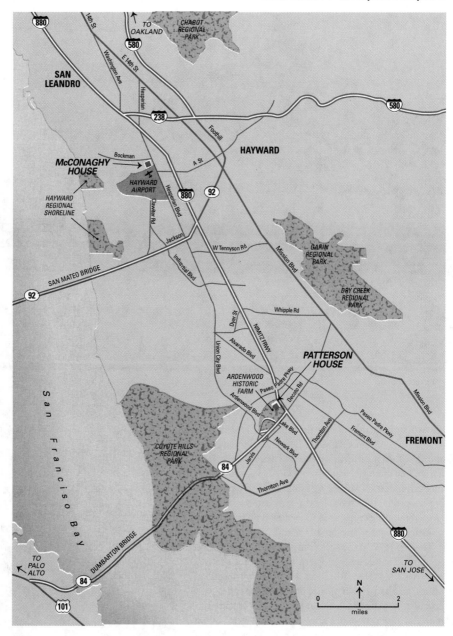

a piece of land. In this he was so successful, earning as much as $1,000 in some months, that in 1856 Patterson purchased his first 291 acres of land for $9,748 cash. According to Patterson's biography, this initial acreage provided the basis for all of his later wealth, as he had chosen it well: "The land was very fertile, ideally situated for obtaining water for irrigation from Alameda Creek, and strategically located for transporting produce by water to San Francisco. He had been attentive

and observant during his apprenticeship years." He never sold this initial land, but simply added to it by purchasing adjacent acreage, almost invariably buying his new land with cash.

In 1857 family illnesses took him back to Indiana, and he brought his mother and one brother, Henry, back to California with him. A second brother, Andrew, who had come out earlier, also rejoined the family, and George promptly organized his brothers to build a sim-

Patterson House

ple two-story farmhouse for the family. This well-built 1857 house contained about two thousand square feet, and it still stands, forming the rear wing of the later house. For the next twenty years George continued in single-minded pursuit of farming, regularly reinvesting his profits into more land purchased for cash. He farmed multiple crops, so as to avoid ruin if there was a disastrous year for any one of them.

Then in 1877, at the age of fifty-five, George decided to marry. He had known Clara Hawley since she was nine years old. Her father was a friend and neighbor. Little Clara had grown up and become a schoolteacher. Friendship turned to love, and the couple decided to marry without anyone's knowledge; it is not certain why, but George had been shy with women and may also have been embarrassed by their age difference. They eloped to Sacramento to marry and quickly started their family. By 1880 they had two young sons, and the farm's size had grown to almost three thousand acres.

When their older son was about ten years old, George and Clara decided they needed a new and larger home. They chose one of California's leading architects, Samuel Newsom. Along with his brothers Samuel had designed some of northern California's finest Vic-

torian homes (see the "William Carson House," page 33). The new house he designed for the Pattersons was in the Queen Anne style and had about five thousand square feet of living space. Newsom skillfully joined it to the older home, using a side porch to help soften the junction. Unfortunately, George had only six years to enjoy his fine home.

George Patterson died in 1895, leaving an estate that included 6,478 acres of prime land worth close to one million dollars and over thirty-one thousand dollars in gold. Clara continued to live in their fine new house and ran the farm. Within a few years their elder son, Henry (1878–1955), was an adult and took over the management of the farm, sharing it with his younger brother. The family managed to keep the farm intact until 1952, when they finally began yielding to pressure from development interests. Gradually land was sold off, and in 1971 the remaining heirs banded together to try to sell the 400 acres around the house in a manner that would save the house and surrounding farmland for historic interpretation. It took until 1985 for this to be accomplished, with 46 acres being donated to and 160 acres being purchased by the city of Fremont. Today, these 200-plus acres are administered by the East Bay Regional Park District, and the mansion is operated by the city of Fremont.

A visit to Ardenwood Historic Farm is a treat for both adults and children. There is still enough acreage surrounding the home to give an authentic country feeling. Many of the original outbuildings remain in place, among them a ca.-1890 hay barn, blacksmith shop, and equipment shed. The barn is filled with antique farm equipment, including a remarkable Best tractor, which stands almost ten feet tall and is still operated several times a year. The farmyard is mulched with walnut shells from the walnut grove, tiger butterflies flit about the garden, blooming shrubs give off scrumptious smells, and farm cooking is for sale. Volunteers plant, harvest, wash, cook, and even play croquet on the lawn. So far the farm feeling is quite real, and the operation has not gained the "cutesiness" that sometimes creeps into similar operations as volunteers decide to add new frills. Tours of the house are on a first-come, first-served basis, so ask at the admissions booth if tour slots are available.

The house, which sits as a remarkable survivor in the midst of all the farm activity, is in much its original state, with a fine restoration having been completed in 1991. It is a wonderfully picturesque 1889 Queen Anne home with a tower, Free Classic details, and a Richardsonian Romanesque-influenced round-arched entry porch and a second-story porch above. Inside, there are high ceilings, original fireplaces, and handsome inte-

rior finishes. The rear wing, which was the original 1857 farmhouse, still has its low ceilings and simple finishes.

The house has about 90 percent of the original furnishings and accessories, which were preserved and added to for the more than a century that two generations of the Patterson family lived there. Every room has something of interest. One little-seen artifact is a Victorian lady's equivalent of today's Day-Timers—an ivory fan on which she wrote, and later erased, her engagements for each week.

Two recent changes could indicate an unfortunate trend to portray the home's interior furnishings as more grand than they were. A fine set of donated Victorian furnishings has been placed in the formal parlor, and the family's original "best parlor" furniture removed and put into the less formal family parlor across the hall. This change gives a doubly misleading feeling for how the family truly lived by taking two of the home's major rooms—the one used to impress guests and the one used for family gatherings—and furnishing each more grandly than it actually was. In addition, various elaborate dishes and table settings are being brought in, with romantic touches like perfect breakfast trays of fancy dishes set about on beds—quite likely giving an erroneous view of how this energetic farming family actually lived. In the majority of house museums throughout the country, curators have to seek donations of furnishings and try to imagine how things were. But here where a remarkable percentage of the original material is in place, something most house museums in the United States can only dream about, it is unsettling to see such changes creeping in so early in its history as a museum property.

With its two hundred acres, almost the size of George's original farm, and original home, furnishings, and outbuilding, the Ardenwood Historic Farm and the Patterson House are unusually valuable assets for the Bay Area. With the help of many volunteers, this site demonstrates how and where food was grown for early San Franciscans. It is an important reminder of the beginnings of California's agricultural empire and agribusiness. And it is a unique reminder of the way much of the East Bay looked and functioned until the last half of the twentieth century.

McConaghy House, 1886

18701 Hesperian Boulevard; 510-276-3010.

It is interesting to compare the history of the McConaghy House, originally a rural farm dwelling, with that of the Patterson House. Neal McConaghy (died 1914) sailed to America from Scotland in 1848. Soon, like many before him, he decided to try his hand in

California's goldfields, leaving Philadelphia in 1853 to travel to San Francisco via boat. For five years he held odd jobs and tried working the mines near the Salmon River. In 1858 he arrived in the Hayward area with only five dollars to show for his efforts and took a job on a nearby ranch. McConaghy saved his money and built a gristmill. The mill did quite well, and in 1863 he felt ready to marry Sarah McCaw. Just two years later the McConaghys were able to purchase 167 acres of land on either side of San Lorenzo Creek, and there they built a small house and proceeded to have five children. They farmed their acreage, growing first grain and later high-value fruits and other crops that they shipped to San Francisco from a dock on San Lorenzo Creek. In 1886 they decided to build a large new home just a few miles down the road from their farm. When they moved their almost-grown family into it, their youngest son, John, was fifteen years old. He was to stay until he was one hundred years old.

In looking at the Patterson House and the McConaghy House, we follow the parallel lives of two men who came to California to try their luck in the goldfields, who emerged with almost nothing, who took farm-related jobs, and who saved their money until they had enough to purchase their own land. Each proceeded to prosper from his land, reaping bounteous harvests that were shipped via boat across the Bay and directly to San Francisco. Each married and had a family, and each decided to build a grand house later in life—although Patterson decided to add on to his original house, and McConaghy to build his house down the road. And each had a son who took over management of the family farm after the father's death and kept things, including the family home, intact.

In McConaghy's case it was his youngest son, John (1872–1972), who took over the care of his family and management of farm affairs when his father could no longer manage. John had continued to live in the family home, along with his unmarried sister Mary. When he married Florence Smyth in 1912, the couple lived in the family home so that John could continue to care for his ailing parents. They never moved away and the threesome occupied the house until Florence died in 1939 and Mary in 1940. This left John and a hired housekeeper in the family home, where he remained until his death in 1972, having lived in the same home for eighty-five years. As the curator pointed out, "When he moved in everything moved by horse and buggy and by the time he died, he had seen a man land on the moon."

The McConaghys did not hire an architect to design their home; instead, they relied on local builder John Haar Sr., who later became a mayor of Hayward. The house is built in the West Coast Stick style and has the squared bay windows, window surrounds, and long extended roofline brackets that are typical of the style. The entry is enhanced by a fine pair of stained-glass doors with matching threshold. Inside, the house centers around a large central stair hall lighted by a skylight over the stairs. Downstairs rooms include a company parlor, family parlor, library, dining room, kitchen, and pantries; upstairs are four family bedrooms, the single bath, and two servants' rooms.

Although almost all of the furnishings were removed from the home before it was purchased by the Hayward Area Recreation and Park District, the home has been well furnished with appropriate donations. Remarkably, there has been only one set of significant interior changes since the house was built. These came in about 1915 when, after John's parents' death, Florence had the chance to put her own stamp on the house. She elected to change almost all of the wallpapers and to paint the woodwork, but everything else was left as it was, including some carpets that appear to be original. Today Florence's wallpaper and color choices are almost as historic as the rest of the house. They well demonstrate the reaction against the natural wood of the Victorian era and the return to lighter colors that was urged by the leading decorators of the early twentieth century. Her decision to leave everything else just as it was and her husband's never changing anything in later years have left some intriguing items. It is fun to see the original pump still mounted by the kitchen sink, where it brought in water directly from the family's artesian well. A 1902 "on-demand" water heater sits in the corner. And in the back hall is a rarely seen convenience, a dial that automatically adjusted the damper of the

McConaghy House entry

McConaghy House side view and outbuildings

basement furnace; it has numbered settings much like a thermostat that allowed the family to easily control the amount of heat coming into the house.

McConaghy descendants have returned many personal items to the house. It is fun to see the children's eighth-grade-graduation certificates proudly displayed, as today a high school or college diploma might be. In the nineteenth century, eighth grade was considered a fine level of education, and most educated children stopped there, including John McConaghy and three of his siblings. Only one of the McConaghy brothers went on to obtain a higher education. Another family treasure is a set of original photographs taken shortly after the house was completed. All twelve of the main rooms were photographed and provide an unusual and accurate record of how the family lived. Although extensive interior photographs are often found for very grand

houses, or for one or two rooms of a slightly more modest house, it is much more unusual to find such an early and complete interior record for what was essentially a very large, but not overly grand, farmhouse.

Today, the house remains on its original site and still has its early carriage house and water tank. But unlike the Patterson House, which miraculously sits on a piece of land large enough to help visualize the early countryside, the McConaghy House has been completely surrounded by the town of Hayward. An early exterior photograph on display shows the house standing alone along a long, narrow dirt road. Today, that road is one of the main commercial streets of Hayward, a divided six-lane street lined with newish commercial uses. Yet still, once behind the shrubs that help separate the house from the twentieth century, one has a feeling of stepping back into time in visiting the McConaghy home.

MARTINEZ

FOUNDED 1849

Population Growth:

1860 ....NA

1900 1,400

1940 7,000

1990 32,000

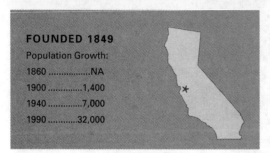

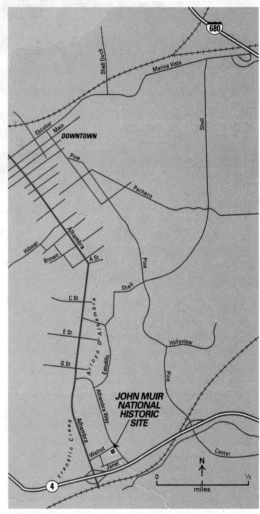

The town was founded by, and named for, Ignacio Martinez, a former commander of the San Francisco Presidio who in 1836 established a rancho on a large land grant adjacent to the narrow, northeasternmost extension of San Francisco Bay. With the coming of the gold rush, Martinez platted a new Bay-side town at the point where the old wagon road leading northward from San Jose reached the Bay. Here, northbound forty-niners could board small riverboats headed for the goldfields. Soon a ferry was also established to transport wagons en route to Sacramento across adjacent Carquinez Strait. In 1850 the bustling small town became the seat of the new state of California's huge Contra Costa County, a distinction that it still holds today.

In subsequent decades, Martinez became a small agricultural trade center for a rich fruit-growing hinterland. Still later, it served the area's railroad-based Bay-side industries. Its principal surviving historic landmark is a fine Italianate museum house, two miles south of town, that was built by one of the region's prosperous fruit growers and later associated with his son-in-law, the famed naturalist and conservationist John Muir.

John Muir House, 1882

4202 Alhambra Avenue; 510-228-8860;
Wolfe and Son, San Francisco, architects.

"Wildness is a necessity. Mountain parks and reservations are useful not only as fountains of timber and irrigating rivers, but as fountains of life." So wrote John Muir (1838–1914), a largely self-educated botanist, biologist, geologist, and glaciologist, who was the father of America's conservation movement. His lifelong approach to learning was to wander in wild places and observe closely the flora, fauna, and rocks. He might sit for a day by a newly discovered plant and try to understand it. Or lie atop a boulder envisioning its path to that place. His insights were profound, and he made valu-

able scientific contributions, primarily as a glaciologist. But his greatest contribution was to help awaken and solidify a conservation ethic in the United States. He wrote movingly about nature, with ten books completed between 1894 and 1914. He was one of the founders of the Sierra Club and served as its president from its beginning in 1892 until his death. And he played a crucial role in the formation of several national parks.

Muir was born in Scotland in 1838 and as a child had roamed the countryside. Then his family moved to Wisconsin in 1849, and he was put to work by his father, helping to clear and farm the virgin land, giving Muir a young introduction to this backbreaking work. Yet even with his work in the fields, Muir could not stop his creative thinking, and during his teenage years he began to invent things at night. In 1860 he took some of these inventions to the Wisconsin State Fair at Madison. There his most famous invention, the self-rising bed, an alarm clock that tilted his bed up on end, made front-page news. While in Madison, Muir was drawn to the University of Wisconsin and enrolled for two years of scientific study. But then he quit school and began to roam the countryside, "botanizing" as he called it, stopping here and there to work in factories to support himself. At age twenty-nine his cornea was pierced as he worked at a sawmill, and he made the decision to forget factories and to devote his life to his passion. He took off to walk, to study, and to write in his journal, which he inscribed, "John Muir, Earth Planet Universe." He walked over a thousand miles south from Wisconsin and sailed to California, ending up in the Sierra Nevada and Yosemite Valley in 1868. These rugged mountains entranced him, and he spent most of the next eleven years in wilderness areas.

In 1874 mutual friends finally convinced him to meet Louisa (Louie) Strentzel (1846–1905), daughter of Dr. John Strentzel, a well-known California horticulturist. They were well suited to each other and married in 1880, when Muir was forty-two and his bride was thirty-three. The day after their marriage Muir threw himself into working in his father-in-law's orchards and vineyards—grafting, cultivating, and eventually managing the 2,600-acre Strentzel farm. He was extremely successful in these endeavors and within seven years had put aside enough money that he felt he could take care of his family, which now included two young daughters, and return to his beloved writing and to somewhat-shortened versions of his earlier wilderness treks.

It was not until this point, as he was approaching fifty, that Muir's years of book writing and conservation advocacy could begin in earnest. Although ever since Henry Thoreau wrote about Walden Pond, American authors had written about our country's natural beauty, Muir was the first to have studied the wilderness firsthand throughout a lifetime. This gave his books and articles an immediacy and authenticity that readers responded to. And added to this was his passion for the subject. He came to say, "I care to live only to entice people to look at nature's loveliness."

The first germ of a national system of wilderness parks had begun in 1864 when President Abraham Lincoln signed a bill to protect our country's first wilderness park—Yosemite Valley and the Mariposa Big Tree

John Muir House

Grove, "jewels of rock and wood"—which was placed under the control of a small volunteer state commission. Ariel Rubissow describes what followed in the booklet *John Muir National Historic Site:* "Without a precedent or a reward for good park management, the commission was soon catering to local politics and private interests. Butcher shops, lumber yards, pigsties, hotels, hay fields and saloons sprang up all over Yosemite's once-pristine floor. When a local entrepreneur adjusted the flow of Nevada Fall for some mercenary purpose, Muir lost patience." He saw that not only was the nation's only protected natural area not protected, but that fully saving it required greatly enlarging it, looking at the entire watershed and the forests upriver. In 1889 he walked through Yosemite with Robert Underwood Johnson, editor of the prestigious East Coast magazine *Century,* showing him the valley floor with its "hogs and hotels" and going on to higher reaches where what at first seemed to be wilderness had been trampled by livestock. The two men formed a plan to create a large and well-run park at Yosemite. Between Johnson's political clout and Muir's articles for *Century* and for local papers, they were successful in creating a large national park around the smaller state-managed

John Muir House

coaxed to support the fledgling environmental movement. For the next twenty-four years, until his death, this was Muir's home.

It is unlikely that Muir would have ever built such a large and commanding home for himself. A large hipped-roof Italianate house, it sits upon a small hillside overlooking the Alhambra Valley. In form, the house is a particularly grand version of the cube-and-cupola house, and its large centered cupola offers a wonderful view out across the valley. The third-floor attic story has small windows that form a part of the broad bracketed cornice. Dr. Strentzel built well; atop a brick foundation are walls of redwood, with an interior lining of brick to provide insulation. The house was fully plumbed and "piped for gas (should its use ever be desired), hot and cold water, and provided with speaking tubes and electric bell signal wires. All the closets are arranged for free ventilation and in other features the latest conveniences and improvements are applied in the building," according to an article in the October 28, 1882, *Martinez Gazette.*

Inside, the finishes are relatively simple, except for several elegant Italianate marble fireplaces. The house is built of redwood, while the floors are of fir grained to look like oak, and the stairway is black walnut. Only a few of the furnishings are original, most notably the above-mentioned desk. Most of the collection is made up of simple Victorian pieces of the type that the Strentzels and Muirs might have had. The one major change that Muir made to the home is the fireplace in the family parlor. He apparently was thrilled when the 1906 earthquake ruined the marble fireplace that had been here. This gave him the opportunity to replace it by building a large brick fireplace with a round-arched opening—its simplicity and straightforwardness more closely matched Muir's personality than did much of the rest of the fine house.

Outside, the orchards and plantings that were here during Muir's lifetime are being re-created. At 8.8 acres, the site is just barely large enough to get some feeling for its early farm appearance. Located on the site, but beyond the orchards, is the important **Martinez Adobe.** Built in 1849 by Don Vincente Martinez, son of Don Ignacio Martinez, holder of the 17,700-acre Rancho El Pinole Mexican land grant, this is a typical 1840s Spanish Colonial–style home. It has a rough stone foundation topped with adobe-brick walls from twenty-four to thirty inches thick. The roof is covered with sawed wood shingles. The adobe had many owners before Dr. Strentzel purchased it in 1874. Strentzel used the house for storage and likely as a residence for some of his overseers. Many years later, from 1907 until 1915, the Muirs' daughter Wanda Muir Hanna and her

preserve in 1890, and a few years later Muir succeeded in adding the state's portion to the larger park.

As an outgrowth of the drive to save Yosemite Park, he joined with others to form the Sierra Club. This extension of his conservation passion offered a way to involve others in the conservation issues that he felt so deeply about. Encouraged by these major initial successes, in his later years Muir hiked Teddy Roosevelt and countless others through Yosemite, winning their support for conservation. He played a crucial role in preserving several other national parks, among them Grand Canyon, Sequoia, and Mount Rainier. Shortly after his death, the National Park Service was formed to oversee our nation's emerging park system.

His home base during these influential years in his life was the Muir House. This large Italianate house was built by his father-in-law, Dr. John Strentzel, in 1882, and in 1890, upon his death, Muir and Louie moved into the big house with her mother. Here, in an upstairs study, on a simple desk that is now back in its rightful place, Muir did most of his influential writing. In addition, the house provided a base from which to entertain influential visitors who needed to be educated and engineer husband, Tom Hanna, lived here with their children. They moved only when all of the farm was sold after John Muir's death.

Luckily, the Muir House remained structurally unaltered after its sale, and in 1964 it became a national historic site. Since then, the adobe and adjacent grounds have been acquired. The National Park Service has been hard at work restoring all aspects of the site. If you are interested in hearing excerpts from Muir's writings and seeing some of the sheer beauty of the natural sites he was working to save, be sure to allow time to view the introductory film at the visitor center.

Martinez Adobe

OAKLAND

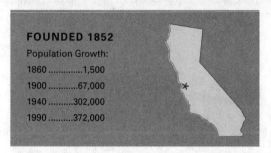

FOUNDED 1852

Population Growth:

1860 1,500

1900 67,000

1940 302,000

1990 372,000

As San Francisco's largest neighbor, Oakland has always been closely tied to its sister city directly across the Bay. Founded in an oak grove on a gently sloping plain at the base of the Contra Costa Range, in the 1850s and 1860s Oakland became a trade center for farms and orchards supplying food to booming San Francisco. In 1869 Oakland gained a unique economic prize when it became the western terminus of the newly completed Central Pacific Railroad, the nation's first transcontinental rail line (see pages 139 and 213).

Rail Terminus and Bedroom Suburb

Like other railroad barons farther east, the Central Pacific's Sacramento-based builders, known as the Big Four, preferred to locate their valuable urban facilities on undeveloped tracts of land that they owned, rather than buying expensive building sites and rights-of-way near established town centers. A typical strategy was to purchase farmland at the edge of town for their passenger stations and freight depots and then profit from land sales as new commercial buildings grew up around these facilities. San Francisco, as the West's largest city and principal seaport, would clearly be the final destination or shipping point for most of the railroad's passengers and freight. To ensure control of land-based traffic in and out of San Francisco, the Big Four made three important acquisitions that set the stage for their long dominance of the California railroad system. Either before or shortly after the transcontinental line was completed, they obtained controlling interests in (1) several previously built short-line railroads providing local service to Bay Area towns; (2) the California Steam Navigation Company, which had long dominated ferry service between San Francisco and other Bay Area towns; and (3) the entire, and mostly undeveloped, five-hundred-acre waterfront of Oakland, then a small agricultural trade center with about five thousand inhabitants.

The local railroads were connected to provide round-the-Bay service to San Francisco, but the train schedules and terminal facilities were geared toward local commuters and shipments. The bulk of transcontinental rail shipments, including passengers, arrived and departed from new railroad-built terminal facilities on the Oakland waterfront. Passengers and freight then reached San Francisco aboard large, railroad-controlled steam ferryboats that continuously traversed the four-mile water crossing. Oakland thus became a key component in the western long-distance transportation network, and its population steadily increased, reaching thirty-five thousand in 1880 and sixty-seven thousand in 1900.

While some of this population growth resulted from the expansion of Oakland's commercial and industrial waterfront activities, much of it also resulted from the city's, and adjacent Berkeley's (see page 170) and Alameda's (see page 162), new roles as pleasantly spacious "bedroom suburbs" of crowded San Francisco. The regular ferry service provided a convenient commute to the heart of the larger city's financial district, while the East Bay's milder and sunnier climate, sheltered from Pacific winds and fogs by the rugged San Francisco Peninsula as well as by the warmer and more tranquil Bay waters, made these East Bay towns ideal family homesites. In 1887 a San Francisco journalist wrote that Oakland was

> essentially a city of homes [with] an appearance of comfort and quiet elegance about the residences which reminds one of some of the older cities of New England. Nearly all of the houses are built on lots sufficiently large to give room for a garden, and great care is shown in the cultivation of rare and beautiful flowers.

Earthquake Refuge

As in most Bay Area cities, some large Oakland buildings suffered toppled chimneys or collapsed front facades in the massive earthquake that shook the region in 1906. Structural damage in San Francisco was more severe, but even there such damage was minor compared to the uncontrollable three-day fire that followed and destroyed all of the city's commercial district and two-thirds of its dwellings (see page 214). Mercifully, other Bay Area towns escaped such fires. As its largest and closest neighbor, Oakland was to play a central role

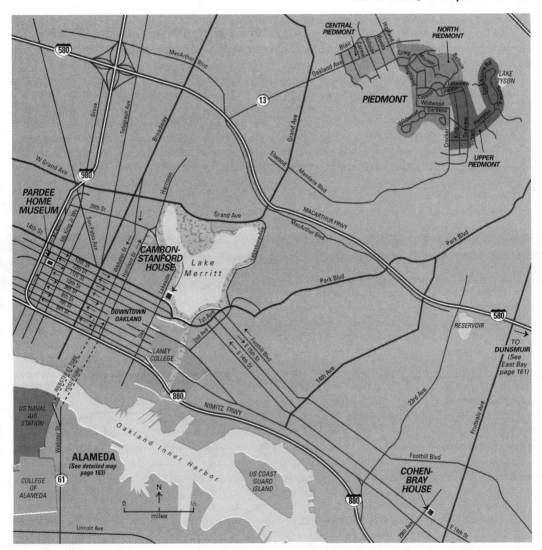

in caring for the estimated 300,000 San Franciscans who lost their homes in the conflagration. About half of these came by ferry to Oakland, whose citizens went to heroic lengths to feed, clothe, and house them. Not surprisingly, many decided to resettle in their friendly host city on the East Bay.

Of even greater long-term significance was the earthquake's role in changing the economies of the two cities. In a half century, San Francisco had developed a large and diverse industrial base as the principal manufacturing and food-processing center of the Pacific coast. Now crowded in aging buildings along the city's narrow waterfront, many factory owners preferred to build modern facilities on Oakland's spacious harbor rather than repair their damaged San Francisco quar-

ters. Thus began Oakland's shift toward becoming the industrial center of northern California. This trend was accelerated in the next decades when many of the nation's booming automobile manufacturers established West Coast assembly plants in Oakland. By the 1920s the city was becoming known as the Detroit of the West. General Motors even added a new Oakland line to emphasize its West Coast presence. By 1930 the city's population was 284,000, an almost-fourfold increase over its 75,000 inhabitants at the time of the earthquake twenty-four years earlier.

Arsenal of the Pacific War

Oakland was to have still-another population surge as San Francisco Bay became a nerve center for military operations against Japan after the surprise attack on Hawaii's Pearl Harbor in December 1941. That attack destroyed most of the U.S. Navy's Pacific Fleet, leaving the entire West Coast vulnerable to attack by Japanese submarines and carrier-based aircraft. As protective warships were diverted from duties elsewhere, the United States began a massive program of emergency shipbuilding, much of it accomplished in new and expanded shipyards in Oakland and nearby towns at the northeastern end of San Francisco Bay. In addition to wartime industries, new and expanded military installations—army and navy bases, supply centers, airfields, and hospitals—filled most of the buildable sites near the northern Bay.

All of this frantic activity led to a massive influx of workers, well described by historian Beth Bagwell in her excellent book *Oakland: The Story of a City:*

> Huge numbers of jobs were available, not only in private industry, but also on the military bases, where civilians filled many jobs. The acute labor shortage in the Bay Area attracted workers from all over the country who leaped at the opportunity after the hard years of the Depression.

As in the postearthquake period, many of these new Oakland area workers stayed on as residents after the war ended in 1945. In 1950 the city's population was 385,000, an increase of 83,000 since 1940.

Modern Oakland

Through much of the period since 1950, Oakland suffered many of the same traumas as did the older industrial cities of the northeastern states. Plant closings and modernizations eliminated many blue-collar jobs, while expanding suburban towns lured many middle-class families away from the inner city. In addition, massive "urban renewal" programs in the 1960s destroyed much of the city's historic fabric. More recently, the city has begun a revival based on its original attractiveness as a lower-cost and milder-climate alternative to crowded San Francisco.

While many of Oakland's once-fine Victorian neighborhoods have not survived, three superb museum houses, one each from the 1860s (see the following entry), 1870s (see page 192), and 1880s (see page 192), provide remarkable insights into the period when it was a renowned "city of homes." A fourth museum house, a fine early-Eclectic-era country estate, is located about eight miles southeast of downtown. In addition, a delightfully elegant Eclectic-era suburb, with the appropriate name of Piedmont, looks out over Oakland from the adjacent Contra Costa Hills (see page 194).

Pardee Home Museum, 1868

672 Eleventh Street; 510-444-2187; John J. Newsom and William C. Hoagland, San Francisco, architects.

This unique museum house was built and preserved by three generations of the civic-minded Pardee family over a period of more than 120 years. During this time the family, especially Helen Newhall Penniman Pardee (1857–1947), filled the grand dwelling with a remarkable collection of fine decorative objects from the late nineteenth and early twentieth centuries. These include furniture, glassware, minerals, ceramics, paintings, pipes, fans, teapots, candlesticks, scrimshaw, and countless other items, many with an ethnographic focus. At the same time, the house itself—a centered-gable Italianate design with a cupola offering splendid views of Oakland, the Bay Bridge, and San Francisco—was preserved on its original half-block site with its original carriage house and water tower. The interiors remain just as they were when the last surviving third-generation daughter, also named Helen, died in 1981. She, in turn, had kept many areas of the house, such as drawers and medicine cabinets, in exactly the same condition as they were when *her* mother, collector Helen Penniman Pardee, died in 1947.

The house was built in 1868 by Dr. Enoch H. Pardee (1827–1896) for his wife, Mary Pardee (she was a distant cousin), and their only son, George C. Pardee (1857–1941). Young Dr. Pardee had left his native Ohio to join the California gold rush in 1852. After some success in the goldfields, he turned to his earlier medical training and become a prominent San Francisco physician, specializing in the eye, ear, and throat. Enoch sent for Mary in 1855, and the couple finally married, culminating a seven-year courtship via mail (many of their early letters remain with the house). Mary developed tuberculosis in the 1860s, and Enoch felt the sunnier Oakland climate would be good for her. Unfortunately, it proved not to be the full solution, and Mary died in 1870. Enoch threw himself into civic affairs, serving as state assemblyman and mayor of Oakland in the 1870s and as state senator in the 1880s. He also had a strong interest in public health and served on the health board, concerning himself particularly with the water supply.

In the meantime their son, George, graduated from the University of California at Berkeley at the top of his class and then spent four years in Germany studying medicine. In 1887 George married Helen Newhall Penniman, who was to become the family's most avid collector of fine decorative objects. While she pursued her varied collecting interests, and raised their four daughters, George joined his father's medical practice in San

Pardee Home Museum

Francisco and also became active in civic affairs. He served as mayor of Oakland in the 1890s and governor of California from 1903 to 1907. As governor he gained national recognition for his skillful management of the recovery from the 1906 earthquake.

Only two of George and Helen's daughters lived past early adulthood—Madeline (died 1980) and Helen (died 1981). Neither ever married, and they lived together in the Pardee Home until their deaths. "The sisters" zealously guarded the house, saving it from urban renewal efforts and from the path of nearby Interstate 980. They actively pursued local and national landmark designations and set up a foundation to maintain the house after their deaths, thus becoming the third generation of the Pardee family to leave lasting contributions to the city of Oakland.

Today, the house is one of the most intriguing Italianate homes surviving in California. Inside, the architectural detailing is relatively simple; the color scheme throughout much of the house—grayish-green paint and carpet—dates from the early 1950s. Dominating the interior is its remarkable collection of rare decorative objects. An example is a striking light fixture made of panels with photographs from the collection of Carlton Emmons Watkins, the Ansel Adams of the nineteenth century, whose exquisite work convinced Congress to make Yosemite a national park. His many wet-collodion photographs created a unique record of early California, and Governor Pardee had arranged for all of Watkins's plates to be transferred to Sacramento for permanent preservation. Just four days before the scheduled move, his entire studio was consumed by the great 1906 fire. This light fixture, happily, was already in the governor's possession.

The collections contain around forty thousand ob-

jects, a number that is difficult to visualize. Mrs. Pardee delighted in arranging displays from her collection. Today the staff continues this tradition by arranging, at the house, shows of objects drawn from the collections. One exhibit called "Fandango of fans" exhibited forty-five fans. These included ethnographic fans from Japan, Korea, China, India, and the South Pacific; fans actually used by the Pardee women and therefore not part of Mrs. Pardee's "collections"; three fans from the 1893 Chicago Columbian Exposition; and a few fashion fans, such as one of ostrich feathers that went with an elegant beaded dress.

Another exhibit, called "The Witching Weed," included about seventy-five objects representing tobacco use by the Pardee family, their employees, and other societies around the world. Exotic versions, such as a Maori pipe from New Zealand, were displayed, as were U.S. presidential-campaign pipes from the 1840s and 1850s, candy boxes made to look like tobacco boxes, tourist pipes from world's fairs, and spittoons used by Pardee employees. With perhaps forty thousand objects to choose from, exhibits like these could be mounted every month for many years with no repetition!

The Pardee Home also provides an instructive glimpse at lifestyles in early Oakland. Something as simple as the fact that both Enoch and George Pardee maintained their medical practices in downtown San Francisco while living here demonstrates Oakland's important early role as a commuting town for affluent San Franciscans. A horse-drawn trolley line passed nearby and ended at the ferry pier. From the pier it was but a twenty-minute ride to downtown San Francisco. Compare this with the plight of modern commuters crossing the Bay Bridge at rush hour in their own automobiles!

Camron-Stanford House, 1876

1418 Lakeside Drive; 510-836-1976.
Large Victorian homes once surrounded the shores of Oakland's picturesque Lake Merritt, but the Camron-Stanford House is now the sole survivor. A large, asymmetrical Italianate design, it has handsomely detailed windows featuring framed segmental arches upstairs and framed full arches downstairs. There is a two-story slanted bay window on the left front and a partial-width one-story porch on the right, a combination of features that was particularly popular in northern California versions of the style.

Will and Alice Camron built the home. He was a cattleman and real estate developer, and during the thirty years it was used as a residence, from 1876 until 1907, four additional families lived here; the Josiah Stanford family—he was the brother of Big Four railroad magnate Leland Stanford (see page 199)—stayed the longest and is commemorated, along with the original owners, in the modern name of the house. In 1907 the widow of the last private owner sold the house to the city for use as the Oakland Public Museum, which opened in 1910. Over the next several decades, the house was frequently altered for expanding museum uses. After the museum moved to spacious new quarters in 1967, the house sat abandoned for four years until the Preservation Association was formed to restore the house and grounds.

Early newspaper accounts and letters were used to guide the well-researched restoration efforts. Entire parts of the house had to be re-created, including marble fireplaces, tin roof, mantelpieces, newly woven Kidderminster carpets, and wallpapers. The results of this unusually extensive restoration is a picture-perfect high-style 1870s interior. A particularly interesting, though brief, exhibit in the basement documents the many steps that were undertaken in this huge project.

Although the results may seem a bit too perfect, it is rare to find a house of this period that re-creates almost every detail of a high-style 1870s dwelling. The David Hewes Art Gallery Room is particularly fascinating, for here nineteenth-century art, sculpture, and exotic novelty furniture have been collected and displayed just as they were in many homes of the era.

Cohen-Bray House, 1884

1440 Twenty-ninth Avenue; 510-532-0704 (limited visiting hours).
This fine Stick-style dwelling was a joint wedding gift for Emma Bray and Alfred H. Cohen—the land and house were given by Emma's parents and the furnishings by Alfred's. The young couple loved their new home and elected to leave it almost unmodified, either

Camron-Stanford House

inside or out, through the rest of their long lives (Alfred died in 1925 and Emma in 1945). Their heirs followed the same policy, so that today the home is a wonderfully intact time capsule of the Victorian era's high-style Aesthetic interiors fashionable in the mid-1880s. This is one of the finest such interiors surviving anywhere in the United States.

The Aesthetic movement was one of a sequence of late Victorian "reform" movements in interior design (Eastlake, Art Nouveau, and Arts and Crafts were the others) that originated in England. These movements were a reaction against the flood of ornate decorative objects and materials produced by the factories of the Industrial Revolution during the preceding decades. As homes were filled with elaborate and standardized machine-made objects, critics such as Charles Eastlake, William Morris, and others advocated a return to simpler, handmade designs.

The exterior of the Cohen-Bray House is a fine example of a Stick-style design with a square tower and a steeply pitched front-gabled roof, features that are more typical of eastern rather than West Coast examples of the style. From the street, the home looks relatively unprepossessing, but inside some dramatic surprises await the visitor. As a wedding present, Emma Bray received from her father's good friend and neighbor, Henry Weatherbee, what seemed a strange present—a charred log. Henry, however, was a good lumberman and knew what was inside that log. It was the butt end of a very old and very large redwood tree. Over the thousand years or more that a tree such as this one grew, it became very heavy, and as a consequence the fibers in the lower portion of the tree's trunk would slowly buckle or become distorted from their normal straight grain into a wavy or curly pattern. It was this redwood that was fashioned into a dramatically paneled entry hall reflecting the "Modern Gothic" interiors made popular by books such as Clarence's Cook's *The House Beautiful*. The room is organized into panels of curly redwood (laid horizontally, vertically, and diagonally) and bounded by decorated redwood battens. The coffered ceiling, cornice brackets, and spindlework all feature the curly redwood. Contributing to this unique interior are the stylized sunflowers carved into the door panels of this and other first-floor rooms.

The parlor is a soft French gray color with the original bordered wall-to-wall carpet and above, a cove-cornice ceiling with several applied borders. This was very much in keeping with the feeling of the day—that the ceiling is a large surface that can be seen all at once, and is thus a fine place to concentrate decorative enhancement within a room. Both the dining room, with its elegant built-in walnut-and-marble sideboard, and

Cohen-Bray House

the library, with its equally elegant Minton-tile fireplace opening, are fine examples of quality cabinet making. The ceiling wallpapers and friezes in the parlor, dining room, rear portion of the front hall, and library are all the original hangings dating from the 1880s. Most of the designs feature Anglo-Japanese motifs. The light fixtures are the original gas ones that were later electrified. Alfred A. Cohen, Alfred's father, an Alameda-based financier (see page 162) who later became an attorney for the Central Pacific Railroad, purchased the furniture for the front parlor from Pottier and Stymus, the premier decorating and manufacturing firm in New York.

Very few changes to the original home have occurred over the years. A large sun porch and a breakfast room for informal meals are the notable additions, both of which were incorporated prior to the turn of the century. The other major change was the rebuilding of the smoking room in the Arts and Crafts style after its total destruction by the collapse of its fireplace chimney during the 1906 earthquake. In 1926 some other miscellaneous pieces of Victorian-era furniture, including two very large mirrors, were brought into the home from Fernside, the grand Alameda estate of Alfred's father.

After Emma and Alfred died, their youngest daughter Emelita lived in the house until her death in 1988, preserving its original interiors through both inclination and longevity. After her death the remaining heirs recognized the home's unique architectural and decorative integrity and formed a foundation to preserve the home as an educational center. Because only one family and its heirs have lived here continuously, the home still has the feeling of "home" rather than that of a museum. Because its interiors are in relatively fragile state, tours are held only once monthly, and reservations are essential. This house is recommended for those with a serious interest in Victorian homes and interiors, rather than for more informal touring and family groups.

Piedmont, ca. 1900–1930

The hills immediately to the east of Oakland began to be settled shortly after 1850, mainly with small farms. In 1870 a grand resort hotel was built on hot springs near Piedmont Park, and this was quite popular until it burned in 1893. By the late 1890s, subdivision had begun, and a few houses were constructed in Piedmont. Not until the aftermath of the 1906 San Francisco earthquake and fire did Piedmont begin to assume its present role as one of the premier upscale residential communities of the East Bay. The tragedy led many wealthy San Franciscans, some of whom had previously summered in the delightful Piedmont Hills, to build their permanent homes there. The town of Piedmont was incorporated in 1907, and a decision was made to keep it strictly a residential community, with no commercial districts. Only three years later the 1910 U.S. Census reported that Piedmont had thirty-two millionaires, giving it the highest per capita income of any similar community in the country.

Central Piedmont centered around an early trolley line that ran along Oakland Avenue and was the first area of Piedmont to develop. Houses were built on a small street grid between Carmel and Highland Avenues. Most of Piedmont's homes dating from the 1890s and the first decade of the twentieth century are found here, along with its handful of public buildings. **North Piedmont** lay just to the east of a second trolley line that ran along Highland Drive. From about 1907 to 1920, fine homes were built on North Piedmont's large lots, and these include many large architect-designed examples of the early modern styles. **Upper Piedmont,** the more deeply shaded area east of Crocker Avenue on the map (see page 189), was accessible mainly by automobile, and its homes were generally built just a bit later than North Piedmont's, primarily during the late 1910s and 1920s. These reflect a variety of Period styles and include some of the largest homes in the entire East Bay area. Many of the town's largest homes are in Upper Piedmont. All of the houses featured below are located there, but the entire town is worth exploring. (For much of the information included here we are indebted to Mark A. Wilson's fine book *A Living Legacy: Historic Architecture of the East Bay*.)

11 Glen Alpine Road (private), Sweetland Estate, 1927–1929; Frederick H. Reimers, architect. According to Mark Wilson, this forty-five-room mansion is the largest historic home in the East Bay and was built for "the man who invented the automobile oil filter, electric timer and electric-eye door opener." It is an asymmetrical French Eclectic design with the huge, high-pitched roof, but little else, visible from the road.

17 Sotelo Avenue (private), Buck House, 1924. Built for Senator Frank Buck, this is a fine example of a side-gabled-roof Colonial Revival design. Notice the use of double-hung windows with single panes in the lower sash and multipane glazing in the upper. The door gives just the hint of an entry porch by using freestanding columns rather than pilasters to support the triangular pediment above. The actual covered entry is created by a recessed area rather than an external porch.

370 Hampton Road (private), ca. 1925–1930; Albert Farr, San Francisco, architect. Light-peach-toned stucco covers this lovely towered French Eclectic home. The tower is on the right side, and the smaller rounded "tower" on the left side is actually a turret. Towers extend all the way down to the ground, while turrets cantilever out from the wall surface and are therefore generally smaller. Note the basket-handle arch above the entry door and first-floor windows, and the handsome metal grillwork.

320 Hampton Road, at Indian Road (private), ca. 1920s. A rounded tower and exceptional carved- or cast-stone entrance distinguish this fine Spanish Eclectic design.

246 Seaview Avenue (private), Ayer House, 1914; Julia Morgan, San Francisco, architect. The pair of front-facing gables here has a lower pitch than those found on most Tudor homes. This low pitch, combined with the corner window on the left and the unusual distribution of half-timbering (only below the upstairs windows and in the top of the gable), gives this house an early modern aspect that contrasts with its Tudor detailing. Among these details are the Tudor arched entry, carved vergeboards, casement windows, parquetry, and front chimney.

250 Seaview Avenue (private), ca. 1925–1930. This large French Eclectic house is in the asymmetrical subtype and is clad with rough-textured stucco walls. The corner quoins are stuccoed, but painted a deeper tone than the house. Note the two circular roof dormers.

260 Seaview Avenue (private), ca. 1925–1930. This is a towered French Eclectic, or Norman French, design with the dominant half-timbering that is typical of this subtype. The wood used to form the half-timbering has been given "antique" imperfections; note how the upstairs window tops break the roofline and the characteristic French combination of stuccoed walls with brick quoins.

62 Farragut Avenue (private), Lombard House, 1916; Julia Morgan, San Francisco, architect. This massive Tudor home has more typical steeply pitched front-facing gables than does Morgan's house at 246 Seaview (see above). Like

Piedmont

246, this house has very fine detailing. Note the semihexagonal bay windows and how the gables form an overhang above them.

205 Crocker Avenue, at Farragut Avenue (private), ca. 1910–1920. This elegant Italian Renaissance design of the flat-roofed subtype has refined and carefully proportioned details.

55 Seaview Avenue (private), McCandless House, ca. 1910 and later; Albert Farr, San Francisco, architect. This large home is a fine example of a Tudor design of the parapeted-gable subtype. The dormers are parapeted and, rather than having a main front-facing gable, it has a dominant flat-roofed two-story bay with a castellated parapet, a common elaboration in this subtype. The carriage entry has a similar castellated section above. There are several tall chimneys, all with multiple shafts and chimney pots above. Note the absence of half-timbering, a feature rarely seen in this subtype that is based on the more formal English building traditions of the late-Medieval period.

25 Seaview Avenue, at Lincoln Avenue (private), Knowland House, 1912; Edson F. Adams, architect. Built for William F. Knowland, publisher of the *Oakland Tribune* and a U.S. senator, this is another fine flat-roofed Italian Renaissance design similar to 205 Crocker Avenue (see above). Note the flat glass hood that fans outward above the entry.

Dunsmuir, 1899

2960 Peralta Oaks Court; from North Bay take 580E going south; take exit 106th Ave.; take three quick lefts under the freeway, and go immediately right on Peralta Oak Dr. Follow the signs. From 580W take the Foothill/MacArthur Blvd. exit; take a right on 106th Ave.; 510-615-5555; J. Eugene Freeman, San Francisco, architect.

This dramatic Neoclassical home, built on an original tract of over six thousand acres of rolling foothills, was a wedding present from Alexander Dunsmuir to his bride, Josephine Bower Wallace. The wedding had been a long time coming. Alexander had arrived in the Bay region in 1878 to run the California branch of his wealthy father's coal empire, which was centered in Victoria, British Columbia. He soon met Josephine, the wife of a friend, and they fell in love. Josephine divorced her husband, and she and her young daughter, Edna, moved in with Alexander. But Alexander's mother forbade him to marry a divorced woman; it took twenty years before she finally consented to the marriage that would legalize Alexander and Josephine's relationship.

Alexander promptly built this handsome home for his bride-to-be, and the couple set off on a long-delayed honeymoon to see daughter Edna, now grown and an actress, perform in New York. Tragically, Alexander died on the trip east, and Josephine returned to the home alone, only to die of lung cancer in 1901. Her daughter, Edna, inherited the thirty-seven-room home, but discovered she could not afford to keep it up.

In 1906 Dunsmuir was sold to Isaias W. Hellman Jr., the son of a wealthy San Francisco banker and financier (see also "Ehrman Mansion," page 274), who used it mostly as a summer house. He, his wife, Frances, and their family lived here year-round, however, for a period following the 1906 earthquake. Mr. Hellman died in 1920, the same year as his father, but his wife, along with their children and grandchildren, continued to enjoy summers at Dunsmuir until her death in December 1959. The estate was then purchased by the city of Oakland for use as a conference center. In 1971 a nonprofit organization was formed to restore and preserve the historic estate for "public benefit."

The house is an excellent Neoclassical design of the full-height-entry-porch-with-lower-full-width-porch subtype. The broad lower porch is extended out to the side to form a large porte cochere. A most unusual feature of the house is the use of three colossal Corinthian columns for the full-height entry porch. Such porches typically have an even number of columns—usually two, four, or six—arranged symmetrically on each side of the entry steps. The broad one-story porch is supported by Ionic columns. The design features extensive roofline balustrades—above the broad one-story porch and on portions of the main roofline. One of these, a square rooftop balustrade, surrounds a skylight that illuminates a handsome interior dome of stained glass. Ten feet in diameter and with over seven thousand individual pieces of glass, this is located in the exact center of the house.

Here, as in many Neoclassical houses, the entryways and interior details are of Colonial Revival inspiration. The main entry door has the sidelights with a large elliptical fanlight above that is typical of the Adam (Federal) style. Inside, the same theme continues, and there are many mantelpieces with Adamesque ornament.

Dunsmuir

The large, roomlike entry hall is in the tradition of the Victorian-era living hall and has a Colonial Revival stairway with simple turned balusters. The floors here and throughout the first floor are made of varied woods laid in patterns that create a unique design for each room. The majority of the furnishings on display belonged to the Hellmans.

The parlor is paneled in mahogany with a beamed ceiling and has a mantelpiece featuring garlands, wreaths, and Olympic torches. Behind it is a large game room that has had billiard, Ping-Pong, and card tables at various times in its life. The library contains unusual Hellman furniture with back-to-back sofas. The dining room, kitchen, and service rooms are remarkably unchanged; Mrs. Hellman even had gas piped into the huge early wood-and-coal stove in the kitchen, rather than having it replaced by a new one. A pastry pantry, butler's pantry, servants' dining room, and back hall complete this service wing. In the basement are still more service rooms, including a wine cellar and laundry. It is reported that when the Hellmans were residing in San Francisco, the laundry was shipped out to Dunsmuir to be done, and of course the farm and green-

houses provided fresh produce and flowers for the family while in the city.

Upstairs, there are many bedrooms, some reconfigured by the Hellmans to accommodate their children. Many of the early beds were found stored on the third floor. Of particular interest are the bathrooms. All of the unmodified original bathrooms have marble splash slabs and drains under the basins, tubs, and toilets. The lack of these make it easy to distinguish the slightly newer added bathrooms. Both Mrs. Hellman's bath and one of the guest baths have delicate tile borders. The guest bath border features shells and gold accents. Mrs. Hellman's border has ribbons and garlands of flowers. The elaborate showers added by the Hellmans to their baths are typical early-twentieth-century additions.

Of the original six thousand acres, only about forty remain, and today, these are handsomely landscaped. They include some original farm outbuildings—chicken coop, milk barn, coal shed, stable, "swayback building," and carriage house. These are of high historic value as fast-vanishing reminders of the time when much of San Francisco Bay was surrounded by large farms.

PALO ALTO

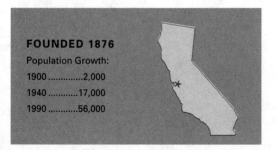

FOUNDED 1876

Population Growth:

1900 2,000
1940 17,000
1990 56,000

Palo Alto and the Peninsula

Because of the national reputation of Stanford University, Palo Alto is perhaps the most widely known of the several towns that lie directly south of San Francisco, or "down peninsula," as locals call the area. Palo Alto (which means "Tall Tree") is about thirty miles south of the city and was originally the most southerly of a string of small railroad towns that served the country homes of San Francisco's wealthiest citizens. As the West's financial capital and, until the 1920s, its largest city, it also had the region's highest concentration of wealth. Here, as elsewhere, many of these affluent families chose to supplement their city homes with elaborate rural estates. The sheltered and scenic Bay-side slopes of the San Francisco Peninsula became favored sites for these estates because of their mild, sunny climate and large tracts of undeveloped land.

They were also conveniently accessible via the Southern Pacific line that ran southward to connect San Francisco with San Jose at the southerly tip of the Bay. The price of a commuter train ride to and from small peninsula towns to San Francisco was considerably higher than the cost of ferry commuting to the East Bay bedroom suburbs of Berkeley, Oakland, and Alameda, and this also helped to restrict the peninsula towns to more affluent residents. Not until paved automobile roads were built in the 1920s and 1930s did the peninsula begin to receive more dense residential development, a trend that accelerated rapidly after 1950.

An East Coast parallel to the San Francisco–peninsula relationship is New York City (the financial capital of the East Coast), which had two similar areas of great estates—northern Long Island and the Hudson River Valley. Both were served by relatively expensive early train service and had particularly pleasant natural settings. As a result, many grand estates were located around a string of small towns that radiated out from

the city along the rail lines. Like the San Francisco Peninsula, both of these areas had huge population increases as the automobile opened them to large-scale suburban development. In both areas most of the original estates have now been subdivided into smaller homesites, although some of their grand early dwellings still survive, mostly now converted to institutional uses.

Here we have included one street, in the still-affluent town of Hillsborough (see the following entry), that provides a brief but instructive look at how the great estates were subdivided. Professorville, in the town of Palo Alto (see page 199), is included as a charming early neighborhood of smaller homes—the sort that could be afforded by educators and others of more modest means. Also included are the area's two grand museum houses—Ralston Hall, in the town of Belmont (see page 202), and Filoli, near the smaller town of Woodside (see page 204), which clearly demonstrate the affluence of many of the peninsula's early residents.

Hillsborough, ca. 1890 to present

Hillsborough, located about halfway between San Francisco and Palo Alto, was the premier "great estate" town, as it was closest to the city and incorporated early to try to protect its upscale status. Today, most of its great estates, as well as those on the rest of the peninsula, are no longer intact. They have either been destroyed, converted to other uses, subdivided into smaller tracts, or at the very best surrounded by neighborhoods of smaller houses. Hillsborough has remained determinedly residential and is an instructive example of a town once made up of multiple large estates that today have mostly been subdivided for "smaller" homes and lot sizes (the adjective "smaller" must be taken in a relative sense, as Hillsborough remains one of the ten wealthiest towns per capita in the entire United States).

The subdivision of Hillsborough's estates began with the Bay Area housing shortage of the First World War and still continues. Most of the homes you see there were built after 1930, with the majority after 1945. But those with a serious interest in how the estate subdivision process has worked will be intrigued by visiting Hillsborough's **Eucalyptus Avenue.** Enter Eucalyptus from its south end, off Ralston Avenue (note that this is *not* the same Ralston Avenue that is the site of Ralston

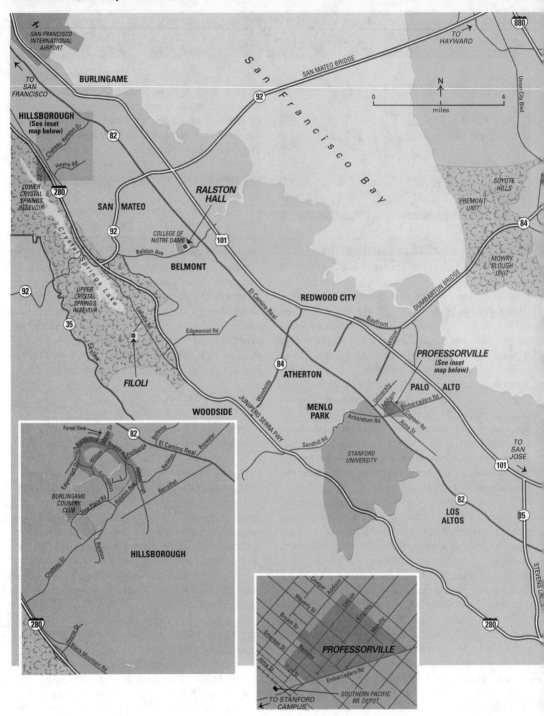

Hall, which is in the town of Belmont; see page 202). The first left off of Eucalyptus at a small triangle intersection (a very hard left) takes you through the original estate gates to New Place, which is now New Place Road

and is lined with newer houses. Almost at the end and on the right, you will see the dramatic rear facade of New Place (private), the country home of William S. Crocker, built in 1911 with Lewis Hobart as the archi-

Hillsborough

tect. This original estate home, now part of the Burlingame Country Club, looks out over the club grounds, most of which were also once part of its large gardens. Bruce Porter, who designed these original, and now mostly lost, gardens for New Place, also designed those that can still be visited at Filoli (see page 204).

Returning to and continuing along Eucalyptus Avenue, you will pass through the grounds of the grand Burlingame Country Club, established in 1893. Note that Eucalyptus Avenue is still framed with its original eucalyptus trees. Amid the newer houses are retained occasional handsome gates that once led into the large estates that were sprinkled along Eucalyptus's length when it was still a country road. (Today, these lead into neighborhood streets for the now subdivided estates.) Just after Eucalyptus Avenue changes into Sharon Road, watch for Manor Drive to the left. As before, you will enter Manor Drive through the original estate gates and pass a number of new homes before you come to 1761 Manor Drive (private) on the right, which was the George Newhall House, built in 1914 with Lewis Hobart as architect. As at New Place, the former long entry drive to this great estate house is now lined with newer homes. Although this brief drive is not a detour the casual house watcher is likely to enjoy, those with a special interest will find it an illuminating lesson in the rural-suburban evolution of houses for the wealthy.

Professorville, ca. 1890–1910

Palo Alto was the site of the nine-thousand-acre stock farm of one of San Francisco's most wealthy and powerful citizens, railroad magnate and politician Leland Stanford, president of the Central Pacific Railroad and United States senator from California (see also pages 139 and 142). In 1885 Californians were to discover a new dimension to the hard-driving leader of the fabled Big Four. The previous year the Stanfords' only child,

sixteen-year-old Leland Stanford Jr., had died of typhoid fever while in Florence, Italy, on a family trip. His grieving parents now announced that "the children of California shall be our children," and, to this end, they were donating their Palo Alto land and an endowment of $21 million for the founding of the Leland Stanford Jr. University, today known simply as Stanford University. This was, in buying power, probably still the most generous private gift to American education ever made. Some indication of its value was the fact that six years later John D. Rockefeller's gifts of only about $1.5 million were enough to establish the distinguished University of Chicago.

Work began almost immediately. The first cornerstone was laid in 1887, faculty were recruited, and classes began on October 1, 1891. The students had new dormitories, and key administrators new on-campus houses, but when faculty families arrived at the fledgling campus, they found it surrounded mostly by large grain fields; local housing was not readily available. Further complicating the housing situation were the

199

Leland Stanford (seated to left of tree) with family and friends at his Palo Alto stock farm, ca. 1880

stipulations of the Stanford endowment—five thousand acres had been set aside for the campus, but none of the remaining four thousand acres could be sold outright as homesites; only leasehold interests were permitted.

Leland Stanford was sympathetic to those professors who preferred to buy land outright, rather than building on the leasehold land belonging to the university. To solve this problem, Stanford instructed Timothy Hopkins to purchase about 700 acres of vacant land across from the campus and subdivide it into "for sale" lots. The location was highly desirable, as it was adjacent to the Southern Pacific depot, established in 1876, mostly to serve the Stanford farm. Like the farm, the new town came to be called Palo Alto. Here, many of Stanford's early faculty chose to build their homes in a new neighborhood known as Professorville.

In building their homes, many of the early faculty, like their counterparts in Berkeley, chose the avant-garde, wood-shingle designs now known as First Bay Tradition (see page 170). Those built during the 1890s favored the Shingle-style version, while later examples have more Craftsman stylistic influences. Scattered among these First Bay Tradition homes are houses of other contemporary styles.

Throughout Professorville, you will find many front yards enclosed with low hedges or short wooden fences

and entered through front garden gates. It is not certain when this practice began. Some gates are constructed of natural wood with a small roof above, a favored First Bay Tradition landscape element (and one that had been actively promoted by Gustav Stickley's magazine, the *Craftsman*). The garden gate at 221 Kingsley Avenue (private) is an excellent example.

Although Professorville is still remarkably intact, it is currently facing the same threat as many historic neighborhoods in particularly desirable locations—affluent buyers who want to purchase well-maintained smaller historic dwellings as "teardowns," to be replaced by much larger structures that are out of scale, and often stylistically incompatible, with the rest of the neighborhood. Once this trend begins, each huge new home dwarfs the historic homes nearby, destroying the intact fabric of the neighborhood. This then causes the original houses to seem smaller and less significant and therefore more like teardowns. In historic neighborhoods not yet protected by strong conservation or historic district ordinances, this sort of replacement can spread almost like wildfire once begun.

1130 Bryant Street (private), Rendtorff House, 1904. Professor and Mrs. Karl Rendtorff chose to build a front-gabled Craftsman house in the Swiss-chalet mode. From Kiel, Germany, both earned Stanford degrees, after which he became a professor of German. The house is clad with wood

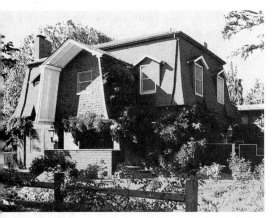

Professorville

shingles above and clapboard below. The most prominent decorative detail is the full-width upstairs balcony with the distinctive railing, flat with a jigsaw cutout design that indicates Swiss inspiration. This same railing is repeated on the front porch. The three prominent front brackets have interesting fishhook-shaped extensions, and the rounded ends of the exposed rafters do not extend beyond the edge of the roof.

1061 Bryant Street (private), Kellogg House, 1899; Bernard Maybeck, Berkeley, architect. Here the gambrel-roofed Shingle style is reinterpreted by the creative Bay Area architect Bernard Maybeck (see page 172). He adds an unusual wide overhang to the style's typical front-facing gambrel, thus earning the house its local nickname of "the Sunbonnet House." The main body of the gambrel roof has been exaggerated to form more of a mansard roof and is covered in the same shingles as the house walls. Notice the irregular widths of the shingles and how the upstairs windows extend into the mansard.

1033 Bryant Street (private), Smith House, 1899. This house features a front-facing gambrel roof of unusual proportions—a very short length along its upper slope and a very long length along the lower one—which gives the house a lot of character. The gambrel is symmetrical with a pair of windows in the center and small windows to each side. Beneath the gambrel is a long bay window with prominent pilasters on each end. The shed dormers on the side slopes look like they might be newer additions. This home was built by Stanford geology professor James Perrin Smith. His wife, Frances Norris Rand Smith, was an authority and writer on the California missions.

1017 Bryant Street (private), Murray House, 1893. This Shingle-style house has a side-gambreled roof with three large dormer windows across the front—a shed-roofed central dormer flanked by two gambrel dormers. The fact that the house has been painted, coupled with the wide-columned entry porch, adds an early Colonial Revival influence. This was built for Professor August Taber Murray, a classics scholar on Stanford's first faculty.

1005 Bryant Street (private), Angell House, 1893. Frank Angell, another member of Stanford's original faculty, was the head of the psychology department and the first track coach. His Shingle home is a classic example of the style. The gambrel roof shape is of the typical proportions. Note the fine brickwork in the broad first-floor chimney, which

then disappears behind the shingled upper story. The use of shed dormers and the round oval window to the side of the entry are both typical of the style.

334 Kingsley Avenue (private), Slonaker House, 1903. This excellent hipped-roof early Colonial Revival house long belonged to Professor James Rollin Slonaker, a leading Stanford physiologist. It is perfectly symmetrical, with full-height pilasters at its corners and on each side of the one-story entry porch. Matching balustrades atop the entry porch and the matched pair of slanted bay windows help to reinforce the picturesque Colonial imagery.

457 Kingsley Avenue (private), Nutting House, 1914. Half-timbering with stucco infill covers almost the entire front facade of this large Tudor house.

1336 Cowper Street (private), Pettigrew House, 1925; George Washington Smith, Santa Barbara, architect. This fine Spanish Eclectic house was designed by one of the masters of this style, George Washington Smith (see "Casa del Herrero," page 259). Smith's very first house, built for himself near Santa Barbara, featured a relatively severe street facade of Andalusian inspiration. Such simple and very private public fronts were often found in Spain, where private life tended to occur inside and in rear gardens. Here, the facade is enlivened only by a deeply recessed door and

Professorville

Professorville

a few windows with ornamental iron grillwork. A few decorative touches like the front steps faced with decorative tiles and the decorative iron light fixture beside the door hint at the nicely ornamented interior one would expect to find in a Smith house. Don't miss the heavy wood entry door with a rectangular design of raised wood panels.

1247 Cowper Street (private), Norris House, 1927. This large Spanish Eclectic house is fun because, even though it presents a very private front facade, the rear portion of the house is higher and therefore visible, allowing you a hint of the courtyard that the house wraps around. Notice how the entry gate of decorative wrought iron with a round arch and hanging lantern echoes the shape of the simple round-arched courtyard entry.

Ralston Hall, 1864

1500 Ralston Avenue, on the campus of College of Notre Dame, in the small town of Belmont, about ten miles northwest of Palo Alto on California Highway 82 (after entering the main campus gates from Ralston Avenue, make an immediate hard left—almost a U-turn—and pass between stone pillars); 415-508-3501 (open only by advance appointment); John Painter Gaynor, San Francisco, architect.

Ralston Hall is undoubtedly the finest surviving Italianate house in the West and one of the best in the entire United States. Built by William Chapman Ralston (1826–1875), the founder of the Bank of California and one of San Francisco's most influential early citizens, and designed by Irish-American architect-engineer John Painter Gaynor, the architect for San Francisco's fabulous first Palace Hotel, Ralston Hall contains 55,360 square feet and has almost all of its extraordinary original interior fixtures and fittings. Among its large and ornate public rooms is what is probably the earliest private ballroom remaining on the West Coast.

William Ralston was born in Ohio, became a partner in a steamship company, and as such arrived in San Francisco in 1854. Enthusiastic, entrepreneurial, and farsighted, Ralston rapidly became one of the most important men in the West. He was involved in the first phase of the Comstock Lode, gaining great personal wealth in the process, and in 1864 he founded the highly respected San Francisco–based Bank of California, which made loans and investments in Virginia City, Nevada, mines—and in turn became the bank where much of the wealth pouring forth from these mines was deposited (see page 424). Ralston, who loved San Francisco and was one of its most avid boosters, used both his personal funds and the lending power of the Bank of California to finance projects designed to turn San Francisco into a major city—mills, factories, a water company, and major buildings, chief among them the California Theater and the Palace Hotel. The latter was, according to the book on San Francisco architecture by Roger Olmsted and T. H. Watkins called *Here Today,* "the most lavish hostelry in the world. The seven-storied, bay-windowed hotel, built around a central court that piled tier upon tier of marble colonnades, contained 800 rooms, all furnished with the best that . . . money could buy." It occupied a full square block, its huge hulk dominating the skyline of a town filled mostly with smaller-scale two- and three-story buildings.

Ralston's personal mission in life was convincing others to move to and invest in his adopted city of San Francisco—and the Palace Hotel was planned to play a major part in this. But before Ralston had begun to build this grand hotel, he had built and used Ralston Hall as a suitable backdrop from which to promote the city. When important visitors arrived, Ralston would invite them to visit his country home. Here he entertained admirals, financiers, vice-presidents, and even the first Japanese diplomatic delegation to the United States—with a retinue of one hundred. These goals and aspirations make the size and elegance of Ralston Hall understandable. Ralston began by purchasing a fifteen-

Ralston Hall

acre estate from Italian count Leonetto Cipriani. It had a comparatively modest Italianate villa on it, and this was incorporated into the right wing of Ralston's extraordinary new home. At the same time, the grounds were gradually expanded to over one hundred acres.

Ralston Hall's large and elegant rooms are designed for entertaining. One enters into a large entry hall, and beyond this is a two-story stair hall lighted by a skylight and encircled with a second-floor gallery of "opera boxes," a design perhaps inspired by Mrs. Ralston's visit to the Paris Opera House. This stair hall with open gallery above is superb—it must be indelibly impressed into the memories of generations of College of Notre Dame graduates (see page 204) and to the current generation of students, many of whom ascend these stairs to apply for admission. The second-story gallery may have served as a family room for the Ralstons, and today contains a number of original Ralston pieces, among them photographs, furniture, dishes, a Thomas Hill portrait of Ralston, and a megalethoscope—a large and rare three-dimensional stereopticon.

The long first-floor wing to the left of these central halls has a unique floor plan. This consists of a long elegant parlor that is sandwiched between a large double solarium in front and an elegant dining room be-

hind—seating seventy-five, which gives you some idea of the scale. Punctuating the long walls between these three rooms is a set of extraordinary dividers, made of etched glass set into wood frames that slide up into the ceiling. This works much like raising the lower sash of a window—only these sash/dividers are almost thirteen feet tall and up to twenty feet wide. It is said that Ralston greatly enjoyed entertaining a group in the parlor and then, at the appropriate moment, raising the huge dividers to reveal a long and perfectly set dining room table. Joining the ends of these three parallel elongate rooms is the curved Half Moon Room, an elegant semicircular secondary entry hall that terminates the left side of the house. This is on axis with the parlor and connects to it through a pair of large curved sliding doors with silver inlay. On each side are large folding doors that lead to the double solarium on the right and the dining room on the left.

The wing to the right of the central halls features an extraordinary twenty-eight-by-sixty-one-foot ballroom. The very earliest ballroom in Newport, Rhode Island, dates from only 1854, making this a remarkably advanced room for California in the mid-1860s. This room is surrounded by a dozen fourteen-foot-high mirrors, contains elegant moldings, and is painted in the original soft-peach and blue-green colors. There is a music shell in the center and a large curved bay at the end with its original curved banquette seating and window cornices. The rest of this wing is built around Cipriani's original house. The music room has the home's only painted ceiling, which has been lovingly restored. In it is a fine grand piano that has never been out of the house, custom-made for Ralston by Jacob Zech of San Francisco of laurel wood trimmed with rosewood. The rooms in this side of the house were likely those used regularly by the family.

The home's magnificent spaces are all the more important because of their original fixtures. These include all of the elegant silver-plate and crystal chandeliers hanging from handsome ceiling rosettes; dramatic parquet floors throughout created from dark walnut and an unidentified light wood; silver-plated hardware and custom moldings. A design motif that unifies the house is an unusual arch, the typical Italianate "flattened" arch, but with a smaller, shallow rectangular shape notched up above it. This is found above windows, doors, arched openings, mantels, mirrors, and even a built-in sideboard.

When one first looks at the exterior of Ralston Hall, an immediate supposition might be that the broad wraparound one-story porches have been enclosed with glass at a later date. But instead these windows are original and the rooms planned to be solaria by day and suitable for entertaining at night, when Pacific breezes are often too cool for outdoor comfort. These rooms exhibit the same level of interior finish as the rest of the house.

As it turned out, Ralston was able to enjoy his home for only a few years. He had committed the Bank of California to some Comstock Lode loans and to other ventures that began to seem shaky, thereby causing a flurry of withdrawals from the bank on August 26, 1875. The concerned board of directors forced Ralston to resign the next morning. A couple of hours later, he went for his regular swim in the Bay, and his body was found drowned. It will never be known if it was a suicide or an accident. His Virginia City, Nevada, agent and partner, William Sharon, is thought to have played an active part in explaining Ralston's problems to the bank's board of directors. When Ralston died, Sharon inherited most of his assets, including Ralston Hall. He owned Ralston Hall for ten years, after which it became briefly a school and then a sanitarium.

How did Ralston Hall become such a miraculous survivor? It is because of the long and dedicated stewardship of the sisters of the College of Notre Dame. In 1922 they were looking for a place to move their college campus, as the original location was fast being surrounded by downtown San Jose. They purchased Ralston Hall, and from the first worked to preserve it. The sisters lived on the fourth floor, and they put their chapel in the ballroom. But rather than convert that fine room to a permanent chapel, they vowed to raise the money for a new chapel and to keep the ballroom intact in the meantime. They stored the large banquette in the barn and carefully covered over the mirrors and windows, leaving everything intact. They put a runner on the floor and added benches on which to worship. It took them thirty-eight years, but in 1961 they moved into their new chapel, rolled up the carpet, uncovered the mirrors and windows, and had the ballroom back.

In 1979, Sister Catharine Julie Cunningham, a historian and third-generation Californian who served as the college's president from 1956 to 1980, began a restoration fund. By 1987 there was enough to do long-needed repairs and restoration. The upper floors are adapted to college uses, as they have been since 1923. But the downstairs and the wonderful gallery have been kept intact, filled with handsome Victorian furnishings donated by the families of graduates of the San Jose campus (established 1851). This allows Ralston Hall's large and elegant spaces to continue in use as Ralston first intended—for parties, events, and even concerts. The only real change the sisters made in 1923 was when they were advised to stucco over the wood exterior cladding, as the cost of keeping up the wood would be prohibitive to them. The College of Notre Dame has just celebrated its seventy-fifth year on the Belmont campus. The sisters have lived in, used, and cared for this fine home far longer than any other owner. And we all owe them a debt of gratitude for saving this extraordinary landmark house and for allowing others to see its public spaces by advance appointment.

Filoli, 1917

Entrance on the west side of Cañada Road and just north of Edgewood Road, about 4 miles northwest of the small town of Woodside, which is about seven miles west of Palo Alto; advance tour reservations required; 650-364-2880; Willis Polk, San Francisco, architect.

"To fight for a just cause, to love your fellow man, to live a good life." This credo was so admired by William Bowers Bourn II (1857–1936) that when he and his wife, Agnes Moody Bourn (died 1936), finally built their great country house, they named it Filoli—from the first two letters of "fight," "love," "live." Their home reflected the integrity inherent in this credo, and it remains today as a rare intact early 1900s country estate—important for its architecture and architect; for its gardens and landscape designers; and for the two prominent families who made Filoli their home. It is

Filoli

the last surviving great estate on the San Francisco Peninsula that remains completely intact—house, furnishings, grand gardens, and the original unspoiled setting for which they were designed. It was Filoli's second owner, Mrs. William P. Roth (1890–1985), known for her horsemanship, her gardening skills, and her philanthropies, who generously gave Filoli to the National Trust for Historic Preservation. Today, Filoli Center, a local nonprofit organization, operates this extraordinary museum property for the National Trust.

William Bourn's father had invested in and then later purchased the Empire Mine (see page 131), a remarkable gold mine that was to produce for 106 years and was the chief source of Bourn's wealth. Bourn was but seventeen years old when his father died. The following year he left for Cambridge, England, to finish his education, where he distinguished himself as a student. During his fourth year, in 1878, a crisis happened at home—the Empire Mine bottomed out, quit producing, and was pronounced defunct by three separate mining engineers. Bourn returned to California to take over management of the mine and the family vineyards and other interests. But along with his cousin, George Starr, Bourn refused to give up on the Empire Mine; they continued to explore it and eventually found a gold vein even richer than the first, assuring him even greater wealth. Along with mining and the vineyards, Bourn found time to be president of the San Francisco Gas Company beginning in 1890, and in 1908 he purchased and became president of the Spring Valley Water Company, which supplied San Francisco's water.

In 1910, shortly after the water company purchase, the Bourns' only daughter, Maud, married Arthur Rose Vincent, an Irish barrister and judge for the Judicial Service of the Foreign Office. Vincent had just been appointed judge for His Majesty's Court in Zanzibar when he and Maud met. The Bourns refused to have their daughter live in Zanzibar, so Vincent resigned from the Judicial Service, and four months after their marriage Bourn purchased a huge estate in Ireland for the couple—a great house, Muckross, built in 1843 in County Kerry on the Lakes of Killarney and surrounded by over eleven thousand acres. On its grounds were the picturesque ruins of Muckross Abbey, destroyed by Cromwell in 1649. It was here at Muckross, during frequent visits to their daughter, that he and his wife learned to love the Irish countryside and the British country house way of life. They might also have begun to wonder why they had provided their daughter and her husband with this spectacular great house and setting and so far neglected to obtain the same for themselves!

Soon the Bourns decided to build their own country home and found the perfect setting for it—near the shores of Crystal Springs Lake on the large undeveloped watershed of the Spring Valley Water Company. Bourn felt the area resembled the Irish countryside, and his company even owned the land he desired for a homesite. He soon discovered that laws prevented the private purchase of any of his water company watershed, so Bourn had his attorney begin looking for nearby property. In 1915 he was able to purchase 1,800 acres near the southern end of Crystal Lake, 1,085 of which he sold to the water company, and the rest he retained for Filoli. By building in this remote and protected watershed setting, he both saved Filoli from the encroachment of future development and added miles of beautiful "borrowed scenery" to its gardens.

Bourn knew just the architect he wanted, Willis Polk (1867–1924) of San Francisco, who had already designed several properties for the Bourn family, including the 1897 cottage at the Empire Mine in Nevada City (see page 131) and his 1896 San Francisco home on Webster Street in Pacific Heights (see page 231). Polk had designed many houses in the 1890s, bringing to them his fresh architectural perspectives. After 1900 Polk had concentrated mainly on more lucrative commercial work. He had moved to Chicago in 1900 and worked in Daniel Burnham's office until 1904, when he returned to San Francisco to help with Burnham's master plan for San Francisco. Before this was implemented, the 1906 earthquake and fire destroyed a large part of downtown San Francisco, and Polk was the architect for much of the rebuilding. Then in 1915, he had been the chairman of the architectural committee for the Panama-Pacific International Exposition. Just as this was winding down, he began working on Filoli—his last house and one of his finest.

Polk preferred to combine influences in his architecture, and Filoli was no exception. Here he added a tile roof and two long frontal wings to a Georgian Revival main house block. The understated exterior design is quite handsome, as the two long symmetrical wings embrace a lovely entrance courtyard, one almost large enough to give a feeling for the completely enclosed and carefully landscaped courtyards that are a staple of the Colleges in Cambridge. The dominant architectural feature is a large and beautifully proportioned white glazed terra-cotta entry porch that stands out against an almost-monochromatic background of soft terra-cotta-colored redbrick walls and a pleasingly irregular roof of similarly colored tiles (these are called thigh tiles because they were originally shaped around the maker's thigh, rather than in identical molds, which gives the roof its irregular feeling). The soft gray-greens of the casement windows and the copper roof dormers

Filoli Gardens

recede into the background. A cornice with modillions, matched pairs of chimneys connected with arches, understated round-arched downstairs casement windows, and mock-brick quoins on the two wings provide other stylistic notes, all of which yield center stage to the entry porch.

One of the most important things about Filoli is the integration of its architecture and its landscape features. Two things make this difficult to understand on the spot. First, the need to keep ultraviolet light out of the interior means that the sparkling exterior views that once were focal points of the main rooms are now dimmed. Second, the interior floor plan of Filoli necessitates a somewhat-circuitous tour route, which makes it more difficult to understand how the house was planned to work.

Standing in Filoli's entry court, facing the front door, is a good place to begin thinking about how the house and gardens were planned as a whole and how they relate both to the surrounding countryside and to the Bourns' preferences. Begin by realizing that the long wing to your right contains only the ballroom and that the long wing to your left contains only the kitchen and other service rooms. The main rooms for family use are all lined up along the far side of the house facing away from you, west toward the mountains. It is easiest to talk about Filoli's plan and gardens by thinking of the entry court facade as facing due east and the garden terrace facade as facing due west, even though the estate is slightly askew of this. The most dramatic feature of Filoli's natural setting is the coastal mountain range to the west, which the Bourns loved. Polk carefully sited Filoli to run parallel to this range. In Bourn's time there was also a north view to Crystal Lake that Bourn enjoyed, but trees have grown up around the lake and now hide it from view. Because the Bourns preferred to have a natural foreground through which to enjoy views of the mountains and the lake, Filoli's main gardens were all placed to the south of the house, where they did not interfere with either the mountain or the lake views. What this means to you, standing in the courtyard, is that straight ahead of you, on the other side of the house, is a beautiful mountain range. To your right, beyond the ballroom, there was once a lake view, which can no longer be seen, but which in 1917 prevented formal gardens from being designed in that direction. Slightly ahead and to your left are Filoli's fine gardens, which begin on the left side of the main house and extend southward from there.

You enter into a large domed foyer with marble floor and small rooms to each side, one for ladies and the other for gentlemen to "organize" themselves for their visit. Ahead are two important rooms, the Transverse

Filoli Gardens

Hall and the reception room. When you first step into the stunning reception room, it is almost unnoticeable that you are also standing in the Transverse Hall, which provides a 175-foot-long north–south axis around which the entire house is organized. The hall is beautifully designed, and its long length is disguised by its handsome moldings and detailing, including alternating sections of barrel-vaulted ceiling with flat ceilings. It passes through the ends of the dining room at the far left, as well as the end of the reception room, and it is also a part of the stair hall, which is out of sight to the right. If you walked down to the left (south) end of the hall, through the dining room and out the door, you would be directly on a straight path that runs along the east side of the long expanse of southern gardens.

If you were a family member using the house, rather than on a tour, you would be delighted to realize that the two rooms designed for your daily use, the library and the study, are both to the right of the reception hall, next to each other and handy to the stairway upstairs. If you were a dinner party guest, you would most often be entertained in the two rooms to the right of the reception hall—the dining room and the drawing room, which are handy to the kitchen and service areas. All five of these main rooms—dining room, drawing room, reception hall, library, and study—face the west side of the house and the mountain range beyond. With

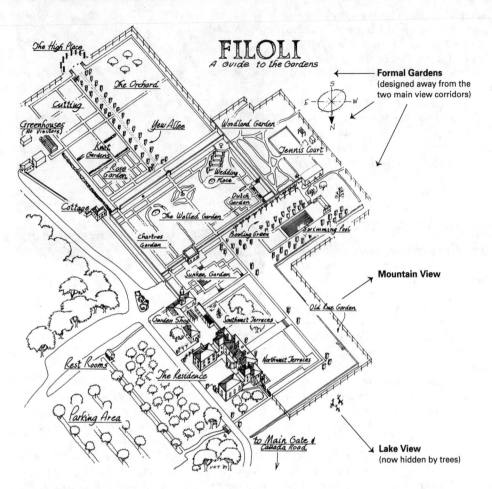

FILOLI
A Guide to the Gardens

Formal Gardens
(designed away from the two main view corridors)

Mountain View

Lake View
(now hidden by trees)

Plan of the Filoli Gardens

the curtains opened, you would have lovely views out across the terrace to the mountains in each of these rooms.

The interiors at Filoli are exquisite and not enough talked about. They were planned to accentuate outward views of distant sky and scenery, and these can best be appreciated from a house if the interior colors are dark or muted. The reception room is covered with its exquisite original wall covering, a silk-screened version of grass cloth in sage greens with taupe and stone accenting it—a superbly muted color scheme that would complement mountain views beyond. This room has its original curtains and many fine Oriental pieces. Wood paneling provides a naturalistic frame for exterior scenery views, and at Filoli the dining room, library, and study are all paneled in wood. The drawing room, sometimes called the French Room, is the only room not planned with the view foremost in mind.

Here, soft-beige linen walls are accentuated with the original Italian silk curtains in an exuberant floral pattern. As might be expected, the furnishings are mostly French. Seventeen-foot ceilings, parquet floors, handsome moldings, and beautiful door surrounds, most featuring a pediment of some sort, are found throughout Filoli. A great many of the furnishings are original to either the Bourn or the Roth families, and where needed fine pieces have been donated to the house or are on loan from San Francisco's Fine Arts Museum.

The large ballroom is somewhat apart from the rest of the house in the north front wing. It is painted a lovely blue-green that Mrs. Bourn referred to as "water green," accented with gold, and has five large panels containing mural paintings by Ernest C. Peixotto (1869–1940) that feature the beautiful Irish Muckross estate which had first inspired the Bourns to build a country house. These paintings make this room delightfully personal, a rare touch in a formal ballroom! One of Polk's most original architectural touches in the house is found at the landing of the main stair. Here, a solid paneled door, crowned with a triangular pediment, is set into a two-story, high-arched glass window that leads out onto a rooftop garden.

Perhaps the greatest compliment that could be paid to the interiors is the fact that Mr. and Mrs. William P. Roth, the home's second owners, who had traveled extensively and who could afford to make any changes to the house that they wished, elected to leave the interior virtually intact. In 1937 Mrs. Roth and her husband moved into Filoli, a home completed twenty years earlier, and decided to leave the wood finishes, the wall coverings, many of the curtains, and most of the furnishings intact, a decision they never changed during the thirty-eight years the family lived there. Mrs. Roth made some judicious additions, as she did in the garden, to reflect her tastes and interest, but always deeply respected the underlying integrity of the integrated whole. She was the daughter of Captain William Matson, founder and president of the Matson Navigation Company and a principal in the Honolulu Oil Corporation. Her husband served as both president and as chairman of the board of Matson.

Filoli's gardens have a unity and subtlety that is rare in American landscape design. This quality reflects the fact that they were carefully observed by two sophisticated gardeners over many, many seasons and were gradually refined and improved by them, something that is extremely rare in the United States. The gardens were originally planned by Bruce Porter (1865–1940), who integrated them with Willis Polk's design for the house. Porter laid out approximately sixteen acres of formal gardens in a series of parterres, terraces, lawns, and pools. These are in the Italian-French gardening tradition and are united by strong architectural themes, including almost a thousand feet of brick walls and the use of 223 towering Irish yews kept trimmed at sixteen feet. The initial plantings and most subsequent ones were supervised by Isabella Worn (1869–1950), a floral designer and third-generation horticulturist, who was involved with the gardens from the time they were designed in 1917 until her last visit three weeks before her death in 1950. Mrs. Roth was a master gar-

dener who worked carefully, in consultation with Miss Worn, as she gradually added more color to the gardens to reflect her love of flowering plants and shrubs. Filoli's gardens are today called the Lurline B. Roth Gardens, after Mrs. Roth.

Filoli was built on a four-foot raised platform. This is reflected today in the upper terrace that stretches across the front of the house with a lower terrace below, both beautifully yet subtly planted so as not to obscure the mountain views beyond. The multiple garden rooms begin just beyond the south end of the upper terrace and are centered along a straight north–south axis that begins with the lower terrace walk and extends south from it. First come the sunken garden on the east, designed by Porter, and the swimming pool garden on the west, added by Roth and Worn. Next you enter a large (278-by-169-foot) walled garden with several different rooms, including the Chartres Garden on the east and a Dutch garden and the Wedding Place on the west, with a naturalistic woodland garden just beyond the end of the wall. When you exit the walled garden, you enter a long yew allée which terminates in the High Place lookout. As you walk along the allée, the long Panel Gardens are on the east, so-called because they are made up of many different rectangular sections, much like the panels on a front door (these include rose gardens, knot gardens, and cutting gardens). To the west of the allée is a meadow and orchard.

The sunken garden in late June provides but one tiny example of how the genius of the original design combined with later refinements to produce the artistry of these gardens. Porter's original pond design has been enhanced by Mrs. Roth's judicious addition of the Lead Water Carrier Maidens, which belonged to her mother. At this season the small color beds around it look like sophisticated flower arrangements in soft yellow, blues, and white—rather than typical annual color beds. This remarkable color combination likely reflects many seasons of experimentation by Roth and Worn. If you imagine this kind of informed attention to detail spread over much of sixteen acres and multiplied through the four seasons of the year, you will understand why Filoli is special both inside and out, and why so few gardens anywhere in the United States have this level of sophistication.

SAN FRANCISCO

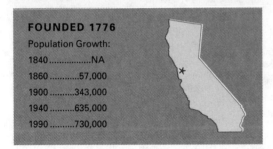

FOUNDED 1776

Population Growth:

1840	NA
1860	57,000
1900	343,000
1940	635,000
1990	730,000

Precocious child of the 1849 California gold rush, San Francisco quickly matured into the nation's principal Pacific seaport and the first large city in the American West. Today, in spite of fires, earthquakes, and a century and a half of urban growth, San Francisco retains the West's largest assemblage of Victorian houses as well as several unusually fine Eclectic-era neighborhoods. Many of its historic houses are enhanced by spectacular hillside settings overlooking the waters of San Francisco Bay and the mountains beyond.

Hispanic Beginnings

San Francisco was built on an unlikely site for one of the world's great cities. A foggy, barren, and windswept peninsula of jagged peaks partially covered by thick deposits of blowing sand, it had been a remote outpost of Spanish settlement since 1776. In that year a modest presidio (fort) was established facing the Bay entrance, as was an equally modest mission located on

a more sheltered Bay-side site three miles southeast of the presidio. These were served principally by wagon roads from the Hispanic capital of California at Monterey, 115 miles to the south (see page 115).

In 1835 the presidio and mission were joined by a beachside "port," located on a cove near the mission, where some of the hides and tallow produced by the region's Hispanic cattle ranches were delivered in small boats to the sailing ships of New England traders anchored offshore (see page xi). Originally called Yerba Buena (Spanish for the herb known in English as "mint"), the port's name was changed to San Francisco (the original Spanish name for both the Bay and the mission) by the captain of the U.S. naval vessel that took possession of the region in 1847, during the final months of the Mexican War. At that time it was a village of about one hundred inhabitants. Three years later it was a city with a population of thirty-five thousand.

Gold Rush Boomtown

The initial gold discovery that set off this frenzied stampede was made in 1848 in the foothills of the Sierra Nevada, about forty miles east of what was soon to become the city of Sacramento (see page 136). The site was adjacent to California's Great Central Valley, whose surrounding mountains offered two principal access routes to the hordes of arriving gold seekers.

Cheapest, but most arduous, was the overland route from Missouri and Iowa, then the westernmost limits

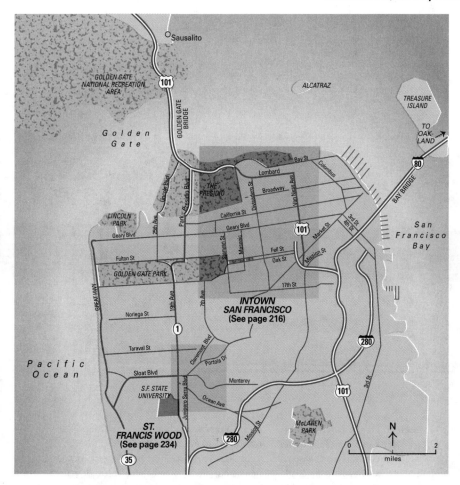

San Francisco in 1851. Note the distant forest of sailing-ship masts, many of them on abandoned vessels whose crews had departed for the goldfields.

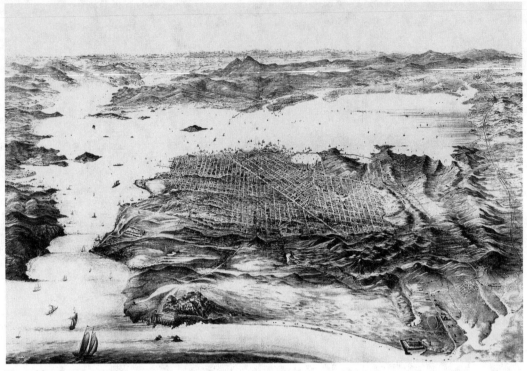

View of San Francisco, 1868

of the nation's Anglo settlement. This involved first following the earlier Oregon Trail, which crossed the Indian-dominated plains of Nebraska and eastern Wyoming and then proceeded through relatively gentle passes over the Rocky Mountains to southern Idaho. Here the California Trail diverged from the route to Oregon, heading southwestward across dry and desolate Nevada to the most formidable barrier of all—the steep eastern face of the Sierra Nevada, a virtual wall of granite that towered four thousand feet above the adjacent desert as if to guard the golden treasure that lay just beyond. Fortune seekers taking this route departed by wagon, horseback, or on foot in the early spring in order to reach the high and rugged Sierra Nevada passes before they were blocked by autumn snows.

About half of the forty-niners, and their successors in the following years, braved the overland journey. The other half came to San Francisco in sailing ships. This was less arduous but more expensive and almost as long, since the vessels had to either sail around the tip of South America or, sometimes a bit faster, deposit their passengers in Central America for a dangerous overland journey before proceeding northward on another ship. In either case, the ships' destination was the deepwater anchorage off the formerly sleepy port town of San Francisco, which was conveniently near the entrance to San Francisco Bay.

In San Francisco the passengers boarded smaller boats that transported them through narrow straits that bisect the mountains at the Bay's northeastern end and into either the Sacramento or San Joaquin Rivers, which drain California's vast Central Valley. The boats docked at the river-port towns of Sacramento or Stockton, from which relatively short wagon roads led into the nearby goldfields (see page 159 and map there).

The seaport of San Francisco was quickly crowded not only with ships loaded with anxious gold seekers, but countless other vessels were also arriving bearing the food, clothing, and supplies needed to support the army of new arrivals in what was previously a sparsely settled frontier. The first ships, like their hide-trading predecessors, had to anchor offshore and have their contents transferred across shallow mudflats to the sandy shore in small boats. Soon long wooden wharves were being extended across the shallow flats to deeper water, thus permitting the oceangoing ships to dock alongside for faster unloading. As the city grew, nearby sandy hills were leveled and the sand used to fill the shallow waterfront cove, thus making possible shorter wharves. This process of shoreline filling toward deeper water was to continue for many decades; the modern seafront Embarcadero, completed in 1914, lies several blocks east of the town's original Montgomery Street waterfront.

The endless flood of workers and goods that poured through early San Francisco to the expanding mining districts was balanced by a much simpler return flow of the world's most valuable currency—dust, nuggets, and ingots of pure gold. These yielded large profits to many San Francisco merchants, financiers, and bankers. By 1854 California gold had quadrupled the world supply of the valuable metal; the same year a new United States mint opened in San Francisco, making the young city a key component of the nation's monetary system.

Silver Bonanza

In the mid-1850s the Sierra Nevada's easily recovered gold deposits began playing out, and San Francisco's hectic expansion was replaced by a serious economic decline. By 1857 more than half of the city's wage earners were unemployed. Relief came two years later when a second remarkable discovery ignited a new San Francisco boom. This was the fabled Comstock Lode silver deposit, one of the world's largest, which was found just beyond the Sierra Nevada's crest at Virginia City, Nevada (see also page 424).

Unlike the "placer" gold dust and nuggets that the forty-niners found scattered in stream gravel along a 150-mile stretch of the Sierra foothills, such "lode" deposits of precious metals occur embedded in narrow veins of hard and massive quartz rock. These require expensive underground mining of ore followed by crushing and chemical processing to release and purify the enclosed metals.

Even though individual prospectors are generally the first to find promising surface exposures of such metal-bearing quartz veins, they rarely have the financial resources to develop the discovery themselves. Instead, their "claim" is normally sold to investors who raise the capital needed for the new mining venture. By this process the Comstock silver deposits quickly passed into the hands of San Francisco financiers. As one commentator later noted, "Virginia City was San Francisco's most solvent and essential suburb."

One of the principal Comstock beneficiaries was banker William C. Ralston (see page 202), the tireless San Francisco booster whose Bank of California financed a multitude of civic improvements during the 1860s. Among these were theaters, an opera house, the monumental Palace Hotel, the beginnings of Golden Gate Park, as well as numerous factories, mills, and a new city water company. His vision of San Francisco as "the Paris of the West" must have appeared accurate to

much of the nation as the ravages of the Civil War unfolded. Nominally pro-Union, silver-rich San Francisco was isolated from the actual conflict by two thousand miles of Indian-dominated plains, mountains, and deserts. As a result, it became a refuge for many war-weary citizens who could afford the price of the long ocean or stagecoach journey. During the decade of the 1860s, the city's population almost tripled, from 57,000 to 149,000.

Emporium of the West

San Francisco's isolation was soon to be ended by the 1869 golden spike that signaled the completion of the first transcontinental railroad line (see page 140). The western, trans–Sierra Nevada segment of the line, known as the Central Pacific Railroad, was an engineering marvel improbably built by four modestly affluent shopkeepers of gold rush Sacramento: Leland Stanford, Collis Huntington, Charles Crocker, and Mark Hopkins (see also page 139). Among them they were to dominate the economic life of both San Francisco and California for the rest of the century.

Having connected the eastern rail network to remote California with a single narrow ribbon of steel tracks spanning mostly formidable mountains and empty deserts, the Big Four, as they came to be called, quickly set about providing their Central Pacific line with more profitable California destinations. Anticipating its arrival, several short-line railroads had already been built by local investors to connect Sacramento with the principal Bay Area centers of Oakland, San Jose, and San Francisco. Following the pattern of the northeastern rail barons, the Big Four purchased these struggling independent lines before deciding on a site for the principal Bay-side terminus of the Central Pacific. This was resolved in 1868, when Leland Stanford obtained five hundred prime acres on the then-largely-empty Oakland waterfront for the principal Central Pacific terminus (see page 188). There the Big Four would build a new transcontinental seaport. To further consolidate their influence on Bay Area transportation, in 1871 they also gained control of the California Steam Navigation Company, which dominated the important ferry services between San Francisco, Oakland, and other Bay-side ports.

All of these developments were, however, but the preliminaries in a much larger vision the Big Four held for the future of California transportation. In 1873 they moved the Central Pacific headquarters from Sacramento to San Francisco and began extending one of their local railroad purchases, the Southern Pacific line, southward through California's Great Central Valley. They also obtained a sixty-acre site on the San Francisco waterfront as the principal terminus for the Southern Pacific's north–south California traffic, while the Oakland terminal just across the Bay remained focused on the interstate traffic of the Central Pacific. In 1872 they also founded the Occidental and Oriental Steamship Company, which was to dominate the Bay's Far Eastern trade for the next twenty years.

The Southern Pacific reached Los Angeles in 1876, opening that soon-to-be-booming metropolis to transcontinental rail service (see page 66). Equally important, this new rail line opened California's fertile Central Valley to irrigated agriculture, a cornucopia whose value would ultimately dwarf the state's total yield of gold and silver (see page 67). As the headquarters for the railroad that was pioneering all of these developments, San Francisco, already the West's center of banking and finance, continued its boomtown growth. During the next three decades, the population surged from 150,000 in 1870 to 343,000 in 1900, making it the nation's ninth-largest city. In the eloquent words of historian John Reps in *Cities of the American West*:

A visitor to the urban West in the 1890s wishing to save the best for last would wisely have scheduled his final stop in San Francisco. Then, as now, it stood out as the most attractive, diversified, and cosmopolitan of American western communities, and even then it was often mentioned as one of the great cities of the world. . . . A half-century of growth had covered its steep hills with houses, filled Yerba Buena cove and pushed out its shoreline elsewhere, lined Market Street . . . with lofty stores, offices, and hotels, witnessed the reclamation of a stretch of barren dune sand into one of America's finest parks, bordered its bay waterfront with wharves, docks, and warehouses, stamped a ubiquitous grid street pattern nearly everywhere and solved part of the resulting transportation problem on its precipitous thoroughfares by a system of cable cars that toiled up the slopes and braked cautiously down the other sides.

It was a city that had built museums, an opera house, theaters, churches, libraries, and an imposing city hall, and whose men of wealth had erected stately mansions on Nob Hill overlooking the business district. It was a city of breath-taking views up and down its steeply pitched streets and out to the water of the bay or ocean.

Disaster and Recovery

Vibrant San Francisco was soon to be the scene of one of the most tragic natural disasters in the nation's history. After several days of small earthquakes, a long-familiar occurrence caused by minor movements on

the nearby San Andreas Fault, at 5:12 on the morning of April 18, 1906, a massive series of shocks, lasting only a minute but seeming like an eternity, shook the entire Bay Area, toppling countless chimneys and steeples, collapsing some wooden buildings, and tumbling heavy cornices and scattered masonry facades into the street as piles of rubble. San Franciscans, mostly still at home, rushed outside to survey the damage, which was widespread but generally repairable. The city had survived a similarly massive quake in 1868 and somewhat less damaging shocks in 1892 and 1898. The mood was almost lighthearted that morning as crowds dressed for work took an unexpected holiday.

Most noticed the small wisps of smoke that arose from isolated sites around the city, but were confident that their highly trained firemen, rushing to the fires on powerful four-horse steam pumpers, would promptly extinguish the blazes. Ordinarily that would have been the case, but by midmorning a fateful new development was emerging. As the firemen connected their hoses to the city's elaborate system of hydrants, they found mostly trickles of water instead of gushing torrents. The large mains that connected the city to its water-supply reservoirs many miles to the south had been severed and telescoped by the massive quake. As the priceless flow surged uselessly down remote canyons, the people of San Francisco looked on with disbelief as the small blazes grew steadily larger.

For three days the massive flames, fanned by an easterly wind, marched relentlessly across the city, destroying everything in their path. All would have been lost save for a merciful wind shift to the west on the fourth day, which blew the blazes back toward the previously burned area. The residential neighborhoods west of Van Ness Avenue were spared. In the rest of the city—including all of the commercial core and 60 percent of the residential districts—only the burned-out hulks of masonry structures remained standing. Now 300,000 newly homeless citizens had to find temporary shelter in tent cities, or doubled up with relatives, friends, and generous strangers throughout the Bay Area.

Many thoughtful observers predicted that such massive destruction would mark the end of San Francisco's remarkable record of growth. They were wrong. The embers were barely cool when an equally massive reconstruction began, this time with an emphasis on fire- and earthquake-resistant structures as well as on fire hydrants that could be fed directly from San Francisco Bay in the event the city water supply failed.

These efforts were so successful that only four years later the 1910 census showed the city's population, in spite of much postearthquake migration elsewhere, to have grown by 74,000 inhabitants since 1900 to a total

Watching the spreading fires from Alamo Square after the 1906 earthquake; the blazes ultimately destroyed much of the city, but this area was spared.

of 417,000. Still-larger gains were made in the next decade when the 1914 opening of the Panama Canal was celebrated in San Francisco by the widely acclaimed Panama-Pacific Exposition held in 1915. By 1920 the population had climbed to 507,000.

San Francisco's seemingly eternal population boom continued through the 1920s with help from the automobile. The only undeveloped land within the city now lay in the southwestern quadrant, where convenient access from the commercial core had long been blocked by the rugged Twin Peaks barrier. In 1916 the completion of a two-mile automobile tunnel beneath the peaks abruptly doubled the city's potential residential area. This set the stage for an expansion of new automobile-oriented suburbs, many of which were developed during the nationwide economic boom of the 1920s. By 1930 San Francisco's population had leaped by another 127,000 to a total of 634,000.

Depression and World War II

The nationwide Great Depression of the 1930s marked the first decade without a dramatic population increase in San Francisco's long history. The 1940 census counted 635,000 inhabitants, a scant thousand-person increase over 1930. The effects of the depression were, however, muted in San Francisco by its continuing im-

portance as an international seaport and regional financial center. In addition, during the 1930s the city gained two remarkable civic improvements that permanently altered its skyline and ended its long isolation from Bay Area neighbors. The first of these was the eight-mile-long **San Francisco–Oakland Bay Bridge,** a twin-suspension structure anchored in the middle by a deep concrete pier more massive than the largest Egyptian pyramid. Begun in 1933 and completed in 1936, it required what was then called "the greatest expenditure of funds ever used for the construction of a single structure in the history of man."

The next year the Bay Bridge was joined by another state-of-the-art engineering marvel, the graceful **Golden Gate Bridge,** which, towering dramatically above the Bay's narrow entrance, quickly became a beloved San Francisco symbol. In 1939 to 1940 the city threw an exuberant world's fair, called the Golden Gate International Exposition, to celebrate these accomplishments. Built on a newly-dredged-up island adjacent to the Bay Bridge, the exposition soon became known by the more intriguing name of its site—Treasure Island. Designed around the theme "A Pageant of the Pacific," the fair attracted 17 million visitors to its exotic wonders just before the dark clouds of World War II descended on the Bay. In 1941 Treasure Island's fantasy buildings were

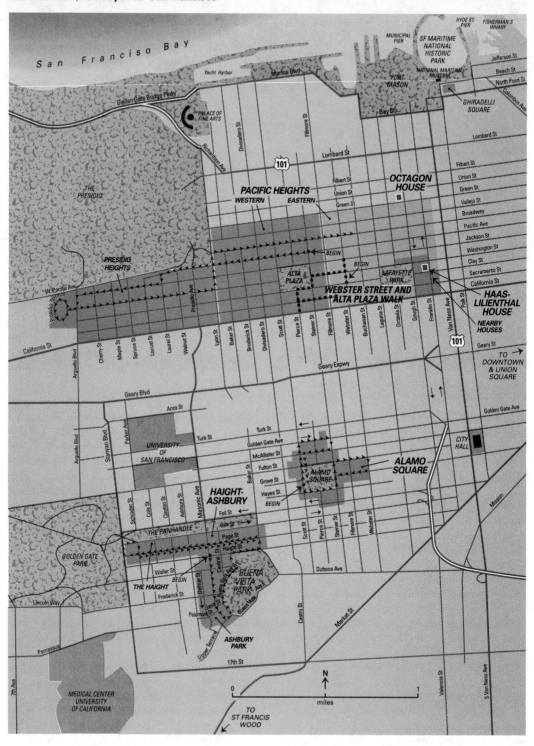

replaced by the battleship-gray structures of a U.S. naval base.

The Japanese bombing of Hawaii's Pearl Harbor in December 1941 brought the United States abruptly into World War II. As the nation's principal Pacific Ocean port, San Francisco and the Bay Area were to play a central role in the many Pacific battles that ultimately led to the Japanese surrender in August 1945. More than a million and a half soldiers, sailors, and marines passed beneath the Golden Gate Bridge during the war, as did 23 million *tons* of equipment and supplies. As new factories, shipyards, and military bases sprang up around the Bay, more than 150,000 new war-industry workers somehow squeezed into the already-crowded city of San Francisco.

Modern San Francisco

Many of these new residents chose to remain in San Francisco. Five years after the war's end, the 1950 census recorded a population of 775,000, an all-time high that has not since been exceeded. During the following decades, fully built-up San Francisco stabilized at about 700,000 inhabitants, while its previous pattern of explosive growth shifted to other Bay Area towns. As a result, San Francisco today retains the West's most important assemblage of urban neighborhoods from the Victorian and Eclectic eras.

The city's historic commercial core was destroyed by the 1906 earthquake and fire, as were almost all of its surviving pre-1870s houses. With the introduction of cable cars in the mid-1870s, new residential suburbs quickly spread beyond steep Nob Hill to the mostly vacant lands beyond fashionable Van Ness Avenue, where the 1906 conflagration was finally contained. Today, several blocks of 1870s Italianate dwellings scattered through the Western Addition are the city's oldest Victorian survivors (see page 220). Much more of the unburned area beyond Van Ness was built out in the population boom of the 1880s, when fashionable Stick-style urban dwellings replaced their simpler Italianate predecessors. By the 1890s these were giving way to still-newer Queen Anne designs as well as to early versions of the Colonial Revival, Neoclassical, and other Eclectic-era fashions that were to fill newly opened neighborhoods farther west in the early twentieth century.

Several important nonresidential historic sites from the nineteenth century survive today either because they were located beyond San Francisco's 1906 burned area or were rebuilt after the fire on their original sites. In the first category are the many historic buildings of the **Presidio,** site of the original Spanish fort guarding the Bay entrance that later grew into a large U.S. Army post. Now operated by the National Park Service as a part of its huge, multicomponent Golden Gate National Recreation Area (GGNRA), two Presidio highlights are **Fort Point,** a pre–Civil War brick fortress now tucked under a giant arch of the Golden Gate Bridge, and the **Presidio Army Museum.** Near the main Presidio entrance is a later landmark, the reconstructed colonnade of the **Palace of Fine Arts,** originally the baroque centerpiece of the 1915 Panama-Pacific Exposition and now its only surviving structure.

Located along the Bay front to the east of the Presidio is the **San Francisco Maritime National Historic Park,** another important component of the GGNRA. This includes the shiplike Art Moderne **National Maritime Museum** (Beach Street at the foot of Polk, 415-556-3002); docked nearby on the **Hyde Street Pier** are several "museum ships," which can be visited to provide a fascinating real-life glimpse of the sort of vessels that were the lifeblood of San Francisco's growth. Among these are an 1886 square-rigged Cape Horn sailing ship; an 1895 schooner built to transport lumber from the Pacific Northwest to booming San Francisco; a massive 1890 trans-Bay steam ferry; and a 1914, side-wheel paddle tug described as "reminiscent of those that towed ships into San Francisco Bay during Gold Rush times."

One of the city's most remarkable historic survivors is its early cable-car system, invented here in the 1870s as the world's first practical means of mechanical mass transit. Designed by mining engineer Andrew Hallidie, this replaced the horses that pulled the city's trolley cars with a continuously moving cable located beneath a street-level iron slot between the tracks. The cable-car operators, called gripmen, put the cars in motion with a lever that closes a plierslike device that "grips" the moving cable; to stop, the gripman releases the pliers and brings the car to a halt with wheel brakes. The continuous cable is driven from a central powerhouse that originally used steam engines; these were later replaced with large electric motors.

Hallidie's invention was so successful that by the mid-1880s San Francisco had eight cable-car companies and more than a hundred miles of line. It was this system that made possible the rapid development of the formerly remote suburban tracts too distant from the central city to have been served by horse-drawn trolleys. Soon other cities were following San Francisco's lead as cable-car systems were installed in New York, Chicago, Denver, and numerous other locations, including nearby Oakland. By the next decade, however, cable-car lines were being converted to a still-more-efficient transit system using self-propelled trolley cars powered by electric motors.

By the early decades of the twentieth century, electric trolleys had replaced many of the San Francisco cable-car lines, and by 1947 the remaining lines were scheduled for replacement by buses. After much public protest, the final three surviving lines, with about nineteen miles of line in the northeastern corner of the city, were saved in 1955; in 1964 these were declared a national historic landmark. In addition to rides on the cars themselves, fascinating insights into cable-car operations and history are provided by the **Cable Car Barn and Museum** (1201 Mason Street, 415-474-1887). The museum building is also the central power plant of the surviving lines; in its basement, one can view the large electric motors and moving understreet cables that propel the cars.

OVERVIEW OF SAN FRANCISCO NEIGHBORHOODS

San Francisco's original street grid was laid out by traditional surveyors, who stuck closely to the north–south/east–west grid plan that dominated town planning in the American West. Following the example of ancient Roman road builders, they built San Francisco's streets in straight lines even up the sides of the site's many steep hills. Only in a few totally hopeless cases did they dead-end a street and resort to a flight of steps to connect it to the next, up-slope section. Lombard Street had such an impassable section until 1922, when a now-famous serpentine roadway was constructed between Hyde and Leavenworth Streets. Several other originally impassable areas throughout the city were later connected by tunnels.

Walking some of San Francisco's steep streets inspires admiration for the Roman armies marching on similarly inclined straight roads. One advantage of this system is that, unlike the complex mazes of curving streets found in most hilly cities, it is almost impossible to get lost in the older parts of San Francisco. Another bonus is the spectacular long views down the hillsides. It was not until after about 1900 that the hills in the southwestern part of the city began to be developed, and these have curved streets that loosely follow the contours of the hills rather than continuing the rigid grid of the earlier city (see "St. Francis Wood and Ingleside Terrace," page 234).

House watchers visiting San Francisco can sometimes feel like kids in a candy store—in parts of the city almost every vista and block face offer striking views of intriguing houses. In an attempt to provide a sampling of these marvels, we have included one short introductory walking tour and four driving tours through representative neighborhoods. These can be completed in about a half day of touring. San Francisco's narrow-lot urban houses have some distinctive stylistic features that are uncommon outside of the Bay Area (see page 38 for nonurban variations). Also, "San Francisco Town House Styles" (see page 220) provides a brief introduction to the six most common styles that are repeated over and over in rich variation throughout the older parts of the city. The short introductory walking tour to the Alta Plaza neighborhood (see the following entry) includes examples of each of these styles.

Two of the driving routes, Alamo Square (see page 223) and Haight-Ashbury (see page 225), treat neighborhoods renowned primarily for their Victorian-era homes. Alamo Square features four grand landmark dwellings and several fine block-face rows of more modest structures, one of which is the "photographers' favorite," a view of Queen Anne homes with the city skyline in the background that has become a San Francisco signature.

Haight-Ashbury, which gained a reputation as a "hippie hangout" during the 1960s, still has many fine Victorian homes of both the freestanding and row-house types. Many of these can be seen along a street that is, except during rush hours, generally quiet enough to permit leisurely viewing, a rarity in hectic San Francisco. The streets around nearby Buena Vista Park have Eclectic-era homes mixed with still more Victorians.

Two additional driving routes visit neighborhoods renowned for their fine Eclectic-era homes—Pacific Heights (see page 227), which also has some choice Victorian landmarks, and St. Francis Wood and Ingleside Terrace (see page 234). Pacific Heights has slightly more urban homes built on San Francisco's early grid street system. St. Francis Wood and Ingleside Terrace, in the later-developed southwestern quadrant of the city, has a more suburban feel, with homes built along curving streets.

In describing San Francisco neighborhoods, we have relied for construction dates, architects, and other data on the many fine books about the city's architecture prepared by such authors as Randolph Delehanty, John Woodbridge, Sally Woodbridge, and others (see "For Further Reference," page 707).

Alta Plaza Walk, ca. 1875–1910

This short walk, shown on page 216, conveniently begins at a public parking garage at Webster and Clay Streets, and has examples of most of San Francisco's Victorian and early-Eclectic-era urban house styles. If you do not yet understand these frequently repeated house types, this is the best place to start your touring (see "San Francisco Town House Styles," page 220).

From the parking garage the walk proceeds north-

Alta Plaza Walk

ward through the **Webster Street Historic District,** a small city landmark area of only about two dozen residences, almost all built from 1878 to 1880 in the Italianate style. The houses represent the typical middle-class houses of the period and have been nicely preserved. These homes were originally part of house "rows"—groups of similar houses that were constructed by the same builder. At first such rows had almost-identical houses; later, it became more fashionable to alternate two or more closely related designs and floor plans.

From Webster Street the walk proceeds westward, down two blocks of Washington Street that have a rich mixture of Victorian styles, to Alta Plaza. Alta Plaza was one of a series of parks that the city established in 1855 as a part of its large new Western Addition. Alamo Square (see page 223) and Lafayette Park were established at the same time. Located at the tops of steep hills, these park sites were not originally considered to be desirable for development. With the invention and immediate success of San Francisco's cable-car system during the 1870s (see page 217), these hilltop locations became easily accessible, making the block faces around the parks highly desirable as homesites. The parks are still visually connected—each can be seen from the top of the others.

2209 to 2229 Webster Street (all private), 1878; Henry Hinkel, builder. Italianate designs with slanted bay windows

were the most common town houses built in San Francisco during the 1870s. This is a fine row of five such town houses with their identifying slanted bay windows and elaborate bracketed cornices. The elaborated cornice continues down the left side of each house and across the one-window-wide rear wing. This "cornice" is actually a false front that extends above the actual roofline, something it is easiest to see looking back at the right-hand side of a house. There are subtle differences among these houses—some original and some due to later alterations. Original differences include the flattened-arch window tops upstairs and the segmental-arch window tops downstairs at 2209; these alternate with the opposite combination (segmental arch up and flattened arch down) as you go along the row. Later differences include the varied treatments of the basement story, which, for example, has been kept a room at 2209 and made into a garage at 2217. Number 2229 has had a Colonial Revival remodeling.

2245 to 2253 Webster Street (all private), 1879; Henry Hinkel, builder. This group of five slanted-bay Italianate houses by the same builder are true row houses with common walls, unusual in San Francisco. If you stand back far enough, you can see what San Franciscans call a French cap atop the cornice—a miniaturized mansard-type roof.

2315 to 2321 Webster Street (all private), ca. 1875; John Remer, architect. This fine row of slanted-bay Italianate row houses was built by the Real Estate Associates, a prolific Victorian-era building company that constructed almost a thousand San Francisco homes, of which about two hundred survive.

2405 to 2461 Washington Street (all private), 1888; Charles Hinkel, builder. Originally a row of Stick-style urban houses, several have had later modifications. The style is most easily recognized by the squared bay windows; it dominated San Francisco homebuilding during the boom-

Flat-front
(ca. 1860–1870)

- No bay windows
- Brackets at cornice
  line

Bay window
(ca. 1870–1880)

- Bay windows
  with slanted sides
- Decorative brackets
  at cornice line
  (do not always align
  with corner boards
  and sides of
  windows)

Italianate Style (ca. 1860–1880)

This style appears in two distinct versions: the flat-front Italianate, which was most popular during the 1860s, and the bay window Italianate, which dominated in the 1870s and featured a dominant two-story bay window with slanted sides. Both have identifying features similar to those of Italianate designs throughout the country. Both versions typically have roofs that appear to be flat when viewed from the street. In most cases the tall bracketed cornices are only thin parapets that conceal a front-gabled roof behind. The tall and narrow windows often have some sort of arch or curve above and are frequently elaborated with window crowns. However, the hooded, full-arched window (which looks like an inverted U and was often found in other parts of the country) is unusual here. Flattened and segmental arches with pedimented and/or bracketed crowns are more common. The flat-front version is, in general, earlier and has simpler detailing. The bay window version is usually later and has more elaborate detailing. Shallow false-mansard roofs called French caps are sometimes added above the cornice.

San Francisco Town House Styles

From about 1870 until about 1900, most homes in San Francisco were built by developers who quickly filled entire blocks as the city's population surged during those three decades. The houses they built were often almost identical, and these groupings of similar houses, constructed by the same builder, are called house rows. Early rows were commonly made up of almost-identical houses, while later it became more fashionable to alternate somewhat-different variations of the same general plan.

Until the 1906 earthquake and fire, most San Francisco homes were built of redwood. This remarkable wood is resistant to rot, termites, and many of the other ills that affect wooden houses—a ready supply was available in the vast redwood forests of the northern California coast (see "Eureka," page 32). The refinement and spread of factory techniques to shape the raw wood into endless intricate variations made it progressively easier to provide an elaborated front facade as the late nineteenth century progressed. Thus the city was the unique beneficiary of a readily available quality building material, the fruits of machine-age technology, and an extraordinarily rapid city growth that combined to produce its wealth of Victorian homes.

From the 1860s until about 1920 San Francisco's urban houses exhibited a remarkably consistent sequence of changing architectural styles. All were variations of housing fashions popular in other parts of the country modified to suit San Francisco's deep narrow lots, typical house form, and the abundance of rot-resistant redwood. This sequence had five principal phases.

- Front-gabled
  roof
- Decorative
  wood shingles
  and/or other
  ornamental
  surface texture
- Slanted-side
  bay windows
  are common
- Usually combines spindlework and Free
  Classic details

Queen Anne Style
(ca. 1890–1900)

Queen Anne designs of the front-gabled subtype were the most typical house style built here during the decade of the 1890s. These generally combine elements of both Free Classic and spindlework detailing. Porches are usually only of partial width and commonly have an arched entry and are supported by Classical columns. Slanted-side bay windows are common, and textured wood shingles are usually present, as in the style throughout the country. Along with these, other types of ornamental surface texture is frequently found, often now made of plaster rather than the wood of the earlier two styles. Towers are sometimes added.

- Bay windows with straight (squared) sides
- Decorative brackets, which form upper extension of vertical window strips
- Vertical strips along sides of windows and on corner boards on wall surface

Stick Style (ca. 1880–1890)

It would be hard to recognize San Francisco's Stick-style houses simply from knowledge of their eastern counterparts—Stick houses here have their own unique set of identifying features. Most prominent is an almost-universal square-sided bay window, which was probably simpler to construct than its slant-sided Italianate predecessor. Cornice-line brackets line up with the side framing of the windows, and the two elements are connected with vertical trim on the intervening wall. Commonly, the rectangular areas above and below the windows are also filled with ornament (panels and so on), and the squared-bay window ensemble thus becomes a continuous decorative element from cornice line to foundation. False gables are sometimes added above the cornice over the square-sided bay window.

About "Eastlake"

By the 1880s the nation's factories were spewing forth a plethora of decorative architectural detailing, much of which was popularly called Eastlake trim—after the English furniture designer and author Charles Eastlake, whose designs often featured turned spindles and incised floral designs. Automatic lathes and milling machines made possible the inexpensive mass production of these "Eastlake" details, which would previously have required time-consuming handcrafting. In addition to the dry wood's being mechanically shaped, redwood was sometimes soaked, and the incised designs were simply stamped into it. Columns and pediments and other variations of Classical detailing could also now be inexpensively machine produced. Although some of these exuberant details (in particular the columns) were used on some late-Italianate homes, by the Stick-style era they were the preferred fashion for most new San Francisco houses. For this reason the term "Stick/Eastlake style" is often used for this California-based substyle.

- Uniform wall cladding of dark-stained wood shingles with no interruption at corners
- Wide variety of other details

Shingle Style, or "First Bay Tradition" (ca. 1900–1915)

The San Francisco–area version of the Shingle style, sometimes called the First Bay Tradition (see page 170), was clearly inspired by the Shingle style that was first popularized by high-style architects in northeastern coastal resorts more than a decade earlier. Here, it has been adapted to narrow city lots, something rarely if ever attempted in the East. The style is easily recognized by the uniform wall cladding of dark-stained wood shingles with no interruption at the corners. As in the East, curved wall surfaces, inventive dormer shapes, simplified entry details, strips of windows, and Palladian window patterns are all part of the architectural vocabulary. What is missing in the city version are the extensive porches and steeply pitched roofs commonly seen in eastern examples of the style.

- Rounded bay windows
- Dentils and modillions at the cornice line
- Classically inspired details such as pilasters, columns, and/or garlands at the entry
- Often found on three-floor flats

"Edwardian" Style (ca. 1900–1920)

This simplified style of town house with Classical ornamentation was the most common San Francisco replacement for the Queen Anne style in the first decades of the twentieth century. Here it is usually called the Edwardian style, borrowing a British term for fashions popular during the reign of Queen Victoria's son and successor, King Edward VII. In these designs, rounded bay windows are combined with pilasters, Classical columns at the entryway—and often garlands, dentils, and other Classically inspired details. Some parts of San Francisco were almost entirely rebuilt after the 1906 earthquake with homes and, more commonly, three-floor flats with these distinctive features. In some cases slanted-side bays are combined with a large rounded bay window at the corner. This style reflects the simplified Classical designs inspired by Chicago's 1893 World's Columbian Exposition. In other parts of the country, this influence first produced Free Classic Queen Anne designs. These were followed by Neoclassical houses in a variety of subtypes and by contemporaneous four-square Colonial Revival houses (hipped-roof-with-full-width-porch subtype), with their porches supported by simple Classical columns.

Alta Plaza Walk

ing 1880s. Stick-style designs tend to be more elaborately decorated than their Italianate predecessors; they are sometimes called Stick/Eastlake houses because of their spindlework and incised-pattern detailing. Numbers 2405, 2411, and 2447 appear much as they must have when first built. At 2447, note the king post truss made of spindlework above the window over the entrance and also the small mansard-roofed French cap. The others have had later stylish updates; 2455, for example, has been converted to the Spanish Eclectic style but is still visually related to its neighbors by its identical scale and squared bay window.

2506 Washington Street (private), ca. 1880. A fine example of the slanted-bay Italianate style, this has a modern, added-on garage in front, a common San Francisco modification. Note the fine detailing of the cornice, with small inset panels, mock dentils above, and incising on each of the brackets.

2548 Washington Street (private), Thayer House, 1881; W. F. Smith, architect. This Stick-style house is much more like its eastern counterparts than are most of San Francisco's urbanized Stick-style designs. Rather than the usual flat roof, it has a front-facing gable with a simple king post truss. The characteristic upside-down-picket-fence pattern is used as a wide band of trim under the eaves, as are many elaborated triangular trusses. The bricked-in front patio and the garage are later additions, as are all such features along this street.

2560 Washington Street (private). This house looks as if the mansard roof is original, making it the Second Empire style, quite unusual in San Francisco. More often San Francisco Italianate or Stick-style designs have a much narrower, mock mansard above the cornice, which is locally called a French cap. (See 2245 to 2253 Webster Street, page 219.)

2561 Washington Street (private), 1885; Charles Geddes, architect. This Queen Anne house with a tower is an early example of the style for San Francisco. The front-facing gable has octagonal shingles and overhangs the second story, supported by four large brackets. The second story is clad with an unusual pattern of rectangular shingles, and the front porch is handsomely detailed. Note that there have been changes to the porch to accommodate the basement

garage; the left half of the porch floor has been removed and a decorative window filled in with siding.

2576 and 2580 Washington Street (both private), ca. 1908. This large double house, originally built for two sisters, illustrates an architectural style that became popular in the Bay Area at the turn of the century. Known locally as the First Bay Tradition (see page 170), this is actually the West Coast version of the Shingle style, which was popular in the Northeast a decade earlier; the style is easily identified here by the house's uniform wall cladding of dark wood shingles. The broad overhanging eaves, the long second-floor flower box, and the first-floor overhang are all supported by lines of simple brackets. Note the Palladian-type windows in the dormers and the recessed entry with the strikingly elaborated triangular pediment. The actual entry doors are not easily visible, as they are to each side.

As you reach Alta Plaza and turn the corner, you have an excellent view to the south of Alamo Square (see page 223), giving you a feeling for the visual connection that exists between the three large Western Addition parks— Alta Plaza, Lafayette Park, and Alamo Square.

2334 and 2336 Steiner Street (both private), ca. 1905. These are good examples of the Edwardian style of urban house, which features rounded bay windows and understated, Classically inspired ornamentation. Such houses dominated San Francisco house building in the first decade of the twentieth century. They were more often designed with several apartments than for single-family occupancy.

2302 Steiner Street (private), 1896; W. H. Lillie, architect. This large Colonial Revival house was built on a choice corner overlooking Alta Plaza. Clad in wood, it features many of the slightly exaggerated Georgian details that are typical of early examples of the style. Note the high-arched window over the front door, the central Palladian window on the shallow bay, and the three second-floor balconies with elaborate railings above supported by large brackets. The cornice line is enlivened by a decorative frieze of torch-and-wreath designs connected by floral garlands.

2637 to 2673 Clay Street (all private), 1875; Real Estate Associates, builders. This excellent row of seven Italianate houses alternates simple, flat-front designs with more typical, slanted-bay-window facades. Flat-fronted Italianate houses were generally built a bit earlier in San Francisco than were the bay-windowed versions, which typically had more elaborate detailing. Here the two types were built at the same time by the same builder and have similar detailing.

2695 Sacramento Street (private), Bacon House, 1894; J. J. Manseau, architect. This choice Queen Anne design is in the hipped-roof-with-lower-cross-gables subtype, which is rarely seen in San Francisco. It has a rounded tower, an upper story covered with patterned wood shingles, and elaborate areas of wall ornament, probably made of plaster. The architect even squeezed in a long "porch" (in this case more of a garden) under the side overhang, although its porch supports look like modern replacements.

2006 to 2010 Pierce Street (both private), ca. 1875. This double house is a large and relatively simple flat-front Italianate design. Comparing it with the double house next door at 2002 to 2004 Pierce Street (see the following entry) gives a quick feeling for how the surface decorative detailing of Italianate houses from the 1870s differs from that of the Stick-style houses built in the next decade. It is easy to see here because one is not distracted by the differences between the squared and slanted bay windows. On this house the windows appear as distinct units on a wood-clad wall, as was most often the case with Italianate houses. In the following pair, the windows are incorporated into a basement-to-roof decorative treatment, which is typical of West Coast Stick–style houses.

2002 to 2004 Pierce Street (both private), 1882. This unusual double house combines the flat-front Italianate shape of the 1870s with the elaborate redwood detailing typical of Stick-style houses in the 1880s. The cornice-line brackets are placed in line with the sides of the windows and extend downward to form strong vertical elements that bound both the second-floor and first-floor windows. Ornamented elements are then added in the rectangular spaces above and

below the windows. All together, this creates a tall and highly ornamented vertical architectural element that extends from roof to foundation and contains the windows. Compare this to 2006–2010 Pierce, next door, where the windows are distinct units on a wood-clad wall, the most typical Italianate-style treatment.

From here return to Sacramento Street and turn right to reach the parking garage. The two blocks of Sacramento on the way to the garage have still more examples of many of the San Francisco house types you've just been seeing.

2687 and 2691 Sacramento Street (both private), ca. 1895. These two adjoining houses illustrate the kind of front-facing-gable Queen Anne houses that were typically built on San Francisco's narrow urban lots during the decade of the 1890s. Areas of shaped wood shingles, a partial-width entry porch, and a highly elaborated gable are always present. Slanted-side bay windows and porches with arched entries and Classical columns for porch supports are also typical. Many were two-story flats, as seen here, and many others were single-family houses. The difference is noticeable only in the number of doors—and even here you must distinguish between the paired doors often found on single family houses and the two separate doors that lead to upstairs and downstairs flats.

Alamo Square, ca. 1875–1915

Alamo Square was created in 1855 as a part of the same Western Addition planning effort as Alta Plaza (see page 218). The blocks around the square, now a city historic district, retain many fine Victorian homes built from the 1870s to 1900, some of them designed by San Francisco's most distinguished architects. One view here, located along the block face at the eastern edge of

View from Alamo Square

Alamo Square neighborhood

the park, may look familiar. This highly photogenic row of Queen Anne homes (see photograph page 223), with San Francisco's skyline beyond, has become almost a trademark symbol of the city that appears in countless publications. In order to actually photograph this view, you must climb toward the top of the Alamo Square Park.

This is a rather-short driving route. In addition to the view, it features a pleasing combination of architect-designed landmark houses (both Victorian and Eclectic) as well as some fine Victorian "builder's rows" of the sort that provide so much of San Francisco's historic architectural character.

1198 Fulton Street at Scott (private), Westerfield House, 1889; Henry Geilfus, San Francisco, architect. This large and extremely fine Stick-style dwelling features a square tower and exhibits a very high level of architectural detail throughout. Notice the cornice line with a deep frieze of panels and intermittent windows. Below this is a tall band of the style's distinctive upside-down-picket-fence ornamentation. The two squared bays are heavily decorated and form a solid four-story composition extending from basement to attic. Note the corners of the house and how the corner boards are ornamented to mark each story. This is one of the most handsome examples of the style in the West.

1513 to 1531 Golden Gate Avenue (all private), 1875; Real Estate Associates, builders. This fine row of slanted-bay Ital-

ianates, like most such rows, has had various later modifications, including a few, like 1517, that have been stuccoed in a complete stylish update.

1400 to 1412 Golden Gate Avenue (all private), 1884; John P. Gaynor, San Francisco, architect. All seven of these attached Stick-style dwellings were built for thirty thousand dollars for a single original owner and remain wonderfully intact today. Note the peaked roofs that form mock towers over the bays.

1057 Steiner Street (private), Chateau Tivoli, 1892–ca. 1900; William Armitage, San Francisco, architect. This fantasy of a Queen Anne structure, which first comes into view on Golden Gate Avenue and then continues around the corner onto Steiner Street, was built as an apartment house. It features an amazing potpourri of Free Classic ornamentation, including Corinthian columns and large areas of floral decoration. The corner tower has hints of its namesake Chateauesque style in the basket-handle ornament above the windows, the through-the-cornice wall dormer, and the high-pitched candlesnuffer roof topped with an elaborate pinnacle.

1347 McAllister Street (private), ca. 1915; James F. Dunn, San Francisco, architect. Several of this architect's Beaux Arts town houses and apartment buildings, featuring unusual Art Nouveau detailing, survive in the city. Once you've seen one, you will likely recognize the others. Note the sinuous curves of the front door, of the hood and crown above it, and of the tops of the windows on the first two floors.

1443 to 1451 McAllister Street (all private), 1885. Each of these three Stick-style homes has slightly different, but equally elaborate, ornamentation. Two, 1443 and 1451, have original false gables. Numbers 1447 and 1451 both have upper window sashes featuring large panes of glass bounded by small rectangular panes, a window type most often found in Queen Anne designs.

1463 McAllister Street (private), 1880. This Stick-style house has an unusual, diagonally placed bay window. Angels peek out from segmental pediments both in this bay and above the entry porch.

1201 Fulton Street (private), ca. 1895; Edgar Matthews, San Francisco, architect. According to Sally B. Woodbridge et al., in their excellent book *San Francisco Architecture,* this one-of-a-kind house is "a cottage inspired by the English Arts and Crafts movement, which drew inspiration from medieval building types like the Cotswold cottage."

710 to 720 Steiner Street (all private), 1895. This carefully preserved row of Queen Anne dwellings is the "photographers' favorite," featured in countless publications about San Francisco (see page 223). The houses were originally sold for $3,550 each by developer Matthew Cavanaugh. All are front-gabled examples of the style, and each has small variations in detailing that distinguish it from its neighbors. All have two-story, slanted bay windows. Upstairs, the roof overhang creates a characteristic cutaway-bay-window pattern to one side with a recessed balcony on the other side. The entry porches alternate between those with round arches supported by shorter columns and those with full-height columns and no arch.

1000 Fulton Street, at Steiner Street (private), Archbishop's Mansion, 1904. Built by Roman Catholic archbishop Patrick Riordan to "reflect the stateliness of the archdiocese," this is an extremely simplified Beaux Arts design of the mansard-roof subtype. The style is indicated by the symmetrical shape, the mansard roof (which normally occurs on no other style except for the much earlier Second Empire), the paired columns at each side of the entry, and the long line of decorative garlands on the low roofline railing. Round-arched windows (on the first floor) and pedimented windows (in the dormers) are both typical of this style.

921 Fulton Street (private), ca. 1895; Martens and Coffey, San Francisco, architects. This is a good example of a towered Queen Anne design with Free Classic detailing. Another towered Queen Anne is next door at 915 Fulton Street (private). Both appear to have had major ground-floor modifications. Just ahead, looking straight down Fulton, is a fine view of San Francisco's domed city hall.

926 Grove Street (private), Koster House, 1897; Martens and Coffey, San Francisco, architects. This imposing Neoclassical home is set on a large lot with a front garden that looks out toward city hall. The unusual design combines a one-story entry porch set in front of a two-story facade graced with a series of full-height, half-round pilasters (technically called engaged columns) beneath a pedimented central gable. Note the multiple, rounded-corner bays.

957 Grove Street (private), 1886; Samuel and Joseph Newsom, San Francisco, architects. Despite many later alterations, it is still possible to grasp the unique exuberance that the Newsom brothers (see page 180) brought to this Queen Anne design. The recessed porch above the entry, with its rounded overlook clad in decorative wood shingles, is a typical example of their creative innovations.

Haight-Ashbury, ca. 1870–1915

Probably no other historic neighborhood in the West has a name with more notoriety than Haight-Ashbury, named for the street intersection that lies near its center. Ironically, it is not the neighborhood's many handsome Victorian homes that gained such attention but rather its role as a focal point for the "hippie" movement of the 1960s. Although Haight Street, the neighborhood's principal shopping area, still has a somewhat-bohemian

flair, neighborhood zoning changes in the 1970s began to attract new home owners interested in reclaiming its deteriorating Victorian dwellings. Today, many have been delightfully restored.

The double name hints at the fact that Haight-Ashbury really has two distinct parts. There are the flatlands called the **Haight** (along Haight, Page, and Oak Streets); south of these is the slightly later hillside neighborhood of **Ashbury Heights** (which includes Buena Vista Park, Buena Vista Avenue West, Masonic Avenue, and Delmar and Ashbury Streets among others).

The Haight grew up along the **Panhandle** of Golden Gate Park, a long, narrow access sliver of parkland that began to be landscaped together with the rest of the park in 1870. In 1883 a cable-car line was built along Haight Street that ended at Stanyan Street, the park's eastern boundary. San Franciscans rode this line to visit both Golden Gate Park and the Chutes, a small nearby amusement park. These were the sort of end-of-the-line amenities used by streetcar and cable-car entrepreneurs to attract lot buyers, and thus future customers, to new neighborhoods developed along their lines (see page 156).

During the 1880s a carriage drive, called the Avenue, ran through the Panhandle extension of Golden Gate Park. This became a favorite place for the wealthy to "promenade" in their expensive carriages in order to see and be seen. The local newspapers reported on who was riding with whom and in what kind of clothes and carriage—much as a society column today might report on who attended an event and what they wore. Fifth Avenue in New York and Commonwealth Avenue in Boston, Massachusetts, were similar Victorian promenade sites. As in those cities, elegant homes soon

Haight-Ashbury

Haight-Ashbury

began filling the lots near to the Panhandle. By the 1890s the Haight district was almost completely developed with fashionable dwellings, most of them in the popular Queen Anne style.

Just as development of the Haight was spurred by the landscaping of the adjacent Panhandle parkland, the development of Ashbury Heights centered around hilly Buena Vista Park. Although set aside as parkland in 1867, this was a barren hilltop until the first modest landscaping efforts began in 1880. Scattered Victorian homes were built over the next two decades, but it was not until 1913 that these early residents were able to get substantial improvements for the park and its surrounding road. The park improvements included staircases, paths, and tennis courts. These stimulated the construction of new Eclectic-era dwellings on the vacant lots between their Victorian predecessors.

The Haight began to lose its upscale image when the 1917 Twin Peaks Tunnel and 1928 Buena Vista Tunnel opened the previously remote southwestern quadrant of the city to new automobile-oriented housing developments (see page 215). In San Francisco, as elsewhere, the trend toward suburban living accelerated during the 1950s as many inner-city residents moved to new, large-lot suburbs. Home ownership in neighborhoods like the Haight dwindled as its large, single-family dwellings were divided into multiple apartments. By the 1960s the area was sufficiently deteriorated that the state planned to build an elevated freeway down the Panhandle. Concerned residents rallied in the "Freeway Revolt of 1962," as San Francisco became one of the first American cities to stop a proposed urban freeway.

Antiestablishment sentiment was still running high in the neighborhood when in January of 1967 the Human Be-In/Gathering of the Tribes was celebrated in Golden Gate Park. Janis Joplin, Grace Slick and other members of the Jefferson Airplane, and the Grateful Dead rented houses and apartments in the area. *Time* magazine pronounced Haight-Ashbury the "vibrant epicenter of America's hippie movement." And as spring semesters ended across the country, about seventy-five thousand young people flooded into the neighborhood, producing the 1967 "Summer of Love," a happening that indelibly etched Haight-Ashbury into the national consciousness. In the early 1970s the city enacted more restrictive zoning for the area, and home ownership and restoration began to rise, a trend that continues today.

The driving route shown on the map keeps you mainly on the quieter residential streets where, outside of rush hours, one can generally drive slowly enough to enjoy the fine houses. Oak and Fell Streets, which bound the Panhandle, are a one-way couplet filled with cars expecting to move very fast, thus making house watching problematic from a car. Page Street, between busy Oak Street and the Haight Street commercial district, is the best spine from which to view the Haight's homes. Many fine houses are also located on the north–south cross streets, where stop signs may give one a chance to linger and look. It is worth making a return drive down Page Street to view the west-facing homes on these side streets.

Although the route through Ashbury Heights goes up Masonic Avenue, nearby Delmar and Ashbury Streets are both worth driving if you have the time. Busy Haight Street, site of the neighborhood's original cable-car line, once had many residences but is now Haight-Ashbury's main commercial street. It features mostly small, locally owned establishments, some with offbeat merchandise that your mother might not approve of.

Ashbury Park: 1214 to 1256 Masonic Avenue (all private), 1896–1897; Cranston and Keenan, builders. This is a highly unusual row of Queen Anne houses, all eight of which have towers, or more precisely "turrets," the name for small towers, particularly those that emerge from the middle of a house rather than beginning at ground level. A couple of these homes have had unsympathetic remodelings.

Ashbury Park: 1301 to 1335 Waller Street (all private). The two houses closest to the corner (1301–1303 and 1307–1309) were constructed in 1901, while their four neighbors with rounded arches at the entry (1315, 1321–1323, 1327–1329, and 1333–1335) were all built in 1896 by developer J. A. Whelan. The entire row is set on high foundations, and together the houses produce the typical San Francisco Queen Anne roofline that looks like a silhouette cut with a pair of old-fashioned pinking shears. Although all of the homes have lavish ornament, the two built in 1901 are slightly more restrained and fit rather neatly into the Free Classic category of Queen Anne detailing. This is unusual in San Francisco, where most Queen Anne designs combine both Free Classic and spindlework details.

Ashbury Park: 615 Buena Vista Avenue West (private), ca. 1915. This fine Tudor-style home is clad in wood shingles and has unusual windows (at least for this style) gracing its handsomely detailed front-facing gable. As you drive down the hill, notice how many of the homes lining the park are Eclectic-era designs built in the first decades of the twentieth century.

Ashbury Park: 737 Buena Vista Avenue West (private), Spreckels House, 1897; Edward J. Vogel, architect. Depending on the source, this was built for a son or nephew of Claus Spreckels, the sugar magnate, whose son Adolph built the Spreckels Mansion in Pacific Heights (see page 233). Whichever, it is a fine example of an early Colonial Revival design in the hipped-roof subtype. It features a handsomely detailed semicircular entry porch and four sets of paired windows beneath an elliptical arch, the whole encased by pilasters and crowned by an entablature. The central dormer is probably original, while the other two dormers are almost certainly later additions.

The Haight: 1080 Haight Street, at Baker Street (private), Spencer House, 1896; Frederick P. Rabin, architect. This large Free Classic Queen Anne design is quite unusual for San Francisco because it is freestanding rather than being part of a closely spaced row. It has the hipped-roof-with-lower-cross-gable shape rather than the front-gabled form that dominates in Queen Anne town houses. It features a triple-arched entry and Palladian motifs in the first-floor windows of the octagonal tower. Note the ornament above the upstairs cutaway bay windows on the side; this kind of deeply curved surface ornamented with stylized leafy or floral detail is used in different ways on a number of San Francisco houses, but is rarely seen in the rest of the country.

The Haight: 15 to 19 Baker Street (all private), 1890; Hugh Keenan, builder. This unusual row alternates designs having Stick-style squared bay windows with those featuring Italianate slanted bay windows. Decorative detailing on both is a mixture of Italianate and Stick elements.

The Haight: 1321 Page Street (private), ca. 1910. Mission-style urban houses such as these are uncommon. Note the visor roof, shaped parapet with miniature bell towers at the sides, open quatrefoil, and varied bay window designs.

The Haight: 1390 and 1392 Page Street (both private), ca. 1900. Although from the front it looks like a house, this Shingle-style structure was built as an apartment building. Note the Moorish-shaped windows in the first-floor bay.

The Haight: 1550 Page Street, at Ashbury Street (private), 1891; Cranston and Keenan, builders. This is the best remaining example in a row of five Queen Anne designs that extends from 1542 through 1550. It features Romanesque arches at the entry and framing the second-floor recessed porch. Returning down Page Street permits one to see the side facade and also get a better view of the entire row, two of which have been remodeled with Missionesque stucco facades. The round-arched upstairs porches unmistakably relate these to their siblings.

The Haight: 1901 Page Street, at Schrader Street (private), 1896; Edward J. Vogel, architect. This striking hipped-roof Colonial Revival design has a long and carefully detailed side facade along Shrader Street. It was designed by the same architect as the Spreckels House (see "737 Buena Vista Avenue West" of Ashbury Park). On the narrow front facade Vogel used some of the same elements—a semicircular entry porch and, upstairs, similar paired windows under an elliptical arch encased by pilasters and an entablature. This is the earlier design and has more floral ornamentation.

The Haight: 156 to 160 Central Street (all private), ca. 1899. These three houses combine the front-gabled Queen Anne form with the beginnings of the Edwardian rounded bay windows that dominated San Francisco in the decade from 1900 to 1910.

The Haight: 142 to 152 Central Street (all private), 1899; Daniel Einstein, builder. Here the front gable has disappeared, and the bays are definitively rounded, as are the dormers above. These houses are yet-another step en route to the typical San Francisco Edwardian town houses and flats of the next decade.

Pacific Heights, ca. 1875–1920

Pacific Heights was at the hilly northern edge of the city's large Western Addition of 1855. Originally too remote and rugged to be attractive to home buyers, after the introduction of cable cars in the 1870s it became San Francisco's premier upscale neighborhood. By the early 1880s, the blocks around Lafayette Park and Alta Plaza (see also page 218) were among the city's most prestigious addresses.

Fillmore Street, running between the hilltop sites of the two parks, divides Pacific Heights into two sections. **Eastern Pacific Heights,** centered around Lafayette Park, is closer to downtown and by 1900 was almost completely filled with Victorian houses. Beginning in the 1910s, the houses of Eastern Pacific Heights began to be replaced by upscale apartment buildings. Today, the neighborhood's surviving single-family houses, some of them Eclectic-era replacements of earlier Victorian homes, are scattered amid larger-scale apartment and commercial buildings. Among the most

Pacific Heights

important survivors are the Haas-Lilienthal House, the city's only Victorian museum house, and several important nearby dwellings (see page 231). These give a feeling for the large and fine Victorian homes that once filled the area. Many of the finest were located along Van Ness Avenue, its eastern boundary and the widest street in the city. These homes were dynamited in 1906 to provide a broad firebreak that helped prevent the enormous postearthquake conflagration from spreading farther westward.

The blocks stretching westward from Fillmore Street, centered around Alta Plaza Park, make up **Western Pacific Heights.** Here, single-family houses still dominate. Victorian-era homes are mostly confined to the southern portion—the blocks between California and Jackson Streets. Located farther from downtown, and thus requiring a longer cable-car commute, than Eastern Pacific Heights, the lots and houses here tended to be smaller than their now-rare eastern neighbors. The Alta Plaza Walk (see map, page 216) visits typical Victorian houses in this part of Western Pacific Heights.

The northern part of Western Pacific Heights, located north of Alta Plaza along Pacific Avenue and Broadway Street, was farthest from the cable-car lines and filled later with unusually fine, automobile-oriented Eclectic-era dwellings. Many of these have spectacular views northward across the Bay. Immediately to the west, adjacent to the parklike Presidio grounds, is a still-younger neighborhood called **Presidio Heights.** This is a treasure trove of fine early-twentieth-century houses in a variety of styles and sizes. All of these Pacific Heights neighborhoods not seen in the Alta Plaza Walk are visited by the driving route shown on the map, page 216. Some of this area's many fine homes seen along this route are:

2501 and 2505 Pacific Avenue and beyond (all private), ca. 1890s. On your left as you begin the tour is a row of quite-varied late Queen Anne– and Shingle-style houses. Number 2501 is a striking Queen Anne design with rounded corners and a ground-to-gable composition of windows and surface texture on the Pacific Avenue facade. Note the wide band of trim beneath the cornice that unites the composition. Number 2505 Pacific Avenue is a fine example of a front-gabled Shingle-style design. Notice the typical shingled porch support; the simple, rounded corners of the porch entry; the multilevel eaves; and the two-story rounded bay window. The remainder of this row has variations of the late Queen Anne style, some with towers, and some with Shingle influence.

2799 Pacific Avenue (private), ca. 1900. This striking early Colonial Revival house is complete with a roofline balustrade, paired dormers, and an elaborate entry porch. It has a rounded two-story bay window on one corner and an angular one on the other. Note also the wide band of floral trim beneath the cornice.

2800 Pacific Avenue (private), 1899; Ernest Coxhead, architect. It is fun to contrast this early brick Colonial Revival house, designed by one of San Francisco's most inventive architects, with the more typical wood-clad example diagonally across the street at 2799 (see the preceding entry). Rather than using lots of ornamentation as at 2799, Coxhead concentrated on a few bold elements—the broken segmental pediment over the front door, supported on dramatic quoins; unbroken segmental pediments over the two downstairs windows; and a bold projection of the entry area, accentuated by a few balusters inserted into the otherwise solid roofline balustrade. There has been an addition on the roof.

2810 and 2830 Pacific Avenue (both private), both built in 1910; designed by Albert Farr, architect. These are later, and more typical, interpretations of the Colonial Revival style. Squeezed in between these two, and set far back on its lot, is a 1912 Italian Renaissance house designed by Willis Polk and Company.

2889 Pacific Avenue (private), 1890, Arthur Brown Jr., architect. This inventive house combines some Shingle-style elements (the shingle cladding and the corner tower, which blends into the main body of the house) with a remarkably exaggerated two-story entry area that incorporates both Beaux Arts elements and a Colonial Revival–type recessed entry porch crowned by a segmental pediment.

3198 Pacific Avenue (private), 1892; Samuel Newsom, architect. This is an excellent example of a Shingle-style design of the gambrel-roofed subtype. Here the style looks as it does throughout the rest of the country. The two blocks ahead (see the following entry) show how the Shingle style was adapted to narrower urban house lots by San Francisco's talented architects.

3200 and 3300 blocks of Pacific Avenue, from Presidio Avenue to Laurel Street (all private). This great collection of Shingle-style houses (known in the San Francisco area as the First Bay Tradition; see page 170) features houses by many fine architects and shows the many guises of this style when adapted for San Francisco's urban houses. Number 3233 (private) was designed in 1909 by Bernard Maybeck; 3234 in 1902 by Ernest Coxhead; 3235 and 3236 to 3240 (all private) around 1910 by William F. Knowles; 3333 (private) in 1903 by Albert Farr; and 3377 (private) in 1908 by Julia Morgan.

3500 Jackson Street (private), Roos House, 1909; Bernard Maybeck, architect. This wonderfully idiosyncratic Tudor-style house by one of the Bay Area's most innovative architects uses his favorite Gothic motifs in the balcony design and in the quatrefoil "windows" hanging from the roof brackets.

Presidio Terrace (all private). This small cul-de-sac was developed by Fernando Nelson beginning in 1905 and is filled with architect-designed houses, mostly built during the period from 1905 to 1915. Developer Nelson did not build his own home here until 1930, when he had it designed by W. R. Yelland. It is the large and picturesque false-thatched-roof Tudor house just to the left of the main entry at 30 Presidio Terrace (private). It has a remarkable roof texture and elaborate half-timbering. The homes built around the rest of the circle form a rather-complete collection of early-twentieth-century styles, with the Mission, French Eclectic, Pueblo Revival, Craftsman, Italian Renaissance, and Prairie styles all represented.

3800 Washington Street (private), Koshland House, 1902; Frank von Trees, architect. The Petit Trianon beautifully transplanted from Versailles to San Francisco.

3690 Washington Street (private), 1928; Arthur Brown Jr., architect. This is an excellent example of the formal, symmetrical subtype of the French Eclectic style. It is clad in a light stone, and, although the same style and subtype as 3450 Washington Street (see the following entry), its facade has little ornament and is very formal and restrained in comparison.

3450 Washington Street (private), 1929; Willis Polk, architect. Another symmetrical French Eclectic design, this is more informal than 3690 (see the preceding entry) because of its composite walls. In the French originals, two wall materials were sometimes combined to add structural strength. Thus, a brick house might be reinforced by using stone for corner quoins, a tabbed window, and bands around the house. A stuccoed house of rubble stone might give the opposite effect, with brick used as the reinforcing material. Here, the primary facade material is brick (proba-

Pacific Heights

bly cladding, not solid masonry), and the areas of stone "reinforcing" have been deliberately exaggerated, leaving only small areas of brick.

3340 Washington Street (private), 1912; Oliver Everett, architect. This is an excellent example of the mansard-roof subtype of the Beaux Arts style. Note the rusticated first story, the floral elaboration of the brackets, and the wide balustrade beneath the windowsills—all typical Beaux Arts features.

2800 and 2900 blocks of Broadway (all private). The base of Lyon Street, where you must turn right onto Broadway, offers a spectacular view of the East Bay and Bernard Maybeck's Palace of Fine Arts, originally built of stucco for the 1915 Panama-Pacific International Exposition and rebuilt in the 1960s of more permanent concrete. On a nice day it is worth parking here and walking down Broadway for a block or two. All of the grand houses in the 2800 and 2900 blocks overlook the same spectacular view you've just seen, and most do not display their addresses. The odd-numbered side of the street has houses perched up high and out of sight if you stay in the car.

Two houses you'll be able to find because they are distinctive, side by side, and located just past the Baker Street steps are 2998 Broadway (private), 1913, Walter Bliss, architect, and 2880 Broadway (private), 1900, Willis Polk, architect. The first, which overlooks the Baker Street steps, is a

San Francisco Town House Plans

Ground Plan

Most of the city's older homes are town houses—tall, skinny dwellings adapted to the narrow and deep lots of San Francisco's early street grid. Town houses come in many different forms—freestanding houses, attached side-wall houses, and double houses being the most common types (see illustration). Double houses (sharing one side wall with a neighbor) and true row houses (with both side walls attached, such as those that fill much of New York City) are infrequently found here. Instead, San Franciscans settled on a general pattern of closely spaced freestanding houses separated from the adjacent structures by a few feet on one side and only a few inches on the other. The side windows in the principal rooms faced the more open side. San Francisco's cool summers made the one-sided window placement, and resulting lack of cross ventilation in some interior rooms, quite bearable (see below).

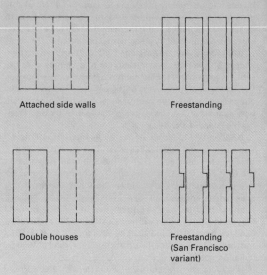

Attached side walls   Freestanding

Double houses   Freestanding (San Francisco variant)

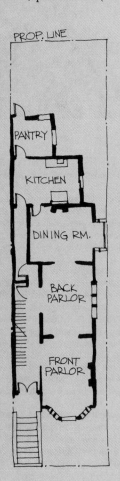

PROP. LINE

PANTRY

KITCHEN

DINING RM.

BACK PARLOR

FRONT PARLOR

Floor Plan

The typical floor plan is one room and a hall wide (see illustration) and is simply described by Randolph Delehanty in his *Victorian Sampler: A Walk in Pacific Heights and the Haas-Lilienthal House:*

> The common two-story row house plan consisted of a long hall with no windows on one side of the house from which branch three interconnected principal rooms: a rarely used formal front parlor, a second, or family parlor, and a dining room with a projecting bay window. Behind the dining room were the kitchen and pantry. Ten foot high sliding doors connecting the ornamented front rooms rendered the lower floor of such a house admirably suited for receptions. The second, or bedroom floor, repeated the plan of the first floor without the interconnecting sliding doors. The master bedroom was usually in the front and had a bay window. The children's bedrooms were in the middle, and servants were housed in the rear rooms or in the attic. The bathroom was placed over the kitchen to minimize plumbing.

Pacific Heights

grand brick Colonial Revival design of the gambrel-roofed subtype. The gambrel roof faces Broadway and has an entry porch with paired columns and a simple flat entablature above; a Palladian-motif window sits above this; and two distinctive quarter-round windows are tucked under the sloping sides of the gambrel roof in the third story. The second house, just beyond, is a fine flat-roofed Beaux Arts design. Architect Polk elected to omit the typical floral ornamentation and concentrate instead on paired columns and pilasters and other Renaissance-based details. The roofline balustrade, the arched windows, the balustraded windowsills, and the right-rear wing's pedimented windows are all typical Beaux Arts features.

2222 Broadway (private), James Leary Flood Mansion (Second), 1912; Bliss and Faville, architects. This is the finest of three exceptional homes that are owned and used by the Convent of the Sacred Heart School. It is built with a steel frame clad in Tennessee marble. Every detail of the home is subtle, refined, and exhibits a high degree of craftsmanship. This was the second home built by James L. Flood, the son of a Nevada silver baron (see "2120 Broadway" below), and looked out over the grounds of the Panama-Pacific Exposition.

2200 Broadway (private), Grant Mansion, 1910; Hiss and Weekes of New York, architects. This is an outstanding mansard-roof Beaux Arts design.

2550 Webster Street (private), Bourn House, 1896; Polk and Polk, San Francisco, architects. This house, visible to the right as you cross Webster Street, is the town house designed by Willis Polk for William Bourn (see also "Filoli," page 204, and "Bourn Cottage," page 130). Here, Polk deftly uses clinker brick and his usual "few but bold" details for a high-style interpretation of the Colonial Revival.

2120 Broadway (private), James Leary Flood Mansion (First), 1901; Julius Krafft, architect. Loyalty to Italian architecture ran high in the Flood family. James Leary Flood's father, James Clair Flood, made a fortune in the mining business while tending bar near the financial district. During the late 1860s he and his partners, one of whom was John Mackay (see page 427), quietly accumulated stock in several then-declining Comstock Lode silver mines. In 1872 they formed the Consolidated Virginia Mine and began deeper exploration in the earlier mines. The result was the Comstock's largest "bonanza" discovery of all, a find that reenergized Virginia City, Nevada, and poured enormous new

wealth into San Francisco. The elder Flood quit bartending and in 1886 commissioned architect Augustus Laver to build him a great Italianate mansion atop fashionable Nob Hill, now adjacent to the city's downtown commercial district. Constructed of brownstone, this was the only one of the Hill's grand Victorian mansions that was not built entirely of wood. As a result its walls were the only Nob Hill survivors of the 1906 fire. The house was then rebuilt by the Pacific Union Club and still stands at 1000 California Street (private).

Flood's son built this Italian Renaissance home in Pacific Heights only five years before the fire. It has wooden walls, finished to look like stone. Although it survived the conflagration, the son decided to take less risk in the future. Soon after the fire he built an equally grand second Italian Renaissance home, this time made of steel and marble, at 2222 Broadway (see above). This first home was then occupied by his maiden sister. Today it has been well preserved by the Hamlin School, a nonsectarian private institution for girls.

Haas-Lilienthal House, 1886

2007 Franklin Street; 415-441-3004;
Peter R. Schmidt, architect.

The Haas-Lilienthal House is one of those rare museum houses that was only occupied by three generations of a single family. In 1973, eighty-six years after it was built, the family generously donated the grand home and all of its principal furnishings and fixtures to become a public museum. Here, the visitor has a rare and accurate glimpse into the lifestyles of upper-middle-class San Francisco at the turn of the twentieth century. This view is enhanced by a charming book written by Alice Haas Lilienthal's niece, Frances Bransten Rothmann, called *The Haas Sisters of Franklin Street: A Look Back with Love.* This affectionate account tells how the two sisters, Alice Haas Lilienthal (1885–1972) and Florine Haas Bransten (1881–1973), ran their houses, entertained family and friends, shopped, courted, and traveled in the first decades of the century, and then the story continues through World War II and after, when they lived to a gracious old age.

The home was designed for their father, William Haas, by architect Peter Schmidt, who was born in Germany and had a long and successful career in San Francisco. They chose the Queen Anne style, then the most popular style in the rest of the country, but one that would not become common in San Francisco row-house design for another few years. Schmidt's design has typical Queen Anne features in its asymmetrical facade, dominant front-facing gable, textured shingle surfaces, and asymmetrically placed porch with simple spindlework supports. It also has the typical round tower used on Queen Anne houses, rather than the square towers favored for Stick-style houses. Only the straight-side bay windows in Schmidt's design reflect the then-popular Stick style, which dominated San

Haas-Lilienthal House

Francisco house building during the 1880s. The avant-garde nature of Schmidt's facade can be seen by comparing it with the Westerfield House at 1198 Fulton Street (private) in Alamo Square (see page 224). That is a Stick-style house of similar size and grandeur built three years later than the Haas-Lilienthal House.

It is interesting that the floor plan of the large Haas-Lilienthal House, which includes 11,500 square feet (excluding the garage and bedroom wing added in 1929), is very similar to that of the typical smaller San Francisco row house (see page 230). As in the smaller houses, Haas-Lilienthal has a long stair hall at the side with three rooms opening off of it—a front parlor, a second parlor, and a dining room, with kitchen and service rooms behind. Upstairs, the same pattern is repeated. The primary difference in the two floors is that the downstairs rooms open into each other with broad double doors, which facilitated entertaining, while the upstairs bedrooms are both interconnected and served by a side hall.

Entering the house, you are struck by the quality of the construction, beginning with the marble mosaic floor of the entry and the double set of paired doors that lead to the entrance hall. Here, the walls are covered with faux leather bordered by a geometric design in gold leaf. The fireplace that originally graced the entry hall was removed in an 1898 remodeling when new fireplaces were added in the front parlor and in the second parlor. Architect Frank von Trees was hired to do this remodeling, which included a stylistic updating of the front parlor. He added a mahogany dado and a Classical cornice with dentils, egg-and-dart molding, and a Classic design of laurel leaves wrapped with ribbon.

The original Lincrusta Walton wall covering remains in many of the halls and original dual gas-electric light fixtures are found throughout the house. Most of the furnishings are original and give the home an authentic and comfortable lived-in feeling. The front parlor features an exquisite antique Oushak carpet, an electrical grand player piano, and furnishings that are mostly late-nineteenth-century American copies of European antiques. The second parlor features red tones, including a Oushak carpet, a fireplace faced in red Numidian marble, and an Edwardian plush chair. The dining room is filled with golden oak—including a faux golden-oak dado, oak coffered ceiling and fireplace, and the late-Victorian favorite, a golden-oak dining table and chairs. The room's original Anaglypta wallpaper is finished to imitate Spanish leather.

Upstairs, several rooms are open for tours. These include the original front master bedroom that was later changed to a family sitting room; the small room used by Bertha Haas's maid; a bathroom with the original tub, tiles, and vanity; and a smaller bedroom used by Alice Haas Lilienthal when she and her husband moved back into the house in 1916 to live with her widowed mother. This holds Alice's striking ten-piece oak Arts and Crafts bedroom suite.

The basement was used as a ballroom and as a special-occasion dining room for large and festive holiday dinners. Today, it is used as an entry area from which the house tours begin and end. It also features a bookstore and small exhibit.

Nearby Houses

By walking nine short blocks from the Haas-Lilienthal House (only two of which are steep), one can comfortably see four houses that belonged to relatives of the Haas-Lilienthal family and end up with a view of the grand Spreckels Mansion, the model for the Beaux Arts "Identifying Features" illustration in *A Field Guide to American Houses* and likely the finest Beaux Arts house in the West. These will give you a feeling for the grand Victorians that once filled Eastern Pacific Heights. From the Haas-Lilienthal House turn right (south) and walk four blocks down Franklin Street to California Street; go right along California for one block; and then turn right (north) on Gough Street returning north to Washington Street. Turn left, and the Spreckels Mansion is on the right at the end of the block.

1735 Franklin Street (private), Bransten House, 1904; Herman Barth, San Francisco, architect. This redbrick Colonial Revival home is where Florine Haas Bransten, one of the subjects of *The Haas Sisters of Franklin Street* (see page 231), lived with her husband, Edward. Note the segmental pediments on both the street facade and above the side entry.

1701 Franklin Street (private), Coleman House, 1895; Salfield and Kohlberg, architects. This large Free Classic Queen Anne design dominates the corner and has two towers, one rounded and one hexagonal. The many applied surface details are mostly of plaster, not wood.

1818 California Street (private), Lilienthal-Pratt House, 1876. Samuel Lilienthal, Alice Haas's future husband, grew up in this handsome Italianate home. Samuel's maternal grandparents built it as a wedding present for his parents. Note the corner quoins and use of bay windows not only on the front facade, but on the right side as well, this made possible by the unusually wide lot.

1834 California Street (private), Wormser-Coleman House, 1876 and 1895. This unusual house was built in two stages. The first produced the Italianate-style right-hand section. The second, undertaken when a family with ten

Haas-Lilienthal House vicinity

children purchased the house and an additional lot in 1895, added a side garden and the left side with rounded tower that is more Queen Anne in character.

2080 Washington Street (private), Spreckels Mansion, 1913; MacDonald and Applegarth, architects. This commanding mansion across from Lafayette Park was built by Adolph Spreckels, the son of the wealthy sugar-refining magnate, and his wife, Alma de Bretteville Spreckels. Constructed of reinforced concrete faced with white Utah limestone and decorated with paired engaged columns and floral garlands, it is one of the country's great Beaux Arts landmarks. The entrance was originally on the front, but his widow moved the main entrance to the east side and added a porte cochere after Mr. Spreckels's death. Climbing up the steps to the north side of Lafayette Park gives the best view of this massive and dramatic house.

Octagon House, 1861

2645 Gough Street; 415-441-7512.

This fine structure was built by William C. McElroy (1819–1870) and his wife, Harriet Shober McElroy (1820–ca. 1899). McElroy was originally from Virginia and arrived in gold rush San Francisco in 1851. His wife, a native of Lancaster, Pennsylvania, had arrived two years earlier with the forty-niners. The McElroys must surely have read Orson Fowler's popular book promoting the Octagon style, called *A Home for All, or the Gravel Wall and the Octagon Mode of Building*, which was published in 1848 and reprinted at least seven times over the next decade.

Fowler was a phrenologist, a practitioner of a kind of nineteenth-century pseudoscience that purported to be able to tell people's personality traits from the shape of their heads. This unusual background did not stop him from also concluding that he knew exactly the sort of home everyone needed to build—one with eight sides. This shape would, in his opinion, save building materials and heating costs and, at the same time, add light and ventilation and simplicity to one's home life. He further advocated construction of these octagonal houses with a type of concrete wall.

The McElroys followed Fowler's advice on almost everything except the construction material, for here

Octagon House

and at the top is a semicircular terrace with a second grand fountain. The entrance gates at Junípero Serro Boulevard and the fountains were designed by John Galen Howard and Henry Gutterson. This subdivision had the latest suburban amenities, including underground utilities. Deed restrictions gave the community a pleasing unity of house setbacks and construction materials. Olmsted also prescribed lush landscaping, which was first achieved with the installation of many trees purchased at the close of the 1915 Panama-Pacific Exposition.

It was difficult to reach this neighborhood until the early 1920s, when the new Twin Peaks Tunnel made it more readily accessible. The development then quickly filled up. The oldest homes in St. Francis Wood are built along St. Francis Boulevard and on the long blocks to each side of it. Just south of St. Frances Wood is Balboa Terrace, which lies in the blocks south of Monterey Boulevard and north of Ocean Avenue. Balboa Terrace features a delectable assortment of smaller houses, where many common Eclectic-era styles are interpreted in homes with stucco walls finished in a variety of textures.

Just south of Ocean Avenue is Ingleside Terrace, named after the mile-long racetrack that opened here in 1885. Urbano Drive still marks the path of the old track. Ingleside Terrace was platted for development in about 1905, and, although the majority of the homes appear to have been built in the 1920s, there are a few earlier Craftsman- and Prairie-style homes.

they wisely chose native California woods. This was a lucky decision, for in 1952, after going through a succession of earthquakes and tenants, the house was scheduled to be torn down by the Pacific Gas and Electric Company. It was at this point that the National Society of Colonial Dames of America in California purchased the historic home and moved it directly across the street from its original site. They changed the first-floor plan, opening it almost entirely into one large room, in which they hold functions and display their small but fine collection of eighteenth-century American decorative arts. The stairway was also moved from the center of the house, under the cupola, to its present rear location. Upstairs, other displays of decorative arts and historic documents of the Colonial and Federal periods continue, but the floor plan has been kept as close to the original as the moved stairway made possible. Three of the original large, square second-floor rooms, separated by small triangular storage or service rooms, remain.

The West has very few surviving Octagon-style houses. Even though altered, it is lucky that the Colonial Dames were able to save this most unusual dwelling for the enjoyment of future generations.

St. Francis Wood and Ingleside Terrace, ca. 1905–1930s

The handsome St. Francis Wood neighborhood was one of the new early-twentieth-century neighborhoods developed in the previously inaccessible southwestern quadrant of the city (see page 215). It was laid out by Frederick Law Olmsted Jr. in 1912 with gently curving streets intersected by a grand central parkway, with a landscaped median, called St. Francis Boulevard. Midway up the boulevard is a circle with a fountain,

Ingleside Terrace: 35 Lunado Way (private). This simple false-thatched-roof Tudor house is clad with stucco textured in an unusual horizontal pattern seen elsewhere in the neighborhood.

Ingleside Terrace: 153 Lunado Way (private). Another false-thatched-roof Tudor design that appears to retain its original, wavy-layered roofing material. This is complemented by the rough-finished stucco texture of the walls.

Ingleside Terrace: 140 Cedro Avenue (private), ca. 1915. This intriguing home combines the dissimilar Prairie and Colonial Revival styles. The red sandstone first story has horizontal lines typical of the Prairie style, as is the wide, boxed-in roof overhang and the squared piers of the second-story terrace. The segmental pedimented hood over the entry and the balusters for the terrace are of Colonial Revival inspiration. The stucco cladding and tile roof were used on pre-1920 homes in both the Prairie and Colonial Revival styles.

Ingleside Terrace: 90 Cedro Avenue (private), ca. 1910. This lovely Craftsman home with wood-shingled wall cladding and foundation and chimney of stone makes a striking contrast to its many stucco-clad neighbors.

Ingleside Terrace: 244 Moncada Way (private), ca. 1920. A Spanish Eclectic design clad with a rough-finished stucco and ornamented with spiraled entry columns and round-arched windows, it overlooks a small park surrounded with homes in an assortment of Eclectic-era styles.

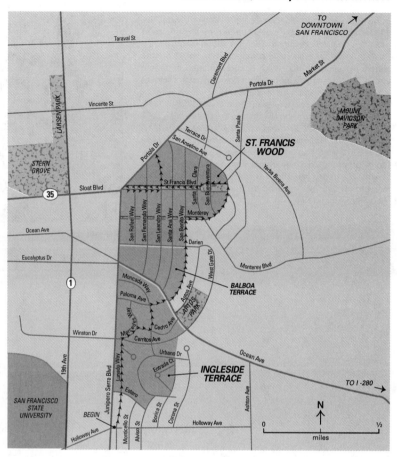

Ingleside Terrace

Balboa Terrace: San Benito Way, from Ocean Avenue to Monterey Boulevard (all private), ca. 1920s. These two long blocks in this more modest neighborhood south of St. Francis Wood are filled with small Spanish Eclectic homes, all nicely landscaped and mostly having red tile roofs and stuccoed walls. These blocks are quite uniform because of the neighborhood's comprehensive deed restrictions.

St. Francis Wood: 1600 Monterey Boulevard (private), ca. 1910s. This stucco-clad Tudor design has a handsome brick chimney topped with elegant copper chimney pots. Note the subtle half-timbering, fine leaded windows in the downstairs, and small wall dormer on the right wing.

St. Francis Wood: 98 St. Francis Boulevard (private), 1917; Henry Gutterson, architect; remodeled 1929 by Masten and Hurd. This elegant and understated example of the Spanish Eclectic style combines a low hipped-roof section to the rear with a side-gabled entry block. The arrangement of entry door, recessed balcony, and windows shows a studied asymmetry. The entrance features sculpted stucco that curves into a deep recess with colorful tiles around the door and striking door hardware. An unusual feature is the way the side garden fence curves in to become one side of the sculpted door recess.

235

St. Francis Wood: 55 San Leandro Way (private), ca. 1910s. Here the Colonial Revival is interpreted in stucco to meet the deed restrictions (which the wood-clad Colonial Revival next door must have somehow avoided). Note the handsome entrance door with open segmental pediment above. The two large window openings downstairs feature a broad central window with narrower windows to each side, a favored window treatment from about 1905 to 1920, which allowed much natural light into the interior.

St. Francis Wood: 67 San Leandro Way (private), 1917; Julia Morgan, architect. Morgan turned this large and understated stucco Tudor home sideways, placing the entrance off of the driveway (rather than on the front facade) to achieve a more usable house interior on a narrow lot. This side-turned floor plan is used on a number of St. Francis Woods's larger homes.

St. Francis Wood

SAN JOSE

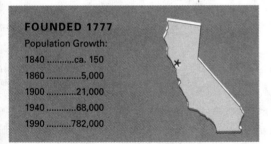

FOUNDED 1777

Population Growth:

1840 ....ca. 150
1860 5,000
1900 21,000
1940 68,000
1990 782,000

With only two important exceptions, all of the early Spanish settlements in California grew around one of the twenty-one coastal missions that were established to convert the local Indians to Christianity (see page ix). The Spanish *Laws of the Indies* provided that, when needed to accommodate Spanish citizens, new towns, or pueblos, could be founded in addition to the more numerous missions and their protecting presidios (forts). The two principal nonmission-based settlements were the pueblo of San Jose de Guadalupe, established in 1777, and the pueblo of the Reina de los Angeles (Queen of the Angels), established in 1781 (see page 65). The Spanish authorities chose well when they picked the sites of these civilian towns, for they grew to become modern Los Angeles and San Jose, now California's largest and third-largest cities.

San Jose was founded as an agricultural center in the fertile riverside lowlands at the southern end of San Francisco Bay. Nearby was the Mission Santa Clara de Asis, which was founded in 1777 along with the new pueblo. The civilian pueblo was needed principally to supply food for the soldiers at the important seaport presidios of Monterey, founded in 1770, and San Francisco, established in 1776. Normally the missions, which were agricultural communities worked by their Indian converts under the supervision of the padres, were expected to supply not only their own food but enough surplus for the garrisons of protecting soldiers. Unfortunately, the missions at San Francisco and Monterey had rocky, coastal soils and a cool, foggy climate that limited their self-sufficiency.

The San Jose agriculturists performed their job well, and by 1781 they were producing enough food, mostly wheat, to more than supply the entire needs of the two presidios. In the following decades, San Jose prospered as a wheat-growing center and by the early 1800s was Spanish California's most important inland town.

In the early 1840s a small trickle of Anglo settlers

began arriving from the East via the California Trail. San Jose was the first Mexican town they encountered after making the perilous crossing of the Sierra Nevada. In most cases the Mexican authorities permitted the newly arrived Anglos to become California residents, and many remained in the fertile San Jose area as farmers or traders. When California became a part of the United States in 1848, most of its residents, both Anglo and Hispanic, considered this an inevitable change that could benefit both. San Jose, more centrally located and Anglo oriented than the venerable Spanish capital of Monterey, was quickly made the new capital of the U.S. province of California.

Unfortunately, Anglo-Hispanic cooperation in building agricultural California was truncated the following year when the great gold rush brought in hoards of restless Anglos intent on finding a quick fortune. Soon burgeoning San Francisco became California's dominant city, the capital was moved to several new towns farther north before finally landing permanently in the gold rush center of Sacramento, and San Jose reverted to its role as a center for wheat growing and its reputation as the loveliest inland city of California. By the 1880s high-value fruit orchards had mostly replaced the wheat fields, as San Jose became a major center for the growing, canning, and drying of plums, apricots, and pears.

By 1940 San Jose was the largest fruit-canning and dried-fruit-processing center in the world; no one could then have guessed that only forty years later it would be transformed into the booming capital of a vast new industry built around something as seemingly insubstantial as bits, bytes, chips, and software, terms that were then either unknown or had a far more limited meaning. Today, the fertile Santa Clara Valley, named for its early mission, which was surrounded first by the wheat fields of Spanish farmers and later by the orchards of Anglo fruit growers, has become Silicon Valley, jammed with electronics factories, office complexes, and residential suburbs that sprawl northwestward from San Jose all the way to Palo Alto and beyond.

While the San Jose area has lost most of its rural character over the past four decades, the city itself, now the nation's eleventh largest, retains many important remnants of its earlier incarnations. It is, for example, one of the only cities in the entire West with house museums representing each of its eras of architectural design—Colonial, Romantic, Victorian, and Eclectic. Interpreted together, and both on their original loca-

tions, are the Colonial-era Peralta Adobe, built in 1797, and the two-story Romantic-era Fallon House (see the following entry), built in 1855. The Victorian-era Winchester Mystery House (see page 240), constructed from 1884 to 1922, began as a fine Queen Anne rural residence and then continued to grow in more and more unusual ways. Quite nearby, in Campbell, is the Eclectic-era Ainsley House (see page 242), built in 1925, which still has almost all of its original furnishings and fixtures. Just a bit farther afield in the small

Peralta Adobe

Fallon House

town of Saratoga is an Eclectic-era great estate, Villa Montalvo (see page 243), with a fine Italian Renaissance–style dwelling built in 1912 and today adaptively reused as a performing arts center.

Most of San Jose's older neighborhoods have been engulfed by its fast-growing downtown, but some large homes survive around its edges, now mostly converted to office uses. One early-twentieth-century neighborhood that has survived intact is the Hanchett Residence Park (see page 241), which is mostly filled with smaller homes built from about 1910 to 1920.

Peralta Adobe, ca. 1797, and Fallon House, ca. 1858

San Pedro Square, on the corner of San Pedro and West Street John Streets; 408-993-8182.

These two houses, both recently restored, tell a compelling story of California's three earliest periods—the Spanish Colonial, the Mexican, and the post–gold rush American. This is accomplished by looking first at the modest two-room adobe in which Don Luis Maria Peralta (1759–1851), holder of the 44,800-acre Peralta Spanish land grant, lived until his death. The sleeping room is furnished to illustrate California's Spanish Colonial period, from the first California mission in 1769 to the year Mexico won its independence from Spain in 1821. The main room is furnished to reflect California's Mexican years, which lasted from 1821 until the United States effectively controlled the state in 1846.

Then you cross the street and enter into the immediate post–gold rush American years, demonstrated in the home built by Captain Thomas Fallon (1824–1885), an Irishman who grew wealthy in the goldfields and by marrying Carmelita Lodge, the half-Irish and half-Spanish daughter of Martina Castro, holder of the

thirty-four-thousand-acre Rancho Soquel land grant. He later gained his own wealth in the early California gold rush, a wealth this house was built to reflect. These two houses are both well restored and furnished, although with few items that belonged to their original owners, and together they visually interpret the lifestyles that accompanied these three important eras.

Don Luis Maria Peralta participated fully in the early Spanish and Mexican periods of California and lived to see the province become part of the United States. He first arrived in San Jose in 1778 with his father, Corporal Gabriel Peralta, one of the fifteen Spanish soldiers chosen to establish a Spanish civilian pueblo here in the rich Santa Clara Valley to produce food for Spain's nearby missions and presidios. Don Luis enlisted in the service of the king of Spain when he reached twenty-one and served with the Escolta (guards) at the missions of Santa Clara and San Jose. In 1805 he became recognized as an Indian fighter by killing and taking as prisoners a group of Indians that had been attacking Mission San Jose.

This success led to his being appointed the *comisionado* in charge of Pueblo San Jose in 1807, making him the highest-ranking secular figure in the town. While serving in this capacity, he was given two of the farm lots that had been distributed to the pueblo's original settlers and moved into this adobe, which was built in 1797. It and its gardens were not part of the large 44,800-acre land grant that Don Luis was later awarded in 1820. These lands were located to the north of San Jose, and his ownership was reaffirmed a few years later by the new Mexican government. Don Luis's four sons oversaw these lands to the north, while he continued to live in this two-room adobe. In 1842, when he was eighty-three years old, he officially divided his large land grant among his sons, and they were the ones to face the trauma of trying to hold on to even a small portion of their land and wealth under the Anglo on-slaught after 1849.

The sleeping room of the Peralta Adobe has a dirt floor and simple furnishings that reflect the Spanish Colonial period. Almost everything is made of indigenous materials, as the Spanish were reluctant to allow foreign trade. Leather, from the great cattle herds on the Spanish ranchos, was a plentiful and much used material. The bed is supported on a foundation of interwoven leather straps, and a small Indian bassinet hangs from the ceiling, suspended by strips of leather. Light is provided by tallow candles, extracted from beef fat, and the floor has an animal skin on it. This room also has a replica of the type of "armor" Spanish soldiers like Don Luis wore when they fought hostile Indians—a multi-layered leather jacket and a deerskin shield, both relatively effective against the bow and arrow.

The adobe's main room shows the far greater material prosperity of the Mexican period after the new government opened up California to foreign trade; its officials had realized they could levy taxes on the ships' cargoes to help support the fledgling government. There is an 1840 American Empire style table to reflect this trade, while a pen and inkwell demonstrate Don Luis's literacy, unusual for this period. The pictures of the Virgin of Guadalupe and Saint Joseph are copies of the originals that hung in the Peraltas' living room. It is the only adobe from San Jose's Spanish Colonial era to survive, miraculously saved by being used as a warehouse in the early twentieth century.

Across the street, the ca.-1858 Fallon House survived by being converted to a hotel and then later a restaurant. The basement now houses an audiovisual presentation and exhibit on the history of this area. The Fallon House needed extensive restoration to be returned to its original form. It has fifteen-foot ceilings, bay windows, fine moldings and a staircase, wall-to-wall carpeting, and many handsome furnishings that visually demonstrate how much life in California changed during the few short years after the Americans arrived and gold was discovered.

As a young man, Thomas Fallon was known for his good looks and charm. He immigrated to Canada from Ireland as a bound apprentice to a saddle maker and at age eighteen took off to seek his fortune in the West. He went first to Texas, and then he and a group of similarly adventurous young men decided it would be a "novel enterprise" to march to the Pacific coast. What was really novel was that they made it and arrived in Santa Cruz in the spring of 1844. Two years later, he gathered a troop of about twenty and crossed the Santa Cruz Mountains north to San Jose to "help" in the Bear Flag Revolt of 1846.

Soon Fallon made a fortune in the early goldfields and married Carmelita, the daughter of Martina Castro, holder of the thirty-four-thousand-acre Rancho Soquel land grant. Carmelita inherited one-ninth of this ranch in 1850. Fallon became mayor of San Jose in 1859 and sometime between about 1855 and 1859 built this fine Italianate house—which was extremely advanced for California in the late 1850s. To put it into context, remember that it was not until the 1870s that slanted-bay-window Italianate houses became common in San Francisco. And at this time in San Jose, there was no railroad, which meant that everything in this house had to be either locally produced or brought in by ship and wagon. For its place and time, this was a remarkable house. The Fallons later fell into marital difficulties over his rumored infidelities and divorced. Fallon remarried in 1875 and finally left this home to move to San Francisco in 1882. Apparently his great charm never deserted him, and when he died at age sixty, he was being sued for breach of promise; litigation over his estate would continue until the 1920s.

Winchester Mystery House, 1884–1922

525 South Winchester Boulevard, between Interstate 280 and Stevens Creek Boulevard; 408-247-2101.
Sarah Pardee Winchester (ca. 1840–1922) was the forty-three-year-old widow of William Wirt Winchester when she left her native New England for California. Her husband was the son of Oliver Winchester, founder of the Winchester Repeating Arms Company, manufacturer of many guns and other products, with the most famous being the Winchester Model '73—a repeating rifle known as the "gun that won the West." Sarah had visited a psychic after her husband's death and was apparently advised that as long as she kept building, day and night, she would be safe from the ghosts of the many soldiers and Indians that her husband's rifles had killed.

Mrs. Winchester moved to San Jose in 1884, where she purchased an eight-room farm house on about forty-five acres and began to enlarge it. Although she owned about 10 percent of the company stock when she came west, in 1904 she inherited about $20 million, which represented most of the Winchester family's shares. After this date, construction picked up its pace, and many of the largest additions appear to have been built between 1904 and her death. To the end she kept the exterior of the house in the Queen Anne style. Sarah Winchester acted as her own architect for all of the expansions of this house and for its gardens and many outbuildings. She strongly believed that friendly spirit

Winchester Mystery House

guides were always telling her what to build next to elude the spirits who would wish to do her harm because of her late husband's guns. Although she was afraid of unfriendly spirits, she was not afraid of technology and incorporated some remarkable features into her house, including three elevators and a small outdoor plant that produced gas for lights and other purposes.

Inside is an amazing amalgamation of some relatively normal rooms, now with appropriate furnishings added, coupled with all kinds of odd-sized rooms, stairs, and passageways that can only be explained by her desire to confuse the evil spirits and provide a hospitable environment for the friendly spirits that she believed to be guiding her efforts. By the time she died, the house had 160 "rooms," 47 fireplaces, 13 bathrooms ("13" was Mrs. Winchester's favorite number), and 10,000 windows spread over six acres. Included with the bizarre are many fine examples of art glass, wall coverings, and Victorian-era architectural details. Mrs. Winchester's storeroom, at the beginning of the tour, has a dazzling array of art glass, light fixtures, and wall coverings that had been collected to incorporate into the house. There is also a particularly intriguing collection of outbuildings, including a dehydrator, pump house, garage and car wash, gas plant, aviary, and a handsome greenhouse with 13 glass cupolas. The gardens include a number of Mrs. Winchester's original plants and many fountains and fine pieces of garden statuary from J. L. Mott Company in New York; all are made of a corrosion-resistant metallic blend of zinc and tin. Although with its large gift shop, food court, and many visitors, this has a more commercial feeling

than most museum houses, there are countless architectural highlights to intrigue house watchers.

Hanchett Residence Park, ca. 1910–1920

This neighborhood was developed by T. S. Montgomery and Sons in about 1910 and was laid out by landscape architect John McLaren, whose role as the landscape architect for Golden Gate Park helped land him many of the most choice commissions in the Bay Area. Montgomery and Sons provided their development with the most up-to-date amenities, including streetlights, concrete sidewalks, modern septic tanks, curbs and gutters, and street trees. Craftsman-style houses predominate, but a number of Italian Renaissance houses and a sprinkling of other styles are also found. Magnolia Avenue, just beyond the Hanchett Park boundary, has a nice collection of Queen Anne cottages, some of which are beginning to be restored.

1148 Martin Avenue (private), ca. 1915. Martin Avenue is full of fine Craftsman-style houses in many variations. This one has a cross-gabled roof, heavy squared porch supports atop square brick pedestals, twin attic-story windows with pointed tops, and a secondary gable added to the side-gabled roof for both decorative effect and attic ventilation. Notice how the pattern of window lights in the front door echoes the pointed tops of the twin windows above. This house has a choice Craftsman-style porch railing.

1163 Martin Avenue (private), Coe House, 1910; Wolfe and Wolfe, architects. This is a rare one-story Prairie-style house; it is architect designed and has a flat roof rather than the more usual hipped one. The design is strongly symmetrical and features a centered front entry, which is only slightly disguised by placing the sidewalk and front steps to one side. Note the three horizontal rows of windows, with

Hanchett Residence Park

the central bank containing the angular geometric art glass inspired by Frank Lloyd Wright's window designs. The strong horizontal lines of this house have been nicely emphasized with color along the porch coping and overhanging eaves. Number 1208 Martin (private) was also designed by Wolfe and Wolfe.

1249 Martin Avenue (private). This cross-gabled Craftsman house has a pair of pointed-top windows similar to the ones at 1148 Martin Avenue (see page 241), but with quite different window surround detailing. Each porch support combines an inward-sloping pedestal of rounded cobblestones that begins at ground level with four squared wood supports above. These are joined together by a "pierced arrow" detail.

295 Sequoia Avenue (private). One of the largest houses in the neighborhood, this is a symmetrical Italian Renaissance house with a bit of Spanish influence in the wrought-iron balconets and the two-story decorative motif at the entry.

Ainsley House, 1925

330 Grant Street, Campbell Historical Museum, between city hall and the library, Campbell, about six miles southwest of downtown San Jose; 408-866-2119.
As the owner of the local fruit-canning factory, John Colpitts Ainsley (1860–1937) was one of the most important men in Campbell, then a growing small town in the heart of Santa Clara Valley's fertile orchard country. Ainsley had emigrated from England and in 1893 established the John C. Ainsley Packing Company, selling all of his factory's output direct to English markets rather than in the United States. The cannery provided as many as eight hundred jobs for the town of Campbell.

Mr. Ainsley's concern for the well-being of his workers was as great as his concern for the quality of his product. He was the first employer in the area to supply

a nurse for his workers, establish a day care center for their young children, and provide a hot lunch at low cost. In 1912 he helped to alleviate the annual housing shortage faced by seasonal cannery workers by building cottages for them to live in during the canning season.

In May 1894, Ainsley married Alcinda Shelley (1875–1939), a nineteen-year-old woman whose parents had come to Campbell from Kansas ten years before. The new Mrs. Ainsley worked as a bookkeeper in her husband's cannery until the birth of their first child, Gordon, in 1896. A daughter, Dorothy, followed in 1900. It was not until their two children had grown up that the Ainsleys decided to build this spacious new home. A contract was let in January 1925 and they moved in the following December.

The Ainsley House is a fine example of a false-thatched-roof Tudor design. It still has its original roof, made of cedarwood soaked in linseed oil and then expertly applied by J. C. Spencer, a local roofer who created a number of similar roofs and then disappeared from the area. Like many homes of this subtype, it is a symmetrical house, but it is unusual for a 1920s Tudor house in having no prominent front-facing gable. A picture of Anne Hathaway's cottage, near Stratford-on-Avon, that still hangs in the house suggests this as the likely inspiration for this house form. Ainsley's love of English interiors shows in the squared wood paneling in the main hall and library and in the many Tudor arched openings with rectangular molding above, the areas between the arch and molding filled with an oak-leaf motif.

The Ainsley House is quite special in that it still has almost all of its original floor coverings, wall finishes, fixtures and fittings (including some handsome tiled bathrooms), kitchen appliances, dishes, and most pieces of the original furniture, all of which came from Grand Rapids, Michigan. The house was little used for forty years after Ainsley's death. Mrs. Ainsley never returned to the house after his funeral, and her daughter and granddaughters kept all of the original furnishings. Stepping into the Ainsley House today is, therefore, much like walking right into a mid-1920s *House and Garden* magazine.

The Ainsley House has been moved about one mile from its original site, but the entire house was moved completely intact—a remarkable 285 tons of house and roof—and nothing was injured in the move. When the house was resited, the grounds around it were laid out and planted according to the original plans of landscape architect Emerson Knight, even to the extent of using the old rose varieties he had specified. This gives Ainsley House a feeling of fitting very comfortably into its immediate setting—a perfect house and surrounding garden now looking out on Campbell's modern civic center.

Villa Montalvo, 1912

Entrance on Montalvo Road, approximately ⅓ mile south of Saratoga, just off California Highway 9 and about twelve miles southwest of San Jose; 408-961-5800; William Curlett, San Francisco, architect.

The Honorable James Duval Phelan (died 1930), who served three terms as the mayor of San Francisco and was California's first popularly elected United States senator, was a great lover of San Francisco. He followed in William Ralston's footsteps (see page 202) in his unabashed promotion of good things for his native city—with a particular interest in good government and farsighted planning for the city. He also loved the arts. He had hoped to be a poet, but followed his father's

wishes and became a part of the family real estate and banking business, where he managed to double its worth. Phelan completed Villa Montalvo about the time he was elected senator and delighted in entertaining accomplished authors, writers, painters, and musicians there. Upon his death he left his estate for use as a public park, but one that would be used also for art, music, literature, and architecture.

Today, Villa Montalvo, a handsome Italian Renaissance design, sits in the middle of a 175-acre arboretum and bird sanctuary that features several miles of nature paths. It still has some of the gardens laid out by John McLaren, who had been the landscape designer for Golden Gate Park. This estate, a rare survivor of the many that used to dot the peninsula (see page 197) has been saved by its adaptive reuse as an arts center that has performances on its huge front lawn, in the more intimate Garden Theatre, inside the carriage house, and on a nearby mountain winery stage. There is a gallery and gallery shop in a side wing, while the artist residency program occupies the main house, which is not regularly open to visitors.

Visits to Villa Montalvo are thus generally only to its parklike gardens and the handsome terraces surrounding the house—which usually give a good view of the interior. The house itself is only open for special receptions and events and during certain brief seasons. However, if you enjoy wandering at will around the grounds of a great estate, this is a pleasant setting and retreat. But be forewarned that the grounds are closed for many of the larger performances, so when planning a visit check to see if an event will interfere—or if you can attend one and enjoy Montalvo in the way envisioned by Senator Phelan. If so, be sure to ask about the receptions held in the villa in association with some performances.

Villa Montalvo

SAN RAFAEL

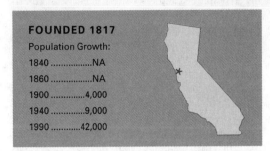

FOUNDED 1817

Population Growth:

1840	NA
1860	NA
1900	4,000
1940	9,000
1990	42,000

This was the site of Mission San Rafael Arcángel, the first of two missions that extended the earlier chain of Spanish missions northward from San Francisco in the early 1800s (see page xi; the other was at Sonoma—see page 266). Built in a less foggy, more healthful site than the San Francisco mission, San Rafael was a sort of outpost sanatorium for aging and ailing Indian converts from San Francisco. Virtually abandoned after the mission was secularized in 1833, the site took on new importance as a local government center when it was made the seat of remote Marin County in 1850. It remained a small town until the 1950s, when it began a new life as the focus of woodsy suburbs designed to attract San Francisco commuters. In spite of its rapid subsequent growth, it retains remnants of its Victorian past, the most important of which is a rare museum

house in the half-timbered version of the Queen Anne style.

Falkirk, 1888

1408 Mission Avenue; 415-485-3328; Clinton Day,
San Francisco, architect.

Queen Anne houses with half-timbered decorative detailing were always unusual, comprising about 5 percent of all Queen Anne homes. Falkirk is the only half-timbered Queen Anne house in the West, and perhaps in the entire country, that is open to the public. It sits on its original eleven acres of land and is a cultural center for the city of San Rafael. In the process of conversion to this use, the fine fixtures and finishes on the first floor have been left intact, but with few furnishings, while the upstairs rooms function as art gallery exhibition spaces. The quality of the house and its lush setting make it worth visiting.

Falkirk was originally built by Ella Nichols Park (1847–1905), who as a child summered in this area. In 1886, now a wealthy and reclusive widow, she purchased this eleven-acre tract, tore down the existing home, and commissioned Clinton Day (1846–1916) to build her home. Day is best known as the architect of San Francisco's beloved City of Paris department store, which was demolished by Neiman Marcus's parent

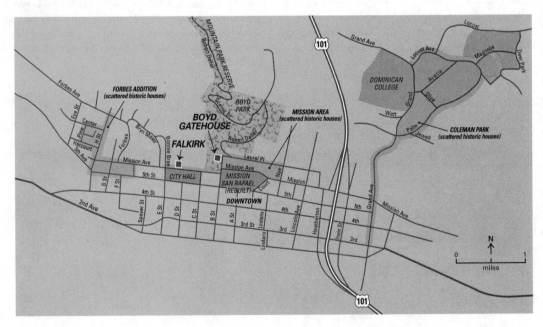

Falkirk

firm, Carter Hawley Hale, after great public outcry and preservation pleas. After Park's death the house was purchased by Robert Dollar, and his family remained here until the home passed into public hands in 1974 after the citizens of San Rafael voted to tax themselves to purchase it.

Day did a fine job of designing this house, which he made look deceptively large from the outside, yet gave a pleasing domestic scale inside. Located on a hill overlooking the San Rafael Valley, the house is imaginatively massed, with an irregular roof shape and two front-facing gables—both gables and the home's upper story are half-timbered. Multiple materials are used on the wall surfaces—including stone, brick, terra-cotta, half-timbered stucco, wood siding, and wood shingles. As is typical of this decorative subtype, the porch supports are very heavy turned posts, and the spandrels between them are solid, in this case shingled. There are also lines of three or more windows typical of this subtype; the rounded oriel window under the central gable has one such grouping.

You enter the house through the wraparound porch, then a recessed area surrounded by squared wood panels, and finally the fine Eastlake doors with art glass above. Inside is a living hall with a tall fireplace and overmantel and square paneled wainscoting. Three

major rooms open off the living hall, each at a different angle. Parquet floors, ornate redwood, ash, and oak paneling, and coffered ceilings ornament the downstairs. The stairway, which has a built-in seat on the landing and an unusually elegant Victorian balustrade, is dominated by a large stained-glass window of flowering vines, executed in an unusual palette of soft gray, brown, mauve, beige, and blues. Upstairs, the rooms have been painted white to accommodate changing art exhibits.

A tour of Falkirk's handsome grounds and interior spaces makes it easy to see why Robert Dollar (1844–1932) and his wife, Margaret Proudfoot Dollar (ca. 1854–1941) decided to purchase the home in 1906 and why their descendants stayed until about 1970. Robert Dollar had been born in Falkirk, Scotland (the source of the house's name), and had come to Canada as a youngster. From there timbering had taken him across the Midwest, harvesting the virgin forests of Michigan and Minnesota, until coming to the seemingly inexhaustible stands of the Pacific Northwest. He gained an interest in shipping and particularly to the Orient. He became so knowledgeable that he was revered by Chinese businessmen, traditionally slow to accept Westerners, and built up a large Oriental trade. Then at age eighty Dollar launched his newest and most radical idea, an around-the-world passenger and shipping line. It was the first steamship line to publish a schedule of arrival and departure times and stick to it. And it was the first around-the-world scheduled service. For his last eight years of life he expanded the line, which had been an instant success. Dollar Line passengers could purchase an around-the-world ticket and get off at any stop, secure in the knowledge that another Dollar ship would arrive in two weeks and they could board and continue on their way. In his last decade he had played a key role in opening the East to travel. Robert Dollar, a man of few but well-chosen words, summed up his life as follows:

First ten years of his life: Helped his mother
Second ten years of his life: Bought a farm for his father
Third ten years: Rose from chore boy to lumber camp owner
Fourth ten: Extended his lumber business
Fifth ten years: Found new lumber markets
From age 50–60: Added shipping to the lumber business
From age 60–70: Developed shipping and foreign trade
From age 70–80: Developed shipping in the Far East
Last eight years: Established the greatest passenger and freight fleet in the world.

Although looking at Dollar's birth date and the year he purchased Falkirk it would be easy to imagine that he had purchased it for his later retirement years, in fact the last decades of his life were among his most active

and creative. During these crucial years he and his wife and an ever-changing cast of children and grandchildren lived here.

Boyd Gatehouse, 1879

1125 B Street; 415-454-8538.

This charming Gothic Revival cottage was built as a guest house or gatehouse to the estate of John Boyd, a successful mining engineer. It has flattened pointed-arch windows and drip molds over the windows and doors. Shaped wood cresting is found along the porch and bay rooflines. A very late example of this style, it has some Stick influence in the trusslike detailing in the gables, but this is arranged into Gothic lancet and trefoil shapes, rather than more geometric Stick lines. Today, this house is used as the Marin County Historical Museum and houses artifacts and photographs. Note the handsome iron-and-stone fence.

Nearby Houses

333 G Street (private), Bradford Manor, 1883. This is an outstanding Stick-style house that beautifully combines the features typical of both eastern and western Stick houses. Note the decorative truss above the porch entry and in the gable, the horizontal and vertical bands of trim, the small shed roofs above the windows supported by decorative brackets, and the overhanging eaves with vertical board-and-batten beneath. Typical of western interpretations are the cornice-line brackets, which line up with the sides of the windows and extend downward to touch them. Except for the glassed-in right porch, this house looks wonderfully original.

828 Mission Avenue (private), McCarthy House, 1884. A straightforward Stick-style house, this has a picket fence modeled after the original fence. It has a pure example of the upside-down-picket-fence design beneath the cornice.

SAN JUAN BAUTISTA

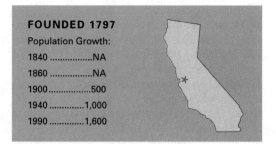

FOUNDED 1797

Population Growth:

1840	NA
1860	NA
1900	500
1940	1,000
1990	1,600

This small town grew up around the fifteenth mission established in the chain of twenty-one, which were founded by Spanish friars to convert coastal California Indians into Christian citizens of New Spain (see page ix). Its location, about halfway between earlier missions at Monterey and Santa Clara, was part of a plan to make each mission in the chain no more than a day's horseback journey from its neighbors. Located adjacent to a fertile river valley in an area with a large Indian population, San Juan was once the largest of California's mission settlements.

After its mission was secularized in 1834, the small town of San Juan Bautista became an important crossing of two principal stagecoach routes—San Francisco to Los Angeles and the route east from Monterey to California's Central Valley. After San Juan Bautista was bypassed by the Southern Pacific Railroad in 1876, it lapsed into a sleepy trade center for local ranches and farms, a role that it retains today. As is so often the case, this economic stagnation had a silver lining, for modern San Juan Bautista also retains much of its early character as a former Spanish mission site turned Anglo stagecoach stop.

The mission church still survives on its picturesque bluff-top site overlooking the irrigated fields of the adjacent river valley. Along the base of the bluff is what may be the only surviving unpaved section of the original Camino Real that linked California's early missions. Unfortunately, this picturesque bluff is also the site of California's notorious San Andreas Fault, whose motions account for many of the state's most severe earthquakes. As a result the mission church and adjacent structures have been repeatedly rebuilt after earthquake damage. The 1906 San Andreas earthquake that destroyed much of San Francisco also collapsed the roof and many of the adobe walls of the large mission church. These were fully repaired only in 1950 after decades of fund-raising efforts. Most recently, in 1976, the historic church, which still serves the local parish, underwent a major earthquake-resistant rebuilding. Today, the arcaded padres' quarters adjacent to the church contain an interesting local museum treating several aspects of its earlier history.

The mission church and padres' quarters line the west side of the town's central plaza. On the plaza's south and east sides are a number of important early buildings that are now preserved as the **San Juan Bautista State Historic Park** (408-623-4881). Two of these are important museum houses. A third remarkable survivor is the 1858 **Plaza Hotel,** a renowned center of hospitality

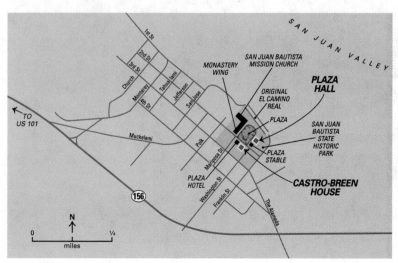

during the town's stagecoach era. Elsewhere in town, the streets near the historic plaza retain numerous modest, one-story folk and styled houses built over the hundred-year span from the 1850s to the 1950s; descriptions follow of several of these. Similar in scale and siting, these modest dwellings, combined with the historic plaza and a small "downtown" with many early storefront structures, make San Juan Bautista one of California's most delightfully authentic historic towns.

Castro-Breen House, ca. 1838

Second Street and Washington Street, facing the plaza, San Juan Bautista State Historic Park; 408-623-4881.
This was originally built by José Tiburcio Castro, the secular administrator of the mission, for his son, José Maria Castro, the prefect of the northern part of Alta California. Young Castro intended this building to serve both as his home and as the judicial and administrative headquarters for the northern half of Alta California as soon as he was confirmed as its governor. This confirmation never came, and Castro instead became commanding general of the Mexican troops in northern California, which required him to constantly travel rather than settling in this home as he had planned. In 1848 he invited the Breen family to stay in his home in his absence.

Patrick Breen (born 1790), his wife, Margaret (born 1810), and their large family were members of the ill-fated 1846 Donner Party, which was stranded snowbound in the Sierra Nevada for 111 days. The exhausted Breens arrived in Sutter's Fort in April of 1847. Then, in February of 1848, the family, now penniless, moved to this house at Castro's generous invitation. Four months later came news of the gold strike on Sutter's land, and the Breens' sixteen-year-old son, John, immediately traveled to the newly discovered goldfields. The following March, he returned home with over ten thousand dollars in gold dust. With this bonanza the Breens were able to purchase the Castro home and four hundred acres of prime farmland in the San Juan Valley. Descendants of the Breens continued to live in the house until 1933, when it became part of the state historic park. The house has been restored to reflect the period of the Breens' occupancy.

It is a handsome pitched-roof Spanish Colonial house, built of thick adobe walls right up to the sidewalk line, as was the Hispanic tradition. It has a narrow cantilevered second-story porch and Greek Revival front-door surround—both of which reflect later Anglo influence, as does the wood-clad addition on the right side. The large rear courtyard is kept swept clean in the Hispanic manner, and today it displays two of the enormous tubs used to render the tallow for the hide and tallow trade that was so much a part of the early California economy and that of San Juan Bautista.

Inside, there is a display of the Breen family history and many of the items they used in ranching activities. The three main downstairs rooms are appropriately furnished, and there are a few Breen family items, including a handsome short-keyboard piano that was

Castro-Breen House

shipped from New York for son Simon Breen. When you pass through the front entry hall, note the Greek Revival door surrounded by a narrow line of transom and sidelights; the light from these floods the front hallway—which was the original reason for adding so much expensive glass around an entry. Typically, entry halls were too narrow to have windows, and since electricity and gas were not yet available and candles were expensive, glass areas added around the door were the only way to light them. Today, passage up the narrow front stairway (which is an Anglo feature rather than a Hispanic one) is barred, and you reach the upstairs via a rear stairway in the west addition. At the top of these stairs is a study with son Judge James Breen's desk and other 1860s office furnishings. There are three bedrooms, one with the original bed, one with Mrs. Breen's delicate 1852 Wheeler-Wilson sewing machine and Breen family parlor rug, and a third with the wedding dress of Isabella Breen, the Breen's only daughter.

Plaza Hall, 1868 and earlier

San Juan Bautista State Historic Park, facing the plaza opposite the Monastery Wing of the mission; 408-623-4881.

It is confusing to discover that what looks like a commercial or office building from the exterior is furnished as a residence inside. However, this interpretation quite accurately reflects what actually happened with this building. In 1868 Angelo Zanetta, who already owned and operated the nearby Plaza Hotel, purchased an old

adobe on this site. He included its adobe-brick walls in the first floor of this larger two-story structure, which he designed to hold the offices for the county seat that he hoped to win for San Juan Bautista.

When the county seat was awarded to Hollister instead, Zanetta converted the downstairs for his family to live in and used the upstairs for community activities—with many meetings, dances, and shows held there over the years. The rear yard was developed to serve his household, and it still has its washhouse—with one room for people and the other for clothes. In about 1861 the Plaza Stable was built next door to accommodate the multitude of stagecoaches and wagons that were passing through San Juan Bautista in the late nineteenth century. Today, the stable and sheds behind it house an interesting display of coaches, specialty wagons, an old fire engine, and a wheelwright's shop, which shows clearly how the old wood-and-metal wheels were made.

Nearby Houses

Most of the houses in San Juan Bautista are only one story high, which gives the town a feeling of neighborhood continuity. These one-story homes include both folk houses (such as hall-and-parlors and shotguns) and styled houses (such as Queen Anne, Craftsman, Spanish Eclectic, and Ranch houses).

705 Third Street (private), ca. 1950s. This simple Ranch-style house has a low-pitched roof and only the lower one-

Plaza Hall

third is clad with brick, a feature often encountered on Ranch houses in California.

609 Third Street (private). Side-gabled folk houses like this one are called hall-and-parlor houses because they have two rooms in the main section of the house—which in Britain were called the hall and the parlor. Part of a folk-house tradition that began in that country and came to America with early English colonists, hall-and-parlor houses became one of our country's most persistent folk-house forms and were built up until the early 1900s. Although they are most common in the southeastern United States, there are a number of examples here in San Juan Bautista.

607 Third Street (private), ca. 1930. This small Spanish Eclectic home has a cross-gabled roof, while the one next door has a flat roof surrounded with parapeted walls finished with a row of tiles.

506 and 504 Third Street (both private), ca. 1920. A pair of small front-gabled Craftsman houses are mirror images of each other. Number 506 looks relatively unmodified, while 504 looks like it has newer windows.

Near 500 Third Street (private). Next door to 504 is another hall-and-parlor. This one has squared Classical porch supports and a side wing. Note the two different kinds of wood siding on the hall-and-parlor and on the left side wing—strongly suggesting that these were built at two different times. More folk-house forms have been added behind.

503 Third Street (private), "Honeymoon Cottage," 1890. Now adapted to commercial uses, this is a nice board-and-batten clad example of the narrow front-gabled folk-house form that is called a shotgun house. Note the tall narrow windows that are divided vertically into two panes per sash.

800 Second Street (private), Lovett House, 1852. Board-and-batten clads this side-gabled folk house that is extended with both a front porch and a rear addition. It would be called an extended hall-and-parlor, but the side-gabled section looks wide enough to contain more than two rooms.

SAN SIMEON

FOUNDED CA. 1865

Population Growth:

1900 ....ca. 1,000

1940 ....ca. 100

1990 ....ca. 300

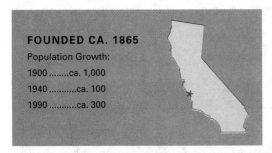

This early sailing-ship anchorage on California's isolated and rugged central coast was later to become renowned as the site of the West's most spectacular country estate.

Hearst Castle, 1919–1947

California Highway 1, about halfway between San Francisco and Los Angeles; 800-444-4445 or 800-444-7275; Julia Morgan, San Francisco, architect.

Hearst Castle, like its owner William Randolph Hearst (1863–1951), has many different dimensions. First came the breathtaking site, which inspired Hearst to build a home there. Next there was Hearst himself, with his ever-enlarging and sometimes-capricious vision for life at San Simeon and his enormous and continually growing collections of art and historical architectural elements. Hearst then sought out the brilliant and prodigiously productive architect Julia Morgan (1872–1957), who was inspired by Hearst and perfectly complemented him. She was the architect, landscape architect, planner, and overseer of the entire project. The final ingredient, and the one that secured Hearst Castle's public renown, was the continual parade of stars and celebrities who visited it.

The land was acquired by George Hearst (1820–1891), William Randolph's father and a renowned mining expert and investor (see page 427). The Hearst family gradually acquired 250,000 acres of land with

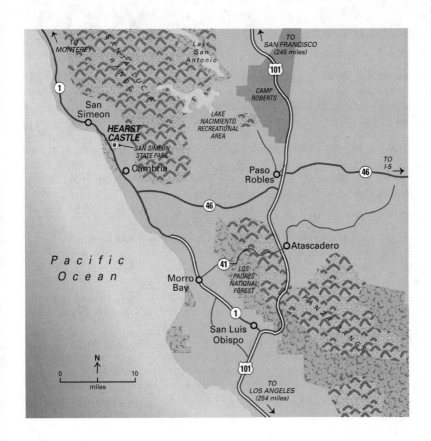

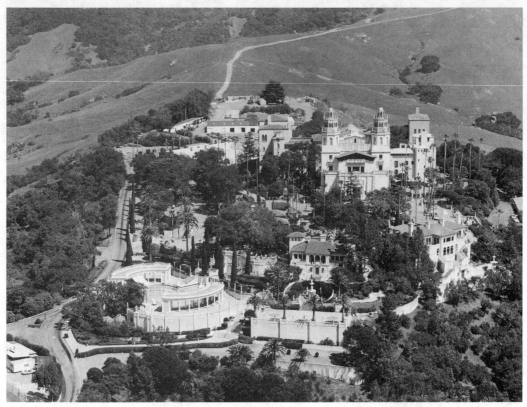

Hearst Castle complex

50 miles of frontage along the Pacific Ocean, which stretched out to cover the adjoining foothills, valleys, and mountains. George Hearst enjoyed bringing his family here, and eventually William Randolph did the same with both family and friends. The hillside called Camp Hill was a favored picnic spot and in time had a rather elaborate tent village for overnight stays. Years after his father's death, Hearst declared his affection for the site in a 1906 letter to his mother, Phoebe Apperson Hearst (1842–1919):

> I love this place. It is wonderful. I love the sea and I love the mountains and the hollows in the hills and the shady places in the creeks and the fine old oaks, and even the hot bushy hillsides—full of quail—and the canyons full of deer. It is a wonderful place. I would rather spend a month here than any place in the world. And as a *sanitarium!* Mother, it has Nauheim, Carlsbad, Vichy, Wiesbaden, French Lick, Saratoga, and every other so-called health resort beaten a nautical mile.

Hearst must have long planned to build on this site, for his mother died in April of 1919, and he had his first meeting with Morgan in the same month. Morgan first walked the site in August of that year, and on November 21 the materials to begin construction were sent by ship from Oakland. Because of the hilltop location, a winding five miles from the San Simeon dock, everything about construction was complicated. Some said it could not be done. But Julia Morgan was more than equal to the challenge. After obtaining a degree in engineering from the University of California, she had become the first woman ever accepted to the architectural program at the École des Beaux-Arts in Paris. While it had taken her over two years in Paris to convince the school to accept her, she had graduated in about one-half the usual time and earned, as she later commented, "her fair share of medals and mentions" in the school competitions she entered. She was extraordinarily talented, possessed an encyclopedic memory, and had an excellent grasp of organization and business. During her remarkable fifty-year career she designed and built more than seven hundred structures. The buildings at Hearst Castle were surely the most demanding and varied of all of her jobs. Here Morgan did prodigious design work for almost every detail—site work and planning, complex landscape design, the four hillside houses with their compli-

Hearst Castle

changes!) and the means to build it. With the financial support of his wealthy parents, Hearst had energetically created a vast and influential media empire. He owned major newspapers in more than twenty American cities, owned magazines such as *Good Housekeeping, Cosmopolitan,* and *Connoisseur,* and was outspoken about his political beliefs, which made him a very controversial character. His mother's death gave him the additional fortune needed to create San Simeon. Together he and Morgan decided to build in the Spanish tradition, which had gained a renewed impetus with the 1915 Panama-Pacific Exposition in San Francisco and the Panama-California Exposition in San Diego. At the latter, its architect, Bertram Grosvenor Goodhue, who had authored a detailed study of Spanish Colonial architecture, emphasized the richness of the Spanish precedents found throughout Latin America. This had sparked an interest in the Spanish originals as well and also spawned the Spanish Eclectic style of houses. San Simeon is essentially in this style, with Morgan drawing from all kinds of Spanish and Italian precedents, each reinterpreted through her unique eyes. The gardens she designed were more Italian than Spanish in origin. The gardens of southern Spain were restrained in their use of water and eschewed the use of figurative art. Such was hardly the case at Hearst Castle, where the landscape owed more to the gardens of Italy with their emphasis on sculpture, stone- and marblework, and water. To these, Hearst and Morgan added prodigious numbers of colorful flowering plants.

cated handcrafted details, and innumerable outbuildings, including a zoo, chicken coops, stables, and warehouse buildings. In addition she "ran the job." According to Sara Holmes Boutelle, her biographer:

> Running the job included hiring, firing, and settling disputes, arranging lodging, food and working quarters for the laborers; making trips to interview specialists such as a cheese maker, a chicken man, gardeners, and housekeepers; procuring special plants and materials; creating various crafts centers on site; arranging transportation by ship, rail and truck to the remote hilltop; building warehouses and cataloging objects to be incorporated in the project; checking on thousands of details; and satisfying the whims of artists and the client. That all this was taken care of by the architect was most unusual, but the physical remoteness of the site and the rare sense of partnership between architect and client in a venture cherished by both made it work.

And she did all this while spending only her weekends at the site, a pattern she maintained for many years until switching to only Mondays on-site.

William Randolph Hearst was a remarkable client—one with a strong vision of what he wanted to accomplish (even if the vision was subject to frequent

Hearst Castle is not at all a typical museum house. It is rather a grouping of four houses, three smaller "cottages" and the main house. An 8,000-square-foot cottage called Casa del Mar faces the Pacific Ocean and is where the Hearsts stayed while the main house, Casa Grande, was being built. The other two cottages are Casa del Monte, with 3,600 square feet and northern mountain views, and Casa del Sol, with 6,500 square

Hearst Castle, Neptune Pool

feet and a terrace with evening sunset views. These guest cottages are to one side of a large landscaped terrace, and Casa Grande, the big house with its twin towers and carillon, commands the other. The setting is reminiscent of a small hillside village, with the cathedral facing out onto the plaza and houses across the way. Construction of Casa Grande began in 1922, and Hearst, along with his companion, actress Marion Davies, was able to move into the third-floor suite in late 1928. Work on the house continued until 1937, when Hearst's financial situation became dismal (he owed about $130 million). His finances improved during World War II, and construction commenced again in 1945 and continued for two years until Hearst's health forced him to move to Los Angeles.

All of the houses incorporate parts of Hearst's prodigious art collection. Antique ceilings, Greek pottery, tapestries, marble sculptures, wellheads, paintings, antique furnishings, rare books, manuscripts, and letters—all these and more were gathered by Hearst, who was a compulsive collector. He bought things for which he likely had no room and even placed rush orders for items that then sat unpacked in warehouses for years. Two of the primary rooms in Hearst Castle, the Assembly Room and the Refectory (the room where guests assembled to await dinner and the room used for dining) were built to a height to accommodate the antique woodwork with ancient tapestries hanging above. When there was not quite enough of a historic ceiling or door, skilled workmen simply added onto it, leaving new additions indistinguishable by all but experts.

Where ancient objects were not being incorporated, Morgan drew plans for elaborate period detailing and oversaw the craftsmen executing them. The stunning Roman Pool, an interior plunge decorated with mosaics of blue and gold leaf, is but one example of her talent for beautiful design and execution. She designed it, chose the craftsmen, and supervised both their production and setting of the mosaic pieces. The numerous craftsmen she worked with had high praise for her knowledge and abilities; she knew enough to demand and get their best work.

The landscape design for Hearst Castle was every bit as demanding as the house itself. The breathtaking views of the Pacific Ocean that had originally inspired Hearst had to be maintained and the native oak trees carefully preserved. Elegant terraces, gardens, fountains, and an esplanade walk surrounded and linked the four houses and the Neptune Pool. Marble statuary, columns, and even a temple front were incorporated into the designs. Thousands of trees were brought to the site, both to enhance the formal gardens and to cover the hillside, where their planting holes had to be dynamited in the rock. A demanding program of outbuildings was executed, including Hearst's zoo. Designs were often changed, both indoors and out, as Hearst either added new acquisitions or new demands. The beautiful Greco-Roman Neptune Pool was changed twice to accommodate Hearst, but in the process became one of the most stunning sights on the hillside. Particularly indicative of Hearst's grandiose outdoor vision was the pergola he had built. Wide and tall enough to accommodate Hearst as he cantered along on his favorite steed, this winds sinuously for over a mile along the crest of Orchard Hill and had almost a thousand trees and vines planted along its length.

All of this then became a stage on which to entertain his friends and, through this, the world. Marion Davies had many friends in the movie business, and the film stars of the 1920s and 1930s coveted an invitation to the Enchanted Hill, as it was often called. Hearst had a special train that left Los Angeles Friday evening for an overnight ride, breakfast aboard the railroad car, and a fleet of unmarked taxis, financed by Hearst, that then delivered them to the hilltop. Here they were assigned to a guest suite or cottage and had all of San Simeon's pleasures to enjoy, including other guests, often politicians, writers, minor royalty, and such. They strolled around the grounds, rode, swam, played tennis, visited the zoo, and picnicked. In the evenings they gathered in the Assembly Room for dinner in the Refectory with Hearst and Davies and afterward for a film in the theater. These gatherings were filmed, photographed, written about, and, during the late twenties and early depression years, this exotic Shangri-La captured the public's imagination.

Entire books have been written about the Hearst Castle at San Simeon, its history and its collections. A 1994 interpretive history, *Hearst Castle,* by Nancy E. Loe, is extremely well done, has many historic and contemporary photos, and gives an excellent overview of the undertaking. There are five separate tours of San Simeon: three are year-round, and two are seasonal. Each originates at the well-equipped visitor center, where visitors board a bus for the gorgeous five-mile ride up the mountainside. Tour 1 is a basic introduction that includes the main downstairs rooms of Casa Grande and Casa del Sol. If you are in a hurry, taking this (or any of the tours) is very gratifying. But if you want a fuller understanding of Hearst Castle, going on one tour in the afternoon to get a feeling for the site and its structures, followed by an evening perusing Nancy Loe's (or some other) book on the site and taking another tour the next morning, would allow time to begin to absorb Hearst Castle, the most grandiose museum house complex in the West.

SANTA BARBARA

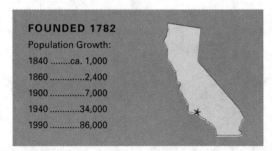

FOUNDED 1782
Population Growth:
1840 ....ca. 1,000
1860 2,400
1900 7,000
1940 34,000
1990 86,000

Located on one of California's few stretches of relatively sheltered, east–west–trending coastline, Santa Barbara's beachside harbor area was the site for one of the four Spanish presidios built in the late 1700s to protect the province's newly established chain of missions; the others were at San Diego (see page 149), Monterey (see page 115), and San Francisco (see page 210). Founded near the waterfront in 1782, four years later the presidio was joined by a new mission, the tenth in the California chain of twenty-one, which was located about a mile northwest of the presidio, on higher ground at the base of the nearby Santa Ynez Mountains.

Queen of the Missions

The scenic Santa Barbara coastline, a gently sloping strip of beach-lined flatlands bounded on the north by the sheltering Santa Ynez Range, has been called America's Riviera. This unique setting was apparently appreciated by the early Spanish colonists and their Indian converts, for Mission Santa Barbara Virgen y Martir was to become the largest and most successful of all the California missions. Fed by bountiful crops irrigated with waters from the adjacent mountain streams, by 1803 the agriculture-based mission community had almost two thousand baptized Indian neophytes.

After the California missions were secularized and their lands distributed for civilian use in the 1840s, the mission buildings were mostly abandoned. Those built of maintenance-intensive adobe soon decayed into formlessness. Even the missions built of stone required regular repair as roofs and walls collapsed in coastal California's frequent earthquakes. The result was that almost all of the California mission chapels and related buildings that can be visited today are early-twentieth-century reconstructions, many of them so romanticized that they do not closely resemble their early counterparts.

Picturesque **Mission Santa Barbara** (Upper Laguna Street, 805-682-4149) is the outstanding exception. Built in its present form with massive stone walls in 1820, it has miraculously remained under the continuous control of the Franciscan Order since that time. The mission was severely damaged several times by earthquakes, and the friars have each time carefully restored the historic structure so that today it is the most authentic survivor of California's Hispanic Mission era. Other important Spanish Colonial survivors in Santa Barbara are a landmark 1820s dwelling, which was among the finest in Hispanic California, and parts of the original Spanish fortress, now preserved as **El Presidio de Santa Barbara State Historic Park** (123 East Canon Perdido Street, 805-965-0093).

Spanish Revival

After the American takeover of California in 1848, the narrow, mountain-bounded Santa Barbara coastline became a small agricultural backwater far removed from the state's principal travel arteries. The only overland access was a dead-end roadway along the coast from Los Angeles. Even the town's first railroad, which arrived in 1887, was a spur line that served a small community made up mostly of health seekers and part-time residents escaping from cold midwestern winters. Not until the early automobile era did larger numbers of travelers and residents begin to discover this American Riviera. By 1920 Santa Barbara's population had jumped to thirty-four thousand, almost a 300 percent increase since 1900.

Many of the city's newcomers were attracted not only by its scenery and climate, but also by its important Spanish Colonial heritage. By the early 1920s many new structures in the growing city were being designed in the Mission Revival or Spanish Eclectic styles to reflect this heritage. In 1925 Santa Barbara was struck by a major earthquake that destroyed or seriously damaged much of its older commercial district. The city government responded with a bold initiative that required all major repairs and new construction in the central city to be in a "Mediterranean" style consistent with the city's Hispanic heritage. The result is one of the nation's most architecturally unified downtowns.

Modern Santa Barbara

As Sunbelt population booms overwhelmed the historic centers of most California towns in the last

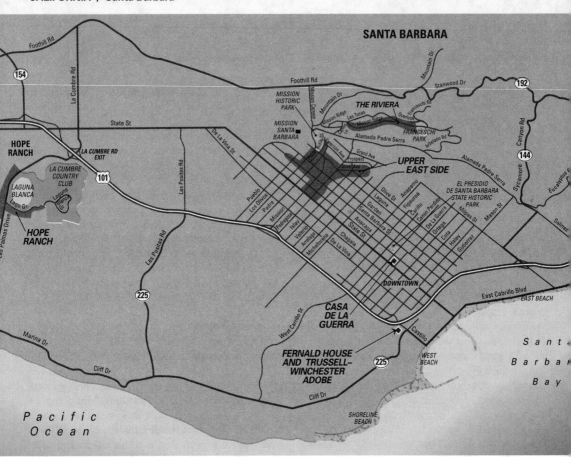

Casa de la Guerra

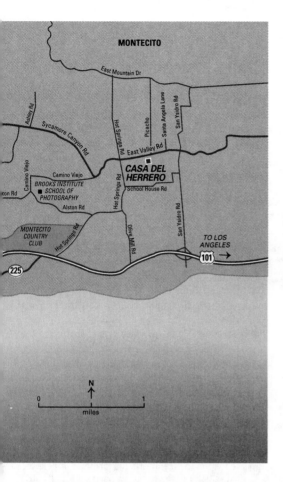

served as *comandante* of the Presidio de Santa Barbara, one of California's four presidios. His business acumen made him a wealthy and respected merchant and also led the padres at Mission Santa Barbara to seek his financial advice and make him their treasurer. His position, personality, and good works made him one of the most respected men of the day, and his home, Casa de la Guerra, was the economic, political, and social center of Santa Barbara until his death.

At a time when a typical adobe home was but one or two rooms, Don José and his wife, Maria Antonia Juliana Carrillo y Lugo (1786–1843), were able to build this large twelve-room house, which was under construction from about 1818 until 1828. It is one room deep and built in a U shape, which was the favored plan for large Spanish houses. A portale (narrow porch) was built along all three sides of the U. When completed, the house contained a level of detail unusual for even grand Spanish Colonial homes.

The Santa Barbara Trust for Historic Preservation has spent almost a decade researching the history of this grand house—through archaeological evidence, archival documentation, and fieldwork. Through this they were able to determine the home's appearance during Don José's lifetime with an unusual degree of accuracy. The east wing and the main rooms of the house have been restored to the highly significant period when Don José lived here, with various rooms finished and furnished to different decades of that tumultuous thirty years of California's history (Don José and Maria and the surviving of their thirteen children lived in Santa Barbara through the Spanish period, the Mexican period, and into statehood). The west wing is a museum that presents the family's long history, the history of the house in its later years, and changing exhibits.

Casa de la Guerra had four different lives before the restoration. First came the Spanish Colonial home of Don José and his family. Second, after an 1857 earthquake, the home was restored and Victorianized with wood cladding and an Anglo-influenced porch. Third, Francis Underhill (1863–1929), an architect born in Oyster Bay, New York (and apparently with significant family money), married a de la Guerra descendant and "restored" the house to its Hispanic appearance between about 1910 and 1914. This he did with a fair degree of accuracy, but he added Craftsman-influenced details. Fourth, the home was incorporated into the Paseo, a Spanish Eclectic shopping district, and for this it was encased in chicken wire and cement stucco. Ironically, this covering helped preserve much of its early fabric. The Santa Barbara Trust has peeled away these later layers. In doing so it has discovered original

decades of the twentieth century, the city of Santa Barbara adopted a limited-growth policy intended to stabilize its size at about eighty-five thousand inhabitants. Although this number has been exceeded in the 1990s, the city's percentage size increase since 1970 has been minuscule in comparison with most of its California peers. Not surprisingly, Santa Barbara retains fine Eclectic-era neighborhoods as well as several important museum houses. Unfortunately, only one of these, the Spanish Colonial Casa de la Guerra (see the following entry), has regular hours for visits. Casa del Herrero (see page 259), a Spanish Eclectic masterpiece built a century later, requires long advance reservations, and the Fernald House complex (see page 259) is open only once a month.

Casa de la Guerra, 1820s

15 East de la Guerra Street; 805-965-0093.

José de la Guerra y Noriega (1779–1858) was one of the most powerful men in Alta California when he built this grand Spanish Colonial home in the 1820s. He

wooden window grilles and window framing (these have been replicated in the rest of the house). In one room the trust found the original rafter poles, complete with the original leather ties (still with tannic acid stains) holding them together. About 80 percent of the original adobe brick was still in place, as was much of the home's early iron hardware, some salvaged from a ship that had run aground in the harbor. The trust decided to retain glass windows. Although the evidence for their being present in 1828 is scant, many would likely have been added during the home's long period of importance. The house also had an uncommon *altito* (tower) added in the rear; this served as Don José's office and library and may someday be rebuilt. An unusual, but original, feature of the de la Guerra home is that the court enclosed by the house opens *toward* the street rather than *away* from it as was the Hispanic custom.

As was typical of Spanish Colonial homes of the wealthy, Casa de la Guerra was built right on Santa Barbara's main plaza. This had been laid out in compliance with the *Laws of the Indies,* and its corners pointed (*almost* directly) to the cardinal points of the compass, as the laws prescribed. Although the *Laws of the Indies* also prescribed straight wide streets leading away from the plaza and throughout the town, the streets away from Santa Barbara plaza were not aligned with any particular compulsion as was typical in remote colonial towns. In the 1850s, following statehood, a strict new Anglo street grid was superimposed on the meandering Hispanic streets. This was positioned to carefully avoid taking any part of the home of the powerful Guerra family, a nicety not extended to many other adobe owners. An instructive map showing Santa Barbara's old Hispanic street pattern (and houses) with the new Anglo grid streets superimposed hangs as part of the east wing's exhibits.

Although the de la Guerra family was slower to lose control of its lands and properties than were many other wealthy Californios, the combination of Don José's death, sibling squabbling over the estate, devastating drought in the 1860s, and a series of unfortunate business dealings left the family in much the same shape as their neighbors. As more and more Anglos moved to Santa Barbara, the political control, and with it much of the city's wealth, passed to them.

Today, Casa de la Guerra has regained its rightful position as the domestic heart of Hispanic Santa Barbara and shares this elegant past with all who visit. The *sala* was the main reception room where Don José received and entertained important guests. It has been restored to the 1840s, when it sported a dashing dado of Prussian blue. To the right was the *sala*'s antechamber, where Don José could retire for a brandy or private conference. To the left of the *sala* is the dining room, restored to about 1828, the earliest part of the era of significance, when written descriptions of its simple furnishings exist. The zaguan is next to this, providing a passage from the front court to the rear of the house. Next is a bedroom, with a reconstruction of the oft-pictured de la Guerra bed, followed by visitor facilities. Finally, the last room in the west wing, adjacent to the street, is interpreted to about 1858. Originally a storeroom (and also the room in which the original rafters and leather ties were uncovered), by 1858 it had family members living in it—and with the room next door made a two-room suite. Five layers of wallpaper were found on the wall. The earliest, a French paper, has been re-created and the room furnished as the salon of the family members who occupied this part of the house.

Although the general rule in historic preservation is to freeze everything just as it is found (an approach that is almost always preferable and saves the most historic fabric), rules are made to be broken when circumstances warrant. California has a rich Hispanic past, yet the job of researching and reconstructing adobes has been spotty. A great many were "restored" in the early part of the century with much romanticized accouterments. Only a few show what the early structures looked like and how people actually lived in the Spanish Colonial and Mexican periods. Where a home of this importance has already gone through four architectural lives (and where this degree of archaeological and archival evidence about the original appearance exists), it makes little sense to decree that it shall always remain encased in a romanticized skin of chicken wire and plaster. Here was a chance to show, with a high degree of authenticity, an era that is often poorly interpreted throughout the entire state because of these many later alterations and the great difficulty of determining the past of most earth-wall buildings (see "Santa Fe," page 444).

The opportunity to undertake this major work appeared in the 1970s when the Santa Barbara Trust received a gift of the entire Paseo and Casa de la Guerra. By reselling the remainder of the Paseo with easements, they were able to generate a large trust fund, which has allowed them to undertake this work. The entire town of Santa Barbara participated in the decision to take this home back as close to its original appearance as possible—and to tell the story of when it was the most important home in the city and one of the most important in Alta California. Casa de la Guerra is a place where one can learn much about the way wealthy Californios lived in the latter years of California's Hispanic rule.

Fernald House

Fernald House, 1862 and 1880, and Trussell-Winchester Adobe, 1854 and later

414 West Montecito Street; 805-966-1601; limited hours.
The Fernald House is a restoration in process. Built as a simple brick home in 1862, this home received a complete stylish update in 1880 to be ready for a visit from Queen Victoria's daughter. The entry hall and master bedroom have been thoughtfully restored, and the entire upstairs creatively arranged and interpreted by the current curator (these rooms await Period wallpaper). The downstairs has been intensively researched for the additional work needed there. The house contains a great many of the Fernalds' original furnishings and personal objects, and much of their family history comes alive in the house.

The adjacent Trussell-Winchester Adobe was built in 1854 by Captain Horatio Gates Trussell (born 1808). It was sold to the Winchester family in 1882, after the captain built a large house where the Fernald House now stands. The adobe received additions in the mid-1880s and again in 1904. The current furnishings belonged to Katherine Hastings, a granddaughter of the Winchesters, who purchased the adobe in 1926. Her belongings have a bit of a New England feel and are a great reminder of the late 1920s and 1930s period when a number of easterners "rediscovered" their California roots

and moved to the old family home with their eastern antiques (the Larkin House in Monterey is another great example of this phenomenon; see page 117). Even those *without* California roots participated in much the same movement. *Town and Country* wrote a classic article about Mrs. Hastings in her California adobe, which of course encouraged others to follow in her footsteps.

The adobe's interior is today interpreted just as Mrs. Hastings left it—a 1930s eastern vision of what a proper adobe home should contain. The Trussells' new home, originally built behind this adobe, was eventually demolished, and in the 1950s the Fernald House was saved from demolition by being moved onto the same site. These homes are open only one weekend a month, but as restoration is completed, open hours will likely extend.

Casa del Herrero, 1925

1387 East Valley Road, just barely west of Picacho Lane; 805-565-5653; long advance reservations required for visit; George Washington Smith, Santa Barbara, architect.

Casa del Herrero is one of our nation's architectural treasures. Built for George F. Steedman (1871–1941) and his wife, Carrie Howard Steedman (died 1963), it was by all accounts Mr. Steedman who devoted twenty

Casa del Herrero

years of his life to building an "authentically Spanish" home. Having been forced by ill health to step down as head of St. Louis' Curtis Manufacturing Company (a very successful family business that manufactured saws, pneumatic equipment, and, during World War I, shell casings), Steedman had the time, the taste, and the financial means to pursue this dream.

He commissioned architect George Washington Smith (1876–1930), California's master of the Spanish Eclectic style, to design their house and engaged Arthur Byne (1882–1935), an American expert in Spanish art and architecture, to purchase its fine Spanish architectural antiques and furnishings. Landscape architects Ralph T. Stevens, Peter Riedel, and Lockwood de Forest Jr. worked on the garden plans. The professionals involved were kept constantly challenged by their client, an extraordinarily talented man with a lifelong interest in architecture. Together, Steedman and his design team produced perhaps the finest intact early-twentieth-century Spanish home in the country—one where house, furnishings, and garden were planned as a whole.

Steedman carefully researched all of his projects. He visited Spain in 1923 and produced sketches and measured drawings for details he might want to include in his home (the dining room fireplace, copied from the fourteenth-century Castle Guadamor, and the master-bedroom fireplace, copied from a simple peasant home, are both details sketched by Steedman). On this same trip he traveled with Byne (accompanied also by Byne's wife and professional partner, Mildred Shipley) and purchased prodigious amounts of fifteenth-, sixteenth-, and seventeenth-century Spanish antiques (furniture, rugs, and textiles) and architectural artifacts (ancient tiles, wrought-iron window grilles, and hand-carved doors). This sort of "buying trip" was a common practice among those who seriously aspired to build great houses in the early twentieth century. The results inevitably reflected the expertise of both client and consultant.

As might be expected, Steedman and Byne did extraordinarily well. Many of the furnishings and architectural antiques in Casa del Herrero are of museum quality. Steedman and Byne concentrated on obtaining items from Spain's golden age—the era when the country was a world colonial power, ruled much of the Americas (including the U.S. Southwest), and prospered from the gold and silver wealth of Mexico and South America. The results of a similar buying trip just a few years later would have been greatly curtailed; in 1926 Spain passed a law forbidding the export of such national treasures. As it was, Steedman returned to Santa Barbara with many treasures, and architect Smith began working to incorporate them into his plans for the casa. As new items were discovered (such as the fifteenth-century ceiling from a cloistered walk at the Convento de San Francisco, northeast of Madrid, which now graces the casa's entry hall), Smith would rework the plans to include them. Where antiques were not available, new items were sought out. Among these were thousands of tiles produced by the Chemla family in Tunis and additional metalwork, some produced by Steedman himself in his large workshop. Casa del Herrero means "House of the Blacksmith," for Steedman's former business had been a foundry, and one of his hobbies continued to be producing many kinds of fine metalwork.

The antique furnishings at Casa del Herrero are superb. Choir stalls, *fraileros* (those austere Spanish chairs that often have leather seats and backs), beautifully inlaid *vargueño* chests, Flemish tapestries, Spanish paintings, religious statuary, and tables are particularly in evidence. Thirty hand-carved doors, 2,600 sixteenth-century geometric tiles, 150 seventeenth-century figurative tiles, and 200 eighteenth-century figurative tiles are among the architectural treasures.

The gardens received equal attention. They are organized along two axes: one stretches to the east and is

Casa del Herrero

aligned with the cross axis of the casa, the other flows to the south and is aligned with the main axis. The easterly gardens consist of a series of formal garden rooms, while the southerly ones are a bit more loosely organized along a broad allée. Both are primarily Spanish in inspiration. Muslim Moors, who ruled much of Spain for seven hundred years (A.D. 711 until expulsion from their final Granada stronghold in A.D. 1492) did not allow figurative sculpture for religious reasons, and their influence lingered long after they had departed. As a result, Spanish garden focal points tend to be fountains, arches, and tiled walls, rather than the garden statuary of Italian and French gardens. Water was a precious commodity in arid southern Spain, so water features are small scale compared to the lakes of England and the gushing fountains of Italy. Grass was difficult to grow, and broad open lawns were not a viable option. Spanish gardens tended to have enclosed garden rooms with "floors" of tiles, pebbles, or compacted clay. These were then ornamented with plants in pots. All of these features are incorporated into the casa's lovely gardens, which include many garden rooms, Moorish fountains and pools, garden seats, and walls—most of which contain lovely tiles. For more history about Casa del Herrero and its many fine features, *Casa de Herrero*, by Jean Smith Goodrich, the source of many of the facts included here, makes up the entire contents of the summer 1995 *Noticias* publication of the Santa Barbara Historical Society and is available at the Santa Barbara Historical Museum shop.

Casa del Herrero survives because of the stewardship and generosity of Steedman's daughter, Medora Steedman Bass, and her family, who created and endowed the Casa del Herrero Foundation to preserve this beautifully integrated and intact estate. A visit there today requires advance reservations. Only four tours a week are given: two tours on two days each week. These are opened for booking every six-month period until all the available spaces are filled; then one must wait for the next six-month cycle. It is hoped that at some point in the future it will be possible to have slightly more frequent small groups visit this treasure. Many museum houses operate regularly with such small timed groups and have an imperceptible neighborhood impact (unlike unendowed house museums, which often host special events and endure peak hours). The tour is ninety minutes long and visits the house, garden, and Mr. Steedman's beloved blacksmith shop.

Nearby Montecito Houses

It would be wonderful to be able to list a number of nearby houses, for there are some quite grand ones. But this is estate country, complete with walls and massive hedges and private roads. Even if you know where the homes are (and David Gebhard and Robert Winter's excellent *A Guide to Architecture in Los Angeles and Southern California* can tell you just that), they are generally impossible to see. For simply appreciating the feeling of being amid grand estates without annoying rapid through traffic, Picacho Lane and Hot Springs Road *north* of East Valley are good bets. With your curiosity aroused by the tempting near views of great houses, head to a Santa Barbara bookstore and find a copy of the latest edition of *Santa Barbara Architecture*, by Herb Andree and Noel Young, for lovely photographs by Wayne McCall.

1321 Alameda Padre Serra. Here is housed the Brooks Institute School of Photography and Photo Gallery (805-966-3888) in a ca.-1920s Spanish Eclectic estate home. If you are interested in photography, you can visit the constantly changing student photographic exhibits and a collection of antique photographic equipment.

695 Ashley Road (house private; gardens open by reservation), Lotusland Gardens; 805-969-3767. This thirty-seven-acre estate surrounds a Spanish Eclectic house that was designed by Reginald Johnson in 1919 and enlarged by George Washington Smith in the 1920s. Its gardens were designed by many of the same people as Casa del Herrero: Peter Riedel, Ralph Stevens, Lockwood de Forest, and Joseph Knowles Jr., with Smith as a consultant. Beginning in 1941 opera singer Madam Ganna Walska transformed them with her exotic and original botanical collecting. Only the gardens are open for tours, and this requires reservations made about one year in advance.

Upper East Side, ca. 1885–1930

Somehow adjacent to one of California's most historic missions (the only one that has remained always in the Franciscans' hands) one expects to find a Hispanicized neighborhood name. This is not the case, twiceover. This area, just below the mission, has apparently always been called the Upper East Side. Many easterners moved to Santa Barbara for their health, and perhaps

Upper East Side

Upper East Side

those who first built in this neighborhood were home-sick for their native New York City. The canted grid blocks of the Upper East Side are filled with a few late-nineteenth-century and mostly early-twentieth-century homes. Craftsman, Mission, Spanish Eclectic, Colonial Revival, and Italian Renaissance are all found.

Not only do we have the Upper East Side just below the mission, but the **Riviera** is the name of the neighborhood located along a steep foothill just northeast of the mission. In this kind of topography, contour-curved streets are almost always used, and this neighborhood is no exception. Mission Ridge Road is the straightforward name for a not-so-straight street that creates a long spine through it. Like most steep hillside areas in the United States, the Riviera did not become popular as a building site until people could reach their homes via automobile. The view from **Franceschi Park** (see page 264) will make obvious the genesis of the neighborhood's name.

Upper East Side

Upper East Side: 1920 Laguna Street (private), ca. 1910. A cross-gabled Craftsman home with excellent proportions and use of material. The porch railing incorporates a version of the "lift-line," which was popularized by the Greene brothers and symbolized a line of clouds.

Upper East Side: 1910 Laguna Street (private), 1897. A wonderful late-Victorian Swiss chalet with a superb second-floor porch featuring a flat cut-out patterned railing; both porch and railing are typical of this style. Patterned stick-work decoration on exterior walls is also common on Swiss-chalet houses; in this late example, the house is encased in half-timbering instead. Note the matching open trellis downstairs.

Upper East Side: 1741 Prospect Avenue (private), Bentz House, 1911; Greene and Greene, Pasadena, architects. The garden facade is visible uphill from Olive Street, and the Prospect Street facade is hidden. Designed by the Greene brothers, masters of the Craftsman-style house, this house is clad in wood shingles, their favored material. Note how the roof on the left side steps just slightly down to another level and how the gable's five vertical windows are also stair-stepped.

Upper East Side: 2010 to 2052 Garden Street (all private), Crocker Row, ca. 1895; A. Page Brown, architect. A rare group of five Mission-style houses, built for William Henry Crocker and designed by A. Page Brown, the architect who won the commission for the Mission-style California Building at the 1893 World's Columbian Exposition. Crocker built these for family vacation homes (and perhaps for speculation as well), and when built, nothing stood between them and the Mission Santa Barbara. Number 2010 is particularly striking. A shaped Mission Revival parapet stretches across the entire side of its side-gabled roof, and art glass gleams from the trefoil windows on each side of the front door.

Upper East Side: 31 East Pedregosa Street (private), Storke House, 1886. Except for a two-story wing added on the right side, an early photograph reveals that this house is remarkably unaltered. It is a very forward thinking house for 1886. The Classical detail over the windows, the arcaded front porch (clad with wood siding, not shingles), and the windows set out to the corners of the front extension are all unusual features. The house is an interesting blend of the contemporaneous Shingle and Queen Anne styles. Despite its lack of an overall coating of wood shingles, its feeling is more Shingle style, which is evident in its overall form and massing, unornamented gable verges, arcaded porch, overlapping front gables, and creative window placement. The cut-away bay window, flared band of shingles wrapping the midsection, and wraparound porch are typical Queen Anne features.

Upper East Side: 400 block of Plaza Rubio (all private), ca. 1925; Mary Osborne Craig, Santa Barbara, architect. Although Mary Osborne Craig (1889–1964) had never had formal architectural training, Mrs. J. A. Andrews trusted her to design this streetscape of Spanish Eclectic houses, which were carefully planned to complement the mission by defining the southern edge of a plaza in front of it and complementing its style. Craig succeeded in varying the size, shape, and details so it is not immediately obvious that all were built at the same time by the same person. For her own home, which terminates the street at 530 Plaza Rubio (private), Mrs. Andrews turned to George Washington Smith.

The Riviera: 1849 Mission Ridge (private), Burke House, 1923; George Washington Smith, Santa Barbara, architect. This handsome home by Santa Barbara's talented Spanish Eclectic architect George Washington Smith presents a severe facade to the road and opens out to a rear garden. Note the tall chimney (and mailbox) that are shaped like miniature Spanish houses. The cacti in front provide an appropriate setting.

The Riviera: Franceschi Park. To enter, from Mission Ridge Road, turn north on Franceschi Road and then left into the park. Although this is not a house, if you are driving you will appreciate a quiet place to enjoy the great view this offers of Santa Barbara Bay (and it also is a simple place to turn around and head back to the mission if desired). Pausing in the park will quickly clarify why this neighborhood is called the Riviera (both Rivieras share similar dramatic views out over the ocean)—and what attracted so many to build here (most houses enjoy this view from their garden facades).

Hope Ranch, ca. 1928–1960s

Although platted in 1887, it was not until after it had been acquired by the La Cumbre Estate Corporation in 1924 (and the country club and other amenities added) that this large development began to be built out. Las Palmas Drive, the main road through it, is lined with palms planted in the early 1900s and passes by the La Cumbre Country Club and picturesque **Laguna Blanca.** Beautifully laid out with carefully contoured roads, the setting is actually far grander than many of the houses. Large Ranch-style homes are the norm, which could be a great treat (since California is the birthplace of the Ranch style), but a number appear to have already been altered. A few slightly earlier Monterey-style homes are located on Lago Drive, just south of the golf course and overlooking the lake.

Hope Ranch

SONOMA

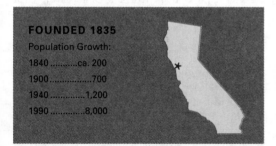

FOUNDED 1835

Population Growth:

1840 ....ca. 200
1900 700
1940 1,200
1990 8,000

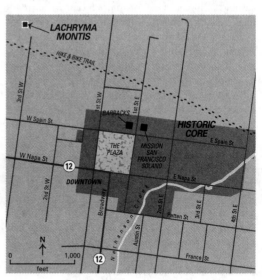

The small town of Sonoma has had a disproportionately large role in the history of California. Like Napa, its larger neighbor to the east (see page 124), Sonoma is best known today for the fine wines produced from its nearby vineyards. Many visitors to this unpretentious town fail to appreciate that it was the actual *birthplace* of both the California wine industry and of American-controlled California. Each of these events revolved around a larger-than-life Mexican army officer named Mariano Guadalupe Vallejo (1807–1890), the founder of Sonoma.

In 1846 the widely respected Vallejo, by then the highest-ranking Mexican official in the region, became the central target in the Bear Flag Revolt, an almost-comic-opera operation during which thirty-two opportunistic American frontiersmen "captured" undefended Sonoma during the opening days of the Mexican War. Loosely attempting to follow the precedent set in Texas a decade earlier (see page xii), the Bear Flaggers declared California an independent republic with themselves as its leaders. To strengthen their position, they then kidnapped the already pro-American Vallejo, along with his brother, his American brother-in-law, and several of their associates, transported them sixty miles eastward to Sutter's Fort on the Sacramento River (see page 136), and held them there in closely confined captivity for the next two months. Fortunately, all were released unharmed when California's capital city of Monterey was occupied by official U.S. naval forces, who quickly ended the Bear Flaggers' dream of making California their own personal fiefdom.

Vallejo was a Jeffersonesque figure—a distinguished statesman who was also multitalented, curious about everything, and a voracious reader with a twelve-thousand-volume personal library. Like Jefferson, Vallejo was fascinated by farming and horticulture. One of his first concerns after founding Sonoma was to have the abandoned orchards and vineyards of the

early mission dug up and replanted on his own lands, where he could ensure that they would be carefully nurtured in the future.

In 1856 Vallejo, now the mayor of Sonoma and already one of California's revered elder statesmen, sold four hundred acres of land near his vineyards to Agoston Haraszthy, a Hungarian nobleman who was also a talented and farsighted wine maker. Haraszthy had come to California several years earlier in search of the perfect site for growing fine European varieties of wine grapes in America. Convinced that he had now found it, he acted on his convictions by planting eighty-five thousand European vines in his new Sonoma vineyard, which he named Buena Vista. The 1939 *WPA Guide to California* summarizes what happened next: "When he

General Mariano
Vallejo, 1850

265

[Haraszthy] wrote an article on viticulture and wine making in 1858, Sonoma was deluged with a flood of inquiries; overnight it became the State's chief center for distribution of viticultural knowledge and nursery cuttings of foreign vines." A more recent writer notes that Haraszthy "undertook the experimental plantings which established northern California forevermore as a worthy second home for the great wine grapes of Europe" (Robert Finigan, *Essentials of Wine*, 1987, Alfred A. Knopf).

Vallejo clearly had an important role in these events, for, on June 1, 1863, a festive double wedding was held at Lachryma Montis (see page 267) between Haraszthy's sons Attila and Arpad and Vallejo's daughters Natalia and Jovita (both fathers favored heroic names for their sons—Vallejo's were called Andronico, Napoleon, Platon, and Uladislao). After many changes in ownership and facilities over the years, Haraszthy's historic **Buena Vista Winery** (about three miles northeast of the Sonoma Plaza at 18000 Old Winery Road, 707-252-7117) is still active and open to visitors.

Sonoma State Historic Park

Modern Sonoma is second only to Monterey (see page 115) in surviving buildings dating from California's Hispanic era. The most important of these are now preserved in the **Sonoma State Historic Park** (information center in the restored **Sonoma Barracks**, Spain Street at First East Street, 707-996-1744), which centers around the northeastern side of the town's unusually large, Spanish-style plaza. This was laid out by Vallejo in 1835 adjacent to **Mission San Francisco Solano**, which had been founded eleven years earlier as the youngest and most northerly of California's chain of twenty-one Hispanic missions (see page xi). Among the park's important buildings are the much reconstructed and redesigned mission buildings, the original adobe barracks completed by Vallejo in 1840 to house the garrison of Mexican soldiers he commanded, and, one-half mile westward, the splendid Gothic Revival dwelling, called Lachryma Montis, that Vallejo built for his large family in 1852. About twelve miles westward, the park also administers Petaluma Adobe, the large and remarkably preserved 1836 headquarters building of the first of Vallejo's several huge ranches in the region (see page 134).

Historic Core

After winning independence from Spain in 1821, the new Republic of Mexico was plagued by a series of political and economic crises that made it increasingly difficult to support the remote chains of forts and missions that had long protected its northern frontier. In 1834 the government decided to close the missions and distribute their vast landholdings for civilian development. Vallejo was among the principal beneficiaries of this new policy. Son of a Spanish soldier of aristocratic ancestry stationed in the venerable California capital of Monterey (see page 115), the talented young Vallejo joined the army there and began a fast-track military career.

As a twenty-four-year-old lieutenant, he was made commander of the presidio of San Francisco in 1831. Three years later the governor of Alta California received orders to "secularize" the province's missions and chose Vallejo to deal with the Solano Mission. Promoted to captain, Vallejo was sent with a garrison of troops to found a civilian town adjacent to the mission and to encourage civilian development of the region's lush grasslands. To further the second objective, Vallejo was given a personal grant of sixty-six thousand acres of prime land west of the Sonoma River (see "Petaluma Adobe," page 134).

As the region's highest-ranking government official, Vallejo erected an impressive official dwelling on the north side of the large central square that he laid out for the new town of Sonoma. Called Casa Grande, the main house was destroyed by fire in 1867, but the Monterey-style rear servants' quarters still survive as a part of the Sonoma State Historic Park. Many of Vallejo's relatives, friends, and associates in developing the region built adobe houses around the square. Some were one-story structures, and others were two-story dwellings with either upper-story Monterey-style cantilevered porches or full two-story Anglo-type porches.

Several of these still survive as hotels or commercial buildings, but all have been much modified over the years. One-story houses became two-story, some adobe walls were covered with wood, larger windows were typically added, and so forth. Despite these changes, the north and west sides of the plaza still maintain the feeling and scale of an early Hispanic town. On the streets just around the square, a few less altered examples of early dwellings still survive. Among these are:

205 East Spain Street (private), Ray/Adler Adobe, ca. 1846–1851. This Spanish Colonial–style home remains remarkably unmodified. It was built in two stages by John Ray, a native of Virginia. The east front (of wood) was constructed in 1846. In 1851, after prospering in the gold rush, he constructed the west front section with adobe walls twenty-two inches thick. The rear wood section is a later addition. The gabled roof seen on the wooden end is most typical of the Spanish Colonial style, while the hipped roof seen on the adobe end is more typical of French Colonial design. Note the Anglo influence in the broad verandah stretching across the front and side of the house.

245 East Spain Street (private), Cook/Hope House, ca.

1855. This hall-and-parlor folk house is thought to be the oldest wood-frame dwelling in Sonoma; the original portion measured eighteen by thirty-six feet. It has casement windows and a front facade clad with wide-board siding made from redwood and applied with simple butted joints. This smooth wood finish on the front facade was considered more formal for the entrance front than more typical lapped-wood cladding seen on the sides. An addition was built in the 1940s.

579 First Street East (private), Nash-Patton Adobe, ca. 1847. Purchased in 1848 by Donner Party survivor Nancy Bones Patton and her husband, this Hispanic folk dwelling was carefully restored to its original appearance by their great-granddaughter in 1931. Note the roof of thick wood shakes, the simple front doors, and the textured finish of the protective stucco covering applied over the adobe bricks. The porch beams are hand-hewn redwood. The double-hung windows reflect early Anglo influence.

564 First Street East (private), Poppe House, ca. 1860. This very small Gothic Revival house has the board-and-batten siding typical of the style. Note the decorative fringe of trim and the tiny, Gothic-arched window and cross brace in the side gable.

531 Second Street East (private), Clewe House, ca. 1878. This striking Italianate design is unusually well preserved. Both the main roof and the porch roof are actually very low mansards topped with iron cresting. Note the segmental arched window tops—those in the second story have brackets and pediments above. There is a two-story bay window facing the right side and a one-story bay window at the right front.

156 East Napa Street (private), Granice House, ca. 1880s. This is an excellent small Queen Anne design of the hipped-roof-with-lower-cross-gable subtype with a spindlework

porch. Every detail of the house looks remarkably original. Stick-style influence is seen in the diagonal siding applied both on the top of the gable and in the panels underneath the paired windows. It also is evident in the shed roofs with spoked brackets above many of the windows.

Lachryma Montis, 1852

Third Street West north of West Spain Street, a geographically distinct part of Sonoma State Historic Park; 707-996-1744.

This charming Gothic Revival house was the home of Sonoma's founder, Mariano Vallejo (see page 265), and his large family for more than thirty-five years. He purchased the 228-acre site, located about one-half mile northwest of Sonoma's main square, in 1850 and was particularly attracted by a wonderful, free-flowing hillside spring that the Indians had called Chiucuyem, which meant "Crying Mountain." Vallejo simply translated this into Latin and called his new home Lachryma Montis. It was approached from the south by a straight, quarter-mile-long entrance drive. Vallejo lined this with Castillian roses and cottonwood trees; even today the original splendor of the approach is still evident.

Vallejo immediately began to develop his new property by planting large vineyards and orchards with many kinds of fruit. He also sent to Europe for the prefabricated timbers of a large building to be used to store casks of wine, olives, and other products. Once assem-

Lachryma Montis, storehouse

Lachryma Montis

Lachryma Montis, guest house/retreat

bled, the timbers were infilled with brick—the result is a unique "Swiss chalet" storehouse that was later used as a residence and today is an interpretive museum for the site.

Vallejo also ordered his picture-perfect Gothic Revival home shipped unassembled around Cape Horn from New England, as were many Anglo-type dwellings in early California. Upon the house's arrival, the timber frame was infilled with adobe bricks, which provided extra strength, insulation, and fire protection. The front porch faces a small entry courtyard that connects to the Swiss-chalet warehouse. A similar rear porch looks out on a small garden. Matching dormer windows and carved vergeboards complete both facades. Outbuildings include a Gothic Revival cookhouse and a Gothic Revival guest house/retreat off of the rear garden. The original Gothic Revival barn and other outbuildings are no longer standing.

Inside, the house has simple interior finishes with understated wood trim around the doors and windows. The marble fireplaces are Italianate in design; a large Gothic window dominates the upstairs master bedroom. About 60 percent of the furnishings belonged to the Vallejos or their children.

The historic dwelling, furnishings, and twenty surrounding acres were acquired by the state of California from Vallejo's youngest daughter in 1933 as a permanent monument to a remarkable pioneer who was truly the "Father of Northern California."

SOUTH LAKE TAHOE

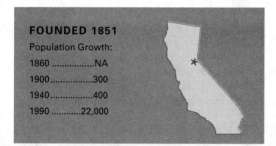

FOUNDED 1851

Population Growth:

1860 ....NA

1900 300

1940 400

1990 22,000

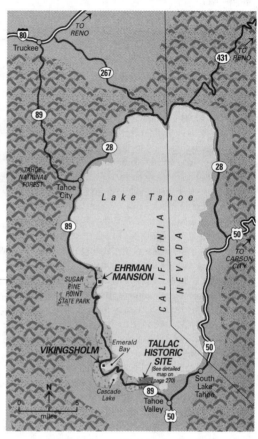

Perched 6,200 feet high in a bowl-shaped valley amid snow-clad Sierra Nevada peaks, Lake Tahoe is one of the scenic wonders of the West. Measuring 22 miles long, 12 miles wide, and 1,600 feet deep, it sits astride the California-Nevada border and was a familiar sight to early wagon-trail immigrants using the nearby Johnson Pass across the rugged Sierra Nevada.

Lake Tahoe and its surrounding timber-covered mountain slopes remained an unsettled wilderness until 1859, when the massive silver and gold deposits of the Comstock Lode were discovered at Virginia City in the Nevada desert, twenty-five miles northeast of the lake (see page 424). In the next two decades the frenzied Comstock mining activities, and the expanding town of Virginia City, consumed enormous amounts of wood—not only for dwelling construction and firewood for heating in the town, but also to fuel the steam engines that powered the mine operations and the local railroads that served them. In addition, the deep mines themselves, dug through unusually soft ore bodies, required a massive underground framework of closely spaced timbers to support their hundreds of miles of shafts and tunnels. To meet this demand, Lake Tahoe became the center of a remarkably engineered timber industry.

Ox-drawn wagons first brought the massive logs of pine and fir down to the lakeshore from the surrounding mountainsides. The logs were then floated across the lake in huge, tugboat-drawn rafts to several lakeside milling towns, the largest of which was Glenbrook on the Nevada side. From the mills the finished lumber was hauled by ox wagons or small local railways to the top of the Sierra Nevada's easternmost slopes, where it was literally floated downhill for more than five miles in V-shaped, water-filled wooden flumes to vast lumberyards in the Carson Valley below. From there, a narrow-gauge railroad transported the lumber through lower desert hills to its final Virginia City destination.

The rich ores of the Comstock Lode and the virgin forests of Lake Tahoe were to have about the same life expectancy—both were declining by the 1880s. Lake Tahoe then slowly reverted to its original wilderness splendor with the regrowth of its surrounding forests. Beginning in the 1890s wealthy Californians, mostly from San Francisco and Sacramento, began to build summer homes along the lake's scenic shores. By the 1920s the first ski resorts were opening to take advantage of the area's deep winter snows. Until the late 1940s, however, this remained a rustic resort area with a very small permanent population.

This pattern began to change in the late 1940s, when the first gambling casinos appeared on the Nevada side. Today, Lake Tahoe is one of the West's most popular vacation destinations—a booming year-round resort area whose largest city, South Lake Tahoe, resembles a miniature Las Vegas transported to a setting not unlike the Swiss Alps. A completely modern urban center, South Lake Tahoe provides a convenient base for visiting several nearby museum houses, all of them delightful survivors from the lake's earlier and quieter resort decades.

The houses are today owned by either the California Department of Parks and Recreation or by the U.S. National Forest Service, which acquired them primarily for their vast surrounding acreage that borders Lake Tahoe. The grounds of each are open and provide a variety of outdoor activities. Hiking, biking, boating, and picnicking are the primary focus for most visitors, and the early houses, which are little advertised, seem to present themselves simply as delightful additional surprises. They have only recently come to be recognized as important attractions in their own right. This is fortunate for both historians and house watchers, for few such fine Eclectic-era resort homes are available for public enjoyment anywhere in the country. Fewer still retain, as these do, enough of their surrounding lands to give visitors a feeling of the strong relationship between house and natural environment, which was the reason they were originally built.

Visits to see the interiors of these houses is seasonal, as indeed was their occupancy from the beginning. In midsummer it is hard to visualize the fierce mountain blizzards that normally begin in late fall. Or to grasp that parts of the parking lot one is using might have just been rebuilt following destruction by a savage winter avalanche. The opening of the houses each summer was always, according to guides, a journey of discovery. The park rangers and dedicated volunteers who work on these houses today are still greeted by these annual spring maintenance surprises.

Tallac Historic Site

North side of California Highway 89, about ten miles west of the Nevada state line; 916-541-5227.

This historic site, managed by the U.S. Forest Service, has three important historic houses along with numerous contemporaneous outbuildings and the archaeological ruins of the famed nineteenth-century resort hotel from which the site takes its name. Each of the three houses has a different use today. The **Baldwin Estate** is a museum and interpretive center; the **Pope Estate,** with its extraordinary set of remaining outbuildings, is being restored as a museum house; and the third, **Valhalla,** also called the Heller Estate, is used for both public and private performances and events. All are set in a large park that is open during daylight hours with a hiking and biking trail that passes all three houses, thus making the setting of the estates and their

exteriors accessible year-round (at least to those with snowshoes!).

The site's name comes from Lake Tahoe's first resort, a small timber-era hotel built in 1875 and called the Tallac Point House. In 1880 this became the property of Elias Jackson "Lucky" Baldwin (1828–1909), a San Francisco stock speculator and real estate investor who had made a fortune of $7.5 million from his stock in the Ophir Mines (see page 428), in nearby Virginia City, Nevada. Baldwin immediately began improvements to the hotel that made it a popular destination for his wealthy friends. As its reputation grew, additions were made in the early 1890s, and a large new building, the Tallac Hotel, was added in 1895. The promenade between the original Point House and the Tallac Hotel soon became a popular place where ladies strolled and men ogled. Affluent bachelors from Virginia City came to regard "trolling for schoolmarms" at Tallac as a great way to spend the weekend. In 1902 a casino was added for "games and entertainment," including illegal gambling.

During the 1890s Baldwin began selling pieces of his land as homesites for prominent California families, which of course also increased the prestige of his adjacent resort. Visitation dwindled following the First World War, and in the 1920s Baldwin's daughter and heir, Anita Baldwin, concerned among other things about the environmental impact the hotel was having on the lake, had the remaining commercial structures razed, leaving only the privately owned dwellings. By then numerous large summer estates had been developed along the scenic lakeshore, but by the 1950s, many of these expensive luxuries were falling into disuse. At the same time, the area's population boom aroused concern about how little of the lake's dramatic shoreline was accessible for public enjoyment. This led, during the 1960s, to the purchase of several of the larger

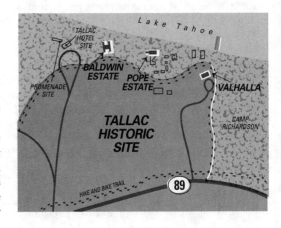

Tallac Historic Site, Pope Estate

estates for use as park conservation lands by the state and U.S. Forest Service.

The first private home to be built on the Tallac site was the Pope Estate, erected on land sold by Lucky Baldwin in 1894. Three influential California families eventually owned this property and gradually developed the estate as seen today. The first owner, George Payne Tennant, was a prominent San Francisco banker who built a part of the main house and the kitchen unit in 1894. In 1899 he sold the property to Lloyd Tevis, a founder of Wells Fargo Bank who had that year received $8 million for the sale of his interest in Montana's huge Anaconda Copper Company (see page 374). Over the next twenty-one years Tevis extensively remodeled and expanded the house to its present appearance and added most of the outbuildings. In 1923 the estate, which then consisted of thirty-eight acres and seventeen structures, was deeded to George A. Pope Sr. of San Francisco, chairman of the board of the Pope and Talbot Lumber Company, whose principal operations were at Port Gamble, Washington (see page 666). The combination of three prominent owners, extensive outbuildings, and some unusual interior features gives this house exceptional historic importance.

The main house of the Pope Estate is a Shingle-style design with gambrel roof and "Adirondack Lodge" touches, which include bark-clad logs used as porch supports and in a nearby rustic honeymoon cottage. This has exotic curved branches elaborating the gable and a bark exterior finish. In the Northeast, several wealthy Victorian-era financiers had built rustic summer homes in New York's Adirondack Mountains with these kinds of details, which were then adopted in occasional summer homes elsewhere, as well as in larger resort structures, including some in several national parks.

Among the many other surviving outbuildings on the Pope Estate are an icehouse, dairy, laundry, and several furnished servants' quarters. Most of these have high-pitched gable roofs, sometimes with a small centered cross gable, and appear to mimic the post-Medieval cottages in a seventeenth-century New England village. One two-room house served Lavinia, the cook and the seamstress; another the butler and the gatekeeper; yet another housed the tutor and the head gardener. Several other cottages provided quarters for additional guests. The Tevises loved gardening and planted many exotic trees in a small garden they called the Arboretum. Recently restored, it has a rustic gazebo, fishpond, and bridge.

The interior of the large main house is being restored room by room. One enters a sweet-smelling cedar-paneled entry hall with a coffered ceiling. The spacious living room has a pool table that belonged to the Tevises and handsome hand-carved redwood bookshelves. The dining room has been completely restored. Its handsome original Mission-style table and sideboard, finished a deep forest green, were recently returned to the house by a Pope family member and inspired the restoration. Deep-green sisal mats cover the floor, and the original wicker chairs are cushioned with the original grape-and-vine-patterned fabric that has also been reproduced to make a dramatic wall covering above the chair rail.

Upstairs are a number of bedrooms, some of which have the original French linen wall fabrics attached with brass tacks. Many closets are tucked under the slope of the gambrel roof, and the openings to them echo the shape of the roof. One closet even has a wonderful collection of early-twentieth-century wool bathing suits on display. The children were housed over the kitchen and servants' dining room, detached from the main house and connected by a curved breezeway. The servants' dining room has a table, chairs, and sideboard that belonged to Lucky Baldwin.

The next house constructed on the site was the Baldwin Estate, built in 1920 by Anita's daughter and Lucky's granddaughter Dextra Baldwin, who managed to retain the property through five divorces. Built in a U shape, it also has an Adirondack flair. Most of the interior has been converted to a museum and interpretive center for the Tallac Historic Site. But the main large room, at the base of the U, remains intact. It is open to the roof and has rustic support beams, an upstairs loft, and a huge fireplace constructed of small boulders. The kitchen also maintains its 1920s feeling.

The third house built was Valhalla, a Norse word for "heaven," constructed by the Walter S. Heller family in 1924. It is a gambrel-roofed Shingle-style house, and its wonderfully rustic Adirondack touches include porch supports and a balustrade of bark-covered logs and limbs. The porch wraps around three sides of the house, and a large stone fireplace opens out onto the porch and also into the main hall of the house where a large hearth area surrounds it. Much of the house is dominated by a large main hall, which extends the entire width and height of the building, facilitating the adaptive reuse of this structure for events. Outbuildings include a gambrel-roofed boathouse, sided with bark-clad wood, and a pair of small gambrel-roofed buildings connected by a breezeway.

Worth noting is the extensive volunteer program that maintains these Tallac site houses each summer season. Retirees with construction or maintenance experience are offered free scenic campsites in return for work on restoration and maintenance of the houses. Some stay as little as two weeks and others as long as three months.

Vikingsholm, 1929

Emerald Bay State Park, California Highway 89, about fifteen miles west of the Nevada state line, or about seventeen miles south of Tahoe City; house accessible only via a one-mile downhill trail or by rented boat; 916-525-7277 or 916-541-3030; Lennart Palme, Rye, New York, architect.

Approaching Vikingsholm from South Lake Tahoe, you pass a high divide with beautiful Emerald Bay, the largest bay on Lake Tahoe, on one side and Cascade Lake on the other; the Inspiration Point scenic view area is here, and one can look far down on the bay and its tiny island. Just about one-half mile farther down the road is a small, subtly marked parking lot for Vikingsholm. This is the trailhead for a one-mile trail that leads down to the home. At first one thinks that the house, of course, could not possibly be as far down as the lakeshore and that surely it is perched up on a high bluff overlooking the lake. Since it is a beautiful walk down, filled with small waterfalls and streams and wildflowers, the mind dwells on these, but as the trail continues to lead down closer and closer to lake level, it begins to become apparent that the house *is* at lake level. The steep return trip requires either recent aerobic training or *very* slow walking.

Heiress Lora Josephine Knight (1864–1945), who built Vikingsholm, would have had very firm views on this matter. She entertained frequent summer guests and insisted that no one participate in activities such as swimming and hiking in their first few days after arriving at Vikingsholm, since "everyone, regardless of age, should be thoroughly rested from their trip and acclimatized to the altitude before engaging in any form of strenuous endeavor." Her custom was to take a long walk after dinner when she and her guests were driven by limousine *up* the steep roadway to Highway 89, which was followed by the pleasant stroll *down* the hill to Vikingsholm.

These and many other facts are remembered in a lovely small book called *Vikingsholm: Tahoe's Hidden Castle*, written by Helen Henry Smith (privately published in 1973 and available at the site), who spent fourteen consecutive summers visiting Vikingsholm as a child. Her insights into the rhythm of the summer life there and how Mrs. Knight managed her home, her business, and her house guests all at once are brief but warmly personal.

Mrs. Knight's equally firm ideas on the design of her summer house and the preservation of its natural landscape make Vikingsholm a rare treasure. She was born in Galena, Illinois, the daughter of a corporate attorney. He took on two young partners, brothers William

Vikingsholm

Henry Moore and James Hobart Moore. Eventually, Lora Josephine married James, and Ida, one of Lora's three sisters, married William. The brothers were uncommonly successful and in time had large or controlling interests in National Biscuit, Continental Can, Diamond Match, and Union Pacific and Rock Island Railroads. Lora and James lived mainly in Evanston, Illinois, and Lake Geneva, Wisconsin, and enjoyed extensive travels together. They had just purchased a retirement home in Montecito, California, when Lora was widowed in 1916. A second marriage to Harry French Knight in the early 1920s ended in divorce.

It was then, at about age sixty-five, that Mrs. Knight, who had owned a summer house on the north shore of Lake Tahoe for sixteen years, decided to build a larger summer home of what might be called "Scandinavian Eclectic" architectural inspiration. In this choice she was inspired by a Nordic home built in Rye, New York,

for her niece's family and designed by the niece's architect husband, Lennart Palme. The Palmes and Mrs. Knight set out on a research and buying trip to Scandinavia in the summer of 1928. With camera in hand, they visited old homes and eleventh-century wooden churches in Norway, stone castles in Sweden, and other ancient buildings in Denmark and Finland.

Palme must have worked as they traveled, for the foundation of Vikingsholm was laid late that same summer. As soon as the snows melted the following spring, a small army of two hundred workmen descended on the site. By the first snows of fall, the house had been completed for occupancy the following season. In this brief period not only was a large home constructed, but its many custom-designed and hand-crafted architectural details were executed. These included complex exterior and interior wood carvings, wrought-metal hardware, broad hand-planed interior wallboards, and intricate light fixtures. Many of the craftsmen were of Scandinavian descent, and they built sections of the house in traditional ways, without nails or screws. The Swedish custom of earthen roofs was even followed on Vikingsholm's lower wings, and wildflowers still grow atop these wings.

Despite this breakneck schedule and the fine craftsmanship and unusual construction techniques required, architect Palme later said that his most difficult task in building Vikingsholm was finding a site that fulfilled Mrs. Knight's dictum "not to disturb the trees." She was a committed conservationist and respected the beautiful natural setting that remains intact today. Inside Vikingsholm, she and the Palmes created a calm oasis of soft colors, natural wood walls, and intricate yet understated furnishings that have a rare coherence of design. Some unusual Scandinavian antiques were purchased during their trip, and others, on display in museums, were measured and carefully copied. Traditional hand-carved dragon beams hang in the living room, Nordic corner fireplaces have screens custom designed by Palme, and handwrought latches are on the outside of the bedroom doors, in honor of the Viking custom of the chieftain's locking all guests into their rooms and then locking his own door behind him.

Today, Mrs. Knight's legacy still sits in the midst of a lovely forest of pine and fir trees, with small meadows of wildflowers nearby. She never felt a need to create man-made gardens. In retrospect, the walk down the natural beauty of the hillside was almost as lovely as the tour of the home. Those who are physically unable to make the round-trip by foot can make advance arrangements for vehicle transport by the park staff.

Ehrman Mansion, 1902

Sugar Pine Point State Park, California Highway 89, about twenty-three miles northwest of the Nevada state line, or about nine miles south of Tahoe City; 916-525-7982; Bliss and Faville, San Francisco, architects.
In 1897 Bavarian-born San Francisco resident Isaias W. Hellman (1842–1920) began to acquire a 1,016-acre estate with two miles of water frontage on the west-central shore of Lake Tahoe. Hellman was one of the financial geniuses of his day and played a strong role in the development of West Coast banking, amassing a fortune in the process. Highly respected, at his death in 1920 at the age of seventy-eight, he was still either president or director of six different banks.

In 1901 Hellman hired the well-known San Francisco architectural firm of Bliss and Faville to design a large summer home for his family and guests. The result was this handsome Shingle-style dwelling, originally called Pine Lodge, which could host as many as

fifty houseguests during the season. The home retains most of its original fixtures and fittings. Unfortunately, it does not still have the original furnishings, which were offered to the state of California as a part of the 1965 sale of the property. The state declined to buy them, and now that the importance of the home has been recognized, replacement furnishings, based on extensive research and oral histories of family members and former guests, have had to be purchased. Less than a handful of family pieces are in the house, but the spirit of the replacement furnishings is true to that of the originals. It is hoped that original furnishings still in the hands of family members or sold in a 1965 auction will gradually be returned to the mansion.

One enters the house from a broad, slate-floored porch with stone railing, pebbled ceiling, and bark-clad log porch supports. This was originally furnished with wicker furniture, scattered Oriental rugs, and even a billiard table. Each end of the porch opens into the first-floor room of one of the twin towers to form what were called the north and south circular porches. The north circular porch was where servants served large buffet lunches on warm summer days. The south circular porch was a game room with facilities for bridge and dominoes, a phonograph, and an early pinball machine.

Inside is a large central hall with a curving staircase. To the left is a large living room with floral chintz drapes dating from a 1920s remodeling by Florence Ehrman, a Hellman daughter. She also changed the walls from their original cranberry red color to their present white at the same time. This has lightened the room and accentuated the dark wood-patterned walls and beamed ceiling. The large fireplace is of the same locally quarried granite that is found in the basement, chimney, and first floor of the towers.

The huge dining room on the right of the entry hall is stunningly unusual. The focal point is a large fireplace surrounded with handsome Oriental-design tiles made in Holland. The walls are covered with thin strips of redwood woven into an extraordinary basket-weave design. The heavy chandeliers in all three of these main downstairs rooms are original.

Many upstairs bedrooms are also on view, as is the kitchen area, which retains many of its original fixtures. The grounds are spacious and well groomed. One can dock at the long pier and swim and picnic on the grounds. Although this looks like a large pier, the original one stretched far out into the lake so it could accommodate the deep draft of the lake steamship, which had to bring all of the early materials for construction and later the supplies for the household. Several wonderful outbuildings also survive. The original boat-

Ehrman Mansion

house still has one of the family's huge, sleek wooden speedboats, as well as an assortment of smaller boats used for summer sport. Other buildings include a caretaker's cottage, a butler's house, and maids' quarters, a children's house, a carriage house, and a tall tank house where water for the house was stored (it arrived via flume from General Creek one mile away). Beneath the

tank is a room housing wood-fueled steam electricity generators. There is also an original icehouse where Mrs. Ehrman had ice cut from the lake each winter and stored, a practice she continued until her death, as she preferred its taste. She had reluctantly allowed the introduction of a commercial refrigerator in 1945. Prior to this the kitchen staff had only an icebox for food storage.

Isaias Hellman's will divided his large fortune among his three children, Clara, Florence, and Isaias Jr. Florence received Pine Lodge, of which she was particularly fond, while Clara and Isaias Jr. received other compensating property. Florence, who married Sidney Ehrman in 1904, had long managed the Lake Tahoe summer home for her father. After she became the owner, it gradually became known as the Ehrman Mansion. She kept it up in the grand manner, with elaborate openings each summer, until her death. Her daughter, Ester Lazard, inherited the property and sold it to the state of California for a generously low price in 1965.

UKIAH

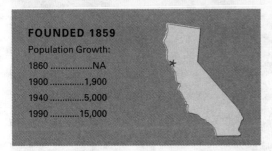

FOUNDED 1859

Population Growth:

1860 ....NA

1900 1,900

1940 5,000

1990 15,000

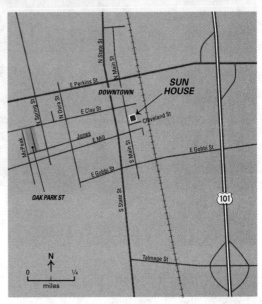

The seat of northern California's Mendocino County, this small agricultural marketing and trade center is home to one of the nation's few architect-designed museum houses in the avant-garde Craftsman style of the early twentieth century.

Sun House, 1911

Grace Hudson Museum, 431 South Main Street; 707-462-3370; George Wilcox, Berkeley, architect.

This small gem of a Craftsman house perfectly reflects the ideals of its creative and energetic builders—painter Grace Carpenter Hudson (1865–1937) and her ethnologist husband, Dr. John W. Hudson (1857–1936). Charmingly intact, with its original interior finishes and furnishings unmodified, Sun House is a rare survivor of the period, from about 1905 to 1915, when an architect-designed Craftsman "bungalow" represented the cutting edge of modernism for creative and far-thinking owners like the Hudsons.

Grace and John were a remarkable couple. She was a painter, renowned for her portraits and studies of the local Pomo Indians, whom she had known since her childhood in Potter Valley, fifteen miles northeast of Ukiah. These won her many prizes and a national reputation. He was a Nashville-born physician who immigrated to Mendocino County in 1889, where he and Grace met and were married in 1891. John's first love was anthropology, not medicine. Fascinated, as was Grace, by the local Pomo people, by 1896 John had given up his practice to pursue his deep interests in collecting the rapidly vanishing artifacts—particularly baskets—of the California Indians and in writing about their tribal life. He became widely respected in these pursuits and worked for many years as a collector and researcher for the Chicago Field Museum of Natural History. Their joint love of the native peoples of California drew the couple together in a marriage that lasted for more than forty-five years.

The Hudsons had been painting, collecting, and writing in cramped quarters for almost twenty-one years when they set out to build a new home. Their somewhat-bohemian lifestyle did not provide them with a large income, and most of their earnings had gone into John's voluminous collections. To raise the $3,500 needed to build Sun House, they sold a large portion of his superb basket collection to the Smithsonian Institution, where the baskets would remain together and be permanently available for study and public display. The $3,500 payment was a small fraction of what the Hudsons could have obtained by selling the baskets in small lots to private collectors.

Architect George Wilcox provided a fine, front-gabled Craftsman design clad in board-and-batten. Entry is through an understated front door with a trellis above that is dramatically accented with a tall Indian totem pole (this is a duplicate—the original pole is now in the adjacent museum building). Enormous redwood timbers support the inset side porch, which was used as an outdoor living and dining room. This porch overlooks a small garden with a fishpond and natural stone benches. The Hudsons so loved this small side garden that it was replicated in their large private cemetery plot. Near this garden is an original wisteria-draped trellis. Vines were also encouraged to grow on the front of the house. The extended grounds were originally left

Sun House

naturalistic, rather than being carefully groomed and tended as today. The Hudsons' architect became so taken with Ukiah while working on Sun House that he left Berkeley to build his own home here (see page 278).

Inside the house, redwood is used for beamed ceilings and in shallow, narrow strips that form geometric patterns on the walls. The living room walls are covered with a heavy-weave "friar's cloth," or burlap, while the friar's cloth covering in the other rooms is of a much finer weave. Only in the bedroom was one of these simple cloth walls enhanced when Grace covered it with white paint and a simple stenciled flower pattern. The home's two fireplaces are quite uncomplicated in design, with redwood beam mantels. As was the habit of many early modern architects, Wilcox also designed several pieces of furniture for the home. The only one of these to survive is the sideboard in the dining room.

John also had much influence on the house. He designed, and himself built, the massive redwood front door. He built an unusual wall-mounted hat rack in the front hall, with a pronounced Oriental influence. He also designed—and in this case had specially manufactured—the unusual light fixtures and sconces that survive throughout the house. These feature four-sided opaque glass pyramids that are suspended upside down to diffuse the glare of the bulbs.

In this home, finally, the couple had space enough to efficiently pursue their respective professions. Grace had a large studio, with a skylight above (later removed by her niece), a bank of north-facing windows, and a large adjacent dressing room for her subjects to use. A large fireplace in the studio made the room comfortable on chilly winter days. John had not only a study off of the living room but also the entire attic—one huge room with built-in shelves—in which to house the fruits of his continuing collecting activities.

The house has an eclectic collection of furnishings, almost all of which belonged to the Hudsons. Their dishes, books, family photos, and other small objects are still in place. There are a number of Chinese objects, many of them gifts from members of the Wong family, who kept house for the Hudsons for almost fifty years and brought them from occasional visits to their homeland. When the Hudsons lived here, many Indian baskets and artifacts were displayed throughout the home. Today, these are housed in the Grace Hudson Museum, unobtrusively located behind Sun House.

A contemporary description of Sun House, written by Grace's aunt, Mrs. Hale McCowen, reads:

The studio is a large, airy, well-lighted room, which is most admirably adapted for the purpose it was intended. A visit to this home is a pleasure long to be remembered. The floors are polished oak and every nook and corner is filled with rare curios, antiques, rare, old hand-carved furniture and souvenirs from every part of the world. Although unusually well adapted to entertaining, only once has Mrs. Hudson thrown her home open to the public. This was upon the occasion of a Belgian tea. Many people availed themselves of the opportunity to obtain a view of such art treasures that are seldom seen in such an isolated section of the country. (Searles R. Boynton, *The Painter Lady: Grace Carpenter Hudson*)

Toward the end of their lives, money became an increasing problem for the Hudsons. Occasional sales of Grace's paintings provided their only support. She complained to a friend that she "couldn't buy a powder puff," yet they tried to keep their valuable collections together. They succeeded, and today, in addition to parts of the collection's being at the Smithsonian, the Field Museum, and the Brooklyn Museum, many of John's most prized Indian baskets and artifacts belong to the Hudson Museum, along with a number of Grace's exquisite and irreplaceable paintings. Together these make a fitting memorial both to the handsome and proud Pomo people and to the Anglo couple who so appreciated and understood them.

Related Neighborhood (Oak Park Street)

Located about a half-mile west of Sun House (see the map, page 276) is Oak Park Street, the 400 block of which preserves a picturesque sample of the rustic neighborhoods envisioned by Craftsman architects for their houses. It was here that George Wilcox, the designer of Sun House, built his own home after deciding to move from Berkeley to rural Ukiah, then a small town of only two thousand inhabitants. Other like-minded modernists joined him on this block. Unfortunately, the Wilcox home, unnumbered but directly across the street from 404, was later modified and its original natural wood finish painted over. Still, the block as a whole—with its small-scale houses constructed of natural materials and enhanced with rustic outdoor spaces, wooden fences, and lush planting—evokes the landscape qualities sought by many practitioners of the Arts and Crafts movement (see figure 42, page 705).

Near 400 Oak Park Street (private), ca. 1910s. The robust pebble porch supports are most easily viewed from the side facade on Clay Street. Note the jigsaw cutout design used in the porch gable and the line of windows in the broad-gabled dormer.

404 Oak Park Street (private), ca. 1910s. Only the thick wood-shake roof of this house is visible behind the lush landscaping. A side garden is indicated by a delightful wooden garden gate.

417 Oak Park Street (private), ca. 1910s. This house effectively disguises its large size with a narrow, understated street facade. The variegated wood-stake fence and the large adjacent private "park" enhance the streetscape's rustic atmosphere.

527 Oak Park Street (private), ca 1950. This is an excellent flat-roofed Contemporary design, the 1950s incarnation of the 1930s International style. The use of a high ribbon of windows (on the left) was a favorite device of 1950s architects, particularly for street facades. This arrangement let in light, ensured privacy, and provided interior wall space against which to place furniture. Note the interesting way the bricks are laid to form the porch supports. The prominent carport was another favored 1950s feature.

VENTURA

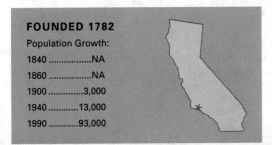

FOUNDED 1782

Population Growth:

1840	NA
1860	NA
1900	3,000
1940	13,000
1990	93,000

This fast-growing coastal city near the far northwestern fringe of Los Angeles urbanization was the site of Mission San Buenaventura, the ninth of the twenty-one Spanish missions established along the California coast from 1769 to 1823 (see page xi). Through most of its postmission history, the settlement was a small agricultural trade center whose official name was also San Buenaventura, later shortened to simply Ventura. A carefully researched modern restoration of the stone-walled mission church can be seen near the center of town, at 225 East Main Street. Surrounded by parklands at the edge of the modern city is a fine Hispanic-era ranch dwelling that is now a locally popular museum house.

Olivas Adobe, 1847–1853

4200 Olivas Park Drive, in the Olivas Adobe Historical Park; 805-658-4728.

Although U.S. statehood and the difficulty of proving their land grants wiped out the fortunes of a great many Hispanic Californios, some were able to prosper under the new system. Don Raymundo Olivas (1809–1879) was one of these. The illegitimate child of a poor mother, Olivas was born in Los Angeles and joined the Mexican army when he turned sixteen. Assigned to the presidio at Santa Barbara, where he served in the cavalry, Olivas somehow managed to learn to read and write. These skills led to his promotion to the equiva-

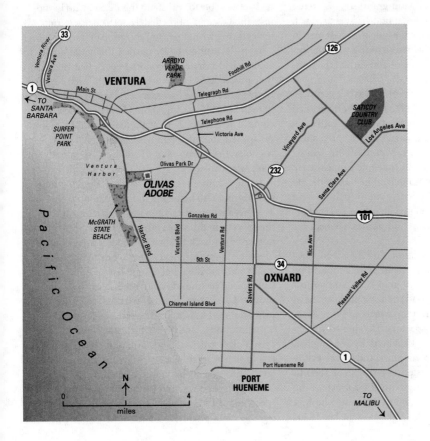

Olivas Adobe

lent of master sergeant, a rank that required completing paperwork. In 1841, as a reward for his service to the army, Mexican governor Juan Alvarado gave Olivas one-half interest in a small land grant of 4,670 acres. Utilizing this modest start, Raymundo Olivas used wit, initiative, and skill to become the fourth-richest man in Ventura County. Over the next thirty-five years, he enlarged his rancho to 30,000 acres and earned the honorary title of *Don* Raymundo.

As soon as he received the grant, Olivas began ranching operations, and, crucial in the future, he diversified to raise sheep, oxen, and horses as well as cattle. He planted fifteen acres of apricots and even ran a small dairy. When California became part of the United States in 1848, Don Raymundo adapted quickly. He hired two Anglo attorneys to defend his land title. He became a Republican, active in local politics and county government, and invited judges and elected officials to his home for fiestas and parties. He kept his land grant.

With his ranching operation thriving, Don Raymundo began building the first part of his adobe home in 1847. Then came the 1849 gold rush, and almost overnight his cattle, which had been worth $2.50 a head for hides and tallow, were now worth $75 a head as meat for the hungry prospectors. He shrewdly marketed his cattle and enlarged his herd; by 1853 he had finished the second story of his home and was a wealthy man. Then came the devastating drought of 1860 to 1861, which provided the death knell for much of the lingering Californio culture; many of those who had successfully defended their land grants in the late 1850s

watched their cattle (and fortunes and often lands as well) lost to drought in the early 1860s. But because Don Raymundo's ranching operation was well diversified, he was able to withstand this period with his holdings intact—and immediately set out to recoup his losses through a higher concentration on raising sheep.

Don Raymundo badly needed this large home. In 1832 he had married Theodora Lopez (died 1895), and they proceeded to have twenty-one children together. By 1853 the couple had married daughters, daughters of marriageable age, and more children of their own to come. The curator here at the Olivas Adobe recently discovered that the family's patron saint was Saint Nicholas, the patron saint of children. Apparently this was a wise choice.

Local Chumash Indians worked on Raymundo's ranches and also helped to build this adobe. They had been freed when the mission was secularized in 1833. In the short term this was a mixed blessing, for they could not easily go back to their previous Native American lifestyle. Many employers took advantage of their plight and paid them only two dollars a month for their labors; Don Raymundo paid three dollars a month and provided an entire "benefits package" (as it would be called today). His workers also received food and clothing allocations, land to farm on for themselves, and even a place where they could build their own home. His Indian workers were also invited to worship and give confession in his home chapel. By all accounts, Don Raymundo was an outstanding man in every respect, not just financially. The curator reported that in eight years of research he had found not one ill word against Don Raymundo, which he considered rather remarkable for such a wealthy man.

The home that Olivas built is remarkably near its original condition today. Spanish Colonial in style, it has Anglo-influenced porches (with supporting columns) on both the front and rear facades. The original window and door surrounds remain, and these are typical of the early period of Anglo influence. Thirty percent of the adobe's original window glass is still in place. Even the setting is much as it was during Don Raymundo's lifetime. The old road passed where Olivas Park Road is today. Early photographs reveal that a long trellis always graced the front yard, which has 100-year-old fuchsias and a 140-year-old grapevine. Don Raymundo also built the adobe wall that surrounds the large well-swept rear yard (although a later owner added the gate's quaint bell tower).

This amazing state of preservation (for an adobe house) exists because the home was continuously occupied, well cared for, and never had a major renovation. Rebecca Olivas lived here until her death in 1899, and then it was purchased by a Mr. Alvord, who ran a dairy nearby. In 1917 it was acquired by the Old Adobe Gun Club, which used it as a hunting lodge. In 1927, Major "Max" Fleischmann purchased the house for a duck-hunting lodge. Fleischmann was the yeast king, maker of Fleischmann's yeast products. He loved the house and, although he hunted here only a couple of weeks a year, he could afford to keep it well staffed year-round until his death in 1951. It then passed to the Fleischmann Foundation, which gave it to the city of Ventura in 1963. In 1972 the Olivas Adobe opened as a museum house.

The house has six main rooms and two small one-story wings. Because it is only one room deep, the traditional Spanish depth, it is smaller than it first appears and has only three rooms upstairs and three rooms down. The curatorial staff has succeeded in finding some treasured Olivas family furnishings for these. In the *sala* (formal parlor) there are many photographs of the Olivas family, but the search continues for a photograph of Don Raymundo Olivas himself. The *sala* does hold one of his greatest treasures, El Cilindro, an 1850 upright music maker, which was made in Brooklyn and plays eight different tunes with its amazing toy band "performing" as it plays. This must have enlivened many an evening. Next to this is the dining room, filled with Fleischmann furniture, including his 1927 Magnavox radio. The third downstairs room was a sewing room and occasionally an extra bedroom. Upstairs, there is a large chapel, with quite accurate furnishings that were guided by an 1870s photograph. The master bedroom is in the center and has a handsome red chest

Olivas Adobe

that was in the Olivas family. The third upstairs room was the girls' room (since they were spaced apart in age, all eight did not live in this room at the same time).

There were also thirteen boys in the family. Those under twelve slept in an enclosed part of the porch (now removed), and those over twelve were sent out to the *garçonnière* at the back of the rear yard. A girl's virginal status was necessary to ensure a good marriage and large dowry; parents therefore kept their sons' friends far from the young women of the house. One of the small wings was used for extra bedrooms, and the other contained the kitchen and pantry.

Author Helen Hunt Jackson's 1880s description, in her novel *Ramona*, of the use of the broad porches helps in understanding how twenty-three people lived together in only a few rooms (with the two largest devoted to chapel and formal entertaining). According to her, the "verandahs . . . were supplementary rooms to the house. The greater part of the family life went on in them. Nobody stayed inside the walls, except the actual cooking was done here . . . babies slept, were washed, . . . and played, on the verandah. The women said their prayers, took their naps and weaved lace there." In the southern California climate, this sounds like a great way to live.

Colorado

BOULDER

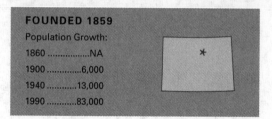

FOUNDED 1859

Population Growth:

1860 ....NA

1900 6,000

1940 13,000

1990 83,000

Most of Colorado's major cities are lined up along the base of the steep mountain front that bisects the state from north to south. In this rather-narrow belt the adjacent mountain streams and lakes provide a reliable water supply in the otherwise arid plains that dominate the eastern half of the state. Rather remarkably, each of the half dozen or so principal mountain-base towns has played a different role in Colorado's economic history. Taken in south–north order, Trinidad was a coal-mining center; Pueblo specialized in heavy industry, particularly steel making and ore smelting; Colorado Springs became a fashionable resort; Denver, the first of the mountain-base towns, become the region's center of trade, finance, and government. Boulder, founded as a small gold rush supply center, was picked in 1861 as the site for the future University of Colorado. The projected university remained largely unfunded until 1875, when a grant of forty-six thousand acres of federal land permitted its first building to be constructed and several professors hired. Most of the town's subsequent history has revolved around its importance as a regional center for higher education.

Boulder remained a small university town until the 1950s, when its scenic surroundings and cool, mile-high summers began to make it a favored site for new federal laboratories and high-tech industry. In spite of pioneering citizen attempts at population control, in subsequent decades the Boulder area has mushroomed into an urban complex with a quarter-million inhabitants.

As in most small university towns, early Boulder had few grand mansions, but the city does retain a delightful and unusually diverse turn-of-the-century neighborhood as well as a museum house offering a rare visit inside a four-square dwelling of the sort that dominated many of the nation's early-twentieth-century housing developments. In addition, the city's **Chautauqua Park** (entrance at Eleventh and Baseline Streets) is a unique western survivor of many such "chautauquas," which were sort of family- and educa-tion-oriented summer camps that flourished throughout the country in the late nineteenth and early twentieth centuries. This one was founded in 1898 by Texans seeking escape from that state's oppressive summer heat. Still active, the Boulder chautauqua retains many of its early buildings, including an auditorium, a dining hall, a community house, and dozens of delightful small-scale folk and Craftsman dwellings.

Mapleton Hill, ca. 1895–1910

This large residential area, located just to the north of Boulder's historic downtown, was the town's first district planned for upper-middle-class families. The Boulder Land and Improvement Company purchased most of the land in 1882 and laid out the Mapleton Addition in what was then West Boulder. Located on a hill, it offered good drainage, fresh air, and beautiful views. Unfortunately, it was also quite barren, and the development company immediately planted two hundred silver maples and cottonwoods to make it more attractive. Today, some of these and later plantings have grown into towering tree tunnels that add a distinctive character to the neighborhood.

The handsome Mapleton School was built in the middle of the still-sparsely-built-up addition in 1889 and spurred more rapid development. Of the five hundred homes in Mapleton Hill, about 28 percent were built from 1895 to 1900 and another 57 percent from 1900 to 1910. These featured a wide spectrum of sizes and styles. Most common are one-story Queen Anne cottages with Free Classic detailing and two-story Colonial Revival designs of the hipped-roof-with-full-width-porch subtype. Many of these are American four-squares in shape, but others are wider and appear to have the centered stair hall that is absent in four-square interiors.

745 Highland Avenue (private), Moorhead House, 1903; Watson Vernon, Boulder, architect. An unusual Neoclassical design, this appears to be front gabled at first glance although it actually has a broad, full-width triangular pediment coming off of a hipped roof behind. Some of the things that make this house different are the corner windows (with a short column at the corner and matching pilasters on each side), the two shallow bay windows on the front (deliberately not placed as a symmetrical pair), the recessed bay window in the front-facing gable, and the carefully articulated side facade along Eighth Street. Note the many window transoms with diamond lights.

903 Pine Street (private), Earhart House, 1879. One of the neighborhood's earliest houses, this fine three-bay, hipped-

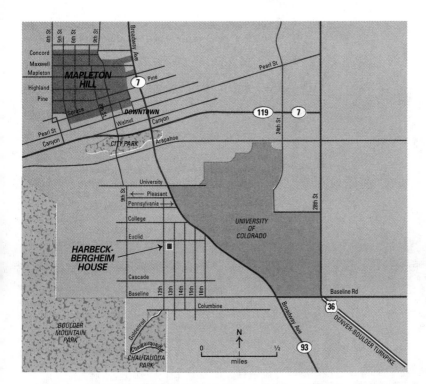

roof Italianate design has a restored porch and added oval window on the left side.

1015 Pine Street (private), ca. 1905. Although this Prairie-style house has the overall look of the hipped-roof, symmetrical, no-front-entry subtype, it actually does have a front entry. This is reached from the side, producing a hybrid between the symmetrical, no-front-entry and the symmetrical, with-front-entry subtypes of the style.

2135 Eighth Street (private), Fonda House, 1901. This is a creative example of an early Colonial Revival design in the hipped-roof-with-full-width-porch subtype. The porch features an unusual stone entry arch, a touch borrowed from the Richardsonian Romanesque style. Notice the elaborate broken-ogee pediment of the centered dormer, the recessed second-story porch, and the subtle sculptural chimney on the right side. The porch columns are replacements.

516 Mapleton Avenue (private), ca. 1905. This is a pleasantly simple example of an early gambrel-roofed Colonial Revival design. Such front-facing gambrels were mostly built from about 1900 to 1915. Note the notched brickwork on the corners of the bay window.

534 and 550 Mapleton Avenue (both private), ca. 1895 and Mitchell House, 1908. This side-by-side pair demonstrates the two most typical house styles on Mapleton Hill—one-story Queen Anne cottages like 534 and two-story Colonial Revival designs in the hipped-roof-with-full-width-porch subtype as at 550. Some of the Queen Anne cottages have hipped roofs with lower cross gables, as at 534, while many others are front-gabled examples. Almost all of them have Free Classic decorative detailing.

604 Mapleton Avenue (private), Eastman House, 1913; Arthur Saunders, Boulder, architect. Like 535 Mapleton Avenue (see page 286), this is an excellent example of a pre-1915 Tudor house. These houses often have front porches with heavy, squared supports borrowed from the contemporaneous Prairie style and also tend toward a slightly stilted, somewhat-boxy look. Two front-facing gables are arranged symmetrically, a form frequently found in pre-1915 examples and rarely in later examples. This house is handsomely detailed with sandstone Tudor arches at the porch entry, above the front door, and over the porte cochere. Crenellations appear over the front-porch entry.

920, 928, and 930 Mapleton Avenue (all private). This is a pleasant row of three Free Classic Queen Anne cottages.

1020 Mapleton Avenue (private), McInnes House, 1905; William Redding and Son, architect/author of plan book design. Banker John McInnes had determined to build his dream house before he was married, and he was in his fifties before he simultaneously completed both goals. His grand Neoclassical landmark home was sometimes called

Mapleton Hill

Mapleton Hill

ends; and the heavy sandstone porch supports (on the left side) that appear to pierce the roof to form the corners of the balustrade above. Nearby at 1014 Mapleton Avenue (private) is a fine front-gabled Shingle design in which the shingled wall of the front-facing gable curves into a recessed bay window. On the left rear facade, one can glimpse a tower porch that seems to grow out of the main body of the house. Both houses have stone first floors with shingled walls above.

607 Mapleton Avenue (private), ca. 1940. A pleasant Minimal Traditional design, this has the style's characteristic close eaves; low-pitched, front-facing gable; and stone chimney. This example adds a section of stone to the front facade and features one of the small octagonal windows that were popular on several styles built from about 1935 to 1955 (circular versions were also common).

545 Mapleton Avenue (private), ca. 1960. This is a typical gabled-roof Contemporary-style house. Note the low roof pitch and wide eave overhang. The front windows that extend right up through the gable to the roof indicate that the rooms inside have pitched ceilings and that the house was probably built after 1950.

535 Mapleton Avenue (private), ca. 1910. This fine early Tudor design has a wide front porch with heavy, squared roof supports borrowed from the contemporaneous Prairie style and widely overhanging open eaves of Craftsman-style inspiration. Like 604 Mapleton Avenue (see page 285), it has the slightly stilted, boxy look common in pre-1915 examples of the style.

Harbeck-Bergheim House, 1900

1206 Euclid Avenue; 303-449-3464.

Two-story cube-shaped houses were so popular early in the twentieth century that they have been given the special name "American four-squares." Varying kinds of stylistic detailing were usually added to the basic four-square form, and the term is thus best used to describe the *shape* rather than the *style* of such houses. Whatever their style, very few four-squares have so far become museum houses, and thus the Harbeck-Bergheim House, an upscale but only slightly enlarged version of this house form, offers a rare opportunity to visit what is locally called a Denver Square (see also page 304).

Typical four-square features seen on the front facade of the house are the pyramid-shaped hipped roof, the centered hipped dormer, and the entry to one side rather than into a central hallway. Instead of the more usual full-width front porch, however, the architect chose to put a smaller entry porch on the right side balanced by a two-story bay window on the left. The window added space and light to the rooms behind. The entry porch has typical early Colonial Revival detailing. The front door is overwide and divided into separately opening upper and lower halves. This was a relatively unusual Colonial Revival detail inspired by early Dutch Colonial houses in New York's Hudson River region.

Inside, the Harbeck-Bergheim is not a typical house museum, but rather an essentially unmodified dwelling

the Wedding Cake House to commemorate his success. It is an elaborate and highly unusual design that takes the full-height-entry-porch-with-lower-full-width-porch subtype and goes it one better by adding a second full porch on the upper story. The two-story columns have Corinthian capitals, while their one-story neighbors are crowned with exaggerated Ionic capitals. Note the columned porte cochere, the highly elaborated cornices, and the beautiful original entry with double doors and beveled-glass surround.

1040 Mapleton Avenue (private), Giffin House, 1891. This, the largest of several Shingle-style houses in Mapleton Hill, features low, understated hipped roofs—unusual for a style in which hipped roofs are normally tall and accented with lower cross gables. Notice how the shingles have been applied to form a subtle horizontal pattern; the very unusual way that the open eaves have pieces of wooden trim applied at their edges to mimic exposed rafter

Harbeck-Bergheim House

used to display the collections of the Boulder Museum of History. The museum's curators have been careful to install their exhibits in such a way that the house's basic plan, original woodwork, fittings, and built-ins can still be admired. Interiors of American four-square houses were most commonly based around either Colonial Revival or Prairie-Craftsman detailing. As the exterior suggests, the handsome interior detailing here is Colonial Revival in derivation and has been well preserved.

You enter into a large living hall complete with fireplace and a particularly large and elaborate stairway—this is the 1900 to 1915 Edwardian version of a favorite late-Victorian room. The woodwork is a very light, almost-blond, version of the popular golden-oak interiors of the period. The focal fireplace is surrounded by Italian tile; there is a built-in seat beneath the stairs; and a dramatic stained-glass window with a design of leaves and flowers is at the stair landing. The living room is to the left through double pocket doors. Here is a second fireplace and the large bay window designed to enlarge the room and add light.

The dining room is directly behind and also features a large bay window. Quite typical of the period is the large built-in buffet in the same original blond-wood finish. Now comes the modification to the typical American four-square, for the kitchen would ordinarily be located in the quadrant of the house just behind the entry hall. Instead, this house plan adds a fifth room behind the dining room for the kitchen, and two small rooms, now used as office space, in the area that would typically be occupied by a kitchen.

Upstairs, the plan is much the same. The area over the entry hall was used as a sitting room; the master bedroom is over the living room; another large bedroom is over the dining room; another bedroom is over the kitchen and the identical small rooms in the right-rear corner where ordinarily the fourth bedroom would be. Note the original floor tile and accessories in the upstairs bathroom.

The house was built for H. Harbeck, a New York City stockbroker and chain-store owner, and his wife, Katherine Ardell Hammell Harbeck, for use as a summer home. After Mr. Harbeck died in 1910, his wife did not return, and the house was left essentially vacant for over twenty years. Local merchant Milton Bergheim purchased the house in 1939 and in 1969 sold it to the city of Boulder for permanent preservation as a museum.

COLORADO SPRINGS

FOUNDED 1859

Population Growth:

1860 ....NA

1900 21,000

1940 37,000

1990 281,000

Colorado Springs was not founded for any of the usual reasons—transportation junction or center of industry, trade, government, or education. Instead, it was one of those rare towns designed from the beginning solely to provide escape from life's everyday cares—an elegant pleasure resort. Like industrial Pueblo thirty-five miles to the south (see page 323), Colorado Springs was the creation of the visionary railroad builder William Jackson Palmer (1836–1909); the town was to become the treasured crown jewel of his hard-won railroad empire (see also "Glen Eyrie," page 292).

Palmer first learned railroading when, as a talented young Philadelphia Quaker, he served as personal secretary to the president of the pioneering Pennsylvania

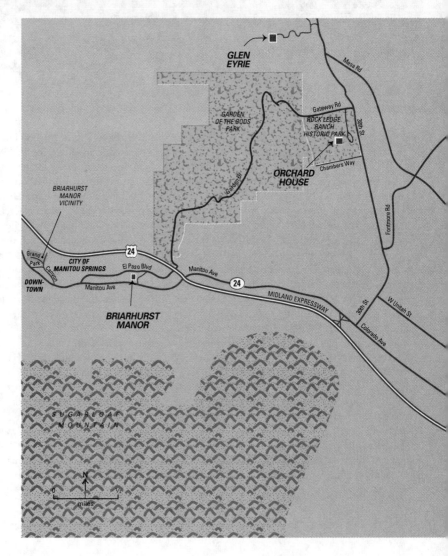

Railroad from 1858 to 1861. With the outbreak of the Civil War, Palmer, in spite of his pacifist Quaker background, decided to serve the Union cause by organizing the Fifteenth Pennsylvania Cavalry Regiment. With many of his aristocratic young friends as junior officers, Palmer led the unit to a distinguished battle record and ended the war as a twenty-nine-year-old brigadier general. He was later awarded the Congressional Medal of Honor for his wartime valor.

After the war, Palmer became treasurer of the recently organized Kansas Pacific Railroad and embarked on a new career in western railroad building that was to occupy the rest of his long life. Hoping ultimately to link Kansas City with distant California, he personally surveyed the new railroad's route across the plains to Denver, then southward through Colorado and across

Raton Pass to cross northern New Mexico and Arizona en route to San Francisco. With Palmer supervising construction, the Kansas Pacific reached Denver in 1870, but the line's organizers lacked the funds to proceed any farther. Instead, Denver backers built a short connecting line northward to link the city with the Union Pacific's newly completed transcontinental tracks at Cheyenne, Wyoming.

Still convinced of the importance of a rail line connecting southern Colorado with the Southwest and Mexico, Palmer now boldly organized his own Denver and Rio Grande Railroad to accomplish this goal. One seemingly insurmountable obstacle stood in his way. Both the Union Pacific's and Kansas Pacific's construction had been largely financed by mortgaging vast tracts of land granted to them by the federal government along their routes through the unsettled West. This policy was by now receiving criticism as an overly generous giveaway of federal lands. As a result, no such subsidy would be available to finance Palmer's dream.

With characteristic ingenuity, he came up with an alternate plan. In the cattle-boom years of the late 1860s, much of the West's best rangeland near the base of the Rockies had been acquired, for pennies an acre, by wealthy British investors seeking new rangelands on which to expand Britain's traditional cattle industry. Palmer's proposed railroad would dramatically increase the value of some of this land, so why not seek financing from the overseas investors who would profit most from its construction?

Realizing that he might need an additional "hook" to convince aristocratic absentee landlords of the long-term development potential of this remote corner of the frontier West, Palmer and his advisers came up with another bold plan. Why not create a European-style resort and spa at the base of picturesque Pikes Peak, where nearby mineral springs and dramatic mountain scenery could provide a wealth of exotic diversions for the idle rich. The plan worked beyond all expectations. Palmer's "Colorado Springs," with wide boulevards, public parks, and Pikes Peak views, was platted in 1871 adjacent to a small, and by then mostly abandoned, 1859 mining supply center named Colorado City. By the mid-1880s Palmer's new resort town counted two thousand Englishmen among its seven thousand or so residents and was jokingly known as Little London.

Some of these did indeed help finance Palmer's railroad dream, which, frustrated by the competing Atchison, Topeka, and Santa Fe, never reached Mexico or California but did become a very profitable narrow-gauge line serving the expanding mining centers of western Colorado and adjacent Utah (see also page 323). As the aristocratic Palmer prophetically expressed

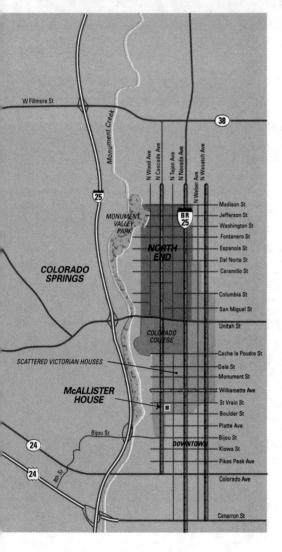

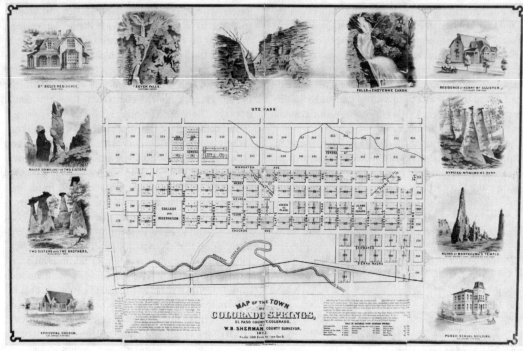

Plan of Colorado Springs, 1874; note the illustrations, in the upper corners, of the McAllister House and Briarhurst Manor ("Dr. Bell's Residence").

it in 1869, "how fine it would be to have a little railroad a few hundred miles in length, all under one's own control with one's friends, to have no jealousies and contests and differences, but be able to carry out harmoniously one's view of what ought and ought not to be done."

By the 1890s Colorado Springs's upper-class Britons were being joined by a more local group of wealthy pleasure seekers. In 1891 an enormous, and previously overlooked, gold discovery was made near the small mountain ranching center of Cripple Creek, located on the opposite side of Pikes Peak only thirty miles west of Colorado Springs.

By the first decades of the twentieth century, Colorado Springs was losing some of its upscale image as it became a favorite vacation, summer home, and retirement site for middle-class midwesterners, many of them attracted by Palmer's Quaker insistence on deed restrictions prohibiting the manufacture and sale of alcoholic beverages. Colorado Springs still maintained much of this resort-town character until the 1950s, when it began an exponential growth, based in part on new light manufacturing, which has today made it one of the nation's fastest-growing urban centers.

As is usual in such cases, much of the town's Victorian architectural heritage has disappeared, although scattered grand houses, usually now adapted for commercial or apartment use, occur around the central business district. Good places to find these are along Weber Avenue from the 400 through the 1600 block; along Wasatch Avenue from the 400 through the 1300 block; in the blocks of Cascade Avenue, Nevada Avenue, and Tejon Avenue just south of Colorado College; and on the many cross streets that run between these avenues. More improbably, the town and its nearby sister city of Manitou Springs have four important early dwellings, all now open to the public, each of which is directly related to General Palmer, the town's visionary founder and longtime patron. In addition, an early-twentieth-century neighborhood retains many fine Eclectic-era houses.

McAllister House, 1873

423 North Cascade Avenue; 719-635-7925;
George Summers, Colorado Springs, architect.

This remarkable survivor was one of the first permanent dwellings built in Palmer's new resort town of Colorado Springs. Throughout his post–Civil War career, the former Union cavalry general often called on his loyal wartime field commanders when he needed a difficult task performed by someone he could trust. To handle the on-site responsibilities of promoting and building Colorado Springs, the centerpiece of his new railroad empire, he chose one of his closest wartime associates, Major Henry McAllister (1836–1921).

McAllister was born in Kent County, Delaware, on September 14, 1836—exactly the same state, county, year, and month as Palmer himself. The two men were both Quakers, and both moved to Philadelphia when young; nonetheless they apparently didn't meet until 1862, when Henry joined Palmer's carefully picked troop of young Philadelphians who led the Fifteenth Pennsylvania Cavalry Regiment. From that moment until their deaths, the two were fast friends. After the war, Henry and his wife, Elizabeth Cooper McAllister (1836–1912), were delighted when Palmer asked them to move west to build his dream resort town.

The major's first job on arrival was to supervise the planting of five thousand irrigated cottonwood trees to help soften the dusty plains landscape of the barren town site. Next, McAllister hired the Denver and Rio Grande's architect, George Summers, to design his and Elizabeth's home. It was the first brick dwelling in Colorado Springs and was intended to set a high standard for the quality of construction expected in the new town. To help ensure this, Summers's architectural services were offered free to all Colorado Springs homebuilders.

The McAllisters built an elegant Gothic Revival cottage with an uncommon hip-on-gable roof that may have been inspired by a similar design in George E. Woodward's 1865 pattern book *Country Homes*. While the house was under construction, one of the region's periodic chinook winds swept down from the adjacent mountains with such fury that it overturned a Denver and Rio Grande train. The major, concerned for his family's future welfare, had the walls reinforced with an extra layer of brick and with steel rods to tie the roof more securely to the massive walls.

Inside, the house is finished with notch-and-knob-patterned moldings in both the living room and stairway. This decorative work was done by a talented and eccentric local carpenter, Winfield Scott Stratton (1848–1902), who was later to become the first multimillionaire in the nearby Cripple Creek goldfields.

Elizabeth McAllister did all of the housework and cooking for the major and their family of three children. Originally, the kitchen was separate from the main house, but soon after construction a new kitchen wing was added. The large lot around the house had fruit and vegetable gardens whose excess produce Elizabeth preserved for the long Colorado winter. Most of the original lot has long been sold and the gardens gone, but the apple tree in the backyard was planted by the McAllisters.

After the major died in 1921, the home became rental property until 1958, when it was sold for a parking lot. This caused community concern over the threatened loss of the historic structure, and in 1961 the National Society of the Colonial Dames of America

McAllister House

in the State of Colorado acquired the house, restored it to the period of its first ten years of occupancy, and has since operated it as a museum house. A number of family furnishings and household items are in the home, either left through the rental period or tracked down during the restoration. A visit takes one back to the very beginnings of Colorado Springs and clearly demonstrates the refined lifestyles of some of its earliest residents.

North End, 1890–1920

Early Colorado Springs's most elegant residential district was located to the north of the downtown commercial district along wide north–south streets and boulevards lined with stately trees and lush landscaping. Many have an unusual pattern of street tree planting; rather than the typical location between sidewalk and curb, the trees instead line the house side of the sidewalk, which makes the wide streets appear to be even broader. By the 1890s the lots north of the original town site, which centered around the McAllister House (see page 290), were becoming filled, and the town's broad streets were extended farther northward into a new North End development, whose fine turn-of-the-century houses remain largely intact today. This district also retains many early ornamental fences, including a good cross section of the iron fences produced by a local foundry called the Hassell Iron Works. Look also for stone foundations and porch supports that were readily available from nearby quarries. Colonial Revival houses are very popular in the North End, perhaps reflecting the tastes of the many easterners who built summer and retirement homes here during the early twentieth century. Permanent residents included many who made fortunes from the nearby Cripple Creek gold bonanza, which lasted from about 1892 to 1915, as well as those who had become wealthy as a result of Colorado Springs's increasing popularity as a health resort and center for summer tourism.

1228 Wood Avenue (private), ca. 1910. This handsomely detailed Italian Renaissance house belongs in the hipped-roof-with-projecting-wings subtype. It features two small wings at either end of the facade with a recessed central block in between. Rather than the triple arches most commonly seen on recessed porches in the style, this has quintuple arches. Four different kinds of elegantly detailed windows grace the front facade. The side wings have tall arched windows downstairs and triangular pedimented windows with balconets upstairs. The recessed central block has shorter arched windows with diamond-pattern glass on the first floor; the upstairs windows have the same attractive pattern in their upper sashes. Note the imposing pair of front doors.

1922 North Cascade Avenue (private), ca. 1905. This hipped-roof, shingle-walled early Colonial Revival design

North End

has a simple entry porch and a full Adamesque doorway with elliptical fanlight and sidelights. Despite the absence of a full-width porch, the prominent roofline balustrade above both the entry porch *and* the bay windows on each side gives the feeling of having one.

1230 North Cascade Avenue (private), ca. 1905. Another of the North End's many early Colonial Revival houses, this is more highly decorated than 1922 North Cascade (see the preceding entry). Note the gabled dormers with arched windows located not only on the front but also on the side roofs. The cornice has a solid line of floral swags, and on the soffit above are closely spaced flat pieces of wood that resemble a row of greatly elongated dentils. The side facade, easily visible from the side street, has similarly stretched-out, flat headings above the windows and a single oval window for accent. There is a full-width porch, which places this in the hipped-roof-with-full-width-porch subtype of the style. The width of the house and the prominent centered front door indicate that this likely had a center-hall interior plan, rather than the American four-square plan that is very common in this subtype. The porch has paired columns, a railing of very closely spaced and simple balusters, and a picket fence out front, which combine to create a thoroughly New England feeling.

Glen Eyrie, 1904

3820 North Thirtieth Street; 719-634-0808, 719-574-2285, or 719-598-1212; Frederick J. Sterner, Denver, architect.

Railroad builder and former Civil War general William Jackson Palmer (see page 288) first visited the Pikes Peak area in July 1869 while surveying the route for his new Denver and Rio Grande line and was immediately entranced by the region's spectacular scenery. The thirty-two-year-old bachelor was probably then in an especially romantic frame of mind, having become engaged only a few months earlier to nineteen-year-old Mary Lincoln "Queen" Mellen (1850–1894), the precociously elegant and cultured daughter of a prominent New York City attorney. Before their marriage the following year, Palmer chose what he considered to be the most beautiful place in his entire ten thousand acres of holdings in the Pikes Peak area as their new homesite, a secluded thousand-acre Garden of the Gods glade that he called Glen Eyrie. This was to be the busy general's beloved home base for the rest of his life.

Palmer's young bride was less enthusiastic about her new home. When she arrived in 1871, both his nearby resort town and his finances were still in an embryonic state. He could afford only a large but simple wooden house at Glen Eyrie where Queen, accustomed to a more luxuriously urbane lifestyle, rarely stayed for long. In 1880 she suffered a mild heart attack and her doctors advised a permanent move to a lower altitude. The couple chose to raise their three small daughters in England, which Palmer frequently visited on business trips. When at Glen Eyrie he led a lonely bachelor's life in his idyllic glade. Palmer's second chance for family happiness began in 1894, when Queen died prematurely at age forty-four, and their three English-reared daughters, now ages twenty-two, fourteen, and thirteen, joined him in a by now much improved Glen Eyrie and Colorado Springs.

With his lively daughters around, the somewhat-reclusive Palmer became more outgoing and began to have parties. In 1901 he sold his interest in one of his railroads, the Rio Grande Western, for $6 million. Now, at age sixty-five, Palmer suddenly found himself with the time, the money, the family, and the inclination to replace his much modified earlier Glen Eyrie with one of the grandest houses west of the Mississippi. Planning for the massive undertaking began almost immediately, and in 1904 to 1905, Palmer and his daughters cruised the Mediterranean and toured Europe, while at home their parapeted Tudor dream castle was being built—large and romantic, with Gothic Revival undertones that must have come from his years of visiting Britain and of staying in his suite at the Bells' lovely Briarhurst (see page 295) and from visits to his good friend Major McAllister's Gothic Revival cottage (see page 290).

Architect Sterner "hired platoons of decorators and sent them abroad to gather ornamental stone for fireplaces. . . . [A] one-ton silver-alloyed bell to hang in the top of the four-story crenelated stone tower . . . was cast in Germany." Sixty-seven rooms, hidden from the main road, were constructed. A book hall was in an enormous wing, twenty-five feet tall and large enough to seat three hundred people. Billiards and a bowling alley filled the basement.

The house was sold by Palmer's heirs in 1916, and since the 1950s the estate has been owned by the Navigators, a nondenominational religious training group. Often the grounds are open for a car tour, and the house is also opened regularly to visitors. Tours are by

Glen Eyrie

reservation only, and since we were not there on the correct day, we cannot comment on the interior other than to say that it should be of great interest to the house watcher, as are the vast grounds and the richly detailed exterior of the remarkable dwelling.

Orchard House, 1907

Rock Ledge Ranch Historic Park, east entrance of Garden of the Gods Park, off of Thirtieth Street; 719-578-6640 or 719-578-6777; MacLaren and Thomas, Colorado Springs, architects.

In 1900 Colorado Springs founder William Jackson Palmer bought this 160-acre ranch near his Glen Eyrie estate (see the preceding entry) in order to ensure that it remained open space rather than eventually becoming a housing subdivision. Retaining the earlier ranch house and outbuildings, in 1907 Palmer added a new Mission-style dwelling at the south end of the tract as a home for his sister-in-law Charlotte Sclater and her ornithologist husband, William Sclater, who had recently moved to Colorado Springs from his native South Africa. Now called Orchard House, this is open to the public as a part of a living history park that interprets the three different eras of the ranch's settlement.

The initial Homestead Era (1867 to 1874) is represented by a reconstructed cabin and an impressive demonstration garden irrigated by Camp Creek, the stream that made this a desirable homestead site for pi-oneer Walter Galloway. The second period, or Working Ranch Era (1874–1900), is interpreted through the original on-site Folk Victorian house of the Chambers family. During these years the family kept a dairy herd, raised specialty produce for the town's elegant Antlers Hotel, and kept boarders who were in the area to recuperate from illnesses. The house is unfurnished and features recorded messages and displays.

The final Estate Era begins when the Chambers family sold the ranch to Palmer in 1900 and is interpreted by tours through the Mission-style Orchard House, which has slightly more flamboyantly shaped parapeted gables than are usual on Mission-style houses, in order to mimic Flemish gables of Dutch South Africa. They may have been used by the architects to make the Sclaters feel more at home. Despite the gesture, they moved to England in 1909 after General Palmer's death. Sclater wasn't idle during his two-year residency. In 1912 his classic book *A History of the Birds of Colorado* was published in London. The ranch was sold with Palmer's Glen Eyrie in 1916 and went through a series of owners until it was purchased by the city of Colorado Springs for its current use. None of the original Orchard House furnishings survived, but it now has appropriate period pieces. During restoration in the early 1990s the original paint colors were matched. In the spirit of the park's living-history theme, much of the house's interpretive emphasis is on the lifestyle of the Sclaters.

Orchard House

Manitou Springs, 1880–1900

Despite its name, Palmer's open-plains town site for Colorado Springs was in fact almost completely devoid of springs. For these, one had to go several miles into the nearby mountain foothills, where a number of natural mineral springs bubbled out of the ground. These had long been used as a healing oasis by the area's Indian tribes. The first Anglo settlers called the site Soda Springs until 1871, when William Blakemore, one of the English financiers who invested heavily in Palmer's new railroad and land development ventures, visited Soda Springs. Blakemore saw Ute Indians sitting nearby and, having recently read Longfellow's *Hiawatha,* promptly christened the area Manitou Springs after the poem's Algonquin Indian spirit.

With this poetic name, the area's healing qualities were soon being publicized by another newly arrived Englishman, this one a physician named Dr. Samuel Edwin Solly. In 1875 Solly published a booklet entitled *Manitou, Colorado, Its Mineral Waters and Climate* that helpfully explained for visitors the potential healing powers of the various waters. In the same year Helen Hunt Jackson, whom Ralph Waldo Emerson once called the "greatest poet in America," came to Manitou for a cure, married a fellow patient, and stayed on for

several years writing articles, poems, and books that informed her millions of readers about the virtues of the Manitou Springs. Soon the town was a bustling center for tourism and "taking the waters."

Still a favorite tourist destination, modern Manitou Springs retains a number of Victorian buildings, many of which have been unsympathetically modified over the years. One of its first grand dwellings survives relatively intact through adaptive reuse as a restaurant (see the following entry), while a handful of nearby houses, and the town's still-compact downtown, provide some feeling for its early years as an elegant European-style spa.

Briarhurst Manor, 1888

404 Manitou Avenue (restaurant, 719-685-1864); Frederick J. Sterner, Denver, architect.

General Palmer had two principal associates in developing early Colorado Springs. One was his former Civil War cavalry comrade, Major Henry McAllister (see page 290), who, like Palmer himself, was a no-nonsense organizer of military-style efficiency. Palmer's other partner in building his new town and railroad had just the opposite personality.

Dr. William A. Bell (1840–1921), the builder of Briarhurst, was the charismatic and adventuresome son of

Briarhurst Manor

an aristocratic English physician. Shortly after completing his own primary medical training, young Bell crossed the Atlantic to attend a series of professional lectures in St. Louis, Missouri. The year was 1867, and the local newspapers were filled with reports that field surveys for the new Kansas Pacific Railroad were about to commence. Rather than return to England, Bell applied for a job as physician on the survey party. Informed that the only unfilled position was that of photographer, he took a crash course in the subject and was hired.

General Palmer was the survey's director, and the two men soon developed a mutually beneficial friendship that was to become lifelong. It was through Bell and his family that Palmer met many of the influential British investors that helped finance his grand vision. Bell, himself a physician familiar with European spas, convinced Palmer of the resort potential of Manitou Springs and promoted it tirelessly during the "Little London" period of the area's development.

In 1872 Bell and his new English bride, the lively and outgoing Cora Georgina Whitemore Scovell Bell (died 1938), built the first Gothic Revival Briarhurst on this site. It was soon the bustling social center of the local British colony. When their home was severely damaged by fire in the 1880s, the Bells immediately replaced it with a much expanded version, using some of the same foundations. They retained the style of the earlier structure, which explains the somewhat-late date for this picturesque Gothic Revival home built of soft peach-colored stone.

Lovely carved vergeboards and decorative chimney pots are used here with great abandon. The peak of the roof is accentuated with terra-cotta cresting and gargoyles at the gable peaks. There is a double entryway in which a stone Gothic arch leads into a small anteroom, where the handsome Tudor-arched main doorway is revealed. Inside, several of the downstairs rooms still have their original Gothic detailing. Upstairs, fewer of the original finishes survive. The house is now quite large, for a later rear addition was built specifically for General Palmer with its own separate entrance. When he rode over from Glen Eyrie, he used this as his office and residence while in Manitou.

Briarhurst Manor is now an upscale restaurant with visitations limited to dinner guests.

Nearby Houses

Grand Avenue, a short hillside street near central Manitou Springs, retains several fine turn-of-the-century dwellings.

2 Grand Avenue (private), ca. 1905. This late Queen Anne design has a stone tower with a bell-shaped roof and entrance steps that face diagonally toward the corner. It appears to have had major additions.

26 Grand Avenue (private), ca. 1895. This fine front-gabled Shingle-style house has a gable ornamented with two shallow pent roofs, two layers of recessed windows with shingles curving into them, and a change in shingle pattern to each side. The balcony porch on the right has huge scalloped brackets beneath and looks as if it was originally designed without additional supports. Asymmetry is accentuated by the fat, rounded oriel window squeezed into the right upper story.

32 Grand Avenue (private), ca. 1895. This rare example of the Exotic Revival's Swiss-chalet style is just barely visible from the street. Note the varying shingle surfaces, the stylized vine incised into the middle section of the vertical stickwork, and the wide overhanging open eaves. The triangular braces underneath the eave have a leaf shape cut out of them. The garage at street level is likely later, but has been matched to the house style.

DENVER

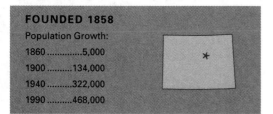

FOUNDED 1858

Population Growth:

1860 5,000
1900 134,000
1940 322,000
1990 468,000

Denver was the focus of the West's second great gold rush, which took place in 1858, almost exactly ten years after the Sutter's Mill discovery drew the hordes of forty-niners to the California goldfields (see page xx). Reports of gold-bearing sands along Cherry Creek, a small tributary of the South Platte River at the base of the Colorado Rockies, set off an almost equally frantic rush of "fifty-niners" across the Kansas and Nebraska plains to the small mining camp of Denver. Their rallying cry of "Pikes Peak or Bust," as historian Rodman Paul has wryly noted, "was as inaccurate as to geography as it was correct in the alternative it offered." The Denver area's deposits of stream-gravel gold proved to

be heartbreakingly small, and a great many of the arrivers returned home with nothing but empty pocketbooks to show for their efforts.

Within a few months, however, more promising gold discoveries began to be made in the rugged mountains to the west of Denver (see page 315). As a wagon-road junction situated on the accessible open plains at the foot of the precipitous Rockies, Denver was ideally located to become the principal supply center for these new mountain mines. Soon an endless stream of "bull trains" was bringing massive loads of wagon-borne freight across the plains to the warehouses of Denver merchants that served the burgeoning mining camps.

Of the very small handful of early western mining camps destined for permanent prosperity, Denver became the absolute grand champion. Two years after its 1858 founding, the town's five thousand inhabitants made it the second-largest urban center in the western interior, exceeded in size only by long-settled Salt Lake City. In 1867 it became the permanent capital of the Colorado Territory and, when two competing railroad

Ox-drawn freight wagons dominated downtown Denver in the 1860s; the trees in the distance are along the South Platte River.

lines arrived in 1870 to replace the bull trains, Denver's position as the Queen City of the mountains and plains was assured.

Victorian Boomtown

As in Montana, whose gold and silver boom years closely resemble those of Colorado (see page 382), arrival of the railroads brought a dramatic increase in the state's mining prosperity. Gold is commonly found as a pure metal—either in stream sands and gravels, where it is rather easily separated from the lighter particles by moving water, or in massive quartz veins, where it can be directly extracted by mining, crushing, and chemical processing. Silver production is an entirely different matter.

Many gold-bearing regions also have deposits of silver, which, unlike gold, only rarely occurs as a free metal. Instead, silver is found combined with other elements—typically lead, copper, zinc, carbon, oxygen, or sulfur—in chemically complex ore minerals. These require not only mining, crushing, and chemical processing, as does quartz-vein gold, but also complex smelting operations that melt the processed ores to separate the silver from the less valuable "base metal" companions. Such large-scale mining and processing require massive machinery that was very difficult and costly to transport in the era of ox-wagon freighting. The newly arrived railroads could not only deliver such bulky equipment, but also made possible the rapid movement of large quantities of ore from mines to distant mills and smelters. As a result, the railroads brought Denver, and its mountain hinterland, an unprecedented twenty-year silver boom as the previously intractable ores yielded their precious treasure. Already an important market and trade center when the railroads arrived in 1870, Denver had a sevenfold increase in population, to 36,000 by 1880, and another surge to 107,000 by 1890, making it second in size only to San Francisco in the entire trans-Mississippi West.

Denver's phenomenal early growth was also rooted in a peculiarity of Colorado's rail network. The mainline railroads that connected the city with Omaha, Kansas City, and the factories of the eastern states had tracks laid four and a half feet apart, the standard gauge that was by then almost universal in the eastern rail network. Railroads traversing the narrow valleys and canyons of Colorado's rugged mountains, on the other hand, required narrow-gauge tracks, spaced only three feet apart. This meant that all long-distance rail cargo going into or out of the mountains required reloading into the appropriate railcars in Denver.

Beginning in the early 1870s, a vast spiderweb of narrow-gauge mountain rail lines converged on Denver from the flourishing mining districts. At first these mostly carried machinery, lumber, hardware, food, and other necessities from Denver's proliferating warehouses to the mining camps. Large return cargoes began in 1878, when a massive smelter was completed on Denver's north side. By 1890 two additional smelters plus numerous foundries, machine works, flour mills, and breweries had added a large industrial component to the city's marketing-based prosperity.

Economic Diversification

The great silver boom in the mining states of the West came to an abrupt end in 1893, when a collapse in world silver prices led to a worldwide recession. Colorado's economy fared better than most, however, because of an enormous 1891 gold discovery made about one hundred miles to the south at Cripple Creek, located in a mountain valley just behind Pikes Peak (see page 290).

As the Cripple Creek gold bonanza faded in the first decades of the twentieth century, Denver's importance as a center of regional agriculture was increasing. Large-scale irrigation projects dammed mountain streams and conveyed the water in artificial channels to the fertile but arid soils of the foothills and plains. At the same time, new techniques of dryland farming were yielding abundant harvests of grain in parts of Colorado's eastern plains, much of which was sent to Denver for milling and distribution over its massive rail network. Finally, the development of refrigerated railroad cars revolutionized the western cattle industry, as shipment of live animals for local slaughter was replaced by vast centralized stockyards and packing plants, which shipped the far-less-bulky sides of dressed beef directly to urban wholesalers and retail butcher shops. Denver, surrounded on the east by vast ranchlands, became a principal center for this new meatpacking industry.

The City Beautiful

Real estate developer Robert Walter Speer (1855–1918), who served as Denver's mayor from 1904 until 1912 and again from 1916 until his death two years later, had attended the Chicago World's Columbian Exposition in 1893. Dazzled, as were so many, by its Neoclassical "Great White City" theme, Speer returned to the dark Victorian buildings and smoky industrial districts of his hometown and became a tireless advocate of the "City Beautiful" movement that was inspired by the exposition. When elected Denver's mayor in 1904, Speer immediately undertook an ambitious three-part campaign to beautify the city. This involved creating a large Neoclassical civic center; laying out a farsighted system of landscaped parkways and associ-

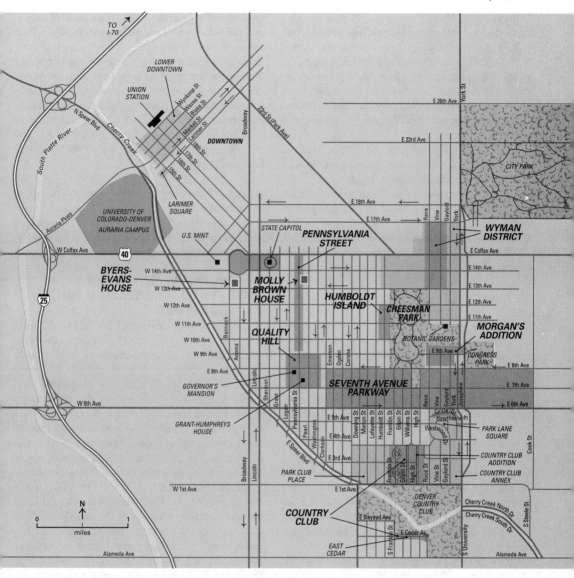

ated parks to accommodate the city's future growth; and acquiring large blocks of outlying acreage to create a mountain park system. Enough of these goals were eventually achieved to make Denver one of the West's best examples of visionary City Beautiful planning.

The most frequently encountered results of Speer's efforts are the city's remarkable number of neighborhoods that are centered around, and interconnected by, handsome "parkways"—divided roadways separated by a landscaped median strip. Among these are the Seventh Avenue Parkway (see page 308), Monaco Street Parkway, East Sixth Avenue Parkway, Speer Boulevard, Martin Luther King Jr. Boulevard, and East Seventeenth Avenue Parkway.

Many of Speer's plans were continued long after his death, a result he encouraged in one of his last speeches (quoted in Noel and Norgren, *Denver*, 1987):

Ugly things do not please. It is much easier to love a thing of beauty—and this applies to cities as well as persons and things. Fountains, statues, artistic lights, music, playgrounds, parks, etc., make people love the place in which they live. Every time a private citizen, by gift or otherwise, adds to a city's beauty, he kindles the spirit of pride in other citizens. One man truly proud of his city is worth a hundred well-meaning but indifferent persons.

Denver Since 1940

As it did for other large western cities, Washington's policy of decentralizing critical industries during World War II brought new, defense-related manufacturing to the Denver area. This period also saw the beginning of a policy to locate western branches of many federal agencies in Denver, a move that added a new regional dimension to its traditional role as the center of state government.

Since the 1950s Denver has chosen not to annex neighboring small towns as they have grown to become a part of its residential suburbs. For this reason, the city's relatively modest population increase in the last half of the twentieth century masks the fact that its metropolitan area had surged to a total of 1.6 million inhabitants by 1990. Perhaps because so much of the area's residential growth has taken place elsewhere, Denver retains one of the western interior's best assemblages of Victorian and Eclectic-era neighborhoods and houses; two of the latter are now important museum houses (see pages 301 and 304).

Contributing to the survival of so many early dwellings is the fact that Denver is almost exclusively a city of masonry houses, with brick far more common than stone. This is a combined result of the excellent brick clays that underlie the region (which mostly produce bricks of a deep-red or red-orange color), the expense of harvesting and shipping timber from the rugged Colorado mountains, and fireproof construction ordinances.

Greater Capitol Hill

In looking at Denver's historic neighborhoods, one frequently sees or hears the term "Capitol Hill" used to refer to what seem to be different parts of the eastern sections of the city. The original Capitol Hill neighborhood was a prestigious, upscale residential development located just to the south and east of the state capitol. It encompassed about eighty blocks and was roughly bounded by Broadway on the west, Downing Street on the east, Colfax Avenue on the north, and Seventh Avenue on the south. This Old Capitol Hill district is now dominated by later apartment buildings but also retains some of Denver's finest houses in its Quality Hill and Pennsylvania Street subdistricts (see the following entry).

Today the term "Capitol Hill" is also applied to a much larger area served by the Capitol Hill United Neighborhoods, an active neighborhood support group. This Greater Capitol Hill district is bounded by Broadway on the west, Colorado Boulevard on the east, Twentieth Avenue on the north, and Cherry Creek on the south. This definition encompasses something close to twelve square miles and includes all of the historic neighborhoods featured in the following sections. This entire area has intriguing houses, some within intact blocks, some in blocks shared with low-rise or even high-rise apartments, and some standing as lonely sentinels amid parking lots. Many are still single-family homes; others have been divided into apartments or converted into offices. The oldest houses, some of them built before the Silver Crash of 1893, are mostly near the capitol, and the houses get progressively younger as one travels eastward.

A constant traffic alert is strongly suggested while visiting these Denver neighborhoods. Many have narrow one-way streets along which high-speed traffic zooms, often quite unexpectedly, through what might otherwise appear to be a tranquil residential district.

Pennsylvania Street, ca. 1885–1910, and Quality Hill, ca. 1895–1920

Grant Street between about Eighth Avenue and Twelfth Street was Denver's Millionaire's Row during the Victorian era; most of its fine dwellings were razed throughout the twentieth century to provide sites for apartment buildings, some of which are now fascinating landmarks in their own right. Logan and Pennsylvania Streets, located immediately to the east of Grant Street, were almost as desirable addresses and have retained more of their original houses. Pennsylvania, in particular, provides the most intact Victorian streetscapes in Old Capitol Hill. Even so, it has many later intrusions.

Quality Hill, located just to the south of Old Capitol Hill, developed a bit later, mostly from about 1900 to 1910, and has superb Eclectic-era houses. Even in those early years, Old Capitol Hill residents were concerned about creeping intrusions into their neighborhood, and Quality Hill's lots were sold with deed restrictions that have helped to preserve its original houses.

The most effortless way to see this area, whose streets are very congested, is first to park and visit the Molly Brown House (see the following entry) and then drive slowly down Pennsylvania Street before parking again near its dead end in Governor's Park. From there, a short walk takes one by a number of Denver's finest early Eclectic-era houses. A more energetic plan, for those comfortable in slightly transitional urban areas, is to walk the five blocks from the Molly Brown House to Eighth Avenue and Governor's Park, which affords a more leisurely look at the dozen or so remaining Victorian houses scattered along Pennsylvania Street. If you choose this option, Logan Street provides an alternate return route.

Traffic travels very fast on the narrow east–west streets that you must cross on this route, and caution, whether walking or driving, is strongly advised.

Molly Brown House, 1889

1340 Pennsylvania Street; 303-832-4092;
William Lang, Denver, architect.

The Unsinkable Molly Brown of Broadway musical and Hollywood film fame was Denver's Margaret Tobin Brown (1867–1932), who, during her lifetime, was actually known as Maggie, never Molly. This minor discrepancy would not have bothered Maggie, who once told a friend, "I don't care what the newspapers say about me, just so they say something."

Maggie Tobin was born to Irish-immigrant parents in Hannibal, Missouri, where she grew up in a four-room cabin with her parents and her five siblings. Seeking new horizons, in 1886 nineteen-year-old Maggie moved west to live with her brother in Leadville, Colorado, then one of the West's hottest "get-rich-quick" mining towns. A few months after arriving, Maggie married a successful, but not yet wealthy, mining superintendent named James Joseph (J.J.) Brown (1854–1922). By 1892 J.J. had a share of the Ibex Mining Company, which obtained a seemingly-played-out mine called the Little Jonny. As superintendent, J.J. figured

out a way to stabilize and expand the Little Jonny and the following year hit a large vein of high-grade gold and copper ore. Soon he and Maggie had a comfortable fortune.

In 1894 the Browns moved to Denver and purchased this house on fashionable Pennsylvania Street. Built five years earlier for mining investor Isaac Large, it was a very "modern" home, with electricity, central heat, and hot and cold running water. Maggie immediately set about improving both the house and herself. She spent a semester at New York's Carnegie Institute studying languages, literature, and drama. She wore fashionable clothes and gave elaborate parties. Her reputation first soared with newspaper raves about her charities; later, as the press focused on family squabbles with J.J., she preferred extensive travels on the East Coast and in Europe, often with their two children in tow, while he preferred a quieter life in Denver.

Maggie and J.J. separated in 1909, and by 1910 she was holding court alone in the house on Pennsylvania Street. That year she gave a typical party at which guests could wander both inside and outdoors, and tents with Oriental carpets and live music added an exotic touch. Maggie had her house, complete with floral party decorations, photographed for this event, and it is to this

Molly Brown House

1910 period that the home has now been restored, using this remarkable series of photographs for reference.

Just two years later, fate made Maggie an international celebrity. Returning from Europe on the maiden voyage of the *Titanic* as it headed for its tragic encounter with an iceberg, she led her lifeboat companions in rowing clear of the sinking ship and then used her command of languages to work with immigrant survivors on the rescue ship. In addition, she raised a large sum of money to help destitute steerage passengers, most of them women and children whose husbands and fathers had gone down with the *Titanic*. On coming ashore, the legend is that she was asked how she had survived. "Typical Brown luck," she reportedly replied, "we're unsinkable."

Unfortunately, the rest of her life was not quite so charmed, and Maggie remained a controversial figure, entertaining the Newport and European social set with her wit and outspoken opinions, some of which brought on libel suits. She died in New York City in 1932, after which her house and its contents were sold and the dwelling began a long decline. In 1971 Historic Denver, Inc., was formed to purchase and restore the house, which today looks almost exactly as it did in 1910.

Constructed of multicolored, rusticated stone, the house was designed by the unusually creative architect William Lang (1846–1897), of whom art historian Richard Brettell has written:

> He was certainly the finest and most complex eclectic architect who worked in Denver and, though his work is not at all well-known, he may have been one of the best late eclectic architects in the United States (*Historic Denver*, 1973).

Few biographical details are known about Lang. He arrived in Denver in 1886, apparently after receiving some architectural training in Chicago, and over the next seven years designed more than 150 Denver buildings, most of them upper-middle-class houses of extraordinary originality. Lang left Denver in 1894, after the depression and Silver Crash of 1893 had halted new home construction in the city, and died in obscurity three years later.

Lang's designs were unique stylistic creations that typically mixed a cupful of Richardsonian Romanesque with heaping spoonfuls of two or more other styles—Queen Anne, Shingle, Colonial Revival, or just about anything else. The Molly Brown House is no exception. Here, Richardsonian rusticated stone walls and rounded upstairs arched windows are mixed with a typical Queen Anne shape and gable trim to which is

Pennsylvania Street

added a simple front porch that could easily grace a Shingle-style design.

Inside, the entry "living hall" still has the original Anaglypta (heavy pressed paper) wall covering, with Lincrusta Walton (similar in appearance but made of a more durable pressed linseed and fiber) on the stair dado. The original golden-oak stairway, mantel, and wainscoting still survive. The Turkish corner that Molly added has been restored. The formal parlor has Molly's original horsehair couch, and the library features many original bookcases that have recently been returned to the house. The dining room ceiling, originally painted to give the room a light and airy look by mimicking a glass conservatory overhead, has been restored. The stained glass in the dining room and on the stair landing is original; it was manufactured locally to Lang's specifications.

Upstairs, the stair hall doubled as a sunroom for restorative private rest during the day, when the beds weren't to be disturbed. Three of the bedrooms have fabric-covered walls, a practice Molly liked because these added warmth, insulation, and quiet. Outside, the small garden area is planted with Victorian favorites like hollyhocks and lilacs. The carriage house, which Molly had doubled in size so that she could keep her own team of horses, is now used for a gift shop and museum display.

Among the other fine houses along Pennsylvania Street and in nearby Quality Hill are:

1200 Pennsylvania Street (private), Dunning House, 1889; William Lang, Denver, architect. In this commanding design, architect Lang (see above) concentrated on his favorite style, the Richardsonian Romanesque with walls of rough-faced, square-cut gray stone laid in regular courses and a typical rounded tower. For variety, he added Tudoresque castellations (also called battlements or crenellations) around the top of the tower rather than the usual conical roof. The house has a number of other typical Richardsonian elaborations, such as the line of arched windows in the front gable, the deeply recessed windows, the stone transoms over the rectangular windows, the heavy post-and-lintel front porch, and the diaperwork balustrade above the porch.

1207 Pennsylvania Street (private), Keating House, 1891; Reiche, Carter, and Smith, Denver, architects. This Richardsonian Romanesque design makes a handsome pair with its across-the-street neighbor at 1200 Pennsylvania Street (see the preceding entry). It is of similar stone, but laid here in alternating narrow and wide courses. The tower has the more typical conical roof, and there is an inset balcony. The windows are not as deeply recessed as those of its neighbor. Both houses appear to have their original front doors.

428 Eleventh Avenue, at Pennsylvania Street (private), Croke-Patterson House, 1891; Isaac Hodgson, architect. Chateauesque houses, one of our most elegant domestic styles, are rare throughout the country and are particularly unusual in the western interior. This one has been converted to office use. Notice the corbeled corner turrets with their tall "candlesnuffer" roofs, the multiple wall dormers, and the gracefully arched front door.

945 Pennsylvania Street (private), Taylor House, 1900; David W. Dryden, architect. This is the type of rare experimental design from around 1900 that we informally call an Early Eclectic What's It? Denver has a number of good examples of these almost-indefinably-varied stylistic experiments. This one takes the shape of an American four-square, stretches it out, adds a Denver favorite through-the-cornice dormer and Craftsman open eaves with exposed rafters, and then encases almost everything with Romanesque arches—some with a bit of Sullivanesque detail.

450 Ninth Avenue, at Pennsylvania Street (private), Weckbaugh House, 1908. This symmetrical French Eclectic design was built for Mrs. Eugene Henry Weckbaugh by her father, John Kernan Mullen. Mrs. Weckbaugh must have been fond of French architecture, for, when building a later home for herself (see "1701 East Cedar Avenue," page 309), she chose to have an even larger and grander French prototype. This 1908 design is an outstanding and unusually early example of the French Eclectic style. Note the gabled wall dormer, the pair of small, arched roof dormers, and the lines of quoins enframing windows and doors. Beaux Arts influence is seen in the handsome metal entry canopy (unfortunately, at last visit missing the glass-paneled top) and

the elaborate decorative panels featuring various floral swagged designs. These are most likely made of terra-cotta.

Quality Hill: 770 Pennsylvania Street (house private; grounds open to the public), Grant-Humphreys House, 1902; Theodore Boal and Frederick Harnois, architects. This Neoclassical landmark, originally built for James B. Grant, a smelter tycoon and former Colorado governor, was purchased in 1917 by oilman Albert E. Humphreys. It was Humphreys's son, Ira, who donated the mansion and grounds to the Colorado Historical Society in 1976. Although at one time open for regular house tours, it is now used primarily for special events and must be admired while freely strolling through Humphreys Park. The park, formerly the grounds of the house, occupies almost a full city block and includes a handsome pergola with a Craftsman-influenced roof supported by Classical columns. Humphreys Park now merges into Governor's Park, which originally faced the house on the opposite side of Pennsylvania Street. The street was later closed and converted to park use.

The most notable feature of the Grant-Humphreys House is the extensive use of glazed terra-cotta trim in window surrounds, porch balusters, roof urns, chimney tops, corner pilasters, and even the full-height fluted columns. The row of three second-story windows with lion surrounds on the north side are great examples of the elaborate decorative detailing made possible with glazed terra-cotta.

Terra-cotta (Italian for "baked earth") is one of the oldest building materials in western architecture. Made of clay packed into decorative molds, it requires a higher grade of clay than brick and is fired at higher temperatures. In Renaissance Italy, a refinement of this process added an outer coating, or glazing, of special clays that fired into a very hard and durable glasslike surface. During the early twentieth century, glazed terra-cotta (called faience in England to distinguish it from the more common, unglazed type) became a very popular material for the surface ornamentation of commercial buildings. Usually custom designed and expensive, it was less commonly used on houses of that era.

Five principal terra-cotta companies supplied much of the country's demand for the material. One of these was the Denver Terra Cotta Company, which used fine clays found in the nearby Rocky Mountain foothills between Boulder and Golden. This firm was undoubtedly responsible for the unusual number of Denver houses that boast glazed terra-cotta ornamentation. The Grant-Humphreys House is among the most striking of these.

By the 1930s more simplified architectural styles and the perfection of cast-stone details (made by molding a mixture of cement, water, sand, and coloring materials) led to the decreasing use of both glazed and unglazed terra-cotta in buildings, and the Denver Terra Cotta Company ceased producing its handsome architectural details.

Quality Hill: 500 East Eighth Avenue (private), Malo House, ca. 1921. Attributed to both Harry Manning and J. J. B. Benedict as the architects (see page 309), this is an unusually formal Spanish Eclectic design and also includes some features from the contemporaneous Italian Renaissance style. Among these are the wide roof overhang with large modillions and the triple-arched recessed front door. Such high-style mixtures were often called Mediterranean designs by architects of the period. Note such Spanish details as the hand-painted tiles tucked just under the eaves, the wrought-iron upstairs balconets and window grilles, the

Quality Hill: Grant-Humphreys House

window in the chimney, and the detail applied over the middle entry arch.

Quality Hill: 777 Pearl Street (private), Porter House, 1917; Varian and Varian, Denver, architects. This understated parapeted Tudor house has a symmetrical facade, which is uncommon in this style. The brick walls are appropriately laid in English bond, with alternating rows of header and stretcher bricks. The roof and dormers are clad with flat shingle tiles.

Quality Hill: 555 East Eighth Avenue (private), ca. 1915. A large and highly elaborated version of the Denver Square, the local name for the brick-walled, four-square-shaped dwellings that dominate many of the city's early-twentieth-century neighborhoods. Here, the stylistic detailing suggests a hipped-roof-with-full-width-porch Colonial Revival house. But the porch is slightly rounded and not totally full width; many atypical features are present, among them the through-the-cornice dormer, elaborate glass-paneled canopy over the upstairs windows, and the horizontal lines around the lower story created by an inset course of brick. Don't miss the matching carriage house with the same horizontal brick detail and through-the-cornice dormer.

Quality Hill: 400 East Eighth Avenue (private), Colorado Governor's Mansion, 1908; Willis Marean and Albert Norton, Denver, architects. Originally built by the widow and daughter of Walter Scott Cheesman (see "Cheesman Park Neighborhoods," page 306), this Colonial Revival landmark was later the home of Claude and Edna Boettcher, who donated it to the state for use as the Governor's Mansion in 1958.

Quality Hill: Governor's Mansion

The house is an early and handsomely detailed example of the centered-gable Colonial Revival subtype. Even if one did not know the date of this house, it would be easy to guess that it was built before 1915 because of the slightly exaggerated quality of its details—such as the broken-ogee pediment over the upstairs center window, the heavy corner pilasters with exaggerated Ionic capitals, the cornice of dentils combined with very blocky modillions. The one-story entry porch has similarly heavy details. Note also the side portico with its colossal columns.

801 Logan Street (private), Sayre House, 1892; Franklin Kidder, Denver, architect. Hal Sayre, a respected surveyor and civil engineer, named his Exotic Revival house Alhambra. The ogee arches seen in several forms above the win-

dows of this house are the key identifying feature of the Oriental version of the style. This was most frequently built in the 1840s and 1850s with scattered examples persisting until about 1900. Sayre is reported to have been inspired to use Moorish detailing for his home after a trip to Morocco. He might also have seen such details in southern Spain, home of the house's namesake, which was built by Moors near Granada in the thirteenth and fourteenth centuries.

Byers-Evans House, 1883 and later

1310 Bannock Street; 303-620-4933.

This important Italianate landmark, located a few blocks southwest of the state capitol, is now on the edge of the city's expanded civic center and sits in the shadow of the starkly modern Denver Art Museum. Occupied successively by two of Denver's most enterprising and civic-minded pioneer families, the home is interesting less as a pure architectural monument than as a demonstration of the evolving lifestyles of the city's leaders from the 1880s through 1930s.

The house was built by William N. Byers (1831–1903), influential founder of the *Rocky Mountain News*, and his wife, Elizabeth Sumner Byers. The Byerses had come from Omaha in the first wave of fifty-niners, but, instead of bringing picks and shovels, their wagon contained a small, hand-operated, printing press with which they produced, only eight days after arriving, the region's first newspaper. Byers was to spend the rest of his long life as a tireless advocate for his adopted Colorado.

The couple apparently enjoyed changing homes, for they built and occupied a series of Denver dwellings over the years, of which this is the only survivor. In 1889, only six years after its completion, the Byerses sold the house to William G. Evans (1855–1924), the eldest son of another Colorado pioneer, their close friend Dr. John Evans (1814–1897). The new owners didn't share the Byerses' fondness for moving—William Evans and his children were to occupy the house for the next ninety-two years.

In 1924 the *Rocky Mountain News* said of William Evans: "he was not a politician in the customary sense . . . he was in politics because his inheritance and what he conceived to be his responsibilities required him to be a silent, patient, and resourceful player at the political chessboard." And indeed William's inheritance was a heady one, not so much in dollars but in the tradition of civic responsibility. His father, Dr. John Evans, was appointed by Abraham Lincoln as the second territorial governor of Colorado to provide guidance for the mineral-rich territory through the turmoil of the Civil War and the Indian Wars that accompanied and followed it.

Byers-Evans House

Known for the rest of his life simply as the Governor, the elder Evans had been a stellar citizen farther east before arriving in Colorado. He is best known as the founder, in 1851, of Northwestern University in Evanston, Illinois, a town named for his family. In addition, he helped organize railroads, taught at Rush Medical College in Chicago, promoted the American Medical Association, founded the first asylum for the mentally ill in Indiana, and served with distinction in fighting a midwestern cholera epidemic.

In early Denver, Governor Evans immediately began the same tradition of community service, for he firmly believed that without farsighted volunteer leaders any new town in the West was in real trouble. Cooperative citizen involvement was necessary, he felt, not only to achieve economic goals, such as attracting railroads and new businesses, but also to establish and nurture organizations dedicated to art, education, religion, and other types of civic improvement.

This tradition of community service was instilled in the governor's children, two of whom, William and his spinster sister, Anne, lived out much of their adult lives in the Byers-Evans House and used it as a base from which to influence Denver affairs. The governor, Anne, and William, in differing combinations, either founded or served as president, chair, or long-term board member of such diverse projects as the University of Denver, the Denver Park Plan, the Moffat Railroad, the Moffat

Tunnel, the Denver City Tramway Company, the Denver Art Commission, the Denver Public Library, the Central City Opera House restoration, the Denver Planning Commission, several Methodist churches, the Denver and Pacific Railroad, the Denver Art Museum, and the Denver Civic Center Extension Plan.

An instructive specific example is the last-mentioned project, a 1923 plan to acquire the land for the City and County Building, a major part of Mayor Speer's original Civic Center Plan (see "The City Beautiful," page 298). Both Anne and William served on the committee, and, in addition, William's son, John, served as treasurer and his son-in-law, Roblin Davis, served as chairman.

How Anne came to live in the house is a fine example of redesigning a dwelling to meet changing family needs. Shortly after the governor died in 1897, William and his wife, Cornelia, invited William's mother, Margaret Patten Evans, and his sister, Anne Evans, to live with them. The families' comfortable finances allowed them to build, in 1902, a two-story rear wing to house the two women. Additional changes were made to the main house during the next nine years—another bedroom was added, the service wing was extended to meet the garage, and the living room was enlarged and redecorated. In 1911 the house as seen today was complete. When Margaret Evans Davis, the last of William and Cornelia's children, died in 1981, the historic dwelling and its furnishings were turned over to the Colorado Historical Society for restoration as a museum house and memorial to this remarkable family of Denver civic leaders.

The original house built by the Byerses was a simple Italianate structure that was not designed by an architect but planned from pattern books in consultation with the builder. Its exterior is still very much intact except for the later enclosing of an upstairs porch on the front facade. Inside, the original stair hall and the left side of the parlor have been enlarged and changed to create a large living hall in Edwardian colors. The right front parlor is left in more Victorian garb. Other rooms in the house have been restored to their probable appearance in about 1912 to 1924. The overall effect is of a remarkably large, intact, and well-lived-in family home that tells an important story about the kinds of individuals that built the West and about the extended manner in which close-knit families sometimes lived for several generations.

Adjacent to the house is a small gift shop and Denver history exhibit. The latter features two interactive touch-screen stations where a large collection of historic photographs tells many stories of the early days and development of the city.

CHEESMAN PARK NEIGHBORHOODS

Cheesman Park was Denver's first cemetery, established in 1859 on rural land distant from the bustling town center. Before the national movement for municipal parks began in the late nineteenth century, cemeteries were considered the green breathing spaces for a city, a place for quiet outdoor contemplation. By 1890 two new private cemeteries, more lushly and romantically landscaped than the old City Cemetery, had been developed, and the owners of these pushed for the competing city burial ground to be closed and changed to parkland. This was quickly accomplished, many graves were moved, and the former City Cemetery became Congress Park. It remained as a relatively undeveloped parkland until 1907, when the widow of Walter Scott Cheesman, a wealthy Denver real estate developer and industrialist, donated $100,000 to build a Classical marble pavilion and rename the park in Cheesman's honor.

Three important historic neighborhoods are located around the park. On the west is Humboldt Island, to the southeast is Morgan's Addition, and to the north is the Wyman District. Each has its own history and architectural character.

As in Quality Hill, discussed earlier, traffic on east–west streets here travels very fast, and visibility is limited by *on-street parking. Caution, whether driving or walking, is essential, particularly when crossing the one-way east–west streets that subdivide the area.*

Wyman District, ca. 1888–1893

The earliest of the three Cheesman Park area historic districts, Wyman District was platted in 1882, but sales of lots did not begin in earnest until the entire subdivision was sold to Porter, Raymond, and Company in 1887. The installation of a streetcar line along Colfax Avenue in the mid-1880s made the Wyman District very desirable, and many houses were built in the area over the next six years. Construction stopped with the Silver Crash of 1893, and when it resumed again, late in that decade, the single-family Victorian houses were joined by multifamily houses and apartments. Today, the neighborhood retains this mixture of housing types. The most prolific pre-1893 architect in this and other upscale Denver neighborhoods was the inventive William Lang (see page 302).

Wyman District

1500 block of Vine Street (all private). This block has many simple four-square-shaped dwellings with walls of brick rather than the more usual wood siding seen in this house form. Known locally as Denver Squares, these come in a variety of stylistic detail. The lack of trees here makes it easy to see the details.

1617 Vine Street (private), 1908; T. Robert Wieger, Denver, architect. This symmetrical Prairie-style design has handsome art-glass windows with the geometric patterns so favored by Prairie School architects. There is much subtlety of detail here. The upstairs windows are carefully spaced and ornamented, there is a handsome frieze of dark geometric brickwork beneath the roof eaves, the porch columns have understated brick detailing, and the broad, welcoming front door and sidelights are still wonderfully intact.

1544 Race Street (private), Schlessinger House, 1890; William Lang, Denver, architect. A lavishly detailed front-gabled Queen Anne by Denver's premier Victorian residential architect. Here the detailing is of the half-timbered subtype. Note the extraordinary porch supports, which look at first glance like turned spindles but are actually four sided, with each surface ornamented. They and the solid brackets between them are typical of the half-timbered Queen Anne subtype. So also is the squared pattern in the balustrade and frieze of the upstairs porch. Rather than a more typical half-timbering pattern in the gable, this simply has large squares. The quality of the art glass, the stonework, and the other details is extraordinarily well preserved. Numbers 1540 and 1560 Race Street (both private) are also by William Lang, and 1541 Race Street (private) is attributed to him.

1453 Race Street (private), 1892; Balcomb and Rice, architects. This front-gabled Queen Anne design is typical of the Free Classic subtype. Note the Palladian window in the front gable, the Classical columns for porch supports, and the floral swags.

1359 Race Street (private), Adams House, 1890; Kedder and Humphreys, Denver, architects. This side-gabled Shingle-style design has an "embedded" tower whose conical roof appears to have pierced upward, rather like an emerging mushroom, through the adjacent main roof. Note the typical rusticated stone first story, polygonal dormer, and shingles curving into a recessed balcony in the right-hand gable. The design of the iron porch railing is quite wonderful.

1456 Vine Street (private), 1892; William Lang, Denver, architect. Here the inventive Lang uses orangy redbrick that is so prevalent in Denver in an unusual Queen Anne design. This block has four more handsome Lang houses at 1451–1453, 1435, 1429, and 1415 Vine Street (all private).

Humboldt Island, ca. 1895–1920

This two-block-long stretch of Humboldt Street contains a miraculously intact streetscape of early single-family homes, thanks to a vigilant neighborhood group and a 1972 local historic designation. Located on the western edge of Cheesman Park, the houses on the eastern side of Humboldt Street have rear yards that adjoin the park. This practice was later decried by the distinguished Boston landscape planner Frederick Law Olmsted Jr., who, hired as a consultant to the city in 1912,

Humboldt Island

wrote numerous letters insisting that Denver's public parks be bounded by city streets, not by houses, which limit public views and access. In the case of Humboldt Island, and of Morgan's Addition (see page 308), he was not successful (see also "Country Club," page 309). Humboldt Island's first house was built in 1895, the next in 1899, and the majority in the years immediately following.

1075 Humboldt Street (private), Sweet House, 1906; Frederick J. Sterner, Denver, architect. This exuberant early Colonial Revival design has details inside of details. Note the inventive front entry that draws on Federal-style precedents but inventively combines a semicircular-arched front door with an elliptical fanlight and sidelights. The architect has continued to play with this same theme in the window to the left of the entry, where two round-arched windows are incorporated into an elliptical fanlight shape. On the second floor, the dominant Palladian window has its taller round-arched window set inside a segmental pediment.

1070 Humboldt Street (private), Thompson-Henry House, ca. 1905. This is a more traditional interpretation of Colonial Revival than its neighbor across the street (see the preceding entry). An early hipped-roof example of the style, it features three Palladian window motifs. The two first-floor windows are each crowned by decorative wooden arches that simulate the Palladian window shape. The third is in the wall dormer where the roof shape and the windows beneath create a Palladian motif. Highly unusual is the "secondary cornice line" below the main roof.

1061 Humboldt Street (private), Tammen House, 1909; Edwin H. Moorman, Denver, architect. This unusual Italian Renaissance design was built for Harry H. Tammen, co-founder of the *Denver Post.* It has a brickwork frieze under the eaves, small terra-cotta cherubs peering out below, banded porch-support columns, and light-colored brick quoins and window surrounds. The open eaves with exposed rafter ends are a hallmark of the contemporaneous Craftsman style, appropriate since architect Moorman first introduced the Craftsman style to Denverites in a series he wrote for the *Denver Times* in 1901 to 1902.

Morgan's Addition, ca. 1906–1930

Tucked into the southeast corner of Cheesman Park just south of the Denver Botanic Gardens is this small development of forty-five homes. Both the Botanic Gardens and Morgan's Addition are located adjacent to the old City Cemetery on a small square of land that was originally the Mount Calvary Catholic Cemetery. In 1887 the church sold the southern twenty acres of this land to Samuel B. Morgan. This prompted a lawsuit that was not settled until 1903, when a ruling of the U.S. Supreme Court upheld the sale. The first house went up in 1906, but the majority were built between 1915 and 1930. The rear yards of the houses along the northern side of East Ninth Avenue open directly into the grounds of the Botanical Garden in a pattern similar to that of Humboldt Island and decried by Olmsted (see page 307).

817 Race Street (private), Neusteter House, 1924; J. J. B. Benedict, Denver, architect. This one-of-a-kind beige stucco house of Mediterranean inspiration has an understated exotic flair that some Denverites called Benedictesque, after its flamboyant designer (see "1701 East Cedar Avenue," page 309). Note the pointed arch over the front entry that is incorporated into a subtle outward curve. The left side facade is strongly articulated with a deep metal balcony, which forms a hood over the garage doors, and with a matching metal finished roof over what appears to be a conservatory.

801 Race Street (private), Sullivan House, ca. 1925; J. J. B. Benedict, Denver, architect. Another unique, Mediterranean-inspired design by the same architect as in the preceding entry, this one has soft-pink stucco walls that contrast with the beige walls of 817. Notice the curved entry walk, the delicate metal-and-glass entry hood, and the line of small arched windows above the entry.

820 Gaylord Street (private), ca. 1910. This early symmetrical Tudor design features heavy, squared columns, simple half-timbering, and a single front-facing gable, a typical pre-1915 combination of features.

840 Gaylord Street (private), Campbell House, ca. 1925.

This asymmetrical brick Tudor design is typical of 1920s examples of the style.

Seventh Avenue Parkway, ca. 1905–1940

This landscaped parkway was part of Mayor Speer's original 1907 Parks and Parkways Plan (see page 298) and is today a prime example of this extensive system of boulevards that lends beauty and dignity to many Denver neighborhoods. Speer hired the very talented St. Louis designer George Kessler to prepare this plan, which worked masterfully with Denver's existing street grid. With Speer's backing, much of it was implemented, and today's Seventh Avenue Parkway is among its most delightful survivors. It is lined with Eclectic-era houses of many different styles, but Colonial Revival and Italian Renaissance seem to be particularly favored. When visiting, note that Seventh Avenue is the central spine for a long series of side streets, each with an instructive collection of Eclectic-era houses dominated by Denver Squares (see page 304) or Craftsman bungalows. At the end closest to town, from Clarkson to Williams, the boulevard drops out and more of the houses face onto the side streets. As you approach Quality Hill (see page 300), the houses on the side streets become larger.

2133 East Seventh Avenue (private). This is a very straightforward example of the Colonial Revival designs that are popular along this parkway. Note the Adamesque elliptical fanlight and sidelights around the front door, the entry porch, the double-hung sash windows with multipane glazing, and the side wing with sleeping porch above. The eyebrow dormer peeking out of the roof adds a touch of wit to an otherwise formal facade.

2101 East Seventh Avenue (private). A broad front terrace is featured in this symmetrical Italian Renaissance design. Note the detailing of the terrace rail, with brick and balustraded sections at both ends and a graceful curve at the front steps. The low-pitched tile roof and wide overhanging eaves with decorative brackets are standard features of the style. An unusual frieze of brick and decorative squares (probably terra-cotta) wraps around the house above the upper-story windows.

740 High Street (private). Through-the-cornice dormers are seen with unusual frequency in Denver. This is one of a row of four American four-squares that share this feature that is relatively unusual in most of the nation. This particular house combines Craftsman-style open eaves and exposed rafters with heavy, squared Prairie-style porch supports. A touch of half-timbering above the porch entry and a tile roof are thrown in for good measure. Although many four-squares are clothed in one primary architectural style, others, like this one, combine features from several contemporaneous styles.

1010 and 1020 East Seventh Avenue (both private), ca. 1905. This is an instructive pair of American four-squares. Each is clad in brick and has a through-the-cornice dormer, both typical four-square features in Denver. In each house the through-the-cornice dormer is extended forward to form a second-story porch under the "dormer" element. At 1020, note the second-story Moorish quatrefoil windows and the theme of paired columns. Pairs of columns support the full-width porch, pilasters paired with columns support the upstairs recessed porch, and paired pilasters are on each side of the dormer. At 1010, the through-the-cornice dormer has a gabled roof rather than the more typical hipped roof. Here, the second-story windows are ovals, single columns support the full-width porch, and a Palladian window (modified by placing arches above the two lower side windows) fills the gabled dormer.

Country Club, ca. 1905–1935

In 1901 a new Denver Country Club was incorporated to provide "golf, tennis, and other games" for its members. In 1902 the club's founders purchased a 240-acre suburban farm as the club site. Following the example of Kansas City's exclusive Country Club Addition, the club's president and several other prominent Denverites then formed the Fourth Avenue Realty Company, which in 1905 opened Park Club Place just across East First Avenue from the club grounds. This first component of the Country Club neighborhood was bounded by East First and East Fourth Avenues and Downing and Humboldt Streets. The next year, the even more exclusive Country Club Addition opened, offering landscaped parkways and spacious lots with deep setbacks along two blocks of High, Gilpin, and Franklin Streets. Handsome Mission-style entry gates were built along East Eighth Avenue, and the area was dubbed Denver's "Spanish Suburb."

Country Club neighborhood

Not everyone approved of the handsome gates, for they served a dual purpose. Not only did they announce the entry to the exclusive Country Club Addition, but they also blocked the proposed Williams Street Parkway. In 1913 urban planner Frederick Law Olmsted Jr. (see page 307) wrote to Denver's park superintendent stating that the "gates will have to be removed sooner or later as they stand upon public property and come out to the curb line and will prove a serious obstruction." The gates were still standing in 1996.

As for its designation "Spanish Suburb," only a handful of Spanish Eclectic houses were erected here, but the Italian Renaissance found great favor. Many variations of Italian Renaissance designs, most of them relatively simple in their details, can be seen in the Country Club Addition. Colonial Revival designs are also frequent. Note that some of the houses here front on the cross street, East Third Avenue.

The blocks just to the east were a third addition, called Country Club Annex, which developed slightly later and has many houses dating from the 1930s, 1940s, and 1950s. A fourth distinctive part of the Country Club neighborhood is Park Lane Square, which lies to the north of Country Club Annex and was opened for development in 1926. It is easily recognized on a map because it was laid out not in a grid like the rest of area but with curving roads designed by landscape architect S. R. DeBoer. Its main street is Circle Drive, and the centerpiece became 475 Circle Drive (private; see below). Other streets around the Country Club grounds, like East Cedar Avenue just to the south, were also developed later.

1701 East Cedar Avenue (private), Weckbaugh House, 1933; J. J. B. Benedict, Denver, architect. Flamboyant Denver architect Jules Jacques Benois Benedict (1879–1948) spent four years as a student at the prestigious École des Beaux Arts in Paris accompanied by his own personal valet. Upon completing his studies, he practiced first in Chicago and then in New York with Carrère and Hastings before moving to Denver in 1909. Here, he cut quite a swath with his strong designs and equally strong opinions. It is not surprising that when Mrs. Eugene Henry Weckbaugh wanted a new French-style home, she turned to someone who had trained in France. Benedict produced a superb French Eclectic design of the asymmetrical subtype, complete with an appropriately steep slate roof, multiple dormers of both gabled and round shapes, through-the-cornice windows, a five-sided tower, and an elaborated entry. Travertine marble is used for much of the exterior trim, and the grounds are entered by an elegant wrought-iron entry gate. Most of the grounds are not visible from the street, but instead overlook the spacious Country Club golf course behind. This is among the finest French Eclectic houses in the West.

475 Circle Drive (private), Reed House, 1931; Harry James Manning, Denver, architect. This remarkable Tudor landmark, like 1701 East Cedar Avenue (see the preceding entry) completed two years later, is among the finest late-Eclectic-era houses in the entire West. It was built for a wealthy widow, Mrs. Verner Z. Reed, and it is said that architect Manning, an eligible bachelor, was in love with his client and continually asked to marry her. This she would not do, but the two did travel together on trips to Europe, where they studied architectural details to be included in her home and purchased furniture and artifacts for the grand dwelling.

When construction began, Mrs. Reed insisted that the garage and servants' quarters be finished first so she could move in and watch their plan take shape. Both Reed and Manning, who was one of Denver's most talented architects, lavished great attention on this home, and the result is a true delight for the house watcher. The house has tapestry brickwork accented with Indiana limestone details. Four soaring chimneys with elaborate chimney pots rise from its slate roof. The recessed entry, with its wrought-iron door and elaborated Tudor arch, is exceptionally elegant. Some gables are parapeted, and others are finished with intricate carved vergeboards and feature half-timbering with pargeting (the stucco infill incised with ornamental designs). Windows and screens are made of solid bronze.

380 High Street (private). The neighborhood theme of "a Spanish Suburb" was taken to heart in this refined hipped-roof Spanish Eclectic design. Most of the detail centers on the handsome entry pavilion, which has an elaborate door surround incorporating an upstairs window and is finished with a subtly shaped parapet.

350 Gilpin Street (private). This is a typical example of the many simplified Italian Renaissance designs seen in the Country Club Addition. It is asymmetrical, has a simple rounded-arch entry, blind arches over the first-floor windows, and an overhanging tile roof. A similar Italian Renaissance house is next door at 360 Gilpin (private).

FORT COLLINS

FOUNDED 1864

Population Growth:
1900 3,000
1940 12,000
1990 88,000

Fort Collins, the northernmost city of Colorado's Front Range corridor, was founded as a center for irrigated farming, watered by the rushing Cache la Poudre River as it descends onto the plains from its origins high in the adjacent Rockies. The town's agricultural roots were strengthened when it became the site for the state's new Agricultural College, which complemented, with more applied studies, the mission of the University of Colorado at Boulder forty miles to the south (see page 284). Still an important agricultural marketing center, the town's early college, now Colorado State University, has made Fort Collins a regional center for the study of engineering and other branches of applied science.

As with other Front Range cities, Fort Collins's population has mushroomed in the decades since 1940. Its principal pre-1940 architectural attractions are an important early museum house and an early-twentieth-century streetcar suburb that is one of the nation's very few to have a fully restored electric streetcar. This operates during the summer weekends as a local tourist attraction.

Avery House, 1879 and later

328 West Mountain Avenue; 970-221-0533.

In 1869 Horace Greeley, the powerful editor of the *New York Tribune*, visited this region and was so impressed with its agricultural potential that he began a promotional campaign to interest "proper persons in establishing a colony in the Colorado Territory." The *Tribune* widely advertised the proposed colony, and Greeley, who popularized but did not coin the phrase "Go west, young man," enlisted the aid of Nathan Meeker, the *Tribune*'s agricultural editor, in his new project. Quickly becoming a convert, Meeker decided to lead the immigrants himself in founding the Union Colony, which centered around the new town of Greeley, named for his inspirational boss.

Among those convinced by the *Tribune*'s enthusiasm was twenty-year-old Franklin Capen Avery (1849–1923), an upstate New York farmer and surveyor who came west to help survey and plat the new town of Greeley. Soon rival agricultural colonies were springing up in the region. One of these, located twenty-five miles west of Greeley and named Fort Collins for an abandoned U.S. Army post on the site, was surveyed and platted by Avery in 1873. In the process he provided the new town with exceptionally broad streets that are still admired today. Young Avery apparently preferred this new location, for he ended up spending most of his long life as a Fort Collins banker, rancher, and civic leader.

In 1876 Avery returned to New York to marry Sara

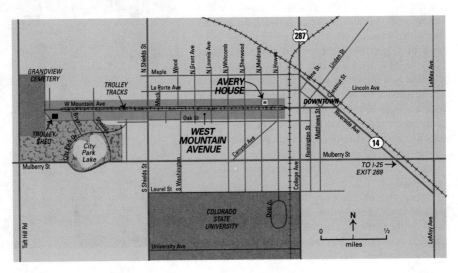

Avery House

Edson (born 1851) and bring her to Fort Collins to make their home. The stone-walled Victorian house the couple built three years later is a great example of a fashionable dwelling that grew and expanded in stages—in this case six additions and modifications over a twenty-five-year period. So skillfully were these made that it has required a great deal of modern detective work to sort them all out.

Franklin and Sara began their home in 1879 by building just the gable-front-and-wing section that makes up the left side of the present facade. In 1881 they added a kitchen wing behind and, in about 1883, came the right wing that created a centered-gable whole. In 1893 the back parlor, right side tower, and wraparound porch were added. In 1904 the stairway and entrance area were remodeled and the left-rear bedroom received a turret-type window. Also in 1904 a matching carriage house to the rear was built to replace the original barn. A back porch and upstairs sleeping porch were added in 1906. Somewhere along the line, no one is certain when, the gazebo and front fountain were added.

Because the same local sandstone was used for all of the work, and all of the exterior details were carefully matched, the house appears as if it were built as a single unit. It is a centered-gable Gothic Revival design with a bit of asymmetry introduced by the wraparound side

Avery House

porch. An unusual note is added by the windows that, rather than having pointed-arch Gothic detailing, are handsome Italianate forms with flattened arches and framed surrounds of red sandstone that contrasts with the lighter stone color of adjacent walls.

The porch and Queen Anne–style tower are the main exterior clues that the house has had later additions. Because the exterior has such a Victorian look, it is a surprise to walk inside and see a light and simple 1904 stairway rather than the dark and ornate versions that were popular twenty years earlier.

Members of the Avery family lived in the home until 1962, after which the house was rented until being purchased by the city of Fort Collins in 1974. The restoration of the interior has been the responsibility of a local nonprofit group, the Poudre Landmarks Foundation. For more than twenty years, the group has been researching the house and carefully restoring it step by step. Reproduction of some of the original wallpapers has been a recent project. The foundation has also devoted much effort to obtaining appropriate furnishings, including many Avery family pieces.

West Mountain Avenue, ca. 1880–1920

West Mountain Avenue has what is probably the only operative residential trolley line in the western United States. Restored and managed by volunteers on summer weekends, this provides visitors a rare opportunity to sample the kind of transportation that dominated American cities from about 1890 to 1950.

A typical pattern for trolley-era town expansion and development was to initiate a streetcar line into vacant countryside but with a park or entertainment destination at the end of the line to attract immediate riders. The trolley builders then platted and sold house lots adjacent to the line, which, as they were developed, ensured increasing numbers of long-term customers for the trolleys (see, for example, Washington Park in Seattle, page 671).

Here in small-town Fort Collins, the trolley system was begun in 1907 and discontinued in 1952. When the trolley was first installed, some of the crucial parts of the usual system were already in place. West Mountain Avenue was then a favored carriage drive because at its end lay both a large cemetery, which in the nineteenth century was much used as tranquil, parklike open space, and Prospect (now City) Park, then the site of races, fairs, and other active events. Fort Collins's inaugural trolley trip delivered riders to a "Race Meet and Stock Show" in Prospect Park.

The new streetcar line encouraged the sale of lots along and near West Mountain Avenue, many of which had languished empty since the development's first house, at 121 Grant Street (see below), was given away in an 1888 lottery intended to spark a rush of lot sales and housing starts. This didn't happen—a drive down West Mountain Avenue today reveals only a few late-nineteenth-century houses. The district instead contains mostly small dwellings that were built either shortly before or after the completion of the trolley line in 1907. Simple Free Classic Queen Anne cottages, Craftsman bungalows, and small hipped-roof National Folk and Folk Victorian houses are most common.

West Mountain Avenue is important not for containing large and elaborate homes, but rather as a perfect (and still-operating) example of the streetcar-based subdivisions that dominated late-nineteenth- and early-twentieth-century America.

402 West Mountain Avenue (private), Edwards House, 1904; Montezuma Fuller, Fort Collins, architect. Sara Avery's sister (see pages 311–312), Phoebe Edson Edwards, and her husband built this fine home. Many members of both Sara's and Franklin's families followed the couple west and settled in the same general area, a pattern that was typical of western settlement. The house is a fine early Colonial Revival design in the popular hipped-roof-with-full-width-porch subtype. The windows in both the first and second stories have the very broad shape that was common between about 1900 and 1915; these typically have taller sashes below and short, transomlike sashes above. These upper sashes feature diamond-shaped panes separated by leaded glass downstairs and wood mullions upstairs. This same diamond pattern is found in the centered Palladian window and in the sidelights and transom surrounding the front door.

121 Grant Street (private), Patterson House, 1888. This, the show home for the then-new Loomis Addition, was given away as a prize in a lottery to attract lot buyers. It is an adorable, small cross-gabled Queen Anne design with a Richardsonian Romanesque touch added by the arched brick entry porch. Note the slight flare to the band of decorative fish-scale shingles that encircles the house and pro-

West Mountain Avenue

vides a transition between the brick first story and the shingle-clad, upper half story. This kind of false overhang was typical on Queen Anne houses and was intended to give the effect of an upper story cantilevering out above the lower story.

938 West Mountain Avenue (private). This pyramidal Folk Victorian house has the centered gable commonly seen on this subtype. There are many similar examples along West Mountain Avenue. This one is of brick and has new front windows and a simple stone lintel over the front door.

1006 West Mountain Avenue (private). This is a wood-clad example of the same style and subtype as number 938 (see the preceding entry). The front door here looks original. To its right is a window with a diamond-patterned upper sash similar to those at number 402 (see page 313).

1120 West Mountain Avenue (private). The gable of this simple, front-gabled Craftsman design has an unusual pattern of shingles laid in alternating broad and narrow rows.

1150 West Mountain Avenue (private). This front-gabled Craftsman house appears to have retained all of its original detailing. Note the pattern in the upper sash of the two sets of triple windows. It is echoed in the small window in the lower-front gable. The gables have the same unusual wood-shingle pattern, with rows of alternating depth, seen at 1120 (see the preceding entry). The "empty pedestal" to the left of the porch is typical of the style and was never intended to have a porch support above it.

1416 West Mountain Avenue (private), ca. 1990. This modern Neo-Victorian house has vinyl siding, a flat left side with a "chimney" of boxed vinyl siding, and noticeably contemporary windows and door. Another Neo-Victorian is at 1307 West Mountain Avenue (private).

GEORGETOWN

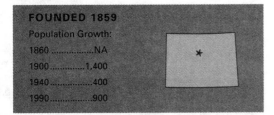

FOUNDED 1859

Population Growth:

1860 ....NA
1900 1,400
1940 400
1990 900

Reports of stream-gravel gold discoveries on Cherry Creek, located on the open plains near the base of the Colorado Rockies, touched off the misnamed "Pikes Peak or Bust" gold rush of 1858. Pikes Peak, the region's most familiar landmark, actually lay sixty miles south of the Cherry Creek discovery, which became the site of the town of Denver (see page 297). The creek's gold deposits were disappointingly small, and many of the fifty-niners soon returned across the Kansas and Nebraska plains to their homes farther east. Some, however, began prospecting along the adjacent mountain streams with greater success. By 1860 several important gold discoveries had been made due west of Denver along rugged Clear Creek. As a result Denver became the principal supply center for rich mountain mining camps at Black Hawk, Central City, Idaho Springs, Georgetown, and elsewhere.

A rare combination of circumstances has made Georgetown a unique survivor among Colorado's many early mining towns. Founded as a stream-gravel gold camp in the initial rush of 1859, five years later it was the site of the state's first major silver strike. Although later overshadowed by the enormous silver deposits found at Leadville in 1877, Georgetown's mines had the unusual virtue of longevity. For more than forty years they consistently yielded several million dollars per year in silver and associated gold, a mining record that a 1908 U.S. Geological Survey report praised as "one of the most steady and reliable in the country."

The architectural result of this continuing prosperity was that the usual jerry-built cabins, shacks, and tents that housed the transient prospectors and laborers in most mining towns were steadily replaced in Georgetown by more permanent family dwellings. Equally remarkable was the fact that the town never experienced the devastating fires that regularly swept through the crowded wooden structures of mining towns. By 1890 Georgetown was a prosperous Victorian community of substantial commercial buildings and tidy residential streets.

As the output of its nearby mines finally declined after about 1915, Georgetown's population dwindled, and some Victorian commercial buildings were abandoned and ultimately demolished. The town's attractive houses, on the other hand, began to take on a new life as second homes for Denverites and other plains dwellers seeking a cool mountain retreat from oppressive summer heat. By the 1960s the town's unique architectural heritage of over two hundred Victorian structures was recognized by designation as a national

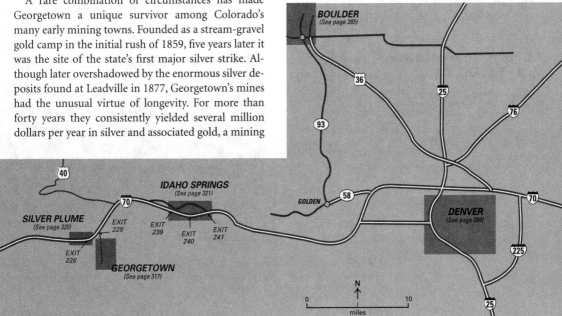

historic landmark. Most of these are dwellings, two of which are now important museum houses.

Recent preservation efforts have focused on making the Georgetown area a unique interpretive center of Colorado's silver-boom era. In 1983, exactly a century after its original construction, the Colorado Historical Society completed restoration of the historic narrow-gauge **Georgetown Loop Railroad** (1106 Rose Street, 303-569-2403). From June through September, this offers visitors a spectacular trip to the nearby mining center of Silver Plume, with an optional stop to tour the otherwise inaccessible **Lebanon Silver Mine and Mill Complex,** one of the region's most prolific and best-preserved producers.

Georgetown's small residential neighborhoods include many different house types but are dominated by National Folk and Folk Victorian dwellings as well as simplified Gothic Revival and hipped-roof Italianate designs. The Gothic Revival houses were primarily built in the 1860s and 1870s and are found in the centered-gable, front-gabled roof, and asymmetrical subtypes. As in the Hamill House, decorated vergeboards are commonly absent, and in some examples the typical Gothic-shaped gable window may also be absent. But the shapes of the houses, the tall narrow windows and the steeply pitched roofs, leave no doubt about their original stylistic inspiration. During the late 1870s and 1880s simplified Italianate houses were more common. These have low-pitched hipped roofs, a boxy shape, and usually such Italianate details as eave brackets or decorative window crowns. Both South and North Georgetown are filled with fences—wire fences, stone fences, picket and other designs of wood fences.

South Georgetown, ca. 1860–1900

This residential area, located just to the south of Georgetown's historic downtown, is anchored by the Hamill House museum.

203 Argentine Street (private). This is a typical front-gabled National Folk house, one and one-half stories tall. Note the lower-rear section indicating that the house has been expanded—either a small one-story house had a large front addition or the front house received a smaller rear addition. The long side porch unites the two parts and is probably newer still. Number 204 Argentine Street (private), across the street, is another front-gabled folk house, this one a full two stories tall and slightly broader.

200 Argentine Street (private). This is a basic centered-gable Gothic Revival design. Vergeboard ornament is omitted but not really missed; the shape and the central Gothic window make the intended style clear, as in the Hamill House (see page 317).

Argentine Street at Fourth Street (private). Located just next door to the Hamill House, this brick Italianate design

South Georgetown

has the typical cubic shape of simple-hipped-roof examples of the style. White-painted brick is effectively used to create segmental-arched hoods over the rectangular windows. The porch and cornice details, nicely painted to highlight them, are typical of the style. A similar nearby example is at 311 Rose Street (private).

Fourth Street just north of Taos Street (private), Maxwell House, 1870; tower and front facade, 1891. This very late, one-of-a-kind Second Empire design was built in two stages. The front facade is unusual in that the mansard roof is not continued across the front as is typical of the style.

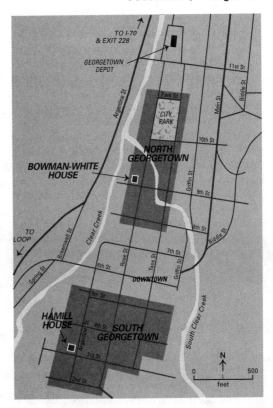

Hamill House, 1867 and 1879–1885

Third Street and Argentine Street; 303-569-2840.
This beautifully preserved, centered-gable Gothic Revival home is the result of two periods of building. The front section of the house was built in 1867 by merchant Joseph Watson. In 1874, after some financial reverses, Watson sold the house to his brother-in-law, William A. Hamill (died 1904), who had better luck in his silver-mining ventures.

In 1879 the increasingly successful Hamill hired Denver architect Robert Roeschlaub to undertake a long-term remodeling that wasn't completed until 1885. During this period, the home was greatly enlarged, a conservatory with curved glass windows was added, and several outbuildings and a large outdoor fountain were built on the property. Hamill lost heavily in the great Silver Crash of 1893, after which he moved to Denver to try to recoup the family fortunes while his wife and youngest son remained behind in their home.

Hamill House

The last Hamill occupant sold the house in 1914, and it passed through many hands before being acquired by Historic Georgetown in 1971. Although most of the furnishings had been removed, the interior fixtures and finishes remained remarkably intact. The society is doing an excellent job of tracking down original Hamill furnishings for the house and has filled in with appropriate period pieces where needed.

The four main downstairs rooms, although of only moderate size, were finished with voluptuous detailing that has miraculously survived—including the downstairs wall and ceiling papers, the walnut woodwork, elegant fireplace mantels, and the original gas-light fixtures that were later electrified. Each room was finished in a different bold color scheme. The parlor wall and ceiling papers are in soft dusky pinks and blues, in the library they are browns and deep golds, and in the dining room deep blues and golds are used. The electrified gas-light fixtures hang from the original large painted ceiling medallions. Both the parlor and the dining room open onto the small conservatory, where an elaborate iron fountain still works and provides a focal point for both rooms.

Outside there is a larger and even more elaborate iron fountain. Outbuildings include a washhouse, a stone carriage house, and an original outhouse complete with Gothic Revival detailing. It has six holes and is divided into a servants' side and a family side. A second stone building opens directly onto the side street and served as Hamill's office. It and a long matching low stone wall are built with a nicely finished stone quarried in the Hamill Granite Quarry near Silver Plume. The office has two downstairs rooms, one the public office and one Hamill's private office. Although little is known about the latter, the public office still has all of its massive original fixtures. This includes a large walk-in vault, a massive curved wood counter that dominates the room, and a particularly exuberant black-walnut stairway. All seem designed to let the visitor or customer know that here is a man who can afford to buy or invest in whatever you are offering, but also a man who can easily afford to say no if your terms are ungenerous.

North Georgetown, ca. 1860–1900

City Park provides a centerpiece for the residential district located just to the north of Georgetown's historic downtown, which preserves many fine Victorian commercial buildings. In 1890 the town purchased thirteen city lots for this park, and many hours of volunteer labor went into leveling and clearing the land and planting it with trees. In July 1891 the local newspaper editor asked, "What other mountain town in Colorado has a park enclosed with iron fence and surrounded with stone flagging? Hurrah for Georgetown!" The marvelous old fence and many of the trees still survive; a gazebo was added in the 1970s. The Rose Street side of the park is lined with larger styled houses similar to those found in South Georgetown, while the Park, Taos, and Tenth Street sides have many small National Folk houses originally built for miners and other working-class families. The Bowman-White House museum (see page 319) represents the former, and the associated Tucker-Rutherford House represents the latter.

1000 block of Taos Street (all private). This block, which faces City Park, has many small National Folk houses. Some continue into the 900 block of Taos (all private), but closer to downtown larger, styled houses predominate.

1010 Taos Street (private). This unusual variation on the gabled-front-and-wing National Folk house has hipped, rather than gabled, roofs at each end of its L-shaped form. The combination of board-and-batten siding on the front facade and clapboard siding on the long, side facade is also

North Georgetown

Downtown Georgetown

break, very high pitched gabled roof, shapely finial piercing the peak of the gable, and tall narrow windows extending up into the gable—indicates its stylistic origins. The entry porch shows Stick-style influence. Note also the incised Eastlake detailing over the windows and the decoratively shaped brick chimney. Next door (located between this house and the Bowman-White House, see below) is the Blackman House (private), built in 1882, which is a similarly simplified late-Italianate-style design. It has the shape and massing of an Italianate house, but lacks the decorative brackets at the roofline and the style's usual window and porch-support detailing. The double door *is* a very typical Italianate feature.

806 and 808 Rose Street (both private). This is an instructive pair of one-story, gable-front-and-wing Folk Victorian cottages, 806 built of wood and 808 of brick. Note the slight variations in window and porch detailing.

unusual. As with many folk houses, this one looks as if it has grown in stages.

507 Tenth Street (private). This is a minimal example of a side-gabled, one-story National Folk house.

921 Rose Street (private), Church House, 1877; Robert Roeschlaub, Denver, architect. This lovely late–Gothic Revival design, like many later examples of the style, lacks decorated vergeboards in the gables. Instead, the basic form of the house—wall surface extending into the gable without a

Bowman-White House, 1892

Rose Street at Ninth Street; 303-569-2840
(scheduled to open in the summer of 1998).

Historic Georgetown has established a farsighted program to illustrate a variety of the town's Victorian lifestyles in different museum houses. In addition to the upscale Hamill House, home of a wealthy mining

Bowman-White House

investor (see page 317), the group owns this fine Queen Anne structure that interprets the upper-middle-class lifestyles of its managerial and professional families. This home has its original woodwork, the wallpapers are reproduced, and about half of the furnishings are from the Bowman and White families. Two more modest earlier houses, whose original sites were purchased for new construction, have been moved to the grounds behind the Bowman-White House. The ca. 1880 Tucker-Rutherford House represents a typical miner's home. Originally a two-room, gabled-front-and-wing National Folk house, a shed-roofed bedroom was added in the 1890s. The log cabin is thought to be pre-1870 and is representative of the homes built by Georgetown's earliest settlers.

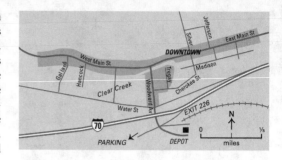

Silver Plume, ca. 1870–1930

As Georgetown grew to become the principal marketing and trade center for the region's many mountainside silver mines, the smaller community of Silver Plume, located higher in the Clear Creek gorge, about two miles to the west, grew up as a workingman's town in the heart of a rich cluster of mines. Many of its early dwellings survive, most of them one-story National Folk houses of different shapes and vintages. Some have Victorian detail added, which puts them into the Folk Victorian category. The downtown area is similarly small scale and consists primarily of one-story storefronts, rather than the two-story versions typical

of Georgetown. The western end of Main Street, Hancock Street, Cherokee Street, Woodward Avenue, and Tregay Street (accessible only by foot at the bandstand footbridge) are lined with delightful folk houses, all of which are private. Among these are:

73 West Main Street (private). This is a classic one-room, one-story, side-gabled National Folk house.
98 West Main Street (private). Here is another one-story, side-gabled National Folk house, but this is two rooms wide. Note the stylish flair added by the shutters.
107 West Main Street (private), ca. 1870s. This probably began as a small, gabled-front National Folk house that was later modified to provide storage for the town's fire carts. The entrance for these is on the right rear. Note the one-and-a-half-story National Folk I-house across the street, with a through-the-cornice dormer.
414 and 416 East Main Street (both private). These illustrate two slightly differing versions of gabled-front-and-wing Folk Victorian dwellings.

Silver Plume, ca. 1880

Silver Plume

Idaho Springs, ca. 1880–1930

Idaho Springs, located in the Clear Creek gorge, about twelve miles east of Georgetown, was the site of one of the region's first significant gold strikes in 1859 (see page 315). It later became an important silver-mining and trade center and retains some fine turn-of-the-century houses along Colorado Boulevard, the northernmost of the town's two main streets. These run parallel to Interstate 70 between exits 241 (on the east side of town) and 239 (on the west side of town); sim-

ply take whichever one comes first in the direction you are traveling. Because this is the old highway, it is not particularly easy to pause to look for addresses and get a closer look. Although interesting houses appear on both sides of Colorado Boulevard, the larger ones tend to be on the north side, which gave them a commanding downhill view.

500 and 700 blocks of Colorado Boulevard (all private). These two blocks have many front-gabled National Folk houses.

940 Colorado Boulevard (private). This is a one-and-a-half-story Queen Anne design clad in brick with spindlework detailing. Windows in the secondary front gable help add light to the upper half story. The detailing of the handsome

Idaho Springs

main gable includes stained glass in the upper window sashes.

1200 block of Colorado Boulevard (all private). Located between Twelfth Avenue and Thirteenth Avenue, this block includes several Queen Anne and American four-square designs.

1435 Colorado Boulevard (private). Another one-and-a-half-story brick Queen Anne design, this one has Free Classic porch detailing, stylized half-timbering in the gable, and a hooded, round-arched window added for good measure.

Idaho Springs

PUEBLO

FOUNDED 1842

Population Growth:

1860 ....NA

1900 28,000

1940 52,000

1990 99,000

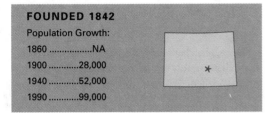

Rising from the adjacent plains in a towering line of snowcapped peaks, Colorado's mountains have only one gap that affords a gradual ascent into the state's rugged western half. This was carved over countless millennia by the waters of the Arkansas River as they plunged downward from their mountaintop source to flow across the plains toward a distant junction with the Mississippi. Long a favored east–west route for Indians, explorers, and trappers, this Arkansas River gateway was later to make the town of Pueblo a unique crossroads when railroads first spread through Colorado in the 1870s.

Pueblo had been founded beside the Arkansas River three decades earlier as a wagon-road junction and trade center for trappers working in the remote mountains to the west. Although only a small village, it was Colorado's most important settlement until the 1859 gold rush brought hordes of immigrants to the Denver area. As Denver boomed during the 1860s, Pueblo, like Trinidad to the south (see page 329), languished as a small trading center for local farms and ranches producing food for the booming mining centers to the north. In 1870, two years before its first railroad arrived, the town had only seven hundred inhabitants.

Modern Pueblo, like Colorado Springs forty miles farther north (see page 288), was the brainchild of the colorful General William Jackson Palmer, youthful Civil War commander of the Fifteenth Pennsylvania Cavalry Regiment who next became a visionary railroad builder and Colorado booster. When the westward-building Santa Fe line preempted Palmer's plan to build his Denver and Rio Grande line directly southward to New Mexico, Palmer used the Arkansas River gateway as a route for building his line through the mountains. Palmer platted the new railroad town of South Pueblo just across the river from the older settlement to serve as the focal point of this new plan.

Palmer's first narrow-gauge trains reached Pueblo in 1872. Construction then continued southward only to Trinidad, reached in 1876. Westward progress through the rugged mountains went more slowly; the line reached Salt Lake City in 1883. Meanwhile, fate handed Palmer, and Pueblo, an unexpected prize. In 1877 an enormous bonanza of silver ore was discovered at Leadville, located high in the Central Rockies near the source of the Arkansas River. Along the relatively easy gradient up the Arkansas Valley, the Denver and Rio Grande's tracks were the first to arrive of three railroads racing to serve booming Leadville. As a result, Pueblo became a principal supply and smelting center for the rich, high-altitude mining district.

Realizing that Pueblo's mountain hinterland had rich deposits of coal, iron, and other industrial metals, Palmer had, from the time he founded the Denver and Rio Grande, planned to make the city the center of the region's heavy industry. The Leadville discoveries accelerated his plans. In 1879 he and his associates organized

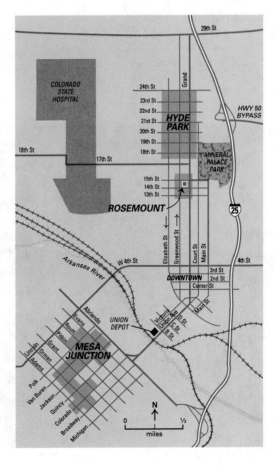

the Colorado Coal and Iron Company (soon renamed the Colorado Fuel and Iron Company and familiarly known as the CF&I). The next year Palmer began constructing blast furnaces on a two-square-mile site adjacent to his Denver and Rio Grande's tracks in South Pueblo. Using nearby lime deposits, coal from the Trinidad area (see page 329), and iron ore from more distant sources, this was the West's first steelmaking facility and became one of the nation's most successful. By 1906 CF&I's mines, ore-supply railroads, and steel mills employed 10 percent of the workforce in the entire state of Colorado. Still active today after several changes in ownership, it remains one of the region's largest employers.

Probably because of its industrial heritage, modern Pueblo has escaped the exponential population growth of its Front Range neighbors to the north. Still retaining much of the relaxed flavor of a mid-twentieth-century city, it's a delightful place for house watching with one of the West's finest Victorian museum houses and two important neighborhoods of both Victorian and Eclectic-era dwellings.

Rosemount, 1893

419 West Fourteenth Street; 719-545-5290;
Henry Hudson Holly, New York City, architect.
This spectacular Richardsonian Romanesque landmark seems to have been the one great indulgence in

the lives of conservative banker-investor John A. Thatcher (1836–1915) and his devoted wife, Margaret Henry Thatcher (1848–1922). Son of a Pennsylvania merchant, young Thatcher left home at age twenty-one to seek his fortune in the West. After five years working as a store clerk in Missouri, he came to booming Denver in 1862, where he continued his clerking career. Hearing that the remote village of Pueblo lacked a general store, Thatcher, with the backing of his Denver employer, left the next year with a wagonload of goods to open his own modest store in a Pueblo mule stable. Two years later he moved into a more suitable building and invited his younger brother to join him in running Thatcher Brothers, Merchants. Soon the pair developed an enviable reputation for honesty and fair dealing; their customers called them "the squarest men that ever lived." As a result they became the community's trusted bankers and began being asked to open banks and general stores in other small Colorado towns. As these prospered, the brothers carefully invested their profits in cattle ranches, mines, smelters, and other opportunities of the developing frontier. In spite of their growing wealth, however, they led unpretentious lives. For twenty-five years, John, his wife, and their five children shared a small but comfortable five-room cottage not far from his downtown bank.

In 1890, with two eligible but unmarried daughters and a five-year-old son still at home, the Thatchers de-

Rosemount

cided that a new lifestyle was called for. Both John and Margaret had been schoolteachers in their youth, and they planned this change with academic thoroughness. Their investigations apparently led them to one of the most popular home-making manuals of the period, architect Henry Hudson Holly's (1834–1892) *Modern Dwellings in Town and Country: Adapted to America's Wants and Climate,* an 1878 book that helped popularize the Queen Anne style in the United States.

Holly had strong opinions and expressed them on every aspect of house design, construction, and interior decoration. His knowledgeable concern for quality building materials and careful construction, no matter what one's budget, would have appealed to John's conservative yet farsighted banker's instincts. On the other hand, Holly's chapter on women's artistic achievements would have struck a chord with Mrs. Thatcher, who was Pueblo's first schoolteacher and an artist whose works still hang in Rosemount. Having become Holly converts, the couple next made an uncharacteristically grand decision. They would invite the distinguished New Yorker himself to design for them a splendid new dwelling on a full-block site at the north edge of town. Holly didn't betray the Thatchers' trust, creating, in what was to be his last commission, a remarkable synthesis of all of his aesthetic ideals.

Holly's Richardsonian Romanesque styling is a bit less obvious in the finished house than in the original drawings, since some exterior details, such as a rounded tower with a conical roof and a third-floor balcony, were ultimately omitted. Nevertheless, it remains an extraordinary monument. The exterior walls are of pink rhyolitic granite from Castle Rock, Colorado; the roof is of red Vermont slate; the steps are of sandstone; the main entry is set off with five pink granite columns; the verandah is basswood painted to imitate stone; and the gutters, cornice, and flashing are all made of solid copper.

Details of the house's construction are very well documented. The basic structure, built by a Leavenworth, Kansas, contractor, cost $60,750. To this was added $19,850 of interior woodwork from the renowned Herts Brothers of New York City; $2,110 of stained- and painted-glass windows from Charles Booth of New York; $3,025 of carpets (mostly Oriental) from W. and J. Sloane of New York; and chandeliers and wall sconces (powered by both gas and electricity, since the electric company in Pueblo shut down at 9 p.m.) from Tiffany and Co. of New York. Finally, the furniture was purchased both from Herts Brothers and from Wanamakers in Philadelphia. All of the lavish interiors were designed under Holly's specifications and supervision.

One missing note is a record of the artists that cre-

Rosemount

ated the exquisite decorated ceilings seen throughout the house. Many different materials and designs were used for these. Some, like the living hall, have beamed and coffered wooden ceilings that were no doubt supplied by Herts Brothers. Others, like the sitting room, are executed in *buon fresco* (water-based paint on fresh plaster), while Mr. Thatcher's bedroom was done in *fresco secco* (water-based paint on dry plaster). In the elegant parlor, a painting on canvas is set in a frame and set off with gilded plasterwork. Stenciled borders and intricate cornices complement many of the hand-painted ceiling decorations.

Touring Rosemount is a special treat, because the Thatcher family, appropriately respectful of Holly's creation, left it virtually unaltered until it was given to the city of Pueblo to become a museum in 1968. It thus provides a rare opportunity to study an original, rather than later-restored, work by one of the nation's master Victorian architects and interior designers.

One enters into a large golden-oak living hall with a massive fireplace, stairway, and stained-glass window. Off of this is an exquisitely "feminine" parlor in ivory, gilt, and rose. The dining room is paneled in golden oak and the library with mahogany—all with coordinated furnishings. Each of the upstairs bedrooms has its own personality, and most retain the original matching furniture. The two upstairs baths have their original fixtures, while the kitchen still has the coal-and-wood range, sink, and oak drain board that were first installed. This authenticity continues throughout the entire house—even photographs, mementos, and dishes are still in place. Outside, a large matching carriage house survives, now converted for adaptive reuse as a restaurant.

One of the reasons Rosemount remained so intact was that the Thatchers' son Raymond (1885–1968), thirteen years younger than his closest sibling and the only child to grow up in the house, never married and lived here until his death. A Yale graduate, he became the chairman of the board of the family bank after his father's death. As a bachelor interested primarily in breeding fine racehorses, he seems to have been perfectly content to leave the grand house just as he knew it as a child. His only heirs were his brother's three children, who chose to donate Rosemount to the community for all to enjoy in memory of their remarkable grandparents, John and Margaret.

Hyde Park

Hyde Park, 1890–1920

This upscale north-side residential neighborhood once centered around Rosemount, but today relatively few houses survive in its immediate vicinity, having been replaced by commercial and other intrusions. A few blocks farther north, the Hyde Park neighborhood is more intact and contains a mixture of houses with varying ages, sizes, and styles. Brick American four-squares with Classical-columned full-width porches are frequent, as are Queen Anne and Neoclassical one-story cottages. Scattered among these are occasional front-gambreled Shingle-style designs as well as Craftsman and other Eclectic-era fashions. As in Denver, one-way streets with fast traffic intrude on what could be a peaceful neighborhood atmosphere.

1801 North Greenwood Street (private), Gast House, 1892; F. V. Newell, architect. This grand Queen Anne design has a commanding four-story stone tower with a bell-shaped roof. The basic house is built of brick, but this is liberally accented with stone, terra-cotta, and areas of both wood shingle and siding. Note the paired-column porch supports on stone pedestals and the large cantilevered bay window.

2121 North Elizabeth Street (private), Frazier House, 1915; designed by owner. Frazier was a famous saddle maker whose design talents clearly extended beyond his chosen profession. Approached from the right side, this large brick Craftsman house features a dramatic swoop where the side-gabled roof extends out over the front porch; the front-gabled dormer has a similar swoop on one side. Note the scalloped roof beams under the gables, art glass in

the upper sash of the main upstairs windows, leaded glass around the front door and in window transoms, and the unusual stone porch supports with horizontal bands.

2102 North Elizabeth Street (private), ca. 1905. Smaller examples of gambrel-roofed Shingle-style houses, such as this one, tend to be narrow and look at first glance as if there were only a single, front-facing gambrel. A closer look usually reveals a narrow cross gambrel located toward the rear that helped enormously in adding usable second-story space. Note here the recessed balcony in the dominant front gambrel. Other good examples of this house type are scattered through both of Pueblo's featured neighborhoods (see also the following entry).

1912 North Elizabeth Street (private), ca. 1905. Here is another charming gambrel-roofed Shingle-style design (see also the preceding entry). As in most larger examples of this subtype, the main roof is a side gambrel, with a front-facing gambrel added to enhance the effect from the street. Again, the front gambrel has a recessed balcony.

409 Eighteenth Street (private), ca. 1910. This symmetrical Mission-style design has all of the style's identifying features except that the roof tiles are green rather than the usual red. Note the quatrefoil windows and the characteristic arcaded entry porch with pier, arch, and wall surface all in a single plane. The symmetrical effect is achieved by balancing the porch arches on the right with carefully recessed window arches on the left.

423 Eighteenth Street (private), ca. 1910. Pueblo's two featured neighborhoods have many brick Colonial Revival designs of the hipped-roof-with-full-width-porch subtype. Most are American four-square shapes, and the full-width porches are supported by Classical columns. Some have modest Colonial Revival details added, such as the row of

Hyde Park

dentils on the porch roof and the fanlight above the front door, seen in this example.

Mesa Junction, 1890–1920

General Palmer's new railroad town of South Pueblo (see page 323) included not only the large industrial tract on which the CF&I plant was built, but also its own residential neighborhood closer to the river, where many of the executives of the nearby steel plant and ore smelters, as well as their more affluent workers, lived. This neighborhood now takes its name from the nearby commercial center located near the river, where trolley lines serving the downtown commercial center terminated and connected with lines serving South Pueblo.

Most of the neighborhood's houses are of moderate size. Some of the larger homes are on Orman Street near Colorado Street, on West Abriendo Avenue just west of the commercial area, and along the south side of the 300 block of West Pitkin Avenue. The latter is now the Pitkin Place Historic District, with six historic homes built for senior CF&I executives shortly after the company was acquired by New York industrialist John D. Rockefeller in 1892. These combine to make an unusually fine Victorian streetscape. The houses range in style from pure Richardsonian Romanesque to pure Queen Anne, but the majority combine elements of both styles. All are either brick or stone, and some feature unusually handsome brick chimneys.

326 West Pitkin Avenue (private), Mechen House, ca. 1895; G. W. Roe and E. W. Shutt, architects. This brick Queen Anne house has Richardsonian influence in the Syrian-arched window in the gable. Syrian arches are very typical of the Richardsonian Romanesque style and spring directly from "floor" level rather than from higher piers, giving them a very broad and dramatic appearance. Another feature here is the monitor roof on the tower, raised to allow more light. The porch of this house has been modified. Craftsman-era porch supports replaced the originals; more

recently spindlework detailing was added to try to make the later supports look more Victorian.

318 West Pitkin Avenue (private), 1895. Like 326 (see the preceding entry), this is a brick Queen Anne design but with a prominent Romanesque-arched window in a front-facing gable. Note how the round balcony on the left side of the house echoes the curve of the arched window. This house has Free Classic porch supports that look original and an intriguing combination of details in the main gable.

310 West Pitkin Avenue (private), Brown House, ca. 1895. Built for the manager of CF&I's rail mill, which supplied tracks for the Denver and Rio Grande and other western railroads, this is pure Richardsonian Romanesque design except for the spindlework Queen Anne porch. Note the rough-faced ashlar stone, the round tower with Romanesque arch, diaperwork railing, and squat witch's-cap roof.

306 West Pitkin Avenue (private), Robinson House, ca. 1895. C. S. Robinson was CF&I's assistant superintendent. His brick Queen Anne home includes a shingled Syrian arch on the upstairs balcony. Typical spindlework detailing ornaments the main gable, but the Palladian window below is more typical of the Free Classic, rather than spindlework, subtype of the style. The original porch supports have been replaced with Prairie-style square piers of brick.

302 West Pitkin Avenue (private). A pure Richardsonian Romanesque house built of rough-faced ashlar and with a wonderful Romanesque-arched porch with diaperwork railing above. The tower here has an unusual double roof, but it is not raised for a row of windows as at 326 (see above). Fine carved stone detailing is used on this house. Note the lovely interlacing floral detail with a face above it located between the two front-porch arches, the pair of stretched-out lions beside the front steps, and the small dragon crawling over the corner of the porch roof railing. The stone of the main body of the house is laid without courses, while the porch is laid in regular courses. There has been a large rear addition.

129 West Orman Avenue (private), ca. 1910. This is one of Pueblo's many brick Colonial Revival designs in the hipped-roof-with-full-width-porch subtype. Here the American four-square shape is more heavily ornamented with additional Colonial Revival details than in most Pueblo examples. Notice the unusual entry-door design with a beautiful leaded-glass fanlight above. Ordinarily the door would be

Mesa Junction: Pitkin Place Historic District

Mesa Junction

era residential architect (see also page 302) was brought to Pueblo to design this large and handsome Richardsonian Romanesque house for a future Colorado governor. Lang took advantage of the corner site to give both of the street-facing facades a high degree of detailing. Tall, vertically modeled chimneys rise high above a roof clad with tiles that carefully match the unusually bright color of the sandstone walls. The house has three towers. The main tower on the right front is three stories high with an unusual distribution of window types. The windows on the first floor have one transom above them, the ones on the second floor have two transoms above them, and the ones on the third floor have no transoms. This tower's roof has the same squat witch's-cap shape seen at 310 West Pitkin Avenue (see page 327). A smaller secondary tower has a recessed balcony and is incorporated into the corner of the house. The third tower is at the rear of the side facade. The matching carriage house has its own small tower and a stepped parapeted roof.

101 East Orman Avenue (private), Stickney House, 1890; William H. Ward and F. A. Hale, architects. This remarkable design clearly demonstrates the close relationship of the Shingle and Richardsonian Romanesque styles. The Shingle elements at the top of the house—an unusual-shaped and balconied front-facing gable and two oriel windows of differing shapes and sizes—fit effortlessly onto the more Romanesque lower portion of the house with its rough-faced ashlar stone and broad Romanesque-arched entry. As if to emphasize the asymmetry, the rounded oriel window has two window designs hung together in one row.

centered beneath the elliptical fanlight, and there would be decorative sidelights on each side. Here, the designer opted for an unusual asymmetry—one broad decorative sidelight with an off-center door to the side. There are two additional elliptical-arched window designs—one in a transom on the left that balances the entry transom and the other in a larger half window centered in front of the entry steps. The one-story garage matches the main house.

102 West Orman Avenue (private), Orman House, 1890; William Lang, Denver, architect. Denver's premier Victorian-

TRINIDAD

FOUNDED 1859

Population Growth:

1860 ....NA

1900 5,000

1940 13,000

1990 9,000

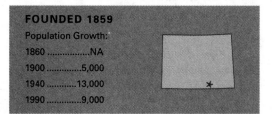

The Trinidad area, long a favored camping site on the northern or "Mountain" branch of the Santa Fe Trail (see page xx) at the southern end of Colorado's Front Range corridor, was first permanently settled in the 1860s by both Anglo and Hispanic farmers and ranchers. The region's lush grasslands were soon converted into large ranches while farmers of fertile riverside fields grew wheat and vegetables. Much of the area's agricultural produce was first marketed in the Denver area's gold-rush boom (see page 297).

Still a small local trade center when Colorado's first railroads arrived in the 1870s, Trinidad soon paired with Pueblo, eighty-five miles farther north, to create one of the nation's great steel-making centers. The scenic mesas around Trinidad contained thick layers of high-grade coal, and the city quickly became a prosperous financial and trade center for nearby small mining towns that supplied fuel for Pueblo's blast furnaces (see page 324).

Trinidad's coal-mining boom peaked about 1920. As the area's economically extractable deposits played out, the Pueblo steel makers shifted to coal mines elsewhere in the Rockies, and Trinidad once again became principally an agricultural trade center. In recent decades the town has also become an important focus for tourism, based both on the area's scenic lakes and mountains and on its surviving concentration of historic architecture. In addition to many fine turn-of-the-century commercial buildings, Trinidad boasts two important museum houses, one of them a rare, large-scale, Hispanic-influenced structure.

Baca House, 1870

East Main Street at Chestnut Street, entrance at 300 East Main Street; 719-846-7217.

The Baca House and the adjacent Bloom House are shown and interpreted together. They were built only twelve years apart, and during that period the first railroad came through Trinidad, bringing with it a wealth of fashionable manufactured goods and stylish building materials from the East. The Baca House represents the town's prerailroad era and shows how a very large and elaborate house looked in a remote corner of the West when all goods and materials had to be either produced locally or hauled great distances in animal-drawn wagons.

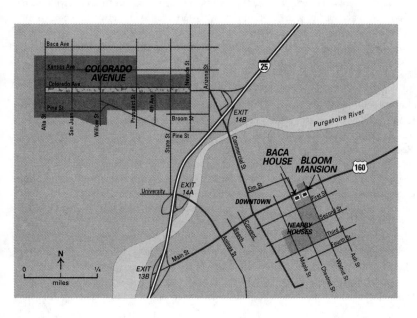

Baca House

time, the simple triangular wooden pediments above the windows and both exterior and interior doorways are typical of the early Anglo-influenced period of Spanish Colonial houses called Territorial. The Victorian-era front porch is clearly a later addition.

The interior of the Baca House is also charmingly simple. The stucco-coated and whitewashed adobe-brick walls are two feet thick. Ceilings are simple planks of wood, and the furnishings are appropriately sparse. The grand piano was hauled over the Santa Fe Trail by wagon, a very expensive proposition. Upstairs, look carefully at the level of detail on the Renaissance Revival furniture in the large front bedroom. You will want to compare it with the more ornate interpretations of the same furniture style in the bedrooms of the Bloom House. Furnishings throughout the house combine both early Hispanic and newly arrived Anglo influences. Outside, across the courtyard, is the *corrillera*, where the Bacas' workers lived. This typical Hispanic outbuilding today houses the informative Santa Fe Trail Museum.

Bloom Mansion, 1882

East Main Street at Walnut Street,
entrance at 300 East Main Street;
719-846-7217.

Shown and interpreted together with the Baca House (see the preceding entry), this elegant Second Empire structure shows what a difference just twelve years made in life on the edge of the western frontier, particularly if the first railroad was built through your town during that period! In 1878 the Atchison, Topeka, and Santa Fe came through Trinidad, linking it with the nation's vast eastern railroad network. Local home-builders could now take advantage of a wealth of fashionable factory-made and relatively inexpensive architectural details, fixtures, and furnishings.

The house was built for merchant and cattleman Frank G. Bloom and his wife, Sarah Thatcher Bloom. Bloom was a Pennsylvania friend and brother-in-law of the wealthy Pueblo industrialist John A. Thatcher (see page 324). He came to Trinidad in 1867 to manage the Thatchers' local mercantile business, and later, with investment capital from the Thatcher family, he incorporated the Bloom Cattle Company, which became a huge operation with ranches in several states.

Among the house's countless factory-made and rail-delivered architectural details are the ornamental metal cresting atop all the roof ridges, the rows of brackets and dentils both outside and inside the huge wrap-around porch, the hood over the upstairs tower window, and the two elegant sets of entry doors. Inside are piped-in-gas-fueled elaborate light fixtures that were

The house was originally built by John Hough, a local merchant and cattle trader. A year after its completion, he left Trinidad and sold the house to Felipe Baca, one of the town's leading citizens, at a price of $7,000 for the house and $1,500 for the furnishings, all paid for with a trade for wool of that value. Originally from Mora, New Mexico, Baca first visited Trinidad in 1860 as a trader taking flour and other goods to Denver-area miners. He noticed the area's fertile grasslands and in 1861 returned with his family to homestead nearby. He raised both cattle and sheep, but his fortune came from his sheep herds and their wool. Baca was one of Trinidad's most respected citizens, serving as a member of the territorial legislature and as president of the school board and donating land for a church and convent.

The basic building material at Baca House is locally made, sun-dried adobe bricks finished with an outer coating of adobe plaster. These form a typically Anglo house shape—a squared box with a hipped roof similar to contemporaneous Italianate houses. At the same

Bloom Mansion

designed to anticipate soon-to-arrive electrical service. Interior details, such as wallpaper, carpeting, fancy hinges and doorknobs, and elegant mantels, could be readily ordered and shipped from the catalogs of distant suppliers. The mantels used here are of wood painted in a faux marble finish. The pair in the two downstairs parlors are fun because their black-and-gold pattern is simply reversed in the two mantelpieces.

Of course not everything was imported from the East. The brick clay and sandstone were obtained nearby, and local pine, painted to resemble imported hardwood, was used for much of the interior detailing.

In spite of its grand exterior, the house inside lacks the usual central stair hall typical of such large and symmetrical designs. Instead, guests enter into a small foyer at the base of the tower from which a pair of doors leads directly into each of two large parlors that dominate the first floor. Behind the spacious parlors are a smaller kitchen and dining room.

Upstairs, the bedrooms have some pieces of furniture acquired by the Blooms. It is instructive to compare the highly elaborated Renaissance Revival furniture seen here with the far simpler interpretations in the Baca House next door. Larger Renaissance Revival pieces, such as headboards or dressers, are usually crowned by an architectural-style "pediment" with varying degrees of elaboration. As in the pediments over Classical doorways, these may be triangular, broken triangular (interrupted at the apex), segmental (curved top), or broken segmental in basic form.

Nearby Houses

Baca House and Bloom House are located in the Corazon de Trinidad Historic District, which covers the heart of old Trinidad, now principally a commercial district. A handful of grand early houses still survive in the area, mostly on what was once called Aristocracy Hill immediately behind the Bloom and Baca Houses. Among these are the following:

Main Street, directly across from Bloom House (private), Chappell House, 1883. This exceptionally creative design interprets the Shingle style with more stone and fewer shingles than is usually the case. The inventive shapes and many simplified details point to Shingle as its primary stylistic inspiration, but the front porch owes much to spindlework Queen Anne designs. Analyzing this unusual house is challenging, as it has had both a new rear addition and some changes to the front porch. Concentrate first on the porch where the slanted Craftsman-era supports on each side of the entry steps are definitely later additions; so is the metal porch railing. But what about the Classical columns on slender pedestals? These could be original, but then again if you look at the Walnut Street facade and up at the small porch tucked under the front upstairs gable, you will see a very heavy turned spindle with an identical one used flat against the house to the rear. These are almost certainly original to the house and seem to be more in the exuberant spirit of the main front porch. So a good first guess would be that all the porch supports might have once looked like these. A porch detail that looks original is the closely spaced, rounded brackets under the cornice. These also continue around the side of the house where they "support" the second-story overhang. The wavy frieze of the porch is strikingly unusual and probably original. Note the line of ornamental stepped windows on the left facade (toward the post office). These likely indicate the location of an original interior stairway. You can continue in this fashion looking at all of the myriad details on this exceptional house. The carriage house is new, but built in the spirit of the main house.

212 Second Street (private), Van Fleet House, 1900–1904. This is a classic example of what we call an Early Eclectic What's It? Prairie-style squared porch supports combine with flared roof eaves on both the main roof and dormers. The gables are covered with shaggy shingles applied in lines of three to form a horizontal pattern. The overall form is that of an early Tudor house, but then there is the anomaly of the flared eaves and shingled gables. The porch supports and flared eaves could be on a Prairie-style house, but the shape of the house is not typical, and there is little roof overhang. After a long hard look, one realizes that if the gable faces were half-timbered the house would be immediately classified as a 1900 to 1910 Tudor house—a time period during which this style so often included a full-width porch with Prairie-style columns. (See also the following entry.)

312 Second Street (private), ca. 1905. Another Early Eclectic What's It? reflecting Trinidad's early-twentieth-century coal-mining prosperity, this house has the same flare to the eaves as 212 Second Street (see the preceding entry), and the front-facing gables are also shingled, although in a slightly different pattern. Here, the house is symmetrical and has a full-width porch, Classical porch supports raised on pedestals, and quoins at the corners. Except for the anomalous flared and shingled gables, this would look like a large and elaborate variation of an early full-width-porch Colonial Revival house.

Colorado Avenue, ca. 1890–1920

Colorado Avenue is the main spine for a large neighborhood, across the river from the original town, which is filled with a typical small-town mixture of houses of various sizes and ages—Queen Anne, Shingle, Craftsman, Spanish Eclectic, and Tudor styles are all found here.

723 Willow Street (private). This side-gabled Shingle-style design has a first floor of uncoursed, uncut rubble stone. Note the long recessed balcony on the side facade facing Colorado Avenue. The two broad dormers on the front facade are each quite different; one is gabled with a balcony recessed beneath; the other has rounded corners

Colorado Avenue neighborhood

and a conical roof. The Classical porch-support columns and the Palladian window show a bit of early Colonial Revival influence. Notice the elaborate brick carriage house behind with the Romanesque-arched carriage entrance that has been adapted to a garage entry.

216–218 Colorado Avenue (private). A rare example of a Shingle-style duplex.

431 Colorado Avenue (private). A rather-funky Italian Renaissance design borrows its open eaves and shaped rafters from the contemporaneous Craftsman style. The house is symmetrical and has unusual massing. A full two-story entry section gives the feeling of an Italian bell tower. This then steps down to one-and-a-half-story wings on each side and then down again to one-story side wings. A full two-story stands behind this carefully composed and "stair-stepped" entry section. Note the red tile roof, the ornamented blind arch above the entry, and the yellow brick, which was favored for Italian Renaissance houses because it gives more of an appearance of stone than does redbrick.

603 Colorado Avenue (private). This one-story Queen Anne cottage features a very slender decorative tower perched unsupported on the porch roof above the entry. Note the notched brick detailing at the corners of the bay window that leaves open spaces that look as if the two planes of the brick wall could simply be fitted back together into a straight wall. Diamond lights enliven the transom of the main bay window.

711 Colorado Avenue (private). This Queen Anne cottage features a tower that is as exaggeratedly fat as the one at 603 (see the preceding entry) is skinny. Note how the front porch wraps around the base of the tower.

Idaho

BOISE

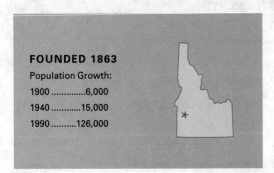

FOUNDED 1863
Population Growth:
1900 6,000
1940 15,000
1990 126,000

Idaho, like its mountainous neighbors Montana and Colorado, received its first large influxes of Anglo settlers in a series of post–California gold rushes that were concentrated in the four-year period from 1858 to 1862 (see page 297). The Idaho strikes were made both in the rugged terrain of its narrow northern panhandle as well as in the southwest, along mountain streams that unite to form the Boise River, a short tributary of the larger Snake River that makes an arcuate slash across southern Idaho. The Oregon Trail, active since the 1830s, followed the relatively flat Snake River Plain

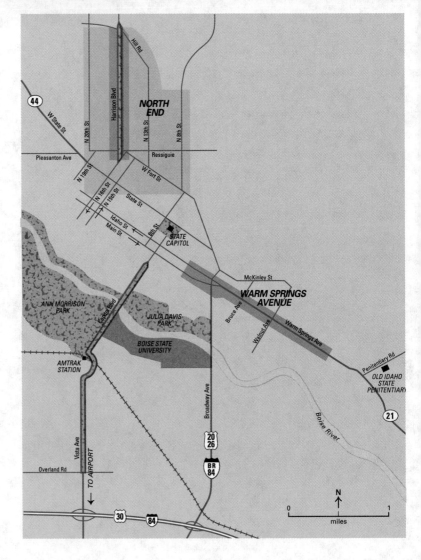

through southern Idaho and provided a well-known wagon route to the nearby Boise River discoveries. These were in territory controlled by Indians who had been tolerant of travelers to Oregon but soon became hostile as a horde of gold seekers arrived to stay in their homeland. As a result, a new military post, called Fort Boise, was established in 1863 to protect the mining camps. By 1870 Boise City, founded adjacent to the fort, was a bustling town of about a thousand persons as well as the capital of the new Idaho Territory.

Boise's location had many advantages—a fertile and well-watered valley for crops and livestock, wooded bottomlands and nearby mountain slopes for lumber and firewood, and, most important of all, a ready market for these products in both the region's numerous mining camps and among its Oregon Trail travelers. The town's principal disadvantage was its isolation. When it was founded, steamboats provided service from Portland up the Columbia and Snake Rivers to the Washington-Idaho border, but the closest of these river ports were separated from Boise by two hundred miles of rough and arduous wagon roads. Equally distant was the first transcontinental rail line of 1869, whose nearest wagon-road connection was at Kelton, in northern Utah.

The Railroads Arrive

Southern Idaho's isolation ended abruptly in 1884 when the Oregon Short Line Railroad, following the venerable Oregon Trail route along the Snake River, completed a main-line connection from northern Utah to Portland. With the railroad, and its many branch lines, came the heavy equipment needed both to expand the state's mining industry and to build dams and canals to make the Snake and Boise River Valleys into large-scale oases of irrigated agriculture. The railroads also made it possible to transport valuable timber, harvested from the vast stands that covered Idaho's mountain ranges, to distant and profitable markets. As both the state capital and the commercial center for this railroad-based prosperity, Boise became Idaho's principal urban center. By 1940 it was a small city of fifteen thousand people.

Modern Boise

As with so many western cities, Boise's population has expanded almost exponentially in the decades since 1940. World War II first brought light industry to the town, and manufacturing has since increased to become a major contributor to the local economy. Expanding state government, and the growth of several local agricultural and forest-products industries into giant corporations, have also been factors in the city's

800 percent growth since 1940. These changes have left Boise with only a handful of architectural survivors from the Victorian city of 1900. Most important of these is the **United States Assay Office** (210 Main Street), a small but handsomely designed sandstone structure built by the Treasury Department to purchase and store, for shipment to distant federal mints, the gold and silver production of Idaho's mines. Completed in 1871, the building retained its original function until 1933 and today houses the Idaho State Historic Preservation Office. Two instructive neighborhoods preserve a few fine late-Victorian houses along with many Eclectic-era dwellings.

Warm Springs Avenue

This historic district stretches for more than a mile southeast from the outskirts of downtown along the route of an 1890s streetcar line. It includes most of Boise's surviving upscale homes from the turn of the century. Late-Victorian and Eclectic-era styles are freely mixed with the greatest concentration of Victorian homes closest to downtown. The avenue takes it name from a small surface spring that, when supplemented by artesian wells drilled in the 1890s, produced a bountiful supply of 171-degree water. This was used for heating houses in the Warm Springs area as well as downtown Boise buildings, reportedly the first such use of geothermal energy in the country.

929 Warm Springs Avenue (private), Anderson House, 1925; Kirtland K. Cutter, Spokane, architect. This fine Tudor design is by one of the region's most distinguished architects (see page 676). Note the parapeted wall on its dominant front-gabled section, which also has an excellent Tudor-arched (flattened-point) entry and a story and a half of tall, narrow windows above. It was built for the owner of Idaho's largest retail store.

1009 Warm Springs Avenue (private), Regan House, 1911; Tourtellotte and Hummel, Boise, architects. An unusual front-facing-U plan characterizes this handsome design. Italian Renaissance in inspiration, it also shows some influence of the contemporaneous Mission style and does not fit neatly into either style. Both typically have tile roofs with a wide eave overhang; in this example, the overhang is boxed in, rather than open, an Italian Renaissance feature. So too are the porch balustrade and Doric columns supporting the entry porch (square columns have replaced the original round ones). On the other hand, the Craftsman-influenced top of the entry porch would more often have been found with the Mission style.

1109 Warm Springs Avenue (private), Moore House, 1891; James King, architect. This dwelling was built for the president of Boise's hot-water-heating company, and his was the first house in Boise to have natural hot-water heat, thereby demonstrating its practicality for more widespread use. It was designed by an early Idaho architect who created a substantial Queen Anne home with an unusual square

Warm Springs Avenue

corner tower set on the diagonal. This has a very high-pitched hipped roof, which gives the house a bit of Chateauesque flair.

Old Idaho State Penitentiary, 2445 Penitentiary Road; 208-334-2844. Located off Warm Springs Avenue about a mile beyond the historic district is this intriguing and sobering complex of historic prison buildings, built from 1889 to 1950 and now operated as a museum by the Idaho Historical Society. Self-guided tours with clear interpretive signs provide a rare look at how a typical state prison functioned from 1872, when the first building, now destroyed, was erected here, until 1973, when, following a destructive riot,

the old complex was abandoned for more modern facilities elsewhere. Located just outside of the prison are three historic dwellings—the Warden's House (private), 1902, Tourtellotte and Hummel, Boise, architects; the Bishop's House (rarely open), 1880s with 1890s addition; and the domestic-scale Guard's House (private), 1912. The Warden's House is a simple four-square design, while the later guard's dwelling has Prairie-style detailing. Both are constructed of local sandstone quarried by convicts. The Bishop's House, a fine Free Classic Queen Anne structure also made of local sandstone, was moved here in 1975 from its original near-downtown location.

Warm Springs Avenue

North End

North End, ca. 1905–1940

The neighborhoods north of downtown are composed of a series of small historic districts, most of them subdivisions platted in the late nineteenth century that continued being built out until 1940 and even after. Many of the homes are of modest size. The portion of North End closest to downtown has had commercial intrusions, and the houses are more scattered.

The showcase of the North End area is tree-lined Harrison Boulevard, whose divided roadway, separated by a landscaped median, was inspired by the turn-of-the-century City Beautiful movement, which emphasized grand, Beaux Arts city planning (see page xxxviii). The boulevard's developer, Walter E. Pierce, was the force behind many of the North End's neighborhoods. It is said that each time he opened a new subdivision he had a fine house built for himself and one for each of his partners. He soon ended up selling these and building new houses in his next subdivision. Harrison Boulevard developed slowly and thus shows a wide spectrum of housing styles ranging from Queen Anne and Neoclassical to post-1940s Ranch houses. The houses become smaller and more modest at the end farthest from downtown. Among the boulevard's many fine designs are:

1305 Harrison Boulevard (private), Looney House, 1905; Tourtellotte and Company, Boise, architects. This is a typical example of a two-story Free Classic Queen Anne design with a round tower. The local architectural firm of Tourtellotte and Company, which later became Tourtellotte and Hummel, designed dozens of these throughout Boise, and the towers on them were such staples of the firm that they became known locally as Tourtellottes. The first floor is of stone, a feature typical of Boise Queen Anne designs. Note that the large through-the-cornice dormer does not overlap the tower and how the double-column porch supports are on stone pedestals with a balustrade connecting the pedestals.

1409 Harrison Boulevard (private), Wyman House, 1908; Tourtellotte and Company, Boise, architects. This house should be compared with the preceding example by the same architects. Many features distinguish this as a very late Queen Anne design. The pitch of both the tower roof and the house roof is lower. The porch is not enclosed by a balustrade, but rather by a solid railing, a feature that was favored in newly fashionable Craftsman designs. Rather than the single windows most often used on Queen Anne houses, there is one double and one triple window. Finally, instead of being separate elements, the squat hexagonal tower interlocks with the dormer, a rare feature in Queen Anne designs.

1505 Harrison Boulevard (private), Bond House, 1911; Tourtellotte and Hummel, Boise, architects. This unusual Mission-style design has its full-width porch recessed into the body of the house and supported by stocky columns. The upper windowpanes have a mullion pattern made of

North End

Colonial Revival. Regency houses are based on English rather than American precedents and are very simplified in detail and appearance. They were popular in the 1930s, probably because their stripped-down appearance made them a more traditional way to emulate the avant-garde Modernistic styles that were in vogue during that decade. Note the parapet at the roof-wall junction and the brick pattern that decorates it. The quadruple casement windows and built-in garage on the front facade are typical 1930s details.

1100 block of West Fort Street (all private). This block includes an unusual group of almost-identical cross-gabled Queen Anne houses, undoubtedly built by the same builder or developer. Each has slight variations of original detailing and later changes.

2312 Pleasanton Avenue (private). Art Deco stylistic detailing was common on public and commercial buildings in the 1920s and 1930s but was rarely found on domestic architecture. This modest north-side dwelling has the distinction of being one of the few such houses the authors have seen anywhere in the country.

curved diamond shapes, with the same pattern found in the lights surrounding the front door. The open roof overhang has shaped rafters that end at the roof edge. The upstairs corner windows are cantilevered out beyond the walls of the house and are supported by handsome brackets in a squared geometric design (see page 668 for related illustration).

1201 Harrison Boulevard (private), Oaks House, 1913; Nisbet and Paradice, architects. This is one of several Boise examples of Neoclassical houses with a full-height entry porch with a lower full-width porch, a subtype most often found in the southern states. Built of brick with stone trim, the side windows, particularly those on the right, have very elaborate keystone lintels above. The column capitals are inventive, with an Egyptian influence. The front porch is partially enclosed, probably a later alteration. A simpler, wood-clad version of the same design can be seen at 1403 Harrison Boulevard (private), Golden House, 1908.

1107 Harrison Boulevard (private), Orr House; 1937. This house is an excellent example of the Regency variation on

North End

Kansas

ABILENE

FOUNDED 1861

Population Growth:

1900 3,500

1940 6,000

1990 6,000

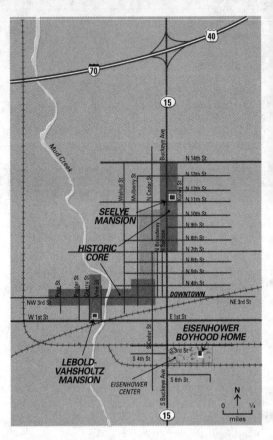

Abilene was the first of the fabled Kansas railhead towns where trail-driven cattle from Texas met the westward-building Kansas Pacific tracks to provide massive railroad deliveries of beef to a war-starved nation. This enterprise was promoted by Illinois cattleman Joseph G. McCoy (1837–1915), who, sensing a unique opportunity, in 1867 purchased 250 acres adjacent to the sleepy village of Abilene shortly before the arrival of the Kansas Pacific tracks. Here he built a large stockyard complex, complete with a hundred-room frontier hotel for trail bosses and cattle buyers and, at the same time, blanketed the Texas cattle lands with advertisements of his new facility.

McCoy's gamble was a roaring success. The vast herds of half-wild Texas longhorns were worth only about four dollars each in their home state, which at the time lacked national railroad connections. Eastern cattle buyers, on the other hand, were happy to pay fifteen dollars or more per head for stock that could be quickly shipped by rail to a meat-hungry nation. Within months, Abilene was a frenzied boomtown

Abilene's cattle drovers'
hotel and stockyards,
ca. 1870

340

with thirty-five thousand animals awaiting shipment and dozens of potential buyers, bankers, and promoters arriving every week.

Abilene's cattle-boom era created large profits for Texas cattlemen and local bankers but was to last only five years. By 1871 farmers had discovered that the area's rich prairie soils grew fine crops of winter wheat, which was easily destroyed by the trampling of large herds of free-ranging livestock. That year marked the end of the town's large-scale cattle shipments, which moved to more westerly Kansas railroad towns, among them Wichita (see page 365). Abilene then assumed the role that it still retains today—a small market center for a prosperous wheat-growing region, supplemented in recent decades by tourism focused around its most renowned citizen, former general and president Dwight D. Eisenhower (1890–1969; see page 343).

Although only reconstructed buildings survive from Abilene's brief and hectic cattle-boom years, the town's agriculture-based prosperity and stable population have given it an unusually fine collection of Victorian and early-Eclectic-era dwellings, three of which are important museum houses (see pages 342, 343, and 344).

Historic Core, 1877–1925

As in so many western towns, Abilene was laid out in a simple grid of north–south streets. Third Street, which runs east–west, was a favored location for upscale Victorian homes—indeed, it was once named Grand Avenue. Around 1900, North Buckeye Avenue, which runs north–south, replaced Third as the most popular street for large new houses.

Abilene Historic Core

Abilene's long period of agricultural prosperity has led to stylish updates on many of its numerous Victorian-era houses. The most common change was the addition of a new and "more stylish" front porch. Most common, a Victorian structure, as revealed by a high-pitched, multigabled roof and upper-story decorative detailing, has received a more simplified Eclectic-era porch with Classical supporting columns.

205 Northeast Third Street (restaurant, 785-263-7336), Kirby House, 1885. After a long period of neglect this large Italianate house underwent an extensive restoration in 1986. Both the front porch and the tower had to be entirely reconstructed from early photographs. Thomas Kirby, the banker who built the home, must have admired the earlier Lebold House (see page 342), for he built a smaller but remarkably similar wooden version of that structure. Both houses have centered towers with concave mansard roofs, paired windows in the tower, and a deep hood over the second-story tower door. The centered location for a tower, while common on Second Empire houses, is relatively unusual in Italianate designs.

515 Northwest Third Street (private), Barber House, 1902. This Colonial Revival house is of the hipped-roof-with-full-width-porch subtype, one of the most common early forms of the style. The entry door placed slightly off-center indicates that this example probably has a typical American four-square interior plan (see also "1100 North Buckeye Avenue," page 342). This style and subtype are always two stories tall and come in three basic widths, often dictated by lot width. The narrowest is adapted to city lots and has a hall on one side with two or three rooms lined up front to back on the other. The widest examples have a centered entry hall with formal rooms to each side. Four-squares, with two front rooms placed side by side and no real circulation hall, make up the midwidth category.

Note the cutaway bay windows on the right side, a holdover from the earlier Queen Anne style. The porch railing covered with Queen Anne–type patterned shingles is quite unusual; it would be interesting to know if it is original. The front door has a lovely oval window of beveled glass, a type of door popular from about 1900 to 1910.

813 Northwest Third Street (private), Rogers House, 1886; porch, ca. 1905. Here is an excellent example of the kind of porch remodeling that took place on so many of Abi-

Abilene Historic Core

Lebold-Vahsholtz Mansion, 1880

106 North Vine Street, at First Street; 785-263-4356; advance reservations required.

Rarely does one house share the combined distinction of being unquestionably the finest Victorian house in a town full of Victorian houses *and* of having incorporated within its walls the home of the town's first settler. But such is the case with this handsome Italianate structure, a miracle of architectural ambition when it was built in this small western town. It is on the site where the town's founder, Timothy Hersey, built a stone-walled dugout home. In 1869 Hersey sold his home and the surrounding land to Conrad Lebold, a prosperous cattle-boom banker. When Lebold later built his grand Italianate dwelling on the site, he incorporated Hersey's dugout into the base of its five-story tower.

Lebold's prosperity did not last long; his bank failed in 1889, and in 1894 his home, which had cost eighteen thousand dollars to build, was sold for three thousand dollars. The home was eventually used as a residence for young women who worked as telephone operators, as an orphanage, and was finally divided into seventeen apartments. When purchased by Merle and Fred Vahsholtz in 1975, the house had been abandoned by all but "pigeons, rats, mice, snakes and skunks." Mrs. Vahsholtz had always wanted "an old derelict mansion that no one else could do anything with and to fix it." Here, she found just what she had been looking for, and as a "retirement" project the couple undertook a massive restoration that included replacing missing bits of exterior trim, rebuilding the porte cochere, adding a new copper roof, and preparing and painting a long-neglected exterior.

The interior presented equal challenges. Many extra walls, baths, and loads of pigeon manure had to be hauled away before the actual restoration could start. Only then could the multiple coats of peeling paint, dingy brass hardware, and parquet floors black with dirt and pockmarked with missing pieces be tackled. Happily, most of the structure's fine original detailing, both interior and exterior, had survived the years of neglect; missing pieces were restored with unusual skill and dedication.

Fifty feet wide by fifty feet deep and containing twenty-three rooms, the house actually has six stories. The basement story was considered the first floor because it was finished and held the main kitchen as well as many servants' rooms. Above this are the two main living stories and a finished attic that is a treat to visit. Finally, the dramatic center tower rises up an additional two stories, one of which is within its mansard roof.

lene's early houses. It is easy to discern the original Italianate house by a look at the upper story with its widely overhanging eaves supported by decorative brackets and by the tall, squared tower. New owners purchased the house in 1901 and shortly afterward added the massive front porch with its gabled roof angled out to the corner. The stone porch railing is a "checkerboard" pattern typical of the Richardsonian Romanesque style and the massive squared porch supports with geometric caps are of Prairie-style inspiration.

214 North Walnut Street (private), Johntz House, 1880. This fine Italianate house commands the corner of North Walnut Street and Northwest Third Street. Its three-story squared tower is embraced by two identical wings of the house, one facing each street. The porch wraps around half of both street facades, and steps lead out from it onto each street. The house has had only three owners, and all have appreciated its architectural integrity and kept it in pristine condition. Note the intricate detailing of the tower—it has a mansard roof with mansard wall dormers featuring roundels (small round windows), decorative roof cresting, and a belt course made from the same decorative trim as the bracketed cornice on the main body of the house.

400 North Cedar Street (private), Gordon House, 1877. This is a fine asymmetrical Gothic Revival design. Built of bricks manufactured in Abilene, it has its original porch with delicate porch supports and matching frieze. Note the cross bracing in the gable, typical of post-1860 examples of the style, and the window crowns with the slight triangular lift in the center.

1100 North Buckeye Avenue (private), Ley House, 1905. Here the Prairie style clothes an American four-square house, forming an excellent example of the Prairie in its most typical vernacular form.

1202 North Buckeye Avenue (private), Shockey House, 1924. This is a familiar interpretation of the Colonial Revival style with its paired windows, Adamesque elliptical fanlight over the front door, and entrance porch with a roofline balustrade. The low-pitched hipped roof and wide eave overhang are holdovers from the American four-square form (see the preceding entry), which was dying out by about 1920.

Lebold-Vahsholtz Mansion

The exterior provides a visual feast of fine details. The walls are of yellow-brown stone quarried at Hays, Kansas, about a hundred miles to the west. Contrasting white quoins and window hoods provide dramatic accents to the darker stone. The fine Italianate porch supports and window hoods are all ornamented with incised Eastlake detail. Tall, floor-length, walk-through windows lead out onto the porch. The paired front entry doors are elaborately detailed. You enter through these into a small anteroom and then into a center hall with thirteen-foot ceilings and a handsome walnut stairway.

From the very first, the Vahsholtzes intended to open their home to the public and to live in it as well. An unusual program, but fortunate because people were flocking to see their resurrected home anyway. Today, it is filled with the Vahsholtzes' large collection of antiques, which includes an exceptionally large collection of tapestries, many fine antique dresses and toys, and an entire houseful of antique furniture, mostly Victorian. The challenging program of living in a tour house has worked well for almost twenty years, perhaps because the tour, always given by a family member, is as lively and rare as the house itself.

Eisenhower Boyhood Home, 1887

201 Southeast Fourth Street,
in the Eisenhower Center; 785-263-4751.

This small Italianate house was built by schoolteacher Ephraim Ellis in 1887 and then purchased by Dwight D. "Ike" Eisenhower's grandfather just five years later. He then sold it to Ike's uncle, who in turn sold it to Ike's father in 1898. Ike was eight years old when he, his four brothers, his parents, and his grandfather came to live in what was then a four-room house. Still on its original site and kept exactly as it was when the Eisenhower family lived there, this home offers a rare look at the furnishings and lifestyle enjoyed by an early-twentieth-century middle-class household in a small western town.

The original Italianate house with its side hall and two rooms on each floor is easily discernible from the exterior. As was often the case, as the Eisenhower household prospered, its home grew. In 1900 two downstairs rooms—a small room for Ike's grandfather and a larger bedroom for his parents—were added to the east side of the main house. In 1906 a new porch

Eisenhower
Boyhood Home

with more stylish Classical columns replaced the Italianate original, as in so many Abilene homes. A few years later, after grandfather Jacob's death, his bedroom was turned into a bathroom, for city water and sewer lines were now available. Finally, in 1915, four years after Ike had left to study at West Point, the rear kitchen and back porch were added.

Ike's parents died in the 1940s, and their sons gave the house and its contents to the Eisenhower Foundation with the condition that it remain just as it had been when the family lived there. What they could not have foreseen was that brother Ike would become president, and that the library and museum commemorating his life would be built around it, changing its entire setting and bringing an international audience that can permanently visit the modest but typical turn-of-the-century setting that helped mold a remarkable American soldier and statesman.

Seelye Mansion, 1905

1105 North Buckeye Avenue; 785-263-1084.
Dr. A. B. Seelye (died 1948) and his wife, Jennie (died 1951), built this handsome Neoclassical home with money earned from Dr. Seelye's patent medicines. He began making these products in his mother's kitchen and went on to employ twenty wagon-driving salesmen to distribute his popular remedies across fourteen states. Seelye's most famous and lucrative item was a cure-all known as Wasa-Tusa, which was recommended for a multiplicity of conditions afflicting both man and beast. Joining it were over a hundred other

products such as Ner-vena and Fro-Zona. These were produced in a downtown Abilene factory that until the mid-1990s remained much as it was at Dr. Seelye's death almost fifty years earlier. Today a small building erected behind the Seelye Mansion houses a time-capsule selection of his manufacturing equipment, sales records, and unsold stock of medicines.

In 1904 the Seelyes were earning a large income, and Mrs. Seelye decided it was time to build their family a suitable new home. She commissioned a New York architect, whose name appears to be lost, and then took the family to the 1904 World's Fair in St. Louis to inspect all of the latest things available for the new home. Upon their return, working drawings were completed. Construction began in April 1905 and was finished in time for the family's Christmas celebrations. Mrs. Seelye herself supervised every detail of construction, checking each day's work against the blueprints with measuring tape and level.

The home is set on an entire city block. It has a finished basement, two main floors, and a third-floor ballroom, which also provided quarters for the traveling salesmen as they returned to replenish their wagons. In the basement is a Box Ball (similar to bowling) alley purchased at the St. Louis fair. Other discoveries of Mrs. Seelye at the fair were early Edison light fixtures and bulbs. She purchased these for the entire house, where they remain in place.

Most of the home's furnishings are original, as the house remained in the family until 1993. The Seelyes had two daughters—Marion (1895–1988) and Helen

Seelye Mansion

(1897–1993)—who never married and spent their entire lives in the family home. In 1982 the sisters sold the house and its entire contents to twin brothers Terry and Jerry Tietjens, who agreed to undertake their lifelong care as a part of the purchase agreement. The Tietjens began opening the home for regular tours in 1985, but also continued to care for their "honorary" grandmothers in the home until their deaths at ages ninety-three and ninety-six—old enough to make one a believer in Wasa-Tusa. Today, after his brother's death, Terry lives alone in the grand home.

The house is an intriguing example of the Neoclassical style in the full-height-entry-porch-with-lower-full-width-porch subtype. What makes it unusual is the sinuous inward swing of the one-story porch, which is echoed by the shape of the recessed entry facade. Handsome Ionic pilasters, echoing the grand columns of the entry porch, ornament the facade. Inside, much of the detailing is Colonial Revival in inspiration and includes a handsome fireplace that dominates the entry hall and a fine open stairway that ascends three full stories to the top-floor ballroom. Particularly unusual is the accessory stair leading directly from the dining room to the Box Ball alley in the basement, thus providing easy access to after-dinner entertainment.

ATCHISON

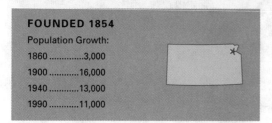

FOUNDED 1854

Population Growth:

1860 3,000
1900 16,000
1940 13,000
1990 11,000

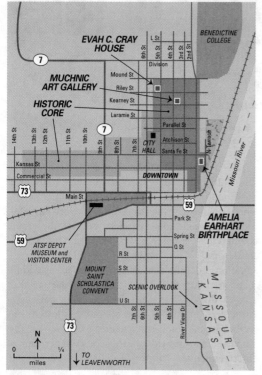

EVAH C. CRAY HOUSE

BENEDICTINE COLLEGE

MUCHNIC ART GALLERY

HISTORIC CORE

Mound St
Riley St
Kearney St
Laramie St

L St
6th St 5th St 4th St 3rd St 2nd St
Division

Parallel St
Atchison St
CITY HALL   Santa Fe St

14th St 13th St 12th St 11th St 10th St   9th St 8th St 7th St

N Terrace

Missouri River

Kansas St
Commercial St

DOWNTOWN

Main St

59

Park St
Spring St

AMELIA EARHART BIRTHPLACE

Q St

ATSF DEPOT MUSEUM and VISITOR CENTER

R St
S St

MOUNT SAINT SCHOLASTICA CONVENT

SCENIC OVERLOOK

U St

7th St 6th St 5th St 4th St

River View Dr

M I S S O U R I   K A N S A S

N

0   ¼
miles

↓ TO LEAVENWORTH

rian John Reps, in his *Cities of the American West*, clearly summarizes the situation in both Atchison and nearby Nebraska City, Nebraska (see page 404):

> Atchison and Nebraska City had much in common: a favorable location with respect to the wagon routes west, an initial prosperity depending almost exclusively on the overland freighting business, . . . a utilitarian grid plan, . . . ambitious town promoters, and wildly optimistic predictions of a glorious future. Yet by 1880 the seemingly prosperous cities had already lost some of their momentum. . . . Omaha to the north and Kansas City to the south succeeded in capturing the major railways, river traffic dwindled, and Atchison, like Nebraska City and Leavenworth, was left as a small city serving mainly the manufacturing and trading needs of the immediate vicinity.

Such early growth followed by a more modest economic role can sometimes, as in both Atchison and Nebraska City, lead to long-term population stability and the resulting survival of an unusual number of important early buildings.

Historic Core, ca. 1865–1920

Atchison retains a remarkable collection of fine Victorian houses clustered in a picturesque hillside historic district located just to the north of the downtown commercial and industrial area. Many of the district's larger homes have received stylish updating during their long period of prosperous, single-family occupancy. These provide a rare and historically significant look at a spectrum of upscale Victorian house alterations. Also included in the district are three important museum houses.

305 North Terrace Street (private), Howard House, 1885. Brick houses with Stick-style detailing are relatively rare; the Howard House is an excellent example. Note the diagonal porch-support braces behind the screen of the front porch and in the one-story side bay window, and also the upside-down-picket-fence pattern used beneath the side gables. The main side gable has curved-wood trusswork set out from the brick face of the house.

203 Second Street (private), Pease House, 1880. This late Italianate design has relatively simple detailing. Closely spaced brackets at the roofline, simplified flat window hoods, a handsome entry porch, and a pair of doors with narrow vertical windowpanes are among its important features.

503 North Second Street (private), Glick House, 1873; remodeled, 1913. The slightly unusual shape and form of this

Atchison and Leavenworth, its neighbor twenty-five miles to the south (see page 353), were the principal Missouri River ports founded in the new Kansas Territory when it was opened to Anglo settlement in 1854. Both towns quickly became important centers for wagon freighting of steamboat-delivered supplies bound for the military posts and frontier settlements served by the venerable Oregon-California Trail, a branch of which crossed northeastern Kansas from a long-established terminus farther east at Independence, Missouri. As with their river-port rivals along the Missouri in adjacent Nebraska, this wagon-freighting prosperity was to prove short-lived. Histo-

Tudor house is explained by the fact that it is a remodeling of a large 1873 Victorian design. The original house was built by J. W. Glick, the first Democrat to be elected governor of Kansas. In 1913 his daughter, Jennie Orr, and her husband undertook an almost-complete stylish update, which gave it the Tudor exterior seen today.

805 North Fourth Street (private), Brown House, 1879; remodeled, 1890. This house has distinctive dual-color window tops that are typical of high-style polychrome Gothic Revival houses. The steeply hipped roof and ornamented gabled dormers in the right wing are also Gothic Revival features. In 1890 the house received a stylish update that included the addition of a front porch with Richardsonian Romanesque arches in its railing. The entire porch could have been designed at that time, but it is possible that the porch-support columns, which appear a bit slender for the square plinths above them, could have been added at a still-later date.

806 North Fourth Street (private), ca. 1910. This Colonial Revival design has an unusual feature seen in several Atchi-son houses. The entry door is set out from the main facade by ornate curved windows on either side. A similar example is on a typical four-square shape at 609 North Fifth Street (private). Here the decorative windows are much shallower, with curved brick below.

819 North Fourth Street (private), Waggener House, 1886; H. R. Prudden, architect. This imposing Queen Anne house was built for W. P. Waggener, a railroad attorney and politician. It is a measure of Atchison's late-Victorian prosperity that its 1886 downstairs wooden porches, probably of spindlework, received a stylish update in 1896 when they were replaced with elegant Romanesque porches, designed by architect George Washburn. The third-floor balcony porch under the front-facing gable gives a feel for the kind of wooden detailing that likely graced the original porches. The earlier house and the Romanesque porches fit together so well that it is not immediately obvious that they have been changed. It takes a second look to begin to realize that their Romanesque detailing is later than the spindlework porches above. Like the Muchnic Art Gallery (see page 350), this house has several fine open upstairs porches and balconies. The extensive patterned brickwork was executed by John Fletcher Thompson and enlivens much of the surface of the house and its massive chimneys. A serious pair of gargoyles sits atop the roof.

820 North Fourth Street (private), ca. 1880s; remodeled, ca. 1930s. This is one of the more unusual stylish updates we've encountered. Someone found themselves in possession of a large Queen Anne house and yearned for a Modernistic design of the Streamline ilk. All along the side, one can see surviving Victorian features—cutaway bay windows, stepped stained-glass windows marking what must have been the original stairway, and other bits of assorted detail. In order to achieve the desired Modernistic look, the roof was lowered, glass block was added in the corner window, an octagonal window and curved front porch were added, and everything was painted white.

519 North Fifth Street (restaurant, 913-367-4996), 1864–1894. This unusual house was begun in 1864 by Elijah Norton, then enlarged in 1869 by Otis Gunn, and not finally completed until 1894 by George Pennell. The long period of construction and the tastes of three successive builders have given it a distinctive character all its own.

1301 Kansas Street (private), McInteer Villa, 1890. John McInteer was an Irish immigrant who earned a handsome living outfitting departing wagon trains and wisely invested his profits in income-producing real estate that survived the decline of wagon freighting. Some of his later earnings went into this grand and individualistic Victorian home. The Stick-style porch is rather modest, but is only the underpinning for a design that gets progressively more exuberant with each story. The roof has a tower with a witch's-cap roof, rounded dormers, open spindlework balcony, and bulging chimneys. The tower has two overhangs, one at each story and both with curved overhangs below. Despite the Stick detailing of the porch, the house is not Stick style; it is a one-of-a-kind creation dominated by builder Owen Seip's unique wall patterns of stone-accented brick.

Amelia Earhart Birthplace, 1861

223 North Terrace Street; 913-367-4217.

One of Atchison's earliest surviving styled dwellings, this charming Gothic Revival house is a memorial to

Atchison Historic Core

one of the town's most avant-garde natives—the pioneering aviatrix Amelia Earhart (1897–1937). Perched high on a bluff overlooking the Missouri River, with grounds that once extended all the way down to the river's banks, the house was built by her grandparents, Judge Alfred Otis and his wife, Amelia Harres. Amy Otis Earhart, the Otises' fourth child, chose to return here for the birth of her first daughter, who was named Amelia after her grandmother. But this house was not only Amelia's birthplace, it was also where Amelia and her younger sister, Muriel, spent much of their young lives, as their mother frequently traveled with their father.

Not until Amelia was eleven did her father have a desk job and the girls move elsewhere to stay with their parents. It was, however, a nomadic existence, as the family moved almost yearly, following the father from job to job. Atchison was therefore Amelia's only real childhood home. Here she built her famous "roller coaster," a kind of early skateboard made from roller skates and wood. Here she and her sister roamed freely, walked on stilts, and played baseball in their advanced "bloomers" while their classmates stood by primly in long skirts.

Standing in the window of Amelia's bedroom, one can easily imagine how she might have yearned to sail out the window and through the air, swooping down and along the river. But it was to be many years before she developed her love affair with flying. Always fiercely independent, she had quit the Ogontz School near Philadelphia before graduation to serve as a nurse to the men returning from the First World War. She took a year of premed work at Columbia before her mother talked her into coming home for a summer in Los Angeles—a summer that turned into a fateful two-year stay.

Having nursed many young pilots, Amelia found herself visiting nearby airfields and air shows, finally paying one dollar for a ten-minute ride. As she later wrote, "By the time I had gotten two or three hundred feet off the ground, I knew I had to fly." It cost an expensive one thousand dollars to learn, and her family did not have the money. So for the next two years, Amelia worked at a full-time job to pay for weekend flying lessons. In 1922 she earned her international pilot's license from the Fédération Aéronautique Internationale and became one of the first women in the world to be so licensed. She had saved up funds as well during this period, and these, combined with gifts from her mother and sister, purchased her first plane. Almost immediately Amelia set a women's altitude record.

Soon her parent's long-troubled marriage ended, and Amelia sold her plane to move to Boston with her mother. After a rare interlude of confusion about her goals, she got a job as a social worker in a Boston settlement house where she was an immediate success with the young girls that it served. But the expensive business of flying was still much on her mind; she joined the Boston chapter of the National Aeronautic Association and on weekends demonstrated aircraft to potential buyers in order to be able to fly.

Then, in April 1928, Amelia received an unexpected invitation to become the first woman to cross the Atlantic in a plane, although she would only be a passenger. The flight was an enormous success, and its tumultuous publicity completely changed her life. Practically overnight Amelia became a lecturer, author, and role model for young women of the 1920s. At the same time, she was filled with guilt over her fame—a fame she felt was not deserved, as she had, in her view, done nothing more than ride as a passenger in a plane piloted by others. She now actively set out to *earn* the recognition she was already receiving.

In late 1928 Amelia became the first woman to fly solo across the United States. In 1929 she was a founder and first president of the Ninety-Nines, Inc., an international organization of women pilots that today owns the Earhart Birthplace. She married her publisher-manager, George Putnam of G. P. Putnam and Sons, in 1931, and other triumphs followed. She became the first woman to fly solo over the Atlantic Ocean in 1932. In 1935 she was the first person of either sex to fly solo from Hawaii to California and later that year the first to fly solo from Burbank, California, to Mexico City to Newark, New Jersey. She lectured constantly, sometimes in more than a hundred cities in a single year. In 1935 she became an aeronautical adviser and career counselor at Purdue University.

Then in 1937, after massive preparations and one false start, Amelia Earhart embarked on her ill-fated round-the-world flight with Fred Noonan as her navigator. World press followed her feverishly from stop to stop for the next month as she successfully completed twenty-five of twenty-eight long legs of the trip. The twenty-sixth leg was to be 2,556 miles, from Lae, New Guinea, to Howland Island, a tiny island in the midst of the Pacific. It was the most dangerous part of the trip and the one requiring the most exact navigational skills.

She and navigator Noonan took off on July 2. The radio communications with the Coast Guard, planned to assist them, were not well organized. They were passing near Japanese territory at a time when many were expecting war with the Japanese. A series of enigmatic radio messages came from Earhart as she should have been approaching Howland Island, requesting posi-

Amelia Earhart Birthplace

tions and weather. The time for her to arrive passed and then the messages stopped. A massive and fruitless air search followed. The logical assumption was that they strayed off course, ran out of fuel, and went down. But the impending war, the necessary State Department and U.S. military support of the trip, and the other circumstances created a mystery around the flight and its end that still continues. Many believed she had been on a mission for the U.S. government or that the Japanese had captured her. A definitive answer has never emerged.

During the 1920s and 1930s Amelia was a central figure in promoting both the emerging field of aviation and the multifaceted roles that courageous women could play in society. She had strong views on many subjects and was a committed feminist as well as pacifist. Speaking to the Daughters of the American Revolution in Washington, D.C., she said, "You know you really shouldn't have invited me here. I always say what I think and you may not like it." She discussed war. "You glorify it. You applaud the marching feet and the band and you cheer on the military machine. You really all ought to be drafted." Applause was tepid. In school, accused of not believing in God when she defended a Hindu poet's right to worship as he pleased, Earhart replied, "God, to me, is a power that helps me to be good. The way we worship isn't a bit important." And about women's roles, she said, "I am not one to set any

boundaries upon the work of men or women nor restrict them except by the natural laws of individual aptitude." Her high school yearbook described her as "the girl in brown who walks alone."

Here in the Earhart Birthplace, it is her life and accomplishments that are celebrated and the role she played both in the development of aviation and women's rights. The house itself was long out of the family when it was purchased by prominent Atchison physician Dr. Eugene R. Bribach, who donated it to the Ninety-Nines, the international women pilots association that Earhart had helped found. This group has undertaken a lengthy and still ongoing restoration of the house.

The house is a two-story, centered-gable Gothic Revival cottage, a style and subtype that was quite popular along the Missouri River in the 1860s and 1870s. The front entry door has a typical Gothic drip-mold decorative crown. Upstairs, double doors, constructed to look like a pointed-arch Gothic window, open out from the hall onto the porch roof, which provides a dramatic view over the Missouri River. The original house is wood clad and has simple interior detailing, but a later dining room addition has elaborate Eastlake-inspired woodwork, stained-glass windows, and angled corners. Built of brick, the dining room addition was probably added in 1873 and is connected to the house via an enclosed breezeway. Looking about the grounds and down toward the river, one can imagine the free-spirited Amelia, accompanied by her younger sister, Muriel, in their new bloomers and with their stilts and footballs, mildly shocking their less adventuresome neighbors.

Muchnic Art Gallery, 1888

704 North Fourth Street; 913-367-4278;
W. F. Wood, architect.

Don't be confused by the name of this handsome museum house, for although three upstairs bedrooms have been converted for the use of a popular community art gallery, the remainder has been beautifully preserved as a house museum. The home was purchased in 1922 by Mr. and Mrs. H. E. Muchnic, who owned the prosperous L. F. M. Foundry. The Muchnics were hospitable people and enjoyed sharing their extraordinary home with the community while they were alive. After their deaths, it was left to the Muchnic Foundation so that it could continue to be enjoyed by the public.

This was indeed fortunate, for the house is a rare survivor of such once-common grand spindlework Queen Anne designs. These houses, with their many open porches and extensive exposed woodwork, are notori-

ously difficult to maintain. In most remaining examples, the open porches and balconies have been enclosed and deteriorating wooden detailing removed without replacement. Here the Muchnic Foundation has kept the home not only intact, but beautifully preserved in pristine condition.

Purchased by the Muchnics in 1922, the house was originally built for George W. Howell, a wholesale lumber merchant. For several years before construction began, Howell used his business connections to gather fine woods for the house's interior detailing. This explains the home's extraordinary parquet floors of walnut, mahogany, and oak and its handsome wood paneling and carved wooden details. The parquet floors are in the large living hall, the upstairs hall, the dining room, and the library. These areas also retain their original wood paneling, hand-carved details, and lovely stained-glass windows. Cast-bronze hardware and original fireplaces and surrounds occur throughout the house. The upstairs hall has very unusual tooled leather used as wainscoting and also in panels above the doors. A small downstairs conservatory is beautifully preserved with its original glass-top roof and stunning stained-glass panels with appropriate floral designs.

Muchnic Art Gallery

The huge living hall has an English baronial feel with its heavy, carved stairway and heroic fireplace.

The furnishings in the house belonged to the Muchnics. They were able to repurchase a few of the house's original pieces, like the mirrors in the upper and lower halls, but most are from the 1920s and reflect the comfortable, overstuffed sitting pieces popular in that period. A huge triple parlor fills the entire left side of the house, and here the Muchnics indulged their love of French antiques. The three rooms are connected by broad, segmental-arched openings, and all of the Victorian woodwork is covered in light paint. A period photograph on display shows the same rooms with Victorian furnishings and the woodwork already painted. It is thus likely that the room, either originally or very early in its history, was decorated in the light "feminine" look that was often favored for the parlor even in the most heavily paneled of Victorian-era houses. The Muchnics simply created their own 1920s variation.

The exterior of the house is equally well preserved. It has its original wraparound spindlework porch, an elegant design with paired spindle supports with cutout panels between, a frieze and railing that echo each other, and solid carved spandrels. Standing on the porch, you get a feeling for the fine construction of the entire house. The porch floor slopes gently downward, to drain water away from the house, and even the porch ceiling is nicely detailed as it wraps around the corner tower. In addition to the main porch, there are three other porches. One, in the third story of the tower, is a very unusual survivor. Such open tower porches were a favored high-style Queen Anne feature, but because of their constant exposure to wind and water damage, most were later enclosed. This one remains intact, with doubled porch supports and solid spandrels that are miniature versions of those on the front porch. An unusual walkway connects the porch with an attic-story ballroom. Both the front and side-facing gables have additional balcony porches tucked under them, a third-floor version on the front facade and a large second-floor example on the side.

Evah C. Cray Historical House Museum, 1882 and later

805 North Fifth Street; 913-367-1948 or 913-367-2427; Alfred Meier and John Peterson, architects.

The original part of this house and the matching carriage house behind were built in 1882 in a late-Victorian interpretation of a rear-towered Second Empire design. The carriage house remains relatively unmodified, but the house has had at least two major stylish updates. The first was the addition of the large tower on the right front of the house. This was added

Evah C. Cray Historical House Museum

early by the W. W. Hetherington family who built the house and whose descendants lived here until 1962. Mr. Hetherington won a trip to Europe, and on this trip Mrs. Hetherington is reported to have decided that she had to have a Scottish-type tower on her house. Soon after their return (the exact date is uncertain), she added the large castellated tower.

The broad front porch looks like it was added in about 1905 to 1910, likely to replace an earlier one. One of the most striking exterior features of the house, the remarkably detailed spindlework porte cochere, is still a mystery. Was it a part of the original house, a part of the tower addition, or yet-another addition? Did it originally connect directly into a similarly lavish front porch? Another interesting exercise is to look at the two different kinds of windows on the mansard roof. The paired window on the left front has a late-Gothic influence, while the right-front window, which has a mate on the side facade on the other side of the tower, looks like a more typical Second Empire window. This intriguing house badly needs a detailed historic-structures report to unravel its past and guide future restoration efforts.

The interior of the Cray house is more easily understandable, as most of the original 1882 woodwork and fireplaces still survive. The downstairs woodwork has

Eastlake incising, and the house's five fireplaces are faced with tile. Many of the original art-glass windows and chandeliers are still in the home. Throughout the upstairs, the detailing is much simpler. The slightly later tower has sunny rooms on each floor; its first-floor interior woodwork was imported from Scotland.

From 1962 until 1978 the house had a series of owners. Its present life as a Victorian house museum began when Evah C. Cray (1901–1992) needed a Victorian house to hold her growing collection of Victorian furniture and artifacts. There is only one piece of furniture original to the house—a huge and elaborate hall piece with griffins on which to hang one's hat. This was apparently too massive to be sold at auction like the rest of the furnishings. Many of the larger pieces of furniture on display came from the large Victorian home of one of Mrs. Cray's friends. A few other items are from the Atchison County Historical Society, but everything else in the home was collected by Mrs. Cray, wife of the founder of Midwest Grain Products, one of Atchison's largest industries. Spry and energetic, she collected everything that appealed to her, even into her late eighties. The home today is owned and administered by the Evah C. Cray Charitable Trust.

LEAVENWORTH

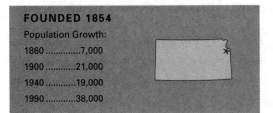

FOUNDED 1854

Population Growth:

1860 7,000

1900 21,000

1940 19,000

1990 38,000

The town of Leavenworth, like its neighbor Atchison, twenty-five miles to the north (see page 346), was founded as a Missouri River port immediately after the new Kansas Territory was opened for Anglo settlement in 1854. Leavenworth had one important advantage over its nearby rival—it was named for, and located adjacent to, an early military post that had already served as the region's center of Anglo activities for almost three decades.

Founded in 1827, **Fort Leavenworth** was one of the first government outposts in the then-largely-unexplored West. From its initial role of protecting wagon traffic along the recently established Santa Fe Trail (see page 442), the fort went on to play crucial roles in both the Mexican and Civil Wars before becoming one of the nation's most important military training centers, a distinction it still holds today.

The promotional founders of the 1854 *town* of Leavenworth, located three miles south of the fort, deliberately chose the name to suggest to potential lot buyers its proximity to the protective garrisons and supply de-

pots of the familiar military post. This strategy was a great success. By 1860 Leavenworth was the largest town in Kansas and a principal organizing point for wagon trains of river-borne supplies destined for the distant mining towns, agricultural settlements, and military posts of the western plains and mountains.

Leavenworth was to maintain its dominance until 1880, when its population reached twenty thousand. With the rapid spread of the western rail network and the decline of wagon freighting, Kansas City, Missouri, then became the region's principal rail junction and transportation hub, and Leavenworth's growth came to an abrupt end. Now principally a service center for three nearby federal institutions—military fort, penitentiary, and veterans' hospital, the town retained its 1880 population size until the 1940s. Regrettably, much of its Victorian architectural heritage has disappeared in the post-1950 decades; among the survivors are a fine museum house and some of its grand early neighbors. Fort Leavenworth has fared better than the town and retains a delightful collection of historic officers' dwellings.

Carroll Mansion, 1867 and 1882

1128 Fifth Avenue; 913-682-7759;
George McKenna, Leavenworth, architect.
This handsome Victorian home is owned by, and sometimes advertised as, the Leavenworth County Historical Society Museum. This might suggest that the house's

View of Leavenworth, 1857

Carroll Mansion

interiors have been remodeled for museum displays. This is not the case, for the society early recognized the architectural and historical importance of the house itself and has devoted great effort to furnishing and interpreting it as a house museum. Other types of exhibits are confined to the former garage and two upstairs bedrooms.

The home was built in three stages. First, in 1858, came a simple two-story, wood-framed cottage. In 1867 its owner, building contractor John McCullough Foster, incorporated this earlier home into a large, brick-walled Italianate house. Three bays wide and four bays deep, this is still visible today behind the porches and tower added as part of the third and final stage. This took place when Lucien Scott, the first president of the First National Bank of Leavenworth, purchased the house and wanted to make it more impressive. From 1878 to 1882 he carried out a remodeling campaign with the help of local architect-builder George McKenna. They installed bay windows, parquet floors, indoor plumbing, and gas lighting. A broad Stick-style porch and open tower were added. Most important of all was the handsome new interior woodwork, much of it hand-carved by McKenna. Although the wall coverings have been changed, most of the rest of the 1882 interior remains intact today.

In 1888 Scott sold the mansion to Edward Carroll, an important citizen of Leavenworth who was president of the Leavenworth National Bank. Carroll moved into the mansion with his wife and their six children. The Carrolls were a conservative family that loved their house just as it was, and carefully preserved its 1882 character. It remained in their family until 1964 when Ella Carroll, a daughter and the last owner of the home, donated it to the society. The house was then almost empty, and the Historical Society has gradually furnished it with appropriate Victorian pieces from the Leavenworth area. Some were manufactured locally, and some were shipped up the Missouri River. One bedroom suite belonged to the Carroll family and another to architect-builder McKenna.

McKenna's heroic wood carvings are a Carroll Mansion highlight. The dining room has a matching carved sideboard and fireplace, the latter with a built-in warming oven. The library has beautifully carved wood transoms and built-in shelves. The stairway, entry hall, and the many door surrounds are all equally handsome. Combination gas-electric light fixtures remain throughout the home. Yet-another feature preserved from McKenna's interior remodeling is the art-glass transoms found throughout, all in striking turquoise tones. Even early plumbing features, among them a copper sink in the kitchen and a metal tub upstairs, are still in their original places. A 1911 gas-and-

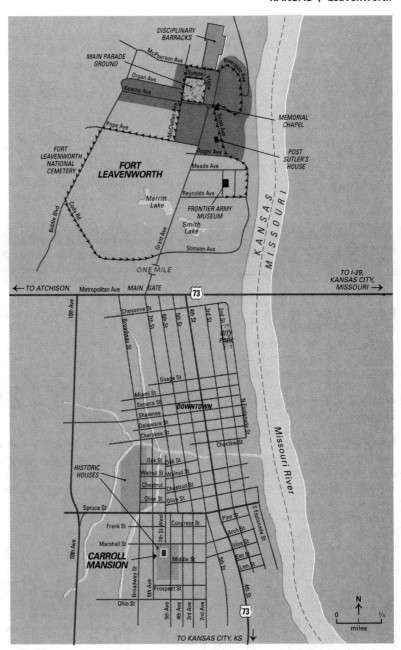

wood stove from the local Great Western Stove Company is in the kitchen. It was manufactured by the next-door neighbor.

Nearby Houses

Other fine Victorian houses are scattered in the blocks near the Carroll Mansion. The most concentrated cluster is on South Broadway Street between Cherokee and Spruce Streets.

1200 South Fifth Avenue (private), Burt House, 1895; William P. Feth, architect. This large home, next door to the Carroll Mansion, is built on land purchased from the Carrolls by Nathaniel H. Burt, the president of Great Western Stove Company, an important Leavenworth industry. This unusual house, with its fat, rounded tower with conical roof and parapeted wall dormer, looks at first glance like it should be Richardsonian Romanesque. But no Romanesque arches are in sight. Perhaps the porches, with their Classical columns, are later additions, or perhaps the house was built as a stylistic combination. It is particularly intriguing that the foundation of the porch and the pedestals on which the columns sit are all made of rusticated stone, which would have been perfect for a more Romanesque porch design.

714 South Broadway Street (private), Angell House, 1884. Queen Anne houses of the half-timbered subtype are unusual outside of the northeastern states, so this large but simplified example is a rare find. It has half-timbering in some of its many gables and also features groups of triple windows, a detail that is most frequent in this subtype. The simple wooden porch supports are typically a bit heftier, but these may be later replacements. Note the low retaining wall around the extensive grounds and what may be the original iron fence.

508 South Broadway Street (private), Abernathy House, 1867; remodeled, 1916; H. Hamblin, architect; Wight and Wight, Kansas City, architects for the remodeling. Here an 1867 towered Italianate house received a skillful stylistic update in 1916 that added the tile roof and the broad colonnaded porch and porte cochere. It all blends together into a remarkably unified whole, perhaps because Italianate and Italian Renaissance houses were inspired by the same Old World sources.

Fort Leavenworth, ca. 1840–1900

Established by Colonel Henry Leavenworth in 1827, Fort Leavenworth is today a national historic landmark; the National Park Service's book *Soldier and Brave* (1971) calls this fort "the oldest active Army post west of the Mississippi [and] one of the most historic in the West and in the Nation." It was founded on the then-remote Missouri River frontier as one of a sparse line of fortifications that guarded the West's "Permanent Indian Frontier." Its location near the eastern termini of the Santa Fe and Oregon Trails soon gave it an important role in protecting wagon trains from Indian attacks.

As mining settlements sprang up and wagon-train traffic increased in the distant West, new forts were established at strategic points along the major trails. By the 1850s Fort Leavenworth had become the principal supply depot for these remote forts. The civilian wagon-freighting firm of Russell, Majors and Waddell was awarded a contract for transporting the supplies and established a large headquarters in the booming town of Leavenworth. According to Horace Greeley, "They counted their oxen by the 10,000s and their wagons by the acres." Even allowing for exaggeration, this enterprise was responsible for the rapid expansion of both town and fort during the 1860s and 1870s.

Indians were not the only business of western forts. During the Mexican War (1846–1848), Fort Leavenworth was the base of operations for the Army of the West, which occupied what were to become the southwestern states. Leavenworth also played a delicate role

during the years leading up to the Civil War, when its soldiers were called upon to keep peace among warring pro- and antislavery Anglo settlers in Kansas.

Had Fort Leavenworth's business ended with the taming of the West, it would today be either in ruins or reconstructed as a historic site like so many of its western contemporaries. In 1881, however, the School of Application for Infantry and Calvary was begun here, and today this has evolved into the U.S. Army's renowned Command and General Staff College, the principal center for training talented midcareer officers for higher responsibilities. In addition, the U.S. Disciplinary Barracks, a military prison, was established here in 1873 and displays the surprising motto "Our Mission—Your Future" over the entrance. But the motto is accurate, as this prison is widely recognized for the success of its rehabilitation programs. Fort Leavenworth National Cemetery, established in 1846, was one of the original twelve national cemeteries designated by Lincoln in 1862. General Henry Leavenworth himself is buried here. These events and much more of the fort's distinguished history is interpreted in the post's **Frontier Army Museum** (see map on page 355 for location; 913-684-3191).

Houses for senior military staff, built in many different eras, are scattered around the fort's eight thousand acres. The army's suggested tour route, shown on the map, takes you past the earliest and most important of these. Italianate, Gothic Revival, and Folk Victorian are the most common styles and frequently occur in unusual combinations. All along the route are signs displaying the construction dates for many of the early houses, all of which are in private use by base personnel.

611 Scott Avenue (private), Post Sutler's House, 1841; enlarged to present appearance, 1860s. Traditionally sutlers were peddlers who followed armies to sell goods and food to the soldiers. In 1841 a log cabin was built here by Hiram Rich, the civilian merchant who sold Fort Leavenworth's soldiers luxury goods like tobacco, writing paper, and liquor and was called the post sutler. In the 1860s a second story and wood cladding were added, creating the front-gabled Greek Revival house you see today. Fairly late in date for this style, the Post Sutler's House has Italianate eave-line brackets, a common feature on late–Greek Revival designs.

620 Scott Avenue (private), 1865. This asymmetrical Gothic Revival house has Italianate hoods above its windows. The cross bracing in the top of the main gable is found almost exclusively in post-1860 examples of the style. Note the lovely side porch, which has a dramatic view overlooking the Missouri River to the rear.

Riverside Avenue, northern end (all private), 1855–1895. This is a rare grouping of simplified Gothic Revival cottages, all clad in wood and painted soft yellow with cream trim. Most are simple, front-gabled forms, but there is at least one gabled-front-and-wing example. At the end of Riverside Av-

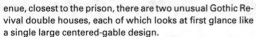

Fort Leavenworth

enue, closest to the prison, there are two unusual Gothic Revival double houses, each of which looks at first glance like a single large centered-gable design.

Sumner Place, just south of the Rookery, two matching duplexes (both private), 1855; E. V. Carr, Syracuse, New York, architect. This matching pair of Italianate double houses is called the Syracuse Houses because they were built by a designer-craftsman-workman from that city. This may explain why they have a bit more stylistic flair than is usual in early military housing.

14 Sumner Place (private), the Rookery, ca. 1834. Reported to be the oldest building in Kansas continuously occupied as a residence, this was originally bachelor officers'

quarters and later became a double house for officers. In the 1850s it served as the first executive mansion for the governor of the newly created Kansas Territory. Future general Douglas MacArthur once lived here.

22 Sumner Place (private), Original Post Commander's House, 1840. This impressive side-gabled brick structure has handsome paired-end chimneys of a type seen on some high-style Georgian houses. Greek Revival details include the full-facade porch, doorways, and three-part windows that open out onto both the upstairs and downstairs porches. Dual-level porches like this were less common on Greek Revival houses than porches featuring dramatic two-story columns.

MARYSVILLE

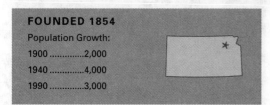

FOUNDED 1854

Population Growth:

1900 2,000

1940 4,000

1990 3,000

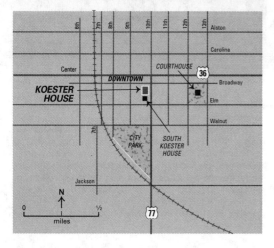

This small agricultural marketing center and county seat grew from a ferry site where the southern branch of the Oregon Trail crossed the Big Blue River. Its principal architectural attraction is a remarkably preserved Victorian museum house.

Koester House, ca. late 1850s and 1874

919 Broadway Street, at Tenth Street; 913-562-2417.

Families frequently moved westward in several stages, and often in family groups. Such was the case with the first two generations of the Koester family, who were ultimately to make Marysville their home. The first generation, Charles Daniel Koester (1796–1866) and his wife, Ludowine (1807–1874), came to America from Germany in 1850 with their two children, Jane Amelia (1834–1928) and Charles F. (1841–1902). The early family history is not entirely clear, but it is certain that daughter Jane married Frank Schmidt in 1856 in Keokuk, Iowa, where their first two children were born. A third child was born in St. Joseph, Missouri, in 1859, and their fourth and final child was born in Marysville in 1860. Jane's parents and brother arrived in Marysville at about the same time. Here Jane's husband

founded a bank and her brother, Charles F., soon joined him in what was to be known for more than a century as the Exchange Bank of Schmidt and Koester.

The Koester House was owned by Jane's parents, then passed to her brother and his family, and, finally, to her nieces. Two fourth-generation Koesters, Jane's great-niece and great-nephew, donated the historic dwelling and all of its contents to the city of Marysville in 1972. The house is located on the northeast quarter of a square block owned by the Koester family. Behind it on the southeast corner is the South Koester House (see page 359), built in 1904 for Charles F.'s only son, Charles John Daniel Koester (1881–1965). The northwest corner of the block is occupied by a group of 1880 storefronts known as the Koester Commercial Block, and the southwest corner is now a city park. In 1977 the family gave the remainder of this square block to the city.

The Koester House was built in two sections. First came the large front-gabled section on the left of the house as seen today. This large folk dwelling was built before the family arrived in 1860, and was purchased by the elder Koesters. After they died, their son, Charles F., expanded it into a vernacular Gothic Revival structure during the period from 1872 to 1874 by adding the two smaller and steeper gables on the right and the broad front porch. The expanded home was completed in time for his marriage to local schoolteacher Sylvia C. Broughten (1848–1883). The couple had three children, Tinnie, Jennie, and Charles J. D.

Sylvia died of tuberculosis when the youngest child was but two years old, after which Charles F. remained in the house with his three children and never remarried. He served as mayor of Marysville and held many other responsible positions. Charles F. particularly loved landscaping, and today one of the unique features of the Koester House is its small Victorian garden accented with many pieces of original nineteenth-century garden statuary and outlined paths. An early brick wall surrounds the house and garden because the picket fence that had been erected by the elder Koesters allowed occasional torrential rains to wash away Charles F.'s tidy paths and plantings. He also added a number of outbuildings, among them a summer kitchen, icehouse, and carriage house. In addition, there was a greenhouse and a gardener's cottage, which was demolished in 1902 to make room for the South Koester House.

Koester House

After Charles F.'s death, his daughter Jennie Lee Koester and her husband, Arthur J. Scott, moved in and kept things much as her father had left them. Later, her widowed sister, Tinnie, moved back into the house with Jennie, whose husband had also died. Unfortunately, after the death of the two daughters, the house was left mostly empty and some deterioration occurred before the house was donated to the city in 1972. Much restoration was then undertaken. Many of the wallpapers and carpets were replaced under the direction of two local antique lovers. Some of the curtains were resewn to the original pattern in new fabric, but one complete original window treatment survives in the dining room. Another unique feature of the house, also found in the dining room, is a large walk-in dish cupboard with a glass wall, so that the family collection of dishes was visible from the dining room as in a more traditional display case, but was exceedingly easy to get out and put up.

The Koesters were a thrifty German family, and the three generations who lived in the house rarely threw anything away. When the fourth generation donated the house, they generously included all of the fixtures, furnishings, and contents. Today, only original furnishings are on display. In addition the house is filled with original family photographs, needlework, dishes, and everything else that went into a well-run household. A storage room adjacent to the summer kitchen still holds a chronology of children's bicycles and tricycles. Another interesting part of the house's collection is Sylvia Koester's wardrobe, which her husband boxed up and labeled when she died in 1883. A Victorian maternity dress was one of the pieces on display the day we toured the house.

908 Elm Street (restaurant, 913-562-2279), South Koester House, 1904. Located just behind the original Koester House, this was built for Charles and Sylvia's only son, Charles John Daniel Koester, on a corner of their lot that held the gardener's cottage, which was demolished to make room for the new house.

This one-story Free Classic Queen Anne design has some Shingle-style elements. These include the two shingled gables with recessed porches—one with a Palladian motif and one with a broad Romanesque arch. The smooth brick walls, the oval-glass front door surrounded with sidelights and transom, and the broad downstairs windows are all typical features of early-twentieth-century designs. This house remained in the family until it was donated to the city of Marysville along with the rest of the block in 1977. Today, it is being adaptively reused as the Koester House Restaurant.

TOPEKA

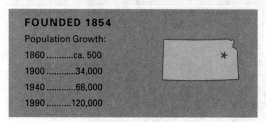

FOUNDED 1854

Population Growth:

1860	ca. 500
1900	34,000
1940	68,000
1990	120,000

Topeka was founded on the Kansas River sixty miles west of its junction with the Missouri River, the region's principal transportation artery in the prerailroad era. Unlike the shallow and sandy Platte River of adjacent Nebraska, the Kansas River was deep enough to accommodate steamboats and thus facilitated early settlement of the eastern interior of the new Kansas Territory. In 1861 Kansas voters made the small town of Topeka the capital of their new state, and its future importance was thus assured.

In the following decade Topeka was to become an unusually important railroad junction. In 1866 the Kansas Pacific (later a part of the Union Pacific) was built through en route to Denver. By 1871 this line gave the town direct rail service to San Francisco. More important, in 1868 Topeka's founder, former Pennsylvania railroad builder Cyrus K. Holliday (1826–1900), began westward construction of his Atchison, Topeka, and Santa Fe Railroad with its headquarters and principal shops in Topeka. Although his visionary goal of linking Kansas with the Pacific and Gulf coasts was not finally achieved until 1885, from then until 1909 the much expanded "Santa Fe" line was the only railroad running on its own rails all the way from Chicago to California.

Because of its importance as a railroad and government center, Topeka had explosive population growth during the 1870s and 1880s. By 1890 its thirty-one thousand inhabitants made it the seventh-largest city in the western interior region, exceeded only by Omaha,

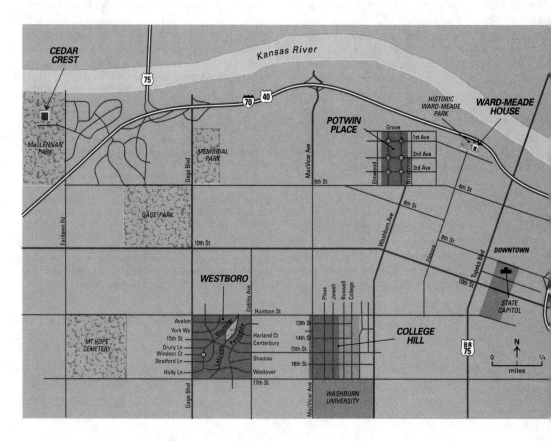

Denver, Lincoln, Salt Lake City, Dallas, and San Antonio. In subsequent decades it has grown less dramatically, and its economy is today dominated by its role as the center of state government.

Most of Topeka's boom-era Victorian neighborhoods have succumbed to later expansions of the commercial core and adjacent government complex, but one small Victorian suburb (see the following entry) survives to provide remarkably intact streetscapes of late-Victorian dwellings. Topeka also has two instructive Eclectic-era neighborhoods (see page 363) and two museum houses (see pages 362 and 364).

Potwin Place, ca. 1885–1915

Most Victorian residential subdivisions were aggressively advertised with phrases such as "Double your money in six months" and "Better than gold-mining stocks" that were designed to encourage speculative purchases of lots for later resale. Potwin Place's developer, C. W. Potwin of Zanesville, Ohio, had a different approach. Seeking a stable neighborhood of home owners rather than land speculators, he relied on word-of-mouth advertising and sold only to those who agreed to build on their lots. Indeed, he would only issue the final deed to the lot as construction was commenced. Potwin's approach clearly worked, for it is exceedingly rare to find such a large concentration of Victorian homes in a single subdivision; most were filled more slowly with mixtures of Victorian and Eclectic-era dwellings.

Two streets, Woodlawn and Greenwood Avenues, form the heart of Potwin Place. These have unusually large building lots, 122 feet wide and 205 feet deep. To vary the grid street pattern, Potwin had large, landscaped circles installed at each intersection; today, these slow traffic and provide visual interest. The original brick streets still remain, and huge trees form graceful tree tunnels. Another unusual feature is the exceptionally broad landscaped area between the sidewalk and the street.

The neighborhood is dominated by Queen Anne houses and includes an unusual number of cross-gabled examples. Added shutters and remodeled front porches are common later additions, but happily many houses have recently been undergoing sympathetic restoration.

303 Woodlawn Avenue (private), Weir House, 1886. This Queen Anne house has an unusually low pitch to its gabled roof, perhaps due to a later rebuilding. It is likely that the entire house originally had spindlework detailing; the downstairs porch supports probably echoed those remaining on the upstairs porch. Note the texture provided by the overlapping rectangular shingles on the second story.

Potwin Place

421 Woodlawn Avenue (private), McLellan House, ca. 1885. This simple-hipped-roof Italianate design is recognizable by its overall shape and the modest paired brackets under the eaves. It originally had a typical Italianate porch that has been replaced by a simpler porch with Classical columns. Although at first glance this might look like an American four-square, it can be distinguished by the shallow eave overhang, the lack of the centered dormer typically present on four-squares, the arrangement of the windows into three regular ranks, and by the Italianate paired brackets.

238 Woodlawn Avenue (private). An excellent example of a spindlework Queen Anne design with a cross-gabled roof, this house appears to have most of its original detailing. The large front-facing gable is ornamented with several different wall patterns—hexagonal textured shingles, grooved boards laid in different directions, and a diamond pattern at the very top. Half-round curves in the corners of the panel above the highest pair of windows echo similar half-round curves in the top section of the somewhat-unusual porch railing. The paired front doors have their upper panes of glass bounded by smaller colored panes.

224 Woodlawn Avenue (private), Nowers House, 1887. This is a simple half-timbered Queen Anne design of the hipped-roof-with-lower-cross-gables subtype. The solid brackets on each side of the paired porch supports are typical of the half-timbered decorative subtype. Note the patterned brick chimney in the center of the roof.

125 Greenwood Avenue (private), ca. 1905. Very simple front-gabled Tudor houses were built mainly before 1915; this one has particularly large areas of half-timbering.

333 Greenwood Avenue (private), Updike House, 1885. The elaborate corner two-story bay window with the overhanging porch above it is a rare Queen Anne feature. This large home originally had much more elaborate spindlework porches, one in the location of the present porch and a second one, of about the same size, facing the side street (in the side rear area that is now enclosed and much modified). Despite the changed porches, this house still has enough original detailing to provide a feeling of its original grandeur.

400 Greenwood Avenue (private), ca. 1910. Most examples of the Prairie style's hipped-roof, symmetrical, with-front-entry subtype are relatively simple American four-square designs. This is a large, handsome high-style version of the subtype, with hard-to-miss massive porch supports, very deep eave overhangs, and a broad one-story side porch on the right. Upstairs the horizontal row of five windows has a continuous sill line that extends across the entire house. These and other windows are ornamented with Wrightian angular geometric designs of colored glass. The left-side facade has a built-in planting box and a long horizontal row of windows in the second story.

338 Greenwood Avenue (private), ca. 1980s. This Neo-Victorian house has done a good job of picking up decorative details seen in the district's original Victorian dwellings. Here the detailing is just a bit flatter and less lush than the originals upon which it is modeled. This subtle difference is quite valuable, as it allows one to recognize this as a modern house. If this characteristic Neo-Victorian flatness is hard to visualize, try comparing the diamond pattern found in the gable with the original textured diamond pattern in the top of the gable at 238 Woodlawn Avenue (see page 361). Next door to the left, at 330 Greenwood Avenue (private), is another Neo-Victorian, as is the house to the right of 338, which appears to incorporate a 1925 chimney.

Ward-Meade House, 1870 and later

124 Northwest Fillmore Street; 785-368-3888.
Located in Historic Ward-Meade Park, near the Kansas River a few blocks east of Potwin Place, is the pioneer dwelling of Anthony and Mary Jane Ward, who paid a Pottowatamie Indian one hundred dollars for a 240-acre farmstead at the edge of the small settlement that was incorporated as Topeka just a few months after they arrived in 1854. The Wards found three one-room log cabins on their property that they moved to this location and joined together to form a more spacious three-room dwelling in which they and their children lived for almost twenty years. The southernmost branch of the

Oregon Trail, and an expensive ferry crossing over the Kansas River, were adjacent to their property, and Mrs. Ward, sometimes called the "Mother of Topeka," is said to have always kept a candle burning in her window to lead weary travelers to her door.

The family led a typical pioneer lifestyle of gradually increasing affluence and in 1870 began construction of a larger and more fashionable new home. Built of brick and stucco with twelve-inch-thick walls, this was in the Italianate style and took the Wards four years to complete. In 1897 one of the Ward daughters, Jennie, inherited the family home. She and her husband, John Mackey Meade, who worked as a civil engineer with the Atchison, Topeka, and Santa Fe Railroad, decided to add a new Neoclassical porch to the Italianate house—a typical ca.-1900 stylistic update.

Today, this house, now known as the Ward-Meade House, is still standing on its original site and forms the core of the historic park. Nearby, the Wards' three-room log cabin has been reconstructed. A tour of the family's two homes focuses on the differences in lifestyle between the frontier era of the early cabin and the luxury of the "new" house. The 1874 house has a few family pieces and many family photographs, but both properties are primarily furnished with appropriate donations. Unfortunately, a decision was made to hold weddings and large events in front of the Ward-Meade home. As a result, the former front yard has been modified. This change in context makes it difficult to fully appreciate the original residential character of the home. Other parts of this small historic park feature moved-in and reconstructed buildings. An arboretum covers part of the five-acre site.

Ward-Meade House

Ward Cabin

College Hill, ca. 1915–1930

This small grid-plan neighborhood is located just across Seventeenth Street from Washburn University. Originally founded in 1865 as a denominational college, Washburn was later taken over by the city of Topeka. MacVicar, Plass, and Jewell Avenues offer the most intact streetscapes, with a bit more campus-housing character creeping in along Boswell and College Avenues. The neighborhood has a pleasing mixture of early-twentieth-century styles—Craftsman cottages, American four-squares, and various styles of period houses all intermingle. Its mostly midsized dwellings provide an instructive chronological transition between the earlier Potwin Place and the later and grander Westboro neighborhoods.

1617 MacVicar Avenue (private), ca. 1925. Modestly but carefully detailed with keystones over the windows, upper windows touching the cornice line, and shutters wide enough to actually close, this side-gabled Colonial Revival house has a quintessential Revival doorway. The broken segmental pediment, complete with pineapple, rarely, if ever, appeared on original Georgian houses but was a great favorite with Colonial Revival architects. In addition, the small fanlight, set into the rectangular window above the door but beneath the pediment, was not found on either Georgian or Adam houses, but was often incorporated into Revival designs. The side wing with the screened-in porch below, seen on the left, was also a favored Revival feature. The attached garage in the right-side wing, if original, was very advanced for 1925.

1625 MacVicar Avenue (private), ca. 1922. False-thatched-roof Tudor houses are among the most picturesque of Eclectic-era houses; this small design is one of the more charming examples we've encountered. The roof shape—with paired, almost-elliptical, gables—combined with the rough stucco texture, casement windows, shapely entry, and perfect centered chimney combine to give it unusual character.

1626 MacVicar Avenue (private), ca. 1929. Built by an architect as his own home, this side-gabled Colonial Revival design combines Colonial features with a high-pitched front-facing gable and a dominant chimney—two features most often associated with the contemporaneous Tudor style. But as used here and by other architects building similar houses,

like architect John F. Staub's own home in Houston, Texas (see "3511 Del Monte Drive," page 612), these features were meant to evoke the feeling of a transitional Medieval-Renaissance English house. Number 1427 MacVicar Avenue (private) has a somewhat-similar combination of features and shows what happened when builders imitated the architect's designs. They tended to take a more obviously Tudor form, here with a side-gabled roof swooping off to the left, and simply added a Colonial Revival entrance.

1517 Plass Avenue (private), ca. 1915. This is an excellent small Prairie-style design of the hipped-roof, symmetrical, with-front-entry subtype. It features the typical massive, squared porch supports and low-pitched hipped roof with broad eave overhang. Less common for a small four-square-shaped house in this subtype are the line of four windows and the continuous sill line that wraps around the house. A similar but more elaborately detailed Prairie design can be seen at 400 Greenwood Avenue in the Potwin Place neighborhood (see page 361).

1619 Jewell Avenue (private). This delightful Tudor cottage features a main gable swooping off to the right, eyebrow dormer, casement windows, and heavily textured stucco walls ornamented with brickwork and half-timbering.

Westboro, ca. 1925–1950s

Curving streets, planted islands at many intersections, and large irregular lots give this subdivision a distinctive character. It contains a wide variety of house styles, including Colonial Revival, Neoclassical, Tudor, French Eclectic, and Ranch. These are, in general, large and late examples of these styles; most appear to have been built from the 1930s into the early 1950s.

3237 Southwest Westover Road (private). This unusual Colonial Revival house of the second-story-overhang subtype has a rare combination of a brick first story and stucco second story. The facade is asymmetrical and the side-gabled roof is relatively high-pitched; both features are true to the spirit of the original post-Medieval houses this subtype is based on, but are rare in Colonial Revival interpretations. The house at 3225 Southwest Westover Road (private) is another example of the same style and subtype. It is a more typical interpretation with a symmetrical main house block. Note the small pendants underneath the overhang at the corners.

1535 Pembroke Lane (private). This Italian Renaissance home appears to be one of the earlier houses in Westboro.

College Hill

Cedar Crest

Light-colored brick was typically used in this style to more closely mimic the stone of the Italian originals. Here the triple-arched entry porch is recessed, and tall double casement windows are used throughout, made to look larger on the first floor with handsome cast-stone surrounds.

1518 Southwest Lakeside Drive (private). We had a hard time deciding when this large Neoclassical house, with nine vertical rows of windows, was built. The cupola and the rounded dormers treated as vents were not generally used in early-twentieth-century houses. Neither were the shallow or simulated window muntins. These clues, along with the not-yet-mature trees, indicate that it is likely a Neoclassical Revival house, built sometime in the last twenty years. It is so carefully proportioned and handsomely detailed that an argument could also be made for an earlier home with newer windows and landscaping.

3200 Southwest Westover Road (private), ca. 1930. Covered in masses of ivy, this large and sprawling towered French Eclectic house angles to follow the irregular shape of its large lot.

Cedar Crest, 1928

1 Cedar Crest Road, off Interstate 70 and Fairlawn Road; 785-296-3636; William D. Wight, Kansas City, architect.

Originally built for Frank P. MacLennan, publisher of the *Topeka State Journal*, and his wife, this became the Kansas Governor's Residence in 1962 after Mrs. MacLennan willed it to the state for that purpose. The house is beautifully sited on a 240-acre hill overlooking the Kansas River. Today, the grounds are a private park open to the public with nature and jogging trails, and from some of these the residence can be viewed at a distance; the home itself is open during limited hours each week.

Cedar Crest is a handsome example of a towered French Eclectic house, a type often called Norman French. It is an unusually formal and symmetrical example of this subtype; the tower, a modified octagon in shape, is centered on the front facade and includes the front entry. The walls are mostly of stucco accented with native stone and some brick. Except for the formal entry, the stone is left with a rough quarry face. The roof is of Pennsylvania slate.

The main rooms preserve much of their 1928 appearance; the natural woodwork remains on the entire first floor. A large central entry hall opens into a twenty-by-forty-foot wood-paneled library that housed the MacLennans' personal book collection. Mr. MacLennan's study is decorated with hand-carved replicas of fifteenth-century printer's marks, and with frescoes showing bookplates used by famous authors. Many of the furnishings seen in the house today were moved here from the original Governor's Residence. Others have been donated to the state.

WICHITA

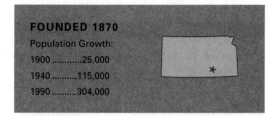

FOUNDED 1870

Population Growth:

1900 25,000

1940 115,000

1990 304,000

Like its neighbor Abilene, ninety-five miles to the north (see page 340), Wichita began as one of Kansas's fabled railhead cow towns, where vast herds of trail-driven Texas longhorns were shipped to a beef-hungry nation after the Civil War. As in Abilene, Wichita's frenzied cattle-boom era was to last only a few years. By 1875 fence-building farmers, growing bountiful wheat crops on the region's rich prairie soils, had pushed the cattle drives farther westward. Abilene had settled into sedate prosperity as a local grain-marketing center after its cattle boom ended, but Wichita was to have a different destiny. Soon it became involved in a second, and still-larger, boom, one that paved the way for it to become Kansas's largest city through most of the twentieth century.

Wichita's original cattle-shipping railroad was the southwestward-building Atchison, Topeka, and Santa Fe, which arrived in 1872. In 1880 the town got a coveted second rail line, the westward-building St. Louis, Wichita, and Western, better known as the Frisco line. When yet a third railroad, the Missouri-Pacific, was built through Wichita in 1883, the town's future as a principal rail center of the southern plains was assured. As wholesalers and manufacturers, attracted by its excellent transportation network, began pouring in, Wi-

chita's population jumped almost fivefold, from five thousand in 1880 to twenty-four thousand in 1890.

Slowed by the nationwide depression of the 1890s, Wichita entered a third boom era in the early twentieth century. New meatpacking plants and large-scale flour mills doubled the 1900 population to over fifty-two thousand inhabitants in 1910. The next decade added a new bonanza when, in 1914, oil was discovered in adjacent Butler County. Spurred by the fuel demands of the First World War, the Butler County fields, among the largest then discovered, brought enormous new wealth to Wichita, which became the financial and residential capital of this new petroleum province.

By 1920 Wichita's population had reached seventy-seven thousand, yet even the town's most ardent boosters could not have predicted what happened next—by 1930 the town had become the pioneering capital of the nation's fast-growing civil-aviation industry. The seed for this development was planted in 1919 when wealthy local oilman and flying enthusiast Jacob M. Moellendick persuaded Chicago aircraft builder E. M. Laird to make Wichita the base for building his new Swallow design. This was a modest commercial success with forty-five planes sold over the next four years.

Far more important was the Swallow factory's role as a training ground for the next generation of legendary aviation pioneers. Walter Beech, Clyde Cessna, and Lloyd Stearman were all talented Laird associates who, by the mid-1920s, had each formed his own innovative Wichita-based aircraft company. By the time Charles Lindbergh made civilian flying into a national obsession with his epoch-making solo across the Atlantic in 1927, Wichita was already the nerve center for such fly-

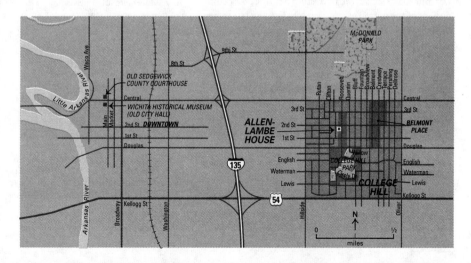

ing. In 1929 the city could boast of sixteen aircraft plants, its own airline, thirteen flying schools, almost three square miles of "flying fields," and six aircraft-engine factories.

The nationwide depression of the 1930s slowed Wichita's progress but was made less severe by new oil strikes nearby and by the continued, if slower, expansion of civilian aviation. Just ahead lay another boom as the Second World War propelled Wichita's previously small-scale aircraft plants into major industries. As the European war intensified in 1940, Beech, Cessna, and Stearman received massive orders for their small planes to be used as trainers for military pilots. Soon their expanded plants were also assembling components for larger military fighters and bombers. Wichita's role in military aviation was not, however, to end there.

Even before the Japanese aircraft carrier attack on Hawaii in December 1941, the U.S. government had begun locating new wartime industries in less vulnerable midcontinent sites. Wichita was to be a principal beneficiary of this policy when, in late 1940, Seattle-based Boeing Aircraft, which specialized in military bombers, began building an enormous supersecret plant on the edge of town to produce its newest and largest B-29 bombers. These were later to play a critical role in the defeat of Japan, including dropping the fateful Hiroshima atomic bomb in 1945.

The huge new bomber plant required 30,000 workers, and these, coupled with Wichita's many other war-production facilities, fueled an unprecedented migration into the city, whose population jumped from 115,000 in 1940 to 225,000 in the metropolitan area only three years later. Many of the newcomers lived in temporary government housing, but most were squeezed into spare bedrooms and newly partitioned apartments scattered throughout the city and nearby countryside.

Some of these new residents went elsewhere after the war, but many stayed on as Wichita became a key component of the nation's Cold War–era defense strategies. Boeing Wichita, as the huge plant came to be called, was to produce several more generations of Boeing bombers, and in 1951 the huge McConnell Air Force Base was built nearby to provide specialized training for their pilots. At the same time, Beech and Cessna became dominant players in the postwar light-aircraft industry.

Wichita's post-1950 population has grown steadily with its aerospace-dominated economy, and today only scattered remnants of the Victorian-era boomtown survive. Much of the city's upscale Eclectic-era housing, reflecting its early oil and aviation boom years, is concentrated in the delightful College Hill neighbor-

hood (see the following entry), which also boasts one of the West's most important museum houses, a seminal 1915 masterpiece designed by Frank Lloyd Wright (see page 367).

College Hill, 1887–1930

One would expect a neighborhood named College Hill to be located near a college or university. Indeed, in the 1880s, when these eastern neighborhoods of Wichita were being platted along new trolley lines, there were seven separate colleges under construction or being promoted in the area, hence the name. Today, only one of these survives—Wichita State University, located about two miles north of College Hill. Probably of more importance than the projected colleges was a 1901 decision to locate the new Wichita Country Club here, which clinched the neighborhood's long-term attraction to affluent home owners.

The large area typically referred to as "College Hill" is shown in a light tint on the map (see page 365). The smaller sections with the greatest concentration of important early houses are more darkly shaded. These include Belmont Place, a small, upscale subdivision marked by large entry gates and centered on a four-block stretch of Belmont, Crestway, and Terrace Streets.

Belmont Place: 401 North Belmont Street (private), ca. 1920s. This unusual house form, three units arranged like three sides of an octagon into a sort of "bay-window" shape, is found on a number of corner lots in Belmont Place. Here the style is Italian Renaissance, and much of the house's character comes from the atypical entry tower and unusual shape, rather than from elaborate architectural detailing. A large open terrace is enclosed by the two outer wings. Houses of differing styles but sharing this bay-window shape can be seen at 254 North Crestway Street (private), ca. 1920s, Tudor style; 301 North Crestway Street (private), ca. 1920s, Spanish Eclectic style; and 300 Terrace Street (private), ca. 1920s, towered French Eclectic style.

Belmont Place: 304 North Belmont Street (private), ca. 1910s. This fine symmetrical Italian Renaissance design has very wide eave overhangs and a broad terraced porch. Prairie stylistic influences are seen in the simple slab balusters and handsome flattened planters.

Belmont Place: 312 North Belmont Street (private). This excellent wood-clad Colonial Revival design has a side-gabled roof, three dormers with triangular pediments, and a very distinctive front gate and fence.

Belmont Place: Next door to the north of 312 North Belmont Street (private), ca. 1920s. This brick-clad, parapeted Tudor house has a diamond-shaped brick pattern in the left gable, the original Tudor-arched front door with squared panels, and unusual asymmetrical stone trim down one side of the entry pavilion.

Belmont Place: 444 North Belmont Street (private). The paint scheme used on this stuccoed Tudor design, which has extensive half-timbering, gives it a very jaunty air.

Belmont Place: 300 North Crestway Street (private), Butts House, 1929. Automobile dealer J. Arch Butts built

College Hill

area of pebbled texture, all arranged asymmetrically to balance the rounded entry porch.

330 Circle Drive (private), Aviary, 1887; George Bird, Wichita, architect. As a whimsical touch, architect Bird named his home Aviary and proudly announced this, perhaps to intrigue prospective clients, in both a large chimney escutcheon and etched into the glass of the front door. The design combines Queen Anne massing with many Shingle-style details. Note the first floor of squared cut stone, such as was used in many of the firm's public-building designs. Unlike his partner's more unusual home (see the preceding entry), which remained a one-of-a-kind creation, Bird's design is reported to have been reused for several clients. Perhaps they were attracted by the Aviary labels.

Allen-Lambe House, 1918

255 North Roosevelt Street; 316-687-1027;
Frank Lloyd Wright, Spring Green, Wisconsin, architect.
This exquisite home was considered by its renowned architect to be "among my best." The last of Wright's influential Prairie-style designs, the Allen-Lambe House also introduced some of the important concepts later used in his futuristic "Usonian" homes.

The survival of this landmark house, filled with many of its superb original fixtures and furnishings, has been a long-term labor of love on the part of Wichita architect Howard W. Ellington, who, along with Liz Koch, formed a foundation dedicated to saving the house. He was able to convince the Claude R. Lambe Charitable Foundation to provide substantial initial support for his vision, and to enlist the cooperation of the Wichita State University Endowment Association, which owns many of its furnishings. Ellington's six years of championing this unique treasure, raising funds from farsighted donors, and overseeing its restoration have preserved one of the nation's finest remaining early modern homes and its interiors for the enjoyment of all.

The home was built for Henry J. Allen, owner of the *Wichita Beacon* newspaper and onetime governor of Kansas, and his wife, Elsie J. Nuzman Allen, an active arts patron. They began working with Wright on the design ideas for the house in 1915 and occupied their new home in 1918. Howard Ellington's *1995 Newsletter* for the Allen-Lambe Museum and Study Center includes a concise and authoritative description of the house:

Stylistic exterior features include a horizontal gray carthage marble "water table" as a transition design element between the prairie floor and the house, white raked horizontal brick joints and flush ocher head joints, red clay tile roof with emphasis on horizontal lines and a unique ridge, hip ridge and lower stating course with a Japanese flavor.

this large Italian Renaissance house in the hipped-roof-with-projecting-wings subtype. It has a low front terrace and blind arches above the first-floor windows.

3755 Douglas Street (private), ca. 1910. Douglas Street appears to have been College Hills's most fashionable early-twentieth-century address, originally lined with the large mansions of the very affluent. As was so often the case, what began as a desirably convenient location along a street with a trolley line later became troublingly noisy and dangerous when crowded with fast-moving automobiles. As a result, many of the grand houses were later torn down for, or converted to, apartment and commercial uses. This very large Colonial Revival house, a little-altered survivor now occupied by a lodge chapter, has four handsome brick chimneys, dormers with exaggerated broken-ogee pediments, and Palladian windows adorning both the front and side facades. Note also the elaborately detailed entry.

303 Circle Drive (private), Hillside Cottage, 1887; Willis Proudfoot, Wichita, architect. This delightful Shingle-style house was designed as his own home by a partner in the local architectural firm of Proudfoot and Bird. Not to be outdone in advertising his talents, Proudfoot's partner also built *his* new home the same year at nearby 330 Circle Drive (see the following entry). In 1901 Proudfoot's house was leased as the club house for the new Wichita Country Club; after the club moved to another location in 1913, a part of its golf course became College Hill Park. The house is a very fine small example of its style, with a cross-gambreled roof and stone first floor. The design of the front-facing gambrel is quite elegant; it combines a small oval window, a tall round-arched window, two rectangular windows, and an

Allen-Lambe House

Interior features include the continuity of the exterior brick which is a blend of ocher and tan colors with all horizontal joints gilded gold. This detail was only used elsewhere at the Martin house in Buffalo, New York, 1904, and the Imperial Hotel in Tokyo 1915–1923.

The living room and dining room wrap around a sunken garden with a large water garden filled with water lilies and Koi fish from Japan. The other two sides of the garden are defined by a garden house and wall capped by large concrete vases with oyster shell aggregate.

The quarry tile terrace extends into the living room and dining room with access from both rooms through glass doors to the terrace. This continuity of floor material along with the brick, plaster colors, etc. establishes a strong indoor/outdoor design relationship.

Views to the exterior are through "light screens" which consist of clear glass doors and windows with terminal windows or side windows framing the view with art glass.

Exterior window flower boxes raise the prairie floor up to establish a strong visual relationship to nature.

Lighting is integrated into the environment with the living room ceiling lanterns in wood and mulberry paper or wood and art glass as in the dining room.

Radiator grilles, built in furniture, bookcases and movable furniture are all interrelated designs for a harmonious whole.

The furniture was a collaborative effort between Frank Lloyd Wright and George M. Niedecken who worked with Frank Lloyd Wright on 12 projects over a 15-year period, which included the Coonley House, Robie House and the Meyer May House. Twenty-three pieces of original furniture are on long-term loan from the Wichita State University Endowment Association. The balance of the furniture is owned by the Allen-Lambe House Foundation.

Most of the interior woodwork is of red gum. Extensive analysis of the interior paint colors has been undertaken, and they have been restored to their original appearance with a "scrumbling" technique that blends many different paint shades into a harmonious whole.

Wright's fascination with technology is evident throughout the house. The glorious water garden was kept at the correct level with a copper float valve that automatically refilled it; the house also had a central vacuum system. Even the home's original security system was retained and upgraded to current art museum standards.

Montana

BILLINGS

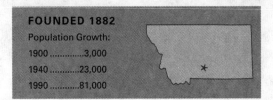

FOUNDED 1882

Population Growth:

1900 3,000

1940 23,000

1990 81,000

Billings was a creation of the Northern Pacific Railroad, which was built across Montana in the early 1880s to complete a transcontinental link between Minnesota's Great Lakes ports and those on Washington's Puget Sound. Named for the railroad's president, the new town was clearly expected to become the principal financial and trade center of the south-central Montana plains. Its founders were right. Building on a base of cattle and sheep ranching supplemented by irrigated agriculture along the fertile Yellowstone River Valley, in the 1920s the town also became the refining and marketing center for the region's newly discovered oil and gas fields. Billings is today the state's largest city.

Having experienced much of its growth in the decades since 1940, Billings has few historic neighborhoods but is the home of one of Montana's several fine turn-of-the-century dwellings that have survived to become important museum houses.

Moss Mansion, 1903

914 Division Street; 406-256-5100;

Henry Janeway Hardenbergh, New York City, architect.

In 1892 twenty-nine-year-old Preston Boyd Moss (1863–1947) arrived in this bustling railroad town to seek his fortune, which he found rather quickly. Within a year he was vice-president of the First National Bank and four years later became its owner and president. Soon he was helping build Billings's early utility company. Shortly after completing this grand dwelling for himself, his wife, Martha, and their six children, Moss added eighty thousand head of sheep, the Northern Hotel, and the *Billings Gazette* to his growing financial empire.

Architect Hardenbergh created a suitably solid dwelling for his banker client. Built of reddish-brown sandstone, the house is Chateauesque in inspiration, as seen in its dominant, through-the-cornice dormers. Other features are less typical of that style, among them the symmetrical design of the front and side fa-

Moss Mansion

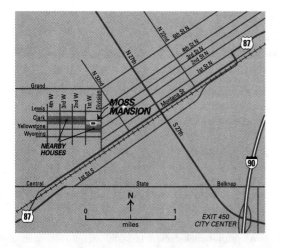

cades, the rough-faced wall stone, the red tile roof, and the severely simple front entrance. These features combine to give the house a singularly impregnable appearance.

The interior preservation is quite extraordinary. Some of the original window treatments survive in excellent condition. In the dining room, where the windows are shaded by an adjacent greenhouse, even the fragile transparent lace panels remain. The portieres (draped fabric hung at the doors between rooms) are still in place. Many of the original rugs remain—choice Persians in some rooms, custom-made Aubussons in the parlors, and a large Wilton in the upstairs hall. Wall fabrics and coverings are also well preserved, including striking rose silk damask in the adjoining Louis XVI parlors. Interior fixtures are similarly intact. Particularly impressive are the specially commissioned combined gas-and-electric light fixtures made by the Gibson Gas Fixture Company of Philadelphia.

Hardenbergh was best known as a designer of grand hotels and apartment buildings, among them the Plaza in New York City, the Willard in Washington, D.C., the Copley Plaza in Boston, and New York's famed Dakota apartments. This unusual design is one of his few private residences. Hardenbergh's commercial design background can be sensed in some of the interior spaces, which have a slightly hotel-like feeling. This is most apparent in the scale of the large entry hall and the very large downstairs and upstairs main halls. The architect even called the individual bedrooms "apartments," a label that continued to be used by the family.

Almost all of the rooms retain their original furniture. Highlights of the interior include the Moorish entry hall (inspired by the Alhambra), a library with the original leather upholstered pieces, the Louis XVI twin parlors, a family sitting room with a charming "Art

Nouveau" frieze, the original conservatory, and the family's "apartments."

Nearby Houses

The blocks immediately behind the Moss Mansion have scattered large dwellings along with many of the smaller houses typical of early-twentieth-century neighborhoods. The larger homes are primarily along Yellowstone Street between Division and First Streets and along Clark Street between First and Fourth Streets. Among the neighborhood's highlights are:

105 Clark Street (private). This late Free Classic Queen Anne design has a second-story oval window above the entry that is almost identical to one at 142 Clark Street (see the following entry). That house and this clearly demonstrate the stylistic transition from very late Queen Anne to early Colonial Revival. Here the roof pitch is higher and pyramidal, and there is a tower and a wraparound porch—all typical of the Queen Anne style. In contrast, the floral garland detailings mark the beginnings of Colonial Revival influence. Note also the Shinglesque dormer and Craftsman-like open eaves of the tower roof.

142 Clark Street (private). This is a nicely detailed example of the earliest Colonial Revival subtype, the asymmetrical. It is easy to see how this house, with its lower hipped roof and front-facing gable, evolved from the earlier Queen Anne style (see the preceding entry). Here the hipped roof is not pyramidal in shape, there is only one cross gable, the porch does not wrap, and the details are all typical of the Colonial Revival. Note the front door with a garland in the bottom panel and clear glass design above with matching sidelights. Complementary garlands are in the triangular pediment on the porch above the entry. The entire second story is covered with cut shingles in two different patterns. The oval window above the entry is used on several houses in these blocks.

123 Clark Street (private). Here we see an early example of the Colonial Revival's gambrel-roof subtype. From about 1895 to 1915 this subtype typically had a front-facing gambrel, occasionally with a cross gambrel at the rear, as seen here.

83 Yellowstone Street (private). Yet-another early Colonial Revival house, this is in the hipped roof with full-width-porch subtype. It has a roof dormer with an exuberant broken-ogee pediment and another of the oval windows seen also at 105 and 142 Clark Street (see the preceding entries).

106 Clark Street (private). This is a highly detailed example of the many houses built from about 1900 to 1920 that blended both Prairie- and Italian Renaissance–design influences. In this house the Italian Renaissance detailing dominates. The squared porch supports and pedestals above are the Prairie-style contribution. There is an almost-lavish use of brackets under the closed eaves of the house and porch roofs. Note the use of two colors of brick for the house wall surface and a third color to add details of quoins, mock-keystone lintels, and so on. The front door, with sidelights and transoms above, and the open eaves in the dormer, a Craftsman-style contribution, are found more often in Italian Renaissance houses built before 1915. A much simplified version of the same design can be seen at 39 Yellowstone Street (private).

BUTTE

FOUNDED 1864

Population Growth:

1900 30,000

1940 37,000

1990 33,000

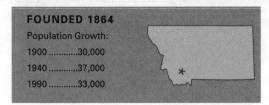

Most early western mining camps rather quickly became ghost towns as their easily worked, near-surface deposits were depleted and the restless miners moved on to the next potential bonanza. A favored few became centers of regional government or commerce and thus survived the almost-inevitable decline of their nearby mines. Among these are such state capitals as Helena, Boise, Denver, and Carson City. Rarest of all are a very small handful of early mining centers located on the true bonanzas—deposits so rich and extensive that they lasted not just for months or a few years, but for decades or even centuries. Butte, situated atop what has with only slight exaggeration been called the richest hill on earth, is one of these. Since its discovery in 1864, the hill has produced an incredible $25 billion worth of gold, silver, and copper and is still being mined today, although on a much reduced scale.

Butte's enormous potential remained undeveloped by its first prospectors, who arrived with the initial Montana gold rushes of the 1860s. These first miners found only modest amounts of easily worked placer gold in the stream gravel along the base of the hill. Some also noticed that the hill itself was crisscrossed with prominent ledges of dark-stained quartz rock that resembled the rich silver-bearing ores of Nevada's fabled Comstock Lode, which had been discovered in 1859. Several attempted to extract silver from the quartz veins using primitive grinding and "roasting" techniques, but the complex Butte ores yielded very little. By 1870 Butte was a near ghost town where a few miners retained their claims by struggling with the recalcitrant quartz veins. Then appeared two remarkable entrepreneurs who were to shape the destiny of Butte, and much of Montana, for the next century.

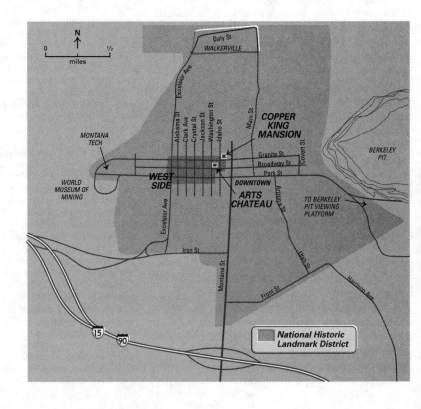

The Silver Boom

First to arrive was William Andrews Clark (1839–1925; see also "W. A. Clark House," page 376), a former Missouri schoolteacher who, with the outbreak of the Civil War, preferred to take his chances in the western goldfields rather than on the battlefields. After a stint in Central City, Colorado, in 1863 Clark arrived in Bannack City, Montana's first gold camp. Within a year Clark's diggings there had yielded a two-thousand-dollar profit. Realizing that such windfalls were very rare in the mining camps, the conservative yet fiercely ambitious young man invested his earnings in bringing ox-drawn wagons filled with trade goods from Salt Lake City to the Montana camps.

Soon Clark's trading profits allowed him to open general stores at Helena and at Elk City, Idaho. By 1872 he had expanded into banking, with headquarters in the thriving livestock center of Deer Lodge (see page 378). There, as a former prospector, Clark became intrigued by Butte's tantalizingly difficult ores, which lay only forty miles south of Deer Lodge. In the summer of 1872, he purchased, for modest sums from their still-struggling owners, four of Butte's most promising mines. Then, with schoolteacher thoroughness, he left his banks and stores to be run by subordinates during the slow winter months while he became a special student at New York's prestigious Columbia School of Mines to learn firsthand about making his new purchases yield their precious silver.

On his return, Clark opened a branch of his bank in Butte and began developing his mines by shipping the highest-grade ores by wagon and rail to Utah or Colorado for smelting, a costly process that consumed much of the profit. By 1876 he had completed the first local mill and smelter to successfully process the intractable ores. Thus began a new silver boom as Butte's rich ores attracted a flood of prospectors and potential investors to the town.

By far the most important of these newcomers turned out to be Marcus Daly (1841–1900; see also "Daly Mansion," page 380), who needed no professors to help him understand what he found. Daly had emigrated from potato-famine-decimated Ireland to New York as a penniless boy of fifteen. After two years of laboring on the city's docks, he had saved enough to buy a sailing-ship ticket to the California goldfields. By 1862 he had become a laborer in the booming Comstock Lode silver mines of Virginia City, Nevada. Soon the resourceful and energetic young Irishman was a foreman with a reputation for "being able to see farther into the ground than any mining engineer."

Daly's first big break came in 1870, when Salt Lake City's wealthy Walker brothers, learning of his unusual

William A. Clark

talents, hired him as manager of a rich silver discovery made near their hometown. In 1876 the brothers sent Daly to evaluate Butte's Alice Mine, a modest silver producer that was being offered for sale. He liked what he saw, and the Walkers purchased the mine and made Daly its superintendent with a one-fifth-ownership interest. Under his capable management, the Alice became one of Butte's most profitable and renowned silver producers.

By 1880 Daly was ready for new challenges and decided to take a bold gamble on his X-ray vision into the earth. Most of the quartz veins on Butte Hill were stained black by their silver-bearing ore minerals. In a much smaller area on the east side of the hill, the veins also showed the yellowish stains of copper-dominated ore. Clark and others had previously been intrigued by these veins, but near-surface mining failed to produce commercial quantities of copper. Daly believed that these disappointing veins were likely to change at depth into massive deposits of valuable copper ore. He also realized, as probably did Clark and others, that the local silver-bearing ores were of the type that tend to be richest near the surface and then diminish with depth, which meant that the silver bonanza had a limited future. Putting these insights together, Daly sold his share of the Alice Mine for a reputed $100,000 and used some of the proceeds to buy the Anaconda Mine, a modest silver producer situated in the very heart of the yellow-stained outcrops.

The Copper Bonanza

Daly faced formidable challenges in his gamble on copper becoming the ultimate jewel in Butte's crown. Much of the U.S. supply then came from northern Michigan's massive deposits of the pure native metal. Long used directly for tools, weapons, or ornaments by the region's Indian tribes, the Michigan copper required almost no processing, whereas Butte's complex ores would demand expensive concentration, smelting, and refining. On the other hand, the nation's burgeoning telegraph industry had dramatically increased demand for the red metal, and Edison's newly invented electrical lighting systems held promise for requiring enormous quantities for wires, generators, and motors. Furthermore Butte's first railroad line, fast building northward from Utah, would soon make possible truly large-scale mining and ore processing. In any event, producing the Butte copper at competitive prices would require unprecedented investment for expensive deep mining, costly state-of-the-art processing plants, and local railroads to connect mines and plants. And of course Daly's theory of bonanza copper ores at depth still remained to be proven!

To provide capital for his bold venture, Daly turned to one of the deepest pockets in American mining—San Franciscan George Hearst (see pages 251 and 427), an acquaintance from his Comstock Lode days. Daly presented Hearst with a carefully staged plan. They would first concentrate on the *silver* potential of the Anaconda Mine, which Daly felt could be made to yield substantial profits. While doing this, they would also construct deeper shafts to test for valuable copper ores.

In view of Daly's almost-unparalleled successes in operating silver mines, Hearst and his associates agreed to general funding of the first stage of the plan. Daly would receive a comfortable manager's salary as well as a one-fourth-ownership interest in the enterprise. Sinking of deep exploratory shafts and shallow cross tunnels for silver ore began in the summer of 1881. Less than a year later, at the three-hundred-foot level, workers reported hitting a thick vein of "some new material." Daly rushed down to discover the exceptionally rich copper ore that he had predicted.

Daly's vision into the earth had not failed him, yet ahead lay another large gamble—expenditures on adjacent mines to protect and extend the discovery as well as the costs of deep tunneling, mills, smelters, and interconnecting rail lines to produce the copper. To their credit, Daly's partners, by now fully convinced of the soundness of his vision, gave him a blank check to proceed, and Butte's copper boom was on. Within a decade Butte's many deep copper mines, led by the large Anaconda holdings, had replaced the declining silver veins as the principal source of the city's wealth.

By 1906 Butte was furnishing 20 percent of the world's copper and ranked second only to South Africa's gold-rich Rand district in the value of its mineral output. Daly's partners were handsomely rewarded for their faith and loyalty. In addition to many millions in distributed profits over the years, they and their heirs divided $40 million in payments when their Anaconda holdings were sold to eastern financiers in the 1890s. Daly himself did equally well (see page 380). W. A. Clark's early purchases of several key mines in Butte's copper belt became, after Daly's discovery, the cornerstone of an even greater fortune (see page 376).

Modern Butte

Butte remained a relatively small town during the pre-railroad silver boom of the 1870s. In 1880 it had a population of only three thousand, which was to more than triple to eleven thousand in 1890 after the arrival of the railroad-based copper boom. With continued expansion of copper production, the size tripled again during the 1890s and has mostly remained in that 30,000 range ever since. As a result, Butte still retains many buildings from its late-Victorian and early-Eclectic-era past. These are concentrated in both the original "Uptown" commercial district, as well as in the mostly middle-class residential streets immediately to the west, which, with their narrow brick town houses, resemble a northeastern factory town more than a typical western mining center. Butte's mining origins are otherwise unmistakable, for the surrounding hills are dotted with mine spoils and abandoned gallows frames, the aboveground pulley supports for cables that lowered men and equipment down the deep mine shafts and brought back up the valuable ore for loading into railroad cars.

Butte's labor-intensive underground mining, which ultimately reached depths of over a mile and honeycombed the hill, was already declining by 1955 when the Anaconda Copper Company began open-pit mining on the copper-rich east side of town. When this ended in 1982, the resulting mile-wide **Berkeley Pit,** which has an observation area near the eastern end of Park Street (406-494-5595), had consumed not only many of the most productive early copper mines, including the legendary Anaconda, but several early residential neighborhoods as well. East of this vast abandoned hole, a smaller pit remains in operation today. On the opposite side of town, at the far western end of Park Street beyond Montana Tech College, is the **Orphan Girl Mine,** an important silver producer that operated from 1875 until 1956. It is now the nucleus of the **World Museum of Mining** (406-723-7211), which offers many fascinating glimpses into Butte's colorful past.

All of early Butte, a large area of 4,600 structures that covers almost the entire hill north of Interstate 90, is today a national historic landmark. Early vernacular and folk houses are found throughout this district. At the turn of the century Butte had three principal neighborhoods: Uptown, East Butte, and the West Side. "Uptown" was the name applied to the downtown area dominated by commercial buildings, many of which still survive. East Butte was the neighborhood in which thousands of mine workers lived; it has now been mostly eaten away by the huge Berkeley Pit. A smaller mining center called **Walkerville,** located at the top of the hill just north of town, gives a less densely built-up suggestion of the working-class folk houses that once dominated East Butte. In Walkerville several of the gallows frames that once provided access to the mines survive, still surrounded by the houses of their former miners.

West Side, ca. 1885–1930

This is the principal survivor of the city's early residential districts and was always the preferred setting for homes of its more affluent residents. Even here, these were intermixed with numerous working-class homes. The mostly intact core of the West Side includes the several blocks of Granite, Broadway, and Park Streets between Idaho Street on the east and Excelsior Avenue on the west. The larger homes here tend to be concentrated at the tops of hills at each end of the area (around Washington and Idaho Streets and again around Alabama Street and Excelsior Avenue), while smaller homes are more numerous in the hollow between. All of the houses are tightly spaced, and most have no front or side yards. Some are urban town houses, often with flat roofs. Brick was the preferred building material. This type of house with small-lot spacing is rare in western towns and, indeed, is uncommon anywhere outside the older cities of the northeastern states.

105 North Excelsior Avenue (private), Ryan House, 1899; west wing, 1906. This early Colonial Revival design is unusual in having both a centered gable section and a full-width porch. Note the atypical design of the dormers—a smallish window with a broken-pediment crown is placed within a dormer topped with a triangular pediment. Ordinarily the window would fill the dormer with only a single pediment above. Also notable are the quoins, the Palladian window over the entry, and the slightly bayed triple windows to each side. John Ryan was the president of both the Anaconda Copper Company and the Montana Power Company. He was the second owner of the house and added the west wing.

829 West Park Street (private), Kelley House, ca. 1905. This Neoclassical house has a full-height entry porch with a lower full-width porch, a subtype that is unusual outside of the southern states. This example has particularly elegant porches; the full-height one is rounded, and the one-story element has paired columns and a handsome roofline balustrade. Con Kelley was an attorney who later became president of the Anaconda Copper Company. Next door at

West Side

W. A. Clark House

847 Park Street (private) is a very similar house, but here the porches are executed with stacked one-story columns.

301 West Granite Street (private), Connell House, early 1880s. This charming Second Empire house has a copper-covered mansard roof with through-the-cornice dormers. The curved front porch is echoed by the windows of the curved sitting room to the right.

W. A. Clark House (Copper King Mansion), 1888

219 West Granite Street; 406-782-7580;
C. H. Brown, architect.

Clark, among the earliest of Butte's wealthy mining magnates, commissioned this large and elaborate patterned-masonry Queen Anne home after some of his former silver mines began yielding an even-richer bonanza of high-grade copper ore (see page 374).

Clark and Marcus Daly, both workaholic mining geniuses, became arch rivals in the development of Butte's copper industry. The two men had strikingly different personalities. Daly, largely self-educated, was a gregarious, generous Irishman who shunned personal publicity and devoted most of his life to building a single grand monument—the remarkably engineered and loyally paternalistic Anaconda Copper Company. Clark, in contrast, was a vain and restless intellectual. Cold and unapproachable in personal relations, he had an almost-pathological need for public notice and acclaim. Clark tirelessly sought high-profile political of-

fices and even bribed his way into the U.S. Senate, a responsibility that, once attained, apparently bored him, for his lackluster Senate record was marked by frequent absences.

After Clark's Butte-based fortune was secured in the mid-1880s, he used some of his rapidly increasing wealth to build this house. The year it was completed, he also purchased a small and remote Arizona silver mine, the United Verde at Jerome, whose ores Clark felt might duplicate his Butte copper bonanza. He was right. By 1900 the United Verde, and other investments made from its vast profits, had made him one of the world's richest men, with a $50 million fortune that had the buying power of about $2 billion today. By then Clark had mostly abandoned Butte for still more lavish homes in the social and political worlds of Los Angeles, New York, France, and elsewhere. Amazingly, this Butte house is one of the few surviving monuments to his extraordinary career.

The house has a very high level of detail in the elaborate wooden porches and in the white stone and brown terra-cotta ornament seen in belt courses, cornice, window crowns, and dormers. The interiors still have almost all of their original finishes as well as many original fixtures. Of particular interest is the extraordinary "combed" plasterwork in the main halls and elsewhere in the house. The area above the stairs is the most elaborate and exhibits a great variety of pattern. An up-

West Side:
C. W. Clark House on left

stairs bath has an example of this technique at its most playful. Many walls in the house have their midsections wrapped with a molded plaster frieze. This is painted to resemble copper in the billiard room, silver in the dining room, and bronze in the hall. Painted ceilings are found throughout, as is handsome wood detailing. In the billiard room, these details interpret the theme of the room. Few of the furnishings are original; most are from the current owner's private collection but feel at home in their adopted setting.

C. W. Clark House
(Arts Chateau), 1899

321 West Broadway Street; 406-723-7600;
McKim, Mead, and White, New York City, architects.
William Aldrich of this famous architectural firm served as lead architect for the Chateauesque design built for the eldest son of W. A. Clark (see the preceding entry). The main entertaining rooms are on the second floor, as was the custom in Manhattan town houses. Despite its imposing exterior, the house is relatively small, with 4,200 square feet of floor space. The ceilings are much lower than had been usual during the Victorian era.

The first floor has a reception area and an adjoining "male retreat" that retains its original fine satinwood wall paneling. Two rosewood chairs that belonged to W. A. Clark are displayed here. The second floor, the main living area, has a salon, library, petit salon, dining room, and chapel. The rooms are decorated in the softer colors and early antique furnishings that became popular at the turn of the century. The decor of these rooms makes a dramatic contrast with that in the nearby home of Clark's father that was completed only a decade earlier.

A bedroom and bath on the third floor and a fourth-floor ballroom complete the furnished rooms on view. The remainder of the house, mostly the original service areas, is now used as a community arts center and museum.

DEER LODGE

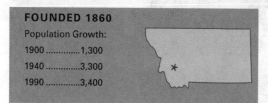

FOUNDED 1860
Population Growth:
1900 1,300
1940 3,300
1990 3,400

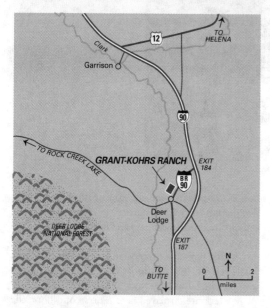

Rather surprisingly, Montana's vast cattle industry had its beginnings not on the endless short-grass plains that make up the eastern half of the state but in the mountainous west. Until the 1880s the eastern plains remained dominated by buffalo herds and nomadic Indians, but thirty years earlier some enterprising "mountain men"—the West's small contingent of early trappers and fur traders—developed a profitable cattle trade based on the needs of west-bound immigrants along the Oregon Trail.

Many of these travelers carried their belongings in ox-drawn wagons. After a thousand miles of hard pulling and hurried grazing, most of the oxen reached southern Idaho in very poor condition. There the mountaineers-turned-cattle-traders offered to swap a single strong and fresh animal for two thin and trail-weary ones. These they then herded northward into Montana, where several small mountain valleys offered both lush grasses and light winter snowfalls. Here the exhausted cattle were revitalized by almost a year of restful grazing before being moved southward the next summer to begin the cycle again and, not incidentally, double the size of the traders' Montana herd after the two-for-one swaps.

One of the most successful of these trapper-cattlemen was Johnny Grant, a Canadian whose base ranch was in the fertile Deer Lodge Valley. By 1862, when the first Montana gold rushes initiated serious Anglo migrations into the area, Grant's valuable herds numbered 4,000 cattle and 2,500 horses. That same year the prosperous rancher built a new Greek Revival dwelling (see the following entry) that was considered a palatial novelty in this sparsely settled frontier.

Important early gold discoveries were made in the mountains around Grant's ranch, and soon the small town of Deer Lodge was established near his home as a supply center for the local mines. The mining boom brought Grant still more profits, as he supplied the miners with much-needed beef, for which he was paid in gold. In 1866 Grant sold his ranching operation for nineteen thousand dollars and moved to Manitoba, Canada.

The Deer Lodge ranch's purchaser was Conrad Kohrs (1835–1920), a young German immigrant and former butcher who, after trying his luck in the western goldfields, had become a trusted supplier of beef to the Idaho and Montana mining camps. A man of remarkable energy, integrity, and vision, Kohrs went on to become not only an innovative and successful cattleman, but also one of early Montana's most respected citizens. The former Grant ranch was to remain the center of his far-flung operations for more than fifty years. Remarkably, much of this pioneering ranch survives today as a unique national historic site operated by the National Park Service.

Grant-Kohrs Ranch, 1862 and later

West side of Interstate 90 Business Route immediately north of the Deer Lodge town center; 406-846-2070.
The main ranch house, the "palatial" home built by Johnny Grant, is a simple side-gabled folk-house form with some modest Greek Revival details in the door surround and small entry porch. Originally only the upstairs was used as a dwelling, while the downstairs was Grant's trading post. When Conrad Kohrs bought Grant's "spread" in 1866, he began using the entire house as a dwelling.

In 1868 Kohrs married nineteen-year-old Augusta Kruse in Davenport, Iowa, after a brief courtship. Her introduction to her new home began with a seven-week riverboat trip up the Missouri, during which both the water level in the river and the food on board the boat ran low. This was followed by a one-week wagon trip from Fort Benton to Deer Lodge in pouring rain. Augusta's first two nights at the ranch house resulted in massive numbers of bedbug bites, which led to an intensive program of extermination with kerosene and boiling water.

Despite all this, Augusta was determined to be a proper mistress of the house and refused to have the male cook continue to prepare meals for the ten men who worked with her husband on the ranch. She insisted on taking over the large extended household herself, roasting coffee, making soap, scrubbing floors, cooking, and then producing her first child just ten months later.

Augusta's tenacity showed in her improvements to their home. As her husband's prosperity increased, she set about acquiring the stylish furnishings that remain in the house today. The first large purchases came in 1882. Returning from an extended stay in Germany with her young children, she and her husband shopped first in New York, where they bought Rogers silverware, and then in Chicago, where the parlor furniture, several bedroom sets, and new carpets were added.

In 1890 the house was expanded by adding a large brick extension at the rear. As noted in Kohrs's autobiography, "The new addition to the house proved a great comfort. The furnace, waterworks and gas plant gave us all the conveniences of the city and lightened the burdens of the housekeeper perceptibly—no carrying of wood for six or seven stoves and filling of lamps."

Augusta continued her improvements to the ranch house until 1900, when the family moved to Helena, where they purchased two large homes—one for themselves and one for their daughter Anna Kohrs Boardman and her husband, John (see page 384). After the move, the old ranch house was left unchanged with all the furnishings Augusta had accumulated over the years. She continued to spend part of her summers in the house until her death in 1945 at age ninety-six. In the meantime, her grandson, Conrad Warren, assumed management of the ranch in 1932, purchased it in 1940, and, knowing that he would like to see it permanently preserved, worked with his wife, Nell, to gather important documents and records related to the historic property.

Both the ranch house and its many outbuildings survive intact. The early bunkhouse row, icehouse, thoroughbred barn, Leeds Lion Barn (a special stallion barn), buggy shed, draft-horse and oxen barns, and the Bielenberg Barn (named for Kohrs's half brother and lifetime partner who also lived at Deer Lodge) are still standing. Newer outbuildings were added by Con Warren in the 1930s. These include a garage, blacksmith shop, chicken coop, dairy, and granary.

The most magical part of a visit to Grant-Kohrs today is that it is still a working ranch rather than a static museum. One can wander at leisure through the corrals and feedlots filled with horses, cattle, and chickens. This is made possible by the careful stewardship of the National Park Service, which assumed ownership in 1972. On the excellent tour one also gains an understanding of how the cattle business evolved from open range to carefully controlled breeding herds during the many decades in which this pioneering enterprise was operated by Johnny Grant, Conrad Kohrs, and Con Warren.

Grant-Kohrs Ranch

HAMILTON

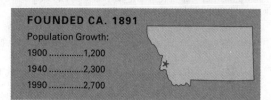

FOUNDED CA. 1891

Population Growth:

1900 1,200

1940 2,300

1990 2,700

This is the smaller of two paternalistic company towns founded by Irish immigrant Marcus Daly, a self-made mining genius who built Montana's Anaconda Copper Company into one of the world's premier mining enterprises (see page 373). Daly's greatest pride was the model industrial city of Anaconda, twenty-five miles west of Butte, where he built state-of-the-art mills and smelters to process the prodigious ores that flowed from his Butte mines. In 1894 the city of Anaconda narrowly lost out to Helena in a popular vote to determine the permanent capital of Montana.

Hamilton was a more intimate love of Daly's, for it

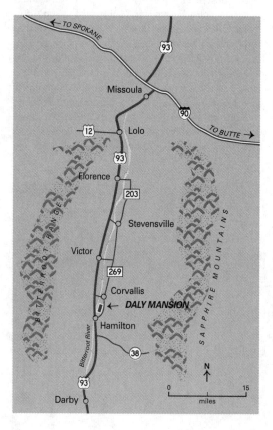

was here, in the lush grasses of the Bitterroot Valley, that he built a vast stock farm that specialized in breeding the fine racehorses that were his principal hobby. Daly's twenty-two-thousand-acre spread also included much of the adjacent wooded mountain slopes. To ensure a continuous supply of low-cost timber to his mines and smelters, which consumed enormous quantities of wood, Daly also built a large sawmill near his ranch, and this became the industrial nucleus of the small town of Hamilton. The town's principal historic interest lies not, however, in Daly's mill but in his stock farm, important parts of which survive as the most personal monuments of his extraordinary life.

Daly Mansion, 1910 (extensive remodeling of an earlier Victorian house)

251 Eastside Highway (Montana Highway 269); 406-363-6004; A. J. Gibson, Missoula, architect.

Marcus Daly first visited Montana's remote and beautiful Bitterroot Valley in 1864 while still a young mine superintendent at Virginia City, Nevada. Perhaps the lush wild grasses reminded him of his native Ireland, for he is said to have vowed that, if he could ever afford it, he would make the valley his home. In 1888, after the enormous flow of copper from his Butte mines and Anaconda smelters had given him great wealth, he began buying Bitterroot Valley land to fulfill this youthful dream.

The one great personal indulgence of his life, Daly developed his Bitterroot stock farm with the same meticulous thoroughness as his mining ventures. A state-of-the-art irrigation system provided water to his vast pastures and hay fields during droughts. Tree-lined gravel roads gave ready access to all parts of his thirty-four-square-mile empire, whose fields were bordered by white wooden fences rather than the usual barbed wire. His horse-breeding facilities, the heart of the enterprise, resembled a small town and included both open and closed racetracks to provide year-round exercise for his thoroughbreds. These responded to such indulgences by winning every major U.S. race except the Kentucky Derby. These successes Daly attributed to the stamina and lung power developed from training his horses in the thin mountain air.

The racing facilities were supplemented by an equally impressive agricultural enterprise that included pure-bred dairy and beef cattle as well as hogs,

Daly Mansion

sheep, poultry, and other livestock. Gardeners brought from the northeastern states and Europe tended orchards, truck farms, and greenhouses for winter produce. In 1891, a year for which records exist, the greenhouses and hot beds had 10,000 strawberry plants, 20,000 celery plants, 225,000 tomato plants, and 12,000 cauliflower plants. The farm's products regularly won top prizes in world's fairs. Among its entries in the 1893 World's Columbian Exposition in Chicago were three heads of cabbage weighing sixty-five, seventy-three, and seventy-eight pounds.

Today, the principal survivor of all this activity is the Daly home, which was remodeled by his devoted widow ten years after her husband's death. A visit to the house begins with photographs and discussion of how the present structure evolved from earlier dwellings on the site. First came a simple two-story gable-front-and-wing Folk Victorian house built in the 1870s by pioneer rancher Anthony Chaffin. In 1886 Daly's brother-in-law purchased the house and surrounding acreage, which later became the nucleus of Marcus Daly's vast stock farm. The Dalys steadily expanded the original structure, which was remodeled in 1897 into a massive Queen Anne design.

Daly is said to have disliked this pretentious dwelling from the first moment he saw it (he had been away during the construction). He and his wife, Margaret, discussed changing the house, and finally in 1909, nine years after Daly's untimely death, she proceeded with another extensive remodeling that obliterated most traces of the earlier home, at least on the exterior. Thus the Neoclassical house that we see today is very much Mrs. Daly's creation.

Such grand Eclectic-era mansions are rare in Montana, where most great houses were completed prior to the silver-panic depression of 1893. Daly's vast copper-based fortune survived the panic; Mrs. Daly continued to operate their vast stock farm until her death in 1941. She made only one substantial change in the farm's operations. Her husband's racehorses, a man's sport, were replaced by huge herds of wool- and mutton-producing sheep.

The house has much Colonial Revival detailing on the interior. All of the original wall treatments survive, as do many of the original window treatments, light fixtures, floors, and even some rugs. Five of the mantelpieces are hand-carved Italian marble. The decor in many of the bedrooms, with coordinated wallpapers and window treatments, is particularly enlightening about taste in 1910.

The kitchen is remarkably intact, complete with a wood-and-coal cookstove in working condition and a rather-amazing rubber-based floor covering. The butler's pantry still has its call button and warming oven. The servants' dining room, pastry rooms, and coolers are all intact. It is in the kitchen area that details from the earlier houses are most visible.

The most conspicuous feature of the grounds is the grand allée of trees that leads to the front of the house. Daly was fond of trees and planted them along most of his roadways throughout the valley, and many survive. There are a number of domestic outbuildings, including a three-quarter-scale playhouse, a carriage house, laundries, grape arbors, greenhouse, icehouse, boat house, and a 1911 swimming pool called the Plunge, which measures 120 by 135 feet.

The house was unoccupied and boarded up from Mrs. Daly's death in 1941 until 1986, when it and fifty surrounding acres were acquired by the state of Montana. Unfortunately by then the original furnishings had been dispersed. These are gradually being donated to the house, and the property is now being restored with funds raised by a nonprofit corporation, the Daly Mansion Preservation Trust.

HELENA

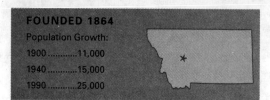

FOUNDED 1864
Population Growth:
1900 11,000
1940 15,000
1990 25,000

Few cities have such a vivid reminder of their origin as does Helena, whose principal downtown street takes it name from, and still winds along, the bottom of Last Chance Gulch. In 1864 rich deposits of gold-bearing gravel were discovered here, and other strikes quickly followed in the nearby Rocky Mountain foothills. Soon the original Last Chance Gulch discovery site, which had the advantage of a relatively flat, Missouri River Valley location near the region's principal wagon road, was renamed Helena and became one of Montana's first boomtowns.

By 1870 many of the important early gold strikes made elsewhere in the Montana mountains were playing out while new discoveries in the Helena area were enhancing the town's importance as a supply and trade center. In 1875 the small town became the capital of the Montana Territory, a distinction that it managed to maintain, despite many challengers, when the territory became the forty-first state in 1889. Still Montana's capital, modern Helena, and nearby Butte (see page 372), are among the most fascinating survivors from the hundreds of early mining camps that blossomed in the western mountains during the post–California gold rushes of the 1860s.

The evolution of Helena as a mining center, first for gold and then for silver, was not an easy one. Because of Montana's sparse population and rugged mountains, the railroads were late in arriving. For more than a decade after the 1869 completion of the first transcontinental rail line, Montana's mining communities were still served by long wagon roads. From Helena it was more than 400 miles south to the nearest railhead at Corinne, Utah, and about 150 miles north to Fort Benton, Montana, which offered only high-water (spring and summer) steamboat navigation down the shallow Missouri River. Not until 1883 did the Northern Pacific Railroad finally complete its tracks across Montana, and through Helena, to forge a new transcontinental route connecting Minnesota with Tacoma, Washington. With this railroad, a second mining boom came to the Helena region.

In prerailroad days, all shipments of heavy machinery for working the region's mines and refining its ores were limited by the cost and weight restrictions of transport in wooden wagons drawn by horses, mules, or oxen. Similarly limited were the movements of bulky ores from the mines to distant smelters for processing. These problems disappeared with the coming of the railroads. In the Helena region, railroad-delivered heavy equipment now made it possible to mine rich lodes of gold embedded in massive quartz veins, which required powerful crushing mills to separate the small amount of gold from the much larger volumes of enclosing rock. Other types of railroad-delivered machinery made possible the region's first large-scale silver production.

Unlike gold, which is commonly found as the pure

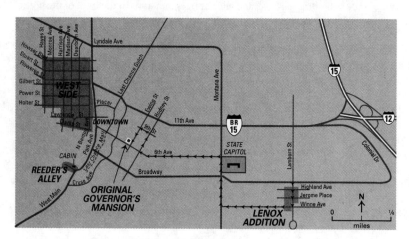

metal, pure silver rarely occurs in nature. Instead it is normally found combined with other chemical elements, such as copper, lead, zinc, sulfur, and oxygen, in complex ore minerals. These minerals, in turn, are usually embedded in a much larger volume of worthless rock. Successfully producing silver thus requires two steps. First, the small volume of silver-bearing ore minerals must be separated from the surrounding rock. Then the concentrated ore minerals must be processed to release the valuable silver. This second step requires both a sophisticated knowledge of metallurgy as well as large-scale machinery for transporting, concentrating, and refining the ores. Lacking such facilities, the Helena region's rich silver-bearing ores had been mostly a nuisance in the search for gold during the prerailroad years.

When the railroad finally arrived in 1883, Helena was already the financial, governmental, and cultural capital of Montana and had a population of about four thousand people. Local financiers, bankers, stockmen, and gold mine investors then quickly supplied much of the capital to build the railroad spurs, crushing mills, and smelters needed to tap the long-neglected nearby silver ores. The following "silver decade" brought enormous wealth to the region. By 1893, when a worldwide economic depression ended the ten-year Montana silver boom, Helena was reputed to have more millionaires per capita than any city in the country.

Overshadowed by nearby Butte as the state's financial center in the decades after 1900 (there the silver boom began somewhat earlier and followed a very different course; see page 373), modern Helena remains a small governmental center whose population has barely doubled in the last century. As a result it retains an unusually large fraction of its Victorian architectural heritage. Several important early commercial buildings still survive in Last Chance Gulch among younger neighbors. Many others were lost in a frenzy of 1960s urban renewal. More spectacular are the surviving grand dwellings of the silver-boom years, which, in the West Side neighborhood (see the following entry), make up one of the prime concentrations of large Victorian houses in the interior West. In addition, two smaller Helena neighborhoods (see pages 384 and 385) and the fine former Governor's Mansion (see page 385), now a museum house, provide instructive historic insights.

West Side, ca. 1880–1915

This large and elegant neighborhood has long been the preferred home of both affluent Helenans as well as more rural Montana ranchers and entrepreneurs who desired a second, more urban residence. As a result, the neighborhood has a remarkable mix of well-preserved houses of many styles and sizes. The spirit of the neighborhood is such that a small Folk Victorian cottage might be located adjacent to one of the district's many Victorian mansions, most of which date from the Helena silver-boom decade of 1883 to 1893.

Few such concentrations of large Victorian homes have survived with so few later modifications. This has undoubtedly been aided by the cool and dry Montana climate, which is well known for preserving delicate architectural detailing of wood or metal. Victorian house styles stressed such complex exterior ornament, but in less favorable climates, which include much of the country, this has commonly deteriorated and been either simplified or removed. Here original details survive in like-new condition. Among the neighborhood's many outstanding dwellings are:

400 Dearborn Avenue and 418 West Lawrence Street (both private), Kaufman House and Stadler House, both 1888. These large patterned-masonry Queen Anne houses share a carriage house that lies between them. Alike in feel, the two homes were built at the same time by ranching partners. Note the similar shape of the windows on the two houses—long rectangular sashes in slightly arched brick openings. Each window is crowned by a decorative pattern at each upper corner that looks a bit like horns. One house has a squared tower and one an octagonal. The roof cresting, double front doors, and porch detailing are remarkably intact.

600 Harrison Avenue (private), Power House, 1891. Built of rose-colored granite, this is a striking interpretation of the Richardsonian Romanesque style. It was commissioned by Thomas C. Power, who arrived in Montana in 1869 to open a general store at the Missouri River port of Fort Benton and ended up owning steamboat and stagecoach lines, sheep

West Side

West Side

and cattle ranches, as well as many blocks of valuable Helena real estate. Power became one of Montana's two original senators when the territory gained statehood in 1889.

Note the intricate stonework detail of the house's arcaded side porch. Between the arches, small squares of alternating smooth and rough stone create what is called a diaper pattern; this same theme is picked up in the stone railing above. Many of the windows have transoms above with a stone ledge dividing these two elements. Several huge blue spruce trees partially hide the front facade, but it is still possible to see the Romanesque arches of the entry and the porte cochere. The arches are supported by a cluster of squat columns with "cushion" capitals made of cast terra-cotta. The matching carriage house, visible behind, once housed Power's handsome team of black horses and his fine carriages that are now displayed at the Original Governor's Mansion (see page 385).

529 Floweree Street (private), Tatem House, ca. 1890. This early Tudor mansion occupies a full half block that provides excellent views of all facades. The basement and first-floor walls are of rusticated stone that is replaced by half-timbering in the upper story and gables. Note the cutout Gothic arch shape that ornaments the gable ends of the roof and dormers; there is also an unusually broad overhang of the roof in the gable ends. In some gables this is supported by stone brackets. The broad front porch with heavy squared columns is often seen on Tudor houses built before about 1915, but the embellishment of the porch roof with small twin gables is unusual. Two cantilevered through-the-cornice dormers dominate the second-floor portion of the house, which juts forward above the porch.

702 Madison Avenue (private), Boardman House, 1889. This is an impressive Shingle-style design of the hipped-roof-with-cross-gables subtype. Note how the upper corner porch, which would have been a separate element in Queen Anne designs, here blends into the main roof. The supports of this upper porch are unusual, as is the use of a second open porch between the two roof dormers. The side gable that faces Floweree Street has intricate wood detailing that visually extends it down into the second story.

Records of the original owner are sketchy. In 1900 Conrad Kohrs (see page 379) purchased this house for his daughter,

Anna, on her marriage to John Boardman. Boardman died shortly thereafter, but Anna continued to make it her home. In 1900 Kohrs, then sixty-five, also purchased a West Side home at 804 Dearborn Avenue for himself and his wife. Their longtime ranch home at Deer Lodge then became their summer residence.

642 Dearborn Avenue (private), Ashby House, 1886. This imposing patterned-brick Queen Anne home occupies a full block. Surviving outbuildings include a carriage house and brick playhouse. The facade ornamentation features a molded terra-cotta belt course that incorporates several different design patterns. This is echoed in a decorative band of brickwork around the second story and in a line of molded trim that runs above the first-floor windows.

The grounds were designed by the State Nursery and Seed Company, a distinguished Helena firm that landscaped much of the neighborhood and popularized the now-mature blue spruce trees seen scattered throughout. A low granite wall still surrounds the property, and an early hitching post survives in front.

404 North Benton Avenue (private), Evans House, 1877. This is a picture-perfect one-story Second Empire design with a tower. Note the paired brackets along the cornice line and how the dormer windows cut through the cornice line. The unusual dormers are crowned with small mansard roofs that are completed by a forward extension of the molded cornice at the ridge of the roof. The rooftop cresting is intact, as are the original entry porch and the Italianate window crowns. Second Empire and Italianate houses share similar architectural details everywhere except on roofs, roof cresting, and dormers.

Reeder's Alley, 1860s–1890s

Louis Reeder, a brick mason from Philadelphia, constructed these irregularly sited folk structures to house some of Helena's early gold prospectors. The picturesque grouping was restored as small shops and a restaurant in 1962. Some of the flavor of life in the mining camps is found in the early, two-room log house at the base of Reeder's Alley, which was built in 1864 to 1865 and is probably Helena's oldest surviving building. Visitors are admitted to the house on request.

Lenox Addition, 1891

This suburban development was opened at the end of a streetcar line located just four blocks from the proposed site for the new state capitol building. The developer's timing was unfortunate, for the financial panic of 1893 was accompanied by a crash in silver prices that stopped affluent homebuilding in Helena for many years. Most of the thirteen early homes remaining in the Lenox Addition were either under construction or completed when the panic hit (an additional five homes were destroyed in an early fire). Rarely does one get to see so clearly what was valued in a residential building site in the early 1890s. Here the prime lots (those that were first purchased and built on) were those closest to the Lamborn Street streetcar line. In addition, the early houses were built on the south side of the street, their front porches offering a wonderful view out across the valley floor to the mountains beyond. Most of the homes are in the Shingle or Queen Anne style. Some blend features of both.

1823 Highland Avenue (private), Kleinschmidt House, 1892; W. E. Norris, architect. The largest of the Lenox Addition homes is a fine Queen Anne design with a square tower having a graceful reverse-curved roof. The house is reported to have cost $112,000 in 1892. One of the developers of this addition was T. H. Kleinschmidt. It is not certain whether he built this large house for himself, a common practice for developers wanting to make their subdivisions look grand, or constructed it for someone else and then ended up having to move in himself when the 1893 financial panic hit.

Original Governor's Mansion (Chessman House), 1888

304 North Ewing Street; 406-442-3115;
Hodgson, Stem, and Welter, St. Paul, architects.
The designers combined an amazing blend of stylistic influences in their home for entrepreneur William A. Chessman.

The rear facade has a dominant Richardsonian Romanesque arch; the side facade facing Sixth Avenue has a handsome Shingle-influenced gable end; the front facade, with its Colonial Revival porch with balustrade above, looks like the hipped-roof-with-full-width-porch subtype of that style. That is until one notices the high-pitched, almost-Chateauesque, centered dormer and Romanesque arched first-floor window. To further complicate this creative mixture, the side facade toward the carriage house sports a typical Queen Anne tower and side gable. One might suspect some of this to be later stylistic remodeling, yet an 1890 photograph shows it all to be the original design. The result is a skillful blending of several then-fashionable design influences into a single dwelling.

The profusion of design influences continues inside the house. The entry hall is of golden oak, a late-

Reeder's Alley

Original
Governor's Mansion

nineteenth-century favorite. The hall features a "Moorish" carved-wood frieze, columns on each side of the stairway, and an open-grain floor in shadow design. Perhaps the most unusual room in the house is the dining room, which has one wall covered with a striking built-in sideboard and display cases made of dark mahogany. Added in 1900, this has Colonial Revival detailing. A library–sitting room has another interesting built-in, this one a combination of fireplace, glass bookcase, and display shelf supported with Classical columns.

In 1913 the state of Montana purchased the house as the official governor's residence. Nine governors had made it their home, when it was replaced in 1959 by a modern dwelling near the state capitol. The earlier structure is now operated as a museum house by the Montana Historical Society, which has tastefully furnished it with appropriate pieces from many sources.

KALISPELL

FOUNDED 1891

Population Growth:

1900 3,000

1940 8,000

1990 12,000

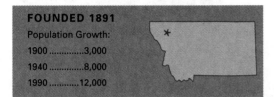

This is one of many towns founded by the Great Northern Railway as it was built along a route near the Canadian border to link Minneapolis with Seattle in 1893. Principally a trade and supply center for the region's farms and lumber mills, Kalispell is also a summer tourist destination as a gateway to Glacier National Park. The small town's principal historic interest is as the site of one of the Northwest's most important Victorian museum houses, which also has a surrounding neighborhood with many fine early-twentieth-century dwellings.

Conrad Mansion, 1895

313 Sixth Avenue East; 406-755-2166;
Kirtland K. Cutter, Spokane, architect.

This superb Shingle-style home retains almost all of its original fixtures and fittings as well as about 90 percent of its original furnishings. It remained in the Conrad family until 1975, when it was given to the city of Kalispell by Alicia Conrad Campbell, daughter of the original owner, Charles E. Conrad (1850–1902), who was the founder of Kalispell.

Charles Conrad entered the Civil War at age thirteen when he and his older brother, William, rode with the 43rd Virginia Cavalry. The war ended the boys' formal education and devastated the family's Virginia home—so the youthful brothers decided to head west. Traveling down the Ohio River to St. Louis, they then journeyed up the Missouri River to remote Fort Benton, Montana, the head of river navigation. There the boys took jobs at the I. G. Baker Company, which operated riverboats and freight wagons. These hauled supplies to the early mining camps and then carried a return cargo of hides and furs back downriver to St. Louis.

Within four years Charles and his brother owned a half interest in the company. Four years later they bought the entire enterprise. During these years of frontier trading, Charles became a close friend and trusted representative of many of the local Indian leaders, a rare accomplishment among western pioneers of

that era. When the Conrads sold their prosperous freighting company in 1891, its thousand oxen and hundreds of mules were hauling 30 million pounds of merchandise each year.

By then Conrad also owned several banks and cattle ranches scattered through western Montana. He and his wife, Alicia, planned to leave rustic Fort Benton and establish a new home and financial headquarters in the region's principal city, Spokane, Washington. En route to Spokane, the Conrads stopped to visit the ranch of Alicia's brother, which was located in the scenic, mountain-surrounded Flathead Valley of western Montana. Both Conrads fell in love with the remote and beautiful region and decided to make it their new home. Learning that the Great Northern Railway would soon build across the valley, Conrad, in partnership with several others, purchased land and incorporated a new town that he named Kalispell, an Indian word meaning "Grassy Place Above the Lake."

The Conrads retained a seventy-two-acre homesite and hired the renowned Spokane architect Kirtland K. Cutter, who had designed many of that booming city's finest dwellings (see page 676), to plan their new home. Construction began in 1892, and the Conrad family moved in during the spring of 1895.

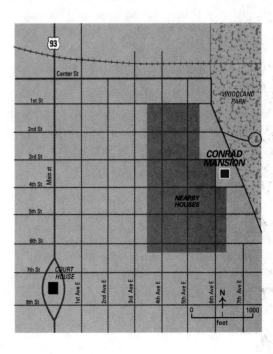

Conrad Mansion

A recent biography of Cutter by historian Henry Matthews provides these insights into the architect's interactions with his clients:

> Charles Conrad wanted to recreate the southern plantation house of his youth. Alicia, invoking her English heritage, preferred to think of something in the Tudor style. Cutter, seeing the wooded 72-acre site with beautiful views of the Flathead range of the Rocky Mountains to the east, envisioned another romantic rambling mansion such as he had designed for Glover and Moore [in Spokane].
>
> He must have charmed them as they discussed proposals, for he won them over . . . and left Kalispell with the understanding that he would have "a free hand and no restrictions in cost" . . . The drawings were done by him, personally.

Thus was born one of the finest Shingle-style dwellings in the American West, one with a striking facade of dark shingles accented by a harmonious assortment of the gables, dormers, oriel windows, and Romanesque arches that are typical of the style.

Inside is a particularly grand example of the living halls that were so popular in late-Victorian designs. Known here as the great hall, this one is overlooked by a second-story balcony and features a heroic Romanesque-arched passageway under the staircase. A visit to the Tudor/Richardsonian Romanesque Glover Mansion in Spokane (see page 683), also by Cutter, shows an almost-identical use of arches and balcony. Coincidentally, Glover was the founder of Spokane, as Conrad was of Kalispell.

The interior of the house remains almost exactly as when first occupied in 1895. The woodwork, light fixtures, and fittings are unchanged. Even the kitchen was never updated and retains the original range and soapstone sink. Many of the furnishings are also original, and even many toys and pieces of clothing survive. The furnishings were divided among the Conrads' three surviving children at their parents' death. Alicia donated all of her share along with the house itself to the city of Kalispell as a museum commemorating her parents. Other family members have also been remarkably generous in returning original pieces to the home.

The third floor of the house is open and features a fully equipped washroom, with both old-fashioned scrub-board tubs as well as 1910-vintage "modern" automatic washers. A central fire-hose system was installed in the house, and the original hoses remain in their central positions on each floor.

The house still is surrounded by its original low stone wall. Recently archaeological work has uncovered the locations of garden walkways, and these and the original planting beds have been replaced.

Nearby Houses

Most of Kalispell's upscale early homes are located along three streets near the Conrad Mansion. These are Fourth Avenue East, Fifth Avenue East, and Sixth Avenue East. The houses are concentrated in the blocks between First and Sixth Streets East. Here one sees the mixture of house styles and size that are typical of America's turn-of-the-century small towns. Several of the neighborhood's more striking houses were designed by a talented local architect named Marion Riffo, who seems to have delighted in analyzing the typical styles of the day and then adding some sort of different twist to the design.

505 Sixth Avenue East (private), Elliot House, 1910; Marion Riffo, Kalispell, architect. This unique house combines open eaves and Craftsman-style details with a balanced, symmetrical facade, a rarity in Craftsman designs.

305 Fourth Avenue East (private), Conlon House, 1914; Marion Riffo, Kalispell, architect. This design has a symmetrical facade and is quite similar to the house by the same architect at 505 Sixth Avenue East (see the preceding entry).

Here, however, it is embellished with Colonial Revival detailing, including stone quoins and a dramatically curved one-story entry porch.

535 Fifth Avenue East (private), Sickler House, ca. 1913. This fine Prairie-style house features a ribbon of five windows on the second story. Although difficult to see behind the storm windows, the upper sashes of these are glazed with striking, Prairie-style geometric designs. Local historians believe this house was built from a pattern-book design.

538 Fifth Avenue East (private), Keith House, 1911; Marion Riffo, Kalispell, architect. This is one of those wonderful mixtures of stylistic influences that were built near the turn of the century. At first glance, it simply looks like an asymmetrical Colonial Revival house. Then one notices the Tudor-style half-timbering in the gables and the Craftsman-style stone porch supports.

604 Fifth Avenue East (private), Agather House, 1910; Marion Riffo, Kalispell, architect. This looks like a Shingle-style design of the gambrel-roofed subtype. But, as in many of Riffo's houses, there is a twist. Here it is that most of the main body of the house is brick rather than shingled! Note the curved window growing out of the front-facing gambrel and the rounded section of house in the right corner that is truncated and tucked under the main roof, rather than having a tower roof as one might expect.

Nebraska

BROWNVILLE

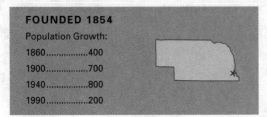

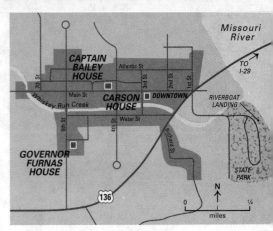

Brownville is a unique survivor of the numerous, and now mostly vanished, small, and ambitious Missouri River ports founded in 1854, the year the Nebraska Territory was first opened to Anglo settlement (see also "Omaha," page 410, and "Nebraska City," page 404). Never larger than about 1,300 inhabitants, Brownville is today a remarkable time capsule that retains more than a dozen modest and relatively unmodified Romantic-era houses, mostly in the Gothic Revival or Italianate styles. The town is now a center for small-scale heritage tourism, and, as a result, three of these unpretentious Brownville houses are now public museums that provide an opportunity, rare anywhere in the West, to visit several such mid-nineteenth-century dwellings.

Brownville Historic District, ca. 1859–1879

Once promoted as the City of Seven Hills, the entire village of Brownville is today a historic district with an informal rural flavor reinforced by the lack of streetside curbs. The houses built on its many hills often have lower stories that are not visible from the street. Three early brickyards provided the dominant building material, but the local clays made relatively soft bricks that usually required a coat of paint to protect them from crumbling and to prevent moisture from seeping into the walls.

Brownville Historic District

Southeast corner of Atlantic Street and Second Street (private), Muir House, 1870. This large, cube-shaped Italianate house has had a recent oversize cupola added to the roof, but the rest of the exterior appears to have been authentically restored. Scotsman Robert Valentine Muir (1827–1917) immigrated to the United States with his family as a child. Arriving in two-year-old Brownville in 1856, the entrepreneurial Muir was soon operating a sawmill, flour business, and ferry. He also dabbled in real estate, published the *Nebraska Advertiser,* one of the territory's first newspapers, and ran for governor as the Prohibition Party candidate.

In 1868 Muir began construction of this fashionable brick home, a simple-hipped-roof Italianate cube. Two bay windows were added to the basic cube on the right side and one on the left. The narrow doubled windows and the slightly wider single windows give a pleasantly alternating rhythm to the front facade. The single and paired decorative brackets along the cornice line add another rhythmic pattern. Note the upside-down fleur-de-lis in the keystones of the stone window hoods.

Water Street at Fourth Street, on northwest corner (private), Gates House, 1859. Abbot Gates, who owned one of Brownville's early brickyards, built this pleasing front-gabled National Folk house, which is thought to be the first brick structure in Nebraska. Like so many other homes in Brownville, it has a second story tucked downhill at the rear.

Carson House, 1860, 1864, and 1872

Main Street (south side) between Second and Third Streets; 402-825-6001 or 402-825-4131.

This Italianate house and most of its original furnishings were given to the Brownville Historical Society in 1953 with the stipulation that only the original contents would ever be displayed in the home. This has given us a rare intact survivor of an earlier age that is a true "preservation" rather than a later "restoration." The society's efforts are aimed at keeping the original property and furnishings intact, rather than trying to re-create a period of history.

The house was built in three distinct phases. First came a simple, two-room brick structure built in 1860 by Brownville's founder, Richard Brown. A few years later, John Lind Carson, who was born in Mercersburg, Pennsylvania, in 1832, purchased the home and moved in with his wife, Mary Masters Brown. They first added the side-gabled addition at the rear of the house. Then, in 1872, the house assumed the form seen today with the construction of the wood-clad right wing and the entire upstairs of the main house. From the front exterior, the two different wall materials make it easy to distinguish the original house from the large 1872 addition. When this was added, the entire exterior of the house was remodeled with Italianate detailing. The

porch was updated and the shape of the addition made the home a typical asymmetrical example of the style. The windows were also topped with "flattened" arches and surrounded by a frame with a decorative keystone in the top.

Captain Carson was a "dealer in coin, uncurrent money, land warrants, exchange and gold dust." He also served as president of both the Carson National Bank of Brownville and the First National Bank of Lincoln. He wanted the finest of furnishings for his young family and purchased many choice pieces in St. Louis that he brought upriver by steamboat. The house eventually ended up in the hands of their daughter Rose who deeded it to the Brownville Historical Society at her death. With the exception of a few pieces she donated to the Nebraska State Historical Society for a Carson Room, the house still has its original furnishings.

The house is actually three stories tall. Because it is built into the side of a hill slanting down to Whiskey Run Creek at the back of the lot, from Main Street you enter the middle story of the house—into a central hall with a prominent stairway. On the left is the library and to the right is the first of two parlors. This, the family parlor, has wonderful floor-to-ceiling windows almost ten feet tall. Each window is hung with a handsome, deep-maroon-colored lambrequin. This is a flat piece of material cut into an ornamental shape. The lambrequins here are partially original, and their festive scallops are accentuated with bits of the original gold braid

Carson House

and tassels. Everything in the family parlor is original except for a replacement rug and chandelier.

The rear parlor was the most formal room and contains the house's only fireplace. Here even the original carpet is still in place. The rest of the house is heated by potbellied, Franklin-type stoves that still sit on their original metal pads. The Carsons' master bedroom is also on this level, across the hall from the formal parlor, and today still has its original carpet and the Carsons' handsome bedroom furniture.

Upstairs, the Carsons' two daughters shared a huge and airy thirty-two-by-eighteen-foot room. Their one surviving son (a second died of whooping cough) had his own smaller room. The lower floor, downstairs from street level, has the dining room, kitchen, maid's room, cook's room, and some smaller service rooms. Like the rest of the house, these still have their original contents, including a lovely Chicago Gold Coin cookstove with a decided Art Nouveau influence. What is particularly unusual is that the cook's and the maid's rooms are both still amazingly intact. The two men servants, a gardener, and a doorman, lived in the three-story carriage house.

Captain Bailey House, 1877

Main Street (north side) between Fourth and Fifth Streets; 402-825-6001.

The Captain Bailey House is a fine example of a centered-gable Gothic Revival design. In this case the centered gable has smaller cross gables on each side. While relatively modest by national standards, for a town at the edge of western settlement this was a good-sized home. It began as a four-room, center-hall house with two rooms on each floor. Later, a T-shaped extension was added to the rear. This was a fairly common way of adding space to houses of this style and can be seen on other houses in Brownville, such as the Governor Furnas House (see the following entry).

This house was purchased unfurnished by the Brownville Historical Society to house its local-history museum. While not strictly a museum house, the structure's original interior architectural detailing remains intact and is easily visible. Note how much simpler the detailing in the T addition is than that in the front section of the house. Also, from inside the two upstairs front rooms, one can see an excellent example of one

Captain Bailey House

Governor Furnas House

kind of "false shaping," which was used to create pointed-arch Gothic windows in the smaller cross gables. Inside the house one sees simple rectangular sash windows; outside only a Gothic arch is visible because the exterior cladding covers the remainder of the window sash.

Governor Furnas House, 1868

Sixth Street (east side), about two blocks south of Main Street; 402-825-6001.

This small, quaint Gothic Revival house is one and a half stories high on the street facade but is set into the hillside and also has a lower story on the rear facade. It is interesting to compare the floor plan of this with that of the larger Captain Bailey House (see the preceding entry). Rather than having a central hall with a stairway, this house has simply an enclosed stairway right in front of the entry door and no hall. Both houses are enlarged

with a T extension at the rear. The rooms here are smaller; there is only one room per floor in the T; and the two smaller side gables that add space and light to the second floor of the Captain Bailey House are absent.

Thirty-two-year-old Robert W. Furnas (1824–1905), a native of Ohio, arrived in Brownville in 1856 and went on to a distinguished career as a newspaper editor, Civil War colonel, politician, and agriculturalist. From 1873 to 1875 he served as the third governor of the state of Nebraska. Retiring from public service to devote the rest of his life to his beloved Brownville experimental plant nursery and farm, Furnas purchased this modest home in 1878 and died here in 1905. The house had many occupants after Furnas's death but is now owned by the Nebraska State Historical Society. Several Furnas-owned objects have been obtained for the house, and one of the front rooms has an instructive exhibit on the talented governor's multifaceted life.

KEARNEY

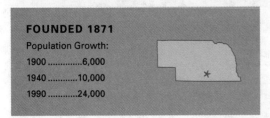

FOUNDED 1871

Population Growth:

1900 6,000

1940 10,000

1990 24,000

In 1865 the Union Pacific Railroad began building westward from Omaha toward its historic transcontinental junction with the eastward-building Central Pacific in Utah four years later (see page 140). Like the wagon trails that carried earlier immigrants to California and Oregon, the railroad crossed Nebraska along the well-watered valley of the Platte River. Kearney is one of the many agricultural marketing and trade centers that grew up along the Union Pacific tracks near the river in the 1870s. The town's principal architectural attraction is a remarkably avant-garde museum house built by one of its visionary promoters.

Frank House, 1889

2010 West Twenty-fourth Street
(West U.S. Highway 30); 308-865-8284;
George W. Frank Jr., Kearney, architect.
The presence of this unusually early and sophisticated Shingle-style dwelling in what was, when it was built, a small and remote agricultural town requires some explanation. The home was designed by architect Frank for his parents, George Washington Frank (1830–1906) and Phoebe McNair Frank (died 1900). George Sr., son of a successful merchant on the early frontier of western New York State, had left home in 1869 to pursue a similar career in the post–Civil War railroad boom of the western states. He relocated to Corning, in southwestern Iowa, which at that time was the western terminus of the expanding Chicago, Burlington, and Quincy Railroad. Soon George Frank Sr.'s talents had made him one of the most successful land brokers and investors in that rapidly developing region.

In 1871 Frank accompanied railroad officials on a visit to the site, in Nebraska some 250 miles west of Corning, where the westward-building Burlington line would soon connect with the Union Pacific, which had been completed only two years earlier to become the nation's first transcontinental railroad. Sensing great potential for the new town of Kearney, then being platted at the junction site, Frank bought several large

tracts of farmland immediately west of the town site as a long-term investment.

Continuing his activities in Iowa, Frank watched Kearney grow to become a small agricultural marketing center of 1,700 inhabitants by 1880. Five years later a growing influx of farmers into central Nebraska had doubled the town's population, and new housing construction was beginning to approach Frank's lands at the western edge of the original town site. The veteran town builder by then had conceived a bold plan to make the booming railroad crossroads into a major center for heavy industry. The key to this was a proposed "Kearney Canal" that would divert some of the Platte River's waters at a higher elevation to the west of town and channel them through Frank's acreage to power new mills, factories, and hydroelectric plants.

By now Frank's youngest son, George W. Frank Jr. (born 1861), had completed studies in architecture and civil engineering at New York's prestigious Rensselaer Polytechnic Institute. In 1884 he moved to Kearney to help with on-site supervision of the family's properties, which soon became the site of the new town of West Kearney. His father's long-term vision began to be real-

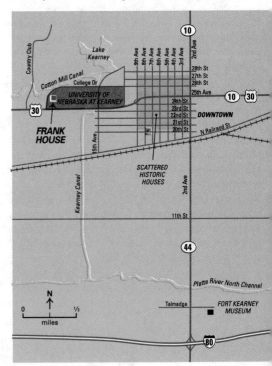

Frank House, early view

ized when the Kearney Canal was completed two years later. Soon mills and factories, as well as a railroad depot and new businesses and homes, began sprouting up in West Kearney.

So promising was this new venture that Frank Sr. and his wife decided to move their home from Iowa to Kearney. Throughout his career the father had maintained close contacts with wealthy New York City financiers, who supplied much of the capital for his town-development ventures. Frank now asked his son to design an appropriately fashionable and elegant new home where the couple could entertain eastern industrialists and bankers in grand style while encouraging them to invest in Kearney. The result was this Shingle-style landmark, built to a standard of quality that was rare even in the northeastern states, where the style originated and was most popular.

The Franks planned for this to be their final home, and it was designed with unusually permanent materials. The first floor is of sandstone quarried in Wyoming and then cut to fit on the site. The large, swooping roof is clad with clay tiles from Holland, rather than the wooden shingles that are typical of the style.

Handsome and expensive detailing was used throughout. The front door has horizontal panels below, small panes of glass above, and is enhanced by heavy metal ornamental hardware with a handcrafted look. The stairway landing features a large Tiffany stained-glass window. Authenticated by the original work order, it includes an early example of Tiffany's famed iridescent glass. Woodwork throughout the house is of oak, hand-

Frank House

carved by John Lindbeck, a local Swedish craftsman who included innovative variations in almost everything he carved. The house was built with nine fireplaces, six of which survive; with electricity; with steam heat; and with several bathrooms. The original brass hardware survives throughout. Furnishings are mostly donations, although Frank family pieces are finding their way back and are easily visible because each has an attached red ribbon.

Unfortunately, the Franks' final visionary dream was to be short-lived. The nationwide depression of 1893, coupled with a devastating Nebraska drought in 1894, forced them into bankruptcy. Most of the grand house's furnishings were sold at auction, and it is these pieces, many of which remained in Kearney, that are gradually being returned. The house itself first became a clinic and in 1907 was purchased by the state of Nebraska for use as the staff residence of an adjacent State Hospital for the Tubercular. The hospital closed in 1972, and the grounds and buildings were then converted for use by the University of Nebraska at Kearney.

The university now maintains the historic Frank House for official functions and is restoring it, mostly through private donations, to its original grandeur. This has been a heroic task—the Tiffany window had to be painstakingly disassembled and restored; the unique and costly tile roof had to be replaced; the enclosed porches reopened; a later garage built within the original porte cochere removed; most of the inside woodwork stripped and refinished; lowered ceilings removed; and much more. Work is ongoing, and the restoration of the remaining windows is now a high priority.

The appearance of this delightful house today is a testament both to the very high quality of its original design and to the care that has gone into its restoration. On display is a long-term landscape plan that looks as if it will replace the original spacious lawns with a more modern and confining context. It is hoped the work finally undertaken on the grounds will be of the same sensitive quality as that done on the house itself. Part of the beauty and history of the home is its unique setting on the broad western plains—a symbolic sentinel of its builder's faith in the future.

Nearby Houses

Scattered Victorian houses are found in the city's west-side neighborhood that now adjoins the campus of the University of Nebraska at Kearney. The campus today occupies the heart of what was once the Franks' new town of West Kearney. Most of the neighborhood's houses are painted white, a nostalgic reminder of the visual unity preferred in most small American towns through the middle decades of the twentieth century. Beginning with the historic preservation movement of the 1970s, many owners of historic houses in larger cities have switched to the more lively colors originally used on Victorian and Craftsman dwellings.

621 West Twenty-seventh Street (private), 1889; George W. Frank Jr., Kearney, architect. This is the home that George Jr. built for himself and his young family, completed the same year as his father's grand new Kearney dwelling (see page 396). Here we have a typical, wooden-walled example of the Shingle style with the upper story clad in shingles and the lower in narrow wood siding without corner boards. This combination is seen in several other houses in the neighborhood. Originally, the porch extended across and beyond the left side of the house. This area was later enclosed to create an attached garage.

LINCOLN

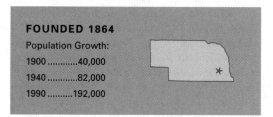

FOUNDED 1864

Population Growth:

1900 40,000

1940 82,000

1990 192,000

Lincoln is one of the rare U.S. capital cities that, like Washington, D.C., or Austin, Texas, was planned from the beginning to be a seat of government. The Nebraska Territory, formerly unorganized Indian lands, was created by Congress and first opened to Anglo settlement in 1854. In that year the territory's first towns were established along the Missouri River, its eastern boundary where regular steamboat service provided convenient access (see "Omaha," page 410; "Nebraska City," page 404; and "Brownville," page 392). As pioneer farmers moved westward from the river over the next decade, pressure grew to move the territorial capital from Omaha to a more central inland location; many small towns vied for the honor. The matter was settled

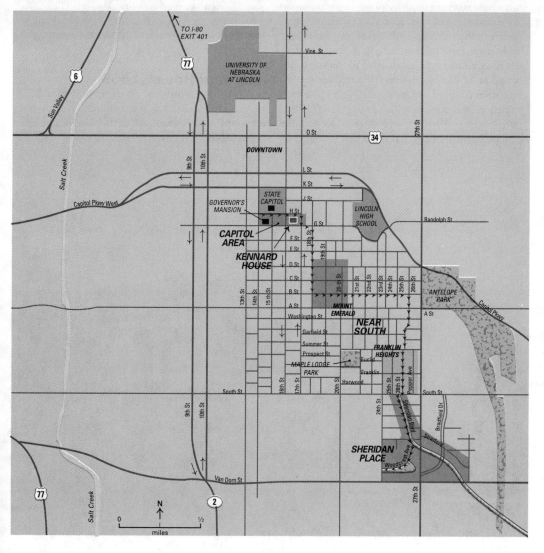

in 1867 when Nebraska was admitted to the Union as the thirty-seventh state. The new governor then headed a three-man commission that chose a capital site on the open prairie about fifty miles southwest of Omaha. The new capital was called Lincoln, in honor of the recently martyred president, and was also to be the home of a new state university.

A plan for the new town was drawn up by surveyor Augustus F. Harvey, who advised the governor's commission on the capital site and was also a lawyer and politician. Harvey was clearly a very talented surveyor, for historian John Reps, a scholar not easily moved to such statements, has this to say about Harvey's plan in his book *Cities of the American West*:

> [It is] by all odds the most successful of any adopted for a Nebraska community. In its generous provision of public sites and open spaces; its recognition that major public buildings could be so located as to provide vistas down major streets; its differentiation of lot sizes between those intended for business and those to be used for residential purposes; and its variation of street widths depending on proposed functions, this plan ranks high among those of western America. Moreover, and more important, the three-dimensional city that developed on this two-

dimensional plan became one of the most impressive and pleasant communities of the country.

Over the years since its founding, Lincoln has steadily grown into a midsized city but still retains much of the feel of a smaller government center and university town. Dominating the central city is the skyscraper-like tower of the magnificent **Nebraska State Capitol** (entrance at Fifteenth and K Streets), a Modernistic classic considered to be one of the seminal landmarks of American architecture. Designed by New York–based Bertram Grosvenor Goodhue (1869–1924; see also page 253) after his conceptual drawing won a national competition, the grand structure was built slowly, from 1922 until 1932, on a frugal "pay as you go" basis. Inside are handsome murals and interiors that can be seen on regular tours. Modern Lincoln also retains an important Italianate museum house and several fine neighborhoods of late-Victorian and early-twentieth-century dwellings.

Kennard House, 1869

1627 H Street, at Sixteenth Street; 402-471-4764;
John Keyes Winchell, Chicago, architect.

One of the three members of the governor's Capital Commission that picked the site for the state capital in

Kennard House

1867 was Nebraska's new secretary of state Thomas P. Kennard. When he built this picturesque Italianate home two years later, railroads had not reached the area, and every part of the house had to be either manufactured locally or brought by wagon from Missouri River ports. Clearly committed to making the barren site into a proper capital city, and to having a suitable setting for his new duties, Kennard spared no expense in constructing this stylish and substantial home on the remote Nebraska plains. The house was located adjacent to the site of the first State Capitol Building, which was completed only a year before the house.

The house is an asymmetrical Italianate design with a prominent rooftop cupola encircled by a balustrade. The cornice has paired decorative brackets combined with a row of dentils. Both round and segmentally arched window hoods are used, as are three typical bay windows. Originally, there was a rear wing that contained the kitchen and dining room; this was removed in 1923.

Over the years the historic dwelling was modified for a variety of uses and by the 1960s was about to be demolished by the state for a parking lot when local preservationists persuaded the state legislature to save it as a historic landmark. It was restored by the Nebraska Historical Society from 1966 to 1968. Remarkably, some of the early interior detailing still survived, including metal coal-burning fireplaces, a walnut staircase, and folding interior shutters also made of walnut. Furnishings appropriate to the 1870s are displayed throughout. As with most museum houses, restoration is ongoing; goals here include rebuilding the rear wing and additional structural work and repainting the exterior.

Capitol Area

Capitol Area

In addition to the Kennard House (see the preceding entry), the blocks immediately to the south and southeast of the state capitol building include several other important historic dwellings. Among these are:

740 South Seventeenth Street (private), Atwood House, ca. 1900. A lovely Neoclassical design, this features a full-height entry porch with triangular pediment above. The frieze is lavishly detailed with oval windows and floral swags and continues around the entire main house, a very unusual feature in Neoclassical designs. Both the front door and the upstairs balcony door are set into a Palladian motif, the latter opening onto a graceful wrought-iron balcony. Also note the fluted columns with elaborate Corinthian capitals and the overhanging eaves with closely spaced brackets. You may want to retain a mental image of this house to compare with the Governor's Mansion (see "1425 H Street").

700 South Sixteenth Street (state offices; quick interior viewing allowed), Ferguson House, 1911; Seales, Hirsch, and Gavin, Cleveland, architects. This handsome Italian Renaissance design is built of narrow, Roman-style bricks

brought in from St. Louis despite the fact that its entrepreneurial builder owned, among many other enterprises, a local brick company. The quoins, lintels, and belt course are of Vermont marble. The design takes full advantage of its corner lot by placing the living room, with its broad terrace and arched windows, along H Street and the main entry facade on South Sixteenth Street. This facade has a central wing projecting forward to an entry porch that shelters a round-arched doorway. An unusual Palladian motif dominates the second floor of this wing. This features not only a blind arch, but also a mostly blank expanse of brick below the arch.

720 South Sixteenth Street (private), Yates House, ca. 1893. Very fine porches are the dominant feature of this beautifully detailed spindlework Queen Anne design. These include a porte cochere, a large wraparound porch, and many small second-story porches and balconies. The exterior has been recently restored to its early appearance.

1425 H Street (open for occasional tours); Nebraska Governor's Mansion, 1958; 402-471-3766. It's instructive to have this 1950s Neoclassical house to compare with the ca.-1900 version at 740 South Seventeenth Street. Both are in the same full-height-entry-porch subtype, and both have triangular pediments above the entry. Yet here, on a larger and more formal home, the level of detailing is far simpler than in the earlier design. Such scaled-down and simplified detailing is typical of mid-twentieth-century Neoclassical houses. The columns are unfluted shafts with simple Doric capitals, and the entablature does not extend around the house as at 740. The cornice has dentils that are relatively sparsely spaced; only a single keystone ornaments each window. Inside, the ceiling heights are lower, a 1950s fashion that is obvious even from the exterior. The house is normally open weekly for tours.

Near South, ca. 1885–1930

Following the early precedent set by Nebraska secretary of state Kennard (see page 400), Lincoln's upscale Victorian and early-twentieth-century residential neighborhoods developed to the southeast of the state capitol in a large district now known as the Near South. This area, which encompasses about a square mile, bounded by G, South, South Thirteenth, and South Twenty-seventh Streets, is unusually well documented thanks to two guidebooks by Lincoln city planner Ed Zimmer called *The Near South Walking Tours: Volumes 1 and 2.* The district grew as a series of small subdivisions that opened throughout more than three decades, from the 1870s to about 1905. Not until the 1920s were all of the platted lots finally filled with houses. The result is a large area with homes of varying ages. Some of the district has now been intruded on by later apartment buildings, particularly along its northern and western margins.

On the map (see page 399) we have shown a suggested driving route that provides a representative sampling of the Near South's diverse housing stock. Beginning at the Kennard House (see page 400), the route passes through the district's most intact concentration of larger houses in the **Mount Emerald** subdivision, developed in 1905 on the grounds of what was previously a single large estate. Leaving the Mount Emerald neighborhood, which includes all of the addresses listed below, the route passes through **Franklin Heights,** an intact neighborhood of middle-class homes built from 1906 to the 1920s, many in the Craftsman and Prairie styles. Adjacent to Franklin Heights, and beyond the limits of the large Near South district, is the younger Sheridan Place neighborhood (see page 403).

1845 D Street (private), Phillips Castle, 1889; John H. W. Hawkins, Lincoln, architect. This rare survivor was originally the centerpiece of one of the Near South's large Victorian estates. A Richardsonian Romanesque design, it is built of quarry-faced red sandstone laid in several different patterns. The handsome side facade on South Nineteenth Street is the more easily visible. Note the copper-ornamented dormer on the far right and the elegant stained-glass windows.

1946 D Street (private), Steckley House, 1921; Fiske and Meginnis, Lincoln, architects. This similar house by the same architect who did 1950 C Street (see the following entry) is rather late for this type of Tudor design.

1950 C Street (private), Meeker House, 1916; Ferdinand Fiske, Lincoln, architect. Such Tudor designs with squared, Prairie-inspired porch supports and a somewhat-blocky appearance were common in the first two decades of the twentieth century. Overhanging eaves with exposed roof rafters and beams add a Craftsman touch.

1965 B Street (private), Whitney House, 1917; Ferdinand C. Fiske, Lincoln, architect. A handsomely detailed Italian Renaissance design, this retains its original wall finish of rough, natural-gray stucco. Notice the fine cornice and eave detailing. The underside of the eaves (soffit) is coated in stucco and accented with heavy dentils and paired brackets. All of the windows are narrow vertical pairs (sometimes called French doors), with those upstairs opening onto decorative balconets. Architect Fiske (1856–1930) arrived in Lincoln in 1890 after professional training at Cornell University in Ithaca, New York; shortly after this design was completed he entered into a decade-long partnership with Harry Meginnis. These few blocks of Mount Emerald demonstrate Fiske's great facility with such popular Eclectic-era fashions as the Italian Renaissance style, seen here, and several varied approaches to the Tudor and Prairie styles (see the following entries).

1953 B Street (private), Love House, 1916, Fiske and Meginnis, Lincoln, architects. This subtle and unusual Tudor house was built in the same year as the more typical early Tudor house at 1950 C Street. Note the original gray stucco walls and the Tudor-arched door and entry porch. Brick is used to clad a contrasting two-story bay window topped with castellations. Matching brick is used as trim on the entry porch and windows.

1944 B Street (private), Burkett House, 1914; Fiske and Meginnis, Lincoln, architects. This house was built for Elmer J. Burkett, an attorney who served as both a U.S. congressman and senator. He spent twenty thousand dollars on his large home, almost twice the cost of the other houses on the block. Here Fiske and his partner used a unique combination of Prairie and Craftsman details. Borrowed from the Craftsman style are the open eaves with exposed rafters, the gable dormers, and the triangular knee braces in the dormers and gables. Prairie features include the change of wall materials in the upper third of the house and the many horizontal-line details, including those in the stuccoed upper walls. A particularly distinctive feature is the original

Near South: Mount Emerald

Near South: Mount Emerald

feet wide with ample space for a streetcar line down its broad, landscaped median, Sheridan Place quickly became a favored site for upscale homes and is still one of Lincoln's most desirable neighborhoods. The original plan was for Sheridan Boulevard to run all the way to Calvert Street, as it does today, but the actual construction proceeded in several shorter stages, with the first being completed in 1909. At the end of this first four-block section are two later developments, each designed by a different landscape architect. Woodscrest, laid out to the west in 1916, had unusually large lots and was designed by the talented Jens Jensen of Chicago, whose work stressed native plant materials. The blocks to the east were laid out in 1917 by Lincoln landscape architect Ernst Herminghaus, who followed the topography of the land with Stratford Avenue and Bradfield Drive.

2221 Sheridan Boulevard (private), Spaulding House, ca. 1910. This symmetrical Mission-style house is clad with stone, an unusual material for this style. The house probably originally had a tile roof. It also had the exposed rafter ends so typical of Mission-style houses, which were being hidden by the addition of a fascia board the day we visited the neighborhood.

2636 Woodcrest Avenue (private), Miller House, 1927; Davis and Wilson, Lincoln, architects. This towered French Eclectic design is reported to have been inspired by the sixteenth-century French country estate later owned by the duke and duchess of Windsor. Notice the varied massing of the handsome slate roof, the use of tall and narrow leaded-glass windows in the entry area, and the elegantly understated ornament surrounding the front door. Ernst Herminghaus, who laid out the subdivision to the east of Sheridan Boulevard, designed the landscaping for this house.

2465 Woodcrest Avenue (private), Campbell House, 1935; Meginnis and Schaumberg, Lincoln, architects. This gracefully symmetrical French Eclectic design is clad in rough-faced limestone. Note the arched windows with tops breaking the roofline, the corners trimmed with contrasting smooth limestone, the low wings on each side of the main house block, and the full-height floor-to-ceiling windows with shutters on the first floor. The metal canopy entrance would have been very avant-garde in 1935. They were never very common and appear occasionally on houses built from about 1935 to about 1955, usually on simplified Colonial Revival Regency designs and on symmetrical French Eclectic houses such as this one.

3035 Sheridan Boulevard (private), Lord House, 1928; Davis and Wilson, Lincoln, architects. What an original interpretation of the Tudor style this is. The main front-facing gable swoops down to the right, leaving an immense expanse of roof ornamented with two levels of shed dormers before it terminates over an attached garage. There are two huge chimneys, both with triple chimney pots. Although masses of ivy hide most of the front facade, the front door with its elaborate hinges of wrought iron and the glimpses of leaded-glass windows give a good idea of the quality of the detailing. The house is complemented by a brick driveway and low retaining wall.

glass-and-metal canopy over the front entry, a feature typical of Beaux Arts houses rather than the more "modern" Prairie and Craftsman styles. Note how the porte cochere is set at a rakish angle toward the right rear.

1941 B Street (private), Robbins House, 1908. Ida Robbins (1869–1947) was an early suffragist and lifelong volunteer for humanitarian causes who was eulogized as "a woman of fine intellectual ability, active in public and world affairs to the day of her death." She earned a master's degree from the University of Nebraska in 1901 and seven years later built this avant-garde Prairie-style home. There is no record that she hired an architect, but the builder was T. P. Harrison, who constructed many of the homes designed by Fiske in Mount Emerald. The walls are finished in rough-textured stucco, a material favored in this neighborhood and which Harrison must have excelled at applying because of its amazing survival in almost-new condition. What is most remarkable about this design is the dramatic through-the-cornice dormer of the type that was, in 1908, just becoming fashionable among Chicago's innovative Prairie School architects. Could the independent Ms. Robbins have explored Chicago's new suburbs looking for inspiration? The porch supports and railing look like they could be later alterations.

1930 B Street (private), Watkins House, 1916; Fiske and Meginnis, Lincoln, architects. A handsome symmetrical Prairie-style design, this has distinctive horizontal lines formed by rows of upright (soldier course) bricks. Early photos show that the original shingle roof also had a horizontal-line motif. The width of the house is exaggerated by including the sleeping porch under the main roof. The use of a different wall material for the upper third of the house is a typical Prairie feature, as is the distinctive low arch with horizontal wings used in the entry-porch roof.

Sheridan Place, ca. 1910–1950s

Developed in the early twentieth century at the southeast corner of the older Near South grid of streets, Sheridan Place introduced to Lincoln such early twentieth-century planning concepts as curving streets and landscaped boulevards (see also pages 298 and 337). Centered around heroic Sheridan Boulevard, 160

NEBRASKA CITY

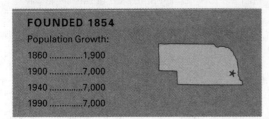

FOUNDED 1854

Population Growth:

1860	1,900
1900	7,000
1940	7,000
1990	7,000

Of the several dozen new Missouri River towns founded when the Nebraska Territory was created from former Indian lands in 1854, only two—Omaha and Nebraska City—were serious contenders to become the new territory's dominant metropolis. Omaha had the advantage of being directly opposite long-established Council Bluffs, Iowa, a traditional starting point for travelers heading westward along the Oregon-California Trail, which followed the south bank of the Platte River across Nebraska. Nebraska City's location also had advantages. Located forty miles south of Omaha on the opposite side of the Platte's junction with the Missouri River, it provided a more direct route westward to a southerly bend in the Platte's channel. This route also avoided the difficult problem of crossing the Platte, which was too shallow for dependable ferries and generally too soft to ford with heavily laden wagons.

Nebraska City's advantages were to become crucial when gold was discovered in the Denver region in 1858 (see page 297). Soon a constant stream of wagon freight was leaving the city's docks en route to Denver with heavy loads of mining equipment and trade goods bound for Colorado's booming gold camps. By 1865 Nebraska City rivaled Omaha as a river port and center of wagon freighting. Within only a few years, Nebraska City's advantages were to disappear as the first Union Pacific trains, following the early Platte River route from Omaha, forever replaced animal-drawn freight wagons. As its population growth clearly shows, Nebraska City was destined to become a small agricultural marketing and trade center whose population of about seven thousand has remained remarkably constant throughout the twentieth century. Not surprisingly, the town retains a fine collection of historic dwellings, three of which are museum houses.

Nebraska City Historic District, ca. 1860–1940

The Nebraska City Historic District is a huge, fifty-eight-square-block, mostly residential area. As is typical in small towns, it includes intermingled houses of many different sizes, ages, and styles, a charming characteristic that contrasts with the normally more homo-

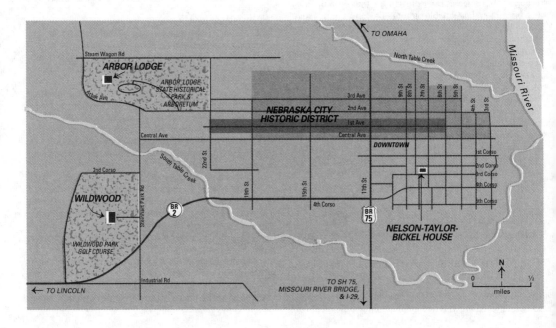

View of Nebraska City, 1865

geneous neighborhoods found in larger cities. Here, as in many small towns, a single street has a disproportionate share of the larger, upscale houses. In this case it is First Avenue, which is still paved with bricks and has a shady tree tunnel along most of its length.

806 First Avenue, Taylor-Shewell-Gilligan House, 1882. This fine Italianate house (home of the Chamber of Commerce) is a relatively late example of the asymmetrical subtype of the style. The deep band of cornice trim is elaborated with molded panels and fine vertical brackets featuring decorative pendants dripping from their tops. The wraparound porch has Italianate porch supports with vertical brackets above but adds a touch of the Queen Anne style with an open spindlework frieze. Note the iron balustrade above the porch roof and the early iron fence at the sidewalk.

815 First Avenue (private), Green House, ca. 1871. Built for the minister of the Cumberland Presbyterian Church, this is a simple one-and-a-half-story Gothic Revival cottage. As was often the case in the western states, this has a Greek Revival entrance with the front door surrounded by a narrow line of small windowpanes called lights. The entry porch is reported to have been added in the 1880s, but is Gothic Revival in character. The iron roofline balustrade above the porch and the wooden shutters are recent additions.

1014 First Avenue (private), Dillon House, ca. 1864. This three-bay design, and its five-bay companion at 1118 First Avenue (see the following entry), are excellent examples of the vernacular Greek Revival houses built just after the Civil War. These were commonly of the simple entry-porch-less-than-full-height subtype, as seen here. The front door is surrounded by a narrow line of rectangular windowpanes, the small entry porch has simplified Doric columns, and simple

stone lintels crown the windows. The usual wide band of trim beneath the roofline, typical of Greek Revival houses, is absent here, and the widely overhanging eaves were borrowed from the contemporaneous Italianate style. Early locally made bricks, which were probably used here, were very soft and almost always were soon painted to help preserve them and prevent moisture from seeping into the walls.

1118 First Avenue (private), Rottman House, 1868. This vernacular Greek Revival house is essentially a five-bay version of 1014 First Avenue (see the preceding entry). Its roof eaves do not have as wide an overhang as 1014, making them more typically Greek Revival. The balustrade above the entry porch is likely a later addition; the wide spacing of the individual balusters is an almost-certain indicator of this.

1520 First Avenue (private), ca. 1900. This front-gabled two-story house form is often called a homestead house; this shape was most common in large northeastern cities where high land costs and very narrow city lots were the norm. This particular version was built beginning in the 1890s and has been quite precisely described in Herbert Gottfried and Jan Jennings' most useful book *American Vernacular Design, 1870–1940* as having a bay window to one side and a closed gable (to make a full triangle), and "a distinctive Palladian window was placed in the closed gable, and the entire gable now overhung the main body of the house. The entrance porch [was of full-] facade width, columns were introduced with an order of architecture and dormers were placed on the side elevations." In addition this example has elegantly narrow wood siding and decorative transoms over what appear to be newer windows.

1714 First Avenue (private), ca. 1905. This is a unique variation of the one-story, pyramidal-hipped-roof houses that were very popular in the early years of the twentieth century. Most styled examples of this house form have

Nebraska City Historic District

either Colonial Revival, Neoclassical, Prairie, or Craftsman detailing. This house is unique in combining a prominent rounded Shingle-style dormer with three different textures of cast stone—a cobblestone texture used for a base and two different widths of "rusticated stone" used in alternating courses for the main body of the house.

1820 First Avenue (private), ca. 1950. One-story Colonial Revival houses, or Cape Cod cottages, as they are commonly called, have been built relatively continuously from the 1700s right up through today. But there was a period from the late 1930s to mid 1950s when they were especially popular. Minimal Cape Cod cottages were used for large subdivisions of small houses, and in more expensive suburbs they offered a simple way to impose a traditional style on the one-story house form being popularized by Ranch houses.

Here we have an instructive example of this trend. The house was designed to appear as if built in several stages, as were many Colonial-era houses. The section just to the right of the entry door has a slightly lower roof than the main house; beyond and to the rear is an even lower gabled-roof section. The house has an enclosed garage that faces the side street and is topped by a small cupola, a favorite Colonial Revival elaboration from the ca. 1940s period. The main house and garage were probably originally connected by a breezeway, now enclosed, another favored feature of the ca. 1940s period. Breezeways were an interesting transition between the completely detached garages of the 1920s and 1930s and the completely attached versions that were almost universal by 1960. This house appears to have later vinyl siding.

2110 First Avenue (private), ca. 1950. Another one-story

Colonial Revival Cape Cod similar to 1820 First Avenue (see the preceding entry). This is a minimal builder's interpretation; the garage problem has been solved by adding a later carport. Next door is an even simpler interpretation of the same type, this sided with aluminum and with added metal shutters and an attached garage. It would be interesting to know if the garage is original to the house.

Arbor Lodge, rear, 1855–mid-1880s; front, 1903

Second Avenue west of Twenty-second Street, in Arbor Lodge State Historical Park and Arboretum; 402-873-7222.

Arbor Lodge has to be one of the West's best, and best-documented, examples of a "little house that grew and grew." The four-room, side-gabled folk cabin, built in 1855, received three major enlargements that transformed it into the grand Neoclassical home you see today, with a facade dating from 1903.

The original cabin was built by J. Sterling Morton (1832–1902) and his bride, Caroline Joy "Carrie" French (1833–1881), on their 160-acre homestead claim in the newly created Nebraska Territory. Its four rooms and wooden-framed construction (as opposed to walls of sod or logs) made it an extremely fine home when built. The Mortons, who had grown up in Michigan and Maine, had set out for Nebraska from Michigan on the very day of their wedding in October 1854. They chose the highest point on their land, which was then treeless prairie, as the site of their first home. As their family grew to include four sons, so did their home—into a larger and larger and still-larger Folk Victorian dwelling, always with broad porches. In 1879, to celebrate their twenty-fifth wedding anniversary, handsome Eastlake woodwork was added throughout the interior of the house. Because this earlier portion of the house remains intact, with many original furnishings, a visit to Arbor Lodge lets you see interiors from two different eras in one house.

As soon as they moved in 1855, Carrie set about designing drives and walkways and planting the first trees. Sterling obviously shared her interest, and on April 10, 1872, he was instrumental in creating the first Arbor Day observance. It was held in Nebraska, and it is said that over a million trees were planted in Nebraska on that one day. It is easy to see why the couple, arriving from the forested part of the continent, would have missed trees. But rather than simply planting them on their claim, as most would do, or even throughout their town, as a few others did, they set about trying to correct the situation for the entire state of Nebraska. From this base, the idea of a special tree-planting holiday spread throughout the nation. Morton, who had both a journalistic and political career, was in a unique position to promote the holiday. In Nebraska he held many offices, including acting governor of the territory from 1858 to 1861, and nationally he was the nation's first full-time secretary of agriculture during Grover Cleveland's second term, from 1893 to 1897.

After Sterling's death in 1902, his eldest son, Joy, inherited the house and almost immediately began his own large and final addition to the historic structure. To design this, he hired the well-known Chicago architect Jarvis Hunt (1858–1941), nephew of New York's Richard Morris Hunt, a renowned designer of opulent Victorian mansions. To redesign the large grounds he commissioned Warren H. Manning (1860–1938), a distinguished Boston landscape architect who had apprenticed under the pioneering Frederick Law Olmsted. Manning was a specialist in the choice of plant materials and was particularly skilled in the use of native American plants. Peter Holm of Chicago designed the addition's interiors. Joy was well able to afford this expensive remodeling, since he had made an independent fortune as the founder of the highly successful Morton Salt Company.

The easiest way to understand what you are seeing at Arbor Lodge is to begin by walking all the way around the outside of the house. The Victorian house will be easily distinguishable from the 1903 addition simply by looking at the cornice line. When you hit the cornice with Italianate brackets, you are looking at the pre-1903 house. Even though the walls of this house were stuccoed over, the roof-wall junction was left un-

Arbor Lodge

touched, as is so often the case with stylistic remodel-ings (this is why looking at the roof and cornice line of a house can be such a useful key to later modifications).

When you enter the house, first look at the series of exterior photos on display, which are also reproduced in the guide pamphlet. Finally, look around at the huge entry hall of the 1903 addition and note that it sits com-pletely in front of the 1882 house illustrated in the pho-tograph. That house's porches were removed and this broad new addition was substituted. The doorway to the right of the grand stairway leads into the center hall of the Victorian-era house. The front wing is broader than the Victorian house and forms a T shape in front of it. Most of the small T-shaped houses you see in Nebraska City and nearby Brownville were formed the opposite way. An earlier styled front section of a house had a later narrower rear wing, often only one room wide, added.

One enters into a huge symmetrical hall, with a very wide central stairway as its focal point. The carpet is forest green, and the walls a sponged sky blue, repre-senting the green carpet on earth and the skies above. To the right is a handsome library filled with striking Mission furniture. Dark wood beams, reddish-orange walls, a gold ceiling, and a large brick fireplace give the room its character. Across the hall and to the left as you enter is a large reception room, its huge fireplace sur-rounded with a diamond dust mirror above and elabo-rate pilasters to each side. Just behind this is a long, narrow conservatory with a dramatic Tiffany-glass ceiling that features a trellis-and-grapevine motif, giv-ing the room the feeling of an ever-productive grape arbor. Beyond these four major 1903 rooms is the 1879 house with its lovely Eastlake woodwork, including a dining room and the Red Parlor, both with striped hardwood floors made from alternating boards of black walnut and honey maple.

Up the main 1903 stairway, on the landing, a dra-matic four-by-nine-foot 1897 oil painting depicts the signing of the Table Creek Treaty of 1857; the elder Mortons stand in the background as the Pawnee cede their Nebraska lands to the United States. The new ad-dition has four bedroom suites upstairs, and behind these, down a couple of steps that make clear the divi-sion of the old and new parts of the house, are the fully furnished Victorian bedrooms of the earlier house.

A closer look at the exterior is now useful once the interior context has been seen. The dominant 1903 ex-terior detailing is Neoclassical. There are three almost-identical full-height entry porches—each rounded and supported by six colossal unfluted columns with Com-posite capitals. One faces the front entry with the grand allée of trees leading to it, and the other two are on each side, leading out into gardens. The front and side entry doors all have broad elliptical fanlights above and those on the two side porches have a large broken-ogee pedi-ment crowning the fanlight. Each upstairs porch has doors opening onto a broad, balustraded balcony.

Today, the house is a national historic landmark and sits in the middle of the Arbor Lodge State Historical Park. Naturalistic woodland landscaping dominates the large park, with more formal gardens on each side of the main house. A handsome Shingle-style carriage house was built in 1901. It includes a house for the grounds superintendent that is connected to the car-riage wing by an open breezeway. A fascinating chrono-logical collection of coaches and carriages is housed here, all used by various members of the Morton fam-ily, some here at Arbor Lodge and others in Chicago.

The park surrounding the home has a seventy-two-acre arboretum with more than 260 varieties of trees and shrubs and a half-mile Tree Trail winding through a portion of it. Another area is the Pine Grove, where Morton proved to Governor Furnas (see page 395) that white pines would grow in Nebraska.

Wildwood, 1869

Steinhart Park Road north of the city route of Nebraska Highway 2; 402-873-6340.

Built as the suburban estate of Nebraska City banker Jasper A. Ware, this is another of the centered-gable Gothic Revival houses that were popular along this stretch of the Missouri River (see also "Governor Fur-nas House," page 395, and "Captain Bailey House," page 394, in Brownville, and "Amelia Earhart Birth-place," page 347, in Atchison, Kansas). One and a half stories high, Wildwood has unusual small windows that light the upper half story. Of solid brick construc-tion, the main section of the house is one room deep and two rooms wide with a center hall. There is a T wing behind, as is also seen in the Gothic Revival houses in nearby Brownville. There is a Gothic-arched window in the center gable, but the front door and its narrow glass surround are holdovers from the earlier Greek Revival.

The interior has little Gothic detailing but features a lovely hand-hewn stair rail. There are only a few origi-nal furnishings; other appropriate pieces have been gathered from the Nebraska City vicinity. Among these are an étagère made with a scroll saw by a local crafts-man and a dining room table made locally. Also on dis-play is a rather-fabulous opera dress made for a Nebraska City woman. Featuring lace and chinchilla, it provides a feeling for the level of personal elegance that could be obtained even at the edge of the frontier.

Wildwood

Nelson-Taylor-Bickel House, 1857

711 Third Corso; open by appointment only; 402-873-5287.

This Greek Revival dwelling is probably the best example of the style in Nebraska and one of the state's oldest homes. It is worth driving past to view the exterior simply because it is so unusual for this part of the country. It is built of brick and has a parapeted end wall, quite rare for the West at this early date. A broad cornice with stylized dentils distinguishes the front of the house. The front door and its handsome surround of transom and sidelights is slightly recessed with simplified pilasters on each side of the entry door. From the front, you can see the low windows that light the basement story. The old iron fence that encloses the yard was brought in to replace the original, which was deteriorating.

Built with Nebraska City–made bricks for local businessman and politician William H. Taylor, the house was restored by Mr. and Mrs. Karl Nelson from 1976 to 1980. The Otoe County Historical Society now uses the basement story for a research center. The interior has a center-hall plan and twelve-foot ceilings. A parlor, living room, and bedroom are furnished with walnut Victorian-era pieces collected locally and donated to the house. Interior detailing is very simple; the two large fireplaces have their original surrounds.

OMAHA

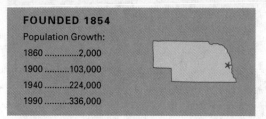

FOUNDED 1854

Population Growth:
1860 2,000
1900 103,000
1940 224,000
1990 336,000

For many years before the town's founding, the Omaha area had been a principal gateway for travelers venturing into the American West. Located due west of Chicago and Des Moines at a ferry crossing on the Missouri River, Council Bluffs, on the Iowa side of the river, became the final assembly and supply center for wagon trains heading westward along the Oregon Trail in the 1830s. This flow increased in 1846 when three thousand Mormons, fleeing persecution in Illinois (see page xix), established their Winter Quarters in what is now North Omaha before departing to found Salt Lake City the next spring. Over the next twenty years eighty thousand additional Mormon pioneers assembled here for the journey westward to their new Zion. Beginning in 1849, still another large wave of immigrants began passing through, these en route to seeking their fortunes in the California goldfields.

Until 1854 permanent Anglo settlement on the vast plains west of the Missouri was illegal because the lands were reserved by treaty for the use of the resident Indian tribes. In that year Congress created the Kansas and Nebraska Territories and opened their easternmost regions to Anglo settlement. Within a few months land promoters from the long-settled adjacent states of Iowa and Missouri founded dozens of speculative Nebraska towns along its Missouri River boundary. Most of these quickly disappeared, but a few, such as Nebraska City (see page 404) and Brownville (see page 392), became local trade centers that still survive today. All had hoped to become the dominant metropolis of the Nebraska Territory, but Omaha, founded just across the river from the venerable immigration center and wagon-road junction of Council Bluffs, Iowa, had an important head start.

All doubts about the ultimate winner of this metropolitan sweepstakes were removed in 1863, when President Lincoln chose Omaha–Council Bluffs to be the eastern terminus of the new Union Pacific Railroad, the

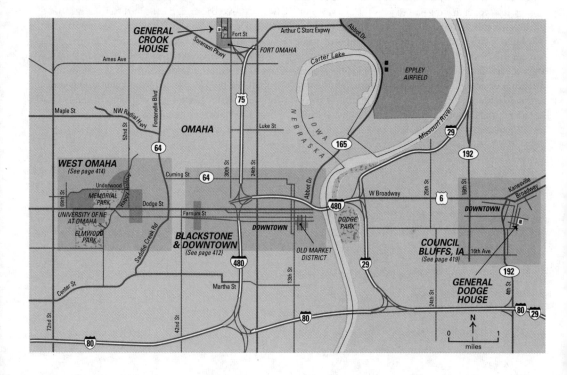

eastern half of the nation's first transcontinental rail line. Construction began in Omaha in 1865 as the Union Pacific built westward toward its historic "golden spike" junction with the eastward-building Central Pacific in northern Utah in 1869 (see also pages xxvi and 140). By 1880 Omaha, now the Union Pacific's headquarters city served by eight other railroad lines, was a thriving rail junction, agricultural marketing, and manufacturing center with 30,000 inhabitants. Ten years later its population had grown to 140,000, making it second in size only to San Francisco among the cities of the American West.

The decade of the 1890s reversed the fortunes of both Omaha and much of the West. Drought and blizzards caused widespread crop failures and massive losses of livestock. In addition, the collapse of silver prices in 1893 led to a worldwide depression with rampant bank closings and business failures. A great many of the nation's railroads passed into the hands of bankruptcy receivers who severely curtailed operations. All of these factors contributed to Omaha's population decline to 103,000 in 1900.

The new century brought a gradual return to prosperity. The perfection of refrigerated railroad cars permitted the distant shipment of dressed meat rather than the temperamental and more bulky live animals. As a result, huge packinghouse and stockyard complexes grew up at several major rail junctions in the ranching lands of the eastern plains. Omaha was a principal beneficiary of this development and by the mid–twentieth century was the world's largest livestock market (see also "Fort Worth," page 588). Equally important was the importation of hardy varieties of winter wheat from the Russian steppe, as well as the discovery of other grain varieties that thrived in the cold winters of the central plains. Omaha's rail connections made it a major center for the distribution and processing of this new wheat bonanza.

Omaha's economy continued to be dominated by its traditional roles as a railroad and food-processing center throughout the twentieth century. As a result it did not experience the explosive post-1950 growth seen in many larger western cities. Today, an important concentration of the city's early commercial buildings survives in and near the downtown **Old Market District** (1880–1915; Eleventh and Howard Streets). Some of these buildings now house a lively collection of restaurants, shops, and theaters.

Omaha's principal residential districts spread westward from the riverfront industrial and commercial areas. Most of this area's Victorian-era neighborhoods have now been consumed or massively intruded on by expansion of the downtown commercial district. Far-

ther west, several fine early-twentieth-century neighborhoods still survive intact (see the following entry). In addition, the Omaha area is the site of two important Victorian museum houses (see pages 417 and 418).

West Omaha, the Gold Coast, ca. 1900–1940

From the late nineteenth century on, Omaha's most desirable residential neighborhoods were built on the hills to the west of downtown. Rather imprecisely following the lead of Chicago, Omaha citizens called this group of neighborhoods, all several miles from the nearest waterway, the Gold Coast, a name that persists today. Sometimes it refers to the entire group of older West Omaha neighborhoods, and sometimes it is used more specifically for only Blackstone, the oldest of the original west hills neighborhoods, which was the city's most fashionable address in the earliest years of the twentieth century.

A bit to the west of Blackstone lay the eight-hundred-acre farm of John Nelson Hayes Patrick, which was gradually subdivided into three fine Eclectic-era suburbs—Dundee, Happy Hollow, and Fairacres. Patrick purchased his farm in 1870, where he built a thirty-three-room mansion. In the late 1880s Patrick began subdividing his farm by platting the first part of Dundee. The area attracted little development through the economic and population decline of the 1890s, but about 1905 it rapidly became so popular that Dundee South was quickly added. This was soon followed by Happy Hollow, located across Fifty-second Street just west of Dundee, which was laid out with curving streets in the naturalistic style pioneered by Boston planner Frederick Law Olmsted. Happy Hollow was soon fully developed and was followed by Happy Hollow West, whose unusual street pattern forms a nested series of quarter circles. Last to develop was Fairacres, another naturalistic neighborhood located still farther west and featuring unusually large, estate-size lots. This continued to be built up through the 1950s.

These three nearby West Omaha neighborhoods are great places to see the subtle differences in early-twentieth-century subdivisions developed at slightly different times and with houses in differing price ranges. Although there is considerable overlap in house style, age, and size from one area to the next, the overall flavor of each neighborhood—Dundee, Dundee South, Happy Hollow, Happy Hollow West, and Fairacres—is slightly different. Dundee is the earliest, with many Craftsman and American four-square-shaped houses, often clad in wood. Dundee South and Happy Hollow were developed almost contemporaneously, with larger homes and lots in Happy Hollow than

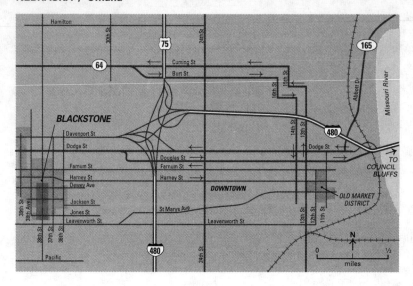

in Dundee South. Both areas have many Period homes based on historical styles, but these often show "modernist" Craftsman and Prairie influences. This is particularly true in Dundee South, where the less expensive homes were mostly builders' versions of the period styles. Happy Hollow West, mainly developed after 1920, is filled with "pure" period styles. Fairacres developed last and, along with a few earlier homes, has mostly architect-designed houses built from the 1930s through 1950s. Each West Omaha neighborhood is discussed individually below.

When house watching in the older grid sections of West Omaha, notice that there are sometimes, but not always, two parallel streets with the same name distinguished only by whether they are labeled "Street" or "Avenue." For example, Thirty-eighth Street and Thirty-eighth Avenue are parallel and adjacent to each other. Also note that Farnum Street, an important but narrow east–west spine through the area, has reversible lanes at rush hours.

Blackstone, ca. 1895–1920

This area, once the home of many of Omaha's wealthiest families, has lost much of its original fabric from demolition and apartment-house intrusions. It also does not have a generally agreed-upon name. It is often called the Blackstone neighborhood after the grand **Blackstone Hotel** (Thirty-sixth and Farnum Streets, 1916), long the site of Omaha society events. Other names for the neighborhood include "West Farnum," after its principal east–west residential street, and also simply the "Gold Coast," a term that is now also used for *all* of the West Omaha neighborhoods discussed here.

A number of the Blackstone area's grand mansions still survive but are now mostly scattered among larger areas of vacant lots and younger apartment buildings. The map above shows this large National Register historic district in light color and the district's most intact concentration of important houses (on Thirty-eighth Street) in a darker color.

518 South Thirty-eighth Street (private), Morsman House, 1923; F. A. Henninger, Omaha, architect. Now owned by the Omaha Women's Club, this is a superbly detailed example of the Tudor style. It has brick walls constructed of larger-than-normal paving bricks, with extensive half-timbering in its upper story and multiple gables. Note the leaded-glass windows, carved vergeboards, and elaborate cast-stone trim that is irregularly "tabbed" into the brickwork around the door and windows.

3727 Jackson Street (private), Kirkendall House, 1901; Thomas R. Kimball, Omaha, architect. This extraordinary Italian Renaissance house was designed by one of the Midwest's most gifted Eclectic-era architects. Thomas Kimball

Blackstone

Blackstone

Blackstone: Joslyn Castle

(1862–1934) was born near Cincinnati, Ohio, and received his architectural training at the Massachusetts Institute of Technology. He was also an accomplished painter and studied art as well as architecture in both Paris and Boston. In 1889 he became a partner with Walker and Best in Boston, and when this firm was appointed supervising architect for Omaha's 1898 Trans-Mississippi Exposition, Kimball was sent there to open an office. When the exposition was over, Kimball resigned from the Boston firm to open a private practice in Omaha.

In his long career Kimball designed many fine buildings and residences both in Omaha and throughout the Midwest. The quality of his work was nationally recognized, and he served as president of the American Institute of Architects from 1918 to 1920. Kimball was a master of many architectural styles, but the Italian Renaissance was apparently his favorite. In this house he drew more from precedents he had used in the Omaha Public Library (designed in 1891 to 1892) than from the more typical residential interpretations of the style. Here is a public-building version of the style translated to a residential design. Of particular note is the striking attic story with variegated marble panels topped by an elaborate cornice similar to that used on his landmark library building. The walls are of precisely laid, buff-colored brick with limestone trim.

500 South Thirty-eighth Street (private), Brandeis-Millard House, 1904; Albert Kahn, Detroit, architect. This is a fine parapeted Tudor house that is the only Nebraska work by the distinguished Kahn (1869–1942), who gained a national reputation for his innovative designs for both automobile assembly plants and Eclectic-era mansions to house their owners. Notice the two-story semihexagonal bay, the cast-stone trim, and the parapeted gables. The steeply pitched gable dormers introduce an informal note to what is otherwise a very formal exterior.

608 South Thirty-eighth Street (private), Hamilton House, 1910. This fine Prairie-style design was apparently inspired by the work of the Chicago architect George W. Maher (1864–1926), a contemporary of Frank Lloyd Wright who had his own unique way of approaching the style. Here, as in Pleasant Home (a Maher design that is now a museum house near Oak Park, Illinois), there is a long, shallow parapet along the roofline. Maher loved to repeat the same design element, and the same shallow curve is repeated in the

central dormer, over the porch entry, in the striking fence design, and even in the chimney top. The quality of all the architectural details is superb—everything from the tops of the porch-support piers and the ornate cornice lines to the small vertical detail on the chimney. Unfortunately, the left side of the porch has been enclosed.

3902 Davenport Street (open to visitors one day per month; 402-595-2199); Joslyn Castle, 1903; John McDonald, Omaha, architect. This striking Chateauesque home sits on a wooded five-acre site. It was built for George A. Joslyn, wealthy president of the Western Newspaper Union who, along with his wife, Sarah, was also a generous patron of the arts. The stone walls, parapeted wall dormers topped with pinnacles, and basket arches of the entry porch are all Chateauesque hallmarks. Architect and client also apparently wanted a touch of Scottish baronial castle to add strength to the home's Renaissance facade. Thus, we have the large castellated tower on the right with a miniature version at the far left. The house was originally donated to the Society of Liberal Arts of the Joslyn Art Museum and is now owned by the state of Nebraska. This is an unusual landmark dwelling in a pivotal location and is reported to have a well-preserved interior.

413

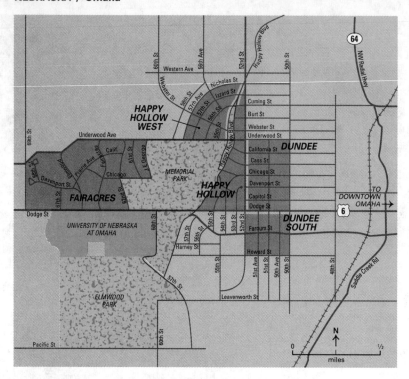

Dundee, ca. 1900–1915, and Dundee South, ca. 1910–1925

West Omaha's Dundee neighborhood, with a traditional grid street plan, was originally subdivided in the 1880s and given the name of Dundee Place. By 1893 there had been relatively little development, and the project was incorporated as the independent village of Dundee (the boundaries were Forty-eighth and Fifty-second Streets and Dodge and Cuming Streets) in an attempt to encourage homebuilding. Almost immediately, the nationwide depression of the 1890s stopped all construction. Not until about 1905 did Dundee begin to fill with houses, all of which had to be set back twenty-five feet from the street and cost a minimum of $2,500.

Dundee's success soon led to the opening of Dundee South, located in the blocks south of Dodge Street. The original Dundee street grid (north of Dodge Street) has houses facing due north and south. These are mostly Craftsman and four-square homes clad in wood. The slightly later blocks of Dundee South have houses that face due east and west thus making it easy to distinguish the two phases of the development. Here there are more brick-clad homes, mostly in the Tudor or Colonial Revival styles, many of which have Craftsman and Prairie features added. Note that few of the houses here, which were built on relatively narrow lots, have side wings or

porches. In 1915 the independent town was annexed by Omaha.

Dundee: 5124 Cass Street (private), ca. 1910. This two-story Craftsman design has a fine original front porch. A close look reveals that all of the dramatic exposed rafters and roof beams, which would have enlivened the original roofline, have later been enclosed.

Dundee: 5102 California Street (private), ca. 1910. An American four-square-shaped house, this example combines open Craftsman-style eaves, an enclosed porch railing, and the Classical columns typical of Colonial Revival four-squares. Note the intriguing quadrant cross in the center of the upstairs.

Dundee South: 105 South Fifty-first Street (private), ca. 1915. Prairie and Craftsman details indicate the likelihood of a pre-1920 date for this side-gabled Colonial Revival house. These include the wide roof overhang without a formal cornice, the continuous sill line below the upper-story windows with a change in material above, the mullion pattern in the upper window sash, and the exposed roof beams on the entry porch. Notice the paired windows both down and up, the centered one-story entry porch, the window boxes and the brick quoins around the upper-story windows in lieu of shutters. At 105 South Fiftieth Avenue (private), ca. 1915, is a similar side-gabled Colonial Revival design with a one-story entry porch. It is clad in wood and has Craftsman-type overhanging eaves with exposed rafters and a three-part door typical of vernacular Prairie-style houses. These features suggest that it too was built before about 1920.

Dundee South: 108 South Fifty-first Avenue (private), ca. 1915. This handsome symmetrical Prairie design is completely in the spirit of the style except perhaps for the balusters of the porch railing, which look a bit out of character. If they are original they show a touch of originality on the part of the builder, or perhaps they were just on sale the day he went to the lumberyard to get balusters! Either way should be treasured as an indication of the liberties that builders often took and the countless variations that these created. If the balusters are later replacements, they'd have to be judged as stylistically inappropriate. Early photographs, original plans, or structural evidence of replacement could solve the puzzle.

Dundee South: 113 South Fifty-first Avenue (private), ca. 1915. This is a good example of a pre-1920 builder's version of the Tudor style. Note the wide eave overhang and the large, square porch supports borrowed from the Prairie style. The shutters are a later addition. Another early builder's version of the Tudor style is at 118 South Fifty-first Avenue (private), here with a strong dose of Craftsman style added in the shed dormer, the exposed roof rafters, and the exposed roof "beams" above the porch entrance. Number 310 South Fifty-first Avenue (private) is a larger version of this same type of early-Tudor-style home with Prairie and Craftsman influences that was so popular with builders from about 1905 to 1920.

Dundee South: 113 South Fiftieth Avenue (private), ca. 1915. This is one of a cluster of gambrel-roofed Colonial Revival houses (often called Dutch Colonial) on the odd side of this street, some of which have added aluminum siding. This example has a side gambrel and the typical shed dormer that added a half story of upstairs space. Here the roof has flared eaves, and the entry door has a Palladian motif in its surround, which is reinforced by the arch of the porch. Note the robust porch supports and the rough-finished stucco cladding the first story, and the window boxes. At 317 South Fiftieth Avenue (private), ca. 1915, is the same style and subtype but with a front-facing cross gambrel. Number 313 South Fiftieth Avenue (private), ca. 1915, adds a pair of front-facing gambrels to a hipped-roof house with full-width porch.

Happy Hollow, ca. 1910–1925, and Happy Hollow West, ca. 1920–1940

As the original village of Dundee was successfully building out, two real estate developers began laying out a more naturalistic residential area just to the west. They began by filling in a creek (creating the "happy hollow") and surrounded it on each side with Happy Hollow Boulevard. They then developed the land from Happy Hollow Boulevard to Fifty-second Street to the east. This neighborhood has a wide range of house styles, built at about the same time as Dundee South but with slightly larger homes placed on larger lots. When this original portion of Happy Hollow began to fill up, the land west of Happy Hollow Boulevard was developed in an unusual, concentric quarter-circle street pattern to create Happy Hollow West. Lots here tend to be a bit smaller than in the original.

Happy Hollow West was built up mainly in the late 1920s and early 1930s. The Tudor style was the most fa-

vored; the neighborhood has an unusually fine collection of two-story Tudor houses with an amazing repertoire of variations and details. Colonial Revival, French Eclectic, and other styles are also found here, but Tudor rules. Like most houses from the 1920s and early 1930s, the homes in Happy Hollow West show almost none of the Craftsman and Prairie features (such as wide front porches, heavy squared piers for porch supports, and exposed roof rafters) that appear on these same styles in Dundee South. In general the larger houses are along Fifty-sixth and Fifty-seventh Streets, with the houses getting slightly smaller as one moves farther out and away from the "center of the circle." There are many attached garages in Happy Hollow West, a relatively rare residential feature prior to 1940.

In Happy Hollow West, Omaha's unusual practice of having parallel streets and avenues with the same number takes on a new twist, for Fifty-sixth Street and Fifty-sixth Avenue both curve in different directions toward Happy Hollow Boulevard and cross each other. To increase the confusion, Fifty-sixth Avenue marks the change in street name from the north–south numbered streets to the east–west named streets.

Happy Hollow: 109 North Fifty-third Street (private), ca. 1925. This hipped-roof Colonial Revival house has a broken triangular pediment accentuating the front door, a row of modillions along its Georgian-inspired cornice line, and a two-story side wing added to its basic five-bay house block. It is larger and has slightly more "correct" details than its mates in Dundee South.

Happy Hollow: 115 North Fifty-third Street, at intersection/curve into Davenport Street (private), ca. 1915. This lovely Prairie-style design (hipped-roof, symmetrical-with-front-entry subtype) has a continuous sill line below its second-story windows. This is accentuated by a row of brick marking a change in the wall-cladding material to stucco on the upper third of the house, which contrasts sharply with the brick walls below. Note the long horizontal row of windows downstairs and the four triple windows used upstairs and in the dormer. The broad roof overhang is elegantly detailed; the underside of the eaves (soffit) is coated in stucco

Happy Hollow

Happy Hollow

and accented with widely spaced decorative brackets that wrap around and actually clasp the fascia board. The square porch supports have contrasting caps.

Happy Hollow: 5201 Davenport Street (private), ca. 1930. A large, seven-ranked, centered-gable Colonial Revival design, this is an uncommon example of this subtype in that the central gable covers three ranks of window and door openings rather than the more typical single rank. Note the round window in the front-facing gable, an embellishment that is often found on this subtype when the base of the gable is closed to form a complete triangle as seen here. Other embellishments include a belt course, keystones above many of the windows, and an entry porch that has both squared and rounded columns.

Happy Hollow: 305 North Fifty-fourth Street (private), ca. 1920. This simple-hipped-roof Italian Renaissance house has two one-story side wings, each with a Palladian motif. What is unusual here is that the main entrance is into the right one-story wing. This probably allows the living room to sweep across the entire front of the main house block and to open into a sunroom in the matching one-story wing.

Happy Hollow: 110 North Fifty-fourth Street, at North Fifty-fifth Street (private), ca. 1915. This commanding false-thatched-roof Tudor design occupies a large and prominent triangular lot and has extensive half-timbering in the upper story. Note the open porch on the right side and the curved

roofline of the broad shed dormer above it. Miniature roofs top the pair of short piers that mark the street entrance to its walkways from both Fifty-fourth and Fifty-fifth Streets.

Happy Hollow West: 703 Fifty-sixth Street (private), ca. 1920s. This brick Tudor house is almost symmetrical, with three equally dominant front-facing gables. The cast-stone door surround has a Tudor arch, as does the door itself. The half-timbering is filled with both stucco and brick on different sections of the house.

Happy Hollow West: 5404 Cuming Street (private), ca. 1930. A location at the curved intersection where Fifty-sixth Street runs into Cuming Street makes this house an important focal point, a role it admirably fills with its tall, steeply pitched, hipped roof, a primary identifying feature of the French Eclectic style. The prominent round tower with its tall conical roof places it in the towered subtype. The round-arched front door is of vertical boards and is surrounded with brick accentuated with unusual flat pieces of stone radiating outward. Note the similar, but less ornate, secondary entrance to the left with a second, smaller tower.

Happy Hollow West: 735 Fifty-seventh Street (private), ca. 1920s. In contrast to 703 Fifty-sixth Street (see above), this Tudor design has asymmetrical massing. It is highly detailed and combines portions of stucco-clad wall with walls of brick. A one-story entry wing projects from the main body of the house.

Happy Hollow West: 681 Fifty-seventh Street (private), ca. 1920s. This lively asymmetrical Tudor house features informal cladding materials. An unusual rough-finished brick is used in combination with pieces of stone that accentuate the peak of the gable, the front door, the windows, and are also randomly placed over the entire wall surface. A diamond brick pattern is used in the left wing, and a small metal oriel window is above the entrance.

Happy Hollow West: 5406 Izzard Street (private), ca. 1920s. This hipped-roof Colonial Revival design is unusual in having two features that were found in original Georgian houses built only in Pennsylvania and the Middle Colonies— a pent roof separating the first and second floors and a hooded front door.

Fairacres, ca. 1920–1955

This 160-acre section of the Patrick Farm was platted in 1907, but its distance from downtown, lack of public transportation, and the availability of good building lots in Happy Hollow all combined to delay its development until much later. Fairacres has a naturalistically irregular street pattern with much larger lots than the other Gold Coast neighborhoods; they range from one to seven acres in size. The streets are paved in brick, and the setting is quite lavish. Development here continued through the 1930s and into the 1950s, as evidenced by several Ranch-style houses.

412 Elmwood Street (private), ca. 1930. This large and impressive Tudor house occupies a prominent lot in the center of Fairacres. It is built of multihued, terra-cotta-colored bricks topped by a roof of reddish-colored flat tiles. The door has a round-arched surround of cast stone. Most of the windows have casement sashes, many with decorative diamond-shaped panes of leaded glass. The massive front chimney divides into two shafts topped by chimney pots. The extensive half-timbering in the upper story is filled with brick laid in different directional patterns. A new wing has been added on the left.

321 North Sixty-eighth Street (private), ca. 1990. This striking Neo-International-style house plays two geometric forms off against each other. A "wave" form on the left is juxtaposed against a "cube" form on the right, each with recessed balconies and the wave with a full-facade recessed porch. Glass-block walls and horizontal railings add Modernistic touches.

Just west of 321 North Sixty-eighth Street (private), ca. 1940s. This large, one-story Colonial Revival cottage (a form often called Cape Cod) probably has a half story of living space in the attic. The likelihood of the ca. 1940s date is indicated by the pair of bay windows with flared sloping roofs and by the understated detailing on a relatively large house. Note the simplicity of the gable dormers and the overall "flatness" of the pilasters and moldings that form the front door surround and its broken triangular pediment.

6421 Chicago Street (private), ca. 1940s. This Italian Renaissance house is constructed of (or clad in) rough-cut, irregularly coursed stone. Solid stone construction is very expensive, but from the 1930s through the 1950s there was a fad for cladding houses with a thin stone veneer applied over less expensive wood-framed construction in a manner similar to the brick veneers that became popular on even very small houses in the 1920s. One would have to look closely at this house's construction to know which technique was employed here. The plain rectangular shape and relatively few and simple openings could indicate solid-masonry construction, or it could simply indicate a simplified version of the style more appropriate to the 1930s, 1940s, or 1950s. The latter is more likely because in solid-masonry houses the windows are more often deeply recessed into the thick stone walls, forming what are called

deep reveals. Here the windows are instead set almost in the same plane as the exterior wall, making it more likely that the house is simply clad in stone. Note the broadly overhanging tile roof, the very simple recessed entry, the iron balconies, and the recessed triple-arched upstairs porch.

General Crook House, 1878

Thirtieth Street at Fort Street, Fort Omaha (now Metropolitan Technical Community College campus); 402-455-9990; George Field, architect.

The Omaha metropolitan area has two splendid Victorian museum houses, both of them named for U.S. Army generals. The two houses have both similarities and differences. The General Crook House is less personal, for it was built as a residence for the commander of the army's Department of the Platte, which included much of the northern plains. Now named for its first occupant, Brigadier General George Crook (1828–1890), who directed many campaigns against the Plains Indians in the 1870s and 1880s, the fine Italianate dwelling was later occupied by a succession of twenty-six commanders of Fort Omaha. The General Dodge House (see the following entry) was, in contrast, the longtime home of a man who served in the army only during the Civil War and devoted most of the rest of his life to other endeavors; his home remained in his family for eighty-one years.

The General Crook House is far larger than it at first appears, and indeed the first and second floors are of almost the same scale as the grand General Dodge House

General Crook House

across the river. If you are going to visit both houses, you will have a chance to see how closely the exteriors of Italianate (Crook) and Second Empire (Dodge) houses can approximate each other from the roofline down. Both houses are built of redbrick with hooded windows; those at the government-built Crook House are quite simple, while the window hoods at the Dodge House are far more elaborate. Both are asymmetrical, five-rank designs, with the right two ranks pushed forward into a front-facing wing featuring a first-floor bay window (a squared bay of brick here and a slanted-side wooden bay at the Dodge House). Both have a porch inserted in the L formed by the main house and wing; both also have handsome double entry doors that enter into a broad central hall. Not surprisingly, the Dodge House has far more elaborate interior detailing, and its restored decor is more luxuriant than that in the army's version from approximately the same period. Taken together, the two houses today provide an instructive contrast between the upper-middle-class lifestyle of a military general and the decidedly upper-class lifestyle of one of the West's wealthiest Victorian railroad builders.

The U.S. Army planned to spend $10,000 on General Crook's new dwelling, but the thrifty commander rejected and altered the original plan, and the house as seen today cost only $7,716—a considerable savings but still a hefty amount for army housing! Crook had a rare reputation as a compassionate Indian fighter who genuinely understood his adversaries and used force only as a last resort. He much preferred diplomacy to bloodshed and seen in this light the impressive house was almost certainly a bargain. Here Crook sought to reason with visiting leaders from both sides—Indian war chiefs as well as hawkish Washington generals and politicians.

One of Crook's cost-cutting measures was pine interior woodwork grained to look like hardwood. The handsome interior arches are also cleverly made of plaster, not of more expensive wood. But no corners were cut on the basic construction—massive walls of solid brick with heavy timbers supporting the floors and roof. The floors are dramatically striped with alternating light and dark planks surrounded by simple geometric borders in each room. Like any home that has had numerous occupants, the interior of the house was much modified over the years. In 1976 the Douglas County Historical Society began the home's ongoing restoration to its early appearance. The handsome furnishings are excellent examples of the fine but not extravagant Victorian pieces likely to have been found in an important government dwelling in the frontier West.

One of the great charms of visiting the General Crook House is its tree-lined setting overlooking a parade ground surrounded by other historic buildings at Fort Omaha, which served as an active military base for almost a hundred years. Since 1975 the grounds have served as the home of Omaha's Metropolitan Technical Community College, which has carefully preserved the fort's historic integrity.

General Dodge House, 1869
605 Third Street, in Council Bluffs, Iowa (across the Missouri River from Omaha); 712-322-2406; William W. Boyington, Chicago, architect.

This grand Second Empire dwelling was the home of one of the nation's most remarkable railroad builders—Major General Grenville Mellen Dodge (1831–1916). During his long lifetime, Dodge surveyed and supervised the construction of an incredible sixty thousand miles of railroad lines in the Midwest, West, and Cuba.

Born near Boston, Dodge studied military and civil engineering at Norwich College in Vermont and by 1854 was already a merchant and railroad construction contractor in Council Bluffs, which became his lifelong home base. With the outbreak of the Civil War, Dodge was commissioned a colonel and organized the Fourth Iowa Infantry Regiment, which he led with great distinction. In addition to fighting in many important battles (he was severely wounded at Atlanta in 1864), the multitalented Dodge also organized a sophisticated and accurate behind-the-lines intelligence-gathering system for General U. S. Grant. In the crucial latter years of the war, Dodge's specialty became the rapid repair of mangled railroad tracks and the reconstruction of ruined bridges so that the Union armies could again use the railroads as supply lines. His rebuilding feats were remarkable—in one case Dodge's crews bridged the Chattahoochee River with a 710-foot-long, 14-foot-high double-tracked structure in just three days. Now a major general, he spent the final year of the conflict as military governor of war-ravaged Missouri.

In 1866 Dodge had a unique opportunity to return to his principal passion of railroading when he was appointed chief construction engineer for the Union Pacific as it built westward toward its historic junction with the eastward-building Central Pacific at Promontory Point, Utah, in 1869. Dodge was later to refer to this difficult project as "my greatest achievement." Still only thirty-eight years old, the now-legendary Dodge was much in demand by newly organized railroads. He ultimately made substantial contributions to the building of seventeen different railroads and was a valued consultant to many others, including Russia's fabled Trans-Siberian line. At the same time Dodge found

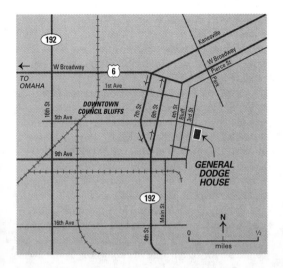

time to invest his railroad earnings in profitable banking, real estate, and other ventures.

When Dodge completed the Union Pacific in 1869, he decided to build a new Council Bluffs home appropriate to his status as a wealthy railroad builder and Civil War hero. Another of Iowa's wealthy citizens, Benjamin F. Allen, had just completed a grand new mansion called Terrace Hill (now Iowa's historic Governor's Mansion) in nearby Des Moines. Allen had chosen Chicago architect W. W. Boyington, who designed his home in the very latest architectural fashion of the day, the French-inspired Second Empire style. Dodge followed Allen's lead by choosing both the same architect and style.

With an eye for terrain honed by years of surveying the West, Dodge had earlier purchased a prime site for his new home—nine acres along the rising bluff of what is today Third Street. It was high enough to overlook Council Bluffs and is still visible today from downtown. Originally the lot sloped down to the street, but a later lowering of Third Street required adding the retaining wall seen today. Boyington's elegant design has fifteen-foot ceilings, a finished third floor under the massive mansard roof, and interior detailing of choice woods and fine architectural fixtures and fittings. Dodge moved in with his wife, the accomplished Ruth Anne "Annie" Brown Dodge, and their three young daughters. The last family member left the house in 1950.

The exterior of the Dodge House has had only one major change since it was built. At some time in the early 1900s, the porch, which originally covered only the left three ranks of the front facade, was extended along the left side of the house to add exterior enter-

General Dodge House

taining space; at this time the entire porch design was modified with the Classical-columned porch supports, the enclosed railing, and the Palladian motifs at the corner. The museum knows this was added after 1901 and is still seeking evidence to determine if it was added during or after General Dodge's lifetime. The original porch would have been a more typical Italianate/Second Empire design. Other than this minor early change, the exterior is just as Boyington and Dodge planned it.

Inside, the general insisted upon the most up-to-date systems, and the house had central heat, hot and cold running water, and even large closets. Today, one enters the home through the original black-walnut double doors and a large center hall with heroic fifteen-foot ceilings. Butternut wood dominates the hall, along with the handsome cherry-wood stairway. The main rooms downstairs include double parlors, a reception room, a dining room, and General Dodge's library. All rooms have original Dodge furnishings, but the library is the most completely authentic, as the Council Bluffs Library had purchased all of its furnishings when the contents of the house were auctioned, and the room was later returned to the house intact. Walnut and butternut woods are used together here for contrasting wood tones. The double parlor has the original pair of pier mirrors and many of the Dodge family's chairs. The dining room features the original table and many family dishes, silver, and goblets. There are seven original fireplaces remaining, but only one chandelier. The service-oriented basement and all three floors of the house are visited on the tour.

Despite the fact that the general's many railroad-building obligations took the Dodges away from Council Bluffs for long periods of time, they never lost their love for the city and spent their last years here. After the elder Dodges' deaths in 1916, their daughters kept the house and used it occasionally until the last died in 1950. At this point, the house underwent a tragic period. The city of Council Bluffs turned down the chance to acquire the home with all its furnishings, and a major auction was held, with not only furniture but architectural artifacts sold. The house was subdivided into apartments, but luckily its basic structural framework remained intact.

In 1963 the house was purchased by the Historical Society of Pottawattamie County and given to the city of Council Bluffs. In 1964 it became a national historic landmark. Because the Dodges traveled extensively, and lived for periods in New York, Washington, D.C., and abroad, the decision was made to restore the house to the level of opulence that such a wealthy and well-traveled Victorian family would have displayed, not to the more modest standards of most frontier houses of the Victorian era. By 1968 the house was essentially restored, and acquisition of original Dodge furnishings continues today. Entering the home, one is not aware of the years of painstaking restoration required, nor of the efforts involved in returning so very many of the Dodges' personal possessions and furnishings to their original setting.

Next door to the Dodge House at 621 Third Street is the **Augustus Beresheim House** (1899), which serves as the orientation center for the tour of the General Dodge House. Built just thirty years after its more famous neighbor, it is an intriguing house in its own right. It is an unusual Colonial Revival design of the hipped-roof-with-full-width-porch subtype, with an added center roof gambrel on the front. Inside, a large and dramatic central stairway leads all the way up to the widow's walk. In addition to an orientation center and gift shop, the upstairs rooms display some of the fine period clothing collection that belongs to the Dodge House.

There are a number of interesting houses along nearby Third Street and its cross streets. Also, be sure to see the description of the General Crook House (see the preceding entry) for additional descriptions of the Dodge House exterior and for similarities and contrasts to look for if visiting both homes.

RED CLOUD

FOUNDED 1871

Population Growth:

1900 1,600

1940 1,600

1990 1,200

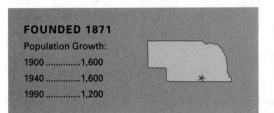

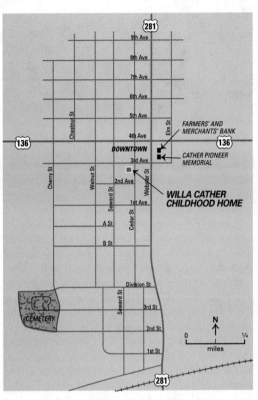

This modest Great Plains county seat and agricultural trade center is one of the rare small towns to have become immortalized by the words of one of its residents, in this case the distinguished novelist and short-story writer Willa Cather (1873–1947), who moved here with her family from distant Virginia when she was nine years old. Her subsequent experiences in this small, railroad-era Nebraska town provided the background for many of her most important stories. Because of its importance as a literary shrine, many Cather-related early buildings in Red Cloud have been lovingly preserved, among them her remarkable childhood home, with interiors that remain today much as she eloquently described them in several of her stories.

The Willa Cather Pioneer Memorial and Educational Foundation, which operates the Cather Home in cooperation with the Nebraska State Historical Society, also provides tours and literature that interpret the entire town of Red Cloud and its surrounding countryside as they were presented to the world in Cather's vivid descriptions and characterizations.

Willa Cather Childhood Home, 1879

245 Cedar Street, at Third Avenue (tours originate at 326 North Webster Street, Willa Cather Pioneer Memorial's Art Gallery and Bookstore); 402-746-2653. In 1883 Cather's parents moved from the green and mountainous Shenandoah Valley of Virginia to the flat Nebraska plains near the pioneer farm of her father's parents. She explained her initial shock in a 1913 interview:

I shall never forget my introduction to it. We drove out from Red Cloud to my grandfather's homestead one day . . . the land was open range and there was almost no fencing. As we drove further and further out into the country I felt a good deal as if we had kind of ended everything. It was a kind of erasure of personality. I would not know how much a child's life was bound up in the woods and hills and mead-

ows around it if I had not been jerked away from all these and thrown out into a country as fair as a piece of sheet iron.

But it was not long before Cather began to understand the quiet beauty of her new home, where she "knew every farm, every tree, every field in the region around my home and they all called out to me." Her new Nebraska friends and neighbors similarly impressed her.

Cather finished high school in Red Cloud in 1890, graduated from the University of Nebraska at Lincoln in 1895, and then moved to Pittsburgh and New York to write for magazines and journals. As she later explained: "I searched for books telling about the beauty of the country I loved, its romance, the heroism and strength and courage of its people that had been plowed into the very furrows of its soil and I did not find them. And so I wrote *O Pioneers!*" This, her first novel set in the West, was published in 1913. Others followed, most notably *The Song of the Lark* in 1915 and *My Ántonia*, consid-

Willa Cather
Childhood Home

ered by many critics to be her masterpiece, in 1918. These and many of her short stories featured the landscapes, the houses, the churches, the shops, and the inhabitants of her fictionalized Red Cloud, which went by many different names in her stories.

A tour of Cather's modest childhood home gives unique insights, not only into the writer's formative years, but also into how the family of a middle-class midwestern insurance salesman lived in the late nineteenth century. The home has been faithfully preserved and restored to reflect Cather's lyrical descriptions, recordings of which are played to visitors as a delightful introduction to each room.

The house itself is a small, front-gabled Folk Victorian design that she described as "a low story-and-a-half house, with a wing built on the right and a kitchen addition at the back, everything a little on the slant—roofs, windows and doors." Here Cather, the eldest child, lived with her parents, her maternal grandmother, her six young brothers and sisters, and a young servant girl, Marjorie Anderson, who came from Virginia with the family and is buried with them. Everyone lived and functioned in six moderate-sized rooms, five downstairs and one in the upstairs half story.

The main floor had a parlor, a dining room, the parents' bedroom, a small room for the grandmother, and a kitchen. The parlor was filled with the symbols of cultured middle-class living. A piano, a family Bible, whatnot shelves filled with mementos, and a Brussels carpet were among the family treasures that were carefully transported from Virginia and then protected from the chaos of seven active children. Their grandmother's room became a favorite children's gathering spot and is restored as Cather lovingly described it—with a small bed, a potbellied stove, a rocker with curved arms, and a rocking horse.

The upstairs consisted of a single larger room for the children. Cather wrote:

Upstairs was a story in itself, a secret romance. No caller or neighbor had ever been allowed to go up there. All the children loved it—it was their very own world where there were no older people poking about to spoil things. . . . Bracing the long roof rafters were cross rafters on which one could hang things—a little personal washing, a curtain for tableaux, a rope swing. . . . In this spacious and undivided loft were two brick chimneys, going up in neat little stair steps from the plank floor to the shingle roof—and out of it to the stars!

Eventually, Cather's mother insisted that she have her own small and private room, which was partitioned off from the rest of the loft. This rare treasure has survived just as Cather left it, sealed up and unused by those living in the house after the Cathers left and before its purchase by the Cather Foundation. Here Willa, like Thea in *The Song of the Lark,* "papered the room, walls and ceiling, in the same paper, small red and brown roses on a yellowish ground." There are "white cheesecloth curtains . . . hung on tape." And "an old walnut dresser with a broken mirror. Her own lumpy walnut single bed and a blue washbowl and pitcher which she had drawn at a church fair lottery." This survives today as a wonderful tribute to the decorating prowess of a talented teenage girl seeking to create her own personal kingdom.

A wealth of similar Cather surprises awaits the visitor elsewhere. The 1889 **Farmers' and Merchants' Bank,** on Webster Street two doors south of Fourth Avenue, contains the Cather archives and changing exhibits, while tour pamphlets for the town and countryside, available at the adjacent bookstore, reveal the inspiration behind many of the characters, places, and events in the writings of one of the American West's most gifted storytellers.

Nevada

VIRGINIA CITY

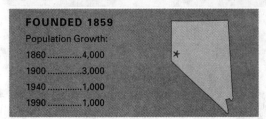

FOUNDED 1859
Population Growth:

1860	4,000
1900	3,000
1940	1,000
1990	1,000

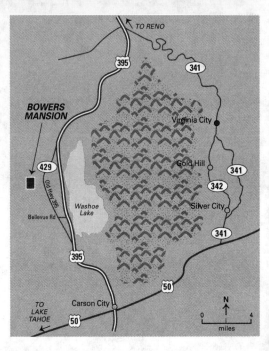

The mining town of Virginia City sits atop the fabled Comstock Lode, one of the world's richest deposits of silver ore. Discovered in 1859, eleven years after the goldfields on the opposite side of the Sierra Nevada set off the great California gold rush (see page 136), the Comstock, as it came to be called, was to become a similarly crucial turning point in the history of the West.

The geologic setting and subsequent development of these two prodigious bonanzas were strikingly different. The gold of the Sierra Nevada's western foothills was scattered in stream valleys and quartz ledges spread throughout an enormous area 30 miles wide and 150 miles long. As a result, it was exploited by many tens of thousands of individual miners and thousands of mining companies, both small and large. In contrast, the Comstock riches, located just beyond the eastern edge of the Sierra Nevada, were concentrated in a single ore-bearing quartz vein within an area of only two square miles. During its twenty-year productive life, this vein yielded precious metals whose value totaled more than half that produced by all of the California goldfields combined for more than fifty years after their discovery.

Founded in 1859 on the site of the original Comstock discovery, Virginia City became an instant city as thousands of California prospectors, miners, and speculators, reversing the westward flow of the forty-niners a decade earlier, crowded the Sierra Nevada passes en route eastward to the "Comstock diggin's." Most were to be disappointed. Although small amounts of easily mined surface gold occurred in the Comstock vicinity, the true treasure lay in complex, bluish-gray ore minerals that required deep, hard-rock mining, followed by expensive mechanical crushing and chemical processing before the silver, and its smaller quantities of gold, could be released.

Soon the thousands of small surface claims staked along the mineralized vein by the first arrivals were being sold to traders and speculators, many of whom organized mining companies that sold stock to the public to finance their expensive mining ventures. Un-

fortunately, only a few favored claims were located on the richly productive ore bodies that were widely scattered throughout the vein, rather as if only a dozen chocolate chips had been baked into a single, tabletop-sized cookie. These became the legendary "bonanza mines" of the Comstock. Most were developed by San Francisco–based financiers who then used their fortunes to greatly enhance the city's role as the financial capital of the West. Their massive investments, not only in local banking, real estate, and civic improvements but also in new mining enterprises throughout the western states, were to dominate the region's economy for several decades.

Development of the Comstock's rich bonanza mines took place in two phases. The first-discovered, near-surface bonanza ores were playing out by the mid-1860s, and Virginia City appeared on the way to becoming just another boom-and-bust ghost town. Then in 1872 John Mackay and his associates (see page 427), in a bold gamble, began a series of deep and expensive exploratory shafts and tunnels in a previously barren zone between two of the earlier near-surface bonanzas. The following year they discovered the biggest bonanza of them all, the legendary Consolidated Virginia Mine, which, over the next seven years, produced one-third of all the Comstock silver and paid its four principal owners more than $74 million in profits, an amount that then ranked them among the world's wealthiest individuals.

By 1880 even the Consolidated Virginia was in decline. As the Comstock's shafts and tunnels were pushed still deeper in search of new bonanzas, the already-difficult problems with debilitating heat and frequent incursions of near-boiling underground waters became insurmountable. By 1900 Virginia City, which reached a peak population of twenty-one thousand in 1876, had declined to three thousand inhabitants, most of them supported by reworking the previously discarded tailings of the rich bonanza mines to extract their small remaining amounts of silver and gold.

Few mining towns have ever produced the enormous wealth found in the Comstock, and for this reason Virginia City boasted an unusual number of fine Victorian commercial buildings and dwellings during its boom years. Enough of these still survive to make it one of the West's best-preserved mining towns. Now a national historic landmark, modern Virginia City thrives on heritage tourism. Among many other historic attractions, one can ride on the **Virginia and Truckee Railroad,** the town's restored narrow-gauge steam line, and visit two museum houses (see pages 427

and 428) associated with important developers of the bonanza mines. A third museum house built by a Comstock pioneer is located twenty-five miles west of Virginia City in the Washoe Valley (see page 430).

Beyond C Street, ca. 1860–1910

The ore-bearing Comstock quartz vein was exposed as a five-hundred-foot-wide north–south band of weathered rock on the side of a desert mountain. Virginia City's early commercial district developed along a terracelike level roadway graded about five hundred feet downslope from, and parallel with, the mine-covered quartz. This roadway came to be called C Street as two more long, terraced streets, called A and B, were soon added upslope, between the commercial district and the mines, while parallel D, E, et cetera streets were added farther downslope. Underground mining quickly showed that the surface quartz vein plunged downward into the earth in an easterly direction at an angle of about forty-five degrees and thus passed directly under the commercial district as it deepened to the east. Soon vertical shafts to reach the rich deeper ores were developing along and near F Street. Ultimately, a third line of deeper shafts was dug still farther downslope beyond the city limits to reach the deepest ore bodies.

View of Virginia City, 1865

As the industrial district, with its mills, mine dumps, railroad yards, and associated miners' cabins and small houses, moved downhill to the east, the "uphill" streets to the west, nearest to the first shallow diggings, became the favored homesites for the city's more affluent, white-collar workers. It is here, in the "beyond C Street" neighborhood, that most of the town's remaining Victorian houses are concentrated. Small front-gabled shapes, some simple unembellished folk houses and others with added Italianate, Gothic, or Folk Victorian detailing, are most common. Italianate is the favorite style for the neighborhood's scattered larger dwellings.

Locating specific houses in Virginia City can be a problem. After we noticed that duplicate addresses seemed to appear on the same street, and indeed that addresses did not seem to necessarily be in numerical order, a visit to the local post office turned up this explanation: "At one time the residents of Virginia City were allowed to simply pick out their own addresses,

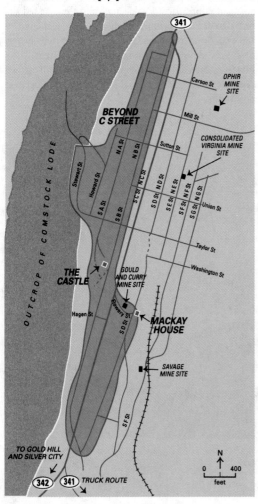

and some of them picked out the same numbers or ones that were not exactly in order. Sure does confuse new postmen when they first start on a route." It will also confuse house watchers searching for an address. Viewing the situation as a charming local custom, and a reliable recipe for looking carefully at even more houses than one might have expected to see, helps put this inconvenience into a more endearing perspective.

Summit Road (all private). This newer street, developed highest up the hillside from C Street, is lined with new Neo-Victorian homes. Notice the features that help one recognize that these are new houses rather than old ones—things like metal chimneys, new windows, the type of siding, and so on.

53 and 60 Stewart Street (both private). This pair of one-story front-gabled houses demonstrates the range of architectural trim seen on this typical Virginia City shape. Number 53 has extensive detailing, including a segmental-arched door transom and windows. The windows are crowned by a small triangular pediment supported by brackets, a typical Italianate feature. The modillions along the cornice line are also of Italianate inspiration, and this combination of detailing makes it reasonable to call this a front-gabled Italianate cottage. Next door, 60 Stewart Street is elaborated only by the very simple spindlework porch and is best called a front-gabled Folk Victorian design.

66 Howard Street (private), King House, ca. 1875–1880. The dormers have been added, but they only slightly detract from the many handsome details on this landmark Italianate dwelling. Note the doors, entry porch, roof cresting, and fence.

99 and 81 North A Street, on the east side of the street, just south of Sutton (both private). This side-by-side "Mutt-and-Jeff" pair of three-bay, front-gabled Italianate houses has almost identical bracketed hoods over the windows and doors.

118 and 63 North A Street, on the west side of the street, north of Sutton (both private). This side-by-side pair of small one-story houses contrasts the simple Gothic Revival styling of number 63 with the simple Italianate styling of number 118. Note 118's hipped roof, corner quoins, and framed windows, the latter similar to the window surrounds on the Castle (see page 428); 63, in contrast, has a front-gabled roof with cross bracing in the gable apex and a typical Gothic Revival front porch. A pair of rounded-arch windows had to be substituted for more appropriately Gothic pointed-arch designs, likely because the rounded versions were locally available at the right price.

168 North B Street (private). This small, centered-gable Italianate design has paired windows with bracketed tops, quoins, copious roofline brackets, and an elaborately hooded entry porch. In the gable is a small round window of a type that is seen frequently in Virginia City.

56 South B Street (private), Cole House, 1887. Note the corner quoins, the paired Italianate brackets under the cornice, and what could easily be the original porch railing cut with a jigsaw from flat boards. These details contrast with those of the Gothic Revival house next door at 158 South B Street (private).

146 South D Street (private), Savage House, 1861. This elegant Second Empire structure, like the Mackay House (see the following entry) was built to serve both as a mining of-

Beyond C Street neighborhood

fice and as the mine superintendent's house. Here the office of the Savage Mining Company, whose principal shaft was just down the hill between E and F Streets, occupied the building's first floor, with the residence on the two upper floors.

Mackay House, 1860

129 South D Street; 702-847-0173.

This remarkable survivor, built in the second year of the Comstock frenzy, was owned at different times by

two of the most colorful of the Lode's dozen or so multimillionaires. An attractively simple, brick-walled structure of cubic shape with a low-pitched hipped roof, Italianate porches, and Greek Revival doorways, it was built by George Hearst (1820–1891) as the combined headquarters and superintendent's house for his nearby Gould and Curry Mine, the third of the Comstock bonanza discoveries that helped launch Hearst on one of the most profitable careers in the history of American mining.

As a boy Hearst had become fascinated by the challenges of hard-rock mining while helping his father work on small lead mines near their farm in southeastern Missouri. Like so many midwesterners, as a young man Hearst joined the California gold rush. Arriving in 1850, he worked the stream-gravel deposits for several years with marginal success. By 1859 he had a small, hard-rock mine in the quartz-vein gold center of Nevada City, California (see page 127). In that year the first Comstock silver ores were sent to the Nevada City assay office for analysis. Hearst was among several local miners who learned of their rich silver content and hurried over the Sierra Nevada passes to see for himself. Quickly convinced of the Comstock's potential, Hearst returned to Nevada City, sold his mine, borrowed an additional thousand dollars from a local hotel keeper,

Mackay House (also known as Mackay Mansion)

and then used the proceeds to purchase a one-sixth interest in the Ophir Mine, the first of the Comstock's bonanza discoveries.

The Comstock's sulfur-bearing ore minerals were unlike those that dominated the California goldfields but similar to the lead-bearing ores that Hearst had carefully studied in his native Missouri. Soon his re-markable insights into the true values of the Com-stock's thousands of small surface claims became legendary. W. W. Allen and R. B. Avery noted in the *California Gold Book*, published in 1893:

There was no one who could so correctly estimate the character of a mine nor develop it to greater ad-vantage than he. He had no equal in these respects. All that was of practical value regarding minerals and mineral formations he knew . . . he became a master miner, and was so recognized by all.

By 1865 Hearst's interests in Comstock mines had al-ready made him a fortune, yet the restless mining ge-nius, now in great demand as a fair-minded evaluator of mining prospects throughout the West, continued his search for new bonanzas elsewhere. Having begun his wealth-building with the country's richest silver de-posit, at his death in 1891 Hearst and his partners owned both the nation's richest gold producer, the Homestake Mine in Lead, South Dakota (see page 539), as well as its richest copper deposit, the Anaconda Mine in Butte, Montana (see page 373). Today, Hearst is mostly remembered as the father of the flamboyant newspaperman and politician William Randolph Hearst, builder of the spectacular Hearst Castle at San Simeon, California (see page 251).

As the first Comstock bonanza mines played out in the 1860s, Hearst sold his interests and focused his re-sources on more promising discoveries elsewhere. In 1873, John W. Mackay (1831–1902) and his partners acquired the old Gould and Curry Mine, along with its headquarters building, as a part of their search for a deeper bonanza in the relatively barren stretch of rock between the rich Ophir discovery of 1859 and the equally rich Gould and Curry discovery of 1861. Mackay was a gold rush veteran who arrived in Virginia City from California in 1859 and quickly worked his way upward from ordinary miner to mine superinten-dent and, ultimately, to owner of several profitable smaller mines. He was the senior partner, with about two-fifths ownership, of the four-man group that dis-covered the enormous Consolidated Virginia bonanza in 1873 (see page 424). By the late 1870s Mackay was the wealthiest of all the Comstock silver barons. He also remained the most loyal to his adopted home of Vir-ginia City as this, its last bonanza, faded in the early 1880s.

In 1875, after their home and almost 90 percent of Virginia City was destroyed by fire, Mackay and his wife, Louise, moved into this unassuming house, which was not damaged, and made it their home until 1888. It is from their occupancy that the house now takes its name. The Mackays made a number of improvements designed to turn the house into a more luxurious home. Since their departure the structure has had nu-merous owners; the current one, who operates it as a museum house, is making an effort to track down orig-inal furnishings that long ago left the home.

An unusual exterior feature of the house is the porch that wraps completely around all four facades. On the downhill side, this provided an overlook that allowed the early mine superintendent to watch the nearby sur-face operations from his home and office.

The house is actually smaller than it looks—only one full room deep and two rooms wide. It is built into the hillside and has the old mining office and a formal par-lor on the middle, entry floor, with bedrooms on the floor above and the dining room, kitchen, and laundry on the floor below. Original features include two large ore cabinets and gold cornices above the draperies in the mining office, light fixtures and ornamental tran-soms, and some of the Mackay furnishings traced and repurchased by the current owner.

One of the special features in the home is the upstairs bathroom, which is thought to date from the original 1860 construction. It was the first bath in Virginia City and was gravity fed from a five-hundred-gallon tank in the attic. This was kept full by servants who had to hand carry the water up to it in buckets. The surrounding garden area is very pleasant, and its lower level offers a prime view of the arrivals and departures of the re-stored Virginia and Truckee Railroad below.

The Castle, 1868

70 South B Street; 702-847-0275.

This intriguing home is not a restoration but rather a preservation. All of the original furnishings have twice been sold with the house. Since early in the twentieth century, these have been kept intact by four generations of the McGuirk family, which now operates it as a mu-seum house. The family's care, coupled with the very dry air of Virginia City, has preserved a rarely seen col-lection of original Victorian wallpapers, carpets, fix-tures, and furnishings.

The house was built by Robert N. Graves, a young mining engineer from London who became a local mine superintendent and stockholder. He brought with him an English taste for European antiques and

The Castle

decorative objects, and, as his earnings increased, Graves built and furnished this fine home for his young family. It took five years, hardly surprising since most of the things in it had to be shipped from Europe to San Francisco, then taken by smaller boat to Sacramento, and from there transported by wagon to Virginia City. Graves, his wife, and two young daughters had lived here for only four years when they moved to San Francisco. The house stayed with its second owners for over forty years before being purchased intact by the McGuirks in 1916.

Although undoubtedly some of the specific details of the home and its furnishings have been confused after 128 years of oral tradition about Graves's efforts, the big picture is very clear—he set out to build a very fine home for this remote location, imported many of the fixtures and furnishings and even the workmen, and the result has been remarkably preserved. The first treat is simply standing at the front door in the recessed, round-arched entry alcove and admiring the cabled moldings and the handsome pair of entry doors. These swing open to reveal the original, hand-blocked French wallpapers and ceiling papers with gold and silver leaf. Brussels lace curtains hang at the windows. The large formal parlor and dining room have matching Czechoslovakian crystal chandeliers, original drop-border wallpapers, wool Brussels carpet, and an eclectic collection of European furniture. The Italian white Carrera marble fireplaces throughout the house have been closed up because of downdrafts; early stoves were added in front of them where needed. Enormous French gold-leaf overmantel mirrors rise above the fireplaces.

The house's architectural fittings are equally elaborate. The hinges throughout are of German bronze, the doorknobs of French silver, and the original chandeliers in the rest of the house are made of French metal with enormous Czechoslovakian etched globes; each chandelier has a different theme. Sliding louvered shutters inside each window still work perfectly.

The exterior of the house, while impressive, barely hints at the riches inside. It is an Englishman's version of an Italianate design with clipped, jerkin-head gables and a mansard-roof tower. All of the windows are framed with an unusual "eared" pattern, resembling that seen on some Greek Revival door and window surrounds. One of the round windows so favored in Virginia City is seen in the front-facing gable. Highly unusual is the use of the same "corrugated" molding pattern on both the horizontal cornice line and the vertical corner boards. The prominent bay window features the same molding. The overall impact of the facade is increased by the house's hillside site, which necessitates a massive stone retaining wall and a long flight of steps leading upward to the entry.

Bowers Mansion, 1864

4005 Old U.S. Highway 395 North
(Nevada Highway 429), in Bowers Mansion Park;
702-849-0201.

Although located about twenty-five miles west of Virginia City in the Washoe Valley, this large Italianate dwelling was built by the couple thought to have been the Comstock Lode's first millionaires, Lemuel Sanford "Sandy" Bowers (1833–1868) and his wife, Alison "Eilley" Oram Bowers (1826–1903).

Eilley was the more colorful of the pair, and Sandy was her third husband. She was born and first married, at age fifteen, in Scotland, where her first husband, Stephen Hunter, converted to Mormonism. In January 1849 the couple traveled to Liverpool to embark on the maiden voyage of the Mormon ship *Zetland* bound for New Orleans. The shipload of converts endured sixty-three days of cramped quarters (six-by-three-foot berths shared by two people) and meager rations (oatmeal, rice, potatoes, and biscuits cooked by each family) before arriving at their destination. Two days later they boarded the Mississippi steamboat *Iowa* for an eight-day trip upriver to St. Louis. Five days later came a seventeen-day journey up the Missouri River in a smaller steamboat to Council Bluffs, Iowa, near the site three years earlier of the Mormon's famed Winter Quarters. Here, under Brigham Young's leadership, the original Mormon pioneers had paused on their heroic initial trek westward to found Salt Lake City (see pages 642 and 647).

In May the couple headed west on the Mormon Trail as part of an immigrant wagon train and finally arrived in Utah in September, nine months after leaving England. The couple separated shortly thereafter. Eilley, who never herself converted to Mormonism, stayed in Utah until 1855 when she and her second husband moved to a remote Mormon trading outpost, later named Genoa, in the Carson River Valley of what is now western Nevada.

In 1857 Mormons throughout the West were called back to Utah to help defend against a threatened attack by the federal government. Eilley, an energetic and enterprising woman, elected to remain behind to manage their properties rather than return with her Mormon husband. Later, when it was clear that he was not coming back to Nevada, she obtained a divorce. Eilley also ran a popular boardinghouse and restaurant serving gold prospectors working the modest stream-gravel deposits of Gold Canyon, which is about twenty miles southeast of their ranch.

One of Eilley's boarders, lacking cash, had offered to settle his account by giving her a small mining claim near the canyon's northern end, and she accepted this offer. Another of her customers was Sandy Bowers, a struggling miner who owned the claim adjacent to hers and became "the love of her life." The two were married in August 1859, just as the first discoveries of the Comstock Lode's rich silver ores were being made. The now-united "Bowers Claim" proved to be in the very heart of the Lode's second bonanza discovery, made shortly after the original Ophir Mine strike but this time at a location about one and a half miles south of Virginia City, known as Gold Hill.

Soon the newlyweds' Gold Hill Mine was yielding substantial amounts of silver and gold each month. To escape the frenzied chaos of the Virginia City area, they decided to build this, their grand dream house, on Eilley's peaceful Washoe Valley ranch. As construction began in May 1862, the couple left on a ten-month trip to Europe to purchase furnishings. They must have preferred French interiors, for while in Paris they reportedly drew drafts totaling more than $250,000 on their Wells Fargo account. By 1864 their new home was ready for occupancy.

Multiple tragedies were soon to strike the Bowerses. Their mine began playing out in 1867. The following year Sandy died of silicosis, a lung disease afflicting many miners. In 1874 their beloved adopted daughter, Persia, died at age twelve of a ruptured appendix. Eilley tried to save her home by converting it to a luxury hotel,

Bowers Mansion

but finally, in 1876, this too failed, and her land, house, and furnishings were lost to creditors. Until her death twenty-seven years later, Eilley lived in relative poverty, making her living by telling fortunes as the "Washoe Seeress."

From 1876 to 1946 the estate had nine different owners. In that year it was purchased as a public park by Washoe County. With the assistance of the Reno Woman's Civic Club, the historic house was maintained until it could be restored to its original appearance. The last phase of the restoration was made possible by a 1966 county bond issue, and in 1968 the grand dwelling was opened to the public as a museum house.

The house has exterior walls made of massive granite blocks that are enlivened both by stone quoins and window surrounds as well as by a picturesque roof cupola and a broad, one-story porch that wraps around the front and sides. Stone houses were very rare in the boomtown atmosphere of early Carson County, where even the largest houses were typically built of wood. Perhaps Eilley had absorbed Brigham Young's belief in

the importance of building with permanent materials during her years in Utah. And indeed the house's solid construction helped it to survive many years of neglect. The loss of most of the original furnishings has been offset by donations of appropriate Victorian antiques by over five hundred Nevada families. Among these are some handsome original Bowers pieces that have now returned home.

Downstairs the reception room has the Bowerses' original matching settee and chairs. The formal parlor is furnished with donated pieces, except for the contents of the center parlor table, that ubiquitous feature of Victorian parlors. Here is displayed Eilley's fascinating crystal ball, her sole means of support during her later life. The dining room features some of the Bowerses' original silver flatware.

Upstairs there are matching master bedroom suites—one for Sandy and one for Eilley—across the hall from each other. Sandy's has his original bedroom set of walnut bed, bedstand, washstand, and dresser. Eilley's suite has a similarly elaborate Renaissance Revival bedroom set. Persia's bedroom has her doll carriage and small walnut rocker. And the original upstairs billiard room, which was groaning under the weight of a billiard table, is now shown as a music room with several Bowers pieces. It still has its original oak-grained wainscoting.

Today, Bowers Mansion Park, where Washoe County offers picnicking, swimming, and other recreational activities, surrounds the historic home. If some of the grounds now lack their original grandeur, they are nevertheless in keeping with Eilley's attempt to save her home by opening it as a hotel, where others could enjoy its nearby springs and rural setting.

New Mexico

ALBUQUERQUE

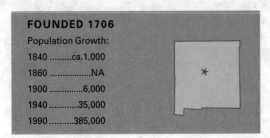

FOUNDED 1706

Population Growth:

1840	ca.1,000
1860	NA
1900	6,000
1940	35,000
1990	385,000

Now a Sunbelt boomtown, Albuquerque, like Santa Fe, Los Angeles, and San Jose, was among the small handful of Spanish-era settlements originally founded as civilian towns rather than the more usual missions or forts. The provincial capital of New Mexico at Santa Fe is located on a relatively small river, which restricted the amount of irrigated land available to grow food for the town. As new settlers began to cause it to outgrow its agricultural potential, the provincial governor in 1706 founded the new settlement of La Villa Real de San Francisco de Alburquerque, named for the duke of Alburquerque who was then the aristocratic viceroy in charge of all of New Spain (the first *r* has been subsequently dropped from the original spelling of "Alburquerque"). The new town was located about sixty miles southwest of Santa Fe along a broad and fertile stretch of the Rio Grande Valley.

Agricultural Village

In the Hispanic era the small town of Albuquerque was never as important as the rich surrounding farmlands, which stretched for many miles along the Rio Grande. Spanish land policies encouraged irrigated farming by making long-lot grants to settlers. These narrow tracts had only a small river frontage, behind which lay an ample strip of fertile valley land to be watered from the river by irrigation ditches (see "Casa San Ysidro," page 439). The area's farmers preferred to live directly on, or very near, their farms, since neighbors were generally close enough to discourage raids by nomadic Indians. As a result, relatively few chose to make their homes in Albuquerque. Seventy years after Albuquerque's founding, a visitor reported (as quoted by Marc Treib in his excellent 1993 book *Sanctuaries of Spanish New Mexico*):

The villa itself consists of 24 houses near the mission. The rest of what is called Albuquerque extends upstream to the north, and all of it is a settlement of ranches on the meadows of said river. . . . Some of their lands are good, some better, some mediocre. . . . The crops taken from them at harvest time are many, good and everything sown in them bears fruit.

As a result of this dispersed living pattern, population estimates for Hispanic Albuquerque, which are usually in the two thousand to five thousand range, refer mostly to rural occupants spread along many miles of the river valley. The population of the village of Albuquerque itself is thought to have been no more than several hundred during the Spanish era but may have been somewhat larger when it became an important stop on the Anglo trading route from Missouri to Chihuahua after Mexican independence (see page 442).

Anglo Railroad Center

Sleepy Albuquerque rapidly awakened when the Atchison, Topeka, and Santa Fe Railroad built through northern New Mexico en route to California in the 1880s. In spite of its name, the Santa Fe, as it was universally called, ended up with only an inconvenient, dead-end spur serving its namesake city (see page 443). Instead, the railroad chose Albuquerque, with a more central location and prosperous agricultural hinterland, as its New Mexico headquarters. As was usual in such situations, the railroad preferred to locate its facilities on nearby rural sites, which became the nuclei of new towns growing up on land owned by the railroad.

The Santa Fe built through the Albuquerque area in 1881; in 1880 railroad officials had joined with several wealthy locals in the purchase of farmland two miles east of the early town. Here they platted the city of New Albuquerque, constructing their depot and rail yards near its center. In the first year of rail service, 3 million pounds of New Mexico wool were shipped from Albuquerque—and that was just one product.

Albuquerque soon outdistanced Santa Fe in population and took on a much more Anglo character. By 1910 about two thousand of its eleven thousand inhabitants were working "in some capacity" for the Santa Fe Railroad, which was also the city's largest landowner.

Route 66

In 1926 a different kind of transportation boon came through town with the building of Route 66, the first "all-weather" U.S. highway across the American Southwest, which connected Chicago with Los Angeles. The original roadway traversed Albuquerque from north to south, but in 1937 a more direct east–west route through the city was completed. Remarkably, much of this highway's early roadside architecture survives as **Historic Route 66,** a delightfully intact collection of fast-disappearing Americana. About one-half of the tourist courts (today called motels) built in the 1930s and 1940s still exist, and efforts are under way to save these, along with historic neon signs, service stations, theaters, drive-ins, cafés, and commercial strips. It is fun to drive west from the city on Route 66 to Ninety-eighth Street (which is toward the top of Nine Mile Hill). From there one has a great view to the east across the Rio Grande Valley and the city of Albuquerque. Driving from that overlook eastward through the city to the Route 66–Interstate 40 intersection on the east, one sees numerous examples of 1930s, 1940s, and

1950s roadside architecture. Crossing the Rio Grande heading eastward, the highway passes the early Hispanic plaza of Old Town, the "new" (1880–1960s) Anglo downtown with the Santa Fe tracks on the eastern edge. Past the tracks, in chronological order, are the three featured Anglo-style neighborhoods treated below—Huning Highlands (1880–1915; see page 436), Spruce Park (1920–1940; see page 438), and Nob Hill (1925–1950; see page 438).

Old Town

Early Hispanic Albuquerque centered around a plaza with the parish church, to which a Victorian facade was added in the 1870s, on its north side. Low adobe houses and shops originally occupied the other sides of the plaza, but these were later replaced by, or remodeled into, Anglo-style "storefronts," which today, along with

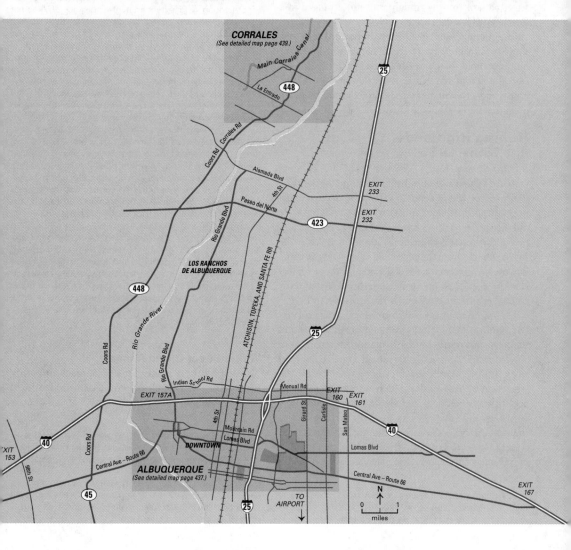

Old Town

the area's few surviving adobe dwellings, house mostly tourist-oriented shops and restaurants. Although few Hispanic-era facades survive in Old Town, its early street pattern (mostly straight, but not arranged in a formal grid) is still in place.

The Albuquerque area's most important Hispanic survivor is an authentic re-creation of a riverside farming household of the 1870s located in the village of Corrales, about ten miles north of downtown. The house, and its fascinating agricultural outbuildings, are open to visitors by appointment (see page 439).

Huning Highlands, ca. 1890–1915

It is hardly surprising to discover that Franz Huning, who had helped assemble the land around the Santa Fe Railroad's proposed depot location, also opened Huning Highlands, Albuquerque's very first subdivision. He did this in 1880, the same year the railroad arrived, and his subdivision was strategically located just across the railroad tracks from the depot and what was to become downtown Albuquerque. It is remarkable that with this close in-town location the neighborhood survived intact to become the city's first historic district in 1978.

Huning Highlands was developed in a strict grid system, with the long blocks running north and south. Rather than a north–south orientation, its streets were aligned parallel to the slightly canted Santa Fe Railroad track. The neighborhood has planting strips next to the street and wide sidewalks. The front yards tend to be about twenty feet deep and are often enclosed by low fences along the sidewalk line, a pattern that began early in the neighborhood's history. Huning Highlands has a wide range of house styles and sizes, including a number of one-story Queen Anne and Folk Victorian houses.

324 Southeast Edith Boulevard (private), Walker House, ca. 1901. Paired columns on pedestals and an unusually wide entablature are found on this one-story Neoclassical

cottage. Note the unusual oval trim on each side of the gabled dormer.

502 Southeast Silver Avenue, at Edith, and 602 Edith Boulevard (both private), ca. 1910. Both of these houses are built of concrete blocks cast to resemble quarry-faced stone. Number 502 Silver still has the original fence along the sidewalk—a simple iron design on a continuous low base of concrete blocks. These two houses are quite similar in shape; each has one and one-half stories, with the second story under a high-pitched hipped roof and with large dormers extending out to the wall in several directions. At 502 Silver, the dormers have parapets, and the roof has a slight outward flare along the edges; it also has a porch that wraps around the house. At 602 Edith, the dormers are gabled, the roof does not flare, and there is a simple entry porch. A 1909 house-pattern book, *Radford's Cement Houses and How to Build Them,* helped to popularize this kind of construction for a brief period. Plans for houses similar to these were published in many of Radford's pattern books; nonetheless, they were never common and were rarely built after 1920.

629 Southeast Edith Boulevard (private), ca. 1900. The Folk Victorian style is defined by the presence of Victorian decorative detailing on simple folk-house forms. This Folk Victorian house begins with a pyramidal folk house and adds a spindlework porch and centered gable—a typical Folk Victorian elaboration that provided a handy place for additional decorative detail, such as the textured wood shingles seen here. Pyramidal folk houses such as this one were built across the South and into New Mexico during the late nineteenth and early twentieth centuries; their rapid spread was hastened by the railroads.

302 Southeast Walter Street (private), Whitney House, ca. 1907. This house has an unusual combination of features: three rounded arches at the entry, paired Classical columns supporting a full-width porch, a flat roof with a stepped parapet (which looks a bit like a 1907-era commercial building), and a cantilevered cornice with dentils and modillions. Mr. Whitney was the proprietor of the Whitney Hardware Company, which looks quite elaborate in an early photograph: a floor of stone or marble, palm trees, and a row of bathtubs, set at a slant, down the middle (sinks, toilets, and basins hang from the walls). With this wealth of builder's supplies, he perhaps had access to less common pattern books. For a style, it probably comes closest to being a flat-roofed Italian Renaissance, but with so many modifiers about the atypical stepped roof parapet and the full-width colonnaded porch that our fallback "Early Eclectic What's It?" is likely better.

Walter Street Queen Annes

The 300 block of Walter Street has many one-story Queen Anne houses, mostly Free Classic designs with Classical columns.

316 Southeast Walter Street (private), Watson House, ca. 1908. On this Free Classic brick Queen Anne with bay windows, each window in the bay has a simple segmental arch above.

306 Southeast Walter Street (private), Wickstrom House, ca. 1898. A more elaborate design, this house has a squared tower over the entry, a side sweep to the porch, and a row of dentils along the porch roof.

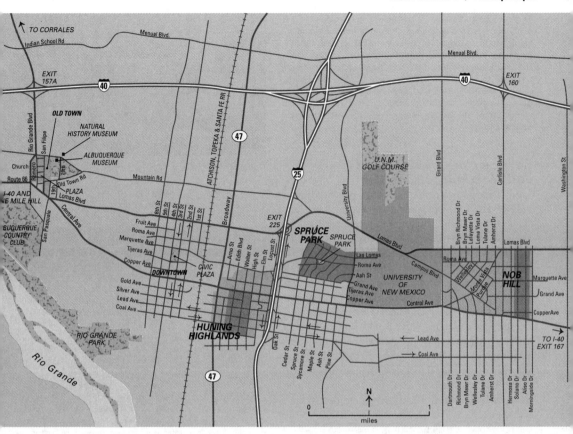

301 Southeast Walter Street (private), Stroup House, ca. 1902. Another Free Classic Queen Anne, this looks like it might incorporate a half story in the attic. (Note that the front-facing gable begins higher above the first floor than that at 316, page 437.) At one point in its life, this was covered with fake stone, and its removal damaged the face of the brick. The owners carefully removed every single face brick, turned it around, and relaid it—thus restoring the home's original brick exterior appearance.

416 Southeast Walter Street (private), Lembke House, 1894. Local preservationists have thoroughly researched this house. It was originally built of a soft, hand-molded brick that was later covered by brown stucco. From the street the segmental arches over the windows indicate that the stucco is applied over brick. The only other change on this house is the porch supports. An early photograph shows that they were originally spindlework and later were replaced by the Classical columns seen today. The delightful fence was carefully replicated from a ca. 1900 photograph. It uses square pickets and alternates two high ones with two low ones. The gate is set off with finials. Creative painting accentuates the shingles in the gable and the gable-on-hip roof's small gable.

123 Southeast Walter Street (private), Cornish House, 1901. The builders in Huning Highlands were definitely inventive. The most immediately striking feature of this house is the unusual cove cornice that wraps all around the house, continuing up into and across each centered clipped gable. The porch supports had been covered with fake stone and

Huning Highlands

have now been restored to quite close to the original. The front door and transom are new. It is both frustrating and intriguing to find two houses within three blocks (see also 302 Southeast Walter Street, page 436) that are so distinctive and that both defy any easy stylistic classification. Local preservationists have called this a late Second Empire because of the mansard roof. A late and atypical Free Classic Queen Anne also springs to mind, but like 302 Southeast Walter Street, the house really defies an overall stylistic classification.

Nob Hill

Spruce Park, 1920–1940, and Nob Hill, 1935–1950

Spruce Park, just west of the University of New Mexico, and Nob Hill, just to the east, are both located in Albuquerque's East Heights, a large community of neighborhoods near the university. Spruce Park, closest to downtown, is the earlier neighborhood. It has Albuquerque's best collection of 1920s and 1930s Period houses, the more historically "correct" Eclectic-era houses built between World War I and World War II. This neighborhood has Olmstedian curved streets and incorporates a planned park, from which it takes its name. The houses here are greatly enhanced by the many mature trees that form tall street tunnels and by lot sizes that are generally larger than those in Nob Hill.

Nob Hill is a far larger area, with the oldest houses concentrated between Girard, Morningside, Central, and Lomas. Here little was built before 1926, and the neighborhood was almost fully developed by 1942, with much of it being built during the 1930s. It is a neighborhood of primarily one-story houses set twenty feet back from the street and with five-foot side yards. One street, North Aliso, is particularly interesting because a great many of the houses there were built in 1939 and show many different versions of how the Pueblo Revival style looked in the hands of builders of small houses just before World War II. Mixed in with these are a few small builders' versions of Modernistic- and International-style homes. A 1939 newspaper article on the street calls these "Southwestern style and Modern type" homes. A few of the houses have a one-car attached garage, which would have been an up-to-date luxury in 1939. Solano is the next street toward downtown from North Aliso and has a number of Spanish Eclectic houses that are probably slightly earlier than those on North Aliso Drive. It has considerably more landscaping than North Aliso Drive, and houses that generally appear to be just slightly larger.

Spruce Park: 600 Cedar Street, at Roma Avenue (private), ca. 1920s and later. This one-story Pueblo Revival house received an entirely new stepped-back second-story addition in 1996.

Spruce Park: 1517 Cedar Street (private), ca. 1920s. Wood survives well in the dry New Mexico climate. This towered French Eclectic house has what looks like its original carefully applied false-thatched roof. The roof curves over the edges on the gable ends and otherwise depends only on the roof texture for its effect. The house is clad with a rough-finished stucco and is accented with brick and stone trim. Note the double side-gabled roof.

Spruce Park: 1315 Las Lomas (private), ca. 1920s. Spanish Eclectic houses were particularly popular in this neighborhood, and this house is one of the grander examples.

Nob Hill: 224 North Aliso Drive (private), ca. 1939. The five horizontal lines and the curved corner of the entry porch are enough to indicate that this builder had an Art Moderne (also called Streamline Moderne) house in mind. The carport has been added.

Nob Hill: 228 North Aliso Drive (private), ca. 1939. This Pueblo Revival house is particularly elaborate for this neighborhood. It has exposed vigas above a portale (porch), which is supported by rustic porch supports with shaped corbels. There is a side garden gate on the left with a typical Hispanic pattern of cutout wooden grille. It is possible that the stepped-back second story was added later.

Nob Hill: 237 North Aliso Drive (private), ca. 1950. Hipped-roof Ranch houses like this one are unusual for this neighborhood; this was probably built after World War II.

Nob Hill: 316 North Aliso Drive (private), ca. 1940. A screened-in porch appears to be the main modification to this Minimal Traditional house.

Nob Hill: 328 North Aliso Drive (private), ca. 1939. Corner windows, a flat roof, a cantilevered section, and a front entry porch supported by a single pipe (à la Walter Gropius's own house in Lincoln, Massachusetts) lets you know that this builder was working to achieve the International style.

Nob Hill: 332 North Aliso Drive (private), ca. 1939. A slight inward slant to the stucco wall and a small entry porch with a corner corbel and a *canale* (rainspout) announces this small house as Pueblo Revival.

Nob Hill: 341 North Aliso Drive (private), ca. 1939. Creative use of wood trim and paint make the screened-in porch seem like an integral part of this house's Pueblo Revival style.

Nob Hill: 412 North Aliso Drive (private), ca. 1939. The full-facade portale with corbels gives this Pueblo Revival house the look of a miniature Palace of the Governor (see page 449).

Nob Hill: 445 North Aliso Drive (private), ca. 1939. A line of brick trim at the cornice line indicates that this builder wanted to create a slightly less common Territorial Revival house.

Nob Hill: 539, 535, and 533 Solano Drive (all private), ca. 1930s. These are three examples of the small Spanish Eclectic houses that were popular on this street.

Nob Hill: 446 Solano Drive (private), ca. 1930; addition, 1996. What started out as a one-story Pueblo Revival house received a large second-story addition in 1996. It was built of wood-frame construction covered with a coat of stucco.

Casa San Ysidro, ca. 1875 and later

Old Church Road, Corrales, about twelve miles north of Albuquerque (Old Church Road is about .8 mile north of the Corrales Post Office; go west, and the house is about .2 mile directly across from the San Ysidro Church); 505-898-3915.

Casa San Ysidro is located on land that was awarded to the Guttierez family as a result of service in Spain's 1793 reconquest of New Mexico. In about 1875 an adobe-brick house was constructed on the property. It remained in the hands of Guttierez descendants until purchased by Alan and Shirley Minge in 1950, by which time the adobe house had six rooms.

This remarkable couple then devoted the next forty-five years of their lives to maintaining the exterior just as they had found it, restoring the home's interiors, and building additional rooms in the traditional manner to enclose a rear courtyard. They used only historic tools in doing this and incorporated early wooden elements throughout. They lovingly maintained the home's soft mud plaster exterior coating and even in the interior they eschewed paints and instead coated the walls with colored clays (of soft red, sage green, and yellow tones) from pits traditionally used by Indian and Hispanic builders.

The front landscape was kept naturalistic, much as the Minges had found it, and the interior courtyard was planted as traditionally as possible. Quince, berries, apricots, pears, herbs, old roses, and trumpet vine are

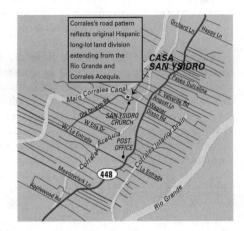

Casa San Ysidro

incorporated into the plantings. Behind the courtyard there are workrooms, sheds, and working gardens.

The glory of Casa San Ysidro is its fine collections of New Mexican decorative arts, household arts, and working tools. The Minges began collecting at a time when there was little interest in the traditional arts and crafts of northern New Mexico and consequently were able to acquire a broad collection of important objects. There are eighteenth-century chests, numerous fine pieces of nineteenth-century tinwork, early woven *jergas* (throw rugs), simple New Mexican pine furniture, and many carved wall cabinets (*alacenas*). A mica-covered photograph is a reminder of the era when it was almost impossible to obtain glass (before the opening of trade with the United States in 1821).

The Minges' wide-ranging interests also led to a large collection of working tools. Included are oxen yokes, oxcarts, and even the kind of bells worn by the lead oxen in a train. Traditional woodworking, metalworking, and gardening tools are also part of the collection, as are many typical household utensils. The Minges continued to use many of these items until 1996, when the house was purchased by the city of Albuquerque. Today, it is operated by the Albuquerque Museum, which opens this house for tours by advance reservation only.

Casa San Ysidro

SANTA FE

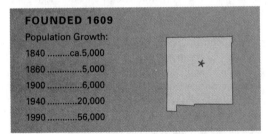

FOUNDED 1609

Population Growth:

1840	ca.5,000
1860	5,000
1900	6,000
1940	20,000
1990	56,000

The Spanish missions founded to convert the Pueblo Indians in what is now northern New Mexico came more than a century before the mission chains of Texas and California (see page xi). Indeed, Santa Fe, the provincial capital of Spanish New Mexico, was only the third permanent European settlement made anywhere in what is now the United States, the others being at San Augustine, Florida, founded by Spain in 1565, and at British colonial Jamestown, Virginia, first settled in 1607.

Conquest of the Pueblos

Early Spanish-Indian relations in New Mexico more closely resemble the conquests of the gold- and silver-rich Aztecs and Incas in the 1500s than the relatively benign establishment of the Texas and California missions in the 1700s. Seeking other advanced and wealthy Indian cultures to exploit, early Spanish exploring expeditions discovered the numerous (about thirty, with an estimated total population of about twenty thousand) agricultural towns (*pueblos,* in Spanish) of the Pueblo tribes, which clustered around the fertile valley of the upper Rio Grande. While these lacked the gold and silver of their counterparts in central Mexico and Peru, the area seemed ideal for the establishment of a rich grazing and farming province at the far edge of Spain's arid northern frontier.

In 1595 the Spanish king authorized a colonizing expedition led by a wealthy colonial aristocrat named Juan de Oñate, who in 1598 set out for the upper Rio Grande with a party of 129 soldier-settlers, their families, ten Franciscan friars, and herds of livestock. At first the Indians were generous in supplying the newcomers with food and assistance; a small provincial capital was established on the Rio Grande near the San Juan Pueblo, and eight of the friars set off to establish missions at other Pueblo towns. Soon, however, tensions developed as the colonists, accustomed to a more comfortable European lifestyle, made increasing demands on the Indians' limited resources.

Oñate spent much of his time leading exploring expeditions around the Southwest, rather than managing his new colony, and complaints from its settlers led to his replacement as provincial governor in 1607. The new governor apparently decided to make the settlers more self-reliant, and the Indians less accessible to their demands, by moving the provincial capital to a more remote site on a plateau about twenty miles east of the Rio Grande. There, in late 1609 or early 1610, he founded the new town of Santa Fe, which after almost four centuries is still the capital of New Mexico.

As additional Mexican settlers arrived in the region over the next decades, the Pueblo Indians here, as throughout the New World, suffered devastating epidemics of European diseases to which they had no natural immunity, particularly smallpox. This loss of population, coupled with the increasing demands of the settlers, led to insurrections at several pueblos that were harshly suppressed by the Spanish soldiers.

This explosive situation reached a tragic climax in the Pueblo Revolt of 1680, when, led by the most northerly pueblo at Taos, the tribes united in a revolution against their Spanish conquerors. Settlers and priests in outlying districts were massacred, and the survivors fled southward, first to the larger Spanish settlements at Santa Fe and Albuquerque. When these were massively attacked by the enraged Indians, the survivors fled once again, crossing the deserts of southern New Mexico to the safety of the important Spanish settlement at El Paso del Norte, today's Ciudad Juárez, Mexico.

For the next twelve years formerly Spanish northern New Mexico was once again ruled by its original Indian inhabitants, who occupied the Spanish Palace of the Governor (see page 449) in Santa Fe and attempted to form a permanent Pueblo alliance to prevent a Spanish reconquest. This was to be thwarted by internal rivalries intensified by a massive cultural change that had recently altered the centuries-old balance of power among the Indian tribes of the American Southwest.

"The World's Best Light Cavalry"

The New Mexico pueblos, both before and after the coming of the Spaniards, were agricultural islands surrounded by a sea of hostile nomads. To the east and south were the Apache, who specialized in quick raids to capture food, livestock, and women and children slaves from settled villages. Scarcely better were the nomadic Navajo and Ute to the west and north. As long as the raiding was being done by warriors traveling on foot, the defending warriors in and around the semi-fortified pueblos made such encounters risky enough to keep losses within acceptable limits.

In the mid-1600s some of the nomadic tribes mastered the art of bareback horsemanship using simple rope bridles. The horses had been introduced by the Spanish conquerors in the 1500s and could either be stolen from them or captured from wild plains herds descended from escaped animals. Soon these equestrian techniques spread through the nomadic tribes, whose warriors could ride three hundred yards and discharge thirty deadly arrows in the time it took a mounted European soldier to reload his single-shot firearm. As a U.S. Army officer later noted, this made a band of mounted Plains Indian warriors "the world's best light cavalry." Now the former on-foot raids of the Apache and other nomadic tribes became lightning-fast encounters that were all but impossible to defend against.

Such attacks on the more remote New Mexico pueblos had already led to their abandonment before the Pueblo Revolt. At the more clustered pueblos along the Rio Grande, the Spanish officials had followed a prudent policy of preventing raids by bribing the Indians with food and livestock. They presumably kept obtaining slaves in the traditional way. With the Spanish gone, the Pueblo tribes, partly Hispanicized after almost a century of occupation and protection by armor-wearing soldiers, fell easy prey to the raiders. When a small Spanish army moved northward to reoccupy Santa Fe in 1692, it had to fight not a single battle with the formerly hostile Pueblos. As large numbers of colonists began returning the next year, there were some spirited local outbreaks of Indian resistance, but by 1700 both Indians and Spaniards had settled into a relatively peaceful, bicultural partnership that emphasized the importance of self-sufficiency in their isolated domain surrounded by potentially hostile neighbors.

Mexican Independence and the Santa Fe Trail

The American and French Revolutions of the late 1700s planted the seeds of independence throughout Spain's vast New World colonies. As the suppliers of such high-value raw materials as silver, sugar, coffee, and cocoa, the colonists particularly resented the scarcity and high cost of imported manufactured goods. These were strictly controlled through Spain's iron-clad policy of permitting trade only with the mother country. By the early 1800s, this and other restrictive policies were fueling revolutionary movements and conflicts throughout the Spanish colonies. These would result in

independence for most of the larger colonies during the 1820s. Central Mexico was wracked by a civil war from 1810 until the defeat of the last Royalist holdouts in 1821, when it became an independent republic. These distant events would soon end northern New Mexico's century-long slumber as an all-but-forgotten frontier outpost of New Spain.

Independent Mexico closely followed the policies established by Spain with one crucial exception. Whereas the Spanish authorities prohibited outside trade by arresting any foreigner found trespassing on its territory, cash-poor Mexico reversed this policy and encouraged foreign trade as a source of much-needed customs duties. Soon the sailing ships of Yankee traders were calling at long-forbidden ports in Hispanic California. In 1821, only a few months after Mexican independence, a Missouri trader with a small load of goods bound for the Rocky Mountains ventured across Raton Pass into Mexican territory. There he was met by Mexican troops who, instead of arresting him, escorted him to Santa Fe to trade his wares for silver pesos.

The Santa Fe authorities urged the trader to return and bring his friends. Soon dozens of Anglo traders were bringing caravans of cotton cloth, hardware, silk shawls, books, paper, pens, and countless other manufactured items along the Santa Fe Trail to supply the demands of the goods-starved New Mexicans. Some idea of the profits involved can be seen in the records of the first large trading caravan, which left Missouri with twenty-three wagons and eighty-one men in 1824. The trade goods had cost $35,000 in Missouri and sold for the equivalent of $180,000 in Santa Fe.

By the 1830s the Santa Fe market was becoming saturated, and many caravans continued down the Camino Real to the larger Mexican interior town of Chihuahua, where their prices were lower than those of local merchants supplied from faraway Europe. Soon affluent Santa Feans became involved as middlemen in this flourishing trade, and the ancient town was reenergized as a center of commerce. It was also on its way to becoming tricultural, as Anglo merchants opened stores and became permanent residents. As in the California capital of Monterey, many of these Anglos, who were mostly young, single males, married into prominent Hispanic families and became Mexican citizens.

Anglo-Hispanic relationships soured somewhat throughout the Southwest after the successful revolution of the Texas Anglos in 1836 (see page xii). In 1841 things became particularly tense in Santa Fe when a hot-blooded band of about three hundred ill-prepared and ill-advised Anglo Texans marched toward Hispanic Santa Fe to "liberate" it. The Mexican governor led an army of three thousand eastward to meet the Texans,

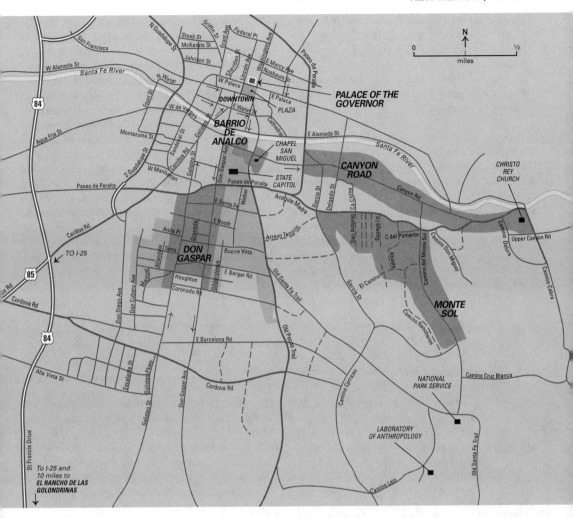

who were found half starved and lost. The governor sent them all to prison in Mexico City, but the New Mexicans' subsequent distrust of *tejanos* still lingers today.

In 1848 Santa Fe's tricultural status became official, as New Mexico, California, and adjacent areas were ceded to the United States following the Mexican War (see page xx). Santa Fe's importance as an Anglo trade center and transportation junction was soon enhanced by the California gold rush, many of whose participants traveled westward via the "southern route" through Santa Fe and then southwestward across New Mexico and Arizona.

The "Santa Fe" Railroad

It was the building of the transcontinental railroads in the twenty years from 1870 to 1890 that transformed the primitive wagon-road West into an integrated part of the national economy (see page xxix). Among the four transcontinental lines completed before 1890 was the Atchison, Topeka, and Santa Fe, which began building westward from eastern Kansas in 1868 along the route of the Santa Fe Trail. By 1879 the line had reached the town of Las Vegas, in eastern New Mexico. There it stopped while the citizens of Santa Fe debated whether to pay the substantial subsidy demanded by the railroad builders to divert its main line onto the high plateau where its namesake city was located. The answer was no, and in 1880 the main line was built through Albuquerque, which was to become the principal rail junction and financial and trade center of New Mexico (see page 434). Santa Fe was left with only an inconvenient, eighteen-mile dead-end spur line. Now the venerable capital city had neither its namesake trail nor main-line railroad. In 1884 a magazine journalist correctly predicted Santa Fe's future:

The mining districts are all at a distance. No livestock country is tributary. Agriculture is limited to the possibilities of irrigation in a small valley. Santa Fe is destined to be renewed as a picture of the past—a peaceful seat of learning, a quiet health resort, and a mecca for the antiquarian (quoted in John W. Reps, *Cities of the American West*).

Modern Santa Fe

The journalist was right. Throughout the more than a century since he wrote, Santa Fe has remained a small government center with a unique Indian-Spanish culture that has made its principal industry what is today called heritage tourism. This began with the railroad, which first gave health seekers, artists, vacationers, and retirees convenient access to the city's charms. The idea of deliberately preserving and enhancing northern New Mexico's historic character seems to have begun in 1901, when archaeologist William G. Tight was appointed president of the University of New Mexico in Albuquerque. Concerned that newer Anglo-style construction was diluting the region's architectural heritage, Tight remodeled several university buildings in a "Spanish Pueblo" style. By 1912 the Santa Fe Chamber of Commerce was encouraging the use of this historically based style for new construction to help preserve the historic capital's tourism appeal. Many of the city's important public and commercial buildings were to use the style in the following decades, and it also became popular for Pueblo Revival houses. In 1957, Santa Fe was among the first cities in the country to adopt a historic preservation ordinance with stylistic guidelines for new construction in its historic core. Ironically, the design review ordinance allowed historic buildings to be demolished and replaced with new buildings that followed the "historic" design guidelines.

Many longtime residents and visitors now feel that

The Dilemma of Looking at Earth-Wall Houses

Earth-wall houses are different. Those of us accustomed to looking at typical Anglo houses (with walls of wood, brick, or stone), and judging their antiquity and originality by a set of visual clues learned over the years, find our skills inadequate for earth-wall houses.

First, an earth-wall house of fairly new vintage can look old in just a dozen or so years if neglected—making the mere appearance of age an inaccurate guideline.

Second, the exterior walls of well-maintained earth-wall structures of almost any age can look quite similar. Traditionally, adobe bricks were covered with a coat of soft mud "plaster," which bonded perfectly to the wall but had to be replaced yearly. Today, almost all of Santa Fe's oldest structures have been covered either with a coating of a hard plaster of lime and sand (which does not perfectly adhere to the walls and creates areas for water to run into wherever it begins to crack away) or, more common today, a coating of cement stucco (which will only adhere to the wall if the adobe bricks have been covered with chicken wire or a similar product and creates water penetration problems at cracks similar to those of hard plaster). Thus, a new coating might well cover an old wall or, less likely, old soft mud plaster can cover a new wall—making the exterior cladding material an inaccurate age guideline.

Third, wood elements, such as simple windows and doors, are often not reliable guides. It has long been a common practice to incorporate old windows and doors into newer houses. Old vigas and corbels are also treasured additions. This was an excellent way to recycle scarce wood and save labor in the early days and in the twentieth century offers a great way to achieve an "ancient" look in new Pueblo Revival dwellings. In addition, expensively constructed Pueblo Revival houses can succeed in making even new windows and doors look old at a distance—so the appearance of old wood elements is a problematic age guideline.

Fourth, just as a newer Pueblo Revival house may incorporate old elements to achieve an old look, the residents of an older structure may be proudly updating their adobe with newer windows or doors. Many structures with visibly new or remodeled features may well include ancient walls.

Fifth, determining modifications and changes in houses meant to be easily expanded and contracted is difficult, and perhaps less meaningful, than in homes of other materials. One of the great advantages of earth walls is that they are easily changeable. Their smooth wall surfaces, covered by an all-forgiving coat of plaster, can be added onto and changed with little visible trace. Windows and doors can be moved from one place to the other; openings can be enlarged or filled in. New additions can meld almost seamlessly into older structures. Old wings can be abandoned, and all traces of the city's historic attractiveness has been almost *too* successful, as its population has almost tripled since 1940, leading to traffic congestion on its narrow streets and conversion of many historic houses into upscale shops and restaurants. Fortunately, Santa Fe still retains a number of historic buildings, even if they must now be enjoyed in the context of a much larger city. In addition to its unique, almost four-hundred-year-old Governor's Palace, several surviving neighborhoods retain important examples of its Colonial, Victorian, and Eclectic-era dwellings.

Barrio de Analco, 1760s and later

Loosely translated, Barrio de Analco means the "District on the Other Side of the River," and it was here, across the river from the Governor's Palace and Plaza, that Tlaxcalan Indian servants (brought from Mexico City by Santa Fe's early missionaries and officials) settled in the 1600s. Ransacked in the Pueblo Revolt of 1680, the barrio was rebuilt around 1700 for *genízaros* (Native Americans who had been converted to Catholicism by the missionaries) and other servants of the returning Spaniards. Much of the barrio was washed away in a flood in the 1760s, but it was again rebuilt. Today, it is still possible to get a feeling for an early Hispanic streetscape here, even though only a handful of early houses remain. The street is narrow and winding, and some houses are built to the edge of the narrow sidewalk. Anchoring the district is the **Chapel of San Miguel,** which served the barrio's residents. It was rebuilt in 1710 on the site of an earlier one (damaged in the Pueblo Revolt) and has been modified several times since.

129–135 East de Vargas Street (private), Tudesqui House, pre-1840 with later additions. A small Victorian entry hood is located over the door of a part of this house, nicely re-

their connecting point can disappear under a new coat of plaster (or at least those visible without archaeological investigation). Thus, beneath the wall surface and belowground inspection is necessary to unravel the history of even a known historic dwelling. (One can't look in the attic and basement for construction history clues.)

There are a few clues. Most early earth-wall buildings have an irregular surface and handmade look that give them a distinctive visual character. During the early years of the Pueblo Revival (1910s to 1930s), architects often effectively mimicked these irregularities, even though the basic structure might be hollow tile and/or brick. The larger and more romanticized a "handmade"-looking structure is (with ladders, a second story step-back, broad portales, and so on), the more likely it is to be a Pueblo Revival dwelling rather than an earlier survivor.

Pueblo Revival houses are still being built today. These often use bricks, concrete blocks, or even a balloon-frame structure covered with concrete plaster to imitate an earth-wall dwelling. Unlike earlier Pueblo Revival dwellings (which went to great expense to provide a handmade look), today's Pueblo Revival houses more often have a "new" look. The straightness of the walls, the sharpness of the corners, and the regularity of the right angles all provide important clues that one is looking at a new dwelling. So do the less authentic doors and windows that may be used. Still, one can be fooled even here, particularly when the walls are made of adobe brick.

For all of the above reasons, it is difficult to make "from-the-street" guesses about the ages of earth-wall houses (or even houses built to appear like earth-wall houses). In addition, even when an earth-wall house is known to be old, deciphering the date and original configuration takes sophisticated archaeological and historical analysis. This is the only way to estimate the age of the adobe bricks themselves, to find the location of early walls now washed away, or to tell when a viga was cut by tree-ring analysis. Even the latter won't tell you for certain if it was salvaged from an earlier house. Wills can tell if a house was on the property, but not necessarily if it was this particular house or an earlier one. And the fact that Spanish Colonial houses were often built in stages simply adds to a challenge that is best left to earth-wall-house experts.

It is better, perhaps, while house watching in Santa Fe, to just enjoy the environment and look for historic Santa Fe's plaques, which identify some of the oldest (mostly Spanish Colonial style) buildings. *Old Santa Fe Today,* published by the Historic Santa Fe Foundation and with a foreword by John Gaw Meem, features photographs, history (including tree-ring dates and mentions in wills), and maps of about seventy plaqued historic buildings.

Barrio de Analco

Brito, a Tlaxcalan Indian who helped in the 1693 reconquest of New Mexico. He and his brother contributed 1,500 adobe bricks (out of 21,000) to the 1710 rebuilding of the Chapel of San Miguel. This house has its side turned to the street and faces right, onto a side garden. The entry gate opens onto the portale and has a typical Hispanic wooden grille at the top. The stone foundation, needed to prevent absorption of ground water, is exposed. This house has had many changes and additions, including a Territorial-era brick cornice and, of course, the Anglo windows.

214 East de Vargas Street (private), "Oldest House," ca. 1760s. This house has been called the "Oldest House" for more than a century. Tree-ring dating of the downstairs vigas indicates dates of between 1740 and 1767. A second story was removed in the early twentieth century and then added back later. The left side of this structure has the low door, low ceiling, thick adobe walls, and dirt floors associated with very early structures in Santa Fe. Note how the doors are raised above street level, a feature typical of Spanish Colonial houses.

Canyon Road, ca. 1780–1942

This "residential arts-and-crafts zone" features many shops, galleries, and restaurants located in former homes along Canyon Road—which still retains a residential scale. When the Spanish first arrived in Santa Fe, this was already a trail that led from Santa Fe to the Pecos Pueblo, an important trading area where Native American tribes from all over the Southwest gathered to exchange goods. (Today, Pecos Pueblo is preserved as a ruin but is no longer reachable via Canyon Road.)

Canyon Road, located on high ground above the Santa Fe River, became a favored place to build houses because it offered a beautiful view out across the river valley, and it allowed access to water from a location comfortably above flood level. The former homes along the road are mostly twentieth-century Pueblo Revival houses, along with a handful of earlier Spanish Colonial–style homes. To the east of the gallery and restaurant area, Canyon Road continues as a narrower and still-residential road for another several miles. John Gaw Meem's 1940 **Cristo Rey Catholic Church** (located where Canyon Road turns and becomes Upper Canyon Road) is built of adobe brick in the spirit and style of Spanish-period New Mexico missions; it makes a nice terminus for a Canyon Road walk or drive.

flecting how it has changed over time. There is a narrow street to the left of the house that leads down to the Santa Fe River. Walking down it and looking back uphill give you both a glimpse of the rear garden of the house and an understanding of why Barrio de Analco was a favored early building site, located on the river yet high enough to be above all but the most tremendous flood.

132 East de Vargas Street (private), Crespín House, ca. 1750s. Here the great thickness of the adobe walls and tree-ring dating of the vigas indicate a construction date of before 1750. The land was part of a land grant to Juan de León

724 Canyon Road (private), Borrego House, ca. 1770. The earliest parts of this house are in the rear. Most visible today is the late-nineteenth-century front room built by the prominent Borrego family, probably to provide a proper room for entertaining and political events. The gracious portale may have been added at the same time. The squared vernacular Greek Revival porch supports, the roof parapet crowned with brick, the casement windows, and the door surround with a minimal triangular "pediment" above are all typical of the Anglo-influenced architectural changes that began taking place during New Mexico's Territorial period, and

Canyon Road

buildings with this combination of features are called Territorial style. Placing a portale (porch) across the front of the house (rather than in a more private interior location) also shows a strong Anglo influence.

545 Canyon Road (apartments private; garden open), El Zaguán, ca. 1850s. In 1849 James L. Johnson, a merchant who prospered during the days of the Santa Fe Trail, purchased an earlier home that had several rooms with four-foot-thick adobe walls. With this as a beginning, he added rooms (these with three-foot-thick walls) until he had twenty-four, including a "chocolate room" for grinding chocolate and preparing and serving afternoon hot chocolate, a delectable alternative to afternoon tea. This wonderful house is now owned by the Historic Santa Fe Foundation, which has its office here.

All of the large east wing of the building contains private apartments, but to the west (on the left side of the house) is a large garden and portale that are open to the public. To reach it, walk through the entry garden and turn left through the zaguan, which runs from left to right. The garden offers not only mature plantings, but also a view out over the river, where one can actually see the canyon of Canyon Road. The lower terrace behind would have held orchards, livestock, and a vegetable garden.

Monte Sol, ca. 1912–1942

This district is still quite rural in character, with unstudied native landscape and many unpaved roads to each side of its two main streets—Camino del Monte Sol and Acequia Madre Street. Acequia Madre Street runs alongside Santa Fe's Acequia Madre (Mother

Ditch), which was built by Spanish colonists over three hundred years ago. The Spanish brought to America the engineering knowledge needed to build elaborate irrigation systems to deliver water for everyday use and to grow crops in arid climates. They also brought an established body of law about who owned the rights to these waters. And along with the rights came responsibilities, among them helping with the annual upkeep needed to maintain such a system. Today, this acequia is still functional after three hundred years of use, a remarkable testimony to the Spaniards' sophisticated engineering.

Acequia Madre Street is shaded by the tall cottonwood trees that grow along the acequia. The long, unpaved dead-end streets off of Acequia Madre are typical of the long-lot land division that was used along both rivers and acequias. At first those who owned land along the waterway had long, narrow lots stretching back from the acequia, since the cost of the land was determined by the amount of water frontage (which in turn determined the size of one's ownership of the water rights). Later, short lateral irrigation ditches could be added—and smaller lots created to front along these. This created the distinctive street pattern seen today south of Acequia Madre, with the length of the cross streets generally limited by the length of the secondary irrigation channels. Alternatively, original long lots were purchased later for subdivision without a secondary irrigation ditch ever being added. This same kind of long-lot land-division pattern can also be seen along the Rio Grande Valley in the small town of Corrales (see page 439).

Camino del Monte Sol, which climbs the hill, has a quite-different character. Unlike the shaded Acequia Madre, this street has fewer trees and an arid look more typical of New Mexico. Monte Sol began to gain prominence in 1912, right after New Mexico statehood, when many members of Santa Fe's early-twentieth-century colony of nationally important artists and writers chose Camino del Monte Sol for their homes. Although at that time many of the artists had small galleries in their homes, today the Monte Sol district is almost entirely residential (the galleries are now concentrated in other parts of Santa Fe). The majority of homes here are Pueblo Revival in style and were built before 1940.

Throughout the district, a varied streetscape is produced by the many different ways in which houses are sited relative to the street. Some are built right to the street line, while others are barely set back from it; some have their side turned to the street, and others are set far to the back of the lot; a handful are placed at angles. There are no curbs or sidewalks (except for a narrow path adjacent to the roadway). Driveways tend to be of gravel, and most of the landscape is natural. When the house is set back from the street, the resulting courtyard is almost always surrounded by an enclosure. Most commonly, this is a thick plaster-stuccoed "pueblo"-style wall supported by buttresses; these are built in all heights and frequently incorporate characteristic stepped height changes. Stone, unfinished adobe brick, and a distinctive Hispanic coyote fence (made of thin, unpeeled pieces of aspen that are placed vertically in the ground and lashed together) are also used to enclose courtyards. When metal was still scarce, coyote fences were lashed together with leather, but wire has been used since railroads made this product affordable. Attractive gates offer glimpses of the courtyards and houses beyond, and these are interesting in and of themselves. According to Nancy Hunter Warren in *New Mexico Style* (Museum of New Mexico Press, 1995), "wooden garden gates have probably been the most popular decorative architectural element in northern New Mexico during [the twentieth] century." Some are based on older Hispanic designs, and others are new interpretations of Southwest themes. Cutout patterns applied to a solid piece of wood are common, as are areas of open wooden grillwork. Wrought-iron gates, which are less common except for newer driveway entrances, were introduced about 1900.

The only streets recommended for driving in the Monte Sol district are the paved ones. Even then, you will have a difficult time getting more than a fleeting glance from a car, as the streets are narrow, and the local traffic tends to be in a hurry. But when walking, one must take care because of the lack of sidewalks and the same hurrying traffic. The handsome Pueblo Revival **National Park Service Administration Building** (about one-fourth mile south of the historic district boundary) makes a visual terminus for Camino del Monte Sol; and John Gaw Meem's 1931 **Laboratory of Anthropology** and a cluster of associated museums are only about a quarter mile beyond on Camino Lejo.

506 Acequia Madre, at Garcia Street (private), pre-1938. An elaborately detailed entry gate marks the entrance to this one-story Pueblo Revival home. It even has a small second-story area complete with a setback and a picturesque ladder.

569 Garcia Street (private). The brick parapeted roof and porch identify this as a Territorial Revival, less common than Pueblo Revival.

421 and 429 Delgado Street (both private), Meadors-Staples-Anthony Commission, 1925; John Gaw Meem, Santa Fe, architect. Here is a pair of early small houses by one of the region's most prominent Pueblo Revival architects. Number 433 Delgado (private), built about 1941, is a Territorial Revival located on the same dead-end street.

408 Camino del Monte Sol, at Poniente (private), 1912 and 1920s; Frank Applegate, Santa Fe, architect for remod-

Monte Sol

eling. This picturesque house, which began as a one-story structure and then had the second story added in the 1920s, turns its back to Poniente and faces a large courtyard along Monte Sol. It is behind a stepped wall, but the prominent corner buttresses, battered wall, and roof ladder hint at its richness.

538 Camino del Monte Sol (private), pre-1938 and later. This Pueblo Revival house features the kind of upper-story setback encouraged by Carlos Vierra (see 1002 Old Pecos Trail, page 449). Much of the woodwork on the main house looks old, making one guess that it is part of the original design. The double garage between the house and the road is likely a later addition (almost any two-car attached garage on less than the most grand of houses here is a later addition). But such semieducated guesses are always suspect for earth-wall houses (see page 444).

550 Camino del Monte Sol (private), ca. 1920s. This cute one-story house has a prominent front chimney (carefully shaped to look old), a stepped buttress against the right front, and a simple buttress against the left front. The top of the wood-plank front door is cut at a jaunty angle, intended (along with the iron hardware) to add to the picturesque handcrafted appearance. Even a novice builder of the early pueblos could likely have created a more level opening than this one. Frank Applegate, who designed 408 Camino del Monte Sol (see above) may have been the architect for both this house and 558 Camino del Monte Sol (see the following entry).

558 Camino del Monte Sol (private), ca. 1920s. This symmetrical Pueblo Revival house is set back from the road with a front courtyard that is more Anglo than Hispanic. On each side, a one-story wing extends out to the road, and a low fence stretches between them forming the front courtyard. The projecting vigas were carefully designed to look old and irregular.

566 Camino del Monte Sol (private), Nash House, ca. 1920–1925; Frank Applegate, Santa Fe, architect. This was the home of Willard Nash, one of Santa Fe's Cinco Pintores—a group of five radical 1920s painters (Fremont Ellis, Walter Mruk, Joseph Bakos, Will Shuster, and Nash) called themselves. They were an important part of Santa Fe's early colony of artists and built their homes together here on Monte Sol, which helped attract other Santa Fe artists and writers to the street. Nash and Applegate (an architect, sculptor, watercolorist, and tile maker who lived just down the street) collaborated on the design of this, Nash's own home.

Don Gaspar, ca. 1890–1942

This large historic district contains about 450 houses, with different styles prevalent in different parts of the district. The two earliest streets are Galisteo Street and the Old Santa Fe Trail, both of which appear on maps by 1766. Many of the earliest houses are along these streets—low adobe structures of Spanish Colonial descent. Most have been modified and do not generally read as a unified Hispanic streetscape.

Don Gaspar Avenue features a concentration of early-twentieth-century Anglo houses, a rarity in Santa Fe. These were built mainly from about 1895 to 1920. Before this brief period, houses of Spanish Colonial descent predominated, and after this period Pueblo Revival houses have reigned, encouraged by the city's design review ordinance.

Several streets (Allandale, Anita, and Don Cubero) are filled mostly with 1920s and 1930s bungalows, primarily in the Pueblo Revival style, with stuccoed walls, parapeted flat roofs, and projecting vigas and drainpipes. Many of these are built in the two-room-wide and three-room-deep floor plan that was popularized in Craftsman bungalows during the 1910s and early 1920s; many have three windows set into a single wall opening, a common Craftsman feature.

Don Gaspar

505 Don Gaspar Avenue (private), Salmon House, 1907. Although the main entrance is on Don Gaspar, a similar facade faces Paseo de Peralta, and both facades feature a pyramidal hipped roof, centered hipped dormers, and an arcaded porch. Originally of redbrick, the walls were later covered with stucco. The stylistic inspiration, revealed by the wide arched porches and simulated tile roof, was Mission Revival. The house and large garden (which faces the Acequia Madre on the south) are surrounded by a picturesque wall. Built in the 1920s, this is designed with reverse echoes of the porch arches, filled with graceful wrought iron.

610 Don Gaspar Avenue (private), Clossen House, ca. 1920. This large brick Craftsman-style house has a smaller second story and unusually tall pedestals beneath the inward-sloping wood porch supports.

614 Don Gaspar Avenue (private), Andres House, ca. 1920. This early Pueblo Revival design is symmetrical and constructed of adobe brick with its flat roof hidden behind a thick and undulating parapet. Its squarish shape and full-width porch are similar to those found on contemporaneous American four-squares.

644 Don Gaspar Avenue (private), ca. 1915. This large front-gabled Craftsman-style house is clad in stucco. Note the brick trim over the tripled windows and around the segmental arched recessed entry. It is easy to see where a side porch has been enclosed and stuccoed. Upstairs, there is a line of four windows in both the front-facing gable and the gabled dormer on the left side; wood trim extends vertically from the window frames into the eaves, giving the effect of half-timbering.

661 and 665 Don Gaspar Avenue (both private), ca. 1910. Both of these hipped-roof Craftsman houses are constructed of the same brick. Number 661 has a hipped-roof dormer, stone lintels over the windows, and a simple front door with transom. Number 665 has no dormer but has segmental brick arches over the windows and a more elaborate door surround.

1002 Old Pecos Trail (private), Vierra House, 1918; Carlos Vierra, architect. Although located just beyond the official boundary of the Don Gaspar district, the house that Carlos Vierra, one of the earliest and most vocal proponents of the Pueblo Revival style, designed for himself is a joy to see. In many ways it is the prototypical Pueblo Revival house. Vierra was not an architect but rather an artist and a staff member of the Museum of New Mexico and the School of American Archaeology and was involved with the restoration of the Governor's Palace. John Gaw Meem, one of Santa Fe's most prolific Pueblo Revival architects, once credited Vierra's large collection of original early New Mexico architectural photographs as his most useful source material.

Palace of the Governor, ca. 1610 and later

East Palace Avenue between Lincoln and Washington Avenues on the north side of Santa Fe Plaza, 505-827-6483.

Never simply a domestic structure, the Palace of the Governor was originally built in 1610 to house most of the needs of the fledgling Spanish government, including private apartments, offices, barracks for the soldiers, and stables for horses. The Governor's Palace was much larger at this early date and included a ten-acre enclosed courtyard with vegetable gardens. From 1680 to 1693, the palace was occupied by the local Indians after the Pueblo Revolt (see page 441). They tore down parts of the palace, added lookout towers, and converted much of it into small living apartments, such as those used in their pueblos (see "Taos," page 453).

When the city was recaptured, the palace was returned again to the varied uses of the Spanish government officials. Over the next 217 years its many rooms held a regular "fruit-basket turnover" of functions. An

Palace of the Governor, circa 1955

Sena Plaza, near Palace of the Governor

apartment under one administrator might be an office under the next, or it might be used as a reception room or library or council room or whatever the need was at the time. During the years 1909 to 1913 the palace was converted into the Museum of New Mexico. And in the intervening years there have been sophisticated archaeological investigations and many changing displays.

Without paying a fee, one can look around the spacious entry area and see examples of both a Spanish Colonial door and a Territorial door and a simply furnished early Spanish conference room. Within the museum itself, there is a photographic exhibit of the history of the palace, which shows the portale (this was not a part of the original building but was added at some later date) around the 1870s, then around the 1890s with a delicate Victorian porch substituted for the portale, and then again after the 1909 to 1913 restoration with today's portale in place.

Two other exhibits aid in understanding more about early life in northern New Mexico. The first is "The Hispanic Residents of New Mexico, 1790." Based upon the findings of the Spanish census of 1790 (the most complete ever undertaken during the 223 years that New Mexico was under Spanish rule), the exhibit highlights and explains the everyday lives of ordinary Nuevo Méjico civilians in 1790 by featuring the primary occupational activities found in the census. Artifacts and information explain domestic life and food preparation, farming and irrigation, cattle and sheep raising, carpentry, weaving, blacksmithery, and common day labor.

A second and even larger exhibit is "Spanish Life on the Upper Rio Grande." This illustrates the adaptation of the Spanish colonists, through time, to conditions in northern New Mexico. Drawing from artifacts found in archaeological excavations here in the Palace of the Governor and at other Spanish Colonial sites, it beautifully illustrates the kinds of goods and belongings that were central to each era of Spanish inhabitants of New Mexico (with the primary emphasis on the years before

1821). The end of the exhibit features the L. Bradford Prince Period Room, which duplicates a photograph of the room taken in 1893 when Prince was the territorial governor. A simple sketch outline of the 1893 photograph is color coded to convey the provenance of every item in the room—one glance tells if you are looking at the exact item in the photograph, an "of the period" similar item, or a new reproduction.

El Rancho de las Golondrinas, 1700s and later

334 Los Pinos Road (Santa Fe County Road 54), fifteen miles south of Santa Fe; 505-471-2261 (general information) or 505-473-4169 (guided tour reservations).

The small valley created by Cienega Creek was inhabited for many centuries before the Spanish arrived. Fertile soils and marshlands (or ciénagas) created by the valley's small springs helped produce reliable crops both for the earlier Native Americans and for the Spanish families who followed. The Camino Real passed near the rancho, and it served as the first stop south of Santa Fe and the last stop on the return trip. The recorded history of the present dwelling begins with the 1727 will of Diego Manuel Baca, and the property stayed in the hands of his and Maria Vega y Coco's descendants for over two hundred years.

The name Rancho de las Golondrinas, which in English means "Ranch of the Swallows," was first mentioned in a Spanish official's journal on November 9, 1780. New roads gradually bypassed Las Golondrinas, and in 1932 the last of the Baca-Piño descendants sold the rancho to the Curtin family. It was Leonora Curtin, author of *Healing Herbs of the Rio Grande,* and her husband, Y. A. Paloheimo, a Finnish consul (see also Pasadena's "Fenyes Mansion," page 101), who decided to restore the rancho and create a living-history museum of agricultural life in northern New Mexico. They restored the original Golondrinas *placita* (courtyard) and the later rear *placita,* including moving in small agricultural outbuildings around the latter.

Next, across the Acequia Madre irrigation ditch, which serves the valley, and well away from the original rancho, they moved in a number of mostly log structures to create a typical northern New Mexico mountain village. On the hill above they built a copy of a Penitente meetinghouse, or *morada,* a copy of a *morada* at Abiquiu. (Penitentes were lay Catholics who ministered to needs in rural areas that had no priests.)

Today, the fields are farmed with old strains of seeds and the original irrigation methods. Standing in the midst of these fields that have been farmed for untold hundreds of years, and watching them being irrigated with an acequia constructed by Spanish colonists growing antique strains of seeds, is an awe-inspiring experience. In addition to traditional farming methods, many related crafts are demonstrated when volunteers are available.

Livestock has also been reintroduced into Las Golondrinas, including a program of back breeding for churro sheep. These sheep are the descendants of the culls (which is the meaning of "churros"), which the Spanish sent aboard ship to America. Ironically, their long and low-lanolin hair proved particularly well

El Rancho de las Golondrinas

suited to weaving, and when their fuller and "more desirable" antecedents, merino sheep, began making their
way to New Mexico, the quality of woven goods declined. Today, only a few pure-bred churro sheep remain, all in the care of Navajo shepherds.

Rancho de las Golondrinas first opened to the public in 1972, and title was transferred to the El Rancho de
las Golondrinas Charitable Trust in 1982. A visit here
clearly demonstrates the agricultural life practiced by
many generations of New Mexicans. It is a lifestyle that
continues today, in only a slightly updated version, in
many rural areas of Mexico.

El Rancho de las Golondrinas

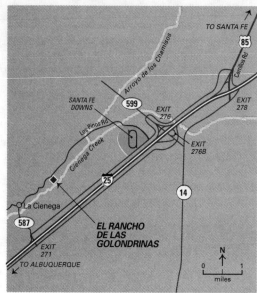

Las Golondrinas is fifteen miles south of Santa Fe
and forty-five miles north of Albuquerque, off Interstate 25. From Santa Fe, take Interstate exit 276 and
bear right on New Mexico Highway 599. Turn left at the
first intersection on the Frontage Road and right on Los
Pinos Road (you reach it just before the racetrack). The
museum is a bit more than three miles from this intersection. There is a Y intersection just before you reach
the museum; bear left at the Y and you will soon see the
museum entrance on the left.

From Albuquerque, take exit 276B and bear right on
New Mexico Highway 599. Turn left on the Frontage
Road and right on Los Pinos Road, which is just before
the racetrack, and follow the preceding instructions
to the museum, which is about three miles from this
intersection.

TAOS

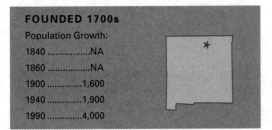

The spectacular "apartment house" Indian dwellings of the Taos Pueblo, the most northerly of New Mexico's Puebloan towns, are one of the most familiar images of the American West. Although more than a dozen of New Mexico's early pueblos are still occupied by the descendants of their original occupants, only at remote Taos do the Pueblo Indians' once-typical multistory, mud-walled houses still survive (see the following entry).

The early Spanish missionaries to the Taos Pueblo built their chapel and houses adjacent to the semifortified Indian dwellings for mutual protection during raids by the surrounding nomadic tribes, which were frequent at such outlying locations (see also page 441). By the late 1700s the local Hispanic population was establishing its own small agricultural villages well beyond the limits of the Indian pueblo. For defense against nomadic raids, these were built as semifortified "plazas," in which a continuous perimeter of adobe houses and buildings surrounded a large central square. The adobe structures had openings only onto the square, and thus served as an external defensive wall for the village. The square itself was entered only through a single wide passageway, which could be closed off with massive wooden gates. When hostile nomads were in the area, the village's horses and cattle were herded through the gateway into the protected inner square.

The first such fortified plaza town was Ranchos de Taos, located about seven miles south of the pueblo, but the most important was to become Fernando de Taos, which was about halfway between Ranchos and the pueblo. This was the nucleus of the small town known today simply as Taos. Even in the pre-Spanish era, the Taos Pueblo, located near the junction of important north–south and east–west Indian trails, had become the site of yearly trading fairs at which the region's many tribes suspended their usual hostilities to barter dried meat, animal skins, and slaves, supplied by the nomads, for corn, squash, cotton cloth, and pottery from the Pueblo. The Spanish continued and enlarged the trading tradition, adding small manufactured items as well as large quantities of food and livestock to the trading mix. By the 1800s the trading fairs had spilled beyond the early pueblo into the nearby town of Taos, and by the 1830s Anglo traders were adding an endless diversity of new items to the fairs. Some of these also opened year-round stores in Taos, which soon became the commercial center of mountainous northernmost New Mexico.

Too small and remote to warrant a railroad connection, Taos remained a difficult-to-reach backwater of mixed Indian, Hispanic, and Anglo cultures until the first improved automobile roads were constructed in the 1920s. By then picturesque Taos had been "discovered" by Anglo artists and was the center of a lively arts colony, which it remains today.

Like Santa Fe, in recent decades Taos has seen a dramatic upsurge in heritage tourism, now augmented in winter by several popular nearby ski resorts. In spite of some incompatible new construction, the small town retains much of its historic character, including an extraordinary collection of unusual museum houses. The crown jewel of these is the great Taos Pueblo, whose unique history is sensitively interpreted to visitors by knowledgeable native guides. Taos also has New Mexico's most intact and thoroughly documented rural hacienda constructed in the Spanish era (see page 455), as well as important dwellings reflecting its early Anglo years (see page 457) and its later incarnation as an avant-garde art colony (see pages 458, 459, and 461). Also in Taos are the now much modified remnants of its early, fortified plaza, as well as a more intact small plaza nearby (see page 462). Four miles southwest at Ranchos de Taos are the remnants of the region's first such plaza.

Taos Pueblo, ca. 1350 to present

Approximately 2.7 miles north from the Taos Plaza on Paseo del Pueblo Norte; 505-758-1028 or 505-758-9593. The inspiring Taos Pueblo has been continuously occupied from sometime around A.D. 1350 until today. Despite the early arrival of Spanish missionaries and the late coming of Anglo culture to the Taos area (although some argue it is *because* of these occurrences), this pueblo has kept its Native American culture and religion alive. Its tribal rolls have grown from 830 in 1942 to more than 2,000 today; of these around 150 live in

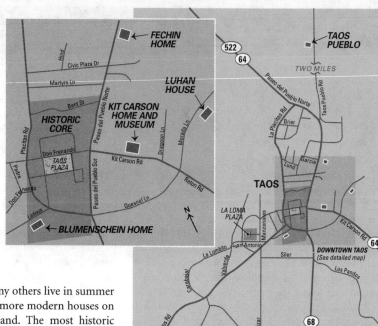

the pueblo full-time, and many others live in summer homes near their fields or in more modern houses on other parts of the pueblo land. The most historic dwelling featured in this book, in 1992 the Taos Pueblo was designated a world heritage site by the World Heritage Foundation of the United Nations, joining such peers as the Great Wall of China and the Vatican.

Taos Pueblo and its buildings and lifestyle reflect a different worldview than that of Anglos. A simplistic overview is that they (along with many other Native Americans) believe humankind is from and of the earth and shares a oneness with all living things. Humankind was created and born from mother earth and will return to it. Therefore we do not own the earth, and indeed are not even capable of owning it. The mountains and the lakes and the streams and all other life are supreme gifts from a greater being and are therefore to be protected, not exploited. As Tony Anella writes in his essay "Learning from the Pueblos" in *Pueblo Style and Regional Architecture* (Van Nostrand Reinhold, 1990):

The profound lesson we can learn from the Pueblos and their architecture is precisely the one suggested by the satellite image of the earth against the backdrop of space: that man is part of nature, not separate from it. The architecture of the Pueblos should not be seen merely as the picturesque perception of a simpler world. . . . By learning from the Pueblos, architecture can begin to complement the land by helping man to live with the land, and not merely on or in spite of it. The sublime beauty of the New Mexican landscape is its ultimate indifference to man's presence. It is an indifference that should remind us of our place within nature.

Some elements of this worldview are reflected in the pueblo plan, which is organized around the crystal-clear Rio Pueblo de Taos, which runs through the midst of the pueblo and is its primary source of water. A large communal space has been left on each side of the river

Taos Pueblo

and it opens out to a view of the Sangre de Cristo Mountains, which provide wood, plants, fish, and game. High in the mountains, between the prominent Taos Mountain and Mount Wheeler behind, is the river's source—the sacred Blue Lake, which was made a part of the Carson National Forest by Teddy Roosevelt in 1903. Shocked to discover that the Forest Service allowed tourism near the lake, the Taos Indians fought for its return to their reservation for sixty-four years and in 1970 won back 48,000 acres, including Blue Lake.

On one side of the central space is the North-Side Pueblo and on the other the slightly smaller South-Side Pueblo. Each of these is a multistoried communal structure made up of many rectangular rooms; exterior rooms are used for living quarters and interior rooms for food storage, eating, and some cooking. These structures are built of thick adobe walls. Their packed-earth roofs are supported by massive horizontal timbers brought down from the mountains and placed on top of the walls. The supporting timbers are then covered by a uniform layer of smaller wood pieces called *latillas* before the earth is added. Because of the difficulty of cutting the roof timbers, or vigas, to precise lengths with stone tools, the ends were normally allowed to project somewhat beyond the wall surface, where they provided useful exterior places to hang things.

Each primary family has its own rooms within the pueblo, most often two for the uses described above. Each of these dwelling units is discrete and does not open to the units either behind or on either side, but only through its exterior door. The original exterior entrance was not through doors, but rather through openings in the roofs with ladders leading to them that could be pulled up to afford protection. Ladders are still used to reach the upper stories. As late as 1900 there were few windows, but today many have been cut into the walls. The interiors are covered with a thin wash of white earth, or *tierra blanca,* a mixture of locally occurring white mica clay and cooked wheat paste, which gives the rooms a very bright finish. A number of shops are located at ground level, which give you the opportunity to go inside some rooms of the pueblo.

Other visible elements include the large beehive ovens, or *hornos,* traditionally used for baking, and large wood drying racks for food. Beyond the pueblos you may see fences with tall poles projecting into the air behind them. These mark the locations of the pueblo's six kivas, which are sacred ceremonial chambers. These large underground rooms are used for religious rituals and are inviolable; non-Taos should never approach them. The Catholic San Geronimo Chapel, completed in 1850 to replace the original church, is also on the grounds. About 90 percent of the Taos Pueblo Indians are Catholic, a religion that is not in conflict with the ancient Indian religious rites and that is practiced along with them.

The Taos Pueblo has elected not to allow electricity or running water or plumbing within the pueblo walls. This is a reminder that while the Taos Indians have incorporated many Hispanic and Anglo customs and objects into their lives, they have withstood being engulfed by either of these cultures. They maintain today a life of community and of family that has been deeply rooted to the soil and to their ancestors for thousands of years in the lands of the Southwest.

Martinez Hacienda

Martinez Hacienda, 1804 and later

Ranchitos Road (New Mexico Highway 240) about two miles southwest of the plaza; 505-758-0505.

This early Spanish Colonial hacienda (rural house) has excellent self-guided explanations of the rugged life-styles on the northern edges of Spanish colonization. Eighteen of the hacienda's twenty-one rooms are open to the public (the eight rooms located in the rear *placita* are reconstructions based on archaeological evidence). Almost every room relates to some aspect of everyday life and the regional economy around Taos. The small booklet *La Hacienda de los Martinez: A Brief History,* by Skip Keith Miller, is a recommended accompaniment to a tour, as it is based on relatively new research in Spanish borderlands history.

Antonio Severino Martinez (1761–1827) was born in northern New Mexico and purchased his original piece of land in 1803; it was sixty varas (a vara equals about thirty-three inches) in length along the Rio Pueblo and stretched from the river up to a ridge one and a half miles to the west. A piece of land in a long narrow shape like this included water from the river for irrigation of riverside crops, as well as grazing land for cattle and sheep on the drier uplands. This practical "long-lot" method of parceling out early agricultural lands was a typical Spanish practice. The irrigated fields were mostly devoted to growing wheat, a crop brought to New Mexico by the Spanish. The cool Taos area was ideal for this crop and is often called the Breadbasket of Northern New Mexico. Martinez built this home, or at least the front *placita* (courtyard), almost immediately. Although nomadic Indian tribes from nearby were engaging in fewer raids at this time, Martinez was taking no chances and built a completely enclosed house with central courtyard. The essential water well is safely in-

Martinez Hacienda

side the courtyard, and the exterior walls have no windows. The parapet walls about the roof have openings for guns, thus giving the family the safety of a fort. Almost every aspect of everyday domestic and work life was carried out within the hacienda, called the *casa major* by Martinez. Surprisingly few of the rooms were used for family living. A large *sala* was the primary living, dining, and even bedroom for the family. Furnishings were fairly sparse in the early years and would have been slowly added over time. There were two other rooms likely used primarily for sleeping in the early days and later several others, now private, for the grown children and their families. There is also a small room interpreted as a chapel, a use found in many of the wealthier Spanish Colonial homes. The kitchen, grain storage room, and cold storage room were used to store and prepare food for the hacienda.

The largest room in the front *placita*, called La Sala Grande, had many uses. Its importance is made clear by its wooden floor, a very expensive and time-consuming luxury to produce in a period with few metal tools. This room was provided for community events such as meetings and fandangos (dances). Martinez occupied an important place in the Taos community, serving as *alcalde* (mayor) twice and three times as the northern New Mexico delegate to the Republic of Mexico's Territorial Assembly for New Mexico. This room, like many in the hacienda, is covered with *tierra blanca* (see page 455).

But this hacienda was more than just a home; it was also a trading post for the Taos area. Don Martinez was an important merchant in early Taos, and many of the rooms are interpreted to reflect this important role. Martinez invested in (and at least once accompanied) the trade caravan that traveled annually between Santa Fe and Chihuahua. This was the major way that supplies came into northern New Mexico and that goods produced there could find a market. Cloth, raw iron bars, paper, medicines, tobacco, books, mirrors, and glass were some of the kinds of goods coming from Chihuahua. It was then a barter, rather than a cash, economy, and the New Mexicans traded hides of buffalo, deer, and antelope; corn; piñon (pine) nuts; wheat; sheep; and many locally woven woolen products, such as blankets and *jergas,* for the Chihuahuan goods. These annual caravans began around 1724 and continued until 1821, when the new government of independent Mexico allowed American goods to be brought in via the Santa Fe Trail, and trade could then go in both directions. When this happened, Don Martinez could obtain goods from the United States for his trading post. This freer trade with the United States that opened a second market for New Mexican products is what finally gave New Mexico a cash economy. The Trade Room displays some of the kinds of goods that would have been bartered, bought, or sold here.

The rear *placita* has been restored based on archaeological evidence and today contains displays that relate to nineteenth-century life in northern New Mexico. It includes a weaving room (which has an illuminating explanation of how churro and merino sheep related to the quality of Indian woven goods and the local economy), Santos display, tack room, servants' quarters, and

Martinez Hacienda

blacksmith's shop. The latter was likely never included in the hacienda while Don Antonio Martinez was alive. Metal was very scarce in northern New Mexico. The only way to get it was to import bars of iron from Spain to Mexico and then up the trail to Taos. A measure of its scarcity is the fact that Martinez mentioned every nail that he owned in his will! Metal tools were even more precious during his lifetime. However, such a shop was likely to have been added after 1827, when his son took over the ranch.

One of the reasons that Martinez Hacienda has survived is that Martinez's youngest son, Pascual Bailon Martinez, eventually became the sole heir to the hacienda and continued to build up the ranch and trade operations until his death in 1882. The hacienda then stayed in his heirs' hands until 1931. It began to fall into disrepair at about the time of World War II, and in 1964 Jerome and Anne Milord purchased the home with the intent of restoration. When they could not complete this massive undertaking, they sold it to the Kit Carson Historic Museums, which completed the restoration and interpretation of this very important site.

Kit Carson Home, 1825

Kit Carson Road; 505-758-0505.

Kit Carson (1809–1868) was one of the mythic figures of the American West, and this home gains its landmark status because he purchased the front three rooms in 1843 as a wedding gift for his wife Josefa Jaramillo (1829–1868). They lived here for twenty-five years. Carson was born in Kentucky and at seventeen left his saddle-making apprenticeship to go to Santa Fe where he was a cook and mountain man (as the fur trappers who came to the western mountains were called) until 1842. That year he became John C. Frémont's guide and companion in many adventures, including participating in the Bear Flag Revolt of 1846 (see page 265). Frémont's books about these adventures are what made "Kit Carson" a household name. Subsequent to this Carson became, in rapid succession, a sheep rancher, an Indian agent, a brigadier general in the Civil War, a tactician in campaigns against the Indians after the Civil War, and, finally, the superintendent of Indian Affairs for the Colorado Territory. He had a working knowledge of Spanish and eleven Indian languages as well as the universal sign language. He had eight children with Josefa, who died from the complications of childbirth just one month before Carson died of an aneurysm. His varied career spanned almost all of the major phases of the settlement of the American West.

He met success in many different endeavors, but Carson's great success as a sheep rancher between 1847 and 1853 was one of the most economically rewarding. In his final year of ranching, 1853, Carson herded 6,500 sheep from Taos to Sacramento, California, using his accumulated knowledge of western trails and Indian culture to shepherd the herd through this long and treacherous journey. The sheep, which had been purchased for 50 cents a head in the sheep-raising center of northern New Mexico, brought a premium price of $5.50 a head in the gold rush supply town of Sacramento—giving Carson a handsome profit of more than $32,000.

The Carson House underwent its first restoration in the early twentieth century. Today it is joined to an older rear house by a new side wing, and archaeological work is being done on this rear house (which was never the Carsons'). Their three front rooms are furnished as domestic living spaces but contain only a few personal possessions, among them one of Carson's desks. Varied exhibits are on display in the other rooms.

Blumenschein Home, ca. 1800 and later

222 Ledoux Street; 505-758-0505.

Ernest L. Blumenschein (1874–1960) was one of the six cofounders, in 1915, of the famous Taos Society of Artists, which was formed to exhibit their works in galleries throughout the country. Blumenschein had first visited Taos by accident—a wagon wheel broke nearby as he and a friend were driving their surrey to Mexico City on a sketching trip. The time it took for the wheel to be repaired was enough for them to fall in love with Taos and decide to stay here rather than continue on to Mexico. This was the first of many such visits. For many years Blumy, as he was called, and his wife, artist Mary G. Blumenschein (1869–1958), brought their daughter Helen Blumenschein (1909–1989), who became an anthropologist and artist as well, to Taos for the summer. In 1919 the family decided to move here permanently and purchased four rooms of this house; it was easy to divide adobe houses and sell parts of them to different people and this was a typical practice at that time.

Blumenschein Home

Over the years the Blumenscheins bought the remaining parts of the house as they became available until they had a lovely twelve-room dwelling. They furnished it with a creative combination of fine antiques, furniture made here in Taos, and an eclectic group of decorative objects, which includes works by all three of the Blumenscheins and Indian pieces collected during the twenties, thirties, and forties. After the death of her parents, Helen donated the home to the Kit Carson Historic Museums, furnished just as the Blumenscheins had left it. Artistic variety mixed with an intimately personal feeling give the house great charm.

The Blumenschein House is an excellent example of how incredibly changeable adobe houses are (see page 444). Their smooth wall surfaces, covered by an all-forgiving coat of plaster, can be added onto and changed almost at will and with little visible trace. Windows and doors can be moved from one place to the other, openings can be enlarged or filled in. Here the earliest part of the house is thought to date from 1797. Other parts were added later, a ceiling was raised, and windows enlarged. Some rooms were redone in the 1930s, in others the vigas sag with age and floor levels change.

Throughout the entire house, each room is both comfortable and unique, reflecting the creativity and relatively simple lives of the Blumenscheins. In the dining room the ceiling has ancient split cedar *rajas* laid over the heavy vigas, and a mock fireplace was designed to hide the relatively new hot-water heater (1928). It is furnished with Taos-made table, buffet, bed, and firewood box, and many pieces of Indian art hang on the walls. In contrast, the library has Anglo antiques, an Oriental rug, and new *latillas* laid over the ceiling vigas. The kitchen has its original electric *and* wood stove and a rather-amazing California Cooler for storing food. Blumenschein's large studio is made of two rooms joined together, with the ceiling raised and large windows added. At the end of the tour is a display of Taos School paintings and a history of the Blumenscheins' lives.

Luhan House, 1922 and earlier

240 Morada Lane, half mile east of Kit Carson Road; 800-846-2235 or 505-751-9686.

Mabel Dodge Luhan (1879–1962) had what one author heard as "a talent for talent" and another heard as "talons for talent." Easy to be confused—since this unusual woman possessed both the ability to identify the most creative artists and writers of her era and the creativity to lure them to Taos. She and her fourth husband, Tony Luhan, from the Taos Pueblo, created this large and welcoming Pueblo Revival home just for the purpose of bringing talented individuals to the American Southwest. In an interview (*Taos Magazine*, Jan.–Feb. 1990, p. 8) her biographer, Lois Palken Rudnick, said that Mabel "hoped that she and [Tony] together could articulate for the white race, of Anglos, a whole new way of conceiving culture. . . . She wanted to help Anglos and Western civilization to understand that it needed to reintegrate body and mind." She felt that Anglo civilization was both fragmented and materialistic. "Her analysis of what is healthy about Pueblo culture, although romanticized, still demonstrates a great deal of insight about why it is that when you have a community in which play and religion and work are integrated, you have the basis for a healthier society."

Mabel had a great deal of money to indulge these beliefs, and her interest in the arts had been nurtured through two earlier "lifetimes." She had remodeled a Medici villa in Florence while married to her second husband, architect Edwin Dodge, and entertained great artists and musicians while there. Later she had lived in Greenwich Village where she was involved in the 1913 Armory Show and been involved in cutting-edge causes like psychoanalysis. Promoting Taos and the world view of the pueblos was her third artistic "life," one into which she felt she had been reborn.

The rolls of those who passed through their home reads like a who's who of the arts in the 1920s and 1930s. Georgia O'Keeffe, D. H. Lawrence, and Nicolai Fechin were three who left highly visible legacies. O'Keeffe had established her reputation in New York City. It was Mabel Luhan who first brought O'Keeffe to New Mexico, where Mabel's husband, Tony, introduced her to some of New Mexico's scenic churches and mountain and desert views. What resulted are some of O'Keeffe's most extraordinary works, the products of summers spent painting New Mexican subjects during the rest of her long life.

Mabel's pursuit of D. H. Lawrence and his wife, Frieda, included glowingly descriptive letters and gifts of Indian jewelry, blessed by Tony, sent to Frieda. The Lawrences came twice in the early 1920s, and his paintings (for he painted as well as wrote, if perhaps not so well) are still visible on the windows of Mabel's second-floor bathroom. Mabel tried to give Lawrence a ranch in the hills north of Taos, but he refused, not wanting to be in her debt. Frieda, however, happily traded an original manuscript of *Sons and Lovers* for the ranch. Lawrence's love of northern New Mexico helped attract many other writers and artists to Taos. He wrote of his stay:

I think New Mexico was the greatest experience from the outside world that I have ever had. It certainly changed me forever. . . . In the magnificent fierce

Luhan House

morning of New Mexico one sprang awake, and the old world gave way to a new.

For Fechin's legacy to Taos, you will have to visit his extraordinary house (see page 461). His daughter, Eya, described the first summer she and her parents spent in one of the Luhans' guest houses in an article for *American West* magazine in 1984:

> There was a parade of visitors coming through Mabel's houses, all "famous" and all "special." I was used to seeing such people around my father; so this was a familiar scene for me—just many times multiplied and in a wonderful mountain setting where the air was so clear that everyone's foibles or beauty, cruel gossip and back-biting, as well as radiant originality stood out vividly.

When they returned for a second summer, her mother, Alexandra, had a "quarrel with Mabel [over rent] and insisted on moving at once." This was when the small house that was to be transformed into the Fechin Home was purchased. Mabel Luhan, who brought so many to her home, could be difficult at times and often ended up driving people away as well. But in this, as in so many cases, the original purpose had been more than fulfilled.

When Mabel purchased this property, it had an old adobe dwelling—three rooms all in a row. These comprise the long one-story wing with portale in front. The Luhans added various pieces to the house, including the Big Room (which Mabel's solarium is atop) in 1920

Luhan House

and the colorful Rainbow Room in 1924. The windows in this room are installed low, so you only see out when seated. The large dining room was influenced by Mabel's Italian-villa days. Only two other rooms are open to the public, the kitchen and the library off of the Big Room.

The home is on the edge of the Taos Pueblo lands and

adjacent to a main irrigation ditch for the Taos Valley that is lined with cottonwoods. A large inviting flagged terrace, which still has its early pigeon houses intact, lies between the parking areas and the house. When the Luhans lived here many of the nearby houses were part of the property, including a row of guest houses along the road. The Luhan House was designated a national historic landmark in 1991 and today houses a bed-and-breakfast and conference center. But to maintain the spirit of the home's earlier hospitable owners, the five major downstairs rooms are open to the public, and a small gift shop has a number of books both by and about Mabel Dodge Luhan. The furnishings in the public rooms are not original, although Mabel's hand-carved double bed remains in a guest room.

Fechin Home, 1927–1933

227 Paseo del Pueblo Norte; 505-758-1710;
Nicolai Fechin, architect and builder.

Tolstoy once wrote, "A Russian with nothing but an axe could build a house or shape a spoon." He was paying homage to the long tradition of wood-carving and craftsmanship that allowed northern Russians to create striking buildings in wood with only the most primitive of tools, an ax and perhaps a few simple wedges. Nicolai Fechin (1881–1955), an internationally known artist, grew up within this tradition. From his father, a master craftsman who carved elaborate interiors for churches and other buildings, in his earliest years Fechin learned about carving and carpentry. This early

training was then greatly enhanced by an intensive six-year course at the Petrograd Academy, which included architecture as well as painting and sculpture. It was in painting that Fechin made his reputation, but he only painted by natural light. When that began to wane in the afternoon, he turned to other arts, and while in Taos he chose to build and furnish this house. The somewhat-cool-looking exterior, which combines elements of 1930s modernism with the Pueblo Revival, barely hints at the warmth and life that lie within.

For six years Fechin joyously devoted himself to creating this house and to carving every piece of exposed wood in it—doors, columns, beams, cabinets, and furniture. Preferring to paint only by bright sunlight, on cloudy days, he worked at carving. He first used an adze to texture each piece of wood and then carved it in shallow bas-relief, hand sanded, and finished each piece. Even more impressive than the individual pieces is the manner in which they are assembled. Everything is asymmetrical, no two windows or doors are alike, yet all flows together with harmony. Every single view is carefully composed—as you look from one room into the next, each opening frames a perfect composition beyond. The effect is beautiful yet singular and is a testament to Fechin's multiple talents. He even worked with a Taos blacksmith to make all of the hardware, lanterns, and light fixtures.

And then in 1933 Fechin's wife, Alexandra Belkovitch, abruptly sought a divorce. He and his daughter, Eya, left Taos immediately in a quite painful separation from

Fechin Home

Taos Plaza area

their life and his work, living briefly in New York and then moving to southern California. But Eya had fallen in love with Taos, continued to visit there, and moved back in 1964. It is through her efforts that the Fechin Institute, a nonprofit cultural and educational foundation, was established. Under its auspices the Fechin Home, a remarkable work of art and architecture, has been restored and opened to the public. Almost every item in this extraordinary house is original to it.

Taos's Plazas, 1797–ca. 1810

The *Laws of the Indies* prescribed a central plaza for each Spanish Colonial town plan (see page ix). The plaza took on a slightly different twist in northern New Mexico. Here nomadic tribes of Native Americans had historically raided the food supplies of the agricultural Pueblo people in years of drought or hardship, and there was a need for Spanish settlers to protect themselves from similar raids. This was sometimes done in a single house, as in the enclosed courtyard plan of the Martinez Hacienda (see page 456), and it was sometimes accomplished in a small village that was also called a plaza. Here a continuous ring of houses was built around a central open space and had no windows or openings on the exterior facade. A central gate was provided and in times of danger all of the livestock could be herded into the plaza area and the gates closed;

making a very effective small fort out of the town. **Ranchos de Taos,** just south of Taos, began as such a fortified plaza. Today it is best known for the **Church of St. Francis of Assisi,** which has been made famous by legions of artists and photographers. The many houses that once formed the fortified ring around the plaza have mostly been turned into shops. Their rear walls, which once were solid, now have newer openings, and streets have been cut leading into the plaza. Nonetheless, it is easy to see how this was first designed to function and is quite instructive for that reason.

The original **Taos Plaza** was also a fortified plaza. Authorized in 1796 and built in 1797, the original plaza was quite large and covered an area that encompassed about eight blocks of downtown Taos. Remnants of the original fortified wall have been found in the Blumenschein Home (see page 458), which will help to give you an idea of its original extent. By the early 1900s much of the interior of this original plaza had been filled with newer structures and the more compact Taos Plaza you see today had begun to take shape. Then, a series of fires in the early 1930s destroyed all of the structures on the east, west, and north sides of this now smaller plaza. Most of today's Taos Plaza is lined with shops behind newer pueblocized facades. In addition, most of the older houses remaining in Taos's historic core have been converted to shops, restaurants, or bed-and-breakfasts. Nearby Ledoux Street, location of the Blumenschein Home, still has a very residential feel to it, despite the many conversions. The Kit Carson Home (see page 458) is another of the historic core's Spanish era residences.

A third plaza, **La Loma Plaza,** begun in 1800, is the only one of Taos's old plazas to remain residential. It has a large gravel courtyard with a small plaza in the middle and is surrounded by a variety of houses—older, newer, and modified—but the plan is still essentially intact. The Inn on La Loma Plaza is located just south of the entrance to the somewhat inconspicuous plaza.

Ranchos de Taos, historic view

North Dakota

BISMARCK

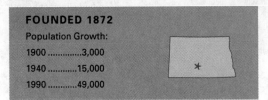

FOUNDED 1872

Population Growth:

1900 3,000

1940 15,000

1990 49,000

Bismarck is a railroad town founded by the westward-building Northern Pacific as it reached the Missouri River, the region's principal prerailroad gateway from St. Louis and Kansas City to the Dakota and Montana Territories. "Navigable" in this instance requires qualification, for the wide-but-shallow upper Missouri was an unusually capricious and unpredictable river, given to destructive flooding as spring thaws melted the snows in its mountainous source regions, then dwindling to a mere trickle by early fall. Even in the summer "steamboat season," the river was notoriously difficult to navigate. The river was nicknamed "Big Muddy," and the mud played havoc with steamboat boilers, which had to be shut down and laboriously cleaned at regular intervals. Even worse, the periodic flooding altered the river's channels and left behind a multitude of navigational hazards—hidden sandbars, half-buried trees, and, on its uppermost reaches, large boulders and exposed bedrock.

Several adventuresome steamboat captains tested the upper Missouri's waters in the 1830s and 1840s,

often losing their boats in the process. By the late 1850s specially designed shallow-draft stern-wheelers were making occasional ventures across the Dakotas and into the adjacent Montana Territory. These increased dramatically in the 1860s as new military outposts, and a Montana gold rush (see "Helena," page 382), made summer steamboat travel a principal means of transportation into this otherwise remote region.

St. Louis, Missouri, was the most important supply point for steamboats making the winding, 1,600-mile journey up the Missouri to Fort Benton, Montana Territory, the seasonal head of navigation. Bismarck soon changed this pattern as the Northern Pacific, with direct rail service to Minneapolis and Chicago, made the town a principal supply center for upriver destinations by eliminating a thousand miles of slow riverboat travel from St. Louis. Bismarck's importance as a transportation center increased still further after 1874, when gold was discovered in the Dakota's Black Hills. Soon hordes of gold seekers began arriving by both train and steamboat before embarking on a 200-mile stagecoach or wagon ride to the boomtown of Deadwood, center of the gold fever (see page 539). Bismarck's fortunes further improved when, in 1883, the bustling young city replaced Yankton (see page 541) as capital of the Dakota Territory. The former territory became two new states in 1889, with Bismarck as the capital of "North" Dakota.

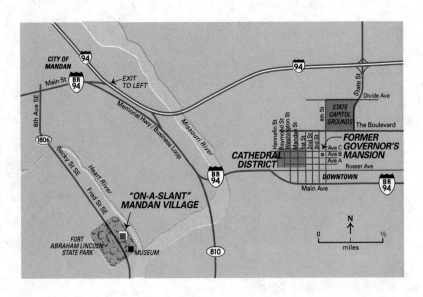

Cathedral District

Modern Bismarck

After this romantic beginning, the small city settled into a more workaday role as the seat of government, supplemented, after North Dakota wheat farming was established in the late 1800s, by its growing importance as an agricultural marketing center. Post-1950 growth has left little record of the pre-1900 river port town, but the city has an instructive Eclectic-era neighborhood, a Victorian museum house, and a nearby reconstruction of the earth-lodge dwellings of the Mandan Indians, the region's original inhabitants.

Cathedral District, ca. 1900–1940s

This small Eclectic-era neighborhood is regularly serenaded by the chimes of the modernistic Art Deco Catholic Cathedral of the Holy Spirit, built from 1942 to 1945, with a dramatic white tower that provides the neighborhood with both a visual center and a name.

304 West Avenue A (private). This handsome Shingle-style house, now owned by the Catholic diocese, occupies a quarter block and has a matching carriage house. The entire first story is built of rough-faced stone, cut and laid in different patterns on different parts of the house. Note the round porch supports constructed of uncut rubble stone and the fat, round tower, which anchors the corner of the house. The side elevation is carefully composed with a small first-floor oriel window balancing a large second-floor cantilevered bay window.

519 First Street (private). This carefully detailed, stucco-walled Craftsman bungalow has an unusual front-gabled roof, with jerkin head, intersected by a lower cross-gabled roof. Rock is used for the foundation and extends upward into a front-facing chimney, which contrasts with the adjacent stucco walls. The trellised front porch and window box add interest.

220 West Avenue B (private). A combination of Colonial Revival and Tudor elements is seen here, an association that is not uncommon in early-Eclectic-era designs. Most often a symmetrical house with a Colonial Revival–inspired entrance area is combined with a false-thatched roof and other Tudor elements; as seen here, a Palladian window above the front entrance combines with half-timbering ornamenting the side wings. (Two houses in the same general theme can be found in photographs 4 and 5 on page 369 of *A Field Guide to American Houses*.)

Former Governor's Mansion, 1884

Avenue B at Fourth Street; 701-328-9529.
This fine Stick-style home was built by businessman Asa Fisher in 1884. Nine years later the state purchased it for five thousand dollars and made it the official governor's residence. Twenty-one governors lived here between 1893 and 1960, when a new official residence was built five blocks north, and this home was converted to office use.

In 1975 the state decided to restore the early dwelling, much modified over the years, as a museum house, which is administered by the State Historical Society of North Dakota as a state historic site. The question then became what period to restore it to and how to furnish it. A general rule of historic preservation is to restore buildings to their period of greatest significance. With governors' homes this can be a difficult question, as there is usually little agreement on which governor should be so honored. Even choosing a general period can be complicated by the evolution of uses and furnishings in a house that has been the temporary home to many disparate families. Typically each family was allowed to modify and redecorate the house to suit

Former Governor's Mansion

its own tastes. Many occupants even brought their own furniture.

With these challenges, it was wisely decided to restore the exterior of the house to its appearance in 1893, the year it was purchased by the state. The house's interior was not made to resemble a typical house museum but is instead a "museum of the house," which demonstrates how the historic dwelling was used over time. For example, each room has a record of the many different wallpapers that have been used in it. The many layers of different-colored paint used on the woodwork are similarly displayed. Even the house's construction details are exposed in one place.

Also interesting is the history of the main windows in the rear parlor. Those seen today are reproductions of the tall, narrow windows that were originally used in this location. During the administration of Governor John Burke (1907–1912), these were replaced with a single large window with transom above; this remains on display in the house. This type of early "picture window" was very popular from about 1900 to 1915 and little used outside this period.

The house's only furnishings consist of several well-chosen pieces from different eras housed in Lucite displays in the middle of each room. Accompanying these are informative explanations of the room's use during different administrations and a history of the furniture on display.

"On-a-Slant" Mandan Village

Fort Abraham Lincoln State Park, four miles south of Mandan on North Dakota Highway 1806; 701-663-9571.

In addition to the partially reconstructed site of an important U.S. Army post dating from the 1870s, this state park includes the archaeological remains and partial reconstructions of a Mandan Indian village that was occupied from the late 1500s to the late 1700s. During this time the Mandan lived in villages made up of many large, dome-shaped, earth-covered lodges, each housing an extended family. The villages, as here, were usually located on high ground overlooking the riverside agricultural lands. The locations were also chosen to facilitate defense against raids by hostile tribes. Here the river offers protection from the east, two ravines protect the north and the south approaches, while a palisade and ditch were added for protection on the west. Originally the village contained about eighty-five earth lodges.

This was but one of many such villages built by the

Mandan and their village-dwelling neighbors, the Hidatsa and Arikara tribes. These tribes built up a complex system of trade among themselves and other more distant Indian tribes. Trade items included tobacco (which only men were allowed to grow in special gardens), other crops, and handcrafted wares. European-introduced smallpox, to which Native Americans had no natural immunity, had all but obliterated these tribes by the mid-1800s.

In the 1930s the Civilian Conservation Corps (CCC), guided by a Mandan Indian named Scattered Corn Holding Eagle, reconstructed a small part of the village. Here one gets a powerful feeling for the site and the proud people who lived here, as well as a look at the homes in which they lived. This is still a sacred site for the Mandan, and visitors are asked to respect this.

About an hour's drive north of Bismarck is the Knife River Indian Villages National Historic Site, where the remains of two other villages variously occupied by the Mandan and Hidatsa are preserved and interpreted.

"On-a-Slant" Mandan Village

FARGO

FOUNDED 1871

Population Growth:

1900 10,000

1940 33,000

1990 74,000

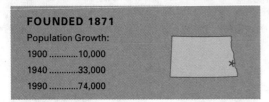

Fargo, like Bismarck 190 miles to the west (see page 464), was founded where the westward-building Northern Pacific Railroad crossed an important waterway, in this case the Red River of the North, which marks the boundary between North Dakota and adjacent Minnesota. This is the western United States' only large northward-flowing river. It empties into Canada's Lake Winnipeg 250 miles north of Fargo and, with the arrival of the railroad, became an important steamboat route into the Canadian province of Manitoba.

Fargo's river-cargo boom years were to be brief, for by 1880 new north–south railroad lines along the Red River Valley had largely replaced the steamboat traffic. By then, Fargo was developing a more permanent source of prosperity. The alluvial soils of the wide Red River Valley were proving to yield extraordinarily large crops of wheat, and a rush of "bonanza farmers" was making the region one of the nation's premier agricultural districts, a distinction it still holds. Fargo also

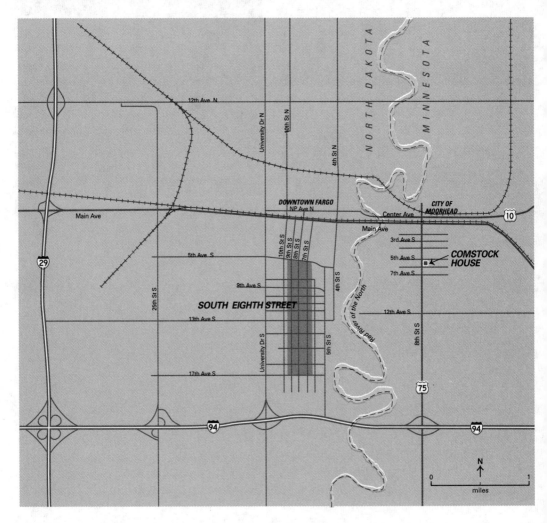

prospered as the region's principal trade and market center, a fact demonstrated by its steady growth as North Dakota's largest city. This growth has obliterated most of its Victorian-era architecture, but it retains a fine Eclectic-era neighborhood as well as an instructive Victorian museum house across the river in adjacent Moorhead, Minnesota.

South Eighth Street

South Eighth Street, ca. 1880s–1950s

Now an official historic district, this has been Fargo's most fashionable neighborhood since the late nineteenth century. Stretching for a dozen blocks due south of downtown, Eighth Street features a tall and majestic tree tunnel, an unexpected delight on the Dakota plains. Its many fine homes were built in approximate chronological order, with the oldest near downtown and the newest farther out. Thus a drive down South Eighth Street, and its adjacent Seventh and Ninth Streets, takes you from a handful of late-nineteenth-century houses in the blocks closest to downtown, through Craftsman bungalows and American foursquare homes built during the early twentieth century, to blocks of Tudor, Colonial Revival, and other period styles from the 1920s and 1930s, and ends with post–World War II Ranch houses at the district's southern boundary.

611 South Eighth Street (private), Roberts House, ca. 1885. This late-Victorian dwelling is an unusual combination of stylistic influences. If pressed for a style, we would choose Gothic Revival—making this a late example of the relatively unusual paired-gable subtype. A post-1870 date is indicated by the presence of cross bracing in the gables and the simplified ornament on the vergeboards. Several other styles have contributed to the design. Note the mansard roof behind the paired gables, a roof form rarely found in this style and obviously borrowed from the Second Empire style. The windows, with their segmental arches, are more Italianate than Gothic. The paired entry doors are particularly striking—their lower wood panels have Stick-style wood ornament. Finally, the shaped shingles of the paired gables are most typical of Queen Anne designs.

1115 South Eighth Street (private), ca. 1880. This large Italianate dwelling now has an enclosed front porch, a particularly common modification in northern, cold-winter neighborhoods.

1515 South Eighth Street (private). This is a delightfully asymmetrical example of the French Eclectic style. Most unusual is the side facade to the south. Here you can easily see the typical high-pitched roof, enhanced with two levels of dormers, the lower a row of three, through-the-cornice, hipped-roof dormers above which is a single hipped-roof dormer. Such double rows of dormers reflect French prototypes in which the high pitch of the roof made possible two levels of attic rooms. Another, smaller French Eclectic house is nearby at 1546 South Eighth Street.

1550 South Eighth Street (private). Frank Lloyd Wright's influence can be seen here superimposed on the later and more stark International style (see the following entry). This interpretation was likely done in the 1950s, when the style was often softened by the use of brick or wood wall cladding rather than the white stucco of most 1930s examples. Note the broad, flat chimney on the right front corner of house and the use of a sunscreen panel on the side rear.

1500, 1506, and 1510 South Ninth Street (all private). It is highly unusual to find such a streetscape of International and Modernistic houses. These are graduated in size, with the largest and grandest at 1500 and the smallest and simplest at 1510. The two smaller houses at 1506 and 1510 are International in style; 1500 is Modernistic. Note the prominent attached garages at 1506 and 1510. In the 1930s one was proud to show off such an up-to-date addition to the home. The garages held only one car, as few families then had more. At 1500 note the curved front corner with two glass-block windows wrapping around; the round window; and the horizontal line of the balustrade on the upstairs deck. The facade facing the side street received a second curved corner.

Comstock House, 1882

506 Eighth Street South (U.S. Highway 75), Moorhead, Minnesota (across the river from Fargo); 218-291-4211.

This large and welcoming Queen Anne home is a beautifully preserved example of an entire family's way of life. It is remarkably original in both architecture and contents. Inside are the furnishings, the china and crystal, the books and clothing, and even the doll clothes and children's games of the Solomon Comstock family. Comstock was an attorney who made his fortune developing land along the proposed route of the Great Northern Railroad. He highly valued education and donated time, influence, and land to founding nearby Moorhead State University.

All three of Comstock's children became educators. Most renowned was Ada Louise Comstock, president of Radcliffe College from 1923 to 1943 and the woman who engineered a crucial part of Radcliffe's merger with Harvard University. Both Radcliffe and the University

Comstock House

of Minnesota, where she served as the first dean of women, have buildings named Comstock Hall in her memory. Indeed, one of the authors spent four years living in Comstock Hall and dining every night underneath Ada Louise's portrait. Therefore, one of the treats of this particular house museum visit was to see Ada Louise's fine 1920s and 1930s evening garments and find it easy to imagine her wearing them to understated dinner parties where she set about convincing the Harvard faculty to allow Radcliffe women to attend their all-male classes.

The Comstock House's location on a main thoroughfare was typical of Victorian days when affluent families wanted easy access to downtown amenities. The house was built on a large corner lot, and its spacious side yard still survives. Upon stepping inside the home, one is greeted with warm oak and butternut woods, period wallpaper, and hundreds of books. The house is only two rooms wide and three rooms deep. Upstairs it is interesting to see that the family occupied one side of the house and a narrow hall and the servants' rooms the other—meaning that the family and the household help lived in very close proximity.

This closeness extended into the kitchen, where Mrs. Comstock herself oversaw the cooking. As in the rest of the house, the kitchen is remarkably original with an early stove and the family's pots and pans all still in place. The many personal items that remain with the house make it possible to give every room a lived-in feeling that is totally authentic, not re-created, making this a particularly warm and personal museum house to visit.

Oklahoma

ANADARKO

FOUNDED 1878

Population Growth:

1900 ....NA

1940 3,500

1990 7,000

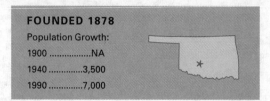

This small agricultural trade center and county seat was among the "overnight" towns settled by land rushes or lotteries when parts of the former Indian Territory were opened to unrestricted Anglo settlement from 1889 to 1906 (see also page 478). Located on lands previously reserved for the nomadic Kiowa, Comanche, and Apache, Anadarko was platted in 1901 adjacent to an important federal Indian agency established in 1878 to serve the Plains tribes.

Unlike some of its land-rush counterparts, modern Anadarko has honored its Native American past by becoming a focal point for the preservation and celebration of Plains Indian culture. It is the site of a weeklong American Indian Exposition, held each year in August, and also has such year-round attractions as the Southern Plains Indian Museum and, most important from an architectural perspective, a remarkable museum village that contains what is probably the nation's most di-

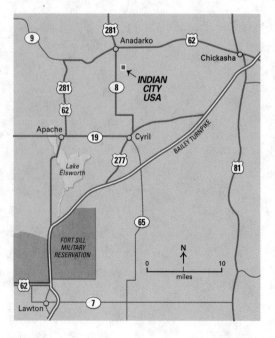

Comanche tepee village in western Texas

verse and authentic collection of reconstructed, pre-European Indian dwellings.

Indian City U.S.A.

Oklahoma Highway 8, two and a half miles southeast of Anadarko; 800-433-5661 or 405-247-5661.

This fascinating complex of reconstructed dwellings and associated structures is organized into seven "villages," each depicting the lifestyles of a different Plains or Southwestern Indian tribe (see the map, page 473). Planned and constructed under the supervision of the University of Oklahoma's Department of Anthropology, these range from the temporary, brush-hut wickiups of the nomadic Apache to the complex, multicomponent "apartment" structures of their town-dwelling Pueblo neighbors in the Southwest. Two different styles of wooden-walled hogans are featured in the Navajo village, which also reflects the southwestern culture area.

The dwellings of the four Plains Indian tribes are equally diverse. The Pawnee spent much of the year in large and permanent earth lodges that resemble small, rounded hills from the outside but have an intricate internal supporting frame of logs and timbers (see also page xvii). At the opposite extreme are the familiar tepees of the nomadic Kiowa and other buffalo-following Plains tribes. These were remarkably engineered portable houses, whose frames of light wood, and covering of carefully tanned, fitted, and sewn buffalo skins, could be quickly adapted for cold, hot, or wet weather.

The closely related Wichita and Caddo tribes were village-dwelling agriculturists who fashioned large,

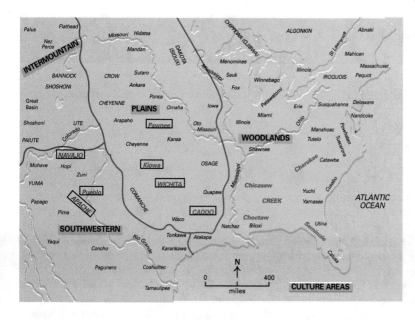

Pre-European distribution of American Indian tribes—Indian City U.S.A. has reconstructed dwellings of the seven outlined Plains and southwestern tribes; also shown in red are the Five Civilized Tribes of the southeastern woodlands that were forcibly removed to what is now eastern Oklahoma in the 1830s (see Tahlequah, page 492).

hemispheric dwellings, up to forty feet tall, made of an interlaced wooden framework covered with thatchlike courses of straw. The Caddo's original homeland at the eastern edge of the plains brought them into regular contact with Mississippi River–based French trappers and traders. From them some Caddo groups learned to adapt their traditional dwellings into rectangular structures with French-style walls of upright posts chinked with clay and covered by high-pitched, hipped roofs of straw or bark. This is the version seen in Indian City's Caddo village.

See also "Tahlequah" (page 492) for a discussion of the Five Civilized Tribes, southeastern woodland dwellers who, in the 1830s, were forcibly resettled to new "nations" located in what is now eastern Oklahoma.

Early Wichita village in Kansas

Indian City U.S.A.

BARTLESVILLE

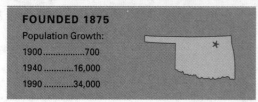

FOUNDED 1875
Population Growth:
1900 700
1940 16,000
1990 34,000

This was the birthplace of Oklahoma's vast oil industry, which, in the years from 1906 to 1928, exceeded even that of its larger neighbor Texas in the production of petroleum. From the early years of settlement, the Indian Territory was noted for its many oil springs, those whose flowing waters also contain small amounts of liquid petroleum that could be skimmed from the surface of ponds and used as a medicinal ointment or taken internally for a variety of ailments.

In 1859 Pennsylvania's Drake Well, drilled near similar oil springs, had ushered in the production of much larger quantities of subsurface crude oil that, refined into high-value kerosene, rapidly replaced candles and whale oil as a lamp fuel for interior lighting. Pennsylvania and adjacent Ohio were to dominate the nation's lucrative kerosene-based petroleum industry for the rest of the century, but, wherever oil springs were found, hopeful entrepreneurs sunk wells that sometimes found subsurface oil deposits. The Indian Territory was no exception; several small discovery wells were drilled

in the Cherokee Nation and elsewhere during the 1880s and early 1890s. Producing only modest amounts of crude oil, and lacking railroads or pipelines to move the oil to distant refineries, these were abandoned as economic failures. The territory's first commercially successful oil well was destined to be drilled at Bartlesville in 1897.

Located near the northwest corner of the Cherokee Nation (see page 492), Bartlesville was named for Indian trader Jacob Bartles, who opened a store and trading post here in 1875. By 1897, Bartlesville was a small village of two hundred inhabitants. In that year, Nebraska oilman Michael Cudahy, attracted by a nearby oil spring, joined local tribal leaders George Keeler and William Johnstone in drilling the Nellie Johnstone Number 1, named for William's daughter. At 1,300 feet, the well penetrated an oil-soaked sandstone that flowed fifty barrels per day, the territory's largest producer to date. Soon this oil-rich sandstone, called the Bartlesville Sand, was found to underlie thousands of adjacent acres. After the Santa Fe Railroad reached Bartlesville in 1899, these were to provide the future state of Oklahoma with its first commercial oil field as a steady stream of tank cars delivered the local oil to a Kansas refinery for conversion to kerosene. By 1910 Bartlesville had a population of six thousand and was the booming center of an important new oil region.

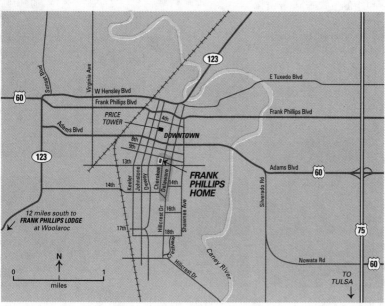

Among those attracted to this bustling boomtown were two talented young brothers from Iowa, Frank and L. E. Phillips, whose legendary careers were later to dominate Bartlesville (see the following entry). Today the city remains the world headquarters of the giant Phillips Petroleum Company, which was founded by the two brothers in 1917. Frank's fine Neoclassical home and rustic country lodge are now magnificent museum houses. Bartlesville is also the home of the **Price Tower** (Sixth Street and Dewey Avenue), architect Frank Lloyd Wright's only skyscraper, a nineteen-story composition in blue-green copper, golden glass, and white concrete that was completed in 1956 as the headquarters for a pipeline construction company.

Frank Phillips Home, 1909; remodeled 1931

1107 South Cherokee Avenue; 918-336-2491;
Walton Everman, architect; Edward Buehler Delk,
Kansas City, architect for the remodeling.

Energetic young Frank Phillips (1873–1950) grew up on his family's farm in Creston, Iowa. Seeking a career as a barber, by age fourteen he had achieved that goal, and by twenty he owned "all of the barber shops in and around Creston." He then married a banker's daughter, and his father-in-law encouraged him to try his hand at selling bank bonds for him. Phillips's second trip took him to Bartlesville in what was then still the Indian Territory.

Challenged by the opportunities of the local oil boom, Frank decided to move to Bartlesville, where he arrived in 1904 with his wife, Jane (1877–1948), and their young son. The next year he was joined by his brother, L.E., and the two began buying oil leases, organized the Citizens Bank and Trust Company in 1905, and then started drilling for oil. After an unpromising beginning with three dry holes, the brothers next drilled a remarkable string of eighty-one producing wells. They later sold their interests in most of these to concentrate on banking, but when the First World War caused oil prices to soar in 1917, the brothers reentered the oil business. In that year they founded the Phillips Petroleum Company with original assets of $3 million and twenty-seven employees. The company then grew rapidly, acquiring interests in the nearby Osage Field, in the Texas Panhandle, and later in the prolific Oklahoma City Field (see page 480). In 1927 they began direct retailing through their own Phillips 66 service stations, and by the 1930s the company's pioneering research and good management had turned it into one of the country's leading petroleum companies.

It was in 1908, after their first string of producing

Frank Phillips Home

wells, that Frank and Jane decided to build this elaborate Neoclassical home near downtown Bartlesville. It is of the full-height-entry-porch-with-lower-full-width-porch subtype that was very popular in Texas and Oklahoma from about 1900 to 1915. The Phillipses built on almost a full city block and surrounded the entire lot with a low stone retaining wall. The home has elaborate Ionic columns, and its relatively high-pitched roof, which houses a third story, is clad with tile. The side facade facing the automobile entrance features a second full-height entry porch, this one in semicircular shape with a flat roof. The front door, with sidelights and transom light above, is typical of the era. The design etched into the sidelights looks symbolic of the tall prairie grasses that covered much of the Indian Territory. The most prominent outbuilding is a large six-car garage that today houses an exhibit on the life and times of Frank and Jane Phillips.

There is little evidence of the extensive 1931 remodeling from the front facade, which retains its 1909 appearance, except for now being slightly asymmetrical. Even though the library on the left side was extended outward twelve feet, materials were carefully matched. Most of the work took place on the interior and on the rear facade, which received a large addition. Inside, the foyer and entry hall, the music room, the dining room, and the butler's pantry all remain close to their 1909 appearance.

A visit to the Phillips Home is a particular pleasure because almost all of the home's original furnishings were included in granddaughter Elizabeth Irwin's 1973 gift of the home to the Oklahoma Historical Society. She had lived in the house for many years and prided herself in maintaining its 1930s appearance. On display in each room is a wonderful series of interior photos taken after the 1931 remodeling that show how close today's house is to that time. Many family photographs are also found throughout the house, and all but three of the home's many Oriental carpets are ones chosen by the elder Phillips.

One enters the house into a grand Craftsman-style entry hall with mahogany beams, paneling, and woodwork and a large staircase, all of understated, early modern design. To the right is the music room, which had the silk damask wall covering and ornamented ceiling added in 1931 but is otherwise in its original state. The original dining room has a dramatic Arts and Crafts fireplace with green-gold tiles.

To the left of the entry hall is the large library, which was extended out twelve feet and had the floor lowered in the remodeling, giving it a hint of the "cube" room appearance that gained popularity in England in the eighteenth-century under the Adam brothers. An Adamesque mantel and other details enhance this feeling. The furnishings include great overstuffed sofas and chairs and a numbered Tiffany lamp to the side of the fireplace. Behind is the sunroom, which was a favorite of both Jane and Frank and was used for many meetings and bridge parties. Jane's needlepoint is seen here to great effect. The Phillipses had nine servants, and four of the service rooms are on display, the butler's pantry, the servants' dining room, the refrigerator and storage room, and the cooking kitchen.

Upstairs are many bedrooms with original furnishings, including Jane's elegant French suite. Two remarkable highlights of the second floor are Jane and Frank's 1931 bathrooms. Jane's is of pink marble with pink fixtures throughout. Most of the fittings are of solid gold. White fur covers the floor, and twenty-five mirrors, fifteen of them hand painted, endlessly reflect the white, pink, and gold color scheme. Frank's is more austere but equally intriguing. It is finished in greens, with a dark green marble sink and fittings of chrome and Lucite. A large shower and bath and "treatment" room surround the room. Mounted smack in the middle is a large commercial barbershop chair. True to his beginnings as a barber, Frank was a believer in having professional shaves. Early every morning a barber and an osteopath arrived to give him his daily "treatment."

Much of the third floor was turned into a recreation room in the 1931 remodeling, and here a Ping-Pong table sat in the middle of a large Oriental rug. Also housed on the third floor was Frank's butler, Henry Eignage, a Japanese immigrant who became a millionaire investing in the stock market, yet continued to work for Mr. Phillips. Tucked around the corner is a rather-nostalgic display of sand pails used by the Phillips children and grandchildren.

Nearby Houses

1200 South Cherokee Avenue (private), ca. 1930s. This late-Tudor house has an uncommon flair to it. Small pieces of flat, unfinished ledgestone form unusual corner quoins and window surrounds. The same stone is in a low retaining wall around the property. Smooth-finished stone of the same color is used for a unique entry porch with a stone parapet. The roof is clad with very thick pieces of slate. The main portions of the house are clad in brick and rough-finished stucco. Even the detailing of the metal downspouts accentuates the attention paid to every aspect of this home's quality materials and construction.

1500 South Hillcrest Drive (private). This Italian Renaissance design is a good example of the corner-facing Eclectic-era houses with slanted side wings that were popular in eastern Kansas and Oklahoma. The entry block that faces the corner has a round-arched entry door typical of the style. Above is a typical round-arched, recessed porch but with an unusual parapeted roof above. While the two slanted wings look symmetrical at first glance, they are actually different, probably reflecting the differing functions contained within each one. Note the corbeling on the chimney top. In this technique, each course of brick or stone extends outward beyond the one below it in order to support a chimney stack, oriel window, or such.

1408 South Hillcrest Drive (private). This towered French Eclectic house (a subtype often called Norman French) bends around the corner on its irregular lot. This informal style was particularly adaptable to irregular lots. Note the through-the-cornice window with a half-timbered gable above, the brick window surrounds, and the scalloped motif over the front door.

Frank Phillips Lodge, 1927

Woolaroc Museum and Wildlife Preserve,
twelve miles southwest of Bartlesville on Oklahoma
Highway 123; 918-336-0307.

This large log lodge was built as the Phillips family's summer home and a place where they could informally entertain guests. The entire home is huge, with nine bedrooms; nothing has been updated since the Phillipses left. Only the large living room and dining room are regularly open to the public, but these are fascinating. The home is a later western interpretation of the rustic Adirondack Lodge style popular in some late-nineteenth-century resort areas (see also "Tallac Historic Site," the Pope Estate, page 270, in South Lake Tahoe). The walls and ceiling beams are all constructed of large Arkansas pine logs with their bark left on.

The two rooms on display still have their original furnishings. A large collection of Indian rugs fills the living room. Animal trophies on the walls are all animals raised at the ranch—Phillips did not hunt. The two large wagon-wheel chandeliers were made at the ranch, while the four chandeliers made of horns were the result of Phillips's investment in the first Waldorf-Astoria Hotel. These are said to be the only things that he got out of that investment. The furniture is rustic, some of it made on the ranch during the 1920s. There is also some "Fort Worth longhorn furniture." Frank Phillips himself invented and reportedly patented a method for applying Arkansas pine bark to the picture frames used here. Then he took this same process and covered a Steinway dual-Art player piano with Arkansas pine bark for a unique instrument that still plays today.

What began as simply the Phillipses' summer home and ranch now has many additional attractions. Among these are the Woolaroc Museum, with western art and many western artifacts, and Native American Heritage Center, which features Indian crafts and a multimedia show, *Arrows Skyward*. There is also a two-mile drive through the wildlife preserve, which holds deer, elk, longhorn cattle, and one of Oklahoma's largest privately owned buffalo herds grazing in tallgrass prairie meadows. The five-mile North Road Tour takes you through more scenic landscapes, while a nature trail allows a more intimate look at the vegetation of Oklahoma's beautiful Osage Hills.

OKLAHOMA CITY

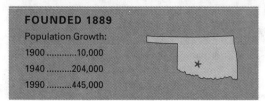

FOUNDED 1889
Population Growth:
1900 10,000
1940 204,000
1990 445,000

Oklahoma's largest city had the rare distinction of being "born grown." Throughout the 1880s, residents of Kansas, Arkansas, and Texas had fomented the "boomer" movement, meant to bring pressure on the federal government to release, for Anglo settlement, about 2 million prime but mostly unoccupied acres near the center of the adjacent Indian Territory. In 1889 federal authorities finally relented. Settlers would be allowed to enter these Unassigned Lands to stake claims to free 160-acre homesteads at noon on April 22, 1889.

Army troops guarded the territory's borders to prevent early trespass. By the next day, Oklahoma City's population had gone from about six people to an estimated ten thousand as vast hordes of immigrants invaded the former Indian lands. Though this 1889 rush was the first, similar events were to open much of western and central Oklahoma for Anglo settlement over the next two decades.

The location of the new town of Oklahoma City was no accident, for, by the time of the rush, the geography of the Unassigned Lands was already well known to non-Indians. In the late 1860s and 1870s, cattle trails from Texas to Kansas had brought many Anglo cowhands through the region. These visitors were followed in the next decade by the Anglo builders of the Atchison, Topeka, and Santa Fe Railroad, which, by 1887, had been completed along the route of the prin-

Site of Oklahoma City early on the day of the land rush, April 22, 1889 (top); downtown scene a few weeks later (bottom)

478

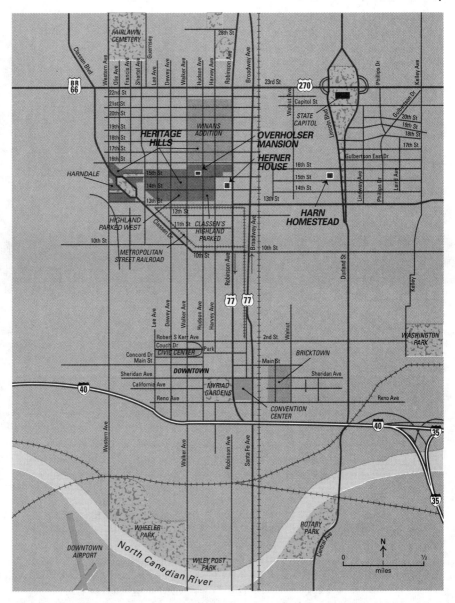

cipal early cattle trail. The point where the Santa Fe tracks crossed the North Canadian River (the Oklahoma Station stop) was recognized by railroad employees as an ideal city site, equipped as it was with both water and transportation. Until the rush of April 22, railroad employees were the only legal Anglo residents of the area. Either some of them, or illegal early arrivers called Sooners, had already staked out some of the new city's lots shortly before the rush began. What happened next was described by the local railroad agent, one of the site's six prerush residents (quoted in John W. Reps, *Cities of the American West*):

The first train from the south came in about two o'clock in the afternoon. It was crowded—people clambered together from the platform, on the car roofs, everywhere. There must have been two thousand persons aboard that train. The rush was on in full. Train load of humanity followed train load, and a city was made in a day.

During the following years Oklahoma City prospered as a market and trade center where the newly arrived farmers and ranchers brought wagon loads of produce to exchange for railroad-imported tools, hardware, cloth, coffee, sugar, and countless other items. By 1907, when Oklahoma was admitted to statehood, Oklahoma City had six rail lines, a population of thirty-two thousand, and was the financial and marketing nucleus for a rich agricultural region emphasizing wheat, cotton, and livestock. Further growth was assured three years later when a public vote moved the state capital to Oklahoma City from the smaller town of Guthrie, located thirty miles to the north.

Still-another boom arrived in 1928 when a wildcat oil well, drilled on the southeast edge of town, discovered the Oklahoma City Field, a supergiant that ultimately produced more than 700 million barrels of oil. The timing of this bonanza was most fortunate, for its development helped moderate the effects of the depression and "dust-bowl" droughts of the 1930s, as oil derricks sprouted in many backyards and even on the landscaped grounds of the state capitol, where oil is still being produced by the rhythmic up-and-down motions of "pump jacks."

Oklahoma City's hectic early growth slowed to a more normal pace in the decades after 1950, tending to rise and fall with the price of oil and the frequency of rainfall. The city's fluctuating fortunes hit a low in 1995, when the A. P. Murrah Federal Building (at the north end of downtown) was infamously bombed, but through its tribulations, Oklahoma City has remained the state's civic and cultural center. As in so many western cities, little of its Victorian architectural heritage survives, but it does retain an unusually fine Eclectic-era neighborhood (see the following entry) and three important museum houses (see pages 484, 485, and 486).

Heritage Hills

Heritage Hills, 1902–1930

Confidence in the "instant city" of Oklahoma hit a low in 1896, and its brash instant population of ten thousand dropped to only four thousand. Then the town began a remarkable comeback. With the 1897 Frisco Railroad junction, the city became a major distribution center, and by 1900 the population was back at the ten thousand mark. It was in August of that year that Anton Classen opened the first of the four main subdivisions that were to eventually make up today's Heritage Hills neighborhood—**Classen's Highland Parked Addition.** Development was slow at first; Classen had platted large lots and required extensive deed restrictions specifying expensive houses. But the momentum of the city and a well-placed new electric trolley line (of which Classen was one of the principal owners) saved him.

In 1902 the Metropolitan Street Railroad (actually an electric trolley) opened a line that ran from down-

town out Broadway Avenue, turned west, and ran along Thirteenth Street to Classen Drive and then down Classen Drive to Broadway and downtown (see the map, page 479). By 1902 the first houses were going up, and in 1903 Classen opened the adjacent **Highland Parked West.** Oklahoma's population boomed to sixty-four thousand by 1910, spurred by two 1907 windfalls—statehood and the discovery of the giant Glenn Pool Field (see page 495). Classen's two subdivisions blended into Oklahoma's most desirable neighborhood, advertised as the Highlands or Highland Park, and it gradually filled with expensive, architect-designed homes.

The remaining two sections of Heritage Hills are **Harndale,** just west of the Highlands and easily distinguished today by its diagonal streets and parklike boulevards, and **Winans Addition,** to the north. Both were opened for development in 1910, but a depression from 1911 to 1917 delayed their development. Oklahoma City's most prolific building partnership—G. A. "Doc" Nichols, formerly a dentist, and his partner, Horace Chandler, who had a Ph.D. in classics, were destined to play a vital role in each of these two neighborhoods.

The partners had begun building homes in 1908, and in 1917 they decided to expand their horizons by purchasing several blocks of Winans Addition. Here they began to perfect mass-production methods to build homes quickly and inexpensively—and modern merchandising to sell them as fast as they could be built. Their goal was to add value to their vacant Winans holdings by building houses—thus making profits through both home sales and the sale of lots made more valuable by the new houses. Chandler died tragically in the 1918 flu epidemic, but Nichols plunged ahead, and by 1921 almost every block of Winans had a Nichols-built home. Some blocks had half a dozen or more. With Winans rapidly being built out, Nichols looked to Harndale, which had only seven houses in 1921. Nichols bought the entire area and proceeded to do the two things he did best—build and promote. Between 1924 and 1929 he built every single house on Classen Boulevard, describing it as "the city's most beautiful and exclusive residential neighborhood" filled with "aristocratic homes." When Nichols completed Harndale, his next project was creating an entire new town, Nichols Hills, which he platted in 1928 to include bridle paths, curving streets, and a country club. It was so successful that it almost proved the end of Heritage Hills.

By the 1960s the majority of Heritage Hills' affluent owners had moved to newer areas like Nichols Hills. Those who remained, beleaguered by nonresidential uses and a street-widening proposal, worked together under the leadership of Oklahoma City mayor George Shirk to win a historic designation for the area in 1969. As soon as this was accomplished, all involved united to form a single group called Historic Preservation, Inc., known as HPI. HPI became a strong and forceful voice for preservation, not only of Heritage Hills, but of numerous neighborhoods nearby. Group members were remarkably successful in this, and today north Oklahoma City has five additional historic and conservation districts. HPI also undertook numerous Heritage Hills improvement projects, from code enforcement to streetlights. Between 1982 and 1984 they undertook a major survey to completely document the neighborhood, which culminated in a book, *Heritage Hills: Preservation of a Historic Neighborhood*, by Bob L. Blackburn and Jim Argo. This book's strength is that it thoroughly documents the builders, architects, owners, and changes of each house and accompanies each description with a photograph. This thorough documentation, rare in post-1900 neighborhoods, has made it possible to have unusually detailed data for the Heritage Hills entries. The architectural descriptions in the book are often not consistent with those in *A Field Guide to American Houses*, so you may find the same house described as one style there and another here.

Heritage Hills

327 Northwest Fourteenth Street (private), Gloyd House, 1912; Smiser Construction Company, builders. Prairie style married with a strong Italian Renaissance influence is a combination often found before 1915. The dark brick, Craftsman-influenced brackets, and a contrasting horizontal line under the eaves tip this example toward the Prairie. See also 325 Northwest Fifteenth Street (page 482) for a similar combination with a bit heavier accent on the Italian Renaissance.

1415 Hudson Avenue, at Fourteenth Street (private), Cooke House, 1904. A house built by Philadelphia publisher Edward Bok provided the inspiration for this superbly detailed early Tudor house. Note the distinctive look created by the close spacing of the half-timbering, a feature sometimes found on early high-style examples of this style; later examples are likely to have more widely spaced timbers.

401 Northwest Fourteenth Street (private), Ames House, 1911; Layton, Wemyss-Smith, and Hawk, architects. This handsome Prairie-style house was heavily influenced by the individualistic work of Chicago architect George W. Maher and particularly by his 1897 Farson House, now a museum in the Ridgeland–Oak Park (Illinois) Historic District. The parapeted edge around the hipped roof, the three-bay organization of the facade, the broad-framed upstairs side window, and the massive porch supports with a geometric decorative element were all used by Maher in that house. Even the broad pedestal urns on the upstairs railing are almost identical to those in early photos of the Farson House. The through-the-cornice dormer (with a ribbon of five windows) and the Sullivanesque detailing uniting the upstairs centered window/door composition are variations on the work of other Prairie School architects. Beautifully built of reinforced concrete, this 13,800-square-foot home is faced with limestone, roofed with Ludowici-Celadon tiles, and features a hand-tooled copper cornice and gutters.

Three Mission-Style Houses

436 Northwest Fourteenth Street (private), Vose House, 1907; James W. Hawk, Oklahoma City, architect. Heritage Hills has a number of fine Mission-style dwellings, among them this example and the two that follow. This symmetrical Mission design has asymmetrical extensions on each side of the main house block: a sunroom and recessed upstairs porch on one side and a porte cochere and sleeping porch on the other.

529 Northwest Fourteenth Street (private), Dunn House, 1917; Stewart and Wilderson, contractors. This Mission-style house has a broad through-the-cornice-shaped

Heritage Hills

dormer and two unusually large quatrefoil windows. The boxed eaves are unusual for a Mission house.

601 Northwest Fourteenth Street (private), Gerson House, 1909. Yet-another Mission-style house, this with unusually heavily textured stucco, squat columns supporting the arcaded porch, and two Mission-style roof dormers.

920 Northwest Fourteenth Street (private), Fitschen House, 1940. It is a treat to find an excellent example of a two-story Minimal Traditional here. Mainly built just before and after World War II, this style is more often seen in one-story houses. The trellis and carport look like later additions.

325 Northwest Fifteenth Street (private), Hogan House, 1912; James W. Hawk, Oklahoma City, architect. Italian Renaissance married with a strong Prairie-style influence is a combination regularly found in homes built before 1915. The light brick, the refined balustrade, and the combination of brick quoins with a quoinlike pattern in the porch supports tip this example toward the Italian Renaissance. See also 327 Northwest Fourteenth Street (page 481) for a similar house with a bit heavier accent on the Prairie style.

1521 Hudson Avenue, at Fifteenth Street (private), Hales House, 1916; Hawk and Parr, Oklahoma City, architects. Two beautifully detailed facades, each with limestone detailing and full-height paired columns, double the drama of this Beaux Arts mansion. The Hudson Street entry facade has a full-height entry porch enhanced by a balustraded terrace. The Fifteenth Street driveway facade has its columns set just out from the wall and a graceful canopy suspended above the door. Tall windows with ornamented blind arches enhance the first story. Note the elaborate cornice, the elegant Hudson Avenue door surround, and the wide frieze with attic-story windows.

501 Northwest Fifteenth Street (private), Noble House, 1906. This Prairie-style home has three thin horizontal lines of rough-faced limestone encircling the house below the porch railing. Exposed rafter tails under the roof and unusual stone ornament on the corners of the porch piers are other prominent features.

Two Italian Renaissance Houses

721 Northwest Fifteenth Street (private), Stewart House, 1929; W. H. Shoemaker, architect. This house has both symmetry and resonance in its design. The recessed entry has triple arches and is flanked by single windows with blind arches. Three groups of triple windows above continue the three-note rhythm.

825 Northwest Fifteenth Street (private), Ward House, 1933. Here the entry porch has a single arch. Double windows provide the theme, with blind arches above the two downstairs pairs and true arches on the upstairs pair.

915 Northwest Fifteenth Street (private), Towler House, 1948. This Colonial Revival–style home reveals its late date by the shallowness of the moldings, the mullion pattern of the downstairs windows, and the general stinginess of the porch detailing.

Three Prairie Houses

301 Northwest Sixteenth Street (private), Lee House, 1916. An American four-square house detailed in the Prairie style.

315 Northwest Sixteenth Street (private), Riely House, 1918. This began as a symmetrical simple-hipped-roof Prairie-style house and had the two-story left wing added in 1924.

316 Northwest Sixteenth Street (private), 1916. The asymmetrical Prairie style of this house is joined by a Mission-influenced tile visor roof.

326 Northwest Sixteenth Street (private), Brown House, 1929; Ray Smitzer, builder. This Spanish Eclectic house has a multicolored tile roof and a Moorish touch in the arched downstairs windows. The recessed entry has four successively smaller segmental arches, each surrounded by a cable mold (so-called because it looks like a twisted cable). The spiraled pilasters are more typical of the Spanish Eclectic and pick up the same "twisted" theme.

400 Northwest Sixteenth Street (private), Vose House, 1912; James W. Hawk, Oklahoma City, architect. Elegant re-

Heritage Hills

straint describes this Italian Renaissance house; a single broad arch on the right echoes the triple-arched window above the front entry.

Three Colonial Revival Houses

424 Northwest Sixteenth Street (private), Halmburger House, 1932; Keene Burwell, builder. This and the next two examples illustrate the diversity of Heritage Hills' Colonial Revival designs. This side-gabled version is more elaborately detailed than was usual in the 1930s.

425 Northwest Sixteenth Street (private), Clayton House, 1912. The detailing of this gambrel-roofed Colonial Revival house is very "correct" for such an early date and built so far from the East Coast. The three dormers, wood siding, and an elliptical fanlight over the entry give this house a lot of character.

439 Northwest Sixteenth Street (private), Flynn House, 1921. Side-gabled Colonial Revival, again.

319 Northwest Eighteenth Street (private), Barrett House, 1926; John McKinney, builder. After the first surprise of the exotic elements (horseshoe-arched entry, the figurative brackets under the balconies, and the sculptural "upside-down-pyramid" elements at the roofline), you will note that this is a fairly typical Italian Renaissance house given a Moorish flair by adding the above-mentioned enhancements. It was built for the owner of the Cascade Amusement

Heritage Hills

Company, who perhaps enjoyed bringing a bit of fantasy home.

G. A. Nichols in Winans Addition

400 Northwest Nineteenth Street (private), 1923; G. A. Nichols, Oklahoma City, builder. Now you are in the heart of the part of the Winans Addition developed by Nichols. This is a slightly smaller builder's version of 316 Northwest Sixteenth (see page 482), a Prairie house with a Mission-influenced tile visor roof.

410 Northwest Twentieth Street (private), Goldstandt House, 1919; G. A. Nichols, Oklahoma City, builder. This is how Nichols was interpreting the Italian Renaissance in a slightly less expensive house than the ones above. A similar house, also built by Nichols in 1919 and now slightly modified, is at 216 Northwest Twentieth Street (private). This was likely a pattern-book design, for there is an almost-identical house in Dallas.

418 Northwest Twentieth Street (private), Lykes House, 1919; G. A. Nichols, Oklahoma City, builder. Here builder Nichols is interpreting the Colonial Revival. It is instructive to compare this to the larger 425 Northwest Sixteenth Street (see above), which was likely designed by an architect. Both houses have a similar pattern to the entry porch, but Sixteenth Street adds an Adam-style door and brackets. This house has the wide roof overhang associated with the Prairie style (on both main roof and dormer), while the house on Sixteenth Street has a more historically correct narrow eave overhang. Next door, 422 Northwest Twentieth Street (private) is another 1919 Nichols Colonial Revival house.

442 Northwest Twentieth Street (private), Leecraft House, 1919; G. A. Nichols, Oklahoma City, builder. Prairie-style porch supports with Craftsman-inspired, exposed, cut-tail rafters were a favorite builder's combination, and here Nichols made good use of it. Wood-clad houses like this one were less expensive than those with a brick veneer.

329 Northwest Twenty-first Street (private), Naden House, 1928. This asymmetrical Italian Renaissance house is another builder's interpretation of that style.

G. A. Nichols in Harndale

1501 to 1618 Classen Drive (all private), 1924–1929; G. A. Nichols, Oklahoma City, builder. With almost all of Winans Addition built out, Nichols tackled Harndale, building all of the homes on this street in just five years. His individualistic variations of styles are intriguing and give this street a singular appearance. Nichols is no longer building the Prairie- and Craftsman-style homes that were a staple in his earlier and less expensive homes in Winans Addition (in the 1920s these styles were no longer fashionable). Instead he is now building Tudor houses such as those at 1508, 1525, and 1530 Classen Drive (all private). Numbers 1601 and 1608 Classen (both private) are examples of Nichols's own flat-roofed interpretation of the Mission style. Nichols must also have become intrigued with clipped gables (often called jerkin-head roofs), since these are seen at 1515, 1525, and 1618 Classen Drive (all private).

Overholser Mansion, 1904

405 Northwest Fifteenth Street; 405-528-8485; W. S. Matthews, architect.

Though he participated in the land rush of 1889, entrepreneur Henry Overholser (ca. 1846–1915) was a more cultured figure than your average western pioneer. Between his arrival in 1889 and death in 1915 at age sixty-nine, Overholser augmented his land and railroad interests by overseeing the construction of the 2,500-seat Overholser Opera House and of this Chateauesque mansion, whose pumpkin-yellow facade lends it an opulent air. Overholser built it to set a high and ambitious standard for the development of Heritage Hills.

Like William Harn (see page 486), Overholser was an Ohio native who landed in Oklahoma to exploit the wealth of land just opened for settlement. Unlike Harn, however, Overholser clearly sought to become a citizen of influence and prestige—an ambition that he admirably fulfilled, earning him the posthumous nickname "the Father of Oklahoma City." Before his entrance into Indian Territory, he had established successful mercantile, mining, and railroad ventures in such disparate locales as Indiana, Colorado, and Wisconsin. When he arrived with the eighty-niners to stake his claim, Overholser had the foresight (and resources) to bring eight prefabricated commercial buildings with him, neatly transported on several railroad flatcars. These were quickly erected, and ten days after the land run he was already renting eight two-story buildings in the new "downtown." He applied this same foresight and practicality to such projects as leading the fight to move the territorial capital to Oklahoma City, recruit-

Overholser Mansion

Hefner House

ing railroads, funding the first state fair, and even stopping a bank run.

In 1901, when Overholser bought the land to build his mansion, the plot lay a good deal north of the town's center—a location for which he was chided. But the four hundred guests who showed up for his opening gala on April 18, 1904, probably didn't notice the distance. Architect Matthews created a simplified Chateauesque design with a dramatic turret that dominates the house's profile. To this he added ornament less typical of this style—such as quoins, the columns that stand at the side entrance, and an unusual cornice.

The interior boasts a similar cultural mélange, and almost all of the furniture is original to the home. Bruges lace curtains, woven by Belgian nuns, hang from the windowpanes. The woodwork and molding were hand done by twelve Belgian woodcutters, who traveled to Oklahoma City to work on-site for two years. The unusual stained-glass windows facing the front staircase were designed by Anna Overholser (Henry's second wife, who died in 1940; when the two married in 1889, she was only eighteen) and made in Paris. Various French and Chinese antiques abound.

Though most of its furniture is original, the second floor has been repainted and rearranged three times since the house's construction. The third floor, once home to a ballroom and some dozen closets, is also open to visitors. The kitchen, with its fabulously retro 1931 Frigidaire electric refrigerator, antique butter churn, and vintage stove, offers the home's most realistic portrait of contemporaneous daily life in Oklahoma City.

In 1972 the home was acquired by the Oklahoma Historical Society, after a concerted communitywide effort to raise the funds and save the house of one of Oklahoma City's most admired early citizens.

Hefner House, 1917

Oklahoma Heritage Center, 201 Northwest Fourteenth Street; 405-235-4458; Albert F. Stewart, Oklahoma City, architect.

Though not technically within the boundaries of the Heritage Hills Historic District, the Hefner House (which sits just outside the Hills southeast border) serves as a fitting entrance to the area. The home's exterior grandeur and fine interior make a nice summation of the Oklahoma oil boom's material rewards.

Stewart built the house for original owner F. L. Mulky, about whom little record has been kept at the house. The exterior is an excellent example of the Neoclassical subtype most beloved in Texas, Oklahoma, and across the South: a full-height entry porch with lower full-width porch. Very unusual for this style are the two massive square Prairie-influenced piers that form two of the porch supports. When the home became a city landmark in 1972, a west wing and office were added to the original structure.

Judge Robert A. Hefner, a Texas native and future Oklahoma City mayor, bought the house when he relocated from Ardmore, Oklahoma, to take a seat on the state supreme court in 1926. The interior furnishings display Hefner's particular passion for antiques that boast a fancy provenance. The drawing room features a Louis XVI plaque table (ca. 1780), which reportedly came from the Palace of Versailles. Elsewhere in the room sits a furniture set from the palace of Archduke Franz Ferdinand, bought from the Austrian government after World War I. "World's fair" pieces include a German bedroom suite from the 1893 Columbian Exposition and a bed shown at the St. Louis World's Fair of 1904.

On the second floor, several wall-mounted glass display cases exhibit Hefner's cane collection—some 171 pieces, many associated with celebrities. A nearby display boasts Hefner's extensive bell collection. Judge Hefner was eclectic in his tastes, and the home's interior reflects many different design aesthetics. The third floor has been completely remodeled to house the Oklahoma Hall of Fame, an ongoing tribute to such native sons as Will Rogers, Mickey Mantle, Jim Thorpe, Maria Tallchief, and Oral Roberts—plus the requisite assemblage of judges, politicians, veterans, and socialites. The home and all of its furnishings were donated to the Oklahoma Heritage Association in 1970.

Harn Homestead, 1904

313 Northeast Sixteenth Street; 405-235-4058.
Reflecting the kind of unpretentious ruggedness characteristic of Oklahoma City's early days, William Fremont Harn (died 1944) purchased this quaint, Queen Anne–style home in 1903 from an 1891 *National Builder* catalog. Harn, an attorney from Mansfield, Ohio, had moved to Oklahoma City in 1891 at the behest of the Department of the Interior, which needed lawyers to settle claim disputes stemming from the

1889 land rush (see page 478). Harn's occupation, which often involved prosecuting unscrupulous Sooners, made him rather unpopular in his new hometown. He received frequent death threats, and hate mail depicting Harn being hung or drawn and quartered can now be found in Oklahoma's State Museum. Despite such perils, Harn lived in Oklahoma City until his death, during which time he owned a trolley line, raised registered Jersey cattle, began a housing development (Harndale), served as railroad attorney for local magnates Henry Overholser (see page 484) and C. G. Jones, and cultivated what he claimed was the largest strawberry patch in Oklahoma County.

The current 9.4-acre site of the Harn Homestead constitutes a mere fraction of the 160-acre tract Harn and his wife, Alice, purchased for $425 in 1896. The site had been the subject of a previous claim dispute, and the Harns themselves were not given the property title until 1902, when they proceeded to build their home. An 1889 two-room cabin already existed on the property, so the Harns catalog-purchased a modified version of the Eagan Cottage Plan to build around it. The home, made of yellow pine, was built in six weeks in early 1904 for a total cost of $2,106; a back porch and room were added a few years later. Though Harn sold much of his original property between 1910 and his death in 1944—even donating the northeast corner of his land to house the current state capitol—the present

Harn Homestead

site remained in the family until the Harns' niece, Florence Wilson, allowed the city to create a park and museum here in 1968. Today, the museum is operated by the William Fremont Harn Gardens, Inc., a private, nonprofit organization.

Though most of the interior's furniture and decorations are period pieces brought to the museum, a few notable exceptions linger. The gasolier light fixtures are original, and the home's Eastlake-style molding remains intact. The family never completed work on the third floor, intended to be a children's playroom. Harn reportedly believed that when his children became old enough to go to school and do chores, they were too old to play; he thus stopped work on the attic playroom.

Of the several outbuildings on the current Harn Homestead, only two are original: the Man's House, where Harn's superintendent lived, and the original outhouse. Of note among the transplanted buildings are the Stony Point School, an 1897 schoolhouse originally located near Guthrie, and the Shepherd House, which constitutes the only remaining building from the 1889 land rush. The two-story, four-room affair housed George T. Shepherd, his wife, and their eight children; the Shepherd House also purportedly represents the first home in Oklahoma City with a built-in staircase. In a nice bit of irony, Shepherd's land claim was one of the first that Harn prosecuted.

PONCA CITY

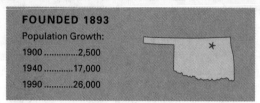

FOUNDED 1893

Population Growth:

1900 2,500

1940 17,000

1990 26,000

Located seventy miles due west of Bartlesville, which was the 1897 birthplace of the Oklahoma oil industry (see page 474), Ponca City was to become a formidable rival to its older neighbor after 1910. During the 1920s both towns came to be dominated by a single giant oil company and its visionary founder—the Phillips Petroleum Company in Bartlesville and the Marland Oil Company, which later became the Continental Oil Company (Conoco), in Ponca City.

Ponca City had been founded in Oklahoma's landrush era (see page 478) as a small agricultural trade center on the Santa Fe Railroad. No important oil pro-

duction had yet been discovered in this region (the principal finds had all been made farther to the east) when thirty-three-year-old Ernest Whitworth (E.W.) Marland (1874–1941) arrived in Ponca City in 1907 (see also the following entries). Unlike his rival Frank Phillips, who was a former barber turned bond salesman, young Marland was already an experienced Pennsylvania oilman and self-taught geologist. He correctly surmised that the lands west of Ponca City would prove richly productive and by the early 1920s had parlayed this insight into a fully integrated oil company, one whose hundreds of service stations were supplied from a massive Ponca City refinery. This impressive facility, now part of the Conoco Inc. complex, is located at South Fourth Street.

Like the industry that still dominates Ponca City's economy, the town's principal architectural sites are also the products of Marland's restless energy. His two Ponca City homes are now important museums, while a nearby neighborhood retains several fine dwellings built by some of his handsomely rewarded associates.

Marland Mansion, 1928

901 Monument Road; 580-767-0420;
John Duncan Forsyth, Tulsa and Ponca City, architect.
This austere Italian Renaissance palace stands as a monument to Marland's aristocratic, generous, and sometimes-unrealistically-optimistic personality. Begun in 1925 at the height of his wealth, it was soon to become his principal asset as his vast oil empire, overburdened by the costs of his visionary projects—many of them designed to improve his adopted hometown and the lives of his workers—passed into the hands of his New York bankers. Ever the civic-minded optimist, Marland then embarked on a new career in politics, and from 1934 to 1938 he served as Oklahoma's tenth governor.

Marland was a complex man. Born to an English father who became a wealthy Pittsburgh industrialist and believed strongly in primogeniture, E.W. arrived as the first and only son in a family that already had seven daughters. He was treated as a young prince by all of the family. Yet the same father also believed strongly in the rights of the common man and instilled this bedrock belief in his son. Pampered and privileged in his youth, as a young adult Marland saw most of his father's wealth lost in the depression of the mid-1890s. Determined to make his own fortune, he soon made his first million exploring for coal and oil in Pennsylvania and

Marland Mansion

West Virginia. In 1907 he lost everything in a financial panic and set off for Oklahoma to seek another oil fortune, which he did with a remarkable sequence of geological insights combined with extraordinary good luck. By the early 1920s he was worth perhaps $100 million (he always refused to compute his actual holdings).

With this enormous new wealth, Marland began to reveal the complexities bestowed upon him by his unusual upbringing. Not only did he provide unusually generous benefits to his workers, but he also began to indulge himself and his top employees with such aristocratic English luxuries as polo games, fox hunts, and game preserves. This palatial mansion originally sat on a 2,500-acre hunting preserve with five lakes, a nine-hole golf course, polo grounds, stables, a large guest house, art studio, and multiple other outbuildings and amenities that were to be shared with his senior associates.

In 1928, the year the mansion was completed, Marland found himself ousted from control of his beloved oil company and had to watch helplessly as his trusted lieutenants were fired by the new owners. That same year was also to bring dramatic changes to his personal life.

When planning began, the mansion was to be the home of Marland and his first wife, Virginia Collins Marland (1876–1926), a native of Philadelphia whom he had married in 1903, and the two children they had adopted in 1916, George (1897–1957) and Lydie (1900–1987). In 1926 Virginia died after a long illness. Two years later a Philadelphia court revoked the adoption of daughter Lydie, changing her legal status and name to that of her birth, Lydie Roberts. Marland then married Lydie, the daughter he and his wife

had adopted when she was sixteen. Lydie thus became the formal mistress of the grand new mansion. The Oedipal overtones, if not the reality, of this marriage aroused considerable gossip and innuendo.

Marland lost most of his fortune with his ouster from Marland Oil. He and Lydie were able to live in their newly completed mansion only briefly before moving into the art studio, where they remained for many years. Marland's most successful and glorious years were over. Yet he remained a political, if not financial, force in his adopted state by becoming first a U.S. congressman and then, from 1934 to 1938, Oklahoma's governor and a champion of the New Deal reforms of President Franklin Roosevelt. Throughout these years, the mansion was opened only for special occasions, such as his inauguration.

Just six months before Marland's death in 1941, the mansion was sold to the Carmelite fathers, who in turn sold it to the Sisters of St. Felix. In 1975 the citizens of Ponca City approved a two-year sales tax increase to permit the city to acquire the historic mansion. Today, a conference center and hotel is run on the grounds in buildings added in the years of church ownership. The mansion itself, now a museum house, remains almost exactly as E.W. and Lydie Marland left it. In Lydie's words, "My own feelings about the place are naturally emotional and personal—but I would like to say this much—to me it is a place of rare beauty and artistic integrity. A structure that is an expression from mind into substance, of the quality, the strength, and the heart of a man."

Built of locally quarried, square-cut limestone laid in irregular courses, the house has an imposing exterior. It is modeled after an early Renaissance palace in Florence, and the entry facade is quite private and urban—in some respects almost fortresslike. Inside, the elaborate original finishes, fixtures, and fittings all remain, although many of the furnishings are gone. A large book of original photographs in the entry foyer shows the rooms as originally furnished. Easily recognized symbols identify the remaining original objects throughout the house.

Highlights of the Marland Mansion include a series of elegant decorative ceiling treatments painted by Italian muralist Vincent Margliotti. The original silver and silver-plate light fixtures, sconces, and locks are still in place. Floors throughout are of polished terrazzo. The curved staircases are of marble with wrought-iron railings. Extensive wrought-iron ornamentation is used throughout the interior and on the exterior of the house.

The entry foyer features handsome stonework and a domed ceiling covered with a painting that looks convincingly like an intricate pattern of mosaic tiles. The downstairs gallery hall just beyond has an elegant vaulted ceiling ornamented with a painted chinoiserie design. At the end of the hall is a ballroom with chandeliers that cost fifteen thousand dollars each when new, along with eighty thousand dollars' worth of 1928-priced gold leaf. The dining room is paneled with English oak and has a large carved-stone fireplace and strapwork ceiling, giving it an "Elizabethan" character. Adjacent is a small octagonal breakfast room. This adjoins the original, and remarkably modern-looking, service kitchen, which is a feast for the eyes with its 1930s decor in grayed lime-green glass and stainless steel. Upstairs are guest and family bedrooms. Mrs. Marland's is of delicately carved limewood with a soft-pink Italian-marble fireplace. Several pieces of her elegant original bedroom suite have been returned. Mr. Marland's bedroom is paneled in oak, and two of his favorite polo mounts are immortalized in the carved-wood mantel. His suite includes an adjacent study and a walnut-clad dressing room.

On the basement floor, which becomes the ground floor at the rear of the mansion, are large informal living spaces. Among these is a large recreation room with a ceiling celebrating the history of surrounding Kay County, Oklahoma. An outer lounge was intended for swimmers and for hunt breakfasts prepared in its cheerful "Dutch" kitchen with colorful tiles. Outside is a broad terrace. Little remains of the extensive gardens that originally enhanced the estate. The focus today is the heroically scaled house, an amazing anomaly in small Ponca City and a fine remembrance of the unusual man that built not only this grand home, but much of the town as well.

First Marland Home, 1916

1000 East Grand Avenue, Ponca City Cultural Center; 580-767-0427.

The first home that Marland built in Ponca City, a less grand but also very fine Italian Renaissance design, has been preserved not as a museum house, but rather as a house that holds a museum. The original home is nicely preserved, but set into its rooms are not original furnishings but instead several exhibits: one on the Miller's 101 Ranch, where Marland found his first Oklahoma oil; one on the four Indian tribes that surrounded Ponca City; one duplicating the New York studio of Bryant Baker, the sculptor who created the Pioneer Woman statue that Marland donated to Ponca City; and the last the D.A.R. Memorial Museum. A highlight of the library, to the right as you enter the house, is a huge canvas of a foxhunting scene featuring Marland and much of his entourage, painted by Randall Davies. It gives a wonderful feeling for how this very English sport, which Marland so diligently pursued, looked when transported to the Oklahoma countryside.

The house has a full-width, extended-roof porch, an unusual feature in Italian Renaissance designs, where porches are mostly incorporated beneath the principal roof of the house. Craftsman influence is seen here in the open eaves with exposed rafters and triangular knee braces. The trelliswork between the paired columns supporting the front porch is also a typical Craftsman detail. The house is unusually broad for a central-hall design, and this appearance is accentuated by the low-pitched roof uninterrupted by a dormer. The broad effect is also enhanced by the one-story wing to the right and the small wing and very broad terrace to the left. This terrace actually covers one of the first indoor swimming pools in Oklahoma, a heroic fifteen-by-seventy-foot version visible from the basement of the main house. Originally the terrace was a grand viewing platform for the home's crowning glory—eighty acres of formal gardens between Central and Grand, which stretched all the way to Fourteenth Street. Marland, in his typically generous fashion, left the gardens unfenced and invited the citizenry of Ponca City to stroll in them as if his gardens were a public park.

Nearby Houses

Many old brick streets remain in the grid-plan neighborhoods near the First Marland Home, where many Marland Oil Company executives lived. Most of the surviving early houses are typical American foursquare shapes with varying stylistic detailing or Craftsman bungalows. Many are given a distinctive look by

First Marland Home

the local limestone, which was used extensively for foundations, porch supports, and porch railings.

417 South Eighth Street (private), Heck House, 1913 and 1920s. This house received a complete stylistic update in the 1920s when the Pueblo Revival facade was added. The family spent a lot of time in Santa Fe, grew to love the style, and decided to use it for their Ponca City home. This style is rare outside of New Mexico, and this is an unusual local interpretation. Note the left side wing with the shaped parapet and bell.

1104 East Central Street (private). This Mission-style design has three shaped parapets on the front facade—twin ones on the roof and a simpler one over the entry porch. The stone porch supports are of the local stone so often used here for foundations and other details. The front door has been modified, and the paint scheme is not likely to resemble the original version.

310 North Sixth Street (private). This is an excellent example of an American four-square-shaped house with foundation, porch railings, and column pedestals all of the local limestone. The pedestals provide bases for simple columns, and the porch wraps to the left. Number 218 North Sixth Street (private) is an almost-identical house with slight variations in the railing and porch-support design and the plan reversed so that the porch wraps to the right.

202 North Sixth Street (private). This gambrel-roofed Dutch Colonial Revival house has a pair of front-facing gambrels. Decorative details visible from the right side include a handsome Palladian window in the right gambrel, a refined roofline balustrade atop the one-story porch, and a pair of pleasing oval windows in the side facade. The front door is surrounded by an elliptical fanlight above and sidelights to each side, accentuated by narrow pilasters. The porch supports are ornate Ionic columns set atop limestone pedestals with stone railings between, in the Ponca City fashion.

TAHLEQUAH

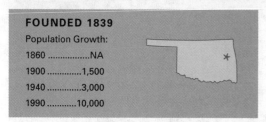

FOUNDED 1839

Population Growth:

1860	NA
1900	1,500
1940	3,000
1990	10,000

Few towns have had such a tragic beginning, or have so successfully turned initial adversity into later success. Tahlequah lay at the end of the Cherokee Indians' infamous Trail of Tears, a brutal 1839 deportation in which armed federal troops abruptly uprooted a peaceful, prosperous, and totally unprepared people from their ancestral homes in northern Georgia and sent them a thousand miles westward to a new "homeland" in what is now northeastern Oklahoma. Four thousand men, women, and children—about one-quarter of the Cherokee people—died from exposure, starvation, or disease during this long ordeal, which remains one of the darkest chapters of our nation's history.

A similar fate befell the Cherokee's southeastern Indian neighbors: the Choctaw, Chickasaw, Creek, and Seminole tribes. Known as the Five Civilized Tribes because so many of their members were already Europeanized and well educated before the deportations, these resourceful and resilient peoples soon overcame the uncivilized outrages inflicted by their oppressors. Indeed, the five semi-independent "nations" they founded were to prosper for more than half a century as part of a formal Indian Territory, which ended, over

much protest from its residents, with incorporation into the newly formed state of Oklahoma in 1907.

As the capital of the semi-independent Cherokee Nation, Tahlequah became the center of the tribe's educational, cultural, and political activities and remains so today. Its central focus, however, changed with statehood, which accelerated the tribe's integration into the surrounding Anglo culture. In anticipation of statehood, in 1901 all members of the five nations received U.S. citizenship, and over the next five years their tribal lands, formerly owned in common by all members of the tribe, were allotted by the federal government to the individual Indians. This made them Anglo-style landowners who could sell their property, but also violated a sacred Indian tradition of joint tribal use for all agricultural and hunting lands.

By that time the spread of Anglo culture had already become inevitable because the Indians were a minority group in their own homeland. From 1889 to 1906, most of the sparsely settled Indian lands to the west of the Five Nations had been reclaimed by the federal government and opened for Anglo settlement as the new Oklahoma Territory (see page 478). At the same time the Five Nations had themselves gained numerous Anglo residents who worked as legal immigrants, either for Indian employers, railroads, or as licensed merchants. Many other Anglos had become illegal "squatters" on the Indian lands. An 1895 census showed that the Five Nations had a total of 350,000 inhabitants, only 70,000 of whom were Indians.

Modern Tahlequah demonstrates the result, for

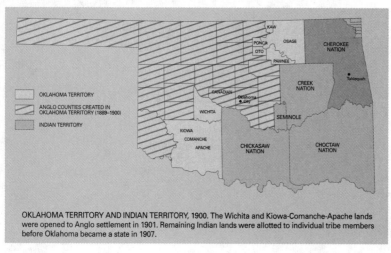

OKLAHOMA TERRITORY AND INDIAN TERRITORY, 1900. The Wichita and Kiowa-Comanche-Apache lands were opened to Anglo settlement in 1901. Remaining Indian lands were allotted to individual tribe members before Oklahoma became a state in 1907.

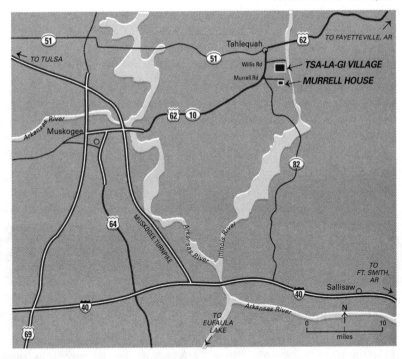

today it resembles any other small county seat and agricultural trade center of the region, but with one important exception. Like Anadarko for the Plains Indians farther west (see page 472), it remains the focus for preservation and celebration of the Cherokee's many remarkable achievements. These activities center around the **Cherokee Heritage Center** (see the following entry), which includes the Cherokee National Museum, a large amphitheater with regular summer performances of the Trail of Tears drama, and reconstruction of a pre-European Cherokee village. Nearby is the large, southern-style dwelling of an important early Cherokee citizen, now preserved as a museum house.

Tsa-La-Gi Ancient Cherokee Village, ca. 1650 (reconstruction)

Cherokee Heritage Center, Willis Road, off U.S. Highway 62, three miles south of Tahlequah; 918-456-6007.

The original homelands of the Cherokee people were in the foothills of the Appalachian Mountains in what was

Tsa-La-Gi Ancient Cherokee Village

to become the western Carolinas and adjacent Georgia and Tennessee. Already an advanced agricultural people when the first Europeans entered the region in the late 1600s, over the next century most of the Cherokee adopted a Europeanized lifestyle. By the time of their forced removal to Oklahoma in the 1830s, they mostly lived in log or wood-framed folk houses that were indistinguishable from those of their English, Scotch-Irish, and German neighbors.

In their pre-European history, the Cherokee lived in small villages of flat-roofed, rectangular-plan dwellings with walls consisting of a framework of small timbers covered with a thick layers of clay. Such a village has been reconstructed here, along with secondary structures relating to the early Cherokee lifestyle. During the summer months, craftsmen demonstrate some of the many skills of their early forebears.

Murrell Home, ca. 1844

Murrell Road, off Oklahoma Highway 82,
three and one-half miles south of Tahlequah;
918-456-2751.

This remarkable Early Classical Revival dwelling is one of the region's few styled houses that survive from the pre–Civil War era. It was built by former Georgia merchant George M. Murrell (born 1808), an Anglo from Virginia who became an adopted Cherokee after his 1834 marriage to Minerva Ross, niece of Principal Chief John Ross. The Ross family survived the Trail of Tears to establish prosperous new homes and agricultural enterprises in this vicinity. Ross's nearby grand Greek Revival home, like most houses of the Cherokee Nation, was destroyed during the Civil War. Although looted by partisan raiders, Murrell's dwelling somehow survived. It has a fine Adamesque doorway and six-over-six-pane windows that clearly demonstrate the taste and sophistication of affluent Cherokee families in both their old and new homelands.

In 1948 the historic structure, then in disrepair, was purchased and restored by the state. In 1991 it was transferred to the Oklahoma Historical Society, which operates it as a museum house. Inside are appropriate furnishings, most of them associated with the Murrell and Ross families. Beside the creek at the rear of the home is an early springhouse, an often-mentioned but now rarely seen southern amenity. Here milk, butter, and other perishables were kept cool by the flowing waters during the long, hot summers.

Murrell Home

TULSA

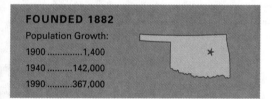

FOUNDED 1882

Population Growth:

1900 1,400
1940 142,000
1990 367,000

One of the West's youngest large cities, modern Tulsa is a product of Oklahoma's amazing early-twentieth-century oil boom (see also pages 474 and 488). The town was founded in the north-central Creek Nation of the Indian Territory (see map, page 492) as a cattle-shipping stop on the westward-building Frisco Railroad. In June 1901 Tulsa, still little more than a village, had the good fortune to be near one of the region's most timely oil discoveries, which was made at Red Fork, three miles to the south.

Five months earlier the nation's industrial leaders had been astounded when another wildcat well, drilled at Spindletop, near Beaumont, Texas (see page 554), blew in gushing an unprecedented 100,000 barrels of oil each *day.* At that time the entire nation's oil production, obtained from countless thousands of wells mostly located in Pennsylvania and its adjacent states, totaled only about 137,000 barrels per day. Here was a single Texas well with the potential of supplying more than half of the nation's oil needs.

Spindletop understandably focused the petroleum industry, and the national press, on the potential oil riches of the southwestern states. Coming so soon after Spindletop, the Red Fork discovery, which turned out to be a relatively small producer like all of the region's previous wells, ignited a firestorm of national interest. This has been vividly described by Oklahoma historian Angie Debo in his book *Tulsa: From Creek Town to Oil Capital* (University of Oklahoma Press, 1943):

The news sprang into headlines throughout the country—"Great Oil Strike," "Greatest Oil Well West of the Mississippi," "A Geyser of Oil Spouts at Red Fork." The well's modest production of one hundred barrels a day was boosted by the press to thirty thousand; it became, in imagination, a "great gusher," spouting "over four hundred feet into the air." Hundreds of investors . . . rushed to the tangle of hills and brush that made up most of the town of Red Fork, and oil men from distant states came to bid for leases. . . .

The greatest excitement of all over the Red Fork strike centered in Tulsa . . . [whose] days as a cow town were over. . . . Its leaders were determined that it should benefit from the oil development. In 1902 they organized a Commercial Club . . . and began to force opportunities to come their way. First they set out to get the railroads that were building so rapidly across the territories. . . .

Even more important was the determination to make Tulsa the headquarters of the oil men whose operations were extending south from Red Fork. W. N. Robinson started a three-story hotel, which served good meals and had a bathtub. The oil men appreciated these conveniences, but the treacherous Arkansas River, with its wide, sandy bed and its sudden freshets, lay between them and the field . . . crossing was still made by ferry or the more dangerous ford. Three Tulsans then constructed a toll bridge with their own capital. It was this bridge that enabled the town to benefit from the first spectacular oil strike made in the Indian Territory.

The initial, and modest, Red Fork well was but a prelude to a later discovery that rivaled Spindletop in importance. It was made in 1905 on the farm of Ida Glenn, about twelve miles south of Tulsa, and came to be known as the Glenn Pool. By 1907 this field had over five hundred wells and was ultimately to become one of the small handful of giant fields that have yielded more than 300 million barrels of oil. Tulsa, with its multiple railroad connections and expanding commercial facilities catering to the oil industry, became the focus of the Glenn Pool bonanza. By 1907 it was a town of seven thousand inhabitants. Three years later, as smaller nearby fields were discovered, Tulsa's population reached eighteen thousand, and it became the financial and administrative center of the prolific new midcontinent oil province, a distinction the city still holds today.

More riches were yet to come, as three additional giant fields were discovered in north-central Oklahoma over the next two decades. As a result, Tulsa's population again soared—to 72,000 by 1920 and 141,000 ten years later. This ended a decade that was, for Tulsa, truly the "Roaring Twenties"—a period of enormous oil-based prosperity and unbridled optimism. This spirit is still reflected in the city's remarkable collection of fine Art Deco commercial buildings added to its downtown from 1920 to 1940.

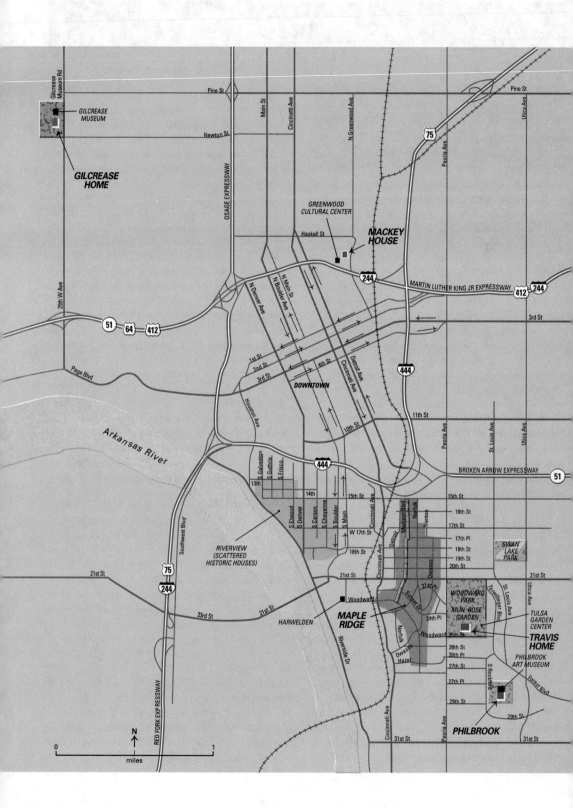

Along with the rest of the country, Tulsa's prosperity was interrupted by the Great Depression of the 1930s, but the petroleum demands of the Second World War revived the Oklahoma oil industry in the early 1940s and also brought Tulsa a giant new Douglas Aircraft bomber plant, which is still an important aerospace manufacturing facility. Tulsa's explosive growth rate has slowed in the decades since 1950, but the city remains a prosperous and handsome "oil capital" with fine Eclectic-era neighborhoods (see the following entry) and four important museum houses (see pages 498, 501, 502, and 503), each of them now associated with other civic activities.

Maple Ridge

Maple Ridge

When this upscale neighborhood opened in 1912, it was still on "the wrong side of the tracks." The wealthy beneficiaries of Oklahoma's 1905 Glenn Pool bonanza (see page 495) had begun building their homes just south of downtown Tulsa, along the bend of the Arkansas River in the Riverview neighborhood that lies immediately west of Maple Ridge. Today, apartment buildings have destroyed much of the Riverview neighborhood's original single-family character. Among the most important surviving houses are five listed on the National Register of Historic Places: 1322 South Guthrie Avenue (private), Clinton-Hardy House, 1920; 2210 South Main Street (private), Harwelden, 1923; 1414 South Galveston Avenue (private), McBirney House, 1928; 1610 South Carson Avenue (private), McFarlin House, 1918; and 228 West Seventeenth Street (private), Moore Manor, 1918. These five homes demonstrate the stiff competition that Maple Ridge faced in its early years when such grand dwellings were still being built in Riverview.

Located literally on the other side of the Texas and Pacific Railroad tracks from Riverview, Maple Ridge was mostly empty prairie, with the nearest streetcar line several blocks away when it opened in 1912. Its one great advantage was that its lots were restricted to upscale houses by protective covenants. As Tulsa's population soared and its commercial core expanded through the 1920s, these restrictions made Maple Ridge a favored site for upscale homes.

In Maple Ridge's initial phase, seventy-five acres north of Twenty-first Street were developed with north–south grid plan streets. A few years later additional acreage south of Twenty-first Street was added, and this second phase was laid out with Olmstedian curved streets. Today most of Maple Ridge's homes still survive, providing a delightful series of 1920s streetscapes that are enhanced by gorgeous mature maple

trees, farsightedly planted by the neighborhood's original developers.

2101 South Madison Boulevard (private), Skelly House, 1921; John T. Blair, Tulsa, architect. This was the home of William G. Skelly, who founded Skelly Oil Company, one of the country's largest independent oil corporations until it merged with the company of his longtime rival and onetime Tulsa citizen, J. Paul Getty, in 1977. It is a Neoclassical design with full-height entry porch—as is 1030 East Eighteenth Street (see page 498). Here the entry door with a tall transom above is remarkably understated for such a large home. The plethora of round-arched windows is unusual for the style. The Skelly House's overhanging eaves with brackets beneath are far more typical of American Neoclassical designs than is the Classically correct cornice, frieze, and architrave detailing seen at 1030 East Eighteenth Street.

2202 South Madison Boulevard (private), Flanagan House, 1923; George Winkler, Tulsa, architect. This delightful Italian Renaissance house is very unusual in its form, with a narrow one-story front entry that steps back and widens to fit neatly onto its triangular lot. The visor roof with parapet above, which tops the front porch, is unusual in Italian Renaissance homes but is common in Mission-style designs.

2222 South Madison Boulevard (private), Farmer House, 1921; George Winkler, Tulsa, architect. By the same architect as 2202 (see the preceding entry), this is a much more typical Italian Renaissance design. It has a hipped roof with a pair of forward-projecting side wings, and its Palladian-motif entry door is accentuated by pilasters and an entry porch with squared piers paired with Classical columns. There is much ornate detailing on the home, including floral swags typical of the contemporaneous Beaux Arts style. Note the double band of trim that stretches from the left side wing all across the front of the house and continues as a railing for

Maple Ridge

both the one-story entry porch and for the one-story right wing. It is accentuated with rectangular areas of floral detail. Some of the details look like they are covered with a thick coating of secondary material that masks their crispness.

2417 South Owasso Avenue (private), 1948. This is an example of the Cape Cod cottage (one-story Colonial Revival style) at its finest. The weathered gray shingle wall cladding is accentuated by windows with twelve panes per sash and solid-white shutters. The front door is crowned by an unbroken segmental pediment with a single line of lights below. The dormers, a typical way of adding light to a second story, indicate that this is actually a one-and-a-half-story cottage. Two lower side wings and a white picket fence complete this picture-perfect small house that is clearly based on New England Georgian precedents.

1016 East Nineteenth Street (private), Kistler House, 1921. This handsomely detailed centered-gable Colonial Revival home has a fine entry that includes a door with elliptical fanlight and sidelights and a one-story entry porch supported with fluted Ionic columns. Above is a Palladian window with deep moldings and small fluted Ionic columns. Notice the "tile" roof that is made of metal, a typical early-twentieth-century roofing material. Number 1008 East Nineteenth Street (private), just next door, is another fine Colonial Revival design, also in the centered-gable subtype and with a Palladian window above the entry area.

1030 East Eighteenth Street (private), Huntleigh, 1916; John Winkler, Tulsa, architect. Owner Dan Hunt wanted his Neoclassical home patterned after a house he had seen in Joplin, Missouri. Huntleigh's full-height entry porch is supported by six thirty-five-foot columns of cypress wood sent from Louisiana on railroad flatcars. The wide, divided band of trim beneath the cornice line is a feature typical of the Greek Revivial but rarely found in Neoclassical designs. It likely was a feature of the Missouri home that had inspired

Hunt. The wide part of the band above is called the frieze, and the narrower part below is the architrave; these two bands, together with the more usual cornice molding above, form the entablature of Classical Greek architecture. Here the frieze is decorated with triglyphs, regularly placed rectangular blocks that are divided into three parts, and guttae, small ornaments resembling drops beneath the triglyphs. This type of frieze decoration was prescribed for buildings using the Doric order. The entire composition of column (with base, shaft, and capital) and entablature (with architrave, frieze, and cornice) was called an order by the Greeks and Romans, and its parts were rigidly prescribed. Huntleigh copies the Doric order with an accuracy rarely seen in American houses. (The house next door at 1020 East Eighteenth Street [private] was built by Hunt for his daughter.)

1132 East Eighteenth Street (private), McGuire House, 1915. When Bird McGuire, a prominent Oklahoma attorney who had authored the enabling bill for Oklahoma statehood and served as the state's first congressman, retired from Congress to practice law in Tulsa, he could not find a suitable lot in Riverview for his new home. Maple Ridge's developers then offered him an entire block for six thousand dollars if he would agree to build a sizable home there. The sale was completed, and McGuire's decision to build this huge home was an important factor in making Maple Ridge an acceptable site for upscale homes. Soon many other prominent citizens were following the lead of the popular McGuire. Every stone in the home was handpicked in the nearby Osage Hills and delivered to the site by mule-drawn wagon, so the house could "look like Oklahoma." Unfortunately, Mrs. McGuire did not like the finished house, and it was quickly sold at a profit. It is a Prairie-style design, a very large but simple version of the hipped-roof-with-front-entry subtype. Although the exterior detailing is quite simple, its size and random stone construction combine to give it an imposing presence.

Philbrook, 1927

2727 South Rockford Road, Philbrook Museum of Art; 918-749-7941; Edward Buehler Delk, Kansas City, architect.

Waite Phillips (1883–1964) always had a wanderlust. He and his similarly named twin brother, Wiate, were only sixteen when they set out from their Iowa home for a three-year trek, during which they worked their way across the Midwest, down the Pacific coast, and returned via the Indian Territory. The twins' adventure ended abruptly when Wiate died of a burst appendix and Waite took his body back to Iowa and gave up traveling for several years. Then, in 1906, his older brothers, Frank and L.E., urged him to join them in their Oklahoma oil operations (see "Frank Phillips Home," page 475). Waite came and learned the oil business from the ground up. In 1915 he sold his shares in their company for twenty-five thousand dollars, and set out on his own. His explanation was that "when you're on a trail, someone has to be in the lead." Evidently he was tired of following.

Waite and his wife, Genevieve Elliott Phillips (1887–

Philbrook

1979), whom he had married in 1909, moved first to Fayetteville, Arkansas, and then to Okmulgee, Oklahoma, and finally to Tulsa in 1918, all the while using his twenty-five thousand dollars as start-up funds to develop new oil properties and build them into an oil company. Waite moved quickly, and in 1925, just ten years later, he sold the company for $25 million. His deep-seated commitment to fairness and philanthropy became evident after the sale, when he distributed 10 percent of the proceeds to his employees.

Waite's next undertaking was to build Philbrook for Genevieve and their two children, Helen Jane, then thirteen years old, and Elliott, then seven. Genevieve had always loved the villas of Italy and wanted a home in the Italian Renaissance style—she played a large role in the design of the house's interiors. As architect they hired Edward Buehler Delk (1885–1956) of Kansas City. Delk had graduated from the University of Pennsylvania, won a prize for a four-month sketching trip through Greece and Italy, and later studied town planning at the University of London. In 1920 he had been hired to consult on the development of Kansas City's Country Club Plaza, one of the nation's first and most influential planned shopping centers. Delk prepared the perspective drawings that were used to guide the project's final development.

As landscape architect, the Phillipses hired the distinguished S. Herbert Hare (1888–1960), also of Kansas City, who had worked with Delk in planning the residential district around Country Club Plaza. Hare was responsible for the siting of Philbrook and for the design of much of the grounds. Waite Phillips was particularly interested in landscaping and had a strong influence on Hare's designs.

From the front, Philbrook is understated and elegant; the more showy elements of Italian Renaissance design are nowhere in evidence. There is no broad terrace with balustrade, no triple-arched entry or recessed upstairs porches. The main front door is at ground level, and the windows are few, creating a simple and restrained entry facade. Only in the side wings did slightly more elaborate elements come into play. The exterior walls are stucco, glittering white because of the crushed marble included in the stucco mix. The refined exterior trim is of Kasota limestone from Minnesota, a soft-pink American equivalent of Italian travertine marble. It was not until one entered the house that its true richness and drama became evident.

With his restless and creative spirit, Waite never stayed long in one place. Just eleven years after they had begun their home, he and Genevieve donated it to the citizens of Tulsa for an art museum and also gave the income from their downtown Beacon and Elliot Buildings to help support it. The house underwent a number of changes over the years to accommodate the museum, but in the early 1990s a large new wing made it possible to restore important parts of the house. Several rooms remain much as built, and the original interior plan is easily understood. The exterior has been beautifully preserved, and the handsome sloping East Garden was restored in 1983.

Today you cannot drive up to the front door as a visitor would have in the 1920s. Instead the house is entered from the large rotunda of a new museum wing added in 1990. An excellent guidebook, on sale in the museum shop, is James Yoch's *A Guide to Villa Philbrook and Its Gardens,* published in 1991 and filled with original photographs and an analysis of the home's history. This book was of great help to us in understanding the home's multifaceted history.

From the museum's main entry area, you walk to the right and enter the original Villa Philbrook from the side, walking down its main hall, which provides a cross axis through the house. Continue until you see the divided stairway and lowered entry area on your right. To begin your visit as would a guest arriving in the 1920s, step down into the entry and stand in front of the original front door. The dramatic view was what greeted the Phillipses' guests.

After the understated, almost-severe, front facade, the richness of the main hall and adjacent Great Hall come as a surprise. Baroque columns, spiraled and entwined with vines and topped with elaborate composite capitals, support the intricately painted ceiling vaults of the main hall. The home is constructed of concrete reinforced with steel beams, and the columns were cast in two parts and put together to hide the steel support beams inside. The Kasota limestone used for exterior detailing is continued on the interior, used for floors and many other enriching details. The Great Hall is separated from the hall by steps and an elaborate decorative railing of steel and brass with panels of dancing girls. This room, built in 2:1 proportions (one of seven ideal room proportions recommended by the great Italian Renaissance architect Andrea Palladio), is twenty feet by forty feet and has a handsome painted ceiling above. A large fireplace is at one end of the room and an organ at the other. Triple doors open onto a loggia with five arches. Beyond this is the Great Terrace that looks out over the spectacular East Garden.

At the far end of the hall, and entered through a pair of striking ornamental iron gates, is the sunroom, which is encircled by full-length, round-arched windows. The room's focal point, which creates a delightful terminus to the hall view, is *Joy of the Waters,* a sculpture

by Harriet Frismuth depicting a girl dancing in a fountain. Beneath the large rug is a dance floor of glass blocks through which alternating colored lights showed from below. This was a last-minute addition by Genevieve Phillips, inspired by a similar floor in a Paris nightclub. Beyond the sunroom is the former South Terrace, originally an open porch but now enclosed.

The living room and music room are on each side of the main hall between the Great Hall and the sunroom. The music room held Genevieve Phillips's harp and is encircled with a mural of dancing girls by Philadelphia painter George Gibbs. Note the names painted on each wall: Andante, Rondo, Allegro, and Scherzo—with the paintings reflecting each musical rhythm.

At the north end of the main hall was the dining room, library, and breakfast room. The large pantry lay right where the house connects to the new museum wing. The decor of the dining room was originally similar to the rest of the downstairs, but in 1942 the Daughters of the American Revolution transformed it into a drawing room typical of Colonial America. Upstairs most of the rooms have been converted to art galleries with little of their original architectural detailing.

Genevieve was responsible for most of the decor on the two main floors of the house, but the basement was Waite's domain. It originally was to have held a billiard room, a gymnasium, and many service rooms. But these were turned into a group of informal rooms focused around Waite's interest in North American Indians and their art. One of these, the striking Santa Fe Room, remains largely in its original state. It is dominated by a huge painting of Philmont, the Phillipses' 800,000-acre ranch at Cimarron, New Mexico, which was painted in 1927 by Oscar E. Berninghaus (1874–1952).

Outside, the large East Garden was the only one fully developed by the Phillipses. Waite was very interested in naturalistic landscapes and leaned more toward informal designs featuring native trees and plants rather than formal, Italian-style gardens. When the East Garden was originally laid out, he insisted that most of the native trees remain in place right in the middle of the formal parterres of the top garden. These have long since disappeared, and it is easy today to appreciate Hare's original plan, which was carefully focused on the pool at the base of the terraced slope. The house and the domed temple at the opposite end of the garden were sited so that each would reflect in the pond when seen from the other, giving a double sense of drama to the views. The area between the house and pond began with the formal parterres just below the terraces of the house and then gave way to a wilder rock garden as it approached the pond. The more distant temple was placed in a grove of trees, and the surrounding areas retained the look of a native woodland.

The Phillipses' generosity continued throughout their lifetimes. Waite and Genevieve later gave their vast Philmont ranch to the Boy Scouts of America and donated to the city the land for the Tulsa Airport. And upon his death, Waite left all of his employees one-half year of salary for every year they had worked for him. All told, about 85 percent of his large estate was given to civic projects. The Phillipses' truly believed in one of Waite's favorite mottoes—"The only things we keep permanently are those we give away."

Nearby Houses

The streets that lead to Philbrook and that define its boundaries are filled with fine homes built mainly during the 1930s, 1940s, and early 1950s. Most are set on very large lots and feature stone wall cladding or trim. Tudor and French Eclectic are the most common styles. Number 1712 Twenty-ninth Street (private) is a stone-clad Tudor example. A towered French Eclectic design, also clad in stone, is located at the intersection of Terwilliger Boulevard and St. Louis Avenue (private). What appears to be a recent stone-clad Neo-French design is at 1332 Twenty-seventh Place (private).

Travis Home, 1921

2435 South Peoria Avenue, Woodward Park Complex; 918-746-5125; Noble B. Fleming, Tulsa, architect.
David Travis and his brother, who built his home next door, were Russian immigrants who came first to Pennsylvania, where David became a carpet salesman, and then moved to Tulsa to participate in its early oil boom. The brothers accumulated large real estate holdings, and David's handsome Italian Renaissance home was later built on eighty acres of suburban land.

Architect Fleming (1892–1937) was born in Oklahoma City and received his architectural license after apprenticing in that city. Here he created a fine example of the hipped-roof-with-projecting-wings subtype of the style. The home had twenty-one rooms and ten baths incorporating white, black, green, and gold marble. Because the Travis brothers were Jewish, and there was not yet a synagogue in Tulsa, the large basement ballroom was used for worship while the Travis family lived here. The mikvah still survives.

The house was sold in 1923 to J. A. Hull, who added the handsome conservatory. The home had only four owners before being purchased, along with ten acres of surrounding land, by the city of Tulsa in 1959. Since that time extensive restoration has been undertaken. The house is not a museum house, but rather the headquarters of the Tulsa Garden Center. A gift shop and extensive horticulture library are housed on the second floor. Much of the home's original interior detailing survives.

The central portion of the design is dominated by a large entry hall with a round curved cornice and a large decorative stained-glass ceiling. A handsome gold-leaf ceiling has been restored in the downstairs library.

Tulsa is known for its Modernistic-style architecture, found in some scattered houses as well as in many surviving commercial buildings. The Travis Home has a striking Modernistic powder room downstairs, added

Travis Home

between 1932 and 1936. It is filled with chrome and reverse painted glass that looks like highly polished marble. Note also the elongated hexagonal ceiling with its Art Deco lights.

The home's entry facade faces a long formal lawn that is appropriate to the style and period of the house. Today, most of the rest of the large block the house sits on has become Woodward Park Complex, which features a five-acre rose garden, designed as five formal terraces and constructed by the WPA (Works Progress Administration) in 1934. Behind this is an All-American Rose Selection Test Garden. Other gardens in the park include a rock garden, iris garden, herb garden, azalea garden, conservatory, and arboretum.

Gilcrease Home, 1914

1400 Gilcrease Museum Road,
Gilcrease Museum; 918-582-3122.

Thomas William Gilcrease (1890–1962) grew up in Wealaka, Oklahoma. He was one-half Creek Indian, and his family had moved to Indian Territory from Louisiana to take advantage of the federal land allotments made to each member of the Creek tribe. Young Thomas received 160 acres, which, in 1905, when he was only fifteen, turned out to be in the heart of the giant Glenn Pool Oil Field (see page 495).

Still a minor, the ambitious Thomas didn't trust his parents' judgment in dealing with his newfound bonanza, so he sued for majority rights that would permit him to manage his own affairs. He won the suit, and by age twenty-one he had been a farmer, a banker, a storekeeper, an oil speculator, and a millionaire. Mostly self-educated, throughout his long life Gilcrease read avidly and taught himself several languages. He also continued to pursue both the oil and banking businesses and traveled extensively as part of his self-education program. It was on a train that he met his first bride, Belle Harlow, who was a citizen of the Osage tribe. Their two sons were born in 1909 and 1911. Gilcrease purchased this home in 1913 for his young family. The house was already under construction when Gilcrease first saw it, on eighty acres and atop the highest hill overlooking downtown Tulsa. Flowers Nelson, a prominent Tulsa attorney, was building the home for himself, but Gilcrease fell in love with the house and location and convinced Nelson to sell it to him. There was no architect, and Nelson's builder, C. W. Kern, continued to complete the home for Gilcrease.

The home is a wonderful example of a one-story Neoclassical cottage. It has the hipped roof so typical of that subtype, which is here covered by green tiles shaped from metal. The shaped "tile" peaks, ridges, and corners have a pagoda-influenced shape that gives the roof an Oriental flair. The home's extensive porches and a porte cochere are all supported by Classical columns. It is built of local sandstone, quarried, cut, and shaped just a few hundred feet from the building site. The porch balustrade is robust, made of slabs of sandstone about twenty-four inches high, fourteen

Gilcrease Home

inches deep, and two inches wide. The entry door appears to still have its original hardware—a lovely Art Nouveau tree branch and acorn door handle and a matching tree-leaf doorbell.

One enters the house into a small entry area that opens into a handsome golden-oak stair hall with a simple Mission-type staircase. To the right are a small living room and dining room in much the same shape as Gilcrease originally built them. To the left are two large rooms, now used as exhibit halls for the Tulsa Historical Society. Originally, there were about five rooms on this side of the house, but these were converted into two large rooms in the 1920s—one for entertaining and one for a master bedroom. Only a few of the home's furnishings are original.

Gilcrease was less successful at marriage than at business and art collecting. He and his first wife divorced in 1926. A second marriage in 1928 was to Norma Smallwood, a Tulsa beauty who had become Miss America in 1926. It was Norma who presided over the home's interior changes during the late 1920s. Their marriage ended in a separation in 1933 and divorce in 1936. From this point on, Gilcrease devoted himself to art collecting. After several trips to Europe, he decided to concentrate on the then-neglected art created in North America rather than collecting the European materials favored by so many of his affluent peers. During the next two decades, Gilcrease assembled an extraordinary treasure that experts have called "the most impressive [private] collection of American painting and Indian art in this country." During these years Gilcrease lived mostly in San Antonio, and this home sat vacant or was occupied by one of his children.

Toward the end of his life, Gilcrease ran into financial difficulties. In 1954 the city of Tulsa voted bonds to purchase his home and collection. Then Gilcrease devoted his last years to organizing the museum and nonprofit society that would own and maintain it. After his death, the house was used as a home for the museum curator, then for a children's museum, then a geology museum, and finally for storage, before the fortunate decision was made to restore the deteriorating home as the headquarters of the Tulsa Historical Society.

Today Gilcrease's collection is housed in the modern Gilcrease Museum, built next door to his early home. As a result of his remarkable efforts, the museum contains 10,000 priceless works of art, 250,000 Indian artifacts, and more than 100,000 books and rare documents. Only about one-fifth of this total is on display, with the rest available for study by scholars. In Gilcrease's unpretentious words, "A man should leave a track of some sort."

Mackey House, 1926

322 North Greenwood Avenue,
Greenwood Cultural Center; 918-582-4185.

The Mackey House is the only home remaining of an extensive freedmanstown that was once located in this part of North Tulsa. Such towns were those developed by and for African-Americans in the late part of the nineteenth century and into the early years of the twentieth century. Many urban neighborhoods where African-Americans live today were first developed and built by some other ethnic group. In contrast, a freedmanstown is an area that was first settled primarily by blacks. Greenwood is a particularly interesting example because many blacks chose to move to the Indian Territory or, later, Oklahoma because of its extensive Indian citizenry and landholdings. This multiracial dimension would, they hoped, help them to be part of a true multiracial society. Still earlier, African-Americans had arrived in the Indian Territory with the Five Civilized Tribes (see page 492) that were relocated here from the southeastern states in the 1830s.

By the time Oklahoma became a state in 1907, many African-Americans had received allotments of land, either as tribe members or in the "runs" and lotteries that encouraged settlement by non-Indian citizens. As a result, some blacks became prosperous farmers, and a lucky few, with farms underlain by the region's oil fields, became very wealthy. By 1920, many of Oklahoma's affluent African-Americans lived and owned businesses in a thirty-five-block area of North Tulsa called Greenwood. This was the name of the district's principal commercial street, Greenwood Avenue, which had so many thriving businesses that it was known as the Black Wall Street of America. The Greenwood district also had a thriving music scene, which helped give birth to the Kansas City style of jazz.

All of this came to a tragic halt on the night of May 31, 1921, when a tragic Tulsa race riot erupted, the most destructive in American history until that time. When the riot ended on June 2, all that was left of the Greenwood business district were a few burned-out shells. In addition, a thousand nearby homes had burned to the ground. The black community vowed to rebuild, and by 1922 more than half of the burned-out churches were holding services again, and about eighty businesses had reopened.

Among the burned structures was the wood-frame home of the Sam Mackey family at 327 North Greenwood Avenue. Like so many others, their loss was not insured because "riot damage" was not covered by their insurance policy. But the Mackeys decided to rebuild. Not among the neighborhood's affluent families, they

Mackey House

were ordinary working people who made their living by doing domestic and yard work for others. It took them until 1926 to be able to rebuild, this time in brick so the house would not burn so easily. By 1930 they had paid off their mortgage. Their home became a symbol of the rebirth of Greenwood's residential district and was also the location for many community social events.

When an urban renewal project and the building of Interstate 244 called for the demolition of the home, the only survivor from Greenwood's 1920s rebuilding, Tulsa's African-American community intervened and saved the important structure. It now houses the Mabel B. Little Heritage Center, named for one of the many women who led the fight to save it from demolition. So important was this home to the African-American history of Tulsa that community leaders were able to raise $7,000 in just one week and over $100,000 in less than a year, primarily from the African-American community. The home is now a part of the Greenwood Cultural Center, where a new adjacent building houses an extensive photographic exhibit about the riot, a jazz museum, and other facilities.

The Mackey House, a two-story, redbrick Prairie-inspired structure provides a rare look at middle-class lifestyles of the 1920s. The floor plan is extremely efficient. A large living room runs across the entire width of the main house block. Behind this are a dining room and kitchen. The stairway runs sideways, dividing the living room from the two rear rooms. The base of the stairway faces the adjacent porte cochere, meaning that it is easy to go from upstairs to outside without passing through any of the main rooms. An adjacent sunporch opens into the living room, providing a pleasant secondary living space. The same room pattern is repeated upstairs, where a large master bedroom stretches across the front of the house, with a small sunroom off of it. Two smaller bedrooms are behind. Unusual for the 1920s are the spacious walk-in closets. The furnishings include a few original Mackey pieces; the remainder are appropriate 1920s items.

Oregon

ALBANY

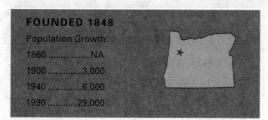

FOUNDED 1848

Population Growth:

1860 ....NA
1900 3,000
1940 6,000
1990 29,000

Albany, like its neighbor Salem twenty-two miles to the north, was one of several dozen small marketing and trade centers founded by 1840s Oregon Trail immigrants to serve the rich agricultural lands of the Willamette River Valley (see also pages 512 and 528). Unlike most of the valley's towns, Albany later experienced much of its explosive post-1940 growth beyond the original near-downtown residential core. As a result, Albany has two of Oregon's most intact late-Victorian and Eclectic-era neighborhoods.

These two complementary districts have an intriguing history that suggests the legendary feud of the South's rival Hatfield and McCoy families. Here the protagonists were two of the town's founding families, the Monteiths and the Hacklemans, who laid out adjacent residential districts around the riverside commercial center.

Their disagreements began even before the town was founded. Abner Hackleman had received the area's first donation land claim (free land offered to Oregon immigrants by the federal government) in 1845, but left the valley after only one year, and his son, Abram, returned in 1847 to take up the family claim. The fol-

lowing year two immigrant brothers from New York, Walter and Thomas Monteith, purchased the adjacent claim on part of which they founded Albany, named for their hometown.

Beat to the punch despite his family's earlier arrival in the valley, young Hackleman was not long in beginning the division of his claim into competing town lots. Hostilities became public in 1853 when residents of the Hackleman side of town successfully petitioned the state legislature to change the name "Albany" to "Takenah," an Indian word for a deep pool of water on the adjacent Willamette River. Many town residents, presumably living on the Monteith side of town, disagreed with the change and translated the name more broadly as "Hole in the Ground," a less picturesque image for the new village. In 1855 the name was changed back to "Albany" by the legislature.

During the Civil War, town rivalries intensified. The Monteith side was dominated by Republican merchants and professionals who staunchly supported the Union. In contrast, the Hackleman side was dominated by working-class Democrats who just as staunchly supported the South. At one time such disagreements were reported to have reached such proportions that a tall hedge was planted down the middle of town near Baker Street as a visual reminder of their separation. In 1881 the only direct contest between the two families took place at an Annual Game Hunt when Duncan Monteith and Denver Hackleman headed up teams to see who could bag the most birds. The Hackleman team won with 990—which probably tells more about the

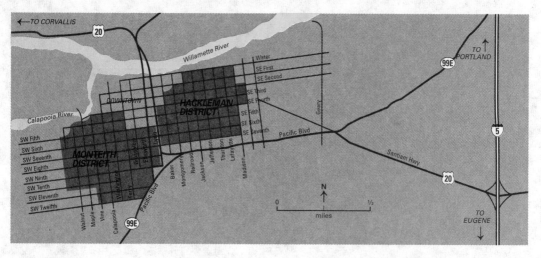

abundance of game than the marksmanship of the participants.

Rivalries aside, both sides of town developed in a balanced manner as the town's population climbed slowly from about two thousand in 1870 to only six thousand in 1940. When a wartime boom of industries and workers began arriving in 1942, both the factories and new housing were happily built away from the main core of town, which remained intact. A later preservation blessing occurred when Interstate 5 was built well to the east of the town's historic core.

Today both the Hackleman and Monteith areas, now official historic districts, retain a wide variety of houses built in most of the major styles popular between 1850 and 1940. It is wonderful to see both large and small examples of almost a century of housing styles interwoven throughout two districts. This is a pattern that rarely survives even in relatively small towns. Today Albany provides a particularly prime example of the rich stylistic blend that once characterized much of small-town America.

Monteith District

Monteith District, ca. 1850s–1940s

Traditionally the Monteith District was the more upscale side of town; the houses here are overall a bit larger than those in the Hackleman District.

518 Southwest Second Avenue (periodically open to the public), Monteith House, ca. 1849; 503-967-8699. This side-gabled folk house was Albany's first dwelling built by the town's founding brothers. It was a very grand home for Oregon in 1849, and is still preserved on its original site. Monteith House is just beginning to come into its own as a volunteer-operated museum house.

540 Southwest Sixth Avenue (private), Marshall House, 1898. This picturesque Queen Anne home is one and a half stories tall, a less common form than the more usual one- or two-story versions. It is of the hipped-roof-with-lower-cross-gables subtype and has simple spindlework ornament. The centered turret and the rounded-corner-porch section with a matching turret roof add character to the design.

138 Southwest Seventh Avenue (private). This design has a funky combination of Prairie-style features—the broad roof overhang and the heavy squared porch supports—superimposed on the porch form often seen in the contemporaneous Neoclassical style—a full-height entry porch with lower full-width porch.

730 Washington Street (private), Cathey House, 1906; A. C. Ewart, Corvallis and Portland, architect. This imposing Neoclassical design is of the full-height-entry-porch subtype. Somewhat unusual in early examples of this style is the use of squared columns, rather than round, with elaborate Ionic capitals. Note the pair of projecting corner bays on each side of the first floor, the one-story curved entry, and the wide overhanging eaves with brackets. This same wide

overhanging eave is also seen on several Prairie/Neoclassical combinations in town, including the house next door and the very similar 138 Southwest Seventh Avenue (see the preceding entry).

425 Southwest Eleventh Avenue (private), 1930s. This simple, early Modernistic-style house is located in an area of mostly small dwellings.

1134 Washington Street (private), ca. 1912. This lovely side-gabled brick-walled Craftsman design features a foundation, porch, chimney, and porte cochere built of stone. It has triangular knee braces under the exposed roof beams, exposed roof rafters with shaped ends, and a shed dormer. Also note the broad and subtle Tudor arch of the front porch.

516 Elm Street (private), Armstrong House, 1868. This small centered-gable Gothic Revival house is built of board-and-batten wood siding, the material widely advocated by pattern books of the day as particularly suitable for Gothic Revival houses because of its verticality. The windows have the characteristic Gothic window crown called a drip mold. Originally designed in the Middle Ages to protect windows from water running down the face of a building, the molding turns outward on each side to deflect water away from the window frame. The porch on this house was added in the 1890s.

Hackleman District, ca. 1860s–1930s

Traditionally the more working-class side of town, the Hackleman neighborhood features folk houses and smaller examples of many different styles, including a number of simple Italianate cottages. Mixed in are a number of large homes, including several of the more elaborate houses in Albany. The Oregon Electric Railroad interurban tracks ran along Fifth Avenue, and in 1912 the railroad built a depot at 133 Southeast Fifth Avenue, which still survives (see below).

Hackleman District

632 Baker Street (private), Ralston House, 1889. An elaborately detailed, one-story western Stick-style house, this combines a more typical Queen Anne shape (hipped roof with lower cross gables) with very elaborate Stick-style ornament. Note the king's post truss in all of the gables, the band of trim below the windows with diagonally applied siding, the squared bay window, and particularly the hoods covered with a picket-fence pattern; the tips of the pickets make a fringe draping off of the hoods. There is also a fine squared tower, set in at a diagonal and with a balcony in the top.

331 Montgomery Street (private), Goltra House, 1893. William H. Goltra was born in New Jersey and worked his way west, finally walking the entire distance from Missouri to Oregon in five months. He began as a farmer and then switched to selling farming implements for this rich agricultural region. He and his wife, Sarah, built this handsome Italianate home in 1893. This was late for Italianate houses, and his home picked up a few of the features used in the western Stick town houses of San Francisco—the squared bay window and the way the roofline brackets line up with the window sides and extend down into them, with the space between window top and cornice filled with a pattern.

118 Southeast Fifth Avenue (private), Althouse House, ca. 1868. This front-gabled Greek Revival house is recognized by the corner pilasters and with a band of trim under the eaves and front-door light pattern. The brackets under the gable are Italianate in origin and could well have been part of the original house design. Italianate trim added to Greek Revival houses was not an uncommon combination. The porch appears to be later.

Samuel Althouse came to Albany with the Monteiths and helped build the Magnolia Flour Mill, the town's first industry. He also owned a tin shop and a planing mill. He is quoted as saying, "My house is even now not a small house as compared to others, but in the early days it was almost a castle." Directly across the street, note the former interurban depot (see above), with its clay tile roof and OER (Oregon Electric Railroad) emblem in the gable.

ASTORIA

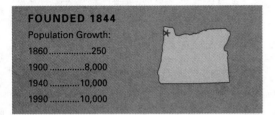

FOUNDED 1844

Population Growth:

1860 250

1900 8,000

1940 10,000

1990 10,000

Astoria was the site of the first American settlement in the Pacific Northwest. This was inspired by the 1804 to 1806 Lewis and Clark Expedition, sent by President Jefferson to explore the vast western wilderness he had purchased from France the previous year. The expedition reached its hard-won goal, the Pacific Ocean, via the Columbia River in November 1805. Unable to begin the return journey over snow-blocked mountain passes until spring, the party spent the winter at a temporary camp of log cabins, which they built about five miles southwest of modern Astoria. An instructive recreation of these buildings can be visited at the National Park Service's **Fort Clatsop National Memorial** (located off of U.S. Highway 101, 503-861-2471).

Lewis and Clark's descriptions of the bountiful wildlife in the region prompted New York's John Jacob Astor (1763–1848), whose American Fur Company has been called "the first U.S. business monopoly," to establish a fur-trading post near the mouth of the Columbia. Founded in 1811 and named Fort Astoria for its founder, the venture was to be very short-lived. After war with Britain erupted in 1812, the remote post was sold to the British North West Company, a Canadian-based Astor competitor, who later moved its base of operations farther inland to Fort Vancouver, near modern Vancouver, Washington.

With the Oregon Trail immigrations of the 1840s (see page 512), the early site of Fort Astoria was resurrected as one of many new waterfront villages that hoped to become the region's principal seaport. Astoria had several serious disadvantages in this competition. Its harbor, facing the wide Columbia River estuary only ten miles from the open ocean, offered too little protection from the Pacific's notoriously dangerous tides, currents, and storms to be an attractive anchorage for large sailing ships. Even more serious was Astoria's location on the wrong side of the low but rugged belt of Coast Range mountains, which restricted landward access to the region's principal area of settlement—the fertile agricultural lands bordering the Willamette River, which lay a hundred miles to the southeast.

By the 1850s Portland had won the seaport race (see page 513), and Astoria was a small fishing village, which it remained until the 1870s. In that decade a new economic dimension was added to the town by the opening of a large cannery to process the prolific salmon that swim up the Columbia and other northwestern rivers every spring to spawn. The cannery was a great success, and Astoria soon became a central processing center for salmon fishing fleets returning with their catch from as far away as Alaska. This boom is most clearly reflected in the town's population figures, which surged from 600 to 2,800 between 1870 and 1880 and jumped again to 6,200 by 1890. Many of these newcomers were experienced fisheries workers who, attracted by Astoria's high wages, emigrated from

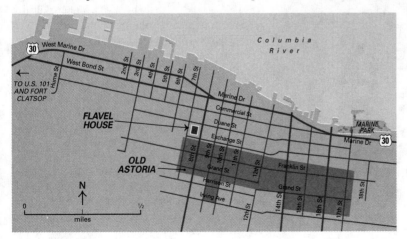

Scandinavian countries, with Finland contributing the largest proportion.

By 1910 Astoria's population had reached almost ten thousand and has remained at about that level ever since. Not surprisingly, this lack of twentieth-century growth has led to the survival of numerous early houses. Because Astoria is principally an industrial town, many of these are modest worker's dwellings, but Astoria also retains many landmark structures, among them a fine Stick-style museum house.

Old Astoria, ca. 1870s–1930s

The hillside that overlooks downtown Astoria is dotted with historic houses, most of which enjoy a spectacular view across the wide Columbia Estuary. Franklin Street was the town's original landward edge. Beyond it, built atop pilings driven into the tidal mudflats, were a series of plank streets lined with commercial enterprises. Later the pilings were replaced by mud and sand dredged from the adjacent harbor, a program that was finished in 1916. After a disastrous downtown fire in 1922, the river was pushed still farther back to its present location as part of the reconstruction.

1393 Franklin Street (private), Page House, 1879. This modest Italianate dwelling, just two window rows wide, was built as a wedding present by Captain Hiram Page for

Old Astoria

his daughter Annie and her new husband, Judge Charles H. Page. The two-story bay window with slanting sides was widely used in San Francisco's many Italianate town houses and likely found its way here through Astoria's close trading ties with that city (see "Flavel House," below).

1555 Franklin Street (private), rectory of Grace Episcopal Church, 1923. This simple but engaging Tudor-Craftsman home superimposes a large Tudor front-facing gable on a typical two-story, side-gabled Craftsman design, which is complete with open eaves, exposed rafters, and a through-the-cornice shed dormer. Detailing on the gable-fronted Tudor wing is equally typical of that style and includes a decorative vergeboard and vertical half-timbering atop two stories of tall, narrow casement windows. The half-timbering between these windows has a subtle Gothic-arch pattern.

Flavel House, 1885

441 Eighth Street; 503-325-2203;
Carl W. Leick, San Francisco and Astoria, architect.

This imposing late-Victorian design occupies a full city block on a steep hill overlooking downtown Astoria and the Columbia River. The house's large grounds are enhanced by many picturesque trees, most dramatic of which is a hundred-year-old giant sequoia at the right rear of the dwelling. The home was built for Captain George Flavel (1823–1893) and his family, which then included his wife, Mary, who was some sixteen years younger, and two unmarried daughters.

Flavel was already an experienced sea captain/merchant when, in 1849 at age twenty-six, he brought a cargo of merchandise from Norfolk, Virginia, around Cape Horn to San Francisco's gold rush frenzy. Finding that too many competitors had arrived before him, he sailed on to less frantic Portland, where he found eager buyers for his cargo. Perhaps it was this, his first crossing of the shifting shoals of sand that made entering the Columbia River an invitation to disaster for sailing-ship captains, that led Flavel to a brilliant career change. The next year he became a licensed bar pilot, skilled at guiding ships through the treacherous sands. With their large gold rush profits, ships' captains could afford to reward Flavel handsomely for a few hours of work that greatly reduced the risks of their voyage.

Flavel used these earnings wisely and expanded into shipping, hotels, banking, real estate, and politics—he eventually served as city councilman and Clatsop County commissioner. When he built this grand dwelling, he was, at age sixty-two, one of the wealthiest men in Astoria.

The house is designed in the West Coast version of the Stick style. This substyle is most common in San Francisco, where it dominated town-house design during the 1880s. Larger, freestanding examples are also scattered around northern California. Astoria had close

Flavel House

for the roof of the entry porch, the open overhanging eaves, and the distinctive upside-down-picket-fence pattern used as a wide band of trim in the gable end and under the eaves. Although the interior of this structure has been converted to offices, the exterior is still amazingly intact.

In about 1896 the house was painted white with red trim to give it a more "Colonial Revival" appearance. It remained white until 1984, when it was repainted in its original colors—antique gold with olive-green and chocolate-brown trim—to celebrate its hundredth anniversary. Color schemes such as this one were the height of fashion when it was applied in 1885. The rage then was for tertiary colors—and the fashionable Victorian home was painted in at least three of these. Most of us learned in grade school about the three primary colors—red, yellow, and blue—and the three secondary colors, orange, green, and purple, made when any two primaries are mixed together. What we were not taught, but likely encountered when randomly mixing paints, was about the tertiary colors—those slightly muddy shades that result from mixing the secondary colors together in various proportions. It is fun to see these faithfully re-created here.

Inside, the house is as imposing as when seen from the street. Its 7,300 square feet of floor space has fourteen-foot ceilings on each floor. The most striking interior features are the six original fireplaces and their surrounds. Each is hand-carved wood surrounded by a unique pattern of imported tiles—those in the library are from Algeria and the wonderful molded tile in the dining room are from Italy. The shallow metal fireboxes in each are for burning coal. Upstairs are an original main bath and built-in sinks and closets in the principal bedrooms.

Unfortunately, most of the light fixtures and Flavel family furnishings have been removed from the house. Among the surviving Flavel possessions are two large 1884 oil paintings of the mouth of the Columbia River by Cleveland Rockwell (1837–1907), which were specially commissioned by Captain Flavel, as was the stained-glass transom of a sailing ship over the front entrance. The citizens of Astoria have admirably filled the house with donations of fine Victorian furnishings.

trading ties with San Francisco, and Captain Flavel, with his many business interests, was a frequent visitor to that city. On one of these visits he commissioned San Francisco–based Carl Leick to design his new home. The architect then apparently opened a branch office in Astoria.

The front facade of the Flavel House clearly demonstrates the West Coast Stick style's characteristic *vertical* stickwork, in which each vertical band terminates in a bracket beneath the overhanging roof cornice. A wide band of horizontal trim is applied between the brackets. The style's typical shallow, square-sided bay window is used above the main entry. Other characteristic features are the window crowns with a molded cornice supported by small side brackets and the squared porch supports, which contrast with the turned spindles seen in early Queen Anne designs.

On the grounds is also a small original carriage house whose design is more typical of the East Coast subtype of the Stick style. Characteristic features are the steep-gabled roof with a king's post truss in the apex of the dominant front gable, the diagonal support

PORTLAND

FOUNDED 1845

Population Growth:

1860 3,000

1900 90,000

1940 305,000

1990 437,000

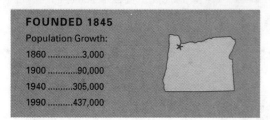

The Portland area was the first magnet to draw Anglo settlers across the scorching deserts and rugged mountains of the interior West to a new life on the verdant Pacific coast. In the 1830s, while California was still an unwelcoming backwater province of northern Mexico, Oregon's fertile Willamette River, glowingly praised by previous government explorers beginning with Lewis and Clark in 1806, prompted a small handful of New England Methodist missionaries to make the arduous journey to Oregon.

Oregon Fever

Unsuccessful in converting the local Indians, the missionaries became enthusiastic publicists for the agricultural and climatic virtues of their newfound homeland. By 1842 these efforts had created "Oregon Fever," as the first wave of what was to become a steady flow of immigrants arrived from the northeastern states. These hearty pioneers gathered in Missouri each spring to begin a grueling, several-month wagon journey along the Oregon Trail, which traversed almost two thousand miles of western wilderness. Their final destination was the frontier village of Oregon City, on the southernmost edge of modern Portland (see map, page 524).

Oregon City is located at a falls near the head of upstream navigation on the Willamette River, which could be reached by oceangoing sailing ships entering from the nearby Columbia River, one of the Pacific coast's few navigable waterways leading inland from the open sea (see page 509). As expected, the fertile Willamette Valley produced bumper crops of grain, vegetables, and fruits, for which, beyond amply sustaining their growers, there was then little demand in the remote and sparsely populated Pacific Northwest. Lacking markets where their surplus produce could be traded for the essential imports of frontier life—tools, hardware, cloth, coffee, tea, sugar, and such—the dispirited Oregon agricultural colony was close to failure by 1848.

View of Portland, 1870

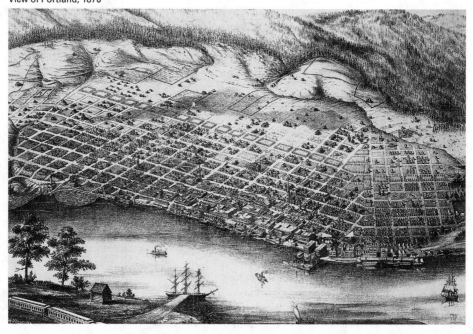

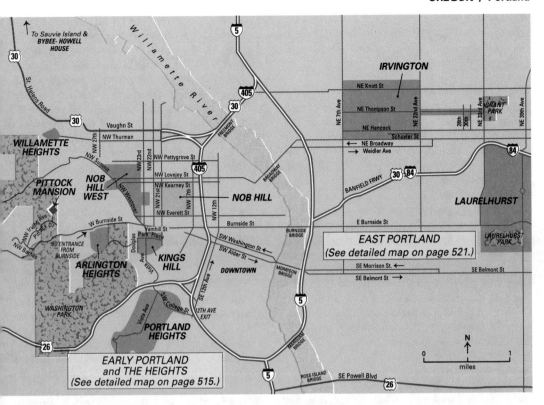

Saved by the Forty-niners

In January of 1848 the rich and easily worked gold deposits of California's Sierra Nevada foothills were discovered, and the greatest of the western gold rushes was on (see page 136). By 1852 California's pre–gold rush population of about 10,000 had increased to 225,000, many of whom were being fed by means of sailing ships arriving in San Francisco with the rich harvests of Willamette Valley farms.

The principal beneficiary of this frenzied trade turned out not to be Oregon City, whose waterfalls provided fine sites for early saw and flour mills but also made the river too narrow to provide wharves for the new flood of oceangoing ships. Instead, this activity centered on the rival town of Portland, a few miles downriver, which had the advantage of a wide anchorage adjacent to deepwater docks, a combination that was to make it the principal port of the Columbia River gateway, a distinction that it still holds today.

Gateway Seaport

Through the late 1850s California's gold rush subsided, and its agriculture expanded toward self-sufficiency. Portland's initial boom faded but was reinvigorated in the 1860s when gold was discovered in the mountains of Idaho. The most direct route to these new goldfields was up the Columbia River, where, as in the Willamette, massive waterfalls prevented oceangoing vessels from proceeding much beyond the Portland area. This time not only did Willamette Valley farms supply food, distributed through Portland, to the mining camps, but the city itself took on the role that San Francisco played in the earlier California rush—it became the entry point for a flood of ocean-borne fortune seekers as well as for most of the supplies that sustained the distant mines. This new bonanza almost tripled Portland's population in the decade between 1860 and 1870.

Railroad Boomtown

Several short-haul local railroads had been built in Oregon during the 1870s, mostly to connect Portland's docks with the Willamette Valley's many small farming centers (see "Albany," page 506, and "Salem," page 528). Transcontinental trains had first arrived in California in 1869 but did not reach the Pacific Northwest until fourteen years later, when the Oregon Short Line, following the route of the old Oregon Trail, joined Portland to the Union Pacific main line in southwestern Wyoming. With this 1883 rail connection Portland became the seaport for a vast interior hinterland, the most important export of which was wheat from the enormously productive soils of easternmost Washington.

This new railroad-based prosperity led to a spectacular population boom, as Portland's inhabitants jumped from 16,000 in 1880 to 46,000 in 1890 and then surged to almost 250,000 by 1910.

World War II and After

The Second World War led to a final period of rapid growth as Portland became a principal supply and embarkation center for operations against Japan throughout the Pacific, as well as a favored site for new wartime industries. The largest of these was the enormous Kaiser Shipyard, which brought seventy thousand new workers to the Portland area.

Unlike most western cities that had experienced rapid wartime growth, the city of Portland in the succeeding decades followed a policy of maintaining its small-city quality of life by restricting suburban expansion. As a result, the 1950 population of 374,000 increased by only 15 percent over the next forty years. Many of Portland's surrounding towns, on the other hand, encouraged new development so that the metropolitan area had a 1990 population of well over a million and is still growing rapidly.

Residential Portland

As can be seen in the view on page 512, the original Portland town site on the west bank of the Willamette was rather closely confined by an arc of steep and rugged hills to the west. Even in 1870, when the population was only eight thousand, the town's street grid covered the entire area of flat riverside land, and scattered dwellings can be seen on the low foothills to the west. By 1880 the street grid covered these foothills, and new residential districts were beginning to develop across the river in East Portland, where a flat landscape stretched many miles eastward before reaching Mount Hood and the Cascade Mountains.

At first served only by ferryboats, with the explosive railroad-based growth of the 1880s East Portland became the principal direction of the city's growth, particularly after the first vehicular and pedestrian bridge spanning the Willamette was completed in 1887. By 1891 Portland officials, noting that the population of Seattle, the city's upstart young rival to the north, was approaching that of Portland, retaliated by annexing East·Portland, a move that added more than twenty thousand of the city's ninety thousand inhabitants recorded in the 1900 census. This figure was comfortably larger than Seattle's total of eighty-one thousand.

Modern Portland

Today more than 80 percent of the city's residents live in East Portland neighborhoods, several of which,

among them Irvington (see page 522) and Laurelhurst (see page 522), retain fine assemblages of Eclectic-era houses. The original town-site area on the west bank of the river, shown in the map below, is now mostly filled by the city's central business district, but the low foothills to the west still retain some Victorian dwellings scattered among younger apartment buildings in the Nob Hill neighborhood (see the following entry), as well as more intact, mostly Eclectic-era, districts in the Nob Hill West (see page 516) and Kings Hill neighborhoods (see page 517).

With the initiation of cable-car access in the 1890s, some of the steeper hills to the west of the early city became the sites of prestigious residential districts, most of them having the word "Heights" in their name to distinguish them from the adjacent "Hill" neighborhoods, which they overlook (see pages 517, 518, and 519).

In addition to these many fine neighborhoods, the Portland area boasts three very important museum houses, two of which, the McLoughlin House (see page 523) and the Bybee-Howell House (see page 526), are miraculous survivors from the region's earliest years of Anglo settlement in the 1840s and 1850s; the third is a rare French Eclectic landmark built in 1914 atop a dramatic peak in the western hills (see page 519).

Looking at houses in Portland's early twentieth-century neighborhoods, one finds an unusually high percentage of Tudor designs with false-thatched roofs and also of stucco-clad Tudor cottages without half-timbering. In addition, two relatively unusual architectural details seem to occur more frequently here than in most cities. These are jerkin heads (gables that are clipped or hipped just at the peak) and the squat, oversized "columns" that were favored in Craftsman movement pattern books but uncommon in executed houses.

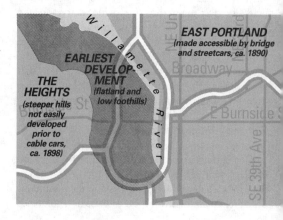

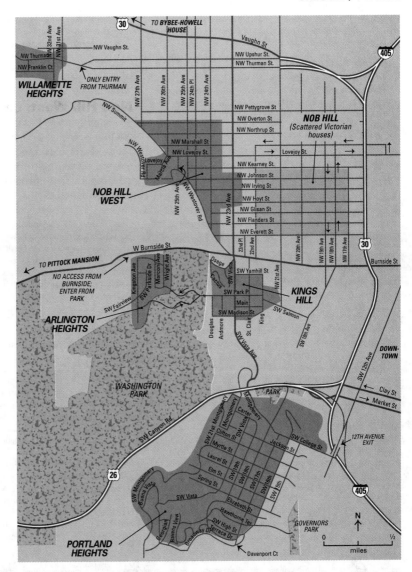

EARLY PORTLAND

These are the surviving neighborhoods developed in the late 1800s on the low foothills to the west of the riverside flats (see map, page 514).

Nob Hill, ca. 1880–1910

Said to have been named by a local grocer who likened it to the more dramatically situated Nob Hill of his native San Francisco, today the district has many Victorian-era homes scattered amid thriving storefronts, funky early-twentieth-century apartment houses, and a mélange of newer buildings. Finding the houses among all this requires do-it-yourself exploration, but those with the time and interest will be rewarded by the discovery of many fine dwellings in several late-Victorian styles—Queen Anne examples dominate, but there are also scattered Italianate-, Stick-, and Shingle-style designs.

Nob Hill has a very tightly packed, urban feel (at least for the Pacific Northwest!), with narrow streets closely bounded by houses built on narrow lots. Keep an eye out for the handful of double and attached houses that survive. Navigation is made somewhat easier by understanding that the east–west streets are in alphabetical order, each named for a leading Portland citizen.

1705 to 1719 Northwest Irving Street and 715 to 719 Northwest Seventeenth Avenue (all private), Campbell Townhouses, 1893. This row of six attached Queen Anne–

style town houses apparently contains the only brick row houses in Oregon. Intact examples of attached Queen Anne town houses are rare throughout the United States. These happily retain most of their fine original detailing. Note the way these details—windows, gable elaboration, and so on—vary slightly from house to house.

615 Northwest Twentieth Avenue (private), MacKenzie House, 1892; Whidden and Lewis, Portland, architects. This fine dwelling demonstrates the close relationship between the Shingle and the Richardsonian Romanesque styles, which often have similar forms executed respectively in either wood or masonry. This example has all of the Richardsonian Romanesque's identifying features but with the upper stories executed in wood shingles rather than masonry. Note the unusual, small front-facing gable that is cantilevered above a large bay window—a very modern-looking treatment. Note also the side facade with its broad-shingled gable and the pair of unusual gabled dormers. The front roof also sports an eyebrow dormer, a type commonly seen in only these two styles.

Whidden and Lewis was apparently the city's first firm of professionally trained architects. William Whidden had studied at M.I.T. and in Paris and was working for New York's prestigious McKim, Mead, and White when he first came to Portland to oversee one of its commissions. His partner, Ion Lewis, was a native of the Boston area and was trained in the Boston office of Peabody and Stearns. Betting their futures on the rapidly expanding city, the young architects formed their partnership in 1889. They brought to the city a thorough knowledge of current East Coast trends and designed in many then-fashionable styles (see also "2381 Northwest Flanders Street," below, and "2359 Northwest Overton Street," page 517).

733 Northwest Twentieth Avenue (private), Mills House, 1908; Shepley, Rutan, and Coolidge, Boston, architects. This is a superb example of the centered-gable Colonial Revival house. Note the parapeted side walls that incorporate paired double end chimneys and the very heavily ornamented central gabled section that extends slightly forward for emphasis as a "pavilion."

209 Northwest Twenty-third Avenue (private), Weist Apartments, ca. 1907. This is an excellent example of the early-twentieth-century apartments that were built right after Portland's 1905 Lewis and Clark Exposition, a period during which the city was growing very rapidly. Note the colossal columns supporting the porticoes located on each side of the entrance. The entrance itself is emphasized with a rather remarkably oversized and heavily ornamented segmental pediment.

Nob Hill West, ca. 1890–1910

To the west of Nob Hill at the base of the steeper western hills is the slightly later Nob Hill West district. Here the residential blocks are more intact and, although the area is a bit younger than its more fragmented namesake, still feature a mixture of late-Victorian and early-Eclectic-era homes.

2377 and 2387 Northwest Kearney Street (both private), Korell Houses, ca. 1890. This fine pair of Queen Anne dwellings features elaborate spindlework detailing. The first-floor porches do not wrap around to the sides of these houses as is common in the Queen Anne style; this is an adaptation to the narrow urban lots.

Twenty-fourth Avenue between Lovejoy and Kearney Streets (all private). This short block face has three contrasting-style houses all in a row—a fine Neoclassical at the corner of Kearney Street, a very late half-timbered Queen Anne in the middle, and a Colonial Revival at the corner of Lovejoy Street.

2355 Lovejoy Street (private). This is a pleasantly simple, one-and-a-half-story, front-gabled Shingle-style design. Notice the outward flare at the base of the front-facing gable.

2381 Northwest Flanders Street (private), Bates-Seller House, 1908; Whidden and Lewis, Portland, architects. This nicely proportioned Neoclassical house has the full-height entry porch with lower full-width porch that is mostly seen in the southeastern states. Amazingly, it seems to have also gained wide acceptance in the Pacific Northwest. This is one of several houses in this block designed by Whidden and Lewis. Another of their houses, built in 1904, is at 2352 Northwest Flanders Street. (See also "615 Northwest Twentieth Avenue," this page, and the following entry.)

Nob Hill West

2359 Northwest Overton Street (private), Holman House, 1898; Whidden and Lewis, Portland, architects. This is one of Whidden and Lewis's more creative designs (see the preceding entry). It has the overall proportions and symmetry of a Colonial Revival house but has a striking bow-front central section with two levels of semicircular balustrades, all crowned by a high central gable with an oval window anomalously near its peak. It is clad with a combination of wood siding on the first story and wood shingles on the second.

Kings Hill, ca. 1890–1930

Like Nob Hill, this neighborhood to its southwest at the base of the steep western hills has had many later intrusions. Originally, Kings Hill was part of 513 wooded acres owned by a tannery boss named Amos King. King gradually and carefully sold off his holdings, mainly to persons he expected to build large houses, thereby raising the value of the rest of his land. Kings Hill thus had generally larger lots and houses than Nob Hill. Today this neighborhood is a mixture of fine historic houses with newer apartments and institutions interspersed between.

2178 Southwest Main Street (private). This is an intriguing gambrel-roofed Shingle-style design. Note the use of both an eyebrow dormer and a gable dormer, a Palladian window with an oval window above, and rough-faced stone porch supports. The house appears to have had a major rear addition.

2220 Southwest Main Street (private). A lively Tudor dwelling that was probably built before 1915. Note the exaggerated details, the blocky massing, and the squared "Prairie-style" porch supports.

2370 Southwest Park Place (private), Holtz House, ca. 1925; Albert E. Doyle, Portland, architect. Contrast this large and elaborate parapeted Tudor house with 2220 Southwest Main Street (see the preceding entry) to see how much more historically "correct" the style had become by the 1920s. Although this house is much larger, the individual details are much more refined and in scale with the house.

2400 Southwest Park Place (private), Barde House, 1926; Carl A. Linde, Portland, architect. This good example of the Italian Renaissance subtype has a hipped roof and a pair of projecting wings on each side. Note the red tile roof, the many round-arched casement windows, and the wrought-iron balconies. The eaves of the roof are unusually close for this style of house (that is, the usual roof overhang is absent).

THE HEIGHTS

By the 1890s Portland's steep West Hills, barriers that had previously confined the city's westward growth, were themselves yielding to residential development. In 1891 the summit of one of the northernmost hills was flattened and its approach regraded to permit a streetcar line to serve a hilltop development called Willamette Heights. This was followed by a whole series of new "Heights" subdivisions along the West Hills.

Most had only scattered dwellings until the great population surge that followed the city's 1905 Lewis and Clarke Exposition. By 1910 these dramatically sited hilltop neighborhoods, now being made more conveniently accessible by narrow and winding automobile roadways, were among Portland's most prestigious addresses, a distinction they still hold today.

Portland Heights, ca. 1898–1930

This large neighborhood is the grande dame of the West Hills developments. Its lower slopes, then accessible only by steep, unpaved roads for horse-drawn vehicles, were a favorite site for Portlanders' "summer retreats" in the 1880s and 1890s. In 1898 a cable-car line was completed to serve the neighborhood, leading more of its residents to construct year-round homes in the scenic hills. As automobiles became more common after 1910, the development spread up the steeper slopes along a challenging set of twisting and turning and dead-end roads.

As the earliest and largest of the Heights neighborhoods, Portland Heights boasts a treasure trove of fine Eclectic-era homes—located both on the older and flatter grid and along the winding roads of its more steeply pitched slopes. Regrettably, few of its original Victorian houses survive, having been replaced by more up-to-date dwellings in the early twentieth century. These are an instructive mixture of house sizes and styles intriguingly situated among lovely stone retaining walls, public footpaths, and stairways. In the words of the Oregon Historical Society's guide to the city, Portland Heights features "narrow twisting streets with the charm of lanes in an English village."

Today Portland Heights is best approached via the old Vista Street Bridge. This leads into the earlier (and flatter) portion of the neighborhood, from which one can explore the more challenging up-slope streets to the southwest.

2040 Southwest Laurel Street (private), Ball House, 1921; Albert E. Doyle, Portland, architect. This elegant home is a landmark example of a false-thatched-roof Tudor home clad in stucco without half-timbering. As noted on page 514, such Tudor designs are unusually frequent in Portland. This home is symmetrical and has a fine entrance. Note the subtle curve of the roof over the entry porch and the jerkin head (clipped gable) in the top of both of the front-facing gables—another feature often seen in Portland.

2156 Southwest Elm Street (private). This simple Italian Renaissance house sits uphill, and its small matching garage is tucked into the hill at the base of the lawn, an early-automobile-era design feature seen throughout the Heights neighborhoods.

1825 Southwest Elm Street (private), Bowman Apartment House, 1916; G. R. Wright, architect. This unusual Craftsman-style apartment house still has most of its origi-

Portland Heights

multigabled form of these adjacent homes. Their architect, Wade Pipes (1877–1961), was one of Portland's several distinguished Eclectic-era designers. Pipes grew up in the Willamette Valley near the city, and except for four crucial years, 1907 to 1911, studying architecture in England, Pipes spent his entire life in the Portland area, where he designed numerous homes from 1912 until 1961—all of them influenced by his English training.

Pipes studied at the Central School of Arts and Crafts in London where he received a thorough grounding in the English Arts and Crafts movement and became familiar with the work of C. F. A. Voysey and Sir Edwin Lutyens, both of whom designed understated "modern" houses loosely based on English vernacular forms. Wade Pipes continued this tradition in Portland for almost fifty years. These two houses, located on a narrow lane at the top of Portland Heights, are excellent examples of his own understated style. Pipes's influence on Portland's Eclectic-era homebuilders is probably responsible for Portland's unusual number of simple, stucco-clad Tudor houses that are unadorned by half-timbering or other visually dominant details usually found in Tudor designs.

Arlington Heights, ca. 1910–1930

A leveled hilltop above Washington Park provides a scenic setting for this very small area of fine Eclectic-era homes. Access to the neighborhood is complex. One follows Southwest Park Place up through Washington Park, avoiding turnoffs to the Japanese Garden and other attractions, and heads toward the Spanish Eclectic house visible at the top of the hill, which is part of the tiny Arlington Heights neighborhood. The district uses several different street names, but each street here seems to meld directly into the next. Going up the hill, you will progress from Park Place to Washington Street, to Southwest Sagijawici to Southwest Marconi to Southwest Kingston. To get back to the base of the hill, exit from the top down Southwest Park Circle. We could find no simple access to Arlington Heights from

nal detailing, including the handsome open porches—semi-elliptical brick arches decorate the downstairs porch, while the upstairs porch features Craftsman detailing in stucco and wood. Note the U-shaped form built around a courtyard to facilitate cross ventilation.

1707 and 1727 Southwest Hawthorne Terrace (both private), Burke House, 1926, and Catlin House, 1927; Wade Hampton Pipes, Portland, architect. Note the simplified,

Arlington Heights

Burnside Street, although it may well be there. Once you arrive at the top of the hill, there are a handful of very nice houses, among them:

122 Southwest Marconi Avenue (private), Bennes House, 1911; John Virginius Bennes, Portland, architect. John Bennes received his architectural training in Illinois, and the influence of Frank Lloyd Wright is clearly visible in this, his own home. It is a delightful Prairie-style design of the hipped-roof-with-no-front-entry subtype. Ornamentation includes a tile roof and other Italian Renaissance features. This was a very typical combination of styles during the 1910s and is seen again in this neighborhood at 226 Southwest Kingston Avenue (see the following entry). Bennes's dexterity in combining elements of these two styles, but with different emphases, is seen in these two examples.

226 Southwest Kingston Avenue (private), Maegly House, 1915; John Virginius Bennes, Portland, architect. A hilltop setting for an elegant Italian Renaissance home built for the co-owner of a local brokerage firm. This design also incorporates Prairie-style elements, such as the tile string course under the upper-story windows, the squared porch supports, and the use of ribbon windows—one set of which is cantilevered. This house originally had twelve porches, a few of which have now been enclosed.

Willamette Heights, ca. 1891–1915

This development opened in 1891 when the Russell, Masland, and Blythe Company extended the Twenty-third Avenue streetcar line up a gently graded extension of Thurman Street to serve its newly leveled hilltop subdivision. The first of the West Hills developments to be served by public transit, Willamette Heights remains a remarkably intact assemblage of pre-1915 dwellings that gives a pristine glimpse into what one writer calls the "Edwardian middle-class lifestyle in Portland." Number 3114 Northwest Thurman Street and 1611 and 1627 Northwest Thirty-second Avenue (all private) are of particular note.

Willamette Heights

Pittock Mansion, 1914

3229 Northwest Pittock Drive; 503-823-3624; Edward T. Foulkes, San Francisco and Portland, architect.

This extraordinary French Eclectic museum house, which overlooks riverside Portland a thousand feet below from a spectacular forty-six-acre hilltop site, is the premier West Hills dwelling. Now a public park, the grounds form an important link in five thousand acres of scenic West Hills highlands that have been farsightedly preserved as parkland by the city of Portland.

The equally remarkable house was built late in life by Portland pioneers Henry Pittock (1835–1919) and his wife, Georgiana (1845–1918), who had both come to Oregon by wagon train when they were children—he from Pennsylvania and she from Iowa. They were married in 1860, when Henry was twenty-five and his bride but fifteen. Their fifty-eight-year marriage produced six children, fourteen grandchildren, this magnificent home, and a legacy of community service and wise investments.

At seventeen Henry, then in his own words "barefoot and penniless," went to work for the local newspaper, the *Weekly Oregonian.* Just seven years later, he was able to buy the paper and soon built it into a successful daily that informed and influenced Portland throughout his lifetime. With this as the basis of his fortune, he also amassed holdings in banking and real estate, railroads and steamboats, sheep and silver, and pulp and paper. At the same time, Georgiana plunged into community service. She helped form the Ladies Relief Society in 1867, which provided help for needy children, and was active in the Woman's Union and helped establish the Martha Washington Home of single, working women. Georgiana also loved flowers, and in addition to tending her own lush flower gardens, she instigated Portland's annual Rose Festival.

Near-downtown residents throughout most of their married life, the couple began planning their hilltop dream home in 1909. They rather daringly picked a young and relatively inexperienced architect named Edward T. Foulkes, a native of Oregon who officed in both San Francisco and Portland, to design their grand dwelling. Remarkably, this was his *first* residential commission. The Pittocks believed strongly in giving promising young people a chance, and many such artisans were hired to work with Foulkes. Fred Baker, the famed light-fixture designer, was then a student and designed all of the lighting in the house. Another young student, William Klingenberg, carved the ornate wood library and lintel details through the house. And Henry Wentz, a young artist, hand painted the embossed ceil-

Pittock Mansion

ing of the Turkish smoking room and executed the gold leaf throughout the house. As a visit to the house will prove, none of these choices could have disappointed their clients.

The Pittocks also took great pride in building the home almost entirely of materials supplied by the Pacific coast region. The outside is clad with Tenino stone from nearby Washington. The main hall and stairway are finished with Columbia marble from California, while the oak and maple flooring and eucalyptus wood of the elevator are from the forests of the Northwest. Indeed, there are only three imported materials in the entire house—Italian marble for accents in the main hallway, French Caen stone for the library and drawing room fireplaces, and Honduran mahogany paneling in the dining room. Planning and building the home took five years—the Pittocks moved in 1914, when Henry was seventy-nine and Georgiana seventy.

The house is an extraordinary example of French Eclectic design of the symmetrical subtype based on formal Renaissance precedents. Built of reinforced concrete, the basic concrete structure is clad with light-colored Tenino stone. A broad terrace with stone balustrade sweeps around the house and provides a dramatic view of nearby Mount Hood. The steeply pitched hipped roof is covered with flat terra-cotta tiles and has two rows of dormers—three tall, narrow hipped-roof dormers below and three small circular dormers above. Tall, narrow chimneys and a matched pair of towers with conical candlesnuffer roofs provide further elaboration.

Inside, the house's central feature is a magnificent three-story marble staircase with a bronze grillwork balustrade. Large leaded-glass windows flood the stair hall with light. Downstairs are three main rooms. The library features oak paneling carved in the style of seventeenth-century England and dramatic cove lighting emphasizing the quatrefoil design in the plaster ceiling.

The drawing room is oval shaped and features an elaborate frieze, a pair of crystal chandeliers and two original Pittock pieces—a piano and an Aubusson-type rug custom loomed for this room. The dining room is less formal and in the Arts and Craft style popular in this era. A small Turkish smoking room, located on the ground floor of one of the towers, is a particular jewel, with very fine plasterwork and parquets. The domed ceiling of embossed plaster retains its original intricate paintwork.

Upstairs are three bedroom suites. The master suite is in the center of the house and includes two bedrooms, a sitting room, and a master bath, which retains its original elaborate shower installation. The house had all of the most up-to-date conveniences of the day, including an intercom telephone system, individual room thermostats, a central vacuum system, and a walk-in freezer.

Don't miss the landscape architect's rendering of plans for the grounds and their gardens that hangs in the lower-level hallway. The plans feature the formal geometric gardens of which the French are so fond. Happily, they were never executed, and the grounds remained more natural and appropriate to the site. A

number of original outbuildings survive, among them a three-car garage complete with its own machine shop for repairs and the Lodge, a charming house, four stories tall and only two rooms wide, that is now used as a tearoom.

Henry and Georgiana were to enjoy their home together for only five years before Georgiana died in 1918. Henry followed her in death just one year later. But their descendants lived here, high in the hills, until 1958, when the sixteen-thousand-square-foot home and its forty-six acres of grounds were put on the market. The still-unsold vacant house was heavily damaged, seemingly beyond repair, in a severe 1962 storm. The potential loss of this familiar landmark led to a community fund drive to prevent its demolition. This prompted the city of Portland to purchase and restore the grand dwelling as a public museum in 1964.

EAST PORTLAND

The area across the Willamette River from early Portland was originally a flat woodland that stretched for twenty miles eastward to Mount Hood and the Cascade Range. By the 1860s the forest immediately across from Portland had been cleared for farmland, centered

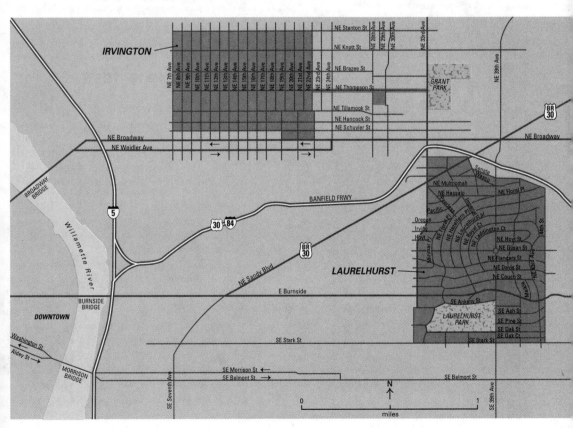

around the village of East Portland, which was served by ferryboats from the Portland docks. Portland's railroad-based population explosion of the 1880s quickly began conversion of these farms into residential suburbs, a process that accelerated with the completion of the first bridge spanning the Willamette in 1887. This carried not only wagons, carriages, and pedestrians, but also Portland's recently installed electric trolley cars.

In 1891 East Portland, now a city of twenty thousand, was annexed to become a part of Portland. By 1910, one thousand streetcars and thirty thousand pedestrians crossed the Burnside Bridge every day en route to and from East Portland neighborhoods and the downtown commercial district. Today about 80 percent of Portland's population lives east of the river. A number of fine and unintruded Eclectic-era neighborhoods are found here, two of the finest and most intact being Irvington and Laurelhurst.

Irvington, 1905–1920

Irvington is a large and cohesive neighborhood mainly filled with wood-clad four-square-shaped houses built from about 1905 to 1920. It is among the largest and most intact districts of this house type in the West. Unlike Laurelhurst (see the next entry), which was planned with a pattern of irregular, curving streets, Irvington has the regular street grid typical of most western cities. Deed restrictions ensured a degree of regularity in the houses placed on the rectangular lots; for most of the district there could be only one house per fifty-foot lot, a minimum building cost of $2,500, and a uniform twenty-five-foot setback from the street. Today, towering tree tunnels enhance most of Irvington's streets.

Stylistic detailing of the neighborhood's many four-square-shaped dwellings reflects a variety of early-twentieth-century fashions, particularly the Prairie, Craftsman, Colonial Revival, and Neoclassical styles. In addition to the many four-squares, a number of larger landmark dwellings are scattered throughout the district; still more are concentrated along the **Thompson Street** corridor (see the map, page 521), which leads toward Laurelhurst.

2110 Northeast Sixteenth Avenue (private), Coleman House, 1916; John Virginius Bennes, Portland, architect. This fine Colonial Revival design features four full-height pilasters paired on each side of the entry. Note the handsome Palladian window above the entry and the round-arched windows in the roof dormers (See "Arlington Heights," page 518, for two additional Bennes designs, one of them his own home, built in 1911).

1627 Northeast Stanton Street (private). This is a wonderfully intact American four-square in the Prairie style. No-

Irvington

tice the broad overhang of all the eaves—on the dormer roof, house roof, and porch roof.

1914 Northeast Twenty-second Avenue (private), Lytle House, 1911; David L. Williams, architect. This design combines elements of both the Italian Renaissance and Neoclassical styles. The tile roof, the first-floor windows, the low balustrade around a platform porch, and the wide eave overhang are typical Italian Renaissance details, but a full-height Neoclassical portico dominates the front facade.

2230 Northeast Thompson Street (private), Kennard House, 1911. Distinguished by its cladding of rock-faced cast stone, this Prairie-style design sports Craftsman-influenced open eaves with exposed rafters and a Mediterranean-influenced roof of glazed tile.

Laurelhurst, 1909–1935

Laurelhurst is a fine example of the artistically planned curved-street subdivisions that became popular in the first decades of the twentieth century (see page xxxv). It was designed by Boston's distinguished Olmsted brothers, sons of the renowned Frederick Law Olmsted (1822–1903), the "Father of American Landscape Architecture" who, shortly before his death, had executed

Laurelhurst

the overall plan for Portland's Lewis and Clark Exposition held in 1905. The brothers used winding streets, a large public park, two roundabouts, and monumental subdivision gates to provide an appropriate setting for 2,880 homesites in Laurelhurst. The centerpiece of the neighborhood is Laurelhurst Park, purchased from the developers by the city of Portland in 1909. Its lake and fine plantings were designed by Emanuel Mische, a former Olmsted employee who moved to Portland to become park superintendent.

Laurelhurst features a mix of small and large homes, all well designed and carefully maintained. The development's original deed restrictions required a minimum construction cost of three thousand dollars. About five hundred houses, occupying 17 percent of the lots, had been completed by 1916; by 1935 only 10 percent of the lots were still vacant. Thus about 75 percent of Laurelhurst's dwellings were built between 1916 and 1935. Common styles include Craftsman, Tudor, side-gambreled Dutch Colonial, and Colonial Revival. Tudor false-thatched roofs and Craftsman designs with jerkin-head roofs and unusually robust porch-support columns are details that occur here with unusual frequency (see the following two entries).

525 Northeast Floral Place (private). This is a typical front-gabled Craftsman design, but with unusually thick and robust columns used as porch supports. Laurelhurst has several homes with these large and simple columns, which were often featured in the pages of the Craftsman movement design magazines and pattern books but are infrequently seen on actual houses.

3600 block of Southeast Oak Street (all private). Facing northward toward Laurelhurst Park, this block has an instructive collection of houses. Beginning on the east corner (Southeast Oak Street at Thirty-seventh Street), there is a false-thatched-roof Tudor design. As one travels west, the third house is a typical side-gambreled Dutch Colonial variant of the Colonial Revival style with a broad shed dormer. This house contrasts with its neighbor four doors west (the seventh house from Thirty-seventh Street), which is another side-gambreled Dutch Colonial, but this time with its porch supported by robust Craftsman columns as at 525 Northeast Floral Place (see the preceding entry). The eighth house in this block (at the corner of Southeast Oak and Thirty-sixth Street) is another false-thatched-roof Tudor.

3206 Northeast Glisan Street (private), Markham House, 1911. This delightful Mission-style design has two large squared towers and widely overhanging street eaves. The porch and porte cochere are arcaded and have a shaped Mission parapet at each end. Set on a corner, the home faces Glisan with its "official" front facade, while the actual entry is on Thirty-second Street; interestingly neither facade reads as a formal entryway.

3316 Southeast Ankeny Street (private), Green House, 1928; Herman Brooman, architect. One of the largest homes in Laurelhurst, this elaborate Spanish Eclectic design has unusual contrasting chimneys of brick rather than stucco. Note the lack of overhang at the roof eaves, which is usually

the quickest and easiest way to distinguish this 1920s and 1930s style from the earlier (1890 to 1920) Mission style seen in the preceding example.

PORTLAND VICINITY
Oregon City

This small village, founded in the 1820s as a Hudson's Bay Company mill site near the base of forty-foot waterfalls on the Willamette River, became nationally famous in the early 1840s as the "end of the Oregon Trail." Here the wagon trains of weary pioneers, arriving in the fall after a several-month journey across forbidding deserts and mountains, could find food and shelter during their first Oregon winter. In the spring, most of them again loaded their wagons and moved southward, past the waterfalls, to establish farms and plant their first crops on the broad and fertile banks of the upper Willamette.

Oregon City's national prominence was destined to be short-lived. By the 1850s, nearby Portland, better situated to serve oceangoing sailing ships (see page 512), was becoming Oregon's principal city, while such up-river towns as Salem (see page 528) and Albany (see page 506) were developing into the principal trade centers for the rich agricultural valley to the south. Oregon City, however, had one valuable asset that its rivals lacked—the tall Willamette waterfalls that could provide the power required to operate very large mills. The first of these, a woolen mill, was built in 1864 and was followed two years later by the first paper mill on the Pacific coast. These were followed by still-other water-powered factories as Oregon City became a small industrial town to the south of burgeoning Portland.

Today, early Oregon City's central role in the first Anglo immigrations to the Pacific coast would be scarcely visible were it not for one early architectural survivor, a museum house with the coveted designation of "national historic site" conferred by the National Park Service.

McLoughlin House, 1846
713 Center Street, Oregon City; 503-656-5146.

This large and unpretentious dwelling, which looks as if it belongs beside a New England village green, is, like Oregon City itself, the creation of an extraordinary Canadian-American named John McLoughlin (1784–1857).

Born in Quebec of Scottish, Irish, and French grandparents, young McLoughlin was but fourteen when he began a five-year medical apprenticeship under his uncle, a prominent Quebec physician. By eighteen he was a licensed physician. Rather than entering private practice, Dr. McLoughlin decided to follow the exam-

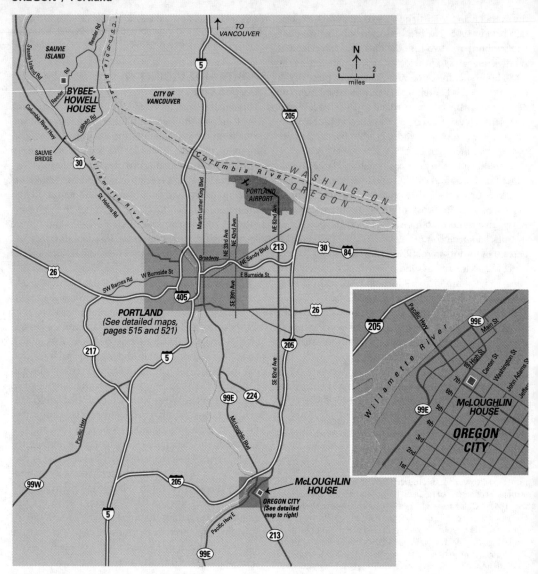

ple of another uncle by joining the British-backed North West Company, a large fur-trading enterprise that operated in western Canada in competition with the older and larger Hudson's Bay Company. Starting out as a company physician, McLoughlin soon demonstrated an unusual talent for working with the company's far-flung and multiethnic trappers and Indian partners. By age twenty-seven he was a partner and field manager of the company.

Ten years later, in 1821, McLoughlin was a leader in negotiating a merger between the two giant fur-trading enterprises. That same year, he became superintendent of the largest and most westerly of the Hudson's Bay Company's remote fur-trapping territories—one that

stretched from the Rockies west to the Pacific coast and from Mexico north to Alaska. As a Hudson's Bay Company partner, he would receive two-eighty-fifths of the profits earned in this vast wilderness territory.

McLoughlin chose the Portland area for his new headquarters and in 1824 oversaw construction of the first buildings of what was to become the first permanent Anglo settlement in the Pacific Northwest. Named Fort Vancouver for the British explorer who discovered the Columbia River, the stockade-protected complex of log buildings was located on the north side of the Columbia in what is now Vancouver, Washington. The new enterprise was soon prospering under McLoughlin's firm but fair-minded leadership.

McLoughlin House

McLoughlin's principal problems with his complex managerial responsibilities originated not in the West, but in faraway Washington and London. Under the 1814 Treaty of Ghent, Britain and the United States were to jointly occupy the disputed Pacific Northwest for ten years, after which a permanent boundary was to be established between the westernmost United States and British Canada. Either side could secure advantages in the boundary negotiations by increasing its presence in the remote wilderness.

McLoughlin's fur-trading activities were the principal British effort in this direction, while the first Methodist missionaries from New England, who arrived in the 1830s, marked the beginnings of a United States presence in the region. As Oregon Fever heated up in the early 1840s, the steady stream of Willamette Valley immigrants arriving from the northeastern states threatened to tip the balance toward permanent United States dominance of the entire area. It was at this point that McLoughlin's wisdom and humanity prevailed.

Ignoring his distant Hudson's Bay Company superiors, who had ordered him to deny food and shelter to the newly arriving, and in many cases desperately needy, Oregon Trail immigrants, McLoughlin instructed his employees to provide generous assistance to all comers. Expecting the new international boundary to be set at the Columbia River, McLoughlin en-

Dr. John McLoughlin

couraged the new arrivals to settle south of the Columbia in a new town that he platted in 1842 just as the first substantial group of Oregon Trail immigrants reached their destination. It was located at the falls of the Willamette where McLoughlin constructed a sawmill and flour mill. He named his new town simply Oregon City and sold a lot to any settler who agreed to build on it. As a result the town quickly became the focal point of Oregon Trail immigration.

The region's political situation changed dramatically in 1846 when Britain and the United States agreed to place the international boundary not along the Columbia River, as many had expected, but more than two hundred miles northward at the forty-ninth parallel. Well before the decision was final, McLoughlin had received much criticism from his British superiors for aiding the large-scale American immigrations that strengthened the American demands for a more northerly boundary. In 1845 he was forced to resign from his Hudson's Bay Company partnership. He was, however, allowed to purchase the still-largely-undeveloped Oregon City town site from the company for twenty thousand dollars, a very substantial sum at that time.

The following year, as the final boundary treaty was negotiated and signed, McLoughlin, still vigorous at sixty-one, moved to a fine new home with his large family in Oregon City. In addition to many undeveloped lots, his purchase of the town site included the two important mills that he had built four years earlier. McLoughlin, who became a United States citizen in 1851, was to devote his considerable energies to managing these and other investments and to helping others develop the territory he had helped to establish, until his death twelve years later.

McLoughlin built his large New England–type dwelling near his riverside mill. By 1900 the narrow riverside section of Oregon City was becoming filled with commercial and industrial buildings. Atop the hundred-foot cliff to the east lay the city's principal residential district, some of which was already platted into homesites by 1849. Threatened with demolition to make room for an expanding paper mill, in 1909 the historic structure was laboriously moved up the steep road to its present location, which, appropriately, is on a block originally designated by McLoughlin to be a public park.

The house is an excellent example of a two-story, massed-plan New England tradition folk house (also called a Classical box or a New England large). This folk tradition gradually moved westward, and the house type continued to be built by settlers on the northwestern edges of the frontier until about 1850. Most have had later alterations or additions. This one remains amazingly original, particularly the sixteen-over-twelve-small-pane windows, a stylish detail usually found accompanied by such definitively Georgian features as Classical door surrounds and cornice-line dentils. Most of this house was made from local lumber, but McLoughlin had the fashionable windows and prefabricated interior trim shipped around the Horn from Boston. A second stylish detail appears on what was once the riverfront side and is now the rear or garden facade, which has Greek Revival–inspired narrow windows surrounding the doorway.

The furnishings reflect an amazingly successful effort to reclaim as many McLoughlin possessions as possible. Of particular interest are the dining room table and chairs, Staffordshire china, a hand-carved bed from Scotland, and the Bible used during services at Fort Vancouver. Gaps have been filled in with appropriate early furniture from other sources.

Sauvie Island

The picturesque mill town of Oregon City (see page 523) is on the Willamette River about fifteen miles southward, or upstream, from downtown Portland. Along the river about the same distance in the opposite direction, northward, or downstream, lies Sauvie Island, an equally picturesque destination with an exactly opposite charm—peacefully rural rather than dynamically urban. Here one finds much of the look and feel of the Willamette region's prerailroad agricultural landscapes, a mood that is reinforced by a visit to a Greek Revival farmhouse, another miraculous survivor built only ten years after McLoughlin's Oregon City residence (see the preceding entry).

Bybee-Howell House, 1856

Howell Territorial Park, off Sauvie Island Road, Sauvie Island; 503-222-1741.

One has only to turn off the main highway and cross the bridge to Sauvie Island to feel that another century has been entered. This magical place, near the Willamette's junction with the larger Columbia River, is one of the largest river islands in the United States; it was formed when the interactions of a midriver ledge of rock and a slow bend in the river worked together to capture deep layers of topsoil that were being washed downstream. This makes the soils of the fifteen-mile-long-by-five-mile-wide island extremely fertile—a favored site for Indian dwellings since pre-Columbian days. Today it remains a landscape of lush farmlands interspersed with river-bottom trees and a stand of ancient oaks on the highest, rarely flooded ground near the island's center.

By the 1830s McLoughlin was using part of the island's lush grasses for Hudson's Bay Company dairying operations, swimming the cows across the river from his headquarters at Fort Vancouver. In 1850 Congress passed the famous Donation Land Act, which provided that each adult man or woman who settled in Oregon before December 1, 1851, could receive a 320-acre "donation" of Oregon land from the federal government. Among the many claimants were "Colonel" James F. Bybee and his wife, Julia Ann Miller Bybee, who together received 642 acres on the south end of Sauvie Island.

The Bybees had arrived in Oregon from Kentucky in 1847 along with their several small children. Before settling on their new land, James had gone to the Califor-

Bybee-Howell House

nia goldfields, where he is reported to have made a small fortune. By 1856 he and Julia were ready to build their dream house, and behind it they constructed a straightaway thoroughbred racetrack. Apparently uninterested in farming, the Kentucky colonel intended to breed and race thoroughbred horses. Like most dreams based on gambling, this one didn't last. By 1858 the colonel needed to seek another fortune and headed for the new goldfields being found in what are today British Columbia and Idaho.

The Bybees left behind an unusually large and stylish dwelling for its time and place. It is a nine-room, center-hall, Greek Revival design with a small entry porch supported by "squared" columns, which were easy to build on-site. The house has paired interior chimneys and the style's characteristic wide band of trim under the eaves, which wraps around each gable end to form a distinctive triangular pediment. The corner boards at each end are finished with capitals at the top to resemble tall skinny pilasters.

The fine house was purchased by the Bybees' neigh-bors, Dr. Benjamin Howell and his wife, Elizabeth, who were serious farmers. They and their descendants owned the home and worked the farm for almost a hundred years. In 1959 the now-deteriorating historic structure was purchased by Multnomah County and carefully restored, largely through volunteer efforts and fund-raising sponsored by the Oregon Historical Society. With help from the local chapter of the American Institute of Interior Designers, the society furnished the house with appropriate Oregon-made furniture. Room settings are fairly simple, as would be typical of a house in the Oregon Territory in the middle nineteenth century. Today the home is a national historic landmark.

Acreage around the house was also acquired so that today it is the focal point of a county park that is both a historical and natural conservancy. The grounds are mostly planted with native Oregon species. An old orchard has been restored by saving as many of the surviving trees as possible and then adding over 150 rare early varieties of fruit, making it a sort of "living-museum orchard."

SALEM

Salem, Oregon's capital city, was founded by the New England Methodist missionary Jason Lee, who was one of the first Americans to make his home in the remote Pacific Northwest. Arriving at the Hudson's Bay Company fur-trading post at Fort Vancouver in 1834, Lee was advised by the post's Canadian superintendent, Dr. John McLoughlin (see "McLoughlin House," page 523), to locate among the Indians living in the fertile Willamette River Valley, where he could "teach them first to cultivate the ground and live more comfortably than they could do by hunting, and as they do this, teach them religion."

Discouraged by their lack of success with the local natives after ten years of effort, the missionaries decided to found a school to educate the children of the Anglo immigrants who began arriving via the Oregon Trail in the 1840s (see page 512). To finance this Oregon Institute (now Willamette University), they sold lots in the new town of Salem, which they laid out in 1846.

By the early 1850s the Willamette Valley's farms were prospering as sailing ships delivered their produce to San Francisco to help feed the hordes of fortune seekers arriving in the great California gold rush. Salem soon became a principal marketing center of this agricultural boom, and in 1851 the town replaced Oregon City as the territorial capital.

Modern Salem remains an important agricultural marketing and processing center as well as the seat of the state's government. In spite of its subsequent growth, the city still has a pleasant small-town feel about it. Some of this is captured in **Mission Mill Village** (1313 Mill Street Southeast, 503-585-7012), a

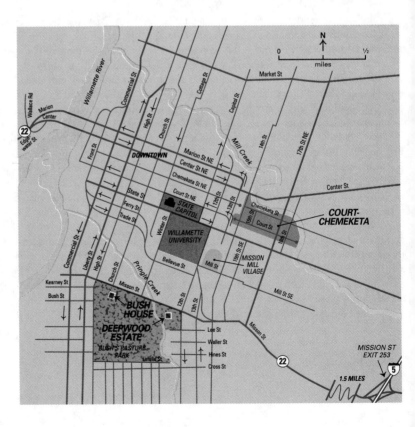

museum complex centered around a remarkably well-preserved and interpreted 1889 woolen mill. Among several moved-in structures on the grounds is Salem founder Jason Lee's 1841 New England–type folk dwelling.

A small cross section of Salem's pre-1940 residential architecture is preserved in the Court-Chemeketa Historic District. In addition the town has two fine Victorian museum houses.

Court-Chemeketa Historic District, ca. 1870–1937

This small historic district has 117 homes that were built over a period of more than sixty years—with the earliest couple of houses constructed in the 1870s and the last lot developed in 1937. The period of greatest activity was about 1908 to 1910, a time when Craftsman bungalows, American four-squares, folk houses, and even late Queen Anne homes were being built. The neighborhood was long called East Salem and housed many of Salem's elite, including lieutenant governors, Supreme Court justices, doctors, bankers, and professors. But the neighborhood always had a mixture of income levels and house sizes—carpenters, stonecutters, and laborers lived here as well.

296 Fourteenth Street (private), Collins House, 1887. This picturesque West Coast Stick-style house has a deep vertical frieze under the eaves. Note the way the windows in the gables pierce this frieze, the lovely wooden detailing surrounding the single windows, and the handsome king's post truss in the top of the side gable.

1547 Chemeketa Street (private), Pooler House, 1910. Jefferson Pooler constructed six houses in this district and lived in this one for ten years. This is a fine example of a one-story, hipped-roof Craftsman design. Note the solid porch railing and the interesting bulge in the porch-support columns, almost as if they were expanding under the

Court-Chemeketa

weight of the roof. Number 1474 Court Street (private), another house constructed by Pooler, is practically identical, right down to the porch supports.

1694 Court Street (private), Steeves House, 1926. This is a fine example of the Colonial Revival's gambrel-roofed subtype, which is often called Dutch Colonial. This house has an interesting cross-gambrel form, with the two wings forming an L, and the entry set into the crook of the L. The entry porch is handsomely detailed and shelters an

Court-Chemeketa

Bush House

Adamesque front door with an elliptical fanlight and side-lights. The two wings of the house are subtly asymmetrical, one roof is slightly lower than the other, and one dormer is slightly smaller. The two end facades, with their gambrel profiles, are each quite handsome. The more traditional one faces Seventeenth Street and is clad in shingles, while the one facing Court Street features a handsome sculptural stuccoed chimney with half-round windows in the second floor. Note the slight flare of the eaves, a feature found in many original Dutch Colonial dwellings in New York and New Jersey, but rarely seen in Revival versions.

Bush House, 1878

600 Mission Street Southeast; 503-363-4714;
Wilbur F. Boothby, Salem, architect.
This understated Italianate design was built by Asahel Bush II (1824–1913), who founded both the *Oregon Statesman* newspaper and the Ladd and Bush Bank and had the largest estate yet probated in Oregon when he died in 1913. This home was originally the centerpiece of a farm complex whose outbuildings included a barn (partially burned and now reconstructed) and the earliest greenhouse in Oregon. It is still surrounded by Bush's Pasture Park, a one-hundred-acre city park that did, indeed, once serve as a pasture for his cattle.

Bush's wife had died in 1863, leaving him with four young children—Estelle (1856–1942), Asahel III (1858–1953), Sally (1860–1946), and Eugenia (1862–1932). It was his second daughter, Sally, who always acted as mistress of Bush House, even traveling to Springfield, Massachusetts, while she was in college to pick out the furnishings for their new home. She lived here until her death, when her brother, Asahel III, moved in. During his occupancy, he prudently arranged for both the house and pasture to be taken over by the city of Salem at his death, despite the temptation of a lucrative sale to a developer. Because of the long tenancy by a single family, including the years of careful tending by "Aunt Sally," as she was lovingly called, today Bush House and its grounds are remarkably intact.

The house itself is a very pleasing and understated asymmetrical version of the Italianate style. Its low-pitched gabled roof is in the gabled-front-and-wing form. There is a substantial partial porch, as was common in L-shaped houses. The windows have full-frame surrounds, rather than simply a hood or pediment above. Those upstairs are topped by segmental arches, while those on the first floor have "flattened" arches.

Most of the house's original fixtures and more than half of the original furnishings remain. Highlights include several wallpapers from France, the original gas-light fixtures (some now converted to electricity), and ten one-of-a-kind hand-carved Italian-marble fireplaces. The house was built with many of the latest comforts—central heating and a marble-topped washstand with hot and cold running water in each bedroom.

Deepwood Estate, 1894

1116 Mission Street Southeast; 503-363-1825;
William C. Knighton, Salem, architect.
This elegant Queen Anne home sits on its original five-and-one-half-acre site—now a picturesque setting of

woodland, stream, and formal gardens. This early residential commission helped launch the career of architect Knighton, who went on to become the first state architect of Oregon and to build some of the finer buildings in the Northwest. He sited Deepwood on the bank of Pringle Creek and designed the home's elaborate porte cochere to angle out toward the creek.

The home was built for Dr. Luke A. Port, a druggist and land speculator. After little more than a year, he sold it to Mrs. Willie Bingham, who, along with her husband, George, a respected attorney, and their young daughter, Alice, lived here until 1925. In that year Clifford Brown and his wife, who was also named Alice, purchased the house and moved in with their two teenage sons. Tragically, Clifford drowned just two years later. In 1929 his widow hired two of her friends, Elizabeth Lord and Edith Schryver, to prepare a garden plan. This was one of the partnership's first commis-

sions—they went on to become highly respected landscape architects.

Both Lord and Schryver had attended the Lowthorpe School of Landscape Architecture for Women in Groton, Massachusetts. Schryver, fourteen years younger than Lord, had additionally worked for Ellen Shipman, the prominent New York landscape architect, for five years. The two women met on a study trip to visit European gardens and decided to form a partnership and practice in Oregon. Shryver concentrated on design, and Lord specialized in plant selection. Their plan for Deepwood, one of their earliest, features several outdoor "rooms," which complement and enhance the surrounding naturalistic setting.

These varied "rooms" still survive today—the garden includes the Rose Arbor, Lilac Walk, Chinese Garden, "Great Room," Tea Garden, and Spring Garden. A handsome gazebo featured in the garden came from

Deepwood Estate

the 1905 Lewis and Clark Exposition in Portland. It seems particularly appropriate here because its roof echoes the jaunty bell-curve design of Deepwood's tower roof.

It was not until 1930 that Alice Brown began calling her home Deepwood, after a favorite book of her children's called *The Hollow Tree and the Deepwood Book,* by Albert Bigelow Paine. Alice not only gave the estate its picturesque name, but also lived in the house longer than any of its previous occupants and left it with its legacy of handsome gardens.

Deepwood's design is the unique creation of a talented architect, and most of it survives unmodified. An exception is the jauntily angled porte cochere, which was enclosed by Alice Brown in 1925 to create a lovely solarium. Notable exterior features include a sculptural stone chimney, a recessed upstairs balcony, and, on the rear of the house, a number of through-the-cornice gabled dormers, a feature that is unusual in Queen Anne designs.

The interior retains most of its original golden-oak woodwork and also the stained glass and beveled glass executed by the Povey Brothers of Portland, Oregon. David Povey was trained at Cooper Union in New York City and was the designer of the three-brother firm, which has been called the Tiffany of the Northwest. Their work survives in major buildings throughout the region, including numerous churches and synagogues in Portland. At Deepwood they created a stained-glass memorial to the Ports' son, Omega, over the parlor fireplace, as well as the glass at the front entry.

The house is attractively but simply furnished, primarily with donated pieces. This approach allows it to be used for community events as well as being open for public tours. A handsome Period carriage house, also designed by Knighton, complements the main house.

South Dakota

SIOUX FALLS

FOUNDED 1857

Population Growth:
1860	100
1900	10,000
1940	41,000
1990	101,000

Founded as a frontier farming community in the fertile agricultural lands of southeastern Dakota Territory, Sioux Falls remained a small village until the western railroad boom of the 1880s. It then had the good fortune to become a junction point for five separate rail lines building northward and westward across the Dakota plains. In a single decade, the town's population jumped fivefold, from two thousand in 1880 to ten thousand in 1890. By that year it had already become the region's principal agricultural marketing and trade center, as well as South Dakota's largest city, distinctions it has maintained ever since.

Sioux Falls also has a more unusual claim to fame, one that is directly reflected in much of its early architecture. The same massive layers of reddish sedimentary rock that form the near-downtown waterfalls that gave the town its name turned out to also make a superb building stone. Exceptionally tough, handsome,

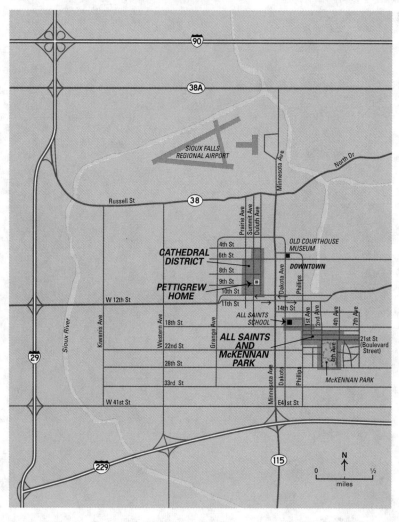

and relatively easy to quarry in uniform-width layers, this Sioux quartzite quickly became a favorite building material for architects and contractors throughout the country. Not surprisingly, it is also a local favorite, used throughout the city not only in the walls or foundations of houses, churches, and public buildings, but also as a paving material for early streets, on some of which it still survives. Among these is the 500 block of West Sixth Street in the Cathedral District (see the following entry).

Among the city's many historic structures built of Sioux quartzite is the **Old Courthouse Museum,** formerly the Minnehaha County Courthouse (1890; Wallace Dow, Sioux Falls, architect). Located at 200 West Sixth Street (605-367-4210), this handsome Richardsonian Romanesque building now houses the main part of the Siouxland Heritage Museums. Among the exhibits is an unusually informative treatment of late-nineteenth- and early-twentieth-century Sioux Falls architecture.

Cathedral District, ca. 1880–1915

Located on a high bluff just west of downtown, there is some confusion about the name of this extraordinary neighborhood. It's official title is the Sioux Falls Historic District, an overly general term in a town with several other fine historic districts. Most residents prefer to call it the Cathedral District, after the handsome St. Joseph Cathedral at 503 North Duluth Avenue (1916–1919; Emanuel L. Masqueray, St. Paul, Minnesota, architect), which provides a strong visual anchor for the neighborhood. This area was for many decades the favored homesite for affluent Sioux Falls citizens. House styles range from a few late Italianates (now with stylish updates) to early-twentieth-century Period houses, with the heaviest emphasis on Queen Anne and early Colonial Revival designs.

Many of the neighborhood's finest homes were designed by an unusually talented Sioux Falls–based architect named Wallace L. Dow (1844–1911). Dow learned his future profession as a young carpenter in New Hampshire. There he had the good fortune to befriend a local politician named Nehemiah Ordway, who, in 1880, was appointed by President Rutherford B. Hayes to the governorship of the remote Dakota Territory. Ordway must have had great confidence in his young friend's abilities, for in 1881 he asked Dow to design the territory's new hospital for the insane in the then-capital city of Yankton (see page 541). Thus began Dow's long career as the Dakotas' premier architect.

Cathedral District

618 West Ninth Street (private), 1903. This fine early Colonial Revival design has a hipped roof with a full-width porch that also wraps around to the right side. Note the use of multiple rounded arches—in the dormer, entry door, Palladian motif above the entry, and on a first-floor window to the far right of the house. Among the notable details is an unusual curved corner window on the first floor right. This same distinctive window appears in several other houses in this neighborhood. Note also the matching railings around the upper and lower porches. The railings have closely spaced balusters and a distinctive reverse curve in the handrail.

215 North Summit Avenue (private), Rogde-Manchester House, 1901. This early Colonial Revival house has strongly exaggerated detailing—a bulky entry porch with Ionic columns, an idiosyncratically high-pitched triangular pediment that is accentuated with a tall, narrow oval window, and a row of unusually deep swags beneath the cornice line.

103 South Duluth Avenue (private), Carpenter House, 1892; Wallace Dow, Sioux Falls, architect. This striking Queen Anne house with exotic overtones is one of architect Dow's finest domestic designs. Its upper story is covered with slate shingles rather than the more typical shaped-wood shingles. Note the way Dow handled the ornament on the cutaway corner window on the lower left of this house—he used a cantilevered stone with an intriguing design cut into the underside. Other unique features include the entry-porch supports, the unusual upside-down broken-ogee pediment beneath the upper-right window, and the deep-jewel-toned trim paint colors, which were carefully researched for the house's restoration.

Cathedral District

109 North Duluth Avenue (private), Hollister/Peck House; ca. 1880 and later. This simple-hipped-roof Italianate house had a stylish update in the late Victorian era when a Queen Anne–inspired wraparound porch was added. Number 335 North Duluth Avenue (private) is another updated Italianate house—this time with both an added porch and a large front-facing gable. The distinctive and telling Italianate window surrounds remain clearly visible on the first floor.

202 North Duluth Avenue (private), Hollister House, 1904. Another of the neighborhood's many early Colonial Revival designs, this one with an unusually high-pitched hipped roof. Garlands are found only above the two main upper-story windows, not around the entire cornice line, as at 618 West Ninth Street (see page 535). Despite the overall symmetrical feeling of this house, note the slightly asymmetrical placement of the front entry door and nearby oval window. These were probably shifted slightly off-center to accommodate an American four-square floor plan and thus allow for a slightly larger living room and slightly smaller entry hall than if the door were centered.

226 North Duluth Avenue (private), Spier House, 1915. This engaging house is a mixture of styles. It takes its tiled visor roof and stucco walls from the Mission style. Craftsman influence is obvious in the exposed rafter ends along the entire edge of the visor roof and in the trelliswork above the side entry porch. The "bowling pin" balusters along portions of the roof parapet and the "blind" arches above the first-floor paired French doors are most typical of the Italian Renaissance style.

227 North Duluth Avenue (private), Mallanney House, 1913. This Colonial Revival design, clad with wood shingles, was built later than the other Colonial Revival houses featured here. Its architectural details are not overly exaggerated, unlike those of the earlier houses.

350 North Duluth Avenue (private), Bailey-Edgerton-Kirby House, 1889; Wallace Dow, Sioux Falls, architect. This handsome Romanesque house is built of native Sioux quartzite. Note the diaper (an overall pattern, often of squares, as seen here) of squared stones in the top of the front-facing gable. This pattern is echoed more inexpensively in wood on at least two of the side-facing gables. The wooden porch supports are elegant and are related to those at Dow's 103 South Duluth Avenue design (see page 535) by their spiraled grooving.

Pettigrew Home, 1889

131 North Duluth Avenue; 605-367-7097 or 605-367-4210; Wallace Dow, Sioux Falls, architect.

Architect Dow (see page 535) created this unusual Queen Anne design for lawyer Thomas McMartin, but it is now most closely associated with the pioneer Sioux Falls entrepreneur and civic leader Richard F. Pettigrew (1848–1926), who purchased the house in 1911. While studying law at the University of Wisconsin, Pettigrew in 1869 took a summer job as part of a federal crew surveying the Dakota Territory and became intrigued with the promise of the Sioux Falls area. He returned the next year, opened a small real estate office, and began building both a fortune and a reputation as a tireless booster of the town's assets. Pettigrew was ultimately to

Pettigrew Home

build two of the five railroads that assured the town's long-term prosperity and was instrumental in the arrival of the other three. In addition, he founded the town's street railway, opened a successful industrial park, donated land for civic improvements, and enjoyed the challenges of Territorial politics. This last pursuit ultimately led to two six-year terms in the U.S. Senate.

Pettigrew's later years were devoted to travel and adding to his extensive collections of art and artifacts. In 1923 he built a large museum wing onto the rear of his home to house these materials. When he died in 1926, his will left the house, museum, and collections to the city of Sioux Falls, which opened the museum and collections to the public in 1930. The house was used for caretaker's quarters and curatorial activities until 1986, when it was restored as a museum house by the city and county. The complex is now a part of the Siouxland Heritage Museums, which also include downtown's Old Courthouse Museum (see page 535).

For the main body of the house, Dow used a hipped-roof, patterned-masonry Queen Anne design but omitted the dominant front-facing roof gable usually seen in the style. Instead, there is a low-hipped-roof dormer. The first story is of Sioux quartzite, with the brick walls above accentuated by bands of lighter quartzite. Other Queen Anne features include three tall decorative chimneys, a tower on the side, and an asymmetrical

front porch with shaped porch supports. Note also the fine window details, some with thresholds above and some with areas of leaded glass. This was an unusually forward-looking house for its day, much quieter and less exuberant than the more typical Queen Anne houses in the neighborhood, such as the one Dow designed at 103 South Duluth Avenue (see page 535).

The fine interiors show a mixture of finishes and fixtures—some original to the 1889 house and others added in a major remodeling undertaken in 1911 when Senator Pettigrew and his wife acquired the house. Striking among the 1889 features is the Lincrusta-Walton wall covering in the large entry, stairway, and upstairs halls. A smaller-scale Lincrusta pattern covers the ceiling. Lincrusta was an embossed linoleum-like product for covering walls, made to imitate stamped Spanish leather. Almost impervious to wear, it was particularly favored by the Victorians for high-traffic halls. Finishes from the 1911 Pettigrew remodeling include silk damask wall coverings in the front and back parlors and painted ceiling canvases.

The furnishings reflect the time period from 1911 to 1926, when Senator Pettigrew lived here. There are a number of original pieces, including many things acquired by Pettigrew on his travels. The most impressive furniture is that in the upstairs study, left as it was by the senator's special request and containing his huge over-stuffed black leather chairs.

All Saints and McKennan Park, ca. 1890–1930

Like the Cathedral District, each of these two adjacent neighborhoods, now city historic districts, takes its name from the most dominant feature within its boundaries. The older of the two is All Saints, which lies directly south of the downtown business district and is named for the landmark **All Saints School,** built as an Episcopalian school for young women and now converted to housing. The five-acre campus retains its original polychromed Gothic building, a remarkable structure designed by Wallace Dow and built in 1884. The presence of this elegant new school for young ladies sparked interest in homebuilding nearby, and about twenty houses were built in the neighborhood by 1900. Most of the neighborhood's development took place between 1900 and 1919 (about 70 percent). The houses were comfortable, and some quite large, but few had the level of detailing seen in many Cathedral District examples.

McKennan Park, just to the south, takes its name from the twenty-acre park that was donated to the city of Sioux Falls by Mrs. Helen Gale McKennan in 1906. Maintenance of the broad median down Twenty-first Street (formerly called Boulevard Street) was taken over by the city in 1910. Development remained spotty, and only eight of the houses remaining in the district were built before 1915. A 1910 description of the area gave this depiction: "Cattle grazed in the open area adjoining the scattered homes and lawns. Prairie chickens were so plentiful in the summer and fall that an energetic boy with a sharp shooting eye and a trusty gun could easily bag enough of these game birds for mamma to serve the family supper." By 1915 the streets were paved, and streetcar service had been initiated. Forty additional houses were built between 1915 and 1925, and construction continued up until 1954, when the last of the neighborhood's fifteen Ranch houses were completed.

1203 South First Avenue (private), Coughran House, 1887. This elegant Queen Anne house has unusual spindlework ornamentation. The porch and porte cochere are enhanced by rounded arches formed by a single piece of curved wood with the resulting corners filled in with beadwork. The porch railing has an uncommon pattern of offset squares made by short turned spindles. Note the extraordinary sculpted design of the tall brick chimneys.

1525 South Second Avenue (private), Fenn-Brown House, 1915. This engaging Craftsman design is clad in brown shingles. Jaunty Oriental-influenced upturned ends enliven the rafters and roof beams as well as the lintels above the front door and main windows. This same motif is used to produce a creative pattern in the front-facing porch roof gable and also to produce a unique variation of the usual triangular knee brace under the side gables of the roof. The original front door is an upside-down variation of the more typical Craftsman door design that places three tall windows above and a blocky wood pattern below.

201 East Twentieth Street (private), Beach House, 1924. This pleasant Prairie-style house has brick walls in its lower two-thirds and stucco walls in the upper third. The stucco is ornamented with a Wrightian geometric cross motif created with tiles. (Look for this distinctive two-thirds/one-third wall-division pattern in other Prairie-style houses in this neighborhood.) Note the lovely pair of stained-glass windows only in the north side of the enclosed entry porch. An interesting question is whether this was originally an open porch with these two glass windows used as sidelights on each side of the front door.

1103 South Phillips Avenue (private). This house has a unique combination of features—Shinglesque rounded arches at the sides of the front porch, large Tuscan columns as porch supports, a Greek key design along the edge of the porch roof and main roof, and the remains of an exotic, but now-enclosed, upstairs side porch.

SPEARFISH

FOUNDED 1876

Population Growth:

1900 1,200

1940 2,000

1990 7,000

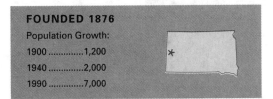

The picturesque Black Hills of western South Dakota were the scene of one of the last, and richest, of the western gold rushes. Considered sacred by the mighty Sioux tribes that long ruled the far Dakota plains, the Black Hills were closed to Anglo prospectors until 1875. The previous year a U.S. Army survey party first confirmed long-standing rumors that the Black Hills held rich gold deposits. The federal government attempted to delay the inevitable rush of prospectors while attempting to purchase entry rights from the Sioux. When these negotiations failed, Washington, already unable to control the flood of unauthorized gold seekers, officially opened the lands to settlement. By 1876 Deadwood Gulch, near the north end of the hills, was proving to be the heart of enormously rich gold-bearing veins. In that same year the small town of Spearfish was established on the nearby plains to serve the many farmers and ranchers who arrived to seek their rewards not in high-risk prospecting, but in supplying food to the hungry miners.

Modern Spearfish is still an agricultural trade center as well as the northern gateway to the scenic Black Hills and its historic mining towns. It is also the site of an unusual museum house, a rare example of a typical middle-class dwelling from the transitional Victorian-to-Eclectic years between 1900 and 1910.

The nearby Black Hills gold rush town of **Deadwood,** magnet for the initial Anglo settlement of western South Dakota, was, like most early mining "camps," dominated by single male prospectors and laborers who lived very spartan lives in tents, shacks, or crowded rooming houses. It thus lacks important historic residential neighborhoods or museum houses but does retain an unusually fine collection of early commercial buildings. The nearby town of **Lead** has the distinction of being the home of the nation's richest and longest-lived gold deposit—the fabled **Homestake Mine**—which is still in full production today. Tours of its aboveground operations are available (605-584-3110), while the nearby **Black Hills Mining Museum** (U.S. Highway 85 and Main Street, 605-584-1605) offers full-size models of the underground workings, which now extend downward to depths of more than eight thousand feet.

Hatchery Superintendent's House, 1905

423 Hatchery Circle, D. C. Booth Historic National Fish Hatchery; 605-642-7730.

Fly-fishing for trout in mountain streams is today a central theme of western sportfishing. But such was not

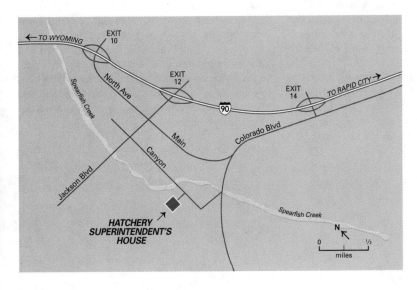

Hatchery
Superintendent's House

always the case. The countless mountain streams of the Black Hills—and other western ranges—originally lacked edible fish. In 1896 the U.S. Fish Commission, later to become the U.S. Fish and Wildlife Service, established a fish hatchery here in an attempt to introduce trout into the many Black Hills mountain streams. The experiment was a resounding success, and the hatchery expanded to become the prototype for the service's subsequent efforts throughout the country. Today the historic hatchery is being restored as a living museum. Among its important structures is an inviting Superintendent's House that provides a seldom-seen glimpse into a typical middle-class home of the early Eclectic era.

The house was occupied for twenty-eight years by the family of the hatchery's first superintendent, Dewitt Clinton Booth, for whom the historic complex is now named. Booth's wife, Ruby, a former music teacher at Spearfish Normal School, now Black Hills State Uni-

versity, made the home a center of the town's social life, hosting a constant stream of visitors and community events.

A two-story, front-gabled form, the unpretentious Colonial Revival dwelling is of the full-width-one-story-porch subtype. It is simply but appropriately furnished with period items, some of them in an attic-story office used by Mr. Booth. Very innovative for the period are the bedroom's walk-in closets, each with its own window.

Elsewhere on the site, the 1899 Shingle-style Hatcheries Building has historical exhibits. Outside are the old ponds and raceways, still filled with brown and rainbow trout that can be fed. There is even an underground viewing room into a pond that contains both species. An early railroad car is being remodeled into the kind of car used to distribute trout eggs and hatchlings throughout the West.

YANKTON

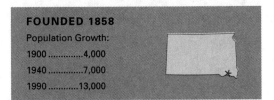

FOUNDED 1858

Population Growth:

1900 4,000
1940 7,000
1990 13,000

Named for a subtribe of the Sioux Indians, who ceded the surrounding area of their tribal lands for white settlement in 1858, Yankton, served by summer riverboat traffic on the adjacent Missouri River (see page 464), soon became the region's principal Anglo town. By 1861 it was the bustling capital of the newly created Dakota Territory. In the words of the town's historian, it was "full of ambitious politicians, fiercely partisan newspapers, and vigorous mercantile firms."

Yankton's prosperity was to be short-lived. In 1881 a devastating Missouri River flood destroyed part of the town. Its steamboat docks, already declining as a result of the region's rapidly spreading railroad network, were never rebuilt. The final blow came when the territorial capital was moved to Bismarck in 1883. Soon Yankton was but another county seat and agricultural trade center among many that dotted the fertile lands of southeastern South Dakota.

Yankton's early success followed by rapid decline has, as is often the case under such circumstances, left it with an unusually rich heritage of historic architecture. Of particular interest is the old **Yankton College Campus** (Douglas Street at Tenth Street), with buildings dating from 1883. In a creative adaptive reuse plan, the college has now been converted to a minimum-security federal prison. Yankton also retains many fine Victorian dwellings, one of which is a handsome Stick-style museum house.

Historic Core, ca. 1870–1885

The majority of Yankton's surviving Victorian houses were built during the decade from 1873 until 1883—when it still served as the territorial capital for the huge Dakota Territory and after the 1873 arrival of the first railroad had substantially increased the town's size and prosperity. Most of these are concentrated in a ten-block area just northeast of downtown, although scattered examples can be found throughout the older parts of town. Italianate designs from the 1870s are most common, but many Queen Anne examples from the 1880s also occur. Most of Yankton's Italianate houses have had some sort of later alterations—keep your eyes peeled for the typical brackets at the cornice line and the distinctive window shapes, both of which commonly survive later modifications.

400 East Sixth Street (private), Nyberg House, 1885. Note the Craftsman-era porch supports on this Italianate design.

416 Pine Street (private), Matthiesen House, 1879. This is another Italianate design with a modified front porch. There are several other modified Italianates along Pine Street. Grandest is number 503 (see the following entry).

503 Pine Street (private), McVay-Gurney House, 1879. Note how the front wall beneath the low-pitched front gable extends forward from the rest of the house to accentuate the gable area. This asymmetrical Italianate looks a bit like someone elected to build only two-thirds of a centered-gable design. The front porch appears to be a modern reconstruction.

517 Mulberry Street (private), Coulson Home, 1878. This is a fine example of a towered Second Empire house. What appears to be original ornamental cresting remains in place

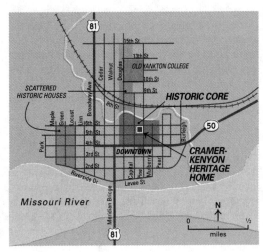

atop the tower. Note the tall narrow windows with unusual surrounds on both the first floor and dormer. A matching carriage house is behind.

16 Capital Street (private), Gamble House, 1890. This half-timbered Queen Anne appears to be unaltered. Note the etched pattern between the half-timbering in the gable.

512 Mulberry Street (private), Ward Home, 1873. An unusual mixture of two Romantic-era styles is found in this large and handsome home built by Reverend Joseph Ward, the founder of Yankton College. The windows have Italianate crowns, while the pair of high-pitched parapeted gables is Gothic in inspiration.

7 Pine Street (private), Purdy House, 1880. Built by a druggist, this engaging one-story Italianate cottage is essentially unaltered. Note the delightful entry hood that is suspended from the house without any porch supports.

514, 516, and 518 Douglas Street (all private), 1879. These matching brick-walled Italianate designs were originally built as rental houses. Today their porches have all been supplied by a modern wrought-iron salesman, and the cornice-line brackets are all missing. But their low-pitched hipped roofs and Italianate window surrounds make their style immediately apparent.

205 Green Street (private), Ohlman Home, 1871. This elegant centered-gable Italianate home sits atop a large lot that must have once afforded a magnificent view of the Missouri River from its cupola. The house's beauty is enhanced by exquisite detailing, a tall raised foundation, and a one-story porch that encircles much of the house.

517 Locust Street (private), Banton House, 1920. Dr. B. M. Banton's hobby was stonework. He did work throughout Yankton, but this, his own Craftsman-style home, is truly a marvel of individual craftsmanship—one of the great charms of this style.

Cramer-Kenyon Heritage Home, 1886

509 Pine Street; 605-665-7470.

This rare Stick-style dwelling is in remarkably original condition. Only two related families have lived here since Nelson J. Cramer and his wife, Alice, purchased it in 1890, just four years after it was built. The Cramers decorated the house to suit their tastes using fine wallpapers, some imported from Germany. In 1930 the Cramers' great-niece inherited the house and its furnishings. Although she used her own furniture, she kept the house itself remarkably intact and stored all of the Cramers' furnishings in the attic. Thus in 1972, after she and her husband died, the makings of an authentic early house museum were already here.

Exact reproductions of the original wallpapers are used in the entry hall and the double parlors. In one of the upstairs bedrooms, an exceptional wallpaper of shells and coral has been reproduced from a scrap of the original. The woodwork has never been painted, and most of the original fixtures and fittings remain in place. Intriguing English Minton tiles from Stoke-on-

Cramer-Kenyon Heritage Home

Trent surround the back-parlor fireplace; these feature Shakespearean scenes hand painted by J. Moyer Smith. Other unusual features include coved cornices, very unusual during this period; an early Murphy bed; and paintings throughout the house done by Mrs. Cramer.

The exterior shows many typical Stick-style details. Some of these appear around and beneath the through-the-cornice-dormer on the right. Flat wooden strips, resembling sticks, are applied to the wall to connect the dormer windows with the upper-story windows below. Two of the resulting squared spaces are filled with diagonal woodwork. A similar element appears on the main front-facing gable, where the space between the upper-story windows and the gable-level windows is filled with a horizontal composition. Even the tiny side wing, toward the right rear, has an area of applied stickwork and diagonal siding, between the upstairs and downstairs windows. A fun exterior feature to notice is the gable-on-hip roof (a tiny front-facing gable perched atop the main hipped roof).

The only major exterior modification has been to the front porch, which received new and simplified porch supports and railings when it was enclosed with screen. Many porches were enclosed with fine-mesh metal screening when this material became affordable. This furnished front porch is a great example of how such screened-in porches were often used—for comfortable outdoor living rooms, protected from insects yet still open to breezes.

Texas

AMARILLO

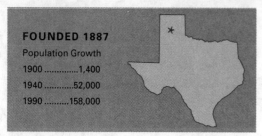

FOUNDED 1887

Population Growth

1900 1,400
1940 52,000
1990 158,000

The principal trade and manufacturing center of the Texas Panhandle, Amarillo is today the state's eighth-largest city. It was founded as a cattle-shipping station on the Fort Worth and Denver Railroad, which opened a vast swatch of northwestern Texas and southern Colorado for new settlement in the late 1880s (see also page 588). The town's future importance was assured when the westward-building Atchison, Topeka, and Santa Fe line built through it in 1898, followed by the Rock Island line in 1902.

Amarillo's cattle-based economy received an enormous boost in 1918 when the giant Hugoton Gas Field was discovered in the northern Panhandle. Still one of the nation's principal producers, the gas in Hugoton's deep reservoirs contains large quantities of dissolved gasoline, which can be marketed directly, rather than requiring expensive refining from heavier crude oil. Some Hugoton wells also contain large amounts of rare helium gas, which has many commercial uses. Amarillo quickly became the principal processing and marketing center for this new bonanza. Between 1920 and 1930 the town's population surged from fifteen thousand to forty-three thousand, and it remains today a major center of the petrochemical industry.

As if cattle and petroleum weren't enough, in the post-1950 decades the Panhandle, drawing on deepwater wells tapping the prolific Ogallala Aquifer, has, like Lubbock to the south (see page 616), become the heart of a bountiful hinterland of irrigated crops. Wheat and feed grains dominate the Amarillo region, where the latter combine with its many cattle ranches to make it a center for quality beef production in large feedlots. The Lubbock area's somewhat-milder climate has given it a different emphasis—the growing of high-value irrigated cotton.

Amarillo's early cattle and petroleum booms provided it with a delightful neighborhood of fine Eclectic-era homes, one of which is now an elegant museum house.

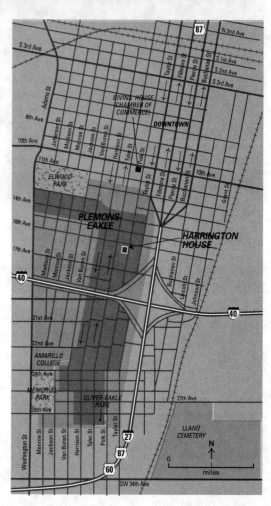

Plemons-Eakle, ca. 1905–1935

Brick streets and mature street trees add distinction to this large neighborhood, which includes parts of two subdivisions—the 1890 Plemons Addition and the 1906 Oliver-Eakle Addition. The first, located north of today's Interstate 40, was platted by Potter County's first judge, William B. Potter, who purchased section 170 in 1887, the year that Amarillo was founded. In 1890 he platted it as Plemons Addition. Mrs. Melissa Dora Oliver-Eakle, an Amarillo businesswoman, platted the second subdivision, the Oliver-Eakle Addition, just south of today's Interstate 40. She was a woman well ahead of her times, as she is the only female land developer encountered in researching this book. Both of their subdivisions have straightforward grid streets, and the line between them can be detected today by a slight shift in the direction of the street grid. The Oliver-Eakle Addition is aligned north–south, while Plemons Addition is at a slight cant. Plemons is closer to Amarillo's downtown, and Potter chose to align his addition's streets with those of downtown Amarillo, which align with the angle of the town's main railroad tracks.

The neighborhood features a typical small-town mixture of sizes and styles (appropriate to a town that had only 1,400 people in 1900 and had boomed to 10,000 by 1910). Although there are a number of large homes, such as the Harrington House (see page 546), smaller Craftsman-style houses are the norm. These include many interesting variations on the Craftsman style and a higher proportion of brick-clad Craftsman homes than is typical. The larger houses tend to be Neoclassical, Tudor, or Craftsman/Prairie mixtures.

1000 South Polk Street (ground floor open), Bivins House, 1905; George Parr, builder. Lee Bivins and his wife, Mary Elizabeth, built this house as a team. She supervised construction while he built up his cattle and natural gas businesses to pay for it. In the 1920s Bivins was reportedly the largest individual cattle owner in the world. He owned over a million acres of ranch land with as many as sixty thousand head of cattle at one time. They chose to build an imposing Neoclassical house of brick with elaborate limestone trim. The basement story, two-story pilasters, and arch surrounding the front door are rough-faced stone, while the remainder of the stone trim has smooth or tooled finishes. The front facade features a handsome full-facade porch approached by a dramatic sweep of stone steps.

The side facade is just as elaborate, with a semicircular full-height porch supported by six colossal stone columns. It has a flat roof with balustrade above and a graceful curved balcony at the second-story level. This facade still has broad special windows (see "1710 South Tyler Street," page 546) with a graceful beveled-glass pattern above. Regrettably, the ones on the front facade have been removed.

The Junior League of Amarillo has restored the large reception hall of this house, which holds the Chamber of Commerce Visitor Center, making it a treat to obtain walking-tour and other information on Amarillo and this house. The woodwork and light fixtures are original, and you are allowed to look around several of the public rooms.

1608 South Polk Street (private), Shuford House, ca. 1913; Shepard, Farrar, and Wiser, Kansas City, architects. Designed by the same architects as Harrington House (see page 546), this was built for Jefferson Davis Shuford, the general livestock agent of the Fort Worth and Denver Railroad. It is a Colonial Revival house in the hipped-roof-with-full-width-porch subtype, which accounted for more than one-third of the Colonial Revival houses built before 1915. It has a strong Prairie influence in the wide overhanging eaves and the massive squared supports located at each end of the porch.

1700 South Polk Street (private), Shelton House, ca. 1914; Joseph Camp Berry, Amarillo, architect. This fine home

Plemons-Eakle

today serves as the headquarters for the Junior League of Amarillo. It is an excellent cross-gabled Craftsman-style house—with open eaves, low-pitched side-gabled roof and centered front gable, exposed roof beams, and shaped triangular braces. The influence of the Prairie style is seen in the massive squared porch supports and the unusual section of hipped roof to each side of the centered gable. Features not particularly typical of either style (but very much at home on this architect-designed house) include the wide arch in the centered gable, the oversize keystones over the windows and front door, and the triangles-in-square pattern in the upper portion of the windows. There is a matching carriage house behind.

1710 South Polk Street (private), Galbraith House, ca. 1912. This unusually large and elaborate hipped-roof Craftsman-style house gains a Prairie-style flair from the horizontal lines at the top and bottom of the broad upstairs porch (which continue on the house as belt courses) and the third horizontal line formed by the long supporting beam underneath.

2104 South Polk Street (private), Eakle House, 1923; Clarence M. House and Guy A. Carlander, Amarillo, architects. Multiple materials (brick, stucco, river stone, and flint) are used in this Craftsman-style house. During the early 1900s, Craftsman houses with this much pizzazz (which here includes dramatic stone porch supports growing out of the ground and an Oriental flair to the eaves) were often called California Craftsman houses. The small second story behind makes this house an airplane bungalow. In the "battle of the grandmothers" one author's grandmother maintained that this was because the second story, sometimes as small as only one room, allowed a good view out to low-flying aircraft on all sides. The other author's grandmother maintained that it was because the small second story looked like an airplane cockpit with the gabled roof looking like spreading wings.

2500 South Van Buren Street (private), ca. 1930s. Smoothly rounded corners, original casement windows (some turning the corners), and two upstairs porches (one covered and one open) lend distinction to this intriguing Art Moderne house. Art Moderne is one of the two Modernistic styles, and this house has all of its identifying features, including a flat roof, a smooth stucco wall surface, an asymmetrical facade, and horizontal lines in the porch railings and in triple bands of trim wrapping the house.

2501 South Van Buren Street (private), Hubbell House, ca. 1923. Note the picturesque jerkin-head roof and eyebrow dormer in this Tudor house, simulating the effect of a false-thatched roof. The Plemons-Eakle neighborhood has a number of houses with jerkin-head or clipped-gable roofs (these are two names for a gable roof that is clipped off at the top with a bit of sloping hipped roof).

2202 South Tyler Street (private), ca. 1920s. This brick Tudor house also has a distinctive jerkin-head roof like that at 2501 South Van Buren (see the preceding entry). Here it is used in combination with a broad-arched entry porch and a roof clad with tiles that form alternating flat and rounded vertical rows.

1710 South Tyler Street (private), Herring House, 1910. A full-height porch combined with a full-width porch was the favorite southern form of the Neoclassical style. Here the full-width porch wraps around to the left side of the house, and the balustrade atop forms a long, open upstairs porch. Note the very broad windows downstairs with smaller patterned upper areas. This type of extra-wide window (with an unequal division in height between the clear lower pane and the decorated upper area) was designed especially for the

front of houses and was popular from about 1900 to 1915. Their presence is an excellent way to date houses to those approximate years.

Many millwork companies carried these windows. The 1908 to 1909 *Official Catalogue* of Adams and Kelly Company (Omaha, Nebraska) featured twenty-six pages of variations. They came in two basic forms—single-sash windows (not designed to open) and double sashes called check-rail windows (these were designed to open). Both varieties came in less expensive "cottage" windows (where the ornamental effect above was obtained by using plain glass set in decorative wood mullions) and as more expensive "special front windows," which featured a variety of leaded-, beveled-, or colored-art-glass patterns for the decorative top.

Harrington House, 1914

1600 South Polk Street; 806-374-5490
(advance reservations required);
Shepard, Farrar, and Wiser, Kansas City, architects.

Amarillo's history as a ranching and petroleum center is reflected in this fine Neoclassical home, which has projecting side wings and other details borrowed from the Italian Renaissance style. Built by cattlemen John and Pat Landergin, the house was purchased in 1940 by the influential oilman Don Harrington and his wife, Sybil. The exterior of the home features unusually handsome detailing—portico with eight fluted Ionic columns; decorative iron balconies; and an elegant, balustraded front terrace. Walls of dark brown brick with contrasting limestone window surrounds add further drama to the facades.

Harrington House

Harrington House

Inside, the fifteen-thousand-square-foot dwelling has the style's typical center hall plan with formal rooms on either side. Among the fine original details are a limestone fountain and arched ceiling in the music room; oak paneling and Gothic strap-work ceiling in the library; and French silk damask wall coverings in the drawing room. The furnishings feature many fine French and English antique items collected by the Harrington's during their extensive travels.

Following Mr. Harrington's death in 1974, Mrs. Harrington continued the couple's generous philanthropic ventures, both in the Amarillo area and elsewhere. In 1995 Harrington House was conveyed to the Amarillo Area Foundation, which operates it as a nonprofit house museum. Tours are currently offered two mornings a week, limited to four persons (minimum age sixteen), and must be arranged in advance by telephone.

AUSTIN

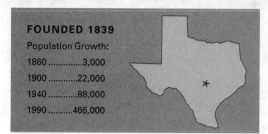

FOUNDED 1839

Population Growth:

1860 3,000
1900 22,000
1940 88,000
1990 466,000

Founded by the leaders of the Texas Revolution to replace Hispanic San Antonio as the capital of their new
republic (see page 622), Austin first languished as a remote frontier village. Then, following Texas's admission to the Union in 1845, the state began attracting an
increasing flow of cotton-growing Anglo farmers from
the older southern states. By the time the first railroads
reached Austin in 1871, it was the bustling capital of an
expanding agricultural empire. In 1883 the city was
chosen as the site for the new University of Texas, which
added the role of educational center to its growing importance as the focal point of state government. By
1940 Austin was Texas's fifth-largest city.

In the last decades of the twentieth century, Sunbelt
population shifts to Texas caused exponential growth
in both the university and the state government. In addition, Austin's mild climate, scenic setting, and laid-
back lifestyle have made it a favored location for new
light industry and corporate relocations. Between 1970
and 1990, the city's population almost doubled, making it one of the nation's fastest-growing urban centers.

As usual, such spectacular growth has taken a heavy
toll on the city's historic architecture. Early residential
neighborhoods, mostly centered around the magnificent 1888 **State Capitol** (Eleventh Street and Congress
Avenue, 512-463-0065) and around the nearby university, have been particularly hard hit by demolition for
new public buildings as well as for many blocks of still-
vacant redevelopment sites. Fortunately, Austin's small

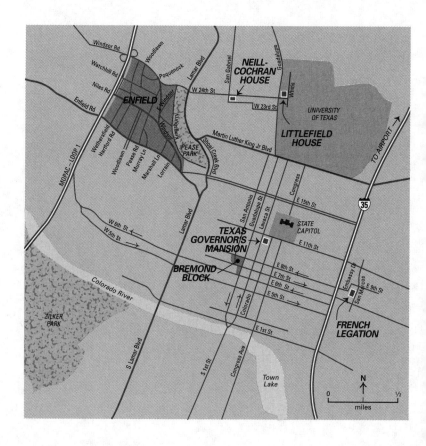

French Legation

collection of antebellum landmark dwellings, the finest in the state, still survive to delight the visitor. These include an 1856 Governor's Mansion (see page 550) that is one of the oldest in the nation still in use for its original purpose.

French Legation, 1841

802 San Marcos Street; 512-472-8180;
Thomas William Ward, architect.

The French Legation is important both as the oldest wood-framed house on its original site in Austin and as one of the few homes remaining in the entire state that date from Texas's interlude as an independent republic.

During the mid–nineteenth century, France provided full-scale embassies with ambassadors for only the most important countries. Smaller "legations" with official "ministers" served less important nations and, for minor emerging ones like the Republic of Texas, the legation had only a chargé d'affaires rather than a minister. As their Texas chargé, France sent the eccentric Jean Pierre Isidore Dubois, who upon his arrival in Austin changed his name to Count Jean Pierre Isidore Dubois de Saligny—adding both the title "Count" and a related place of origin (Saligny) to magnify his local importance. He needn't have bothered, for the urbane Parisian found Austin to be a village of only 856 persons, most of whom lived in simple log houses.

Dubois ended up residing in Austin for only fourteen months, and much of this was spent in extended visits to bustling New Orleans. Despite his brief residence, he managed to cut a wide swath through the town. The chargé combined lavish entertaining and political scheming with bitter complaints about the frontier village and its rustic inhabitants. Among the latter was a neighbor whose roaming domestic animals offended the haughty diplomat. After Dubois instructed one of his servants to kill the intruders, the dispute escalated into a farcical "Pig War" that ended the Frenchman's effectiveness as a local diplomat. His more substantial legacy is the unusually elegant frontier residence he built for his legation.

Architecturally, the house owes much to neighboring Louisiana, a state that its designer had worked in extensively. It has the hipped roof, wide front porch, and multiple exterior casement doors across the front facade that are associated with the French Colonial style as seen in rural Louisiana. It is built of heavy timber construction with plank walls. Manufactured items, such as window glass and hardware, had to be hauled long distances by wagon to the remote Texas capital. The striking hardware, which included oversize hinges and large locks with keys, probably came from Louisiana via a now-vanished port on the Texas coast.

Austin's French Legation became superfluous when the Republic of Texas was annexed to the United States in 1845. By that time, Dubois's fine house had already been sold to private owners. In 1848 Dr. Joseph W. Robertson purchased the home for his large family. His

Texas Governor's Mansion

daughter, Sarah, was born in the house in 1850 and was the last person to live in the historic dwelling when she died there ninety years later. In 1949 the house was purchased by the state of Texas and turned over to the Daughters of the Republic of Texas to restore and manage as a historic museum.

The furnishings are a mixture of original pieces and donations. They include a sofa and chair in the parlor that have a good probability of having belonged to Dubois. A number of Robertson possessions are still in the house, including their 1830 bed and dresser that have been in the master bedroom of the house since 1848, an 1860 spindle-post bed that was used by their children, and an early painting of the house by their daughter Julia.

The property has had varying degrees of restoration. The house itself appears much as it did in Dubois's time. It was never greatly altered by the Robertsons, and the restored colors are as authentic as modern paint analysis allows. The garden is a creation of the 1950s. The separate kitchen building, which houses a fine collection of French country furnishings and cooking utensils, is a modern rebuilding of the original. The carriage house/shop is also a new structure, although there was originally a carriage house on the grounds.

Texas Governor's Mansion, 1856
1010 Colorado Avenue; 512-463-5516;
Abner Cook, Austin, architect.

In 1854 the Texas legislature appropriated $14,500 for building a new governor's residence. An additional $2,500 was allotted for furnishings. Abner Cook (1814–1884), a talented local designer-builder, won the competition to build it and in doing so provided the finest Greek Revival residence in the state. Although a man named Richard Payne is on record as having received $100 for "plans" for the house, it is so similar to Cook's several other large homes in Austin that it seems highly probable that he provided much of the final design. Cook had worked in Nashville, Tennessee, for Joseph Reiff and William Hume, who rebuilt Andrew Jackson's home there called the Hermitage. The Texas Governor's Mansion has many similarities to the Hermitage but lacks the latter's large side wing (see also the Neill-Cochran House [page 551], another very similar house by Cook).

Built of local buff-colored brick fronted by six thirty-foot-high Ionic columns supporting an entablature six feet deep, the mansion became an immediate Texas landmark. Every governor since has made at least minor changes, as is the custom in governors' residences. Cook's original design was so strong, however, that the exterior has kept its integrity through many administrations and a 1914 rear addition.

In 1978, governor-elect Bill Clements and his wife, Rita, determined that the mansion needed either to become a museum, with a new mansion built, or the house restored to its original Greek Revival glory. Restoration carried the day, and a combination of $1 million in state funds and $3 million of private contributions was raised. The restored mansion was officially reopened in 1982. The original interior, with the exception of one back bedroom, was little altered, while the 1914 rear addition, which houses the private quarters upstairs and the kitchen downstairs, had major renovations and functional updating. This trade-off allows the house to remain in full use for both living and official entertaining.

The main rooms of the historic interior—the entry hall, parlors, library, and state dining room—maintain a high degree of architectural integrity. Surviving original details include the keyhole door and window surrounds, staircase, and front door. The restoration committee elected not to furnish the interior only with pieces similar to those that might actually have been present in the mansion's early days in a struggling frontier town. Instead, they chose to amass a museum-quality collection of early-nineteenth-century American furnishings and combine these with historic pieces related to Texas and early mansion inhabitants. Thus the interiors are far grander, and in general a bit earlier, than might be expected in a strict restoration. The elegant result provides a magnificent background for official state entertaining. It is important to remember that the goals here differed from those of most historic house museum restorations.

The spacious grounds, which cover a full city block, have seen many uses over the years—from vegetable gardens and orchards to croquet courts and a small private zoo. Today's landscapes date to the mid-1960s, a look that was kept and enhanced during the restoration. One of the highlights of the grounds is the surrounding iron fence, featuring the Texas star, which originally graced the state capitol and was moved here.

Neill-Cochran House, 1855

2310 San Gabriel Street; 512-478-2335;
Abner Cook, Austin, architect.

Designed and built by the same master builder as the Texas Governor's Mansion (see the preceding entry), this is a very similar house. Instead of brick, however, the eighteen-inch-thick walls are native Austin limestone (probably meant to have been stuccoed). Both houses are dominated by six colossal columns supporting full facade porches. Here the columns are of the

Doric order and constructed of twenty-six-foot-long cypress boards. The upstairs balconies here and in the Texas Governor's Mansion and in 6 Niles Road (see below) all have balusters of the "bundled stick" design that is considered a signature of Cook buildings in Austin. Most of the windowpanes are the original thick, wavy glass.

Inside, the house has door surrounds in the characteristic Greek Revival keyhole design and retains its very simple original mantelpieces. The furnishings were collected from the donations of members of the Colonial Dames (who operate the museum) and reflect a variety of periods and countries of origin.

Enfield, ca. 1915–1950s

The Enfield neighborhood is built on what were once the grounds of a 365-acre plantation purchased by Texas governor Elisha Pease in 1857. Pease named his home Woodlawn, and he called the plantation proper Enfield, after his Connecticut birthplace. In the early twentieth century, Pease's grandsons divided the plantation into two residential subdivisions, Enfield and Westfield. The grander and earlier houses are concentrated in Enfield, near the original Greek Revival plantation house. The area continued to develop through the 1950s, and still today some new houses are being added, like the Neo-Victorian at 1611 Watchhill Road (private). Examples of almost all of the Eclectic-era period styles are found here, but there is an unusual collection of fine Italian Renaissance houses, possibly because of the influence of Dallas architect Henry Bowers "Hal" Thomson (ca. 1882–ca. 1974), who particularly favored that style. The same architect also designed at least one of Enfield's several walled Spanish Eclectic homes.

6 Niles Road (private), Woodlawn, 1853; Abner Cook, Austin, architect. This is the original Pease plantation house once surrounded by 365 acres. It is similar to Cook's other

Enfield

fine Greek Revival homes—the Texas Governor's Mansion (see page 550) and the Neill-Cochran House (see page 551); like them, it has had significant later additions.

2 Niles Road (private), Butler House, 1930; Henry Bowers Thomson, Dallas, architect. A choice setting for a striking Italian Renaissance design.

2210 and 2300 Pease Road (both private). Two elaborate Spanish Eclectic homes made relatively difficult to see by their surrounding walls.

1503 Marshall Lane (private). One of Enfield's finest Italian Renaissance houses, this is an asymmetrical form with a strong Spanish influence in the door surround and roofed chimney. The entry courtyard is also typical of Spanish Eclectic houses. (See also "1706 Windsor Road," below.)

1502 Marshall Lane (private). A smaller and less grand Italian Renaissance house, this is a more typical neighborhood example of the style.

1702 Windsor Road (private). This handsome Italian Renaissance house has a recessed and triple-arched upstairs porch with recessed entry below. The entry is approached by a split pair of entry stairs, an unusual feature in private homes. The house has two distinctive side wings; the two-story one has arched windows on the first-floor level and a colonnade with recessed casement windows above. During the period, wings such as these often housed a sunroom or solarium on the first floor and a sleeping porch on the second. In this house the sunroom may have been in the smaller one-story wing.

1706 Windsor Road (private). Another Italian Renaissance house with Spanish overtones, like 1503 Marshall Lane (see above). This asymmetrical design has an entry courtyard and Spanish influence in the chimney and door surround.

Bremond Block

Bremond Block, ca. 1850s–1940

This striking Victorian assemblage resulted when two intermarried families, that of John Robinson and John Bremond, built six adjacent homes as a center for family activities. Other family members also lived nearby, and the alley area of the Bremond Block, as it came to be called, was used as a play area for the children. Many members of the two families were long prominent in Austin affairs. Over the years several of the houses were remodeled, either to add more space or to gain a more stylish appearance.

Other interesting older houses can be found near the Bremond Block, particularly along the south side of West Ninth Street near Guadalupe and along Rio Grande and Nueces, the streets just west of San Antonio Street.

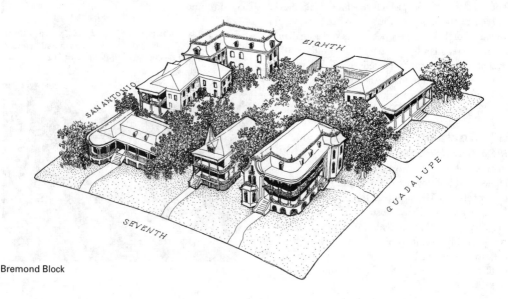

Bremond Block

700 Guadalupe Street (private), John Bremond House, 1886; George Fiegal, architect. This ornate example of the Second Empire style, designed by a native of New Orleans, was built at a cost of forty-nine thousand dollars. The architect's New Orleans heritage is very evident in the exquisite two-story porches of decorative ironwork that wrap around the house. The roof is ornamented with a colored fish-scale pattern and with iron cresting and finials along the ridge. The first-floor window pattern, with a rectangular tab added to the flattened arches of the upper panes, is quite rare.

402 West Seventh Street (private), Pierre Bremond House, 1898. This tan brick dwelling is a good example of the Free Classic Queen Anne style.

708 San Antonio Street (private), North-Evans House (Austin Women's Club), 1874; additions, 1890s; Alfred Giles, San Antonio, additions architect. This fairly simple five-bay, two-story house had elaborate stone porches with Romanesque arches added in its remodeling in the 1890s. Only a small portion of the elaborate porchwork can be seen from street level, and still more has been hidden by later additions.

610 Guadalupe Street (private), Smith House, 1854. This small Greek Revival cottage is built of handmade brick. It illustrates a one-story example of the full-facade porch subtype of the same pattern seen in the grand two-story Texas Governor's Mansion (see page 550), Neill-Cochran House (see page 551), and Woodlawn (see "6 Niles Road," page 551).

Littlefield House, 1894

304 West Twenty-fourth Street; 512-475-9600; James W. Wahrenberger, San Antonio, architect.

Major George Washington Littlefield made a fortune in the Texas cattle business and became one of Austin's leading citizens and financiers. He gave much, both in dollars and in time, to secure the future of the University of Texas. He was one of the school's most generous early philanthropists; it is fitting that his extraordinary Victorian home now houses the university's Development Office upstairs; the downstairs is used for official functions and can be visited by request. Restored for these uses in 1967, the house is the oldest structure remaining on the university campus.

Architect Wahrenberger (1855–1929) studied in Europe, and a fondness for French precedents is suggested by this unusual design. Basically Chateauesque in form, the facade also includes Beaux Arts detailing (garlands and paired columns) as well as a New Orleans–style two-story iron porch. The seventeen-room structure is reported to have cost fifty thousand dollars. The redbrick came from St. Louis and is trimmed with contrasting sandstone detailing. The brick joints are

Littlefield House

pointed with white marble dust, which matches the white marble steps. The tall iron porch wraps around one side of the house and has elegant slender supports and balustrade. The original carriage house is behind.

The interior floor plan features a large central living hall with rooms and halls to both sides. Double parlors and a spacious stair hall are to the left side. Major Littlefield's library is to the right. It contains a settee original to the house and a painting by Mrs. Littlefield. A secondary hall and the dining room are beyond the library.

The interior decoration was done by Marshall Field and Company, the famous Chicago department store. Although the original furniture and window treatments are now gone, this makes it possible to fully appreciate the extraordinary interior wall finishes that have been restored to their original grandeur. The double parlors are in gold and white with a ceiling fresco; they were the location of many family weddings. The rest of the downstairs features more than a dozen different woods. Quite unusual are the large segmental pediments that are found over many of the doorways. Also note the balusters on the stairway—an unusual "block with bull's-eye" adorns each one.

BEAUMONT

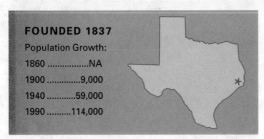

FOUNDED 1837

Population Growth:

1860 .... NA

1900 9,000

1940 59,000

1990 114,000

Founded in the early years of the Republic of Texas (see page xii) near the junction of Texas's coastal prairies and eastern pine forests, by 1890 Beaumont was an important market center for the surrounding cattle ranches, lumber mills, and irrigated rice fields. Few res-

idents of this prosperous Victorian town in 1900 believed the local folklore that oil might someday be found beneath the sulfur-laden springs that bubbled out natural gas on Spindletop mound, four miles southeast of town. Several shallow wells had already been drilled to test this idea, and none had found significant quantities of oil.

Then, on January 10, 1901, yet-another test well shook the mound with a mighty roar and spewed out a six-inch-wide column of oil that reached two hundred feet into the air. Earthen ponds were hastily constructed to capture the enormous flow as it fell back to the ground; by the time the runaway well was brought under control nine days later, the ponds contained a

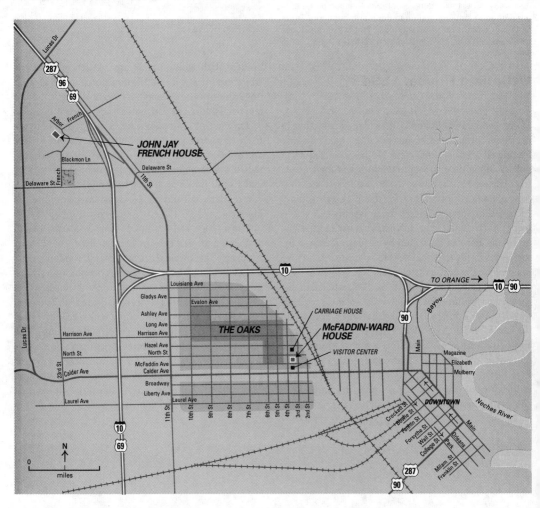

million barrels of oil, more than most oil fields at that time could produce in *years*.

The Spindletop Field, and others soon found beneath similar "mounds" along the coast of southeastern Texas (caused by underground pillars of salt, known as salt domes), ushered in a new era of abundant energy from petroleum. Refined petroleum products not only began replacing coal as a boiler fuel for steam production, but also made possible the widespread use of gasoline-powered internal-combustion engines (see page xxxiv). The extraordinary economic importance of the Spindletop discovery can be gauged by the several giant oil companies, among them Gulf (now Chevron), Texaco, and Humble (now Exxon), that had their beginnings here.

Soon tank farms, refineries, and tanker-loading docks began springing up along the nearby Neches River to process and distribute the enormous flood of Spindletop crude oil. The first large refinery was built by what became the Magnolia Petroleum Company (now Mobil Oil). As new fields were discovered in the region, much of their production was also delivered by railroad tank cars or pipelines to Beaumont-area refineries, and the city quickly grew into an important industrial center. By 1910 its 1900 population had doubled to twenty-one thousand; by 1920 it reached forty

thousand. By then the original Spindletop Field had long been depleted, but in 1925, new deeper drilling on the flanks of the salt dome initiated a second flood of Spindletop oil; in 1930 the city's population was fifty-eight thousand.

The Second World War brought new manufacturing and shipbuilding facilities, and an influx of workers, to Beaumont. In the post-1950 decades the city's population has stabilized at slightly more than 100,000. Today it retains two important museum houses, one a rare survivor from the 1840s (see the following entry), the other a Spindletop-era Neoclassical mansion adjacent to a varied neighborhood of Eclectic-era houses (see page 557). These are complemented by a superb Queen Anne museum house in nearby Orange, Texas (see page 560), and the nearby smaller Heritage House that shows a more middle-class lifestyle, ca. 1920 (see page 562).

John Jay French House, 1845

2985 French Road; 409-898-0348.

John Jay French (1799–1889) and his wife, Sally Munson French (1799–1885), were both from Connecticut. Married there in 1819, they journeyed to Texas to take advantage of free land grants then being offered by the Mexican government. French selected a three-

John Jay French House

John Jay French House

hundred-acre tract just three and one-half miles north of Beaumont and, in 1845, built this fine home, which was quite grand for the Beaumont area—being of sawed and painted lumber rather than logs. It was built in the early I-house folk form (two stories high and one room deep). The basic I-house form was extended with an original one-story shed-roofed extension on the rear and one-story full-width porch across the front. Simplified Greek Revival details include the front door and rear door surrounds, both of which are surrounded by a narrow line of transom and sidelights; the more formal flush boards that clad the front facade; and the hint of boxed cornice returns.

John French opened a trading post here and became quite prosperous from tanning hides and farming as well as from his trading activities. The setting around the house still has a pleasantly rural feeling. The detached kitchen has been rebuilt, and a number of related outbuildings were either reconstructed or moved to this site. There are many large live oak trees, some planted by French, and these are today enjoyed by a large resident population of gray squirrels. The areas immediately adjacent to the house have a clean-swept yard, which was a way to avoid snakes and other creatures being concealed in greenery near the house. A low picket fence also helped in this endeavor.

Inside, the home has a wide central hallway that is well lit by the glass door surrounds at each end. The ceiling of the hallway still has its original coat of buttermilk paint, made blue from added indigo. The ceilings of all the downstairs rooms have been painted to match. A steep stairway is tucked on the left side of the hall and provides passage to the single huge room that comprises the upstairs of the house—making it an excellent multipurpose room for parties, meetings, and dances as well as for storage and activities such as weaving. The home has been furnished to the period 1845 to 1865, and a number of original French family pieces have been donated by descendants. These include an unusual English music box, the French family Bible, a Seth Thomas clock, and, in the kitchen, a handsome pie safe made by John French himself.

The Oaks, ca. 1900–1950

This large historic district, one of the largest in Texas, encompasses a cross section of early Beaumont, from the huge McFaddin-Ward House occupying one square block to small folk houses on the edges of the district. Although there is a handful of Victorian-style homes in the district, they are late examples of their styles. The area includes houses from small to large (with the highest number being midsize) that date from the 1920s and 1930s and even up to the 1950s. It is all developed on a traditional street grid that is oriented north–south/east–west. A number of the largest early homes have been demolished and replaced either by apartments on the interior of the neighborhood or by commercial uses along Calder Avenue. The area shaded in the darker pink screen has a high concentration of interesting houses (see the map, page 554).

2140 Hazel Avenue (private), ca. 1900. This one-and-one-half-story Free Classic Queen Anne house has a gable-on-hip roof and an unusual sawtooth-textured shingle pattern in both of its front-facing gables.

2108 Harrison Avenue (private), ca. 1910. A rare example of a one-and-one-half-story Neoclassical house designed in the full-height-entry-porch-with-lower-full-width-porch subtype. Note how neatly the two-story entry porch is integrated into what would otherwise be a one-story Neoclassical cottage. Whoever built (or remodeled) this must have wanted their home to resemble the nearby McFaddin-Ward House (see page 557). The Ionic column capitals and the porch balustrade railing design both resemble those at McFaddin-Ward.

615 Sixth Street (private), ca. 1910. A Prairie-style house with unusual step-backs in the heavy squared porch supports. Note how the geometric covering of the vents (visible

The Oaks neighborhood

beneath the porch on the right side of the house) echoes the railing of the handrail on the upstairs side porch. This house has been modified by enclosing an upstairs porch and adding new windows.

2301 Long Avenue (private), ca. 1940. This is an example of the Creole French variation of the Monterey style that was popular in the late 1930s and built up until about 1955. Here the influence of nearby New Orleans has not only replaced the typical Monterey balcony railing (cantilevered and covered by the principal roof) with a decorative cast-iron railing, but full-length windows with shutters have been added as well, mimicking the look of the many shuttered exterior doors found on French Colonial homes.

2466 Long Avenue (private), ca. 1950. This Neoclassical house with a full-height entry porch demonstrates the tall, skinny columns that characterize most Neoclassical houses built from the late 1930s into the very early 1950s. Number 2534 Long Avenue (private) is a full-facade porch example from the same era, and with similarly skinny columns.

2550 Ashley Avenue (private), Wilson House, 1935; John F. Staub, Houston, architect. Here well-known Texas architect John Staub introduces New Orleans influence in a large estate house—cast-iron porches, railing, and porte cochere and full-length French doors with shutters. But like so many of Staub's works, this is his own unique blend of influences and does not fall neatly into any particular stylistic category. The Wilson House was used for a period of time as the Beaumont Museum of Art and is still recovering from this use, which subdivided what had been large gardens surrounding the house. Number 2301 Long Avenue (see above) is an example of a more typical builder's interpretation of the same New Orleans influences.

McFaddin-Ward House, 1906

1906 McFaddin Avenue; 409-832-2134;
Henry Conrad Mauer, Beaumont, architect.

Lived in only by two generations of the same family, the McFaddin-Ward House has most of its original furnishings, fixtures, and fittings. Owned by a foundation set up especially to administer the house, it has been maintained just as it was when Mamie McFaddin Ward (ca. 1895–1982) died. Today the McFaddin-Ward House displays not only many original features, but also the many improvements that Mamie Ward and her mother, Ida Caldwell McFaddin (1872–1950), chose to make during the many years they both lived in the home. Thus McFaddin-Ward presents not only an extremely fine example of 1906 architecture (with some rooms and furnishings dating to that period) but a well-researched and documented record of the changes that two women chose to make over a period of several decades. The McFaddin-Ward House has sponsored a number of conferences about changing lifestyles that have resulted in several outstanding publications, among them *American Home Life, 1880–1930: A Social History of Spaces and Services,* edited by Jessica Foy and Thomas Schlereth, and *The Arts and the American Home: 1890–1930,* edited by Jessica Foy and Thomas Schlereth.

McFaddin-Ward House

W. P. H. McFaddin (1856–1935) was a third-generation Texan. His grandfather James McFaddin (died 1845) came to Texas from Tennessee in 1823. W.P.H.'s father, William McFaddin (1819–1897), fought for Texas independence in the Battle of San Jacinto and for this service was awarded 177 acres. William and his wife, Rachel (died 1898), had nine children, of which W. P. H. McFaddin was the seventh. W.P.H. inherited prodigious energy and drive from his father, as well as a passion for accumulating land. For many years he worked with his father and helped diversify the family land and cattle interests to include rice production, meatpacking, and commercial real estate. After W.P.H.'s first wife, Emma, died in 1890, he married Ida Regina Caldwell, the daughter of a wealthy coal magnate and businessman in Huntington, West Virginia. She had come to Beaumont to visit a classmate from the Mary Baldwin Seminary, a school for young women in Staunton, Virginia. Ida and W.P.H. fell in love and were married in December of 1894.

Ida cut quite a swath in Beaumont society, having brought with her an intimate knowledge of a privileged eastern lifestyle. She wasted no time in constructing a new Queen Anne home, which was built and furnished in 1896. But house styles changed quickly at the turn of the century, as did the McFaddins' fortunes. In 1901 Spindletop (see page 554) blew in on some of the land owned by the McFaddins. Although it was actually W.P.H.'s sister and brother-in-law, Di and W. C. Averill, who built the McFaddin-Ward House (beginning in 1905 and finishing in late 1906), they, for some unknown reason, almost immediately traded it to W.P.H. and Ida in return for their Queen Anne home and thirty thousand dollars cash.

The McFaddin-Ward House is a premier example of the South's favorite Neoclassical house type, which combines a dominant full-height entry porch with a one-story full-width front porch of the type beloved by generations of southerners. Here at the McFaddin-Ward House, the broad front porch is as deep as a very generous room and wraps around the house on each side. The porch was used not only as an outdoor living space in which to catch the most gentle of evening breezes, but also for entertaining and teenage dances. The exterior of the home is enhanced by many details borrowed from the contemporaneous Colonial Revival, which was not uncommon in Neoclassical homes. These features include the roof balustrades on both porches and on the house itself, the garlands on the entablature of the full-height porch, the dormers with triangular pediments above, and the elliptical fanlight above the front door.

The McFaddins moved into their new home in January 1907, and Ida immediately began refining its interiors. The parlor remains much as Ida originally planned it, with canvas-covered walls and elaborate hand-carved rococo moldings hand painted with trailing roses. Although some of the furniture appears French in style, these pieces were purchased from the Robert Mitchell Furniture Company in Cincinnati, Ohio (a favorite stop for Ida McFaddin because it was on the train route to visit her family in Huntington, West Virginia), while others are Vernis Martin gold-leaf accent pieces. The room, almost unchanged since 1909, also includes porcelain pieces and marble statues. The McFaddins' daughter, Mamie, married Texas A&M Hall of Fame football player Carroll Ward (died 1961) in this room in 1919. The couple continued to live in this home for the rest of their lives. Mamie took over many of the household duties from Ida after her marriage. From that time forward mother and daughter generally collaborated on shopping for and redecorating the house.

The breakfast room was added on by the McFaddins in 1907, soon after they moved in. Although the room looks like it is full of custom-made paneling, moldings, and decorative glass, in actuality all of it was ordered from the Lecoutour Brothers Stair Manufacturing Company of St. Louis and then installed. The Art Nouveau light fixtures and curved art-glass windows are particularly handsome. The glass grape-cluster light fixtures came from Lecoutour Brothers. The rounded end of this room holds a large marble fountain and statue and forms a wonderful conservatory designed for houseplants.

The library originally contained Arts and Crafts furnishings, but was redecorated in the 1940s by Ida and Mamie. In 1910 the home had even more Arts and Crafts furniture and fixtures, but today these remain mainly in one upstairs bedroom. Tastes had changed by the 1920s, and, for example, the simpler copper wall sconces in the entry hall were replaced with more formal crystal ones. The rugs throughout the house were originally mostly machine made, but beginning in the 1920s these were gradually replaced until today the home has an outstanding collection of more than one hundred Oriental rugs, mostly Persian Kermans or Sarouks.

Mother and daughter completely redecorated several of the upstairs bedrooms during the 1930s and 1940s with the help of popular decorators. These are classic rooms of their period with a subtle 1930s color palette and wonderful use of satin and taffeta—in draperies, quilted and trapunto bedspreads, and dressing table skirts. Some of the bedrooms include furnishings that were altered or more heavily carved in New

Orleans during the 1920s and 1930s, reflecting Mamie McFaddin Ward's interest in more ornate carved-wood pieces.

Those with a serious interest in the decorative arts and interior decoration will admire the remarkably thorough documentation that gives the purchase dates and sources for items in each room. Provided to each docent (none of whom could possibly be expected to remember such a mountain of information), this information is available in notebook form for guides to look up the answers to specific questions at the end of the tour.

After the guided tour, the McFaddin-Ward House's full city block of grounds can be explored. There is also an interesting self-guided tour of the original eight-thousand-square-foot carriage house, which includes servants' quarters, a stable, a hayloft, space for automobiles, and an indoor gymnasium.

McFaddin-Ward House and W. H. Stark House—Parallels and Contrasts

The Queen Anne–style W. H. Stark House (see page 560), built in the nearby town of Orange, Texas, in 1894, and the Neoclassical McFaddin-Ward House (see page 557), built in 1906, make a particularly illuminating pair of houses to visit. Both have been restored and interpreted with the same philosophy—leaving each just as their owners intended them to be. They are shown complete with the changes that the owners made to improve each house to their liking. Both houses contain all of the belongings of the household, including many more items than can actually be displayed in the house. Contents of attics and drawers and cupboards and closets are part of each home's collection. And the owners kept copious records, giving an unusual amount of information about the contents of both homes.

Built only twelve years apart, this pair allows you to see the difference that a dozen short years made in house styles at the turn of the twentieth century. The 1894 Stark House is an exquisite spindlework Queen Anne design with towers. It is very asymmetrical, and with several exterior doors—which one is the actual front entrance can even be a source of slight confusion. Inside, the asymmetry continues into the entry hall, which has a small inglenook tucked behind the last flight of stairs, and into the room arrangement, which centers on both a long central hall and a shorter cross hall.

The 1906 McFaddin-Ward House, in contrast, is symmetrical. Reflecting the stylistic changes that swept the country after the 1893 Columbian Exposition in Chicago, it has Classical columns and is based on Classical Greek, rather than Medieval English, precedents.

There is absolutely no doubt that the entrance is centered behind the dominant two-story entry porch. Inside, the entry hall focuses on a broad centered stairway that continues the exterior symmetry, the main rooms of the house opening off to each side.

The two houses' interior decoration, while by no means the same, is a bit more similar. The Stark House has its original Victorian woodwork and art glass, but the wall finishes and light fixtures reflect changes made in a 1920 remodeling. Both homes have high wood wainscoting in the entry halls, breakfast rooms, and other places. In the Stark House, fabrics were added to fill the fields above the wainscoting in the 1920s remodeling. In the McFaddin-Ward House, wallpaper, fabric, and tapestries can all be found in the wall area above the wainscot.

Both houses have one first-floor room decorated in whites and pinks and with "French" furniture, almost an obligatory feature of upper-class houses built just before and after 1900. At McFaddin-Ward, it is the parlor, which is entirely hand painted with trailing roses and has gilded American "French" furnishings. In the

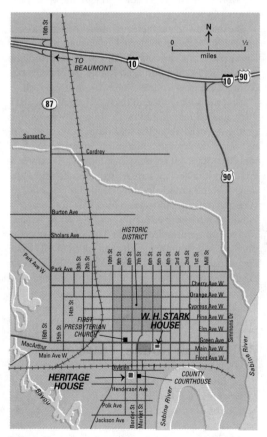

Orange, Texas

Stark House, it is the music room, complete with a hand-painted ceiling panel of angels and a delicate Aubusson rug. It includes a Steinway piano with rare curvilinear legs and "French" furnishings of natural wood finish.

But the general appearance of the houses is quite different, for Mrs. Stark, who began her home during the Victorian era, had a great love of decorative objects, lots of objects, displayed on every surface, often many on any one surface. The McFaddin-Ward House, although it has many fine objects, displays them in the more spare manner typical of the early twentieth century (the house is interpreted to the 1940s). The Stark House keeps its Victorian feeling in everyday objects like fancy decorated wastebaskets and also in the higher percentage of Victorian-era light fixtures and lamps.

The Stark House is restored to its 1920s appearance. Its only mistress died in 1936 and the house never had any 1930s or 1940s influences added. In contrast, the McFaddin-Ward House has a number of rooms that reflect the popular fabrics and color schemes of those decades. Its last owner, Mamie Ward, lived in the home until 1982, and minor changes were made up until at least the 1960s.

The three owners of these two homes each had a deep interest in the decorative arts. Cut glass from the brilliant period, multiple sets of china and silver, and fine table linens are found in both homes. So also are fine decorative objects—porcelains and statues and such.

It is in this latter area, in particular, that Mrs. Stark distinguished herself. Although Mamie Ward and her mother enjoyed shopping and decorating, they were not seriously dedicated lifetime shoppers and collectors. Mrs. Stark, on the other hand, went on many several-month collecting trips, often abroad, where she diligently and knowledgeably shopped for fine porcelains and other decorative arts pieces for her home.

Both houses were primarily creations of the women who owned them, rather than the work of an architect or interior designer (although the McFaddin-Ward House did use decorators in the 1930s and 1940s). They give an excellent insight into the personal tastes, goals, and aspirations of many wealthy women of the period—particularly those who lived far away from the tastemakers of New York City, Chicago, and San Francisco.

W. H. Stark House, 1894

610 West Main Avenue, Orange, about twenty miles east of Beaumont; 409-883-0871; Fred Wilbur, Pennsylvania, architect.

Miriam M. Lutcher Stark (1859–1936) was the daughter of Henry Jacob Lutcher (1836–1912), a Pennsylvania lumberman, and his wife, Frances Ann Robinson Lutcher (1841–1924). Lutcher was attracted to the vast forests of southeast Texas, known as the Big Thicket, and in the 1870s he and his partner, G. Bedell Moore, established a sawmill in Orange and began investing in timberland, as well as purchasing other mills in the southeast.

William Henry Stark (1851–1936) came to Orange in 1870 and proceeded to learn every phase of the lumbering business. After his marriage to Miriam Lutcher in 1881, this knowledge made him a valued partner in the Lutcher and Moore Lumber Company. Stark also branched out into many other businesses and had a knack for succeeding in each, thereby building the family fortune.

In 1894, with business prospering, the Starks built this extraordinary spindlework Queen Anne home, designed by Mrs. Stark's uncle Fred Wilbur, who lived in Pennsylvania. Encircled with two levels of porches and accented with a tall corner tower, the Stark House is one of the largest (fourteen thousand square feet, including porches and basement) and most elaborate Queen Anne houses left in the West. It was constructed of virgin longleaf yellow pine and cypress and has fifteen rooms, nine fireplaces, and three tall chimneys. When the Starks moved in, their only son, H. J. Lutcher Stark (1887–1965), was but seven years old.

After the turn of the century oil was discovered on timberlands owned by Stark and the families' wealth increased. Mrs. Stark had always had an interest in the decorative arts, and she could now afford to collect fine objects, many of museum quality. She sometimes traveled abroad for months at a time, looking for treasures as she went. In 1920 she redecorated the house herself, adding some fabrics and colors typical of the early twentieth century but keeping the home's essential Victorian character intact. She arranged the rooms to show off the many fine pieces she had accumulated over the years. The entire house is interpreted to this 1920s period, and everything in it is original (or carefully reproduced) to that time period, even to the beautiful original lace panels that hang at each window. Fine porcelain, silver, cut glass, lamps, family portraits, and more than eighty Oriental rugs fill the house.

The home is entered through handsome beveled clear glass doors that provide lots of light, and originally great cross ventilation. The stair hall and the home's many long circulation halls have a high wainscot of longleaf "curly" pine set in floating panels. This means that the inset panels are not attached by glue or nails to their frames, which allowed them to expand and contract without cracking. The area above the wainscot is filled with fabric, reproductions of those from the 1920 remodeling.

W. H. Stark House
and, below left, its
carriage house

There are many lovely rooms in the home, each with its own unique character. The elegant music room is discussed on page 560 in comparison with the Mc-Faddin-Ward House. One of the most striking is the breakfast room. Here the restoration was able to use the original fabric, as Mrs. Stark had purchased enough (and prudently stored the additional yardage) to completely redrape, reupholster, and re-cover the walls with the vivid red silk brocade. The wainscot here is of mahogany. This room has handsome cloisonné vases and Art Deco figurines, porcelain pieces, and carved Oriental furniture in combination with American pieces, all skillfully mixed by Mrs. Stark. Down the hall, the Starks' many sets of china are displayed in their original cupboards. Demitasse cups, bouillon cups, chocolate cups, coffee cups, and even individual creamers are all there for one large set.

On the second floor there is a comfortable sitting room, and each of the bedrooms has a different character. Mrs. Stark's sentimental nature is revealed in the master bedroom. Despite her dedication to searching out fine objects, she always retained the Eastlake bedroom set that her father gave her when she was eighteen years old—her son was born in the bed, and she died there. The large third floor is also a part of the tour, and its closet display of beaded purses and fans is a treat. Mrs. Stark kept almost everything she ever purchased, and many excess items are now on display in the upstairs of the large carriage house.

One of the largest rooms is the downstairs library, with its original furnishings set on a large Kashan rug. Mr. Stark had a great love of books, and the huge personal library that he accumulated during his lifetime actually helped to save the house. After both of the Starks died in 1936, their son donated the house and contents to the University of Texas. Three librarians from the University of Texas appeared and spent two years cataloging Stark's books. They removed all of the rare books and first editions to Austin and had the rest of the house contents packed. They had the beveled-glass doors removed, the painted ceiling panel in the music room was taken down, and, along with the multitude of decorative objects, all was crated. Then nothing happened. Nothing happened, in fact, for twenty years. Everything just sat in crates and boxes. The gift's stipulation had been that the contents of the house should be properly housed, and other than the books, the university apparently did not know what to do with the rest of the contents. But due to the librarians' meticulousness, all were carefully stored.

Eventually, the elder Stark son, Lutcher, and his wife established the Nelda C. and H. J. Lutcher Stark Foundation. Their foundation made the decision to restore the house and contents. It undertook a careful restoration that began in 1970 and continued until 1981, when the home was opened to the public. Extensive photographs and documentation meant that everything could be restored to its rightful place. Today a visit to the Stark House, which requires advance reservations, will provide a rare insight into the life and lifestyle of a turn-of-the-century lumber baron and his family.

Nearby Houses

Orange, like Beaumont, was an early lumbering and ranching center that, having missed most of the Spindletop-era oil frenzy, has remained a small city of less than twenty thousand people for most of its history. Today it has a large historic district offering a typical small-town mixture of houses that vary in size, style, and age. There are many National Folk houses, including those in the pyramidal and hall-and-parlor families. Green Avenue was originally the town's grand residential street, but, with the exception of the Stark House, the Victorian homes that lined much of that street are now gone, victims of its increased traffic and commercialization. The district is indicated in pale pink on the map (see page 559); the largest remaining homes are in the area near the First Presbyterian Church. Although most houses here face the streets with tree names, some also face the numbered cross streets.

812 West Pine Avenue (private), ca. 1900. This is a late–Free Classic Queen Anne design with some elements typical of the early twentieth century, producing an unusual combination of features that gives this home a distinctive look. The basic shape of the home (hipped roof with lower cross gables and a porch wrapping around to one side) is Queen Anne, as are the cutaway bay windows, the textured shingles in the roof gables, and the conical roof on the corner of the porch (although the roof pitch is unusually low). Later features include the windows (with their clear lower panes and diamond-patterned upper panes), which were not used until about 1900 and often appear in American four-square homes of various styles and in Craftsman-style houses. The elaborate Corinthian capitals on the porch columns are more typically found in American four-squares with one-story porches and in Neoclassical-style homes. (Most Free Classic Queen Anne homes have Doric or, at

Near the W. H. Stark House

the most, Ionic column capitals.) Note also the eyebrow dormer.

Seventh Street at Cypress Avenue, southwest corner (private), ca. 1900. This Free Classic Queen Anne house has a tower with an open balcony and large Palladian-motif windows in its two broad gables.

802 Cypress Avenue (private). This is an unusually large one-story Neoclassical house.

Heritage House, 1902

905 West Division Street; 409-886-0917.

This home was built in 1902 by J. O. Sims and remained in his family until sold to the city of Orange in 1977 and subsequently moved a few blocks to this site. Originally a two-story T-shaped folk house, it received a large rear addition in 1919. Although a few of the items in the house belonged to the Sims family, the majority of the furnishings have been collected to reflect the general lifestyles typical of upper-middle-class family homes during the years 1900 to 1940, rather than interpreting the life of a single family. Since these are the approximate years during which the McFaddin-Ward House (see page 557) was evolving, a look at this much smaller home provides an illuminating contrast. One point of interest is the preordered brick fireplaces used in both homes. One can compare the large one that dominates the entry hall at McFaddin-Ward with the similar but more modest example here.

COLUMBUS

FOUNDED 1823

Population Growth:

1860 ....ca. 800

1900 2,000

1940 2,500

1990 3,500

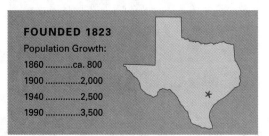

This is the West's oldest Anglo town, platted by Steven F. Austin as one of two riverside trade centers to serve his new colony of Anglo immigrants in Mexican Texas. Austin had persuaded the government of newly independent Mexico that the best way to stop the growing incursions of Anglo frontiersmen into vacant eastern Texas was to permit controlled immigration of more responsible Anglo farmers, who would be given the right to earn large blocks of land in exchange for becoming loyal Mexican citizens (see also page xii). The immigrants were to be recruited, and the agricultural colonies managed, by Anglo land developers called *empresarios*, who were assigned vast tracts to which they earned full title when they had provided the first three hundred families of farmers. Having suggested the plan, Austin was the first, and by far the most successful, of many such Anglo *empresarios*, most of whom were unable to supply enough immigrants.

Austin located his vast colony on 11 million acres of prime cotton land centered around the lower Brazos and Colorado Rivers, an area that lies between the modern cities of Austin and Hous-

ton. Austin's Colony was a great success—by 1831 its prosperous farmers and their families gave it a population of 5,600. By then the volatile Mexican government, alarmed by the growing Anglo dominance, changed its earlier liberal policies. Further immigration was forbidden, while taxation and military supervision of the colonies were increased. These events precipitated the successful Anglo Revolution that led to the independent Republic of Texas in 1836 (see page xiii).

Columbus, on the Colorado River, and San Felipe, Austin's headquarters town on the Brazos River, were the principal Austin's Colony towns; both were small villages throughout the period. Although burned by the retreating Anglos during the Texas Revolution, the two early towns were rebuilt after independence but were soon eclipsed by the newly founded cities of

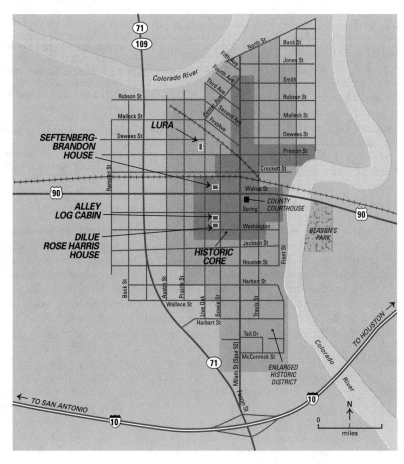

Galveston, Houston, and Austin, which became the principal urban centers of independent Texas.

San Felipe all but disappeared in the succeeding decades, but Columbus has survived as a small county seat and market center. Today it retains several modest folk and Greek Revival dwellings from the 1850s and 1860s, as well as a fine collection of Folk Victorian houses, both large and small, most of them built during an 1880s cotton boom.

Columbus Historic Core

Historic Core, ca. 1850s–1930

Columbus was originally laid out by Austin, aided by friend and associate the Baron de Bastrop and several slaves. Their initial survey created square blocks, which today have been built out with houses facing onto every block face. Compared with the more usual rectangular blocks (see figure 30, page 699), this plan has a slightly disorienting effect, as almost every intersection offers houses or businesses extending uniformly in all directions. One more easily and instinctively navigates a rectangular grid system in which distinctions in street widths and block lengths make it easy to orient yourself. Imagine the prospect of every intersection presenting the same-width street, the same-length block, and the same general mixture of uses in all four directions, and you can begin to understand how a town of similar square blocks is more confusing.

Once you realize that navigating will require a bit of concentration, you can enjoy Columbus's many historic homes. The town was one of the first in Texas and has long maintained a fairly steady population, so many of the homes built during its long history still remain. The map (see page 563) shows the general outline of Columbus's original historic district in the darker shade. Recently a much larger area has been designated—this area has fewer nineteenth-century homes and features mainly early-twentieth-century houses. Columbus's districts offer the wonderful mixture of sizes, ages, and styles of homes, standing side by side, that typifies most older small towns.

A pair of outstanding carpenter-builders, the Wirtz brothers, lived in Columbus. They added spindlework detail to earlier Greek Revival houses (producing houses with a Folk Victorian appearance), and they also built original, symmetrical Folk Victorian houses. The Wirtzes were fond of using elaborately ornamented centered gables, particularly on one-story homes. Their fine work adds distinction to many Columbus homes.

1100 Bowie Street (private), Raumonda, 1887. This handsome two-story Folk Victorian house was built by the Ilse family with a cypress-wood exterior and double wall throughout. The house measures twenty feet by twenty feet and has elegant double porches on both the front and the back. These have distinctive railings and friezes composed of interlocking circles and porch supports with Stick-influenced diagonal braces at the tops. Italianate decorative brackets are placed along the cornice line, above each porch support. Note the handsome paired front doors.

436 Smith Street (private), Luck House, 1898. This gabled-front-and-wing Folk Victorian house has a tiny squared embraced tower.

903 Front Street (private), Crebbs House, 1860s and 1892. This is one of Columbus's many Greek Revival–era homes that had stylish Folk Victorian porches added later.

634 Spring Street (private), Townsend House, 1892; Jacob Wirtz, Columbus, builder. This cross-plan house has exuberant spindlework porches and other Eastlake-inspired details executed by one of the talented Wirtz brothers, who here produced a Victorian-era jewel.

1216 Live Oak Street (private), Bartels House; 1885. A fine one-story Folk Victorian with a centered gable. Note that the porch balustrade and much of the detail have been cut with a jigsaw out of flat wood, rather than being turned spindlework as at 634 Spring Street (see the preceding entry). A Texas Lone Star ornaments the front gable. This house has paired doors, which were apparently much favored in Columbus, perhaps because they allowed more breeze into the central halls.

COLUMBUS MUSEUM HOUSES

Magnolia Homes, a nonprofit corporation formed to save Columbus's historic architecture, has done an excellent job of acquiring four properties that present a continuum of its architectural past. This has always been primarily a volunteer organization, but the town is small and the volunteers are growing weary, so today it tries to limit tours to larger groups. They are happy to try to accommodate individuals and small groups when it is possible, but at the moment their longtime regular tour schedule is on hold, and everything is by appointment. Call the same number to visit all of the houses below. Three of the four homes they show are on their original sites.

Magnolia Homes Tours and the chamber of commerce share offices on the first floor of the restored

Stafford Opera House on the courthouse square. This is an excellent place to get a map and make inquiries.

Alley Log Cabin, ca. 1836

1224 Bowie Street; 409-732-5135.
The one house that has been moved, this belonged to Abram Rawson, the brother of Rawson Alley, the original surveyor for Austin's Colony. The home was built around 1835, with an addition in 1855. It is a prerailroad folk house in the Midland log tradition. The double-pen house has two end chimneys, a dropped-roof front porch, and it is built of squared logs. The interior has local furniture typical of the prerailroad era and includes some fine Texas primitive pieces.

Dilue Rose Harris House, 1858

602 Washington Street; 409-732-5135.
This one-story Greek Revival house has a full-height entry porch and is on a raised foundation. It is built of tabby, a mixture of gravel, sand, and lime formed into large building blocks. These thick walls are scored outside to look like building stone and are plastered inside. The presence of two original front doors is interesting; it is in the tradition of southern hall-and-parlor houses

and helped add both light and ventilation to the home's two front rooms. The inside still has its original moldings and fireplaces and has been appropriately furnished.

Lura, 1872 and 1890s

808 Live Oak Street; 409-732-5135.
Lura, also known as the Keith-Traylor House, is an outstanding example of a side-gabled-roof, one-story Folk Victorian house. It began as a simpler house, but in about 1890 Lester Wirtz, one of the Wirtz brothers, added an elaborate centered gable and spindlework porches (a side porch is on the left, off of the rear kitchen). The full-length windows were added at the same time. This house has all of its original furnishings, including many kitchen utensils and a charming "art square," as elaborate machine-made rugs, like the one in the front parlor, were called locally.

Seftenberg-Brandon House, ca. 1860s and 1890s

616 Walnut Street; 409-732-5135.
The grandest of the group, this house was originally a one-story Greek Revival cottage. In the 1890s it was

Lura

Seftenberg-Brandon House

purchased by the Seftenberg family, who operated the local general store and felt obliged to make a more stylish statement to the community. They added a second story and exterior Stick-style porches as well as Victorian detailing to the interior, although it is still easy to decipher the original Greek Revival plan. The way the local carpenter-builder chose to transform the earlier home's center hall into a "Victorian" stair hall is particularly intriguing. It is filled with Victorian-era antiques, many collected locally.

DALLAS

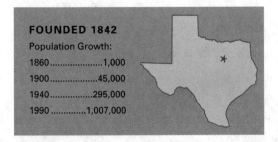

FOUNDED 1842

Population Growth:

1860	1,000
1900	45,000
1940	295,000
1990	1,007,000

Although founded in the days of the Republic of Texas, Dallas remained a small frontier trading post on the north Texas prairies until the eastern railroad network reached the state in 1872. Dallas then had the good fortune to become the junction point where Texas's first two major rail lines crossed each other. These were the north–south Houston and Texas Central (which connected with Kansas City and St. Louis by crossing through the Indian Territory, now eastern Oklahoma) and the east–west Texas and Pacific (which ultimately connected Louisiana and the Gulf South with El Paso and California). These railroads, and their local connecting lines, fueled an enormous agricultural boom on the fertile north Texas prairies. By 1925 an estimated 10 percent of the world's cotton was being grown within a hundred miles of Dallas, and the city, with its excellent rail connections, had become the principal cotton-marketing, wholesale distribution, and banking center for a rich agricultural hinterland.

Petroleum Lending

Dallas had little direct role in the early Texas oil booms. The fertile belt of blackland prairie that surrounds Dallas and stretches south to beyond Austin has yielded little oil or gas compared to the prolific production found both to the east and to the west. As a result, Dallas never had the refineries and drilling services that dominated typical oil towns. The city's bankers made up for this oversight of nature by becoming pioneer lenders for the development of petroleum discoveries, a type of loan that most banks shunned as risky speculations. Dallas-based petroleum geologist Everette Lee De-Golyer (see "DeGolyer House," page 574) helped them eliminate much of the risk by developing sophisticated techniques for evaluating the long-term value of underground reserves of oil and gas. Following his lead, several Dallas banks took the then-unprecedented step of using these estimated reserves as collateral for loans to further develop the fields. As a result, Dallas became a favored location for the region's energy industry headquarters.

The East Texas Field

In 1930 Dallas's petroleum fortunes received an unexpected windfall when a local operator discovered the supergiant East Texas Field about 125 miles east of the city. Subsequent development of this enormous bonanza involved many Dallas oilmen and financiers. With this came a new boom period for Dallas, this

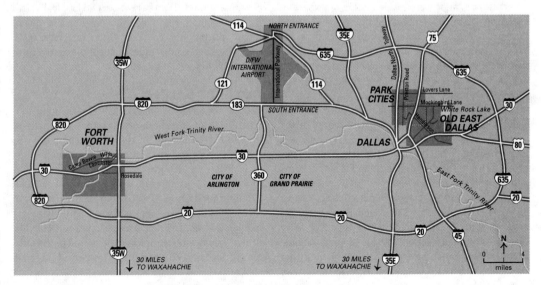

one based on the unprecedented wealth that flowed from this huge resource. The field's size is suggested by the fact that its largest operator, Dallas oilman Haroldson Lafayette Hunt (1889–1974), is said to have supplied a large fraction of the fuel used by the Allied armies and navies in the Second World War. The timing of the discovery also helped shield the city from the most devastating effects of the 1930s depression—several fine residential neighborhoods built in that decade are visible reminders of this new prosperity.

The wealth pouring from the East Texas Field also helped Dallas become the host city for the

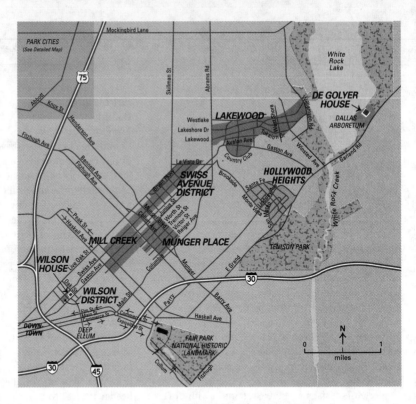

1936 Texas Centennial celebration, a widely publicized great exposition that commemorated the hundredth anniversary of the state's independence from Mexico. It was held at what is now the **Fair Park National Historic Landmark** (Parry Avenue and Robert B. Cullum Boulevard, 214-421-9600), one of the very few great exposition sites that survive intact. The park contains one of the most important collections of Art Moderne architecture, art, and planning remaining anywhere in the world. Its thirty-two buildings built for the 1936 centennial are now home to museums, performance halls, and the State Fair of Texas, held in early October and one of the largest annual events in North America.

Modern Dallas

Along with several other cities in the southern United States, Dallas has been a principal beneficiary of the Sunbelt population shifts of the post-1940 decades. Between 1940 and 1990 the city's population more than tripled as it became a favored location for new light industry and corporate headquarters, both regional and national. Even more spectacular has been the growth of the metropolitan area as Dallas and Fort Worth, its neighbor thirty miles to the west (see page 587), have become linked and ringed by burgeoning satellite towns that increased the area's total population from about five hundred thousand in 1940 to more than

four million today. This expansion has destroyed much early architecture and all but obliterated any trace of the substantial Victorian town that gave rise to modern Dallas. A half-dozen downtown landmark buildings and the carefully restored houses of the Wilson District (see page 569) are some of the principal Victorian survivors. In spite of its modern growth, however, Dallas does retain many fine Eclectic-era neighborhoods that are concentrated in two large areas: Old East Dallas (see the following entry), which lies northeast of downtown, and the adjacent Park Cities (see page 574), which begin about two miles north of the central business district (see map, page 567).

OLD EAST DALLAS

Old East Dallas has some of the best remaining concentrations of historic houses in the city, many of them clustered around the three-mile length of Swiss Avenue, which passes through three instructive historic districts and is adjacent to a fourth. These combine to provide a chronological cross section of Dallas neighborhoods from 1900 to about 1930. Northeast of Swiss Avenue's termination, two slightly younger neighborhoods, Lakewood and Hollywood Heights, provide many fine examples of the period house fashions of the late 1920s to early 1940s period (see map above).

Wilson District, ca. 1898–1902

Swiss Avenue received its name when a group of Swiss and French immigrants from La Reunion, a failed 1850s utopian settlement near Dallas, first settled in the vicinity of the present Wilson District, which is located in the 2800 and 2900 blocks of Swiss Avenue. The two-block historic district is the heart of a multi-block inner-city revitalization project sponsored by Dallas's Meadows Foundation, which today houses more than thirty nonprofit agencies. The entire area is an example of adaptive reuse—single-family houses, warehouses, and even a bottling plant have been converted to office uses.

The 2900 block is composed primarily of original houses built by the Wilson family (see "Wilson House" below). Number 2922 was the Wilson's own home, while 2902, 2906, and 2910 were planned as rental properties so that the Wilsons could "choose their neighbors." The house at 2914 has been moved into what was once the Wilsons' side garden.

The 2800 block of Swiss Avenue is occupied by Victorian dwellings that, originally slated for demolition in nearby Dallas neighborhoods, were moved here and restored by the Meadows Foundation in the 1980s. Except for 2800 Swiss Avenue, all of the houses in the district were built in the Queen Anne style. This is a good place to observe subtle variations in the hipped-with-lower-cross-gable roofs that are so typical of Queen Anne houses. Most commonly there are two cross gables, one front facing and one side facing. Unlike most hipped roofs, in which the ridge runs parallel to the front facade, Queen Anne hipped roofs often look like a pyramid from the front, with no roof ridge visible. Sometimes the roof has no ridge, and the roofs *are* pyramidal. More commonly, a short ridge runs front to back, parallel to the side of the house. Most of the houses in the Wilson District are Free Classic Queen Anne designs in which Classical columns replace the familiar spindlework "gingerbread" on the porches.

2800 Swiss Avenue (private), Beilharz House, ca. 1902. Originally located diagonally across the street from its present location, this is the most architecturally interesting of the moved-in houses. Built by Mrs. Wilson's sister and her husband, it is a good example of a gambrel-roofed Shingle-style home. Theodore Beilharz (1860–1907), a skilled German stonecutter who immigrated to Dallas in 1883, produced the stone used in many fine buildings in the Dallas area. The red sandstone ornament in the side garden was carved by his workers, as, presumably, were the porch-support columns. These are of red sandstone that has now been painted a dark brown. Notice the striking stained-glass transom in the rounded bay and the handsome front door with its early Colonial Revival detailing, a typical feature of Shingle-style houses. The two arched upstairs windows fill in what was originally a recessed open porch.

2902 Swiss Avenue (private), Arnold House, 1902. This house makes a perfect transition between 2922 (see the following entry) and 2800 (see the preceding entry). It is a Queen Anne house like 2922, but has unusual Shingle-style influence in its wraparound porch. Rather than the more common Queen Anne porch elaborations, this house has rounded arches filled with patterned shingles between the Free Classic porch supports. The resulting arched, shingled form bears a striking resemblance to the upstairs porch of 2800. The Arnold House is one of the rental houses built by the Wilsons and was constructed from pattern-book plans.

Wilson House, 1898

2922 Swiss Avenue; 214-821-3290.

Cattleman Frederick Wilson (1863–1923) and his wife, Henrietta, lived in this large corner house, which was completed in 1898. Restored by the Meadows Foundation, it is now open to the public as the home of Preservation Dallas. There is a film and walking tour of the district available. This is not a traditional house museum, but an example of a house adaptively reused for

Wilson House

offices and exhibits. The latter emphasize Dallas's older neighborhoods.

The house is an excellent Free Classic Queen Anne design with shingled corner tower and elegant wraparound porch. Its corner location merited almost-identical porch entries facing both Swiss and adjacent Oak Street. Note the handsome porch balusters and original front door. The carriage house and servants' house in the rear are original but have been moved forward to make room for a parking area behind.

Mill Creek, ca. 1898–1925

Continuing up Swiss Avenue, one enters Mill Creek, which includes the 4300 to the 4800 blocks. These residential blocks are mixtures of multi- and single-family houses, for this area, originally developed without land use restrictions, has had several waves of development.

4301 Swiss Avenue (private). This is a fine, although presently somewhat-deteriorated, example of the most popular southern interpretation of the Neoclassical style—a centered two-story porch coupled with a one-story full-width porch. In this corner house, this distinctive porch arrangement is used on both street-facing facades. Note the elaborate column capitals that are typical of pre-1920 Neoclassical houses.

4409 Swiss Avenue (private). This American four-square house (see the following entry) has fine Prairie-style detailing. Note the wonderful Sullivanesque ornamentation under the eaves and the unusual capitals on the porch supports. Such details were available from catalogs.

Munger Place, 1905–ca. 1920

Munger Place was a side project of inventor Robert S. Munger, who made a fortune designing and manufacturing vacuum-feed cotton gins that were used throughout the world's cotton-growing regions. The first section of Munger's housing development opened in 1905 and was the city's first to include restrictive covenants governing such things as minimum lot sizes, uniform house setbacks and side yards, unobstructed front lawns, two-story construction, and minimum house costs. As the original blocks filled up, additional blocks were added to the development. What is today called the Munger Place Historic District was planned for the development's smaller lots and less costly houses, with construction costs from about $2,000 to $7,500. Adjacent Swiss Avenue (see page 571) was a landscaped boulevard designated for the highest-priced homes (a minimum construction cost of $10,000). The houses on Swiss are mostly of more expensive masonry construction, whereas those in the present-day Munger Place Historic District are mainly handsome two-story wooden-walled structures. Most were built from pattern-book designs in the shape called American four-square (four rooms downstairs and four upstairs). The most common style is a simple, vernacular Prairie design. Next most common is the Neoclassical style. Craftsman, Mission, and Colonial Revival versions also occur.

5205 Reiger Avenue (private), Gibbs House, 1913. An excellent example of the four-square shape with Craftsman stylistic details. Note the pattern cut into the ends of the exposed roof rafters and, above the entry, the exposed porch roof beams with triangular knee braces below. The porch supports have similar triangular pieces to each side; note the unusual pattern of the balusters. This house has the upper story clad with staggered wood shingles rather than the more typical horizontal siding. Although hipped dormers are most typical of four-square houses, those with Craftsman detailing most often have gabled dormers as seen here.

There is a nice juxtaposition of the double dormer windows with the doubled second-story windows and window

Mill Creek

Munger Place

Munger Place

4902 Tremont Street (private), Lane House, 1925. This is a typical Prairie-style version of the four-square shape. The porch supports are large squared brick piers that begin at ground, not porch, level. The dormer has a low-hipped roof with broad, overhanging eaves. Notice how the simple brackets under the eaves are arranged to line up with the sides of the dormer windows, the second-story windows, and the center of the brick piers. Note the typical Prairie door with glass in the upper third and a ledge with three blocks below. To each side are sidelights of tulip-design stained glass.

5124 Victor Street (private), Fay House, 1914. This four-square shape is an excellent example of the Colonial Revival style (hipped-roof-with-full-width-porch subtype) with some Neoclassical influences. Note the pilasters between the paired upper-story windows and the interesting overlapping prism pattern of the muntins in the upper window sashes. The front door has a large and elegant surround with sidelights and a three-part transom above, all with a geometric leaded-glass design. A curious feature is the centered location of the triangular pediment on the entry porch roof, rather than above the steps on the right side. The matching ornaments atop the pediment and the dormer are also unusual.

Swiss Avenue Historic District, 1905–ca. 1930

This carefully landscaped boulevard was the upscale core of the Munger Place development; it is now a separate historic district. In addition to its many fine houses, this district is of interest because of its uniform spatial planning, emphasizing unobstructed front yards and uniform setbacks, that was dictated by the development's original restrictions (see "Munger Place," page 570). Opened in 1905, Munger Place's handsome Swiss Avenue was so successful that additional blocks were added as the preceding ones filled. Prairie-style designs are most in evidence in the earliest blocks (4900 to 5300); next, Prairie homes are interspersed with Period houses in the 5300 to 5700 blocks. By the time the 5800 to 6100 blocks had opened for development, the Prairie style had passed from favor, and this portion of the district has mainly later Period houses of various styles, most of them built in the 1920s.

box with modest geometric pattern below. Note the unusually large windows with thirty lights in the upper sash.

4937 and 5119 Worth Street (both private), ca. 1912. These are two examples of Neoclassical detailing used on four-square-shaped houses. Both are in the same Neoclassical subtype (full-height entry porch with lower full-width porch) and both have the one-over-one pane windows (a single pane of glass in both the top and the bottom sash) that are typical of pre-1920 examples of this style. Number 5119 has elaborate Corinthian capitals on fluted wood columns, with a single pair of colossal columns supporting the entry porch. In contrast, 4937 has square columns, which were easily constructed on-site.

4946 Swiss Avenue (private), Lynch House, 1913. An excellent example of a hipped-roof, symmetrical Prairie design that contrasts with the more high-style Higginbotham House (see the following entry). Note the elegant glass awning over the side entry, which is not typical of the Prairie style. From the front this looks like a typical American four-square house, but a side view shows it to be not "square" but a much larger and deeper rectangular form. The American four-square shape was then so popular that even those building a larger Prairie house sometimes preferred to copy its appearance on the street facade.

5002 Swiss Avenue (private), Higginbotham House, 1913; Lang & Witchell, Dallas, architects. A fine local exam-

Swiss Avenue Historic District

ple of a high-style Prairie design, this is of the asymmetrical subtype with the front door fashionably obscured (it is in the central projecting wing and faces to the left). Note the geometric pattern in the upper sashes of the first-floor window and how this is echoed in the wood mullions of the upper-story windows. These are local interpretations of the full-length geometric glass patterns in the casement windows of the houses of Frank Lloyd Wright and his Chicago-area followers. Most of the other Prairie designs on Swiss Avenue are symmetrical and have a prominent front entry.

5439 Swiss Avenue (private), Greer House, 1916; Hal Thomson, Dallas, architect. A house in the Renaissance tradition that combines both Italian Renaissance and English Georgian features, this was designed by Dallas's most gifted Eclectic-era architect. The Italian Renaissance contributes the handsome recessed entry with arched colonnade and the large front terrace with "bowling pin" balustrade. Most Italian Renaissance houses are of light-colored stone or a material designed to imitate it, like buff-colored brick or stucco. This house is built instead of the deep-red brick more associated with high-style Colonial Revival houses. It also has Colonial Revival shutters and a roof covered in slate, rather than Italian-style tile.

5500 Swiss Avenue (private), Aldredge House, 1917; Hal Thomson, Dallas, architect. Another creative house by the same architect as 5439 (see the preceding entry). This one is in the French Eclectic style, but with a particularly heavy dose of Renaissance details borrowed from the Beaux Arts movement. Note the columns beside the door and in the side wings, the pediment over the entry at roof level, the balustrades on the porch, over the door, and in the roof sec-

tion. The pitch of the hipped roof is lower than in most examples of the style.

5736 Swiss Avenue (private), Womack House, 1923; Bertram Hill, Dallas, architect. This house was clearly inspired by the design of 5439 Swiss Avenue (see above). It is only slightly less elaborate and uses arches above the first-floor windows, not at the recessed entry—exactly the opposite of 5439.

5611, 5417, and 5125 Swiss Avenue (all private). These are three instructive examples of Mission-style designs. Two feature tiled visor roofs; 5125, which was perhaps the best example, accidentally had its green tile roof painted gray, which somewhat obscures the elegant styling of the house itself. Number 5611 still retains its original wall color and roof. Number 5417 has lost the tile on its main roof, making its Mission style less immediately obvious.

Bryan Parkway

This smaller-scale historic district street parallels the upper blocks of Swiss Avenue to the north. The 6000 and 6100 blocks of Bryan Parkway (these are between the same cross streets as the 5600 and 5700 blocks of Swiss) have a wonderful collection of midsized Craftsman houses—6121, 6045, and 6019 (all private) are of particular note, the latter for its still intact trellised verandah. On Bryan Parkway, one can easily see the change in middle-class housing from stucco or wood-clad walls before about 1920 to mostly masonry-walled

Swiss Avenue Historic District

ited Beverly Hills, become enchanted with the Spanish-influenced houses being built there, and returned to Dallas to design and build his own versions. This house originally served as a field office from which he oversaw and promoted his development and was later his own home.

6676 Lakewood Boulevard (private), Vaughn House, 1934. This stately, well-balanced Italian Renaissance house has been a bit unsettled by an unsympathetic addition above the porte cochere and an asymmetrically placed porch awning. It has a fine entry-door surround, elegant cast-stone arches around the first-floor windows, and a double belt course below small second-story windows. The brick is multitoned tan. Fired blue-green roof tiles were sometimes used on Italian Renaissance designs, but these seem to have been painted this color, as traces of underlying terra-cotta are appearing.

houses in the 1920s and later, a change made possible by the perfection of inexpensive brick-veneering techniques that greatly reduced the cost of brick-sided houses. Here there is a transition from mostly wood-clad Craftsman-style houses in the 6000 block, to a mixture of wood-clad and brick-veneered houses in both Craftsman and period styles in the 6100 block, to mostly brick-veneered Period houses in the 6200 and 6300 blocks, which were developed last.

Lakewood, ca. 1920–1940

Munger Place became fully developed in the mid-1920s as the remaining vacant lots in the upper blocks of Swiss Avenue were filled. During the late 1920s and 1930s affluent East Dallas development shifted several blocks northeastward to the Lakewood neighborhood. Its early area was approximately bounded by Abrams Road, Velasco Street, White Rock Lake, and Gaston Avenue—with curving Lakewood Boulevard as its centerpiece. Here can be seen many fine examples of late-Eclectic-era housing fashions. Particularly prominent are the Tudor, French Eclectic, and Spanish Eclectic styles, the latter concentrated in the 7000 block of Lakewood Boulevard. As the street begins to terminate at the end of this block, one can catch a glimpse of nearby **White Rock Lake,** an early water-supply reservoir that is now a city park circled by a popular hiking and biking trail. Overlooking the lake are many fine Eclectic-era estates, among them the important De-Golyer House (see page 574).

7035 Lakewood Boulevard (private), Hutsell Field Office, 1930; C. D. Hutsell, Dallas, architect. This is a small but highly elaborated Spanish Eclectic house of the cross-gabled subtype and has a roofed balcony with a wooden railing, a round tower with a decorative tile cornice, a front courtyard with a tile-capped brick fence, a stained-glass focal window, an intricate wrought-iron arched entry gate, and an exterior staircase. Many of the houses in this immediate area (mostly of similar light-tan brick) were designed by this same architect-builder, who is reputed to have vis-

Lakewood

Lakewood

6758 Lakewood Boulevard (private), Schubert House, 1937. This is a large brick Tudor-style house with the chimney placed on the side. It has two styles of ornamented vergeboards on its two main gables. Each gable has a different pattern of half-timbering infilled with stucco. Most of the second story is half-timbered as well, here infilled with wildly variegated brick patterns. There is a cast-stone door surround and the large bay window has been modified.

Hollywood Heights, ca. 1920s–1940s

This subdivision was opened in the 1920s and is sort of a condensed version of Lakewood—the lots are a bit smaller and the hills a bit taller. Its curving streets are lined with picturesque and well-maintained one-story homes. Most prevalent are "Tudor bungalows," a particular Dallas favorite during the late 1920s and the 1930s. Many of these have brown fieldstone detailing added on the front facade, a Tudor-style elaboration that is almost unique to the Dallas area. In addition there are Minimal Traditionals, Colonial Revival cottages, and even one Pueblo Revival home. Today Hollywood Heights is a conservation district and has one of the most active and effective neighborhood organizations in the city.

Hollywood Heights

DeGolyer House, 1939

8525 Garland Road; 214-327-8263; Denman Scott and Burton Schutt, Los Angeles, architects.

Formerly the carefully landscaped forty-four-acre estate of oilman Everette Lee DeGolyer (1886–1956), and his wife, Nell (1887–1972), the grounds have now become the Dallas Arboretum and Botanical Garden. DeGolyer's grand Spanish Eclectic house, which he called Rancho Encinal, is one of the nation's few museum houses of this style. It was loosely patterned after the Mexican haciendas he had visited during many years of working in that country and further influenced by a 1939 tour of Spanish missions in the Southwest to gather ideas for their home. DeGolyer, an internationally important pioneer in the use of gravity and seismic techniques in the search for oil (see page 567), also had a sense of humor. He is said to have described his home as "a California architect's idea of a Texas oilman's idea of a Mexican ranch house." The house has a severe entry facade, and three of the main rooms look out on and wrap around a rear patio, which overlooks White Rock Lake.

The Arboretum Society, recognizing the importance of this house, conducts regular tours for arboretum visitors. Guided by a fine collection of early photos of the interiors, and aided by a growing number of furniture donations from the family, the home is beginning to reclaim its original look. DeGolyer was an avid book collector and was for many years both the chief stockholder and chairman of the board of the *Saturday Review of Literature.* His large library, built to hold fifteen thousand volumes, is one of the highlights of the house.

Also on the arboretum grounds is the 1936 **Camp House,** an understated design by the distinguished Houston architect John F. Staub (see page 609), who was apparently inspired here by the metal-roofed German folk houses of central Texas (see page 594). The house is now used for offices and meeting rooms.

PARK CITIES

Highland Park and adjacent University Park are two separately incorporated early residential districts, now completely surrounded by the city of Dallas, that are commonly lumped together under the general term "Park Cities." Highland Park, with about nine thousand residents living in its 2.2 square miles, was opened in 1907 amid rural cotton fields as one of Dallas's first fully planned residential suburbs and remains today among the city's most desirable addresses. Its deed restrictions do not even allow churches to be built within its boundaries. Only a country club and the Highland

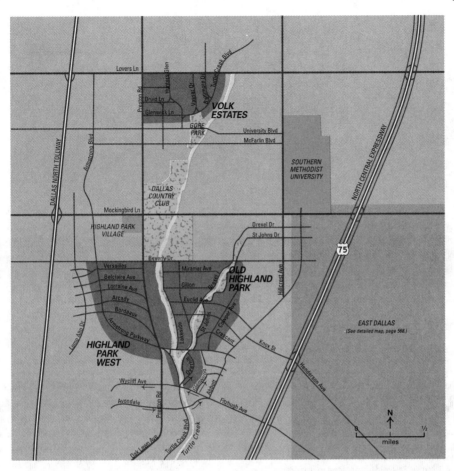

Park Village, one of the nation's first shopping centers, interrupt its residential character.

University Park, Highland Park's larger and slightly younger neighbor to the north, was somewhat less restrictive and includes many churches, Southern Methodist University, apartments, duplexes, a YMCA, and even some strip shopping plus thousands of single-family homes. The town occupies 3.7 square miles and has a population of about twenty-two thousand. Much of the town is filled with relatively modest dwellings built after about 1935.

In recent decades, many early Park Cities homes have been drastically expanded, remodeled, or demolished and replaced with new construction. This began in the older parts of Highland Park but has now spread throughout the two towns. One of the challenges of house watching in Park Cities is picking out the remaining original facades from the many that have been modified, some beyond recognition. Equally challenging can be distinguishing Eclectic-era dwellings from some of their carefully designed Neo-Eclectic neighbors, most of which have been built since the mid-1980s. For example, the blocks of Highland Park's Beverly Drive between Hillcrest Avenue and Preston Road reveal only a handful of original houses amid a remarkable spectrum of alterations and new designs.

Old Highland Park, 1907 to present

The portion of Highland Park east of Preston Road, known as Old Highland Park, was laid out in four phases—1907, 1910, 1915, and 1917. It was designed by New York landscape architect Wilbur David Cook, who, when he began, had just completed a master plan for a part of the exclusive Beverly Hills development in Los Angeles. Here Cook created a series of curving roadways and elegant linear parks focused along Turtle Creek and its smaller eastern tributary known as Hackberry Creek.

The development's largest houses were sited along a small lake created by damming up Turtle Creek. Here along Lakeside Drive was one of the city's finest

Old Highland Park

residential streetscapes, with handsome Eclectic mansions built from about 1910 to 1925. Most of these, like many of the early houses of Old Highland Park, have now been either remodeled beyond recognition or demolished to provide sites for larger houses of varying vintage and design. Some of the more important survivors are:

4205 Lakeside Drive (private), Thomson House, ca. 1919; Anton Franz Korn, Dallas, architect. Bavarian native Anton Korn was a talented architect who in 1916 established a practice in Dallas. He designed homes throughout the Park Cities, including every single house in this block of Lakeside—from Fitzhugh Avenue to Armstrong Parkway—each in a different style. This one is a Colonial Revival design that includes two rarely "revived" features of Middle Colonies Georgian houses—a pent roof between the first and second stories and a hood over the entry.

4321 Overhill Drive (private), 1923; J. Allen Boile, architect. This handsome Spanish Eclectic home, clad in textured stucco, has many refined details. Note the intricate stone door surround, wrought-iron balconies and light fixtures, leaded and stained glass in varied window shapes—the most dramatic a two-story focal window with gently turned columns on each side.

4908 Lakeside Drive (private), Thorpe House, 1915; Thomson and Fooshee, Dallas, architects. The brief partnership between Hal Thomson (see page 572) and Marion Fooshee of the Dallas firm of Fooshee and Cheek produced this commanding house. It is Neoclassical with a full-height entry porch, in this case a curved one. The house has almost every elaboration found in the style—a full-width front terrace with a low balustrade, a roofline balustrade, segmental pediments over the first-story windows, and an elaborately recessed front door with an elliptical Adam fanlight and four miniature Corinthian columns. The dormers are richly detailed with side pilasters, open triangular pediments, and curved muntins.

4704 Lakeside Drive (private), 1915. An excellent hipped-roof Colonial Revival design, this is an early example with a striking oversize dormer topped with a broken segmental pediment. Try putting up a hand to block out the dormer and then remove your hand to see how much life the lone dormer adds to the facade.

3920 Euclid Avenue (private), Riggs House, 1994; Larry Boerder, Dallas, architect. This excellent Neo-French design

illustrates the difficulty of distinguishing some of the Park Cities fine Neo-Eclectic designs from their neighbors built a half century earlier. Note the careful detailing—half-timbering, through-the-cornice windows, a tower, casement windows, and cladding of brick, cast stone, and natural stone. Perhaps the best clue to its modern origin is its expanded scale—few Eclectic-era designs had the vast interior volume seen here.

Highland Park West, 1924 to present

On the opposite side of Preston Road stretches a somewhat-younger neighborhood called Highland Park West, which has curving Armstrong Parkway as its elegant centerpiece. This area was opened in 1924, after the earlier sections of Highland Park were mostly full, and was laid out by the distinguished St. Louis landscape architect George Kessler. Most of the houses here date from the late 1920s and the depression years of the 1930s, a decade when Dallas's oil wealth (see page 567) allowed the continuing construction of the large dwellings that became rare in most American cities. Here the brick-veneered Eclectic fashions of those decades have so far escaped much of the remodeling and demolition that have reconfigured Old Highland Park to the east. Among the area's many fine designs are:

4236 Armstrong Parkway (private), Goodwin House, 1930; Hal Thomson, Dallas, architect. This is a fine example of a French Eclectic design of the symmetrical subtype with Renaissance-inspired detailing. Note the flared eaves of the roof. Nearby at 4248 Armstrong Parkway is a very large example of the same style and subtype—this one with hipped-roof pavilions on each end. The "paint everything one color" decorators have been here.

4271 Bordeaux Avenue (private), 1928; addition, 1992; Hal Thomson, Dallas, architect; Richard Drummond Davis, Dallas, addition architect. This is a very refined interpretation of the Italian Renaissance in light stone. Note the arched entry with its fine metal grille. This house was originally relatively small, with only three bays across the front. It has recently been sympathetically enlarged with a new addition on the adjacent lot.

Highland Park West

4320 Armstrong Parkway (private), Lippitt House, 1938; J. J. Patterson, architect. This creative example of the French Eclectic towered subtype combines natural stone, cast stone, brick, and wood. The pointed Gothic-arched door, entry porch, and balcony door are unusual, as is the close "colliding" juxtaposition of entry, tower, and gable. Notice the arched courtyard entry with iron gate and the handsome two-level wood side porch. There is an asymmetrical French Eclectic house next door at 4330 Armstrong Parkway (private).

4225 Armstrong Parkway (private), Luse House, 1940; Fooshee and Cheek, Dallas, architects. This is a Spanish Eclectic design of the hipped-roof subtype with very formal details of both Renaissance and Islamic inspiration. Note the unusual cornice, door surround, and doubled first-floor window to the left. These all mirror Islamic motifs with their overall geometric patterns. In addition the door and window have shaped arches, mimicking Islamic arches, and pinnacles on each side of the door surround echo the shape of minarets. Renaissance influence appears in the corner

quoins. These have every other quoin vermiculated (that is, looking as if worm eaten).

Volk Estates, ca. 1925 to present

This is the upscale core of the town of University Park, a small area of large homes that include many fine Tudor and French Eclectic designs. Most were built during the 1930s.

6801 Baltimore Drive (private), Lee House, 1929; Hal Thomson, Dallas, architect. This striking Neoclassical design originally had a flat roof, which has been replaced. Everything else is original. There is an unusual portico-in-antis (a portico recessed into the body of the house rather than extending out from it) that is clad with stone rather than the brick of the house proper. The highly decorated broken segmental pediment is particularly elegant. Note the cast-stone cornice, the paired three-panel entry doors, and the almost-hidden side terrace.

6700 Hunters Glen Road (private), Finney House, ca. 1995; Tony McClung, builder. There are many new houses in the Park Cities, and Volk Estates is no exception. This Neo-Tudor has parapeted gables, corner quoins, hood molds on the windows, a cast-stone Tudor arched entry, and even a trefoil window. The extremely wide porte cochere and large size provide clues that it is new.

7000 Vassar Drive (private), Volk House, 1940; I. Gayden Thomson, architect. This is one of this neighborhood's many examples of the Monterey style that was very popular in Dallas from the 1930s into the 1950s. The freestanding columns may be additions.

6912 Vassar Drive (private), Hill House, 1941; D. F. Steele, builder. Louisiana French variations of the Monterey style are common in Dallas. These have New Orleans–style ironwork on the upstairs balconies. This 1941 design has an early example of the large and slightly bowed picture window that became very popular in the 1950s.

3805 McFarlin Boulevard (private), Williams House, 1932; David Williams, Dallas, architect. Built for the mayor of University Park, Elbert Williams (no relation to the architect), this house is revered by Texas architects as a seminal prototype of an indigenous Texas regional style of architecture. In Williams's hands this was characterized by a clean, side-gabled form, a standing-seam metal roof (a characteristic of German folk buildings in the Texas Hill Country; see "Fredericksburg," page 593), a broad Monterey-type cantilevered

Highland Park West

Volk Estates

balcony, and wide wooden shutters. Note the horizontal line of the balcony railing, the subtly multicolored brick, and the custom screen doors upstairs that echo the line of the double doors behind.

The Texas Lone Star, used extensively inside and also as a cutout shape on the side of the downstairs porch, declares that this is a Texas house; the national architectural press of the day called it a "rambling Texas ranch house."

WAXAHACHIE

Named for an Indian word meaning "buffalo creek," this is one of the many cotton-boom towns that flourished on the fertile blackland prairies of north-central Texas with the arrival of railroads in the 1870s. Located twenty-five miles south of Dallas, and now the home of many commuters, Waxahachie, with a 1990 population of 18,000, still retains so much of its Victorian charm that it has become a favorite location for filming period movies. The town's principal landmark is the fine **Ellis County Courthouse** (1895), a Richardsonian Romanesque design by San Antonio architect James Reily Gordon (1852–1937), who specialized in high-style public buildings. The courthouse dominates a town square with several surviving Victorian structures.

Waxahachie's residential districts have many fine Queen Anne houses, most of them located at some distance from the downtown core. Their Victorian occupants traded accessibility for the luxury of large lots, some occupying a full city block, which gave plenty of room for gardens, orchards, chickens, and even a milk cow or two (see "233 Patrick Street," page 580). As the town expanded from a few hundred inhabitants in 1870 to six thousand in 1910, this pattern was made possible by a network of early mule-drawn trolleys, know locally as the "mule-cars," which linked the large-lot residences to the increasingly distant downtown.

Some of their routes are shown on the map, page 579, and today the streets they served (Main, Rogers, and Oldham Streets, and Marvin Avenue) still have a high concentration of early homes. As was often the case, entertainment destinations at the end of two of the lines served to attract additional riders. A fairgrounds was located at the end of the East Marvin Avenue line, and Getzendaner Park was developed at the end of the West Main Street line. This park still has its original 1902 octagonal **Chautauqua Auditorium,** now a very rare building type.

The mule-car lines were converted to electric trolleys in 1913 and then abandoned to the automobile in 1926. The long parallel streets of Main and Marvin still serve as two of the town's principal residential districts, each one discreet and separate from the other—a somewhat unusual pattern dictated by an early railroad line whose railside industries bisected the towns northward expansion.

From 1910 to 1940 Waxahachie's more leisurely growth was mostly accommodated in these original streetcar-served neighborhoods by subdividing the large Victorian lots to accommodate new construction. As a result, the early Victorian streetscapes are now interspersed with younger dwellings, many in the Craftsman and Neoclassical styles.

716 West Main Street (private), Chaska House, ca. 1900. Waxahachie has many one-story Neoclassical houses. These typically have hipped roofs with a prominent central dormer as seen here. This example has particularly handsome architectural detailing. The full-width porch wraps around both sides of the house and has its own separate shed roof (rather than being included under the main house roof). The gabled dormer is accentuated with a pair of corner pilasters, ornamental shingles curving into a recessed window (most typical of the Shingle style), and a pair of columns inset into the recess. The sidelights and transom at the entry feature beveled lead glass in an elegant decorative pattern. Note the two extra-wide special front sash windows that also have decorative transoms above.

Waxahachie

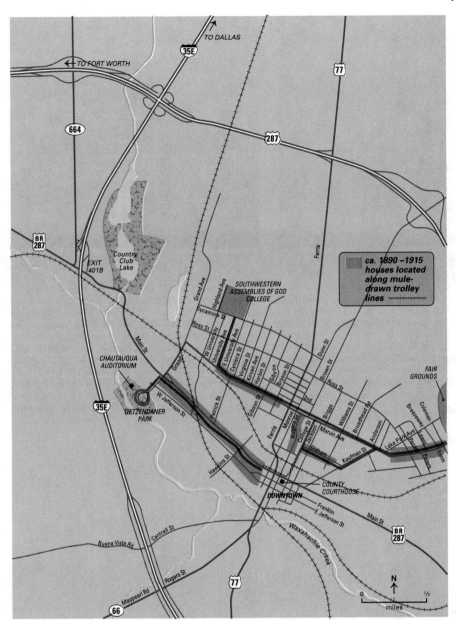

ca. 1890–1915 houses located along mule-drawn trolley lines

Waxahachie, Texas

717 West Main Street (private), ca. 1910. Although not immediately obvious, this house is much the same shape as 716 West Main (see the preceding entry) across the street—a one-story hipped roof design with a prominent central dormer and a full-width porch that wraps around both sides of the house under its own separate shed roof. Here the style is an interesting melding of details drawn from the contemporaneous Prairie style (the heavy, squared brick porch–support piers with geometric detail and the simple brick porch railing design) and Mission style (the shape of the parapeted porch over the entry and the tiled roof).

412 West Marvin Avenue (private), Williams-Erwin

House, 1893. This is among the finest of Waxahachie's many Queen Anne dwellings and has an unusually elaborate spindlework porch. Note that the front facing gable and dormers all have exactly the same roof pitch, but each are a different size and each has different detailing. The handsome front door is ornamented with incised, stylized floral designs of the type called Eastlake after their principal advocate, British interior designer Charles Eastlake. The Craftsman house next door at 414 West Marvin Avenue (private) is built on land that originally was part of this home's large lot.

1201 East Marvin Avenue at Lewis Street (private). Several fine Victorian era homes are clustered in the 1100 and

579

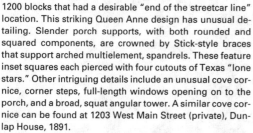

Waxahachie

1200 blocks that had a desirable "end of the streetcar line" location. This striking Queen Anne design has unusual detailing. Slender porch supports, with both rounded and squared components, are crowned by Stick-style braces that support arched multielement, spandrels. These feature inset squares each pierced with four cutouts of Texas "lone stars." Other intriguing details include an unusual cove cornice, corner steps, full-length windows opening on to the porch, and a broad, squat angular tower. A similar cove cornice can be found at 1203 West Main Street (private), Dunlap House, 1891.

500 Oldham Street (private), Strickland Sawyer House, 1897. This is a fine example of a towered Queen Anne design with Free Classic detailing. Note the two-level wrap-around porch. The solid shingle-covered railing of the upstairs porch visually integrates it with the house proper. The low fence around this property is modern.

233 Patrick Street (private), Patrick-Sawyer House, 1899. A rare survivor of a Victorian era "minifarm," this Free Classic Queen Anne–style house with tower still has a barn, windmill house, servants' quarters, and an underground hothouse or "pit" on its spacious grounds. Note where a small extra room (probably a bathroom) has been added on the left, over the front porch.

EL PASO

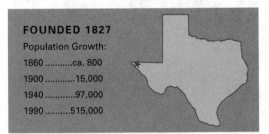

FOUNDED 1827

Population Growth:

1860 ....ca. 800
1900 15,000
1940 97,000
1990 515,000

In the 1600s the El Paso area became an important way station and mission center on the long Spanish wagon road that connected interior Mexico with the prosperous Spanish missions centered around Santa Fe to the north (see page xi). The principal settlement, El Paso del Norte, was on the south side of the Rio Grande, and this has grown to become modern Ciudad Juárez, Mexico's fourth-largest city. Modern El Paso, Juárez's Anglo neighbor across the river, has a much shorter history. It

begins in 1848, when what is now the southwestern United States was acquired following the Mexican War. The discovery of the California goldfields in that same year soon brought a flood of westward-bound Anglo gold seekers through El Paso del Norte, now an international border town with U.S. territory just across the Rio Grande. By 1849 five enterprising Anglo merchants had founded new trading villages across the river. One of these, then called Franklin, was to become the nucleus of today's El Paso.

Franklin remained a modest frontier outpost until 1881 when two important railroads reached the town. These were the Southern Pacific, which was to link Texas and the southern states with distant California, and the southward-building Atchison, Topeka, and Santa Fe, which linked the midwestern states with the populous interior cities of Mexico. El Paso's future prosperity was thus ensured as it became a principal

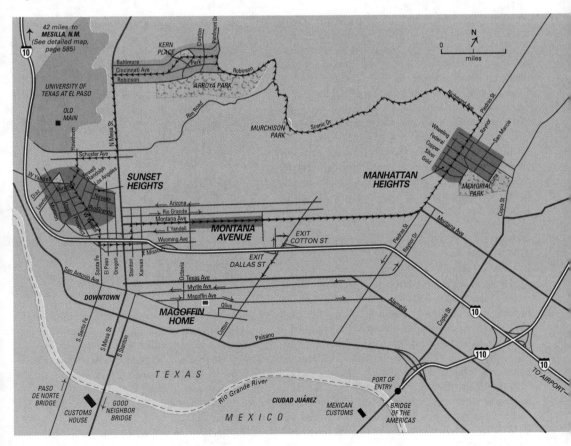

Magoffin Home:
courtyard facade and, below right, main entry

junction for both east–west and north–south railroad traffic. By 1890 the city had 10,000 inhabitants and was the marketing and financial capital of far western Texas and much of adjacent southern New Mexico. El Paso then grew steadily to a population of almost 100,000 in 1940. By 1990 this number had increased fivefold to make it the fourth-largest Texas city. Not surprisingly, this urban growth has destroyed much of El Paso's pre-1940 architectural character. The city does, however, retain an excellent 1875 Spanish Colonial museum house of the rare and transitional Territorial substyle, as well as fine Eclectic-era suburbs that include designs by one of the Southwest's most creative architects of that period.

Magoffin Home, 1875

1120 Magoffin Avenue; 915-533-5147.
James Wiley Magoffin (1799–1868) was one of the five Anglo merchants that established 1849 trading villages on the American side of the Rio Grande across from the historic Mexican city of El Paso del Norte (see page 581). His town, known as Magoffinsville, lay just to the east of Franklin, which was later to become the center of downtown El Paso. Magoffinsville occupied the neighborhood around this historic dwelling.

In 1856 Magoffin's son Joseph (died 1923) joined his father and older brother here to help with the family trading business. Joseph must have been a success, for in 1875, six years before the first railroads reached El

Paso, he built this home, which was exceptionally large and grand by frontier standards. The main house consists of a large entry hall, or zaguan, that was used as a family living area; additional spacious rooms adjoin on each side. Behind the main house are an original carriage house and service rooms that have been connected to the main house to form a semienclosed rear courtyard.

This house is a rare intact example of the Territorial

phase of the Spanish Colonial style. It is built of sun-dried adobe bricks, which about 1887 were covered with lime plaster and scored to look like stone on the three most public facades. This plaster coating helped to protect the adobe mud bricks from the elements. Territorial houses are so named because many of them were built during the prestatehood period, from 1848 until 1912, when New Mexico and Arizona were U.S. territories. These houses typically have flat roofs supported by heavy timbers embedded in the adobe walls, as does this example. Also typical of Territorial houses are simple Anglo-inspired Greek Revival details on doors and windows. Here the front door has side pilasters, a surround of rectangular lights, and a shallow triangular pediment above. Similar pediments are used above the windows. Territorial houses also commonly have roof parapets made of hard-fired bricks, which help protect the softer adobe walls beneath. Magoffin elected to omit these, finishing the parapets with the same hard lime plaster used on the walls.

The Magoffin Home was occupied by Joseph's descendants until 1986 and retains many original family possessions, mostly Anglo-Victorian in origin. These include not only furniture, but paintings, linens, china, and family photos and memorabilia. These authentic furnishings, and the prominent role of the Magoffin family in the early development of El Paso, add to the importance of this unique site.

Sunset Heights, ca. 1900–1925

In 1882 New York financier J. Fisher Sattertwaite began promotion of this steep hillside tract northwest of downtown as an elite, 1,200-lot residential neighborhood. It wasn't until about 1900, however, that the difficult site's many rocky arroyos were filled and graded and the development's street layout fully completed. Navigating the neighborhood is still a challenge, since the hillside streets run at unusual angles. Home to many of El Paso's affluent citizens in the first decades of the century, by the 1970s Sunset Heights was seriously deteriorating, a trend that has begun to reverse since its 1984 designation as a city historic district.

Sunset Heights: three innovative designs by architect Henry C. Trost (bottom two are early views)

1013 West Yandell Drive (private), Trost House, 1907. Henry C. Trost, El Paso, architect. Henry Trost (1860–1933) left his native Ohio in 1880 and spent many years trying to establish an architectural practice in the expanding towns of the West. During this odyssey, about which few facts are known, he spent several years in Chicago, where he met Frank Lloyd Wright and perhaps worked briefly for Louis Sullivan, the father of the modern skyscraper who was also Wright's mentor. After leaving Chicago in 1896, Trost worked in Tucson (see page 22) before moving his practice to El Paso in 1904. By then a highly talented and versatile designer, Trost spent the next thirty years creating a remarkable series of skyscrapers, stores, banks, schools, hotels, apartment buildings, and houses, many of which still richly embellish his adopted hometown. None of these is more spectacular than his own Sunset Heights home that was inspired by Frank Lloyd Wright's then strikingly avant-garde Prairie houses, which had first appeared only a few years earlier. Trost's version is of the gabled-roof subtype and has a Wrightian bas-relief frieze along the cornice line. Note also the matching wide-eaved gabled roof over the entry and the half-timbered upper-story detailing infilled with white decorative panels.

323 West Rio Grande Avenue (private), Williams House, 1905; Henry C. Trost, El Paso, architect. At the turn of the century El Paso was still a small southwestern town where clients interested in expensive architectural experimentation were very scarce. Thus only in his own home could Trost introduce Wright's still-controversial brand of modernism. It's a measure of his skill that he could also produce distinctively original structures in the more traditional fashions of the period, such as this Mission-style design. It is unusual in that it does not have a tiled overhanging roof, but instead a flat roof with a parapet. It also lacks the tiled visor roof that is commonly found on flat-roofed Mission houses. Thus the main house block appears quite stark, with the softening tiled-roof areas confined to the porch roofs.

Two additional Trost houses (see the following two entries) survive on nearby North Mesa Street. Like Montana Avenue (see below), this street was originally a main El Paso transportation artery lined with grand homes. North Mesa, with its many gap sites, is much more typical of how most of these turn-of-the-century residential thoroughfares now appear. Montana is an unusual exception in still retaining several intact residential blocks.

1501 North Mesa Street (private), Schwartz House, 1915; Henry C. Trost, El Paso, architect. This is a striking Italian Renaissance design with some Beaux Arts influence in its porch, which is embellished with paired columns and cartouches. Note the highly detailed attic story, the geometric tilework and brickwork, the two wreaths surrounding the small windows, and the colorful southwestern scene in the arch over the recessed second-story porch.

1712 North Mesa Street (private), Lawson House, 1913; Henry C. Trost, El Paso, architect. A unique house that incorporates fine decorative detailing of both Italian and Spanish origin.

Manhattan Heights, 1912–ca. 1925

This hillside suburban development northeast of downtown has dramatic views overlooking the Rio Grande Valley and El Paso–Ciudad Juárez. First opened in 1912, an undeveloped part of the new addition, located in the vicinity of what is now Memorial Park, had formerly been the site of a smelter for refining some of the rich copper, silver, and gold ores found in the nearby mountains. In 1925 El Paso hired the distinguished St. Louis urban designer George Kessler to prepare a plan for beautifying the city. Among his proposals was a detailed program for reclaiming the old smelter site and its adjacent slag dumps to create Memorial Park, which now marks the eastern boundary of Manhattan Heights. The historic smelter is memorialized in the names of some nearby streets— Gold, Silver, Copper, and Bronze Avenues. Today a city historic district, Manhattan Heights is a pleasant and well-kept neighborhood of mostly midsized houses in the Spanish Eclectic and Craftsman styles. Open trelliswork porte cocheres and porches are found on many of the Craftsman homes, their maintenance and survival facilitated by El Paso's dry climate—the city averages only eight inches of rainfall annually. Many of the Spanish Eclectic houses are of the flat-roofed subtype, appropriate because flat-roofed Spanish Colonial

Manhattan Heights

houses were indigenous here (see "Magoffin Home," page 582).

3003 Wheeling Avenue (private). This unusual Italian Renaissance house has a side entry sheltered by a suspended glass-and-metal canopy. Unusual exaggerated broken pediments are over the lower-story windows in the one-story wings. The ribbon of five windows in the two-story portion is a Prairie-style influence.

3015, 3017, and 3025 Wheeling Avenue (all private). Three delightful small Spanish Eclectic houses in a row. Note the large arched window and courtyard of 3017 and the unusual roofline of 3025 (the two-story portion consists of a three-quarter section of a typical gabled roof).

3115 and 3117 Federal Avenue (both private). A pair of dramatic Craftsman bungalows with Oriental influence in their peaked gables and flared rafter ends. Note the huge elephantine porch supports.

3100 Gold Avenue (private). This large, rambling Ranch house is in the Spanish Eclectic style. It is a highly detailed design with multiple layers of tile on the roof, carved supports for the inset porch (called *portale* in Spanish), and wrought-iron grilles over the windows. Even the garage doors have a Hispanic flair.

1702 Raynor Street (private). This unusual, one-of-a-kind Craftsman-style design is clad in stone with brick detailing. Note the robust, round brick and stone columns.

Montana Avenue, ca. 1895–1915

This is one of the city's principal east–west thoroughfares. It is a rare survivor of the brief posttrolley, preautomobile era when elegant homes tended to be strung out along trolley lines, making for a short walk home. Prior to trolleys, such dispersion was not possible; after automobiles, it was easy to drive to a more distant and less noisy neighborhood. Most of the fine homes that lined these transition-era streets around the country have long since disappeared, replaced either by newer, upscale commercial development or, more commonly, by the roadside blight of used-car lots, shabby commercial buildings, or simply vacant lots. Here on Montana

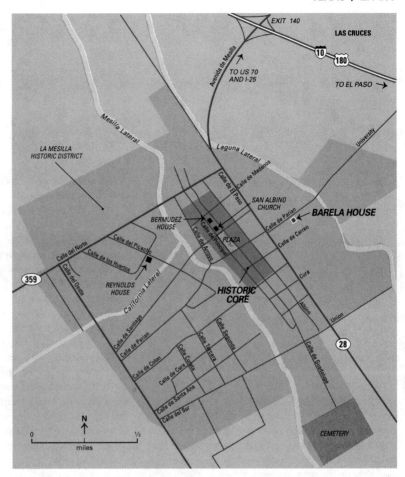

Mesilla,
New Mexico

Avenue, entire blocks of early houses survive, most of them intact and well maintained, even though now converted to commercial uses.

1101 Montana Avenue (private), ca. 1900. This handsome Queen Anne design has Free Classic decorative detailing. Note the unique roof detail added to the main hipped roof. It looks like a miniature hipped roof with a centered gable perched atop the main roof.

1301 Montana Avenue (private), ca. 1910. This nicely detailed, flat-roofed Neoclassical house has an interesting band of Beaux Arts inspired, low-relief carving, complete with a centered cartouche, above its upper-story door. The elegant main-entry door has ornate sidelights with an elliptical fanlight above. The two dominant first-floor windows are of the three-part, Palladian shape.

1514 and 1518 Montana Avenue (both private), ca. 1910. This pair of three-bay Neoclassical houses look like they were built at the same time and are quite similar at first glance. A closer look shows that all of their major details are just slightly different, almost as if they were planned that way. Number 1518 has its porch enclosed under the main roof, Corinthian columns, an offset door with a rectangular line of lights surrounding it, and a broad straight balcony.

Number 1514, slightly larger, has the porch attached with its own roof, Ionic columns, a centered door with an elliptical fanlight, and a smaller curved balcony.

1519 Montana Avenue (private). This is an appealing Mission design. It is a symmetrical example with an arched porch and a pair of bay windows, each topped by a tile roof.

MESILLA

Mesilla, New Mexico, is an historic gem located about forty miles north of El Paso (and less than a mile west of Exit 140 off Interstate 10). The permanent settlement of Mesilla began in 1848 after the Mexican-American War ended, and Texas and the southwest were ceded to the United States (see page xx). At that time what is now the southernmost part of New Mexico, on the west side of the Rio Grande, remained a part of Mexico. Seeking to retain their nationality, some Hispanic families residing on the American side of the river founded the new town of Mesilla on the opposite Mexican side.

Mesilla

Four years later the Gadsden Purchase made Mesilla part of the United States and its mostly Hispanic occupants prospered as the town became an important stagecoach stop and supply center on a new wagon road to California, made possible by the purchase. The town also became the principal agricultural market center for this fertile stretch of the Rio Grande Valley. By the 1860s it was the largest town between San Antonio and San Diego.

Bypassed by the railroad in 1881, Mesilla stopped growing. From then until after the Second World War its relatively few new buildings were all traditional Hispanic vernacular structures. The town's residents didn't like the few modern buildings that were added in the 1950s and 1960s, and quickly adopted an historic zoning ordinance. Through this farsighted action they have managed to maintain much of the scale and feeling that the town had a century ago.

Mesilla is today one of the West's most unspoiled early Hispanic towns. This is reflected not only in its architecture and planning, but in such details as the lack of street addresses for its many lovely homes. To partially circumvent this problem, the locations of the two private houses described here are shown on our Mesilla map; one is an urban house in the town's historic core and the other is in a semirural suburb, where grander houses were traditionally built. Many of Mesilla's houses are of adobe construction, as can be easily seen and studied by looking at some examples in a less-than-perfect state of repair.

The old plaza is at the center of town, with San Albino Church located on the north side. The blocks closest to the plaza have common-wall homes built up to the sidewalk line, with private open space located behind, as was the Spanish custom. The Bermudez House (private), located on Calle de Guadalupe just behind the church, is a good example of this type of house and siting. Freestanding houses were built on the outskirts of town and the fine Territorial-style Reynolds House (private), which is located in the northwest part of Mesilla known as the California District, is an excellent example of this house type.

Barela House, 1860 and 1878

Gadsden Museum, Calle de Parian, just east of Texas Highway 28; 505-526-6293.

The Barela House was built in two stages; the original portion was constructed in 1860 by Anastacio and Rafaela Barela, who were at that time the largest landowners in this part of the Rio Grande Valley. In 1876 their son, Sheriff Mariano Barela, enlarged it into the large Territorial-style home seen today. At that time it faced onto Gran Plaza, another of Mesilla's plazas. In 1936 Albert Fountain II purchased the home and it was his daughter who eventually turned it into the Gadsden Museum. This commemorates the Gadsden Purchase and also holds items relating to several generations of the Fountain family. The authors have not visited this museum, and the description is thus based on published information.

FORT WORTH

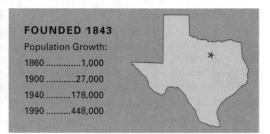

FOUNDED 1843

Population Growth:

1860 1,000

1900 27,000

1940 178,000

1990 448,000

Fort Worth, located at the western edge of central Texas's tallgrass prairies, was founded where an early Indian trail forded one branch of the Trinity River. Like Dallas, founded at another Trinity River ford thirty miles to the east, Fort Worth remained a small frontier village until the first railroads arrived in north Texas in 1872. The boom sparked by the railroads brought differing economic roles to the neighboring towns. Fort Worth looked westward, emphasizing the gathering and processing of bulk commodities—cattle, grain, and oil—from the vast plains of western Texas. Dallas, on the other hand, looked eastward. It became the principal north Texas center for wholesale marketing of manufactured goods from the factories of the midwestern and northeastern states.

Fort Worth first became a cattle town in prerailroad days when it was an important supply center on the fabled Chisholm Trail, the route along which half-wild south Texas cattle were driven to market at Kansas railheads. The brief, and later much romanticized, cattle-drive era began in 1866, when a hungry nation ravaged by the Civil War made beef a prime commodity. It ended in the 1870s, when the expanded eastern railroad network reached into Texas and eliminated the need for the long drives to Kansas.

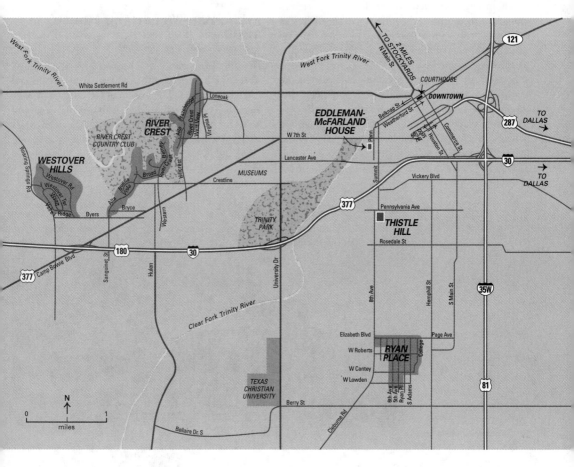

One of these railroads was the westward-building Texas and Pacific line, which opened the endless plains of western Texas for settlement by ranchers and farmers. Fort Worth then became a marketing center for cattle now arriving by rail rather than trail drives. More cattle were added in 1882, when the city became the southern terminus of the Fort Worth and Denver Railroad, which opened still more land for settlement in northwestern Texas. In 1901 Armour and Swift, both giant Chicago-based meatpacking companies, built enormous Fort Worth plants. These made the town the dominant livestock center of the entire Southwest, a position it retained until motor-truck transport decentralized the nation's meatpacking industry beginning in the 1950s. Fort Worth's heritage as a livestock center is today commemorated in the **Fort Worth Stockyards Historic District** (1902 and later; Exchange Avenue and North Main Street, 817-624-4741), which retains some of the spirit of the city's early meatpacking complex.

In the decade from 1910 to 1920 the expansion of dryland wheat farming into the southwestern plains added an important new commodity to the region's economy. Once again Fort Worth was a beneficiary as trainloads of western wheat arrived to unload at new grain elevators and milling complexes that still punctuate the city's skyline.

Fort Worth also played an important role in the Texas oil booms that followed the great Spindletop discovery of 1901 (see page 495). Important early discoveries were made near Fort Worth's western railroad network at Electra (1911), Burkburnet (1917), and Ranger (1918). As a result, the city became an early hub for refining and distributing north Texas's oil. This role has slowly declined since about 1940 as railroad tank cars have been replaced by cross-country pipelines, which now more efficiently transport both crude oil and its refined product over long distances to and from a relatively few centralized refining centers.

As in many southwestern cities, Fort Worth first gained large industrial plants during the Second World War. Today it remains an important center for aerospace-industry manufacturing. Fort Worth has also benefited from the post-1950 Sunbelt population boom that by 1995 had made the Dallas–Fort Worth metropolitan area home to 4 million people.

This population explosion has destroyed much of Fort Worth's early architecture, yet the city has preserved an important fraction of its Victorian downtown. This includes the fine 1895 **Tarrant County Courthouse** (100 East Weatherford Street) and a small nearby commercial district, known today as **Sundance Square,** which occupies the 300 blocks of Main and Houston Streets. The city also retains important Eclectic-era neighborhoods and two fine early museum houses.

Eddleman-McFarland House, 1899

1110 Penn Street; 817-332-5875;
Howard Messer, Fort Worth, architect.
This superb design, with a Queen Anne shape and Chateauesque detailing, was built by the wealthy Mrs. Sarah Ball of Galveston, Texas, who used it as a second home for herself and her son. She died just a few years after its completion, and in 1904 the home was sold to W. H. Eddleman, a Weatherford, Texas, banker and

Eddleman-McFarland
House

rancher. Mr. Eddleman and his wife, Sarah, along with his daughter Caroline (Carrie) Eddleman McFarland and her husband, Frank Hays McFarland, all moved into the house, living together until the elder couple's death. Carrie eventually inherited the house, which she vowed to preserve despite the fact that most of the grand houses around her were being converted to, or demolished for, commercial buildings. When she died in 1978 at the age of one hundred, the house was purchased and preserved by the Junior League of Fort Worth as a combined headquarters and museum house. It was deeded to Historic Fort Worth, Inc., in 1984.

The surrounding neighborhood, now mostly commercial, was once known as Quality Hill and was Fort Worth's most prestigious residential district. Located high on a bluff overlooking the Trinity River, this house, along with its surviving next-door neighbor the Pollack-Capps House, is visible from miles away when approaching the city from the west. The lots along the ridge were long and narrow—seeming like ordinary city lots from Penn Street, but stretching west down the slope to the Trinity River at the rear. Outbuildings and terraced gardens once led down the hill.

The house is built of a handsome pressed yellow brick from Pennsylvania and is ornamented with red sandstone corner quoins and a matching sandstone porch. The high-pitched roof is particularly striking. The tall portion is of slate, while the lower-pitched porch roof and the many ornamental spires and finials of both roofs are of copper.

Inside, all of the original finishes and fittings are still in place—light fixtures, doorknobs and doorplates,

stained glass, and such. Fun to note is the profusion of egg-and-dart molding throughout the home; it appears on everything from doorplates to mantelpieces. The home has extensive oak and mahogany paneling, as was typical of upscale late-nineteenth-century interiors. The floors are particularly lovely, and each room has a different intricate pattern of oak parquet. Both paneling and floors were ordered from catalogs and then installed by local carpenters. The house has appropriate period furnishings. Tours emphasize the home's occupants and their lifestyles and the unusually fine architectural detailing of the interiors and exterior.

Thistle Hill, 1903

1509 Pennsylvania Avenue; 817-336-1212;
Sanguinet and Staats, Fort Worth, architects.
When the Quality Hill area around the Eddleman-McFarland House (see page 588) became completely built up by about 1900, fashionable Fort Worth neighborhoods began to move southward. These first centered around Pennsylvania Avenue, where Thistle Hill is one of the last grand survivors, preserved today as a museum house. Of Neoclassical design, the house was built as a wedding gift from cattle baron W. T. Waggoner to his daughter "the fabulous Electra" and her husband, Philadelphia socialite A. B. Wharton.

The Whartons cut a wide swath in Fort Worth society. Electra's ultra-fashionable wardrobe was maintained by a steady stream of deliveries from as far away as Paris, and the couple was noted for frequent and lavish parties. Anticipating her future inheritance, in 1911 Electra's father gave her $2 million and one of his vast West Texas ranches located near Vernon, a small, and

Thistle Hill

perhaps less socially tempting, town 140 miles north-west of Fort Worth. The Whartons moved to the ranch and sold their house to a cattle baron friend, Winfield Scott (1849–1911), who immediately undertook a major remodeling. Scott died while this was under way, but his widow completed the job and made the house a local showplace, living there until her death in 1938.

The Scotts employed the original architect for the remodeling. The original brick-walled exterior was much as you see it today, but was surrounded by more extensive wooden Neoclassical porches. During the re-modeling, some of these porches were removed, some enclosed, and others substituted brick porch supports for wooden columns. The colossal limestone columns at the entry were most probably carved to replace wooden originals as part of the Scott remodeling. The original roof was wood shingles painted green; the Scotts covered these with more permanent green-glazed terra-cotta tile. Many smaller wooden architec-tural details were replaced by more lasting tile, marble, or stone duplicates. An exception to their taste for ma-sonry materials was an elegant wooden pergola that they added. Many of the details on the main brick house block are of Colonial Revival inspiration—the front door with elliptical fanlight, the corner quoins, and the keystone details over the window to name a few.

One enters the home into a huge symmetrical foyer dominated by a broad centered stairway that curves to both sides at the landing. The foyer has English oak wainscoting and ceiling panels. Such paneling would have been a bit passé by 1912, but was still quite fash-ionable when it was originally installed in 1903. The in-terior has been restored mostly to the 1912 remodeling, which although extensive still retained many elements of the 1903 house. For example, the elegant metallic paint finishes in the library were part of the 1903 house, while the mauve and gray of the drawing room reflect the tastes of Mrs. Scott's 1912 remodeling. Note the contrast between the "feminine" decor of the drawing room and the "masculine" decor of the large billiard room (at the turn of the century such terms were often used in interior design).

By the 1930s many of the once-grand dwellings of Pennsylvania Avenue were being converted into room-ing and apartment houses, shops, or offices. In 1940 Thistle Hill was purchased by the Girl's Service League, a philanthropic organization that provided housing for underprivileged young women. When the league moved elsewhere in 1968, it was one of the area's few surviving grand early dwellings, most of which had been demolished for new commercial development. Thistle Hill was saved from a similar fate by a twenty-

year public relations, fund-raising, and renovation campaign that has now converted it into a carefully restored museum house and source of great civic pride.

Ryan Place, 1911–ca. 1940

Developed in 1911 by John C. Ryan, this was Fort Worth's first neighborhood to have protective cove-nants permanently restricting the lots to single-family houses and thus preventing the commercial encroach-ments that led to the destruction of most of the Qual-ity Hill and Pennsylvania Avenue dwellings. These covenants also mandated only masonry houses with uniform setbacks, side yards, and a minimum cost of construction. Elizabeth Boulevard, named after Ryan's wife, was designated for only the most costly homes. It soon replaced Pennsylvania Avenue as the city's most prestigious address.

Most of the houses in Ryan Place were constructed between 1911 and 1920 in various early-twentieth-century styles. Prairie and Italian Renaissance designs predominate along Elizabeth Boulevard. Many brick Craftsman-style designs are found along the adjacent streets of smaller houses. More typically built of wood in the western states, these brick examples were man-dated by Ryan Place's requirement that all houses have masonry walls.

1001 Elizabeth Boulevard (private), Dulaney House, 1923; Wyatt C. Hedrick, architect. Pale buff or yellow ochre were the brick colors of choice for most Italian Renaissance de-signs. This was considered a close approximation of the light stone used in Italy and was commonly substituted for more expensive stone facing. This elaborately detailed dwelling shows how effective such brick walls can be. Many of the exquisite details are reputed to have been imported from Italy. These include the green-glazed tile used for the columns of the entry porch and a massive bronze interior staircase. The house is of the hipped-roof-with-projecting-wing subtype; two small wings at either end project for-ward, leaving a recessed central block in between. Here this is almost obscured by the deep front entry porch, with the triple arch that is so typical of this style. The modern plate-glass glazing in the arched windows across the first story re-placed paired doors that opened out onto the terrace that wraps around the front and side of the house. Number 1302 Elizabeth Boulevard (private), built in 1914 as the home of the subdivision developer John C. Ryan, is another varia-tion of this same Italian Renaissance subtype.

1306 Elizabeth Boulevard (private), Harrison House, ca. 1915. This unusual Prairie-style design features glazed tiles ornamented with a geometric pattern in terra-cotta and green. These handsome tiles are used as a frieze at the cor-nice line, at the top of the massive rectangular porch sup-ports, and even encircle the chimney top. The broad front door is of solid wood with tall, narrow, rectangular stained-glass windows—the color and design of the glass and those of the tiles echo each other. Brick is used for the upper part

Ryan Place

of the second-story walls and as an accent around the front door and under the windows.

1315 Elizabeth Boulevard (private), Smith House, 1918; Wiley G. Clarkson, architect. This elegant Colonial Revival house has two design themes that are subtly repeated. First, the Palladian window shape used for the central second-story window is repeated in the first story on each side of the entry. On the right side, although the Palladian shape was needed to maintain exterior symmetry, most of what would ordinarily be window is stuccoed. Why? A first guess might be that this hides a fireplace behind, but there is no chimney. Another guess is that the room behind has one of the tile wall fountains that were popular during the teens. A second repeated design theme is the segmental arch. These arches are seen on the side porch on the left, the sunroom windows on the right, and in the glazing of the front door and the line of lights above the door.

A full-width terrace porch adds importance to the house. The upstairs shutters, with their mixture of louvers and a cutout shape above, look like they could be the originals.

1030 Elizabeth Boulevard (private), Long House, 1916. This singular house is Prairie style but with some added Italian Renaissance details in the roofline brackets. Although the architect is unknown, he or she apparently was familiar with the well-known Prairie architect George W. Maher of Chicago, whose work it resembles. Note how broad the house is, even though the main house block only has three window bays. Also notice the unusual curve of the dormer and the long horizontal line formed by the grooved facing along the roof edges—an untraditional place for ornamental trim that many Prairie designers exploited. Green tiles are used here for the roof and also as a facing over the porch entryway. The porch roof serves as an open terrace for the second story.

River Crest, 1911–ca. 1940s

The first attempt to expand Fort Worth westward beyond the Trinity River took place in 1890 when the Chamberlain Development Company of Denver bought two thousand acres and platted them into small homesites. The developers extended Seventh Street across the wide bottomlands of the river to higher ground beyond. There they built a new main street called Arlington Heights Boulevard (now Camp Bowie Boulevard) and added a trolley line to serve their new Arlington Heights development. What they did not provide were water lines, sewer service, and police and fire protection. These were not added until 1917, when the still mostly vacant development was occupied by a large World War I training camp called Camp Bowie. When the camp was abandoned after the war, western Fort Worth, taking advantage of the new services now extended to the area, became the focus of the city's residential growth.

Most prestigious of these new western developments was River Crest, opened in 1911 with a number of large homesites clustered around the golf fairways of the exclusive River Crest Country Club. This was an unusually early example of the now-familiar pattern of an upscale residential development with homesites, mostly on quiet cul-de-sac streets, that face out onto the unfenced fairways of an exclusive golf course. By the 1920s, River Crest was replacing Ryan Place as the city's most fashionable address. Today the area combines a few important landmark dwellings from the pre-1920 era with many fine later Period houses.

4900 Bryce Avenue (private), Fairview, 1893; Sanguinet and Messer, Fort Worth, architects. William J. Bryce, a native of Scotland, moved to Fort Worth in 1863 and developed a brick manufacturing company. His home, one of the neighborhood's earliest, is an interesting combination of the Chateauesque and Richardsonian Romanesque styles, both unusual in the western states. Note the Romanesque rounded arches at the corner porch and Romanesque carved-stone details above the triple window.

935 Hillcrest Street (private), Gartner House, 1929; John F. Staub, Houston, architect. This is a unique design by the distinguished architect of Houston's Bayou Bend (see page 612). In this Eclectic-era masterpiece, Staub took the trademark of the popular Tudor fashion of the day—a dominant front-facing gable—and transformed it into a fanciful, scallop-edged centerpiece of rare delicacy and charm. Note the subtle flair in the surround of the segmental-arched entry and the broad segmental-arched porte cochere. This understated house has an almost-postmodern feeling to it.

4117 West Seventh Street (private), Coffey House, 1929; Ben B. Milam, architect. This Tudor design is clad in polychrome clinker brick (brick that has been misshapen by being fired too close to the heat source), accented with sandstone and cast-stone detail. Identically detailed Tudor

591

River Crest

arches of subtly different sizes support the openings to the porch and porte cochere. A crenulated parapet is above. The main front-facing gable extends strongly out from the house and features a shapely centered chimney with pointed-arch windows to each side, all ornamented with sandstone.

600 Alta Avenue (private), Leonard House, 1936. A restrained Tudor design executed almost entirely of terracotta brick. The brickwork is simple but handsome; it is seen in the diaper pattern in the south gable, the sculptural chimneys, and the round-arched entry. Note that the same subtle brick detail is found in the cornice, over several windows, and repeated in the top of the brick fence.

500 Alta Avenue (private), Thompson House, 1931; Joseph Pelich, architect. This parapeted Tudor design is clad in limestone, a relatively unusual material for Tudor houses. Here it is laid in random courses.

900 River Crest Road (private), Landreth House, ca. 1929. It is unusual to find a symmetrical Tudor house built in the 1920s. This one is ornamented with areas of sandstone wall cladding and a handsome cast-stone door surround. In the main gable the half-timbering features two curved cruck-style timbers—the kind of timbers used to support the roofs of early Medieval English folk dwellings. Note the varied patterns of the brick infill and the handsome oriel window in this main gable. The through-the-cornice dormers are half-timbered but infilled with stucco, not brick. There is a simple brick cornice above the sandstone, and the roof is of polychrome slate.

Westover Hills, 1930 and later

In 1930 two Florida land developers moved to Fort Worth and purchased this bluff-top tract immediately to the west of River Crest, which by then had sold out almost all of its available lots. They incorporated their development as the small island town of Westover Hills. A labyrinth of curving streets and large lots was laid out on the wooded hills, and these lots soon became the city's most prestigious homesites, a distinction they retain today. Divided into two isolated segments by its only through street, Roaring Springs Road, Westover Hills development during the 1930s centered on dead-end Westover Road in the eastern segment. Here can be seen many fine examples of the late-Eclectic housing fashions of that decade. After World War II development shifted to the western portion, which contains an upscale, architect-designed progression of housing styles built from 1950 through the 1980s.

8 Westover Road (private), Westover Manor, 1930; Victor Marr Curtis, architect. Owned by John R. Ferrell, the first mayor of Westover Hills and one of the discoverers of the massive East Texas Field (see page 567), this house was the first large home built in Westover Hills. It is an elaborate brick Tudor design with half-timbering, extensive rough-cut limestone ornament, and cast-stone accents. It has two contrasting chimneys, one with separate chimney pots with hexagonal roofs and one simple and squared with mixed brick and stone cladding. The arched entry to the auto court gives a glimpse of the matching garage behind.

22 Valley Ridge Drive (private), ca. 1935. This is a French Eclectic house of the asymmetrical subtype. This subtype occurs both in picturesque examples based on rambling French farmhouses and in more formal houses similar in detailing to the symmetrical subtype, but with off-center doors and asymmetrical facades. This house falls into the latter group. Note the quoins at the corners, the segmental-arched entry, and the very steep hipped roof, with three asymmetrically placed, hipped-roof dormers. Particularly interesting is the way the hipped roof steps out over the entry pavilion (the part of the house that projects forward at the entrance).

1 Westover Road (private), ca. 1935. This fine towered French Eclectic (Norman cottage) design is clad in multi-toned terra-cotta brick that has a slightly rough finish. The roof is covered with plain shingle tiles in a deep-toned terra-cotta. There is a pair of gabled wall dormers on the right, a pair of gabled roof dormers on the left, and a single shed-roofed dormer. Except for the brick face of the wall dormers, all of the dormers' sides and front are covered with the roof tile. Note the outline of a round-arched "carriage entry" in the brick wall beneath the shed dormer. Casement windows are used extensively.

The conical tower has a candlesnuffer roof with a slight flare at the eaves. A line of molded brick corbels is located about twelve inches below the eave line. The rounded entry arch is surrounded by bricks of varying sizes. These step back to emphasize the thickness of the walls. Elaborate brickwork is also displayed in the chimneys.

56 Westover Terrace (private), ca. 1935. This French Eclectic house is of the third subtype, which includes those with symmetrical facades. This example has a massive hipped roof with its prominent ridge paralleling the front of the house. As is frequently the case in this subtype, there are side wings separated from the main house block itself by lower "hyphen" rooms. This shape is sometimes called a Palladian five-part plan. The main house block has three segmental-arched through-the-cornice wall dormers, a single circular roof dormer (a shape rarely found in any other house style), and corner quoins. The upper third of the house has brickwork in a diamond pattern. The only unusual element is the heavily accented, almost-English door surround.

This house seems quite original when seen from the front, which faces Westover Terrace. When viewed from the rear (or at least what was originally the rear), off Wyatt Road, it appears to have had a major addition. The details have, however, been so well matched that it is difficult to tell exactly what is old and what is new.

FREDERICKSBURG

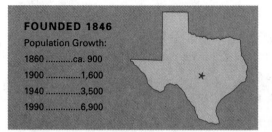

FOUNDED 1846

Population Growth:

1860 ....ca. 900
1900 1,600
1940 3,500
1990 6,900

Fredericksburg was the second of two important Texas towns founded by the Adelsverein, an association of German noblemen that bought land on the Texas frontier for the resettlement of farmers and craftsmen impoverished by their homeland's economic deterioration (see "New Braunfels," page 618). The Adelsverein's first purchase, sight unseen, was the right to settlement of the Fisher-Miller grant, a vast tract of almost 4 million acres in west-central Texas that turned out to be unsuitable for two reasons—the hilly topography, stony soil, and limited rainfall made traditional farming very difficult, and, more immediately, the grant was the homeland of many bands of mounted Comanche, a tribe later described by their military adversaries as the "world's best light cavalry." When the first large contingent of Adelsverein settlers arrived in 1844, their leader, Prince Carl of Solms-Braunfels, belatedly discovered that the original tract was "too remote for immediate settlement." He then bought a far smaller site between Austin and San Antonio, where, in 1845, he founded the town of New Braunfels and then promptly returned to Germany.

The prince had intended New Braunfels to be but the first in a series of supply stations stretching westward to permit the eventual occupation of the enormous Fisher-Miller grant. He was replaced by another nobleman, Baron Ottfried Hans von Meusebach (1812–1897), who established the second link in the proposed chain by founding Fredericksburg, named for the prince of Prussia and located in the limestone hills eighty miles west of New Braunfels. This was to be the last of the Adelsverein's important settlements, for the following year, apparently now aware of the futility of expecting profits from their Fisher-Miller investment, the group declared the project bankrupt, leaving seven thousand Texas immigrants with unfulfilled promises of land and support. Fortunately for them, Baron Meusebach was made of much sterner stuff than was Prince Solms.

Unlike the haughty prince, who demanded royal treatment from his less sophisticated German and Anglo neighbors, Meusebach got off to a good start by abandoning his title and becoming both a Texas citizen and plain Mr. John O. Meusebach. Undeterred by the Adelsverein failure, he spent the rest of his long life as a visionary yet practical leader among his fellow German Texans. Much about his character is revealed in his relations with the Comanche. Fredericksburg was near their traditional hunting grounds, which were foolishly violated in an unauthorized exploring expedition on the part of the newly founded town's resident supervisor. The Indians retaliated with several murderous moonlight raids.

To the amazement of his Anglo neighbors, who warned him he was embarking on a suicidal journey, Meusebach, based in New Braunfels, organized a small party to travel into the Indian lands on a peacemaking mission. When met by Comanche scouts asking the nature of their travel, Meusebach instructed his men to discharge their single-shot firearms into the air, leaving the party defenseless from sudden attack. This show of courage convinced the Indians of Meusebach's sincerity and led to two weeks of negotiations in which the Comanche chiefs agreed to permit exploration and limited settlement in the vast Fisher-Miller tract in return for one thousand Spanish silver dollars and the right to be treated as friends in Fredericksburg and other German settlements. In the words of Texas histo-

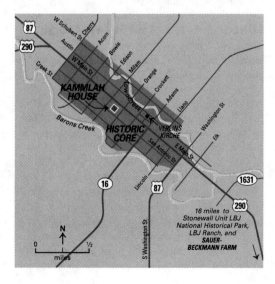

Fredericksburg Historic Core

rian Joe B. Frantz (*Texas,* W. W. Norton, 1976): "The Germans never broke their word to the Comanches, and were so sure of the integrity of the Comanches that they went into the Indians' territory alone and un-armed in search of new farm sites. And the Comanches measured up to the Germans' faith, so that we have that most unusual of treaties in American-Indian relation-ships—a treaty that was never broken by either side."

In the years that followed, Fredericksburg became the cultural and trade center for hundreds of German farms, ranches, and villages scattered among the rocky hills and narrow valleys of the remote Texas Hill Coun-try. This role is reflected in the town's picturesque folk architecture, much of which has survived to add her-itage tourism to its still important functions as an agri-cultural trade and market center.

Historic Core, 1840s–ca. 1940

This large district includes most of early Fredericks-burg, which was laid out along the crest of a ridge bounded by creek valleys. As a result, the early town has a long and narrow grid of streets dominated by a cen-tral and very broad Main Street, which was called San Saba Street until the early 1900s. Residential and com-mercial uses were, and still are, interspersed there, while the parallel streets of Schubert, Austin, San Antonio, and Creek are dominated by houses, many of which are surviving folk dwellings built by the town's early Ger-man settlers. These immigrants came from parts of Germany with no tradition of building with logs, but upon arrival many adopted the building practices of their Anglo neighbors, who favored the Midland log houses that dominated much of the southeastern United States. The main Germanic feature of the Hill

Country version is an exterior stairway placed on the gable end of the house. Chimneys are also less com-mon, as many Germans were accustomed to using more efficient metal stoves for indoor heating and cooking.

Other early German settlers built folk houses with half-timbered walls, called *fachwerk* in German, a tech-nique that was common in their homeland. The infill between the framing timbers was usually either locally made, sun-dried adobe bricks or blocks of the abun-dant local limestone. Both of these were usually cov-ered with a layer of protective stucco. Most of these early *fachwerk* dwellings were later covered with wooden clapboard siding, as were their log-walled, Anglo-style neighbors.

The Fredericksburg pioneers also soon learned to build more durable masonry buildings. The plentiful local limestone was soft when first quarried and was rather easily cut into blocks with a saw. The resulting rock walls then hardened with age, thus providing an ideal, and locally favored, construction technique. An-other permanent building material favored by the Ger-mans was metal roofing sheets, the junctions of which were tightly crimped together in standing seams. These replaced the typical, and less durable, wood-shingle roofs of traditional Anglo dwellings.

Beginning about 1900, some houses in Fredericks-burg were built as "Sunday" houses—small one-room-and-loft homes used to accommodate farm families during temporary stays in town for shopping, church, school, or medical needs. The upstairs loft, often reached by an exterior stairway, was used for sleeping space or hay storage.

A great many early Fredericksburg houses have received later modifications and additions. This is typical of folk dwellings—as the family grew or prosperity increased, new sections could be built or new wood cladding could be added.

307 West Schubert Street (private), Crenwelge House, ca. 1860 and later. This expanded folk dwelling illustrates the three wall–building techniques of Fredericksburg's German pioneers. The one-story unit to the right, which faces the rear yard, is believed to be the original house. It has the Anglo-style log walls (not visible from the street) first used by many of the immigrants. A rear kitchen with a *fachwerk* wall facing Schubert Street was added later. Finally, a much larger two-story addition with limestone walls was added facing Town Creek on the east side of the earlier units.

309 West Schubert Street (private), Knopp House, 1871. This limestone-walled folk dwelling began as a small story-and-a-half structure and has been variously expanded rearward and remodeled over the years.

312 West Schubert Street (private), Crenwelge House, ca. 1903. This simple, wood-framed, hall-and-parlor structure provides an instructive contrast to the earlier stone- and *fachwerk*-walled houses across the street. German influence is evident in the outside stairway to the loft and in the standing-seam metal of the gabled roof. The house was apparently built for a daughter of the early Crenwelge family who lived across the street.

406, 408, and 410 San Antonio Street (all private). These are three typical side-gabled Sunday houses (see page 594), all of them folk dwellings of the hall-and-parlor form with front porches covered by a separate roof extension. All have the locally favored standing-seam metal roofs and exterior stairways leading to an attic hay storage or sleeping area.

Kammlah House (Pioneer Museum), 1849–1910

309 West Main Street; 830-997-2835.

Several of the structures in this museum complex remain on their original sites, including the Kammlah House, barn, smokehouse, and the Fassel-Roeder House next door. Several other structures have been moved in from the immediate area.

The centerpiece of the museum is the Kammlah House, an early stone folk dwelling with stucco-covered walls. Occupied by the same family for four generations, this often-expanded structure provides an excellent demonstration of how folk houses grew and how the uses of their rooms changed over time. In 1859 a large second kitchen was added to the rear of the house. In the 1870s the original house was converted to a store and a large house added behind the "new" kitchen. Finally, in the early 1900s the "new" house received a rear addition. The original house remains furnished as a store with many fascinating early items. The new house displays furnishings that belonged to John Meusebach, the former German baron who founded Fredericksburg and befriended the local Comanche, as well as exhibits about the local German immigrants.

The Fassel-Roeder House next door is also a much modified stone folk dwelling on its original site. A Folk Victorian porch was added in an 1880s remodeling.

Kammlah House

Sauer-Beckmann Farm

The attractive furnishings date from about 1890 to 1920, with an emphasis on the 1915 to 1920 period.

An original wood-framed Sunday house, the 1904 Weber House, has been moved to the museum grounds and is appropriately sited facing Milam Street. Although moved, the house has remained remarkably intact, with all of its original furnishings. It never had the exterior attic stair found in most Sunday houses.

Sauer-Beckmann Farm, 1869 and 1915

Entrance on U.S. Highway 290, in the Lyndon B. Johnson State Historical Park, sixteen miles east of Fredericksburg; 830-644-2252.

Not directly related to the life of President Johnson (see "Johnson City," page 614), this remarkably preserved and well-interpreted farmstead provides a rare glimpse into the lives of the Hill Country's pioneer German farmers. This is a living-history farm in which the guides go about the daily business of the farm family—keeping up the garden; feeding the pigs, chickens, cows, and turkeys; preserving homemade sausages in lard; putting up crocks of sauerkraut for the winter; and cooking meals on a wood-burning stove.

Architecturally, this is an interesting complex because, like the Kammlah House (see the preceding entry), it remains on its original site with many original outbuildings. The Germans were highly skilled farmers who, in the Old World tradition, expanded their farmsteads as their families and resources grew. The Sauer family began life here in 1869 in a one-room log cabin with a sleeping loft above. Soon adjacent rooms were added with half-timbered walls of *fachwerk* filled with local limestone. Still later a detached sleeping room with limestone walls was added; this was later converted to the kitchen. Along the way many outbuildings were constructed, including barns, a smokehouse, and a tank house with a large cypress water tank fed by a windmill.

By 1915 the farm was owned by Emil and Emma Beckmann, who built a fashionable new house adjacent to the earlier folk dwelling. Their dream house, meant to last a lifetime, was a fashionable gable-front-and-wing Folk Victorian design that cost just over a thousand dollars. It was built with wood-stud walls sided with pressed tin, which imitated the stone houses of many of their neighbors. As in most frontier farmsteads, the fenced yard around the house was raked clear of grass both to avoid a potential fire hazard and also to leave no place for snakes and such to hide.

The Texas Parks Department has done an excellent job of appropriately furnishing the farmstead, right down to the nine-by-twelve-foot linoleum "rugs" and furniture of the kind bought by farmers of the period from Sears, Roebuck and Montgomery Ward catalogs.

GALVESTON

FOUNDED 1836

Population Growth:

1860 7,000

1900 38,000

1940 61,000

1990 59,000

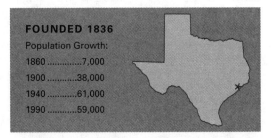

Galveston is one of those rare time-capsule towns that preserves large chunks of its architectural past for the delight of modern visitors. Site of the only reliable deepwater port on the long Texas coastline, the town first flourished in the 1830s, when the newly independent Republic of Texas opened its borders to unrestricted immigration. New settlers from the adjacent South mostly came by wagon through Arkansas or Louisiana, but those from the Atlantic seaboard states, or still more distant Europe, generally arrived in Galveston by sailing ship. With the immigrants came a supporting flood of shipborne manufactured goods from the factories of the Northeast—tools to work the rich farmlands; hardware for new buildings; and cloth, dishes, pots, coffee, tea, and countless other items to supply Texas households. On their return voyages, these ships mainly carried the principal commercial product of Texas's farms—high-value bales of cotton destined for the mills of New England or Great Britain. By 1850 this thriving seaborne trade had made Galves-

ton the "commercial emporium of Texas" as well as the state's largest and most cosmopolitan city, a position it retained for the next forty years.

Galveston and Houston

Galveston, like such early seaports as Boston, New York, Philadelphia, or New Orleans, might still be the dominant urban center of the state were it not for one serious natural disadvantage—it is located on a coastal island separated from the mainland by two miles of shallow ocean (see the map, bottom left). This meant that freight and passengers had to be transferred from large oceangoing vessels into much smaller, shallow-draft boats to make the journey to and from the mainland. To further complicate the situation, the mainland coast is fringed by miles of low-lying marshes and floodplains, where wagon roads became impassable quagmires in rainy weather. So serious was this problem that Galveston's fine natural harbor might never have prospered were it not for an alternative route that avoided the muddy coastal lowlands.

Behind the east end of Galveston Island lies Galveston Bay, a shallow coastal reentrant that, like the adjacent coastline, is bordered by muddy lowlands. At its northwest corner, however, is a narrow but deep river called Buffalo Bayou that flows through the muddy lowlands to reach firmer upland soils about twenty miles from its mouth. Shortly after Texas independence, the new town of Houston, named for the hero of the Texas Revolution, was founded at the head of navigation on Buffalo Bayou to serve as an inland port for the small boats that traversed shallow Galveston Bay carrying a bounty of oceanborne merchandise to the mainland and returning with bales of valuable cotton. This Galveston Bay to Houston route had the great advantage of bypassing the muddy coastal lowlands and

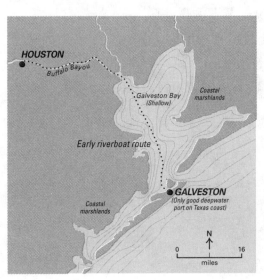

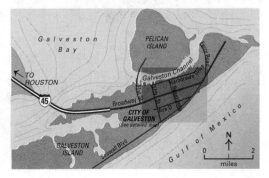

connecting with an inland destination where freight and passengers could proceed by horseback or wagon over dependable roadways. Thus early Galveston and Houston developed close economic ties that benefited both.

The Great Storm

Galveston's long tenure as Texas's principal seaport and the state's financial and cultural capital received a blow from which it never recovered on the night of September 8, 1900. On that fateful evening the low-lying island was struck by a deadly tropical hurricane whose 120-mile-per-hour winds and extraordinarily high tides swept the city with waves that covered even its highest land with eight feet of water. By morning, as the sea receded, most of the buildings in the southern, seaward half of town had been reduced to a thirty-foot-high band of wave-battered rubble scattered with the bodies of six thousand drowned citizens. This still ranks as the most deadly natural disaster in our nation's history.

The city's path to recovery was particularly long and arduous. Not only was there the enormous task of cleanup and rebuilding, but the possibility of such devastating hurricanes in the future led many survivors and businesses to abandon the city, threatening it with economic ruin. To combat this, the city's leaders joined with the U.S. Army Corps of Engineers in one of the most amazing reclamation feats of the twentieth cen-

tury. They decided to raise the entire city high enough above sea level that it could be protected by a wave-breaking seventeen-foot seawall along its ocean-facing southern margin. This required six years of jacking up most of the surviving structures and filling beneath them with sand pumped in from the adjacent seafloor. The depth of the fill required ranged from about fifteen feet immediately behind the seawall to only one or two feet along the higher ground near the commercial district and on the city's north side. Completed in 1906, the seawall and added height have successfully protected Galveston from several subsequent hurricanes, some of which were potentially more damaging than the 1900 giant.

The Houston Ship Channel

Not long after Galveston completed its reconstruction came an economic challenge that ended its long reign as Texas's only deepwater port. In 1914 Houston completed its own massive engineering project—dredging and constructing the Houston Ship Channel and Turning Basin—which allowed oceangoing vessels to dock along twenty miles of a much widened and deepened Buffalo Bayou. Soon the Ship Channel, far enough inland to be safe from the Gulf's periodic storms, was lined not only with wharves, but also with new industrial enterprises, particularly oil refineries. As the new port of Houston thrived, Galveston declined to minor

Pumping in sand, dredged offshore, to raise the grade level of oceanside Galveston, ca. 1905

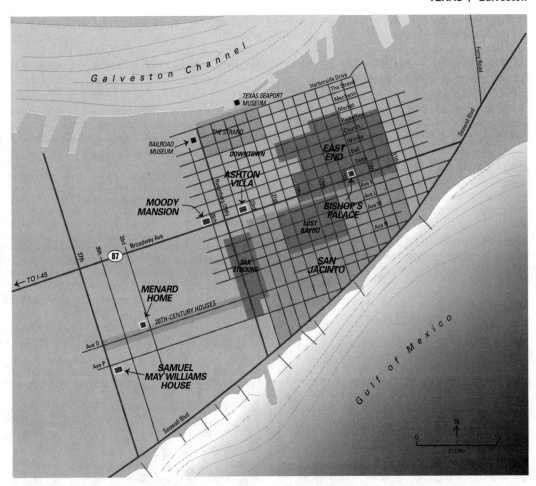

importance as a seaport. As a result, the city's 1990 population of fifty-nine thousand reflects only a modest increase over its thirty-eight thousand residents when the Great Storm struck in 1900.

Modern Galveston

Economic decline—always the great preserver of historic architecture—has left modern Galveston with an extraordinary assemblage of fine Victorian buildings. In the 1960s the city's leaders began to recognize the long-term economic potential of these rare and picturesque survivors. With the help of local foundations and generous citizens, they undertook a massive campaign to preserve and restore the city's historic resources and market them as a unique destination for what is today called heritage tourism. Many blocks of the city's original Victorian commercial district, which is located on the island's inland north side and was protected from the full force of the 1900 storm by the mountainous wall of midisland wreckage, is today the splendidly restored **Strand Historic District.** Adjacent are several tastefully planned historic attractions that emphasize the city's vital role in the development of early Texas. Transportation is the theme of the large **Railroad Museum** (Twenty-fifth Street and Strand, 409-765-5700) as well as of the **Texas Seaport Museum** (Pier 21 on Harborside Drive between Twenty-first and Twenty-second Streets, 409-763-1877), where the 1877 tall ship *Elissa*, a restored sailing ship typical of those that served the early port of Galveston, is docked. A nearby multimedia presentation called *The Great Storm* (Pier 21 at Twenty-first Street and Harborside Drive, 409-763-8808), dramatically portrays both the tragic 1900 hurricane and the city's heroic grade-raising project that followed. All three are within easy walking distance from the **Strand Visitors Center** (2016 Strand, 409-765-7834).

Fortunately, the same midisland wall of debris that protected the downtown commercial district also sheltered many of its finest early homes from the full destructive fury of the 1900 storm. As a result, modern Galveston is a veritable museum of Victorian domestic architecture. An excellent recent guide, the *Galveston Architecture Guidebook* by Ellen Beasley and Stephen Fox, contains clear photographs and authoritative descriptions for more than seven hundred Galveston houses and buildings located throughout the entire island. It is highly recommended for more in-depth exploration.

East End, ca. 1870–1930

The East End Historic District, a national historic landmark that includes about forty square blocks of homes built mostly during the 1870s through 1890s, is one of the nation's largest intact concentrations of Victorian houses and a delight for house watchers. Most are built of wood, and, as is often the case in coastal cities, many are on raised foundations to help protect them from storm flooding. Styles are varied, but elaborate Folk Victorian houses predominate. Most of these are simple front-gabled shapes that fit their narrow urban lots but are embellished with front-porch ornamentation that befits the city's nineteenth-century prosperity (see "1228 Sealy Street," page 601). Stick, Queen Anne, and Italianate are among the other Victorian styles found here. The Chateauesque Bishop's Palace (see page 601) is the most elaborate in the district and, indeed, among the grandest Victorian dwellings in the entire West.

1627 Sealy Street (private), Trube House, ca. 1890; Alfred Muller, architect. This unusual design was built for Danish immigrant John Trube, who arrived in Galveston in 1848 as a penniless eleven-year-old. He is reputed to have retired with a real estate fortune at the age of thirty-five. His home's mansard roof, gabled dormers, and much of the detailing are typical of the Second Empire style, which was most popular two decades earlier. The house's irregular massing, busy facade, and concrete-covered walls rusticated to look

East End

East End

East End

like stone make it a one-of-a-kind interpretation of that style. Local tradition says that Trube wanted something resembling the castles of his homeland.

1826 Sealy Street (private), Sonnenthiel House, 1887. This house is a Galveston favorite because of its extraordinary two-story porch. It was built for a prominent merchant and its style combines Italianate arched windows, wide overhanging eaves, and bay windows with spindlework Queen Anne porch details.

1228 Sealy Street (private), Burr House, 1876; attributed to Nicholas J. Clayton, Galveston, architect. Built for the traveling agent of a large Galveston wholesale company, this is an elaborate, center-gabled, three-bay design in the Folk Victorian style. It combines Italianate details (the double brackets under the wide eave overhang) with a Gothic pointed arch under the central gable. The Lone Stars on the window crowns—taken from the state flag and symbolizing Texas's years as an independent republic—were often used by Clayton and other early Texas builders.

511 Seventeenth Street (private), Heffron House, 1899; Charles W. Bulger, architect. Built of brick for a prominent cement contractor, this design is an interesting transition between the Queen Anne style (one-story wraparound porch and round turret) and the then-just-emerging Prairie style (low-pitched roof and wide eave overhangs). The two different porch support designs are quite unusual.

1722 and 1724 Winnie Street (both private). These side-by-side twins are particularly well preserved examples of the city's many early "shotgun" folk houses.

1604 Postoffice Street (private), Landes House, ca. 1895; Dickey and Helmich, Houston, architects. This unusual brick design with both Queen Anne and Richardsonian Romanesque features was built for H. A. Landes, a cotton buyer, shipowner, and importer. The outbuildings, visible at the rear of the lot and along the alley, are "some of the most characteristic Galveston back buildings in the East End," according to the *Galveston Architecture Guidebook*.

Bishop's Palace, 1893

1402 Broadway Avenue; 409-762-2475;
Nicholas J. Clayton, Galveston, architect.
Among the finest early Eclectic-era houses in the West is this home built for Mr. and Mrs. Walter Gresham. He

had come to Galveston in 1866 to practice law and later became one of the founders of the prosperous Gulf, Colorado, and Santa Fe Railroad. In 1886 Gresham hired the prolific and talented Clayton, architect of many of the city's finest public buildings, to design a home for his family of seven. Before coming to Galveston, Clayton had studied stonecutting in Cincinnati; his familiarity with that trade is quite evident in the house's superb exterior detailing.

The house is in the Chateauesque style with its typical elaborated roofline, through-the-cornice dormer (above the front entrance), candlesnuffer-tower roof, and tall slender chimneys. It also has a few elements of the contemporaneous Richardsonian Romanesque style, particularly the rough-faced stonework and round-arched windows. The gifted Clayton brought his own imaginative detailing to the Chateauesque, then much in favor for homes of the very wealthy. One such telling detail can be seen on the column capitals at the front entrance—carved calla lilies, Mrs. Gresham's favorite flower.

The exterior walls are of reddish-gray sandstone accented with details of granite, both pink and gray, and of light-cream-colored limestone. Mr. Gresham assembled quality components from all over the world for the house's lavish interiors. He was particularly fond of mantelpieces. Installed in the parlor is the first-prize winner at the 1876 Philadelphia World's Fair, which celebrated the centennial of U.S. independence. The music room mantel, crafted of Mexican onyx and silver, was purchased for the then-enormous sum of ten thousand dollars at the 1886 New Orleans Exposition. Each downstairs room has mantelpieces of differing fine woods—white mahogany with satinwood trim in the

Bishop's Palace

music room, black walnut in the library, Santo Domingan mahogany in the parlor, and so on. Other notable interior details include the carved staircase and the domed rotunda ceiling above. The house acquired its popular name when it was sold to the Roman Catholic Church and served as home to the local bishop for many years before the church, which still owns the grand dwelling, opened it as a public museum.

San Jacinto, 1840s–ca. 1940

The large San Jacinto neighborhood, loosely bounded by Broadway, Seawall Boulevard, and Rosenberg (Twenty-fifth Street), has many houses of interest. This part of Galveston Island was lower in grade than the parts of town north of Broadway, making it more subject to flooding and therefore less valuable as building sites. As a result much of San Jacinto was developed with houses built as rental investments or as workers' housing. Scattered throughout are many early folk houses, mostly shotguns or simple side-gabled homes, many of which sit on raised foundations. The parts of the San Jacinto area closest to Seawall Boulevard were completely destroyed by the 1900 storm and then rebuilt shortly afterward. The closer you get to Seawall Boulevard the fewer pre-1900 houses remain.

There are two parts of San Jacinto with unusually high concentrations of historic houses, the Silk Stocking and Lost Bayou neighborhoods, both of which are

historic districts. The four-block **Silk Stocking Historic District** (see map, page 599) preserves a small but important concentration of the neighborhood's pre-storm homes. The Silk Stocking district received its popular name because this part of the San Jacinto neighborhood had a higher concentration of large homes occupied by professionals than most of the rest of the district.

The **Lost Bayou** neighborhood's name refers to the shallow Hitchcock's Bayou, which was filled in to allow its initial development. The district includes a several-square-block area that burned in a fire in 1885 (the area between Seventeenth and Twenty-first Streets). These blocks were quickly rebuilt in the years following the fire, producing more unified streetscapes than are found in most of the large San Jacinto district.

2424 Broadway Avenue (all private), Open Gates, 1889; McKim, Mead, and White, New York, architects. Although located a block north of the San Jacinto neighborhood boundary, this striking design, attributed to the flamboyant Stanford White, is too good to miss. White was perhaps the most creative of the three distinguished partners who founded what was, by 1900, the world's largest architectural firm. The house has a unique combination of Victorian influences with Medieval roots—for example, the turrets and high-pitched, pyramidal roof, which contrast with the more formal Italian Renaissance details, such as the corbeled arches, tile roof, and elaborate cornice with modillions and swags. The house was built for George Sealy, one of Gal-

San Jacinto

veston's many self-made men of the Victorian era. Starting as a shipping clerk, he rose to control a vast financial empire based on cotton brokerage and banking.

2314, 2318, 2322, and 2326 Avenue M (all private), ca. 1840–1870. This instructive group of side-gabled folk houses provides a rare glimpse of a typical pre–Civil War

Galveston neighborhood. They also demonstrate the variety that size differences, raised foundations, or a bit of Greek Revival detailing can add to basically identical folk-house forms.

1916 Avenue K (private), Johnston House, 1886. This fine Folk Victorian house was built by the Johnston family to replace the home they lost in the 1885 fire. Hipped-roof examples of the Folk Victorian style are common in the South, but the roofs are usually shaped like pyramids rather than having a visible ridge as seen here. This home is accentuated by a centered gable and also has porches across both the first and second stories, a pattern typical of Gulf Coast and other warm-climate seaport towns.

Ashton Villa, 1859

2318 Broadway Avenue; 409-762-3933;
after Samuel Sloan, Philadelphia, architect.
James M. Brown, an early Galveston hardware merchant who later made a fortune in banking and railroad building, based his Italianate dwelling, one of the first of Broadway's landmark houses, on a pattern book design. This was Design XXI, entitled "A Suburban Residence" in Samuel Sloan's *The Model Architect* (Philadelphia, 1851; republished in 1980 as *Sloan's Victorian Buildings*). Brown changed several details and added the cast-iron double galleries and elaborate window crowns.

The house grew and changed a bit over the years. About 1877 the space between the original house and the rear kitchen building was enclosed to create a huge family room. Then in 1890 the west parlor was remod-

Ashton Villa

eled to become the Gold Room. Finally, in 1895 the east side of the house was extended to add more room for a Brown daughter returning home with her children.

The Browns finally sold their family home in 1926 and it then served as the El Mina Shrine Temple for more than four decades. The Shriners kept the main house intact, but demolished the detached kitchen and family room, replacing these with a large ballroom. In the late 1960s the Shriners decided to move and were preparing to sell Ashton Villa as a site for a new service station. Happily, the grand house, one of antebellum Texas's most fashionable, was saved from demolition when it was purchased by the city of Galveston and leased to the Galveston Historical Foundation. The foundation's restoration was completed by July 1974.

Given its long years of nondomestic use, Ashton Villa retains an extraordinary number of its original furnishings and fixtures, including most of the medallions, moldings, hardware, and fixtures, as well as Renaissance Revival valences in the dining room and parlor. The furnishings in the dining room and three upstairs bedrooms are almost all original, and other pieces are found throughout the house. Among these is a large collection of oil-on-corduroy paintings by a

daughter, "Miss Bettie" Brown, which is displayed throughout the house. Some of these furnishings have never left Ashton Villa, having been sold to the Shriners along with the house. Others have been generously donated back to the house by the Brown family.

Ashton Villa's Romantic-era interior, quite bright with light-colored woodwork, makes an interesting contrast with the darker late-Victorian interior fashions of its younger Broadway neighbors—the Moody Mansion (see the following entry) and Bishop's Palace (see page 601).

Moody Mansion, 1895

2618 Broadway Avenue; 409-762-7668;
William H. Tyndall, Galveston, architect.
This is a fine example of the Richardsonian Romanesque style and is one of the relatively few houses of this grand style in the entire country that are open to the public. Built of redbrick accented by white limestone trim, it has three turrets, each of a different shape, and a broad wraparound porch and porte cochere supported by Romanesque arches.

Originally completed in 1895 for Narcissa Worsham Willis, a wealthy widow, the home was purchased, at a

Moody Mansion

bargain price, from her heirs by cotton broker and banker W. L. Moody Jr. in 1900, just a few weeks after the Great Storm. The house's fine interiors had been designed by the distinguished New York firm of Pottier and Stymus. Each of the public rooms features a different Revival style, ranging from rococo through Classical to Colonial Revival.

Most of the Moody Mansion's original interior finishes are still intact. The furnishings are those that belonged to the Moody family; many pieces were acquired at about the time they purchased the house and came from the Robert Mitchell Company of Cincinnati, a well-known furniture maker of the day.

Two important interior features are the style's characteristically large living hall, which greets visitors upon entering, and the delicate and light French Rococo parlor, which markedly contrasts with the rest of the downstairs decor. These light, romantic parlors, foreshadowing the Eclectic-era fashions to come, were often used for contrast in high-style Victorian homes near the end of the nineteenth century. (See also "Rosemount," page 324, in Pueblo, Colorado, and the "McFaddin-Ward House," page 557, in Beaumont, Texas, for two other examples of this trend.)

Samuel May Williams House

Samuel May Williams House, 1839

3601 Avenue P (Bernardo de Galvez); 409-762-3933.
This simple Greek Revival cottage is thought by some to have been prefabricated in Maine and shipped to Galveston. More likely it was built locally, but with some materials shipped in from the East. Designed with a massive hipped roof that extends beyond the main house walls to shelter full-facade porches across the front and one side, its shape is typical of Greek Revival houses in the southern states, particularly Louisiana. Financier Samuel May Williams built his home on a twenty-acre site in what was then the island's rural countryside. Today his house is Galveston's second-oldest and is one of only a handful of Texas dwellings that survive from the Republic of Texas period (see also the following entry and "French Legation," page 549, in Austin).

An enigmatic associate of Steven F. Austin in the original Anglo colonization of Mexican Texas (see page xii), Williams, through his banking connections, is said to have provided most of the funds for the Texas Revolution. After the revolution, Williams became one of the founders of the republic's new port city of Galveston and one of early Texas's leading bankers and entrepreneurs. Indeed, prior to the legalization of banking in Texas after the Civil War, he operated the only "quasilegal" bank in Texas, according to the *Galveston Architecture Guidebook*.

Avenue O, a pleasant residential street with several fine Victorian and Eclectic-era houses, is a good route to use in reaching the Williams House.

Menard Home, 1838

1605 Thirty-third Street; 409-762-3933.
In 1838, after the battle of San Jacinto (see page xiii), Michel B. Menard and ten associates (including Samuel May Williams and John K. and Augustus C. Allen, founders of Houston) formed the Galveston City Company for the express purpose of developing a town on Galveston Island. The partners purchased the eastern end of the island and hired a surveyor to divide the portion near the port into narrow and deep (42 feet 10 inches wide by 120 feet deep) urban lots, which they then offered for sale. Menard then promptly built his own home not in the early urban core, but well away from it on a large, ten-acre "outlot" of the original survey. Like Williams, he chose to build a fashionable Greek Revival–style dwelling. Menard greatly expanded his home in 1845 by adding flanking wings and a full-facade porch with colossal Ionic columns.

In 1992 the Galveston Historical Foundation, after ten years of negotiations, was finally able to purchase the Menard Home, which had stood vacant for fifteen years and suffered hurricane damage. The foundation then resold the home to owners willing to undertake its complex restoration. In 1996 the Menard Home won first place in the National Trust's Great American Homes Awards for the quality of its exterior restoration. Today, the owners allow the Galveston Historical Foundation to regularly show the house for the benefit of the foundation.

The present owners have retained as much of the original interior architectural fabric as possible, while updating the kitchen, bathrooms, and other areas for modern living. Panels left in the walls allow the visitor to see the original wood joinery used in constructing the house. Today, the Menard Home contains an impressive collection of Federal and American Empire antiques. The handsome furnishings are appropriate to the period and style of the house, but are of such a high overall quality that they probably originally graced an affluent home located along the eastern seaboard or in the Old South rather than on remote Galveston Island during the 1840s and 1850s.

HOUSTON

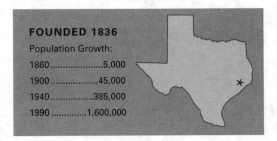

FOUNDED 1836

Population Growth:

1860 5,000
1900 45,000
1940 385,000
1990 1,600,000

Texas's largest city throughout most of the twentieth century, Houston is also one of its oldest urban centers. Founded the year the Republic of Texas won independence from Mexico (see page xii), it first prospered as a river port where small boats traversing nearby Galveston Bay could proceed still farther inland via narrow Buffalo Bayou (see the map, bottom left, page 597). Houston, twenty-five miles upriver from Galveston Bay, was located at the bayou's head of navigation and soon became the favored inland destination for cargoes arriving at nearby Galveston, the

new republic's only deepwater port. Galveston is located on an island separated from the mainland by two miles of shallow ocean, which meant that most goods and passengers had to arrive from, or depart for, the mainland in small boats. Furthermore, the coastal mainland was fringed by miles of marshy lowlands, where wagon roads became impassable quagmires in rainy weather. By making the longer voyage via Galveston Bay and Buffalo Bayou to Houston, the small boat traffic could bypass this belt of muddy coastal lowlands. Thus early Houston and Galveston became symbiotic partners in handling the burgeoning commerce of newly independent Texas (see also page 597). The two cities maintained their partnership throughout the nineteenth century, during which they had similar patterns of prosperity and population growth. Then, in close succession, two dramatic events occurred that catapulted Houston toward its present national prominence while establishing Galveston's destiny as a picturesque survivor from another era.

Houston's modest beginnings—this amazing 1860 photograph shows the steamboat *St. Clair of Galveston* docked on narrow Buffalo Bayou at the foot of Main Street; note the cotton bales, the mainstay of the local economy.

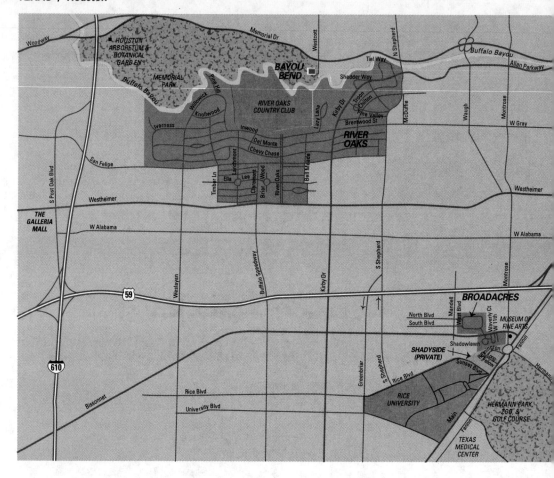

Four Fateful Months

The first occurred on the night of September 8, 1900, when Galveston was devastated by a giant hurricane whose 120-mile-per-hour winds covered even the highest parts of the island under several feet of ocean water. By the next morning large residential neighborhoods on the city's seaward-facing southern side had been reduced to a wave-battered mountain of debris. More than six thousand people, about one-sixth of the city's population, were drowned on that fateful night, which still ranks as our country's most deadly natural disaster. In spite of heroic rebuilding efforts (see page 598), Galveston never regained its former commercial prominence. The second, and more positive, event occurred only four months later near Beaumont, about eighty miles east of Houston. There, on January 10, 1901, the giant Spindletop oil gusher blew in to introduce the world to the enormous petroleum potential of Texas and adjacent states (see page 554).

Oil Capital and Seaport

Houston became an early beneficiary of the frenzied oil exploration that followed the Spindletop discovery. In 1904 a similar giant field was found near the small town of Humble, only seventeen miles north of Houston, and in 1908 came the discovery well of the Goose Creek Field, which lies twenty miles east, near the confluence of Buffalo Bayou with Galveston Bay. Already the region's center of banking and commerce, Houston soon became the financial capital, as well as the equipment supply hub, for the booming coastal oil industry. By 1915 the city was the headquarters for dozens of local oil companies, among them such future international giants as the Texas Company (Texaco), Humble (now Exxon), and Gulf (now a part of Chevron).

Its new status as an oil center led Houston's financial leaders to undertake a long-proposed plan to eliminate the city's dependence on the deepwater port of Galveston by dredging a channel for oceangoing ships across Galveston Bay and up Buffalo Bayou. Financed in part

by city bond issues, construction of this new port of Houston began in 1910 and was completed with much fanfare in 1914. Far enough inland to be protected from the full force of Gulf hurricanes, the Buffalo Bayou segment of the Houston Ship Channel, as it came to be called, was soon lined not only with docks and wharves for traditional cargoes, but also with new refineries for processing the increasing flood of regional oil and with tank farms for storing and shipping the refined products—mostly gasoline, fuel oils, lubricating oils, and specialized petrochemicals—throughout the world in specially designed tankers. Today a drive along the La Porte Freeway (Texas Highway 225) eastward from Interstate Loop 610 provides a remarkable skyline view of these vast Ship Channel industries.

Sunbelt Boomtown

Houston's oil-based prosperity and growth have continued almost unabated throughout the twentieth century; today it is the nation's fourth-largest city, ex-

ceeded in population only by New York, Los Angeles, and Chicago. Unfortunately, the city's explosive 400 percent growth since 1940 has eliminated much of its architectural heritage. Only a few scattered fragments of Victorian Houston survive, a loss that is partially compensated by the extraordinary Victorian neighborhoods of nearby Galveston, its early commercial partner (see page 597). Many Houston landmarks do survive, however, from the early oil-boom decades of 1900 to 1940. Among these are two residential districts that reflect the affluence of its petroleum pioneers. These and the city's many fine post-1950 architectural landmarks are treated in depth by historian Stephen Fox in his excellent *Houston Architectural Guide* (see page 710).

Broadacres, 1920–ca. 1935

Along South Main Street about two miles from downtown is a cluster of Houston's most important public institutions, including Rice University, the Museum of Fine Arts, and Hermann Park, which has a zoo and science museum. Adjacent to Rice University are two small but exceptionally fine Eclectic-era residential districts. The first of these, Shadyside, is focused around short Remington Lane and was developed between 1919 and 1930 by Texaco founder Joseph Stephen Cullinan (1860–1937). Today this small neighborhood is gated and no longer accessible to the public.

Inspired by Shadyside's success, several developers opened small subdivisions nearby on West Eleventh Place, Waverly Court, and Shadowlawn Circle. Adjacent was the larger Broadacres development, centered around easternmost North and South Boulevards. West Eleventh Place has but seven houses on two and a half acres; all but number 8 and number 10 were built between 1920 and 1922. Shadowlawn Circle is a bit larger in scale and had twelve houses, as well as two garage apartments, designed by architect H. T. Lindeberg (see the following entry) to serve two of his large Shadyside dwellings.

Largest of all was the several-square-block Broadacres development, laid out in 1923 by Houston architect William Ward Watkin (1887–1952). Occupying the 1300 to 1500 blocks of North and South Boulevards, it is landscaped by rows of handsome live oak trees planted along the sidewalks and in the boulevard's central esplanade. Their branches have now intergrown to form picturesque tree tunnels reminiscent of the Old South. The houses are mostly Eclectic-era designs from the 1920s.

1400 South Boulevard (private), Kuldell House, 1929; John F. Staub, Houston, architect. Architect John F. Staub (1892–1981) came to Texas to supervise the construction of

four Shadyside homes designed by New Yorker H. T. Lindeberg, one of America's preeminent country-house architects. Staub decided to make Houston his home and established what became a long and distinguished architectural practice (see also "Bayou Bend," page 612). Staub biographer Howard Barnstone notes that: "Lindeberg's working philosophy, which Staub would largely adopt, was that an elegant house need not be an ostentatious house; a simple, traditional design, richly textured and carefully proportioned, was more beautiful than the most magnificent palace."

This Tudor house has handsomely detailed brickwork and extensive leaded-glass casement windows. Compare this to Staub's more austere interpretation of the brick Tudor at 1324 North Boulevard, completed three years earlier in 1926.

1318 North Boulevard (private), Gilmer House, 1926; William Ward Watkin, Houston, architect. This Spanish Eclectic home was William Ward Watkin's only design in Broadacres, even though he planned the subdivision. Its symmetrical form is relatively unusual for this style. Note the two matching upstairs balconets with iron railings. The arched upper-story windows are later additions.

1515 South Boulevard (private), 1928; Birdsall P. Briscoe, Houston, architect. A handsome Italian Renaissance design by one of the city's most prolific Eclectic-era architects.

1405 North Boulevard (private), 1924; John F. Staub, Houston, architect. This Staub version of the Colonial Revival was his first Houston house after leaving Lindeberg (see page 609). It has an elegant broken-ogee pediment over the front door and unusually shallow windows in the upper story of the main house block. Note how the two side wings

Broadacres

project in front of the main house rather than being slightly set back as is more common. As in many Staub houses, it has a wide front facade but is only one and a half rooms deep. This assured good air circulation in Houston's steamy climate.

1505 North Boulevard (private), Tennant House, 1927; John F. Staub, Houston, architect. Another Staub interpretation of the Colonial Revival, this one is a centered-gable example. Most houses in this subtype mimic high-style Georgian and Adam prototypes. In this refined brick home, the Georgian is most in evidence; indeed, it was inspired by the ca. 1720 Tintinhull House in Somerset, England, which was illustrated in one of Staub's favorite reference books. Like Tintinhull, there is a striking segmental pediment over the entry, but here with a single line of lights below. The facade is organized with a subtle asymmetry—added by the tall arched window to the left of the central gable.

River Oaks, 1923 to present

In 1923 Houston's residential development took a quantum westward leap when the wealthy Hogg family (see page 612), and their associate Hugh Potter, established the new River Oaks subdivision. Carefully designed by Houston planner H. A. Kipp, this restricted enclave was located on 1,100 wooded acres in what was then remote countryside well beyond the city limits. By means of a discreet but well-funded long-term public relations effort, the Hoggs convinced many Houstonians that this large but then-distant development would ultimately become the city's most desirable, in part because its carefully drawn deed restrictions ensured against the threat of commercial intrusions. They were right, for the River Oaks lots slowly filled with fine houses that are still among the city's most prestigious addresses.

Faced with luring new residents to an exceptionally large and remote development, the Hoggs wisely designed it to include middle-income houses as well as palatial estates. The latter are mostly located on large lots clustered around the River Oaks Country Club, which borders Buffalo Bayou in the north-central part of the tract—particularly along Lazy Lane (where fences and large lots make viewing difficult), Inwood Drive, and Del Monte Drive.

Many River Oaks houses date from the 1930s and 1940s, decades when first the Great Depression and then the Second World War stifled new home construction in much of the country. Houston's booming oil industry, which played a principal role in fueling the victorious Allied armies, gave the city an unusual degree of late-depression-era and wartime prosperity.

Modern River Oaks is a showcase for the many housing fashions popular during the 1930s, including some modern designs from the 1950s and later. The heaviest emphasis is on late-Eclectic-era styles, particularly

Tudor, Colonial Revival, French Eclectic, and Neoclassical. The latter, evoking images of the Old South in their River Oaks setting of moss-hung pine trees, was a particular favorite. It is especially in evidence along River Oaks Boulevard, the grand entrance road that leads from Westheimer Road to the River Oaks Country Club. Number 1623 River Oaks Boulevard (private), built in 1954, and number 2104 River Oaks Boulevard (private), built in 1940, are but two examples.

3460 Inwood Drive (private), Sewall House, 1926; Cram and Ferguson, with Stayton Nunn, Boston, architects. Typical of River Oaks's many fine dwellings designed by nationally prominent architects is this Spanish Eclectic home by the distinguished Boston firm of Cram and Ferguson, which had earlier planned the Rice University campus and designed many of its first buildings.

3325 Inwood Drive (private), Mott House, 1930; Katharine B. Mott, Houston, with Burns and James, Indianapolis, architects. Mrs. Mott designed and built speculative houses in Houston's more upscale subdivisions, including ten in River Oaks. This was built to be her own family home. It is a wonderful example of the towered French Eclectic subtype that builders often called Norman cottages. It has the high-pitched hipped roof and half-timbered detailing typical of this subtype. Note also the casement windows and fine brickwork. Another of Mrs. Mott's French Eclectic designs, a smaller asymmetrical form, is at 2421 Brentwood Drive (private), which features an Italian Renaissance entrance—a very unusual combination.

3358 Inwood Drive (private), Christie House, 1930; Charles W. Oliver, architect. This was River Oaks's first

River Oaks

River Oaks

bine contrasting sections of white shingle with sections of darker brick, giving an overall impression of an early-eighteenth-century house that was expanded and updated. The combination is most unusual and must have been appealing, for it is one that was often copied. A nearby example is at 3363 Inwood Drive (private).

Bayou Bend (Ima Hogg House), 1928

1 Westcott Street, entrance north of River Oaks from Memorial Drive; 713-639-7750; advance reservations normally required for visit; John F. Staub, Houston, architect.

Largest of all the homes in River Oaks are about a dozen estate-sized lots that border Lazy Lane to the east of the country club; it was off this lane that the Hoggs built their own home, Bayou Bend. Although one of the grand Lazy Lane estates, Bayou Bend is today invisible from the lane; access for museum visitors is now from distant Memorial Drive. Designed by the prolific and talented Staub (see page 609), it is today home to one of the nation's outstanding assemblages of Early American furniture and decorative arts. This was collected over many years by philanthropist Ima Hogg (1882–1975) and donated, along with the house, to the Houston Museum of Fine Arts in 1966.

Miss Hogg and her two elder brothers, who also contributed to the Bayou Bend collections, were the children of James Stephen Hogg (1851–1906), a popular and high-minded civic reformer who served as governor of Texas from 1891 to 1895. Seeking a more secure future for his motherless family after his wife died in 1895, Hogg retired from politics and opened a law practice, the proceeds of which he invested in real estate and the region's new oil industry. The principal fruits of these efforts matured after his death, when a large Brazos Valley cotton farm that he had purchased became, as he had confidently predicted it would, the site of a major new oil field discovered in 1918. Soon Miss Hogg and her brothers were sharing an enormous income from their oil holdings. To their great credit, Governor Hogg's children inherited their father's high sense of civic responsibility and returned most of their fortune to the people of Houston and Texas through a series of philanthropic projects. One of these was, in fact, the River Oaks development, which they conceived as more a model exercise in thoughtful city expansion than as a profit-making venture. Indeed for many years they had to subsidize their visionary but remote new suburb.

It was partly in recognition of the public relations value of attracting some of Houston's wealthy elite to River Oaks that Ima Hogg built this home on its four-

house in the Neoclassical style. It was inspired by the great plantation houses of Louisiana, with its two-level, full-facade porches that wrap around three sides of the house. Such houses were designed for a climate similar to Houston's. For whatever reason, this southern plantation image must have been appealing, because a number of similar houses followed—each with heroic two-story columns supporting either a full-width or a full-height entry porch.

2909 Inwood Drive (private), Heyer House, 1936; John F. Staub, Houston, architect. This large and freely interpreted Colonial Revival home has a facade enhanced with six two-story pilasters, six tripartite windows, and cast-aluminum balconies. Staub also designed 2929 Inwood Drive (private), just next door, in 1934.

3511 Del Monte Drive (private), John F. Staub House, 1926; John F. Staub, Houston, architect. Inspired by the early homes found in his wife Madeleine's native Massachusetts, Staub's own home combines a free interpretation of the high-pitched roofs of Medievally inspired First Period English houses with a Georgian Renaissance-inspired doorway crowned with a broken-ogee pediment. The walls com-

Bayou Bend

teen-acre tract. She engaged Staub and then worked with him to build what she called a Latin Colonial house, loosely blending New Orleans–style French windows, stuccoed walls, and iron balconies, with the beloved, symmetrical shapes and detailing of the English Georgian and Regency periods. It is in the Palladian five-part plan—a central house block with "hyphens" connecting it to lower dependencies. The house is enveloped by the warm tones of its soft-pink stucco walls. Miss Hogg had noted that many houses in Greece were of a soft pink and decided that color was appropriate for a sunny climate like Houston's. The color was created by crushing pink stone into the stucco. Today the walls have been cleaned and lost much of their patina. The house has a copper roof and shutters in a harmonizing color.

The home was called Bayou Bend after a sharp turn in the adjacent river, and Miss Ima, as she was affectionately called by everyone, was also an avid collector of fine American antiques. This enthusiasm was particularly farsighted, for in those days Early American furniture was generally looked down upon as a rather-unrefined country cousin of its sophisticated English and Continental relatives. Collecting with both expert consultation and impeccable taste, Miss Hogg slowly

built up a unique assemblage that was planned from its beginning to ultimately rest in some deserving Texas museum. By the 1950s it was clear that the collection had outgrown the capacity of most museums to fully display it, so she generously added her twenty-eight-room house and grounds, plus a permanent endowment for its maintenance, and donated the entire package to Houston's Museum of Fine Arts, which operates it as a special branch.

In the conversion of Bayou Bend from house to museum, the collection was rearranged under Miss Hogg's direction so that each room now reflects a particular period of American design. Among the most popular rooms are the Federal-style Museum Room (1790–1815), the William and Mary Pine Room (1700–1725), the Chippendale Drawing Room (1760–1790), and the early Victorian Belter Parlor (1845–1870).

The domestic scale of the rooms at Bayou Bend and its worldwide reputation mean that advance reservations, usually available on short notice, are required for the ninety-minute tours. The fourteen-acre grounds are open without reservations. The combination of handsome formal and naturalistic gardens, the refined house exterior, and the choice river setting make even the exterior alone worth a visit.

JOHNSON CITY

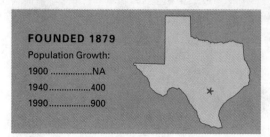

FOUNDED 1879
Population Growth:
1900 ....NA
1940 400
1990 900

This small community fifty miles west of Austin was the boyhood home of Lyndon Baines Johnson (1908–1973), who served as the nation's thirty-sixth president, from 1963 to 1969. The president's grandfather, along with his brother, established a pioneering cattle ranch here in the 1860s. This served as a base for driving herds of wild Texas cattle up the Chisholm Trail to railhead marketing centers in Kansas. The ranch later became the nucleus of the small town of Johnson City, a county seat and trade center for ranches and stream-valley farms scattered through the region's rocky hills. In 1913 the five-year-old future president's parents moved from a remote family ranch into Johnson City, where they purchased what is today known as the Lyndon Baines Johnson Boyhood Home.

His earliest childhood was spent on a family ranch located fifteen miles west of Johnson City near the small village of Stonewall. Always fiercely proud of his frontier heritage, in 1951 Johnson, then a U.S. senator, purchased this Stonewall ranch from an aunt and made it his showplace "L.B.J. Ranch" Texas headquarters.

These two separate properties, the home in Johnson City and the ranch near Stonewall, form the core of what is today the Lyndon B. Johnson National Historical Park. The Johnson City Unit of the park includes the carefully restored and interpreted boyhood home as well as the president's grandfather's nearby log house and other outbuildings that miraculously survive from the original nineteenth-century Johnson Settlement that later became Johnson City.

The second or Stonewall Unit of the national historical park is also instructive. In addition to the L.B.J. Ranch, the grounds of which can be seen on special bus tours, there is a visitor center, the president's reconstructed birthplace, the family cemetery where he is buried, and the nearby Sauer-Beckmann Farm (see page 596) that, although not directly related to the president's life, provides a fascinating look at early farm life in the region.

Lyndon Baines Johnson Boyhood Home, ca. 1900

Ninth Street between F and G Streets, in the Lyndon B. Johnson National Historical Park; 830-868-7128.
This carefully restored Folk Victorian house began as a simple L-shaped, gabled-front-and-wing folk house to which a second L was added a few years later to create a

Lyndon Baines Johnson Boyhood Home

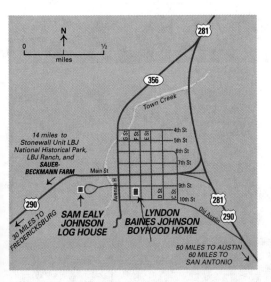

When the young future president lived in the house, it still did not have full indoor plumbing. There was a bathroom with a sink and tub in the house (very early for Johnson City) and an outhouse, an arrangement described as "half-a-bath and path." The house is very appropriately furnished and has some Johnson family pieces.

Sam Ealy Johnson Log House, ca. 1867

In the Lyndon B. Johnson National Historical Park, accessible only by a ten-minute walking trail from the nearby Lyndon Baines Johnson Boyhood Home (see the preceding entry).

This is a rare example of an early southern dogtrot log house that, although restored, is still intact on its original site. The name comes from the roofed open porch that separates the two log rooms, a space where presumably the family dogs liked to linger, shaded from the hot summer sun. The house, which has never had electricity or plumbing, first served as both home and headquarters for the Johnson brothers' extensive cattle operations. Several early barns and outbuildings also survive on the large Johnson Settlement site, which captures some of the spirit of the remote frontier village.

cross-shaped dwelling. This was a good house form for early Texas, as it was only one room deep at any given point, thus allowing each of the four principal rooms to catch cool breezes from three different directions. It also created four separate porches, each with a separate function. There is a front entry porch, a men's porch, a sleeping porch, and a kitchen porch.

Sam Ealy Johnson Log House

LUBBOCK

FOUNDED 1891

Population Growth:

1900 ....<1,000

1940 32,000

1990 186,000

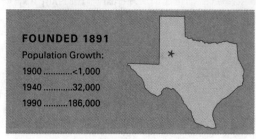

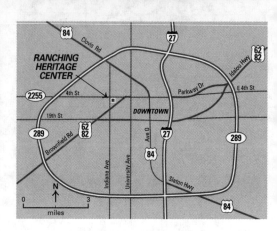

Lubbock is a western Texas market and financial center for a prosperous region of irrigated crops, particularly high-value cotton, watered by wells tapping a deep aquifer (see also page 544). A young city, it has few pre-1940 architectural resources save for one extraordinary attraction—the Ranching Heritage Center at Texas Tech University. This is a museum complex of relocated folk buildings that provides fascinating insights into the lives of pioneer settlers on the western plains.

Ranching Heritage Center

Fourth Street and Indiana Avenue; 806-742-2498.

Much of the western interior region was originally unforested grassland. Long the domain of buffalo herds and the Plains Indians that depended on them, during the 1870s western railroad building, buffalo hunting, and removal of the Indians to reservations all combined to open these vast prairies and plains to Anglo ranching (see page xxvii). The "cattle rush" that followed was far larger, as well as more permanent, than any of the West's many gold and silver bonanzas.

Wood for building ranch houses and service buildings was scarce in the western grasslands, and the earliest ranchers built folk dwellings that minimized the need for logs and lumber, which usually required long wagon hauls from distant rail junctions or from the sparsely timbered banks of the region's few large rivers. As the railroad network, and the rancher's affluence, expanded, these first-generation folk dwellings were replaced by more fashionable styled houses.

In 1970 administrators and faculty at Texas Tech, the principal university center of northwestern Texas, realizing that many of the region's few surviving early folk buildings would soon be lost forever, organized the Ranching Heritage Center on a twelve-acre site adjacent to the campus. Mostly completed and dedicated as

Ranching Heritage Center

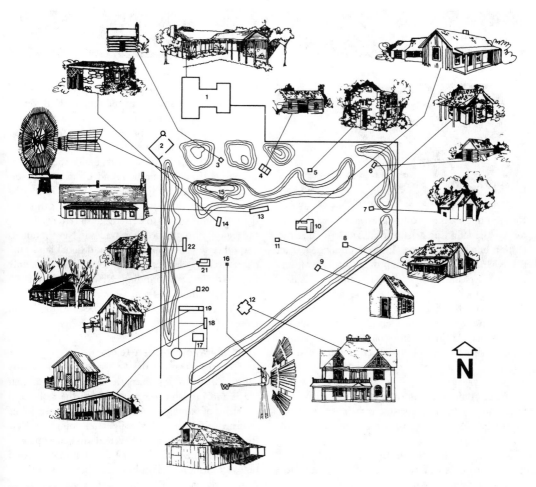

The Ranching Heritage Center

a bicentennial project in 1976, the carefully executed and well-interpreted center now includes more than two dozen structures, about half of them dwellings, moved from throughout western Texas and reinstalled with landscaping similar to that of their original sites. Among the more unusual houses are half dugouts, a fa-

vorite technique for saving wood and gaining wall insulation by excavating into the ground or hillside to create partial walls of earth, and examples of the rarely seen box-and-strip and picket-and-sotol techniques of wall construction.

NEW BRAUNFELS

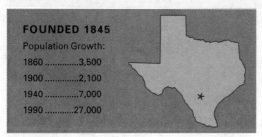

FOUNDED 1845

Population Growth:

1860	3,500
1900	2,100
1940	7,000
1990	27,000

New Braunfels was the cultural and commercial center for a massive mid-nineteenth-century German immigration into central Texas. This began under Mexican rule when an 1831 land grant brought a trickle of German farmers into what is now northwestern Austin County, about seventy-five miles west of Houston. By the early 1840s enthusiastic letters written home by these pioneers had spawned larger schemes for bringing German farmers and craftsmen, increasingly impoverished by overpopulation, crop failure, and factory-made imports, to the sparsely settled Republic of Texas (see page xii).

The most important of these plans was formulated by a group of Rhineland aristocrats who called themselves the Adelsverein (Association of Noblemen). These men saw an opportunity to relieve the suffering of some of their semifeudal dependents and enhance their own wealth by converting cheap Texas land into a valuable agricultural empire. In the summer of 1844 the group sent one of its members, Prince Carl of Solms-Braunfels, stepson of the king of Hanover, to Texas to investigate sites for their new colony. In San Antonio the following spring he purchased a 1,265-acre wilderness tract between that city and the republic's new capital of Austin. There, beside the beautiful spring-fed Comal River, he founded the city of New Braunfels, named for his ancestral home. During the next two years the Adelsverein sent more than seven thousand immigrants to farm the fertile river valleys of the region or to practice their trades in New Braunfels and other towns established on additional land purchases (see "Fredericksburg," page 593). By 1850, only five years after its founding, New Braunfels's 1,700 inhabitants, most of them German, made it Texas's fourth-largest town after Galveston, San Antonio, and Houston.

The Capital of German Texas

As a financial venture the Adelsverein was a failure. Most of its titled organizers were more adept at high ideals and inspiring words than with the real-world problems of taming a distant wilderness. Prince Solms returned to Germany shortly after founding New Braunfels, and soon the Adelsverein was bankrupt. As a social experiment, on the other hand, it ranks second only to Mormon Utah in its success at transplanting a complex agricultural society into the raw wilderness of

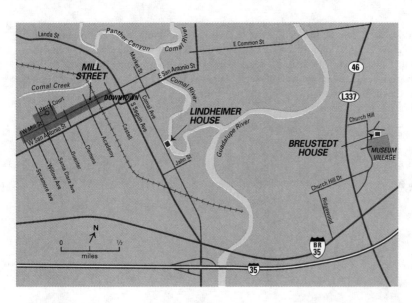

the American West. Following the Adelsverein's lead, thousands of other disaffected Germans from all social classes followed their countrymen to Texas. By 1850 there were thirty-three thousand German Texans who made up one-fifth of the state's population. Many of these immigrants, particularly university-educated professionals and highly skilled craftsmen, settled in the urban centers of Galveston, the state's principal seaport and gateway for German immigration, or San Antonio, the region's oldest and largest town (see page 622). Still more were concentrated in the agricultural counties centered around New Braunfels, which became the unofficial social and cultural capital of German Texas.

Modern New Braunfels still retains much of its Germanic heritage, although this has now been diluted by the region's enormous post-1950 Sunbelt growth. As late as 1940, the town was still a small regional trade center dominated by bilingual German speakers. Today it is a substantial city with light industry, expanding suburbs, tourism emphasizing its German origins, and a predominance of conversations in English.

In physical appearance New Braunfels never closely resembled the mother country, for most of its early settlers adopted the log-building practices of their Anglo neighbors (see also page 594). These were, in turn, later replaced by, or sided over to look like, Anglo wooden-framed dwellings, particularly after the town's first railroad arrived in 1880. Architecturally, New Braunfels is of greatest interest today because of its carefully preserved folk houses dating from both the pre- and postrailroad periods. These include two important museum houses, one of them a rare unaltered survivor of the German-influenced building techniques used in the early years of settlement; the other is an example of German construction with Anglo wood cladding added later.

Lindheimer House, 1852

491 Comal Avenue; 830-606-1512.

This charming folk dwelling was the home of Ferdinand Jakob Lindheimer (1801–1879), one of the central figures in the early German settlement of Texas. Son of a wealthy Frankfurt merchant and cousin of the great writer-statesman Johann Wolfgang von Goethe (1749–1832), young Ferdinand was educated in mathematics and classical languages and became a high school teacher in his native city. In his spare time he pursued two disparate hobbies—politics and botany—that were to dominate his long life. An outspoken opponent of the authoritarian and repressive government of his homeland, in 1834 Lindheimer immigrated to Belleville, Illinois, where a group of similarly disaffected German intellectuals had established a flourishing expatriate community. Soon his restless curiosity and love of botany led him southward to collect the relatively unknown floras of Mexico and Texas, where he supported himself by such odd jobs as managing a distillery, supervising a pineapple plantation, and truck farming near Houston. By 1844 Lindheimer's tireless collecting had made him "the Father of Texas Botany" as well as a familiar figure in the earliest German settlements west of Houston. In that year he was asked to help guide Prince Solms and the first group of Adelsverein immigrants to the site of New Braunfels, where Lindheimer was rewarded with a picturesque

Lindheimer House

riverside lot that was to be his home until his death thirty-five years later.

Lindheimer continued his work as a plant collector from his New Braunfels base until 1852, when he built the more substantial house that survives today and embarked on a new career as the courageous editor of the *Neu-Braunfelser Zeitung,* which was to become one of the most influential and respected U.S. German-language newspapers. Much of its content was written by Lindheimer, who also printed its issues on a hand-press in a small, brick-floored room in his new home, which served as the publication's headquarters.

Lindheimer built his house in the two-room, hall-and-parlor plan favored by Anglo southerners. But instead of the usual squared-log walls, he built with traditional German *fachwerk,* or half-timbering, in which a strong timber framework is filled with clay, brick, or stone and then covered with a protective layer of plaster. Other early *fachwerk* structures remain in New Braunfels and in nearby Fredericksburg (see page 594), but most have been variously rebuilt, restored, or covered with later wooden siding—as in the Breustedt House (see the following entry). Lindheimer's survives in what appears to be its original configuration.

As in most Anglo hall-and-parlor dwellings, Lindheimer later added a rear extension to provide two additional rooms of living space. One was used as an indoor kitchen, replacing a small outbuilding used for cooking, the other a bedroom that made possible a formal parlor next to the fourth principal room, which was the newspaper's office. The house was given to the New Braunfels Conservation Society by Lindheimer's granddaughter and retains many original furnishings. In the picturesque rear garden, the society has gathered a collection of the many species of Texas plants with botanical names that honor Lindheimer's pioneering studies.

Breustedt House, 1858

1370 Church Hill Drive, Museum of Texas Handmade Furniture; 830-629-6504.

This is a fine example of a German farm house with *fachwerk* walls that were originally clad with cypress siding, which still survives. The large attic is open, and there you can observe the pegged timbers and adobe-brick wall filling characteristic of this type of construction. The house has been moved from a nearby location, and, although principally a museum of furniture made by local German craftsmen, the pieces are arranged to give the feeling of an upper-middle-class German household of the period. The focus of the interpretation is, of course, on the furnishings themselves. The work of over twenty German craftsmen is represented, including pieces by such well-known cabinetmakers as Johann Jahn, Heinrich Scholl, and Franz Stautzenberger. Native woods, principally walnut and pine, were lovingly crafted by these masters into fine wardrobes, chests, beds, tables, and chairs for the many local families whose homes they once graced. Some of the smaller decorative objects used in these homes are also on display, including an extensive collection of English ironstone from around 1813 to 1865.

Two other buildings share the museum's grounds—the 1847 Reinenger log cabin, moved here from a nearby site, and a newly constructed cabinetmaker's shop. The furnishings in the cabin show the contrast in living conditions between the Breustedt House (refined) and that of a typical frontier family (more prim-

Breustedt House

Mill Street

itive). The shop houses a wonderful collection of tools and a workbench that belonged to Jahn. An effective display shows the main steps used to produce a single fine chair.

Mill Street, 1840s–ca. 1930s

This street has an unusual concentration of Folk Victorian houses, mostly of either the side-gabled or the gable-front-and-wing form. Most of these appear to be earlier houses to which Victorian decorative detailing was later added. The Victorian elements are predominantly front-porch supports and brackets at the cornice line. But one elaboration, featured in some mid-nineteenth-century pattern books but relatively rarely used, appears on many Mill Street houses. This is a hood (or canopy) built over one of the main windows.

230 West Mill Street (private), Pfeuffer House, 1846. This is a two-story I-house form with a saltbox extension in the rear. It has a Greek Revival–style front door that could have been original in 1846 or added anytime up to about 1860 as a stylish update. The turned spindlework detailing on the full-width front porch would have been added during the late nineteenth century (see the following entry).

256 West Mill Street (private), Geue House, ca. 1860s. This small, three-ranked, side-gabled folk house has a porch with details that could have been original to its construction. The squared porch supports and flat, cutout balusters seen

here were more easily constructed than lathe-turned elements and were featured in many mid-nineteenth-century pattern books. In contrast, the spindlework porch supports and balusters at 230 West Mill Street (see the preceding entry) required a machine lathe to be quickly produced; they were not common in frontier towns until after the coming of the railroads.

392 West Mill Street (private). This gabled-front-and-wing Folk Victorian house has an excellent example of a hood (or canopy) accenting a pair of tall, narrow windows in the front-facing gable. Similar gables are found at 772 West Mill Street (private) and in several other houses in this block.

554 West Mill Street (private), Ullrich House, 1846. This is a simple hall-and-parlor folk house with front porch included under the main roofline. Many of its neighbors, including 256 West Mill Street (see above), have the more usual pattern of a separate shed roof of lower pitch above the porch.

Herry Court (private), ca. 1915. This pleasant "bungalow court," small-lot cul-de-sacs with houses in a single unified style, is located just one and one-half blocks north of Mill Street. Such courts originated in southern California and are unusual outside of that region. They were most commonly built in the Craftsman style, as here, but are sometimes seen in other earlier-twentieth-century styles, particularly Spanish Eclectic or Tudor. Herry Court's yellow brick Craftsman houses are arranged into six matched pairs. A twin pair of cross-gabled forms sits on either side of the cul-de-sac entrance. Next are four identical front-gabled pairs, and the court terminates with a part of side-gabled forms (one of this pair has been altered).

621

SAN ANTONIO

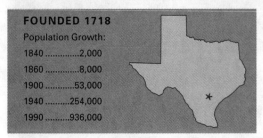

FOUNDED 1718

Population Growth:

1840 2,000
1860 8,000
1900 53,000
1940 254,000
1990 936,000

San Antonio is an underappreciated treasure trove of important historic architecture. Already a bustling Colonial capital when most of the West was unexplored wilderness, the city has miraculously managed to preserve much of its early Spanish heritage through two hundred years of growth and change. In addition, many important structures survive from the town's period as a regional trade center during the Republic of Texas and early statehood eras, before the first railroads reached the city in 1877.

Spanish Capital

San Antonio began as one of a chain of Texas mission-forts established by Spain in an attempt to protect its New World borderlands against intrusions from French Louisiana (see page xi). Mission San Antonio was located near the clear, spring-fed waters of the San Antonio River. The river actually begins just a short distance north of the mission area, where huge springs, fed by the underground Edward's Aquifer, gush out in several different locations to form an instant river of clear, cool water. These prolific springs give the San Antonio River a much steadier flow than most Texas rivers, which often shrink to bare trickles or even disappear during summer droughts.

When hostile Indians and French indifference led to the abandonment of the more easterly Texas missions, which were near the Louisiana border, their founding padres reestablished some of them along the bountiful San Antonio River, downstream from the original Mission San Antonio. By 1731 there were six riverside missions protected by a fort and served by the small town of San Antonio, which was the administrative center of Spanish Texas, a position it held until the Anglo Revolution of 1836 (see page xii).

Its dependable spring-fed flow made the San Antonio River particularly favorable for irrigated agricul-

Looking west along Crockett Street, 1857; at the far right is the Alamo, seen from the rear.

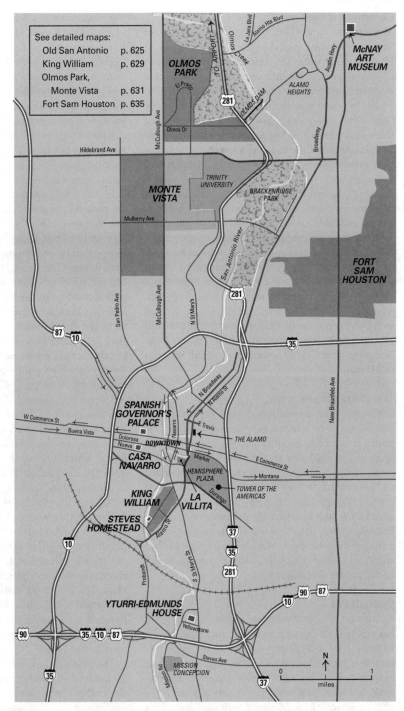

See detailed maps:
Old San Antonio   p. 625
King William   p. 629
Olmos Park,
    Monte Vista   p. 631
Fort Sam Houston   p. 635

ture, an enterprise at which the padres excelled. When the mission lands were parceled out to private owners by the government of the new Republic of Mexico in 1824, the irrigation systems were expanded farther. Eventually they consisted of "seven gravity-flow irriga-tion ditches known as acequias, five dams and an aque-duct [that] were constructed in a network covering over fifteen miles," according to a 1967 historical sum-mary by the San Antonio River Authority.

Commercial Center

Although the Anglo leaders of the new Republic of Texas moved their capital eighty miles northeast of Hispanic-dominated San Antonio to the new town of Austin (see page 548), the venerable Spanish capital long remained the state's dominant inland commercial center. In addition to the river's rich irrigated farms, large cattle, sheep, and goat ranches were located throughout the region. San Antonio became the principal livestock-trading and supply center for these remote ranches. Many ranchers even built second homes in the city.

In 1877 the first railroad arrived, building westward to eventually connect Houston and New Orleans with El Paso and California. During the next decade three more railroads reached the city, and its century and a half of exclusive dependence on wagon trains for long-distance transport abruptly ended. Additional wealth was added in the twentieth century when large oil and gas fields were discovered on many south Texas ranches. As a result of these activities, San Antonio alternated with Galveston as the state's largest city from 1850 until 1890 and then retained first place from 1900 to 1930. Since then it has steadily ranked third, behind Houston and Dallas.

The Army's Hometown

San Antonio's early-twentieth-century growth also resulted from a new role that supplemented its long importance as a commercial center. Beginning with the Spanish-American War of 1898–1899, San Antonio's early military post of Fort Sam Houston was expanded and upgraded to become a principal headquarters and training center for the U.S. Army. The First World War added army aviation with the establishment of nearby Randolph Field. Both facilities were greatly expanded during the Second World War and subsequent Korean and Vietnam Wars, which also added Brooks, Kelly, and Lackland Air Force Bases.

Sunbelt Era

As with other large southwestern cities, San Antonio has experienced explosive growth in the decades since 1940; by 1990 its 1940 population had increased 370 percent to make it the nation's tenth-largest city. Unlike most of its giant Sunbelt neighbors, however, San Antonio has also been working energetically since the 1920s to preserve its architectural heritage. Much of the credit goes to the remarkable San Antonio Conservation Society. Founded in 1924, two years later the group organized a mass protest that prevented the picturesque, horseshoe-shaped river bend at the core of the city from being drained and covered with concrete.

The result is today's delightful downtown **Riverwalk**, which links many of Old San Antonio's landmarks. The Conservation Society next sponsored a successful bond election to purchase and restore the long-neglected Spanish Governor's Palace, the crown jewel of the nation's very few Spanish Colonial dwellings that survive from the eighteenth century (see page 624). Building on these early successes, the society has taken on and completed numerous other preservation projects, a record that has given it unprecedented financial and political clout that it continues to use for enhancing San Antonio's architectural charm.

Probably the Conservation Society's most challenging project has been its long battle to save and restore San Antonio's unique collection of Spanish Colonial mission buildings. In this seventy-year struggle, it has been joined by several powerful allies, particularly the city's Roman Catholic diocese, which owns many of the historic structures, some of which are still used for parish worship. In 1983, after many years of intense lobbying, the federal government took the lead by creating the **San Antonio Missions National Historic Park** (210-229-5701), which includes the four surviving eighteenth-century missions established along the San Antonio River just south of the city. A visit to these, and the still-developing Mission Trail that links them, is a must for understanding Texas's unique Spanish heritage.

No visitor can miss the oldest of the surviving missions, San Antonio de Valero, from which the city took its name, for later events have made it the sacred shrine of Texas tourism. In 1801 the abandoned mission structures, whose stone walls made an ideal fortress, became the base for the local military garrison. In the fortress, by then renamed the Alamo, about two hundred besieged Anglo rebels, who had previously driven out the local Mexican garrison, were martyred during the Texas Revolution of 1836. Today only the mission church survives as the much visited **Alamo** (318 Alamo Plaza, 210-225-1391). These often-dramatized events have made it difficult to remember that more than a hundred years earlier the mission itself, its grounds now mostly covered by modern buildings, was the cradle of urban Texas.

The great significance of San Antonio's unique Spanish Colonial architecture makes it easy to overlook the city's other historic resources, among them a fine assemblage of Victorian-era dwellings and several delightful Eclectic-era neighborhoods on the city's north side. The historic importance of these early-twentieth-century neighborhoods was well summarized by the local chapter of the American Institute of Architects in its 1986 publication *A Guide to San Antonio Architecture:*

For connoisseurs of domestic architecture between 1900 and 1940, north-central San Antonio is a sheer delight. The area contains the largest and most distinguished collection of early- to mid-20th century residential design in all of Texas, spread throughout the neighborhoods of Monte Vista, Laurel Heights, Alamo Heights, Olmos Park, and Terrell Hills. All of the architects responsible for the revamping of San Antonio's architectural character in the 1920s and 1930s designed houses here, and the great majority of these works have survived [unaltered] along with the broad streets and splendid landscaping that are so much a part of this special environment. . . . [The many styles found in] north-central San Antonio span the full range of residential architectural expression, and it merits an extensive driving tour. [See the Monte Vista (page 630) and Olmos Park (page 632) neighborhoods discussed below.]

OLD SAN ANTONIO

Historic San Antonio was concentrated around the horseshoe-shaped bend in the San Antonio River that has become today's picturesque Riverwalk. In addition to the Alamo, which is the only surviving structure from the large mission complex that once occupied much of the eastern side of the river, two important museum houses and a reconstructed village of more humble dwellings survive from the early military fort and civilian town that grew up immediately west of the mission lands.

Spanish Governor's Palace, ca. 1749

105 Plaza de Armas; 210-224-0601.

This remarkable building is among the oldest surviving Spanish Colonial dwellings in the United States. It was once one of several army-built structures that surrounded the Military Plaza of Old San Antonio. The middle of the plaza, where the city hall now stands, was a parade ground, and this house was the commanding officer's quarters (much like the arrangement on the Staff Post and other posts in Fort Sam Houston; see page 634). Although built on the remote northern frontier of Spain's vast New World empire, the house was large and comfortable, befitting one of the ranking Spanish officials of eighteenth-century San Antonio. By the 1780s the house and adjacent military building were privately owned. Among several later owners was the interim governor of Mexican Texas from 1814 to 1817. Although there is no record of his actually living in the old commandant's house, this may help account for its somewhat-misleading later name. Through the efforts of the San Antonio Conservation Society (see page 624), the historic dwelling was restored as a museum house in 1929.

The keystone over the front door announces 1749— SE ACABO (finished) and is inscribed with the coat of arms of Spain's king Philip V. The door itself is of hand-carved walnut and is patterned after an early etching of the original. The exterior facade is rather severe and in

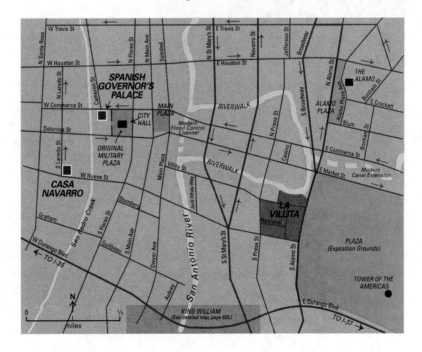

Spanish Governor's Palace

The furnishings are a mixture of Spanish Colonial antiques, reproductions (the dining room table and benches), and scattered display cases. Some rooms give you a feeling of how the house might originally have looked, and others are more museum-like in character.

Casa Navarro, ca. 1850 and later

228 South Laredo Street; 210-226-4801.

Jose Antonio Navarro (1795–1871) was born in San Antonio and at the age of eighteen was exiled to Louisiana for supporting Mexico's struggle for independence from Spain. He returned to San Antonio in 1816, and in 1821, following Mexican independence, he was elected mayor of the city. In 1836 Navarro was one of only two native Texans who signed the Texas Declaration of Independence. He also helped to draft the constitution of the new Republic of Texas. Captured by Mexico as a traitor in 1841, Navarro escaped from prison in 1845 in time to become the only native Texan to participate in the convention that ratified Texas's annexation to the United States. A man of great wisdom and integrity, Navarro became a revered elder statesman of early Texas.

In 1832 Navarro bought this one-acre site, which was then on the edge of town and surrounded by farmlands. Some years later he built the initial structure, which was a small two-room adobe dwelling, probably with a detached kitchen. Beginning about 1853, more rooms, some with limestone walls, were added. The final product is a five-room, L-shaped house with a semidetached three-room kitchen, all connected by rear porches. From the street it looks like a simple side-

typical Hispanic fashion has a door from each main room opening out onto the street, rather than one central entrance. Inside, there are no hallways; each room opens directly into the adjacent rooms, as was the custom in Spanish dwellings. One original interior door remains, that between the living room and the family bedroom. The walls are built of rubblework stone coated with plaster. The traditional roof-support timbers of flat-roofed Spanish Colonial houses have been restored throughout.

Casa Navarro

gabled folk house with a full-width front porch, a typical plan for Texas houses of the period. Most of the doors, windows, and hardware seen today date from the 1964 restoration of the house by the San Antonio Conservation Society. The furnishings are appropriate—simple pieces from early Texas, Louisiana, and Mexico. A few of Navarro's personal effects are also on display.

Two other buildings were constructed over the years on the property. A square two-story stone structure, located at the corner of the lot, was probably used as an office or a store. A smaller three-room house in the rear is now used for offices and interpretation. A transparent panel on the back of this house shows the adobe construction techniques used for the central room. The Casa Navarro became a state historic park in 1975.

La Villita, ca. 1835 and later; restored, 1939 and 1980
Bounded by South Alamo, West Nueva, South Presa and Villita Streets, entrance from the Riverwalk up through the Arneson Theater; 210-207-8610.
This group of early San Antonio folk houses was rescued from demolition in 1939 and restored, with additional modern structures added, to become a popular center for multicultural shops and civic activities.

La Villita, Spanish for "Little Town," was located across the river from the early town center and was San Antonio's original low-rent district. First the home of Spanish foot soldiers' families in the 1700s, it later housed nineteenth-century Anglo pioneers as well as German and Alsatian immigrants. Only the core of the historic neighborhood, by then a big-city slum, was

saved in the 1939 restoration. Surviving early structures, mostly on their original sites, include an 1879 church, several stores, and sixteen folk houses, most of which are side-gabled forms dating from the mid–nineteenth century. The pre-1835 Cos House is considered to be the oldest in the district. All of La Villita's buildings have excellent interpretive markers, and a walking-tour brochure is available in many of the craft shops or at the project's administrative offices in Bolivar Hall.

King William, ca. 1860s–1940
This elegant neighborhood was long dominated by German immigrants, a great many of whom migrated to central Texas in the mid-1800s (see also "Fredericksburg," page 593, and "New Braunfels," page 618). The King William area was originally the Lower Farm, one of the two irrigated tracts developed by the padres of the San Antonio Mission and worked mostly by its Indian converts. The mission's lands began to be transferred to private owners, both Indian families and others, in the 1790s, a process that was completed by independent Mexico in 1824. In 1859 the old Lower Farm became part of the city of San Antonio. In 1866 streets were surveyed and platted by German immigrant Ernst Altgelt, who named the main street King William in honor of Kaiser Wilhelm I of Prussia.

By 1876 San Antonio's stream of Teutonic immigrants had grown to dominance in the city. In that year its total population of 17,314 included 5,630 Germans or Alsatians, 5,475 American Anglos, and 3,750 Mexicans.

Throughout the late 1800s the King William neighborhood was the favored site for San Antonio's upscale homes. Here many prosperous German businessmen and professionals were also joined by a large number of their Anglo counterparts. By the 1930s, most of these affluent families had moved elsewhere, and many of the old neighborhood's fine houses had been converted to semineglected rental properties or to institutional uses. In 1967 the few remaining longtime residents, and a trickle of new home owners, banded together and gained historic designation for their picturesque neighborhood. Today King William's carefully restored houses are once again among San Antonio's most fashionable addresses.

Most of the district's houses date from the 1860s through the 1920s and illustrate a rich variety of sizes and architectural styles. These range from small early folk houses to grand dwellings such as the Steves Homestead (see page 629). The neighborhood's careful landscaping has a lush, almost-tropical feel. Fenced front yards, common in nineteenth-century America to deter errant horses, cows, and pigs, are still much in evidence. These range from elaborate designs of stone or decorative ironwork to simple wooden examples. A complete walking-tour pamphlet on the neighborhood is usually available outside the headquarters of the San Antonio Conservation Society at the Anton Wulff House, 107 King William Street.

King William

116 and 120 King William Street (both private), Joseph and John Ball Houses, ca. 1870. Once these two houses were identical, but number 116 received a second story and a Victorian front porch in about 1903. Number 120 remains relatively unchanged and is an excellent example of the side-gabled folk-house form known as hall-and-parlor, for the two main rooms. Both the hall and the parlor usually have separate doorways opening onto the front porch. The casement window on the right is probably original, while the one on the left is likely a replacement double-hung window. The standing-seam metal roof is common in south Texas folk houses.

217 King William Street (private), Sartor House, 1881; Alfred Giles, San Antonio, architect. Alexander Sartor Jr. was a watch repairman who moved to San Antonio from his native Germany. He hired popular San Antonio architect Alfred Giles to design this delightful one-story Italianate dwelling. The front door and each of the long narrow windows are topped by a segmental arch with a hood mold above. The full-width porch has handsome Italianate porch supports, along with a touch of the Stick style in the open gable with a truss located in the center of the porch roof. On the side, the roof has another bit of Stick-style detailing in the side gable. Note the one-story bay window on the side. The house appears to be built of heavy stone, but this is an illusion. Depending on what source one believes, it is either stucco or caliche block. Whichever, it is mimicking limestone ashlar with pronounced protruding mortar joints.

425 King William Street (private), Kalteyer House, 1892;

James Reily Gordon, San Antonio, architect. Gordon was a very talented designer who, until moving to New York in 1904, specialized in Texas county courthouses. Most of these were in the then-fashionable Richardsonian Romanesque style. Here Gordon applies this same style to a house. The Romanesque arches are accentuated by alternating red and white rough-faced stone used as "voussoirs" (the technical term for the wedge-shaped blocks used to form the arch). Towers are typical of Romanesque houses, and this one has two—a short, squat, round one with a decorative frieze and a tall polygonal neighbor with a recessed balcony. The front entry is nicely detailed with paired front doors, small Romanesque columns supporting the entry arch, and dramatic tilework to the side of the door. Note also the Romanesque-arched porte cochere (with a second recessed balcony above) and the wonderful carved caps of red stone on the fence pedestals.

241 King William Street (private), Joske House, 1900; S. L. McAdoo, San Antonio, architect. Unusually expansive porches surround this large Neoclassical house. Colossal two-story Ionic columns support a full-facade porch across

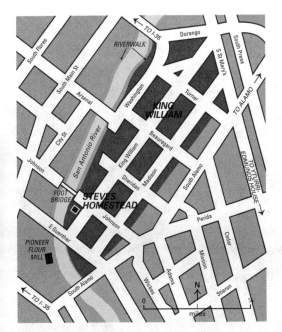

The highlight of the garden is a bronze fountain that the Steveses purchased when visiting the 1876 Centennial Exposition in Philadelphia. There are several outbuildings, including an 1896 washhouse, a carriage house, a servants' house, and a meetinghouse in what was originally a ca.-1900 natatorium, an enclosed swimming pool filled from an artesian well.

Edward Steves (1829–1890) had immigrated from Germany to New Braunfels, Texas (see page 618), in 1848. Only nineteen, he came to this country with his father, who anglicized their name from "Stefes" to "Steves" soon after arriving. Following the Civil War the younger Steves moved to San Antonio and founded the Steves Lumber Company, which soon prospered. In 1876 he built this house for his family, probably assisted by Alfred Giles, the well-known San Antonio architect. The Steveses had three sons and built nearby houses for two of them. Number 504 King William (private), built for son Albert in 1883, is directly across the street, and 431 King William (private), built for son Edward Jr. in 1884, is directly across Johnson, the side street. Their third son, Ernest, lived with his mother until her death in 1930. In 1952 the Steveses' granddaughter, Edna Steves Vaughan, donated the house to the San Antonio Conservation Society, which maintains it as a public museum.

The house is attributed to Alfred Giles (1853–1920), who had studied architecture in his native England but then moved to San Antonio in 1873 seeking a warmer climate for his health, which remained fragile from a near-fatal childhood bout with rheumatic fever. He was first employed by John H. Kampmann, a prominent San Antonio contractor who taught Giles the techniques of working with limestone and other local building materials. Kampmann and Antony Earhart built Steveses' home, and it is thought that the younger Giles, who went on to become one of the region's most distinguished architects, assisted in the house design. It is built of local ashlar limestone, and the mansard roof is clad in slate and topped by iron cresting. Most of the architectural detailing, both exterior and interior, was either ordered from catalogs or copied from architectural pattern books. For example, the elegant main stairway was constructed of mass-produced pieces all ordered from stock catalogs, as were the wooden cornice pieces above the windows throughout the house.

The house is a center-hall plan with two rooms to each side and fourteen-foot ceilings downstairs. The two parlors, located across the hall from each other in the front of the house, have Belter-style furnishings. The right parlor contains a remarkably intricate mosaic table, made from tiny pieces of marble in many different colors. This unique family piece is used as a center

the front and also what looks like a full-height entry porch on the north side. An extensive one-story porch, supported by one-story columns, extends out to cover the porte cochere. It is unusual to find colossal columns set on pedestal bases as seen here. The house also has a strong Colonial Revival influence in its details; dormers with exaggerated broken pediments, tall chimneys, a front door with elliptical fanlight above, and rooftop and cornice-line balustrades. Many Neoclassical houses are found in the King William district and this one—built for German immigrant Alexander Joske of the city's famed Joske Brothers Department Store—is particularly grand.

309 King William Street (private), Hummel House, 1884. Charles F. A. Hummel, born in San Antonio of German parents, was in the sporting-goods business and only twenty-nine years old when he built this fine Italianate home. It is a gable-front-and-wing form constructed of native Texas limestone. This was a common form both for the Italianate style and for Texas folk houses; in both, the porches tended to be placed fronting the "wing" and abutting the "gable front." Two-story houses often had dual-level porches as seen here. Note the slightly different detailing of the upstairs and downstairs porches, the use of paired brackets, and the fine stone quoins at the corners. A very similar, but more elaborated, Italianate house is the 1884 Edward Steves Jr. House at 431 King William Street (private).

Steves Homestead, 1876

509 King William Street; 210-225-5924;
Alfred Giles, San Antonio, architect.

This elegant Second Empire house sits adjacent to the San Antonio River on a large and luxuriantly landscaped lot filled with towering native trees. The grounds are enclosed with a cedar and pine fence that was built in 1875 before construction of the house had begun.

Steves Homestead

parlor table. The left parlor opens into the dining room through a beautiful segmental-arched door frame with operating pocket doors of etched glass. Around 1910 the ceilings throughout the house were stenciled in delicate floral designs. One ceiling is original, and the others are modern restorations.

Monte Vista

This large neighborhood was the principal site for upscale San Antonio dwellings from the late 1890s through the 1920s. Originally a series of smaller subdivisions that spread northward from the central city, Monte Vista is today a carefully controlled historic district that preserves one of Texas's largest and finest concentrations of Eclectic-era houses.

310 West Ashby Place (private), Koehler House, 1900; Carl von Seutter, San Antonio, architect. Located on an imposing site that occupies a full city block, this Queen Anne house is built of light-colored rough-faced ashlar stone laid in random-width courses. It has a fanciful tower with a bell-shaped roof and abundant Free Classic details. Garlands decorate the cornice line of the porch, tower, and main

house. The Palladian window motif (a round-arched window with smaller rectangular ones to each side) is found in the dormer windows, the front door, and the door leading out onto the upstairs porch. Note the two balustrade patterns, checkerboard stone on the first floor and classic "bowling pin" balusters on the second floor. Above the front entry, the balustrade design incorporates a broken-ogee pediment.

102 East Lynnwood Avenue (private). This is a fine stucco-walled Tudor design. It has excellent cast-stone trim in the Tudor arch of the doorway, in the oriel window above, which has diamond-paned casement sashes, and around the other windows of the house. Note the front-facing gable that sweeps down over the porte cochere.

131 East King's Highway (private), Kampmann House, 1922; Henry T. Phelps, architect. The facade here seems a bit confusing stylistically because the nicely detailed Romanesque arch from an earlier, ca. 1890, Kampmann house has been skillfully incorporated into this later design.

114 East King's Highway (private), Reuter House, 1912. This is a striking design with an unusually creative combination of stylistic details. The basic form is the Neoclassical full-height entry porch with lower full-width porch, a subtype that is very common in Texas. But rather than the usual two-story column for the full-height porch, this unique design substitutes pilasters. The overhanging tile roof with

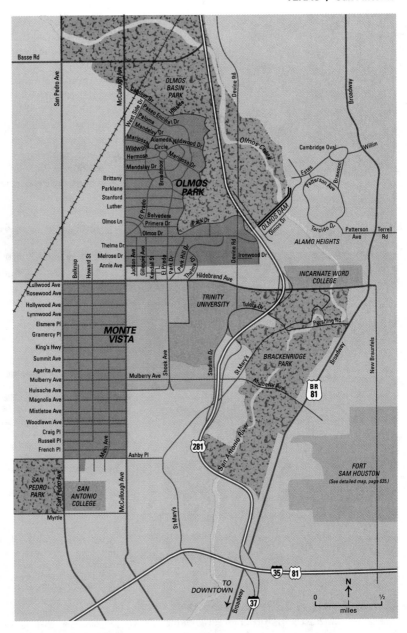

bracketed cornice details is of Italian Renaissance inspiration. The elegant colored-glass entry canopy is most often found in Beaux Arts–style houses. An imposing balustraded front terrace emphasizes the columned porches behind.

118 and 115 West King's Highway (both private). These two houses make an interesting contrast. Number 118 West King's Highway is a high-style Prairie design of the hipped-roof, asymmetrical subtype that is rather unusual in Texas. Note the pronounced white horizontal trim line located just below the upper-story windows. Number 115 West King's Highway is a more typical vernacular Prairie interpretation—with hipped-roof, symmetrical facade, and a conspic-

uous front entry. Note the geometric brick pattern in the columns and the paired brackets under the eaves, common features in this subtype.

108 West King's Highway (private). This is a fine early Tudor–Prairie mix. At first glance it looks like a Tudor house with the typical front-facing, half-timbered gable and a Tudor arch leading to the front door. Then one notices the Prairie influence in the heavy squared piers supporting the front porch and on each side of the bay window, the entry door with its geometric design, and also the horizontal geometric design on the front entry porch. (See "102 East Lynnwood," page 630, for a nearly pure Tudor design.)

Monte Vista

Olmos Park, 1927–ca. 1940s

This large, hilly tract north of Monte Vista bordered flood-prone Olmos Creek, which made it difficult to develop into homesites until the completion of the nearby Olmos Dam and other flood-control improvements in 1926. The next year, developer Herman Charles Thorman bought the 1,600-acre tract, platted it into large, restricted lots, and began marketing it as the most exclusive neighborhood in San Antonio. His restrictive covenants controlled both building materials and the minimum cost of houses. On Stanford Drive, for instance, "brick, brick veneer, rock stucco and hollow tile" were the only building materials al-

lowed. Lots were a minimum of seventy-five feet wide, and no house could cost less than $7,500, more than double that of the nearby Alamo Heights neighborhood to the east.

Olmos Park, not easily accessible by streetcar, was an automobile suburb, and its planners took full advantage of this fact. They laid out the streets in Olmstedian curving patterns that followed the contours of the hilly site. Sidewalks were eliminated. Native trees were retained and picturesque live oaks added. Olmos Park thus has quite a different flavor than the nearby, and only slightly earlier, northernmost sections of Monte Vista.

Most of Olmos Park's houses date from the late 1920s through the 1930s. The area remained an unincorporated town, just outside of San Antonio's city limits, until 1939, when it incorporated as an independent city, likely in an effort to avoid being annexed by San Antonio.

Among the many interesting homes in Olmos Park are:

300 Alameda Circle (private), Morgan House, 1929; Russell Brown Company, architects. This imposing dwelling is even larger than it looks, for it has about twenty thousand square feet of floor space. Its design is a melding of Italian Renaissance symmetry and round-arched first-floor windows with some Spanish Eclectic ironwork and detailing—a combination of styles that architects of the day appropriately called Mediterranean style. This hybrid combination was less common than either of its parental styles.

800 East Olmos Drive (private), Newton House, 1927; Atlee B. and Robert M. Ayres, San Antonio, architects. The same architects designed this and the Jones House (see the following entry) in the same year. Here an asymmetrical facade with informal massing and apparently random window placement, the lack of eave overhang in the entry tower roof, and the Spanish-influenced door surrounds all mark it as a Spanish Eclectic design.

810 East Olmos Drive (private), Jones House, 1927; Atlee B. and Robert M. Ayres, San Antonio, architects. Formal symmetry, a platform front porch with balustrade, and Classical columns at the front entrance all help to identify this as an Italian Renaissance–style house.

300 Paseo Encinal Drive (private), Negley House, 1929; George Louis Walling, Austin, architect. Old stone from a downtown store gives the walls of this Spanish Eclectic design a beautiful patina.

McNay Art Museum, 1928

6000 North New Braunfels Avenue; 210-824-5368; Atlee B. and Robert M. Ayres, San Antonio, architects.

This was originally the Spanish Eclectic home of Marion Koogler McNay, artist, art teacher, and daughter of a Kansas physician who made a fortune when his investments in local farmland became the sites of rich oil strikes. After her father's death, Mrs. McNay assembled a fine collection of nineteenth- and twentieth-

Olmos Park

century art. This included works by such French Post-impressionist masters as Gauguin, van Gogh, Toulouse-Lautrec, and Matisse. Mrs. McNay died in 1950 and left her twenty-four-room house and twenty-three-acre estate to become a museum for display of her personal art collection. Newer acquisitions have resulted in multiple expansions to the house beginning in 1970. In spite of this, the relatively unmodified original dwelling remains the focal point of the museum and still retains much of its residential feeling. The carefully landscaped grounds complete the spirit of a grand 1920s estate.

Of great architectural interest is the house's interior patio. This space and the house facades surrounding it are highly detailed and show almost every elaboration found in Spanish Eclectic designs. In the true Hispanic tradition, this interior patio provides all of the "circulation" for the house. Inside, the rooms open one into the other without adjacent hallways. In order to bypass a room, one must use the courtyard as a passageway.

Stand at the far end of the garden and look back at the original portions of the house to see how the architect re-created a typical feature of Spanish houses—

McNay Art Museum

growing in sections as families expanded or wealth increased. Here we see what looks like such a series of small additions, each with varying roof heights and shapes. Upstairs the exterior circulation is provided through what reads as a series of recessed "balconies," but actually these blend together into a long exterior hall. This articulation of the large house into smaller pieces gives something of the feeling of standing in the plaza of a village in Spain. There are two exterior stairways—one covered and one exposed. Two fountains and a Moorish water channel enrich the courtyard.

Wrought-iron light fixtures and fittings are used extensively in the courtyard and throughout the original portions of the house. Note the fine fixture hanging outside the dining room. Colorful Spanish-style tilework is used abundantly. Although inside the house most rooms have been converted to display galleries, happily the entry hall, living room, dining room, and powder room retain most of their original finishes. Beautiful tile floors, stenciled ceilings, and wrought-iron gates in between the main rooms give a feeling for the quality and detail of the original house, which is one of the nation's relatively few grand Spanish Eclectic houses that are accessible to the public.

Fort Sam Houston, 1876–1940s

San Antonio has been called "the army's hometown" and much of the city's rich military history is concentrated at this venerable post. The first U.S. troops arrived in 1845, when the independent Republic of Texas was annexed to become the nation's twenty-eighth state. The military detachment first rented downtown facilities for housing and supply storage, but after the Civil War the army began looking for a more permanent and secure location. As insurance against a possible army move elsewhere, in 1875 the city of San Antonio donated a ninety-three-acre site just outside the city. This was to become the nucleus of Fort Sam Houston, now one of the nation's oldest army posts still in active service. Through its history, Fort Sam (its local nickname) has played important roles in each of the nation's military conflicts. Teddy Roosevelt's Rough Riders organized and trained here before departing for Cuba during the Spanish-American War. Military aviation began here in 1910 when Lieutenant Benjamin Foulois piloted Army Aircraft Number 1, an early reconnaissance biplane built by the Wright brothers. One-fourth of all the American divisions that served in France during the First World War were organized and trained here—a total of over 112,000 soldiers. The Second World War brought a geometric increase in these numbers, as five of the nation's fifteen massive "armies"

headquartered and trained here before going overseas. In the decades since 1950 Fort Sam's principal role has been the training of medical personnel as home of the renowned Brooke Army Medical Center and related Academy of Health Sciences.

Fort Sam today has over nine hundred historic buildings located on 500 acres (out of a total size of 3,200 acres) that were designated a national historic landmark in 1975. These buildings provide a capsule summary of the major types of American military architecture built since the Civil War.

Most early army posts were designed with a large central parade ground and around this, or at least along one side, were built separate houses for married officers and their families as well as other residential and administrative buildings. Fort Sam Houston has three separate sections built in this pattern: the Staff Post (1881) was built to house the headquarters of the Army's Department of Texas; the Infantry Post (1885–1906) and the Cavalry and Light Artillery Post (1905–1911) added large bodies of resident combat troops to the original headquarters facilities. A later and larger section of officers' quarters is found in the New Post (1928 and later), which, following the dictates of a new 1926 Army Housing Program, more closely resembles the plan of civilian residential neighborhoods (see page 636).

When visiting, it is good to remember that this is a military installation, and, although an "open" one that is generally accessible for anyone to drive into freely, it is a good idea to keep an eye out for any type of military activity that may be taking place and to yield to it. The houses are all private homes, just as in any other neighborhood. There are three buildings open to the general public: the **Fort Sam Houston Museum** (210-221-0019); the **U.S. Army Medical Department Museum**; and the fortresslike, walled **Quadrangle** (1876), the fort's oldest structure, which originally served as a regional supply depot and headquarters of the Texas commanding general, as well as housing a small garrison of troops. It is built of local stone cut out of the city quarries (now Brackenridge Park's zoo and the Sunken Garden). Today the Quadrangle houses a museum shop, restrooms, and small zoo, in addition to administrative offices.

Staff Post, Staff Post Road, 1881; Alfred Giles, San Antonio, architect. Following army guidelines, local architect Giles (see also "Steves Homestead," page 629) produced three coordinated designs for officers' houses in the Italianate style as part of the first expansions of the post beyond the original Quadrangle. Once called the Lower Post, these fifteen houses were built of native limestone. The house at number 6 (private) is the largest and boasts a fash-

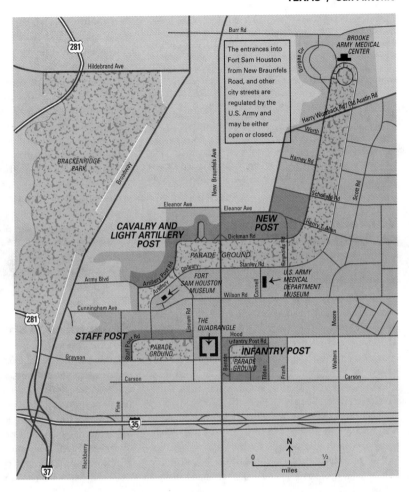

ionable turret. It was built for, and is still occupied by, the fort's highest-ranking officer, the commanding general. It is now called the Pershing House after General of the Armies John J. Pershing, commander of victorious American forces in the First World War. Pershing occupied the house in 1917 before departing for France with his troops. There are eight identical field-grade officers' quarters (numbers 1 to 4 and 8 to 11, all private). Built for majors and colonels (field-grade officers), these centered-gable-plan houses originally had hipped roofs and only a one-story porch. Two-story porches that wrapped around both sides of the house were added to them beginning in 1908 (see "Cavalry and Light Artillery Post," below). The third design is for the six company-grade officers' (lieutenants and captains) quarters (numbers 5, 7, and 12 to 15, all private) and are in matching asymmetrical designs.

Infantry Post (all private), entrance on New Braunfels Avenue, 1885–1906. Also known as the Upper Post, the officers' houses here are simple folk designs with low-pitched hipped roofs. They have two-level, full-width porches and full-length windows that open onto them. This part of Fort Sam had deteriorated considerably after the last infantry unit was housed here in 1941. But beginning in 1988, a long-term program of restoration was begun on the historic

quadrangle. The officers' quarters have been reroofed in the original standing-seam metal material after years of asphalt shingles. The 1885 Long Barracks, which defined the eastern boundary of the original parade ground, are also being restored to their early appearance.

Cavalry and Light Artillery Post (all private), Dickman Road west of New Braunfels Avenue, 1905–1911. The officers' houses here were built from the army quartermaster general's standard designs. Both the commanding officer's quarters (Building 167) and the field-grade officers' (majors and colonels) quarters (Building 104) have two-story porches wrapped around both sides. Three coordinating smaller designs were used for company-grade officers (lieutenants and captains). Some of these are built of yellow brick with gray slate roofs and others are of redbrick with red tile roofs. All five of these designs had two-level porches with the porch roofs supported by simple Classical columns. Some have Colonial Revival Palladian windows in their roof gables.

It is probably no accident that about the time that these newer officers' quarters were being built, the earlier senior officers' quarters on the Staff Post were updated with two-story wraparound porches. These, happily, were built with appropriate Italianate-style porch supports.

New Post (all private), Dickman Road east of New Braun-fels Avenue, 1928 and later. In 1926 a new Army Housing Program was adopted that had several goals. One of these was the creation of more picturesque planned housing communities on military posts. Another was establishing appropriate architectural styles for use in different parts of the country. For San Antonio, the Spanish Eclectic style was chosen and large sections of Fort Sam Houston were then developed in the Spanish idiom. Included were more than three hundred houses of several different sizes, as well as related barracks and community buildings. The division commander's quarters, built in 1934, is quite grand on its central site at the curve of the enormous adjacent parade ground, which was filled with troops in training during the Second World War.

Yturri-Edmunds House, ca. 1840 and 1860

257 Yellowstone, at Mission Road; 210-534-8237.
Originally part of the fields of Mission Concepcion, this land was assigned to Manuel Yturri-Castillo when the mission was secularized in 1824. The house, a typical side-gabled folk form with a full-width front porch, was built around 1840 with additions in about 1860. The house and property were later given to Yturri's daughter, Vincenta Edmunds, as a wedding gift. Later it passed to Vincenta's daughter, Ernestine Edmunds, who bequeathed the historic dwelling to the San Antonio Conservation Society in 1961.

This house is constructed with adobe walls, making it an uncommon survivor in this part of Texas, where many early folk houses look like adobe construction but are actually of stuccoed stone or brick. Like many folk houses, this one was gradually expanded from a two-room house to three large front rooms: music room, parlor, and bedroom. Later the rear addition of kitchen and schoolroom was added. The latter was used by Vincenta to teach local children in the late nineteenth century. She and her daughter both were dedicated educators and became strong advocates for public education in San Antonio.

The grounds are spacious and feature many native plants. A small mill behind the house has been mostly rebuilt and can again grind grain. An unusual feature of the house is that it is built across a small acequia (irrigation ditch) that was part of the mission's pre-1800 irrigation system. This was discovered during excavations for restoring the mill.

Most of the furnishings are family pieces, and the paintings were done by Ernestine herself. Occupied by members of the same family throughout its long history, the dwelling has a still-lived-in character that is rare in museum houses. You can almost feel the students sitting at the piano and working in the small classroom.

Sebastopol, 1854

704 Zorn Street, Seguin, Texas; 830-379-4833.
Located on the scenic Guadalupe River twenty-eight miles east of San Antonio, Seguin is an agricultural and trade center (not shown on map; 1990 population of nineteen thousand) that was founded in the Republic of Texas era. Today a prosperous small city, it has added light manufacturing and servicing the local oil industry onto these original functions, which it also still serves. Seguin's principal architectural attraction is this remarkable Greek Revival museum house.

Yturri-Edmunds House

Sebastopol

Seguin is sited upon coarse gravel deposits adjacent to the spring-fed Guadalupe River. Mixed with the gravels are smaller quantities of fine sand and lime-containing soil. This naturally occurring mixture, when added to water in the proper proportions, hardens into a massive, concretelike building material. The town's early settlers were quick to take advantage of this rare good fortune and built many fences, houses, and even commercial buildings with "limecrete" walls.

Several of these early structures survive, the most important of which is this fine Greek Revival dwelling, built in an unusual T-shape plan. With only four principal rooms on the main floor, the house is smaller inside than its imposing appearance suggests. It is of architectural interest because of its unusual shape and its rare limecrete wall construction technique that is illustrated and explained in detail. A few important pieces of early furniture are also on display.

SAN AUGUSTINE

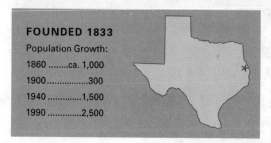

FOUNDED 1833
Population Growth:
1860 ....ca. 1,000
1900 300
1940 1,500
1990 2,500

Located near the Louisiana border in the pine forests of eastern Texas, this settlement was founded at the site of one of several missions established in the region during the early 1700s to discourage French incursions into Spanish Texas (see page xi). The missions themselves had all been abandoned by the 1770s, but they left a more permanent legacy in the early wagon road that connected them with distant San Antonio to the west, the site of Spain's most successful missionary efforts in Texas (see page 622). Spain dealt harshly with foreigners attempting to enter its territory, but after Mexican independence in 1821 the Old San Antonio Road (closely followed by today's Texas Highway 21) became an important route by which Anglo settlers traveled to and from *empresario* Steven F. Austin's large agricultural colony established farther west in 1823 by authority of the Mexican government (see page xii and figure 1, page x). Similar authority for a colony of Anglo immigrants in the San Augustine area was given the same year to another Anglo land developer named Haden Edwards, but his plans were quickly thwarted by the ob-

jections of scattered Mexican nationals who already occupied the region. Soon, however, the eastern San Antonio Road area was receiving a steady influx of unauthorized Anglo squatters. In 1833, with talk of Anglo independence from Mexico in the air, a group of these organized the new town of San Augustine. After Texas independence three years later it became an important early commercial center as well as a principal gateway to the new Republic of Texas, which encouraged further immigration with a generous policy of land grants.

San Augustine's boom was to be short-lived. Anglo immigration surged even more after Texas became a state in 1845, but much of this flow followed new travel routes that were more convenient than the Old San Antonio Road. San Augustine soon became an out-of-the-way county seat and local trade center that today retains some fine antebellum houses and churches.

Historic Core, 1830s–ca. 1940

In 1890 San Augustine suffered a disastrous fire that destroyed its early commercial district and many nearby houses. Fortunately, many of the town's east-side residential blocks escaped the fire, and scattered there today, among younger dwellings, and also along nearby rural roads, are more than a dozen surviving houses built before 1860. Some are simple folk dwellings, and several have had later modifications. A few retain modest to elaborate Greek Revival detailing. Among the most important of the latter are the three houses dis-

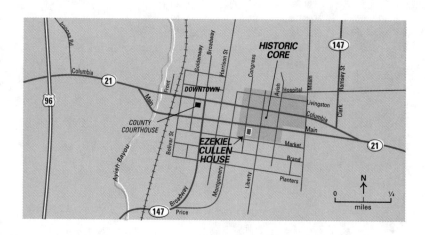

San Augustine Historic Core

cussed here, all completed in 1839 by architect-builder Augustus Phelps. Little appears to be known about Phelps beyond that he was originally from Brandon, Vermont, and came to San Augustine from Philadelphia in 1838 at the age of twenty-four. Over the next two years he left the frontier town with several Greek Revival designs of rare sophistication before departing for Texas's newly founded capital of Austin, where he died in 1841 while working on plans for the new capitol building.

912 Main Street (private), Cartwright House, 1839; Augustus Phelps, San Augustine, architect. This amazingly sophisticated Greek Revival design is a textbook example of the two-story-with-one-story-entry-porch subtype of the style, which was most common in the northeastern states (see figure 9, page xxii). It was originally built for Isaac Campbell, one of the committee that chose the site for Austin, the Texas Republic's new capital city. In 1847 the house was acquired by Campbell's brother-in-law Matthew Cartwright, a prominent local merchant and real estate investor whose descendants still occupy the house. Several early outbuildings survive on the grounds.

501 East Columbia Street (private), Blount House, 1839; Augustus Phelps, San Augustine, architect. This house further illustrates Phelps's versatility as a designer. A one-story-with-full-height-entry-porch plan, it features a wide cornice decorated with hand-carved triglyphs and an arched doorway with a fanlight borrowed from the Early Classical Revival style, as in the Ezekiel Cullen House (see below). The recessed side wings are later additions. The house was built for the Georgia-born local merchant Stephen W. Blount, one of the signers of the 1836 Texas Declaration of Independence.

507 Congress Street (private), Sharp House, ca. 1850. This is a more typical Texas example of an antebellum

Greek Revival house. A characteristic Greek Revival door surround and a porch with a wider-than-average cornice and square "columns" adorn what is otherwise a simple center-hall folk house. The house has been moved here from its original nearby site.

Ezekiel Cullen House, 1839

205 South Congress Street; 409-275-3610;
Augustus Phelps, San Augustine, architect.
The most strictly Classical of the three Phelps-designed dwellings is this large, one-story structure with a heroic front gable accented by a large fanlight in the manner of the Jefferson-inspired Early Classical Revival houses popular in Virginia several decades earlier (the wing at the left is a later addition). The house was built for a Georgia-trained lawyer who became a prominent

Ezekiel Cullen House

judge and civic leader of Anglo Texas. In 1953 it was carefully restored for the local chapter of the Daughters of the Republic of Texas by pioneering preservation architect Raiford Stripling (born 1910), a San Augustine native and resident. The Daughters, who open the historic dwelling to visitors several afternoons a week, have furnished the interior with an eclectic mixture of antique pieces. One room is devoted to portraits painted by artist Seymour Thomas, a San Augustine native. The most striking interior feature is a huge attic ballroom with a coved ceiling and matching front and rear fanlights at each end.

Utah

MANTI

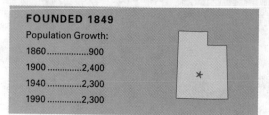

This was the earliest in a series of towns founded by Brigham Young in the Sanpete Valley, about seventy-five miles south of Salt Lake City, soon after he led the Mormons' heroic 1846 trek to their wilderness Zion (see page xix). Although Salt Lake City was planned to be the principal urban center of Young's new Territory of Deseret, he lost no time in sending carefully organized groups of settlers to found additional towns wherever fertile soils occurred on the desert flats adjacent to one of the region's numerous mountain ranges. There the industrious colonists followed the lead of their Salt Lake brethren by building small dams across the nearby mountain streams. These trapped the abundant springtime flow from melting snow to create reservoirs that, by means of carefully constructed irrigation canals, ditches, and gates, provided a summer's worth of water to convert the nearby desert into a verdant agricultural oasis. By 1860 there were 150 of these self-sustaining farming communities, which radiated from Salt Lake City throughout Utah and into adjacent Idaho, Wyoming, Colorado, Arizona, and Nevada. By 1900 their number had grown to more than 500 and constituted one of the most successful attempts at large-scale, planned urbanization in all of modern history. Even more remarkable, most of these towns still exist, although usually with only faint traces of the original Mormon town-planning policies from which they arose. Manti, and some of its neighbors in the relatively isolated Sanpete Valley, are among the few that provide more than a glimpse of the Mormons' remarkable planning skills.

Brigham Young, himself a skilled carpenter-builder, carefully selected the initial settlers who were "called" by the church to found a town. These included not only farmers experienced in the complexities of irrigated agriculture, but also craftsmen familiar with the building trades—masons, bricklayers, carpenters, joiners, glaziers—as well as artisans such as blacksmiths, millers, saddlers, wheelwrights, coopers, and tinsmiths to help make the isolated communities independent of long-distance wagon transport for everyday necessities.

Leaving as little as possible to chance, Young assigned these initial settlers to carefully prechosen sites and gave detailed instructions on laying out the town site and its buildings. The plans followed the well-known practice of using square blocks arranged in a rectangular grid of streets oriented north–south and east–west, but differed in having unusually wide streets, typically one hundred feet or more, which allowed room for streetside irrigation ditches, sheltering rows of tall poplar trees, sidewalks, and a generous roadway that was wide enough for U-turns with horse and wagon.

These towns also differed from their non-Mormon counterparts in a more fundamental way. Most American farmers and ranchers at that time, as still today, lived in widely separated houses located on the lands they worked. Mormon agriculturists, in contrast, lived in compact towns and commuted to work in the surrounding fields. This undoubtedly related to the close interweaving of all aspects of Mormon life—religious,

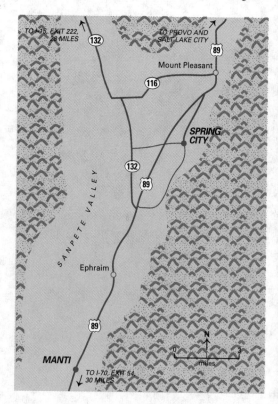

social, and economic—but was probably also a response to decades of persecution, when only nearby neighbors could quickly unite for mutual defense.

The division of the town blocks into building sites reflected the agricultural work patterns of its inhabitants. In newly established towns, where nearly everyone spent at least part-time in the fields, the first houses were built at the four corners of each large, square block (see illustration, page 644). This not only put four families in close proximity, but also gave each a one-acre town lot with room for kitchen gardens, fruit trees, poultry yards, and small outbuildings for horses, wagons, milk cows, and farming equipment. As the towns grew and required more nonfarming workers, these original core blocks, now usually closest to the commercial district, could be subdivided for additional housing while farming families moved to four-lot perimeter blocks closer to the surrounding fields. The nearby fields were, in turn, platted into still more town blocks as the community grew. Much of the charm of Manti and its Sanpete Valley neighbors lies in the fact that they have remained small towns—the largest now has a population of only 3,500—in which some of this distinctive planning pattern is still evident.

Joseph Smith, the founder of Mormonism, always stressed the importance of filling new towns with substantial, permanent buildings built of brick or stone. Brigham Young continued this admonition and added his own personal favorite—sun-dried adobe bricks, which are relatively simple to make and, when covered with a protective layer of plaster, are as durable in the dry Utah climate as are hard-fired bricks and stone. The first permanent Mormon dwellings in Utah were substantial folk houses built of these materials. Most had simple, side-gabled shapes and one-room depths that harked back to the New England and midwestern origins of the Mormon pioneers. Only a handful of unmodified examples of these earliest dwellings survives in the Sanpete Valley. Many others, however, can be recognized as the nucleus of an expanded or stylistically updated house, for, even with increasing prosperity, the thrifty Mormons usually preferred to modify a well-constructed existing dwelling rather than demolish it and build anew.

Manti Temple

Manti, the oldest Sanpete settlement, is located at the southern end of the valley and was planned to be both an agricultural town and the region's religious center, functions that it still serves. In buildings designed for worship, as with houses, the Mormon leaders stressed the importance of constructing with solid masonry

Manti Temple in the final stages of construction, ca. 1887; note the typical Mormon dwellings in the foreground.

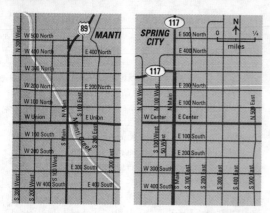

designed to endure for centuries. Among the most impressive of these structures is the Manti Temple, completed in 1888 on a hilltop site that allows it to dominate the lower Sanpete Valley with all the dramatic impact of the great Medieval cathedrals of Europe.

Temples are one of three principal building types used in Mormon worship. Most widespread are meetinghouses, used by local congregations both for regular worship services and for important civic and educational meetings. Serving the same functions on a larger scale are tabernacles, mostly designed for the regional meetings of many assembled congregations. Least common are the temples, such as the one at Manti. These are not used for regular worship but are reserved for occasional rites of special religious significance in Mormon life. Among these are baptisms, weddings, and ordinances, as well as other ceremonies unique to Mormonism. All of Utah's Mormons are served by only four such temples. The other three are located at Temple Square in Salt Lake City, Logan in northern Utah, and St. George in the southwestern corner of the state.

Manti and Spring City Street Names

The typical Mormon system for naming streets can be confusing and requires some explanation. Street signs typically display 100, 200, 300, and so on. Yet in conversation, people often refer to "First," "Second," and "Third Streets." Street 100 converts to "First Street," 200 to "Second Street," and so forth. Next, to make it even more complicated, many of the old Mormon towns have *four* separate streets with the same numerical name. In both Manti and Spring City this is the case. In Spring City the two primary cross streets are not numbered but are called Main Street and Center Street. Just one block away from the intersection of these two streets is 100 South Street, 100 East Street, 100 West Street, and 100 North Street (see maps above). Each of these streets is modified with another "North," "South," "East," or "West" to indicate the quadrant it is in. For ex-

ample, there is both a North 100 West Street and a South 100 West Street.

An additional complication arises from the fact that few of the houses have street addresses, which can make locating an individual structure all but impossible. We've attempted location descriptions for the houses discussed, but if some of these don't seem to work, we suggest reading the principles mentioned and then exploring for other houses that illustrate them—there are many.

Manti Town Planning

Amid overseeing uniform town planning, encouraging permanent construction methods, directing the building of complex irrigation systems, and countless other tasks, Brigham Young was also concerned that his new towns be pleasing to the eye. Planting trees in the barren desert landscape was one way to achieve this. Roadside rows of European poplar trees were encouraged, both for their stately appearance and to relieve the harshness of the desert sun. Some of these are still evident in parts of Manti. The approach from the north along U.S. Highway 89 is particularly dramatic—the handsome temple dominates the hill and poplars line the highway, both suggestive of entering a cathedral town somewhere in rural France.

Many years of prosperity and later infill make it more difficult to discern Manti's original Mormon building pattern of large blocks with dominant corner houses than is the case in the smaller nearby village of

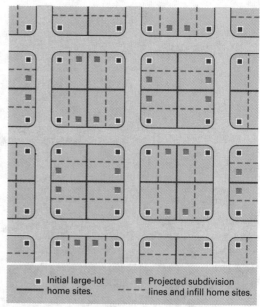

| ■ Initial large-lot | ■ Projected subdivision |
| home sites. | lines and infill home sites. |

Typical Mormon Town Plan

Manti

Spring City (see below). Two areas of Manti that do illustrate traces of its early planning are:

Intersection of North 200 (Second) West Street and West 300 (Third) North Street (all private). Here three early stone houses are located on adjacent corners of their large lots. This gives a feeling for how the early built-up street intersections must have looked. The closeness of the houses gives a sense of neighborhood. Imagine the difference in feeling if each house was instead placed near the center of its large, quarter-block lot. Number 203 North 200 (Second) West Street is a side-gabled folk house with an added center gable. It has three bays (ranks of windows). Directly across North 200 (Second) West Street from 203 is the simplest of the three houses, a gabled-front-and-wing folk dwelling that is two stories tall. Across the side street West 300 (Third) North Street from 203 is another three-bay house, this much more elaborate, with a hipped roof and two favorite Mormon features—three Gothic Revival through-the-cornice wall dormers and a second-story door over the main entrance that leads outward to nothing but open space (see "80 West 300 North Street," page 650).

Main Street South between 200 (Second) South Street and 600 (Sixth) South Street (all private). Along this stretch of South Main almost every corner has a substantial brick, stone, or stucco house; even the later infill dwellings between many of these can't detract from the strong rhythm of the dominant early corner houses. Some are folk houses with occasional stylish touches added; others are styled houses. One of the grander of these is the Crawford House, 1889, a large Queen Anne structure at the southwest corner of 200 (Second) South Street and Main Street South.

Spring City, 1850s and later

Spring City, located eighteen miles to the north and somewhat off the main Sanpete Valley highway, has experienced far less growth than Manti and retains much of its large-block/corner-house Mormon development pattern. The majority of Spring City's dwellings are folk houses, mostly of side-gabled or gable-front-and-wing shape, and are constructed of brick, stone, or stuccoed adobe brick. A few have Victorian-era detailing added. (Note the section on street names in Manti and Spring City [see page 644] before touring Spring City.) Instructive examples include:

218 Main Street South (private). This story-and-a-half brick house of gable-front-and-wing shape has wonderful Victorian detailing. This is most evident in the wing section, where a two-story bay window has a triangular cutaway under the eaves ornamented with Stick-style trusses. The lower part of the bay window is topped by a Stick-style shed roof with trusswork supports. The other windows in this wing are crowned with a unique combination of brick detailing—a typical Italianate segmental-arched window has a brick imitation of a Gothic Revival drip mold above it. The gabled-front section shows less ornament in the brickwork but has two patterns of cut wood shingles in the gabled end. This could have been built in the configuration you see today, or it could have been an original side-gabled house to which the more elaborate wing was later added and cut shingles added in the original gabled end to tie the two parts together. Many gabled-front-and-wing homes began with an original gabled house to which a wing was added later, a favored way of expanding and updating early folk houses.

112 East 200 (Second) South Street (private). This house sits on a large-lot block with multiple agricultural buildings in the center, some belonging to it and some to its neighbors. The house is a fine example of the tendency to build folk houses in stages. The main one-and-a-half-story gabled-front-and-wing house is easy to pick out. To this was added a one-story side-gabled addition adjacent to the gabled front; this addition then had its own addition—a shed section that extends out a few feet beyond the front face of the

Spring City

main house. Yet-another addition, of concrete block, was made behind the wing section. For yet-another possible episode of change and addition to this house, note that the windows in the gabled-front section and in the gabled end of the wing section do not match. This may mean that even the basic gabled-front-and-wing house was built as a composite structure in the way mentioned in the description of 218 Main Street South (see the preceding entry).

East 100 (First) North Street and Main Street North, northeast corner (private), Beck House, 1883 and later; Isaac A. Behunin, builder. The main block of this limestone house (which faces Main Street) is a two-story, hall-and-parlor form elaborated with three gable-topped wall dormers across the front; these represent a Gothic Revival influence seen in many Utah houses. To the rear of this main block is an original T-shaped extension that contains the dining room, kitchen, and office. There is a second entrance to this part of the house that faces East 100 (First) North Street. Although here the T-extension is thought to be original, in many similar houses such extensions are additions.

West 400 (Fourth) South Street at South 100 West Street (private), Johnson House, ca. 1872; additions, 1892. This house, considered by many to be the most ornate in Spring City, demonstrates another way thrifty Mormons expanded their original side-gabled houses. Here the original 1872 side-gabled house faces West 400 (Fourth) South Street. It is built of cut stone lined with adobe for insulation. A large Queen Anne–style addition was annexed behind in about 1892. This changed the main entrance to South 100 West Street. At the same time, the entire home—consisting of the original folk house and the stylish addition—was stuccoed and scored to look like stone. The small stone building that housed the office and courtroom of the builder, Judge Jacob Johnson, still remains on the site, as does a stone barn and granary.

SALT LAKE CITY

FOUNDED 1847

Population Growth:

1860 10,000

1900 54,000

1940 150,000

1990 160,000

Salt Lake City is unique in the annals of American urbanization. Founded in a remote and inhospitable wilderness as a haven from religious persecution, it became an instant city as Mormons from the northeastern and midwestern states flocked to their new Zion (see also page xix). More than 1,700 of the faithful followed leader Brigham Young on the initial thousand-mile trek from Illinois. By 1860, almost a decade before the arrival of the railroads, Salt Lake City's 10,000 inhabitants made it the largest urban center in the entire interior West.

Prosperous Salt Lake City was a natural magnet for the early western railroad builders—the famous "golden spike" that completed the first transcontinental rail line in 1869 was driven at Promontory Point, only sixty-five miles north of the city. The arrival of the railroads was to have a profound effect on the formerly isolated agricultural empire of the Mormons, which

had spread to occupy much of Utah and parts of the adjacent states. Mormon leaders were opposed to large-scale commercial mining, believing its boom-and-bust temporary towns and transient male workers were a threat to the stable, family-based prosperity provided by agriculture. Despite their opposition, with the railroads came non-Mormon prospectors, miners, and industrialists to tap the hitherto inaccessible mineral wealth of the area. Some rich strikes were made in the mountains near Salt Lake City, and by 1880 the town's Main Street was described as "one large mining camp."

Mining also brought concentrated wealth, and by the 1870s Salt Lake City's commercial life was dominated by non-Mormon entrepreneurs. The city and state governments, on the other hand, were controlled by the far more numerous Mormons. This led to two decades of intense political conflict, but by the mid-1890s, compromises on both sides had paved the way for a future of peaceful coexistence between the Mormon majority and their non-Mormon neighbors.

Modern Salt Lake City remains the financial and trade center for a rich hinterland of irrigated farming and mining. The town also has a long history as a manufacturing center. Seeking self-sufficiency for his isolated Zion, Brigham Young encouraged the establishment of woolen mills, iron foundries, shoe and

Salt Lake City in the 1860s

clothing factories, and other basic industries in the early town. Much later, the Second World War brought the city a surge of larger-scale factories, the most important of which was a Remington small-arms plant that employed ten thousand people. Today Salt Lake City is a major industrial center dominated by ore processing and oil refining.

Throughout a century and a half of growth and change, Salt Lake City has steadily fulfilled the central theme of its Mormon founder's remarkable vision. Today it is the spiritual capital for 4 million followers of the Church of Jesus Christ of Latter-day Saints, the official name for the Mormon Church, which is now one of the nation's largest faiths. The principal architectural shrines of Mormonism are concentrated in parklike **Temple Square** (Main and Temple Streets, 801-240-2534). Among these is the extraordinary 1867 **Tabernacle,** a seven-thousand-seat, 250-foot-long oval auditorium roofed with giant wooden arches that eliminate the usual supporting columns. Boasting superb acoustics, the structure is a marvel of early building technology.

Salt Lake City itself has increased only slightly in population during the decades since 1940 and thus might be expected to retain much of its earlier architectural heritage. Unfortunately, this is not the case, for the city's relative stability was accompanied by explosive growth in the surrounding suburban towns served by the central city. In 1950 70 percent of the population of Salt Lake County lived in Salt Lake City;

in 1990 only 22 percent of the county's 725,000 people resided there.

As a result of this expansion, very few structures remain from the large prerailroad town of the 1850s and 1860s. More survive from the late-Victorian decades, including many grand mansions that reflect both the city's mining-based prosperity and the Mormon emphasis on long-lasting walls of stone or brick. The latter is also evident throughout its early residential neighborhoods, which are dominated by masonry-walled dwellings. The three most important of these neighborhoods—South Temple Street (see page 651), Capitol Hill (see page 649), and the Avenues (see page 653)—are now well-preserved historic districts. In addition, three grand early dwellings, including Brigham Young's own home (see the following entry), offer varying degrees of public access.

Beehive House, 1854

67 East South Temple Street; 801-240-2671;
Truman O. Angell, Salt Lake City, architect.
This was the principal home of Brigham Young (1801–1877), the second president of the Church of Jesus Christ of Latter-day Saints and first governor of the Territory of Deseret (now the state of Utah). Completed only eight years after the Mormons' long trek into the desert wilderness, Brigham Young, himself a skilled carpenter, worked with Angell, the official church architect, in planning the large structure as an all-purpose headquarters. Here the Mormon leader

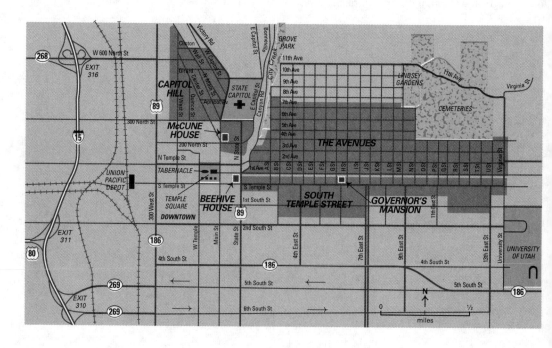

Beehive House

performed his church and state duties as well as raised much of his large family. The house was named for the carved beehive that sits atop its cupola, a Mormon symbol for the industrious cooperative work advocated by its leaders.

Brigham Young grew up in New England, and the core of his home looks like a typical northeastern Greek Revival house with a cupola and widow's walk. This was as useful for spotting travelers on the barren Utah desert as for looking out to sea for arriving ships in New England. The house has, however, two distinctly non–New England features. It is built of Spanish-style adobe bricks, a building technique much favored by Brigham Young for its practical simplicity in the dry desert climate, and it has a two-story, full-facade porch (which also wraps around one side of the house), a feature common only in southern Greek Revival designs.

After Young's death, the Beehive House was purchased by a son who added a large rear addition in 1888. This faced the side street, adding a large side entrance and more space for official entertaining. Later, the house was converted to a home for young women who came to Salt Lake City seeking work. It was restored by the church, guided by the architect's original plans, as a museum house in 1959. The original handcrafted interior detailing was uncovered or reproduced

and, after completion, Young's descendants returned many of the home's original furnishings. Tours begin in Young's large office next door and continue in the Beehive House, where guides offer informed explanations of the family's living arrangements and the functions of the house's many rooms. Among these is the Fairy Castle, a small room at the top of the stairs where a window allowed the children to watch as guests arrived for official functions.

Capitol Hill, ca. 1850s–1940

The Capitol Hill Historic District begins just two blocks north of Temple Square and surrounds the imposing State Capitol Building on the south and west. A remarkably intact near-downtown neighborhood dominated by early dwellings of all sizes, it has probably survived because its hilly terrain and small lots made it an undesirable target for expanding the downtown commercial district.

Capitol Hill has two contrasting subdistricts. Heber's Bench, named after an early Mormon leader, is a small area of large homes on the south-facing slope in front of the capitol. The larger Marmalade subdistrict is a tightly packed neighborhood of smaller working-class homes located on the slopes west of the capitol. This subdistrict takes its name from its street's early names, which commemorated fruits favored by the early settlers—Plum, Peach, Quince, Almond, Apricot, and Currant.

Settlement of the Marmalade area began shortly after Salt Lake City was founded, and some of its early folk houses still miraculously survive, although usually with alterations and additions accumulated over the years. A good example is:

Capitol Hill

80 West 300 North Street (private), Beesley House, ca. 1860s and later. The original two-story portion of this house was built with typical southwestern walls of adobe brick covered by a coat of plaster. In shape, however, it is a typical one-room-deep I-house, the form favored, although with wooden-framed walls, throughout the midwestern states that supplied most of the early Mormon settlers. Behind the original I-house is a one-and-a-half-story rectangular addition, and there is also a third one-story section behind. Note the anomalous upstairs door on the original I-house. These are found on many Utah folk houses, and their function is unclear. Theories include that they were meant to lead to later porch or balcony expansions, or that they facilitated furniture moving, or rug shaking, or even quick escapes.

390 Center Street (private), Jonasson House, 1872. This is an adobe folk form somewhat similar to the Beesley House (see the preceding entry) in shape but with fine Gothic Revival detailing (decorated vergeboard, quoins, and bay window) on its gable end.

355 Quince Street (private), Quayle House, ca. 1885. This Gothic Revival design is one of the most highly styled dwellings now in the Marmalade subdistrict. It was originally built as a downtown rental property and moved to Quince Street in 1975.

93 East 200 (Second) North Street (private), Woodruff House, 1906; Headlund and Wood, architects. Many only slightly less grand dwellings share the small Heber's Bench subdistrict with the McCune House (see the following entry). Among these is this three-story design, partially built into the side of a hill. It is an unusual interpretation of the Italian Renaissance style. The house's brickwork is unusually fine, particularly the corner pilasters and the multipaneled chimney. Note the very unusual coffered-ceiling motif ornamenting the underside of the roof overhang.

McCune House, 1901

200 North Main Street; 801-533-0858; access limited (see page 651); S. C. Dallas, Salt Lake City, architect.
The larger, styled houses in the Heber's Bench subdistrict of Capitol Hill have generally replaced more modest earlier dwellings. The grandest of these replacements is this superb structure built on the site of two smaller houses. Alfred W. McCune was born in Calcutta, India, to British Colonial parents who later became Mormon converts and immigrated to a Utah farm. Young Alfred apparently adapted very quickly to his new homeland, for by age twenty-one he was already contracting to build parts of the new Utah and Southern Railroad. He ultimately made a large fortune as a railroad contractor, a mining investor, and the owner of the Salt Lake City trolley system.

Described by their architect as "persons of innate refinement, highly developed artistic tastes, and definite ideas," McCune and his wife, Elizabeth, spared no expense in making their house a showplace of understated elegance. As but one example, they began by sending the architect on a two-year study tour to the northeastern states and Europe to gather ideas and materials for their house. The result was worth the effort,

McCune House

them the decorative second-floor tripartite window and the bronze porch entry gates with finely crafted metalwork above.

The McCunes moved to southern California in 1920, leaving their remarkable house to the Mormon Church, which used it as an educational center for many years. It was restored by a private purchaser in 1973 and is now a private conference center. Although no original furnishings remain, the lavishly detailed interior finishes and fixtures are remarkably intact. Small-group tours of the interior can be arranged by advance reservation through the Utah Heritage Foundation, 801-533-0858.

for Dallas and his clients produced a structure of rare unity and individuality.

The powerful exterior, with lower walls of dark red-brick accented by brown stone trim, is best described as a Shingle-style design without wooden shingles. Instead of these, Dallas substituted handsome red-brown tiles from Holland, which serve to unify the steeply pitched roof and upper walls, thus achieving the most characteristic design feature of the Shingle style using ceramic tiles rather than wooden shingles. The facade has many unusually fine architectural details, among

South Temple Street, 1850s–1930s

The South Temple Street Historic District includes the entire two-mile eastern length of South Temple Street, from near Beehive House to the hillside University of Utah campus on the east. South Temple's role as Utah's most distinguished residential street began when Brigham Young chose it as the location of his own home, Beehive House, completed in 1854 (see page 648). By the early twentieth century the street was lined with grand mansions designed by the region's finest architects and financed primarily by the profits of Utah's rich silver and copper mines. Although many of these have now been replaced by commercial, institutional, and apartment buildings, particularly in the near-downtown western blocks, enough houses remain to give a sense of the street's original opulence. Styles range from unusually elaborate late-Victorian Queen Anne and Shingle designs to a wide range of Eclectic-era fashions, among them Neoclassical, Italian Renaissance, Colonial Revival, and Prairie. Immediately adjacent and parallel to South Temple is First South Street, which had many similarly grand mansions and is included here as part of the district.

678 East South Temple Street (private), Kahn House, 1890; Henry Manheim, architect. This exceptional Queen Anne design emphasizes fan-pattern ornament. This motif appears as an open fan in the gable of the entry porch, as lines of half-open fans in the frieze surrounding the front porch, in the cresting on top of the front porch, and ornamenting the curved cornice at the roofline. Most of the windows in the house feature a large pane bounded by smaller panes, a typical Queen Anne pattern usually seen only in a house's most prominent windows.

808 East South Temple (private), Downey House, 1893; Frederick A. Hale, architect. This large, cross-gabled-roof Shingle-style dwelling has been lovingly restored—its original weathered-wood shingles, laid in intricate patterns, were once covered with paint. Both the side and the front facades have different shapes of shingles laid in varying patterns. Note the straight shingles laid in a wavy pattern on the gables, the fish-scale shingles surrounding the recessed Palladian window on the front, and the triple row of shingles outlining the round arch over this window. Also of interest are the belt course, made of alternating swirls of shingles in wood frames; the great tower with its S-curve roof; and the entry with its paired doors and large fanlight above. The carriage house and the house next door are also in the Shingle style.

574 East 100 (First) South Street (private), Salisbury House, 1898; Frederick Hale, architect. This early Neoclassical design is built of rough-faced stone with an amazing profusion of garlands in the triangular porch pediment and along its cornice. Also notable are the exaggerated pediment over the front door and distinctive cut-glass transoms over the windows. New additions have been made to accommodate its use as a funeral home.

667 East 100 (First) South Street (private), Armstrong House, 1893; William Ward, architect. This patterned-brick Queen Anne example has fine detailing that includes a diamond-shaped brick pattern at the cornice line and a curved wall at the corner of the house with a small narrow tower inset above.

1172 East 100 (First) South Street (private), Nelden House, 1894; Frederick Hale, architect. This is a good example of the early Colonial Revival, with its curved one-story front porch, hipped roof, and pair of dormers with broken-ogee pediments. A pair of one-story Prairie cottages is directly across the street. Relatively rare elsewhere in the country, similar cottages abound in Salt Lake City's early-twentieth-century neighborhoods. Note how the elaborate

South Temple Street

brickwork emphasizes the horizontal lines in these two examples.

1265 East 100 (First) South Street (private), Neuhausen House, 1901; Carl Neuhausen, Salt Lake City, architect. The architect's own home features an unusual Flemish Baroque parapet on the dominant front-facing gable.

Utah Governor's Mansion

Utah Governor's Mansion, 1902

603 East South Temple Street; 801-538-1005;
Carl Neuhausen, Salt Lake City, architect.

South Temple Street's grandest survivor is this elegant stone dwelling originally built for Thomas Kearns and his wife, Jennie Judge Kearns. The exterior of the house is of mixed-French inspiration with elaborate architectural detailing. Beaux Arts influence is evident in the floral details along the cornice and around the triple arch as well as in second-floor oval windows surrounded by cartouches and draped with garlands. Chateauesque features include the paired "candle-snuffer" towers and the elaborate central wall dormer.

Kearns, who arrived penniless in Utah at the age of seventeen, became a partner in the Silver King Mining Company, which produced his great wealth. He later became a U.S. senator and publisher of the *Salt Lake Tribune*. In 1937, twenty years after Kearns's death, his wife deeded this mansion to the state of Utah for use as the Governor's Mansion.

This use was abandoned in 1957, when the new Gov-

ernor's Mansion was built, and the Kearns' house became headquarters for the Utah Historical Society. In 1977 Utah governor Scott Matheson persuaded the legislature to restore the house to serve as the Governor's Mansion once again. A recent fire precipitated yet another extensive restoration.

The Avenues, 1860s–ca. 1930

The Avenues Historic District is a large (more than one hundred square blocks) residential area. It was developed from the late 1860s up to the 1920s as the city's principal neighborhood for middle-class homes. Examples from the earliest decades of this period have mostly been replaced or are now hidden under later additions and stylistic updates. Many dwellings representing a wide range of sizes and architectural styles still survive from the late-Victorian and early Eclectic decades. Modest Queen Anne and Craftsman designs are the most numerous.

Brigham Young's original plan for Salt Lake City laid out very large, ten-acre blocks and unusually broad streets. The Avenues district was the first to depart from that plan and has narrower streets and blocks of only two and a half acres. Each square block has houses built facing all four block faces. In general, the larger houses face the east–west numbered avenues and the smaller houses face the north–south "alphabet" streets. As would be expected, the blocks closer to downtown have had more intrusions (mainly institutions and large apartments) than those closer to the university on the east. Among the notable examples of the district's large concentration of smaller houses are:

1007 First Avenue (private). This is a fine, cross-gabled Shingle-style design featuring a tower with open balcony, a rough-stone basement story, and an unusual window pattern in the second story of the tower.

1037 First Avenue (private). Although in need of repair, this is a fine Queen Anne design of the hipped-roof-with-cross-gable shape. Note the exaggerated S-curve of the tower roof, the paired Classical columns set on brick pedestals, and the interesting ornament of windows in the front-facing gable—a cutaway bay above and a gable roof over the first-floor window (unfortunately, the window itself looks new).

Copperton, ca. 1925–1940

The small town of Copperton (not shown on map; 1990 population of eight hundred) is located southwest of Salt Lake City (about eight miles south on Interstate 15, then about nine miles west on Utah Highway 48, the Old Bingham Road). It is an excellent example of a planned company town, built for the employees of Utah Copper Company primarily between 1926 and 1941. Designed as a model community by Salt Lake City architects Scott and Welch, it included a park, store, and school as well as many single-family houses. These are small and nicely detailed variations of the Craftsman, Tudor, and Spanish Eclectic styles, with copper detailing subtly integrated into the designs. Although built as rental houses, after the company was taken over by Kennecott Copper the houses were sold to private owners in 1956. Nearby is the famed **Bingham Copper Mine,** a huge open pit that contained one of the world's richest copper deposits. Still in production, the mine is now a national historic landmark with an observation area open to visitors.

Washington

BELLINGHAM

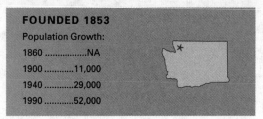

FOUNDED 1853

Population Growth:

1860	NA
1900	11,000
1940	29,000
1990	52,000

Bellingham, fifteen miles south of the Canadian border, is the principal port and trade center of northwesternmost Washington. The modern city began as four separate towns founded in the early 1850s. From north to south these were Whatcom, Sehome, Bellingham, and Fairhaven. The towns went through a series of name changes and consolidations in the late 1800s, and in 1903 all four joined to become the city of Bellingham. By the time they merged, the four towns were already well-developed communities linked by their adjacent locations along the fine harbor of Bellingham Bay.

This multiple birth has left a legacy of historic houses grouped not into one or two compact neighborhoods, but instead scattered along an inland, hilltop road that ran through the towns. Overlooking the harbor below and the scenic waterways and islands beyond, the hills were a favored site for upscale homes. At the beginning and end of this route, in Whatcom and in Fairhaven (the two largest of the four towns), the hilltops developed small neighborhoods of early houses. As an aid in seeing these widely scattered dwellings, the Bellingham map shows a suggested route that winds through the early residential districts of the four towns. Driving along the suggested route from north to south, one moves from houses built in the original town of Whatcom to those of the old town of Sehome to those of ambitious Fairhaven. Today these areas, while still retaining some of their early distinction, nonetheless merge gracefully one into the other.

Old Whatcom

Whatcom's most important surviving houses now make up the **Eldridge Avenue Historic District,** named for the hilltop road that parallels Bellingham Bay. This is a fairly large area—bordered by Squalicum Way, Eldridge Avenue, Broadway, Elm Street, and North—and is fun to explore if time permits. The highest concentration of interesting houses is found along Eldridge Avenue and Utter Street. Most homes in the district

were built between 1890 and 1915. There are many Craftsman designs here as well as multiple examples of the Queen Anne, Stick, and wood-clad Tudor styles. American four-square houses of varied styles and occasional Shingle and Colonial Revival homes are also seen. A few of the four-squares have the recessed porches that were spread by a pattern book published in Seattle (see page 670).

2820 Eldridge Avenue (private), Bolster House, 1891. This was probably the first brick house in Bellingham. It was not a coincidence that it was built by James Bolster, who owned a brick factory and wanted to demonstrate that brick was a fit material for houses as well as for commercial and public buildings. He apparently preferred to build in the fashionable Queen Anne style, but had to improvise a bit because the terra-cotta ornamentation used on East Coast brick Queen Anne designs was not easily available here. Note the square tower at the entrance, the Italianate-influenced window hood over the pair of upper-story windows, the use of wood for patterned shingles in the gable and tower top, the heavy row of brick dentils in the belt course (between the first and second stories), and the king post truss in the gable.

2230 Henry Street, at Washington Street (private), Isensee House, 1893. This transitional design combines Italianate and Stick-style details on a simple gabled-front-and-wing shape. It has Stick-inspired curved king post trusses in the gables and Italianate brackets under the eaves. The slanted bay windows and the window hoods in the gables are Italianate. The entry porch appears to be a more modern reconstruction.

1898 Utter Street (private). Note the way the main roof sweeps down over and curves above the wraparound porch of this simple one-and-one-half-story Queen Anne cottage. There is a recessed window/balcony above the porch. The right side of the house has a single cutaway *corner* rather than the more usual cutaway-bay-window ensemble such as the one seen farther back on the same facade.

2120 Utter Street (private). This simple Free Classic Queen Anne design is nicely painted to highlight the exaggerated moldings above the Palladian window and the dentils that are used liberally across the cornices and above the windows. There is a small and similarly exaggerated triangular pediment that accents the porch above the entry stairs. The handsome front door appears to be original.

Roeder Home, 1908

2600 Sunset Drive; 360-733-6897; Alfred Lee, architect. This large and handsome two-story Craftsman house was built for banker Victor A. Roeder, the son of one of Whatcom's founders. Roeder purchased ten city lots, sold off three of them, and built his home on the spacious grounds provided by the remaining seven.

The finishes and fixtures in the house are of very

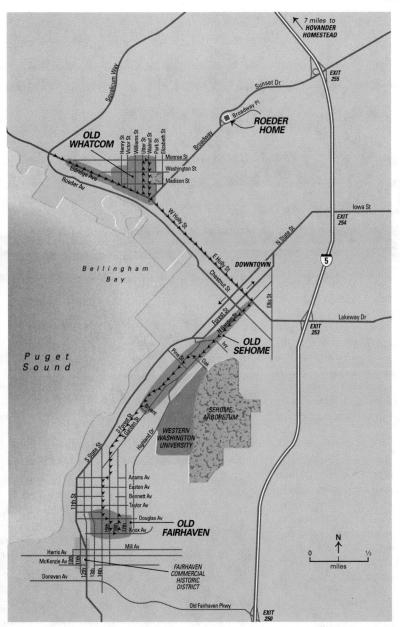

high quality. Both the living and dining rooms have fireplace surrounds of art pottery tile, complemented in the dining room by a wide, hand-painted mural above the squared wall paneling. The living room has a wood-beamed ceiling and handsome built-in bookcases with art glass on each side of the fireplace. The original light fixtures and sconces remain downstairs.

Exterior Craftsman detailing is equally elaborate. Triangular knee braces are placed beneath each of the many exposed roof beams. The house is a side-gabled design with a centered front cross gable that rises above a lower, shed-roofed entry porch below. On the porch, triangular braces are even used not only beneath the roof beams, as is typical, but also beneath the exposed rafter tails, which is very unusual. The address of the house is for the porte cochere entrance, which faces the rear; the main-entry facade fronts on Broadway. This is the grandest home in its immediate neighborhood, the rest of which is mostly filled by smaller Craftsman dwellings.

Roeder Home

The Roeder Home was given to the Whatcom County Park and Recreation Board in 1971, and today it serves as a center for cultural arts and community events. Although classes are held in the upstairs portion and the first floor is available for special events, the house itself is remarkably well preserved. This is a happy occurrence, because Craftsman-style museum houses are unusual, and it is a treat to be able to see an original, high-style interior. Even though the Roeder Home is not operated as a house museum, it is open to visitors.

Old Sehome

The early town of Sehome is now the home of Western Washington University. The need for student housing has led to the preservation of many older Victorian houses near the university—these exhibit the varying degrees of upkeep and condition that typify most such student-housing neighborhoods. Many Victorian and Eclectic-era dwellings farther from the campus are in pristine condition and appear to be still predominantly single-family residences.

1201 North Garden Street (private), Donovan House, 1890. This large and dramatic home was built for lumberman J. J. Donovan. It is a very early and fine example of the Tudor style. Donovan had been active in railroads, and his travels probably gave him a familiarity with this style, which did not become popular in the Northwest until much later.

1014 North Garden Street (private), Morse House, 1896; Alfred Lee, architect. This striking towered Queen Anne design is perched on a hill with a broad view over Bellingham Bay and beyond. Details such as the outward bow of the tower roof, the horseshoe arch around the recessed balcony, and the decorated vergeboards lining the gables let you know that it was originally built to very high standards.

727 North Garden Street (private), ca. 1910. This distinguished early modern house combines the shape of a

Old Sehome

Old Sehome

hipped-roof, asymmetrical Prairie design with open Crafts-man eaves, exposed rafters, and wood shingle wall-cladding. It has casement windows on the first story and horizontal "pivot" windows upstairs in the central two-story towerlike section.

201 North Forest Street (private), Campbell House, 1910. This handsome early Tudor design has the slightly blocky and heavy feeling found in most pre–World War I examples of the style. There is a wonderful bay window—cantilevered out and set asymmetrically into the facade composition. The entry is through an inset porch.

100 North Forest Street, next door to and just south of 201 (private). This lovely, restrained early Colonial Revival house is of the hipped-roof-with-full-width-porch subtype with an oval window centered in the upper story. A decorative balustrade enlivens the porch roof.

Bellingham

The original town of Bellingham was the smallest of the four, and is now the city's commercial core. Relatively few of its early houses survive. It is said that the consolidated town was named Bellingham because neither of the two largest communities—Fairhaven and What-com—wanted to be consumed by the other.

Old Fairhaven

The early town of Fairhaven has a history a bit like Port Townsend's (see page 662). It built up a fine Victorian downtown and scattered large houses in anticipation of becoming the western terminus for a transcontinental railroad, in this case the Great Northern, which, arriving in 1893, chose instead to end its line in the Seattle

area. Today Fairhaven's Victorian buildings house a thriving commercial historic district with shops and restaurants. On the bluff above are several large and distinctive Victorian houses surrounded by a pleasant Eclectic-era neighborhood.

1034 Fifteenth Street, at Knox Avenue (private), Bateman House, 1891. A fine towered Queen Anne design with a wraparound spindlework porch, its tower features a mansardlike roof and a round dormer window.

1103 Fifteenth Street (private), Wardner House, 1890. Longstaff and Black, Bellingham, architects. This is a large Shingle-style design in the hipped-roof-with-cross-gables subtype.

1001 Sixteenth Street (private), Gamwell House, 1892. Longstaff and Black, Bellingham, architects. Real estate de-veloper Roland Gamwell, a Bostonian and graduate of M.I.T., worked to convince Longstaff and Black, fellow Bostonians, to move to Bellingham to design the now-demolished Fairhaven Hotel. Among their next commis-sions was Gamwell's new showcase home, which is one of the most opulent wood-clad Queen Anne houses remaining in the West. Similarly heroic Queen Anne designs crowd the pages of what can be called the "Lost Architecture books"— those with titles like *Lost Baltimore, Lost San Francisco,* or *Lost Cleveland*—publications that make you wonder if such grandly elaborate and exotic wooden structures really ex-isted, since almost none survive today. One begins to sus-pect that some talented model builder moved around the country selling chambers of commerce his photographs of fantastic miniature houses having huge, bulbous domes, el-egant open balconies, and vast art-glass windows. Here we

Old Fairhaven

Old Fairhaven

and their seven children, ranging in age from two to twenty-one when the house was begun. Hakan had an unusual wanderlust that had taken him from his native Sweden to America just after the Civil War. He traveled to San Francisco, Portland, and then Chicago, where, after the 1871 fire, he became a proficient builder and reportedly made a small fortune.

Hakan then returned to Sweden, where he studied architecture, married Louisa, and by 1880 was building an elaborate Beaux Arts dwelling in Stockholm that his family called the Mansion. Sketches on display in the homestead reveal this was not an exaggeration. After a visit to California with his family, they returned to Sweden and sold the mansion to Swedish royalty for $95,000. With this tidy nest egg, the family departed again to settle in Auckland, New Zealand. Just six months later they picked up once more and came to northern Washington where, in 1898, they purchased this site—sixty-five acres of prime Nooksack River bottomland—for $4,700 in gold. At age fifty-seven, Hakan had finally settled down in one place to become a farmer.

have documentary proof that such houses really did exist, in this case with a heroic, squared tower with an exotic bulbous roof. Outdoor balconies for enjoying the local scenery are everywhere—around the tower, beneath a high roof gable, above porch roofs, and elsewhere. Among the many fine details are robust bay windows, shaped brick chimneys, heavy spindlework balustrades and friezes, and beautiful art-glass windows in Art Nouveau designs.

Hovander Homestead, 1901

5299 Neilsen Road, Ferndale, about seven miles north of Bellingham; 360-384-3444; Hakan Hovander, architect.
Hakan Hovander (1841–1915) was a Swedish immigrant who built this unusual home for his wife, Louisa,

The house was begun in 1901 when Hakan and his oldest son laid the brick foundation and completed the brickwork for the chimneys and furnace. The next year Hakan hired a crew to finish the carpentry. This is a one-of-a-kind house, built by an architect with strong Swedish ties, which gives it a rather-unusual feel. In style it is closest to being a symmetrical, hipped-roof Folk Victorian design. Rather than the usual spindlework or Italianate details found on this style, Stick-style

Hovander Homestead

elaborations are used here. Note the trusslike gable details, the squared bay windows, and the areas of applied stickwork.

The interior and exterior finish of the house is quite unusual. In the Swedish tradition, the wood was not painted but finished instead by treating it with raw linseed oil. It still looks remarkably new, with almost every detail preserved intact. Inside, the fixtures, hardware, and even some furniture are just as the Hovanders left them. Only the original interior plaster has been replaced.

The house is a simple center-hall plan with high ceilings and furnishings appropriate to a rural farmstead. There are six main rooms, but each is quite large. Unusual for the day are the large storage closets between most rooms. Downstairs has a library, dining room, and kitchen to one side, and a master bedroom, girls' bedroom, and boys' bedroom to the other. No space is wasted on a formal "parlor." There is also a large second-story room.

Hakan died in 1915, but his family continued to live and farm here until 1971, when the farm was deeded to the Whatcom County Park and Recreation Board. Today the Hovander Homestead is operated as a living farm museum, complete with large barn, lookout tower, many different kinds of domestic livestock, and flourishing vegetable gardens. A number of volunteer groups are active in this effort. They plant and tend the vegetable, herb, and fragrance gardens and staff the house. Another house, the Neilsen Farmstead, is used as an interpretive center for the natural environment of this area.

PORT TOWNSEND

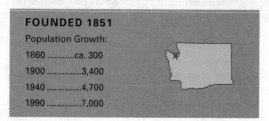

FOUNDED 1851

Population Growth:

1860 ....ca. 300

1900 3,400

1940 4,700

1990 7,000

Port Townsend is a delightful Victorian time-capsule town. Founded, like many Puget Sound communities, as a small timber-shipping village, it became an instant city of seven thousand inhabitants in a single two-year construction frenzy that began in 1888 after the Oregon Improvement Company, a subsidiary of the Union Pacific Railroad, promised to extend its lines northward from Portland to make Port Townsend its new Puget Sound terminus. Few towns have ever gambled so much on a promise. Many blocks of handsome new commercial buildings sprung up in the waterside

downtown area while new Victorian dwellings mushroomed in the adjacent, cliff-top residential district.

What happened next is clearly summarized in the 1941 *WPA Guide to Washington:*

> By 1890 . . . work on the line was beginning to drag; [Oregon Improvement Company] officials seemed more interested in speculating in real estate than in building a rail line. Disquieting whispers of impending failure of the company were confirmed in November when it was learned that the company had gone into receivership. Real estate values fell, thousands of people deserted the town, and everyone knew that the dream was over. A city with the facilities for 20,000 people soon had fewer than 2,000.

Port Townsend never reached that projected population of twenty thousand and, indeed, had only climbed back to the seven thousand residents reported in the late 1880s by the 1990 census, more than a century later. As a result, much of the town's economic base now centers around heritage tourism as visitors come to enjoy the Pacific Northwest's most intact Victorian town.

Historic Uptown, ca. 1870–1892

The original bluff-top residential district adjacent to downtown still retains many fine Victorian houses from the town's brief boom years, as well as a scattering of preboom dwellings (see "Rothschild House," page 664). Here, as in most smaller Victorian towns, the early houses were typically built on large, multilot sites that ranged up to a full city block in size. Initial lot prices were usually relatively low, and homebuilders often purchased several. These served both as a long-term investment as well as providing an immediate "urban farmstead," with room for money-saving gardens, orchards, chicken yards, and milk cows. For this reason, Port Townsend did not have continuous streetscapes of late-Victorian houses; instead, most of the houses were rather widely scattered around the bluff-top residential district. There was also a small bluff-top commercial district centered along Lawrence Street between Fillmore and Taylor Streets, which saved shoppers a trip down the steep roads to the waterside downtown commercial district.

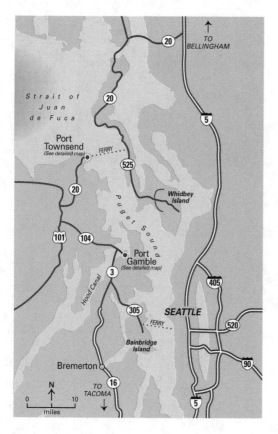

314 Polk Street (private), Bartlett House, 1883. Like most "one-story" Second Empire designs, this one looks deceptively small. A full floor of living space is tucked under the high mansard roof—this house actually has fourteen rooms, some quite large. Note the slightly different bracket designs used under the eaves of the house, the entry porch, and above the dormer and bay windows. The entry porch is very nicely detailed.

502 Reed Street (private), Harper House, 1889. This carefully restored dwelling combines a typical Queen Anne shape with an Italianate two-story bay window and porch details.

313 Walker Street (private), Hastings House, 1889. This fine Queen Anne design has a rounded tower on the front and an octagonal turret in the rear. Note the sweeping porch that wraps around to two sides. It has a porch roof similar to that of the Mutty House (see "640 Taylor Street," page 664), but without the decorative iron cresting.

827 and 834 Pierce Street (both private), Mann House, 1889, and Hammond House, 1890. It's always hard to guess what architectural details will survive on a house. This pair of Italianate cottages, both with simple hipped roofs, were

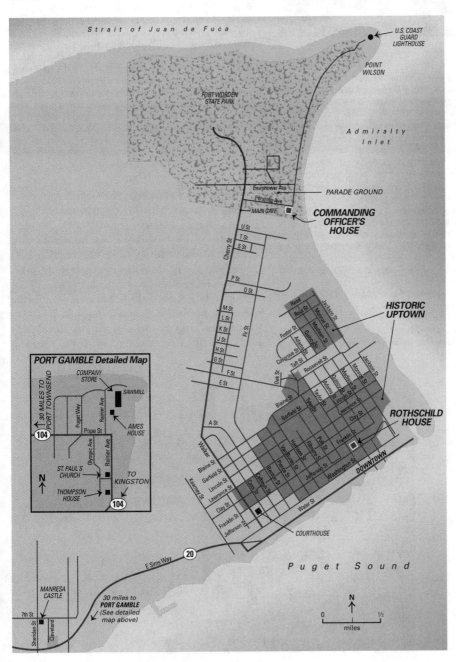

Historic Uptown

originally rather similar. Number 827 still has the tall, narrow paired windows with bracketed tops that are so typical of the Italianate style, but the widely overhanging eaves, with their characteristic decorative brackets, are missing. Number 834, in contrast, has the typical eaves and brackets but the tall narrow windows are missing, having been replaced by two different types of newer window designs.

Sheridan Street at Seventh Street (private), Manresa Castle, 1892; A. S. Whiteway, architect. Port Townsend's first mayor and leading merchant, Charles Eisenbeis, reportedly built this large home to resemble castles along the Rhine in his homeland. It is actually a great example of the Chateauesque style, which was then very fashionable with the well-to-do northeasterners. The original structure had thirty rooms. An even larger, although less highly detailed, wing was added by the Catholic Society of Jesus, which purchased the house in 1925. Today the historic building houses a hotel and restaurant.

640 Taylor Street (private), Mutty House, 1891. This one-and-one-half-story Queen Anne cottage still has its fanciful iron roof cresting. Note the porch roof, which is a shallow mansard shape clad with decorative shingles.

902 Sims Way (private), Saunders House, 1891; Edward

A. Batwell, architect. This large, towered Queen Anne home is set on spacious grounds. It combines spindlework detailing with both Colonial Revival and Shingle-style decorative elements. The former is seen in the broken segmental pedimented dormer, and the latter in the shingles curving into the recessed window and recessed balcony of the main gable.

744 Clay Street (private), Starrett House, 1889. George Starrett was a native of Maine who settled in Port Townsend in 1885 and promptly established himself as a carpenter, builder, contractor, and brick maker. Later, he operated a sawmill. His sterling building credentials enabled him to build this unique home as a gift for his young wife, Ann. It combines Queen Anne massing with lavish Stick-influenced detailing. Note the varied gable details, each with a different pattern of mock trusswork suspended from the overhanging eaves. Also notice how each rank (vertical line) of windows is filled with wood detailing that makes a complete composition from the water table to the cornice line. One enters through the large tower, which contains a rare circular staircase of "free-floating" construction. Such stair towers were uncommon in this country until the early twentieth century, when they were incorporated into many Spanish Eclectic and towered French Eclectic designs.

Rothschild House, 1868

Jefferson Street and Taylor Street; 360-379-8076; A. Horace Tucker, architect.

This immaculately preserved Greek Revival dwelling was built for merchant D. C. H. Rothschild and his family. Rothschild was a German immigrant, who, when asked if he was related to the Rothschilds of European banking fame, replied, "Just enough to get the name, not the money." He was instead a hardworking businessman who in 1858 opened Port Townsend's Kentucky Store, a general merchandise establishment

Rothschild House

located out on a pier so that ships could easily load and unload. After his marriage to Dorrette Hartung in 1863, the couple lived over the store (a common practice in those days) until they had this home constructed. The builder was Horace Tucker, who had come to Port Townsend from Portsmouth, New Hampshire, via the California goldfields. Tucker was an experienced architect/builder and began this house with a heavy stone foundation that formed a food-storage cellar.

The design is a perfect example of a one-and-a-half-story Greek Revival cottage with a front-gabled roof. This was a very common house type in New England, and many similar precut dwellings were shipped from New England ports around Cape Horn to the early coastal towns of the Pacific coast. Here, however, Tucker appears to have brought either plans or strong memories with him to guide in the design.

Rothschild House sits on a high bluff, surrounded by tiny gardens, with a splendid view over the city and bay. But the original interiors are the house's greatest treat. Rothschild's youngest daughter, Emilie, was a librarian who remained a spinster and lived in the house throughout her life, keeping things much as they had been when her parents were alive. In 1958, shortly after Emilie's death, her brother donated the house and all of its contents to the state so it could be preserved intact as a memorial to their parents.

Almost all of the furniture and fixtures throughout the house date from 1860 to 1886. Complementing these are a multitude of family belongings such as dolls, quilts, dishes, fans, clothing, and utensils. The wallpaper in the front parlor and hallway dates from 1885. The original ingrained carpet remains in the master bedroom, and many of the other rooms still have their 1914 carpet, which is composed of twenty-seven-inch lengths stitched together. Most of the woodwork is Douglas fir with the original faux oak hand graining. This small but remarkably complete house provides an unusually authentic look into the lifestyle of an early mercantile family in the West.

Commanding Officer's House, 1904

Fort Worden State Park; 360-385-4730, ext. 0.

Official armed forces architects almost always manage to make their domestic designs related to, but slightly different from, what their civilian counterparts are producing. The fine Commanding Officer's House at Port Townsend's Fort Worden is no exception. It is a simple gabled-front-and-wing design with a one-story porch wrapping around it. Although all the details on the house are familiar and frequently used, this exact combination is rarely seen. If it was a typical 1904 cross-gabled Free Classic Queen Anne house, it would have more elaborate exterior detailing. If it was a 1904 Colonial Revival design with a one-story full-width porch, it would likely be American four-square or front gabled in shape. Yet here is an army architect's somewhat-different domestic vision. One can only imagine how many regulations it had to satisfy and by how many committees it was reviewed and tweaked before it was built. Yet, like many such dwellings on military bases around the country, it and the adjacent row of duplex

Commanding
Officer's House

officers' dwellings manage to project a soundness of purpose and structural integrity that are both cohesive and comforting.

About twenty different families lived in this house before it was decommissioned and put into the hands of the Washington State Parks and Recreation Commission. It has done an excellent job of furnishing the house to reflect the probable lifestyles of the early families that were stationed here. House museums that authentically reflect the lifestyle of typical middle-class and upper-middle-class families are rare anywhere in the country. In Port Townsend, the Washington State Parks system has preserved two such rare jewels—the completely authentic Rothschild House (see the preceding entry) and this fine Commanding Officer's House, built thirty-six years later.

Almost all of the details of this thoughtfully restored house ring true. The pressed-tin ceilings are still extant. The woodwork has never been painted over. The coal fireplaces are still surrounded with Belgian tiles, and the original pocket doors remain. The furnishings have been carefully assembled and include a First World War vintage Underwood typewriter and a diverse assortment of interesting rugs, ranging from a signed Ispahan in the parlor to "moss" rugs made from scraps of wool and silk underwear. There are a few American Indian decorative pieces. Furnishings vary from "parlor best" to Singer sewing machines. There is a refurbished wood cookstove, reported to be the original, and an early Montgomery Ward washing machine that was discovered in a downtown warehouse uncrated and never used.

Fort Worden, overlooking the entrance to Puget Sound, was once a key element in the nation's elaborate coastal defense system. Closed in 1953, the historic fort became a state park in 1973 and is now used for conferences and local recreation.

Port Gamble, 1853

This small company town, located about thirty miles southeast of Port Townsend, provides a storybook glimpse of Puget Sound's many Victorian lumber-mill villages. It was founded in 1853 by lumbermen Andrew Pope and William Talbot, who originally came from East Machias, Maine, where they had both grown up in New England lumbering families. Here the partners gradually created a New England–inspired mill town with many simple side- and front-gabled houses, a town center, and ultimately, in 1870, St. Paul's Episcopal Church, which copied their East Machias parish church. As many as 350 people lived and worked in Port Gamble at its height.

Port Gamble

Today, most of the town residents are still employed by the Pope and Talbot Company. The 1853 lumber mill, now much modernized, is the oldest continuously operating sawmill in North America. Even more remarkably, in the mid-1960s Pope and Talbot faithfully restored most of the village's surviving historic structures, thus preserving a rare example of an early milling center. There are almost no modern intrusions, and even the gas station is appropriately understated. Most of the houses are simple postrailroad folk houses or later Craftsman-style bungalows. The company has put out signs with information on some of the structures, and a guide brochure is available at the company store, which also houses a company museum on the upper levels.

Rainier Avenue, downtown across from Masonic Temple (private), Ames House, 1889. Walker Ames, Pope and Talbot's resident manager, lived in this large Queen Anne dwelling. The main facade faces down the hill to overlook the mill. The side facade facing the company store is nicely articulated (this favorite term of architectural historians as used here means that the window shapes and arrangement on this side facade make a nice composition, or, in Webster-dictionary-ese, the facade is "arranged with coherence").

10 Rainier Avenue (private), Jackson House, 1871. This simple gabled-front folk house belonged to Captain D. B. Jackson, a partner in charge of the company's steamboats, which delivered much of the finished lumber to distant ports. By 1894 there were ten vessels in his fleet.

Rainier Avenue, last house on right as you leave town (private), Thompson House, 1859; addition, 1872. As you continue down Rainier Avenue away from downtown and past St. Paul's Episcopal Church, you will pass several more gabled-front folk dwellings as well as a couple of modest, front-gabled Craftsman houses. The last house in this row, just three past the church, is this simplified Gothic Revival home, reported to be the oldest continuously occupied house in Washington State.

SEATTLE

FOUNDED 1851

Population Growth:

1860 1,000
1900 81,000
1940 368,000
1990 516,000

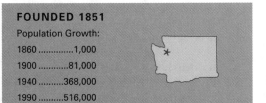

The state of Washington's largest cities—Seattle, Tacoma, and Spokane—are all relative newcomers to the urban scene of the Pacific coast. In 1880, when Portland was already a city with 16,000 inhabitants and San Francisco a metropolis with 235,000, Seattle was a sleepy lumber port of 3,500, while Tacoma and Spokane were mere villages. All three were suddenly awakened by an 1880s railroad boom that ultimately was to make Puget Sound the terminus of three transcontinental railroads.

At first it appeared that Tacoma would be the principal Puget Sound port when the Northern Pacific, the first of the railroads, bypassed hilly Seattle to build its wharves and rail yards farther southward on the flatter waterfront of Tacoma's Commencement Bay. Seattle responded by beginning to build its own eastbound rail line, a development that spurred the Northern Pacific to extend its tracks northward from Tacoma to Seattle's wharves in 1883.

The city also began a long-term program of leveling its waterside hills, which were underlain by soft glacial gravels that could be "washed down" by powerful jets of water, a technique previously perfected for mining California's stream-bank gold deposits. In Seattle the de-

Regrading Denny Hill in order to level that part of the city, 1910

bris from the hills was used to build out the waterfront with new flat land for wharves and rail yards, while the now-flattened adjacent hills provided sites for new factories and commercial buildings. A picturesque fragment of the latter still survives around **Pioneer Square** (First Avenue at Yesler Way), now a historic district whose many restored Victorian buildings feature first-floor shopping and dining.

Seattle's energetic "regrading" program was ultimately successful, largely because its new port facilities were adjacent to a larger deepwater harbor, and were also closer to the waterways leading from Puget Sound to the open ocean, than were those of Tacoma. In 1893 the city's role as the Northwest's principal port and

View of Seattle, 1878

gateway to Alaska, Hawaii, and the Orient was assured when the newly arrived Great Northern Railroad located its principal terminus in Seattle just in time to serve the Yukon's massive Klondike gold rush of 1897–1898. In 1909 still-another transcontinental line, the Chicago, Milwaukee, and St. Paul, arrived to further strengthen the city's dominance of the region.

These events led to an enormous boom as Seattle's population surged from 3,500 in 1880 to 43,000 in 1890, leaped again to 81,000 in 1900, and reached 366,000 in 1930. Subsequent growth has been less spectacular but steady. As in other western cities, World War II brought an influx of workers from the surrounding rural areas to newly expanded war-production factories. Principal among these was the Boeing Aircraft Corporation, now called simply the Boeing Company, founded in Seattle in 1923 to manufacture the trans-Pacific Flying Clippers made famous by Pan American Airways in the 1930s. In 1940 Boeing switched to production of B-17 Flying Fortress bombers, which were to prove decisive in the Allied victory in Europe.

In the post-1950 decades, Boeing became Seattle's principal industry by converting its postwar designs for large, jet-powered military bombers into the first civilian jet airliners. Boeing remains today one of the world's leading manufacturers of commercial jetliners.

Residential Seattle

As the city's population surged in the decades from 1890 to 1930, new residential developments spread steadily over the hills beyond the artificially leveled downtown commercial and industrial districts.

In 1903 the Olmsted brothers were hired to prepare a park plan for the expanding city. Its most dramatic feature was beautiful Lake Washington Boulevard, which linked a chain of parks and also provided views across Lake Washington to the Cascade Mountains beyond for a number of adjacent early-Eclectic-era neighborhoods. Other important early-Eclectic-era neighborhoods still survive intact around more distant Capitol Hill, to the northeast of downtown, and Queen Anne Hill to the northwest.

Capitol Hill, ca. 1900–1940

First Hill, just northeast of downtown Seattle, was the site of the earliest exclusive residential neighborhood in Seattle, but most of its houses have now been replaced by apartments and commercial buildings. Capitol Hill, the next hill to the northeast, was its successor once electric trolleys were introduced at about the turn of the century. The Capitol Hill area is quite large, extending all the way from Interstate 5 on the west to Portage Bay and Interlocken Park on the north, and from Twenty-fourth Avenue on the east to East Pine Street and Madison Street on the south—lovely homes can be found scattered throughout most of this area. The best concentration of upscale houses is much smaller and surrounds the 140-acre Volunteer Park, named to honor the soldiers who fought in the Spanish-American War of 1898.

There are three distinctive subneighborhoods around Volunteer Park. To the west is an area of mixed-size houses but with many large, architect-designed homes scattered throughout. A particularly rich and varied collection of the latter is found along Federal Avenue East. In addition there is a small historic district here, Harvard Belmont, which lies north of East Roy Street and west of Broadway East.

A distinctive Seattle four-square variant

hipped roof, typically with open eaves and exposed rafter tails

centered ornamental window, often with exotic design

projecting square corner windows

porch recessed into main body of house

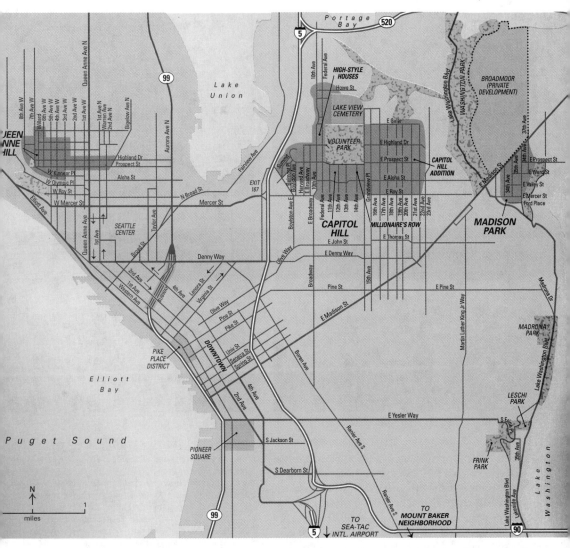

Next, extending southward from the park along Fourteenth Street, was Millionaire's Row. This had an entry gate at Roy Street at one end and a private entrance into the park at the other. Despite the street's relatively small lots, some of Seattle's most prestigious families chose to build their homes here. Finally, to the east of the park is the Capitol Hill Addition, developed by J. A. Moore in about 1905. This large area of upper-middle-class houses was a typical "streetcar suburb" served by a line along Nineteenth Avenue. This district is dominated by particularly well-detailed American four-square houses in many different styles. In addition to Colonial Revival, Prairie, Craftsman, and other types of stylistic detailing found in four-square neighborhoods throughout the country, here can be seen a number of examples of a distinctive Seattle four-square variation.

These designs (see page 668) are found scattered throughout the Pacific Northwest and northern California but are rarely encountered elsewhere. These houses lack the four-square's usual *projecting* one-story, full-width front porch and instead substitute a *recessed* one-story porch, either of full or one-half width. A second feature is the two projecting square corner bays, one on each side of the house. These wrap around the corner of the house and extend slightly out from the body of the house; one large window or a pair of windows is on each facade. The effect from the interior bedroom is a very dramatic expanse of outdoor view that sweeps for 180 degrees. A decorative, and some-

Capitol Hill

times-exotic, shaped window is often inserted in the wide center space left between these two widely spaced upper-story windows (it is interesting to know that these elaborate windows light the closets for the two mirror-image bedrooms on each side). The eaves are usually open with exposed rafter tails that often have rounded ends. The basic design was promoted, and probably introduced, by the *Western Home Builder*, a pattern book by Victor W. Voorhees (Seattle, first published around 1907). In Seattle residents have nicknamed these, and most other styles of the four-square shape, "classic boxes."

948 Harvard Avenue East (private), Peeples House, 1909; Cutter and Malmgren, Spokane, architects. This impressive Swiss chalet is a fine example of one of the rarest styles of American house design. Perhaps for that reason it was a favorite of Spokane's innovative Kirtland Cutter (see page 676), who used it for his own home, Chalet Hohenstein, completed in 1887, shortly after his arrival in Washington after several years of European travel. Note the elaborately shaped corbels and the understated cut trim in a line above the upper-story windows.

1901 Tenth Avenue East (private), Rhodes House, 1911; A. Warren Gould, architect. Extensive grading and a large retaining wall were needed to prepare a flat site for this striking Italian Renaissance house. Note the blind arches above the first-floor windows, the balustraded retaining wall, and the handsome entry. An unusual touch is the way the keystones in the blind arches extend up and out to provide the support for the window boxes. This house is also unusual in that it is entirely clad with terra-cotta. The architect, Augustus Warren Gould (1872–1922), began as a Boston building contractor and had a good understanding of the latest building techniques. These included the extensive use of terra-cotta cladding on the steel frames for high-rise buildings such as downtown Seattle's famous Arctic Building (the one decorated with terra-cotta walrus heads).

1204 Federal Avenue East (private), Scheetz House, 1914; Somervell and Cote, Seattle, architects. This consummate example of the Colonial Revival style, is here interpreted as an understated Federal house. Note the fine brickwork, the elliptical fanlight above the entry, and the interesting way the Palladian window above has been set into an arched opening with oval windows to each side.

923 Fourteenth Avenue East (private), 1902. Although the house is partially hidden behind landscaping, just one glance at the roofline is enough to let you know that this is an unusual design. We'd put it in one of our favorite categories—Early Eclectic What's It?—but scholars have called it a variation of the English Arts and Crafts house. Whichever, it is a great example of the experimental designs that appeared in this country during the first few years of the twentieth century. Notice the open eaves with the remarkable triangular struts underneath, each with a decorative knob. The porch supports are clustered columns, with unusual capitals incorporating leaves as the main decorative element. The stonework is also unusual, with rough-faced stone carefully laid in alternating wide and narrow courses. This section of Fourteenth Avenue East was originally known as Millionaire's Row (see page 669).

1620 East Prospect Street (private), Bucklin House, ca. 1905. This fun early Colonial Revival house has so much detailing it's hard to know where to start. The front door has a lovely elliptical fanlight and sidelights that are set into a slightly recessed one-story columned entry porch, which is set into a slightly extended two-story entry "pavilion" with pilasters on each side and a broad wall dormer above. This entire composition is then encased with a broad wraparound porch with fluted Ionic columns. There is a Palladian window in the dormer and a Palladian door that opens out onto the upstairs terrace. Other details include a garlanded cornice and fine decorative glass transoms over the broad downstairs windows.

933, 937, 943, and 947 Sixteenth Avenue East (all private), Streetscape, ca. 1910. This row of four is just one of many handsome streetscapes found throughout the Capitol Hill Addition, east of Volunteer Park. Note the full-width recessed entry porch (called *in antis*) and modified projecting corner bay windows at 947, the handsome subtly curved bay windows at 933 and 943. Number 943 has upper-story flower boxes that wrap the corner of the house. All have the low-pitched hipped roof with broadly overhanging eaves that is a hallmark of the American four-square house. In Seattle they usually call this kind of house a classic box, but four-squares come in many different styles.

Washington Park, ca. 1900–1930

Located east of Capitol Hill, the Washington Park neighborhood has been a favored location for large, architect-designed homes since the early 1900s. Looking at its location on the map, one can easily imagine an early advertising piece touting Washington Park as "located at the crossroads." It is bisected by East Madison Street, which cuts diagonally across the city's otherwise north–south/east–west street grid, to provide a direct link to downtown. At the same time, an Olmsted-designed landscaped roadway—Lake Washington Boulevard—linked many of early Seattle's most pleasant residential neighborhoods that lie along the city's eastern margin near large and scenic Lake Washington, which limited the town's eastward expansion. Washington Park is at the crossroads of these two key arteries, which give direct access to many city amenities. The area proved to be such a desirable location that in 1927 the large Broadmoor private neighborhood was developed just on the other side of Madison Street.

The history of East Madison Street and its streetcar line (without which Washington Park would not have existed) typifies turn-of-the-century "streetcar suburbs." A Judge McGilvra had purchased much of the land in this area in the mid-1800s, setting aside a twenty-one-acre public park at Lake Washington for picnicking and camping. This could be accessed from downtown by a twenty-five-cent wagon ride. Eventually, the wagon was replaced by a trolley, and an amuse-

Capitol Hill

ment park was constructed at the end of the line, a common technique for assuring passengers in the early years when the streetcar line traversed mostly vacant land. The amusement park attracted riders who, along the route, passed large signs promoting the new neighborhoods, which were to be developed along the way, usually by the trolley company and its associates. Many amusement-park riders became purchasers of residential lots and long-term patrons of the nearby trolley line. The development of streetcar lines and their adjacent residential districts thus proceeded hand in hand. The trolley added value to the land, the sales of which in turn helped pay for the trolley. When all went well this was a great scheme, but not uncommonly insufficient capital, poorly chosen locations, bad timing, or other factors made the early stages of such ventures risky investments.

Washington Park was but one neighborhood along the Madison Street trolley line, but it was the most upscale, and it developed quickly, attracting the attention of those who eventually opened private Broadmoor. Washington Park has been desirable ever since, and today its large lots have lush landscaping and quiet streets sheltered by tall majestic tree canopies. These are mostly lined with early-Eclectic-era Period houses, but there is also a handful of dramatic newer homes.

1117 Thirty-sixth Avenue East (private), Pantages House, 1909; Wilson and Loveless, Seattle, architects. This intriguing house was built for Alexander Pantages, a well-known figure who operated a circuit of vaudeville theaters throughout the United States and Canada. His home adds many twists to its basic Tudor style—most obvious are the two long horizontal areas of very geometric half-timbering with regularly placed windows, one in the upper story and one in the unusual triple-gable dormer, which provides light for the third-floor ballroom. These two areas are balanced by the strongly geometric design of the two-story bay window on the right. Note the handsome tile roof and the unusually

Washington Park

detailed side facades. It was designed by Arthur L. Loveless (1873–1971) who had worked for Delano and Aldrich, New York–based designers of many early-twentieth-century country houses, before coming to Seattle in 1907.

618 Thirty-sixth Avenue East (private). This unusually grand version of a second-story-overhang subtype Colonial Revival–style house could have been built almost anytime from the late 1930s to the 1950s. The attached two-car garage, which looks as if it was built with the house, makes the 1950s a fairly safe bet. Notice the stone-clad central section that contains a careful composition of the entrance, a tall window that probably lights the stairway, and a small octagonal window of a type that was popular during this era. The rest of the house combines a stone-clad first floor with a wood-shingled upper story sporting decorative pendants beneath. One expects this house to be symmetrical, as most houses of this style and subtype are, and at first glance it looks like it is going to be. But a closer inspection reveals there are two windows to the right of the central section and only one to the left; and the four regularly spaced gabled dormers simply emphasize how the elements below them don't really line up.

808 Thirty-sixth Avenue East (private), Walker House, 1907; Bebb and Mendel, Seattle, architects. This Colonial Revival house was designed by a prominent Seattle architectural firm. Today it is the home of the president of the University of Washington. Note the elegant keystone lintels, the lavish use of quoins, the large wall dormer with two arched windows, and the handsome broad front door with sidelights. Changes include the removal of a handsome balustrade that graced the entry porch and the addition of a sun porch over the porte cochere.

815 Thirty-sixth Avenue East (private). This smaller wood-clad Colonial Revival home wonderfully echoes the large, highly detailed, brick-walled Walker House across the street (see the preceding entry). Although many details are quite different, both are three-rank houses with hipped roofs, a centered dormer, an entry door with sidelights, and, most telling, the same dominant large curved entry porch. The smaller house still has its balustrade above the porch.

3727 East Prospect Street (private), ca. 1910; Andrew Willatson, Seattle, architect. A Prairie-style design by Seattle's most competent designer in that style (see also "222 West Highland Drive," page 674).

Queen Anne Hill, ca. 1890–1930

This large hill was the site of Thomas Mercer's 1853 claim of 320 acres that stretched from today's Highland Drive down to Mercer Street and east to Lake Union. He immediately began logging operations, first on the west slope, where logs could be skidded down the hill into Puget Sound and floated to a sawmill. Later, when a sawmill was opened on Lake Union, the same process was used on the east slope. By 1873 Mercer was selling homesites on his portion of the hill. Sometime in the 1880s the foot of the hill began being served by a streetcar line, but the higher parts of Queen Anne Hill remained inaccessible until the First Street Cable Railroad Company began service along Queen Anne Avenue to the top of the hill, where a small commercial district was established. This was in place by 1891, the year the entire hill was incorporated into the city of Seattle. With annexation and transportation solved, more serious development could begin, and by the turn of the century, the southern slope, with its easy access to and view of downtown, was a sought-after site for new homes.

Queen Anne Hill was laid out with the typical east–west/north–south grid of streets, with no particular regard for the steep slopes or views from the hill. In 1906, Queen Anne citizens suggested that a tree-lined boulevard be added to encircle the hill to provide dramatic views of the city and countryside. The streets were not wide enough to accommodate the 150-foot-wide boulevards prescribed by the Olmsted Plan and only a small part of the neighborhood's plan was ever realized—a small segment connecting Highland Drive with Eighth Avenue West. Later, a curved stretch of Bigelow Avenue was added on the east. In 1977 a viewpoint, designed by Victor Steinbrueck, was added to Queen Anne Avenue at the west end of Highland Drive. The retaining walls, steps, railings, and lights along this stretch date from 1913, when residents were still actively trying to get their version of an Olmstedian vision implemented. It is interesting to contrast the layout of Queen Anne Hill, with its grid plan and tiny bit of Olmstedian planning, with the fully realized Olmstedian plan of Mount Baker, which was developed later with streets curving along the contour lines of the hill (see page 674).

If you visit this neighborhood looking for examples of its namesake style—the many Queen Anne houses that are reported to have once dotted its slopes—you will be disappointed, for only a few relatively modest examples of this Victorian style survive. Instead, Queen Anne Hill today has a wide variety of Eclectic-era styles, with the grandest examples mostly dating from 1900 to the 1920s. The flat top of the hill is covered with smaller and more modest houses, while, as might be expected, larger homes dot the slopes with the dramatic views. There is a higher concentration of elaborate houses on the west and south slopes, but Queen Anne Hill has always had a mixture of house sizes on every slope—you don't find a single street lined with grand mansions and another with American four-squares as in Capitol Hill. The older dwellings are joined in places with newer infill houses and apartments.

21–23 Highland Drive (private), Chappell House, 1906; Edgar A. Matthews, San Francisco, architect. The extensive use of unusually decorative half-timbering adds interest to this Tudor design. The overall plan is quite advanced for a Tudor home at this early date. Rather than the boxlike plan of most of its contemporaries, the Chappell House features

Queen Anne Hill

an octagonal main hall with axial room arrangements radiating off of it.

222 West Highland Drive (private), Black House, 1914; Andrew Willatsen, Seattle, architect. Although somewhat altered (by changes that include the replacement of the lower windows), this is still a fine example of the gabled-roof subtype of the Prairie style. Note the long ribbon window across the second story and the change in wall-cladding material just below it. Andrew Willatsen (1876–1974) worked intermittently with Frank Lloyd Wright in his Oak Park Studio from about 1903 until 1907. He designed a number of Prairie-style homes in Seattle, some by himself and some in a brief partnership with Barry Byrne (1883–1967), who had also worked with Wright.

317 and 321 West Highland Drive (both private). This instructive pair of French Eclectic designs contrasts an example of the symmetrical subtype (at 317) next door to one of the asymmetrical subtypes (at 321). Both demonstrate this style's predilection for windows breaking the eave line. At 317 it is with a through-the-cornice gabled dormer, while at 321 the top of an arched window breaks through the roofline.

415 West Highland Drive (private), F. Stimson House, 1904; Bebb and Mendel, Seattle, architects. This house nicely summarizes the general look of many Tudor designs in Seattle. It has a ground floor of massive cut granite, and extensive areas of half-timbering with stucco infill cover the entire upper story and gable. Also note the excellent wood detailing in the gable ends and the shingled square bays that punctuate the ground floor.

Throughout the country, only about 50 percent of Tudor houses have half-timbering at all, and even this is commonly applied to only a small portion of the facade, such as a gable end or dormer. In Seattle a high percentage of Tudor houses have half-timbering, often in *large* areas of the upper stories. This is usually infilled with stucco. The local architectural firm of Bebb and Mendel designed many similar Tudor houses and may have been responsible for its popularity in Seattle. In contrast, Portland, Oregon, has many Tudor designs with stucco walls that completely *lack* half-timbering, again the probable result of a prominent local architect's preferences (see page 514). Number 421 West Highland Drive (private), next door, was very similar to this house before a drastic fire led to remodeling that eliminated the top floor and changed the roof, among other things.

619 West Comstock Street (private), 1924; A. H. Albertson, Seattle, architect. This large French Eclectic design has flared eaves and symmetrical two-story side wings. See "317 West Highland Drive," above, for a smaller version of the same style and subtype.

325 West Kinnear Street (private). The street facade of this Tudor cottage is dominated by a single high-pitched gable with intricate half-timbering. The entrance is to the side, which sports an equally ornate facade.

Mount Baker, ca. 1900–1950s

This was an early planned community, complete with two broad, tree-lined boulevards, dedicated parkland, Olmstedian curved streets laid out to follow the contours of the land, and deed restrictions limiting it to single-family houses with strict setbacks. It also has fine

views to the east over Lake Washington with the Cascade Mountains in the background as well as easy access to landscaped Lake Washington Boulevard, the centerpiece of the Olmsteds' 1903 plan for the city. It also had excellent trolley connections with downtown Seattle.

The Hunter Tract Improvement Company, which developed Mount Baker, hired Edward Otto Schwagerl (1842–1910) to plan the development. Schwagerl was born in Bavaria and educated in Paris until age twelve, when he came alone to New York City. He later worked in Paris in the office of Mons Mulat, the architect designing the grounds for the 1867 Paris Exposition, and also for landscape architect Jacob Weidenmann in Hartford, Connecticut. Schwagerl practiced landscape design in Omaha, St. Louis, Cleveland, and Tacoma before becoming Seattle's superintendent of public parks in 1892. His great ambition was to create a parks and boulevard plan for Seattle, and, in his position as superintendent, he had one almost complete in 1903 when the Board of Park Commissioners decided to hire the high-profile Olmsted brothers to prepare just such

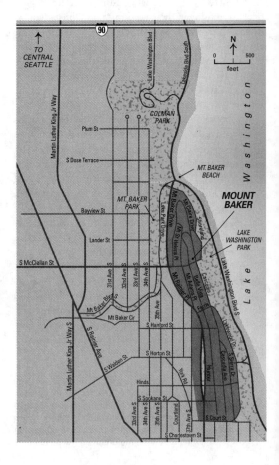

Mount Baker

a plan—their design was later termed "almost identical" to Schwagerl's by the city engineer R. H. Thomson. Ironically, the Olmsted brothers were long credited with the design of Mount Baker, because it was the largest subdivision to be included in their plan for the city.

For Schwagerl, Mount Baker was to be the crowning commission of his career, and perhaps a sweet victory as well, for he was chosen for the commission instead of the renowned Olmsted brothers. He did a superb job, as indicated by the longtime belief that the Olmsteds themselves had planned the district. Not

only did Schwagerl lay out the streets and boulevards, but he also completed a fine, naturalistic design for Mount Baker Park as well. Today, the Mount Baker neighborhood stands as a testament to Schwagerl's skill.

3311 Cascadia Avenue South (private), Phiscator Estate Home, 1907; Ellsworth Story, Seattle, architect. This was one of the earliest houses in the Mount Baker neighborhood and was built to encourage the sale of houses and lots there. The Neoclassical style is not particularly common in Seattle; perhaps this dramatic, colonnaded facade was planned, like a series of towering exclamation points, to attract the attention of potential Mount Baker residents.

3105 Cascadia Avenue South (private), Stuart House, 1913; Elmer Green, Seattle, architect. This large Craftsman house was designed by a local architect who also advertised his own *Practical Plan Book,* which could be purchased for fifty cents. Note the dormer with twin gables, the large triangular knee braces under the eaves, and the small centered upstairs terrace. The triangular knee braces look unusual on this hipped-roof house because, while common on Craftsman houses, they almost always appear on gable ends, usually "supporting" the exposed roof beams.

2540 Shoreland Drive South (private), Bowles House, 1925. This large Tudor design has informal massing, extensive half-timbering, and a prime view over Lake Washington.

3303 Hunter Boulevard South (private), Peterson House, 1913; A. Peterson, Seattle, architect. For his own home, Peterson used a funky Craftsman design with a porch that looks as if it came from an 1870s Stick-style house in New England.

Mount Baker

S P O K A N E

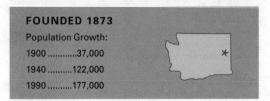

FOUNDED 1873

Population Growth:

1900 37,000

1940 122,000

1990 177,000

Spokane was a Victorian boomtown. Beginning as a village of 350 inhabitants in 1880, its rapid growth began with the arrival of the Northern Pacific Railroad in 1881. The growth accelerated three years later when a gold rush, followed by an enormous silver bonanza in the nearby Coeur d'Alene district of the Idaho Panhandle, made Spokane a booming metropolis of 20,000 by 1890. This figure almost doubled in the next ten years as Spokane also became the marketing center for the newly developed, and enormously productive, wheat farms of Washington's Palouse Hills, which stretch for seventy-five miles to the south of the city. This boom, now based upon both metallic silver and golden wheat, was to build for still another decade. By 1910 Spokane, home to 104,000 people and served by five transcontinental railroad lines, was the capital of what local boosters called the Inland Empire of the Pacific Northwest.

The decade from 1910 to 1920 was to end Spokane's formative boom period. Already overbuilt during the frantic preceding decades, the city was to lose much of its silver wealth in the nationwide industrial reorganizations brought on by World War I. During this period the region's richest mines passed from mostly Spokane-based local ownership into large corporate empires, whose profits flowed directly to eastern financiers. The 1920 census showed a population increase of only thirty-five people from 1910, a startlingly abrupt halt to the exponential growth of the preceding decades.

Marketing the region's valuable wheat, timber, and cattle was to supplement mining as Spokane's economic focus for the next twenty years as the population inched up from 104,000 in 1920 to only 122,000 in 1940. As in most western cities, new World War II industries brought an influx of workers, mostly from the region's smaller towns, and by 1950 the population had surged to 162,000. The city has remained about that size ever since, a fact that makes it something of a time capsule of pre-1950 architecture.

In addition to many fine early commercial buildings in the downtown area, Spokane retains a remarkable turn-of-the-century neighborhood that housed many of the city's silver barons. Two fine Eclectic-era neighborhoods and three superb museum-type dwellings round out the city's fascinating assemblage of historic houses.

Kirtland Kelsey Cutter, Architect

Spokane may be the only American city that has three grand houses, all designed by a single talented Eclectic-era architect, that are open to the public (two are currently restaurants and one is a house museum). These provide a rare opportunity to experience the remarkable facility with which the era's top designers handled a variety of styles.

Spokane's boom-era architectural leader was Kirtland Kelsey Cutter (1860–1939), a self-taught genius who was to design many of the city's most memorable buildings. Cutter is the subject of an important recent biography by historian Henry Matthews, which provided the basis for the following sketch.

Born into a pioneer Ohio family, Cutter was reared in the home of his highly educated great-grandfather, the naturalist Jared Kirtland, who lived until Cutter was seventeen and exerted a great influence on his great-grandson. After Jared Kirtland's death, the young Cutter first studied at the Art Students League in New York City and later traveled and studied art for several years in Europe. Upon his return to the States in 1886, he moved to Spokane, where one of his uncles, Horace Cutter, was a banker.

Educated as an artist rather than an architect, Cutter's first commission was a house for his uncle Horace (homes for family members are a common source of jobs for beginning architects). His next design was a home for himself. His luck soon improved as he began being asked to design new homes for his uncle's business partners in the booming young city.

Among the first of these was Spokane's most prominent citizen, James N. Glover, who had founded the town in 1873 as a mill site adjacent to spectacular waterfalls on the Spokane River. Cutter's innovative design for Glover (see page 683) was quite different from the typical Queen Anne house of 1888, and at first Spokanites did not know quite what to make of it. It took the complimentary comments of a visiting son-in-law of New York's renowned William Henry Vanderbilt to reassure Spokane's leading citizens that Cutter's designs were indeed on the cutting edge of current fashion.

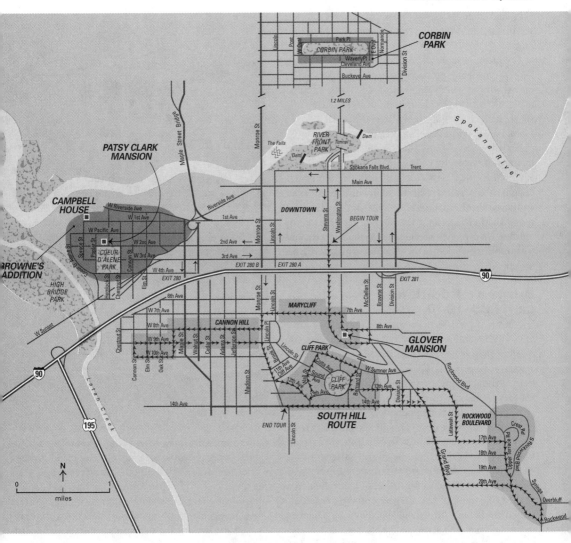

Still greater validation of Cutter's abilities came with his design for the Idaho Pavilion at the World's Columbian Exposition held in Chicago in 1893. He designed the pavilion with a first story of basalt and a second story of timber logs to symbolize the mountains and timber of Idaho. The finished pavilion won rave reviews from both architectural critics and the general public—a rare combination—and was awarded a coveted prize as the building that "best expressed the character of a state."

With this triumph Cutter's reputation was made, and he received the commissions for the important Patsy Clark Mansion (see page 680) and Campbell House (see page 679) as well as for many other residential and commercial designs that remain in Spokane (see both "Browne's Addition," page 678, and "South Hill," page

681). He also took commissions in other cities, among them Seattle, Tacoma, and even Kalispell, Montana, where the Conrad Mansion (now also a house museum; see page 387) survives in pristine condition.

Cutter had two partners during his years in practice—first, John C. Poetz (1859–1932), from 1889 to 1894, and next Karl Gunnar Malmgren (1862–1921), from 1894 until Malmgren's death. Both of these partners added needed construction experience to Cutter's design expertise. But Cutter always remained the lead design partner. The ups and downs of Spokane's economic climate produced corresponding ones in Cutter's finances. Ultimately, he ended up leaving Spokane in 1923 and moving to Long Beach, California, where he designed in the Spanish Eclectic style—executing elegant homes in Palos Verdes, San Marino, Beverly

Hills, and Long Beach—all near Los Angeles. He was still practicing at the time of his death at age seventy-nine.

The great versatility that Cutter displayed over his long professional practice is truly remarkable. He moved with ease between rustic designs with a Craftsman flair (such as the Idaho Pavilion and related work, which included a lodge at Glacier National Park in Montana, an Adirondack camp, and a number of Swiss chalet–style houses) and the Period styles popular at the turn of the century (Tudor, Neoclassical, Mission, and even Exotic Revivals). He then shifted to creative designs in the Spanish Eclectic style, which dominated California in the 1920s and 1930s. All of this Cutter accomplished with no formal training, from a base, for much of his career, in a small, out-of-the-way city, and with only a modest office that fluctuated in size with his fortunes.

Browne's Addition, ca. 1885–1940

It is the rare American neighborhood that reflects most of its city's economic history in its houses. Such is the case here in Browne's Addition. In 1878 J. J. Browne was a thirty-five-year-old Portland lawyer, who, having learned about the great waterfalls of the Spokane River, felt they could provide the power needed to develop a great industrial city in remote eastern Washington. Acting on this belief, Browne came to Spokane, where he negotiated with James Glover, who had, that same year, laid out a town site on land he owned adjacent to the spectacular falls, for a one-quarter interest in the new town, which then had a population of fewer than fifty. At the same time, as a new settler in the government-owned wilderness, Browne filed a claim for a quarter section of land (160 acres) just to the west of Glover's town site. This tract of land, later called Browne's Addition, was to become early Spokane's most fashionable residential district.

With Spokane's railroad boom of the 1880s, Browne's Addition became the site of many fashionable homes in the Queen Anne style, some of which still remain. Building halted abruptly with the nationwide panic of 1893, which caused a precipitous plunge in the price of silver and thus a decline in the fortunes of the many Coeur d'Alene silver barons who made the city their home base (see page 676). By the late 1890s silver prices had stabilized, and rich new mines were being opened in nearby Idaho and British Columbia. Spokane's population boom then resumed with new intensity as the city became a principal beneficiary of this new silver bonanza.

It was during this late 1890s boom that Browne's Ad-

Browne's Addition

dition's grandest houses were built, most of them designed by the talented local architect Kirtland Kelsey Cutter (see page 676). By 1900 Browne's Addition was the upscale core of urban Spokane, with trolleys running downtown every twenty minutes.

As the city's population continued its upward spiral in the next decade, the demand for homesites in the geographically confined Browne's Addition neighborhood began to exceed the supply. As a result, new luxury apartment buildings began to be built. The Westminster Apartments, completed in 1905 (see "West 2301 Pacific Avenue," page 679) are excellent examples of this new trend. Gradually, as Spokane's fortunes declined in the following decades, many of the neighborhood's large houses were divided into several apartments each, and somewhat less elegant new apartment buildings were added. In spite of these changes, Browne's Addition remains a pleasant residential district that retains enough of its grand dwellings to capture the feeling of its earlier glory years.

West 1905 Pacific Avenue (private), Dwight House, 1887. This charming Queen Anne home is typical of Browne's Addition houses built during the late 1880s and early 1890s. Descendants of the original owners lived here until the 1980s.

West 2340 First Avenue (private), Finch House, 1898; Cutter and Malmgren, Spokane, architects. This handsome Neoclassical home was built for the financial backer and partner of mining magnate A. B. Campbell (see "Campbell House," below) and is one of a striking streetscape of three Cutter-designed houses built in 1898, which must have been the neighborhood's most glorious year. Each house is in a totally different architectural style, showing off Cutter's versatility and, presumably, the individuality of his clients as well. This one is Neoclassical, with four Ionic columns supporting the full-height entry porch and pilasters at the corners.

Note the broad band of trim beneath the cornice line, a detail usually found only on Greek Revival houses. This mimics the lower part of the Classical entablature—a flat beam that was laid atop the columns in a Greek temple. These were traditionally divided into two parts, as seen here—the narrower architrave band below and the broader frieze band above. Here the frieze is ornamented with swags above the full-height front porch and with triglyphs above the main body of the house. The molded edge of the roof then acts as the traditional third part of the entablature called the cornice. This home survived as a single-family house only until the 1920s, when it was converted to three apartments.

West 2328 First Avenue (private), Wakefield House, 1898; Cutter and Malmgren, Spokane, architects. This striking Mission-style home was built for an attorney who invested in mines. The roof, which looks like ceramic tile, is actually a lighter-weight metal "tile" that was very popular at the turn of the century. Note the porte cochere and small matching carriage house.

West 2417 Pacific Avenue (private), Bibbins House, 1905. This pleasant American four-square house has a bay window to one side and a wraparound porch. It is indicative of the kind of house most often being built here during the first decade of the twentieth century.

West 2301 Pacific Avenue (private), Westminster Apartments, 1905; Sweatt and Stritesky, architects. This striking Tudor structure is one of the earliest of the luxury apartments built in Browne's Addition to help house the city's rapidly growing population (see page 678).

Campbell House, 1898

West 2316 First Avenue; 509-456-3931;
Kirtland K. Cutter, Spokane, architect.

Amasa Basaliel Campbell (1845–1912) was born in Salem, Ohio, the youngest of ten children. He lived in many parts of the West—Utah, Nebraska, Alaska, and had even mined for a time in Mexico—before coming to investigate the tales of the fabulous Coeur d'Alene district in 1887.

Campbell quickly decided there were still fortunes to be made there and traveled to Youngstown, Ohio, to seek out an old acquaintance, John Aylard Finch (see "West 2340 First Avenue," above), who he felt might be able to raise the capital needed to begin his new mining venture. Finch visited the Coeur d'Alenes, was convinced, and the two men formed what was to be a life-long partnership. In 1889 they invested twenty-five thousand dollars in the Gem Mine, which had been dismissed by mining engineers. They built a mill to work the ores and soon found themselves with over twenty thousand dollars a month in profits. His fortune apparently assured, Campbell returned to Youngstown

Campbell House

and married a thirty-one-year-old schoolteacher, Grace Fox (1859–1924), whom he had known before setting off for the West. They made their first home in Wallace, Idaho, a raucous mining town that was a far cry from the sedate life she had known in Youngstown.

The Campbells' daughter Helen (1892–1964) was born in Wallace the same year that major labor-management conflicts were beginning in the region's many mines. These were soon accelerated by the financial panic of 1893 and the subsequent collapse of world silver prices. The labor disputes came to a climax with the 1905 assassination of Idaho's governor Frank Steunenberg, after which the mining district was placed under martial law.

It must have been a great relief to their families when Campbell and Finch decided to move the center of their mining operations from Idaho to Spokane in 1898. Both hired Cutter to design their new homes, but the styles they chose differed dramatically. Finch, the conservative financier, chose a Neoclassical home, while Campbell, the bold mining venturer, preferred a more rustic and picturesque Tudor-style dwelling.

Cutter provided the Campbells with a handsomely detailed home using multiple wall materials—stucco, sandstone, brick, and heavy timbers. The large main house, an offset service wing, and an adjacent carriage house were all equally carefully detailed—scalloped vergeboards on the gables and a slight overhang of the eaves and of the first story add depth, shadow, and interest to the facades.

But it is inside that the house is most inventive, for the first floor is on two levels, giving the interior a sense of both drama and surprise, since the use of such "split-levels" was an almost-unheard-of residential innovation in 1898. One enters into a dark wood-paneled hall with a beamed and gabled ceiling. To the right is a light, gilded French reception room with wall panels covered in rose moiré silk. To the left is the library/family room with its dark wood beams and fireplace with an inglenook. Ahead are four steps that lead up to the raised level of the remainder of the first floor. Directly on axis is a large dining room with its fireplace surrounded by blue-and-white delft tile and with wood paneling and beams painted white. A deep verandah, barely visible from the front, surrounds the dining room and the end of the library/family room and affords a view over the Spokane River below.

Other features of the house include a basement "game room" designated for male drinking, smoking, and poker; unusually well-planned and -lighted service areas and servants' facilities; and five varied upstairs bedrooms.

Following Mrs. Campbell's death in 1924, the house became a community museum. Happily, most of the home's original interior fixtures and fittings survived this period intact, and, with the opening of a new museum next door, the Campbell House is now undergoing careful restoration as a house museum. Of Cutter's three Spokane houses that can be visited, this is the only one that is now a true house museum with an interpretive tour.

Patsy Clark Mansion, 1897

West 2208 Second Avenue; 509-838-8300; visits require restaurant reservations; Cutter and Malmgren, Spokane, architects.

Patrick Francis Clark (died 1915), known as Patsy, was a penniless Irish immigrant when he arrived in the United States in 1870 and signed on for work in the California goldfields. There he became friends with fellow Irishman Marcus Daly, a mining genius who was to become one of Montana's fabled "Copper Kings" (see page 373). Daly had just been hired as superintendent of a new silver mine at Ophir, Utah, and he asked Clark to help him in his new venture. He was soon one of Daly's most trusted lieutenants and later was made manager of Daly's famed Anaconda Mine in Butte. Still later, Clark and Daly became partners in the Poorman Gold Mine in Coeur d'Alene, and the two joined with Clark's Spokane neighbors Finch, Campbell, Wakefield, and the younger Corbin to exploit newly discovered gold and silver mines in British Columbia.

Clark's remarkably picturesque house is said to be an excellent reflection of his personality. If so, he must have been quite a character, for Cutter's unique design is a flamboyant combination of Romanesque arches and still more exotic architectural details. Cutter's biographer, Henry Matthews, has spent years studying the sources of the various elements of the house, and we'll quote his knowledgeable description from an article he contributed to the book *Spokane and the Inland Empire* (Washington State University Press, 1991):

The Clark Mansion is eclectic, bold in form, and extremely rich in detail and color. Built of warm, honey-colored brick with sandstone dressings, it is covered with a hipped roof of brilliant red tiles. The front, with its central entrance arch and round corner towers, exhibits powerful symmetry. Yet Cutter deliberately broke the symmetry by building one tower higher than the other. The arches fronting the balconies are more Indian in inspiration than Moorish; the brackets under the eaves and the sweeping curve of the roofs appear Chinese. The interior fulfills the promise of the facade; the ornate entrance hall, with cusped arches framing a grand staircase,

Patsy Clark Mansion

betrays a Mughal influence. Rich colors glow against the dark background of carved oak. The focal point of the hall is a pair of superb, Tiffany stained-glass windows, whose warm, subtle colors and flamboyant peacock motif proclaim the extravagance of the gilded age.

The house has for many years been the home of a popular Spokane restaurant appropriately called Patsy Clark's. The owners take pride in their loving care of the grand house and are happy for dinner guests to look all through the home. Ask for the handout that tells you a bit about its many rooms.

South Hill, ca. 1890–1930

By the late 1890s a second fashionable residential district, Marycliff, was competing with Browne's Addition for the houses of affluent Spokanites. Browne's Addition, immediately west of downtown and connected to the city center by frequent trolley service, was the more urban of the two, while Marycliff (or "The Hill" as it was first known) was more rugged and rural, with larger, more countryish, building sites. It was here that James N. Glover, the "Father of Spokane," chose to build his own grand home in 1888 (see page 683). Later, other residential districts spread into the adjacent hills. Today, four of these—the Cannon Hill Historic

District, the Marycliff Historic District, the Cliff Park Historic District, and the Rockwood Boulevard neighborhood—provide an instructive look at the sequence of Eclectic-era homebuilding in Spokane and are visited by the "South Hill Route" shown on the map, page 677.

Marycliff, site of the Glover Mansion (see page 683), was the earliest to develop and still retains its grand centerpiece, which happily remains in its original location, although now crowded in by an expanding hospital complex.

In the 1890s a number of other grand houses were constructed on large lots nearby. Most of these mansions are either gone or have had their large lots subdivided for later houses or commercial buildings. Nonetheless, some very fine late-Victorian and early-Eclectic-era houses remain scattered in the grid area between Marycliff and the Cannon Hill district and are worthy of both a look and a long-term preservation effort by the city.

The Cannon Hill district has houses built primarily during Spokane's decade of greatest growth—from 1900 to 1910—when the population surged from 37,000 to more than 104,000, an increase of 280 percent. The original brick streets remain, as do many large trees. The houses themselves are a mixture of architect-designed and pattern-book structures, both large and small. Most prevalent are Craftsman-style designs and American four-square shapes with varying stylistic detailing. A distinctive unifying feature is the dark stone foundations made of local basalt, a volcanic igneous rock that underlies much of eastern Washington. It is a favored Spokane building material and is exposed in the city's Spokane River waterfalls and in its hillside and riverside bluffs.

The higher basaltic cliffs that lay to the south of the city's original street grid provided a temporary barrier to further development until about 1908, when the cliffs were breached by steep roadways, and new residential suburbs were laid out with curving streets that worked well on the more hilly terrain. Among the most intact of these are the Rockwood Boulevard neighborhood and the Cliff Park neighborhood. These contain an assortment of Eclectic-era styles of different sizes and ages.

Marycliff: West 507 Seventh Avenue (private), D. C. Corbin House, 1898; Cutter and Malmgren, Spokane, architects. This handsome Colonial Revival design with a full-width porch was built for Daniel Chase Corbin, a railroad man and another of Spokane's early founders. He was also Cutter's former father-in-law.

Marycliff: West 701 Seventh Avenue (private), Undercliff, 1896; Cutter and Malmgren, Spokane, architects. This unusual and striking Tudor home was built for investor F. Lewis Clark. Note the distinctive octagonal porch with its Gothic arches and basalt foundation. The nearby outcropping of basalt rock was deliberately left by Cutter as part of the landscape. Next door at 705 West Seventh Avenue is the former gatehouse for Undercliff, built first in 1890 as a bachelor residence for Clark, then converted to a gatehouse when he built the main house, and now converted to a chapel.

Marycliff: West 815 Seventh Avenue (private), Austin Corbin House, 1898; Cutter and Malmgren, Spokane, architects. This striking Neoclassical home, built for Cutter's friend from his days of studying abroad and, later, his brother-in-law, originally stood on seven acres of land. Although today it is in a much reduced site and has been used for many years as a Catholic girls' school, Marycliff is the

South Hill

South Hill

source of the district's name. The house's powerful Ionic portico and grand terrace still dominate the street.

Cannon Hill: West 1725 Ninth Avenue (private), Phair House, 1911; C. Z. Hubbel, architect. Fred Phair, the builder and original owner of this home, was one of Spokane's most successful building contractors. He obviously knew his business well and ensured that his Colonial Revival house, with a full-width porch, had plenty of elegant but understated detailing. Note the paired columns, the nicely detailed cornice molding, and the pair of triangular pedimented dormers symmetrically arranged on each side of a smaller shed dormer. It is currently missing the second-floor balcony railing and some of its other original embellishments.

Cannon Hill: West 1703 Ninth Avenue (private), Bradley House, 1909. This Mission-style design bears a strong resemblance to the Wakefield House in Browne's Addition

South Hill

(see "West 2328 First Avenue," page 679). Both have a low-pitched hipped roof with wide overhanging eaves accented by a single front-facing Mission-shaped parapeted gable with a quatrefoil window. A. L. Lundquist was the builder, but the architect is unknown, and there may well have not been one. A good builder at this time could have looked at the Wakefield House, decided to do something similar, and built it without the help of an architect. Adding the wider front porch would have presented no problem. Although we have featured many architect-designed houses here in Spokane, particularly those designed by Cutter, in actuality most American houses are built without an original architectural design—instead, the building contractors have the plans drafted from pattern-book designs or copied with minor modifications from those of nearby houses.

Cliff Park: West 529 Sumner Avenue (private), Codd House, 1916; Fred E. Westcott, architect. This elegant Italian Renaissance design has blind arches above the first-floor windows, an inviting front terrace, and a round-arched entry. Note the use of casement windows both upstairs and down.

Cliff Park: West 538 Sumner Avenue (private), Hebert House, 1928; G. A. Pehrson, Spokane, architect. Note the dramatic three-story sweep of this Tudor house's main gable. The Tudor-arched entry is of tile. This talented architect worked with Cutter and later had a successful practice in Spokane until about 1968. This is probably one of his earliest commissions.

Rockwood Boulevard: 1835 South Upper Terrace Road (private), ca. 1920s. This well-landscaped and rambling Spanish Eclectic house combines one- and two-story sections to give it the "added onto over the years" look that was so favored in larger examples of the style.

Glover Mansion, 1888

West 321 Eighth Avenue; 509-459-0000;
Kirtland K. Cutter, Spokane, architect.

James N. Glover, "the Father of Spokane," was a business partner of Horace Cutter, the architect's uncle (see also the discussion of Cutter, page 676). He offered the young man one of his first chances to prove himself as an architect, and Cutter responded magnificently with this large Tudor home. The first story of the house is heavy rusticated granite with a wide, rounded Syrian arch, giving the house strong Richardsonian Romanesque overtones. The upper stories are stucco with half-timbering adorning two large front-facing gables. In addition, the house is accentuated with a tall massive chimney adjacent to the entry, making the predominant style Tudor. It is very early for such a refined Tudor design, as these were quite rare before the 1890s.

Inside, the house is dominated by a large living hall. One enters the house into this magnificent two-story

Glover Mansion

room, accentuated by three large Syrian arches, echoing that of the entry. Most prominent is the arch above a large alcove under the stairs with built-in seating on each side. There is also an arch over the dramatic upstairs balcony, which gave the master bedroom a prime view of hall activities. A third arch leads to the upstairs bedroom wing of the house. The living hall's walls are paneled in golden maple, and the ceiling is decorated with a fresco painting. Adjacent is a large library that, in turn, opens into an even larger dining room with an adjacent side porch.

The Glover Mansion was long a part of the Unitarian Church of Spokane, which used it for many church-related and community functions, such as meetings, concerts, and receptions. The current owners continue to seek such events. They welcome house watchers, although, as in the Patsy Clark Mansion (see page 680), there is only a handout, not a formal tour.

Corbin Park, ca. 1900–1920

Much of Spokane's early residential growth took place northward, across the river from downtown, where relatively level land stretched for several miles. Typical of many pleasant north-side neighborhoods is Corbin Park, whose oblong shape reflects its site's former use as the horse-racing track of the Washington and Idaho Fair Association, which was located here from 1887 to 1897. The neighborhood's picturesque central park was once a large, fenced pasture where the horses grazed in the center of the oval racetrack.

The neighborhood was platted in 1900 with building restrictions that required all homes to be constructed thirty-five feet behind the front lot line and to cost a minimum of $2,500 to build. In 1902 the developer, D. C. Corbin, donated the central park to the city. The neighborhood was long enhanced by majestic rows of elm trees, which are now falling victim to disease and being replaced by young saplings for future generations of admirers.

709 Waverly Place (private), Skinner House, 1902; W. W. Hyslop, Spokane, architect. This was the first house in the district, designed by architect Hyslop for his in-laws, Mr. and Mrs. Harry J. Skinner. Hyslop designed this in the pop-

Corbin Park

ular Queen Anne style—a beautiful Free Classic example with its corner entry accentuated by a small tower. It is interesting to look at 525 Waverly Place (see the following entry) to see a more forward-looking house that the architect was designing at the same time.

525 Waverly Place (private), Fox House, 1902, W. W. Hyslop, Spokane, architect. This one-story, Craftsman/Prairie-influenced house, when contrasted with Hyslop's design at 709 Waverly Place (see the preceding entry) built in the same year, clearly demonstrates the drastic changes in housing fashions that took place during the first decade of the twentieth century. This is a one-story design in the "modern" tradition and makes quite a contrast with the Medieval-tradition Queen Anne design of the earlier house. Notice how the roof pitch has lowered and how heavy stone piers have been introduced for porch supports. These piers and the chimney are constructed of stone. Other Hyslop designs in the neighborhood include 403, 615, and 711 Waverly Place, 334, 424, and 614 Park Place, and the architect's own home at 2913 West Oval.

504 Park Place (private), Watson House, 1904. This is a one-story Neoclassical house with Classical columns for porch supports. Think of the typical American four-square house, which commonly has a one-story full-width porch and a centered hipped dormer. Then look at this house. It is simply a one-story version of the same house with a similar dormer and one-story porch.

628 Park Place (private), Robinson House, 1908. This Tudor-style house with its classically inspired wraparound porch was featured in several advertisements for the Ballard Plannery, a source for ready-made house plans.

TACOMA

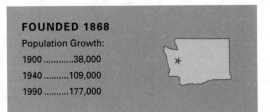

FOUNDED 1868

Population Growth:

1900 38,000

1940 109,000

1990 177,000

Throughout much of its early history, Tacoma was the Northern Pacific Railroad's "company town." In 1873 the small Puget Sound lumber-mill port, founded only five years earlier, was chosen to be the western terminus of the Northern Pacific, the nation's second transcontinental line. Tacoma bustled with anticipation, but the decision turned out to be ill timed. The Northern Pacific's tracks then extended westward only to Bismarck, North Dakota, where construction was abruptly halted only a few months later when the railroad's Philadelphia owners were bankrupted by the nationwide financial panic of 1873. Construction resumed in 1878, but the new owner, New York investor Henry Villard, had financial interests in Oregon and chose to make Portland the railroad's principal Pacific terminus. Tacoma remained a small town awaiting its promised future as an international seaport.

The wait ended in 1887 when a new rail line was completed across the Cascade Mountains to bypass Portland and give Tacoma a direct connection into the eastern railroad network. The Northern Pacific moved its western headquarters into the city, new wharves, warehouses, and grain elevators were constructed, and Tacoma's boom finally arrived. The population jumped from just over 1,000 in 1880 to 36,000 in 1890. Already, however, nearby Seattle's diversified manufacturing and locally financed port facilities were challenging Northern Pacific–dominated Tacoma's goal of becoming the principal seaport of Puget Sound. By 1920 Seattle, with a population of more than 300,000 in contrast to Tacoma's 97,000, had clearly won the race. That same year the Northern Pacific acknowledged defeat by moving its western headquarters from Tacoma to Seattle. In the following decades Tacoma settled into its current niche as a smaller satellite port of Seattle, specializing in the processing and shipping of lumber.

Because of the city's relatively slow growth rate in the decades since 1920, Tacoma retains many fine Eclectic-era commercial buildings and homes, the latter mostly concentrated in the delightful Stadium District to the north of downtown.

Stadium District, ca. 1890s–1930s

This neighborhood, named for the impressive high school stadium that marks its eastern boundary, is spread across a hill overlooking Puget Sound. Its namesake, **Stadium High School,** at 111 North E Street, was begun in 1891 by the Northern Pacific's Tacoma Land Company as a grand luxury hotel for its western terminus city. Built in the elegant Chateauesque style, the hotel occupied a dramatic site overlooking Puget Sound's Commencement Bay. Plagued again by unlucky timing (see above), the Northern Pacific halted work on the nearly completed hotel with the nationwide financial collapse of 1893. The building then sat empty and unfinished for ten years, during which it suffered a damaging fire. Plans for demolition by the railroad were averted in 1903 when the city of Tacoma unveiled ambitious plans to convert it into a high school.

The conversion was completed in 1906, but the school's site was plagued by the precipitous adjacent ravine. The city also needed a new stadium, and the architect hired to design it suggested that the ravine provided a natural setting where a huge stadium could be built more inexpensively than on flat land. Funds were raised, and in 1910 the stadium was dedicated as the second largest in the nation (only Yale University's was larger at the time). Presidents Teddy Roosevelt, Woodrow Wilson, and Warren G. Harding have been here, as have Babe Ruth and John Philip Sousa. The first football game on the West Coast was played here in 1929. The stadium is much beloved by the people of Tacoma, and they have found the funds to restore it three separate times—after extensive damage caused by earthquakes in 1932 and 1949 and by a huge burst pipe in 1981.

While all this was happening, the most elegant neighborhood in Tacoma, and one of the finest in the entire Northwest, was quietly developing to the west. Looking at a map of Tacoma, one can easily see Old Tacoma, the prerailroad town, which had a strict north–south/east–west grid system at the northern tip of the peninsula. New Tacoma is the grid of the downtown area where Northern Pacific surveyors canted the grid to more closely follow the line of the shore. The

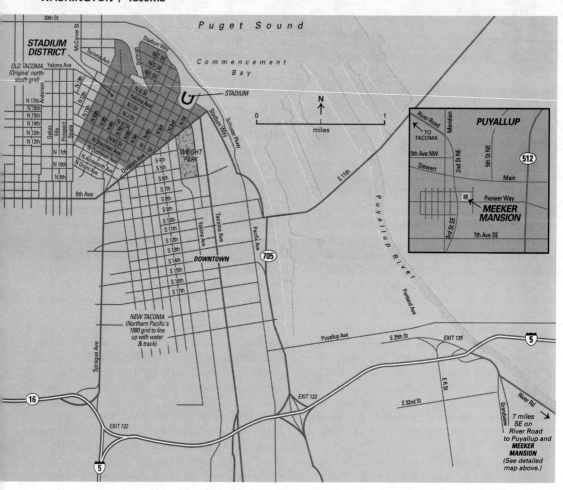

surveyor of the Stadium District introduced yet a third angle of grid streets that connect Old Tacoma and New Tacoma in a surprisingly graceful way.

This was Tacoma's most fashionable neighborhood during its period of rapid early growth, from about 1890 to the 1930s. Here a wide variety of late-Victorian and Eclectic-era housing styles can be found—Shingle, Queen Anne, Craftsman, Prairie, Mission, Neoclassical, Colonial Revival, Tudor, and even Modernistic. Original streetlights and streets paved with cobblestone and brick add an authentic feeling. Beautiful views of Puget Sound emerge as you head down the numbered streets. The larger and more high-style houses tend to be grouped closer to Puget Sound, while many generally smaller (but interesting and often early) wood-clad houses are toward the top of the hill, where there are apartment-house intrusions, some of them quite early.

417 North E Street (private), Gower House, 1906; Ambrose J. Russell and Everett P. Babcock, Tacoma, architects.

This early Colonial Revival design has a lineup of five dormers—all gabled except for a Palladian one in the middle. It has two one-story wings; one is an open porch (so often these have been enclosed) and the other a porte cochere. The large, slightly bayed windows downstairs are unusual. The house was originally covered with brown shingles, had a sleeping porch above the open side porch, and had a porte cochere that extended out into the front yard from the front door and was approached by a circular drive, rather than the more common side-yard version in place today.

501 North Tacoma Avenue (private), Dickson House, 1910; Ambrose J. Russell, Tacoma, architect. It is hard to believe that this very "modern" Craftsman/Prairie house was designed by the same architect as 417 North E Street (Colonial Revival; see the preceding entry), 1001 North I Street (Neoclassical; see page 687), a Queen Anne design at 422 North E Street (private), and many other Washington homes, including the Governor's Mansion in Olympia. Such proficiency with various styles was typical of the best early-twentieth-century architects. Note the flat green tile roof, the horizontal lines of ornamental tile in the stucco, the ribbon windows, and the simple, broad stone chimney.

509 North Tacoma Avenue (private), Betz House, ca. 1915; Russell, Lance, and Muri, architects. This handsome design is Italian Renaissance with Prairie and Colonial Revival overtones. Note the tile roof with wide overhang, the heavy quoins at the corners, and the elaborate window crowns. The hipped dormers and line of trim at the base of the upper-story windows give it a slight Prairie four-square flair, while the dark brick, the entry porch, and the paneled front door have more of a Colonial Revival spirit.

502 North Yakima Avenue (private). This is a Shingle-style house that has had alterations. The two-story wing on the left and the one-story wing on the right are later additions. At the same time, an angular bay window, which echoed the shape of the dormer (over the entry porch), was removed from the front-facing gable; triple windows replaced the original broad windows with transoms; and a shingled balcony in front of the angular dormer was removed, leaving only the dormer. This leaves us with a house that still looks much like an original Shingle-style design but that has lost much of the funky detailing often associated with that style.

517 North Sixth Street (private), ca. 1930. This attractive Modernistic house has walls of white-painted brick. Note how the curved glass-brick bay window is echoed in the reverse curve of the adjacent steps.

705 North Fifth Street (private), ca. 1915. This is a straightforward Italian Renaissance house with a tile-covered hipped roof, broad overhanging eaves, and an arched entry porch with Palladian windows set in blind arches on each side.

1001 North I Street (private), Rust House, 1905; Ambrose J. Russell and Everett P. Babcock, architects. This is an unusually large Neoclassical house of the full-height-entry-porch-with-lower-full-width-porch subtype. Here the two porches are entirely separate. The entry porch is curved and supported by single columns; the lower porch wraps to the side to form a porte cochere and is supported by paired columns. This house is built of sandstone and has extensive detailing, much of it Colonial Revival in inspiration. Note the large central dormer with a broken segmental pediment, the

Stadium District

Meeker Mansion

Adamesque elliptical fanlight above the front door, the elaborate balustrades, and the intricate cornice with triglyphs. Notice also the sunken garden and walkways in the same sandstone.

The house was built by William R. Rust, who, having learned the business of mining and smelting in Colorado, bought a struggling local smelter and built it into the successful Tacoma Smelting and Refining Company, which smelted copper, silver, and gold ores from Alaska and Idaho. Rust sold out to the Guggenheim mining empire for $5 million in 1905, about the time he was building this house for a reported cost of $122,500, with $50,000 more for furnishings.

402 North Sheridan Avenue (private), Murray House, ca. 1905. This unusual Shingle-style design has a very high pitched, side-gabled roof with a pair of highly exaggerated gabled dormers, which tower above small roof balconies. A full-width porch is recessed into the house and supported with pairs of Doric columns. Colonial Revival influence can be seen in the handsome front door, which is paneled below a large-pane window and is surrounded by an Adamesque elliptical fanlight with sidelights.

517 North Sheridan Avenue (private), ca. 1905. A smaller Shingle-style house than 402 North Sheridan Avenue (see the preceding entry), this one is in the gambrel-roofed subtype. Like 402, this has a full-width porch recessed into the house supported with simple Doric columns. The most interesting detail in this house is along the left side, where there is an unusual gambrel dormer and a large cross-gambrel roof that features a Palladian window.

815 North L Street (private), ca. 1910. This is a particularly dramatic false-thatched-roof Tudor house. When the house is approached from the chimney side, five separate gables are visible—a side gable, two front gables, a gabled dormer, and a peculiar little gabled eyebrow dormer in the top of the roof, added for picturesque effect.

Meeker Mansion, 1890

312 Spring Street, Puyallup, eight miles southeast of downtown Tacoma; 206-848-1770; Farrell and Darmer, Tacoma, architects.

The prosperous agricultural town of Puyallup (1990 population 24,000) is the site of the state's only Italianate museum house, a distinctive structure built by a quite remarkable Oregon Trail pioneer who platted the town in 1877. In the spring of 1852, young Ezra Meeker (1830–1928) left his Iowa home with his wife and seven-week-old son to make the six-month wagon journey along the Oregon Trail to a new life in the remote Pacific Northwest. This pioneering experience became Meeker's passion during the last twenty years of his long life, which he spent in tirelessly promoting the memory and preservation of the historic Oregon Trail, which by then had become a fast-fading chapter of western lore.

In the intervening fifty-four years Meeker had several equally passionate obsessions, among them the town of Puyallup, which he platted and named and where he worked tirelessly on civic affairs, including serving as its first mayor. He was also a skilled and innovative farmer. In 1865 he introduced the growing of hops, used in brewing beer, and at that time imported from Europe, to the Puyallup area. His energy and hard work in promoting and marketing the new crop soon made it a mainstay of the local economy and earned Meeker the nickname of "Hops King of the World." In good years his five hundred acres of carefully tended fields produced over ten thousand bales of the valuable plant, which he sold, partly through his own marketing office in London, for an amazing $500,000.

It was after one of these good years, in 1890, that Meeker built his grand late-Italianate dwelling. It was built just in time, for two years later a plague of hops lice wiped out not only his crop, but that of all his neighbors—who had borrowed from him to plant their fields. He forgave their debts with the simple explanation that the loss was not their fault. Then came a second blow—the nationwide banking panic and depression of 1893. Banks everywhere were closing, and Meeker, who owned Puyallup's bank, saw that his was not far behind. He pledged all of his holdings to raise the cash to pay off his depositors. Now penniless, Meeker tried several times without success to regain his fortune. At age seventy-one he returned home from an unsuccessful Alaskan sales trip and turned to a quiet life of writing. It did not last long.

In 1906 at age seventy-six, the ever-energetic Meeker decided to live out a longtime dream and once again walk the length of the Oregon Trail with ox team and wagon. The entire town of Puyallup was upset—even the preacher sermonized on the trip's folly—but Meeker was undeterred. He wanted to mark the trail for all time and also to arouse interest in a transcontinental highway—a remarkably farsighted thought in 1906. This time he traveled from west to east, placing markers and lecturing along the way. The trip was a great success, and Meeker continued to promote the cause of the Oregon Trail—writing about it, lecturing on it, walking it yet again, flying over it, driving along it in a Pathfinder automobile, and following it by train—until his death at age ninety-eight. He was then just preparing to make the trip one more time in a Ford truck outfitted to look like a prairie schooner that he called the *Oxmobile*.

During these later years Meeker wrote movingly about what traveling the trail had been like, trying to stir people to remember and understand one of the great voluntary mass migrations of human history (from Ezra Meeker and Howard R. Driggs, *Ox-Team Days on the Oregon Trail* [World Book Company, 1932], as quoted in *Ezra Meeker*, a booklet published in 1972 by the Ezra Meeker Historical Society in Puyallup):

Worn deep and wide by the migration of three hundred thousand people, lined by the graves of twenty thousand dead, witness of romance and tragedy, the Oregon Trail is unique in history and will always be sacred to the memories of the pioneers. . . .

The pioneer army was a moving mass of human beings and dumb brutes, at times mixed in extricable confusion, a hundred feet wide or more. Like the shifting clouds of summer day the trains seemed to dissolve and disappear, while no one apparently knew what had become of their component parts or whither they had gone. . . .

Sometimes two columns of wagons, traveling on parallel lines and near each other, would serve as a barrier to prevent loose stock from crossing; but usually there would be a confused mass of cows, young cattle, horses and men afoot moving along the outskirts. . . .

The dust was intolerable. In calm weather it would rise so thick at times that the lead team of oxen could not be seen from the wagon. Like a London fog, it seemed thick enough to cut. Then again, the steady flow of wind through the South Pass would hurl the dust and sand like fine hail, sometimes with force enough to sting the face and hands.

The Meeker Mansion has seventeen rooms, most of which have been restored after years of use as a retirement and nursing home. The following are excerpts from some of Meeker's letters describing his home. Among the important details he does *not* mention are the original hand-painted and stenciled ceiling designs that are today being restored, and the six fine original fireplaces:

There is a side entrance from the drive porch. . . . It is a pleasant reception room with very large plate glass for its outer window, with another opening into the wall of special ornamented design. These two, I remember, cost $150. . . .

The first floor consists of a parlor 24 × 14 with large alcove windows on the west, is furnished in walnut (furniture finish) of the highest grade of workmanship. . . .

Opposite the parlor is the library with an adjoining chamber with separate entrances or the whole can be thrown together as one room. . . .

Adjoining this chamber is a bath tub and water closet, stationary wash stand and closet room. . . .

The dining room is furnished in oak and an inlaid floor—a beautiful octagonal room with the east side all glass [no surviving evidence of this inlaid floor has been found].

Meeker also wrote that the exterior of the house had "a stone basement, [and] a stone finish on the weather boarding, of three tons of white sand blown into three coats of pure linseed oil." Using grains of sand to give less expensive wood cladding a look similar to that of stone was a technique advocated by writers of the day. It sounds simple until one reads the sobering statistics in Meeker's letter.

Wyoming

SHERIDAN

FOUNDED 1882

Population Growth:

1900 1,500
1940 11,000
1990 14,000

Sheridan was an early trade center for the surrounding ranches and irrigated farms, a function it still performs today. When the first railroad arrived in the region in 1892, the small community also prospered as a supply center for rich coal mines in the vicinity. The town's principal historic landmarks are the railroad-built **Sheridan Inn** (856 Broadway, 307-674-5440), a remarkable Shingle-style structure later owned by Buffalo Bill Cody, and an equally intriguing Eclectic-era dwelling now operated as a museum house by the state of Wyoming.

Trail End, 1913

400 Clarendon Avenue; 307-674-4589;
Glenn Charles McAlister, Billings, Montana, architect.

Begun in 1908 and finished in 1913, this handsome and individualistic home is a remarkable stylistic combination—flamboyant Flemish gables of Tudor inspiration are placed atop a perfectly symmetrical Renaissance facade with a Beaux Arts entry porch. It was built by wealthy cattleman John Benjamin Kendrick (1857–1933) and his wife, Eula, who served as their own general contractors. The Kendricks hired architects and other designers, but trusted their own tastes and abilities to oversee the process and make it all a reality. They even lived in the carriage house from 1910 until 1913 so that they could closely supervise all aspects of the grand home's completion. The Kendricks' personal touches are seen throughout Trail End, which still retains almost all of its original fixtures and early furnishings, all arranged to give a sense of stepping into someone's 1913 home.

This time-warp atmosphere is likely due to an unusual combination of circumstances. The Kendricks' intense personal attention to every detail of the house during its long construction period was rather abruptly followed by many years during which the home saw little use. Just one year after its completion, John Kendrick became governor of Wyoming, which entailed a move to distant Cheyenne. Two years later, he was elected to the U.S. Senate, a position he held until

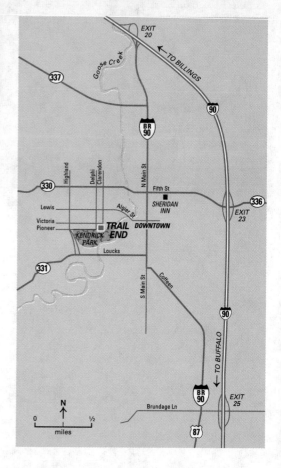

his death in 1933. During this long interval, the Kendricks spent much of their time in Washington, and Trail End was used primarily as a summer house.

After 1933 Eula Kendrick returned to Trail End, where she lived with her son and his family until her death in 1961. The house was then unoccupied for seven years and was saved from demolition by the Sheridan County Historical Society. It is now operated as a museum house by the state of Wyoming.

Much of the decor of the house is "Edwardian" in feeling. This era of English interior design combined dark woods with bright and clear colors, a contrast with the preceding late-Victorian fashion that emphasized light-colored golden oak used in combination with muted tertiary colors, like old gold, olive green, and Pompeian red. Trail End's drawing room is a good example; it combines mahogany woodwork, in a dark

Trail End

"piano finish," with a stunning original rose-colored silk-damask wall covering.

Many of the ceilings of Trail End are subtly hand painted, most often in trompe l'oeil to emulate paneling or coffers. The carefully designed wall panelings, cabinets, stairs, and woodwork were custom-made in Michigan and then shipped to Sheridan for installation. The bills of sale for many of the home's original carpets and Oriental rugs are framed for view.

Original fixtures make even the kitchen and bathrooms a delight. A downstairs powder room, filled with pristine white tile and porcelain, features a double sink with fittings of German silver, an alloy of copper, zinc, and nickel. The kitchen has white tile walls and floors as well as an extensive array of original built-in cabinets and storage bins.

All four floors of Trail End are open to visitors—the basement and three stories of living space. The first floor is the main living area, the second has bedrooms, and the third staff quarters and a large ballroom with a high-pitched ceiling. The basement is mostly service areas. One highlight is the original motor for a built-in vacuum-cleaner system, one of many such up-to-date laborsaving devices built into the house in 1913.

On the second floor, the upstairs landing and hallway feature the Edwardian combination of dark-toned woodwork contrasting with a striking wallpaper in multiple tones of clear green. The stair hall windows have a geometric pattern in clear glass, accented with small areas of emerald-green glass, a feature borrowed from Frank Lloyd Wright's Prairie designs.

Three and a half acres of landscaped grounds include the original 1910 carriage house, now converted to a small theater, a rose garden, and some spectacular views that suggest why the Kendricks originally chose this site for their grand dwelling.

Appendix
Looking at Western Neighborhoods

Dividing Up the Land

This continent's initial occupants, the many tribes of Native American Indians, had a very different concept of land and landownership than the Spanish colonists and later Anglo immigrants who settled the West. The Indians did not believe that individuals owned land, but rather that humans shared the land with all other living things, plant and animal. Although tribes might fight over the right to hunt or gather in certain localities, these disputes were not over ownership.

In contrast to the Native Americans, the Spanish colonists and Anglo settlers who later came to the West brought with them European traditions of individual ownership of specific tracts of land. The modern West still bears many traces of the original land-survey practices of Spain, Mexico, and the United States and of the individual entrepreneurs and settlers who received land from those sovereign entities.

Each government "surveyed" portions of land to establish a system of boundaries in order accurately to trace the ownership of parcels as they changed hands. These initial surveys provided the basis upon which the land of today's United States was first granted to individual owners and could later be sold by them to

fig. 25

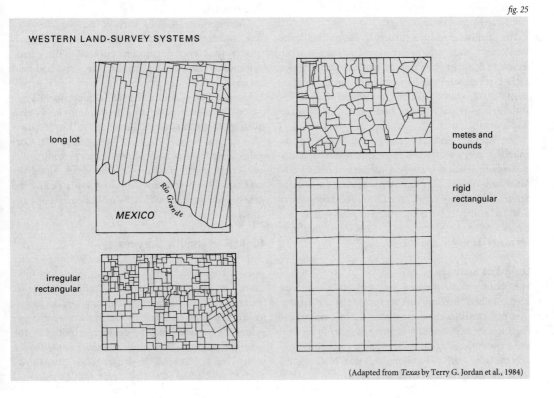

WESTERN LAND-SURVEY SYSTEMS

long lot

MEXICO

Rio Grande

irregular rectangular

metes and bounds

rigid rectangular

(Adapted from *Texas* by Terry G. Jordan et al., 1984)

others. According to geographer Terry G. Jordan's *Texas: A Geography* (Westview Press, 1984), there were four original types of western land surveys (see figure 26). These are often reflected today in the street patterns viewed on maps while one explores western towns and neighborhoods.

Metes-and-Bounds Surveys

The earliest surveys generally used informal landscape features to establish the boundaries of landownership. For example, California's Rancho Malibu (which remained intact until the 1920s as one of the last Spanish land grants to be subdivided) extended from the Pacific Ocean on the south to the ridge of the Malibu Mountains on the north and from a western boundary of Zuma Beach to an eastern boundary of Santa Monica Beach (a distance of approximately twenty-two miles). The use of natural landmarks—such as mountain ridges, the ocean, rivers, beaches, or even rocks, large trees, or river bends—was typical of early land grants. The informality of this early land-apportionment method was appropriate for large grants of what were then low-value lands. Later the distances between landscape features were measured in more formalized metes-and-bounds (measurements-and-boundaries) surveys. In higher-value areas, the distances between landmarks might be measured and recorded from the very beginning—a more exact system that helped to avoid overlapping landholdings.

The Spanish used such surveys to award long-term land leases to those who had rendered military or other service to Spain or to those who agreed to begin making a piece of land productive; the Mexican government actually granted full title to the land in its grants (although in popular usage both are called Spanish land grants).

The use of landscape features and metes-and-bounds surveys was by no means unique to Spanish possessions; it was also used extensively by early Anglo-Americans. Jordan says that Anglo settlers from Tennessee, Kentucky, Virginia, the Carolinas, and eastern Georgia brought this survey system to Texas with them. He goes on to say that southerners knew no other survey method prior to about 1800.

Long-Lot Surveys

The Spanish also employed a second, and closely related, method, the long-lot survey, for apportioning relatively small tracts along waterways. Governed by the colonists' need for reliable water in order to survive and grow crops, long-lot surveys had a short and carefully measured dimension along the valuable waterway, while the longer and less valuable dimension at right

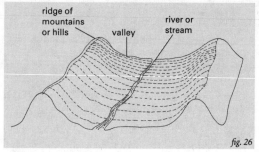

Typical long-lot land survey

angles to the waterway was often less carefully defined. This typically terminated at the crest of the hills or mountains that defined the valley of the waterway (see figure 26). A piece of land in a long narrow shape like this typically included water from the river and woodlands in the adjacent highlands, both essential to everyday agricultural life. Tracts for growing crops could be located close enough to the water to allow irrigation, while cattle or sheep could graze the areas farthest from the waterway (in prairie states the wood would have been in the river floodplain). This is sometimes described as the "riverine long-lot survey." Similar, but generally shorter, long lots were also laid out along Spanish acequias (irrigation canals) as well. Later, secondary acequias could be added and the land still further subdivided.

Like metes-and-bounds surveys, the long-lot survey was not confined to the Spanish colonies; it also was used by the French in parceling out land in the Mississippi River Valley. Under Spanish rule, Texas had land on waterways divided into long lots as early as 1731, according to Jordan, and in the 1830s independent Texas made "this pattern of survey mandatory for lands lying adjacent to major streams." Remnants of this land division can still be seen on local maps today, with **Corrales, New Mexico,** near Albuquerque, providing this book's most striking example. The streets along the acequia in the **Monte Sol** district in **Santa Fe** and the **Martinez Hacienda** in **Taos, New Mexico,** provide additional examples.

Rigid Rectangular Surveys

In 1785, the Continental Congress of the United States passed the farsighted Northwest Ordinance (also known as the Land Ordinance). Drafted by Thomas Jefferson, it defined a more systematic approach to surveying new lands and was inspired by the need to begin selling the lands of Ohio in order to raise money for the new government. The Land Ordinance prescribed a system of continuous 36-square-mile "townships." Each township had 36 sections, each 1 mile square and containing 640 acres. These were surveyed on a strict north–south/east–west grid system. Public roads were to be established at 1-mile intervals along the section lines, and smaller private roads were encouraged at the half-mile, half-section markers. Jordan calls this the rigid rectangular survey.

Beginning with Ohio, federal land managers efficiently surveyed, identified, and mapped most newly acquired territory before it was opened for settlement. The western states that were never under Spanish rule are almost completely covered by this north–south grid survey system.

Even those states that *had* been under Hispanic rule still had large areas that had never been parceled out to private ownership. These remaining public lands were surveyed in the same manner after becoming part of the United States in 1848. It could take a long time to complete these surveys. Arizona, for example, became a territory in 1854, but it took until the 1870s for the federal survey of its unassigned, but habitable, lands to be completed.

Texas was an exception. The former independent republic was allowed to keep its unassigned lands when it became a state, and it handled the surveying and assignation of its own lands. Even Texas, choosing to conform to the norm, eventually surveyed many of the western parts of the state using the federal system of north–south square-mile sections.

As the U.S. government surveys of the West were being completed, newly available lands were granted or sold in north–south–oriented square-mile sections or fractions thereof. Some of these new lands were made available to homesteaders under various homestead acts beginning in 1862. Others were assigned out to entrepreneurs to encourage the building of railroads across the West. No matter by whom the land was first privately owned, the mark of the federal survey system was indelibly stamped across the western states.

Today many parts of the West have roads running due north–south and due east–west at one-mile intervals—an easily visible legacy of these early U.S. surveys. Even where the one-mile pattern has been lost, the north–south/east–west grid has not.

Irregular Rectangular Surveys

In many parts of the West, Anglos arrived in advance of the land's becoming a U.S. territory. These early settlers generally surveyed town sites and neighborhoods in a grid pattern, but their grids rarely conformed to the U.S. government's prescribed north–south/east–west orientation. Texas, in particular, has many areas initially divided into what Jordan describes as "irregular rectangular surveys." He describes these as places where "the individual land holdings are roughly rectangular or square, as in the rigid rectangular system, but they vary greatly in size and lack an orderly grid pattern."

Irregular rectangular surveys evolved in many different ways. Some were adjacent to a river or port, and the direction of their early grids aligns with the orientation of the waterfront (often with "Front Street" or "Water Street" as the name of the street along the river or shoreline). Others align with early railroads or important wagon roads. Still others are relatively arbitrary choices by individual entrepreneurs. In addition, during its years as an independent republic, Texas awarded land grants to veterans of the Texas Revolution, and

fig. 27

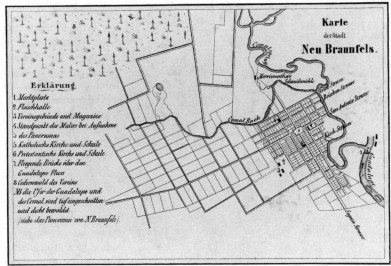

Prince Carl Solms-Braunfels's plan for New Braunfels, Texas, ca. 1845. The main grid is canted to align with the river, and other angles are introduced in the northerly out-lots.

many of these were surveyed on a forty-five-degree southwest-by-northeast angle, perhaps reflecting the *Laws of the Indies* that prescribed this as the favored direction for streets.

Prince Carl Solms-Braunfels's ca.-1845 plan for the town of **New Braunfels** in Texas is an excellent example of a town carefully planned by a group promoting a new town (see figure 27). It has a canted grid, with the angle probably relating to where the streets met the river.

The Modern Legacy of Early Surveys

Different patterns of early land surveys are often obvious on modern city and town maps. This is particularly noticeable when lands assigned by metes-and-bounds or irregular rectangular surveys collide with north–south grid systems relating to later federal land surveys. In many cities of the West, the earliest settled areas are immediately distinguishable on maps by their variously canted street grids (or by the less-than-perfect grids of early Hispanic neighborhoods), which then are surrounded by subsequent north–south grids of streets.

In **Bellingham, Washington** (see the map, page 657), for example, four separate early boomtowns were platted in the early 1850s. Two of them, Sehome and

Bellingham (the downtown area of that map) had surveys that related the angle of the streets to the changing shoreline, while Fairhaven and Whatcom were surveyed with a north–south/east–west street orientation. **Tacoma, Washington** (see the map, page 686), is an unusual example of a town that was initially surveyed in a north–south grid, and then *later* had a slightly canted grid added by the railroad to align with its preferred port. These two grids were connected with yet a third direction of grid bridging between them.

Dallas, Texas (see figure 28 below), is an example we understand because of an unpublished 1990 paper by our friend Constance Adams entitled "The Visible City: Tracing Memory and Character in Dallas' Historical Landscape." While at Yale Architecture School, she was able to trace the varying angles of in-town Dallas streets back to the original land grants. All of the streets that are tilted at a forty-five-degree angle from north–south can be traced back to lands given to Texas War of Independence veterans by the Republic of Texas. Dallas's main downtown streets cut across this to form a second grid surveyed by Dallas's founder, John Neely Bryan—who simply arrived on the banks of the Trinity, laid out a town in 1844, and started selling lots. The angle of his survey related to the bluff along the Trinity River. Lying north of this is a huge area of north–south/east–west streets, all on land that was surveyed at this orientation after Texas became a state. As you move even farther north, the main streets of north Dallas are spaced at one-mile intervals, reflecting their original section-line boundaries.

Building Up the Neighborhood

A primary factor in the character of a neighborhood is the topography and original vegetation of the land upon which it is built. Cities and towns occupy only a tiny fraction of the vast and varied land area of the West. Normally their founders chose relatively level sites near dependable water supplies. In special circumstances, such as mining towns or the deepwater port of San Francisco, it was necessary to build towns on less regular topography. On all nonlevel sites, the neighborhood street plans discussed here interacted with the surface relief to add three-dimensional complexity to the town's neighborhoods.

Much variety results from this interaction of street patterns and local topography (see figure 29). In general, simple grid streets are most at home on flatlands and low foothills; Olmstedian curved streets are most at home on low foothills, but can be easily used in flat areas; and contour curves are typically the only affordable solution to development on steep hills and canyons. There are also three far less common patterns of

Dallas, Texas, street grids reflecting early surveys

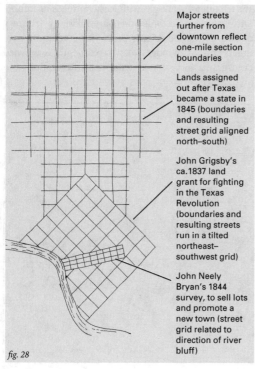

Major streets further from downtown reflect one-mile section boundaries

Lands assigned out after Texas became a state in 1845 (boundaries and resulting street grid aligned north–south)

John Grigsby's ca.1837 land grant for fighting in the Texas Revolution (boundaries and resulting streets run in a tilted northeast–southwest grid)

John Neely Bryan's 1844 survey, to sell lots and promote a new town (street grid related to direction of river bluff)

fig. 28

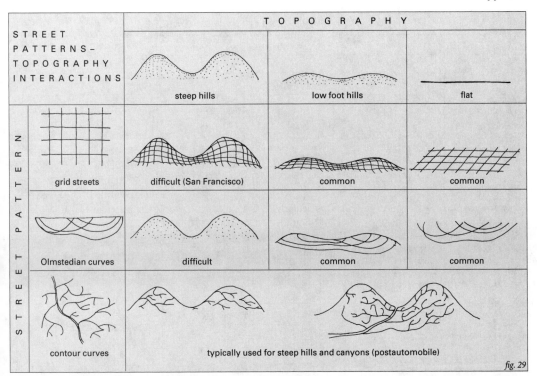

STREET PATTERNS– TOPOGRAPHY INTERACTIONS

T O P O G R A P H Y

steep hills | low foot hills | flat

STREET PATTERN

grid streets | difficult (San Francisco) | common | common

Olmstedian curves | difficult | common | common

contour curves | typically used for steep hills and canyons (postautomobile)

fig. 29

early streets—the irregular "grid" streets found in older Hispanic neighborhoods (see the **Tucson, Arizona,** map, page xvi); the distinctive street pattern that resulted from Hispanic long-lot surveys and water-right practices (see the **Corrales, New Mexico,** map, page 439); and the early-twentieth-century geometric neighborhood plans (see the in-town Phoenix map, page 8). For a discussion of post-1940 street patterns see "Neighborhood Planning in Phoenix," page 7.

Variations in Streets and Blocks

The majority of pre-1940s western neighborhoods were developed with grid streets. A surprising amount of variety is possible with simple grid streets, despite the fact that in map views they may all look identical. The size and shape of the individual blocks are the first place that variety is introduced (see figure 30). Rectangular blocks are the most common, and most often the houses built on these face out in only two directions. The length and depth of rectangular blocks can vary significantly, with the most distinct variation being exaggeratedly elongate blocks such as those seen in **Beverly Hills, California,** below Sunset Boulevard (see the map, page 76). Square blocks, with houses facing out in each of four directions, are the least common pattern (see **"Columbus, Texas,"** page 563, and **"Manti, Utah,"** page 644, for further discussions).

Blocks of identical size and shape may be platted with differing-size lots, adding visual variety from block to block or neighborhood to neighborhood (see figure 31). Lots can be narrow, like the typical twenty-six-foot lots of San Francisco (most often found in urban

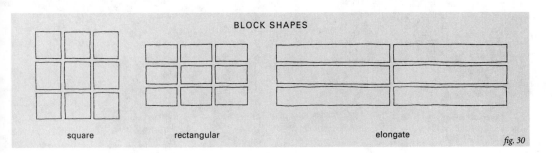

BLOCK SHAPES

square | rectangular | elongate

fig. 30

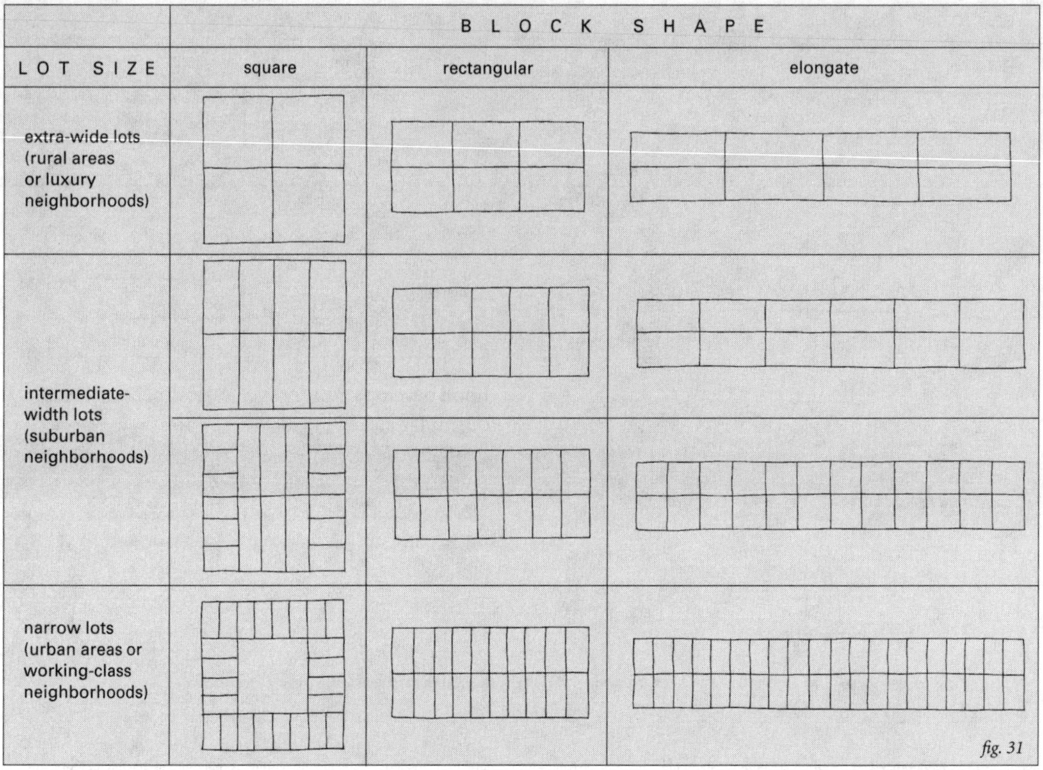

LOT SIZE	BLOCK SHAPE		
	square	rectangular	elongate
extra-wide lots (rural areas or luxury neighborhoods)			
intermediate-width lots (suburban neighborhoods)			
narrow lots (urban areas or working-class neighborhoods)			

fig. 31

environments or lower-income neighborhoods); of medium width (such as the forty-five- to sixty-foot-wide lots found in many neighborhoods of early-twentieth-century American four-square homes or Craftsman bungalows); or generously wide (such as the seventy-five- to more than one-hundred-foot-wide lots found in many upper-income neighborhoods).

Even the width of the streets can be an important contributor to neighborhood character, as street width has strong psychological implications (see figure 32). Wider street widths seem expansive, less intimate, and more likely to carry traffic (even if they do not). Crossing from one side of the street to the other can feel daunting. Narrow streets feel intimate and friendlier to cross. They may impart a rural feel (like a country lane) or a tight urban feel, depending on how close the houses are to the street. Intermediate-width streets balance these extremes and are the most common.

Rhythm of the Street

The size of the houses built on the lots (for example, whether there are small houses on large lots or large houses on small lots) and how they are placed on the lots (either with uniform setbacks from the front and sides of the lot or randomly on the lots) introduce two more sets of variables (see figures 33 and 34).

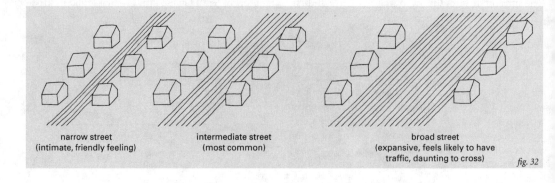

narrow street
(intimate, friendly feeling)

intermediate street
(most common)

broad street
(expansive, feels likely to have traffic, daunting to cross)

fig. 32

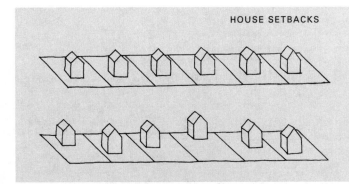

HOUSE SETBACKS

uniform front and side lot setbacks

random front and side lot setbacks

fig. 33

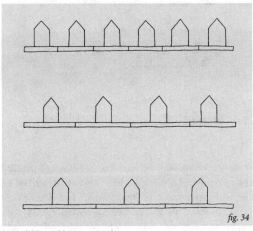

fig. 34

Lot width and house spacing

When all of these factors interact with the ages and styles of the houses, it establishes what planners sometimes call the rhythm of the street. This is actually a very appropriate term. One can have a smooth rhythm (of houses all of the same general age, form, size, and setback) or a syncopated rhythm (of a variety of small and large houses, perhaps set back at different distances from the street) or something in between. The rhythm is most noticeably influenced by whether the houses are of uniform or mixed size and whether or not they are placed in uniform locations on the lots.

A first factor in producing a smooth rhythm (which can also be called a unified streetscape) is whether the neighborhood's initial development restrictions mandated similar lot placement, all two-story houses, or other similarities (see figure 35; see "protective covenants," page xxxv). Streets with a smooth rhythm were rare in the West before about 1900, when larger developments with restrictive covenants became common. A second factor in producing a smooth rhythm is how fast the area filled up with houses. When a neighbor-hood develops quickly, the houses are more likely to be of similar age and form.

Where development was spread over a long period (typical of many smaller towns that never had a major growth period), the streetscape often reflects this (see figure 36). Smaller towns are also less likely to have areas governed by early restrictive covenants, as these were generally used by developers working with larger neighborhoods (which wouldn't be economically viable in a slow-growing small town). Other areas anticipated development over a long period, as with the Victorian mini-farms that could be strung out along early mule car lines (see page xxxii) and Mormon large-block development (see "Manti," page 643). These various factors result in what we often describe in the text as a "typical small-town mixture" of houses.

Interesting rhythmic changes can be seen in neighborhoods that began developing with two-story houses before World War II and did not fill up (see figure 37). After the war, one-story Ranch houses are likely to have been constructed on the remaining lots.

Today one of the problems facing many desirable historic neighborhoods (at least those not protected by

Dallas, Texas: The Swiss Avenue Historic District's unified streetscape and open front lawns are the result of its original protective covenants.

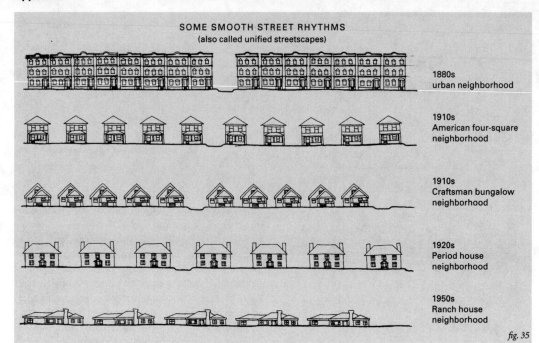

SOME SMOOTH STREET RHYTHMS
(also called unified streetscapes)

1880s
urban neighborhood

1910s
American four-square
neighborhood

1910s
Craftsman bungalow
neighborhood

1920s
Period house
neighborhood

1950s
Ranch house
neighborhood

fig. 35

any type of historic or conservation district designation) is rapid change in a heretofore unified streetscape by the introduction of new houses that are far larger than the older ones that make up the majority of the neighborhood (see figure 38). Mature vegetation and central locations of many older neighborhoods make them prime targets for new and larger infill houses (many of the areas described in this book fall into the category).

The intrusion of just a few behemoths into a smaller-scale neighborhood can have the net effect of making the remaining houses look like what are described in the real estate trade as "teardowns." The description "smaller-scale" in the preceding sentence may well apply to what would generally be considered extremely spacious houses. A street's rhythm is greatly changed by the introduction of just one or two loud drumbeats from out-of-scale houses.

Alternatively, areas that suffer from improper zoning or from unenforced restrictive covenants may have

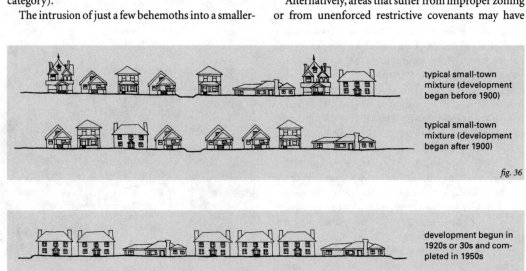

typical small-town
mixture (development
began before 1900)

typical small-town
mixture (development
began after 1900)

fig. 36

development begun in
1920s or 30s and completed in 1950s

fig. 37

formerly unified 1950s
streetscape with newer
out-of-scale houses

fig. 38

formerly unified 1920s
neighborhood with
apartment intrusions

fig. 39

deteriorating
neighborhoods

fig. 40

newer apartments that greatly change the neighborhood rhythm with their greater lot coverage and/or height (see figure 39). At the other end of the scale, historic neighborhoods in less desirable areas may well have their street rhythm interrupted by vacant lots, produced by fire or all too often by code enforcement efforts without any restoration funds or incentives attached (see figure 40).

Street Trees and Landscape

There are all kinds of amenities that can add to the character of a neighborhood. Of these, the one that the authors have been most struck by in preparing this book is the importance of street trees to neighborhood character. Nothing seems to make more of an impression when surveying an area than the absence or presence of street trees. Two side-by-side streets in the same district can be similar in every respect but for an early street-tree-planting program. The blocks with the trees will almost inevitably look more important and inviting. Broad, spreading trees planted along the street line of mid-to-narrow-width streets will eventually form an attractive tree tunnel. (An important exception is the planting of evergreen trees with branches that grow to the ground, such as southern magnolias, that eventually obliterate the views of historic houses.) Trees of varied size and type can have differing effects (see figure 41). The many long north–south streets between Sunset Boulevard and Wilshire Boulevard in **Beverly Hills, California,** had a rather-unusual tree-planting program, and today each street is lined by a single variety of street tree that differs from street to street.

Many early developers worked with landscape architects in laying out their subdivisions and fully understood the importance of landscape on neighborhood character. Restrictive covenants often regulated landscape elements. Street trees, generally planted in the area between the sidewalk and the street, were frequently mentioned as important amenities.

Many neighborhoods have landscaping around the homes that adds to the character of the neighborhood (see figure 42). Broad expanses of front lawns were a symbol of status in the early twentieth century, as they were expensive to maintain. (They still are today—and we now know that, in their current incarnation as monocultures of thirsty, hungry turf grasses, they have a high environmental cost as well.) Still, open front lawns are crucial historic landscape elements in many historic districts. The **Swiss Avenue Historic District** in **Dallas, Texas** (see photo, page 701), is just one example of a neighborhood where deed restrictions prohibited fences or hedges in front of houses, creating a continuous expanse of lawns as one drives down the street. During this era, foundation plantings around the base of a house, typically of mixed shrubs, were popular twentieth-century complements to this pattern. Garages were typically detached.

This was a decided contrast with many earlier Vic-

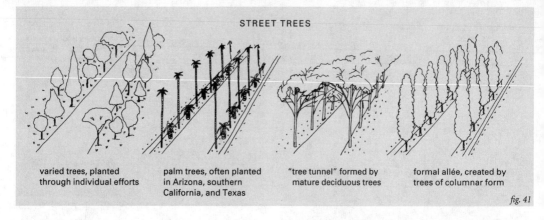

STREET TREES

varied trees, planted through individual efforts

palm trees, often planted in Arizona, southern California, and Texas

"tree tunnel" formed by mature deciduous trees

formal allée, created by trees of columnar form

fig. 41

torian-era neighborhoods that had low or open fences at the sidewalk line, a pattern that has been preserved in the **Huning Highlands** district in **Albuquerque, New Mexico,** and in the **King William** district in **San Antonio, Texas.** Victorian houses were also unlikely to have original plantings along the foundation (they were thought to harbor germs); instead, beds of blooming plants might be set in the middle of the yard.

Some neighborhoods of early Craftsman-style houses, particularly those in northern California (where this style is part of what is called the First Bay Tradition) encouraged hedges or low fences at the sidewalk and sometimes had a distinctive garden gate with a small roof of a type advocated by the *Craftsman* magazine. **Elmwood** and **North Berkeley Hills** in **Berkeley, California, Professorville** in **Palo Alto, California** (see photo below), and **Oak Park Street** in **Ukiah, California,** all have examples of these. The *Craftsman* also encouraged yards filled with bountiful plantings, pergolas, and even ponds.

Curbs, or the lack thereof, contribute to the character of a neighborhood. Streets without curbs seem more rural and small-townish. Streets with curbs seem more urban and suburban. And even within curbs, there is variety. While concrete curbs are the norm today, before about 1900 local stone was often used. The original block of the **Wilson Historic District** in **Dallas, Texas,** has stone curbs around it, but just across the street are more typical concrete curbs, adding a very subtle difference to the two sides of the street. The **Cathedral District** in **Sioux Falls, South Dakota,** has many early stone curbs made with local Sioux quartzite.

Sidewalks are similar in their effect. Their absence seems rural, and their presence seems urban (see figure 43). Post–World War II neighborhoods frequently do not have sidewalks, presuming that almost everyone will arrive via automobile. Although curbs and side-

Hillsborough, California: eucalyptus tree tunnel

Palo Alto, California: Many of Professorville's front yards are enclosed with low hedges and fences.

LANDSCAPE ELEMENTS

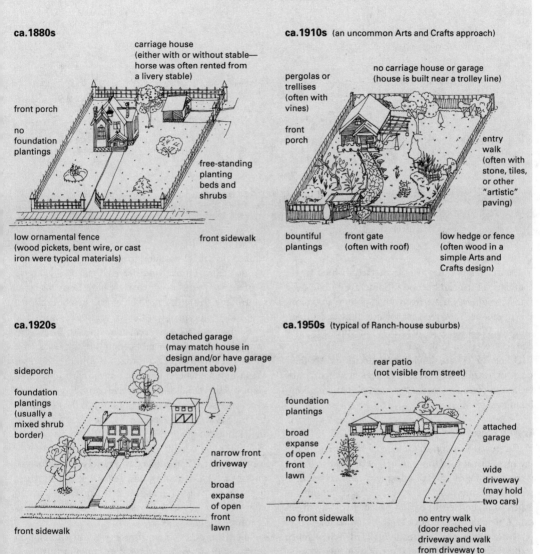

ca.1880s

carriage house
(either with or without stable—
horse was often rented from
a livery stable)

front porch

no
foundation
plantings

free-standing
planting
beds and
shrubs

low ornamental fence
(wood pickets, bent wire, or cast
iron were typical materials)

front sidewalk

ca.1910s (an uncommon Arts and Crafts approach)

pergolas or
trellises
(often with
vines)

no carriage house or garage
(house is built near a trolley line)

front
porch

entry
walk
(often with
stone, tiles,
or other
"artistic"
paving)

bountiful
plantings

front gate
(often with roof)

low hedge or fence
(often wood in a
simple Arts and
Crafts design)

ca.1920s

sideporch

foundation
plantings
(usually a
mixed shrub
border)

detached garage
(may match house in
design and/or have garage
apartment above)

narrow front
driveway

broad
expanse
of open
front
lawn

front sidewalk

ca.1950s (typical of Ranch-house suburbs)

rear patio
(not visible from street)

foundation
plantings

broad
expanse
of open
front
lawn

attached
garage

wide
driveway
(may hold
two cars)

no front sidewalk

no entry walk
(door reached via
driveway and walk
from driveway to
door)

fig. 42

walks are generally found together, many pre–World War II low-to-moderate-income city neighborhoods had sidewalks installed, but not curbs. The sidewalks were considered essential for the many people walking, while the curbs were a luxury.

Because in many of these neighborhoods the original developers did not go to the expense of installing "curbs and gutters," adding them often becomes a neighborhood priority. This sometimes leads cities and towns to believe these amenities should be added to *all* neighborhoods in the city. However, there are many fine neighborhoods where the omission of curbs was a neighborhood-character decision rather than an economic one. Such areas may have large lots and a rolling pastoral quality, and adding curbs negatively impacts the neighborhood's appearance. One neighborhood in this book where curbs were deliberately omitted is **Colonia Solana** in **Tucson, Arizona,** which is also a neighborhood where the native vegetation and drainage topography have been maintained (in an ideal world, this would make it a national model for many of those developing subdivisions today).

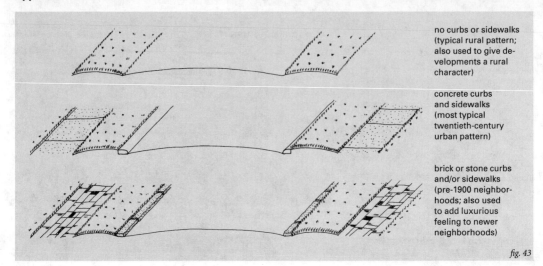

no curbs or sidewalks (typical rural pattern; also used to give developments a rural character)

concrete curbs and sidewalks (most typical twentieth-century urban pattern)

brick or stone curbs and/or sidewalks (pre-1900 neighborhoods; also used to add luxurious feeling to newer neighborhoods)

fig. 43

Other Elements

There are many other details that contribute to the character of a neighborhood. Some are public decisions: Do utilities arrive from street poles placed along the streets or from the rear, or are lines laid underground? What kinds of streetlights are present? What do the street signs look like?

Others are private development decisions: Are there front or rear driveways? Are garages attached or detached? Is there a recurrent type and placement of outbuildings?

Traffic Flow

Traffic flow is also important to neighborhoods. One of the most disruptive things to neighborhood character is the presence of pairs of one-way streets, called couplets. These are designed to carry larger volumes of traffic at higher speeds than a pair of two-way streets can. A neighborhood block lying in between a pair of one-way streets can be greatly affected. When timed traffic lights are added to the equation, remarkably high speeds can result. The many high-speed one-way couplets charging through Denver's older neighborhoods are particularly bad examples of this practice. In Omaha, Nebraska, Farnum Street through the West Omaha neighborhoods has been made reversible, thereby at least confining the problem to one street rather than two—and not affecting an in-between block.

One of the positives of older grid-system neighborhoods is that traffic patterns are much more flexible. Some consider this a negative because it allows more traffic into a neighborhood than is found in newer cul-de-sac areas. (Others find deserted cul-de-sac streets depressing.) Various approaches have been taken to control the greater traffic in older grid neighborhoods. The most widespread is the use of speed tables (or speed bumps) to slow vehicular speeds. These are found in many of the neighborhoods in this book. The most visually dramatic approach is found in **Seattle, Washington,** where in many neighborhoods (like **Capitol Hill**) small traffic circles are present in almost every intersection, allowing the smooth flow of traffic but only at acceptable speeds. A trade-off is the change in neighborhood appearance.

Other older neighborhoods make good use of four-way stop signs. Places like **San Francisco, California,** and the **Park Cities** in **Dallas, Texas,** use a great many four-way stop signs (an approach frowned on by traffic engineers but advocated by some of today's best Neo-Traditional city planners).

There are other, more drastic ways of eliminating traffic, with the most dramatic example in this book being the **Elmwood** and **Claremont** neighborhoods in **Berkeley, California.** Here a number of multiblock sections have been made almost inaccessible (unless you have a detailed map) by a variety of traffic divertors such as forced right turns, closed streets, and such. But the price of protecting these small areas has been to select several streets to carry the additional traffic diverted from the nearby streets. As a result Ashby, Derby, and Claremont Streets carry larger volumes of higher-speed through traffic.

For Further Reference

Most of the published information about American neighborhoods and museum houses resides in leaflets, pamphlets, booklets, and reports meant for local use and thus seldom available in distant libraries. Most museum houses issue giveaway leaflets, and many also have informative longer summaries of their histories available for sale on-site. We urge visitors to take advantage of these important resources, which have also proven invaluable to us in preparing this book. Published information about neighborhoods is more scattered and difficult to obtain. City-planning departments and local-history museums and associations are the best possibilities, but many important neighborhoods remain undocumented. What is needed are more comprehensive and widely available guides to regional architecture of the sort so splendidly pioneered by David Gebhard and Robert Winter for all of California and by Sally Woodbridge and her coauthors for northern California and Washington State. Listed below is a selection of important works that we feel will be among the most helpful to readers seeking additional information. In the state listings, we have placed in brackets the city or state to which the reference is most applicable, when this is not evident from the title. For works treating several architects, those with houses included in this book are listed in brackets.

GENERAL WORKS

Alexander, Christopher, et al. *A Pattern Language*. New York: Oxford University Press, 1977.

The American Heritage Pictorial Atlas of United States History. New York: American Heritage, 1966.

Brown, Dee. *Hear That Lonesome Whistle Blow: Railroads in the West*. New York: Holt, Rinehart & Winston, 1977.

Calloway, Stephen, and Elizabeth Cromley, eds. *The Elements of Style: A Practical Encyclopedia of Interior Architectural Details from 1485 to the Present*. Rev. ed. New York: Simon & Schuster, 1996.

Fishman, Robert. *Bourgeois Utopias: The Rise and Fall of Suburbia*. New York: Basic Books, 1987.

Foy, Jessica, and Karal Ann Marling, eds. *The Arts and the American Home, 1890–1930*. Knoxville: University of Tennessee Press, 1994.

Foy, Jessica, and Thomas J. Schlereth, eds. *American Home Life, 1880–1930: A Social History of Spaces and Services*. Knoxville: University of Tennessee Press, 1992.

Girling, Cynthia L., and Kenneth I. Helphand. *Yard, Street, Park: The Design of Suburban Open Space*. New York: John Wiley & Sons, 1994.

Greenbie, Barrie B. *Spaces: Dimensions of the Human Landscape*. New Haven, Conn.: Yale University Press, 1981.

Grier, Katherine C. *Culture and Comfort: People, Parlors, and Upholstery, 1850–1930*. Amherst: University of Massachusetts Press, 1988.

Jennings, Jan, and Herbert Gottfried. *American Vernacular Interior Architecture, 1870–1940*. New York: Van Nostrand Reinhold, 1988.

Kennedy, Roger G., ed. *Smithsonian Guide to Historic America: The Pacific States* [California, Oregon, Washington], 1989; *The Rocky Mountain States* [Colorado, Idaho, Montana, Wyoming], 1989; *The Desert States* [Arizona, Nevada, New Mexico, Utah], 1990; *The Plains States* [Iowa, Kansas, Nebraska, North Dakota, South Dakota], 1990; *Texas and the Arkansas River Valley* [Oklahoma, Texas], 1990. New York: Stewart, Tabori & Chang.

Lamar, Howard R., ed. *A Reader's Encyclopedia of the American West*. New York: HarperCollins, 1996.

McAlester, Virginia, and Lee McAlester. *A Field Guide to American Houses*. New York: Alfred A. Knopf, 1984.

Maddex, Diane, ed. *Master Builders: A Guide to Famous American Architects*. Washington, D.C.: Preservation Press, 1985.

Paul, Rodman W. *Mining Frontiers of the Far West, 1848–1880*. New York: Holt, Rinehart & Winston, 1963.

Reps, John W. *Cities of the American West: A History of Frontier Urban Planning*. Princeton, N.J.: Princeton University Press, 1979.

Richardson, Ralph W. *Historic Districts of America: The West*. Bowie, Md.: Heritage Books, 1993.

Tishler, William H., ed. *American Landscape Architecture: Designers and Places*. Washington, D.C.: Preservation Press, 1989.

Waldman, Carl. *Atlas of the North American Indian*. New York: Facts On File, 1985.

Winkler, Gail Caskey, and Roger W. Moss. *Victorian Interior Decoration: American Interiors, 1830–1900*. New York: Henry Holt, 1986.

Winther, Oscar Osburn. *The Transportation Frontier: Trans-Mississippi West, 1865–1890*. New York: Holt, Rinehart & Winston, 1964.

For Further Reference

ARIZONA

Brugge, David M. *Hubbell Trading Post National Historic Site.* Tucson: Southwest Parks and Monuments Association, 1993.

City of Phoenix. *Historic Homes of Phoenix: An Architectural and Preservation Guide.* Phoenix: author, 1992.

Cuming, Harry, and Mary Cuming. *Yesterday's Tucson Today.* Tucson: Trillium Enterprises, 1994.

Elmore, James W., ed. *A Guide to the Architecture of Metro Phoenix.* Phoenix: Phoenix Publishing, 1983.

Tucson Planning Dept. and others. *Joesler and Murphey—an Architectural Legacy for Tucson.* Tucson: author, 1994.

CALIFORNIA—General

Abrahamson, Eric. *Historic Monterey: California's Forgotten First Capital.* Santa Barbara: Sequoia Communications, 1989.

AIA Guide to San Diego. San Diego: AIA, San Diego Chapter, 1977.

American Association of University Women, Sacramento Branch. *Vanishing Victorians: A Guide to the Historic Homes of Sacramento.* Sacramento: author, 1973.

Andree, Herb, and Noel Young. *Santa Barbara Architecture: From Spanish Colonial to Modern.* 2nd ed. Santa Barbara: Capra Press, 1980.

Boynton, Searles R. *The Painter Lady: Grace Carpenter Hudson.* Ukiah, Calif.: Sun House Guild, 1978.

Campbell, John Carden. *Houses of Gold* [Nevada City]. Sausalito, Calif.: Deer Creek Press, 1980.

Crane, Clare, and Lucinda Eddy. "Villa Montezuma, 1887–1987." *Journal of San Diego History (Special Centennial Issue)* 33, nos. 2, 3 (1987).

Eureka Heritage Society. *Eureka, an Architectural View.* Eureka, Calif.: author, 1987.

Gebhard, David, et al. *A Guide to Architecture in San Francisco and Northern California.* 2nd ed. Santa Barbara: Peregrine Smith, 1976.

Gebhard, David, and Robert Winter. *A Guide to Architecture in Los Angeles and Southern California.* Santa Barbara: Peregrine Smith, 1977.

Goodrich, Jean Smith. "Casa del Herrero." *Noticias* [Santa Barbara Historical Society] 41, no. 2 (1995).

Hague, Harlan, and David J. Langum. *Thomas O. Larkin* [Monterey]. Norman: University of Oklahoma Press, 1990.

Kamerling, Bruce. *Irving J. Gill, Architect.* San Diego: San Diego Historical Society, 1993.

Kamerling, Bruce, and others, eds. "The George White and Anna Gunn Marston House." *Journal of San Diego History (Special Issue)* 36, nos. 2, 3 (1990).

Kraus, George. *High Road to Promontory, Building the Central Pacific Across the High Sierra* [Sacramento]. Palo Alto, Calif.: American West, 1969.

Loe, Nancy E. *Hearst Castle.* Santa Barbara: Companion Press, 1994.

McCoy, Esther. *Five California Architects* [Gill, Greene and Greene, Maybeck, Schindler]. New York: Prager, 1975.

Michelin Travel Publications. *Touring Guide to California.* Greenville, S.C.: Michelin Tire, 1994.

Regnery, Dorothy F. *The Stanford House in Sacramento.* Stanford, Calif.: Stanford Historical Society, 1987.

Rehart, Schyler, and William K. Patterson. *M. Theo Kearney—Prince of Fresno.* Fresno, Calif.: Fresco City and County Historical Society, 1988.

Rosenus, Alan. *General M. G. Vallejo, and the Advent of the Americans* [Sonoma]. Albuquerque: University of New Mexico Press, 1995.

Winter, Robert, ed. *Toward a Simpler Way of Life: The Arts and Crafts Architects of California.* Berkeley: University of California Press, 1997.

Woolfenden, John, and Amelie Elkinton. *Cooper: Juan Bautista Rogers Cooper, Sea Captain, Adventurer, Ranchero, and Early California Pioneer, 1791–1872* [Monterey]. Pacific Grove, Calif.: Boxwood Press, 1983.

CALIFORNIA—Los Angeles Area

Apostal, Jane. *Museums along the Arroyo.* Los Angeles: Historical Society of Southern California, 1996.

Fogelson, Robert M. *The Fragmented Metropolis: Los Angeles, 1850–1930.* Cambridge: Harvard University Press, 1967.

Gebhard, David, and Robert Winter. *Los Angeles: An Architectural Guide.* Salt Lake City: Gibbs Smith, 1994.

Hoffmann, Donald. *Frank Lloyd Wright's Hollyhock House* [Los Angeles]. New York: Dover, 1992.

Makinson, Randell L. *Greene and Greene: Architecture As a Fine Art* [Pasadena]. Salt Lake City: Peregrine Smith, 1977.

Moore, Charles, and others. *The City Observed: Los Angeles, a Guide to Its Architecture and Landscapes.* New York: Vintage, 1984.

Noever, Peter, ed. *MAK Center for Art and Architecture: R. M. Schindler* [Los Angeles]. New York: Prestel, 1995.

Robinson, W. W. *Los Angeles from the Days of the Pueblo: A Brief History and Guide to the Plaza Area.* San Francisco: Chronicle Books, 1981.

Schad, Robert O. *Henry Edwards Huntington: The Founder and the Library* [Pasadena]. San Marino, Calif.: Huntington Library and Art Gallery, 1963.

Starr, Kevin. *Inventing the Dream: California Through the Progressive Era.* New York: Oxford University Press, 1985.

CALIFORNIA—San Francisco Bay Area

Bagwell, Beth. *Oakland: The Story of a City.* Oakland, Calif.: Oakland Heritage Alliance, 1994.

Boutelle, Sarah Holmes. *Julia Morgan, Architect* [Berkeley]. Rev. ed. New York: Abbeville Press, 1995.

Delehanty, Randolph. *San Francisco, the Ultimate Guide.* Rev. ed. San Francisco: Chronicle Books, 1995.

———. *Victorian Sampler: A Walk in Pacific Heights and the Haas-Lilienthal House.* San Francisco: Foundation for San Francisco's Architectural Heritage, 1979.

Freudenheim, Leslie Mandelson, and Elisabeth Sacks Sussman. *Building with Nature: Roots of the San Francisco Bay Region Tradition.* Santa Barbara: Peregrine Smith, 1974.

Gunn, George C. *Buildings of the Edwardian Period: City of Alameda, 1905 to December 31, 1909.* Alameda, Calif.: Alameda Historical Museum, 1988.

———. *Documentation of the Victorian and Post-Victorian Residential and Commercial Buildings, City of Alameda, 1854 to 1904.* Rev. ed. Alameda, Calif.: Alameda Historical Museum, 1988.

Kennedy, Keith E. *George Washington Patterson and the Founding of Ardenwood* [Hayward]. Cupertino: California History Center & Foundation, 1995.

Longstreth, Richard. *On the Edge of the World: Four Architects in San Francisco at the Turn of the Century* [Coxhead, Maybeck, Polk, Schweinfurth]. Cambridge: M.I.T. Press, 1983.

Margolin, Malcolm. "Historical Introduction." In Don Pitcher, *Berkeley Inside/Out.* Berkeley: Heyday Books, 1989.

Merlin, Imelda. *Alameda, a Geographical History.* Alameda, Calif.: Friends of the Alameda Free Library, 1977.

Richards, Rand. *Historic San Francisco: A Concise History and Guide.* San Francisco: Heritage House, 1995.

Rothmann, Frances Bransten. *The Haas Sisters of Franklin Street.* Berkeley: Judah L. Magnes Museum, 1979.

Scott, Mel. *The San Francisco Bay Area: A Metropolis in Perspective.* 2nd ed. Berkeley: University of California Press, 1985.

Waldhorn, Judith Lynch, and Sally B. Woodbridge. *Victoria's Legacy: Tours of San Francisco Bay Area Architecture.* San Francisco: 101 Productions, 1978.

Wilson, Mark A. *A Living Legacy: Historic Architecture of the East Bay.* N.p.: Lexikos Press, 1987.

Woodbridge, Sally B., and others. *San Francisco Architecture.* San Francisco: Chronicle Books, 1992.

Woodbridge, Sally B., and Richard Barnes. *Bernard Maybeck: Visionary Architect* [Berkeley]. New York: Abbeville Press, 1992.

COLORADO

Barker, Jane Valentine, and Jerry Cleveland. *Seventy-six Historic Homes of Boulder, Colorado.* Boulder, Colo.: Pruett Publishing, 1976.

Brettell, Richard R. *Historic Denver, 1858–1893.* Denver: Historic Denver, 1973.

Dodds, Joanne West. *They All Came to Pueblo: A Social History.* Virginia Beach, Va.: Donning, 1994.

Goodstein, Phil. *The Ghosts of Denver: Capitol Hill.* Denver: New Social Publications, 1996.

Grinstead, Leigh A. *Molly Brown's Capitol Hill Neighborhood.* Denver: Historic Denver, 1997.

Neeley, Cynthia C., and others. *Guide to the Georgetown–Silver Plume Historic District.* 3rd ed. Boulder, Colo.: Johnson Books, 1995.

Noel, Thomas J., and Barbara S. Norgren. *Denver: The City Beautiful and Its Architects, 1893–1941.* Denver: Historic Denver, 1987.

Whitacre, Christine. *Molly Brown, Denver's Unsinkable Lady.* Denver: Historic Denver, 1984.

Wilk, Diane. *The Wyman Historic District.* Denver: Historic Denver, 1995.

IDAHO

Hart, Arthur A. *Historic Boise: An Introduction to the Architecture of Boise, Idaho, 1863–1938.* Boise, Idaho: Historic Boise, 1980.

Shallat, Todd, and David Kennedy, eds. *Harrison Boulevard: Preserving the Past in Boise's North End.* 2nd ed. Boise, Idaho: Boise State University, 1989.

Wright, Patricia, and Lisa B. Reitzes. *Tourtellotte and Hummel of Idaho: The Standard Practice of Architecture.* Logan: Utah State University Press, 1987.

KANSAS

Harris, Cecilia. *Historic Homes of Abilene.* Abilene, Kans.: Heritage Homes Association, 1994.

Kingsbury, Pamela D. *Frank Lloyd Wright and Wichita: The First Usonian Design.* Wichita, Kans.: Wichita-Sedgwick County Historical Museum, 1992.

Peltzer, Theodore F. *Atchison, Kansas: A Photographic Study of Nineteenth Century Architecture.* Atchison, Kans.: Atchison Art Association, 1976.

Sachs, David H., and George Ehrlich. *Guide to Kansas Architecture.* Lawrence: University Press of Kansas, 1996.

MONTANA

Baucus, Jean. *Helena: Her Historic Homes, Volume 1.* Helena, Mont.: J-G Publications, 1976.

———. *Helena: Her Historic Homes.* Volume 2. Helena, Mont.: Bar Wineglass Publishing, 1979.

Malone, Michael P. *The Battle for Butte.* Seattle: University of Washington Press, 1981.

———. "Midas of the West: The Incredible Career of William Andrews Clark" [Butte]. *Montana: The Magazine of Western History* 33, no. 4 (1983): 2–17.

NEBRASKA

Brown, Marion Marsh. "The Brownville Story: Portrait of a Phoenix, 1854–1974." *Nebraska History* 55, no. 1 (1974): 1–141.

Junior League of Lincoln, Nebraska. *An Architectural Album.* Lincoln: author, 1979.

Junior League of Omaha. *Omaha City Architecture.* Omaha: author, 1977.

Peters, Robert C., ed. *A Comprehensive Program for Historic Preservation in Omaha.* Omaha: Omaha City Planning Dept., 1980.

Zimmer, Ed. *The Near South Walking Tours, Volume 1: Franklin Heights and Environs.* Lincoln, Nebr.: Near South Neighborhood Association, 1989.

———. *The Near South Walking Tours, Volume 2: Mount Emerald and Environs.* Lincoln, Nebr.: Near South Neighborhood Association, 1990.

NEVADA

McDonald, Douglas. *Virginia City and the Silver Region of the Comstock Lode.* Las Vegas: Nevada Publications, 1982.

NEW MEXICO

Bodine, John J. *Taos Pueblo: A Walk Through Time.* Rev. ed. Tucson: Treasure Chest Books, 1996.

Bunting, Bainbridge. *Early Architecture in New Mexico.* Albuquerque: University of New Mexico Press, 1976.

———. *John Gaw Meem, Southwestern Architect.* Albuquerque: University of New Mexico Press, 1983.

Bunting, Bainbridge, and others. *Taos Adobes: Spanish Colonial and Territorial Architecture of the Taos Valley.* Santa Fe: Museum of New Mexico Press, 1964.

Fechin, Eya. *Fechin: The Builder* [Taos]. San Cristobal, N.M.: author, 1982.

Historic Santa Fe Foundation. *Old Santa Fe Today.* 4th ed. Albuquerque: University of New Mexico Press, 1991.

Jordan, Louann. *El Rancho de las Golondrinas: Spanish Colonial Life in New Mexico* [Santa Fe]. 3rd ed. N.p.: Colonial New Mexico Historical Foundation, 1993.

Markovich, Nicholas, and others, eds. *Pueblo Style and Regional Architecture.* New York: Van Nostrand Reinhold, 1990.

Noble, David Grant. *Pueblos, Villages, Forts, and Trails: A Guide to New Mexico's Past.* Albuquerque: University of New Mexico Press, 1994.

For Further Reference

Treib, Marc. *Sanctuaries of Spanish New Mexico.* Berkeley: University of California Press, 1993.

Wilson, Chris. *The Myth of Santa Fe: Creating a Modern Regional Tradition.* Albuquerque: University of New Mexico Press, 1997.

NORTH DAKOTA

Heidenreich, Virginia L., ed. *North Dakota's Former Governor's Mansion: Its History and Preservation.* Bismarck: State Historical Society of North Dakota, 1991.

OKLAHOMA

Blackburn, Bob L., and Jim Argo. *Heritage Hills: Preservation of a Historic Neighborhood* [Oklahoma City]. N.p.: Western Heritage Press, 1990.

Goins, Charles R., and John W. Morris. *Oklahoma Homes, Past and Present.* Norman: University of Oklahoma Press, 1980.

Inhofe-Tucker, Marilyn, and others. *Footsteps Through Tulsa.* 2nd ed. Tulsa: Footsteps Through Tulsa L.L.C., 1995.

Yoch, James J. *A Guide to Villa Philbrook and Its Gardens.* Tulsa: Philbrook Museum of Art, 1991.

OREGON

Clarke, Ann Brewster. *Wade Hampton Pipes: Arts and Crafts Architect in Portland, Oregon.* Portland: Binford & Mort, 1985.

Marlitt, Richard. *Matters of Proportion: The Portland Residential Architecture of Whidden and Lewis.* Portland: Oregon Historical Society Press, 1989.

Norman, James B., Jr. *Portland's Architectural Heritage.* 2nd ed. Portland: Oregon Historical Society Press, 1991.

Vaughan, Thomas, and Virginia Guest Farriday, eds. *Space, Style, and Structure: Building in Northwest America.* 2 vols. Portland: Oregon Historical Society, 1974.

SOUTH DAKOTA

Sioux Falls Planning and Building Services Department. *Historic Avenues in Sioux Falls, South Dakota.* Sioux Falls: author, 1983.

TEXAS

Alexander, Drury Blakeley, and Todd Webb. *Texas Homes of the Nineteenth Century.* Austin: University of Texas Press, 1966.

Barnstone, Howard. *The Architecture of John F. Staub: Houston and the South.* Austin: University of Texas Press, 1979.

Beasley, Ellen, and Stephen Fox. *Galveston Architecture Guidebook.* Houston: Rice University Press, 1996.

Burkholder, Mary V. *The King William Area: A History and Guide to the Houses.* 2nd ed. San Antonio: King William Association, 1977.

Carson, Chris, and William B. McDonald, eds. *A Guide to San Antonio Architecture.* San Antonio: AIA, San Antonio Chapter, 1986.

Caswell, Jon, ed. *A Guide to the Older Neighborhoods of Dallas.* Dallas: Historic Preservation League, 1986.

Engelbrecht, Lloyd C., and June-Marie F. Engelbrecht. *Henry C. Trost, Architect of the Southwest.* El Paso, Tex.: El Paso Public Library Association, 1981.

Fox, Stephen. *Houston Architectural Guide.* Houston: AIA, Houston Chapter, 1990.

Friends of the Governor's Mansion, ed. *The Governor's Mansion of Texas: A Historic Tour.* Austin: author, 1985.

Galloway, Diane, and Kathy Matthews. *The Park Cities: A Walker's Guide and Brief History.* Dallas: Southern Methodist University Press, 1988.

Keahey, Kirby, and Allen McCree, eds. *Austin and Its Architecture.* Austin: AIA, Austin Chapter, 1976.

McCullar, Michael. *Restoring Texas: Raiford Stripling's Life and Architecture* [San Augustine]. College Station: Texas A & M University Press, 1985.

McDonald, William L. *Dallas Rediscovered: A Photographic Chronicle of Urban Expansion, 1870–1925.* Dallas: Dallas Historical Society, 1978.

Payne, Richard, and Geoffrey Leavenworth. *Historic Galveston.* Houston: Herring Press, 1985.

Ramsdell, Charles, and Carmen Perry. *San Antonio: A Historical and Pictorial Guide.* 2nd rev. ed. Austin: University of Texas Press, 1985.

Sumner, Alan R., ed. *Dallasights: An Anthology of Architecture and Open Spaces.* Dallas: AIA, Dallas Chapter, 1978.

Williamson, Roxanne Kuter. *Austin, Texas: An American Architectural History.* San Antonio: Trinity University Press, 1973.

UTAH

Angus, Mark. *Salt Lake City Underfoot: Self-Guided Tours of Historic Neighborhoods.* Salt Lake City: Signature Books, 1993.

Carter, Thomas. "The Best of Its Kind and Grade: Rebuilding the Sanpete Valley, 1890–1910" [Manti]. *Utah Historical Quarterly* 54, no. 1 (1986): 88–112.

Carter, Thomas, and Peter Goss. *Utah's Historic Architecture, 1847–1940: A Guide.* Salt Lake City: Utah State Historical Society, 1988.

Churchill, Stephanie D. *Utah: A Guide to Eleven Tours of Historic Sites.* Salt Lake City: Utah Heritage Foundation, 1972.

Rice, Cindy. "Spring City: A Look at a Nineteenth-Century Mormon Village." *Utah Historical Quarterly* 43, no. 3 (1975): 260–77.

WASHINGTON

Kreisman, Lawrence. *The Stimson Legacy: Architecture in the Urban West.* Seattle: Willows Press, 1992.

Matthews, Henry. *Kirtland Cutter: Architect in the Land of Promise.* Seattle: University of Washington Press, 1998.

Niebauer, James W., II. *Port Townsend's Victorian Homes.* Palo Alto, Calif.: Southgate Press, 1984.

Ochsner, Jeffrey Karl, ed. *Shaping Seattle Architecture: A Historical Guide to the Architects.* Seattle: University of Washington Press, 1994.

Acknowledgments

First and foremost, we are much indebted to Jane Garrett, our longtime editor at Alfred A. Knopf, for her enthusiastic and unflagging support of this sometimes dauntingly complex project. We also thank her Knopf colleagues for magically, and patiently, transforming our draft materials into a handsome final product. Design director Peter Andersen helped bring us into the digital age with the photographs and map formats and, along with senior designer Anthea Lingeman, created the overall book design. We are particularly appreciative of the way Anthea was able to integrate the illustrative material and text as she designed each individual page. There are many others on Knopf's outstanding editorial and production staff who have worked hard to complete this volume. In particular we would like to thank managing editor Kathy Hourigan for her encouragement; production editor Dori Carlson for overseeing the project; and editorial assistant Webb Younce for providing coordination.

Family Affair

With a deadline fast approaching and the discovery of some last-minute glitches, our four children were pressed into service. Our journalist son Keven McAlester made time to visit and to prepare final entries for a number of museum houses that we had previously visited in Oklahoma and California. In addition he took photographs for some of these sites and helped edit several chapters. Daughter Martine McAlester became our efficient research assistant, sending out drafts of the museum house entries (and, where possible, other parts of the text) for review by on-site experts. Aspiring Canadian cinematographer Roman Sokal was visiting our son writer-director Carty Talkington at a crucial moment, and spent several days taking photographs in Los Angeles and Pasadena to replace a group of lost film rolls. Carty served as photo-assistant and chauffeur. Movie line producer Zachary Mortensen took photographs of Georgetown, Silver Plume, and Idaho Springs, Colorado, with the assistance of our daughter Amy Talkington, another writer-director. Finally, our parents Dorothy and Wallace Savage cheerfully minded the dog during our many months of research travel.

Maps and Illustrations

Three Dallas graphic artists worked tirelessly on the complex maps for the book. Greg Malphurs and Terry Guyton were responsible for the computer production of the maps. Jerry Guthrie, who had produced maps for two of our earlier books, was map editor for the entire project. Terry and Jerry put in many hours developing the design standards for the maps at the beginning of the project. Greg, who has now joined the Richards Group in Dallas, prepared the maps for the introduction and the California, Oregon, and Washington chapters, as well as the Phoenix Neighborhood Planning maps. Terry produced those for the remaining states.

All of the original drawings for the book were produced by the Dallas architectural firm ArchiTexas. The principals in this firm—Craig Melde as chairman, Gary Skotnicki as president, and coworker Robin McCaffrey—are old friends who served in the Dallas Planning Department during the early days of the city's preservation movement. Today their outstanding firm specializes in historic preservation projects throughout the Southwest. Russian intern Darya Davidenko, from the Moscow Architectural Institute, executed the drawings under the principals' supervision.

The many historic photographs and drawings included in the book were gathered by New York–based photo researcher Laura Straus, who did a heroic job on a very tight deadline.

Special thanks are also owed to Drury Blake Alexander, professor emeritus in the School of Architecture at the University of Texas at Austin, for use of his lovely drawing of the Bremond Block in that city, which is in

Acknowledgments

the university's Architectural Drawings Collection; and to the City of Tucson Planning Department for use of their plan of El Encanto and for leading us to R. Brooks Jeffery, the curator of the Arizona Architectural Archives at the University of Arizona in Tucson, who allowed us to use their drawings comparing Anglo and Hispanic neighborhoods. Also to Douglas Newby for allowing the use of photos from the original promotional booklet of the Munger Place neighborhood in Dallas, Texas; to the Friends of Filoli and the National Trust for Historic Preservation for use of the garden plan for Filoli in Woodside, California; and to the Ranching Heritage Museum in Lubbock, Texas, for use of one of their early plans.

About the Photographs

The authors took most of the photographs in the book, using an aging Nikon camera and either a 35 mm or 28 mm perspective-correcting lens, a polarizing filter, and Kodak Tri-X or TMAX 400 film. The photos were taken in whatever lighting was available during our visits, a less-than-ideal requirement dictated by our tight travel schedules. BWC Imaging Labs in Dallas did all of the photo processing and transferred all of the images onto Photo CDs. Mark Denton of BWC generously took the time to choose the best exposure of each image for this purpose; he and BWC also provided other beyond-the-call-of-duty assistance in our photo efforts.

There were many times during our travels when bad weather, persistent parked trucks, painters' scaffolds, and other such problems prevented our taking any usable images of important sites. For these we turned to the generous help of local photographers, preservation groups, planning departments, and museum curators, who provided the needed photographs. Many did this on short notice and in the midst of a busy holiday season.

Torrents of rain in Houston and Galveston prevented our taking photos while there, and a talented young Dallas photographer, Catherine Wally, made a special two-day trip to provide images for those two cities. Superb art photographer Paul Kozal of Union City, California, accompanied by Virginia Warheit of the City of Palo Alto Planning Department and Karen Holman of Palo Alto–Stanford Heritage, spent hours photographing Professorville in Palo Alto, with a particular emphasis on special neighborhood qualities. The results, along with their insightful questions and comments, helped expand our knowledge about landscape and streetscape qualities of neighborhoods in general, and those of Professorville in particular. We wish that space allowed us to include even more of their fine photographs. San Francisco film student and cinematographer Cynthia

Jane Roessler made two trips to Hillsborough, California, to take photos, after being recruited by a mutual friend, art restorationist Stashka Star.

Several others also generously took the time to shoot one or more rolls of film to fill in major gaps. These include Mark Reavis of the City of Butte, Montana; Jacquelyn Lynch, associate planner in the Community Development Division of the City of Bellingham, Washington; Max A. van Balgooy of the Workman and Temple Family Homestead Museum, City of Industry, California; Lloyd and Connie Chandler of the Governor Furnas House in Brownville, Nebraska; and Marna Porath of the Bush Art Barn in Salem, Oregon.

Others searched through photographic archives, or their own photo collections, and sent us selections of existing photographs for possible use. These included Lawrence M. Kreisman, program director of the Seattle Architectural Foundation; Nancy Gale Compau of the Northwest Room at the Spokane Public Library; Teresa L. Brum, historic preservation officer for the Spokane Historic Preservation Office; Edward F. Zimmer, historic preservation planner for the Lincoln City–Lancaster County Planning Department in Lincoln, Nebraska; David Bush of the Galveston Historical Foundation; Melissa M. Heaver of the National Trust for Historic Preservation; Melisa Harder of Historic Denver; Chuck Petty of the Eureka Heritage Society; Roberta Deering of the Sacramento Department of Planning and Development; the Taos County Chamber of Commerce; and the Heritage Center of Abilene, Kansas.

Catherine A. Horsey and Patsy Stephenson of Preservation Dallas allowed us access to their archives and loaned many photographs, including the fine work done by Dallas photographer David Buffington for the book *A Guide to the Older Neighborhoods of Dallas*. David then let us search his negatives in order to reproduce a missing photograph. Lynn Meyer of the City of Omaha Planning Department loaned us a selection of photographs, including his own work. Nathan Hamm Photography generously allowed us to use their photograph of the Kansas Governor's Residence in Topeka, Kansas. And, finally, Alex McLean, whose splendid available-light color photographs illustrate our book *Great American Houses and Their Architectural Styles*, allowed us to use a number of his outtakes from that project.

Museum Curators, Preservation Professionals, and Other Experts

A great many persons provided invaluable help in preparing this volume—among them museum curators, preservation specialists, city planners, and volunteer preservationists. Some supplied research materials or answered queries; others reviewed portions of the manuscript for accuracy; still others provided us with specific photographs; and a few heroic souls did a bit of each. We very much appreciate all that those listed below have done. Unfortunately, we know that there are others whose names have been misplaced during our travels over the past several years. If you fall into this category, we apologize and hope that you will remind us! Finally, we absolve all of the following for any remaining errors, both of fact and of judgment. The responsibility for these rests squarely, and uncomfortably, upon the authors.

Arizona

Flagstaff: Riordan Mansion State Historic Park—Bill Och. *Ganado:* Hubbell Trading Post National Historic Site—Nancy Stone. *Phoenix:* City of Phoenix, Historic Preservation Office—Roger A. Brevoort, Nancy Burgess; Rossen House—Betty Gleason; Wrigley Mansion Club—Yvonne Roberts. *Prescott:* Sharlot Hall Museum—Richard Sims. *Tucson:* Sosa–Carrillo–Frémont House—Fred McAninch; Arizona Architectural Archives at the University of Arizona College of Architecture—R. Brooks Jeffrey; Tucson Museum of Art—Tisa Rodriguez Sherman.

California

Alameda: Alameda Museum—George C. Gunn, Laura Bayih. *Belmont:* College of Notre Dame, Ralston Hall—Dr. Mary Ellen Boyling. *Chico:* Bidwell Mansion State Historic Park—Paul Holman. *City of Industry:* Workman and Temple Family Homestead Museum—Max A. van Balgooy, Mary A. Roberts. *Fresno:* City of Fresno—Dolores Mellon; Fresno City Historical Society—Thomas Nabe; Kearney Mansion—Adrian McGraw; Meux Home—Linda Impeartrice, Barbara J. McIntosh. *Hayward:* Hayward Area Historical Society—Lois Over. *Long Beach:* City of Long Beach, Department of Planning and Building—Ruthann Lehrer; City of Long Beach, Rancho Los Cerritos Historic Site—Sue McCarty; Rancho Los Alamitos Foundation—Pamela Seager. *Los Angeles:* AIJK Architecture and City Design—John Kaliski; Danielle Brown; County of Los Angeles, Department of Parks and Recreation—Michael Kriste; Hollyhock House—Thomas Stallman; Virginia Robinson Home and Gardens—Ivo Hadjiev; Will Rogers State Historic Park—Nancy Mendez. *Malibu:* Malibu Lagoon Museum—Sandy Mitchell. *Martinez:* National Park Service, John Muir House—David Blackburn. *Monterey:* Monterey State Historic Park—Linda Larson. *Napa:* Napa County Landmarks, Inc.—Dorothy-Dean Thomas. *Oakland:* Camron-Stanford House; City of Oakland, Office of Planning and Building—Betty Marvin; Oakland Heritage Alliance—Steven Lavoie; Pardee Home Museum—David Nicolai, Melissa Rosengard; Victorian Preservation Center of Oakland—Helen and Kenneth G. Gilliland; *Old House Interiors* magazine. *Palo Alto:* City of Palo Alto Planning Department—Virginia Warheit; Palo Alto–Stanford Heritage—Karen Holman, Joan Jack, Carol Murden. *Pasadena:* City of Pasadena—Bill Welch; Cravens House (American Red Cross)—Diane Eyles; Gamble House—Ted Bosley; The Huntington—Lisa Blackburn; Pasadena Historical Museum—Tania Rizzo; Tournament House and Wrigley Gardens—Nancy Atkinson. *Petaluma:* Petaluma Adobe State Historic Park. *Redlands:* Kimberly-Shirk Association and Kimberly Crest House and Gardens—Steven T. Spiller. *Sacramento:* City of Sacramento, Department of Planning and Development—Richard B. Hastings, Roberta Deering; Governor's Mansion State Historic Park—Barbara Baker; Leland Stanford Mansion State Historic Park—Patricia A. Turse; Sacramento Heritage Society—Carol Roland; State of California, Department of Parks and Recreation—Tom Winter. *San Diego:* Alexander D. Bevil; City of San Diego, Planning Department—Bernard Turgeon; Mission Hills Association—Mary-Ann Petino, Max Zaker; Museums of San Diego History—Kathleen M. Eckery, Norma Ferrara, Nancy Jordan, Nancy Lear. *San Francisco:* John Richard Royall; James Sodeman; Octagon House—Nancy P. Weston; San Francisco Heritage—Stacia Fink. *San Jose:* City of Campbell, Recreation and Community Service—Melissa Heyman; Peralta Adobe and Fallon House—Chris Herrara; Villa Montalvo (Saratoga)—Wendy Miller; Winchester Mystery House—Shozo Kagoshima. *San Rafael:* Marin County Historical Society. *San Simeon:* Hearst San Simeon State Historical Monument—James Allen, John F. Horn. *Santa Barbara:* Casa de la Guerra—Patrick O'Dowd; Santa Barbara Historical Museums—David Bisol, Michael Redmon. *South Lake Tahoe:* USDA, Forest Service—Linda Cole. *Ukiah:* Sun House—Betty Fairbanks. *Ventura:* City of Buenaventura, Historic Sites—Richard Senate. *Wilmington:* General Phineas Banning Residence—Michael Sanborn. *Woodside:* Filoli Center—Thomas M. Rogers; National Trust for Historic Preservation (Washington, D.C.)—Melissa M. Heaver.

Colorado

The National Trust for Historic Preservation, Mountain-Plains Field Office. *Boulder:* City of Boulder, Planning Department—Lara K. Ramsey; Colorado Historical Society—Margi Aguilar. *Colorado Springs:*

City of Colorado Springs, Planning, Development and Finance—Timothy J. Scanlon; Glen Eyrie—Len Froisland; McAllister House Museum—Diane Hoover, Joan Bender. *Denver:* Byers-Evans House—Vicky Morton; City of Denver, Planning Office—Ellen Ittelson; Historic Denver, Inc.—Melisa Harder; Molly Brown House Museum—Leigh A. Grinstead; Pearce-McAllister Cottage—Laura Douglas. *Fort Collins:* City of Fort Collins, Planning Department—Carol Tunner; Poudre Landmarks Foundation, Inc.—Jane Hail. *Georgetown:* Historic Georgetown—Ron Neely. *Pueblo:* Pueblo Library District—Joanne Dodds; Rosemount Victorian House Museum—William Henning, Kerry Marie Kramer. *Trinidad:* Colorado Historical Society—Margi Aguilar; Trinidad History Museum—Paula Manini.

Idaho
Boise: Idaho State Historical Society—Ann L. Swanson.

Kansas
Abilene: Lebold-Vahsholtz Mansion—Merle Vahsholtz; Dwight D. Eisenhower Library. *Atchison:* Amelia Earhart Birthplace—Louise Foudray; Atchison Area Chamber of Commerce—Stan Lawson; The Book Station—Rick and Maria Hoecker; Evah C. Cray Historical House Museum—Mickey Parman; Muchnic Art Gallery—Nancy Kaiser-Caplan. *Leavenworth:* Leavenworth County Historical Society Museum—Robert A. Holt. *Marysville:* Koester House—Joy A. Stewart. *Topeka:* City of Topeka, Department of Parks and Recreation, Historic Ward-Meade Park—Anita Wolgast; State of Kansas, Office of the First Lady—Jennie Adams Rose. *Wichita:* Allen Lambe House Museum and Study Center—Howard W. Ellington; Wichita–Sedgwick County Historical Museum Association—Robert A. Puckett; Wichita–Sedgwick County, Metropolitan Area Planning Department—Jeff Tully.

Montana
Billings: Moss Mansion—Ruth Towe. *Butte:* City of Butte—Mark Reavis. *Deer Lodge:* Grant-Kohrs Ranch—Scott Eckberg. *Hamilton:* Daly Mansion—Doug Johnson. *Helena:* State of Montana, Montana Historical Society—Ellen Baumler, Brian Cockhill, Dianne Keller. *Kalispell:* Conrad Mansion—Lynn Redfield.

Nebraska
Brownville: Brownville Historical Society—Don Campbell; Governor Furnas House—Dorothy Broady. *Kearney:* Frank House—Virginia Lund. *Lincoln:* Lincoln City–Lancaster County Planning Department—Edward F. Zimmer; Thomas P. Kennard House—John

Lindahl. *Nebraska City:* Arbor Lodge State Historical Park—Randy Fox; Nebraska City Historical Society—Eric B. Asboe; Nelson-Taylor-Bickel House—Mrs. Karl Nelson; Wildwood—Richard B. and Marcella Wearne. *Omaha:* City of Omaha, Planning Department—Stacey C. Pilgrim, Lynn Meyer; Historical Society of Douglas County—Ann B. Haller; Landmarks, Inc.—Connie Ranald Chandler, Jo Grebenick; Nebraska State Historical Society; *Moorhead, Minnesota:* Comstock House.

Nevada
Virginia City: Bowers Mansion—Betty Hood; The Castle—Marshall Hansen.

New Mexico
Albuquerque: Casa San Ysidro—Alan Minge; City of Albuquerque, Planning Department—Edgar Boles. *Santa Fe:* El Rancho de las Golondrinas—Louann C. Jordan; State of New Mexico, Historic Preservation Division—Mary Anne Anders, Dorothy Victor; City of Santa Fe Convention and Visitors Bureau. *Taos:* Fechin Home—Eya Fechin; Kit Carson Historic Museums—Skip Miller; Mabel Dodge Luhan House—Maria Fortin.

North Dakota
Bismarck: State Historical Society of North Dakota—Janet Daley Lysengen. *Mandan:* Fort Lincoln State Park—Chuck Erickson, Tracy Potter; North Dakota Tourism Department.

Oklahoma
Anadarko: Indian City U.S.A.—George Moran. *Bartlesville:* Frank Phillips Home Site—Susan Lacey. *Oklahoma City:* City of Oklahoma City, Planning Department—Todd Scott; Harn Homestead Museum—Carol Hazelwood; Oklahoma Heritage Center—Gini Campbell; Overholser Mansion—Bill Fullhart. *Ponca City:* Paul L. Prather; Marland Mansion—Kathy Adams; Ponca City Tourism. *Tahlequah:* Cherokee Heritage Center—Tom Mooney; Cherokee National Historical Society; George M. Murrell Home Site—Shirley Pettingill. *Tulsa:* Philbrook—Marsha Manhart; Travis Home—Bonnie Hammond.

Oregon
Katherine Sotka. *Astoria:* Flavel House—Mark Tolonen. *Oregon City:* McLoughlin House—Nancy Wilson. *Portland:* City of Portland Bureau of Planning—Michael S. Harrison, Jeff Joslin; City of Portland Bureau of Parks—Lucy Smith McLean; Historic Preservation League of Oregon—Lisa Burcham, Tibby O'Brien. *Salem:* Bush House—Jennifer Hagloch,

Marna Porath; Historic Deepwood Estate—Michelle Schmitter, George Strozat.

South Dakota
Sioux Falls: Siouxland Heritage Museums—Connie A. Plut, Kevin Gansz; South Dakota State Historical Society Cultural Heritage Center—Jay D. Vogt. *Spearfish:* D. C. Booth Historic National Fish Hatchery—Steve Brim, Randi Smith. *Yankton:* Cramer-Kenyon Heritage Home—Ruby Goeden, Allen Gross; Historic Yankton—Lois Narvel.

Texas
National Trust for Historic Preservation, Fort Worth Field Office—Libby Willis, Jane Jenkins. *Amarillo:* Harrington House—Patty Monroe. *Austin:* French Legation Museum—Sydney Denman; Governor's Mansion—Anne DeBois; Neill-Cochran House—Rachid Moussaid; University of Texas at Austin School of Architecture—Drury Blake Alexander; University of Texas at Austin, Littlefield House—Peggy Kruger. *Beaumont:* City of Beaumont—Stephen Richardson; McFaddin-Ward House—Bradley C. Brooks. *Columbus:* Magnolia Homes Tours—Laura Ann Rau, R. F. "Buddy" Rau. *Dallas:* City of Dallas Planning Department—Jim Anderson; Preservation Dallas, Intown Living Center and Preservation Library—Catherine Horsey, Patsy Stephenson. *El Paso:* Walli Haley. *Fort Worth:* Historic Fort Worth, Inc.—Libby Willis. *Fredericksburg:* Gillespie County Historical Society, Inc.—Paul H. Camfield; Sauer-Beckmann Farm—Donnie Schuch. *Galveston:* Bishop's Palace—Tim Hunter; Galveston Historical Foundation—Peter Brink, David Bush, Christine S. Carl; Moody Mansion and Museum—Margaret Doran, Laura G. Nite. *Houston:* Bayou Bend Collections and Gardens—David Warren; Rice University School of Architecture—Stephen Fox. *Johnson City:* LBJ National Historical Park—Sherry V. Justus. *Lubbock:* Museum of Texas Tech University—Henry B. Crawford; Ranching Heritage Center. *New Braunfels:* Heritage Society of New Braunfels, Inc.—Frances Marquis. *Orange:* City of Orange, Planning and Community Development Department—Dustin Irlenborn; Heritage House of Orange County Association, Inc.; Nelda C. and H. J.

Lutcher Stark Foundation—Walter Riedel. *San Antonio:* Casa Navarro State Historic Park—David McDonald; City of Olmos Park; City of San Antonio, Planning Department—Imogen R. Cooper; Daughters of the Republic of Texas; La Villita; Marion Koogler McNay Art Museum—William J. Chiego; San Antonio Conservation Society; Spanish Governor's Palace—Nora Ward. *Seguin:* Sebastopol State Historic Park—Martha George Withers. *Waxahachie:* Ellis County Museum, Inc.—Marcus Hickerson.

Utah
Salt Lake City: Beehive House—Margaret Adams; State of Utah, Governor's Mansion—Carolynne Lund.

Washington
Henry Matthews. *Bellingham:* Roeder Home—Dana D. Hanks; Whatcom County Park and Recreation Board, Hovander Homestead Park—Dennis Conner; City of Bellingham, Community Development Division—Jacquelyn Lynch. *Port Townsend:* Heritage Group for the Commanding Officer's House; Port Townsend Chamber of Commerce—Rima Phillips. *Puyallup:* Ezra Meeker Historical Society—Andy Anderson. *Seattle:* Seattle Architectural Foundation—Lawrence M. Kreisman. *Spokane:* Campbell House—Marsha Rooney; Glover Mansion—Maria Goodno; Patsy Clark's—Sophia Gorski; Spokane Historic Preservation Office—Teresa L. Brum; Spokane Public Library, Northwest Room—Nancy Gale Compau.

Wyoming
Sheridan: State of Wyoming, Trail End State Historic Site—Cynde Georgen.

Thanks also to NASA architect Constance Adams for information on the development of Dallas street patterns; land use attorney Jonathan Vinson in the Dallas office of Jenkens & Gilchrist for information on the history of zoning; architect Willis Winters of the Dallas Park and Recreation Department for supplying information from his personal library; and Rita Cox of Cox Communications, Dallas, for valuable advice on this book and many, many other preservation projects.

Index

Italicized page numbers indicate illustrations.

Index

Index

Index

Index

Illustration Credits

All photographs not otherwise credited were taken by Virginia McAlester.

Abilene Heritage Center: Robert Paull, 341, both; 342. / Amon Carter Museum, Fort Worth, Tex. Acc. no. 1968.45: 16. / Architectural Drawings Collection, University of Texas at Austin: Drury Blake Alexander, 552, bottom. / Architectural Heritage of the San Antonio Chapter of the American Institute of Architects: xv, bottom. / ArchiTexas: Darya Davidenko, xxxii; 38; 39; 220; 221; 230; 668; 696; 698; 699; 700; 701, left; 702; 703; 704, top; 705; 706. / Arizona Historical Society, Tucson: xvi, top; 18; AHS no. 59715: 19, top. / Max A. van Balgooy, Workman and Temple Family Homestead Museum: 54, both; 55, left. / Courtesy the Bancroft Library, Berkeley, Calif.: 667, bottom. / Banning House Collection, Wilmington, Calif.: 57, left, right. / Dorothy Broady, Governor Furnas House: 392; 395. / Teresa L. Brum, Spokane Historic Preservation Office: 682, right middle and bottom. / State of California, Department of Parks and Recreation: 144. / California History Section, California State Library, Sacramento, Calif.: 138, 265. / California Historical Society, FN-30874: 66. / California State Railroad Museum Foundation, Sacramento, Calif.; photo by Walter P. Gray III: 140, all. / Center for American History, University of Texas at Austin, Map Collection, CN09641: 697. / Cherokee Heritage Center: 493. / Clarke Museum, Eureka; donated by Ann Mendenhall: 34. / College of Architecture, University of Arizona, P.O. Box 210075, Tucson, AZ 85721-0075: xvi, middle and bottom. / Courtesy Colorado Historical Society: 297; 305; 330, bottom. / Corbis/Bettmann Archive: xxix. / Adapted from Randolph Delehanty, *Victorian Sampler: A Walk in Pacific Heights and the Hass-Lilienthal House:* 230, bottom. / Courtesy of the Denver Public Library Western History Department: 290, 320. / Dwight D. Eisenhower Library: 344. / The Fechin Institute: Mark Nohl, 461. / *A Field Guide to American Houses,* drawings by Lauren Jarrett: xiv; xvii; xxii; xxiv; xxx; xxxi; xxxvi; xxxvii. / First Marland Home: 491. / Fresno City and County Historical Society: 44. / Friends of Filoli and National Trust for Historic Preservation: 208. / Galveston Historical Foundation: Robert Rizzo, 601, right. / Nathan Hamm Photography, 320 NW Laurent, Topeka, KS 66608-1469: 364. / Hearst Castle, Hearst San Simeon State Historical Monument: John Blades, 252; Ken Raveill, 253, both. / Historic Deepwood Estate: George Strozat, 531. / Historic Denver, Inc.: 302; 304; Roger Whiteacre, 307, top. /

Historic Ward-Meade Park: 362; 363, left. / Courtesy Houston Metropolitan Research Center: 607. / Hubbell Trading Post National Historic Center, Gannato, Ariz., United States Department of the Interior: 5. / Reproduced by permission of the Huntington Library, San Marino, Calif.: 67, 69, 106, 107. / Indian City, U.S.A.: 473, right three. / Adapted from Terry G. Jordan (with John L. Bean Jr. and William M. Holmes), *Texas: A Geography* (Westview Press: Boulder, Colo., 1984): 695. / Kansas Historical Society, Topeka: 340. / Paul Kozal Photography, 34864 Mission Boulevard, No. 217, Union City, CA 94587: 201, right top and bottom; 202, both; 704, right bottom. / Lawrence Kreisman: 670, all; 671, top and middle; 673, bottom; 675, both. / Reproduced from the Collections of the Library of Congress, Washington, D.C.: 353, 473. / Library of Congress, Division of Manuscripts, Washington, D.C.: xv, top. / Library of Congress, Historic American Buildings Survey: Henry F. Withey, 151, top. / Library of Congress, OWI Collection: John Collier, 462, right bottom. / J. Lynch, City of Bellingham Planning Division: 658, right three; 659, all; 660, top. / Keven McAlester: 27, 480, both; 483, left bottom, right bottom; 484; 485; 486; 546; 547. / McFaddin-Ward House: 557. / Alex McLean, New York City: 100; 260, both; 261, both; 626, both. / Montana Historical Society: Doug O'Looney, 386. / Montana Historical Society Photograph Archives, Helena: 373. / Zachary Mortensen: 316, all; 318, both; 319, both; 321, all; 322, all. / Joe Mullan for *Discover Dallas/Fort Worth:* 569; 589; 592. / Munger Place promotional brochure, ca. 1905, courtesy of Douglas Newby: xxxiv, bottom; xxxv. / Photo courtesy Museum of New Mexico, Neg. no. 6707: 450. / Museum of Texas Tech University: 616. / National Museum of American Art, Washington, D.C./Art Resource, New York: 472. / National Park Service, Lyndon B. Johnson National Historical Park: Bob Greenburg, 614; 615. / National Trust for Historic Preservation: Carol Ivie, 205, 207; Jack E. Boucher, 206; 664, top. / Nebraska State Historic Society: 397, top, 405. / New York Public Library, Map Division, xxxviii. / North Dakota Tourism Department: Clayton Wolt, 467, all. / City of Omaha Planning Department: Lynn Meyer, 412; 413, right, top and bottom; Jim Krance, left top. / Oregon Historical Society, Portland: Neg. no. OrHi26176: 512; Neg. no. OrHi245: 525. / City of Portland, Bureau of Parks and Public Recreation: 520, both. / Port Townsend Chamber of Commerce: 664, bottom. / Preservation Dallas: M. Wayland Brown, 572, right top; 573, left; David Buffington, 570, left; 574, all; 701, right. / Ranching Heritage Center: 617. / Rancho Los Cerritos Historic Site: 60, both. / Mark Reavis, City of Butte: 375, all. / Riordan State Historic Park (Ariz.), Flagstaff Archives, Cline Library: 2. / Cynthia Jane Roessler, 1997: 199, all; 704, middle. / Courtesy of the Rosenberg Library, Galveston, Tex.: 598. / City of Sacramento, Department of Planning and Development: 146, all; 147, all. / Salem Art Association, Bush House Museum: Marna Porath, 530. / Courtesy of San Antonio Conservation Society: 630. / Siouxland Heritage Museums: 537. / Jean Smart: 448. / Roman Sokal: 71, right; 73, all; 74; 75, left, right top and bottom; 77, all; 81, all; 83, all; 84, bottom; 88, both; 89, bottom; 90, right top and bottom; 95, top three; 99, all; 101; 103; 105, second from top. / Southwest Collection, El Paso (Tex.) Public Library: 583, middle, bottom. / Special Collections Division, University of Washington Libraries, Neg. no. uw 4812: 667, top. / Spokane Public Library, Northwest Room: 678, top; 682, left, and right top. / I. N. Phelps Stokes Collection, Mariam and Ira D. Wallach Division of Art, Prints and Photographs, New York Public Library, Astor, Lenox and Tilden Foundations: 425. / Taos County Chamber of Commerce: Bruce Gomez, 455. / City of Tucson, Planning Department (from Joesler and Murphey, 1994): xxxix. / Tucson Museum of Art, David Burckhalter, photographer: 23. / State of Utah, Governor's Mansion: David M. Farr, 653. / Utah State Historical Society, Salt Lake City: 643, 647. / Catherine Wally: 600, all; 601, left; 602; 603, all; 604; 605; 610, all; 611, both; 612, all; 613. / Western History Collection, University of Oklahoma Libraries: 478, both. / Nancy P. Weston: 234. / Whatcom County Park and Recreation Board, Hovander Homestead Park: 660, bottom. / Courtesy of the Witte Museum, San Antonio, Tex.: 622. / Edward F. Zimmer, Lincoln City–Lancaster County Planning Department: 403.

A Note About the Authors

VIRGINIA McALESTER is a graduate of Harvard-Radcliffe College and attended Harvard Graduate School of Design. She is a founding member and past president of Preservation Dallas (formerly called the Historic Preservation League, Inc.) and of Friends of Fair Park, a support group for the Fair Park National Historic Landmark in Dallas, intact site of the 1936 Texas Centennial Exposition. She serves on the Dallas Landmark Commission and is an Adviser Emeritus of the National Trust for Historic Preservation.

LEE McALESTER, a geologist by profession, is Chairman of the Geology Department at Southern Methodist University and was formerly Dean of the School of Humanities and Sciences there. He is the author of several geology textbooks as well as numerous scientific monographs and papers. He has an active interest in architectural history and has been involved in many Dallas preservation projects.

Together the McAlesters are the authors of *A Field Guide to American Houses* (available in Knopf paperback), *Discover Dallas/Fort Worth*, and *Great American Houses and Their Architectural Styles*. The National Trust awarded them a Preservation Honor Award for creating *A Field Guide to American Houses*, and they have recently received the Texas Society of Architects' Flowers Award for excellence in interpreting architecture through the media.

A Note on the Type

The main text of this book was set in Minion, a typeface produced by the Adobe Corporation specifically for the Macintosh personal computer, and released in 1990. Designed by Robert Slimbach, Minion combines the classic characteristics of old-style faces with the full complement of weights required for modern typesetting. The typeface used for the display and subtext of the book is Univers, designed for Deberny & Peignot in 1957 by Adrian Frutiger. Univers is a sans serif with more weights and widths available than almost any other typeface.

Composed by North Market Street Graphics, Lancaster, Pennsylvania
Printed and bound by Quebecor Printing, Martinsburg, West Virginia
Designed by Anthea Lingeman and Peter Andersen, with Arlene Lee